Organizations

Behavior, Structure, Processes

Organizations

Behavior, Structure, Processes

Fourteenth Edition

James L. Gibson
University of Kentucky

John M. Ivancevich
University of Houston

James H. Donnelly, Jr.
University of Kentucky

Robert Konopaske
Texas State University

The McGraw·Hill Companies

ORGANIZATIONS: BEHAVIOR, STRUCTURE, PROCESSES, FOURTEENTH EDITION

Published by McGraw-Hill, a business unit of The McGraw-Hill Companies, Inc., 1221 Avenue of the Americas, New York, NY, 10020.

This book is printed on recycled, acid-free paper containing 10% postconsumer waste.

1 2 3 4 5 6 7 8 9 0 QDB/QDB 1 0 9 8 7 6 5 4 3 2 1

ISBN 978-0-07-811266-9
MHID 0-07-811266-4

Vice President & Editor-in-Chief: *Brent Gordon*
Vice President EDP/Central Publishing Services: *Kimberly Meriwether David*
Editorial Director: *Paul Ducham*
Managing Development Editor: *Laura Hurst Spell*
Editorial Coordinator: *Jane Beck*
Marketing Manager: *Jaime Halteman*
Senior Project Manager: *Lisa A. Bruflodt*
Buyer: *Nicole Baumgartner*
Design Coordinator: *Brenda A. Rolwes*
Media Project Manager: *Balaji Sundararaman*
Cover Design: *Studio Montage, St. Louis, Missouri*
Cover images: *Business Women Sitting in an Interview: © Digital Vision RF; Reflection of Office Building: © CORBIS RF; Global Concept: © Brand X Pictures/Jupiter Images RF*
Typeface: *10/12 Times New Roman*
Compositor: *Aptara®, Inc.*
Printer: *Quad/Graphics*

Photo credits: Ch. 1, Yuri Arcurs/Cutcaster; Ch. 2, Stockbyte/Punchstock Images; Ch. 3, Doug Menuez/Getty Images; Ch. 4, Royalty-Free/CORBIS; Ch. 5, Stockbyte/Getty Images; Ch. 6, © Digital Vision; Ch. 7, Keith Brofsky/Getty Images; Ch. 8, Digital Vision/Getty Images; Ch. 9, Monica Lau/Getty Images; Ch. 10, Manchan/Getty Images; Ch. 11, © Digital Vision; Ch. 12, Ryan McVay/Getty Images; Ch. 13, Photodisc/Getty Images; Ch. 14, Ryan McVay/Getty Images; Ch. 15, Jon Feingersh/Getty Images; Ch. 16, Digital Vision/Getty Images; Ch. 17, Ryan McVay/Getty Images

Library of Congress Cataloging-in-Publication Data

Organizations : behavior, structure, processes / James L. Gibson . . . [et al.].—14th ed.
p. cm.
Includes bibliographical references and index.
ISBN 978-0-07-811266-9 (soft cover : alk. paper) 1. Organization. 2. Organizational behavior. 3. Leadership. 4. Organizational effectiveness. I. Gibson, James L. (James Lawrence), 1935-

HD58.7.G54 2011
658.4—dc22 2010050550

www.mhhe.com

John (Jack) M. Ivancevich (August 16, 1939–October 26, 2009): In Memoriam.

Hugh Roy and Lillie Cranz Cullen Chair and Professor of Organizational Behavior and Management, C.T. Bauer College of Business, University of Houston; B.S. from Purdue University, and MBA and DBA from the University of Maryland.

This book honors the memory of Jack Ivancevich, our finest friend, colleague, co-author, and cancer confidante. He put his heart and soul into this book for 13 editions and although he is not with us now, we know they are very much present in this 14th edition. Not only does he live on in this book, he lives on in our hearts. He was and remains the driving force of this team of authors. We miss you, Jack, and we hope you are proud of this edition.

James L. Gibson and James H. Donnelly, Jr.

The management discipline lost a passionate and award-winning educator, and an influential leader with an incomparable work ethic and sense of integrity. Jack led by example, and those of us who were fortunate enough to know him were inspired to work harder and reach higher than we ever thought possible.

Jack was committed to higher education and the creation and dissemination of management knowledge. He was comfortable in the classroom and would encourage students to think critically about and apply the concepts and theories of organizational behavior and management to their lives. Jack had an "open door" policy, and spent countless hours helping students and answering their questions. His reputation as a tough teacher was softened by his appreciation for the need of many students to balance a desire for education with a full-time job and family demands. Among Jack's most valued honors was the *Ester Farfel Award for Research, Teaching, and Service Excellence,* the highest honor bestowed to a University of Houston faculty member.

Complementing his passion for teaching, Jack loved to write books. He tried to write at least 300 days a year, averaging about 1,200 words per day. Over a 40-year period, Jack reached well over a million students by authoring or co-authoring 88 books about various aspects of management and organizational behavior. Currently in its 14th edition, *Organizations: Behavior, Structure, Processes* (co-authored with James L. Gibson, James H. Donnelly, and Robert Konopaske) continues to be well received by students and instructors alike. In 2005, *Organizations* received the McGuffey Award from the Text and Academic Authors Association. This award recognizes textbooks and learning materials whose excellence has been demonstrated over time. A sample of Jack's other textbooks includes *Human Resource Management, Organizational Behavior and Management* (co-authored with Robert Konopaske and Michael T. Matteson), *Global Management and Organizational Behavior* (co-authored with Robert Konopaske), *Management and Organizational Behavior Classics* (co-authored with Michael T. Matteson), *Fundamentals of Management: Functions, Behavior, Models* (co-authored with James L. Gibson and James H. Donnelly), and *Management: Quality and Competitiveness* (co-authored with Peter Lorenzi, Steven Skinner, and Philip Crosby).

Jack was not only an accomplished educator and book author, but also a prolific and highly respected researcher. Well-known for his highly disciplined work ethic, Jack authored or co-authored some 160 research articles, which were published in such journals as *Academy of Management Journal, Academy of Management Review, Administrative Science Quarterly, Journal of Applied Psychology,* and *Harvard Business Review*. His research was highly influential and explored a range of management and organizational behavior topics, including job stress, white-collar crime, diversity management, global assignments, job loss, absenteeism, job satisfaction, goal setting, job performance, training method effectiveness, and organizational climate. The diversity of Jack's research reflected the complex and inter-related nature of management issues in organizations. In 2000, in recognition of publishing a substantial number of refereed articles in Academy of Management journals, Jack was inducted into the Academy of Management's *Journals Hall of Fame* as one of the first 33 Charter Members. This is an impressive achievement when considering that in 2000, the Academy of Management had approximately 13,500 members.

In addition to teaching, writing books, and conducting research, Jack applied his knowledge of organizational behavior and management to the several leadership positions he held since joining the University of Houston faculty in 1974. In 1975, he was named Chair of the Department of Organizational Behavior and Management, and the following year, Jack became the Associate Dean of Research for the College of Business Administration at UH. In 1979, Jack was awarded the Hugh Roy and Lillie Cranz Cullen Chair of Organizational Behavior and Management, among the most prestigious positions at the University of Houston. From 1988 to 1995, he served as Dean of the University of Houston College of Business Administration. In 1995, Jack was named University of Houston Executive Vice President for Academic Affairs and Provost; a position he held for two years. Through visionary, performance-driven, and principled leadership, Jack left a lasting and meaningful imprint on the entire University of Houston community, including internal constituents, such as fellow administrators, deans, program directors, faculty, staff, and students, as well as external stakeholders, such as legislators, donors, alumni, and area company executives. His accomplishments were even more extraordinary given the fact that Jack continued to teach classes, write books, and publish research articles while holding these myriad leadership positions.

Jack made innumerable contributions to all facets of higher education, all of which will be felt for years to come. Perhaps one of Jack's greatest and longest lasting legacies will be from the many individuals he mentored during his 45 years in higher education. As busy as he was throughout his entire career, Jack was extremely generous with his time and made it a priority to mentor a large number of individuals, including current and former students, junior faculty, colleagues from the publishing industry, and many others. He wanted people to succeed and would do everything he could to help them accomplish their goals. Jack would often invite younger faculty members to collaborate with him on research projects. As a member of 80 doctoral and master's committees, Jack relished his role as mentor and would spend hours with graduate students, helping and guiding them through the process of conducting original research for their theses or dissertations. Jack was always willing to make phone calls and write detailed letters of recommendation on behalf of his students to help them get hired or later in their careers, get promoted or be awarded tenure. He invested heavily in these individuals and expected hard work and commitment to excellence in return. Many of these former graduate students are professors at universities and colleges throughout the United States and now find themselves mentoring and inspiring their own students.

On a personal note, Jack was my mentor, colleague, and friend. Words cannot capture how grateful and honored I feel to have worked so closely with him on several textbooks and research projects over the past 10 years. We became acquainted in 1999, after Jack agreed to be my dissertation chair at the University of Houston. Given Jack's stature and commanding presence, I was a little intimidated by him in the beginning but quickly realized he was a "gentle giant" who could switch rapidly between discussions of research, books, academic careers, teaching, and the importance of being a good family man and father, and achieving balance in one's life. Jack was a great storyteller and especially liked relating tales of his early years in the south side of Chicago. He taught me many things; some lessons were passed along during thoughtful conversations but most came by observing him in action. Jack taught me to take life "head on" with a strong, positive, and can-do attitude, while never losing sight of the importance of being a loving and committed husband and father. He will be sorely missed by all of us who were fortunate to have been touched by his warm friendship and guided by his generous spirit.

Jack is survived by his wife of 37 years, Margaret (Pegi) Karsner Ivancevich; son Daniel and wife Susan; daughter Jill and husband David Zacha, Jr.; and grandchildren Kathryn Diane and Amanda Dana Ivancevich, and Hunter David Michael, Hailey Dana, and Hannah Marie Zacha. Jack was preceded in death by his beloved daughter Dana, and by his first wife, Diane Frances Murphy Ivancevich.

Robert Konopaske

Texas State University

Preface

The 14th edition of *Organizations: Behavior, Structure, Processes* is based on the proposition that managing people, structure, and processes in organizations is a challenging, compelling, and crucial set of tasks. In good as well as in difficult economic times, there is nothing boring about managing organizational behavior. Traditional approaches that worked a decade ago or even a few years ago are currently being questioned, modified, or replaced. This book will provide an opportunity for you to look inside organizations and to develop your own perspective and skills for managing organizational behavior. Your own perspective and approach will serve you in the positions you hold, the challenges you face, and the career choices you make.

This edition of the award-winning *Organizations: Behavior, Structure, Processes* presents theories, research results, and applications that focus on managing organizational behavior in small, as well as large and global organizations. Through the successful history of the book, feedback from students and instructors has suggested that we have succeeded in presenting a realistic view of organizational behavior.

A consistent theme throughout the book is that effective management of organizational behavior requires an understanding of theory, research, and practice. Given this theme, we view our task as presenting and interpreting organizational behavior theory and research so that students can comprehend the three characteristics common to all organizations—behavior, structure, and processes—as they are affected by actions of managers. Accordingly, we illustrate how organizational behavior theory leads to research and how both theory and research provide the basic foundation for practical applications in business firms, hospitals, educational institutions, government agencies, and other organizations.

As dedicated teachers of organizational behavior and management, we are guided by student needs, feedback, and applications in real-world settings. The 14th edition is current, relevant, and offers a variety of techniques to encourage student involvement. The book challenges students to continue to explore the content areas long after they successfully complete their current course. This self-initiated exploration will result in the continuous learning and inquiry so that students' knowledge, skills, and competencies are sharpened at each new juncture.

We incorporate a clear, student-friendly style and presentation in making the management of organizational behavior insightful, meaningful, and realistic. The writing and presentation style used is successful in motivating students to engage in classroom analysis, discussion, and learning.

Special Features

This edition emphasizes that the most successful managers in the global economy will be those who can anticipate, adapt, and manage change. The world and economic conditions change continuously, and the ability to manage behavior, structure, and processes in such a rapidly changing environment will be a premier competency. To help students deal with change better, we have included a significant amount of material on transformational leadership, diagnosing and assessing change, communication effectiveness, information technology, diversity, ethics, global management, organizational culture, offshoring, teams, and team building. Coverage of some of these topics began a few editions back and is further expanded in this edition. Some of the special content and features in this edition include:

- **Opening vignettes** frame the start of each chapter. Real-world situations, events, facts, or problems bring out upcoming issues covered in the chapter's content. These are the circumstances that managers of behavior, structure, and processes face every day.
- A new feature, **OB and Your Career,** is intended to help students apply the concepts of this book to improving their careers. A sample of topics include: finding a job that fits with personality and work style; staying motivated after a layoff; being more efficient with time at work; and acquiring international business experience without relocating.
- Hundreds of **real-world situations, companies, and applied examples** were added to illustrate how OB theory and research can be applied to actual work settings. Students prefer to have real examples to support what academics and researchers are proposing or stating. The real world is reflected in the chapter content, the **OB at Work** features, and the **Cases for Analysis.**
- Student involvement with the World Wide Web is an element designated **Taking It to the Net.** This is an exercise requiring students to perform a specific assignment on the Internet. Each assignment is associated with a theory, research findings, management applications, an organization, or a topic area covered in the particular chapter. By completing the exercise, the student will become more comfortable with conducting research on the Internet and how classmates addressed the exercise.
- Each year organizations become more involved in global business, global joint ventures, and global negotiations. This edition pays particular attention to **global** and **ethical business** issues in each chapter.
- Diversity needs to be examined and managed in all organizations. **Diversity management** and issues such as the changing nature of employees in the workplace and generational differences between Gen Y, Gen X, and Baby Boomers are presented, debated, and analyzed throughout the text.
- **Teams, group dynamics, group decision making, leadership,** and **managing change** are each important topics that are emphasized more in this edition.
- One of the characteristics of every one of our new editions is that the **latest thinking, debate,** and **insight** be included. Content is updated in such areas as managing layoffs and the survivors of layoffs, the MBA oath of managerial ethics, cultural diversity, workplace spirituality, competitiveness, globalization, offshoring, empowerment, mentoring, organizational learning, organizational justice, performance-based rewards, managing information technology, virtual organizations, strategic decision making, innovation, flexible organizational and job design, contingency theory, ethical decision making, sexual harassment, politics and change, communication skills, feedback, entrepreneurship, and motivation.
- Coverage of **ethics** has been greatly expanded. Ethical issues are covered in many parts of the book as well as in our OB at Work features and end-of-chapter material.

As usual, every time we have revised this book there has been an emphasis on responding to the feedback received and the need for updating. The content in the field of organizational behavior and management is constantly changing and expanding. We want to capture currentness along with a sense of history. Thus, the revision work concentrated on using current concepts along with proven approaches to managing behavior within organizations.

Teaching Resources

Continuing attention to **teaching** also went into preparing the supplements for the book. In developing and testing our supplements, we continually focus on needs of both students and instructors. Simply, we want our supplements to add to students' understanding while simultaneously enabling the instructor to teach an exciting course. The *Instructor's Manual, Test Bank,* and *PowerPoint*® Presentation Software comprise a total system to enhance learning and teaching. All of these supplements as well as additional study tools for students are available at www.mhhe.com/gibson14e. In addition, The Organizational Behavior Video DVD offers a selection of videos that illustrate various key concepts from the book and explore current trends in today's workplace.

Also available for purchase with the text, Premium Content includes access to online Test Your Knowledge and Self-Assessments exercises as well as Manager's Hot Seat. Manager's Hot Seat is interactive, video-based software that puts students in the manager's hot seat, where they apply their knowledge to make decisions on the spot on hot issues such as ethics, diversity, working in teams, and the virtual workplace. Resources to support these exercises and videos are located in the Group and Video Resource Manual.

AACSBI International© Guidelines

The guidelines of the American Assembly of Collegiate Schools of Business International (AACSBI) guided the preparation of each revision. This book is used across campuses in business schools, social science disciplines, engineering, hotel and restaurant management, education, and public administration. We are pleased and honored by the many adoptions and the loyalty of instructors in many different disciplines.

The AACSBI guidelines are used as a starting point for synthesizing management and organizational behavior as fields of study. These guidelines call for more of a cross-discipline (e.g., psychology, sociology, engineering) approach. A cross-discipline approach is important because organizations are much more than simply business entities and institutions in which managing behavior, structure, and processes across functional areas poses numerous challenges.

Framework of This Edition

The book is organized and presented in a sequence based on the three characteristics common to all organizations: behavior, structure, processes. This framework has been maintained based on the responses from numerous users of previous editions. However, note that each major part is presented as a self-contained unit and can therefore be presented in whatever sequence the instructor prefers. Some instructors present the chapter on structure first, followed by those on behavior and processes. The text is easily adaptable to these individual preferences. The book concludes with an appendix, which reviews research procedures and techniques used in studying organizational behavior.

Reviewers for This Edition

Julie Bergh, University of Colorado at Denver; Lea Davis, Dallas County Community College; Jeannie Gaines, Brenau University; Bruce Gillies, California Lutheran University; David Leuser, Plymouth State University; Robert Steel, University of Michigan at Ann Arbor; James T. Ziegenfuss, Pennsylvania State University.

Reviewers of Previous Editions

Mel Minarik, University of Nevada-Reno; Dr. Norma Friedman, Indiana Institute of Technology; Consuelo M. Ramirez, University of Texas at San Antonio; Berrin Erdogan, Portland State University; Thomas J. Callahan, University of Michigan–Dearborn; and Robert P. Steel, University of Michigan–Dearborn. Allan E. Pevoto, St. Edward's University; Robin C. Smith, Tarleton State University; David J. Cherrington, Brigham Young University; Mark Fichman, Carnegie-Mellon University; Harry E. Stucke, Long Island University; S. Stephen Vitucci, Tarleton State University; Courtney Hunt, Northern Illinois University; Macgorine A. Cassell, Fairmont State College; James W. Fairfield-Sonn, University of Hartford; Mitchell J. Hartson, Florida Institute of Technology; Mary Giovannini, Truman State University; Monty L. Lynn, Abilene Christian University; Jeffrey Glazer, San Diego State University; Eugene H. Hunt, Virginia Commonwealth University; William D. Murry, State University of New York–Binghamton; Stanley J. Stough, Southeast Missouri State University; William E. Stratton, Idaho State University; Harold Strauss, University of Miami; Harry A. Taylor, Capitol College; Betty Velthouse, University of Michigan–Flint; Diana Ting Liu Wu, Saint Mary's College of California; Peter Lorenzi, Loyola College; Dr. Barry Friedman, State University of New York–Oswego; R. Andrew Schaffer, North Georgia College & State University; Paul Lakey, Abilene Christian University; and Andrzej Wlodarczyd, Lindenwood University.

James L. Gibson

John M. Ivancevich

James H. Donnelly, Jr.

Robert Konopaske

Brief Contents

Contents

PART ONE

Introduction

CHAPTER ONE

Managing Effective Organizations

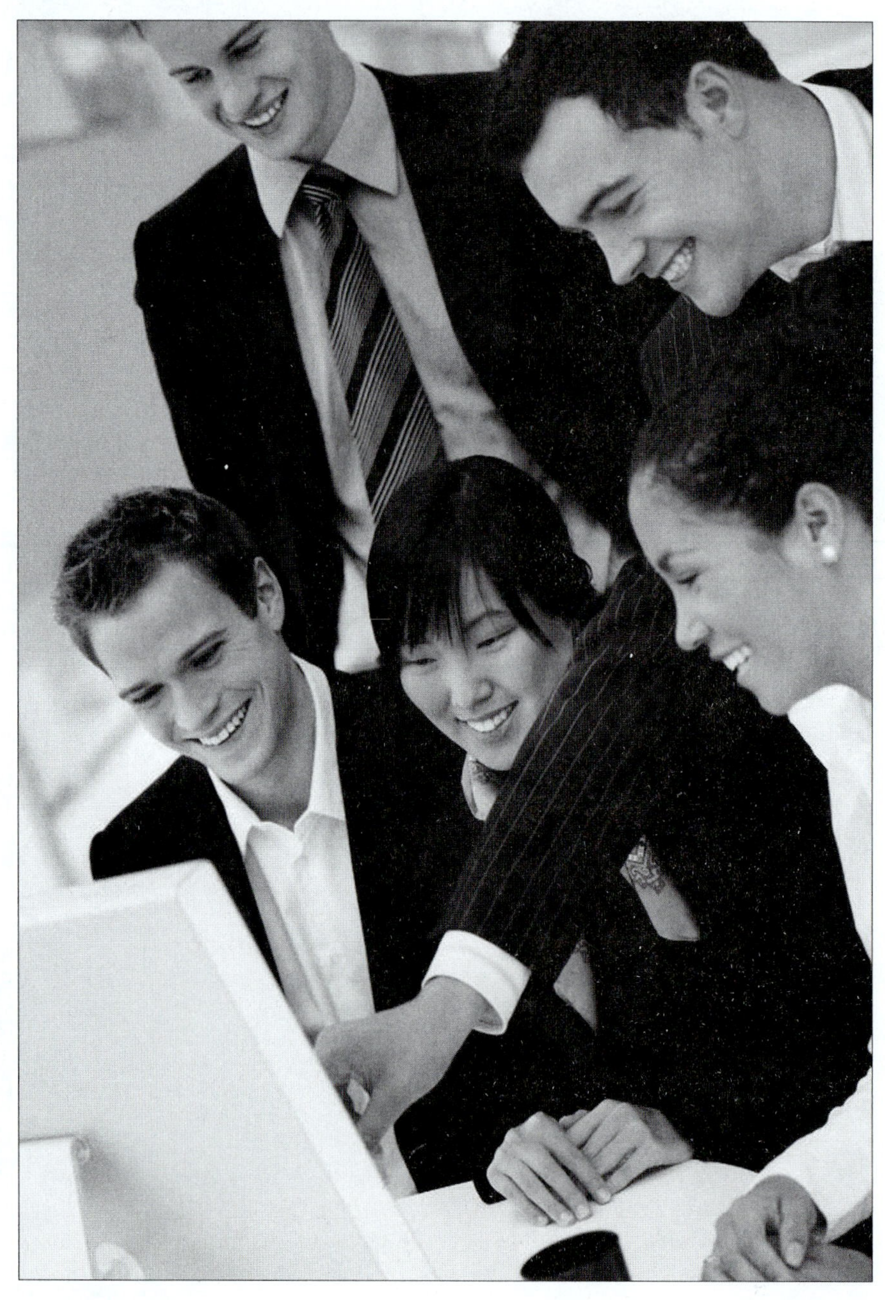

Learning Objectives

After completing Chapter 1, you should be able to

Define
The term *organizational behavior.*

Explain
Why organizations need to manage in an effective manner.

Identify
Why managing workplace behavior in the United States is likely to be different from managing workplace behavior in another country, such as Germany.

Compare
The goal, systems, and stakeholder approaches to effectiveness.

Describe
The type of environmental forces that make it necessary for organizations to initiate changes.

Global Account Managers: Multiple Skills Are Needed

Attracting, retaining, and managing customers in a global marketplace are daunting tasks for even the most astute managers. It is difficult for a company to establish and maintain relationships with customers in their own neighborhood, state, region, or country. In terms of difficulty, the task is multiplied when customers are spread around the world.

As globalization matures and grows, there are more opportunities to find and nurture customers. However, some of the traditional jobs, structures, and systems have to be modified. The notion of a global account manager was not a part of organizational infrastructures a decade ago. However, today the global account manager is center stage and growing in stature.

The global account manager (GAM) in some cases is in charge of a single customer and all of its global needs. The customer's needs, schedules, and interests are the top priority of the GAM. Some believe that it takes more than a decade to develop a responsive, effective, and profitable global account management system.

Studies of DHL, Siemens, SAP, Marriott International, Microsoft, IBM, and others provide some suggestions of how an effective GAM system evolves. Three stages emerge in effective GAM systems: beginner, springload, and embedded.

Beginners identify global accounts, assign managers, and change their structures in terms of communications, decision making, and problem solving to help the GAM succeed. In the *springload* stage, the GAM works with customers to develop new products and find ways to make the customer more competitive. In the *embedded* stage, the entire organization has developed a cooperative culture and global orientation. Serving the needs of the global customer is the top priority of the GAM.

Microsoft started using GAM around 2000. Today, they focus on multimillion-dollar, global customers that rely heavily on information technology. Although size of the customer's revenue is important, Microsoft wants to attract leaders in their industry—customers who are willing to openly share information for the development of new products and processes. Other firms develop their own set of criteria for establishing the GAM program.

Sources: Adapted from "New Company of the Year," *Financial Times*, February 16, 2008, p. 11; Christoph Senn and Axel Thoma, "Global Business: Worldly Wise," *Wall Street Journal Online,* March 3, 2007; and Karen R. Polenske, *The Economic Geography of Innovation* (Cambridge, UK: Cambridge University Press, 2006).

Years ago, change was slow, markets were concentrated in a handful of countries, and stability was the rule rather than the exception. Back then, organizational approaches emphasized top-down hierarchy, rules and regulations, and authority rested in the hands of authoritative executives. Ford Motors, Nestlé, General Electric, and IBM—organizational giants that dominated their respective markets—used a rigid hierarchy system from top management to operating-level employees to accomplish their goals. During the past 30 years, many factors in the environment (such as government regulations, information technology, global competitors, union influence, and customer demands and needs) changed, and as a result, organizations needed to make dramatic adjustments in how they managed their operations. Unfortunately, in the 21st century some organizations have failed to change or adapt to their more turbulent environments. This inability to change with the times has decreased their organizational effectiveness.

The opening vignette on global account managers illustrates how multiple skills are needed to grow operations globally. Adapting to change and flexibility are the requirements for managing effectively in a globally connected marketplace.

This book is about organizations and how they operate effectively in a world that is rapidly changing.[1] We will focus our attention throughout this book on people working within organizations or interacting with them from outside. People working together or contributing individually within organizations, large and small, have built pyramids, city-states, spacecraft, running shoes, automobiles, and entire industries. Each of us spends much of our life working for or conducting transactions with organizations—restaurants, universities, doctors' offices, USAA Financial Services, Amazon.com, Southwest Airlines, United Parcel Service, Target, and the Internal Revenue Service are just a few examples.

People and how they work individually and together are the focus of this book. The story of Aaron Feuerstein in the OB at Work feature on the next page clearly shows that putting people first can have dramatic positive effects for an organization and community.

Another characteristic of the book is that it is globally oriented. That people work in organizations, produce goods and services, and contribute to a society is not a phenomenon found only in the United States.[2] Americans are no smarter than Germans, nor are they better workers than Brazilians. The fact that the United States became such a productive nation is largely the result of the application of sound management practices and techniques. Americans planned efficiently, organized systematically, and led workers effectively. Also, Americans came up with new techniques, new methods, and new styles of management that fit well with the time, the workforce, and the mission. In the past 60 years, productivity improvement has been a major priority for most organizations.

As we move further into the 21st century, managers around the world must recapture the feel, the passion, and the desire for being effective, for producing high-quality products, and for providing outstanding services. Unfortunately, the importance of managing human resources hasn't always taken center stage. It is our strong belief that managing people effectively in organizations is the most essential ingredient for achieving organizational success, retaining a comfortable standard of living, remaining one of the world's economic leaders, and improving the quality of life for all citizens.[3]

Whether we're talking about a pizza parlor in Chicago, a glass manufacturing plant in Monterrey, Mexico, or a cooperative produce shop in Vilnius, Lithuania, management within an organizational setting is important. The clerk in the Lithuanian produce shop wants to earn a fair day's pay for his work, the company president in Mexico has to purchase the best equipment to compete internationally, and the pizza parlor owner must motivate people to show up on time for work. These individuals' work behaviors occur within organizations. To better understand these behaviors, we believe that we must formally study people, processes, and structure in relation to organizations.

organizations
Entities that enable society to pursue accomplishments that can't be achieved by individuals acting alone.

An **organization** is a coordinated unit consisting of at least two people who function to achieve a common goal or set of goals. This is what this book is about—organizations, large and small, domestic and global, successful and unsuccessful. Looking inside the organization at the people, processes, and structures will help enlighten the observer and will also reveal the inner workings of organizations that have been a main contributor to the standards of living enjoyed by people around the world.

OB AT WORK Putting People First

On December 11, 1995, a devastating fire swept through a mill complex in the heart of Lawrence, Massachusetts. Malden Mills, one of the few remaining textile firms operating in New England, owned the factory. The destruction threatened the 1,400 jobs at the mill. Another 1,600 jobs at plants in the community that did business with Malden Mills were also threatened. However, on the morning after the fire, the owner of Malden Mills, Aaron Feuerstein, promised his employees that their jobs were secure. He decided that Malden Mills would rebuild the ruined plant and would continue to provide full paychecks and medical benefits through the holiday season.

The fire and its aftermath generated a lot of national attention. Feuerstein's actions were praised, and he was regarded as a sensitive, caring leader. A few months later, a welder at the plant praised Feuerstein, ". . . with what he's doing with Malden Mills, it's an honor to work in this place."

Feuerstein's philosophy of putting people first is reflected in his statement that

> I have a responsibility to the worker, both blue-collar and white-collar. I have an equal responsibility to the community. It would have been unconscionable to put 3,000 people on the streets and deliver a deathblow to the cities of Lawrence and Matheren. Maybe on paper our company is worth less to Wall Street, but I can tell you it's worth more. We're doing fine.

Putting people first was something that Feuerstein did with ease. In a region of the United States that had witnessed downsizing, reengineering, and outsourcing, Feuerstein's behavior was embraced, applauded, and held in high regard. Feuerstein had faith in his workers and showed how important they were to him.

Since the fire, Malden Mills has fallen on hard times. Economic conditions in Lawrence have deteriorated for the factories in the region. Unfortunately, the years after the fire were filled with debt and bankruptcy. Feuerstein was asked if he would do the same thing again. He said, "Yes, it was the right thing to do."

A memory that citizens will not forget, though, is how managers at Malden treated their employees after an unfortunate fire. This memory continues to be a part of the history of the region even though the factories continue to close down.

Sources: Adapted from In Brief, *Wall Street Journal*, February 21, 2007, eastern edition, p. B.4; www.aish.com, accessed on April 2, 2007; Davis Bushnell, "Maneuvering for Control of Stronger Malden Mills," *Boston Globe*, February 5, 2004, p. D1; "Malden Mills," *Industry Standard*, July 24, 2001, p. 6; www.reputation-mgmt.com/malden.htm; and Richard K. Lester, *The Productivity Edge* (New York: Norton, 1998), pp. 213–14.

As the opening vignette illustrates, the expectations of consumers are changing. Organizations must be prepared to deal with consumer needs for social responsibility, good citizenship, and responsible management and leadership. The array of stakeholders applying pressure suggests that managing organizational behavior can be challenging and rewarding for managers.

Studying Organizational Behavior

organizational behavior (OB)
The field of study that draws on theory, methods, and principles from various disciplines to learn about *individuals'* perceptions, values, learning capacities, and actions while working in *groups* and within the *organization* and to analyze the external environment's effect on the organization and its human resources, missions, objectives, and strategies.

Why does Ric Nunzio always seem to hire older employees for his pizza parlor? Why is Selena Rodriguez the best decision maker in selecting what piece of equipment to purchase for her glass manufacturing plant? Why does Val Kupolus always complain that he's not paid enough to sell produce at the Vilnius produce stand? Such questions are studied, analyzed, and debated in the field called **organizational behavior (OB)**. The formal study of organizational behavior began between 1948 and 1952. This still-emerging field attempts to help managers understand people better so that productivity improvements, customer satisfaction, and a better competitive position can be achieved through better management practices.

The behavioral sciences—especially psychology, sociology, political science, and cultural anthropology—have provided the basic framework and principles for the field of organizational behavior. Each behavioral science discipline provides a slightly different focus, analytical framework, and theme for helping managers answer questions about themselves, nonmanagers, and environmental forces (e.g., competition, legal requirements, and social/political changes).

The multidisciplinary definition of organizational behavior illustrates a number of points. First, OB indicates that *behaviors* of people operate at individual, group, and organizational levels. This approach suggests that when studying OB we must identify clearly the level of analysis being used—individual, group, organizational, or all three. Second, OB is *multidisciplinary;* it uses principles, models, theories, and methods from other disciplines. The study of OB isn't a discipline or a generally accepted science with an established theoretical foundation. It's a field that only now is beginning to grow and develop in stature and impact. Third, there's a distinctly *humanistic orientation* within organizational behavior. People and their attitudes, perceptions, learning capacities, feelings, and goals are important to the organization. Fourth, the field of OB is *performance oriented.* Why is performance low or high? How can performance be improved? Can training enhance on-the-job performance? These are important issues facing managers. Fifth, the *external environment* is seen as having significant effect on organizational behavior. Sixth, because the field of OB relies heavily on recognized disciplines, the *scientific method* is important in studying variables and relationships. As the scientific method has been applied to research on organizational behavior, a set of principles and guidelines on what constitutes good research has emerged.[4] Finally, the field has a distinctive *applications orientation;* it concerns providing useful answers to questions that arise in the context of managing operations.

Organizational Behavior Follows Principles of Human Behavior

The effectiveness of any organization is influenced greatly by human behavior. People are a resource common to all organizations. The pizza parlor, the glass manufacturing plant, and the produce stand employ human assets and interact with people such as customers, suppliers, and job candidates.

One important principle of psychology is that each person is different. Each has unique perceptions, personality, and life experiences. People have different ethnic backgrounds; different capabilities for learning and for handling responsibility; and different attitudes, beliefs, and aspiration levels. We've moved from an era in which large portions of the workforce were middle-aged men who spoke only English to an era of diversity. Today's workforce doesn't look, think, or act like the workforce of the past.[5] To be effective, managers of organizations must view each employee or member as a unique embodiment of all these behavioral and cultural factors.

Organizations Are Social Systems

The relationships among individuals and groups in organizations create expectations for individuals' behavior. These expectations result in certain roles that must be performed. Some people must perform leadership roles, whereas others must participate in the roles of followers. Middle managers, because they have both superiors and subordinates, must perform both roles. Organizations have systems of authority, status, and power, and people in organizations have varying needs from each system. Groups in organizations also have a powerful impact on individual behavior and on organizational performance.

Multiple Factors Shape Organizational Behavior

contingency approach
Approach to management that believes there's no one best way to manage in every situation and managers must find different ways that fit different situations.

A person's behavior in any situation involves the interaction of that individual's personal characteristics and the characteristics of the situation. Thus, identifying all of the factors is time-consuming and difficult; frequently, the task is impossible.

To help us identify the important managerial factors in organizational behavior, we use the **contingency** (or *situational*) **approach**. The basic idea of the contingency approach is that there's not one best way to manage; a method that's very effective in one situation may not work at all in others. The contingency approach has grown in popularity because research has shown that given certain characteristics of a job and certain characteristics of the people doing the job, some management practices work better than others. Thus, the Mexican glass manufacturing plant's manager of operations faced with a poorly performing group doesn't assume that a particular approach will work. In applying the contingency approach, he diagnoses the characteristics of the individuals and groups involved in the organizational structure, and his own leadership style, before deciding on a solution.

Organizational behavior has evolved into an applied set of behavioral science concepts, models, and techniques. The predominant contributors to OB—psychology, social psychology, sociology, political science, and anthropology—have contributed to our understanding and use of OB in organizational settings. Figure 1.1 presents an illustration of some of the major contributions of the behavioral sciences to the study and application of OB.

FIGURE 1.1 **Contributions to the Study and Application of OB**

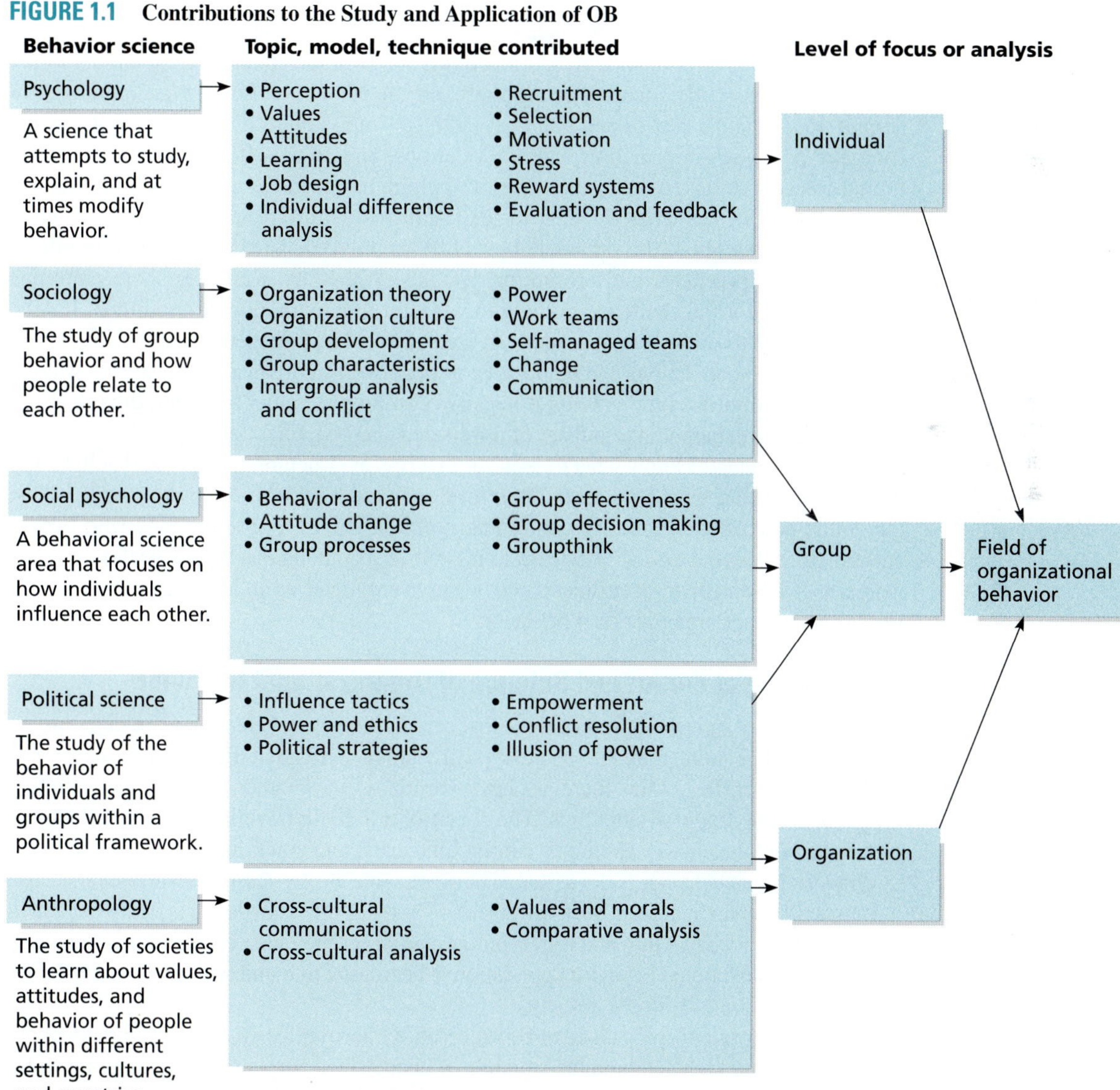

To help you learn how to manage individuals and groups as resources of organizations, this book focuses on *the behavior of individuals and groups, organizational structure and job design, and processes.* Developing the model presented in this book required the use of several assumptions. These assumptions are explained briefly in the following paragraphs, which precede the model.[6]

Structure and Processes Affect Organizational Behavior and the Emergent Culture

structure
Blueprint that indicates how people and jobs are grouped together in an organization. Structure is illustrated by an organization chart.

processes
Activities that breathe life into organization structure. Common processes are communication, decision making, socialization, and career development.

An organization's **structure** is the formal pattern of how its people and jobs are grouped. Structure often is illustrated by an organization chart. **Processes** are activities that give life to the organization chart. Communication, decision making, and organization development are examples of processes in organizations. Sometimes, understanding process problems such as breakdowns in communication and decision making will result in a more accurate understanding of organizational behavior than will simply examining structural arrangements.

The pattern of basic assumptions used by individuals and groups to deal with the organization and its environment is called its *culture*. In straightforward terms, the organization's culture is its personality, atmosphere, or "feel." The culture of an organization defines appropriate behavior and bonds; it motivates individuals; and it governs the way a company processes information, internal relations, and values. It functions at all levels from the subconscious to the visible. A firm's culture has been likened to one of those inkblots in which we see what we want to see.[7] A firm's culture results in shared thoughts, feelings, and talk about the organization.[8] Nike employees share norms about the dress code, business practices, and promotion systems. Wal-Mart associates share emotions about working for the chain and coming to work on time with a positive attitude. It's the sharing that bonds employees together and creates a feeling of togetherness.[9]

Cultures of organizations can be positive or negative. An organization's culture is positive if it helps improve productivity. A negative culture can hinder behavior, disrupt group effectiveness, and hamper the impact of a well-designed organization.

Effective managers know what to look for in terms of structure, process, and culture and how to understand what they find. Therefore, managers must develop diagnostic skills; they must be trained to identify conditions symptomatic of a problem requiring further attention. Problem indicators include declining profits, declining quantity or quality of work, increases in absenteeism or tardiness, and negative employee attitudes. Each of these problems is an issue of organizational behavior.

The Blending of the Art and Science of Organizational Behavior

There is no set of universal prescriptions that can predict every behavior, team outcome, or organizational phenomenon. People are typically unique and unpredictable in some aspects of their behavior. In physics there are laws, formulas, and mathematical procedures that apply to a wide range of situations. The speed of a vehicle traveling down a hill can be calculated, and the answer applies to similar hills, cars, and conditions.

Organizational behavior is not as stable or predictable as physics. OB is different because it deals with human beings in work settings. The body of OB knowledge is being expanded by researchers as they study and report on individual, group, and organizational behavior. The art of organizational behavior application is beginning to blend with empirically-based research.

Managers carry out roles that can be successfully accomplished if they skillfully apply the best available knowledge to the situation at hand. These views of the work of management suggest that art and science can be blended to solve problems. Therefore, effectively

OB AND YOUR CAREER

Research and Managers: Perfect Together!

Many managers make decisions based on intuition and "gut feel." Some of these same managers avoid or undervalue suggestions and tips that originate from empirical studies conducted by researchers from such entities as business schools and/or consulting practices. Although we see the value of intuition, we also feel that science can help managers make better decisions at the workplace. Examples of research findings include:

1. Goal setting is an effective way to improve employee performance.
2. Structured interviews (i.e., ask the same job-related questions of each candidate, use benchmark scoring, etc.) have been found to be more valid than unstructured job interviews.
3. Intelligence is a good predictor of job performance.

What's the bottom line? New and experienced managers alike can be more successful if they take the time to learn and apply some of the key research findings from the management and organizational behavior literatures. Such articles can be found with a few keyword searches using a university library business database or a search engine like Google Scholar. One tip is to look for recent summary articles that review the management and organizational behavior research over the past 10 years or so. Get ahead by being informed!

Sources: John Humphreys, Jennifer Oyler, Mildred Pryor, and Stephanie Haden, "Lost in Translation: From B-School to Business," *The Journal of Business Strategy*, 31, no. 2, (2010): 13–17; Robert J. Grossman, "Close the Gap Between Research and Practice," *HRMagazine*, November 2009, pp. 31–36; Sara L. Rynes, Tamara L. Giluk, and Kenneth G. Brown, "The Very Separate Worlds of Academic and Practitioner Periodicals in Human Resource Management: Implications for Evidence-Based Management," *Academy of Management Journal* 50, no. 5 (2007), pp. 987–1008.

managing in any situation or organization requires the deft touch of an artist and excellent execution of specific and proven behaviors. As the OB and Your Career above suggests, managers who ignore science or art are not likely to be effective or respected.[10]

To be and remain effective, managers must apply knowledge. The application and execution of knowledge can be designated as *competencies*. Included in these important competencies are intellectual capability, a systems orientation, interpersonal skills, flexibility, and self-motivation.

A Model for Managing Organizations: Behavior, Structure, and Processes

The Organization's Environment

Within a society, many factors influence an organization, and management must be responsive to them. Every organization must respond to the needs of its customers or clients, to legal and political constraints, and to economic and technological changes. Environmental forces interact with organization factors.

Economic and market circumstances and technological innovations make up an organization's environment, as do federal, state, and local legislation and political, social, and cultural conditions external to the organization. Together, these components of an environment influence how an organization operates and also how it is structured.

Managers increasingly work in an unpredictable economic environment. It is now important for managers to respond quickly to changing economic conditions in other countries. Also, the dramatic and unexpected consequences of technological innovations require astute management attention and action. For example, since the transistor was invented in 1947, digital technology has been evolving faster and computing devices are getting smaller, cheaper, and more powerful. These devices, combined with databases, multimedia interfaces, and software, are affecting every profession, company, and business practice.

Increased government regulations have affected management's actions in production and employment practices. Foreign trade tariffs, occupational safety and health guidelines, and equal employment opportunities influence the way a firm conducts business.

Behavior within Organizations

The Individual

Individual performance is the foundation of organizational performance. Understanding individual behavior is therefore critical for effective management, as illustrated in the following account:

> Ted has been a field representative for a major drug manufacturer since he graduated from college seven years ago. He makes daily calls on physicians, hospital, clinics, and pharmacies. Ted's sales of his firm's major drugs have increased, and he has won three national sales awards given by the organization. Yesterday, Ted was promoted to sales manager for a seven-state region. He'll no longer be selling but instead will be managing 15 other representatives. His sales team includes men and women, Caucasians, Hispanics, Blacks, and Asians. Ted accepted the promotion because he believes he knows how to motivate and lead salespeople. He comments, "I know the personality of the salesperson. They are special people. I know their values and attitudes and what it takes to motivate them. I know I can motivate a sales force."

In his job, Ted will be trying to maximize the individual performances of 15 sales representatives. In doing so, he will be dealing with several facets of individual behavior.

Individual Characteristics Because organizational performance depends on individual performance, managers such as Ted must have more than a passing knowledge of the determinants of individual performance. Psychology and social psychology contribute relevant knowledge about the relationships among attitudes, perceptions, personality, values, and individual performance. Learning to manage cultural diversity, such as that found among Ted's 15 sales representatives, has become increasingly important in recent years. Managers can't ignore the need to acquire and act on knowledge of the individual characteristics of both their subordinates and themselves.

Individual Motivation Motivation and ability to work interact to determine performance. Motivation theory attempts to explain and predict how individuals' behavior is aroused, sustained, and stopped. Unlike Ted Johnson, not all managers and behavioral scientists agree on what is the best theory of motivation. In fact, the complexity of motivation may make an all-encompassing theory of how it occurs impossible. But managers must still try to understand it. They must be concerned with motivation because they must be concerned with performance.

Rewards and Appraisal One of the most powerful influences on individual performance is an organization's reward system. Management can use rewards to increase current employees' performance. It can also use rewards to attract skilled employees to the organization.

Performance appraisals, paychecks, raises, and bonuses are important aspects of the reward system, but they aren't the only aspects. Ted makes this point clear in the preceding account when he states, "I know what it takes to motivate them." Performance of the work itself can provide employees with rewards, particularly if job performance leads to a sense of personal responsibility, autonomy, and meaningfulness. These intrinsic rewards are also supplemented with extrinsic rewards, or what an organization, a manager, or a group can provide a person in terms of monetary and nonmonetary factors.

Groups and Interpersonal Influence

Group behavior and interpersonal influence are also powerful forces affecting organizational performance, as the following account shows:

> During her two and one-half years as a teller in a small-town bank in Fort Smith, Arkansas, Kelly developed close friendships with her co-workers. These friendships existed outside the job as well. Two months ago Kelly was promoted to branch manager. She was excited about the new challenge. She began the job with a great deal of optimism and believed her friends would be genuinely happy for her and supportive of her efforts. But since she became branch manager, things haven't been quite the same. Kelly can't spend nearly as much time with her friends because she's often away from the branch attending management meetings at the main office. Kelly senses that some of her friends have been acting a little differently toward her lately.
>
> Recently Kelly said, "I didn't know that being a part of the management team could make that much difference. Frankly, I never really thought about it. I guess I was naïve. I'm getting a totally different perspective on the business and have to deal with problems I never knew about."

Kelly's promotion has made her a member of more than one group. In addition to being part of her old group of friends at the branch, she's also a member of the management team. She's finding out that group behavior and expectations have a strong impact on individual behavior and interpersonal influence.

Group Behavior Groups form because of managerial action and because of individual efforts. Managers create work groups to carry out assigned jobs and tasks. Such groups, created by managerial decisions, are termed *formal groups.* The group that Kelly manages at her branch is a group of this kind.

Groups also form as a consequence of employees' actions. Such groups, termed *informal groups,* develop around common interests and friendships. Kelly's bowling group is an informal group. Although not a part of the organization, groups of this kind can affect organizational and individual performance. The effect can be positive or negative, depending on the group members' intentions. If the group at Kelly's branch decided informally to slow the work pace, this norm would exert pressure on individuals who wanted to remain a part of the group. Effective managers recognize the consequences of individuals' needs for affiliation.

Intergroup Behavior and Conflict As groups function and interact with other groups, each develops a unique set of characteristics, including structure, cohesiveness, roles, norms, and processes. The group in essence creates its own culture. As a result, groups may cooperate or compete with other groups, and intergroup competition can lead to conflict. If the management of Kelly's bank instituted an incentive program with cash bonuses to the branch bringing in the most new customers, this might lead to competition and conflict among the branches. Although conflict among groups can have beneficial results for an organization, too much or the wrong kinds of intergroup conflict can have negative results. Thus, managing intergroup conflict is an important aspect of managing organizational behavior.

Power and Politics Power is the ability to get someone to do something you want done or to make things happen in the way you want them to happen. Many people in our society are uncomfortable with the concept of power. Some are deeply offended by it. This is because the essence of power is control over others. To many Americans and a growing number of people around the world, this is an offensive thought.

But power does exist in organizations. Managers derive power from both organizational and individual sources. Kelly has power by virtue of her position in the formal hierarchy of the bank. She controls performance evaluations and salary increases. However, she may

OB AT WORK Raising the Bar on Managerial Ethics

In the wake of corporate and financial scandals, and a persistent recession that has devastated the U.S. job market, corporate leaders and managers have received their share of the blame. This is partly due to the perception that many leaders placed greed and short-term profits well before the needs of their key stakeholders (e.g., employees, customers, and the communities in which they operate). There seems to be a shift in public sentiment over the past few years in that businesses should focus on more than just making a profit. This shift has led to an increase in negative press about the lack of professionalism in the management profession. Caught in this negative fallout are MBA programs that have been criticized for not doing enough to create managers and leaders who take a more humanistic and ethical approach to leading and managing organizations. Students who graduate with MBAs have been criticized for not maintaining strong ethical standards when they reach positions of power in companies.

To address these negative perceptions and critics, in June 2009, a team of Harvard Business School (HBS) graduating MBA students led by Max Anderson and Peter Escher developed an "MBA Oath." The following is an excerpt from the oath:

> As a manager, my purpose is to serve the greater good by bringing people and resources together to create value that no single individual can build alone. Therefore I will seek a course that enhances the value my enterprise can create for society over the long term.

Anderson and Escher's original goal was to collect 100 signatures (or 10 percent) from members of the HBS graduating class but instead collected more than 500 signatures (over 50 percent). Supported by Harvard's dean, the MBA Oath (also referred to as a "Hippocratic oath for managers") concept is spreading to several other business schools throughout the United States and internationally.

Will MBA oaths help change the "greed is good" thinking that has been part of many managers' thinking for many decades? It is too early to tell. The oath seems to underscore the idea that "maximizing shareholder value" may contribute to managerial decision-making that leads to short-term opportunism but damages the long-term prospects, health, and profitability of the organizations. This opportunism seems to be giving way to a more humanistic approach to running enterprises. Perhaps, managers and leaders will reject the "greed is good" mantra and instead support a more ethical and integrity-driven approach to management.

Sources: http://blogs.hbr.org/cs/2009/06/why_we_created_the_mba_oath.html (accessed on June 26, 2010); Michael A. Pirson and Paul R. Lawrence, "Humanism in Business – Towards a Paradigm Shift?" *Journal of Business*, 93, no. 4 (2010), pp. 553–565; "Forswearing Greed: A Hippocratic Oath for Managers," *The Economist*, June 6, 2009, p. 66; Michael Lewis, "Michael Lewis on Wall Street Oath-Taking," *Businessweek*, June 14, 2010, p. 1; Philip Delves, "A Worthy Attempt at Swearing to a Higher Standard," *Financial Times*, April 22, 2010, p. 12.

also have power because her co-workers respect and admire her abilities and expertise. Managers must become comfortable with the concept of power as a reality in organizations and managerial roles.

Leadership Leaders exist within all organizations. They may be found in formal groups, like Kelly's management team at the bank, or in informal groups. They may be managers or nonmanagers. The importance of effective leadership for obtaining individual, group, and organizational performance is so critical that there has been much effort to determine the causes of such leadership. Some people believe that effective leadership depends on traits and certain behaviors, separately and in combination; other people believe that one leadership style is effective in all situations; still others believe that each situation requires a special leadership style.

Quality and leadership concepts have been found to be inseparable. Without effective leadership practices, instilling concern about customer-focused quality is difficult, if not impossible. The OB at Work feature above discusses how some future business leaders are broadening their personal definitions of effectiveness and success.

The Structure and Design of Organizations

To achieve organizational effectiveness, managers must clearly understand the organizational structure. Viewing an organization chart on a piece of paper or frame on a wall, we see only a configuration of positions, job duties, and lines of authority among the parts of an organization. However, organizational structure can be far more complex, as the following account shows:

> Dan was appointed vice president of quality at a small manufacturing shop in Orange, New Jersey. He spent about three months studying the organization that produces generator parts sold throughout the United States, Canada, Mexico, Poland, Hungary, and Russia. Dan wants to instill more of a teamwork concept and an interest in quality improvement. This would be quite a change from the present rigid departmental structure that now exists in the company. His unit leaders are Hispanic, Italian, German, and Vietnamese. They each have voiced opinions that management discriminates against them and isn't ethnically aware. Dan wants to correct this perception and wants each unit leader to be a part of his team. He must change perceptions, redesign the organization, develop a team spirit, and produce high-quality products in an increasingly competitive market.

An organization's structure is the formal pattern of activities and interrelationships among the various subunits of the organization. This book discusses two important aspects of organizational structure: job design and organizational design.

Job Design

Job design refers to the process by which managers specify the contents, methods, and relationships of jobs to satisfy both organizational and individual requirements. Dan must define the content and duties of the unit leader's position and the relationship of the position to each member of his team.

Organizational Design

Organizational design refers to the overall organizational structure. Dan plans to change the philosophy and orientation of the teams. This effort will create a new *structure* of tasks, authority, and interpersonal relationships that he believes will channel the behavior of individuals and groups toward improved quality performance.

The Process of Organizations

Certain behavioral processes give life to an organizational structure. When these processes don't function well, unfortunate problems arise, as this account shows:

> Once Sandra completed her MBA, she was more positive than ever that marketing would be her life's work. Because of her excellent academic record, she received several outstanding job offers. She accepted an offer from one of the nation's largest consulting firms, believing that this job would allow her to gain experience in several areas of marketing and to engage in a variety of exciting work. Her last day on campus, she told her favorite professor, "This has got to be one of the happiest days of my life, getting such a great career opportunity."
>
> Recently, while visiting the college placement office, the professor was surprised to hear that Sandra had told the placement director that she was looking for another job. Since she'd been with the consulting company less than a year, the professor was somewhat surprised. He called Sandra to find out why she wanted to change jobs. She told him, "I guess you can say my first experience with the real world was a 'reality shock.' All day long, I sit and talk on the phone, asking questions and checking off the answers. In graduate school, I was trained to be a manager, but here I'm doing what any high school graduate can do. I talked to my boss, and he said that all employees have to pay their dues. Well, why didn't they tell me this while they were recruiting me? A little bit of accurate communication would have gone along way."

This book discusses two behavioral processes that contribute to effective organizational performance: communication and decision making.

Communication

Organizational survival is related to management's ability to receive, transmit, and act on information. The communication process links the organization to its environment as well as to its parts. Information flows to and from the organization and within the organization. Information integrates the activities within the organization. Sandra's problem arose because the information that flowed *from* the organization was different from the information that flowed *within* the organization.

Decision Making

The quality of decision making in an organization depends on selecting proper goals and identifying means for achieving them. With good integration of *behavior* and *structural* factors, management can increase the probability that high-quality decisions are made. Sandra's experience illustrates inconsistent decision making by different organizational units (human resources and marketing) in hiring new employees. Organizations rely on individual decisions as well as group decisions. Effective management requires knowledge about both types of decisions.

Because managerial decisions affect people's lives and well-being, ethics play a major role.[11] Was Sandra provided with realistic and truthful information about the job? If not, was there a breach of ethics on the part of the recruiter? Managers have power by virtue of their positions, so the potential for unethical decision making is present. With all the newspaper and TV accounts of scandals around the world in business, government, medicine, politics, and the law, there's evidence that ethics in terms of decision making need serious attention.

Ethics suggest that when faced with a problem, situation, or opportunity requiring a choice among several alternatives, managers must evaluate their decision on what course to follow as good or bad, right or wrong, ethical or unethical.[12] Conflicts between an individual manager's personal moral philosophy and values and the culture and value of an organization regularly arise and make decision making a difficult endeavor.

Managerial decision making is permeated by ethical issues. Managers have power and authority; when these factors exist, there is potential for wrong and right, good and evil. Among the indications that managerial decisions are linked to ethics are that managers:[13]

- Make decisions that affect the lives, careers, and well-being of people.
- Make decisions involving the allocation of limited resources.
- Design, implement, and evaluate rules, policies, programs, and procedures.
- Display to others their moral and personal values when they make decisions.

Examples of managerial decision making and their link to ethics and values will become obvious throughout this book. Skilled managers consider ethics to be an important factor to consider when making choices that affect individuals, groups, and organizations.[14] A challenge that managers face is creating a work environment that is ethical, value centered, and performance driven. Some managers unfortunately have concluded that they must make trade-offs. We suggest that being concerned with ethics, telling the truth, and adopting a style that displays integrity in every decision can become the rule, the style—an integral part of managing people.

Managers and others who have interests in whether organizations perform effectively can focus on one or all of three perspectives. The most basic level, *individual effectiveness,* emphasizes the task performance of specific employees or members of the organization.

Perspectives on Effectiveness

Managers routinely assess individual effectiveness through performance evaluation processes to determine who should receive salary increases, promotions, and other rewards available in the organization.

Individuals seldom work alone, in isolation from others in the organization. Usually employees work in groups, necessitating yet another perspective on effectiveness: *group effectiveness*. In some instances, group effectiveness is simply the sum of the contributions of all its members. For example, a group of chemists working alone on unrelated projects would be effective to the extent that each individual scientist is effective. In other instances, group effectiveness is more than the sum of individual contributions (e.g., an assembly line that produces a product or service that combines the contributions of each individual working on the line). The term *synergy* refers to instances when the sum of individual contributions exceeds the simple summation of them.

The third perspective is *organizational effectiveness*. Organizations consist of individuals and groups; therefore, organizational effectiveness consists of individual and group effectiveness. But organizational effectiveness is more than the sum of individual and group effectiveness. Through synergistic effects, organizations obtain higher levels of effectiveness than the sum of their parts. In fact, the rationale for organizations as a means for doing society's work is that they can do more work than is possible through individual effort.[15]

Figure 1.2 reveals the relationships among three perspectives on effectiveness. The connecting arrows imply that group effectiveness depends on individual effectiveness, while organizational effectiveness depends on individual and group effectiveness. The exact relationships among the three perspectives vary depending on such factors as the type of organization, the work it does, and the technology used in doing that work. Figure 1.3 recognizes the three perspectives' synergistic effects. Thus, group effectiveness is larger than the sum of individuals' effectiveness because of the synergies realized through joint efforts.

Management's job is to identify the *causes* of organizational, group, and individual effectiveness. The distinction between causes of effectiveness and indicators of effectiveness can be difficult for both managers and researchers.[16] The term *effectiveness* derives from the term *effect,* and we use the term in the context of cause-and-effect relationships. As Figure 1.3 shows, each level of effectiveness can be considered a variable caused by other variables. For example, a person's motivation, ability, skill, knowledge, attitude, and stress level cause him or her to be effective. There are, of course, many other factors that cause an individual to be effective. The variables in Figure 1.3 are only a sample for illustrative purposes.

Management and organizational behavior literature has reported various theories and research on causes of effectiveness at each of the three levels of analysis. For example, causes of individual effectiveness include ability, skill, knowledge, attitude, motivation, and stress. These individual differences account for differences in effectiveness in individual

FIGURE 1.2
Three Perspectives on Effectiveness

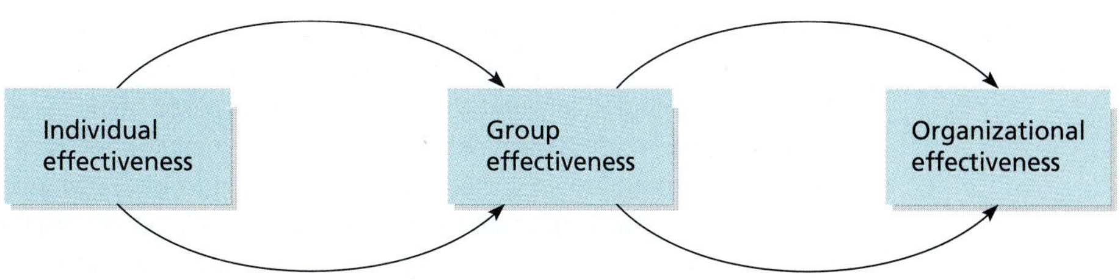

FIGURE 1.3
Causes of Effectiveness

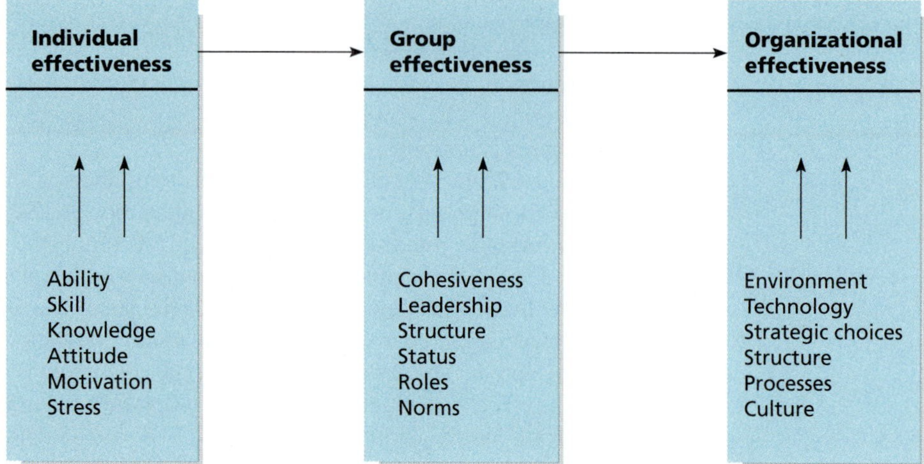

performance. Some of the more usual causes of differences in group and organizational effectiveness are also noted in Figure 1.3.[17] These and other potential causes of effectiveness are discussed at length in subsequent chapters. But the reality of organizational life is that there are few unambiguous cause-and-effect relationships. In most instances, evaluation judgments must take into account multiple causes and circumstances.[18]

How then can managers increase and maintain individual, group, and organizational effectiveness? The following section addresses this question by describing the nature of managerial work.

The Nature of Managerial Work

Many individual writers (far too many to survey completely) have contributed theories describing what managers do or prescribing what they should do.[19] Here we'll rely on the idea of a group of writers who constitute the Classical School of Management.[20] We refer to these writers as *classical* because they were the first to describe managerial work. Writers of the Classical School proposed that managerial work consists of distinct yet interrelated *functions,* which taken together constitute the *managerial process*. The view that management should be defined, described, and analyzed in terms of what managers (functions and processes) do has prevailed to this day, but with considerable modification as management functions and processes change in response to changing times and circumstances.

Henry Mintzberg's influential study identified three primary and overlapping managerial roles: interpersonal role, decisional role, and informational role.[21] Each role has several related activities that distinguish it from the others. Interpersonal role activities clearly involve the manager with other people both inside and outside the organization. Decisional role activities involve the manager in making decisions about operational matters, resource allocation, and negotiations with the organization's constituencies. The informational role involves the manager as a receiver and sender of information to a variety of individuals and institutions.

The concept of management developed here is based on the assumption that the necessity for managing arises whenever work is specialized and undertaken by two or more persons. Under such circumstances, the specialized work must be *coordinated,* creating the necessity for managerial work. The nature of managerial work is, then, to coordinate the work of *individuals, groups,* and *organizations* by performing four management functions: *planning,*

FIGURE 1.4 How Managers Achieve Effectiveness

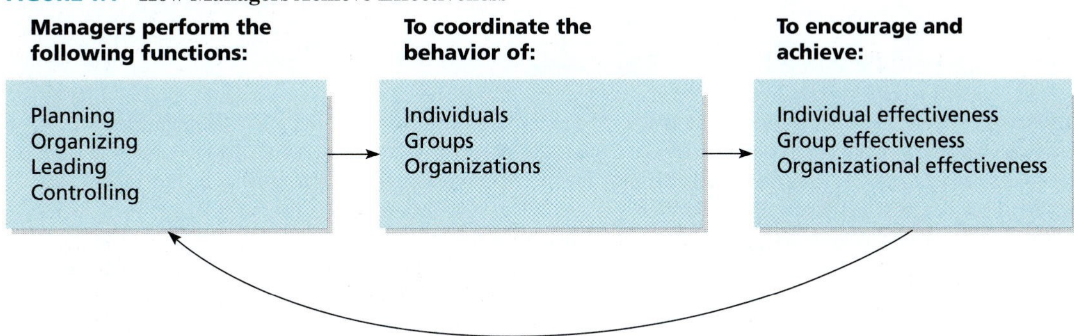

organizing, leading, and *controlling.* Figure 1.4 depicts management's contribution to effectiveness.

The list of management functions can be increased to include other functions, but these four can be defined with sufficient precision to differentiate them and, at the same time, to include others that management writers have proposed. For example, some managers and organizations include functions such as decision making, staffing, coordinating, implementing, and executing. Remember, management and organizational behavior aren't exact sciences with uniform language and definitions. The various definitions of *management* reflect the specific expectations of the people who practice management in specific organizations.[22]

Although the list we propose might be arbitrary, managers at all levels of the organization generally perform these functions. The relative importance of one function vis-à-vis another function differs depending on where the manager is in the organization and what problems and issues the manager faces. But the ability to discern the relative importance of planning, organizing, leading, and controlling may distinguish effective managers from ineffective managers.[23]

The work of a manager is captured in some degree in the next OB at Work feature. It suggests that hectic, frantic, and somewhat chaotic times are what managers know quite a bit about. The manager's day is filled with challenges and with searching for ways to improve the effectiveness of employees.

Planning Effective Performance

The planning function includes defining the ends to be achieved and determining *appropriate means to achieve the defined ends.* The necessity of this function follows from the nature of organizations as purposive (end-seeking) entities. Planning activities can be complex or simple, implicit or explicit, impersonal or personal. For example, a sales manager forecasting demand for the firm's major product may rely on complex econometric models or casual conversations with salespeople in the field.

Planning involves specifying not only where the organization is going but also how it's to get there. In specific terms, alternatives must be analyzed and evaluated in terms of criteria that follow from the mission goals. Thus, managers by their own decisions can affect how they and their organizations will be evaluated. They determine what ends are legitimate and, therefore, what criteria are relevant.[24] And once appropriate means are determined, the next managerial function—organizing—must be undertaken.

Organizing Effective Performance

The organizing function includes all managerial activities that translate required planned activities into a structure of tasks and authority. In a practical sense, the organizing function

OB AT WORK Another Day as a Manager

Hunter (a substituted name) manages a small office that includes an office manager, a business development officer, a researcher analyst, an information technology specialist, and a student intern. The business produces content for books, training programs (traditional and e-learning), and consulting services. The consulting services are provided by individual experts, who serve on the consulting board of the company.

Hunter's typical day is long, 8:00 a.m. to 7:00 p.m. More than 70 percent of his time is spent on the phone, on the computer, or in meetings. He is involved in at least 300 activities a day (e.g., reading and responding to 75 e-mails, talking to 15 different people on the phone, listening to issues or problems brought up by his office colleagues). Variety and interruptions are the norm.

There is little time for Hunter to read reports, white papers, books, or advertising materials placed in his inbox or sent to his e-mail. Reading up on and studying the competition or thinking about the market is a critical activity. Hunter can squeeze in quiet time for such analysis only by coming into the office an hour early. By evening, he is tired after a hectic, frenetic day. Sitting down to read and think when he is tired hasn't been productive.

Hunter relies on social interaction and prefers talking when carrying out his management roles. He is accountable to the owners and the board members of the firm. They want a steady stream of written reports that are not Hunter's favorite work chore. He appreciates the need for written reports, but the 300 daily activities don't leave much time to write, read, and revise reports.

Hunter is so immersed in his daily activities that he loses track of time and commitments. He relies on the office manager to keep him pointed in the right direction and to attend scheduled meetings.

Planning, organizing, leading, and controlling are functions that Hunter knows must be performed. He feels guilty about not systematically fulfilling these functions. He also complains to his office colleagues about not interacting enough with customers, the owners, and other managers. His family and friends indicate that Hunter is just not as available as he once was when he didn't have the responsibility to make his firm a success.

This brief description of a typical manager of a small organization suggests that Mintzberg's classic study years ago still is an accurate portrayal of managers. The interpersonal, decisional, and informational roles performed by managers are hectic, frantic, and challenging. Finding ways to more systematically manage and cope with these role responsibilities is the path of improved effectiveness.

involves (1) designing the responsibility and authority of each individual job and (2) determining which of these jobs will be grouped in specific departments. For example, managers of an engineering firm must determine what each engineer should do and what group each engineer will be assigned to. The organizing function's outcome is the organization structure.

The organization structure consists of many different individuals and groups performing different activities. These different activities must be integrated into a coordinated whole.[25] It's management's responsibility to devise integrating methods and processes. If the differences among jobs and departments aren't too great, then the simple exercise of authority is sufficient to integrate the differences. For example, a small yogurt shop's manager can easily integrate order takers' work by issuing directives. But the manager of a multiproduct, multidivisional organization must rely on more complex cross-functional teams, product and customer services managers, and electronic communication.[26]

Leading Effective Performance

The leading function involves the manager in close day-to-day contact with individuals and groups. Thus, the leading function is uniquely personal and interpersonal. Although planning and organizing provide guidelines and directives in the form of plans, job descriptions, organization charts, and policies, it's people who do the work. And people are variable entities. They have unique needs, ambitions, personalities, and attitudes. Each person perceives the workplace and his or her job uniquely. Managers must take into account these unique perceptions and behaviors and somehow direct them toward common purposes. One thoughtful and sensitive observer of leadership behavior has encouraged managers to become more knowledgeable about human psychology as a means to more effective performance.[27]

Leading involves day-to-day interactions between managers and their subordinates. In these interactions, the full panorama of human behavior is evident. Individuals work, play, communicate, compete, accept and reject others, join groups, leave groups, receive rewards, and cope with stress. Of all the management functions, leading is the most human oriented. It's not surprising that the overwhelming bulk of organizational behavior theory and research relates to this function. And while much of the literature and conventional wisdom affirms the importance of leadership, we must recognize that there's evidence suggesting that leadership's importance is overrated.[28]

Leaders in executive positions represent the organization to its external constituencies. In this role, effective executive leaders use words and symbols to express the organization's abstract ideals and what it stands for. The organization's mission statement provides a starting point for performing this leadership role. But without the ability to use powerful language and metaphors, the executive leader will fail even if she has effective interpersonal skills.[29]

Controlling Effective Performance

The controlling function includes activities that managers undertake to ensure that actual outcomes are consistent with planned outcomes. Managers undertake control to determine *whether* intended results are achieved and if they aren't, *why* not. The conclusions managers reach because of their controlling activities are that the planning function was (and is) faulty or that the organizing function was (and is) faulty, or both. Controlling is, then, the completion of a logical sequence. The activities that constitute controlling include employee selection and placement, materials inspection, performance evaluation, financial statement analysis, and other well-recognized managerial techniques.

The controlling function involves explicit consideration of effectiveness at all three levels: individual, group, and organizational. Performance evaluation involves comparisons of actual personnel performance against standards of performance. Managers judge as effective those employees who meet performance standards. Likewise, when supervisors focus on organizational groups such as production, sales, and engineering departments, they make judgments about whether these units have performed as expected (whether they've been effective). And at the highest level of performance, top managers judge the effectiveness of organizations.

At every level, managers of organizations have the primary responsibility for attaining effective performance. We've seen that they can meet this responsibility by practicing with skill the four functions of management to identify the cause of effectiveness—accentuate the positive ones and eliminate the negative ones. But we must now think about the concept of effectiveness per se. What is it? How can we know it when we see it?

Three Ways to Think about Effectiveness

Thus far, we've assumed a definition of *effectiveness*. But effectiveness means different things to different people, whether in a theoretical or practical sense. Differences in its meaning reflect one's adherence to the goal approach, the systems theory approach, or the stakeholder approach.[30] Managers must be able to use each of these approaches to effectiveness when appropriate.

Goal Approach to Effectiveness

goal approach to effectiveness
Perspective on effectiveness that emphasizes the central role of goal achievement as a criterion for assessing effectiveness.

The **goal approach** to defining and evaluating effectiveness is the oldest and most widely used evaluation approach.[31] According to this approach, an organization exists to accomplish goals. An early and influential practitioner and writer in management and organizational behavior stated, "What we mean by effectiveness . . . is the accomplishment of recognized objectives of cooperative effort. The degree of accomplishment indicates the degree of effectiveness."[32] The idea that organizations, as well as individuals and groups, should be evaluated in terms of goal accomplishment has widespread commonsense and practical appeal. The goal approach reflects purposefulness, rationality, and achievement—the fundamental tenets of contemporary Western societies.

Many management practices are based on the goal approach. One widely used practice is management by objectives. According to this practice, managers specify in advance the goals that they expect their subordinates to accomplish and then evaluate periodically the degree to which they accomplish them. The actual specifics of management by objectives vary from case to case. In some cases, the manager and subordinate(s) discuss the objectives and attempt to reach mutual agreement. In other instances, the manager simply assigns the goals. Management by objectives can be useful whenever there's a strong relationship between job behavior and a measurable outcome, the objective.

The goal approach, for all its appeal and apparent simplicity, has problems.[33] A few recognized difficulties include the following:

1. *Some goals are hard to measure*. Goal achievement isn't readily measurable for organizations that don't produce tangible outputs. For example, a public college's goal is to provide a good education at a fair price. The question is: How would we know whether the college reaches that goal? What's a good education? What's a fair price?
2. *Conflicting goals weaken their impact*. Organizations attempt to achieve more than one goal, but achieving one goal often precludes or diminishes their ability to achieve other goals. A firm states that its goal is to maximize profit and to provide absolutely safe working conditions. These two goals are in conflict because one is achieved at the expense of the other.
3. *Official goals are often not followed*. The very existence of a common set of "official" goals to which all members are committed is questionable. Various researchers have noted the difficulty of obtaining consensus among managers as to their organization's specific goals.[34]

A narrow view of effectiveness defines it as "the financial viability of an organization."[35] A financially viable organization can pay its bills as they're due; the more effective organization will have funds in reserve. This view's proponents state that even though it's narrow, it is still useful because it overcomes the limitations of the wider idea of the goal approach. For example, measuring financial viability is relatively easy compared with measuring management's "real" goals. Return on assets and return on equity are straightforward and readily available measures of firms' financial viability. Nonbusiness organizations have similar measures. Educational institutions can measure financial viability as revenue per student; government agencies can measure it as revenue per employee.[36] The idea that organizational effectiveness can be defined and measured simply has considerable appeal.

The goal approach exerts a powerful influence on the development of management and organizational behavior theory and practice. It's easy to say that managers should achieve the organization's goals. It's much more difficult to know how to do this. The alternative to the goal approach is the systems theory approach. Through systems theory, the concept of effectiveness can be defined in broader terms that enable managers to understand the causes of individual, group, and organizational effectiveness.

Systems Theory Approach to Effectiveness

system
A grouping of elements that individually establish relationships with each other and that interact with their environment both as individuals and as a collective.

The term *system* is used in everyday conversations. A variety of meanings and interpretations are used to describe accounting systems, inventory control systems, a car's ignition system, an ecological system, and the U.S. tax system. Each system consists of elements or characteristics that interact. Thus, a **system** is a grouping of elements that individually establish relationships with each other and that interact with their environment both as individuals and as a collective.[37] Systems theorists propose that systems can be categorized three ways: (1) conceptual systems (a language), (2) concrete systems (machines), and (3) abstract systems (culture of an organization).

Managers in organizations use the notion of a system to view their internal and external world and how the parts relate and interact with each other. By viewing the individuals, groups, structure, and processes of organizations in terms of a system, managers are able to identify common and uncommon themes that help explain the behavior and effectiveness of people. Identification of themes or patterns is important because it helps explain how effective an individual, group, or entire organization is in terms of goals.[38]

Systems theory enables us to describe organizations' internal and external behavior. Internally we can see how and why people inside organizations perform their individual and group tasks. Externally we can assess organizations' transactions with other organizations and institutions. All organizations acquire resources from the larger environments of which they're part and, in turn, provide the goods and services demanded by the larger environment. Managers must deal simultaneously with the internal and external aspects of organizational behavior. This essentially complex process can be simplified, for analytical purposes, by employing the basic concepts of systems theory.

In the context of systems theory, the organization is one element of a number of elements interacting interdependently. The flow of inputs and outputs is the basic starting point in describing the organization. In the simplest terms, the organization takes resources (inputs) from the larger system (environment), processes these resources, and returns them in changed form (output). Figure 1.5 displays the fundamental elements of the organization as a system.

Systems theory also stresses the organization's connection to the larger system of which it is a part. Every organization is part of an industry (a larger system), a society (a yet larger system), and, increasingly, a global economy (perhaps the largest system of all). All these systems make demands on their parts, and they include more than simple demands for products of acceptable quality and quantity. Organizations must also satisfy the demands that their actions contribute to viable environments by promoting clean air and water, internal national stability by rebuilding U.S. cities, and global political stability by investing in the economies of developing countries. Thus, the organization can't simply produce a product or service to satisfy its customers; it must also produce actions and behaviors to satisfy other important components of the larger environment, the larger systems.

FIGURE 1.5
The Basic Elements of a System

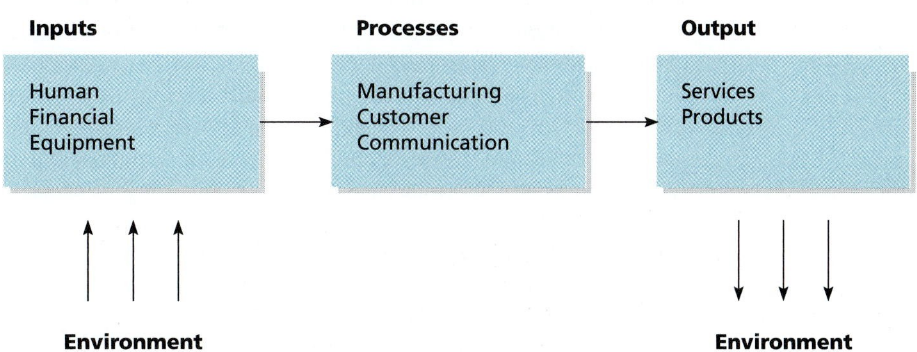

Systems Theory and Feedback

The concept of the organization as a system that's related to a larger system introduces the importance of feedback. As noted already, the organization depends on the environment not only for its inputs but also for the acceptance of its outputs. Thus, the organization must develop means for adjusting to environmental demands. The means for adjustment are information channels that enable the organization to recognize these demands. For example, in business organizations, market research is an important feedback mechanism.

In simplest terms, *feedback* refers to information that reflects the outcomes of an act or a series of acts by an individual, group, or organization. Throughout this text, we'll see how important feedback is for reinforcing learning and developing personality, group behavior, and leadership. Systems theory emphasizes the importance of responding to the content of the feedback information.

Examples of the Input–Output Cycle

The firm has two major categories of inputs: human and natural resources. Human inputs consist of the people who work in the firm: operating, staff, and managerial personnel. They contribute their time and energy to the organization in exchange for wages and other rewards, tangible and intangible. Natural resources consist of the nonhuman inputs to be processed or to be used in combination with the human element to provide other resources. A steel mill uses people and blast furnaces (along with other tools and machinery) to process iron ore into steel and steel products. An auto manufacturer takes steel, rubber, plastics, and fabrics and (in combination with people, tools, and equipment) makes cars. A firm survives as long as its output is purchased in the market in quantities at prices that enable it to replenish its depleted stock of inputs.

A university uses its resources to teach students, to perform research, and to provide technical information to society. A university's survival depends on its ability to attract students' tuition and taxpayers' dollars in sufficient amounts to pay the salaries of its faculty and staff and the other costs of resources. If a university's output is rejected by the larger environment so that students enroll elsewhere and the government uses tax dollars to support other public endeavors or if a university is guilty of expending too many resources in relation to its output, it will cease to exist. Like a business, a university must provide the right output at the right price if it's to survive.[39]

As a final example we'll describe a hospital in term of systems theory. A hospital's inputs are its professional and administrative staff, equipment, supplies, and patients. Patients are processed by applying medical knowledge and treatment. To the extent that its patients are restored to the level of health consistent with the severity of their disease or injury, the hospital is effective.

Systems theory emphasizes two important considerations: (1) the ultimate survival of organization depends on its ability to adapt to the demands of its environment; and (2) in meeting these demands, the total cycle of input–process–output must be the focus of managerial attention. Therefore, criteria of effectiveness must reflect both considerations and we must define *effectiveness* accordingly. The systems approach accounts for the fact that resources have to be devoted to activities that have little to do with achieving the organization's goal.[40] In other words, adapting to the environment and maintaining the input–process–output flow require that resources be allocated to activities that are only indirectly related to the organizations' primary goal.

Stakeholder Approach to Effectiveness

The application of systems theory concepts to the discussion of organizational effectiveness identifies the importance of the external environment. Systems theory also identifies

stakeholder approach to effectiveness
Perspective that emphasizes the relative importance of different groups' and individuals' interests in an organization.

the importance of achieving a balance among the various parts of the system of which an organization is but one part. In practical and concrete terms, the **stakeholder approach** means achieving balance among the various parts of the system by satisfying the interests of the organization's constituency (all those individuals and groups of individuals who have a stake in the organization).[41] But the goal approach emphasizes that organizations are chartered to accomplish goals.

Individuals and groups of individuals having stakes in an organization include its employees (nonmanagers and managers), customers, stockholders, directors, suppliers, creditors, officials at all levels of government, managers of competitive and cooperative organizations, and the general public. Each of these individuals and groups of individuals expects the organization to behave in ways that benefit them; these expectations may or may not be compatible with those of other individuals and groups. Given that an organization can be judged effective or ineffective depending on who's making the judgment, how can managers ever achieve effectiveness in the sense of satisfying all the claims of the organization's constituencies? The chapter's opening vignette pointed out the challenges that face managers in meeting the diverse needs of different stakeholders.

One approach would be to state that there's no way to determine the relative importance of the constituent claims and that there are as many evaluations of effectiveness as there are individuals making judgments. This relative view assumes that all claims on the organization are valid and that no basis exists for ordering their importance, so no basis exists for making an overall judgment of organizational effectiveness.[42]

How then is management to act? One answer is provided by the idea that each of the stakeholders controls resources that are valuable to the organization. At any point in time, the resources they control are more or less important and the organization is effective to the extent that it satisfies the interest of the group controlling the most important resource.[43] Thus stockholders' interests supersede employees' interests when the organization must acquire equity funds to survive. Or a government regulatory agency's interests supersede stockholders' interests when safety regulations require investment in safe working conditions. This new view can be extended to a concept of the organization as an arena in which the different groups negotiate their claims by developing coalitions capable of combining the power of each member of the coalition. Managers of the organization achieve effectiveness by identifying the most powerful coalitions and satisfying the demands of the most influential members of these coalitions.

Whether the organization is effective when satisfying the most powerful group involves value judgment. And we shouldn't lose sight of the fact that all judgments of effectiveness involve value judgment. To state that we should satisfy the most powerful group at the expense of the least powerful group is to make a personal statement of what's ultimately important. Because many different sources of value judgments exist, we shouldn't expect any final answer to the question, Is the organization effective? Nor should we expect any final answer when the focus is individual and group effectiveness. Values reflect human judgments about what's important, but those judgments shift with individuals, place, and time.

One study of the applicability of multiple-constituency theory suggests that it may in fact integrate both the system and goal approaches to effectiveness.[44] The study documents that some constituencies favor outcomes related to means (the process element in systems), while others favor outcomes related to ends (the outcome element in systems). Thus, it's possible to use the multiple-constituency theory to combine the goal and systems approaches to obtain a more appropriate approach to organizational effectiveness. But even if we can resolve the differences between the goal and systems approaches with respect to what different constituencies desire from organizational performance, we still must recognize that these desires can change with and over time.

Organizational Change and Learning

An examination of the stories of how IBM changed or how Harley-Davidson changed from companies that were losing market share and profits to become beacons for success reveals two important patterns. First, successful change is associated with a multistep process that creates power and motivation to continue. Second, the change process is driven by top-quality leaders who exert a lasting influence on the changes being made. These leaders establish direction; align people with their visions; and inspire people to overcome political, personal, and bureaucratic barriers to change.

As changes occur in workforce technology, the economy, competition, social trends, and world politics, it is inevitable that leaders will have to initiate organizational development interventions. Chapter 17 will examine alternative approaches and interventions for change. Because competition is becoming stronger each day, organizations have no choice—they must change. In all industries, a standard of continuous improvement and learning is becoming the norm around the world.

Each of you reading this book has a viewpoint, a set of assumptions, or some specific ideas about why people behave as they do. Each person attempts to explain, predict, or analyze the behavior of others. How valid and how good are these viewpoints? To help you learn how to develop valid viewpoints, this book will provide suggested frameworks and explanations about behavior of people working in organizations.

Think about the following statements and your personal beliefs:

1. Satisfied workers produce the highest quality output.
2. Women employees work harder for female managers than for male managers.
3. Enriched jobs are preferred by the vast majority of employees.
4. American managers are more stressed about their jobs than their Japanese counterparts.
5. Positively cohesive work groups are usually more productive than noncohesive work groups.
6. Women are more motivated by the amount of pay they receive than men.
7. Personality conflicts are outdated and aren't problems in most work settings.
8. Organizations with no structure are more autonomous, more productive, and more cost conscious.
9. Leaders are born.
10. Most training programs are carefully evaluated for their effectiveness.

These broad comments are subjects for debate. None of them are perfectly true or false. This reflects how difficult behavior is to understand and analyze. As you progress through the course, test your own views against what you read and discuss. Improving your ability to understand, explain, and predict behavior is the road we'll follow in the rest of the book.

Even those students with no interest or motivation to serve as managers will benefit from learning more about behavior in general and organizational behavior specifically. Working for others, starting your own organization, or doing business with organizations (e.g., the Internal Revenue Service, the public utility company, the school in your community) will require an awareness and understanding of the behavior of people. Through a better awareness and understanding, the transactions each of us has in society can be more positive and beneficial than if we remained uneducated about behavior.

Managerial Work and the Behavior, Structure, and Processes of Organizations

The concept of managerial work that we've developed so far is brought into perspective and summarized in Figure 1.6. This text's focus is the *behavior of individuals and groups in organizations*. The purpose of managers in organizations is to coordinate behavior so

FIGURE 1.6
Relationships among the Management Functions and Individual, Group, and Organizational Effectiveness

	Sources of Effectiveness		
Management Functions	**Individuals**	**Groups**	**Organizations**
Planning	Objectives	Goals	Missions
Organizing	Job designs Delegated authority	Department or unit	Integrative methods and processes
Leading	Person-centered influence	Group-centered influence	Entity-centered influence
Controlling	Individual standards of performance	Group standards of performance	Organization standards of performance

that an organization is judged effective by those who evaluate its record. Those who evaluate organizations can be concerned with any number of specific or general criteria and with output, process, or input measures.[45] To coordinate behavior and to satisfy evaluators, managers engage in activities intended to *plan, organize, lead,* and *control* behavior. Major factors in determining individual and group behavior are task and authority relationships.[46] Therefore, managers must design organizational *structures* and *processes* to facilitate communication among employees.

Thus, it would seem that the relationships among management, organizations, and effectiveness are straightforward. Effective individual, group, and organizational performance should be the result of effective planning, organizing, leading, and controlling. However, as will become obvious, organizations and people are not that simple. Managing culturally diverse people in organizations to achieve meaningful goals of individual, group, and organizational effectiveness in a rapidly changing and complex environment is challenging, rewarding, and frustrating. This book will portray the challenge, reward, and frustration in a realistic and contemporary way.

Summary of Key Points

- This book focuses on the developing field of management known as *organizational behavior.* Organizational behavior studies the behavior of individuals and groups in organizational settings. The framework within which this book's contents are presented is based on three characteristics common to *all* organizations: the *behavior* of individuals and groups, the *structure* of organizations (i.e., the design of the fixed relationships among the jobs in an organization), and the *processes* (e.g., communication and decision making) that make organizations "tick" and give them life. The model in Figure 1.1 has evolved from our concept of what all organizations are.
- A major interest is learning about the behavioral sciences that have produced theory and research concerning human behavior in organizations. However, no attempt has been made here to write a book that teaches behavioral science. The continuous theme throughout the book is the effective management of organizational behavior. Given this theme, the task is to interpret behavior science materials so that management students can comprehend the behavior, structure, and process phenomena as these are affected by managers' actions. We intend to provide readers with a basis for applying the relevant contributions of behavioral science to the management of organizations.
- An overriding consideration documented in many studies of managerial work is that the managerial process in inherently a human process—people relating to people. Recognizing this fact establishes the importance of understanding human behavior in the workplace. The behavior of individuals and groups is important for achieving effective organizational performance, but behavior of managers themselves must also be understood.

- The nature of managerial work derives from the necessity to coordinate work in organizations. By their nature, organizations exploit the benefits of specializations, but by its nature, specialization requires coordination. Managers coordinate specialized work by applying planning, organizing, leading, and controlling functions. These functions require that managers determine and influence the causes of individual, group, and organizational effectiveness.
- Two competing concepts of effectiveness derive from two competing theories of organizations. Goal theory is based on the idea that organizations are rational, purposive entities pursuing specific missions, goals, and objectives. Accordingly, how well they function (i.e., how effective they are) is reckoned in terms of how successful they are in achieving their purposes. Systems theory assumes that organizations are social entities existing as parts of larger environments and that, to survive, they function to satisfy the demands of those environments.
- The stakeholder perspective on organizational effectiveness recognizes that organizations exist to satisfy the demands of many different individuals and institutions (constituencies). Each constituency has expectations that the organization must satisfy through its performance.

Discussion and Review Questions

1. What expectations do you have about serving as a manager? What parts of the management job appeal to you, and what parts are unattractive?
2. We sometimes encounter red tape and inefficiency in a generally unresponsive and ineffective organization. One of management's goals is to achieve the opposite: an efficient and effective organization. What management skills are needed to help an organization become effective?
3. This chapter suggested that effectiveness can be viewed from the individual, group, and organizational perspectives. Is it possible for an individual manager to be effective even if her group isn't effective? Similarly, can an organization be effective even if several of its employees are not effective? Explain and give examples to support your argument.
4. What contribution does the concept *multiple constituency* make to our understanding of organizational effectiveness? In particular, does the concept make it easier or harder for a manager to know when she has accomplished effective performance for her group or organization? Explain.
5. What has occurred historically to warrant referring to the management of organizational behavior as a blending of art and science?
6. Should a manager of a small firm (say, 25 employees) be concerned about establishing an organization structure? Explain.
7. Describe how a manager who worked for 15 years in Los Angeles would apply a contingency management approach when he's transferred to a similar managerial position in the firm's Barcelona, Spain, office.
8. The study and application of OB has been described as multidisciplinary in nature. Why is it multidisciplinary? Explain.
9. If you were a training director responsible for instructing managers in the techniques of management, how would you evaluate your training program's effectiveness? Is the goal model of effectiveness useful? Is the systems model useful?
10. One writer on management theory states that management is aptly defined as "getting work done through other people." Compare this concept of management with the one proposed in this chapter.

Taking It to the Net

Traditional versus New Economy Comparison

The Internet provides a rich and endless array of data, information, and Web sites that must be carefully used. Note the emphasis on the word *carefully*. There is no universal screening or validating group, agency, or association that approves the information on the Internet. It is your responsibility to make sure that the information you review, consider for use, and incorporate in your studies, reports, or findings is accurate, reliable, honest, and cited properly.

Using the Internet and your favorite search engine (try www.google.com or www.yahoo.com), examine two different firms. Pick a traditional economy company (automobiles, oil and energy, transportation) and what some refer to as a new economy company (social networking and smart phones), and answer the following:

1. How much of each company's revenue and profit is generated outside of the United States?
2. What does the code of ethics statement for each company say?
3. What changes have the managers made to the organization's product/service mix in the past five years?
4. How effective are the firms? (Describe what basis you use to determine effectiveness.)
5. Would you want to work for either of these firms? Why? Why not?

Case for Analysis: *McDonald's Attempting to Regain Its Effectiveness?*

The McDonald brothers' first restaurant was founded in 1937 just east of Pasadena, California. It didn't serve hamburgers, had no playground, and offered no Happy Meals. The most popular menu item was the hot dog. From that humble beginning, Ray Kroc built McDonald's into a mammoth business that earns over $23.5 billion in annual revenue and employs more than 450,000 people in approximately 32,000 restaurants in 118 countries. For decades, McDonald's growth and profit margins were the envy of the world. McDonald's was considered an effective business with tremendous potential for growth domestically and internationally.

Consumer tastes constantly change, and adults began to get bored with the McDonald's menu in the 1960s. Responding to environmental pressure such as changes in consumer tastes, McDonald's introduced a new sandwich called the Big Mac. As consumers grew weary of beef, McDonald's introduced chicken McNuggets and chicken sandwiches in the early 1980s and within four years was the nation's second-largest poultry seller. In 2000, McDonald's started to accept credit cards to pay for meals. In 2009, the company added new premium items such as the Angus burger and McCafé coffees (lattes, cappuccinos, etc.) to help boost sales during the recession. This last move seems to be helping stabilize sales in the United States and increasing profits overseas. Within-stores sales of U.S. restaurants remained flat (not negative) in 2009, whereas overseas sales grew as much as 4.3 percent in Europe, Asia/Pacific, the Middle East, and Africa.

McDonald's changed as the environment demanded. It became the most recognized brand name and built thousands of Golden Arches restaurants. McDonald's wanted to provide consumers with a quality meal, served quickly, at a fair price. In the past, however, McDonald's attempts at pizza, fajitas, pasta, fried chicken, and low-fat sandwiches have all been failures.

For a company that enjoyed significant growth for five decades based on its ability to read environmental trends, the failures have been shocking. McDonald's has been unable to capitalize on its brand name or move beyond hamburgers and French fries. During a period when Americans are eating out more, McDonald's has failed to capture a growing portion of the market. Still, every single day McDonald's serves a meal to 1 of every 14 Americans. McDonald's has expanded into markets in more than 120 countries serving about 5 million customers each day. McDonald's continues to enter new markets each year. The worldwide expansion has created a problem with quality control: McDonald's is faced with the quality control problem of building an increasing number of stores without carefully checking the quality of the product they serve. In a survey for

Restaurants & Institutions magazine in which 2,800 consumers graded chains based on the taste of their food, McDonald's ranked 87 out of 91. Consumers around the world want taste and quality when selecting a restaurant.

McDonald's, like other fast-food chains, is attempting to address claims that their menu is filled with foods that contribute to obesity. Providing more nutritious menu items is still a challenge for a business that primarily is associated with hamburgers and French fries.

The organizational effectiveness of McDonald's remains a serious concern among franchisers, executives, and stockholders. How or whether McDonald's can make the necessary changes to again be the growth-oriented organization it once was is questionable.

DISCUSSION QUESTIONS

1. How can McDonald's use its powerful brand name to help improve its effectiveness?
2. Are quality and taste important to you when selecting a restaurant? Explain.
3. What environmental forces are the most different as we move through the decade of 2010 to 2020 when compared with the 1950s and 1960s?

Sources: Tess Stynes, "McDonald's Sales Rise Overseas," *Wall Street Journal*, February 10, 2010, p. B.6; Paul Ziobro, "McDonald's Gains Share In Fast Food," *Wall Street Journal*, October 28, 2009, p. B.5; McDonald's Annual Report, 2008; "McDonald's to Start Taking Credit Cards," *Business Custom Wire*, March 26, 2004, p. 1; Seth Godin, "When It Comes to Food, Music, and More, Which Do You Prefer: Ubiquity or Authenticity?" *Fast Company*, July 2001, pp. 84–85; and David Leonhardt, "McDonald's: Can It Regain Its Golden Touch?" *Businessweek*, March 9, 1998, pp. 70–77.

CHAPTER TWO

Organizational Culture

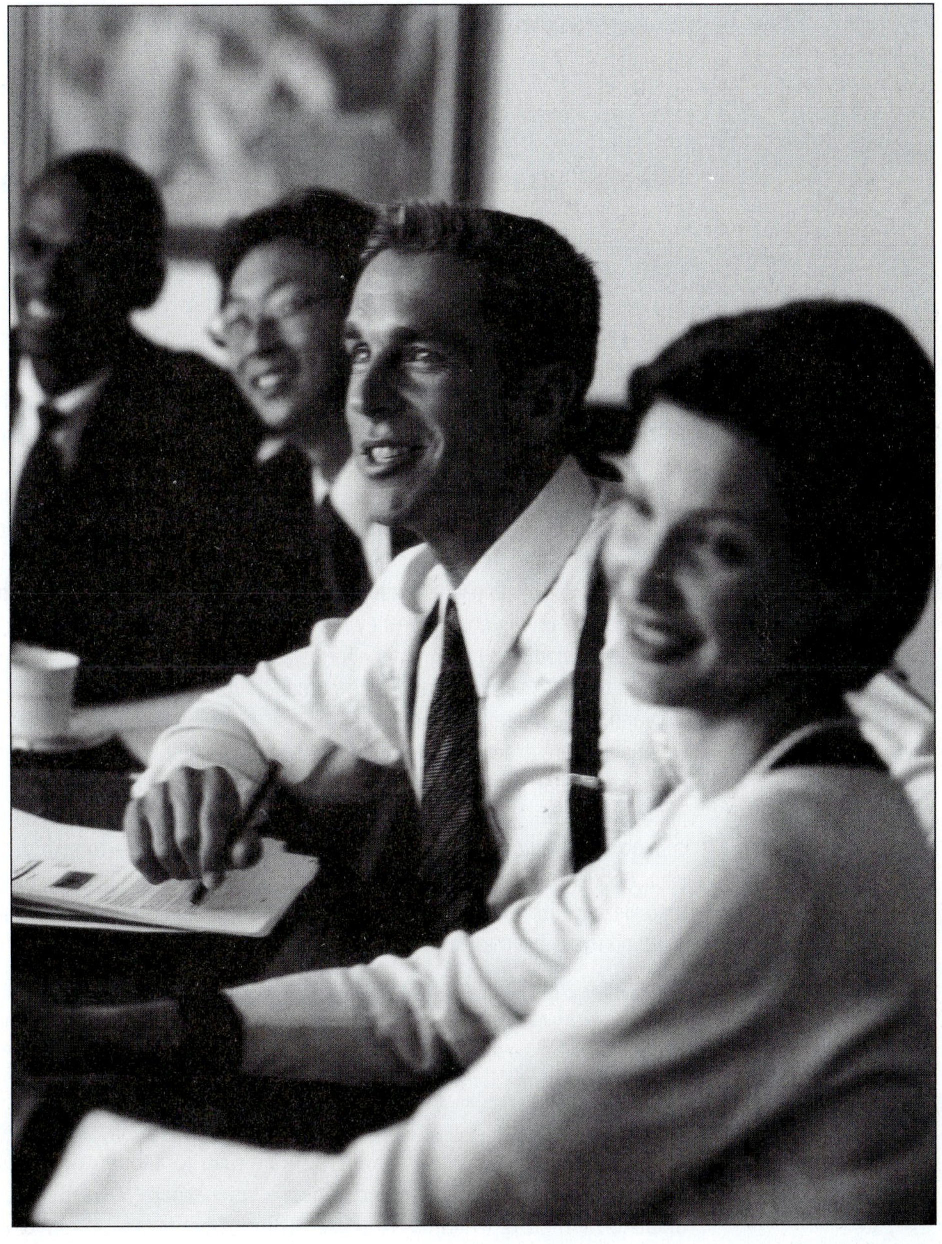

Learning Objectives

After completing Chapter 2, you should be able to

Define
The terms *organizational culture* and *socialization*.

Explain
The difference in how some employees talk about a positive culture and others describe a negative culture.

Describe
The impact of an organization's culture on individual and team behavior.

Explain
Why spirituality is considered to have some positive benefits in the workplace.

Identify
Several types of effective socialization practices in organizations.

Nike's Culture Activists Attempt to Dampen Growth

While earning his MBA at Stanford University, Phil Knight created a business plan that eventually spawned the successful multinational sports and fitness company known as Nike. Looking for ways to expand into the related outdoor gear and clothing sales, Nike performed careful due diligence on The North Face, Inc. Buying The North Face, with its annual $240 million in sales, would have allowed Nike to enter at the top of the outdoor gear sales curve. Nike CEO Phil Knight said no to the purchase and merger, however, because of expected problems in merging The North Face's operation and culture with Nike's. Knight may have been correct to hold off the acquisition because of potential cultural conflict, but not taking chances to expand Nike's growth has dimmed its appeal in financial markets.

Nike's culture is considered to be somewhat insular and protective. Knight was a cofounder and a powerful leader whose style had a major effect on the company's culture. Knight's style, the Nike insular culture, and its hard-charging growth goals set the standard in the sneaker industry for years. However, these same characteristics have contributed to the feeling among current top-level executives that enough is enough—they have left Nike for other jobs. Nike's culture seems to be controlled and modified by Knight's imprint and legacy on how to transact business. When Knight wanted to shift the direction of Nike's product line or make other changes, he reached a final decision and implemented the choice.

Analysts are examining the cultural characteristics of Nike and attempting to decide whether the usual traditional, cautious pace of change and dominating legacy left by Knight will allow the firm to improve its worldwide reach. There are groups such as Adbusters Media Foundation that want to change Nike's culture by slowing its growth and forcing Nike to take the swoosh logo off its products. Adbusters refers to its strategy to slow Nike as culture jamming. Adbusters is concerned that there is too much promotion of consumerism in society and popular national culture. The Nike machine is assumed to be too influential and powerful.

Sources: Adapted from http://www.nikebiz.com/company_overview/executives/phil_knight.html (accessed on April 7, 2010); https://www.adbusters.org/about/adbusters (accessed April 7, 2010); Naomi Rockler-Gladen, "Me Against the Media: From the Trenches of a Media Lit Class," *Adbusters,* March 2007, pp. 1–4; Christoph Senn and Axel Thoma, "Global Business: Worldly Wise," *Wall Street Journal Online*, March 3, 2007; and Karen R. Polenske, *The Economic Geography of Innovation* (Cambridge, UK: Cambridge University Press, 2006).

In most cases a person will move from one firm to another or even from one department to another within the same firm and consequently experience differences between the environments. Attempting to adjust to these different environments involves learning new values, processing information in new ways, and working within an established set of norms, customs, and rituals. The adaptation to new environments is a common occurrence. Although adaptation can be challenging, it can be better understood by learning about organizational culture.[1] As the Nike vignette illustrates, culture provides lessons that continue to affect decision making long after a dominant cofounder has left the day-to-day scene. In addition, organizational cultures can enhance the overall effectiveness and performance of organizations.[2] Companies such as Zappos, Starbucks, Pike Place Fish Market, and Cirque du Soleil have created unique cultures that have contributed to their organizational success.

Organizational Culture

Someone walking into the Broadmoor Hotel in Colorado Springs, the Breakers Hotel in West Palm Beach, or the Westin in San Francisco experiences a certain atmosphere, feeling, and style that is unique. These hotels have a personality, a charm, a feel. They have a cultural anchor that influences the way customers respond and the way employees interact with customers.

Walmart also sends off a powerful cultural message.[3] With over $401 billion in sales in 2009, 2.1 million associates, and 3,600 stores in 50 states, Walmart's singular strategy is to deliver cost savings to customers.[4]

Sam Walton, the founder, instilled these cultural values into the Walmart organization. He had a significant influence on what Walmart is throughout the world—from Tokyo to Chicago to Moscow. Walton projected his vision and his openness about what Walmart would be to customers. He gave the company a purpose, goals, and a cultural base.

Whether the discussion focuses on a grand hotel that exudes culture or a McDonald's restaurant that projects its founder's vision of the business, culture is a part of organizational life that influences the behavior, attitudes, and overall effectiveness of employees. As the opening vignette illustrates, a culture such as Nike's can influence how or whether an organization can grow.

Organizational Culture Defined

Despite being an important concept, organizational culture as a perspective from which to understand the behavior of individuals and groups within organizations has its limitations. First, it is not the only way to view organizations. We have already discussed the goal and systems views without even mentioning culture. Second, like so many concepts, organizational culture is not defined the same way by any two popular theorists or researchers. Some of the definitions of culture describe it as:

- Symbols, language, ideologies, rituals, and myths.[5]
- Organizational scripts derived from the personal scripts of the organization's founder(s) or dominant leader(s).
- A product; historical; based on symbols; and an abstraction from behavior and the products of behavior.[6]

organizational culture
What the employees perceive and how this perception creates a pattern of beliefs, values, and expectations.

Organizational culture is what the employees perceive and how this perception creates a pattern of beliefs, values, and expectations. Edgar Schein defined culture as

> A pattern of basic assumptions—invented, discovered, or developed by a given group as it learns to cope with the problems of external adaptation and internal integration—that has worked well enough to be considered valid and, therefore, to be taught to new members as the correct way to perceive, think, and feel in relation to those problems.[7]

The Schein definition points out that culture involves assumptions, adaptations, perceptions, and learning. He further contends that an organization's culture, such as those of Walt Disney, Twitter, or Apple, has three layers. Layer I includes artifacts and creations

OB AND YOUR CAREER New Job? Learn the Culture

Starting a new job can be both exciting and intimidating. It's exciting because it feels good to land a job, earn an income, and meet new people. It's a little intimidating because new employees often feel like they're under a microscope and don't want to make any mistakes right after bring hired. Our advice is to "hit the ground—*listening*!" Part of the settling-in process happens when new employees get to know their new bosses and co-workers and what their jobs really entail. An equally important step is for new employees to begin learning about the organizational culture. This is important because it will allow new employees to become aware of the invisible glue that holds employees and the organization together. Such knowledge can help new employees fit into the culture and succeed. Here are some specific tips that will help new employees begin the process of learning about the organization's culture:

1. *Read about the organization.* Current and past business news articles, company press releases, and blogs are good sources of information.
2. *Study key organizational documents.* Ask for copies or download from the organization's website the vision and mission statements, annual report, and code of conduct.
3. *Ask questions of people at the organization.* As new employees, individuals can simply ask their supervisor and co-workers about the company culture.
4. *Observe and listen.* New employees can learn a great deal about the organization by observing how managers and fellow employees behave on a daily basis and respond to difficult situations like losing a major customer or discovering a major product defect.

that are visible but often not interpretable. An annual report, a newsletter, wall dividers between workers, and furnishings are examples of artifacts and creations. At layer II are values, or the things that are important to people. Values are conscious, affective desires or wants. In layer III are the basic assumptions people make that guide their behavior. Included in this layer are assumptions that tell individuals how to perceive, think about, and feel about work, performance goals, human relationships, and the performance of colleagues. Figure 2.1 presents the Schein three-layer model of organizational culture.

FIGURE 2.1 **Schein's Three-Layer Organizational Model**

Source: Adapted from E. H. Schein, "Does Japanese Management Style Have a Message for American Managers?" *Sloan Management Review,* Fall 1981, p. 64.

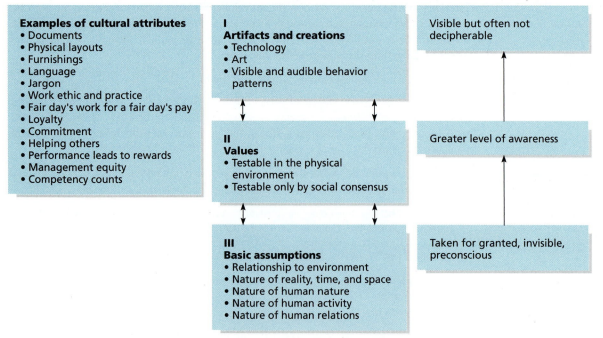

Examples of cultural attributes
- Documents
- Physical layouts
- Furnishings
- Language
- Jargon
- Work ethic and practice
- Fair day's work for a fair day's pay
- Loyalty
- Commitment
- Helping others
- Performance leads to rewards
- Management equity
- Competency counts

I
Artifacts and creations
- Technology
- Art
- Visible and audible behavior patterns

II
Values
- Testable in the physical environment
- Testable only by social consensus

III
Basic assumptions
- Relationship to environment
- Nature of reality, time, and space
- Nature of human nature
- Nature of human activity
- Nature of human relations

Visible but often not decipherable

Greater level of awareness

Taken for granted, invisible, preconscious

OB AT WORK Pfizer

The company in 2009 employed approximately 116,000 individuals and used the skills of over 12,000 medical researchers. Annual revenues are in excess of $50 billion. Each day 38 million patients are helped by Pfizer products.

The Pfizer mission and purpose are as follows:

OUR MISSION

We will become the world's most valued company to patients, customers, colleagues, investors, business partners, and the communities where we work and live.

OUR PURPOSE

We dedicate ourselves to humanity's quest for longer, healthier, happier lives through innovation in pharmaceutical, consumer, and animal health products.

To achieve Pfizer's mission and purpose, the following values are practiced[9]:

- Integrity. We demand of ourselves and others the highest ethical standards, and our products and processes will be of the highest quality.
- Customer focus. We are deeply committed to meeting the needs of our customers, and we constantly focus on customer satisfaction.
- Community. We play an active role in making every country and community in which we operate a better place to live and work, knowing that the ongoing vitality of our host nations and local communities has a direct impact on the long-term health of our business.
- Innovation. Innovation is the key to improving health and sustaining Pfizer's growth and profitability.
- Leadership. We believe that leaders empower those around them by sharing knowledge and rewarding outstanding individual effort. Leaders are those who step forward to achieve difficult goals, envisioning what needs to happen and motivating others.
- Collaboration. We know that to be a successful company we must work together, frequently transcending organizational and geographic boundaries to meet the changing needs of our customers.

Informally asking Walt Disney or Twitter employees about their firm's culture is not likely to reveal much. A person's feelings and perceptions are usually kept at the subconscious level. The feelings one has about a stay at Motel 6 or a stay at the Westin St. Francis Hotel in San Francisco are often difficult to express. The culture of a firm can be inferred by looking at those aspects that are perceptible. For example, four specific manifestations of culture at Walt Disney are shared things (wearing the Walt Disney uniform to fit the attraction), shared sayings (a "good Mickey" is a compliment for doing a good job), shared behavior (smiling at customers and being polite), and shared feelings (taking pride in working at Disney).

The OB and Your Career feature provides suggestions that new employees can employ to learn about their organizational culture.

Pfizer is a large international pharmaceutical company that was founded in 1849 by cousins Charles Pfizer and Charles Erhart. The New York–based firm is the maker of Lipitor, Viagra, and Zoloft. Pfizer is considered a great company in studies of most-admired firms. Bruce Pfau, a vice president of the Hay Group of Philadelphia, states that firms such as Pfizer have unique organizational cultures. He states, "The corporate cultures of high-performing companies are dramatically different from those of average companies."[8] He believes companies like Pfizer stress teamwork, customer focus, fair treatment of employees, initiative, and innovation. The OB at Work feature presents some of Pfizer's values and philosophy.

Organizational Culture and Societal Value Systems

values
The conscious, affective desires or wants of people that guide their behavior.

Organizations are able to operate efficiently only when shared values exist among the employees. **Values** are the conscious, affective desires or wants of people that guide their behavior. An individual's personal values guide behavior on and off the job. If a person's set of values is important, it will guide the person and also promote consistent behavior across situations. Values are a society's ideas about what is right and wrong—such as the belief that hurting someone physically is immoral. Values are passed from one generation to the next and are communicated through education systems, religions, families, communities, and organizations.[10]

A society's values have an impact on organizational values because of the interactive nature of work, leisure, family, and community.[11] American culture has historically given work a central place in the constellation of values. Work remains a source of self-respect and material reward in the United States. Work also serves as a place to achieve personal growth and fulfillment. As the demographics and makeup of the workforce become more culturally diverse, it will become extremely important for managers to learn about the value systems and orientations of the changing workforce.[12] Does the value mix change or is it different for women, African Americans, Hispanics, immigrants, physically challenged workers, and others who are increasingly joining the workforce and contributing to organizational success? This is a question that empirical studies and extensive analysis and debate will need to cover more thoroughly in the next few decades.

Organizational Culture and Its Effects

Because organizational culture involves shared expectations, values, and attitudes, it exerts influence on individuals, groups, and organizational processes. For example, if quality customer service is important in the culture, then individuals are expected to adopt this behavior. If, on the other hand, adhering to a specific set of procedures in dealing with customers is the norm, then this type of behavior would be expected, recognized, and rewarded.

Researchers who have suggested and studied the impact of culture on employees indicate that it provides and encourages a form of stability.[13] There is a feeling of stability, as well as a sense of organizational identity, provided by an organization's culture. Walt Disney was able to attract, develop, and retain top-quality employees because of the firm's stability and the pride of identity that goes with being a part of the Disney team.

In addition to stability and identity, a culture can generate a sense of loyalty and commitment. Individuals by joining an organization and working hard to perform and compete create a sense of "we" and "me." This involves loyalty and remaining committed to the goals of an organization.

It has become useful to differentiate between strong and weak cultures.[14] A strong culture is characterized by employees sharing core values. The more employees share and accept the core values, the stronger the culture is and the more influential it is on behavior. Religious organizations, cults, and some Japanese firms such as Toyota are examples of organizations that have strong, influential culture.

An American firm with a notoriously strong and influential culture is Southwest Airlines. Herb Kelleher, one of the founders, is largely responsible for the strong culture, which generated stability, identity, loyalty, and commitment. Along with Roland King, Kelleher rather impulsively decided to start an airline.[15] At Southwest, employees are expected to learn more than one job and help one another when needed. To show his own commitment, Kelleher pitched in to help employees as he traveled around doing business. Stories about Kelleher's pitching in are legendary at Southwest. One tells of how Kelleher sat next to mailing operators through one night and later into the morning doing the same work they did. He often got off a plane, went down to baggage, and pitched in handling bags. One year, the day before Thanksgiving, which is the busiest day of the year, Kelleher worked in baggage all day despite the pouring rain.[16]

The closeness of the employees at Southwest is expressed by having fun and working hard. One researcher who studied the airline concluded:

> The atmosphere at Southwest Airlines shows that having fun is a value that pervades every part of the organization. Joking, cajoling, and prank pulling at Southwest Airlines are representative of the special relationships that exist among the employees in the company.[17]

OB AT WORK Five Best Places to Work

Annually, *Fortune* identifies and discusses the "100 Best Companies to Work For." Employees evaluate their employers. The "Top Five Best Companies to Work For, 2010" were:

1. *SAS*, Carey, NC (www.sas.com). A $2.3 billion privately owned software company, SAS offers its employees a slew of generous benefits, including low-cost child care, unlimited sick days, comprehensive health insurance, an on-site medical center with doctors and nurses, a free fitness center and pool, and a library.
2. *Edward Jones*, St. Louis, MO (www.edwardjones.com). For the 11th year, this $3.8 billion investment firm was named to Fortune's "Best Companies to Work For" list. With over 7 million investor clients, Edward Jones creates a "family culture" which encourages employees to stay with the organization for the long term.
3. *Wegmans Food Markets*, Rochester, NY (www.wegmans.com). This private grocery chain gets thousand of letters every year from shoppers who want a Wegmans store in their neighborhood. The chain, which has never had a layoff, was founded in 1916 and now operates in 71 stores in five states.
4. *Google*, Mountain View, CA (www.google.com). Google continues to set the standard for Silicon Valley, increasing 401(k) matching and planning to hire thousands of new employees in 2010. Onsite engineers are encouraged to spend 20 percent of their time on creative, independent projects. No wonder Google gets 1,300 résumés from hopeful applicants each day.
5. *Nugget Market*, Woodland, CA (www.nuggetmarket.com). This $287 million supermarket chain helped its employees weather the recent recession by giving them discounts on groceries.

Sources: Adapted from http://money.cnn.com/magazines/fortune/bestcompanies/2010/snapshots/1.htm (accessed April 10, 2010); www.sas.com; www.edwardjones.com; www.wegmans.com; www.google.com; and www.nuggetmarket.com.

The strong culture that has evolved at Southwest Airlines was created by the founder and the employees. They make it a distinct culture that influences everyone within the firm.

Popular best-selling books provide anecdotal evidence about the powerful influence of culture on individuals, groups, and processes. Heroes and stories about firms are interestingly portrayed.[18] However, theoretically based and empirically valid research on culture and its impact is still quite sketchy. Questions remain about the measures used to assess culture, and definitional problems have not been resolved. There has also been the inability of researchers to show that a specific culture contributes to positive effectiveness in comparison to less effective firms with another cultural profile.

Creating Organizational Culture

Can a culture be created to influence behavior in the direction management desires? This is an intriguing question. An experiment to create a positive, productive culture was conducted in a California electronics firm.[19] Top managers regularly met to establish the core values of the firm. A document was developed to express the core values as "paying attention to detail," "doing it right the first time," "delivering defect-free products," and "using open communications." The document of core values was circulated to middle-level managers, who refined the statements. Then the revised document was circulated to all employees as the set of guiding principles of the firm.

An anthropologist was in the firm at the time working as a software trainer. He insightfully analyzed what actually occurred in the firm. There was a gap between the management-stated culture and the firm's actual working conditions and practices. Quality problems existed throughout the firm. There was also a strictly enforced chain of command and a top-down-only communication system. The culture creation experiment was too artificial and was not taken seriously by employees.

The consequences of creating a culture in the California firm included decreased morale, increased turnover, and a poorer financial performance. Ultimately, the firm filed for bankruptcy and closed its doors.

The California electronics firm case points out that artificially imposing a culture is difficult. Imposing a culture is often met with resistance. It is difficult to simply create core values. Also, when a disparity exists between reality and a stated set of values, employees become confused, irritated, and skeptical. They also usually lack enthusiasm and respect when a false image is portrayed. Creating a culture apparently just doesn't happen because a group of intelligent, well-intentioned managers meets and prepares a document.

Cultures seem to evolve over time, as did Microsoft's, Nestlé's, Honda's, and Walt Disney's. Hauser describes this evolution as follows:

> The culture that eventually evolves in a particular organization is . . . a complex outcome of external pressures, internal potential responses, responses to critical events, and probably, to some unknown degree, chance factors that could not be predicted from a knowledge of either the environment or the members.[20]

A model that illustrates the evolution of culture and its outcome is presented in Figure 2.2. The model emphasizes an array of methods and procedures that managers can use to foster a cohesive culture. In examining this model, recall the California electronics firm and the limited method it used to generate a quick-fix culture. Figure 2.2 emphasizes the core factors in creating and sustaining a positive culture, which suggests the importance of history, expectations, groups, and relationships.

FIGURE 2.2
The Core of a Positive Culture

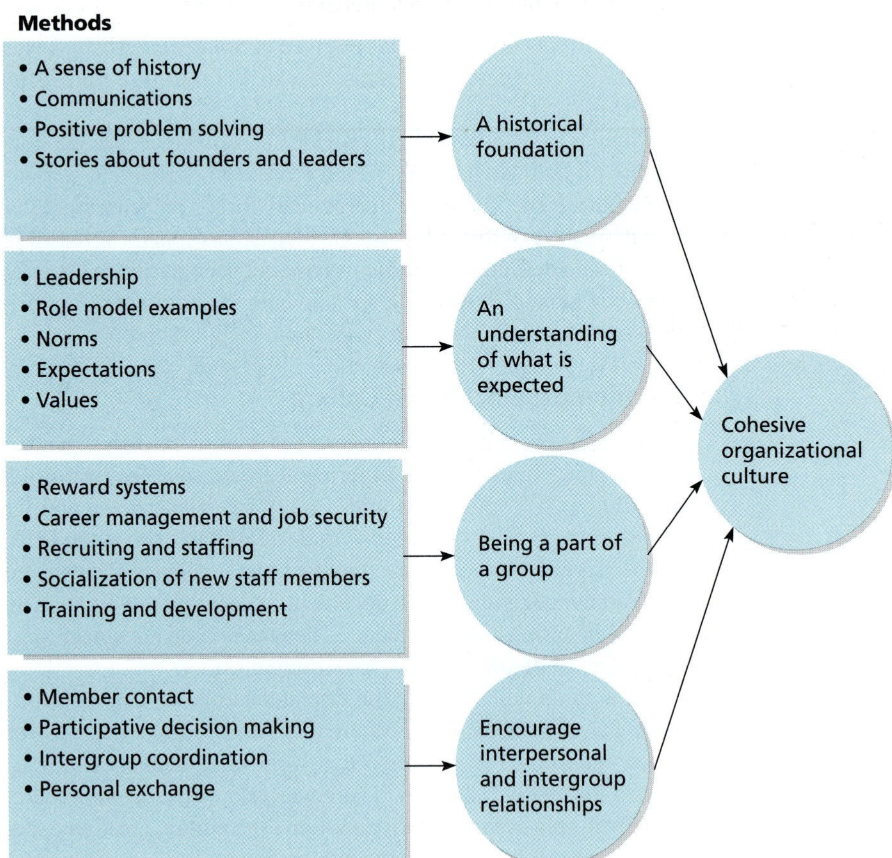

FIGURE 2.3
Four Types of Culture

Sources: Adapted from R. Hooijberg and F. Petrock, "On Cultural Change: Using the Competing Values Framework to Help Leaders Execute a Transformation Strategy," *Human Resource Management* 32 (1993): 29–50; and R. E. Quinn, *Beyond Rational Management: Mastering the Paradoxes and Competing Demands of High Performance* (San Francisco: Jossey-Bass, 1988).

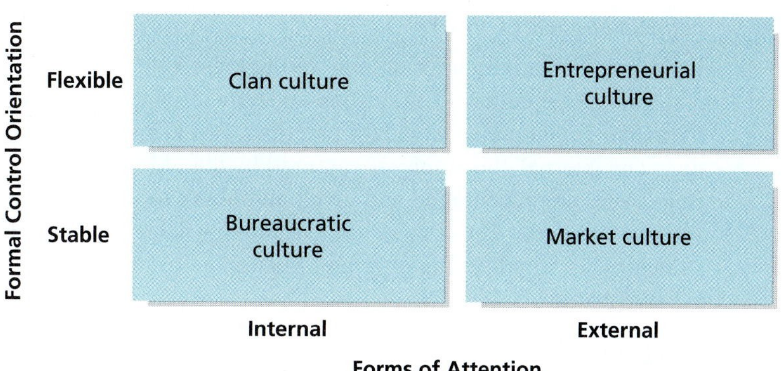

The nearby OB at Work provides some examples of the organizational cultures of five popular places to work.

Types of Culture

Theorists and researches have offered and discussed various listings of different cultures. Such listings and typologies seek to generalize major cultural properties across more than one organization. Figure 2.3 presents a systematic and organized classification of types of culture.[21]

The vertical axis shows the control orientation in the firm or department, ranging from stable to flexible. The horizontal axis depicts the focus of attention from internal to external. The four cells present the four distinct cultures: bureaucratic, clan, entrepreneurial, and market.

Some organizations have a dominant type of culture; other organizations have multiple cultures working simultaneously in different locations, departments, or projects. There is no superior, ideal, or fixed culture. There are, however, preferences by employees for particular cultures. For example, if an employee is working in a bureaucratic culture and prefers a more entrepreneurial culture, difficulties will likely develop. If the person-culture alignment becomes unduly stressful, it will probably result in the individual eventually leaving the organization.

Bureaucratic Culture

An organization that emphasizes rules, policies, procedures, chain of command, and centralized decision making has a bureaucratic culture. The military, government agencies, and firms started and managed by autocratic managers are examples of bureaucratic culture. Some individuals prefer the certainty, hierarchy, and strict organization of such a culture.[22]

Clan Culture

Being a part of a working family, following tradition and rituals, teamwork, spirit, self-management, and social influence are characteristics of the clan culture. Employees are willing to work hard for a fair and equitable compensation and fringe benefit package.

In a clan culture, employees are socialized by other members. Members help each other celebrate successes together. Nordstrom department stores rely on experienced "Nordies" to induct new employees and to show them the way to treat customers. New employees can observe the teamwork, tradition, and rituals that perpetuate Nordstrom's commitment to customer service. Nordstrom is an example of how the clan culture can affect the behavior and performance of employees.[23]

Entrepreneurial Culture

Innovation, creativity, risk taking, and aggressively seeking opportunities illustrate an entrepreneurial culture. Employees understand that dynamic change, individual initiatives, and autonomy are standard practices. 3M is an example of an entrepreneurial culture. The internal philosophy is captured by the 3M motto, "Never kill a product idea."[24] Employees are encouraged and given autonomy to work on projects. 3M intends to invent new markets. The firm's compensation packages, training programs, team-building strategies, and goal-setting programs encourage risk taking, autonomy, and innovation to achieve that goal.

Market Culture

An emphasis on sales growth, increased market share, financial stability, and profitability are attributes of a market culture. Employees have a contractual relationship with the firm. There is little feeling of teamwork and cohesiveness in this type of culture.

Examples of market culture organizations include Nike, Citigroup, Wells Fargo, and Allstate. Employees cooperate and work together to achieve market share and financial performance goals. This results in cooperation when necessary, but not deeply anchored relationships.[25]

Organizational Subcultures

The discussion of bureaucratic, clan, entrepreneurial, and market cultures is addressing the predominant, overarching culture of an organization. Within this dominant culture are subcultures. Teams, projects, divisions, regions, and units may or may not have their own subcultures.[26] Also, subcultures can form around types of work, such as doctors, nurses, and administrators in health care organizations.[27] In some instances the subcultures enhance the dominant culture, while in other cases they may have the opposite effect and actually constitute a counterculture. Subcultures that are opposed to the dominant culture can create conflict, dissension, and frustration among employees.

A subculture that is in alignment with dominant culture can be very rewarding.[28] Programmers, design engineers, technicians, and system integrators work at Microsoft in their own subcultures under the umbrella of the dominant culture.[29] The programmers speak their own language, help other programmers, and establish their own dress codes. In doing so, they still embrace the dominant culture's attributes on innovation, risk taking, and individual self-motivation. The Microsoft entrepreneurial culture is congruent with the various subcultures, and the result is that the firm is a spawning ground for new ideas, products, and experimentation. The congruency allows Microsoft to adapt to changing environmental forces and to be attractive to potential employees who prefer to work in the type of culture and subculture that exists.

Merging Cultures

Research indicates that less than one-quarter of mergers and acquisitions are financially successful in terms of return on investment. A particular merger fails to live up to expectations for numerous reasons. A major reason for joining with another organization is to grow quickly and inexpensively. There is also the notion that by sharing resources and applying leverage, merged companies can create and seize market opportunities better.[30] The analysis to go ahead with a merger usually applies specific financial criteria. When the numbers look right, the deal is completed. Rarely is there any discussion of the cultural compatibility of the merging firms. Culture is considered a "soft" factor that shouldn't be a main consideration. Paying closer attention to the compatibility of cultures, however, would appear to be worth the time and effort.

SmithKline merged with British-based Beecham and both firms checked each other out financially, legally, and culturally.[31] A consulting firm was hired to interview hundreds of managers from both firms to determine values, expectations, styles, and goals. Teams were created to facilitate the merger so that working together from the beginning would be more efficient.

The SmithKline Beecham merger diagnosis, planning, and action steps provide an example of how to bring cultural attributes into consideration. Yet this thorough, diligent, and participative approach is rarely used in mergers.

Before their merger was finalized, Pfizer and Warner-Lambert launched integration planning teams.[32] Although financial issues dominated the negotiations, the teams worked on integration of the two cultures. Neglecting the cultural characteristics of each firm was considered risky and ill-advised by managers in both firms. They had observed many merger failures in their industry category and wanted to carefully focus on cultural issues.

These two examples illustrate that while true due diligence in merger considerations should of course address financial and marketing issues, thoroughly probing cultural compatibility issues seems warranted as well. Other likely candidates for serious consideration of compatibility include the information technology systems, compensation and rewards systems, and the human resource talent pool.

In conducting a thorough analysis of merger partners, SmithKline initially decided against further discussion with Glaxo Welcome PLC.[33] The decision to not pursue the original merger was based on major differences in culture, management style, and managerial philosophy. Eventually though, the merger occurred, creating GlaxoSmithKline in 2000.

As a result of research and available reports, it is recommended that discovery of dissimilar cultures may be sufficient reason not to close a merger deal. The realities of organizations indicate that culture clash can contribute to or cause a merger failure. Rigorously diagnosing and studying the dominant culture and subcultures in the firms considering a merger would be wise before closing a deal. The integration of cultures is a challenge even for managers who understand the significance of culture.[34]

Influencing Culture Change

A limited amount of research has been done on cultural change. The difficulty in understanding culture becomes even more complex when attempting to bring about a significant cultural change. The themes that appear in the literature in discussing change are

- Cultures are so elusive and hidden that they cannot be adequately diagnosed, managed, or changed.
- Because it takes difficult techniques, rare skills, and considerable time to understand a culture and then additional time to change it, deliberate attempts at culture change are not really practical.
- Cultures sustain people throughout periods of difficulty and serve to ward off anxiety. One of the ways they do this is by providing continuity and stability. Thus, people will naturally resist change to a new culture.[35]

These three views suggest that managers who are interested in attempting to produce cultural changes face a daunting task. There are, however, courageous managers who believe that they can intervene and make changes in the culture. Figure 2.4 presents a view of five intervention points for managers to consider.[36]

A considerable amount of knowledge suggests that one of the most effective ways of changing people's beliefs and values is to first change their behavior (intervention 1).[37] However, behavior change does not necessarily produce culture change because of the process of justification. The California electronics example introduced earlier clearly

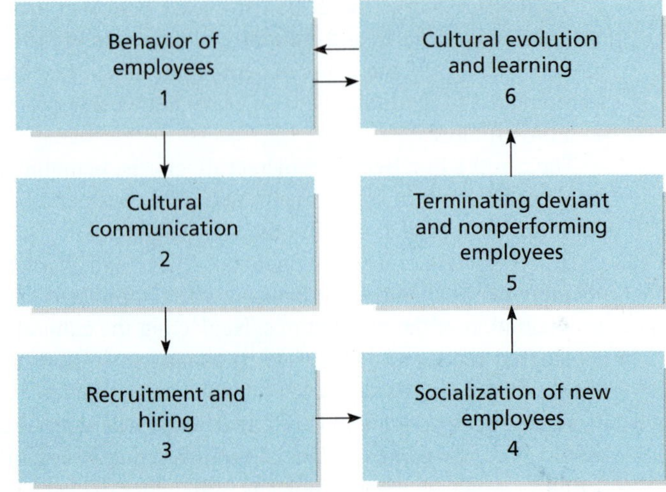

FIGURE 2.4
Changing Culture: Manager-Initiated Interventions

Intervention points	Examples
1	Feedback/discussion of what is expected
2	Discuss history, folklore, and stories
3	Recruit and hire individuals aligned with the culture
4	Training program; mentoring; coaching
5	Terminating problem or nonperforming individuals using appropriate and fair due process

illustrates this point. Behavioral compliance does not mean cultural commitment. Managers must get employees to see the inherent worth in behaving in a new way (intervention 2). Typically, communication (intervention 2) is the method used by managers to motivate the new behaviors. Cultural communication can include announcements, memos, rituals, stories, dress, and other forms of communication.

Another set of interventions includes recruitment and hiring (intervention 3) and then the socialization of new members (intervention 4) and the removal of existing members who deviate from the culture (intervention 5). Each of these interventions must be done after careful diagnoses are performed. Although some individuals may not perfectly fit the firm's culture, they may possess exceptional skills and talents. Weeding out cultural misfits might be necessary, but it should be done only after weighing the costs and benefits of losing talented performers who deviate from the core cultural value system.

Changing an organization's culture takes time, effort, and persistence, especially in firms with strong cultures. Older strong culture organizations have established stories, use symbols, conduct rituals, and even use their own unique language. In a strong culture organization, the core values are widely shared, respected, and protected.

Myths and stories are the tales about the organization that are passed down over time and communicate a story of the organization's underlying values. Virtually any employee of Walmart can tell stories about Sam Walton and his behavior; how he rode around in his pickup truck, how he greeted people in the stores, and how he tended to "just show up" at different times. The Center for Creative Leadership (CCL) has stories about its founder,

H. Smith Richardson, who as a young man creatively used the mail to sell products. Richardson and other early contributors to the CCL believed that leaders needed to be bold and creative so that they could help their organizations adapt to change and avoid the traditional pitfalls of management.[38]

Rituals are recurring events or activities that reflect important aspects of the underlying culture. Mary Kay cosmetics has spectacular sales meetings for its top performers every year. Top-performing saleswomen are awarded an array of gifts—automobiles, diamonds, and fur coats—for achieving sales quotas. This ritual would be an indication of the value placed on high sales and meeting high quotas. Another kind of ritual is the retirement ceremony. Elaborate or modest retirement ceremonies may signal the relative importance an organization places on its people.

Language concerns the jargon, or idiosyncratic terms, used in an organization that can serve several different purposes relevant to culture. First, the mere fact that some know the language and some do not indicates who is in the culture and who is not. Second, language can provide information about how people within a culture view others. Third, language can be used to help create a culture.[39]

Organizational Culture and Spirituality

Scandal and ethical lapses in global organizations have contributed to the increased demand for more attention and focus on spiritual and ethical dimensions in the organizational culture. Many companies are embracing these dimensions as never before. Chick-fil-A restaurants are closed on Sundays, Ford and Xerox sponsor spiritual retreats for employees, and Tyson Foods have workplace chaplains in the plants.[40] The term ***spirituality*** has found its way into the organizational literature. The view of spirituality is that it originates from within the individual. A concise definition is offered by Smith and Rayment:

spirituality
Spirituality is a state or experience that can provide individuals with direction or meaning, or provide feelings of understanding, support, inner wholeness, or connectedness.

> Spirituality is a state or experience that can provide individuals with direction or meaning, or provide feelings of understanding, support, inner wholeness, or connectedness. Connectedness can be to themselves, other people, nature, the universe, a god, or some other supernatural power.[41]

This definition involves inner feelings, being connected to the work and to colleagues. Because work is such a major part of the lives of employees, organizational culture and practices can contribute to a person's spiritual development and growth.

Although research into workplace spirituality is still in its infancy, comprehensive models and empirical research have been developed to explain how spirituality can be facilitated at the workplace[42] and developed to maximize the organization's triple bottom line (e.g., "People, Planet, Profit").[43] Other recent research has explored the linkages between workplace spirituality and organizational behavior concepts such as transformational leadership, organizational citizenship behavior, organizational support, and procedural justice.[44] Many advocates of workplace spirituality suggest that strong spiritual beliefs at work can spawn several important benefits at organizations.

Potential Benefits of Spirituality

Research results suggest that the encouragement and support of spirituality in the work setting can contribute to creativity, honesty, trust, commitment, personal need satisfaction, and improved organizational effectiveness.[45]

For example, Wetherill Associates made *honesty* an important point of attention. The company created and implemented a policy where they promised that they will be completely honest when dealing with customers and suppliers. This emphasis on honesty also carried over into all interactions within the firm. (e.g., group to group, individual to individual). The reported results included higher morale, better job satisfaction, and improved effectiveness in relationships with customers and suppliers.[46]

The spirituality benefits in addition to improved effectiveness include attaining a broader worldview; concern with working with integrity; acquiring a strong sense of community; and a willingness to work to make a positive difference by making contributions to colleagues, stakeholders, and society. In addition to these benefits, there is the individual benefit of creating a more reasonable work/life balance, attitude, and set of behaviors.

Tom's of Maine: A Spiritual Culture

Tom Chappell and his wife, Kate, moved from the corporate world to Maine so that Tom could cofound his own firm.[47] He wanted to create a company that produced innovative, natural personal care products for customers.

Thirty-six years after cofounding Tom's of Maine, Chappell formed a partnership with Colgate-Palmolive Company. He remains as a minority owner and CEO of the 2006 partnership.

The fact that Chappell and his wife decided to produce and sell only products that would not harm the environment is a worthy accomplishment. From the beginning, Chappell emphasized spiritual values and intentions in operating his firm. He adhered to these values and listened to what his customers wanted in their products. The Tom's of Maine seven spiritual values are the following: set aside your ego and connect to a universal force; know who you are and what you care about in life; envision your future in your heart and in your mind; listen to everyone carefully; align your business strategy with your values; use continual assessment to stay on course; and pass your good fortune, gifts, knowledge, and profits to others.[48]

Practicing these values diligently is one of the reasons that Tom's of Maine is an excellent company that does what is right for its employees, customers, and community. By practicing management using the seven spiritual values, the firm has created a unique culture that encourages social responsibility while being profitable.

Critics of Spirituality in Organizations

A number of critics and skeptics have questioned the meaningfulness and practical aspects of spirituality. There are critics who claim that a focus on spirituality means not being able to embrace the diversity of beliefs held by employees and stakeholders. Talking about integrity, honesty, sharing with others, and being open could take on an appearance of preaching. The preaching could turn off many individuals.[49]

The research findings on the positive benefits and problems of spirituality are still sparse. There is a lack of rigor, theoretical foundation, and research design in available studies of spirituality. Until the rigor, theoretical base, and research design can be improved and evidence that is based on scientific inquiry is available, there will be many skeptics of introducing spirituality dimensions in management practices.[50]

One of the key variables in spirituality discussions is the "ability to listen" to others. Such an ability to listen needs to be more carefully studied and analyzed. Is "listening" all that is needed, or must the leader also act effectively on what he or she hears?

There is also the issue of finding the type of spirituality that fits best in the organization. There is not likely to be a single form or template of spirituality. What forms are congruent with an organization's culture? This is still a largely unanswered question that needs to be considered before attempting to introduce spiritual practices and values.[51]

socialization
The process by which organizations bring new employees into the culture.

Socialization and Culture

Socialization is the process by which organizations bring new employees into the culture. In terms of culture, socialization involves a transmittal of values, assumptions, and attitudes from older to newer employees. Intervention 4 in Figure 2.4 emphasizes the "fit" between the new employee and the culture. Socialization attempts to make this fit more comfortable for the employee and the firm.

The socialization process goes on throughout an individual's career. As the needs of the organization change, for example, its employees must adapt to those needs; that is, they must be socialized. But even as we recognize that socialization is ever present, we must also recognize that it is more important at some times than at others. For example, socialization is most important when an individual first takes a job or takes a different job in the same organization. The socialization process occurs throughout various career stages, but individuals are more aware of it when they change jobs or change organizations.[52]

Socialization Stages

The stages of socialization coincide generally with the stages of a career. Although researchers have proposed various descriptions of the stages of socialization,[53] three stages sufficiently describe it: (1) anticipatory socialization, (2) accommodation, and (3) role management.[54] As illustrated in Figure 2.5, each stage involves specific activities that, if undertaken properly, increase the individual's chances of having an effective career. Moreover, these stages occur continuously and often simultaneously.

Anticipatory Socialization

The first stage involves all those activities the individual undertakes prior to entering the organization or to taking a different job in the same organization. The primary purpose of these activities is to acquire information about the new organization, new job, or both.

People are vitally interested in two kinds of information prior to entering a new job or organization. First, they want to know as much as then can about what working for the organization is really like. This form of learning about the organization is actually an attempt to assess the firm's culture. Some individuals attempt to learn about the culture by reading everything they can about the organization, speaking to current or former employees, and asking questions of the recruiters and human resources representatives such as, "How would you describe the culture?" Second, they want to know whether they are suited to the jobs available in the organization. Individuals seek out this information with considerable effort when they are faced with the decision to take a job, whether it be their first one or one that comes along by way of transfer or promotion. At these times, the information is specific to the job or the organization.

FIGURE 2.5
Stages of Socialization

Stage 1: Anticipatory Socialization (Before starting new job)	**Stage 2: Accommodation (After starting new job)**	**Stage 3: Role Management (After settling into new job)**
Gather information about job and organization.	Adjust to people and demands of immediate workgroup.	Manage conflict between work and personal life, and between different work groups.
Key issues: Will I fit there? Will I do the job well? What are the people like?	Key issues: Is this what I expected? Can I relate well to my boss and peers?	Key issues: Can I resolve these conflicts? Will I be able to balance my work and personal life effectively?

We also form impressions about jobs and organizations in less formal ways. For example, our friends and relatives talk of their experiences. Parents impart both positive and negative information to their offspring regarding the world of work. Although we continually receive information about this or that job or organization, we are more receptive to such information when faced with the necessity to make a decision.

It is desirable, of course, that the information transmitted and received during the anticipatory stage accurately and clearly depicts the organization and the job. However, we know that individuals differ considerably in the way they decode and receive information. Yet if the fit between the individual and the organization is to be optimal, two conditions are necessary. The first condition is *realism;* both the individual and the organization must portray themselves realistically. The second condition is *congruence*. This condition is present when the individual's skills, talents, and abilities are fully utilized by the job. Either their overutilization or underutilization results in incongruence and, consequently, poor performance.[55]

Transmitting the culture of a firm such as the Calvert Group, a Bethesda, Maryland, mutual funds company, is a part of the job interview. Determining whether there is congruence between the job applicant and the firm is important because the Calvert Group wants to hire employees who accept its way of conducting business. The firm has pioneered the concept of socially responsible investing. Community involvement is significant at the Calvert Group.[56] The company gives workers 12 days a year off, with pay, to perform community services such as working in a soup kitchen, volunteering at local schools, cleaning up the environment, and delivering food to homebound individuals. The Calvert Group sponsors activities for senior citizens and homeless people, blood drives, Head Start, and a host of similar community-based programs. Becoming an employee who fits Calvert Group's culture requires a fit between a person's values and the organization's need to be involved with the community.

Firms such as Nordstrom, Johnson & Johnson, and Hewlett-Packard have worked extremely hard, like the Calvert Group, to attract and retain employees who have values congruent with the firms' unique cultures. For example, Nordstrom has built so strong a culture around serving the customer (letting go any employee who fails to become socialized) that the entire employee manual is a 5-by-8-inch card with one rule on it: "Use your good judgment in all situations."[57]

Accommodation

The second stage of socialization occurs after the individual becomes a member of the organization, after he or she takes the job. During this stage, the individual sees the organization and the job for what they actually are. Through a variety of activities, the individual attempts to become an active participant in the organization and a competent performer on the job. This breaking-in period is ordinarily stressful for the individual because of the anxiety created by the uncertainties inherent in any new and different situation. Apparently, individuals who experience realism and congruence during the anticipatory stage have a less stressful accommodation stage. Nevertheless, the demands on the individual do indeed create situations that induce stress.

Four major activities constitute the accommodation stage: all individuals, to a degree, must engage in (1) establishing new interpersonal relationships with both co-workers and managers, (2) learning the tasks required to perform the job, (3) clarifying their role in the organization and in the formal and informal groups relevant to that role, and (4) evaluating the progress they are making toward satisfying the demands of the job and the role. Readers who have been through the accommodation stage probably recognize these four activities and recall more or less favorable reactions to them.

If all goes well in this stage, the individual feels a sense of acceptance by co-workers and supervisors and experiences competence in performing job tasks. The breaking-in period, if successful, also results in role definition and congruence of evaluation. These four outcomes of the accommodation stage (acceptance, competence, role definition, and congruence of evaluation) are experienced by all new employees to a greater or lesser extent. However, the relative value of each of these outcomes varies from person to person.[58]

Acceptance by the group may be a less valued outcome for an individual whose social needs are satisfied off the job, for example. Regardless of these differences due to individual preferences, each of us experiences the accommodation stage of socialization and ordinarily moves on to the third stage.

Role Management

In contrast to the accommodation stage, which requires the individual to adjust to demands and expectations of the immediate work group, the role management stage takes on a broader set of issues and problems. Specifically, during the third stage, conflicts arise. A common conflict is between the individual's work and home lives. For example, the individual must divide time and energy between the job and his or her role in the family. Because the amount of time and energy is fixed and the demands of work and family are seemingly insatiable, conflict is inevitable. Employees unable to resolve these conflicts are often forced to leave the organization or to perform at an ineffective level. In either case, the individual and the organization are not well served by unresolved conflict between work and family.

Another source of conflict during the role management stage is between the individual's work group and other work groups in the organization. This source of conflict can be more apparent for some employees than for others. For example, as an individual moves up the organization's hierarchy, he or she is required to interact with various groups both inside and outside the organization. Each group can and often does place different demands on the individual, and, to the extent that these demands are beyond the individual's ability to meet them, stress results. Tolerance for the level of stress induced by these conflicting and irreconcilable demands varies among individuals. Generally, the existence of unmanaged stress works to the disadvantage of the individual and the organization.

Characteristics of Effective Socialization

Organizational socialization processes vary in form and content from organization to organization. Even within the same organization, various individuals experience different socialization processes. For example, the accommodation stage for a college-trained management recruit is quite different from that of a person in the lowest-paid occupation in the organizations. As John Van Maanen has pointed out, socialization processes are not only extremely important in shaping the individuals who enter an organization, they are also remarkably different from situation to situation.[59] This variation reflects either lack of attention by management to an important process or the uniqueness of the process as related to organizations and individuals. Either explanation permits the suggestion that while uniqueness is apparent, some general principles can be implemented in the socialization process.[60]

Effective Anticipatory Socialization

The organization's primary activities during the first stage of socialization are *recruitment* and *selection and placement* programs. If these programs are effective, new recruits in an organization should experience the feeling of *realism* and *congruence.* In turn, accurate expectations about the job result from realism and congruence.

Recruitment programs are directed toward new employees, those not now in the organization. It is desirable to give prospective employees information not only about the job but also about those aspects of the organization that affect the individual. It is nearly always easier for the recruiter to stress job-related information to the exclusion of organization-related information. Job-related information is usually specific and objective, whereas organization-related information is usually general and subjective. Nevertheless, the recruiter should, to the extent possible, convey factual information about such matters as pay and promotion policies and practices, objective characteristics of the work group the recruit is likely to join, and other information that reflects the recruit's concerns.[61]

Effective Accommodation Socialization

Effective accommodation socialization comprises five different activities: (1) designing orientation programs, (2) structuring training programs, (3) providing performance evaluation information, (4) assigning challenging work, and (5) assigning demanding bosses.

Orientation programs are seldom given the attention they deserve. Sometimes referred to as "onboarding," the first few days on a new job can have very strong negative or positive impact on the new employee. Taking a new job involves not only new job tasks but also new interpersonal relationships. The new person comes into an ongoing social system that has evolved a unique set of values, ideals, frictions, conflicts, friendships, coalitions, and all the other characteristics of work groups. If left alone, the new employee must cope with the new environment in ignorance, but if given some help and guidance, he or she can cope more effectively.[62] Avon doesn't believe in this "sink or swim" mentality when it comes to socializing new employees. Newcomers are thoroughly educated about Avon's organizational culture and ways of doing business. Similarly, when new employees join Citigroup, they are immediately told about the 37 employee networks (e.g., Hispanic, working parents, etc.) that help socialize newcomers within the 320,000-employee firm.[63]

Thus, organizations should design orientation programs that enable new employees to meet the rest of the employees as soon as possible. Moreover, specific individuals should be assigned the task of orientation. These individuals should be selected for their social skills and be given time off from their own work to spend with the new people. The degree to which the orientation program is formalized can vary, but in any case, the program should not be left to chance.

Training programs are invaluable in the breaking-in stage. Without question, training programs are necessary to instruct new employees in proper techniques and to help them develop requisite skills. Moreover, effective training programs provide frequent feedback about progress in acquiring the necessary skills. What is not so obvious is the necessity of integrating formal training with the orientation program.

Performance evaluation, in the context of socialization, provides important feedback about how well the individual is getting along in the organization. Inaccurate or ambiguous information regarding this important circumstance can only lead to performance problems. To avoid these problems, it is imperative that performance evaluation sessions take place in face-to-face meetings between the individual and manager and that in the context of the job the performance criteria must be as objective as possible. Management by objectives and behaviorally anchored rating scales are particularly applicable in these settings.

Assigning challenging work to new employees is a principal feature of effective socialization programs. The first jobs of new employees often demand far less of them than they are able to deliver. Consequently, they are unable to demonstrate their full capabilities, and in a sense they are being stifled. This is especially damaging if the recruiter was overly enthusiastic in "selling" the organization when they were recruited.

Assigning demanding bosses is a practice that seems to have considerable promise for increasing the retention rate of new employees. In this context, "demanding" should not be interpreted as "autocratic." Rather, the boss most likely to get new hirees off in the right

TABLE 2.1
A Checklist of Effective Socialization Practices

Socialization Stage	Practices
Anticipatory socialization	1. Recruitment using realistic job previews 2. Selection and placement using realistic career paths
Accommodation socialization	1. Tailor-made and individualized orientation programs 2. Social as well as technical skills training 3. Supportive and accurate feedback 4. Challenging work assignments 5. Demanding but fair supervisors
Role management socialization	1. Provision of professional counseling 2. Adaptive and flexible work assignments 3. Sincere person-oriented managers

direction is one who has high but achievable expectations for their performance. Such a boss instills the understanding that high performance is expected and rewarded; equally important, the boss is always ready to assist through coaching and counseling.

Effective Role Management Socialization

Organizations that effectively deal with the conflicts associated with the role management stage recognize the impact of such conflicts on job satisfaction and turnover. Even though motivation and high performance may not be associated with socialization activities, satisfaction and turnover are, and organizations can ill afford to lose capable employees.

Retention of employees beset by off-the-job conflicts is enhanced in organizations that provide professional counseling and that schedule and adjust work assignments for those with particularly difficult conflicts at work and home. Of course, these practices do not guarantee that employees can resolve or even cope with the conflict. The important point, however, is for the organization to show good faith and make a sincere effort to adapt to the problems of its employees. Table 2.1 summarizes what managers can do to encourage effective socialization.

Mentors and Socialization

mentor
A friend, coach, adviser, or sponsor who supports, encourages, and helps a less experienced protégé.

In the medical field, young interns learn proper procedures and behavior from established physicians; PhD students learn how to conduct organizational research from professors who have conducted studies. What about the process of learning or working with a senior person, called a **mentor**, in work settings? In Greek mythology, the mentor was the designation given to a trusted and experienced adviser. Odysseus, absent from home because of the Trojan Wars, charged his servant, Mentor, with the task of educating and guiding his son. In work organizations, a mentor can provide coaching, friendship, sponsorship, and role modeling to a younger, less experienced protégé. In working with younger or new employees, a mentor can satisfy his or her need to have an influence on another employee's career. The OB at Work feature on the next page illustrates that mentoring occasionally can become problematic, however.

Research has indicated that a majority of managers report having had at least one mentoring relationship during their careers.[64] Considered a best practice, mentoring programs are used by approximately 71 percent of Fortune 500 firms.[65] Kram has identified two general functions of mentoring: career functions and psychosocial functions. The career functions include sponsorship, exposure and visibility, coaching, production, and challenging assignments. The psychosocial functions are role modeling, acceptance and confirmation, counseling, and friendship.[66]

OB AT WORK Mentoring Can Go Haywire

Mentoring involves a person with experience, knowledge, and a network who attempts to help, guide, and support a protégé (mentee) with career, problem solving, and development. Unfortunately, the mentor–mentee relationship doesn't always go according to plan.

Some estimate that approximately 70 percent of the largest firms in the United States have some type of mentoring program. The "script" claims that everyone—the mentor, mentee, and employer—will benefit from a good mentoring program.

One of the most common problems, especially with a formal mentoring program, is simply that the mentor and apprentice are incompatible. As we all know, there's no perfect way to account for individual differences and, especially, emotions. Even the best intentions and most thorough questionnaires can't always identify what might really irritate you about the other person. Different personality quirks, needs, goals, schedules, work/life balance preferences, and backgrounds can quickly frustrate a relationship.

Sometimes the mismatch goes deeper, though. One young woman who didn't want to be identified left a company within a year of joining, in part because she thought her mentor wasn't doing right by some of their smaller, less significant clients. "Those weren't skills I wanted to cultivate," she says.

Respect isn't enough, though. Ideally, both people know what they want out of the arrangement. "I haven't seen a real powerful relationship that didn't have specific goals," says Kim Wise, the head of Mentor Resources. These might include how to manage a project or a team or a budget; or developing an expertise that makes a promotion more likely. And once any of that happens, it's usually time to move on, maybe to another mentor. The most successful of these relationships last no more than a year.

That doesn't mean the mentee can't go back for advice or keep in touch. "Don't obliterate the relationship. Change the intensity," says Sheila Wellington, author of *Be Your Own Mentor,* who has outgrown a few mentors herself. Her other piece of advice: try to end gracefully, but unequivocally.

Things can get ugly when mentors won't accept that a mentee no longer needs them. This is particularly common when male mentors get too comfortable in their role as career coach, especially when working with women. When the mentee gains confidence, experience, and knowledge, he or she wants more autonomy to act alone. Pretty soon the relationship deteriorates. The mentee wants to move forward without constraints.

Mentors can run into serious problems as well, none more so than the ulterior motive. Sometimes the protégé simply wants the mentor's job. That's what happened recently to a female executive who has been mentoring women for 30 years. She describes the experience as being "thrown under the bus."

She had been working with a young woman for several months when her boss began asking pointed questions about her own performance. She couldn't figure out why until colleagues told her that her "student" was whispering in the boss's ear. "I didn't want to believe it," says the executive. "No one had been that duplicitous or self-serving before." Now she wants the young woman fired.

Some displays of ambition aren't quite that raw, but they still do damage, like when the young charge thinks he knows more than the mentor. Richard Laermer, the 46-year-old chief executive of RLM PR and co-author of the book *Punk Marketing,* was developing a talented protégé who seemingly could do no wrong. Then, one day, the young guy decided that a client's business model wasn't sufficiently impressive to warrant attention. Laermer says he didn't realize what was happening until the client fired his firm. He was chagrined by the incident. "Who taught him that?" he wondered. Laermer never raised the matter with his protégé, and weeks later the man left the company of his own accord.

Sources: Adapted from Garry Kranz, "More Firms Paying Mind to Mentoring," *Workforce Management* 89, no. 1 (January 2010): 10; Susan Berfield, "Mentoring Can Be Messy," *Businessweek,* January 29, 2007, pp. 80–82; and John J. Sosik, Veronica M. Godshalk, & Francis J. Yammarino, "Transformational Leadership, Learning Goal Orientation, and Expectations for Career Success in Mentor-Protégé Relationships: A Multiple Levels of Analysis Perspective," *The Leadership Quarterly* 15 (2004): 241–261.

reverse mentoring
A process by which junior-level employees support, encourage, and help senior-level managers. A common focus of reverse mentoring is technology, an area with which junior-level employees often have more experience and knowledge.

Although mentoring functions can be important in socializing a person, it is not clear that a single individual must play all of these roles. New employees can obtain valuable career and psychosocial influence from a variety of individuals—managers, peers, trainers, and friends. Also, there is some anecdotal evidence that suggests that **"reverse mentoring"** can be equally beneficial for the mentors, protégés, and the organization. Some organizations like General Electric ask the younger, more technologically savvy employees to "mentor" their senior managers on issues regarding social networking, online trends, and so forth.[67] At Ford Motor Company, a study was conducted to develop guidelines to socialize new management trainees.

TABLE 2.2
Evolution of the Mentor Relationship

Phase	Definition	Turning Points*
1. Initiation	The relationship gets started and begins to have importance for both the mentor and mentee.	Fantasies become concrete expectations, Expectations are met; mentor provides coaching, challenging work, visibility; mentee provides assistance, respect, and desire to be mentored.
2. Cultivation	The career, developmental, and personal growth of the mentee occurs.	Both mentor and mentee benefit from the relationship. Opportunities for meaningful and more frequent interaction increase. An emotional and personal bond develops.
3. Trial Separation	Mentee goes it alone in problem solving, completing work, and developing networks.	Mentee goes it alone; has some success and some failure; consults and receives feedback from the mentor. Mentor and mentee experience separation anxiety.
4. Separation	The structural role relationship and/or the emotional experience of the relationship changes.	Mentee no longer wants or seeks guidance. Mentor is less available to provide mentoring functions.
5. Redefinition	A period afterthe separation phase during which the relationship is ended or takes on significantly different characteristics, making it a more equal relationship.	Stresses of separation diminish and new relationships are formed. The mentor relationship is no longer needed in its previous form.

*Examples of the most frequently observed psychological and organizational factors that cause movement into the current relationship phase.

Most mentor–mentee relationships develop over time, and there appear to be several distinct phases of mentor–mentee relationships. Table 2.2 presents a model that highlights some of the key phases of the mentor–mentee relationship. The reasons that cause movement in the relationship are described as turning points. Initiation, cultivation, separation, and redefinition cover general periods of six months to more than five years.

The benefits that result from mentoring can extend beyond the individuals involved. Mentoring can contribute to employee motivation and retention and the cohesiveness of the organization.[68] The organization's culture can be strengthened by passing the core values from one generation to the next.

The increasing diversity of the workforce adds a new dimension to the mentor–mentee matching process. People are attracted to mentors who talk, look, act, and communicate like them. Gender, race, ethnicity, religion, and availability of computers can all play a role in matching. If mentor–mentee matching is left to occur naturally, women, African Americans, Hispanics, and Asians may be left out.[69] The underrepresentation of these groups in management-level positions needs to be evaluated in each firm that considers using mentor–mentee matching. One study showed that cross-gender relationships can be beneficial. The results of 32 mentor–mentee pairings (14 male–female; 18 female–female) found that male–female mentor matchings can be as successful as female–female mentoring.[70]

Socializing a Culturally Diverse Workforce

The United States consists of people with many religions, many cultures, and many different roots: African, European, Asian, South American, Middle Eastern, and Indian. Today, African Americans, Asian Americans, and Hispanics constitute about 30.3 percent of the U.S. labor force.[71] In 2009, about 43.2 percent of the total workforce was female.[72]

We hear a lot about diversity, but what it means is sometimes confusing.[73] Diversity is not a synonym for equal employment opportunity (EEO), nor is it another word for affirmative action. **Diversity** is the vast array of physical and cultural differences that constitute the spectrum of human attributes. Six core dimensions of diversity exist: age, ethnicity, gender, physical attributes, race, and sexual/affectional orientation. These are the core elements of diversity that have a lifelong effect on behavior and attitudes.

diversity
The vast array of physical and cultural differences that constitute the spectrum of human attributes.

Secondary forms of diversity—the differences that people acquire, discard, or modify throughout their lives—can be changed. Secondary dimensions of diversity include educational background, marital status, religious beliefs, health disabilities, and work experience.

Valuing diversity from an organizational and leadership perspective means understanding and valuing core and secondary diversity dimension differences between oneself and others. An increasingly important goal in a changing society is to understand that all individuals are different and to appreciate these differences.[74]

Management's Ability to Capitalize on Diversity

Due to the changing demographics in the United States, differences in the employee pool are going to continue to increase over the next few decades. Managers will have to study socialization much more closely and intervene so that the maximum benefits result from hiring an increasingly diverse workforce. Studying the ethnic background and national culture of these workers will have to be taken seriously. The managerial challenge will be to identify ways to integrate the increasing number and mix of people from diverse national cultures into the workplace. Some obvious issues for managers of ethnically diverse work-forces to consider include these:

- Coping with employees' unfamiliarity with the English language.
- Increased training for service jobs that require communication skills.
- Cultural (national) awareness training for the current workforce.
- Learning which rewards are valued by different ethnic groups.
- Developing career development programs that fit the skills, needs, and values of the ethnic group.
- Rewarding managers for effectively recruiting, hiring, and integrating a diverse workforce.
- Focusing not only on ethnic diversity but also learning more about age, gender, and workers with disability diversities.

Socializing an ethnically diverse workforce is a two-way proposition. Not only must the manager learn about the employees' cultural background, the employee must also learn about the rituals, customs, and values of the firm or the work unit.[75] Awareness workshops and orientation sessions are becoming more popular every day. For example, Merck has an educational program to raise its employees' awareness of and attitudes about women and minorities.[76] The program emphasizes how policies and systems can be tailored to meet changes in the demographics of the workplace. Procter & Gamble has stressed the value of diversity. The firm uses multicultural advisory teams, minority and women's networking conferences, and "onboarding" programs to help new women and minority employees become acclimated and productive as quickly as possible. Ortho Pharmaceutical initiated a program to "manage diversity" that is designed to foster a process of cultural transition within the firm. Northeastern Products Company established an onsite English as a Second Language (ESL) program to meet the needs of Hispanic and Asian employees. A buddy system has been established at Ore-Ida. A buddy (English speaker) is assigned to a new employee (whose first language is not English) to assist him or her with communication problems.

The Seattle-Times Co. (newspaper publisher), with 24 percent minority employment, conducts a two-day training session called "Exploration into Diversity" 10 times a year. The training program covers such issues as diversity, multiculturalism, and pluralism. The trainees define terms, discuss obstacles to achieving pluralism, present experiences, present concepts of stereotyping and prejudices, and cover methods to overcome obstacles. Follow-up sessions are also a part of the Seattle-Times's approach to improving diversity awareness.[77] The Seattle-Times Co. has won several awards for being a national leader in inclusivity and equality.[78]

Global competition, like changing domestic demographics, is placing a new requirement on managers to learn about unfamiliar cultures from which new employees are coming. The emphasis on open expression of diversity in the workforce is paralleled by a social movement toward the retention of ethnic roots. The "new ethnicity," a renewed awareness and pride of cultural heritage, can become an advantage of American firms operating in foreign countries.[79] Using the multicultural workforce to better compete, penetrate, and succeed in foreign cultures is one potential benefit of managing diversity effectively.

Summary of Key Points

- *Culture* is a pattern of assumptions that are invented, discovered, or developed to learn to cope with organizational life. *Socialization* is a process by which organizations bring new employees into the culture.
- Simply declaring that "this" will be the culture is not realistic. Culture evolves over time. It can be influenced by powerful individuals such as Ray Kroc at McDonald's or Walt Disney, but it typically evolves and becomes real when people interact and work together.
- Organizations can achieve effectiveness only when employees share values. The values of an increasingly diverse workforce are shaped long before a person enters an organization. Thus, it is important to recruit, select, and retain employees whose values best fit the value of the firm.
- Four dominant cultures can be identified: bureaucratic, clan, entrepreneurial, and market. These cultures vary in terms of control and focus of attention.
- Spirituality has become a topic of interest in discussing management practices. The way a person feels and thinks about life and work is starting to be included in some organizations as a crucial lever for optimizing performance.
- Socialization is the process by which organizations bring new employees into the culture. There is a passing of values, assumptions, and attitudes from older to newer workers.
- Mentoring is an important approach for developing protégés under the guidance of a mentor.

Discussion and Review Questions

1. Organizational culture is a difficult concept to define. How would you define the culture of an organization you have been employed by or observed?
2. A growing number of Americans work for internationally-owned firms that operate in the United States. Do you think that these American employees are being influenced by the international owner's approach to management and the culture of the country of the owner?
3. Identify the three main socialization stages. Which of these stages is most important for developing high-performing employees? Explain.
4. If the process of organizational socialization is inevitable, why is it important that it be managed?
5. How can a leader or founder help create a strong culture in an organization? Can any founder create a culture? Explain.
6. Why is it so important that organizations keep trying to encourage productive mentoring relationships between senior- and junior-level employees? What are some of the challenges associated with mentoring programs?
7. What should managers of diverse workforces know about differences in values among individuals?
8. What do advocates claim about the influence of spirituality on the performance of employees?
9. Why is it so difficult to change an organizational culture that is considered strong or influential in affecting the behavior of employees?
10. In what ways does organizational culture influence a company's effectiveness and performance?

Taking It to the Net

One of the Best Firms

This chapter discussed diversity in the workforce and its impact on organizations' culture. First, visit the U.S. Bureau of Labor Statistics Web site and examine information about diversity and demographics forecasts. Second, secure a hard copy of or view online the most recent *Fortune*'s "America's 50 Best Companies for Minorities." Last, select one of the firms and determine why it is considered favorably in the ranking. Prepare a brief presentation explaining what you learned from reviewing the information and statistics of one of *Fortune*'s 50 best companies.

Case for Analysis: *Toyota's Culture and the "Sticky Pedal" Recall*

Toyota is an extremely successful automaker that has built a reputation for quality by fostering a culture of continuous improvement and long-term relationships with employees, vendors, customers, and other key stakeholders. With such a strong organizational culture, how did the company reach a point in which it was criticized for not sharing enough information about the unintended acceleration problems that were documented in the form of complaints as far back as March 3, 2004? Six years later in 2010, Toyota paid a steep price for initially ignoring or not proactively dealing with the acceleration problem; it conducted a massive recall of more than 8 million vehicles to fix the faulty gas pedals. Not only did the company's reputation take a large hit, but U.S. Transportation Secretary Ray LaHood slapped a $16.4 million fine against the automaker.

Many people were upset with Toyota's handling of the crisis and apparent lack of transparent communication about the extent and cause of the problem. For some time after complaints of unintended acceleration were filed with authorities and the company, Toyota maintained that the cause of the acceleration was poorly fitting floor mats. It took until January 2010 for the company to make the decision to replace the faulty accelerator pedals.

Toyota's organizational culture may be partly to blame for the ill will that was created over the handling of the faulty accelerators problem. First, Toyota's culture of keeping potentially negative information locked tightly within the firm is at odds with what many organizations do during a crisis in the U.S. For example, the leaders of Johnson & Johnson made it a point to communicate with the public major developments regarding the cyanide-laced Tylenol capsule tamperings in 1982. Second, Toyota's leadership may be too insulated to allow it full or timely access to negative information. This problem may be due to the fact that Toyota has a formal, hierarchical organizational structure that prevents negative information from reaching the top.

Will Toyota rebound and regain its global prominence as a top quality automaker? Some experts suggest that the company will eventually work through and resolve these accelerator-related problems. However, another question remains: Will the company also attempt to modify its culture so that it can handle future crises in a more open and timely manner?

QUESTIONS FOR ANALYSIS

1. Why did Toyota wait so long to publically acknowledge and replace the faulty accelerator pedals?
2. Changing a culture from one that rewards secrecy to one that is more transparent (especially in a crisis) appears to be difficult. Why?
3. If you were the president of the Toyota Motor Corporation, how would you have handled the unintended acceleration problems? Explain.

Sources: Adapted from Josh Mitchell and Kate Linebaugh, "Toyota Faces $16.4 Million U.S. Fine," *Wall Street Journal* (April 6, 2010); Laurie A. Harbour, "Toyota: Crisis & The Importance of Culture," *Automotive & Design Production* 122, no. 2 (March/April 2010): 12–13; Norihiko Shirouzu and Mariko Sanchanta, "Support Wavers At Toyota For Chief," *Wall Street Journal,* February 23, 2010, p. A.4; "Leaders: Accelerating Into Trouble, Toyota," *The Economist,* February 13, 2010,, p. 14; Kate Linebaugh, Dionne Searcey, and Norihiko Shirouzu, "Secretive Culture Led Toyota Astray," *Wall Street Journal* (February 10, 2010), p. A1.

Experiential Exercise: *Testing National Culture Knowledge*

OBJECTIVES

1. To test your understanding of cultural differences.
2. To compare your understanding and international experiences with classmates.

STARTING THE EXERCISE

1. Each student should complete the seven-category survey.
2. Score your individual answers with the answer key.
3. Form groups of five or six and compare international experiences. Did individuals with more international experience score better?
4. Within the group, discuss steps that could be taken to improve individual knowledge of cultural differences.

GOING GLOBAL? TEST YOUR BUSINESS ETIQUETTE KNOWLEDGE (SOME QUESTIONS HAVE MORE THAN ONE ANSWER)

1. During business meetings, use first names in
   a. Great Britain, because everyone is so chummy.
   b. Australia, because informality is the rule.
   c. China, because the first name is the surname.
   d. Japan, because the last names are easy to mispronounce.
2. In China, offer expensive gifts to your hosts
   a. Every time they ask for one.
   b. When you need help getting out of the country.
   c. Never. If they can't reciprocate it, they'll lose face.

3. In which country is a business card an object of respect?
   a. Japan. An executive's identity depends on his employer.
   b. Taiwan. It explains a person's rank and status.
   c. France, especially cards describing a man's experience.
4. When doing business in Japan, never
   a. Touch someone.
   b. Leave your chopsticks in the rice.
   c. Take people to pricier restaurants than they took you to.
   d. All of the above.
5. Power breakfasts are inappropriate in all but
   a. Italy. The natives like to bring the family along.
   b. Mexico. People don't bother to get to work till 10 a.m. anyway.
   c. the United States. We invented them.
   d. France. People are at their most argumentative in the morning.
6. In some countries, colors are key. Which is true?
   a. For Koreans, writing a person's name in red signifies death.
   b. In China and Japan, gifts wrapped in white or black should be presented only at funerals.
   c. Purple suits in Great Britain represent lack of taste.
7. Which of these choices are obscene gestures?
   a. The okay sign in Brazil.
   b. A hearty slap on the back in Switzerland.
   c. Doing anything with the left hand in Saudi Arabia.
   d. Thumb between second and third finger in Japan.

ANSWERS

1—b, c; 2—c; 3—a, b; 4—d; 5—c; 6—a, b; 7—a, c, d.

Source: *Business World,* May 1990, p. 27.

CHAPTER THREE

Managing Globally

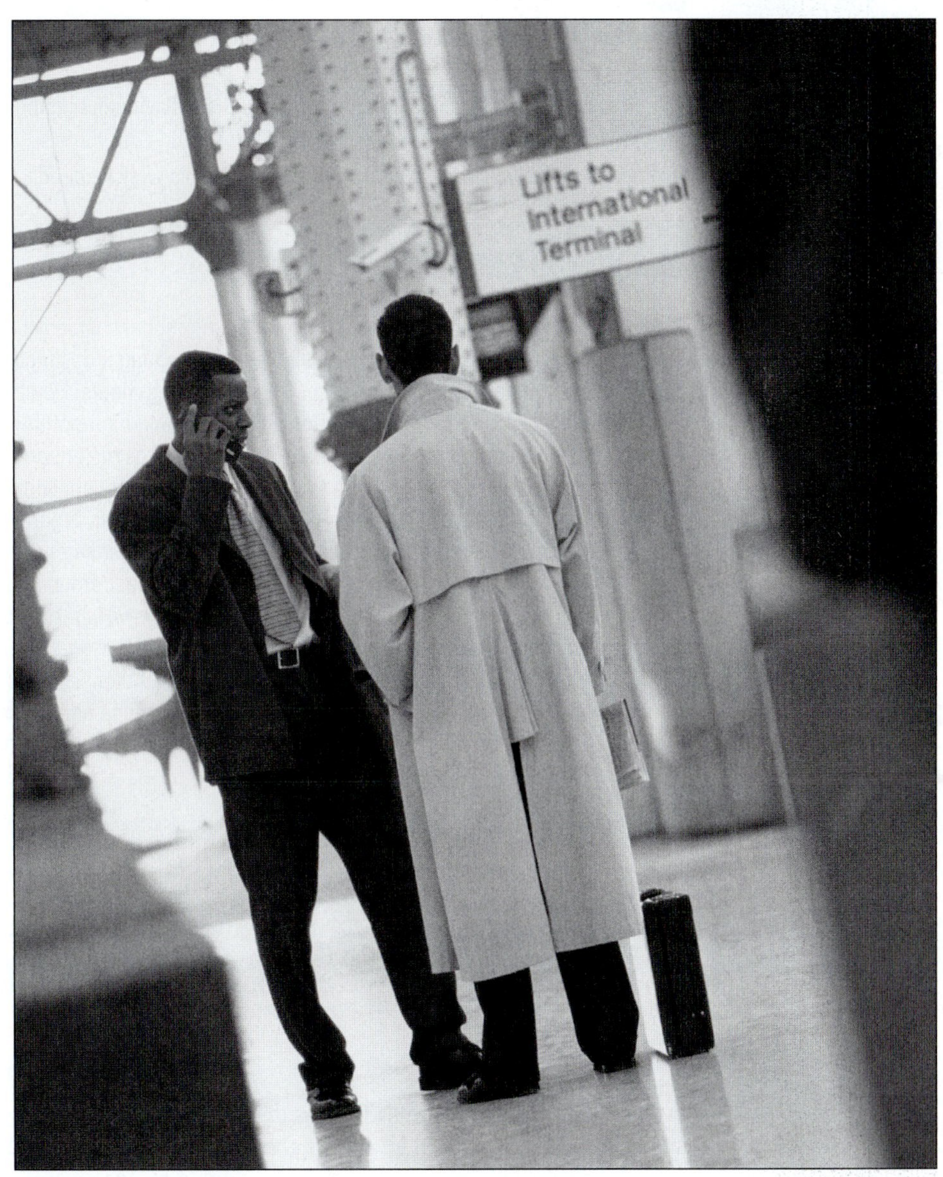

Learning Objectives

After completing Chapter 3, you should be able to

Define
What is meant by *globalization.*

Understand
Why the study of cross-cultural management is important.

Discuss
The global skills managers must learn and apply to deal with a changing world.

Compare
How the characteristics of culture can influence the behavior and attitudes of employees.

Identify
Hofstede's original cultural dimensions and research his work inspired.

The Virtual Expatriate

Robert Adams, an American, has worked for a multinational company headquartered in the United States for over seven years. Perceived as a fast-track manager destined for executive-level status, Adams has performed well in a variety of domestic assignments. However, his supervisor has just asked him to take a three-year expatriate assignment in a high-potential foreign subsidiary some 7,000 miles from headquarters. Although Adams recognizes the importance of developing international language, cultural, and business skills, he has several concerns regarding this long-term assignment: It could make him "out of sight, out of mind" with regard to promotions and politics back at headquarters; his spouse may not be willing to put her career on hold; and his children are about to enter high school and do not want to leave their peer groups. Adams solved this potential dilemma by suggesting to his manager that he become a *virtual expatriate,** meaning he would commute back and forth between the international subsidiary and headquarters. Even though he would be away from home for several days each month, Adams and his family would not have to sell their house and relocate overseas. This way, he would be able to protect his career interests at headquarters while not disrupting his spouse's career or children's social development by relocating overseas.

*Note: The "virtual expatriate" is a popular type of global assignee that has been referred to by a number of authors, including David G. Collins, Hugh Scullion, and Michael J. Morley, "Changing Patterns of Global Staffing in the Multinational Enterprise: Challenges to the Conventional Expatriate Assignment and Emerging Alternatives," *Journal of World Business* 42, no. 2 (2007): 198–213; Shailaja Neelakantan, "India Looks beyond Outsourcing as Technology Firms Innovate," *Wall Street Journal*, December 3, 2003; Steve Bates, "Study Discovers Patterns in Global Executive Mobility," *HRMagazine* 47, no. 10 (October 2002); 14–15; Stephanie Armour, "Commute a Chore? Try USA to London—Quick Trips Can Make More Sense than Relocating for Short-Term Jobs," *USA Today*, November 9, 2000; and Julia Flynn, "E-mail, Cellphones and Frequent Flier Miles Let 'Virtual' Expats Work Abroad but Live at Home," *Wall Street Journal*, October 25, 1999.

In the world of business, organizations that manage the myriad of global interrelationships and interdependencies will achieve higher levels of organizational effectiveness and competitive advantage.[1] Products, capital, and human resources are becoming interdependent as business entities increasingly consider their market areas as being global rather than simply domestic.[2] An increasing number of enterprises search for markets, resources, and human assets in every corner of the globe. Fast-track managers like Robert Adams need to be encouraged to acquire global skills and experiences. Today, fewer and fewer entrepreneurs and businesses find that they can prosper and grow solely within the confines of a domestic market with employees who lack an international perspective.

As the globalization of business continues, organizations must be analyzed and managed in a new way.[3] Simply considering how office workers behave and perform at Apple headquarters in Cupertino, California, and then attempting to generalize findings and conclusions and apply them to office workers at Lenovo Group (which purchased IBM's PC business in 2005) in Beijing, China, is not sufficient. American office workers and Chinese office workers definitely think and behave in different ways. Behavior, structure, and processes are all crucial to the successful operation of an enterprise. However, as globalization spreads, it is important to acknowledge, study, interpret, and manage differences across countries and groups of employees in these areas.[4] In this chapter, we examine organizational behavior from a globalization perspective, starting with an introduction of the requirements for the global manager who must operate in the 21st century. The chapter focuses primarily on culture and cultural variation, areas that managers must understand to compete effectively in a world that's undergoing rapid transformation.[5]

In his book, *The Work of Nations,* Robert Reich notes that "we are living through a transformation that will rearrange the politics and economics of the 21st century. There will be no national products or technologies, no national corporations, no national industries."[6] Reich points out that many corporations are becoming "global webs" in which products are international composites. He also argues that a nation's commitment to developing its people is the prime way to ensure global competitiveness. If development of people is vital on a national level, it is certainly vital on an organizational level.

Globalization

globalization
The interdependency of transportation, distribution, communication, and economic networks across international borders.

International businesses have existed for years. Today, however, economic and business activity includes global strategic alliances, worldwide production and distribution, and regional integration agreements such as the European Union, Asia-Pacific Economic Cooperation, and North American Free Trade Agreement. **Globalization** is defined as this interdependency of transportation, distribution, communication, and economic networks across international borders. As the OB at Work feature illustrates, one controversial example of globalization is outsourcing (offshoring) of jobs to international locations.

Marketing scholar and researcher Theodore Levitt maintains that the existence of truly global markets demands a new type of corporation.[7] He believes the global corporation has replaced the multinational corporation as the most effective international competitor. The multinational corporation conducts its business in various countries, adapting its products and practices to local conditions by customizing products for specific markets. In contrast, the global corporation avoids the high relative costs of the multinational corporation by offering universal standardized products for a homogeneous world market.

Developing successful global strategies and approaches to managing diverse workers has become a new requirement for managers.[8] It is often the case that management practices in an organization relate to the nationality of its ownership rather than to the particular locations of its facilities.[9] However, it is no longer enough to simply assume that a motivational approach, job design technique, or performance review system will have similar results for all workers in all settings.[10] The evolution of business from being primarily domestic oriented to more globally oriented will require new thinking and new managerial skills.[11] Table 3.1 traces changes since 1945 (when a domestic orientation dominated the American manager's attitude) to the present in such areas as competitiveness, structure, and cultural sensitivity. Take, for example, the Ford Motor Company, which was founded in 1903. Although it enjoyed widespread success in the U.S. domestic market, it was not until the 1960s that the company evolved from phase I to phase II by aggressively pursuing international expansion. In 1967, Ford of Europe was established, which eventually helped

OB AT WORK

Offshoring: Does It Create or Replace Jobs in the Global Marketplace?

There's a good chance that recently you have seen a nightly newscast or read a blog or news summary on your smartphone reporting that another U.S. company is "offshoring" or "outsourcing" part of its back-office, customer service, or computer operations to a vendor in an international location such as India. The trend is real. An increasing number of firms are sending a part of their operations—software development, call centers, payroll, loan and insurance claims processing, and so forth—to an offshore location. U.S. firms such as General Electric, Oracle, Motorola, Cisco, Intel, and Prudential engage in offshore activities. Opponents of offshoring argue that such decisions cost Americans their jobs. These critics claim that bottom-line-oriented American executives are too willing to lay off Americans to save some money in labor costs (an individual working at a call center in Bangalore, India, makes considerably less than her counterpart in Cleveland, Ohio). They contend that exporting jobs will have the unintended effects of increasing unemployment and transferring wealth to workers in other countries.

Do the statistics support these claims? The data provide mixed results. On one hand, companies that provide outsourcing services in India (e.g., Infosys Technologies Ltd., Wipro Ltd., and Tata Consultancy Services) have experienced very rapid growth in recent years. These and other companies make up part of the $3.5 billion call-center and back-office industry in India. This high-growth (and high-profit) industry has led to a recent wave of acquisitions, including one made by IBM, which agreed to pay $150 million for Daksh eServices, the third-largest call-center and back-office service provider, with revenues of $60 million. In a similar move, Citigroup is increasing its ownership stake in another Indian outsourcing firm, e-Serve International Ltd. Certainly, it could be argued that such trends will lead to job growth for Indian workers, most likely at a cost to American jobs.

On the other hand, proponents of free trade argue that outsourcing is an economically healthy and acceptable practice that should be allowed to flourish. These individuals point out that such free trade practices have led to job growth and profits for U.S. organizations that provide such services as legal work, computer programming, telecommunications, banking, engineering, management consulting, and other private services to the world market. The U.S. Department of Commerce reported in December 2009 that the value of such U.S. exports of services had reached $507.5 billion. This far exceeded the amount of service imports (e.g., outsourcing of such private services as call centers and data-processing operations to other countries), which totaled $371.2 billion in 2009. In essence, U.S. companies that successfully sell services to the rest of the world are much more likely to be able to grow their businesses and employ larger numbers of U.S. employees. In addition to the trade surplus argument, proponents of free trade point to the number of large Indian companies that have set up large operations in the United States. For example, Tata Consultancy Services (part of Tata Group) has established 47 worksites in the United States to serve customers that include American Express Co., Citigroup Inc., ChevronTexaco Corp., and Eli Lilly & Co. This translates to the creation of more U.S. jobs.

In sum, outsourcing/offshoring is a controversial business practice that represents one aspect of how the globalization of business across national borders is occurring in today's economy. To be effective, managers should understand how globalization affects their domestic operations and influences the effective management of their human resources around the globe.

Sources: Dave Blanchard, "Making It Work Overseas," *Industry Week* 259, no. 3 (2010: 51; "U.S. International Trade in Goods and Services—December 2009," U.S. Census Bureau, U.S. Bureau of Economic Analysis, U.S. Department of Commerce, Washington, DC (February 10, 2010); Steve Hamm, "How Accenture One-Upped Bangalore: It Leads the Pack in Tech Services, Melding Offshoring and Classic Consulting," *Businessweek,* April 23, 2007, p. 98; Manjeet Kripalani and Steve Hamm, "Merger Fever Breaks out in Bangalore," *Businessweek,* April 26, 2004, p. 56; Joanna Slater, "IBM to Buy Indian Call-Center Firm," *Wall Street Journal,* April 8, 2004, p. B.6; Jay Solomon and Elena Cherney, "A Global Journal Report: Outsourcing to India Sees a Twist," *Wall Street Journal,* April 1, 2004, p. A.2; and Michael M. Phillips, "More Work Is Outsourced to U.S. Than Away from It, Data Show," *Wall Street Journal,* March 15, 2004, p. A.2.

Ford to enter phase III of corporate evolution, the multinational stage.[12] Phase IV of evolution, the global stage, emphasizes that firms need to understand their customers' and other stakeholders' needs, quickly translate them into products and services on a least-cost basis, and market them effectively. Ford is attempting to accomplish this by selling off its luxury brands (i.e., Jaguar, Land Rover, and Volvo) so that it can meet tougher carbon emission guidelines in different countries.[13] The ability to diagnose customers' and stakeholders' needs, manage cross-cultural transactions, manage multinational teams, and form and manage effective global alliances is crucial to succeeding in the fourth phase.

cross-cultural management
The study of the behavior of individuals in organizations around the world.

Cross-cultural management involves the study of the behavior of individuals in organizations around the world. The study describes organizational behavior within countries and

TABLE 3.1 Corporate and Cross-Cultural Evolution

Sources: See N. J. Adler and F. Ghadar, "International Strategy from the Perspective of People and Culture: The North American Context," in A. M. Rugman (ed.), *Research in Global Strategic Management: International Business Research for the Twenty-First Century: Canada's New Research Agenda,* vol. 1, (Greenwich, CT: JAI Press, 1990), 179–205. (3) Phases I–III are based on R. Vernon, "International Investment and International Trade Product Cycle," *Quarterly Journal of Economics* (May 1966): 87.

	Phase I Domestic	**Phase II International**	**Phase III Multinational**	**Phase IV Global**
Primary orientation	Product/service	Market	Price	Strategy
Competitive strategy	Domestic	Muitidomestic	Multinational	Global
Importance of world business	Marginal	Important	Extremely important	Dominant
Product/service	New, unique	More standardized	Completely standardized (commodity)	Mass-customized
Technology	Product engineering emphasized Proprietary	Process engineering emphasized Shared	Engineering not emphasized Widely shared	Product and process engineering Instantly and extensively shared
R&D/sales	High	Decreasing	Very low	Very high
Profit margin	High	Decreasing	Very low	High, yet immediately decreasing
Competitors	None	Few	Many	Significant (few or many)
Market	Small, domestic	Large, muitidomestic	Large, multinational	Largest, global
Production location	Domestic	Domestic and primary markets	Multinational, least cost	Global, least cost
Exports	None	Growing, high potential	Large, saturated	Imports and exports
Structure	Functional divisions Centralized	Functional with international division Decentralized	Multinational line of business Centralized	Global alliances Coordinated, decentralized
Cultural sensitivity	Marginally important	Very important	Somewhat important	Critically important
With whom	No one	Clients	Employees	Employees and clients
Level	No one	Workers and clients	Managers	Executives
Strategic assumption	"One way"/ "one best way"	"Many good ways"	"One least-cost way"	"Many good ways" simultaneously

cultures; compares organizational behavior across countries and cultures; and attempts to understand and improve the interaction and behavior of co-workers, clients, suppliers, and alliance partners from different countries and cultures.[14] Cross-cultural management attempts to extend the study of domestic management to encompass global and multicultural considerations.

The global manager is a person who views markets, production, service, and opportunities globally and who seeks higher profits for the firm on a global basis. The truly global manager is at home anywhere in the world. He or she is considered open to national ideas and free of prejudices or attachments to one community, country, or culture. The global manager is aware of and understands the major cultural differences from

FIGURE 3.1
Managerial Skills for the Global Marketplace

country to country. This awareness and understanding is acquired by observation, learning, participation, and involvement with people from many different countries and cultures. Like those in other types of managerial positions, global managers can experience tension when their international work and extensive travel schedules impinge on their personal lives.[15]

Leaders of global enterprises in such emerging markets as the BRIC countries (i.e., Brazil, Russia, India, and China) will need to possess local sensitivity and global knowledge. At times, senior management positions in emerging countries are staffed with nationals from the company's home country.[16] Do these home-country senior managers have the necessary skills, both those mentioned earlier and others, to help their firms achieve and sustain competitive advantage? In addition to having language and extensive host-country and global networking skills,[17] global leaders will need to master many other skills, as illustrated in Figure 3.1.

Providing acceptable products to the gigantic emerging BRIC country markets requires making timely and relevant decisions. For example, consumers in China appear to be very concerned about the price–performance equation. Philips Electronics introduced a combination video-CD player in China when there was no market for this product in the United States or Europe. More than 15 million units have been sold because the Chinese quickly adopted a positive view of the two players (video and CD) for one bargain price.

Companies have learned that consumers in India are different from those in the West. Single-service packets, or sachets, are very popular in India. They allow consumers in India to buy only what they need, try out the products, and save their money. Products as varied as shampoos, pickles, cough syrup, and laundry detergents are sold in sachets in India, and it is estimated that they make up 20 to 30 percent of the total sold in their categories.[18]

Global Strategic Skills

Managers operating in a globally shifting work environment will need a working knowledge of international relationships and foreign affairs, including global financial markets, international law, and exchange rate movements. Understanding global economies of scale, work ethics of employees, and host government policies and procedures will be required to formulate feasible, fair, legal, and effective strategies.[19]

Levitt's view of standardized world markets was presented earlier. Although the global market view is widely publicized, there is a need to be sensitive to local customs, preferences, and idiosyncrasies.[20] A few examples illustrate the strategic importance of local preferences and global standardization:

- Procter & Gamble's liquid detergent failed in Europe when it was introduced because European washing machines were not equipped for liquid detergent. Modifications to the detergent were made and sales subsequently improved.
- Kellogg's Corn Flakes were eaten primarily as a snack when introduced in Brazil. With educational advertising, Corn Flakes gained acceptance as a breakfast food.
- L'Oréal markets its hair care and cosmetic products in more than 100 countries. It has adopted and implemented a strategy to produce local products adapted to local markets, while it reaps world economies of scale in research and development, raw materials sourcing, and productivity balancing.
- Wyeth Pharmaceuticals and Hitachi Data Systems develop training programs from their headquarters' locations but then send the programs to worldwide experts so that the training programs can be tailored to fit the needs and requirements of different local markets.[21] For example, Wyeth may develop a new training program that describes a new prescription drug, but local affiliates would need to review the program to make sure that local issues like price controls, packaging and labeling requirements, and reimbursement policies are "localized" to fit that particular market.
- Nestlé has tailored products to what the Chinese consumer wants and needs—instant noodles, seasonings for Chinese cuisine, mineral water, and a popular live-lactobacillus health drink.[22]

These five examples suggest that global success requires striking a balance between capitalizing on resources and needs within a nation and capturing a vision of a globalizing world.

Local requirements such as customer satisfaction must be met. But local managers also will need to think in global terms so that economies of scale and competition can be addressed.

Team-Building Skills

The increased complexity of global operations will require more use of work teams, including culturally diverse groups. The need for global teamwork is obvious when considering how accounting and auditing are conducted in various parts of the world. In one country, financial statements are used to reflect the economic conditions of a firm, and the audit is an accuracy check of the condition. In another country, the audit is conducted to make sure that legal requirements are met. Imagine how the audit could be interpreted in different countries and why teamwork is needed to ensure a clear understanding of its use.

In operations management, it is important to develop systems, processes, and procedures across subsidiaries. Many companies have subsidiaries in different countries. Determining if the system that is so valuable in one country can be applied or modified to fit another country requires teamwork.

Teams should not ignore or minimize either cultural differences or the difficulty faced in trying to develop and manage multicultural teams.[23] In the context of a global organization, it becomes even more critical that team members become aware of their own stereotypes without allowing them to limit their expectations and actions. There is also an urgent need for teams to avoid cultural dominance (disproportionate power vested in members of one culture over those from other cultures). Managers should distribute power according to each member's ability to do the task, not according to some preconceived notion of relative cultural superiority.

Organization Skills

The management philosophy of North America for the vast majority of the 20th century reflected Douglas McGregor's Theory X. Theory X held that workers are irresponsible and unwilling to work and must be persuaded to perform their obligations to their employers. Thus, the Theory X–based management approach to organization is to structure the job, closely supervise, and reward good performance and punish poor performance. This approach encourages a carrot-and-stick, hierarchically controlled approach to management. The emphasis is on short-term compliance and profitability. Is this really the way U.S. workers are? Certainly some American workers and workers in other countries fit the Theory X mold perfectly. However, others respond better to a Theory Y approach, the opposite of Theory X. Theory Y managers create an environment that encourages self-control and the willingness to take responsibility. They assume that most employees want to work and do not have to be coerced to do a good job. The employees who react positively to this style want autonomy, recognition, and an opportunity to display their skills, creativity, and commitment.

In addition to cultural diversity, managers must consider individual differences when organizing firms, units, and jobs. Minimum requirements for managers operating in a globally shifting world would include

- Creativity and inventiveness in designing organizations and jobs.
- High tolerance for ambiguity and cultural differences.
- Ability to coordinate finance, marketing, operations management, and human resource interdependencies.

Communication Skills

In the global environment, managers will need to be able to communicate with diverse groups of people. The communication task would be easier if managers possessed multilingual skills and high levels of cross-cultural awareness and sensitivity.[24] Within the global business environment, strategy formulation, decision making, motivating, team building, organization and job design, leading, and negotiating are all based on managers' ability to communicate with each other and with subordinates. Achieving effective communication in a culturally homogenous setting is extremely difficult. However, it is much more challenging and difficult when a variety of nationalities, languages, and cultures are represented within the same organization.[25]

Cross-cultural communication often results in misunderstanding caused by misperception, misinterpretation, and misevaluation. When the sender of a text message, e-mail, report, or policy comes from one culture and the receiver comes from another, the chances of an accurate transmission of a message may be quite low. People often understand and interpret the message differently. As the OB at Work feature illustrates, these same communication issues can occur when working in virtual teams.

Continually working to improve communication skills that work with culturally diverse employees will become mandatory. It will not be easy, but awareness of the difficulty of cross-cultural communication is a starting point.[26]

Transfer of Knowledge Skills

The increased competitiveness throughout the world has placed a special emphasis on technological advances for product and process innovations. This emphasis has increased the need to transfer knowledge. Learning about a practice, technique, or approach in one country that can be transferred elsewhere is a skill that managers can apply on a regular

OB AT WORK Communicating in Global Virtual Teams

Used by many different types of organizations such as PricewaterhouseCoopers, Whirlpool, and IBM, global virtual teams are cross-functional teams that operate across time, space, organizational boundaries, and cultures whose members communicate mainly through electronic technologies (texting, e-mail, videoconferencing, voice-mail, etc.). With infrequent face-to-face contact, these teams are faced with the challenge of building and maintaining trust as they work toward accomplishing the team's objectives and goals. In particular, miscommunication between team members from diverse cultures and backgrounds can create a roadblock to the development of trust and, ultimately, effective team functioning. Internationally savvy companies can manage this potential problem by providing each member of their virtual teams with cross-cultural training.

The first part of cross-cultural training should focus on helping each team member understand his or her own cultural beliefs; verbal and nonverbal communication styles; and attitudes toward time, space, and work ethic. The rationale behind this "inward-looking" portion of the training is based on the research of Edward T. and Mildred R. Hall, anthropologists and pioneers in the field of culture and communication who wrote:

> Like people all over the world, Americans take their culture for granted. Indeed, it's only in juxtaposition with other cultures that Americans begin to understand the influence of their own culture on their behavior.

The second part of the cross-cultural training for virtual team members should focus on learning how to work effectively with teammates from diverse cultures. Team members should learn how to interpret the verbal and nonverbal communication styles and cultural backgrounds of teammates and how to respond effectively to these unique cues.

For example, assume an American is placed on a global virtual team with individuals from Mexico. First, she would learn about her own cultural biases and communication style. Like many Americans, she prefers the following approaches to business: likes to tackle projects in monochronic fashion (i.e., one thing at a time); has a strong work ethic; favors direct, get-to-the point communication; and likes to keep work and home life separate. In contrast, her Mexican counterparts tend to be more polychronic (i.e., juggle many activities at once), work hard but spend more time with family and friends, prefer a less direct approach to communication (to allow ample time to build trust), and do not refrain from discussing family issues at work.

Without some amount of cross-cultural training, these global virtual team members are going to have a difficult time communicating and building trust. Without such trust, the likelihood of the team performing at an optimal level will be greatly diminished.

Sources: F. Siebdrat, M. Hoegl and H. Ernst, "How to Manage Virtual Teams," *MIT Sloan Management Review* 50, no. 44 (2000): 63–68; Arvind Malhotra, Ann Majchrzak, and Benson Rosen, "Leading Virtual Teams," *The Academy of Management Perspectives* 21, no. 1 (2007): 60–70; Douglas N. Ross, "Electronic Communications: Do Cultural Dimensions Matter?" *American Business Review* (June 2001): 75–81; Lee Gardenswartz and Anita Rowe, "Cross-Cultural Awareness," *HRMagazine*, March 2001, pp. 139–42; Maurice Cleasby, "Managing Global Contact," *The British Journal of Administrative Management* (March/April 2000): 4–12; Steven L. McShane and Mary Ann Von Glinow, *Organizational Behavior* (Boston: Irwin McGraw-Hill, 2000); Sirkka L. Jarvenpaa and Dorothy E. Leidner, "Communication and Trust in Global Virtual Teams," *Organizational Science*, (November/December 1999): 791–815; and Edward T. Hall and Mildred R. Hall, *Understanding Cultural Differences: Germans, French, and Americans* (Yarmouth, ME: Intercultural Press, 1987).

basis. Research on Capital One Financial suggests that the firm is competing globally by being flexible in the way it develops knowledge and how it applies this learning to other parts of the organization.[27] Capital One Financial is embracing and leveraging knowledge as a way to increase its organizational effectiveness and competitive advantage.

For years, Americans appeared to be oblivious and arrogant about using knowledge, information, or techniques initiated and practiced in other countries. The quality movement initiated in Japan by an American, W. Edwards Deming, after World War II, however, has changed the historic practice of ignoring what other countries and companies are doing. **Benchmarking** (analyzing how well a firm is doing compared with its competitors) is now a widespread practice around the world. Benchmarking attempts to answer the question: How are we doing in terms of strategy, quality of product, compensation program, job design, or teamwork?[28]

benchmarking
A standard of excellence or achievement against which a firm's products or practices are measured or judged.

The Japanese have become experts at transferring knowledge. Although U.S. manufacturers were the first to design both monochrome and color televisions with transistors replacing slower-starting, shorter-lived electron tubes, they failed to implement the newer technology in their main product offering. By 1963, most Japanese sets exported to the United States were transistorized.[29] On the other hand, although they had the capability earlier, U.S. producers did not move to complete transistorization of their monochrome sets until the late 1960s. The Japanese moved aggressively to solid-state color designs, first in their home market and then for export sales. Through learning and transfer of knowledge, they reduced the cost and improved the quality of TV sets. Today, such firms as Toshiba, Samsung, Sony, Panasonic, Philips, and Sharp dominate the television manufacturing industry.

How can managers develop such knowledge transfer skills? Although it doesn't happen overnight, managers must learn how to identify best practices from domestic and overseas-based operations and then cross-pollination will improve organizational learning and, ultimately, the firm's ability to achieve and sustain competitive advantage.

Culture

National Culture

national culture
A set of values, attitudes, beliefs, and norms shared by a majority of the inhabitants of a country.

A ***national culture*** is a set of values, attitudes, beliefs, and norms shared by a majority of the inhabitants of a country. These become embodied in the laws and regulations of the society, as well as in the generally accepted norms of the country's social system. People in a society learn what to notice and what not to notice, how to behave with each other, and how to handle responsibility, success, and failure. Most people are unaware of just how their culture has influenced their values, attitudes, beliefs, and norms. In most countries, a dominant national culture exists. However, even the most homogenous nations such as Japan contain subcultures with distinct characteristics. In the United States, powerful subcultures exist among many groups such as the Amish in Pennsylvania, the Cajuns in Louisiana, the Russian immigrants in Brighton Beach, New York, and the Pueblo Indians in Colorado. Another internally diverse nation, Brazil, has four major subcultures that have been shown to influence employee motivation and performance.[30]

History and Culture

A country's history provides insight into the development of a national culture. The U.S. culture has been shaped by such factors as Native Americans, pioneers, immigrants, its vast size, and abundancy of natural resources. The importance of the individual has been embedded in American history and folklore for centuries.

The Atlantic and Pacific oceans, separating the United States from other continents, have created a tendency toward isolationism, a distrust of alliances, and a general lack of concern about political issues and policies in other countries. Americans have viewed their country as an island, separate from world conditions, problems, and politics. However, as the world became more interdependent and global media, communications, and transportation systems evolved, Americans were suddenly brought into contact with world problems such as hunger, disease, religious and ethnic conflicts, collapsing regimes, environmental degradation, and territorial disputes.

National culture, subcultures, organizational culture, and history all influence behavior patterns of employees and the structures and processes found in organizations. The complexity of these patterns, structures, and processes requires careful analysis of many different variables. Despite such complexity, it is more important than ever for managers to attempt to unravel the dimensions that differentiate cultures. To motivate, lead, reward, structure, evaluate, and change behavior patterns, cultural variation must be studied and understood, particularly as it relates to performance, attendance, satisfaction, and ethical behavior.

Cultural Dimensions

There are many cultural dimensions that differentiate cultures. These cultural dimensions can influence behavior that can cause misunderstandings, disagreements, or conflicts.[31]

People's Relationship to Nature

In some countries, people attempt to control their natural environment. Americans and Canadians use manmade fertilizers and insecticides and technologically sophisticated equipment to improve crops and crop yield. Middle Easterners view events as fated to happen. When a flood or typhoon wipes out a village, it's seen as God's will. Far Eastern countries attempt to deal with nature on nature's terms, to work in harmony with it.

These three perspectives can be referred to as dominance, preordained, and harmony. In terms of organizational practices, these three perspectives could result in significantly different responses to poor performance. In a culture in which dominance is practiced, poor performance often results in sanctions or punishment. In a preordained cultural setting, poor performance is expected from some people. In a harmony-oriented culture, poor performance is likely to be met with recognition that it or the system in which it occurs must be improved.

Individualism versus Collectivism

Americans place a high premium on the concept of individualism that describes the attitude of independence of a person who feels a large degree of freedom in his personal life and decisions. In American culture, individualism may motivate personal accomplishment or striving for self-fulfillment. This ingrained cultural factor may help to explain why many Americans are willing to change jobs and undertake geographic moves to pursue better career opportunities. On the other hand, China and Japan are categorized as *communitarian societies*.[32] This term reflects a premise that the individual is an integral part of the whole and that the best chance of self-fulfillment is in the context of the nation's goals. In an individualist society, it is generally accepted that each person's highest priority is his own welfare and that of his family.

As you might expect, the organization charts of firms in individualistic and collective societies differ. For example, in the United States, organization charts generally specify individual positions by title, job description, and job responsibilities and accountabilities.[33] By contrast, organization charts in more group-oriented societies specify only sections, units, or departments. In group-oriented societies, assignments are provided in collective terms.

Time Orientation

How is time perceived in a society? In many countries, employees are not accustomed to specific scheduling of work on an hourly basis. Time might be considered in terms of seasons or projects rather than in hours or workdays. Americans are meticulous about time—arriving at work, starting a meeting, beginning a sporting event. Being late for a meeting in northern Europe might be considered so disrespectful as to sever a business relationship. On the other hand, in parts of Latin America or Africa, being late is considered the norm.

Americans tend to perceive time as a resource that is scarce and must be used wisely. This perception is captured in the old saying "time is money." This view of time results in impatience about delays and attempting to fit as many activities as possible in the allotted time. In contrast, Eastern cultures view time as unlimited—an unending, inexhaustible resource. These differences in cultural views of time help to explain behavioral differences among people from different societies and the problems that may result when individuals with different orientations must interact.

Activity Orientation

In cultures such as the United States, emphasis is placed on taking action. Accomplishing results and being recognized for one's achievements are considered important. Managers in results-oriented cultures can motivate employees with promotions, merit-based raises, bonuses, and public recognition.

In contrast to a results-oriented culture is a *being culture*. Being cultures emphasize enjoyment, living in a balanced way, enjoying the company of others, and being gratified for the moment. Employees in a being culture work for today, and when the job becomes troublesome or detracts from their enjoyment or interferes with their personal lives, they may quit.

Understanding a culture's activity orientation can provide insight into how employees view work and leisure, what is rewarding, and how they make decisions regarding the job. The results-oriented culture suggests that employees work to accomplish specific goals. The being-oriented culture finds employees working to enjoy life more fully.

Degree of Formality

Americans do not ordinarily have a high regard for tradition, ceremony, and social rules. This informality has caused problems in business dealings and negotiations with people from other cultures. Latin Americans tend to enjoy and expect more pomp, circumstance, and ceremony than do most Americans. They tend to like public receptions, lavish meetings, and formal introductions. Americans faced with such events are often ill at ease, but they need to adjust in order to relate to and build trust with their Latino counterparts.

In negotiations, Americans have acquired a reputation around the world for not taking the time to first establish a relationship. Some consider the American style as brash, arrogant, and distant. Americans want to get to the problem, solve it, and get on with business. However, negotiators from the Middle East, Latin America, and southern Europe find it customary to converse first about nonbusiness areas and topics. They believe that first some degree of rapport must be established between negotiators. In many countries, being blunt and informal is considered impolite and nonprofessional.

Language

Languages present barriers to conducting global transactions. There are more than 3,000 languages spoken in the world. Language reflects what the society values in its culture. In some European and Asian countries, a number of languages are spoken. It is not correct, however, to conclude that when only one language exists, there will be only one culture. People in the United States and Australia speak English, but both countries have distinct cultures.

Canada provides a unique case of how language can play a significant role in business. Canada's heated controversy about the English and French languages has resulted in a joint government–industry committee producing typewriter and computer keyboards including accented French letters. Although the Canadian government is officially bilingual, English remains the dominant language.

When communication in organizations involves translation from one language to another, the problems of meaning that arise become significant.[34] It is difficult to translate from one language to another. Many managers have been surprised to find that nodding and yes responses from their Japanese counterparts did not mean the deal was accepted. The Japanese word for yes, *hai,* can also mean "I understand you," or "I hear you." And indeed, in some countries nodding the head means disagreement while shaking the head means agreement, exactly the opposite of what is seen in most cultures.

Examples of language problems in business transactions have filled books.[35] An example that illustrates barriers and misinterpretations involved a Monterey Park, California, medical office building with the numbers 941–943 emblazoned in three-foot characters. These are merely the building's address. However, to the many Chinese-Americans who pass by or see the building, the numbers have a different meaning. In Mandarin or Cantonese dialects, they sound like a common Chinese saying: "Nine die; one lives." To the Chinese, a medical building with such numbers suggests that the possibility for surviving is almost zero. In contrast, numbers can be used for good luck in business. An affiliate of Tang Frères, the largest Asian grocer in Paris, France, began offering a package of 14 Chinese television channels for the monthly price of 8.88 euros, with "8" being one of the luckiest numbers in Chinese numerology.[36] Chinese numerology is an amalgam of linguistic interpretation and age-old superstitions that have been brought to America.[37]

Religion

In many cultures, religion is a dominant factor. As such, it can have a significant effect on how and what business is conducted, work schedules, and attitudes about ethics. Baptists honor Sunday as a day of rest, whereas in Islamic countries, it's Friday, and in Israel, it's Saturday.

Islam also forbids "excessive" profit, which is considered exploitive. Islam preaches moderation and the sharing of wealth with others less fortunate. The concept of sharing wealth is manifested in one form called *zakat,* an annual tax of 2.5 percent collected from individuals and used for the benefit of the community. Banks in fundamentalist Islamic nations take equity in financing ventures, sharing profits as well as losses in the joint ventures. For example, Saudi Arabia's Al Rajhi Bank, the largest Islamic bank in the world, doesn't pay its depositors with a fixed interest rate (which is forbidden by Islamic law), but rather compensates by sharing some of the bank's profits (or losses).[38]

Muslims are expected to pray facing the holy city of Mecca five times every day. Companies and managers must be aware of this religious ritual and might consider making adjustments that would permit employees to stop working during prayer time. Are American, British, or French managers aware of this ritual, and are they willing to provide their Muslim workers with the opportunity to practice it?

In certain countries, religion may require its followers to dress in a particular manner that may conflict with organizations' norms of appearance. These customs may have to be examined in terms of the individual, the religion, and the organization.

Cross-Cultural Research Findings

An increasing body of research attempts to empirically investigate cultural variation and its effect on behavior and styles of management. The research continues to attempt to deal with cultural dimensions that are difficult to reliably and validly measure and that are difficult to translate in various languages. The studies presented in the section aren't without their limitations and problems. However, they are major attempts to study cross-cultural issues.

Hofstede's Research

Geert Hofstede, a Dutch researcher, studied how cultures in countries are similar and different. He developed a survey instrument and administered it in IBM offices in 40 countries. A total of 116,000 survey instruments were returned and analyzed. The initial Hofstede survey data resulted in four dimensions being identified as explaining differences and similarities in cultures: uncertainty avoidance, masculinity–femininity, individualism–collectivism, and power distance.[39]

uncertainty avoidance A dimension identified by Hofstede that concerns the degree to which people are comfortable with ambiguous situations and with the inability to predict future events with accuracy.

Uncertainty Avoidance

The **uncertainty avoidance** dimension concerns the degree to which people are comfortable with ambiguous situations and with the inability to predict future events with accuracy. People with low uncertainty avoidance feel comfortable even though they are unsure about future events. Their attitudes are reflected in statements such as

- Life is inherently uncertain and is most easily dealt with if taken one day at a time.
- There should be as few rules as possible, and rules that cannot be kept should be changed or eliminated.

In contrast, people with high uncertainty avoidance are uncomfortable when they are unsure what the future holds. Their attitudes are reflected by statements such as

- The uncertainty inherent in life is threatening and must be fought continually.
- Having a stable, secure life is extremely important.

In cultures characterized by high uncertainty avoidance, behavior is motivated to some degree by fear of the unknown. People in such cultures attempt to reduce or avoid uncertainty by establishing rules, policies, and procedures. In Japan, for example, where lifetime employment has been somewhat common in large organizations, there is high uncertainty avoidance.

masculinity–femininity A dimension uncovered by Hofstede. High masculinity in a culture designates assertiveness, dominance, and independence. High femininity in a culture designates interdependence, compassion, and emotional opinions.

Masculinity–Femininity

Hofstede used the term ***masculinity*** to designate the degree to which a culture emphasizes assertiveness, dominance, and independence. People in a culture that has a high masculinity orientation believe that

- Sex roles in society should be clearly differentiated; men are intended to lead and women to follow.
- Ambition and assertiveness provide the motivation behind behavior.

Femininity describes a culture's tendency to favor such values as interdependence, compassion, and emotional openness. People in a culture oriented toward femininity hold the following kinds of beliefs:

- Sex roles in society should be fluid and flexible; sexual equality is desirable.
- The quality of life is more important than personal performance and visible accomplishments.

Work in cultures can be divided on the basis of a masculine–feminine dimension. In masculine cultures, men possess jobs that contain power, authority, and responsibility. In feminine-oriented cultures, the roles of teaching, caring for patients, and helping the less fortunate are valued. There would also be a more equality-based norm between the sexes. Neither men nor women would be expected to be better managers or leaders. Individual talents and skills, and not gender, are the focus for acceptance and recognition in the feminine-oriented national culture country.

individualism–collectivism A dimension uncovered by Hofstede. Individualism emphasizes pursuit of individual goals, needs, and success. Collectivism emphasizes group need, satisfaction, and performance.

Individualism–Collectivism

The **individualism–collectivism** dimension refers to the tendency of a culture's norms and values to emphasize satisfying individual needs or group needs. Individualism emphasizes pursuit of individual goals, needs, and success. It is assumed that if each person takes care of her or his personal needs, then the entire society will benefit. The individualism philosophy is that

- *I* is more important than *we*.
- Success is a personal achievement. People function most productively when working alone.

In contrast, the collectivist perspective emphasizes group welfare and satisfaction. The individual is willing in a collectivist culture to make personal sacrifices to better the stature, performance, and satisfaction of the group. The collectivism philosophy is that

- *We* is more important than *I*.
- Every member of society should belong to a group that will secure members' well-being in exchange for loyalty and occasional self-sacrifice.

People's attitudes and behaviors lie somewhere between these poles of individualism and collectivism. Individualists are committed to their own development, quality of life, and rewards. In collectivist national cultures, the group and its accomplishments take precedence over anything else. There is a strong sense of group commitment.

Power Distance

power distance
A dimension determined by Hofstede. It refers to the degree to which members of a society accept differences in power and status among themselves.

Power distance refers to the degree to which members of a society accept differences in power and status among themselves. In national cultures that tolerate only a small degree of power distance, norms and values suggest that power differences should be minimal. Such cultures prefer participative management and worker involvement in decision making. Individuals in such cultures believe that

- Superiors should be readily accessible to subordinates.
- Using power is neither inherently good nor inherently evil; whether power is good or evil depends on the purposes for and consequences of its use.

On the other hand, in national cultures characterized by a large degree of power distance, norms and values based on hierarchical distribution predominate. People in these cultures use authority and power to coordinate individual work and behavior. Individuals in large power distance cultures believe that

- Power holders are entitled to special rights and privileges.
- Superiors and subordinates should consider each other to be different kinds of people.

Authoritarian manager styles are more likely to exist in a high power distance culture than in a low power distance culture. Decentralization, participation, and worker involvement are more likely to exist in a low power distance culture than in a high power distance culture.

Figures 3.2, 3.3, and 3.4 show how select countries cluster on the basis of Hofstede's proposed cultural differences. As shown in Figure 3.2, the Scandinavian countries Denmark and Norway are feminine (i.e., low on masculinity), while Germanic countries Germany

FIGURE 3.2 **Country Classifications: Uncertainty Avoidance and Masculinity**

Source: Based on Geert Hofstede, Gert Jan Hofstede, Michael Minkov, *Cultures and Organizations, Software of the Mind,* (3rd rev ed.) (New York: McGraw-Hill, 2010).

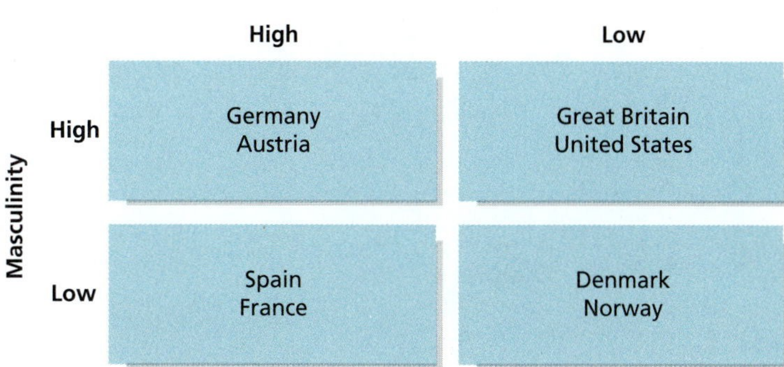

FIGURE 3.3 **Country Classifications: Uncertainty Avoidance and Power Distance**

Source: Based on Geert Hofstede, Gert Jan Hofstede, Michael Minkov, *Cultures and Organizations, Software of the Mind,* (3rd rev ed.) (New York: McGraw-Hill, 2010).

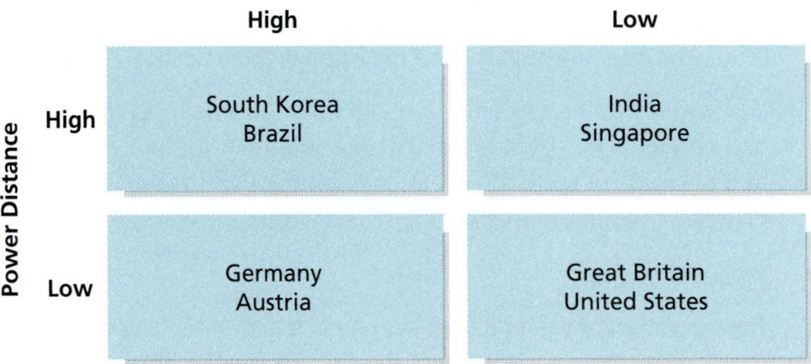

and Austria are highly masculine. In Denmark, Norway, Sweden, and Finland, both men and women are expected to have jobs outside the home and to help with household and child-rearing activities within the home. Quality of life is an important goal in feminine cultures. In terms of uncertainty avoidance, Spain and France, which are Latin European countries, use rules and bureaucratic policies to try to control uncertainty in everyday life and unpredictable future events. The United States and Great Britain are relatively less bureaucratic and tend to be more comfortable with uncertain situations.

Figure 3.3 illustrates that a country such as Great Britain that is low on power distance and uncertainty avoidance has very little hierarchy and much interaction among people. Employees in high power distance and low uncertainty avoidance cultures such as India view their organizations as families. Employees in countries such as South Korea and Brazil tend to consider their organizations as pyramids of people. Roles and procedures in countries with low power distance and high uncertainty avoidance, such as Germany, tend to work in highly predictable settings.

Figure 3.4 shows that the United States rates low on power distance. Japan and India rate high on power distance and low on individualism. In these countries, bypassing or arguing with a superior would be considered insubordination.

FIGURE 3.4 **Country Classifications: Individualism and Power Distance**

Source: Based on Geert Hofstede, Gert Jan Hofstede, Michael Minkov, *Cultures and Organizations, Software of the Mind,* (3rd rev ed.) (New York: McGraw-Hill, 2010).

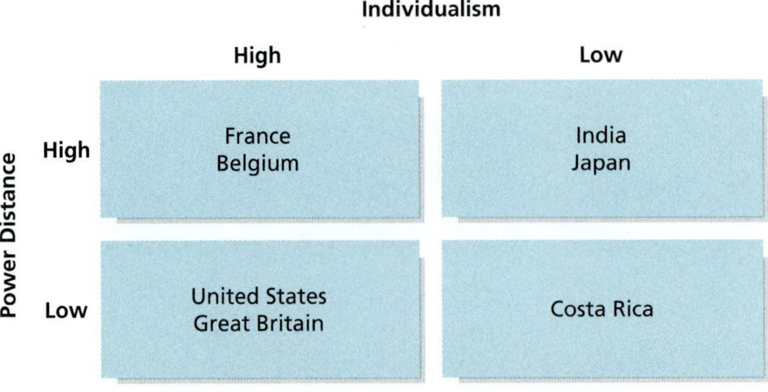

TABLE 3.2
Scores on Four Hofstede Dimensions

Source: Based on Geert Hofstede, Gert Jan Hofstede, Michael Minkov, *Cultures and Organizations, Software of the Mind,* (3rd rev ed.) (New York: McGraw-Hill, 2010).

National Culture	Uncertainty Avoidance	Masculinity–Femininity	Individualism–Collectivism	Power Distance
Argentina	86	56	46	49
Australia	51	61	90	36
Austria	70	79	55	11
Belgium	94	54	75	65
Brazil	76	49	38	69
Canada	48	52	80	39
Chile	86	28	23	63
Colombia	80	64	13	67
Denmark	23	16	74	18
Finland	59	26	63	33
France	86	43	71	68
Germany	65	66	67	35
Great Britain	35	66	89	35
Greece	112	57	35	60
Hong Kong	29	57	25	68
India	40	56	48	77
Iran	59	43	41	58
Ireland	35	68	70	28
Israel	81	47	54	13
Italy	75	70	76	50
Japan	92	95	46	54
Mexico	82	69	30	81
Netherlands	53	14	80	38
New Zealand	49	58	79	22
Norway	50	8	69	31
Pakistan	70	50	14	55
Peru	87	42	16	64
Philippines	44	64	32	94
Portugal	104	31	27	63
Singapore	8	48	20	74
South Africa	49	63	65	49
Spain	86	42	51	57
Sweden	29	5	71	31
Switzerland	58	70	68	34
Taiwan	69	45	17	58
Thailand	64	34	20	64
Turkey	85	45	37	66
United States	46	62	91	40
Venezuela	76	73	12	81
Yugoslavia	88	21	27	76

Note: Larger numbers signify greater amounts of uncertainty avoidance, masculinity, individualism, and power distance.

Table 3.2 presents scores for the 40 initial countries studied by Hofstede on each of the four dimensions. Larger numbers indicate greater amounts of uncertainty avoidance, masculinity, individualism, and power distance. Note that the United States has the highest individualism score (91), a moderate masculinity score (62), a low uncertainty avoidance score (46), and a low power distance score (40).

In addition to Hofstede, other researchers have examined attitude information and concluded that eight basic clusters of nations exist.[40] The attitudes (work goals, needs, and values) of each nation in a cluster were more similar to each other than to attitudes found in other clusters. The United States is found in the Anglo cluster, which includes the *English-speaking* nations of Canada, New Zealand, Ireland, Australia, the United Kingdom, and South Africa. Countries found in the other clusters include:

- *Germanic:* Austria, Germany, and Switzerland.
- *Nordic:* Finland, Norway, Denmark, and Sweden.
- *Arab:* Bahrain, Abu Dhabi, United Arab Emirates, Kuwait, Oman, and Saudi Arabia.
- *Near Eastern:* Turkey, Iran, and Greece.
- *Far Eastern:* Malaysia, Singapore, Hong Kong, South Vietnam, Thailand, Philippines, Indonesia, and Taiwan.
- *Latin American:* Argentina, Venezuela, Chile, Mexico, Peru, and Colombia.
- *Latin European:* France, Belgium, Italy, and Spain.

Four nations—Brazil, Japan, India, and Israel—did not fit into any of the eight country clusters and are considered independent cultures.

Hofstede-Inspired Research

long-term orientation
A cultural dimension that refers to the degree to which a given culture values persistence, thrift (savings), having a sense of shame, and ordering relationships by status.

short-term orientation
A cultural dimension that refers to the degree to which a culture values respect for tradition, the exchange of favors and gifts, protecting "face" (i.e., avoiding shame), and personal steadiness and stability

Informed by Hofstede's research, Bond and Chinese scholars developed a Chinese Value Survey that was administered to Chinese students who were living in 22 countries.[41] The results suggested a fifth dimension along which a culture could be classified: **long-term orientation.** This fifth dimension has also been referred to as Confucian Dynamism. Basically, it measures the degree to which a culture values persistence and thrift (savings), has a sense of shame, and orders relationships by status.[42] It has been suggested that cultures with a long-term orientation are more likely to experience stronger economic growth and entrepreneurial activity. China is a country with a long-term orientation. In contrast, cultures that display a short-term orientation value respect for tradition, the exchange of favors and gifts, protecting "face" (i.e., avoiding shame), and personal steadiness and stability.[43] The Philippines is an example of a country with a short-term time orientation.

Hofstede has proposed that not only management practices but also management theories are constrained by the national cultural environment in which they were created.[44] He claims that management as an activity and a class of people is an American invention. In the United States, the manager is a culture hero. However, other cultures have different views of management and managers.

In Germany, the engineer rather than the manager is the hero. An effective apprenticeship program both on the factory floor and in the office is in place. Germans expect their boss, or *Meister,* to assign their tasks and to be a technical expert. They do not, however, rely on a manager, American style, to motivate them.

The manager in its U.S. version does not exist in Japan. In the United States, the core of the enterprise is the managerial class. In Japan, the core consists of a permanent worker group. University graduates in Japan first join the permanent worker group and subsequently fill various positions. Japanese workers are to a large extent controlled by their peer group rather than by their manager.

Hofstede believes that history and cultural characteristics explain clearly why American managers behave as they do in terms of managing employees, structuring of organization, designing jobs, making decisions, and engaging in communications.[45] Nothing is inherently wrong or right in American managerial behavior, just as nothing is necessarily good or bad about Chinese, German, Mexican, or Nigerian managerial behavior. Each managerial or cadre group has its own peculiar idiosyncrasies.

A study of American and Japanese managers examined the influence of national culture on budget control practices in manufacturing firms. Budget control practices included communication and coordination processes used in budget planning, the time horizon used, the rules and procedures followed, the amount of budget slack built into the system, the degree of managerial control over the budget, and the budget performance evaluation period.[46] Because Japan has been identified as a highly collectivist nation and the United States has been found to be very individualistic, it was proposed that differences in budgetary control would be found. As hypothesized, U.S. companies, compared with Japanese companies, tend to use communication and coordination more widely, build more budget slack into considerations, and use a short-term performance evaluation. The findings are compatible with the view that the United States practices more hierarchically oriented management and uses a shorter-term perspective for evaluation and review.

Critiquing Hofstede

The original Hofstede research was conducted in only one organization, IBM, which limits its generalizability. In addition, questions are still raised about the validity and reliability of the measures used by Hofstede. Is he accurately measuring cultural dimensions? Are these the most important cultural dimensions? Can a survey measure cultural dimensions? Since culture is such a subtle characteristic, can it be measured at all? These are questions raised about any survey-based research.[47]

Cultural tendencies can lead to respondents' minimization or exaggeration of their feelings on a rating scale.[48] There is also the issue of subcultural influences on respondents. If Canadians completed the survey, wouldn't there be differences in responses in British Columbia as compared to Quebec? Are mean values, averaged across all subjects, accurate representations of a national culture?

There is also the problem of whether four or five dimensions can conceivably explain a national culture.[49] What dimensions are missing, if any? Explaining such a complex phenomenon as culture is not an easy task.

Despite these criticisms and limitations, Hofstede's research and the studies that it has stimulated have called attention to national culture and its possible impact on behavior and style. He has finally introduced into the organizational sciences a word of caution about generalizing from one setting and one country to other settings and other countries. Hofstede has increased interest in conducting more internationally relevant organizational science, research, and applications.

The GLOBE Project

The GLOBE (Global Leadership and Organizational Behavior Effectiveness) project, conceived by Robert House of the University of Pennsylvania, is a large international research project involving 150 researchers who have collected data from more than 17,000 managers from 62 different cultures.[50] One of the goals of this large-scale study is to identify and understand managers' perceptions of cultural practices and values in their respective countries. In other words, the research aims at understanding which cultural variables influence leaders and organizational cultures in different countries.[51] Most of the researchers involved in the project are from the host countries in which data are collected, so they are experts in the culture, language, and so forth. Also, the GLOBE project is ongoing in that researchers continue to collect data and publish interesting research findings.

As can be seen in Table 3.3, the GLOBE project classified cultures based on their scores on the following nine cultural dimensions:[52]

1. *Uncertainty avoidance:* The degree to which members of a society or organization use rules, regulations, and social norms to avoid uncertainty or unpredictable future events.
2. *Power distance:* The extent to which a society accepts unequal distribution of power.
3. *Societal collectivism:* The extent to which an organization encourages and rewards group outcomes as opposed to employees pursuing individual goals.
4. *In-group collectivism:* This captures the degree to which individuals express loyalty, pride, and cohesiveness in their organizations and families.

TABLE 3.3 Cultural Comparisons of Three Country Clusters from the GLOBE Project

Source: Based on Geert Hofstede, Gert Jan Hofstede, Michael Minkov, *Cultures and Organizations, Software of the Mind,* (3rd rev ed.) (New York: McGraw-Hill, 2010).

Cultural Dimensions	Anglo Cluster[1]	Confucian Cluster[2]	Latin European Cluster[3]
Power distance	Medium-high	High	High
In-group collectivism	Medium	High	Medium-high
Institutional collectivism	Medium	Medium-high	Medium
Uncertainty avoidance	Medium	Medium	Medium
Future orientation	Medium	Medium	Medium
Gender egalitarianism	Medium-Low	Medium-low	Medium-low
Assertiveness	Medium	Medium	Medium
Humane orientation	Medium	Medium	Medium
Performance orientation	Medium	Medium-high	Medium

[1]Anglo cluster: Australia, Canada, Ireland, New Zealand, South Africa, United States, and United Kingdom.
[2]Confucian cluster: China, Hong Kong, Japan, Korea, Singapore, and Taiwan.
[3]Latin European cluster: France, Switzerland, Israel, Italy, Portugal, and Spain.

5. *Gender egalitarianism:* The extent to which an organization avoids gender discrimination and role inequalities.
6. *Assertiveness:* The degree to which members of organizations are aggressive and confrontational in social relationships.
7. *Future orientation:* The extent to which members of a society plan, invest in the future, and delay immediate gratification.
8. *Performance orientation:* The degree to which individuals in a society are rewarded for performance improvement and excellence.
9. *Humane orientation:* The degree to which individuals in an organization are rewarded for being friendly, altruistic, fair, caring, and kind to others.

Table 3.3 compares the scores of three clusters of countries—Anglo, Confucian, and Latin European—on the nine cultural values in the GLOBE project. This gives future expatriates who are not familiar with the cultures from these clusters a research-based snapshot of how the people from that culture will behave. The GLOBE project, although still a work in progress, is a comprehensive and valid resource for improving our understanding of the similarities and differences between cultures around the world.

Based on their studies and review of the literature, scholars like Hofstede and House believe that managers' national origin significantly affects their views and style of managing. Just as there's an American bias in some managerial approaches, there's an Indian bias in other practices. No nation, group of managers, or set of researchers is perfectly free of any bias or ethnocentric tendencies. Cross-cultural understanding will come about only if managers and researchers are willing to increase their global perspectives and knowledge bases about diverse groups of employees. Global approaches to managing behavior, structure, and processes will eventually become a top priority around the world. The era of domestically bound approaches to managing what occurs in organizations is ending.

Cross-Cultural Transitions

multinational corporation
A firm with operations in different nations with each viewed as a relatively separate enterprise.

Although the terms are often treated as the same, Table 3.1 pointed out important distinctions between a **multinational corporation** and a **global corporation**. A multinational corporation (MNC) might have operations in different nations, but each operation is viewed as a relatively separate enterprise. Key human resources are usually sent out from the company's home offices, and most decision making remains at corporate headquarters. Thus, although the MNC is largely staffed by people from the nation in which a particular facility

global corporation
An enterprise structured so that national boundaries become blurred. The best people are hired irrespective of national origin.

is found, managers from the corporation's home country retain most authority.[53] The multinational corporation does not yet see its potential market as the world. Rather, it views each of its foreign operations as a specialized market for a particular product. In other words, each foreign subsidiary concentrates its efforts on the nation in which it is located. An example of an organization in the multinational stage of internationalization would be Baker & McKenzie, a large legal services firm headquartered in Chicago. This firm has 3,900 local lawyers in 67 offices worldwide, including in Beijing, Abu Dhabi, Milan, and São Paulo. Due to the fact that the practice of law varies considerably from one country to the next, each country's law office will function as a relatively autonomous enterprise.

In contrast to an MNC, the global corporation (GC) is structured so that national boundaries disappear and it hires the best people for jobs irrespective of their national origin. The global corporation sees the world as its labor source as well as its marketplace. Thus, the global corporation will locate an operation wherever it can accomplish its goals in the most cost-effective way.[54] The true global corporation also believes in a world market for essentially similar products. Moreover, the national affiliation of an employee becomes rather unimportant. For example, Mars Inc. Spain has had an English general manager, a French finance manager, and a Swiss human resources manager.[55]

Human Resources for International Assignments

Generally speaking, three sources provide employees for an international assignment. For key managerial and technical positions, all three sources of workers are frequently used in global organizations. Which source is used the most depends, however, on the perspective of the company. The organization might choose to hire

host-country nationals
Workers from the local population where an operation is located.

parent-country nationals
Individuals sent from the country in which the firm is headquartered. Often called *expatriates*.

third-country nationals
Employees from a country other than where the parent company is headquartered or where the operation is located.

- **Host-country nationals**, who are workers from the local population. A worker from Ireland employed by a U.S. firm operating in Dublin would be considered a host-country national. Sometimes they are referred to as local nationals.
- **Parent-country nationals**, who are sent from the country in which the organization is headquartered. These persons are usually referred to as *expatriates*. A U.S. manager on assignment in Ireland is an expatriate or parent-country national.
- **Third-country nationals**, who are from a country other than where the parent organization's headquarters or operations are located. If the U.S. firm employed a manager from Canada at facilities in Ireland, she would be considered a third-country national.

The tendency to be ethnocentric (a belief that your nation's cultural values and customs are superior to all others) is strong for new and even for many well-established foreign organizations conducting business in the United States. There is an assumption that most executive-level positions in Japanese-owned businesses in the United States are occupied by Japanese nationals. Only about 31 percent of the senior management positions in such firms are occupied by U.S. managers. More commonly, local nationals are used for specific functions such as liaison, but Japanese organizations have a reputation among some people for showing little regard for these persons' career development. (See the end-of-chapter case.) In contrast, some researchers suggest that foreign companies in Japan hire local Japanese managers for nearly 80 percent of their management needs.[56]

The Expatriate Manager

expatriate manager
A manager from the firm's home nation who's on an overseas assignment.

Perhaps one of the most important tasks for the multinational or global corporation is managing the expatriate adjustment process. An **expatriate manager** is a manager from the corporation's home nation who is on a foreign assignment. The focus for the company will therefore be on the selection, training, appraisal, and compensation of the expatriate. Significant efforts will also be placed on career management as it relates to the expatriate's

OB AND YOUR CAREER

Acquire International Experience the "Easy Way"

In order to get international experience twenty or thirty years ago, most managers would have to uproot their families and relocate to another country for several years. These long-term expatriates would immerse themselves in the host country culture and language, but they ran the risk that they, their spouse or partner, and their family would not adjust to living in the host culture (and would have to return home early). Similarly, the expatriate took a career-related risk by being "out of sight, out of mind" from key decision makers back in the home or corporate office. A natural outgrowth of these risks was the increase in the number of candidates turning down these long-term international assignments. However, there is considerable evidence that many organizations value managers with international skills and experience. So, how can a manager acquire international experience without taking the risks associated with long-term international assignments?

Managers who want to build some international skills (in a short period) should consider taking traveling international assignments (IAs). Traveling IAs come in many forms, but a typical traveling IA would not require relocation; rather, it would consist of a manager being given both domestic and international job responsibilities. The manager would be expected to travel for a few days or weeks at a time to one or more international locations to visit customers, suppliers, subsidiary employees, alliance partners, and other host country stakeholders. His job could include negotiating joint ventures, resolving export issues, securing new clients, and so forth. In contrast to long-term expatriates, the manager in a traveling IA would still have to perform some domestic job responsibilities in addition to these international duties. For example, a manager from Apple who is helping to coordinate the launch of the iPad might be responsible for marketing activities in the southwestern United States while also covering Mexico, Brazil, and Chile. She would have to split her time across these four countries. These traveling IAs are a great way to rack up some international experience and language skills without have to relocate overseas. By being based out of the home country, managers in traveling IAs can stay in the loop with regard to changes in home office politics and other career-related issues.

Here's how to increase your chances of being chosen for a traveling IA:

1. *Get on the record.* Discuss your interest in taking a traveling IA with your supervisor and the human resources department. If the organization has a skills and interests database, be sure to update your profile.
2. *Be persistent.* You'll need to remind your supervisor periodically of your interest in gaining international skills. These traveling IAs tend to be coveted positions, so you will need to be patient but proactive in getting one.
3. *Volunteer.* If you hear that an international client or supplier (or other stakeholder) will be visiting the United States or the firm needs someone to attend a trade show overseas, volunteer to help out. Although these activities may not fit with your regular 9 to 5 p.m. job responsibilities, you will demonstrate that you're committed to gaining international skills. This "hustle" will get you noticed when that next traveling IA position becomes available.
4. *Study a foreign language.* Saying that you're interested in a traveling IA is one thing, demonstrating it is another. If you want an IA that would allow you to travel to China, start studying Mandarin; for most of Latin America, study Spanish; and so forth. You won't become fluent overnight, but you will certainly send a strong message to your manager and others at the organization that you're serious about working internationally.

return to headquarters. The OB and Your Career feature provides some suggestions on how an individual can acquire international experience without taking a long-term expatriate assignment.

Figure 3.5 lists the factors that seem to be most commonly associated with expatriate success and failure. Clearly, selection for expatriate assignments is a complex, sensitive task. Many factors related to a successful expatriate assignment are difficult to measure, and managers' success in domestic operations may have very little to do with their success overseas.[57] One major reason that expatriate failure rates are so high for many companies is that these companies believe that a manager's domestic performance will always be related to her overseas performance. As a result, they frequently overemphasize technical competency and disregard more important factors when selecting the expatriate.[58]

As Figure 3.5 shows, the real keys to a successful expatriate choice are finding managers who are culturally flexible and adaptable, who have supportive family situations,

FIGURE 3.5
Factors in Expatriate Managers' Success and Failure

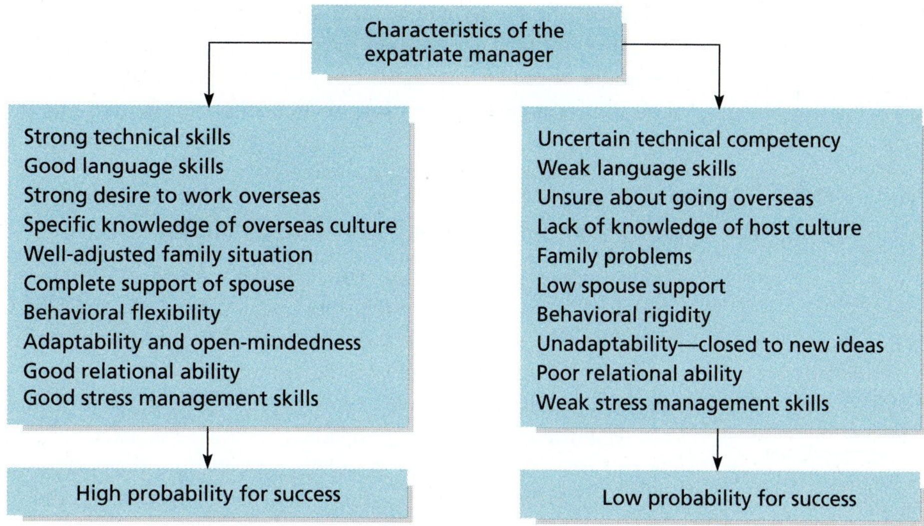

and who are motivated to accept the overseas assignment. Other factors such as cultural familiarity and language fluency are also apparently more important than technical competency.

Staffing an international joint venture with expatriates can be challenging since the partners in the venture might disagree about the necessary qualifications for a manager. For example, a Japanese partner might be looking for a manager who is a real team player, whereas a U.S. partner might be seeking a highly aggressive self-starter for the same position. Such disagreements are one reason that joint ventures using one partner's management philosophies seem to work better than shared systems.[59]

Motivation to accept an overseas assignment is also a factor in the expatriate's success. Without a strong commitment to completing the assignment, the expatriate's chances of success are small. The organization can help create this motivation in several ways. Compensation programs that are attractive to the expatriate can help. Perhaps more important, however, is creating a system where the overseas assignment is beneficial to the expatriate's long-term career objectives. For example, global assignments are an expected part of employees' career progression at companies like Procter & Gamble.[60] One of expatriates' most commonly mentioned concerns is that their position in the home offices may be jeopardized if they are away too long. That is, many expatriates believe that accepting a lengthy overseas assignment will derail any successful career path they had established in domestic operations.[61] Recent research suggests that factors such as the expatriate's (and organizational leader's) previous experiences and the organization's career development practices can have a positive outcome on the expatriate's career within the organization.[62] For example, if the expatriate has already had a successful posting overseas, the CEO of the firm has previous international experience, and the organization provides repatriation adjustment assistance, then the returning expatriate is more likely to have a career success within the firm.

The role of the expatriate's family shouldn't be underestimated when deciding about overseas assignments.[63] Research indicates that a dissatisfied spouse can significantly affect the expatriate's performance. Some evidence even suggests that a spouse's inability to adjust to the overseas assignment is the single most common factor in expatriate failures.[64] For an expatriate with children, worries over schooling and leisure activities can add to the stress associated with the assignment. Eventually, if these worries aren't resolved, the assignment might end with the expatriate's early return to her parent country.

Because the family can be such an important factor in expatriate manager failures, the temptation for many companies may be to send only single managers. Although this practice might eliminate one problem, it could easily create many others. For example, it's likely that a greater proportion of men than women are single in certain occupational groups. If a company selects only single persons for desirable overseas assignments, it might unintentionally discriminate against women.

Culture Shock and the Expatriate Manager

culture shock cycle
A three-phase cycle (fascination and interest, frustration and confusion, and adaptation) that most individuals sent to another culture experience.

A trip to a foreign culture can cause expatriate managers and their families to go through a predictable series of reactions to their unfamiliar surroundings. Figure 3.6 illustrates the **culture shock cycle**.[65] First, there is a period of fascination during which all of the different aspects of the culture are viewed with interest and curiosity. This first reaction to a new culture is generally a positive experience.

Next, however, comes a period known as culture shock. Culture shock refers to the frustration and confusion that result from being constantly subjected to strange and unfamiliar cues about what to do and how to get it done.[66] Notice from the exhibit that culture shock doesn't typically occur during the earliest days of a trip overseas. Thus, while many expatriate managers' assignments begin very positively, their experiences often turn negative soon after.[67]

The successful expatriate must cope effectively with culture shock. It's a period in which the manager may miss the familiar surroundings of the home office. Simple, daily events can become sources of stress and dissatisfaction. For example, being denied access to a favorite snack food or leisure activity because it's unavailable in the host country may not seem important, but to the expatriate on a lengthy overseas assignment, it can become extremely frustrating. What may be even more difficult to deal with is active resentment of the expatriate by host country nationals, such as that which may be faced by African-American managers taking positions in South Africa.[68] Negative feelings such as this resulting from the perception that the expatriate is taking away a job that could be held by a native of the country may be overt or subtle but can influence many aspects of an expatriate's tour of duty.

The final stage of coping with a new culture is an adaptation stage. During this stage, the expatriate has made reasonable adjustments to the new culture and is able to deal effectively with it. Although this stage seldom returns the expatriate to the heights of excitement that

FIGURE 3.6
The Culture Shock Cycle

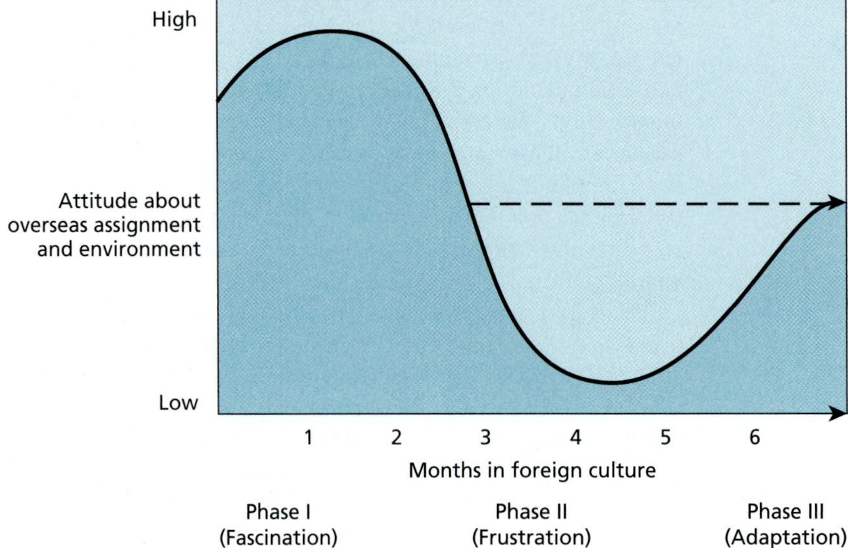

he first experienced, a successful transition to a new culture does return the expatriate to manageable levels of a "normal" lifestyle.

Training the Expatriate Manager

Once the groundwork for a successful overseas assignment has been laid by choosing expatriates with good chances of succeeding, the next step toward ensuring success is for the organization to properly train and prepare these managers for their upcoming assignments. As with selection, expatriate manager training programs need to focus on issues that are not typically dealt with in domestic training programs. For example, members of global virtual teams not only have to work well together but also need to navigate a variety of unknown and unpredictable issues (e.g., how to resolve a particular Brazilian client's needs in a timely manner). Training for global virtual team members may focus more on dealing with the unknown as opposed to learning facts and predetermined information about cultures.[69]

Intercultural training has a positive effect on expatriate adjustment and performance while on an overseas assignment.[70] There are several different kinds of training to choose from, including "documentary" and "interpersonal" training. Documentary training involves relatively passive learning about another culture and its business practices; interpersonal approaches focus on intercultural role playing and self-awareness exercises. Both can be valuable forms of preparation for the expatriate manager.[71]

According to Tung,[72] two primary factors determine how much and what kind of training expatriate managers should receive. These are the level of contact with the host culture that the expatriate will encounter and the degree of dissimilarity between the home and host cultures. As either of these increases, the expatriate will require more in-depth training for the overseas assignment.

Figure 3.7 shows the content and structure of an integrated expatriate manager training program. Its three phases have specific objectives for helping the expatriate to be successful.

Before discussing the specific elements of each phase of expatriate manager training, it's important to describe some scenarios where such training should be more or less intensive. Under those situations where a U.S. expatriate manager is being assigned for two to three years to such dissimilar cultures as those found in Saudi Arabia, China, India, and Brazil, then managers should receive all three phases of cross-cultural training. Moreover, it is recommended that the employing organization provide the manager's spouse/partner and children with language and cultural orientation training. While overseas, it is extremely important that the manager's family adjust to the host culture. A well-adjusted family is important to the overall success of the expatriate manager. On the other hand, if a U.S. manager is being sent to London or Sydney or some other English-speaking location for a relatively short time period (e.g., a month or two), then a less intensive training program is more appropriate. In sum, the intensity and duration of a cross-cultural training must be tailored to fit the nature and length of the expatriate assignment.

FIGURE 3.7
Phases of an Expatriate Manager Training Program

Source: Adapted from Edward Dunbar and Allan Katcher, "Preparing Managers for Foreign Assignments," *Training and Development Journal* (September 1990): 47.

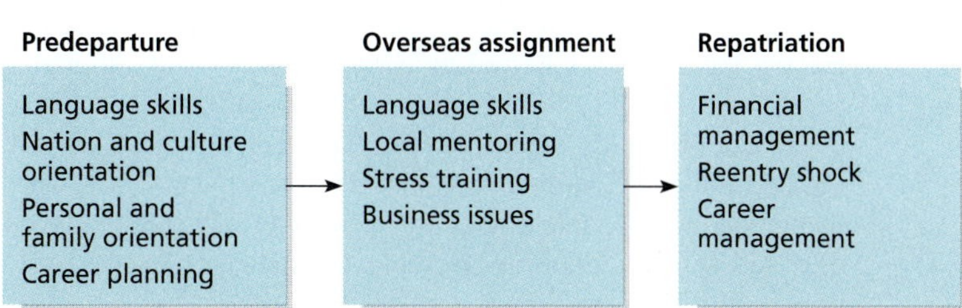

TABLE 3.4
Expatriate Self-Awareness: Being Prepared for Culture Shock

Source: Adapted from P. R. Harris and Robert T. Moran, "So You're Going Abroad Survey," in *Managing Cultural Differences,* 3rd ed. (Houston: Gulf, 1991).

Prospective global managers should prepare satisfactory answers to the following questions before going on an overseas assignment:

1. How will living abroad affect me and my family?
2. What will my spouse do in terms of work and home life?
3. Are my children prepared for living abroad?
4. What assistance and support will be available to us?
5. What will happen to our home and other personal property while we are gone?
6. What arrangements can be made for family pets?
7. How will we handle health care while we are overseas?
8. Can we expect to encounter any anti-Americanism? What about the threat of terrorism?
9. What security measures should we take?
10. What kinds of recreational opportunities are available?
11. Will language barriers present problems for me?
12. What is the proper form of dress for various occasions?
13. How will we handle transportation at the overseas location?
14. What kinds of food can we expect to eat?
15. Are there any experienced expatriates from the organization available who can "show us the ropes?"

Predeparture training includes the critical activities of preparing the expatriate for the overseas assignment. Its purpose is to reduce the amount of culture shock that the manager and his family encounter by familiarizing them with the host country. Among the most important predeparture activities are language training and cultural orientation training.

Self-awareness is an important aspect of preparing for an international assignment. Assessment techniques such as the ones in Table 3.4 can be very helpful to the expatriate. Responding to these kinds of questions can help the manager to know just where she's most likely to encounter the ill effects of culture shock. This kind of advanced preparation can go a long way toward reducing the negative effects of being transplanted to a new culture.

The second phase of an expatriate manager training program occurs at the host country site. Some expatriates prefer postarrival cross-cultural training because after they "unpack their suitcases" and are settling in, their motivation is high to learn the language and how to adjust to working and living in the host country.[73] In other words, expatriate training does not stop just because the manager has her boarding pass in hand. As seen in Figure 3.6, language instruction continues to be a priority during this phase of training. In addition, mentoring relationships have proven to be effective expatriate training tools. Many organizations with several expatriates at the same overseas location have developed local support groups to help the entire family of a newly arriving expatriate. Some organizations even make participation and leadership in such support groups a part of senior expatriates' jobs.[74]

The final phase of an integrated expatriate training program occurs when the manager is preparing to return to the parent country. The process of being reintegrated into domestic operations is referred to as *repatriation.* And although it may seem straightforward, repatriation can cause culture shock similar to the shock that occurred when the expatriate originally went overseas. Some of the more critical issues that repatriation training must deal with are contained in Figure 3.6. These include the financial adjustments that must be made since the expatriate will frequently lose overseas living subsidies and salary premiums. Helping the manager to get back on career track is also important for repatriation.[75]

The Global Theme for Organizations: Behavior, Structure, and Process

The majority of theory, research, practice, and concepts that deal with organizations have been proposed by Americans, using American subjects (mostly male), with U.S.-based firms.[76] However, globalization has now become a reality. The remaining chapters should be viewed in terms of this global transformation. American-made organizational prescriptions are not superior or inferior to the perspectives offered by others. They are, however, limited in their value. The United States is just one of many important countries in which organizations play a significant role in a nation's social-political, economic, and technological process.

The world's dramatic shifts require more than culture-bound approaches to managing behavior, structure, and processes. The more a country's history and culture deviate from America's, the more caution we need to exercise in evaluating the material in the rest of the chapters in this book. The cultural foundations and influences of this chapter are intended to assist readers in recognizing differences and similarities across cultures.

Summary of Key Points

- Globalization has become a reality. It describes the interdependency of transportation, distribution, communication, and economic networks across international borders.
- Cross-cultural management describes organizational behavior within and across countries and attempts to understand and improve the interaction and behavior of coworkers, clients, suppliers, and alliance partners from different cultures and countries.
- The American Society for Training and Development has aptly listed a number of skills that global managers will need to compete effectively in the 21st century. These skills are global strategy, cultural diversity management, team building, organization, communication, and transfer of knowledge.
- Culture consists of patterns of behavior acquired and transmitted within a society. Culture is learned, shared, transgenerational, an influence on perception, and adaptive.
- National culture consists of a set of values, attitudes, beliefs, and norms shared by a majority of the inhabitants of a country.
- Cultural dimensions that differentiate one culture from another include people's relationships to nature, individualism versus collectivism, time orientation, activity orientation, informality, language, and religion.
- Geert Hofstede, a Dutch researcher, has conducted a number of studies that examine national cultures. His initial studies have resulted in the identification of four dimensions that explain some differences and similarities in cultures. The dimensions are *uncertainty avoidance* (the degree to which people are comfortable with ambiguous situations and with the inability to predict future events with accuracy), *masculinity–femininity* (masculine cultures are assertive, with dominance practiced and independence valued; feminine cultures are interdependent, compassionate, and emotionally open), *individualism–collectivism,* and *power distance* (referring to the degree to which members of a society accept differences in power and status among themselves).
- Successful expatriate managers have strong technical and language skills, want to work overseas, are flexible, are supported by their families, and manage stress effectively.
- The culture shock cycle involves an initial period of fascination; then a period of shock, confusion, and frustration; and finally a stage that involves adaptation and the ability to cope with the new culture.

Discussion and Review Questions

1. What are three long-term effects of globalization on businesses, workers, and consumers? Who benefits most/least from globalization?
2. Assume that you want to develop your global skills so that you can pursue international assignments with your company. Identify five skills that you would want to develop, and describe how you would go about improving these skills.
3. Based on Hofstede's findings, which countries do you believe are most different from the United States? Defend your answer.
4. What is meant by the term a *culture-bound theory of motivation?*
5. What can a newly assigned expatriate manager do to avoid or diminish the intensity and negative effects of culture shock? Explain.
6. If you found yourself in Robert Adams's situation (see opening vignette), would you take the three-year expatriate assignment? The virtual expatriate assignment? Or, would you decline both opportunities and remain a domestic employee at the home office?
7. Describe the attitudes a manager would need to be successful and effective in managing in India, China, and Saudi Arabia.
8. Can domestic cultural diversity in the United States help American firms better understand and deal with global cultural diversity? Explain.
9. How does a national culture differ from what is referred to as an organization's culture? Which "culture" exerts more influence over the behavior of a global company's employees?
10. Why is religion often incorrectly ignored in discussions and analyses of business, negotiations, and culture?

Taking It to the Net

Offshoring: What's It All About?

Earlier in the chapter, three different Indian outsourcing firms were mentioned, Wipro Ltd., Infosys Ltd., and Tata Consulting Services. You'll also recall that the activity of offshoring is controversial in that some believe it costs American jobs, while others believe that offshoring is a natural byproduct of free trade and should be left to flourish. To learn more about these successful companies and the controversial offshoring industry, please visit these companies' Web sites and research the following questions:

1. What do these three firms do? What services do they offer?
2. Which industries do they serve?
3. How do these Indian outsourcing companies save U.S. companies money?

The companies' Web sites can be found at:

- Wipro Ltd.: www.wipro.com (click on "Corporate" and then "About us")
- Infosys Ltd.: www.infosys.com (click on "About us")
- Tata Consulting Services: www.tata.com (click on "About us")

Case for Analysis: *Building a Global Outsourcing Powerhouse*

Nagavara Ramarao Narayana Murthy (also known as "NR") and six co-founders of Bangalore-based Infosys Technologies had to borrow US $250 to start their IT outsourcing and software company in 1981. Back then, the idea of Infosys competing with world giants such as IBM in global markets was just wishful thinking. In 2010, Infosys had nearly 114,000 employees in 50 offices and development centers in India, China, Australia, the Czech Republic, Poland, the United Kingdom, Canada, and Japan. Although the company is still relatively small (about US $4.8 billion in annual sales) compared to IBM (US $95.8 billion annual sales), Infosys has become a global powerhouse.

NR and his co-founders created Infosys on what are considered the principles of globalization. He found capital where it was the cheapest, produced in a location that was cost effective, and sold services and products where they were most profitable. The sprawling Infosys campus in Bangalore, India, reflects the firm's global perspective with its high-end restaurant and clocks displaying different time zones.

In the past 10 years, repeat business, high-quality software developed in India at a fraction of the cost of European or American development, and investment in research and development have made Infosys a global success story. For example, Belgian mobile communication operator Belgacom Mobile wanted to develop a customer loyalty program that would handle data storage in different languages and provide flexibility for clients. Infosys delivered the program ahead of schedule, providing Belgacom with a high-quality, first-mover product.

Building on their early success in software development, over the years Infosys has expanded its list of services and products to include:

- Business and technology consulting,
- Business process outsourcing,
- Systems integration,
- Application services,
- Product engineering, and
- Testing and validation services.

Infosys has attracted business from Europe, Latin America, Canada, and the United States. NR gained the confidence of customers, some of whom were anxious about using foreign software outsourcing, by meeting quality standards and schedules. Today, Infosys has the reputation of being one of the best software firms in the world.

NR stresses quality in every phase of producing software. His quality initiative is a part of the Infosys company culture. He matches or benchmarks his quality against the world's most recognized multinational firms. Foreign and institutional investors who in the late 1980s were wary of investing in India are no longer reluctant to invest in Infosys.

NR is proudest of Infosys's ability to compete with any firm, anywhere. He wanted to make a difference in India and throughout the world. Obviously, he has done so through a management system that requires employees to focus on quality production as the top priority. It's no wonder why NR is considered the "father of the country's information technology outsourcing industry."

DISCUSSION AND REVIEW QUESTIONS

1. Which principles of globalization did NR and his colleagues follow when they were growing Infosys into a global powerhouse?
2. According to Hofstede's research, India has a high score on the power distance dimension. To what degree could this high score help to explain Infosys Technology's success in the global marketplace?
3. Refer to Table 3.1 in the chapter. Which phase of corporate and cross-cultural evolution do you think Infosys is currently finding itself? Phase I Domestic, Phase II International, Phase III Multinational, or Phase IV Global?

Sources: Adapted from Joe Leahy, "Eulogy Barely Scratches the Surface of the New India," *Financial Times*, January 21, 2010, p. 10; Joe Leahy, "Infosys Heir with a Mantra for Growth," *FT.com*, July 8, 2007 (accessed on April 20, 2010); http://www.infosys.com/about/what-we-do/pages/index.aspx (accessed on April 20, 2010); http://www.ibm.com/annualreport/2009/2009_ibm_annual.pdf (accessed on April 20, 2010); Anthony Sibillin, "The Best of Both Worlds," *Eurobusiness*, April 2002, pp. 40–42.

Experiential Exercise: *How Important Is Your Family?*

OBJECTIVES

1. To illustrate that within different cultures and subcultures the family unit exerts various degrees of influence.
2. To compare your family experience with that of your classmates.

GROUP SIZE

Create diverse groups of three to five students; vary groups in terms of age, gender, nation of birth, and so forth.

TIME REQUIRED

Approximately 30 minutes.

EXERCISE

Families play various roles in the decisions a person makes with regard to occupation, career plans, education, and self-improvement. Each group of students is diverse in terms of personal life experiences, background, and family cohesiveness. As a future global manager, it is important for you to understand and appreciate other people's points of reference.

1. Please read over and consider the "influence" your family has had on your life in terms of
   - Where you go to school
   - Career plans
   - View of international events
   - Work ethic
   - Family responsibility
   - Ethical behavior
   - Motivation
   - Displays of affection
   - Definition of success
2. Write a brief description of how your family influenced you in these areas. Be sure to include positive and negative experiences about family from a national and subcultural context in which you spent most of your development years (birth to 16 years old).
3. Share your observations and thoughts with group members.

Source: Robert Konopaske and John M. Ivancevich, *Global Management and Organizational Behavior* (New York: McGraw-Hill/Irwin, 2004).

Experiential Exercise: *Expatriate Sources on the Web*

OBJECTIVE

To become familiar with a Web site that has information for current and future expatriates and their families.

GROUP SIZE

N/A—to be performed individually.

TIME REQUIRED

Approximately 1 hour.

OTHER

Internet connection and search engine needed.

EXERCISE

Using the Internet, visit www.expatexchange.com and become familiar with its information and hyperlinks. Then research and prepare a 3- to 4-sentence response for each of the following scenarios:

- *Scenario #1:* Assume that your organization is about to send you to Thailand for a 3-year expatriate assignment. Knowing that your spouse would like to do some volunteer work while in Thailand, you decide to do some research on this issue. Using the Web site given earlier, please identify three leads for your spouse that could lead to volunteer opportunities in the host country.
- *Scenario #2:* Assume that you are about to be assigned to São Paolo, Brazil, and would like to "chat" with former expatriates who have lived there to gather information about the quantity and quality of international schools for your children. How would you go about doing that using this Web site? Please describe.
- *Scenario #3:* Assume that you have just been promoted to global marketing manager for a large consumer products company. This new role will require you to visit customers in several countries each year. Please identify five countries that have "travel advisories" for U.S. citizens and summarize why these countries have travel advisories.

Source: Robert Konopaske and John M. Ivancevich, *Global Management and Organizational Behavior: Text, Reading, Cases, Exercises* (New York: McGraw-Hill/Irwin, 2004).

PART TWO

Behavior within Organizations:

The Individual

CHAPTER FOUR

Individual Behavior and Differences

Learning Objectives

After completing Chapter 4, you should be able to

Understand
Why employees make attributions about the causes of behaviors and outcomes.

Describe
How self-efficacy can influence an employee's behavior.

Discuss
Why the increasing diversity of the workforce will require the adoption of a different approach to and style of managing employees.

Compare
The meaning of the psychological contract from the employee and the employer perspectives.

Explain
Why it's difficult to change a person's attitude.

A Grown-Up Risk Taker

Mark Cuban started out as a blue-collar kid in Pittsburgh. He had a knack for selling things—magazines, papers, greeting cards, and garbage bags. He had an optimistic personality and paid his own way through Indiana University (IU). Cuban always seemed to be creative and a risk taker. His current net worth is $2.3 billion.

Personality traits vary among individuals. Not everyone is as outgoing, risk taking, and creative as Mark Cuban. Creativity has been a special attribute that Cuban has used to become successful.

After graduating from IU, Cuban started his own computer consulting company. He worked around the clock to be successful. After seven years of hard work, his firm, Micro Solutions Inc., was grossing $30 million annually. He sold his company to CompuServe.

While living in Dallas he wanted to listen to his beloved Hoosier basketball games. He couldn't get a station from Bloomington. Then he had an idea: Why not broadcast the IU games over the Internet? Broadcast.com was born. The company was a rousing success and eventually was sold to Yahoo! Cuban took away $2 billion from the deal.

Cuban took some of his money and purchased the NBA Dallas Mavericks for $280 million from Ross Perot Jr. This unique NBA owner—who started in Pittsburgh, sold greeting cards, started his own businesses, and took risks—is one of a kind. Individual differences in personality, attitudes, perceptions, values, creativity, and risk taking are displayed in reviewing the Mark Cuban history.

Lately Cuban has shown an interest in shaking up the media world. He is co-founder of HDNet, a high-definition TV network that provides original sports, music, and entertainment programming. Cuban also founded Sharesleuth.com to provide independent, Web-based reporting aimed at exposing securities fraud. It is obvious that Cuban's unique, risk-taking personality has helped to make him a successful entrepreneur.

Sources: Adapted from http://www.hd.net/ (accessed April 24, 2010); Mark Cuban, *Forbes,* March 8, 2007, at www.forbes.com/lists; and Mark Glaser, "Mark Cuban's Sharesleuth Takes Business Reporting to the Ethical Edge," *Mediashift,* August 22, 2006, accessed April 16, 2007, www.pbs.org/mediashift.

Any attempt to learn why people like Mark Cuban, profiled in the opening vignette, behave as they do in organizations requires some understanding of individual differences. As Cuban's story shows, he is unique, a risk taker, and a hard worker who has been very successful. Individual differences are so dynamic in some instances that any list of characteristics is usually incomplete. From his childhood, Cuban displayed behaviors that marked him as being different from others. He just didn't, and still doesn't, fit a particular model.

Managers spend considerable time judging the fit between individuals, job tasks, the firm's culture, and organizational effectiveness. Both the manager's and the subordinate's characteristics typically influence such judgments. Without some understanding of behavior, decisions about who performs what tasks in a particular manner can lead to irreversible long-run problems. On the other hand, managers who can correctly identify the individual strengths (and weaknesses) of their employees are in a much better position to deploy them in a manner that increases their organizations' effectiveness.

Employees differ from one another in many respects. A manager needs to ask how such differences influence subordinates' behavior and performance. This chapter highlights individual differences and dispositions that can make one person a significantly better performer than another person. In addition, the chapter addresses several crucial individual differences that managers should consider.

We also talk about how the environment affects individual differences. It's incorrect to assume that individual differences have no connection at all with the environment (work, family, community, and society). They're inextricably intertwined.

The Basis for Understanding Behavior

The manager's observation and analysis of individual behavior and performance require consideration of variables that directly influence individual behavior, or what an employee does (e.g., delivers training programs, processes loan requests, maintains air conditioners). The individual variables include abilities and skills, background, and demographic variables. As Figure 4.1 shows, an employee's behavior is complex because it's affected by a number of environmental variables and many different individual factors, experiences, and events. Such individual variables as abilities/skills, personality, perceptions, and experiences affect behavior.

Whether managers can modify, mold, or significantly alter their employees' behaviors is a much-debated issue among behavioral scientists and managerial practitioners. Although they usually agree that changing any individual psychological factor requires thorough diagnosis, skill, patience, and understanding on the part of a manager, there's no universally agreed-upon method managers can use to change personalities, attitudes, perceptions, or learning patterns. On the other hand, it is recognized that people's behavior patterns do change, albeit slightly, sometimes when managers would prefer that they remain stable. For example, an employee who used to be a star performer has slowed down and is now just an average employee. Managers must recognize the inherent difficulty in trying to get people to do and think about the things that are desirable to the organization.

Managers today face sweeping demographic changes in the workplace. There are more women, African-American, Hispanic, and Asian job applicants and employees. As baby boomers start to retire and demand for qualified applicants increases, more attention must be paid to attracting and retaining the most talented individuals and improving the performance of a diverse workforce.[1]

Because many workers may lack needed skills, managers will probably have to devote more time to educating, training, mentoring, and creating a positive motivational atmosphere for employees. Managers must determine how to make work more interesting, rewarding, and challenging. Unless they can accomplish this agenda, the outcomes associated with work—such as quality, quantity, and service—will suffer.[2]

Employees' behaviors lead to outcomes. They can result in positive, long-term performance and personal growth or the opposite: poor long-term performance and a lack of

FIGURE 4.1 Individual Behavior Framework

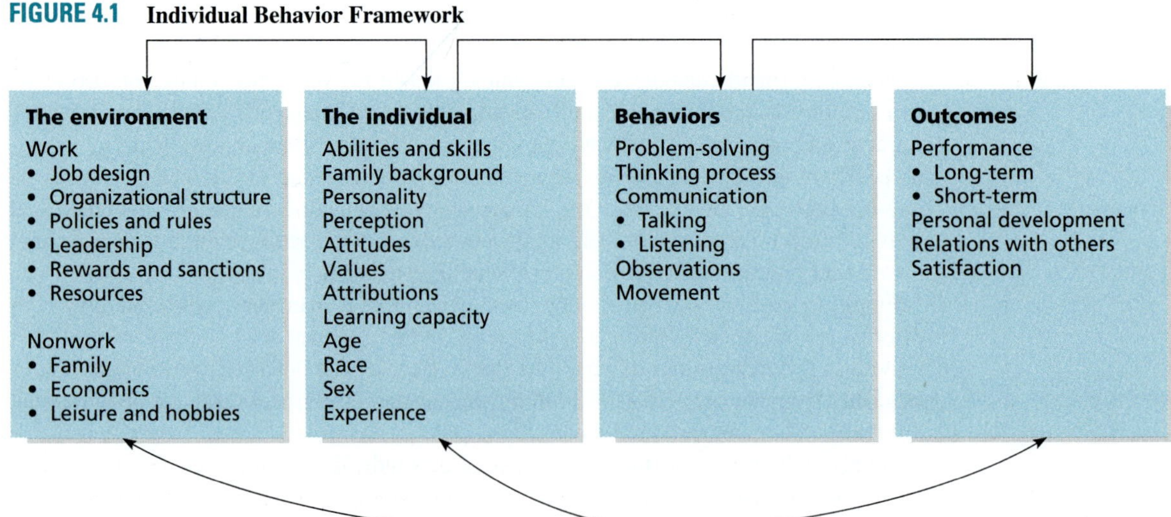

growth. As Figure 4.1 also shows, behaviors and outcomes serve as feedback to the person and the environment.

Human behavior is too complex to be explained by one sweeping generalization. Figure 4.1 gives only a sampling of the relevant variables that influence human behavior. Because coverage of each of the variables in this figure is beyond the scope of this book, most of our attention is given to three major psychological variables: perception, attitudes, and personality. These three form the foundation for our discussion of motivation, group behavior, and leadership. Learning and motivation variables are discussed in Chapters 5 and 6; other chapters of the book present the organizational variables.

Figure 4.1 suggests that effective management requires that individual behavior differences be recognized and, when feasible, taken into consideration while managing organizational behavior. To understand **individual differences**, managers must (1) observe and recognize the differences, (2) study variables that influence individual behavior, and (3) discover relationships among the variables. For example, managers are in a better position to make optimal decisions if they know employees' attitudes, perceptions, and mental abilities as well as how these and other variables are related. It is also important to know how each variable influences performance. Being able to observe differences, understand relationships, and predict linkages facilitates managerial attempts to improve performance.

individual differences
Individuals are similar, but they are also unique. The study of individual differences such as attitudes, perceptions, and abilities helps a manager explain differences in performance levels.

Behavior, as outlined in Figure 4.1, is anything that a person does. *Talking* to a manager, *listening* to a co-worker, *calling* a customer, *updating* the company's website, and *hiring* a new employee are behaviors. So are *daydreaming* about winning the lottery, *updating* a Facebook page, and *learning* how to use a firm's accounting system. The general framework indicates that behavior depends on the types of variables shown in Figure 4.1. Thus, as Kurt Lewin originally proposed, $B = f(I, E)$: an employee's behavior (B) is a function of individual (I) and environmental (E) variables.[3] The behavior that results on the job is unique to each individual, but the underlying process is basic to all people.

After years of theory building and research, scholars have come to the general agreement that *behavior:*

1. Is caused.
2. Is goal directed.
3. That can be observed (e.g., selling) is measurable.
4. That's not directly observable (e.g., thinking and perceiving) is also important in accomplishing goals.
5. Is motivated.

To emphasize these points of agreement, consider the case of Jim, who usually has been an average performer but recently became a high performer. A manager's analysis (which may be totally incorrect) of this behavior change might be as follows: Jim recently increased his efforts to perform. He has shown more interest in his work and has expressed interest in a vacancy in another department. This suggests that the improved performance occurred because Jim became motivated to work harder to gain a possible promotion.

Another explanation of Jim's behavior change might be that employee cutbacks have him worried. He doesn't want to lose his job, and fear of job loss motivates him to do more work.

The desired result of any employee's behavior is excellent performance. In organizations, therefore, individual and environmental variables affect not only behavior but also performance. An important part of a manager's job is to define "good" performance in advance—that is, to state what results are desired. Performance-related behaviors are directly associated with job tasks that need to be accomplished to achieve a job's objective. For a manager, performance-related behavior would include such actions as identifying performance problems; planning, organizing, and controlling employees' work; and creating a motivational climate for employees.[4]

Focusing their attention on performance-related behaviors, managers search for ways to achieve optimal performance. If employees aren't performing well or consistently, managers must investigate the problem. These six questions can help managers to focus on performance problems:

1. Does the employee have the skills and abilities to perform the job?
2. Does the employee have the necessary resources to perform the job?
3. Is the employee aware of the performance problem?
4. When did the performance problem surface?
5. How do the employee's co-workers react to the performance problem?
6. What can I do as a manager to alleviate the performance problem?

These questions and their answers again call attention to the complexity of individual differences and performance. They also indicate that when performance problems are identified, some form of managerial action is required.[5]

Individual Differences

The individual variables in Figure 4.1 may be classified as abilities and skills, background, and demographic. Each of these classes of variables helps to explain individual differences in behavior and performance.

Abilities and Skills

ability
A biological or learned trait that permits a person to do something mental or physical.

skills
Task-related competencies.

Some employees, although highly motivated, simply don't have the abilities or skills to perform well. Abilities, skills, and other factors play a role in individual behavior and performance.[6] An **ability** is a trait (innate or learned) that permits a person to do something mental or physical. **Skills** are task-related competencies, such as the skill to negotiate a merger or operate a computer or the skill to clearly communicate a group's mission and goals. In this book, the terms are used interchangeably in most cases. Remember that $B = f(I, E)$. Table 4.1 identifies 10 mental abilities that make up what's commonly referred to as intelligence.[7] Intelligence is often the best predictor of job success, but "best" does not mean "only," and many other factors play a role in performance.[8] Thus, managers must decide which mental abilities are required to successfully perform each job. For example, a language interpreter helping a manager put together a business deal with a Hungarian enterprise would especially need language fluency, number facility, and verbal comprehension in both English and Hungarian. The astute manager would search for an interpreter who had these abilities. Intelligence is related to more than just job performance. In a recent longitudinal study, general mental ability, when coupled with physical attractiveness and certain personality factors, was linked to higher levels of income.[9]

job analysis
Process of defining and studying a job in terms of behavior and specifying education and training needed to perform the job.

A laboratory technician's job may especially require memory, perceptual speed, and verbal comprehension, as well as various physical skills (see Table 4.2) to operate computer equipment. Managers attempt to match each person's abilities and skills with the job requirements. The matching process is important because no amount of leadership, motivation, or organizational resources can make up for deficiencies in abilities or skills. **Job analysis** is used to take some of the guesswork out of matching. It's the process of defining and studying a job in terms of tasks or behaviors and specifying the responsibilities, education, and training needed to perform the job successfully.[10]

TABLE 4.1 Mental Abilities = Intelligence

Source: Adapted from Marvin D. Dunnette, "Aptitudes, Abilities, and Skills," in Handbook of Industrial and Organizational Psychology, Marvin D. Dunnette, ed. (Skokie, IL: Rand McNally, 1976), pp. 481–83.

Mental Ability	Description
1. Flexibility	The ability to hold in mind a particular visual configuration.
2. Fluency	The ability to produce words, ideas, and verbal expressions.
3. Inductive reasoning	The ability to form and test hypotheses directed at finding relationships.
4. Associative memory	The ability to remember bits of unrelated material and to recall.
5. Span memory	The ability to recall perfectly for immediate reproduction a series of items after only one presentation of the series.
6. Number facility	The ability to rapidly manipulate numbers in arithmetic operations.
7. Perceptual speed	Speed in finding figures, making comparisons, and carrying out simple tasks involving visual perceptions.
8. Deductive reasoning	The ability to reason from stated premises to their necessary conclusion.
9. Spatial orientation and visualization	The ability to perceive spatial patterns and to manipulate or transform the image of spatial patterns.
10. Verbal comprehension	Knowledge of words and their meaning as well as the application of this knowledge.

Every job is made up of two things: people and job tasks. Matching people with jobs suited for their abilities and skills is often a problem.[11] Why do people end up in jobs in which they aren't productive, satisfied, or fulfilled? The effort to match jobs involves the following activities: employee selection, training and development, career planning, and counseling. To be successful in matching a person's abilities and skills to the job, a manager must examine *content, required behaviors,* and *preferred behaviors.* Content is the "what" of the job—the job description, responsibilities, goals and objectives, and specific tasks. Required behaviors are the "how" of the job—how it must be done in terms of quantity, quality, cost, and timing.

Preferred behaviors are often ignored in matching people and jobs. To be selected, some applicants don't honestly explain their preferences. Because they want the job so badly, they hold back or even mislead interviewers. Managers must attempt to determine a person's preference in terms of goals, style, career values, and achievement motives. An ideal job is one in which a person's skills and abilities can be applied to produce work that's satisfactory, fulfilling, and challenging. This is the goal of matching a person with the job.

Demographics

Among the most important demographic classifications are gender and race. Cultural diversity can also affect work situations.

TABLE 4.2 Samples of Physical Skills

Source: Adapted from Edwin A. Fleishman, "On the Relation between Abilities, Learning, and Human Performance," *American Psychologist,* (November 1972): pp. 1017–32.

Physical Skill	Description
1. Dynamic strength	Muscular endurance in exerting force continuously or repeatedly.
2. Extent flexibility	The ability to flex or stretch trunk and back muscles.
3. Gross body coordination	The ability to coordinate the action of several parts of the body while the body is in motion.
4. Gross body equilibrium	The ability to maintain balance with nonvisual cues.
5. Stamina	The capacity to sustain maximum effort requiring cardiovascular exertion.

Gender Differences

Are men and women different in terms of workplace behavior, job performance, leadership style, or commitment? Are the differences significant? It's generally accepted that from the moment of birth, boys and girls are treated differently. Research has shown that men and women are generally similar in terms of learning ability, memory, reasoning ability, creativity, and intelligence.[12] Despite fairly conclusive research data to the contrary, some people still believe that there are creativity, reasoning, and learning ability differences between the sexes.

There have been debates about male and female differences in terms of job performance, absenteeism, and turnover rates. The job performance debate is inconclusive. There are no compelling data suggesting that men or women are better job performers. The only areas in which differences are found somewhat consistently are absenteeism and leadership style. Women have a higher rate of absenteeism since they are usually the primary caregivers to children, elderly parents, and ill spouses, which makes them absent more from the job.[13] In a study of the preferred leadership style of male and female leaders in 27 countries, it was reported that female managers prefer participative, team oriented, and charismatic leadership dimensions more than males.[14]

Whether changes in society will result in more similarity between men and women is difficult to gauge. When society emphasized the difference between the sexes and treated them differently, there were some differences in such areas as aggressiveness and social behavior. But as society places more emphasis on equal opportunity and treatment, many differences are likely to disappear.[15] Men and women are becoming more alike in terms of workplace behavior.

Racial and Cultural Diversity

diversity
Describes human qualities such as race, gender, and ethnicity that are different from our own and that are outside the groups to which we belong.

Today's workforce doesn't look like the workforce of the past. The workforce is now much more diverse in terms of cultural background, values, language skills, and educational preparation. **Diversity** is a term used to describe the cultural, ethnic, and racial variations in a population. Many culturally diverse groups from around the world (e.g., China, Australia, Colombia, Russia) are spread throughout the workforce. Whether significant differences in job performance across diverse groups exist isn't known. Studies haven't been conducted in sufficient numbers to reach a conclusion.[16]

As a more diverse workforce enters organizations, it will become mandatory to not base decisions, prescriptions, and techniques on white male research results.[17] Generalizing from a research dominant group (white males) to women, African Americans, Hispanics, Asians, and other groups isn't sound. Faulty generalization can lead to making improper assumptions; presenting inadequate solutions; and implementing inaccurate reward, performance evaluation, and team-building programs. Similarly, minority-based study results are also unlikely to be generalizable to a majority group.

Managers aren't yet as diverse as the rest of the workforce. To manage the increasingly culturally diverse workforce will require flexibility, recognition of individual differences, and increased awareness of cultural background differences. There are a wide variety of Asian, European, Latin American, and African workers. The U.S Bureau of Labor Statistics issued a report predicting that ethnic minority share of the U.S. workforce will be approximately 35 percent in 2018.[18]

The OB at Work feature captures the effectiveness of three companies' diversity management approaches.

The proliferation of diverse cultural backgrounds in the workforce brings onto center stage differences in values, work ethics, and norms of behavior. Communication issues, insensitivity, and ignorance are likely to become major managerial concerns. There are

OB AT WORK — Johnson & Johnson, AT&T, and Coca-Cola: Leaders in Diversity Management

More than 300 companies were considered for being rated a top company in diversity management. Now in its ninth year, The *DiversityInc* Top 50 Companies for Diversity list is determined solely from a comprehensive survey of diversity management that measures CEO commitment, human capital, corporate communications, and supplier diversity.

Johnson & Johnson was ranked No. 1 on the 2009 *DiversityInc* top 50 companies for Diversity list. The $61.9 billion healthcare company pursues a number of diversity management initiatives, including linking managerial bonuses to diversification results; maintaining a diverse board of directors; providing benefits for same-sex domestic partners; and reporting that 31 percent of the senior-level executives and 47 percent of the company's highest paid employees are women.

AT&T has practiced diversity management for many decades and its number two rank on the 2009 *DiversityInc's* Top 50 list is not an accident. The composition of the employees reflects the communities in which AT&T does business. For example, 39 percent of its employees and 30 percent of its managers are minority (i.e., African American, Latino, Asian, and American Indian). AT&T has also earned a variety of other diversity-related awards for their advancement opportunities for women and veterans.

Coca-Cola was ranked number nine on the *DiversityInc* Top 50 list. This was the sixth consecutive year in which the company was ranked in the top 10. Coca-Cola has accumulated an impressive list of results as a result of the company's long commitment to diversity management, including:

- 50 percent of its U.S. non-hourly workforce is female;
- 35 percent of its U.S. non-hourly workforce is minority;
- From 2007–2009, women in general management roles in the United States have increased to 20 percent; and,
- 3,100 associates have completed various Diversity Education and Workplace Fairness programs in 2009.

Coca-Cola also established a Women's Leadership Council that is sponsored by Muhtar Kent, the CEO. The council is part of the firm's Global Women's initiative to "help accelerate the global recruitment, development, advancement, and retention of women at the Company."

Sources: Adapted from http://dibp.diversityinc.com/content/1757/article/5478/; http://www.jnj.com/wps/wcm/jsp/showData.jsp?q=2009%20annual%20report; http://dibp.diversityinc.com/content/1757/article/5449/http://www.att.com/gen/corporate-citizenship?pid=17721; http://dibp.diversityinc.com/content/1757/article/5505/; http://www.thecoca-colacompany.com/citizenship/diversity.html (all sites accessed on April 26, 2010).

differences in how individuals from different cultures respond to a request to work harder or to correct a defective product.

Managers must learn how to deal with the differences they'll encounter with a diverse workforce. The increased proportion of people of color and immigrants combined with related educational and linguistic issues will cause managers to work hard to match people with jobs.[19] It will be important to fit people with jobs appropriate to their abilities, skills, needs, values, and preferences. This isn't a new task for managers, but it will be more complex because of the diverse mix of workers. What seems right for the Chinese immigrant may be incongruent for the Brazilian immigrant. If managers can accurately assess and understand the values represented in their work units, they can produce the types of jobs, work atmospheres, and reward systems that result in excellent performance.

Individual Psychological Variables

Unraveling the complexity of psychological variables such as personality, perception, attitudes, and values is a challenge for even experienced managers. Even psychologists have a difficult time agreeing on these variables' meaning and importance, so our goal is to provide meaningful information about them that managers can use in solving on-the-job behavior and performance problems. The manager must continually observe individuals because what goes on inside a person can be easily hidden or masked.

Perception

Individuals use five senses to experience the environment: sight, touch, hearing, taste, and smell. Organizing the information for the environment so that it makes sense is called **perception**. Perception, as Figure 4.2 shows, is a cognitive process. Perception helps individuals select, organize, store, and interpret stimuli into a meaningful and coherent picture of the world. Because each person gives her own meaning to stimuli, different individuals "see" the same thing in different ways.[20] The way an employee sees a situation often has much greater meaning for understanding behavior than does the situation itself. Stated more thoroughly:

perception
The process by which an individual gives meaning to the environment. It involves organizing and interpreting various stimuli into a psychological experience.

> The cognitive map of the individual is not, then, a photographic representation of the physical world: it is, rather, a partial, personal construction in which certain objects, selected out by the individual for a major role, are perceived in an individual manner. Every perceiver is to some degree a nonrepresentational artist as it were, painting a picture of the world that expresses his or her individual view of reality.[21]

Because perception involves acquiring specific knowledge about objects or events at any particular moment, it occurs whenever stimuli activate the senses. Because perception involves cognition (knowledge), it includes the interpretation of objects, symbols, and people in the light of pertinent experiences. In other words, perception involves receiving stimuli, organizing them, and translating or interpreting the organized stimuli to influence behavior and form attitudes.

Each person selects various cues that influence his perceptions of people, objects, and symbols. Because of these factors and their potential imbalance, people often misperceive another person, group, or object. To a considerable extent, people interpret the behavior of others in the context of the setting in which they find themselves.

The following organizational examples point out how perception influences behavior:

1. The manager believes that an employee is given opportunities to use his judgment about how to do the job, while the employee feels that he has absolutely no freedom to make judgments.
2. A subordinate's response to a supervisor's request is based on what she thought she heard the supervisor say, not on what was actually requested.
3. The manager considers the product sold to be of high quality, but the customer making a complaint feels that it's poorly made.

FIGURE 4.2 The Perceptual Process

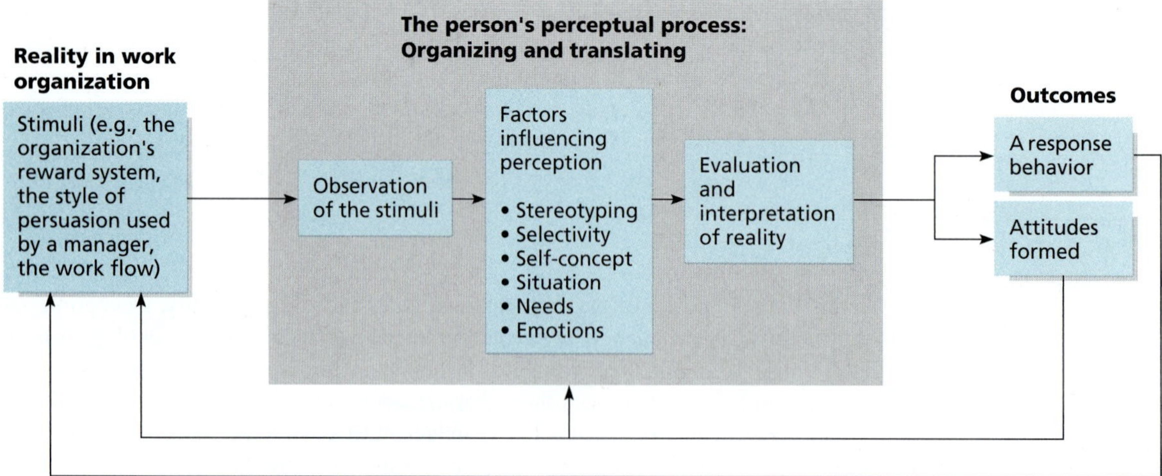

FIGURE 4.3
Perceptual Differences and Behavior

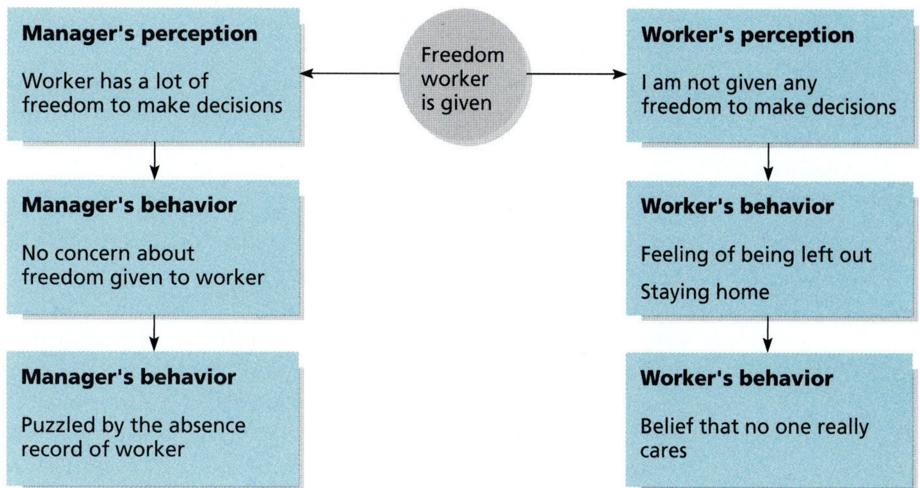

4. An employee is viewed by one colleague as a hard worker who gives good effort and by another colleague as a poor worker who expends no effort.
5. The salesperson regards his pay increase as totally inequitable, while the sales manager considers it a fair raise.
6. One line operator views working conditions as miserable while a co-worker right across the line regards working conditions as pleasant.

These are a few of numerous daily examples of how perceptions can differ. Managers must recognize that perceptual differences exist. Figure 4.3 illustrates how perception works. Suppose the worker in this example has been told that he has the freedom to make decisions about how the job is to be designed. Note that the manager and the employee perceive the job design freedom in different ways; they have different perceptions of the employee's amount of freedom.

Rensis Likert's classic and still informative research study clearly showed that managers and subordinates often have different perceptions. He examined the perceptions of superiors and subordinates to determine the amounts and types of recognition that subordinates received for good performance. Both supervisors and subordinates were asked how often superiors provided rewards for good work. The results (Table 4.3) show significant differences in what the two groups perceived. Each group viewed the type of recognition given at a different level. In most cases, subordinates reported that very little recognition was provided by their supervisors and that rewards were infrequent. The supervisors saw themselves as giving a wide variety of rewards for good performance. Likert's

TABLE 4.3
The Perceptual Gap between Supervisors and Subordinates

Type of Recognition	Supervisor's Perceptions of Frequency	Subordinates' Perceptions of Frequency
Privileges	52%	14%
More responsibility	48	10
A pat on the back	82	13
Sincere and thorough praise	80	14
Training for better jobs	64	9
More interesting work	51	5

Source: Adapted from Rensis Likert, *New Patterns in Management* (New York: McGraw-Hill, 1961) p. 91.

study illustrates how marked differences may exist between superiors' and subordinates' perceptions of the same events.

stereotype
An overgeneralized, oversimplified, and self-perpetuating belief about people's personal characteristics.

The manner in which managers categorize others often reflects a perceptual bias. A **stereotype** is an overgeneralized, oversimplified, and self-perpetuating belief about people's personal characteristics. For example, many people stereotype used-car salespeople, men stereotype female executives, young employees stereotype older managers, and female workers stereotype male managers. Most people engage in some form of stereotyping, both of other people and of occupations.[22] Stereotypes are self-perpetuating because people tend to notice things that fit their stereotype and not notice things that don't.[23]

Age has been a basis for stereotyping employees. Researchers have found that managerial actions against older workers are influenced by stereotyping.[24] Richard Wilson, a former executive of Monarch Paper Company, provides an example of age-based stereotyping. Even after receiving good performance reviews, he was demoted to a warehouse job that required him to perform menial job tasks. The demotion occurred after he rejected a series of early retirement packages from Monarch. A jury awarded Wilson $3.2 million because of age bias in his demotion. The jury indicated that management attempted to intimidate Mr. Wilson as part of their plan to eliminate older workers, who were considered less productive than younger employees.[25]

The inaccuracy of stereotyping can result in unfair decisions related to promotions, motivation programs, job design, or performance evaluations.[26] It can also result in not selecting the best person for a position. In an era of shortages of highly skilled job talent, organizations will suffer from stereotyping that results in the rejection of a limited pool of candidates. Age, race, gender, ethnicity, disability and lifestyle stereotyping can prove extremely costly in terms of lost talent, jury judgments against the firm, and the loss of goodwill and sales from customers in the stereotyped categories.

Selective Perception

The concept of selective perception is important to managers, who often receive large amounts of information and data and may tend to select information that supports their viewpoints. People ignore information or cues that might make them feel discomfort. For example, a salesperson from a pharmaceutical firm is asked by his manager to give her an update on his sales for the current quarter. The salesperson, who always sees things in an optimistic light, tells his boss that his numbers should come in about 10 percent higher than last year's numbers. This assessment seems overly optimistic and unrealistic to the manager who just found out from someone at the firm that this particular salesman just lost sizeable orders from two major clients. It seems the salesperson in question is using selective perception by ignoring this negative information and instead believing that his remaining and potentially new customers will make up the shortfall in sales revenue.

The Manager's Characteristics

People frequently use themselves as benchmarks in perceiving others. Research indicates that (1) knowing oneself makes it easier to see others accurately,[27] (2) one's own characteristics affect the characteristics identified in others,[28] and (3) people who accept themselves are more likely to see favorable aspects of other people.[29] Basically, these conclusions suggest that managers perceiving the behavior and individual differences of employees are influenced by their own traits. If they understand that their own traits and values influence perception, they can probably evaluate their subordinates more accurately. A manager who's a perfectionist tends to look for perfection in subordinates, just as a manager who's quick in responding to technical requirements looks for this ability in subordinates.

Situational Factors

The press of time, the attitudes of the people a manager is working with, and other situational factors all influence perceptual accuracy. If a manager is pressed for time and has to fill an order immediately, his perceptions are influenced by time constraints. The press of time literally forces the manager to overlook some details, rush certain activities, and ignore certain stimuli, such as requests from other managers or from superiors.

Needs

Perceptions are significantly influenced by needs and desires. In other words, the employee, the manager, the vice president, and the director see what they want to see. Like the mirrors in the amusement park's funhouse, needs and desires can distort the world the manager sees.

The influence of needs in shaping perceptions has been studied in laboratory settings. Subjects in various stages of hunger were asked to report what they saw in ambiguous drawings flashed before them. Researchers found that as hunger increased, up to a certain point, the subjects saw more and more of the ambiguous drawings as articles of food. Hungry subjects saw steaks, salads, and sandwiches, while subjects who had recently eaten saw nonfood images in the same drawings.[30]

Emotions

A person's emotional state has a lot to do with perception. A strong emotion, such as total distaste for an organizational policy, can make a person perceive negative characteristics in most company policies and rules. Determining a person's emotional state is difficult. Because strong emotions often distort perceptions, managers need to discern which issues or practices trigger strong emotions within subordinates.

Attribution

Attribution theory provides insight into the process by which we assign cause or motives to people's behavior. Why did something such as "exceptional performance" or "not submitting a budget on schedule" occur? By knowing how people decide among various explanations of behavior, we get a view of how causes of behavior are assessed. Observing behaviors and drawing conclusions is called *making an* **attribution**.

attribution
The process of perceiving the causes of behavior and outcomes.

When causes of behavior are presented, they're usually explained in terms of individual or personality characteristics or in terms of the situation in which it occurred. **Dispositional attributions** emphasize some aspect of the individual such as ability, skill, or internal motivation. Explaining a behavior in terms of something "within" the person such as aggressiveness, shyness, arrogance, or intelligence indicates a dispositional attribution.

dispositional attributions
Emphasize some aspect of the individual, such as ability or skill, to explain behavior.

A **situational attribution** emphasizes the environment's effect on behavior. Explaining that a new worker's low performance was the result of a typical adjustment period in learning the ropes is an example of making a situational attribution. Tardiness at work can be explained by traffic jams or car trouble, which are examples of situational attributions.

situational attributions
Attributions that emphasize the environment's effect on behavior.

In attempting to decide whether a behavior should be attributed to the person or to the situation, Kelley proposed using three criteria:[31]

1. *Consensus.* Would most other people say or do the same thing in the situation? If so, we're likely to attribute the behavior (e.g., low-quality production) to the person's unique qualities.
2. *Distinctiveness.* Is the behavior unusual or atypical for the person? If so (high distinctiveness), then we infer that some situational factor must be responsible. But if the person behaves this way often, we tend to make a personal attribution.
3. *Consistency.* Does the person engage in the behavior consistently? When behavior occurs inconsistently, we tend to make situational attributions.

TABLE 4.4
Criteria and Attributions

Employee	Consensus	Distinctiveness	Consistency	Attribution
Green	Low	Low	High	Person (disposition)
Brown	High	High	Low	Situation
Black	High	Low	High	Mixed (more dispositional than situational)

In many situations, managers have information about employee consensus, distinctiveness, and consistency. Suppose that a manager has three employees, Green, Brown, and Black. Making attributions about their performance is important. A quick review of the record is as follows:

1. *Green:* Currently a high performer. Co-workers are average performers. His record of achievements indicates a history of high performance.
2. *Brown:* Currently a high performer. Co-workers are high performers. His previous job record indicates some average to low performance.
3. *Black:* Currently a high performer. Co-workers are high performers. Her previous record is impeccable with only top performance ratings.

As managers observing and reviewing these behaviors and records, what attributions can you make? Table 4.4 shows how the consensus, distinctiveness, and consistency criteria are applied. Green's performance is low in consensus, is not distinct because he was a good performer before, and is highly consistent for him. This combination would elicit a dispositional explanation that Green is a self-initiator, a highly motivated worker. Brown is inconsistent in terms of performance; is in line or has high consensus with co-workers; and is highly distinctive because, on previous jobs, Brown was only an average to low performer. Black's performance is constantly high, it's similar to co-workers' (so there's low distinctiveness), and there's high consensus.

Attribution Errors

Despite guarding against attribution errors, most individuals have certain biases that can result in making errors. An *attributional bias* is making a judgment with only limited information about the person or situation. Not making a judgment with incomplete information would often be the best action. Research suggests that individuals are more likely to explain others' actions in terms of internal causes rather than external causes. For example, completing a budget late is likely to result in this type of attribution: he doesn't like the budgeting process and puts it off (an internal cause); in reality, however, the true reason for the delay was that the manager didn't provide him with the needed information until an hour before the budget was due (an external cause).[32]

The fundamental attribution error occurs because it is easier to explain behavior in terms of traits (e.g., procrastinator) than to a manager's style, system, or situation. The trait-based explanations can be harmful. The individual can be labeled or singled out in negative terms, which can then result in poor career progress because of the inaccurate judgments.

Other Attributional Bias

Most people tend to make positive evaluations of others. This is referred to as a *general positivity* or *Pollyanna principle.* We generally have an inclination to be positive. Also, people have a tendency to take credit for successful work and deny responsibility for poor work. This is called a *self-serving bias*. Individuals tend to have egocentric recall, in which they keep in mind and recall the good things that were contributed on a project and ignore bad or failed contributions. The excuses people make generally are to blame the problem behaviors on something in the environment instead of something within the individuals.[33] One recent study found that American and Japanese companies use self-serving bias to explain negative information in company annual reports.[34]

Making excuses for oneself often has positive effects because they lower anxiety and keep a person's self-esteem high.

Attitudes

attitudes
Mental states of readiness for need arousal.

Attitudes are determinants of behavior because they're linked with perception, personality, and motivation. An **attitude** is a positive or negative feeling or mental state of readiness, learned and organized through experience, that exerts a specific influence on a person's response to people, objects, and situations. Each of us has attitudes on numerous topics—unions, exercise, dieting, career goals, friends, and tax laws, for example. This definition of *attitude* has certain implications for managers. First, attitudes are learned. Second, attitudes define our predispositions toward given aspects of the world. Third, attitudes provide the emotional basis of our interpersonal relations and identification with others. And fourth, attitudes are organized and are close to the core of personality. Some attitudes are persistent and enduring; yet, like each of the psychological variables, attitudes are subject to change.[35]

Attitudes are intrinsic parts of a person's personality. Several theories attempt to account for the formation and change of attitudes. One such theory proposes that people "seek a congruence between their beliefs and feelings toward objects" and suggests that the modification of attitudes depends on changing either the feelings or the beliefs.[36] The theory further assumes that people have structured attitudes composed of various affective and cognitive components. These components' interrelatedness means that a change in one precipitates a change in the others. When these components are inconsistent or exceed the person's tolerance level, instability results. Instability can be corrected by (1) disavowal of a message designed to influence attitudes, (2) "fragmentation" or breaking off into several attitudes, or (3) acceptance of the inconsistency so that a new attitude is formed. The theory proposes that affect, cognition, and behavior determine attitudes and those attitudes, in turn, determine affect, cognition, and behavior.

affect
The emotional segment of an attitude.

1. **Affect**. The emotional, or "feeling," component of an attitude is learned from parents, teachers, and peer group members. One study illustrates how the affective component can be measured. A questionnaire was used to survey the attitudes of a group of students toward the church. The students then listened to tape recordings that either praised or disparaged the church. As the tapes played, students' emotional responses were measured with a galvanic skin response (GSR) device. Both pro-church and anti-church students responded with greater emotion (displayed by GSR changes) to statements that contradicted their attitudes than to those that supported their attitudes.[37]

cognition
The perception, opinion, or belief segment of an attitude.

2. **Cognition**. The cognitive component of an attitude consists of the person's perceptions, opinions, and beliefs. It refers to the thought processes, with special emphasis on rationality and logic. An important element of cognition is the evaluative beliefs held by a person. Evaluative beliefs are manifested as the favorable or unfavorable impressions someone holds toward an object or person.

behavior
The behavior segment of an attitude.

3. **Behavior**. The behavioral component of an attitude refers to a person's intention to act toward someone or something in a certain way (e.g., friendly, warm, aggressive, hostile, or apathetic). Such intentions could be measured or assessed to examine the behavioral component of attitudes.

FIGURE 4.4
The Three Components of Attitudes

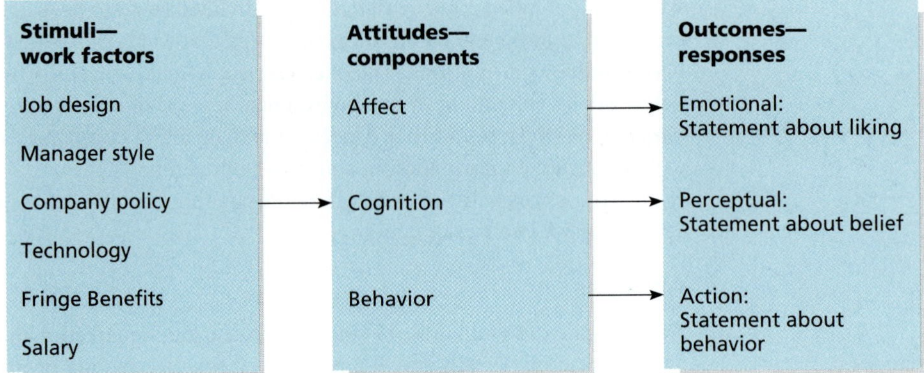

Figure 4.4 presents the three components of attitudes in terms of work factors such as job design, company policies, and fringe benefits. These stimuli trigger affective (emotional), cognitive (thought), and behavioral intentions. In essence, the stimuli result in the formation of attitudes, which then lead to one or more responses (affective, cognitive, or behavioral).

The theory of affective, cognitive, and behavioral components as determinants of attitudes and attitude change has a significant implication for managers. They must be able to demonstrate that the positive aspects of contributing to the organization outweigh the negative aspects. Many managers achieve effectiveness by developing generally favorable attitudes in their employees toward the organization and the job.

Attitudes have many sources: family, peer groups, coaches, society, and previous job experiences. Early *family* experiences help shape individuals' attitudes. Young children's attitudes usually correspond to their parents'. As children reach their teens, they begin to be more strongly influenced by *peers.* Peer groups influence attitudes because individuals want to be accepted by others. Teenagers seek approval by sharing similar attitudes or by modifying attitudes to comply with those of a group.

Culture, mores, and language influence attitudes. Attitudes of French Canadians toward the English-speaking population of Canada, of Americans toward people in England, and of Cubans toward Americans are learned in *society*. Within the United States there are numerous subcultures such as ethnic communities, impoverished sections of large cities, and religious groups that help shape people's attitudes.

Through *job experience,* employees develop attitudes about pay equity, performance review, managerial capabilities, job design, and work group affiliation. Previous experiences account for some individual differences in attitudes toward performance, loyalty, and commitment.

Individuals strive to maintain consistency among the components of attitudes. But contradictions and inconsistency often occur, resulting in a state of disequilibrium. The tension stemming from such a state is reduced only when some form of consistency is achieved.

cognitive dissonance
A mental state of anxiety that occurs when there's a conflict among an individual's various cognitions (e.g., attitudes and beliefs) after a decision has been made.

The term **cognitive dissonance** describes a situation where there's a discrepancy between the cognitive and behavioral components of an attitude.[38] Any form of inconsistency is uncomfortable so individuals attempt to reduce dissonance. *Dissonnance,* then, is viewed as a state within a person that, when aroused, elicits actions designed to return the person to a state of equilibrium.[39] For example, the chief executive officer of a cigarette company may experience cognitive dissonance if she believes that she's honest and hardworking but that cigarettes contribute to lung cancer. She may think, "I'm a good human being, but I'm in charge of a firm producing a cancer-contributing product." These thoughts create inconsistency. Instead of quitting and giving up her successful career, she's more likely to modify her thoughts or cognitions. She could state, "Our firm has manufactured a cigarette that's now very safe and free of cancer-producing products." Or she may think that cigarette smoking actually improves smokers' mental well-being, that it helps them reduce or cope with stress. When inconsistency in attitudes arises, the person can attempt to work the problem out cognitively or behaviorally. Here the CEO used a cognitive process to reduce her dissonance.

Cognitive dissonance has important organizational implications.[40] First, it helps explain the choices made by an individual with attitude inconsistency. Second, it can help predict a person's propensity to change attitudes. If individuals are required, for example, by the design of their jobs or occupations to say or do things that contradict their personal attitudes, they may change those attitudes to make them more compatible with what they've said or done.

Changing Attitudes

Managers often face the task of changing employees' attitudes because existing attitudes hinder job performance. Although many variables affect attitude change, they can all be described in terms of three general factors: trust in the sender, the message itself, and the situation.[41] Employees who don't trust the manager won't accept the manager's message or change an attitude. Similarly, if the message isn't convincing, there's no pressure to change.

The greater the communicator's prestige, the greater the attitude change.[42] The following is an example of how a communicator's prestige can influence attitudes. Sir Richard Branson, CEO of Virgin and a world renowned entrepreneur, used his prestige, creativity, and flare for creating "buzz" among the public and press to build his company into a $17 billion success story that employs more than 50,000 employees in 29 countries. Virgin competes in such diverse industries as air and rail travel, mobile phones, media, financial services, and fitness. Branson is using his prestige to push the envelope once again; he is pursing the relatively untapped market of commercial space travel.[43] In contrast, a manager who has little prestige and isn't shown respect by peers and superiors is in a difficult position if the job requires changing subordinates' attitudes so that they work more effectively. Thus, managers need to be aware of their prestige rating among employees. If they have prestige, they should use it to change attitudes. If they don't have prestige, attitude change may be virtually impossible.

Liking the communicator produces attitude change because people try to identify with a liked communicator and tend to adopt attitudes and behaviors of the liked person.[44] Not all managers, however, are fortunate enough to be liked by each of their subordinates. Therefore, liking the manager is a condition for trusting the manager.

Even if a manager is trusted, presents a convincing message, and is liked, the problems of changing people's attitudes aren't solved. The strength of the employee's commitment to an attitude is important. A worker who has decided not to accept a promotion is committed to the belief that it's better to remain in his present position than to accept the promotion. Attitudes that have been expressed publicly are more difficult to change because the person has shown commitment and changing it is admitting a mistake.

How much people are affected by attempts to change their attitude depends in part on the situation. While listening to or reading a persuasive message, people are sometimes distracted by other thoughts, sounds, or activities. In addition, studies indicate that people distracted while they listen to a message show more attitude change because the distraction interferes with counterarguing.[45]

Distraction is just one of many situational factors that can increase persuasion. Another factor that makes people more susceptible to attempts to change attitude are pleasant surroundings. The pleasant surroundings may be associated with the attempt to change the attitude.

Attitudes and Values

Values are linked to attitudes in that a value serves as a way of organizing attitudes. **Values** are defined as "the constellation of likes, dislikes, viewpoints, shoulds, inner inclinations, rational and irrational judgments, prejudices, and association patterns that determine a person's view of the world."[46] Certainly, a person's work is an important aspect of his world. Moreover, the importance of a value constellation is that once internalized, it becomes (consciously or subconsciously) a standard or criterion for guiding one's actions. The study of values, therefore, is fundamental to the study of managing. There's evidence that values are also extremely important for understanding effective managerial behavior.[47]

values
The conscious, affective desires or wants of people that guide their behavior.

Values affect the perceptions not only of appropriate ends but also of appropriate means to those ends. From the design and development of organizational structures and processes to the utilization of particular leadership styles and the evaluation of the performance of subordinates, value systems are persuasive. An influential theory of leadership is based on the argument that managers can't be expected to adopt a leadership style that's contrary to their "need structures" or value orientations.[48] Moreover, when managers evaluate subordinates' performance, the effects of the managers' values are noticeable. For example, one researcher reports that managers can be expected to evaluate subordinates with values similar to their own as more effective than subordinates with dissimilar values.[49] The effect of values is more pronounced in decisions involving little objective information and, consequently, a greater degree of subjectivity.

Another aspect of the importance of values occurs when the interpersonal activities of managers bring them into a confrontation with different, and potentially contradictory, values. Studies have shown that assembly-line workers, scientists, and people in various professional occupations are characterized by particular, if not unique, value orientations.[50]

Day-to-day activities create numerous situations in which managers must relate to others with different views of what's right or wrong. Conflicts between managers and workers, administrators and teachers, and line and staff personnel have been documented and discussed in the literature of management. The manner in which these conflicts are resolved and integrated is particularly crucial to the organization's effectiveness.[51] (See Figure 4.5.)

Attitudes and Job Satisfaction

Job satisfaction is an attitude that individuals have about their jobs. It results from their perceptions of their jobs, based on factors of the work environment, such as the supervisor's style, policies, and procedures, work group affiliation, working conditions, and fringe benefits. While numerous dimensions have been associated with job satisfaction, five in particular have crucial characteristics.[52]

job satisfaction
The attitude that workers have about their jobs. It results from their perception of the job.

1. *Pay.* The amount received and the perceived equity of pay.
2. *Job.* The extent to which job tasks are considered interesting and provide opportunities for learning and for accepting responsibility.
3. *Promotion opportunities.* The availability of opportunities for advancement.
4. *Supervisor.* The supervisor's abilities to demonstrate interest in and concern about employees.
5. *Co-workers.* The extent to which co-workers are friendly, competent, and supportive.

In some studies, these five job satisfaction dimensions have been measured by the job descriptive index (JDI). Employees are asked to respond yes, no, or can't decide as to whether a word or phrase describes their attitudes about their jobs. The JDI attempts to measure a person's satisfaction with specific facets of the job. Other measures of job

FIGURE 4.5 **Integrating Vision and Values within a Strategic Framework**

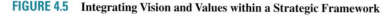

Source: Adapted from Paul McDonald and Jeffrey Gandz, "Getting Value from Shared Values," *Organizational Dynamics* 20, no. 3 (Winter 1992): 75.

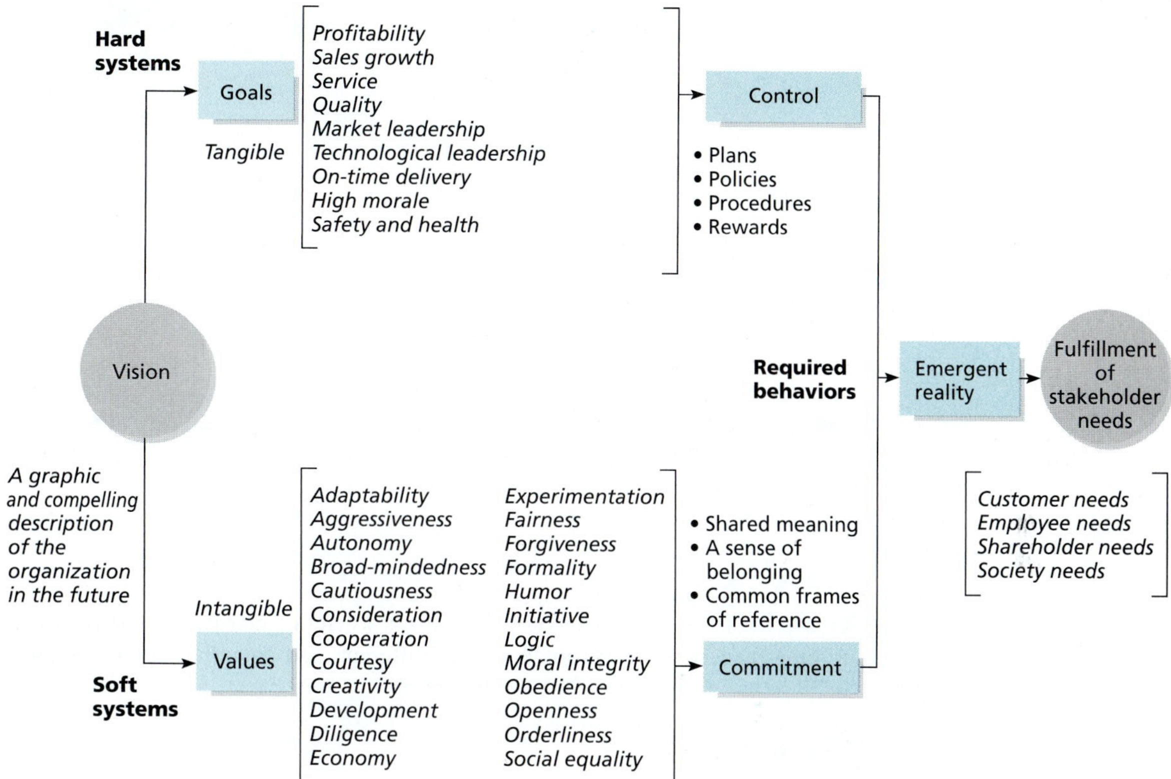

satisfaction, such as the Brayfield-Rothe measures, are more general. Figure 4.6 on the next page presents sample items from four scales measuring job satisfaction.

A major reason for studying job satisfaction is to provide managers with ideas about how to improve employee attitudes. Many organizations use attitude surveys to determine levels of employee job satisfaction. National surveys in the past have indicated that, in general, 75 to 80 percent of workers are satisfied with their jobs.[53]

There is still a general assumption that compensation is the most important factor in terms of the job satisfaction factor. The next OB at Work feature suggests that caution should be the rule when assuming that the way to improve job satisfaction is to use money as the key reward. Job security, communication, recognition, and trust should also be carefully considered by managers.

Job Satisfaction and Job Performance

One of the most researched, debated, and controversial issues in the study of job satisfaction is its relationship to job performance.[54] For years, many managers believed that a satisfied employee was a high-performing employee. Others proposed the opposite; that an employee who performs well is more likely to be satisfied with his or her job. Research into these questions has attempted to clarify the extent and direction of causality (i.e., which variable comes first) of the relationship between satisfaction and performance.

Researchers analyzed 312 samples and over 54,000 respondents from previous research studies on job satisfaction and performance.[55] They identified seven different perspectives

FIGURE 4.6
Sample Items from Four Widely Used Job Satisfaction Scales

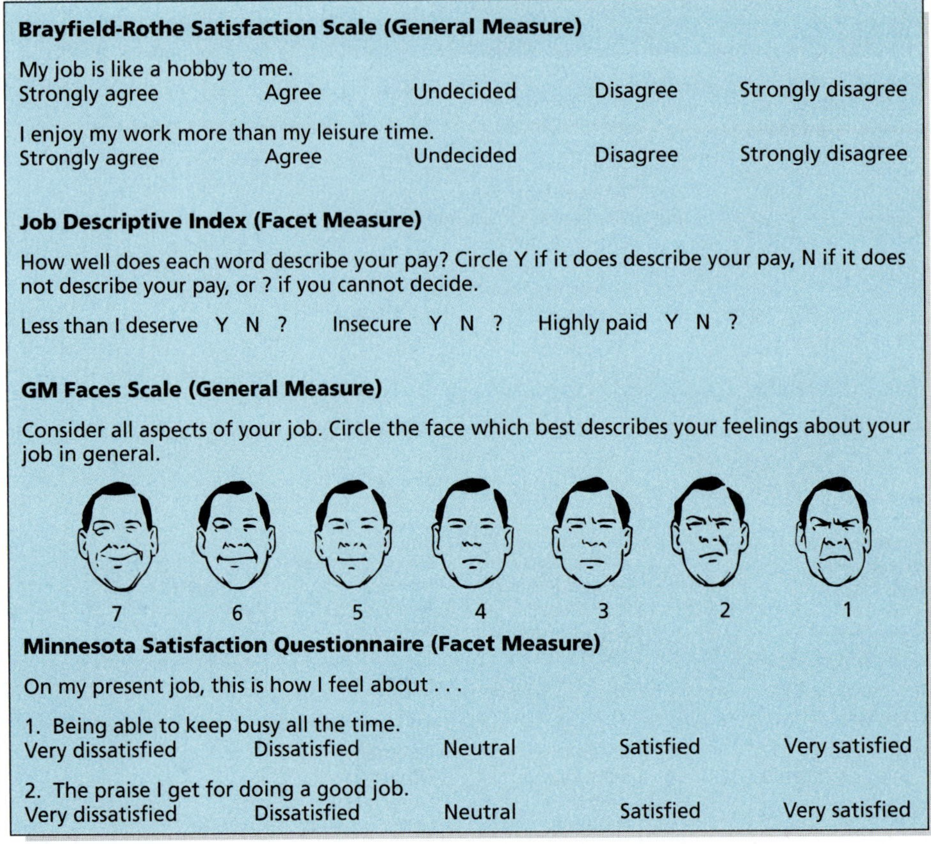

Brayfield-Rothe Satisfaction Scale (General Measure)

My job is like a hobby to me.
Strongly agree | Agree | Undecided | Disagree | Strongly disagree

I enjoy my work more than my leisure time.
Strongly agree | Agree | Undecided | Disagree | Strongly disagree

Job Descriptive Index (Facet Measure)

How well does each word describe your pay? Circle Y if it does describe your pay, N if it does not describe your pay, or ? if you cannot decide.

Less than I deserve Y N ? Insecure Y N ? Highly paid Y N ?

GM Faces Scale (General Measure)

Consider all aspects of your job. Circle the face which best describes your feelings about your job in general.

Minnesota Satisfaction Questionnaire (Facet Measure)

On my present job, this is how I feel about . . .

1. Being able to keep busy all the time.
Very dissatisfied | Dissatisfied | Neutral | Satisfied | Very satisfied

2. The praise I get for doing a good job.
Very dissatisfied | Dissatisfied | Neutral | Satisfied | Very satisfied

that have been used to explain the satisfaction-performance relationship. Three of the more common perspectives include: (1) satisfaction causes performance; (2) performance causes satisfaction; and (3) rewards intervene, and there's no inherent relationship.[56] (Figure 4.7 shows the three viewpoints.) One research study concluded that there is a moderate correlation between job satisfaction and job performance and that some of the seven models have received partial support in previous research studies. The authors of the study also noted that the strength of the relationship between satisfaction and performance varied based on other variables. For example, the relationship between satisfaction and performance becomes stronger when jobs are high in complexity. They propose a model that includes

FIGURE 4.7
Satisfaction–Performance Relationships: Three Views

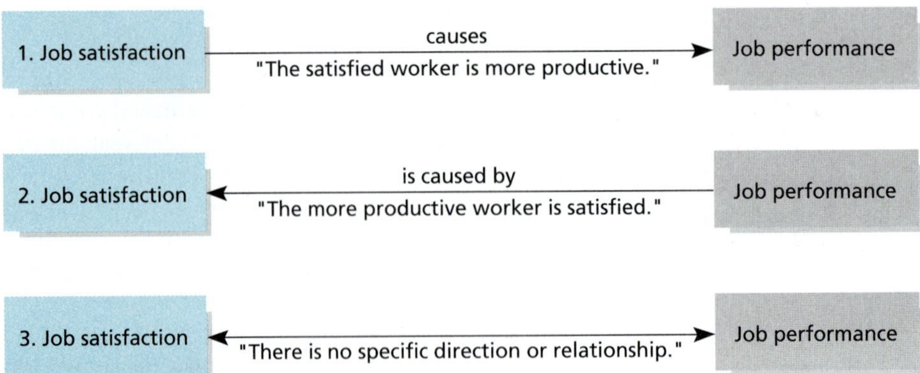

OB AT WORK Is Pay the Most Important Factor?

Pay is often considered to be the main factor that leads to job satisfaction. However, the 2009 Employee Job Satisfaction survey by the Alexandria, Virginia–based Society of Human Resource Management (SHRM) points out that the top concern for employees is job security. Other important predictors of job satisfaction were benefits, compensation and pay, opportunities to use skills and abilities, and feeling safe in the work environment.

Among the human resource professionals who were surveyed, the two most important contributions to job satisfaction were job security and relationship with immediate supervisor. Other important factors included communication between employees and senior management, opportunities to use skills and abilities, and management recognition of employee job performance. Compensation and pay dropped from one of the top five factors to seventh place.

Bill Maness, president of Syndeo Outsourcing LLC, says he's not surprised to see that employees rank benefits so high. "(Benefits) are getting so expensive, so that's understandable," he says. And, he believes job security, in his experience, is different with the category a worker is in. For most blue-collar and gray-collar workers (employees in clerical positions), job security is the overriding concern in a soft economy. The reason is simple, he says: their jobs can most easily be shipped off to other parts of the world. Blue-collar jobs have been lost to Mexico and China, where wages are lower. And gray-collar workers have been facing a steady stream of "offshoring," where jobs are moved to India or other countries where pay is lower.

For higher-paid managerial positions, however, where job loss is more difficult, the concerns are different, Maness says. There, job satisfaction is more important. "For them, job security is not as vital an issue," he says.

Gary Hardman, president of Hardman Benefits, says an often-overlooked factor in job satisfaction is career advancement opportunities within the organization. "The opportunity to grow is a top concern for many," he says. Hardman says he often sees that reason cited for people who are in job or career transitions. But, given current conditions, Hardman, who has more than 20 years of experience in the field, is not surprised that job security and benefits are the top-ranking concerns for employees. Workers have been more concerned recently about benefits as companies have reduced them or, in the case of health care, required higher deductibles, Hardman says. To save costs, some of Hardman's clients, most of whom are in the 25- to 100-employee range, have eliminated once-standard benefits such as dental plans. "Through understanding what employees want, HR professionals can have a great impact on their workforce," he says.

Sources: Adapted from "2009 Employee Job Satisfaction: Understanding the Factors That Make Work Gratifying," A Survey Report by the Society for Human Resource Management—See http://www.shrm.org/Research/SurveyFindings/Articles/Pages/2009JobSatisfactionSurveyReport.aspx (accessed on April 26, 2010); Jeanne Sahadi, "You May Be Paid More (or Less) Than You Think," *CNNMoney.com,* March 29, 2006.

aspects from all seven perspectives and conclude that many factors (e.g., personality, success and achievement, positive mood and performance-rewards contingency) influence the satisfaction-performance relationship.[57]

In sum, managers and researchers alike will continue to be interested in the job satisfaction and job performance relationship. Whenever possible, managers should create an environment in which employees are both satisfied and perform their jobs well.

From a practical standpoint, most managers want employees who are both satisfied and productive. So managers continue to be interested in job satisfaction despite evidence that satisfaction doesn't determine, in any significant way, the level of performance. But some theorists and researchers suggest performance has a broader meaning than simply units or quality of production.[58] Performance also covers a variety of citizenship behaviors, including showing untrained colleagues how to complete a job, helping a fellow worker complete a job when he's not feeling well, making positive comments in the community about the organization, working extra hard to deliver promised goods or services, and not complaining when management doesn't provide resources as promised. These behaviors are more prevalent among satisfied workers.[59]

Another reason for continued management interest is that research has found some indication of a modest correlation between satisfaction and turnover, but this is far from a strong linkage.[60] Evidence also exists of a moderate relationship between satisfaction and absenteeism. Dysfunctional turnover and absenteeism are expensive in terms of costs, lost opportunities, and overall morale. Some evidence shows a relationship between satisfaction and union activity. Dissatisfaction stemming from perceptions of pay inequities, poor supervisor–subordinate relationships, and inadequate working conditions initiate and sustain activities such as voting for union representation.[61]

Although job satisfaction doesn't influence quantity and quality of performance, it does influence citizenship behaviors, turnover, absenteeism, and preferences and opinions about unions. Because of these influences, managers continue to search for techniques and programs that improve employee job satisfaction. Many practicing managers have apparently concluded that performance means more than simply counting the quantity and quality of production.

Job Satisfaction Comparison of Individuals in Work Arrangements

Data indicate that there are more than 10 million independent contractors in the United States. There are also 17.6 million firms with no employees. Few studies have examined self-employed business owners, independent contractors, and organizational employees on job satisfaction. Prottas and Thompson conducted a comparison study of individuals in different work arrangements: self-employed, self-employed with no employees, and organizational employees.

The Prottas and Thompson findings suggest that the self-employed (no employees) group was older and reported higher levels of job satisfaction and lower job stress than the other two groups.[62] The independent owners indicated higher levels of job autonomy and satisfaction, and lower levels of job pressure than small-business owners (that have employees) and organizational employees.

The self-employed (e.g., have employees) reported the greatest amount of job pressure and worked the longest hours. However, they also had the highest levels of income. The independent owners worked the fewest hours of the three groups studied. If autonomy satisfaction is important, the results of this study suggest that self-employment, either as an owner or an independent, is a better career choice than organizational employment.

Job Satisfaction and Customer Satisfaction

More than 75 percent of all businesses in the United States and in other developed countries are service oriented, where it is necessary for employees to interact with customers. It is important for service-oriented organizations to satisfy customers so that they return. To accomplish a goal of high customer satisfaction, employees have to be happy or satisfied with their own jobs. Several companies that provide outstanding customer service were named in the 2008 *Businessweek Customer Service Champions* list, including the Four Seasons Hotel, L.L. Bean, JetBlue, Amazon.com, Chick-fil-A, Fairmont Hotels and Resorts, and Trader Joe's.[63]

Other organizations like Nordstrom, FedEx, Southwest Airlines, and Blue Bell are companies that work extensively to satisfy customers.[64] The theme of what is practiced at these companies is this: "A happy worker who displays a friendly, pleasant or warm demeanor is what is needed to create happy, satisfied, and returning customers." Research shows that satisfied employees increase customer satisfaction and loyalty.[65] Rude, incivil, combative, and complaining customers can leave employees unhappy. The dissatisfied customer appears to increase employee job dissatisfaction. Thus, job satisfaction and customer satisfaction can flow in both directions. To combat the dissatisfied-customer-leads-to-the-dissatisfied-employee situation, organizations such as Southwest Airlines attempt to hire individuals with pleasant, positive, and upbeat attitudes.[66]

Personality

personality
A stable set of characteristics and tendencies that determine commonalities and differences in people's behavior.

Why are some people concerned about the quality of the job they do while others aren't? Why are some people passive and others very aggressive? The manner in which a person acts and interacts is a reflection of his personality. **Personality** is influenced by hereditary, as well as cultural and social factors. Regardless of how it's defined, however, psychologists generally accept certain principles about personality:

1. Personality is an organized whole; otherwise, the individual would have no meaning.
2. Personality appears to be organized into patterns that are to some degree observable and measurable.
3. Although personality has a biological basis, its specific development is also a product of social and cultural environments.
4. Personality has superficial aspects (such as attitudes toward being a team leader) and a deeper core (such as sentiments about authority or the Protestant work ethic).
5. Personality involves both common and unique characteristics. Every person is different from every other person in some respects while being similar to other persons in other respects.

These five ideas are included in this definition of personality: An individual's personality is a relatively stable set of characteristics, tendencies, and temperaments that have been significantly formed by inheritance and by social, cultural, and environmental factors. This set of variables determines the commonalities and differences in the behavior of the individual.[67]

A review of the determinants shaping personality (Figure 4.8) indicates that managers have little control over them. But no manager should conclude that personality is an unimportant factor in workplace behavior simply because it's formed outside the organization. An employee's behavior can't be understood without considering the concept of personality. In fact, personality is so interrelated with perception, attitudes, learning, and motivation that any attempt to understand behavior is grossly incomplete unless personality is considered.

FIGURE 4.8
Some Major Forces Influencing Personality

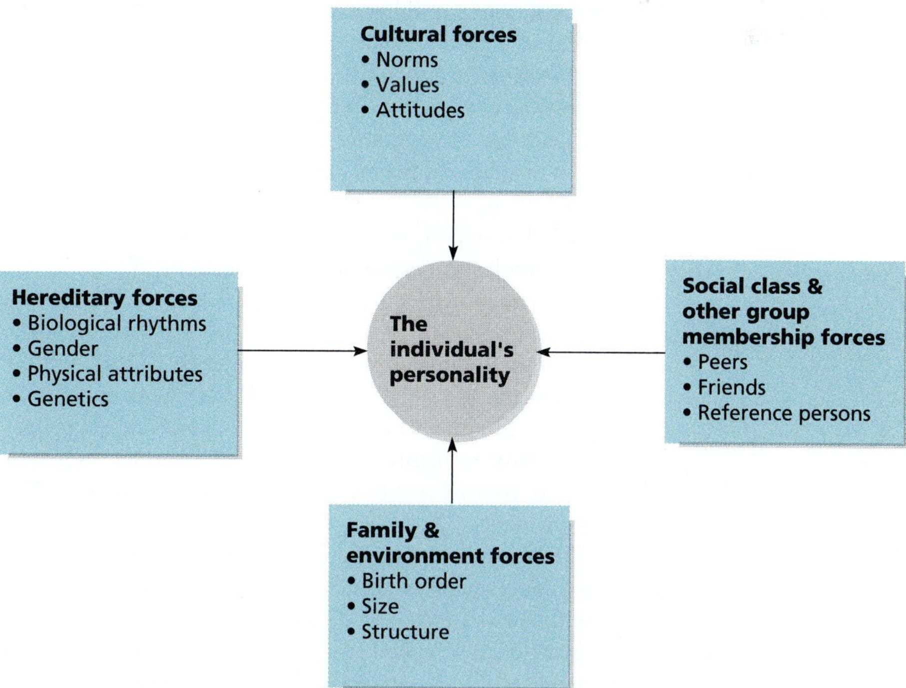

Theories of Personality

Three theoretical approaches to understanding personality are the trait approach, the psychodynamic approach, and the humanistic approach.

trait personality theories
Theories based on the premise that predispositions direct the behavior of an individual in a consistent pattern.

Trait Personality Theories Just as the young child always seems to be searching for labels by which to classify the world, adults also label and classify people by their psychological or physical characteristics. Classification helps to organize diversity and reduce the many to a few. One approach is by using **trait personality theories**.

Gordon Allpost was the most influential of the trait theorists. In his view, traits are the building blocks of personality, the guideposts for action, the source of the individual's uniqueness. Traits are inferred predispositions that direct the behavior of an individual in consistent and characteristic ways. Furthermore, traits produce consistencies in behavior because they're enduring attributes, and they're general or broad in scope.[68]

For decades, psychologist Raymond B. Cattell has studied personality traits, gathering many measures of traits through behavioral observation, records of people's life histories, questionnaires, and objective tests.[69] On the basis of his research, Cattell has concluded that 16 basic traits underlie individual differences in behavior. The research resulted in the development of Cattell's 16 PF (16 personality factors) questionnaire, which measures the degree to which people have these traits. Among the traits he identified are reserved–outgoing, practical–imaginative, relaxed–tense, and humble–assertive. All 16 of Cattell's traits are bipolar; that is, each trait has two extremes (e.g., relaxed–tense).

Trait theories have been criticized as not being real theories because they don't explain how behavior is caused. The mere identification of such traits as tough-minded, conservative, expedient, reserved, or outgoing doesn't offer insight into the development and dynamics of personality. Furthermore, trait approaches haven't been successful in predicting behavior across a spectrum of situations owing to the fact that situations (the job, the work activities) are largely ignored in trait theories.

psychodynamic personality theories
Freudian approach that discusses the id, superego, and ego. Special emphasis is placed on unconscious determinants of behavior.

Psychodynamic Personality Theories The dynamic nature of personality wasn't addressed seriously until Sigmund Freud's work on **psychodynamic personality theories** was published. Freud accounted for individual differences in personality by suggesting that people deal with their fundamental drives differently. To highlight these differences, he pictured a continuing battle between two parts of personality, the id and the superego, moderated by the ego.[70]

The *id* is the primitive, unconscious part of the personality, the storehouse of fundamental drives. It operates irrationally and impulsively, without considering whether what's desired is possible or morally acceptable. The *superego* is the storehouse of an individual's values, including moral attitudes shaped by society. The superego, which corresponds roughly to conscience, is often in conflict with the id: the id wants to do what feels good, while the superego insists on doing what's "right." The *ego* acts as the arbitrator of the conflict. It represents the person's picture of physical and social reality, of what leads to what and of which things are possible in the perceived world. Part of the ego's job is to choose actions that gratify id impulses without having undesirable consequences. Often the ego has to compromise, to try and satisfy both id and superego. This sometimes involves using ego defense mechanisms—mental processes that resolve conflict among psychological states and external realities. Table 4.5 presents some of the ego defense mechanisms used by individuals.

Even Freud's critics admit that he contributed to the modern understanding of behavior. His emphasis on unconscious determinants of behavior is important. The significance he attributed to early-life origins of adult behavior encouraged the study of child development. In addition, his method of treating neurosis through psychoanalysis has added to our understanding of how to get people back on the right track toward effective functioning.[71]

TABLE 4.5
Some Ego Defense Mechanisms

Mechanism	How It's Applied in an Organization
Rationalization	Attempting to justify one's behavior as being rational and justifiable. (I had to violate company policies to get the job finished.)
Identification	Increasing feelings of worth by identifying self with person or institution of illustrious standing. (I am working for Jim, who is really the best manager in the country.)
Compensation	Covering up weakness by emphasizing desirable traits or making up for frustration in one area by overgratification in another. (I may be a harsh manager, but I play no favorites.)
Denial of reality	Protecting self from unpleasant reality by refusing to perceive it. (There is no chance that this company will have to let people go because of the economy.)

humanistic personality theories
Place emphasis on growth and self-actualization of people.

Humanistic Personality Theories **Humanistic personality theories** emphasize the individual's growth and self-actualization and the importance of how people perceive their world and all the forces influencing them. Carl Rogers's approach to understanding personality is humanistic (people centered).[72] His advice is to listen to what people say about themselves and to attend to those views and their significance in the person's experiences. Rogers believes that the human organism's most basic drive is toward *self-actualization*—the constant striving to realize one's inherent potential.

It's hard to criticize theories that are so people centered. Some critics complain, however, that the humanists never explain clearly the origin of the mechanism for attaining self-actualization. Other critics point out that people must operate in an environment largely ignored by the humanists; an overemphasis on self neglects the reality of having to function in a complex environment.

Each major theoretical approach improves our understanding of personality. Trait theories provide a catalog that *describes* the individual. Psychodynamic theories integrate the characteristics of people and *explain* the dynamic nature of personality development. Humanist theories emphasize the *person* and the importance of self-actualization to personality. Each approach attempts to highlight the unique qualities of an individual that influence her behavior patterns.

personality test
Test used to measure emotional, motivational, interpersonal, and attitude characteristics that make up a person's personality.

Minnesota Multiphasic Personality Inventory (MMPI)
A widely used survey for assessing personality.

Myers-Briggs Type Indicator (MBTI)
A scale that assesses personality or cognitive style. Respondents' answers are scored and interpreted to classify them as extroverted or introverted, sensory or intuitive, thinking or feeling, and perceiving or judging. Sixteen different personality types are possible.

Measuring Personality Characteristics

Personality tests measure emotional, motivational, interpersonal, and attitudinal characteristics. Hundreds of such tests are available to organizations. One of the most widely used, the **Minnesota Multiphasic Personality Inventory (MMPI)**, consists of statements to which a person responds true, false, or cannot say. MMPI items cover such areas as health, psychosomatic symptoms, neurological disorders, and social attitudes, as well as many well-known neurotic or psychotic manifestations such as phobias, delusions, and sadistic tendencies.[73]

Managers in organizations aren't enthusiastic about using the MMPI. It's too psychologically oriented, is associated with psychologists and psychiatrists, and has a reputation of being used to help people with problems. A tool some managers find more comfortable is the 100-question **Myers-Briggs Type Indicator (MBTI)**, briefly described in the accompanying OB at Work feature. There is little empirical-based evidence that has dampened the use of the MBTI in organizations. More than 2 million people a year in the United States complete the MBTI.

Projective tests, also used to assess personality, have people respond to a picture, an inkblot, or a story. To encourage free responses, only brief, general instructions are given; for

OB AT WORK The Myers-Briggs Type Indicator (MBTI) Is Preferred by Managers

Hallmark Cards, Apple, ExxonMobil, Honda Motors, 3M, AT&T, and General Electric are using the Myers-Briggs Type Indicator scale to learn about personality. In the 1920s, noted Swiss psychoanalyst Carl Jung developed a cognitive-style theory of personality, which the American mother–daughter team of Katherine Briggs and Isabel Briggs Myers later converted into the MBTI, a scale organizations like to use.

Jung had proposed that two dimensions (sensation and intuition) influence a person's perception. Also, two dimensions (thinking and feeling) affect individual judgment. He believed that an individual's cognitive style is determined by the pairing of a person's perception and judgment tendencies. Myers and Briggs developed a test (Samples: Which word appeals to you more: *build/invent?* In a large group, do you more often introduce others or are you introduced?) so that respondents can discover their personality or cognitive style type. The test identifies people as extroverted or introverted (E or I), sensing or intuitive (S or N), thinking or feeling (T or F), and perceiving or judging (P or J). A person's answers are divided and classified into 16 different personality types.

Four of the combinations and some typical occupations are

Sensation–Thinking: Thorough, logical, practical, and application oriented.

Auditor of CPA firm, quality control supervisor, or safety engineer.

Intuitive–Thinking: Creative, independent, critical. Lawyer, systems analyst, college professor.

Sensation–Feeling: Committed, responsible, conscientious. Union negotiator, social worker, drug supervisor.

Intuitive–Feeling: Charismatic, people-oriented, sociable. Politician, public relations specialist, human resource director.

Can the MBTI be so good that more than 2 million people a year use it to diagnose personality? Jim Talman, vice president of Bayson (a small firm that sells electrical parts in the Southwest and Mexico), believes that it is. It's one of a number of techniques Bayson uses to find the best sales personnel for a job in which language proficiency, cultural sensitivity, and openness in working with customers in Mexico are important. In addition, Bayson has found that the high-scoring sensation-feeling and extroverted salespeople have the best sales records in Mexico.

Bayson hasn't validated the MBTI, but management still believes that it helps them to make better selections. Leaders at Hallmark Cards also feel strongly that this tool can be helpful. A nearly 100-year-old organization, Hallmark has assessed over 1,000 of its managers with a Myers-Briggs type indicator with the hope that the information can help its managers understand better how others perceive their actions and communications. The goal of the company is to become a much more customer-oriented and efficient. Thousands of firms apparently find some value in the MBTI. Is it essentially sound, valid, and reliable? We aren't sure. But even though some researchers have called for cautious use of the MBTI, organizational practitioners continue to charge ahead and use it to identify links between personality types and organizational effectiveness.

Sources: Adapted from J. Overbo, "Using Myers-Briggs Personality Type to Create a Culture Adapted to the New Century," *T + D*, 64, no. 2 (2010): 70–72; David J. Pittenger, "Cautioning Comments Regarding the Myers-Briggs Type Indicator," *Consulting Psychology Journal: Practice and Research* (Summer 2005): 210–21; Ruthann Fox-Hines and Roger B. Bowersock, "ISFJ, ENTP, MBTI: What's It All About?" *Business & Economic Review,* January–March 1995, pp. 3–7; Gregory J. Boyle, "Myers-Briggs Type Indicator (MBTI): Some Psychometric Limitations," *Australian Psychologist* (March 1995): 71–74; Lance Lindon, "Linking an Intervention Model to the Myers-Briggs Type Indicator, Consultancy and Managerial Roles," *Journal of Managerial Psychology* (1995) 21–29; Bonnie G. Mani, "Progress on the Journey to Total Quality Management: Using the Myers-Briggs Type Indicator and the Adjective Check List in Management Development," *Public Personnel Management* (Fall 1995): 365–98; Carol Hildebrand, "I'm OK, You're Really Weird," *CIO,* October 1995, pp. 86–89; discussions with corporate executives in Juarez, Mexico, and Houston, El Paso, and San Antonio, Texas, in summer and fall 1989.

the same reason, the test pictures or stories are vague. The underlying reason for this is that each individual perceives and interprets the test material in a manner that displays his or her personality. That is, the individual projects his or her attitudes, needs, anxieties, and conflicts.

A *behavioral measure* of personality involves observing the person in a particular situation. For example, an individual may be given a specific work situation problem to solve. The person's problem-solving ability is studied in terms of the steps taken, time required to reach a solution, and quality of the final decision.

Each of these measures of personality has drawbacks: Self-report tests have an accuracy problem; projective tests require a subjective interpretation by a trained person; and behavioral measures rely on a small sample of a person's behavior.

The Big Five Model

As a review of the literature indicates, there are many different dimensions of personality that can be used to describe people. Over the past two decades, a consensus has emerged that five dimensions or factors can be used to described a substantial amount of human personality.[74] Organizational researchers have labeled these factors the "Big Five" personality dimensions[75]:

Conscientiousness. The hardworking, diligent, organized, dependable, and persistent behavior of a person. A low score on this dimension depicts a lazy, disorganized, and unreliable person. Research suggests that individuals who score high in conscientiousness tend to have high levels of motivation and perform well across several different types of occupations.[76]

Extraversion–introversion. The degree to which a person is sociable, gregarious, and assertive versus reserved, quiet, and timid. Research has been reported that extraverted people tend to perform well in sales and management jobs, do better in training programs, and have higher levels of overall job satisfaction.[77]

Agreeableness. The degree of working well with others by sharing trust, warmth, and cooperativeness. People who are low scorers on this dimension are cold, insensitive, and antagonistic. People who are high in agreeableness tend be better team players and get along better with colleagues, customers, and other stakeholders.[78] Jobs and professions that require such individuals include customer service, sales, auditing, nursing, teaching, and social work.

Emotional stability. The ability a person displays in handling stress by remaining calm, focused, and self-confident, as opposed to insecure, anxious, and depressed. Recent research suggests that individuals who possess high levels of both emotional stability and conscientiousness (i.e., a "buoyant" personality) tend to have higher levels of performance and are more likely to stay with the organization.[79]

Openness to experience. A person's range of interest in new things. Open people are creative, curious, and artistically sensitive, as opposed to being closed-minded. People high in openness tend to thrive in jobs and occupations where change is continuous and where innovation is necessary. For example, people who create spectacular special effects for large-budget action films (e.g., *Avatar*) need high levels of this personality dimension.

Through a growing number of studies, researchers are finding that the "Big Five" play an important role in workplace behaviors.[80] As the nearby OB and Your Career suggests, finding a job or career that fits your personality is an important step toward achieving success.

Personality and Behavior

An issue of interest to behavioral scientists and researchers is whether the personality factors measured by such inventories as the MBTI, the MMPI, and the 16PF questionnaire; by projective tests; or by behavioral measures collected in controlled settings can predict behavior or performance in organizations. Using a total inventory to examine whether personality is a factor in explaining behavior is rarely done in organizational behavior research. Typically, people try to gain a perspective on personality by measuring different facets of personality such as locus of control, creativity, or Machiavellianism.

locus of control
A personality characteristic that describes people who see the control of their lives as coming from inside themselves as *internalizers*. People who believe that their lives are controlled by external factors are *externalizers*.

Locus of Control The **locus of control** of individuals determines the degree to which they believe that their behaviors influence what happens to them. Some people believe that they're autonomous—that they're masters of their own fate and bear personal responsibility for what happens to them. They see the control of their lives as coming from inside

OB AND YOUR CAREER Finding a Job that Fits

Finding a job or career that fits with "who you are" is probably easier said than done, but it is still very worthwhile goal to pursue. For people who have worked in jobs and careers that didn't fit them, chances are pretty good that they occasionally dreaded going to work and didn't want to go the "extra mile" to achieve high performance. These people probably left their ill-fitting jobs as soon as they could find a job or career that fit better with their personalities and work preferences.

So, how can a person find a job or career that fits well? There's no perfect answer to this question, but a person could take the following steps to increase his or her chances of finding a good fit:

1. Complete several online personality inventories to learn about yourself. Individuals who know their scores on the Myers-Briggs type indicator and the Big Five Personality inventory will be better able to pursue jobs that fit their dispositions. For example, if a person scores high in extraversion and agreeableness, then jobs that require a large amount of interaction with people (e.g., teaching, sales, customer service, etc.) will provide a better fit than those jobs that are more solitary in nature (e.g., research).
2. Ask current and previous co-workers, supervisors, and customers (if possible) to describe your strengths and weaknesses as an employee. Pay special attention to recurring themes across these individuals (i.e., a key strength of the individual is the ability to resolve customer problems), for this suggests that the observations are more likely to be true.
3. Make a list of all current and previous jobs. Next, make a list of the aspects of each job that you liked and disliked the most. Upon comparing the lists, look for themes (e.g., I don't like working on teams) that can help identify what a "good job" looks like relative to the alternative.
4. Seek out people who have jobs that you find interesting and ask them for a 10-minute "informational interview." The purpose of this type of interview is to ask questions about the person's job to see if it's something that really interests you. However, be sure you don't ask for a job; you're there to learn and build your network, not interview for a specific job.

themselves. Rotter called these people *internals*.[81] Rotter also held that many people view themselves as helpless pawns of fate, controlled by outside forces over which they have little, if any, influence. Such people believe that the locus of control is external rather than internal. Rotter called them *externals*.

A study of 900 employees in a public utility found that internally controlled employees were more content with their jobs, more likely to be in managerial positions, and more satisfied with a participative management style than were employees who perceived themselves to be externally controlled.[82] An interesting study of 90 entrepreneurs examined locus of control, perceived stress, coping behaviors, and performance.[83] The study was done in a business district over a 3.5-year period following flooding by Hurricane Agnes. Internalizers were found to perceive less stress than did externalizers and to employ more task-centered coping behaviors and fewer emotion-centered coping behaviors. In addition, internalizers' task-oriented coping behaviors were associated with better performance. The available data have generally indicated that entrepreneurs in most fields, whether male of female, are likely to have an internal locus of control.[84]

Locus of control and other personality traits have been identified as an important trait that differentiates the Gen Y with the other generations in the workplace. The OB at Work feature examines some new thinking about the personality traits and values of the Gen Yers.

In general, research results suggest that internals are more resistant to pressure to conform and are less likely to be persuaded to change their attitudes. Externals appear to be more receptive to structured jobs and seem more receptive to participation in job-related decision making.[85] Evidence suggests that people's behavior changes from one situation to another and that their belief in an internal or external locus of control varies depending on the culture that they have been socialized in[86] and the particular situation they face.[87] In regard to the latter, attempts are now being made to measure a person's specific internal or external locus of control concerning both work[88] and health issues.[89]

OB AT WORK Gen Y Employees: Are They Changing the Workplace?

Research suggests that Gen Y employees (also known as Millennials), who are now in their 20s and early 30s, are different in many substantive ways from members of other generations (i.e., Gen X, baby boomers, etc.). In general, Gen Y workers are thought to be very comfortable with technology, prefer jobs that are defined by task, not by time, and are more individualistic and focused on their own interests and lifestyles. However, there may be deeper level psychological traits and values that differentiate this segment of the workforce from the older generations. Research suggests that the following traits are common among Gen Y workers:

External Locus of Control
- Implications: not taking responsibility for success or failures.
- Organizational response: more work in teams and add accountability for performance.

Less Need for Social Approval
- Implications: casual dress and tone with supervisors, customers, etc.
- Organizational response: dress codes and mentoring.

Higher Self-Esteem
- Implications: high need for praise; less ethical behaviors.
- Organizational response: encourage managers to praise and provide ethics training.

Higher Anxiety and Depression
- Implications: stressed-out and less productive workers; absenteeism and turnover.
- Organizational response: stress management training and mental health services.

Women More Assertive
- Implications: more women in powerful positions.
- Organizational response: provide flextime, childcare; gender equality.

How can Gen Y workers use the above information about the shared personality traits of their generation? They can look for jobs and careers that fit well with these and their individual personality traits. For example, Gen Y workers may want to work for organizations that value work/life balance and a casual work environment, offer meaningful work assignments, have supportive managers who give a lot of feedback, and offer ongoing training and career enhancement opportunities. There are many jobs and careers from which Gen Y workers can choose; a better fit will generally lead to high job and life satisfaction in the long run.

Sources: Adapted from Jean M. Twenge and Stacy M. Campbell, "Generational Differences in Psychological Traits and Their Impact on the Workplace," *Journal of Managerial Psychology* 23, no. 8 (2008): 862–877; Tamara J. Erickson, "Task, Not Time: Profile of Gen Y Job," *Harvard Business Review* 86, no. 2 (2008): 19; Karen Auby, "A Boomer's Guide To Communicating with Gen X and Gen Y," *Businessweek*, August 25, 2008, pp. 63–64; Elisabeth Kelan, "Generational and Gender Transformations," *Personnel Today*, September 16, 2008, pp. 38–40.

self-efficacy
The belief that one can perform adequately in a situation. Self-efficacy has three dimensions: magnitude, strength, and generality.

Self-Efficacy When individuals acquire an internal control orientation that leads them to set goals and develop action plans to accomplish them, they develop a sense of **self-efficacy**. Bandura discusses the self-efficacy concept as a part of social learning theory.[90] He contends that self-efficacy is a belief that we can perform adequately in a particular situation. People's sense of capability influences their perception, motivation, and performance. Most individuals don't even try to do things, such as accept a promotion or use a computer, when they expect to be ineffectual. People avoid others and situations in which they feel inadequate.

Bandura believes that perceptions of one's abilities are best thought of as a host of specific evaluations.[91] Individuals evaluate their past and actual accomplishments, the performance of others, and their own emotional stress. Besides influencing a person's choice of activities, tasks, and situations, these evaluations also influence how much effort is expended and how long the person continues to try to succeed.

Figure 4.9 displays a model of self-efficacy based on Bandura's work. The behaviors of a person with high self-efficacy are positive, success driven, and goal oriented. When they need assistance, they look for tangible aid and not reassurance or emotional support. On the other hand, a person with low self-efficacy sees problems and worries and thinks in terms of failing or not being able to do a high-quality job. Sam Walton, founder of

FIGURE 4.9 Bandura's Self-Efficacy Workplace Application

Source: Adapted from Albert Bandura, "Regulation of Cognitive Processes through Perceived Self-Efficacy," *Developmental Psychology* (September 1989): 729–35; Robert Wood and Albert Bandura, "Social Cognitive Theory of Organizational Management," *Academy of Management Review* (July 1989): 361–84; and Robert Kreitner and Angelo Kinicki, *Organizational Behavior* (Homewood, IL: Richard D. Irwin, 1992), p. 90.

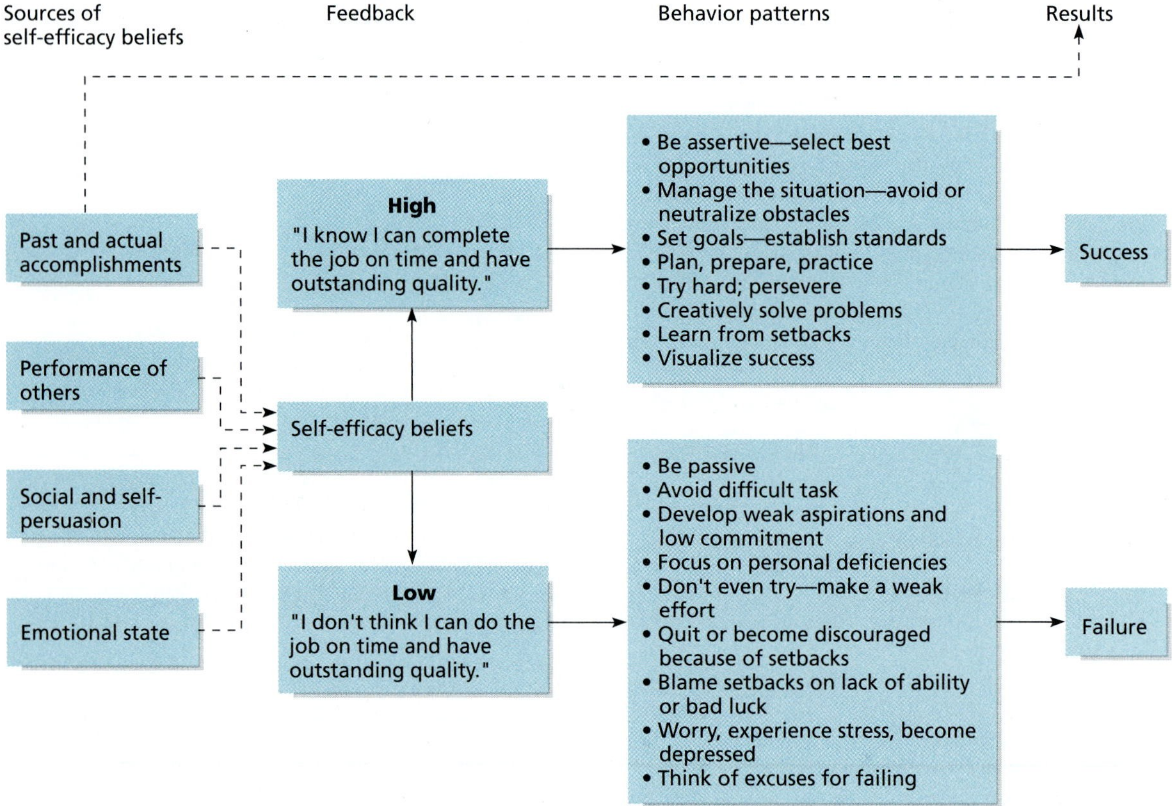

Walmart, was an example of a person with a high self-efficacy belief that he could beat Sears, Kmart, and Target. He selected opportunities, and planned, visualized, and expressed how Walmart would succeed. His speeches and behaviors reveal a person with high self-efficacy.[92]

The organizational behavior implications of self-efficacy are numerous relating to such diverse areas as seasickness among military recruits to job search activities among unemployed workers. Self-efficacy's role in motivation and task performance is obvious. A person high in self-efficacy is more motivated to perform at high levels of achievement. Self-efficacy may be important in terms of training employees to improve skills they believe are inadequate to perform well.[93] Self-efficacy may also be a factor in feedback provided through performance evaluation programs. Individuals with high self-efficacy may respond to the identification of problem areas in a more aggressive, corrective but sometimes self-serving way than those employees low in self-efficacy.[94] In addition, it has been suggested that self-efficacy is relevant to equal employment opportunity. Culture may have a significant effect on self-efficacy,[95] and as a more diverse workforce enters the mainstream, this could become an important issue. Individuals with low self-efficacy could preserve internal barriers to advancement and become passive. The shortage of successful role models among minorities could create self-doubts about advancement. Perhaps efficacy training could help minority group members minimize the self-doubt barrier to success. Chapter 6 discusses self-efficacy in terms of motivation.

Machiavellianism Imagine yourself in the following situation with two other people: Thirty new $1 bills are on the table to be distributed in any way the group decides. The game is over as soon as two of you agree to how it will be divided. Obviously, the fairest distribution would be $10 each. However, a selfish party could cut out the third person, and the remaining two would each end up with $15. Suppose that one person suggests this alternative to you, and before you decide, the left-out person offers to give you $16, taking $14 as his or her share and cutting out the other person. What would you do?

Machiavellianism
A term used to describe political maneuvers in an organization. Used to designate a person as a manipulator and power abuser.

Machiavellianism, a concept derived from the writings of Italian philosopher and statesmen Niccolo Machiavelli (1469–1527), helps to answer the question. Machiavelli was concerned with the manipulation of people and with the orientations and tactics used by manipulators versus nonmanipulators.[96] *Machiavellianism* (a term with negative connotations) is associated with being a political maneuverer and power manipulator.

From anecdotal descriptions of power tactics and the nature of influential people, various scales have been constructed to measure Machiavellianism. One scale organizes questions around a cluster of beliefs about tactics, people, and morality.

In the money allocation game just discussed, the individuals who get the lion's share are those who score high on this scale, the LOW MACH scorers get only slightly less than would be expected by a fair, one-third split. In a job situation, Machiavellianism does seem to have an effect on job performance.[97] HIGH MACH scorers would probably be suited for activities such as selling, negotiating, and acquiring limited resources. LOW MACH scorers would seem to be better suited for structured, routine, and nonemotional situations. They would seem to better suited for planning, conceptualizing, and working out details.[98]

Creativity Many organizations feel that creativity and innovativeness are not only desirable but also should be core competencies and a consistent feature of their cultures.[99] Creativity is the generation of novel ideas that may be converted into commercial opportunities. It is the first step in the innovation process. Firms such as Google, Intuit, Novartis, E Ink, and IDEO demonstrate this very clearly by their support of creative activities by their employees.[100] But it is also the case that creativity may be viewed in many ways.[101] First, you may consider the creative person as mad. The madness of creative artists such as Van Gogh and Nijinsky is often cited as proof of this view. But research evidence offers no support for it. Instead, creative people have been found to have superior ego strength and handle problems constructively. Second, you can see the creative person as being disconnected from the art of creativity. Creativity in this view is a mystical act. Third, you can conclude that to be creative, a person must be intelligent. However, research shows that some intelligent people are creative while others aren't.[102] Finally, you can view creativity as a possibility open to every person, as an expression of personality that can be developed.[103] This view and an increasing amount of research indicate that creativity can be taught. That is, individuals can learn to be creative.[104]

Many studies have examined creativity. Life histories, personality characteristics, and tests are often scrutinized to determine a person's degree of creativity. In a typical test, subjects might be asked to examine a group of drawings and then answer what the drawings represent. Figure 4.10 is a line drawing test used to determine young children's creativity.[105] Novel and unusual answers are rated as being creative.

Organizations can help develop creativity by[106]

1. *Buffering*. Managers can look for ways to absorb the risks of creative decisions.
2. *Organizational time-outs*. Give people time off to work on a problem and allow them to think things through.

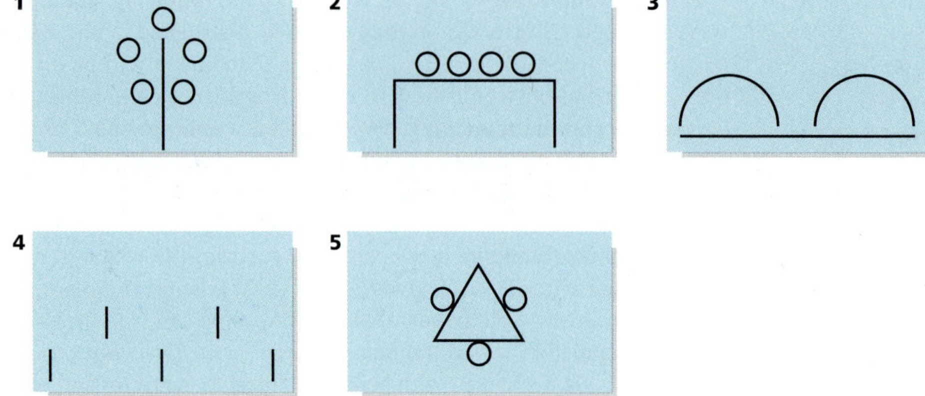

FIGURE 4.10
Testing Creativity

Source: Adapted from T. Proctor, *Creative Problem Solving for Managers* (London: Routledge, 1999).

3. *Intuition.* Give half-baked or unsophisticated ideas a chance.
4. *Innovative attitudes.* Encourage everyone to think of ways to solve problems.
5. *Innovative organizational structures.* Let employees see and interact with many managers and mentors.

Managerial interest in developing creativity seems worthwhile. A review of research findings indicates that creative individuals share important characteristics. They are self-confident and motivated to succeed, they approach life enthusiastically, and they push on even when they must overcome obstacles.[107] The idea that an inexperienced person can look at a problem and immediately be creative is a myth. Mozart was a child genius because he could do what other children couldn't do. But he spent 10 years writing only average music before writing great music.[108]

Emotional Intelligence

The psychologist Daniel Goleman introduced into the discussion of mental abilities the concept of emotional intelligence (EQ). A person's EQ refers to the ability to accurately perceive, evaluate, express, and regulate emotions and feelings.[109] Emotions are difficult to measure.[110] However, Goleman and others suggest that these are five components of EQ: *self-regulation,* the ability calm down anxiety, control impulsiveness, and react appropriately to anger; *motivation,* a passion to work for reasons that go beyond money or status; *empathy,* the ability to respond to the unspoken feelings of others; *self-awareness,* an awareness of one's own personality or individuality; and *social skill,* a proficiency to manage relationships and build networks.

Emotions are the result of a reaction to an object. Individuals display their emotions when they are happy about a promotion, sad about the loss of a contract for work, or angry about unfair treatment received from a manager. There are numerous emotions, but one way to classify them is to discuss positive and negative emotions. Researchers have classified six universal emotions: anger, fear, sadness, happiness, surprise, and disgust.[111]

When employees work or carry out job responsibilities, they often have to express organizationally required emotions. The flight attendant greeting passengers is working when he offers a "Hello, glad to have you aboard" greeting. He is expending emotional labor. Being attentive, happy, welcoming, and courteous are expected. On the other hand, a neurosurgeon is expected to be emotionally neutral or to not provide a scripted response. This, for many physicians, is another form of emotional labor or holding back on showing any positive or negative emotions, which could pose a dilemma: The physician is expected to not be emotional, but she is actually very upset about the patient's prognosis. The felt versus displayed emotions difference creates a strain on the person.

OB AT WORK

Emotional Contagion: A Lesson for the Emotionally Intelligent

Research has discovered that "feelings" can spread from one person to another. For example, an employee's facial expression, posture, eye and head movement, and nervous leg movements are a form of transmission of emotional cues. There is now research that reports that mood can be transmitted from one person to another through voice inflection or emphasis on a particular word or phrase.

Barsade examined the effect of emotional contagion within a group setting.

MOOD CONTAGION WITHIN GROUPS

In her experiment, a trained actor was placed within the group and directed to participate in the group's activities while enacting varying levels of pleasantness and energy. The group was working to assign a pay bonus; they had a fixed amount of money they could spend and had to allocate it based on a set of performance criteria. After the activities were completed, participants were asked to complete self-assessments of their mood. Results of the study clearly suggested that one group member's emotions had an unconscious effect on the mood of the other group members. This held true both for "positive" and "negative" moods.

There are different analyses of the effect of positional power and authority on mood contagion. It may be that those with authority and those who are either liked or respected have a greater effect. What is clear is that leaders affect the group mood:

> In a study of the influence of the contagion of mood of a group leader on group members, the positive mood of the leader positively influenced group members at both the individual and collective level with the opposite for leader negative mood. The leader's positive mood also had a subsequent influence on group coordination and effort.

In proving that mood is contagious, one important consideration is the effect of mood on performance. Some believe the idea that "positive" moods have a positive effect on performance, but in reality sometimes a "negative" mood is appropriate.

In the Barsade study, a negative group member seemed to disrupt the group and reduce efficacy, while having a positive confederate was associated with increased cooperation, fewer group conflicts, and heightened task performance. Likewise, in a similar study, Isen assessed radiologists, finding positive mood enhanced their accuracy. Positive mood has a far-reaching effect on work performance, supervision, decision making, and even on team members voluntarily acting for the good of the organization.

Emotional contagion seems to play a role in the adaptive behavior of individuals to function in groups. This system can enable a rapid communication of opportunity and risk, mediate a group interaction, and help individuals attend to social rules and norms such as maintaining harmonious interaction with a powerful ally.

The evidence that an individual's feelings affect others—and that these feelings in turn affect performance—illustrates the importance of being aware of and managing emotions, especially for leaders. That is, having emotional intelligence can be helpful for leaders to monitor the ability of individuals to function effectively in a group.

Sources: Adapted from Robert I. Sutton, "Are You Being a Jerk? Again?" *Businessweek*, August 14, 2008, p. 52; Sigal G. Barsade and Donald E. Gibson, "Why Does Affect Matter in Organizations?" *Academy of Management Perspectives* February 2007, pp. 36–59; Melissa Bayne and Joshua Freedman, "Emotional Contagion," *Six Seconds*, accessed at www.6seconds.org on April 18, 2007; and A. Isan, "Positive Affect and Decision Making," in M. Lewis and J. Haviland (eds.), *The Handbook of Emotion* (New York: Guilford Press, 1993).

Individuals who have difficulty smiling and appearing happy are likely to have career problems working in service organizations such as Disney, Nordstrom, Hyatt Regency, or TGIFs in the United States. However, smiling and cheeriness don't always work the same way in other countries. For example, in Muslim cultures, a smile is interpreted as a sign of sexual attraction, so women learn not to smile at men.[112]

There are still many unanswered questions and criticisms about EQ research, such as how it affects performance, in what situations it is most important, how it can be measured reliably and validly, and whether training can improve a person's EQ.[113] Despite gaps in research results companies are paying attention to emotional intelligence. L'Oréal places more emphasis on hiring sales agents with emotional intelligence than on traditional technical sales attributes. The company found that sales agents with higher emotional intelligence scores sold approximately $91,000 more than colleagues with lower EQ scores.[114]

The OB at Work feature on emotional contagion suggests that a person with high EQ can use the concept of managing feelings and mood into work situations.

The Psychological Contract

psychological contract
An implied understanding of mutual contributions between a person and his or her organization.

When an individual accepts a job with an organization, an implied psychological contract is established. Because of differences in perception, attribution, attitudes, values, general personality, and emotions, individuals form a personal view of the expectations inherent in the psychological contract. The **psychological contract** is not a written document between a person and the organization; it is an implied understanding of mutual contributions.[115]

The individual has a perception of the reciprocal obligations he or she has with the organization. For example, employees may assume that if they work hard and display loyalty, the organization will provide good working conditions and job security. The psychological contact is a belief that promises have been made by the individual and the organization.

Rousseau has proposed that psychological contracts lie along a continuum ranging from transitional to relational. A transitional contract is based on specific obligations and short time frames. The transactional contract uses financial resources as the primary means of exchange. They are focused self-interest. A relational contract is characterized by long-term relationship development.

In organizations today, a variety of trends such as plan relocation, increased reliance on temporary workers, downsizing and layoffs, demographic diversity, and foreign competition are having a significant impact on how individuals and organizations evaluate their psychological contracts and their fulfillment.[116] As environmental forces become more turbulent and the economy changes, it is likely that individual perception and attitudes about the obligation of organizations will continue to be problematic and uncertain.

Psychological Contract Violations

psychological contract violation
The perception of the person that his or her firm has failed to fulfill or has reneged on one or more obligations.

A **psychological contract violation** is defined as the perception of the person that his or her organization has failed to fulfill or has reneged on one or more obligations. As described by Morrison and Robinson,[117] the perception has a cognitive portion and an emotional or feeling portion. A violation by an employer may affect not only the beliefs of the person but also what he or she feels obligated to provide or contribute to the organization. The majority of research on psychological contracts has not focused on violations of the perceived obligations among parties. Table 4.6 lists a number of possible organizational violations and offers quotes from the perspective of the employee. These types of violations of the psychological contract can seriously undermine the feelings of goodwill and trust held by employees toward the organization.

The seven examples of violation in Table 4.6 indicate how trust is undermined, how the bond between an employer and employee can be weakened, and how perception plays a significant role in psychological contracts.[118] Rousseau believes that violation of a relational contract can produce intense feelings that can result in moral outrage. Minor violations are not so intensely felt. However, a major violation could result in withholding good performance, sabotaging work, absenteeism, or quitting. A sequential pattern of responses to violations has been identified.[119] The first response is *voice:* the person voices concern about the violation and attempts to restore the psychological contract. If unsuccessful, voice is followed by *silence*. Silence connotes compliance with what the employer wants or is doing, but with no commitment. Silence is followed by *retreat,* which is shown by negligence, shirking of responsibility, and passivity. *Destruction* can follow silence. In this stage the employee can retaliate through slowdown of work, sabotage, hiding papers or tools, theft, or even violence. Finally, of course the employee can exit or quit the firm.

This discussion has focused on the psychological contract from the employee's side. This is because most of the research and conjecture in the organizational behavior and

TABLE 4.6 Psychological Contract Violations from Perceptions and Emotions of Individual Employees

Violation	Definition	Employee Statement
Job security	No such thing as security, with good chance of layoff or downsizing.	"When I was recruited I heard on at least four occasions that we (the organization) had not laid off one person in 15 years. What a shock when six of my friends were let go."
Child care benefits	Failing to provide adequate care and services for child care during working hours on- or offsite.	"The firm has refused to improve their skimpy child care benefits even though they brag about this every chance they have. I'm not sure they really care about children and working parents."
Job feedback	Poor attention and little effort to provide meaningful job feedback.	"My boss skips through the feedback session and makes me feel like I am infringing on his time and space."
Merit-based pay raises	No relationship between pay and actual performance.	"I see no effort to link what I do and how I do the job to my pay raises (when I receive them, which is rare)."
Job autonomy	Failure to permit the employee to have the freedom to make job-related decisions about how to perform the job.	"I feel like I am constantly watched and checked."
Computer training	Failure to provide adequate training and coaching on the proper use of computers.	"I have been promised again and again the opportunity to undergo specific computer skills training. This is just not going to happen."
Promotion	Reneging on a specific promise to provide a promotion for excellent performance.	"Time after time I am informed about my superior performance and promotion possibilities. This company just reneges and keeps on going like nothing has occurred."

management literature are from the employee's perspective. We need to increase our understanding and research from the employer's perspective. There is also the need to examine individual, group, and organizational effectiveness in situations, settings, and projects where both employees and employers believe and perceive that the expectations of the psychological contract have been met. Are there unique attributes, techniques, or methods that have a high probability of the psychological contract being achieved? Managers need to be aware of the importance of the psychological contract in committing the employer and employees to a trusting and developing relationship over time.[120] As this chapter has illustrated, how each person views the relationship can significantly vary because of individual differences. Thus, there is no easy method or formula to provide managers for improving their ability to effectively manage the multiple psychological contracts of individuals.

- Employees joining an organization must adjust to a new environment, new people, and new tasks. How people adjust to situations and other people depends largely on their psychological makeup and personal backgrounds.
- There's no compelling evidence that men or women perform better. Some women are better salespeople than some men. On the other hand, some men are better caregivers than some women. Searching for similarities and differences is likely to continue, because historically the majority of organizationally based research has been conducted with male samples.

- Individual perceptual processes help people face the realities of the world. People are influenced by other people and by situations, needs, and past experiences. While a manager is perceiving the employees, the employees are also perceiving the manager.
- Attitudes are linked with behavioral patterns in a complex manner. They're organized, and they provide the emotional basis for most of a person's interpersonal relations. Changing attitudes is extremely difficult and requires, at the very least, trust in the communicator and strength of message.
- Job satisfaction is the attitude workers have about their jobs. Research findings suggest that a satisfied worker isn't necessarily a higher performer.
- Personality, developed long before a person joins an organization, is influenced by hereditary, cultural, and social determinants. To assume that personality can be modified easily can result in managerial frustration and ethical problems. Managers should try to cope with personality differences among people and not try to change personalities to fit their model of the ideal person.
- Personality variables, such as locus of control, self-efficacy, Machiavellianism, and creativity, are associated with behavior and performance. Although difficult to measure, these variables appear to be important personality facets in explaining and predicting individual behavior.
- When a person joins and remains a part of an organization, an implied psychological contract is formed between the employee and the employer.
- Violations of the psychological contract can create dramatic breaks in the relationship between employers and employees. Each person decides what is a minor or major violation of the psychological contract.

Discussion and Review Questions

1. Joan is an accountant who opposes the introduction of a new financial control system. For 15 years she has worked with the old manual system. Now the firm is introducing a new computer-based system. How would you attempt to change Joan's attitude about the new system?
2. Some people believe that perception is a more important explanation of behavior than is reality. Why is this assumption about perception made?
3. Consider all of the topics covered in this chapter, which factors differentiate you the most from two or three of your co-workers? Describe.
4. The chapter focuses on the perspective of the employee in discussing the psychological contract. From the employer's perspective, what is generally expected from employees in terms of the contract?
5. Why is emotional intelligence a difficult construct to measure accurately?
6. What is the relationship between employee satisfaction and customer satisfaction?
7. In the selection of job candidates, what should a manager know about the self-efficacy concept?
8. Why is it accurate to conclude that the study and application of OB are multidisciplinary?
9. Is the "Big Five" model of personality worthwhile in terms of helping explain individual differences?
10. What's the meaning of the notion that, even when differences between the sexes exist, there's overlap between them? Explain this in terms of absenteeism rates and turnover rates.

Taking It to the Net

Evaluating Online Self-Tests

There are many self-test sites for providing immediate feedback at no expense to anyone taking time to take the test. These quick, concise, and informative self-reports are not intended to replace psychometrically derived and rigorous intelligence, personality, or job related tests.

Queendom (www.queendom.com) is an excellent starting place to learn about self-tests to assess individual characteristics. Starting at Queendom, find two other similar sites that provide free self-tests with immediate feedback. Evaluate the quality of the three self-test sites.

1. Which site is the most complete?
2. Which site is the highest quality in presentation and interest?
3. How can the site be improved?

Case for Analysis: *A Potter's Wheel*

Bill Strickland's life changed and began anew on a Wednesday afternoon in Pittsburgh in 1963. Strickland, then a 16-year-old African American, was bored with high school and felt hemmed in by life in this decaying neighborhood. Looking through a classroom door, Strickland saw something he had never seen before: a rotating mound of clay being shaped into a vessel by a man absorbed in his work. He stated, "I saw a radiant and hopeful image of how the world ought to be. It opened up a portal that suggested that there might be a whole range of possibilities and experiences that I had not explored."

Strickland walked into the classroom introduced himself to ceramics teacher Frank Ross, the man at the potter's wheel, and said, "I'd like to learn whatever that is." Ross became his mentor, and Strickland took an entirely new path in life that led to earning a college degree.

Today Strickland applies his potter's hands and is involved in social change. People work with him and come to his programs at the Manchester Craftsmen Guild (MCG) and at the Bidwell Training Center Inc. For nearly three decades, Strickland has worked at his craft back in the same Pittsburgh neighborhood he grew up in—creating a model for turning people with dead-end lives into productive workers. The source of Strickland's unique gift is, according to him, that Wednesday afternoon in 1963. "You start with the perception that the world is an unlimited opportunity. Then the question becomes, how are we going to rebuild the planet?"

Strickland has brought all of his talents, aspirations, and thinking as an artist and applied them to make a change in the neighborhood where he lives. The use of art to change students' attitudes is at the heart of Strickland's vision of education. The goal is not to produce artists or potters. It's to find an individually tailored approach to learning that will redirect young people who are searching for goals and get them interested in education.

Strickland's story and life provide an example of how each person is unique. His background environment certainly had an impact on his individual characteristics. Strickland speaks with a moral authority that should ring true with struggling college students.

DISCUSSION QUESTIONS

1. What environmental factors could Bill Strickland have changed in his life?
2. What moral authority does Bill Strickland speak from to struggling college students?
3. What impact did Strickland's mentor (Frank Ross) have on his goals, self-efficacy, and values?

Sources: Sara Terry, "Genius at Work," *Fast Company*, September 1998, pp. 171–83; and Michael Warsaw, "Have You Got the Right Stuff?" *Fast Company*, October 1998, pp. 219–25.

Experiential Exercise: *Applying Attribution Theory*

OBJECTIVES

1. To examine the cause of a person's behavior.
2. To develop an approach that's best suited to improve unacceptable behavior.

RELATED TOPICS

The concept of perception plays a role in how each of us views other people. Making attributions in terms of dispositional or situational factors is based on how a person views the event, the behaviors of another person, and previous experience.

STARTING THE EXERCISE

Carefully read the following situation facing a manager. If you were this manager, what would you conclude about causes and how would you proceed? Why?

THE LOSS OF EQUALITY

Don Dubose has worked for Maybrooke Manufacturing since its beginning in 1964. He has won four top performer awards during his tenure in the firm. The last award he won was presented to him with a $5,000 bonus check about three years ago. But in the past 18 months, Don's relations with co-workers have become strained. He has never been talkative, but on occasion he has ordered co-workers out of his work area. Don has made it clear that tools have been missing, and he wants to protect his area. His work's quality has also suffered. Until about a year ago, Don's work producing generators was at the "zero-defect" level. Error-free, top-quality generators came from Don again and again. Today when random sample checks are made, Don occasionally produces generators that must be reworked less than 3 percent of the time. He has gone from zero defects to 3 out of 100 defects. His co-workers average about 1.5 defects out of 100 for reworking.

What could be causing Don's behavior changes? They could be caused by:

	1	2	3	4	5	6	7
	Not very likely						Very likely
1. Low motivation	1	2	3	4	5	6	7
2. Low self-efficacy	1	2	3	4	5	6	7
3. Physical health problems	1	2	3	4	5	6	7
4. Family problems	1	2	3	4	5	6	7
5. Poor management	1	2	3	4	5	6	7
6. Lack of creativity	1	2	3	4	5	6	7

Comment on each of your ratings:

1. ______________________
2. ______________________
3. ______________________
4. ______________________
5. ______________________
6. ______________________

Don's behavior has become a topic of concern within the organization. An outstanding worker has become average. What actions would you take as the manager?

	Yes	No	Why?
Transfer Don to a new job.	___	___	___
Fire Don.	___	___	___
Call Don in to discuss your observation.	___	___	___
Suspend Don after informing him about your concerns.	___	___	___
Ask Don's co-workers why they believe his performance isn't up to previous norms.	___	___	___
Leave the situation alone for another six months.	___	___	___
Contact Don's wife to see if there's a personal reason for the performance problem.	___	___	___
Examine your own behavior (as manager) in working with Don.	___	___	___
Send Don to a human resource management counselor to discuss his attitudes about his job.	___	___	___
Promote Don since he has been in the present job over six years.	___	___	___

Other courses of action: ______________________

____

____

____

IN CLASS

After you've analyzed this situation, meet with classmates to discuss their reactions. What did you learn about your attributions process? Are your reactions different from your classmates'?

CHAPTER FIVE

Motivation: Background and Theories

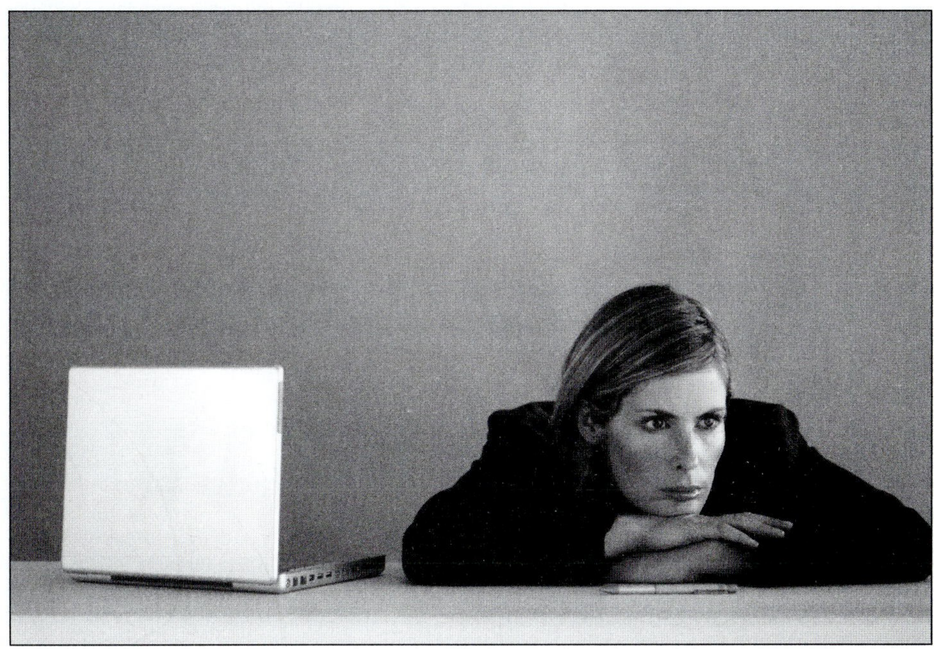

Learning Objectives

After completing Chapter 5, you should be able to

Define
Motivation in practical terms that would be meaningful to managers in organizations.

Differentiate
Between the content and process theories of motivation.

Describe
How equity theory can explain employees' reactions to pay and compensation decisions.

Discuss
Why an individual's needs and preferences will change over the course of his or her work career.

Explain
The motivational force for a behavior, action, or task as a function of three distinct perceptions made by an individual.

Motivating Generations of Employees

Managers have to be excellent at addressing the needs and goals of individual employees. There is no one motivational approach that works for everyone. As motivation theories suggest, individuals differ in their desired rewards, how they attempt to satisfy their needs, and how they view the fairness of what managers attempt to do for them and the work environment.

Four specific generations exist in the workplace. Each generation has its own style, preference, and core values. A starting point in designing motivational systems is to be aware of key generational similarities and differences. For example, *Veterans (or World War II generation),* born between 1922 and 1945, believe in hard work, dedication, sacrifice, and respect for authority. With the youngest of this generation being in their mid-60s, these individuals contain a great deal of organizational knowledge and remain very influential. *Baby boomers,* or those born between 1946 and 1964, are characterized by their optimism, work ethic, teamwork, healthy lifestyles, and personal gratification. These individuals are often willing to "go the extra mile" at work to get the job done and enjoy their work and careers. *Gen Xers,* who were born between 1965 and 1976, understand the importance of diversity, work/life balance, self-reliance, fun, and informality. More cynical than any other generation, their "it's only a job" attitude places them in direct conflict with the boomers. The next big influx of workers is coming from *Gen Y* (a.k.a., Millennials,), who were born between 1977 and 1997. Surveys, focus groups, and research suggest that these are some of the workplace preferences of Gen Y members:

- A fair boss.
- Team-oriented.
- Belief in the company.
- Safety in the workplace.
- Work that is meaningful.
- Training and learning opportunities.
- Flexibility in work schedule.
- Constructive and frequent feedback.
- Timely and fair reward systems.

Ready or not, managers will have to face these millions of new employees in their twenties and early thirties. Knowing the nuances of generational differences before addressing the challenging issue of individual differences is a recommended step in creating a high-motivation work environment. Veterans, baby boomers, Gen Xers, and Gen Yers working side by side make the motivation job complicated. There likely are more similarities than differences across generations. However, paying attention to the specific needs of employees and how these employees sustain high performance is a part of the responsibilities of managers and leaders. It is now a seller's market for talent. Making employees comfortable, satisfied, and compatible with an organization so that talent is retained is an indicator of managerial competence.

Sources: Bruce Tulgan, "Managing in the 'New' Workplace," *Financial Executive*, December 1, 2009, pp. 50–53; James Chen, "Playing the Generation Game in Asia," *The British Journal of Administrative Management* (April/May 2007) 28–29; Lynne C. Lancaster and David Stillman, *When Generations Collide: Who They Are. Why They Clash. How to Solve the Generational Puzzle at Work* (New York: HarperBusiness, 2003); Ron Zemke, "Here Come the Millennials," *Training*, July 2001; Ned Howe, *Millennials Rising: The Next Great Generation* (New York: Vintage Press, 2000); Claire Raines, *Generations at Work: Managing the Clash of Veterans, Boomers, Xers, and Nexters* (New York: AMACOM, 2000); and Bruce Tulgan, *Winning the Talent Wars* (New York: W. W. Norton, 2000).

Why some employees perform better than others is a continual and perplexing problem facing managers. To explain such differences, several interesting and important variables have been used—for example, cognitive ability, emotional intelligence, personality, and aspiration levels, as well as demographic factors such as age, education, and family background. However, one issue that consistently captures the attention of managers and researchers alike is the motivation of people to perform their work. In fact, much of management's time is spent addressing the motivation of their employees.[1] The opening vignette emphasizes that this time investment is necessary because of the many differences that exist across individual employees and generations. By understanding what motivates employees, managers are in a better position to encourage and reward employees and groups to behave in effective ways.

Despite its obvious importance, motivation is difficult to define and to analyze. By one definition, motivation has to do with (1) the direction of behavior, (2) the strength of the response (i.e., effort) once an employee chooses to follow a course of action, and (3) the persistence of the behavior, or how long the person continues to behave in a particular manner.[2] Another view suggests that the analysis of motivation should concentrate on the factors that incite and direct a person's activities.[3] One theorist emphasizes the goal-directedness aspect of motivation.[4] Another states that motivation is "concerned with how behavior gets started, is energized, is sustained, is directed, and is stopped, and what kind of subjective reaction is present in the organism while all this is going on."[5]

A careful examination of each of these views leads to several conclusions about motivation:

1. Theorists present slightly different interpretations and place emphasis on different factors.
2. Motivation is related to behavior and performance.
3. Goal-directedness is involved.
4. It results from events and processes that are internal or external to the individual.
5. Research on motivation is still evolving, and many aspects of human motivation are still unexplained.

Motivating employees was an important topic as far back as 1789. Samuel Slater, a pioneer who introduced textile manufacturing to America, was concerned about creating a work setting where it was comfortable for workers to do their jobs. Other efforts to create a positive motivational work climate ranged from George M. Pullman's company town to Henry Ford's profit-sharing plan. The Edison Electric Illuminating Company of Boston provided tennis courts and bowling alleys. Other firms planted gardens for workers or constructed libraries and athletic facilities.

One reason for corporate generosity was fear of the trade union movement, but there were other motivators. Another reason was greed—the desire to get employees to work harder for less money. Another was humanitarianism, the willingness to treat employees well. And some corporate leaders believed it was simply good business to satisfy workers' needs for good working conditions, a fair day's pay, and social interaction.

Two of the most radical experiments in creating a positive work environment occurred in the late 1800s. Disturbed by reports of worker resentment and sabotage, John H. Patterson, founder of the National Cash Register (NCR) Company in 1884,[6] investigated working conditions himself and found that there was little to motivate employees to achieve or even strive toward doing an adequate job. In response he increased wages, cleaned up the shop floor, improved safety, made company showers and dressing rooms available, and opened a company cafeteria that served hot lunches at reduced rates. NCR provided free medical care at its dispensary, gave additional food to those felt to be underweight, and redesigned the factory buildings to allow in natural light. Patterson also instituted industry's first paid "suggestion" system and provided opportunities for employees to take classes at a company-sponsored night school. These innovations helped to cut turnover and increase productivity and were a significant factor behind NCR's dominance in the cash register business for many years.[7]

Similarly, at the Pullman Company, George Pullman built a company town with houses to rent, stores, schools, a church, and a company plant.[8] He wanted to provide his employees with a feeling of community, a place of employment, and opportunities to practice religion and educate their children. However, when the national economy slid into a depression, events in Pullman, Illinois, turned sour. Pullman cut his workers' wages without lowering rents or prices in the town. What started as an experiment to help workers satisfy various needs eventually spurred workers into attempting to organize a union. Pullman's workers went on strike on May 12, 1894, riots occurred, and federal troops were called in to restore order.[9]

Both of these situations reflect efforts by management to influence the motivation of the workforce, with varying levels of success. Since that time, researchers have learned much about motivation, and managers need to consider these insights when attempting to create positive motivational atmospheres for their employees.

No matter what their nationality or cultural background, people are driven to fulfill needs and to achieve goals. But what are those needs, what goals are desired, and what can motivate people in different countries? This is the complex and difficult-to-answer question. For example, motivational structures among Americans and Japanese need to take into consideration cultural differences that affect attitudes about money, work, incentives, teamwork, and performance reviews.[10] The Japanese tend to confer recognition for excellent performance with plaques, applause, and attention. Japanese employees are likely to be insulted by material incentives because this form of reward suggests they could work even harder. In Japanese firms, bonuses are given because of seniority, gender, and marital status.

In examining each of the motivation theories, remember that cultural differences could be significant and need to be considered. Motivation is a universal concept that must be aligned with the context and cultural background. What proves to be an extremely powerful motivator in one setting or country may be a miserable failure in another setting or nation.

Motivation is the concept we use when we describe the forces acting on or within an individual to initiate and direct behavior. We use the concept to explain differences in the intensity of behavior (regarding more intense behaviors as the result of higher levels of motivation) and also to indicate the direction of behavior (e.g., when you're tired or sleepy, you direct your behavior toward getting some sleep).

What Is Motivation?

motivation
Forces acting on an employee that initiate and direct behavior.

Motivation is an explanatory concept that we use to make sense out of the behaviors we observe. In other words, motivation is inferred. Instead of measuring it directly, we note what conditions exist and observe behavior, using this information as a basis for our understanding of the underlying motivation. For example, you might assume that your friend works overtime because she needs the additional pay. But your inference isn't correct; your friend is actually doing the additional work to help out her boss and because she is fascinated by the specific project in which she is involved. The lesson is clear: we must always be cautious in making motivational inferences. As more and more information is accumulated, however, our inferences should become more accurate because we can eliminate alternative explanations.

One reason our understanding of motivation is important is that high levels of motivation are significant contributors to exceptional performance. Managers prefer highly motivated employees because they strive to find the best way to perform their jobs. They want to come to work and be part of a team; they're interested in helping, supporting, and encouraging coworkers. Self-confident and decisive employees display these and other desirable actions. However, finding a universal set of principles to motivate employees and managers isn't likely to occur, as there is no one approach that works best.

Harvard Business School publishes and circulates thousands of business cases worldwide. The most requested and purchased case is about Lincoln Electric Company of Cleveland. Founded in 1895, the firm produces industrial electric motors and welding products, and it has 39 factories and joint ventures in 19 countries.[11] The Lincoln Electric case is so popular because it illustrates how the company motivates workers. All of Lincoln's 2,000 employees participate in the firm's pay incentive plan. This plan has been a success for decades because it clearly links pay and pay increases to performance.[12]

Lincoln employees receive piece-rate (each piece or product produced results in payment) wages with no guaranteed minimum hourly wage. After two years of employment workers can participate in the year-end bonus plan (one-time lump-sum payment tied to performance). Determined by a formula that considers the firm's gross profits, the employees' base piece rate, and merit rating, Lincoln calculates a bonus system. The average bonus over five decades has been approximately 95 percent of the average wage.

Every six months, the chief executive officer personally reviews each employee's merit ratings. Everyone is rated on output, quality, dependability, and cooperation. Lincoln pays attention to performance, linking pay to performance and the quality of its products. The company has never faced a strike. It has no debt. It believes that success is based on individual accountability and the power of creating a positive motivational atmosphere. As each of the motivation theories in the next two chapters are presented, refer back to the simplicity and popularity of Lincoln Electric's approach to motivation.[13]

The Starting Point: The Individual

Managers are expected to understand the existing types and degrees of motivation in their employees and must also try to enhance the extent of motivation demonstrated in a diverse and in many respects unpredictable group of people. This diversity results in different behavioral patterns that in some manner are related to needs and goals.

need
Deficiency that an individual experiences at a particular point in time.

A **need** is a deficiency or lack of something of value that an individual experiences at a particular point in time. Deficiencies may be physiological (e.g., a need for food), psychological (e.g., a need for self-esteem), or sociological (e.g., a need for social interaction). Needs are energizers or triggers of behavioral responses. The implication is that when needs (deficiencies) are present, the individual will seek to fulfill those needs and may be more susceptible to managers' motivational efforts.

In any discussion of motivation, the importance of goals is apparent. The motivational process, as interpreted by most theorists, is goal directed. The goals, or outcomes, an employee seeks are viewed as forces that attract the person. Accomplishing desired goals can result in a significant reduction in need deficiencies.

As Figure 5.1 shows, people have need deficiencies, which trigger a search process for ways to reduce the tension they cause. A course of action is selected, and goal-directed

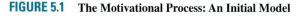

FIGURE 5.1 **The Motivational Process: An Initial Model**

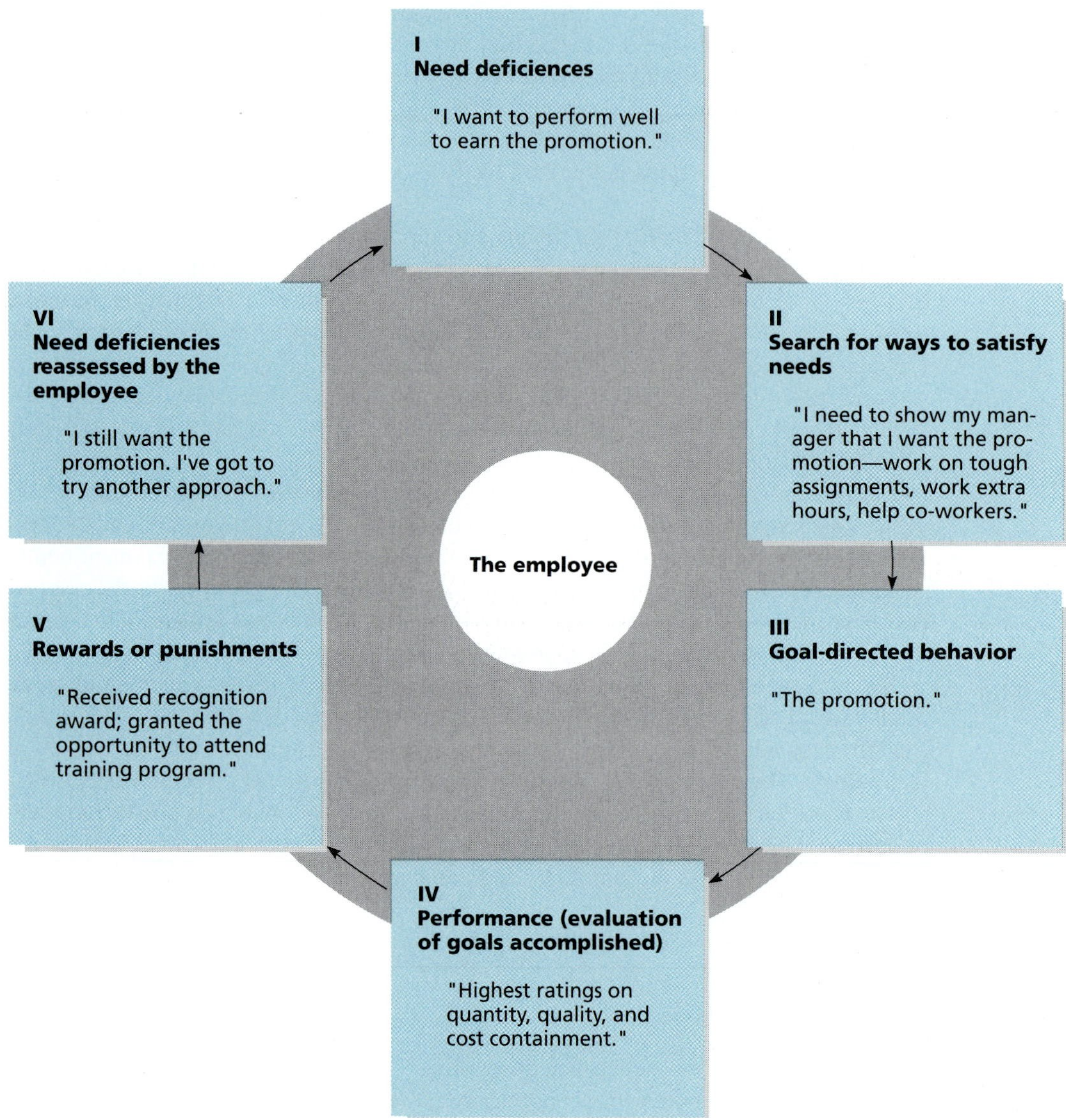

behavior occurs. After a period of time, managers assess that behavior. Performance evaluation will result in rewards or punishments. Such outcomes are weighed by the person, and need deficiencies are reassessed. This in turn triggers the process, and the circular pattern begins again.

Motivational Theories: A Classification System

Each person is attracted to some set of goals. To predict behavior with any accuracy, a manager must know something about an employee's goals and about the actions that the employee has to take to achieve them. Numerous motivation theories and research findings attempt to explain this behavior–outcome relationship.

TABLE 5.1 Managerial Perspective of Content and Process Theories of Motivation

Theoretical Base	Theoretical Explanation	Founders of the Theories	Managerial Application
Content	Focuses on factors within the person that energize, direct, sustain, and stop behavior. These factors can only be inferred.	**Maslow**—five-level need hierarchy. **Alderfer**—three-level hierarchy (ERG). **Herzberg**—two major factors called hygiene-motivators. **McClelland**—three learned needs acquired from the culture: achievement, affiliation, and power.	Managers need to be aware of differences in needs, desires, and goals because each individual is unique in many ways.
Process	Describes, explains, and analyzes how behavior is energized, directed, sustained, and stopped.	**Vroom**—an expectancy theory of choices. **Adams**—equity theory based on comparisons that individuals make. **Skinner**—reinforcement theory concerned with the learning that occurs as a consequence of behavior. **Locke**—goal-setting theory that conscious goals and intentions are the determinants of behavior.	Managers need to understand the *process* of motivation and how individuals make choices based on preferences, rewards, and accomplishments.

content motivation theories
Theories that focus on factors within a person that energize, direct, sustain, and stop behavior.

process motivation theories
Theories that describe and analyze how behavior is energized, directed, sustained, and stopped by external factors.

Theories of motivation fall into two categories: content theories and process theories. **Content theories** focus on the factors *within* the person that energize, direct, sustain, and stop behavior. They attempt to determine the specific needs that motivate people. **Process theories** describe and analyze how behavior is energized, directed, sustained, and stopped by factors primarily *external* to the person. Both categories have important implications for managers, who by the nature of their jobs are involved with the motivational process. Table 5.1 summarizes the basic characteristics of content and process theories of motivation from a managerial perspective.

This chapter covers some of the most publicized content theories (need hierarchy, ERG, two-factor, and learned needs) and introduces two process theories (expectancy and equity) of motivation, while the next chapter discusses several organizational applications of motivation theories. The content theories focus on individual needs in explaining job satisfaction, worker behavior, and reward systems. The theories suggest that within a person, individual need deficiencies activate tensions that trigger a behavioral response.

For managers to be effective, the content theories suggest that they must

1. Determine what needs trigger desired performance, group, and personal behaviors.
2. Be able to offer meaningful rewards that help the employee satisfy needs.

3. Know when to offer appropriate rewards to optimize performance behavior.
4. Not assume that a person's need deficiencies will repeat themselves in a regular pattern. People change because of experiences, life events, aging, cultural and environmental changes, and other factors.

Maslow's need hierarchy, Alderfer's ERG theory, Herzberg's two-factor theory, and McClelland's learned needs theory are four important content theories of motivation.

Maslow's Need Hierarchy

need hierarchy model
Maslow's theory assumes that people's needs depend on what they already have. In a sense, then, a satisfied need is not a motivator. Human needs, organized in a hierarchy of importance, are physiological safety, belongingness, esteem, and self-actualization.

One of the most widely cited and discussed motivation theories is the **need hierarchy model** proposed by Abraham Maslow.[14] The lowest-level needs are the physiological needs, and the highest-level needs are for self-actualization. Maslow defined human needs as

1. *Physiological:* the need for food, drink, shelter, and relief from pain.
2. *Safety and security:* the need for freedom from threat; that is, the security from threatening events or surroundings.
3. *Belongingness, social, and love:* the need for friendship, affiliation, interaction, and love.
4. *Esteem:* the need for self-esteem and for respect from others.
5. *Self-actualization:* the need to fulfill oneself by maximizing the use of abilities, skills, and potential.

Maslow's theory assumes that a person attempts to satisfy the more basic needs (physiological) before directing behavior toward satisfying upper-level needs (self-actualization). Lower-order needs must be satisfied before a higher-order need such as self-actualization begins to control a person's behavior. According to Maslow, a satisfied need ceases to motivate. When a person decides that she's earning enough pay for contributing to the organization, money loses its power to motivate.

One way in which this theory may be of use to managers is in suggesting strategies that the organization can implement to correct need deficiencies. These deficiencies can occur at all levels but are likely to be largest in the areas of self-actualization and esteem—needs that are often ignored in the reward structures of many organizations. Attempts to address these deficiencies may actually have a greater impact in initiating and directing behavior than focusing on lower-level needs that may be closer to fulfillment.

In addition to dealing with individual differences in needs, managers face the issue that needs, work style, and work ethics may differ across cultures. Americans are sometimes perceived by foreigners as lazy and not motivated. The problem often boils down not to laziness but to conflict between culturally different patterns of job behavior, management styles, and work's role in employees' lives.[15] For example, Americans are more "job" oriented than "company" oriented. It is common to see Americans move from organization to organization as they "build their resumes" and develop their career-related skills and experiences. Also, many Americans try to maintain a balance between work and home responsibilities and interests. In China, Japan, India, and some other cultures, work takes on a more central role as individuals attempt to achieve higher levels of economic success and a more comfortable standard of living.

Selected Need Hierarchy Research

A number of research studies have tested the need hierarchy theory. The first reported field research that tested a modified version of Maslow's need hierarchy was by Lyman W. Porter.[16]

Initially, he assumed that physiological needs were being adequately satisfied for managers, so he substituted a higher-order need called *autonomy,* defined as the person's satisfaction with opportunities to make independent decisions, set goals, and work without close supervision.

Since the early Porter studies, other studies have reported that

1. Managers high in the organization chain of command place greater emphasis on self-actualization and autonomy.[17]
2. Managers at lower organizational levels in small firms with less than 500 employees are more satisfied than their counterparts in large firms with more than 5,000 employees. But managers at upper levels in large companies are more satisfied than their counterparts in small companies.[18]
3. American managers overseas are more satisfied with autonomy opportunities than are their counterparts working in the United States.[19]

In general, Maslow's theory hasn't been supported by field research.[20] Maslow himself stated that self-actualization theory in and of itself isn't enough, as the assumptions must be amplified into a more thorough formulation, taking into account such factors as the good of other people and the organization as a whole.[21] Therefore, we don't recommend using the theory to predict behavior. The hierarchy does explain aspects of human behavior in our society. But it's not accurate or thorough enough to explain individual-level behavior.

Alderfer's ERG Theory

Alderfer agrees with Maslow that individuals' needs are arranged in a hierarchy. However, his proposed needs hierarchy involves only three sets of needs:[22]

1. *Existence:* needs satisfied by such factors as food, air, water, pay, and working conditions.
2. *Relatedness:* needs satisfied by meaningful social and interpersonal relationships.
3. *Growth:* needs satisfied by an individual making creative or productive contributions.

Alderfer's three needs—existence (E), relatedness (R), and growth (G), or ERG—correspond to Maslow's in that the existence needs are similar to Maslow's physiological and safety categories; the relatedness needs are similar to the belongingness, social, and love category; and the growth needs are similar to the esteem and self-actualization categories.

ERG theory of motivation
Theory developed and tested by Alderfer that categorizes needs as existence, relatedness, and growth.

In addition to a difference in the number of categories, Alderfer's **ERG theory of motivation** and Maslow's need hierarchy differ on how people move through the different sets of needs. Maslow proposed that unfulfilled needs at one level are of most importance and that the needs on the next higher level aren't activated or triggered until the currently important needs are adequately satisfied. Thus, a person only progresses up the need hierarchy once his lower-level needs have been effectively met. In contrast, Alderfer's ERG theory suggests that in addition to the satisfaction–progression process that Maslow proposed, a frustration–regression process is also at work. That is, if a person is continually frustrated in attempts to satisfy growth needs, relatedness needs reemerge as a major motivating force, causing the individual to redirect efforts toward exploring new ways to satisfy this lower-order need category. Figure 5.2 presents Alderfer's ERG theory.

Consider the case of Mary Higgins, a registered nurse in the pediatric unit in Methodist Hospital in Tampa, Florida. A single parent, Mary is concerned with job security, pay, and co-worker interaction and friendship. She must work to support her family, and she also

FIGURE 5.2 ERG Theory Relationships among Frustration, Importance, and Satisfaction of Needs

Source: F. J. Landy and D. A. Trumbo, *Psychology of Work Behavior*, rev. ed. (Homewood, IL: Dorsey Press, 1980); and, I. Borg and M. Braun, "Work Values in East and West Germany: Different Weights, But Identical Structures," *Journal of Organizational Behaviour*, 17, 1996. pp. 541–55.

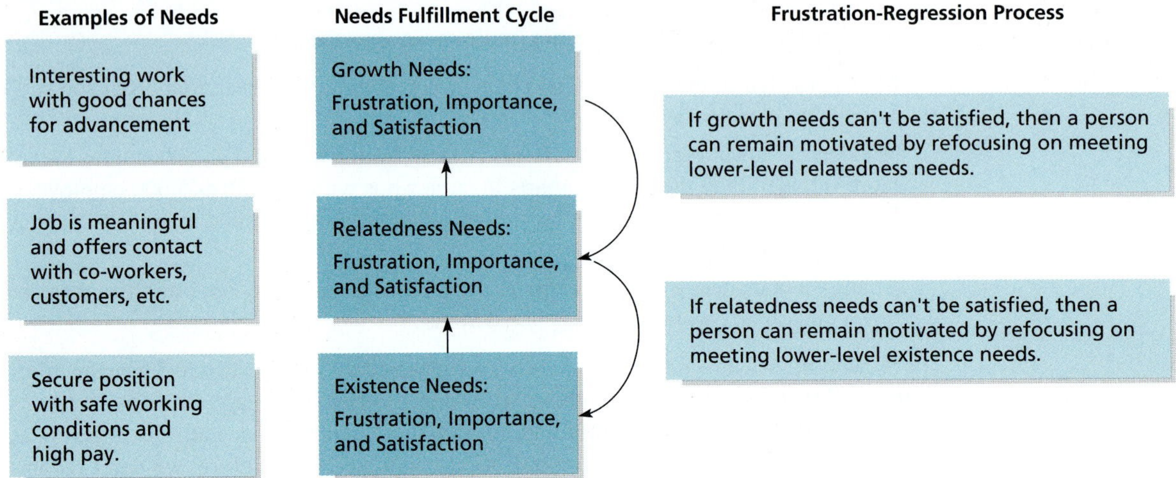

enjoys the social aspect of work. Her performance is outstanding, and she has satisfied her existence and relatedness needs. A head nurse position becomes available in intensive care, a position that would help meet Mary's needs for growth and personal development. But two other candidates have more experience plus outstanding performance records in intensive care. Mary is dropped from further consideration for this job and becomes frustrated, disappointed, and concerned about her future.

Maria Herrera, her supervisor, explains to Mary why she's not being considered, assuring her that other opportunities will occur and that her value to other pediatric nurses is immeasurable. In fact, Maria and three co-workers take Mary to dinner to talk with her. This seems to help Mary refocus her attention on the positive aspects of work, and after a few days of feeling frustrated, she again seems to enjoy her work and her colleagues. Mary has redirected her need for the promotion and the growth it would provide back to the relatedness category.

The ERG theory implies that individuals are motivated to engage in behavior to satisfy one of the three sets of needs. Alderfer's explanation of motivation provides an interesting suggestion to managers about behavior. If a subordinate's higher-order needs (e.g., growth) are being blocked, perhaps because of a company policy or lack of resources, then it's in the manager's best interest to attempt to redirect the subordinate's efforts toward relatedness or existence needs.

ERG: Limited Research Base

The ERG theory hasn't stimulated many research studies. Thus, empirical verification is difficult to claim for the ERG explanation. Salancik and Pfeffer proposed that need models such as Maslow's and Alderfer's have become popular because they're consistent with other theories of rational choice and because they attribute freedom to individuals. The idea that individuals shape their actions to satisfy unfulfilled needs gives purpose and direction to individual activity. Furthermore, need explanations are also popular, despite little research verification, because they're simple, easily expressed views of human behavior.[23] Must need theories be verifiable to be of value to a manager?[24] Or are managers and practitioners less impressed by research-verified explanations than by simple, commonsense explanations?

Alderfer certainly didn't accept Salancik and Pfeffer's critique of need explanations of motivation.[25] He proposed that available research evidence supported at least the conceptualization of the ERG theory. Other evidence to support portions of the ERG theory has been added to the literature since his debate with Salancik and Pfeffer.

One study examined the ERG theory of motivation with regard to the human life cycle, using Levinson's theory of life-cycle development, which includes seven stages (e.g., early adult transition, 18–22 years old; midlife transition, 40–45 years old).[26] Some of the results indicated that (1) individuals whose parents achieved higher educational levels had significantly higher scores for strength of desire for growth, and (2) men had higher scores for strength of existence needs and lower scores for strength of relatedness than did women.

In another study of ERG theory, researchers collected data from 208 employees working in 13 different jobs in a telephone company.[27] In general, the ERG categories were supported. Relatively few individuals (17 out of 208) in this study reported high growth-need satisfaction when satisfaction of relatedness and existence needs was either moderate or low. Also, an examination of how pay can satisfy a variety of needs supported the three need categories proposed by Alderfer.[28] Much work still needs to be done, however, before the ERG theory's value in work settings can be confirmed.

Herzberg's Two-Factor Theory

Herzberg's two-factor theory of motivation
View that job satisfaction results from the presence of intrinsic motivators and that job dissatisfaction stems from not having extrinsic factors.

Psychologist and management consultant Frederick Herzberg developed the **two-factor content theory of motivation**.[29] The two factors are the dissatisfiers-satisfiers, the hygiene-motivators, or the extrinsic–intrinsic factors, depending on who's discussing the theory. The original research testing this theory included a group of 200 accountants and engineers. Herzberg used interview responses to questions such as, "Can you describe, in detail, when you felt exceptionally good about your job?" and "Can you describe, in detail, when you felt exceptionally bad about your job?" Rarely were the same kinds of experiences categorized as both good and bad. This systematic procedure resulted in the development of two distinct kinds of experiences: satisfiers and dissatisfiers.

Herzberg's initial study resulted in two specific conclusions. First, there's a set of *extrinsic* conditions, the job context. They include pay, status, and working conditions. The presence of these conditions to the satisfaction of the employee doesn't necessarily motivate him, but their absence results in dissatisfaction. Because they're needed to maintain at least a level of "no dissatisfaction," the extrinsic conditions are called the *dissatisfiers,* or *hygiene,* factors.

Second, a set of *intrinsic* conditions, the job content, is also present. These conditions include feelings of achievement, increased responsibility, and recognition. The absence of these conditions doesn't prove highly dissatisfying. But when present, they build strong levels of motivation that result in good job performance. Therefore, they're called the *satisfiers,* or *motivators.*

Prior to Herzberg's work, people studying motivation viewed job satisfaction as a unidimensional concept. That is, they placed job satisfaction at one end of a continuum and job dissatisfaction at the other end of the same continuum. If a job condition caused job satisfaction, removing it would cause dissatisfaction; similarly, if a job condition caused job dissatisfaction, removing it would cause job satisfaction. Herzberg's model basically assumes that job satisfaction isn't a unidimensional concept. His research leads to the conclusion that two continua are needed to interpret job satisfaction correctly. Figure 5.3 illustrates the two different views of job satisfaction.

FIGURE 5.3
Traditional and Herzberg Views of Satisfaction-Dissatisfaction

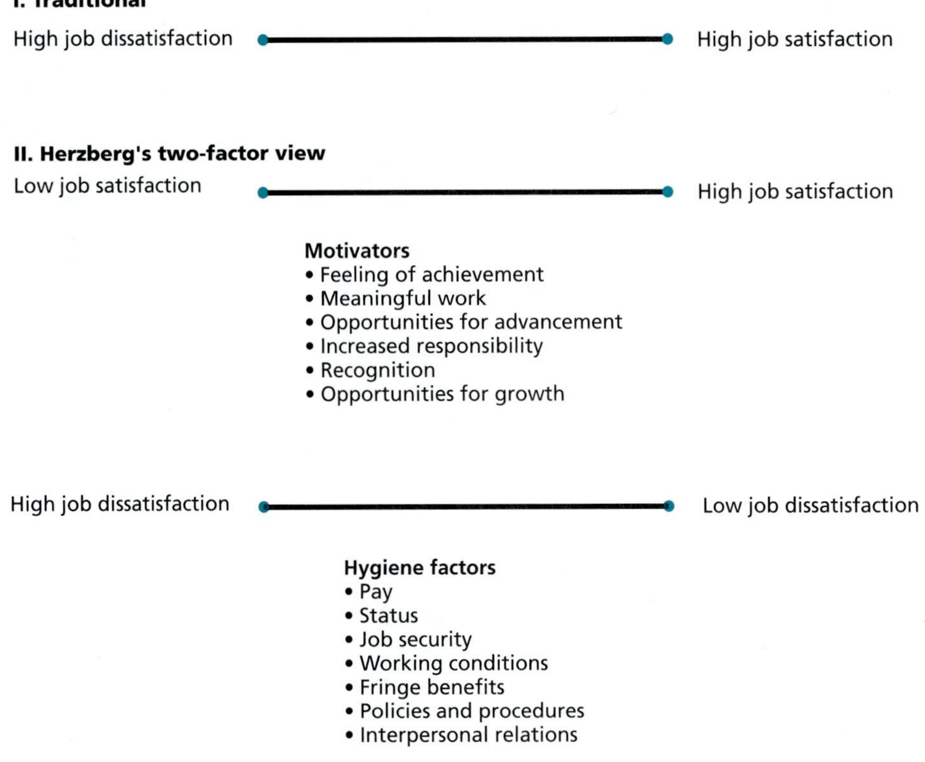

Referring to Figure 5.3, several important managerial implications of Herzberg's two-factor theory are apparent:

1. *Low job dissatisfaction, high job satisfaction:* An employee who is paid well, has job security, has good relationships with co-workers and the supervisor (hygiene factors are present = low job dissatisfaction), and is given challenging duties for which he or she is accountable will be motivated. Managers should continue to assign challenging tasks and transfer accountability to high performing subordinates. Pay raises, job security, and good supervision need to be continued.

2. *Low job dissatisfaction, low job satisfaction:* An employee who is paid well, has job security, has good relationships with co-workers and the supervisor (hygiene factors are present = low job dissatisfaction) but is not given any challenging assignments and is very bored with his or her job (motivators are absent = no job satisfaction) will not be motivated.

Managers should reevaluate subordinate's job description and enlarge it by providing more challenging and interesting assignments. Pay raises, job security, and good supervision need to be continued.

3. *High job dissatisfaction, low job satisfaction:* An employee who is not paid well, has little job security, has poor relationships with co-workers and the supervisor (hygiene factors are not present = high job dissatisfaction) and is not given any challenging assignments and is very bored with his/her job (motivators are absent = low job satisfaction) will not be motivated.

To prevent low performance, absenteeism, and turnover, managers should make drastic changes by adding hygiene factors and motivators.

Critique of Herzberg's Theory

Of all the available content theories, we believe the most criticized is Herzberg's. Several reasons account for this. First, the theory was originally based on a sample of American accountants and engineers. Critics ask whether this limited sample can justify generalizing to other occupational groups and to other countries. The technology, environment, and background of the two occupational groups are distinctly different from those of other groups, such as nurses, medical technologists, salespeople, computer programmers, clerks, and police officers.[30]

Second, some researchers believe that Herzberg's work oversimplifies the nature of job satisfaction, leading to the assumption that a manager can easily change hygiene factors or satisfiers and thus produce job satisfaction. This, of course, isn't an accurate view of how complex and difficult motivation and job satisfaction are in terms of workplace manipulation.

Other critics focus on Herzberg's methodology because it requires people to look at themselves retrospectively. Can people be aware of all that motivated or dissatisfied them? These critics believe subconscious factors aren't identified in Herzberg's analysis. Also, the "recency of events" bias of being able to recall one's most recent job conditions and feelings better than those occurring in the past is embedded in the methodology.[31]

Another criticism of Herzberg's work is that little attention is directed toward testing the theory's performance implications.[32] In the original study, only self-reports of performance were used, and in most cases, respondents were reporting on job activities that had occurred over a long period. Herzberg has offered no explanation as to why the various extrinsic and intrinsic job factors should affect performance.

When the available evidence is reviewed, it's surprising that Herzberg's theory has withstood the test of time. The two-factor theory, not even mentioned by many academic researchers, remains popular with managers, who continue to discuss the theory and attempt to increase motivation by using Herzberg's identified motivators.[33] His theory spells out specific job factors that managers can work with to create a motivational atmosphere. (Job factors are discussed in more detail in Chapter 13 on job design.) Herzberg's theory brings out clearly the differences in perspectives held by practicing managers and academics. Instead of taking sides, we believe that Herzberg's explanation will continue to be cited and used by managers in the United States and around the world.[34] Of course, care must be utilized in applying this or any other theory in international settings, as one study suggests that Herzberg's theory may have applied to a British sample but not to one from Nigeria.[35] However, the general perception of this theory is that it warrants discussion and consideration as a potential applied approach to motivation.

McClelland's Learned Needs Theory

learned needs theory
Theory that proposes that a person with a strong need will be motivated to use appropriate behaviors to satisfy the need. A person's needs are learned from the culture of a society.

David C. McClelland has proposed a **learned needs theory** of motivation closely associated with learning concepts. He believes that many needs are acquired from the culture of a society.[36] Three of these *learned needs* are the need for achievement (n Ach), the need for affiliation (n Aff), and the need for power (n Pow). McClelland suggested that when a need is strong in a person, its effect is to motivate her to use behavior leading to its satisfaction. For example, a worker with a high n Ach would set challenging goals, work hard to achieve the goals, and use skills and abilities to achieve them.

How are these needs such as n Ach measured? It's not enough to assume that those who work hard and long have a need for achievement, while those who work slowly or in spurts

Thematic Apperception Test (TAT)
Projective test that uses a person's analysis of pictures to evaluate such individual differences as need for achievement, need for power, and need for affiliation.

don't. To assess individual differences in the three proposed needs, the **Thematic Apperception Test (TAT)** is used.[37] A person is shown pictures and asked to write a story about what he sees portrayed in them.

For example, a picture would be presented to a respondent. The picture, which is somewhat vague, is of a man who appears to be working at a desk while looking at a small picture on his desk with three vague figures in it. The respondent is then asked to describe what the entire picture illustrates. People tend to write stories that reflect their dominant needs.

For example, individuals with high or dominant achievement typically write a story that reflects this need: maybe that the man at the desk is working long hours and misses his family but nonetheless remains at work to complete an important project. Evaluators reviewing a response to such a picture would search the written stories for recurring themes of hard work, extra effort, gratification received from success, and the setting of challenging goals as indications of a high need for achievement. McClelland believes that achievement, affiliation, and power needs can be inferred from the stories a person writes about a number of such pictures. He states,

> If you want to understand motives behind . . . actions, find out what's on a person's mind. If you want to find out what's on a person's mind, don't ask him, because he can't always tell you accurately. Study his fantasies and dreams. If you do this over a period of time, you will discover the themes to which his mind returns again and again. And these themes can be used to explain his actions.[38]

McClelland proposes that a society's economic growth is based on the level of need achievement inherent in its population[39] and that economically backward nations can be dramatically improved by stimulating the need for achievement in the populace. If McClelland is correct (and some research supports his theory), his approach could have a significant effect on motivation in general, especially in countries where free market economies are beginning to evolve. He also contends that motivation can be taught in organizational and nonorganizational settings.[40]

Research on Learned Needs

Most research evidence offered in support of McClelland's learned needs theory has been provided by McClelland or his associates. For example, a classic study suggested that better managers have a high need for power that is directed toward the benefit of the organization.[41] In general, research on the need for achievement has received the majority of attention from organizational behavior theorists and researchers. This research has provided a profile of the high achievers in society:

> High n Ach persons prefer to avoid easy and difficult performance goals. They actually prefer moderate goals that they think they can achieve.
>
> High n Ach persons prefer immediate and reliable feedback on how they are performing.
>
> The high n Ach person likes to be responsible for solving problems.

Research has pointed out the complexity of the achievement motive. High n Ach individuals who focus on attaining success differ from those who focus on avoiding failure.[42] Those who focus on attaining success tend to set more realistic goals and to choose moderately difficult tasks. Need for achievement has been also found to correlate highly with the need to attain status or wealth, especially for those involved in high-pay/high-status employment groups.[43]

In one ambitious project, researchers tried to raise the achievement motivation of businesspeople in an entire village in India. This program, the Kakinada project, consisted of encouraging the businesspeople to have high-achievement fantasies, to make plans that would help them realize the goals of a successful entrepreneur, and to communicate with one another about their goals and their methods of reaching them. The businesspeople

OB AT WORK Women Managers: Better Motivators Than Men?

Do women have a different management style than their male counterparts, and if so, do the consensus-building, participatory methods that are largely attributed to women work better than hierarchical, quasi-militaristic models? This subject has become increasingly controversial and leads to a deeper issue, namely, whether women managers do a better job of motivating workers than men. Proponents of this theory argue that women are more likely to manage in an interactive style, encouraging participation, sharing information, and enhancing the self-worth of others. Women are thought to use "transformational" leadership, working well with people at all organizational levels, understanding how employees feel, and motivating others by transforming their self-interest into the organization's goals.

A successful example of this kinder, gentler style of management is that of Anita Roddick, founder and owner of The Body Shop Skin and Hair Care stores. "It's just a family here," says Roddick. "We like to say, 'Partnerships, not power trips.'" Her "family" has grown substantially since the company's founding in 1976. Worldwide, The Body Shop has 2,500 stores serving more than 77 million customers in 50 different countries.

Although advocates of these theories argue that women's strengths should be tapped, some critics counter that any type of stereotyping by gender is a form of sexism, one that will only shackle women to their traditional role as nurturer. Some women managers are worried that men are seen as being one way and women another. Others, including Dee Soder (president of the Endymion Company, which advises senior corporate executives on their managerial strengths and weaknesses), believe the distinctions are irrelevant. "I think there is a higher proportion of participative women managers than there is of men," she says, "but the crossover is so high, it is a moot point."

What does research say on this issue? In a review in this area, male and female managers were overall found to be equally effective. However, men were observed to be more effective than women in leadership roles that were defined in more masculine terms (e.g., in the military), while women were generally more effective in roles that were defined in less masculine terms (e.g., in educational or social service organizations). These are generalizations that have many exceptions, of course, such as Deborah Kent, the first woman to head a vehicle assembly plant for Ford Motor Company. Her position in this plant, the third-largest Ford facility in the United States, is one that would typically be described as male in orientation, but while she has been described as tough, focused, and hard working, Ms. Kent has also been noted for her openness and her desire for input and feedback from her workers. Thus, she may reflect the developing redefinition of both jobs and the people who inhabit them.

Whether or not it's a matter of gender, everyone involved in the debate agrees on one thing: It's time to expand the old management model. In the 21st century, there is a greater need than ever to motivate workers. Managers who are nurturers and value driven, be they male or female, will be well equipped for this challenging task.

Sources: See www.bodyshop.com (accessed May 5, 2010); Joan F. Brett, Leanne E. Atwater, and David A. Waldman, "Effective Delivery of Workplace Discipline: Do Women Have to Be More Participatory Than Men?" *Group & Organization Management* 30, no. 5 (2005): 487–514; Barbara Mandell and Shilpa Pherwani, "Relationship between Emotional Intelligence and Transformational Leadership Style: A Gender Comparison," *Journal of Business and Psychology* 17, no. 3 (Spring 2003): 387–404; Susan J. Wells, "A Female Executive Is Hard to Find," *HR Magazine,* June 2001, pp. 40–49; Lena Williams, "A Silk Blouse on the Assembly Line," *New York Times,* February 5, 1995, p. 7; Alice H. Eagly, Steven J. Karau, and Mona G. Makhijani, "Gender and the Effectiveness of Leaders: A Meta-Analysis," *Psychological Bulletin,* January 1995, pp. 125–45; Mary Billard, "Do Women Make Better Managers?" *Working Woman,* March 1992, pp. 68–107; Rose Mary Wentling, "Women in Middle Management: Their Career Development and Aspirations," *Business Horizons,* January–February 1992, pp. 47–54.

became more productive as entrepreneurs, started several industries, enlarged their businesses, and hired more than 5,000 of their neighbors. In a 10-year reassessment of the program, achievement motivation levels and results were still exceptional.[44] Recent work reported by McClelland suggests that at PepsiCo, a high need for achievement was more associated with success than was a high need for power.[45]

Other studies have found that gender differences exist regarding competitiveness and money beliefs. Men are inclined to be more competitive and tend to focus their ambitions toward making money, as capital acquisition is highly desirable.[46] In total, men placed more value on salary, individual achievement, motivation, and directing others, whereas women emphasized good interpersonal relationships, interesting work, feelings of accomplishment, and professional growth.[47] Similarly, successful women may also fulfill their need for power in different ways than successful men.[48] As the OB at Work feature describes, women may be better suited to motivate employees than men.

Based on theory and research, McClelland has made specific suggestions about developing a positive high need for achievement (that is, a high n Ach where there's no fear of success). Using McClelland's prescriptions, a manager would be encouraged to

1. Arrange job tasks so that employees receive periodic feedback on performance, providing information that enables them to make modifications or corrections.
2. Point out models of achievement to employees. Identify and publicize the accomplishments of achievement heroes—the successful people, the winners—and use them as models.
3. Work with employees to improve their self-image. High n Ach people like themselves and seek moderate challenges and responsibilities.
4. Introduce realism into all work-related topics: promotion, rewards, transfer, development opportunities, and team membership opportunities. Employees should think in realistic terms and think positively about how they can accomplish goals.

There are a number of criticisms of McClelland's work. First, use of the projective TAT to determine the three needs has been questioned. While projective techniques have some advantages over self-report questionnaires, the interpretation and weighing of a story are, at best, an art. Validation of such analysis is extremely important and often neglected, but a recent review of research has indicated that the TAT may be as effective in this area as questionnaire methods.[49] A critical-incident technique has been used to examine motivation in a developing country, but more research is needed to determine whether critical incidents or other methods can be used for assessing McClelland-type needs.[50]

Second, McClelland's claim that n Ach can be learned is in conflict with a large body of literature stating that motives are normally acquired in childhood and are difficult to alter in adulthood. McClelland acknowledges this problem but points to evidence in politics and religion to indicate that adult behaviors can be changed.[51]

Third, McClelland's notion of learned needs is questioned on the grounds of whether needs are permanently acquired. Research is needed to determine whether acquired needs last over a period of time. Can something learned in a training and development program be sustained on the job? This is an issue that McClelland and others have not been able to clarify.

A Synopsis of the Four Content Theories

Each of the four content theories explains behavior from a slightly different perspective. None of the theories can or should be used by managers as the sole basis for explaining or inferring motivation. Although some critics are skeptical, it appears that people have innate and learned needs and that job factors result in a varying degree of satisfaction. Thus, each theory provides managers with some understanding of behavior and performance.

Figure 5.4 compares the four theories. McClelland proposed no lower-order needs. However, his needs for achievement and power aren't identical with Herzberg's motivators, Maslow's higher-order needs, or Alderfer's growth needs, although there are some similarities. A major difference among the four content theories is McClelland's emphasis on socially acquired needs. Also, the Maslow theory offers a static need hierarchy system; Alderfer presents a flexible, three-need classification approach; and Herzberg discusses intrinsic and extrinsic job factors.

FIGURE 5.4 **A Graphic Comparison of Four Content Theories of Motivation**

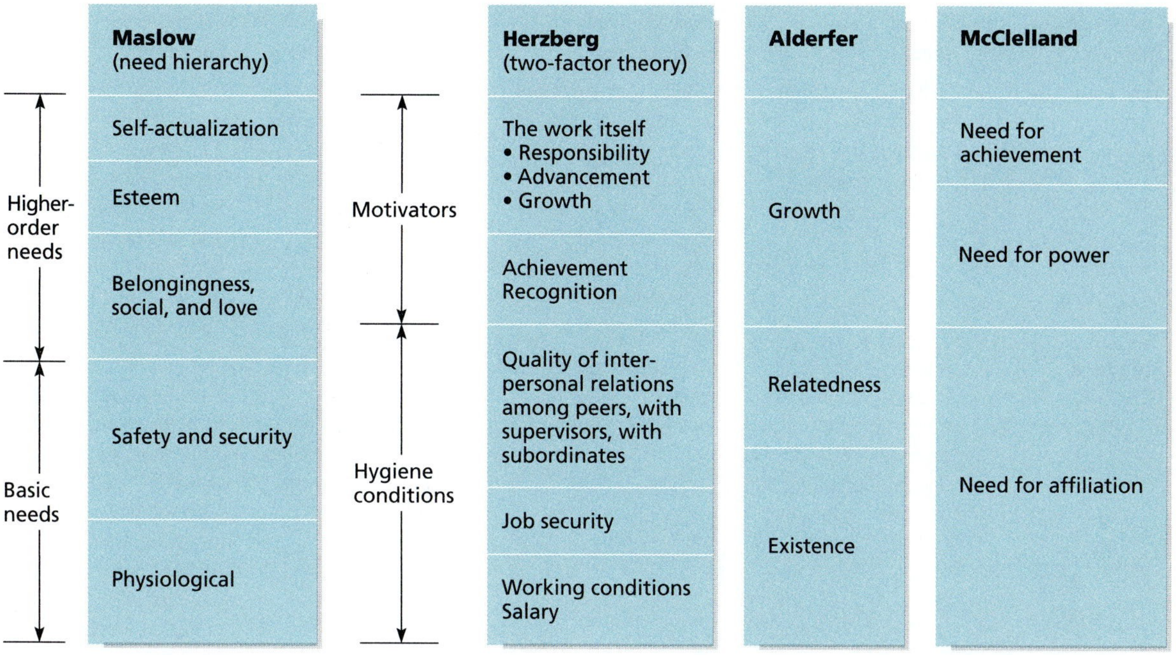

	Maslow (need hierarchy)		**Herzberg** (two-factor theory)	**Alderfer**	**McClelland**
Higher-order needs	Self-actualization	Motivators	The work itself • Responsibility • Advancement • Growth	Growth	Need for achievement
	Esteem				Need for power
	Belongingness, social, and love		Achievement Recognition		
Basic needs	Safety and security	Hygiene conditions	Quality of interpersonal relations among peers, with supervisors, with subordinates	Relatedness	Need for affiliation
			Job security	Existence	
	Physiological		Working conditions Salary		

Each theory has strengths and limitations that practicing managers need to consider and be cautious about. Table 5.2 highlights each model's main characteristics. As is typically the case when competing theories exist, no one theory has clear-cut superiority.

Each of the content theories purports to present the clearest, most meaningful, and most accurate explanation of motivation. One concept that few of the content theories addresses explicitly, however, is the quality of work done by the employee. Do employees have a need to perform so that a high quality of product or service is the outcome? Or is it management's job, to a large degree, to get employees excited about and involved in making high-quality goods? At PepsiCo, parent company of Pepsi-Cola, Frito-Lay, Quaker Foods, Tropicana, Gatorade, and many others, managers feel that the answer to both questions is yes.[52]

PepsiCo attempts to address both areas by encouraging all of its 198,000 employees worldwide to act as if they were the owner of a business, with the rationale that a sense of ownership and involvement in the company will generate the enthusiasm for producing the highest level of goods and services. SharePower is the name of the program at PepsiCo that enables all employees, not just upper-level executives, to earn stock options in the company, each year totaling 10 percent of an employee's pay of the previous year. This program not only gives employees a greater stake in the survival of the company, it also has helped to create a culture where all employees have a sense of both greater responsibility and an opportunity to contribute to the success of their part of the larger organization. The next OB at Work feature further addresses the issue of when and why employees "go the extra mile" for their organizations.

SharePower is PepsiCo's answer to the question, "How can we best become a world-class competitor?" Any theory of motivation claiming to be complete in today's turbulent environment must directly address issues of quality and quality improvement as they are impacted by the strategies of today's organizations.

TABLE 5.2 Comparison of Four Content Theories of Motivation

Content Motivation Theories	Assumptions Made	How Motivation Is Measured	Practical Application Value	Problems and Limitations
Maslow's need hierarchy	Individuals attempt to satisfy basic needs before directing behavior toward higher-order needs.	Maslow, as a clinical psychologist, used his patients in asking questions and listening to answers. Organizational researchers have relied on self-report scales.	Makes sense to managers and gives many a feeling of knowing how motivation works for their employees.	Doesn't address the issue of individual differences; has received limited research support; and fails to caution about the dynamic nature of needs—needs change.
Alderfer's ERG theory	Individuals who fail to satisfy growth needs become frustrated, regress, and refocus attention on lower-order needs.	Self-report scales are used to assess three need categories.	Calls attention to what happens when and if need satisfaction does not occur; frustrations can be a major reason why performance levels aren't attained or sustained.	Not enough research has been conducted; available research is self-report in nature, which raises the issue of how good the measurement is. Another issue is whether individuals really have only three need areas.
Herzberg's two-factor theory	Only some job features and characteristics can result in motivation. Some of the characteristics that managers have focused on may result in a comfortable work setting but don't motivate employees.	Ask employees in interviews to describe critical job incidents.	Talks in terms that managers understand. Identifies motivators that managers can develop, fine-tune, and use.	Assumes that every worker is similar in needs and preferences; fails to meet scientific measurement standards; hasn't been updated to reflect changes in society with regard to job security and pay needs.
McClelland's learned needs	A person's needs are learned from the culture (society); therefore, training and education can enhance and influence a person's need strength.	Thematic Apperception Test (TAT), a projective technique that encourages respondents to reveal their needs.	If a person's needs can be assessed, then management can intervene through training to develop needs that are compatible with organizational goals.	Interpreting the TAT is difficult; the effect that training has on changing needs hasn't been sufficiently tested.

The process theories of motivation describe how employees are motivated or how they select behaviors to meet their needs and determine whether they made the most successful choice. Process explanations of motivation suggest that motivation varies from situation to situation. We will discuss expectancy and equity process theories in this chapter. In the next chapter, other process theories will be introduced. The expectancy and equity process theories are important in explaining goal setting and reinforcement process motivational theories and practices.

OB AT WORK Motivating Employees during a Recession

Although the U.S. economy is recovering from a severe recession, a persistently high national unemployment rate hovering just below 10 percent and an 18 percent unemployment rate for young people aged 16–24 helps to explain why companies and organizations in the United States are not as willing to give large annual bonuses to their employees and executives as in the past. Consequently, many managers are looking for alternative and creative ways to reward and motivate employees.

Some companies, such as FedEx, Hewlett-Packard, Advanced Micro Devices, and The New York Times, have attempted to maintain employee motivation during the recession by bucking conventional wisdom. Instead of instituting large-scale employee layoffs, these companies have opted for companywide reductions in employees' base pay. Leaders of these companies believe that their current executives and employees are willing to sacrifice a portion of their pay for a short time until the firm's financial situation strengthens again. If the pay cut is done in a transparent and equitable manner (e.g., executives give back more than lower-paid employees), then it is hoped that morale will be maintained and forced layoffs of friends and colleagues avoided.

Rhino Foods goes one step further when demand for its dessert products decreases during slow economic times. The Burlington, Vermont, company allows its best employees to voluntarily take other jobs with Rhino's customers with the promise that Rhino will have a job waiting for these individuals once business improves. Rhino officials claim that employees who transfer out to customer companies then return with a new set of skills and stronger relationships with those customers.

Other ways of keeping employees motivated during tough times include a variety of low-cost or "soft" benefits. Here are some examples of low-cost benefits:

- eBay has outfitted two quiet areas at its San Jose campuses with large pillows that employees can use for prayer and meditation during work;
- Microsoft offers its employees dry cleaning at its Redmond, Washington, location and sponsors free grocery delivery to employees' homes;
- Sylvan Dell Publishing set up an on-site kennel to accommodate employees who bring their dogs to work; and,
- Google gives its employees bonuses that can only be used toward the purchase of a hybrid automobile.

During lean times, companies need to retain their talent with fewer financial resources. Some creative approaches such as reduced salaries (instead of layoffs), sharing employees with customers, and providing low cost but meaningful benefits to employees are a good way to keep employees through the tough times.

Sources: See www.bls.gov (accessed on May 5, 2010); A. Mishra, K. Mishra, and G. Spreitzer (2009), "Downsizing the Company without Downsizing Morale," *MIT Sloan Management Review* 50, no. 3 (2009): 39–44; Jena McGregor, "Cutting Salaries Instead of Jobs," *Businessweek*, May 28, 2009, pp. 46–48; Peter Coy, Mark Scott, Lindsey Gerdes, and Kenji Hall, "The Lost Generation," *Businessweek*, October 8, 2009, pp., 32; B. Chapman, "Fun and Games," *Incentive* 182, no. 6 (June 2008): 28–30.

Expectancy Theory

expectancy theory of motivation
Theory in which an employee is faced with a set of first-level outcomes and selects an outcome based on how the choice is related to second-level outcomes. The individual's preferences are based on the strength (valence) of the desire to achieve a second-level state and the perception of relationship between first- and second-level outcomes.

A widely cited process explanation of motivation, developed by Victor Vroom, is expectancy theory. The majority of the early studies (about 50) tested the accuracy of expectancy theory in predicting employee behavior.[53] Since then, additional studies have tested the theory itself.

Vroom defines *motivation* as a process governing choices among alternative forms of voluntary activity. In his view, most behaviors are under the voluntary control of the person and are consequently motivated.

Terminology

To understand the **expectancy theory of motivation**, we must define the terms in the theory and explain how they operate. The most important terms are discussed in this section.

First- and Second-Level Outcomes

The first-level outcomes resulting from behavior are associated with doing the job itself. These outcomes include productivity, absenteeism, turnover, and quality of productivity.

Second-level outcomes are those events (rewards or punishments) that the first-level outcomes are likely to produce, such as merit pay increase, group acceptance or rejection, and promotion.

Instrumentality

instrumentality
Concept in expectancy theory of motivation in which a person's perception of association of first- and second-level outcomes is determined.

This is an individual's perception that first-level outcomes are associated with second-level outcomes. Vroom suggests that **instrumentality** can take values ranging from 1, indicating a perception that attainment of the second level is certain without the first outcome and impossible with it, to 1, indicating that the first outcome is necessary and sufficient for the second outcome to occur. A value of 0 would indicate no relationship between first and second outcomes. This association between outcomes can thus be thought of in terms of correlation.

Valence

valence
Strength of a person's preference for particular outcome.

The preference for outcomes, as seen by the individual, is termed **valence**. For example, a person may prefer a 9 percent merit increase over a transfer to a new department, or the transfer over relocation to a new facility. An outcome is *positively* valent when it's preferred; it's *negatively* valent when it's not preferred or is avoided. An outcome has a valence of zero when the individual is indifferent to attaining or not attaining it. The valence concept applies to first- and second-level outcomes. For example, a person may prefer to be a high-performing (first-level outcome) employee because he believes that this will lead to a merit increase in pay (second-level outcome).[54]

Expectancy

expectancy (probability)
Perceived likelihood that a particular act will be followed by a particular outcome.

This term refers to the individual's belief concerning the likelihood or subjective probability that a particular behavior will be followed by a particular outcome such as level of performance. That is, **expectancy** is the perceived chance of something occurring because of a behavior. Expectancy has a value ranging from 0, indicating no chance that an outcome will occur after the behavior or act, to +1, indicating certainty that a particular outcome will follow an act or a behavior. Expectancy is like a subjective probability.

In the work setting, individuals hold an *effort–performance expectancy.* This expectancy represents the individual's perception of how hard it is to achieve a particular behavior (say, completing the budget on time) and the probability of achieving that behavior. For example, Joan, who's preparing a budget, may have a high expectancy that if she works around the clock she can complete the budget on time; on the other hand, she may perceive that her chances of finishing on time are about 40 percent if she works only during the day. Given a number of alternative levels of behavior to finish the budget (working 8 hours, 10 hours, or around the clock), she'll choose the level of performance that has the greatest motivational force associated with it. In other words, when faced with *choices* about behavior, the person performing the task goes through a process of questioning: Can I perform at that level if I give it a try? If I perform at that level, what will happen? Do I prefer the things that will happen?

Two other terms are worth defining here as well. The term *force* is equated with motivation. The intent of expectancy theory is to assess the magnitude and direction of all the forces acting on the individual. The act associated with the greatest force is the one most likely to occur.

The term *ability* designates a person's potential for doing the job or work; it refers to the person's physical and mental abilities to do the job and not to what the person *will* do. That potential may or may not be utilized.

Principles of Expectancy Theory

Integration of the important expectancy theory concepts generates three major principles:[55]

1. V_1 S(V_2 I). The valence associated with various first-level outcomes is a sum of the multiplication of the valences (V_2) attached to all second-level outcomes with their respective instrumentalities (I).

2. M f(V_1 E). Motivation is a multiplicative function of the valence for each first-level outcome (V_1) and the perceived expectancy (E) that a given behavior will be followed by a particular first-level outcome. If expectancy is low, there will be little motivation. Similarly, if an outcome's valence is zero, neither the absolute value nor variations in the strength of the expectancies of accomplishing it will have any effect.

3. P f(M A). Performance is considered to be a multiplicative function of motivation (the force) and ability.

Figure 5.5 uses numerical values to illustrate how expectancy theory works conceptually. The situation portrayed involves Joan, a budget specialist, facing various performance

FIGURE 5.5 Application of Expectancy Theory: Joan's Situation

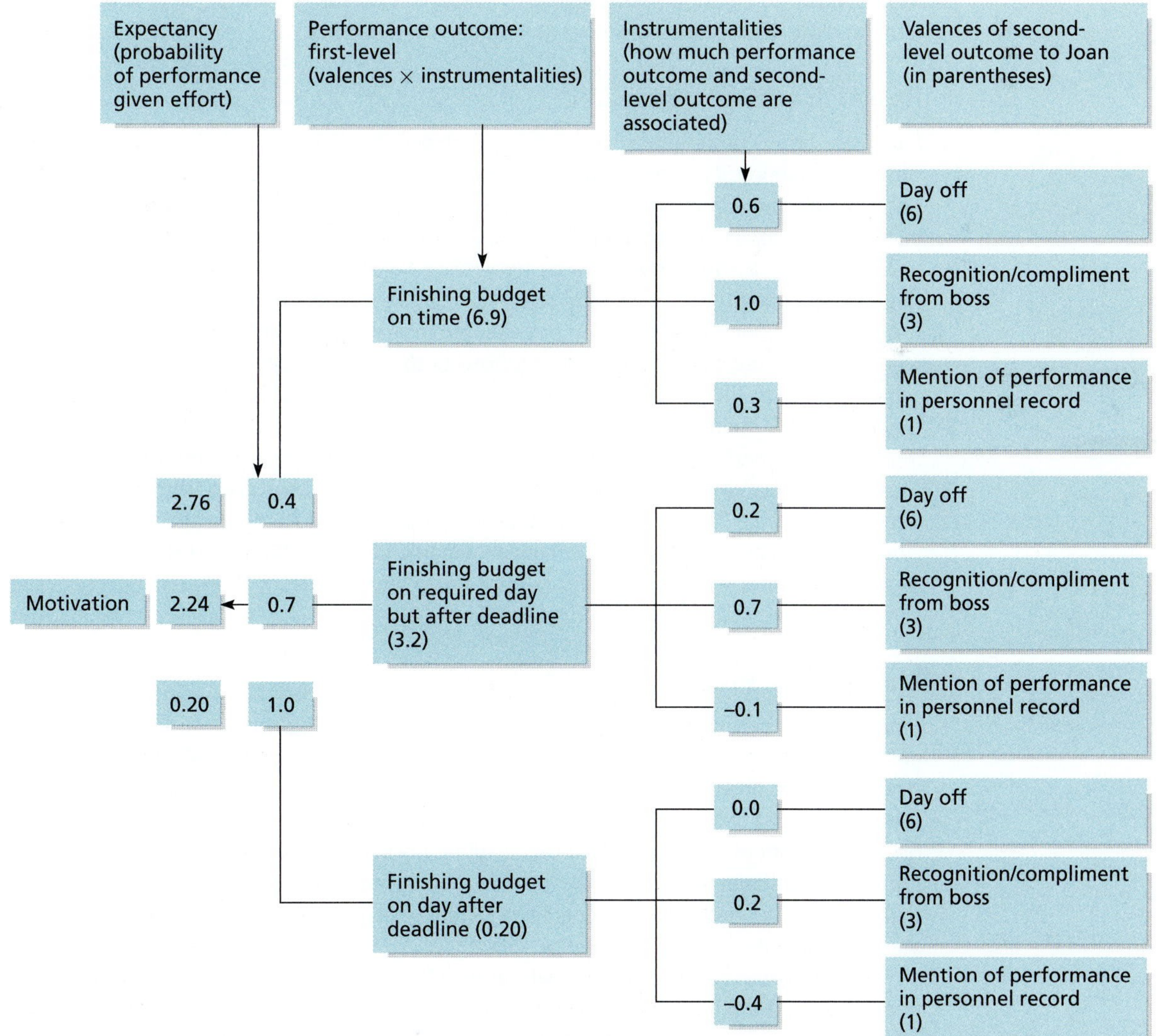

(first- and second-level) outcomes. Starting at the second-level outcome point (the right side), the valence associated with finishing the budget on time is calculated by V_1 V_2 I, or VI (6 0.6) (3 1.0) (1 0.3), or 6.9.

We're assuming that Joan has indicated her preferences, or valence strength, for these three outcomes. She indicates a strength of preference of 6 for a day off, 3 for recognition and compliments from the boss, and 1 for a mention of performance in her personnel file. Her preference ratings indicate Joan values the day off much more than the two other outcomes. Her valences are multiplied by the instrumentalities, her perceptions of the association of performance outcomes, and each of the second-level outcomes. Remember the 6, 3, and 1 valence strengths are set for illustrative purposes. These values indicating strength are subjectively established. Thus, for the "finishing budget on time" performance, this would be 6(0.6) 3(1.0) 1(0.3) = 6.9.

The motivational force for the condition of finishing the budget on time is calculated by M f(V_1 E), or M 6.9 0.4, or 2.76. The motivational force for finishing the budget on the required day but after the deadline is 2.24, while finishing the budget the day after the deadline has a force of 0.20. Thus, the strongest force or motivation would be directed toward finishing the budget on time. Certainly, a manager would not engage in this type of mathematical calculation. However, he or she would attempt to determine how employees think in terms of expectancies, instrumentalities, and valences.

Research on Expectancy

Each year brings more empirical research on expectancy theory. A few studies have used students in laboratory experiments. However, most research has been conducted in field settings. One interesting study, for example, examined performance–outcome instrumentality in a temporary organization.[56] The experiment used either an hourly rate of pay (low instrumentality, or little link between immediate behavior and outcomes) or a piece rate (high instrumentality, or payment based on each piece produced). After individuals worked for three four-hour days under one pay system, they were shifted to the other system and worked three more days. Immediately following the shift in pay systems and for all three subsequent days, the performance of the subjects shifted to the high-instrumentality system was higher than their own performance under the low-instrumentality system and higher than the performance of the subjects shifted to the low-instrumentality system.

Another research area focused on the model's valence and behavior factors. The results have been mixed.[57] However, three conditions apparently must hold for the valence of outcomes to be related to effort. Performance–outcome instrumentalities must be greater than zero; effort–performance expectancies must be greater than zero; and there must be some variability in the valence of outcomes.[58]

Management Practices

Managers can certainly use expectancy theory in developing their own motivation programs.[59] However, some managerial actions must be taken to improve the theory's value. First, managers need to focus on employee expectations for success. That is, do employees feel that they can attain the performance goals that are set for them, or do they perceive that the achievement of these goals and the resultant positive outcomes are beyond their capabilities? If this latter situation is the case, especially in group situations, then low productivity is often the result.[60] Managers need to realign assignments and rewards to facilitate the development of realistic challenge within jobs.

Second, managers must actively determine which second-level outcomes are important to employees. In our example, Joan valued a day off. Simply providing a notation in her personnel file commenting on her performance wasn't as valued as the day off. Managers

OB AT WORK Don't Forget to Consider Nontraditional Rewards

In discussions of expectancy theory outcomes, little attention is usually paid to the preference of employees for flexible work arrangements. This seems to be a mistake. Research data indicate that 85 percent of U.S. wage and salaried workers live with family members and have day-to-day family responsibilities.

If organizations fail to consider the positive benefits of flexible work arrangements and other nontraditional benefits, they will be faced with high absenteeism and turnover. Using strategies for workers with elder care and child-rearing responsibilities would appear to be a powerful motivator. Having valuable employees burn out because of family/work balance issues is costly. SAS—a privately held, $2.3 billion-dollar software firm—is ahead of a lot of firms with regard to retention initiatives, which include onsite and affordable child care and health care, gymnasium facilities, flexible work schedules, and a culture that encourages employees to spend quality time with their families. Treating employees as valuable assets means taking into consideration family, child-rearing, and community responsibilities. SAS believes that because of its progressive programs and the positive motivational climate created it is able to retain most of its 9,000 worldwide employees. The SAS approach works around the world and is preferred by employees because it is fair, meaningful, and flexible. It's no wonder SAS was ranked number one in the Fortune's Best Companies to Work For list in 2010.

Sources: David A Kaplan, "#1 SAS The Best Company to Work For," *Fortune*, February 2010, pp. 56–64; Rick Whiting, "Going Above and Beyond," *InformationWeek*, April 28, 2003, pp. 49–51; John M. Ivancevich and Tom N. Duening, *Managing Einsteins: Leading High Tech Workers in the Digital Age* (New York: McGraw-Hill, 2002); Matt Bolch, "The Coming Crunch," *Training*, April 2001, pp. 54–58; and Robert Reich, *The Future of Success* (New York: Knopf, 2001).

who know what subordinates prefer can attempt to provide the highly valued outcomes. Because (as this kind of outcome preference information points out) individuals prefer different outcomes, motivation programs should be designed with enough flexibility to address such differences in individual preference.[61] The accompanying OB at Work feature suggests that managers must address nonwork outcomes.

Third, managers should link desired second-level outcomes to the organization's performance goals. Showing through example that there's an actual association between performance goals and desired second-level outcomes increases employees' belief that hard work and good performance result in outcomes they prefer.

Expectancy theory assumes employees allocate their behavior according to anticipated consequences of actions. Workers weigh the information available to them and make decisions according to the value of the consequences and their own probabilities of achieving what they prefer. Expectancy theory thus views behavior as the product of what employees believe will happen in the future.

Criticisms of Expectancy Theory

Theorists, researchers, and practitioners (to a lesser extent) continue to work on defining, measuring, and applying expectancy concepts. Many difficulties are encountered when testing the model.[62] One problem involves the issue of effort, or motivation itself. The theory attempts to predict choice or effort. But without a clear specification of the meaning of effort, the variable can't be adequately measured. Typically, self, peer, or supervisor ratings of effort are used. Unfortunately, each study seems to have its own definition, measurement, and research design.

The issue of first-level performance outcomes presents another difficulty. Expectancy theory doesn't specify which outcomes are relevant to a particular individual in a situation. Each researcher addresses this issue in a unique way. Consequently, no systematic approach is being used across investigations.

Furthermore, the expectancy approach contains an implicit assumption that all motivation is conscious. Individuals are assumed to consciously calculate the pleasure or pain they expect to attain or avoid, then make a choice. Although it's generally accepted that individuals aren't always conscious of their motives, expectancies, and perceptual processes, expectancy theory says nothing about subconscious motivation. For the most part, this point has been neglected in the theory.

Most of the available field studies testing the model have relied on employees from a single organization who were doing the same or similar jobs. These studies seriously limit and restrict the range of expectancies and instrumentalities. This type of research also raises the issue of whether results from these studies can be generalized to other samples. Is it valid to make generalizations?

The use of expectancy theory to motivate employees appears to be culturally bound. That is, in cultures where employees believe they have some control over the work context and their own behavior expectancy (e.g., the United States, Canada, New Zealand) expectancy theory explanations appear to have some validity. However, in cultures where the perception of individual control is minimal (e.g., Japan, China, Iraq), the expectancy concepts of preference are not applicable.[63]

Equity Theory

equity theory of motivation
Theory that examines discrepancies within Person after Person has compared his input/outcome ratio to that of reference person.

J. Stacey Adams, while working as a research psychologist with the General Electric Co. in Crotonville, New York, developed and tested an **equity theory of motivation**. The essence of equity theory is that employees compare their efforts and rewards with those of others in similar work situations. This theory of motivation is based on the assumption that individuals, who work in exchange for rewards from the organization, are motivated by a desire to be equitably treated at work. This is significant as authors such as Pfeffer believe that maintaining employee perceptions of equity is a critical aspect of the management role.[64] Four important terms in this theory are

1. *Person:* the individual for whom equity or inequity is perceived.
2. *Comparison other:* any individual(s) or group used by Person as a referent regarding the ratio of inputs and outcomes.
3. *Inputs:* the individual characteristics brought by Person to the job. These may be achieved (e.g., skills, experience, learning) or ascribed (e.g., age, sex, race).
4. *Outcomes:* what Person received from the job (e.g., recognition, fringe benefits, pay).

Equity exists when employees perceive that the ratios of their inputs (efforts) to their outcomes (rewards) are equivalent to the ratios of other similar employees. Inequity exists when these ratios aren't equivalent: An individual's own ratio of inputs to outcomes could be greater or less than that of others.[65] Figure 5.6 illustrates the equity theory of

FIGURE 5.6 **The Equity Theory of Motivation**

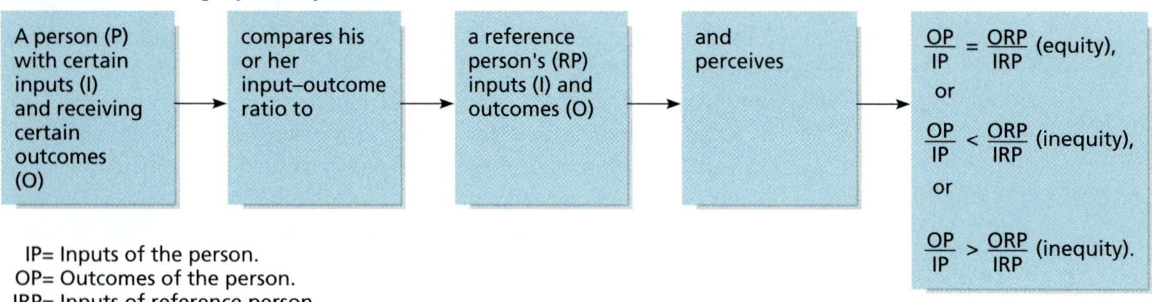

TABLE 5.3
Jeff's Concept of Equity Theory: An Application

Outcomes and Inputs	Weighted Value of Outcomes and Inputs	Jeff	Bob	Weighted Value of Outcomes and Inputs
College degree (input)	1	Yes	Yes	1
CPA (input)	1	Yes	Yes	1
Experience on job (input)	2	18 months	None	0
Executive dining room privileges (outcome)	1	Yes	Yes	1
Annual salary (outcome)	4	$27,000	$31,000	5

$$\frac{\text{Outcomes } (1 + 4)}{\text{Inputs } (1 + 1 + 2)} \quad \frac{\text{Outcomes}(1 + 5)}{\text{Inputs } (1 + 1)}$$

$$\frac{5}{4} < \frac{6}{2}$$

$$\text{(Jeff) } 1.25 < 3.00 \text{ (Bob)}$$

motivation in general; Table 5.3 gives an example. Note that Jeff has considered five points of comparison and has assigned hypothetical values (weights) to the importance of each point. Jeff is assessing his outcomes as 5 and inputs as 4, for a 1.25 index, while Jeff assesses Bob's situation as 6 outcomes and 2 inputs, or 3.0. (The two major differences in this case are Jeff's being paid $4,000 less than Bob and his 18 months' more experience than Bob's.)

Thus, Jeff concludes that he gets less out of the job than does Bob. In essence, he believes that he's being underpaid relative to Bob, he feels distressed or troubled by this unexplained inequity, and he is motivated to resolve this situation.[66]

Alternatives to Restore Equity

Equity theory suggests alternative ways to restore a feeling or sense of equity. Some examples of restoring equity would be

1. *Changing inputs.* Jeff may decide to put less time or effort into the job. Other inputs that could be changed are reliability, cooperation with others, initiative, and acceptance of responsibility.

2. *Changing outcomes.* Jeff may decide to confront his boss and ask for a raise, more time off, or better assignments.

3. *Changing the reference person.* The reference person (Bob) can be changed by making comparisons with the input/outcome ratios of some other person. This change can restore equity.

4. *Changing the inputs or outcomes of the reference person.* If the reference person is a co-worker, it might be possible to attempt to change his inputs. Asking Bob to work harder or to take more responsibility on projects would be examples of such an attempt.

5. *Changing the situation.* Jeff might quit the job to alter his feeling of inequity. He could also transfer to get away from an inequitable situation.

Each of these methods is designed to reduce or change the feelings of discomfort and tension created by inequity. Equity theory proposes that when inequity exists, a person is motivated to take one or more of these five steps.

The value and usefulness of equity theory to managers is evaluated by some in terms of ethical issues. The principle of distributive justice applies equity concepts. Some individuals assume that inequity is acceptable if (1) everyone has the same access to the most favored positions in society and (2) inequities are in the best interest of the least well off in society.[67] Does everyone have equal access to the most challenging, best-paying, or highest-status jobs in society? Should those who are less well off receive greater rewards than the more well off members of society? These are issues that most managers would prefer to not even attempt to resolve; they are part of a broader discussion of ethical, moral, political, sociological, legal, and historical perspectives.

organizational justice
The degree to which individuals feel fairly treated within the organizations for which they work.

distributive justice
The perception of fairness of the resources and rewards in an organization.

In the 1980s and 1990s, equity theory inspired new streams of research to explain employee attitudes and behavior. The concept of **organizational justice**, or the degree to which individuals feel fairly treated at the workplace, attracted a considerable amount of research attention. As Table 5.4 illustrates, there are four main components of this research domain, including distributive, procedural, interpersonal, and informational justice.[68] The first component, **distributive justice**, is the perceived fairness of how resources and rewards are distributed throughout an organization. This concept often deals with compensation and is closely related to the earlier discussion on equity theory. A recent study explored whether high levels of CEO pay violate principles of justice and fairness.[69] However, researchers have applied the concept of distributive justice to a wide variety of workplace situations, including organizational politics, employee smoking policies, university tenure and promotion decisions, taking charge of behavior in organizations, mentoring, and satisfaction with benefit levels.[70]

procedural justice
The perception of fairness of the process used to distribute rewards.

Related to distributive justice is the notion of procedural justice. **Procedural justice** refers to the perceived equity or fairness of the organization's processes and procedures used to make resource and allocation decisions.[71] That is, employees are concerned with the fairness of decision making in all areas of work, including decisions related to compensation, performance appraisal, training, and work group assignments.

TABLE 5.4 Four Dimensions of Organizational Justice

Dimension of Organizational Justice	Definition	Sample of Employee Concerns Related to the Dimension
Distributive	Perception of fairness of the resources and rewards in an organization.	I worked really hard this year but only received a 5 percent raise. I wanted 10 percent. Do I have a right to be upset? I received a 3.0 (out of 5.0) on my performance appraisal this year. I don't think it's a fair rating.
Procedural	Perception of fairness of the process used to distribute rewards.	The way they make pay raise decisions around here doesn't seem fair. The manager's favorites always get the largest raises. I deserved a 4.5 (out of 5.0) on my appraisal. I don't think the appraisal process is fair because it only measures part of what I do at this organization.
Interpersonal	Perception of fairness of the treatment received by employees from authorities.	When I questioned my boss about the 5 percent pay raise, he yelled at me and told me "not to be a cry baby." My boss told me I didn't receive a higher performance rating because I'm a slacker and need to be fired.
Informational	The perception of fairness of the communication provided to employees from authorities.	Can you believe I found out about my 5 percent raise in an email? I was expecting to hear it from my boss directly in a one-on-one meeting.

Procedural justice has been shown to have a positive impact on a number of affective and behavioral reactions at the workplace.[72] In other words, when employees perceive high levels of procedural justice with the organization's resource and allocation decisions, they are more likely to:

- Be committed to the organization;
- Be intrinsically motivated;
- Stay with the organization;
- Engage in organizational citizenship behaviors;
- Trust their supervisors;
- Apply great effort to their work; and,
- Perform their job well.

The aforementioned outcomes are some of the positive consequences of procedural justice when it comes to organizational decision making. Moreover, people are more inclined to perceive decisions to be fair when they have a voice in the decision, there is consistency in decision-making, and the process and procedures used to the make the decisions conform to ethical and moral values.[73] Treating employees, customers, and suppliers in a fair and respectful manner is an important and ongoing managerial goal. In order to be successful, managers must use strong interpersonal and observation skills to be "plugged in" and aware of the perceptions of important stakeholders such as employees.[74]

interpersonal justice The perception of fairness of the treatment received by employees from authorities.

Related to procedural justice is the concept of **interpersonal justice**, which refers to judgments made by employees about whether they feel fairly treated by their supervisors and other authorities in the organization.[75] Perceptions of interpersonal justice are higher when authorities are seen as treating employees in a dignified and respectful manner. However, interpersonal injustice can occur if employees perceive that the authorities treat them in an insulting, embarrassing, humiliating manner in front of others or label the employees as racist or sexist.[76]

Unfortunately, poor treatment by managers and other authorities in organizations appears to be a common occurrence. In a random telephone survey of 1,000 working adults in the United States, approximately 45 percent of respondents reported that they work or have worked for an abusive supervisor.[77] The researchers defined abusive behavior as verbal abuse, intimidation, and threatening gestures. Other researchers analyzed 110 research studies to compare the effects of sexual harassment and workplace bullying on employees.[78] They defined workplace aggression as any behavior that included:

- persistently criticizing employees' work;
- yelling;
- spreading gossip or lies;
- reminding employees of their mistakes;
- excluding or ignoring workers; and,
- insulting workers' habits, attitudes, or personal lives.

The study found that employees who experienced bullying and incivility at work were more likely to quit their jobs, and have lower levels of well-being and job satisfaction. Indeed, research suggests that abusive treatment from authorities and supervisors is associated with lower job and life satisfaction, lower organizational commitment, conflict between work and family, and psychological distress.[79]

informational justice The perception of fairness of the communication provided to employees from authorities.

A final form of organizational justice, **informational justice**, focuses on whether employees perceive that decisions and other communication from authorities are explained in a fair manner.[80] When important decisions are being communicated to employees, do

OB AND YOUR CAREER — Keep Your Surviving Employees in the Loop

Layoffs are a fact of life for many organizations. Unfortunately, there's evidence that companies that engage in layoffs may find that many "survivors" of the layoffs (i.e., employees who don't get let go) end up losing motivation while they wonder if "they're next," voluntarily leave the company, or both. Layoffs, combined with the loss of good employees who jump ship, may leave the firm understaffed when the economy picks up again. What can managers of a company do to lessen the negative impact of layoffs on those employees who survive the personnel cuts? One approach is to communicate and tell the truth when communicating with employees. Managers should keep many channels of communication open and provide information about the financial condition the organization and current and additional layoffs on a frequent basis. Here are some approaches that managers can take to ensure high levels of informational justice during turbulent times:

- Engage in informal "chats" (via text, e-mail, in person, or videoconference) with employees to keep the communication channels open;
- Don't sugarcoat bad news because employees will sense this and lose confidence in decision makers;
- Establish an HR hotline or "800" number for employees to call for updates; and,
- Create a Web page or dashboard that is updated on a daily basis.

In addition, some CEOs are communicating with their employees via blogs. Bill Marriott, chairman and CEO of Marriott International, has a blog called "On the Move," while Mike Critelli, executive chairman of Pitney Bowes, keeps employees up to date with his blog "Open Mike." These blogs and the other communication channels above are meant to convey a sense of trust and inclusiveness while decreasing secrecy and dishonesty when authorities communicate with employees.

Sources: Adapted from Knight Kiplinger, "When Firms Are Hurting, The Pain Should Be Shared," *Kiplinger's Personal Finance* 63, no. 5 (2009): 18; Susan J. Wells, "Layoff Aftermath," *HRMagazine*, November 2008, pp. 37–42; T. R. Tyler, and R. J. Bies, "Beyond Formal Procedures: The Interpersonal Context of Procedural Justice," in J. S. Carroll, (ed.), *Applied Social Psychology and Organizational Settings* (Hillsdale, NJ: Lawrence Erlbaum Associates, 1990): 77–98.

authorities take time to explain their decisions in a thorough and reasonable manner? Or, do they send out a brief e-mail or memo that announces major changes without adequate justification? The former approach will build a sense of informational justice among employees whereas the latter approach will erode it. The OB and Your Career above discusses how important it is to maintain informational justice when organizations undergo difficult periods like layoffs.

In sum, the organizational justice literature suggests that if managers and other authorities treat employees in what's perceived to be a fair manner, then employees are more likely to have higher levels of trust in their supervisors, and be more satisfied with their jobs and organizations.

Research on and Criticism of Equity Theory

Most of the research on equity theory has focused on pay as the basic outcome.[81] One study incorporated workplace elements into an equity theory framework.[82] Employees reassigned to offices of workers two levels above them in the management hierarchy were expected to perform at a higher level than employees reassigned to offices of workers only one level above them. Similarly, employees reassigned to offices of workers two levels below them would be expected to perform at a lower level than employees reassigned to offices of workers only one level below them. The findings indicated that employees assigned to higher-status offices increased their performance (a response to overpayment inequity) while those reassigned to lower-status offices lowered their performance (a response to underpayment inequity). The study supported equity theory's predictions that the reaction to an inequity will be proportional to the magnitude of the inequity experienced. It's also important to note that the workplace environment—not pay inequity—was the focal point in the study. Indeed, a review of the research reveals that pay is not always the outcome considered, as equity theory has shown predicted effects for both organizational citizenship[83] (going beyond the call of duty) and attitudes toward tasks and work groups.[84]

Several individuals have questioned the extent to which inequity that results from overpayment (rewards) leads to perceived inequity. Locke argues that employees are seldom told they're overpaid. He believes that individuals are likely to adjust their idea of what constitutes an equitable payment to justify their pay.[85] Because employer–employee exchange relationships are highly impersonal when compared with exchanges between friends, perceived overpayment inequity may be more likely when friends are involved. Thus, individuals probably react to overpayment inequity only when they believe that their actions have led to a friend being treated unfairly. The individual receives few signals from the organization that he's being treated unfairly.

Most equity research focuses on short-term comparisons.[86] What is needed are longitudinal studies that examine inequity over a period of time. What happens over time as the inequity remains, is increased, or is decreased? Are comparison others always within one's own organization, and do they change during a person's work career? These questions and research to answer them could provide insight into the dynamic character of equity theory and individual responses.[87]

Another interesting criticism of equity theory is that it ignores reactions to experienced inequities. Is it not likely that two people will react somewhat differently to the same magnitude of inequity if they believe different things caused the inequity? Folger has introduced the notion of *referent cognitions theory* to explore the role of the decision-making process in shaping perceptions of inequity.[88] In a work situation, suppose a manager allocates merit raises on the basis of a performance appraisal review. One employee may appreciate this strategy, while another may resent the manager, believing that another approach based on critical incidents and work on difficult assignments *should* have been used to allocate the merit raises. Thus the second employee is more likely to perceive inequity in the appraisal process.

Referent cognitions theory predicts resentment of unfair treatment when procedures yield poor outcomes for a person.[89] A study of manufacturing plant employees found that individual satisfaction with pay was highly related to the perceived fairness of the actual size of pay raises; however, the issues of commitment and trust in the organization were more affected by the *procedure* used to determine the raises. The researchers concluded that, in the allocation of pay increases, concerns other than the specific distribution of the money need to be seriously considered. They thus implied that an equity theory explanation of motivation is too restricted and incomplete.[90] However, because equity theory does seem to be applicable in other cultures such as China, France, and Mexico, it can be a useful explanation of employee behavior.[91]

Summary of Key Points

- Any management attempt to improve individuals' job performance must utilize motivation theories. This results from the fact that motivation is concerned with behavior or, more specifically, goal-directed behavior.
- A major reason employees' behaviors differ is that people's needs and goals vary. Social, cultural, hereditary, and job factors influence behaviors. To understand the nature of motivation, managers must learn about subordinates' needs.
- Theories of motivation can be classified as being either content theories or process theories. This chapter reviews four of the more widely cited content theories. These theories

focus on factors within the person (e.g., needs, goals, motives) that energize, direct, sustain, and stop behavior.

- Maslow's theory assumes that people have a need to grow and develop. The implication is that motivational programs have a higher probability of success if need deficiencies are reduced. Although Maslow's need hierarchy hasn't met rigorous standards of scientific testing, it appears that an adequately fulfilled need doesn't provide a good target for managers in building motivators that can influence performance.
- Alderfer offers a three-level need hierarchy of existence, relatedness, and growth needs. In addition to the satisfaction–progression process proposed by Maslow, Alderfer states that there is also a frustration–regression process at work that plays a major role in motivating people.
- Herzberg's two-factor theory of motivation identifies two types of factors in the workplace: satisfiers and dissatisfiers. One apparent weakness of the theory is that its findings haven't been replicated by other researchers. Despite this and other shortcomings, it does focus on job-related factors in managerial terminology.
- McClelland has proposed a theory of learned needs. The behavior associated with the needs for achievement, affiliation, and power is instrumental in an individual's job performance. Managers should attempt to acquire an understanding of these needs.
- A complex, difficult to assess motivation theory is based on expectancy. This theory examines the processes followed and steps taken by a person in pursuing and attaining outcomes.
- Equity theory of motivation focuses on individuals' perceptions of how fairly they are treated compared with others.

Discussion and Review Questions

1. Think about a current or past job that you held. How motivated were you to do a good job? Which of the theories discussed in this chapter could best explain your high (or low) level of motivation?
2. As a future manager, which of the theories presented in this chapter will be of most use to you in motivating your employees? Explain.
3. Describe the major differences between Maslow's need hierarchy and Alderfer's ERG explanation of motivation.
4. What factors serve to make Maslow's hierarchy of needs theory so intuitively attractive to practicing managers despite its obvious flaws?
5. Why would it be interesting to examine and compare the needs, discussed by McClelland, in young, middle-aged, and older people in the United States, Japan, Germany, Poland, Egypt, Argentina, and Sweden?
6. How would Herzberg's motivation theory help to explain why most people feel a good salary is not enough to motivate someone over the long-term in a job?
7. Based on equity theory, why is it important that decisions about pay or compensations programs have be perceived as fair?
8. In your opinion, should managers attempt to motivate employees with different ethnic backgrounds all in the same manner? Why or why not?
9. Why is it important to understand that a manager must infer the motivation level of subordinates?
10. Why is expectancy theory described as the most complex and difficult to measure theory of work motivation?

Taking It to the Net

Generational Differences

This chapter opened with a discussion of generational differences. Using your favorite search engine, visit the Internet to research answers to the following questions about the different generations in the workplace:

1. Why do the Gen Yers (or Millennials) need a structured work environment, a fair boss, and constructive feedback?
2. What were some of the defining events that happened during the Gen Xers' formative years that made many of them cynical about work, careers, and business?
3. Describe some potential areas of conflict between the Baby Boomers and Gen Xers. Assume that the Baby Boomers are supervisors and the Gen Xers report to them.
4. Thinking about the Veterans, which group (Boomers, Gen X, or Gen Y) do you think they would get along with the best? Why?

Could a manager concerned about motivation use any of your findings?

Case for Analysis: *What Motivates Entrepreneurs?*

For most people, going to work means working for someone else; a select few choose to become entrepreneurs. While TV advertisements depict the good life associated with "being your own boss," the reality may be very different. Small-business owners often risk their homes and life savings to fund a new enterprise, and while they may be the "boss," most work hours well beyond those of a typical employee. A recent Gallup survey found that the majority of small-business owners work an average of 52 hours a week, with 39 percent working 60 or more hours a week. Almost half (49 percent) of the polled small-business owners stated that they work at least six days a week with 19 percent reporting a seven-day workweek.

For some entrepreneurs, this dedication allows them to achieve tremendous financial success and notoriety. For example, consider Max Leeching and Peter Thiel, who founded PayPal in 1998. Their company quickly grew to become the premier Internet payment processing company, and in 2002, less than four years after its inception, eBay purchased PayPal for $1.2 billion. However, few entrepreneurs achieve such stellar success. Most business owners are everyday people: the restauranteur, the convenience store owner, and the dry cleaner. These businesspeople work long hours often for an hourly rate less than they could make working for someone else. What motivates entrepreneurs to take the risk and work these long hours? Just as there may be no single solution as to how to motivate employees, there may be no unique answer to the question of what motivates entrepreneurs. However, the following three accounts of small-business owners provide a glimpse of what keeps entrepreneurs motivated.

THE LUNCH TRUCK

Ivan and Anya immigrated to the United States from Eastern Europe just after the fall of the Soviet Union. They had found life in their old country harsh. Both had been assigned work as laborers in the local government factory. Their particular plant was built to produce war materials during the Second World War, and the large windowless structure had received little maintenance since that time. Beyond the physical conditions, they said the job itself was mind-numbing because workers had no autonomy and little incentive to work harder than the minimum expectations. Their government-assigned apartment was a 200-square-foot studio; its kitchen was a hot plate and sink. A communal bathroom was shared with three other couples on the floor. Hot water seemed like a luxury because most days the building's furnace was not functioning.

They arrived in the United States virtually penniless, sponsored by a distant cousin. Ivan worked for that cousin in his custodial business and moonlighted as a cab driver. Anya secured a job at a local factory and always volunteered for overtime. Within four years, the couple had paid Ivan's cousin back the money they borrowed to come to America and had $15,000 in the bank. When they heard that their friend Gus was selling his lunch truck, they paid $12,000 cash for the 1987 kitchen-equipped Chevy Step Van and the unofficial rights to a particular parking spot on a local college campus.

They had made it! Each morning at 6:00 the couple would restock the truck and drive to campus. When they reached their spot, Anya would jump out and move the 1973 Oldsmobile (that was "saving" their space overnight) to a parking lot approximately one mile away while Ivan parked the truck and set up for breakfast. By the time Anya had completed the walk back, the breakfast crowd was starting to arrive. They served breakfast, lunch, and dinner, and most days it wasn't until 6:15 in the evening before Anya was walking for the car to once again hold their space overnight. When Anya made it back with the car, they were off in the truck to the local warehouse club to purchase supplies for the next day and then it was home, usually by 8:00 p.m. They worked this schedule six days a week, with Sundays "off," although they frequently used that time to address maintenance issues with the truck or the Olds.

Fourteen hours a day, six days a week, the couple worked their lunch truck with the same pride as if it were the best restaurant in town. The money wasn't bad. They purchased a small town home and, in a good month, after paying all of their bills they were able to put $200 or $300 into their savings account.

THE EMPIRE BUILDER

Mary was the brightest student in her high school class and went to the local campus of her state university on full scholarship. While in college, she lived at home and worked 20 hours a week at a dry cleaners to pay her expenses and even save a few dollars. She graduated debt free and to the disappointment of her advisor, who was pushing her to attend graduate school, Mary stayed on at the dry cleaners as the store's manager. She had a plan. Three years after her graduation, the storeowner was looking to retire, and Mary, with help from various relatives, small-business loans, and every penny to her name, scraped together the $435,000 to buy the business. As the owner, Mary was "finally able to market the store properly," and sales grew. With the additional cash flow, within two years Mary purchased a second store, and by the time of her 10-year college reunion she had a dry cleaning empire consisting of eight stores, beating the target of one new store a year. While she still sees growth potential in the dry cleaning business, Mary anticipates that she'll maximize her firm's growth potential after opening 15 stores. She is looking at other businesses as a means of new expansion and has set a goal of matching her projected 15-store revenue with comparable revenue from "new business" by her 25th college reunion.

In addition to her work activities, Mary has been active in the local chamber of commerce meetings and was recently named "Businesswoman of the Year." Through her efforts with her college's alumni association, she was elected president and was planning "the biggest alumni weekend ever!" While Mary has been resisting the gentle encouragement of several chamber members to run for city council, she's beginning to reconsider. City council may be a good first step if she wants to pursue a future political career.

THE SERGEANT MAJOR

Jim was in the army for 28 years. Enlisting at the age of 18, he found that army life agreed with him. His officers recognized his "innate ability to lead" and as a result, he was promoted through the ranks quickly. He eventually earned the highest enlisted rank possible, sergeant major. His uniform was always so crisp and his back always so straight that he personified discipline. His officers knew him to be expert in military procedures and tactics. The sergeant major was not unnecessarily harsh, but he communicated his expectations in such a manner that one private stated, "No sane person would think of doing any thing else but follow."

While in excellent shape, after 28 hard years in the service, Jim's body was finally telling him that he wasn't 18 anymore. The recruits that he had been able to easily intimidate by his prowess in physical training (PT) were starting to keep up on those predawn five-mile runs. The sergeant major could not stomach the thought of a recruit matching him in anything, so he retired.

After a meticulous search, Jim purchased the franchise rights to a local specialized pack and ship company. This was a natural fit for Jim as he told the franchise corporate office, "I've moved troops and equipment on deployments all over the world, I'm sure I can handle packing grandma's lamp to ship to the next town over." Before he even started to look for a location for his store he had the franchise operations and procedures committed to memory. He even submitted improvement ideas to the franchise corporate offices so that he could still be "by the book," but a "better book."

The franchise corporate office was initially intimidated by Jim's "powerful persona" but was quickly impressed with his store's performance. While his first year sales were not the strongest, his operation ran like a clock. He had the lowest loss and complaint record in franchise history. Jim attributed his success to his crew. "You give your men a goal and they will achieve it" was how he explained his success to the corporate staff.

Now, after owning the business for five years, he still has three of his original five employees. One employee had left to join the Army and the other, with Jim's encouragement and financial backing, had left to open his own store. Jim's unit has been a training site for new franchise owners for the past three years. Jim actually wrote the current, new-owner training manual. His one-week pack and ship "boot camp," while intense, has had a 100 percent success rate. At the semi-annual owner meetings, Jim is the man to see if you have operational issues or need help with corporate procedures.

DISCUSSION QUESTIONS

1. How can you apply the motivation theories in this chapter to explain the behavior of the entrepreneurs introduced in this case?
2. When do you think these entrepreneurs will retire? Use the theories in the chapter to justify your response.
3. Is it more challenging to be an entrepreneur rather than work in a large corporation? Explain your answer.
4. What would motivate you to be an entrepreneur? Will that same motivation work in the corporate world?

Sources: Written by Dr. Michael Dutch, Greensboro College, Greensboro, North Carolina (2007); Ed Grabianowski, *How PayPal Works,* December 13, 2005, http://computer.howstuffworks.com/paypal.htm, accessed March 31, 2007; and Dennis Jacobe, "Work Is Labor of Love for Small-Business Owners," Gallup Poll Tuesday Briefing, August 23, 2005.

Experiential Exercise: *Applying Motivation Theory*

OBJECTIVES

1. To evaluate the merits of different motivation theories.
2. To emphasize the decisions that must be made by managers in motivating people.
3. To apply motivation principles.

RELATED TOPICS

The manager's need to make decisions to succeed. The difficulty of diagnosing situations.

STARTING THE EXERCISE

Set up groups of five to eight students to read the facts and the situation facing Margo Williams.

THE FACTS

This chapter discussed several popular content theories. These were among the major points:

Maslow: motivation involves satisfying needs in a hierarchical order.

Herzberg: some job factors are intrinsically satisfying and motivate individuals.

McClelland: motives are acquired from a person's culture.

Alderfer: in addition to the satisfaction–progression process proposed by Maslow, a frustration–regression process is at work.

With these four theories in mind, review the work situation currently facing Margo Williams, project engineer director in a large construction company. She's responsible for scheduling projects, meeting customers, reporting progress on projects, controlling costs, and developing subordinates. A total of 20 men and eight women report to Margo. All of them are college graduates with at least eight years of job experience. Margo has an engineering Ph.D. but only four years of project engineering experience.

Her biggest problems involve the lack of respect and response from her subordinates. Margo's supervisor has considered these problems and assumes that her moderate record of success could be improved if she could correct the situation. Margo is considering a course of action that could motivate her subordinates to show more respect and respond more favorably to her requests.

COMPLETING THE EXERCISE

1. Each discussion group should develop a motivation plan for Margo. The plan should use the content motivation principles discussed in this chapter.
2. After the group has worked together for about 30 minutes, a group leader should present the plan to the class.
3. Discuss each group's plan for the remainder of the class period.

CHAPTER SIX

Motivation: Organizational Applications

Learning Objectives

After completing Chapter 6, you should be able to

Explain
Differences between social learning theory and reinforcement theory.

Learn
How managers can get higher performance out of their employees by reinforcing their employees' sense of self-efficacy.

Describe
How expectancy, equity, and goal-setting theories are used in organizational applications to motivate employees.

Define
Intrinsic and extrinsic rewards and how these rewards influence employee motivation.

Explain
Different reward programs found in high-performance organizations.

Understand
The strengths and weaknesses of using nontraditional reward programs in organizations.

Reward or Punishment: The Saga of Stock Options

Stock options have become a form of reward for executives and employees in a growing number of organizations. They have replaced salary and bonuses as the most significant part of executive pay in more and more firms. For example, Alan Mulally, CEO of Ford Motor Company, received $666,667 in salary plus $8.68 million in stock options and stock-related awards for his efforts in 2006; this was given to Mulally after four months on the job as CEO of the automotive company. While companies' stock price fluctuations (especially the downturns) have robbed options of some of their luster, most option-granting firms are doing more of the same—offering more options at lower prices.

When he stepped down in September 2001, CEO Jack Welch (also see case at end of this chapter) was given a lavish preretirement gift of 3 million company stock options. Valid until September 2010, the securities gave Welch the right to buy GE shares at the stock's gift time price of 57⅜. Although GE's stock price is currently trading below this gift time price, the deal gave Welch the opportunity to make millions of dollars. Stock options are not just granted to GE's CEOs; there are some 36,000 employees currently participating in the company's stock option program. On GE's income statement, giving Welch and employees the nice gift (reward) for a job well done costs nothing. Is this an accounting sleight of hand? Is it motivational to GE employees?

In the real world, stock options are not free. Proxy statements use footnotes to explain options and their true costs. Options involve taking stocks and awarding them to GE employees. This means that wealth has been transferred, and the stock value of company shareholders is diluted. When Welch and other GE employees exercise their options, new shares have to be issued. This means there are more shares in the market, which in turn means the stake of existing shareholders is reduced. When Welch received the gift of stock options, he had a future claim on the company. It was the equivalent of someone putting a lien on your house.

Stock options cost organizations like Ford and General Electric something in the future. From a reward perspective they are good for Welch or anyone else receiving them, but they dilute the ownership stake of others. Those employees in a firm who do not have stock options may not view them as no-cost rewards, but as gifts that primarily go to the top executives and certain managers. A large reward for one person, even Jack Welch, may be distressing to other employees.

Sources: Adapted from http://media.ford.com/article_display.cfm?article_id=24203 (accessed on May 11, 2010); Anonymous, "A Good 4 Months for Mulally: $28 Million," *Automotive News*, April 9, 2007, p. 54; Diane Brady, "GE: When Execs Outperform the Stock," *Businessweek*, April 17, 2006, p. 74; "Jack's Booty," *The Wall Street Journal*, September 10, 2002, p. A12; Justin Fox, "The Amazing Stock Option Sleight of Hand," *Fortune*, June 25, 2001, pp. 86–92; and Geoffrey Calvin, "The Great CEO Pay Heist," *Fortune*, June 25, 2001, pp. 64–70.

In Chapter 5, we examined four *content* (need hierarchy, ERG, two-factor, and learned needs) and two *process* (expectancy and equity) theories of motivation concerning specific motivators of people and the processes people undertake to achieve preferred outcomes. While these issues are critical, it is also clear that most employees want to work and do a good job and that management's role is to provide an organizational environment that facilitates high levels of performance and effectiveness.[1] With that in mind, in this chapter we examine how the motivational process works in organizational settings. The two application-oriented process theories of motivation presented in this chapter are (1) reinforcement and (2) goal setting. However, because behavior and its influences are the focus of these theories, we must first examine the process by which workers acquire these behaviors—namely, how they are learned. Finally, the issue of rewarding employee behaviors will be illustrated and discussed.

Learning

Learning is one of the fundamental processes underlying behavior and, in turn, motivation. Most behavior within organizations is learned behavior. Perceptions, attitudes, goals, and emotional reactions are learned. Skills—for example, programming a computer or counseling a troubled employee—can be learned. The meanings and uses of language are learned.

learning
Process by which a relatively enduring change in behavior occurs as a result of practice.

Learning is the process by which a relatively enduring change in behavior occurs as a result of practice. The words *relatively enduring* signify that the change in behavior is more or less permanent. The term *practice* is intended to cover both formal training and uncontrolled experiences. The changes in behavior that characterize learning may be adaptive and promote organizational effectiveness, or they may be nonadaptive and ineffective. For example, a sales division of a large mobile phone company like AT&T or Verizon may send 100 of its entry-level salespeople to learn skills (e.g., listening, negotiation, relationship building) to enable them to sell more effectively. The goal is to have nearly all of these employees apply and practice the information they learned in training after they return to their regular sales positions. The effectiveness of the training program can be measured in terms of new sales created, value increase of each sale, customer retention rate, and so forth. A number of approaches have been proposed to explain the various ways in which this learning may occur.

Social Learning

social learning
Albert Bandura's view that behavior is a function of continuous interaction between cognitive (person), behavioral, and environmental determinants.

Albert Bandura of Stanford University illustrated how people acquire new behavior by imitating role models (learning vicariously). **Social learning** refers to the fact that we acquire much of our behavior (e.g., hitting a golf ball, giving a speech, using a computer program) by observation and imitation of others in a social context.

The Bandura-inspired view of behavior is that it is a function of both personal characteristics and environmental conditions. According to Bandura, social learning theory explains behavior in terms of a continuous interaction between cognitive, behavioral, and environmental determinants.[2] Bandura stresses the point that cognitive functioning must not be ignored in explaining, understanding, and modifying individual behavior.[3] The opening vignette on stock options emphasizes that social learning among employees may be positive or negative.[4]

Social learning theory introduces vicarious learning (modeling), symbolism, and self-control. We imitate parents, friends, heroes, teachers, coaches, mentors, and other respected leaders because we identify with them. Each of us also uses symbolism as guides for our behavior. For example, we know better than to pull the exit release handle on the airplane because of our mental picture of the consequences of a sudden loss in cabin pressure; we envision successfully achieving personal goals to motivate ourselves; and we use mental reminders to remember a customer's name. We also attempt to exercise self-control by not smoking, not drinking excessively, and not physically throwing out of the office the person who makes a personally disparaging remark about our family or work ethic.

self-efficacy
Belief that one can perform adequately in a situation. Has three dimensions: magnitude, strength, and generality.

A central part of social learning theory, which was introduced in Chapter 4, is the concept of **self-efficacy**, defined as the belief that one can perform adequately in a particular situation.[5] Self-efficacy has three dimensions: *magnitude,* the level of task difficulty a person believes she can attain; *strength,* referring to the conviction regarding magnitude as strong or weak; and *generality,* the degree to which the expectation is generalized across situations. An employee's sense of capability (Can I do the job?) influences his perception, motivation, and performance.[6] We rarely try to do a job or task when we expect to be ineffective. How would you like to try to stop Kobe Bryant (Los Angeles Lakers) from scoring in a basketball game? How would you like to write a speech as emotion-packed as Abraham Lincoln's Gettysburg Address? We often avoid people, settings, and situations when we don't feel up to the required level of performance.

Self-efficacy judgments influence our choices of tasks, situations, and companions, how much effort we'll expend, and how long we'll try. How hard and long a student pursues a course or an area of study depends more on his sense of self-efficacy than on actual ability.

Self-efficacy has been related to other motivation concepts. Edwin Locke and associates suggested that self-efficacy provides an integrating mechanism between learning theory and goal-setting approaches.[7] Feedback is important in formulating efficacy perceptions that interact with goal setting to enhance performance motivation. Self-efficacy may also be related to effort-performance relationships in expectancy motivation theory. Both goal-setting and expectancy theories will be discussed later. The impact of culture on self-efficacy is beginning to be realized.[8]

Pygmalion effect
The enhanced learning or performance that results from others having positive expectations of us.

A concept that has a potential effect on self-efficacy is the **Pygmalion effect**, which refers to enhanced learning or performance that results from others having positive expectations of us. That is, the fact that others believe us capable of high levels of performance may lead us to perform at that level. Some believe that self-efficacy may be involved in the Pygmalion effect through the persuasive influence of others holding positive expectations.[9] A leader's expectations about job performance might be viewed as an important input to the employees' perceptions of their own levels of efficacy.[10] For example, if a manager believes sincerely that her employee is ready for a promotion (even though the employee isn't so sure), then this expectation of success will often bolster the employee's self-confidence that he will in fact succeed in the new position. The strength of the persuasion would be influenced by the leader's credibility, previous relationship with the employees, influence in the organization, and so on. It also may be related to the gender of the leader, as the Pygmalion effect has been found to have more impact among male than among female leaders.[11] However defined and whatever their impact, expectations play a major role in influencing behavior.

Operant Conditioning

operant conditioning
Learning that occurs as a consequence of behavior.

operants
Behaviors that can be controlled by altering reinforcers and punishments that follow them.

In another perspective, learning often occurs as a *consequence of* behavior. This type of learning is called **operant conditioning**. The person most closely associated with operant conditioning is the late world-famous behaviorist B. F. Skinner. Behaviors that can be controlled by altering the consequences (reinforcers and punishments) that follow them are referred to as **operants**. An operant is strengthened (increased) or weakened (decreased) as a function of the events that follow it. Most workplace behaviors are operants. Examples of operant behaviors include performing job-related tasks, reading a budget report, pulling a defective part off a production line, listening to a customer's complaint about poor service, and coming to work on time. Operants are distinguished by virtue of being controlled by their consequences.

In operant conditioning, the desired response may not be present in the subject. Teaching a subordinate to prepare an accurate weekly budget report is an example of operant conditioning. The manager works with the subordinate and reinforces him as he successfully

FIGURE 6.1
An Example of Operant Conditioning

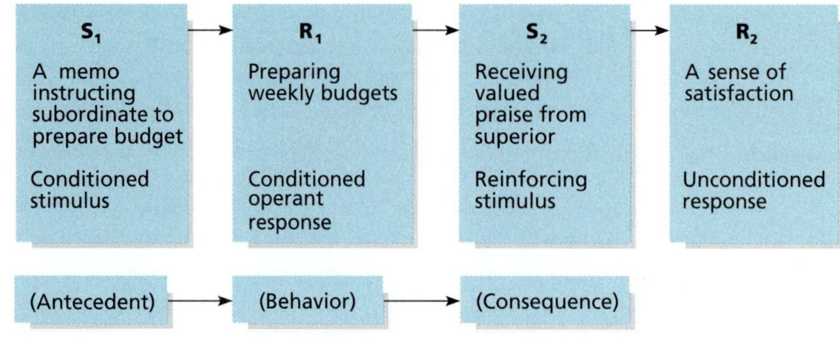

behavior modification
Approach to motivation that uses principles of operant conditioning, achieving individual learning by reinforcement. In this text, used interchangeably with term *organizational behavior modification*.

organizational behavior modification (OBM or OB Mod)
Operant approach to organizational behavior. In this text, used interchangeably with term *behavior modification*.

completes the various steps involved in preparing an accurate budget. Figure 6.1 illustrates the general form of the operant conditioning process. The relationships of $S_1 \rightarrow R_1 \rightarrow S_2 \rightarrow R_2$ are called the *contingencies of reinforcement*.[12]

This sequence is also described as the *ABC* operant mode. *A* designates the antecedent or stimulus that precedes the behavior *B*, while *C* is the consequence, the result of the behavior. Skinner believed that such a sequence will be acted out in the future if it proves to be adaptive for the individual.[13]

The term more often used to describe operant conditioning principles applied to individuals is *behavior modification* (also called *B-mod* and *behavior mod*). Thus, **behavior modification** is individual learning by reinforcement. **Organizational behavior modification** or *OB Mod* (also indicated as *OBM*) is a more general term coined to designate "the systematic reinforcement of desirable organizational behavior and the nonreinforcement or punishment of unwanted organizational behavior."[14] Thus, OB Mod is an operant approach to organizational behavior. *Organizational* has been added to indicate that the operant approach is being used in work settings. In this discussion, the terms *behavior modification* and *organizational behavior modification* are used interchangeably.

Principles of Operant Conditioning

positive reinforcement
Action that increases the likelihood of a particular behavior.

Several principles of operant conditioning can aid managers attempting to influence behavior. *Reinforcement* is an extremely important principle of learning. In a general sense, motivation is an internal cause of behavior, while reinforcement is an external cause. **Positive reinforcement** occurs when a positively valued consequence follows a response to a stimulus. Thus, positive reinforcement is anything that both increases the strength of response and induces repetitions of the behavior that preceded the reinforcement.[15] These positive reinforcers could include items such as raises, bonuses, or promotions or less tangible things such as praise or encouragement. Without reinforcement, no measurable modification of behavior is likely to take place.

Managers often use *positive reinforcers* to modify behavior. In some cases, reinforcers work as predicted; for example, positive reinforcement has been shown to be very effective in reducing accidents and producing safe behaviors at the workplace.[16] However, in other cases, they don't modify behavior in the desired direction because of competing reinforcement contingencies. When the receipt of reinforcers isn't made contingent or dependent on the behavior desired by the manager, desired behaviors don't occur. Also, giving reinforcers long after the occurrence of the desired behaviors decreases the probability of the recurrence of the behavior because the connection between the two is more difficult to make.

Increasingly, organizations are tying rewards and systems of positive reinforcement to corporate values.[17] For example, Conoco made environmental criteria a component of the incentive system. Likewise, Chemical Bank has set up programs to positively reinforce employee actions that lead to better customer service. Mary Kay Cosmetics, as a way to reinforce the importance of sales, lavishes its top saleswomen with rewards, including the famous "pink Cadillac."[18]

Johnson & Johnson rewards its employees by behaving in a manner that reflects the company's credo. The credo (i.e., the firm's moral compass) was written by founding family member Robert Wood Johnson in 1943 and puts the needs of Johnson & Johnson's patients, doctors, and nurses first.[19] Monetary rewards aren't the only type of positive reinforcers shown to be effective. Nonfinancial rewards, such as recognition programs, flexible hours, leaves of absence, time off, and merchandise incentives, can also be used.[20] Peer pressure, involvement, and pride have been shown to be as influential as money in producing desirable actions.[21] The dual powers of financial reinforcement and personal recognition are potent motivational forces.

negative reinforcement
Negative reinforcement strengthens a behavior because the behavior removes some painful or unpleasant stimulus.

Negative reinforcement refers to an increase in the frequency of a behavior following removal of something that is displeasing (e.g., an undesired situation) immediately after the response. An event is a *negative reinforcer* only if its removal after a response increases the performance of that response. A familiar example of negative reinforcement during the summer in Phoenix and Houston is turning on the car air conditioner on a stiflingly hot day. Turning on the air conditioner (the behavior) usually minimizes or terminates an aversive condition, namely being hot (negative reinforcer). This increases the probability of turning on the air conditioning when the car is hot. Similarly, exerting a high degree of effort to complete a job may be negatively reinforced by not having to listen to a nagging boss. By working hard, the employee can keep the nagging boss away. The unpleasant boss is removed because the employee works hard.

punishment
Undesirable consequence that results in the suppression (decrease in frequency) of the behavior that brought it about.

Punishment is an undesirable consequence of a particular behavior.[22] A professor who takes off 10 points for each day a paper is late is using punishment. A mechanic who doesn't hand in his report and is suspended for one day with a loss of pay is being punished. Punishment, when applied, is sending the message to not do something. Some people believe that punishment is the opposite of reward and is just as effective in changing behavior. Others consider punishment a poor approach to learning for several reasons:

1. The results of punishment aren't as predictable as those of reward.
2. The effects of punishment are less permanent than those of reward.
3. Punishment is frequently accompanied by negative attitudes toward the administrator of the punishment, as well as toward the activity that led to the punishment.

Despite the potential costs of using punishment, it has been and will continue to be used as a method of altering behavior. For example, punishing a worker who deliberately treats a customer rudely may be an economically necessary way of altering behavior. (However, there might be ways of dealing with the problem other than punishment.) The point is that punishment and its use depend on the situation and on the manager's style of altering behavior. Punishment is discussed in more detail in the next chapter.

extinction
Decline in response rate because of nonreinforcement.

Extinction reduces the frequency of behavior because positive reinforcement is being withheld. When positive reinforcement for a learned response is withheld, individuals continue to practice that behavior for some period of time. If this nonreinforcement continues, the behavior decreases and eventually disappears. The decline in the response rate because of nonreinforcement is defined as **extinction**. For example, a member of a work team may have gotten into the habit of telling jokes at team meetings because people laughed at them (positive reinforcement). If the team began to feel that the jokes were a time waster and made an effort not to laugh, over time the team member's joke telling is likely to diminish. While extinction is a major form of behavior modification, it is less likely than the other approaches to be used in organizational settings because it is more passive (i.e., withholding of reinforcement) than the active styles preferred in the workplace.

An important base for these four important principles is Thorndike's classic *law of effect:*

> Of several responses to the same situation, those that are accompanied or closely followed by satisfaction (reinforcement) . . . will be more likely to recur; those which are accompanied or closely followed by discomfort (punishment) . . . will be less likely to occur.[23]

The idea that the consequences of behavior—reward or punishment—are critical in determining future behavior remains an important foundation for the use of operant conditioning in organizational settings.

Recall that positive reinforcement occurs when a positively valued consequence (e.g., a promotion) follows a response to a stimulus. Negative reinforcement occurs when a behavior causes an undesirable factor to be taken away (e.g., the nagging boss). Punishment occurs when an undesired behavior is followed by a negative consequence (e.g., loss of pay). In extinction, the behavior is weakened by the withdrawal of something positive.

Behavior Modification: A Managerial Perspective

Behavior modification is based on the assumption that behavior is more important than its "psychological causes," such as the needs, motives, and values held by individuals.[24] Thus, a behaviorist such as B. F. Skinner focuses on specific behaviors and not on such intangibles as esteem needs or personality structure. For example, a behaviorist, told that an employee isn't performing well, would probably ask, "What specific behaviors led to this observation?" Specific and distinguishable behaviors are the most important bases in developing any behavior modification plan to correct a performance problem.

In addition to the attention devoted to these behaviors, there's an emphasis on the consequences of behavior. For example, suppose that all new management trainees are given a two-day training program on preparing budget reports. Shortly after the training sessions, managers notice that most of the reports are still not being prepared correctly. One explanation may be that the training program was ineffective. However, behaviorists might approach the problem from a different direction. First, they could determine whether the trainees understand the importance of correct reports. They might then find out which trainees are turning in correct reports and what consequences, if any, are being received by these trainees. It could be that turning in correct reports results in nothing, that there are no observable consequences. In the same manner, submitting an incorrect report may also result in no consequences, positive or negative. The behaviorists' findings might result in developing a program of positive and negative consequences (e.g., recognition, praise, a meeting with the boss to go over mistakes). Behaviorists believe people tend to repeat behaviors that lead to positive consequences. This principle could serve as a cornerstone in improving the report accuracy of trainees.

The proposed application of behavior modification in organizations follows a five-step problem-solving process similar to that in Figure 6.2.[25]

FIGURE 6.2 Applied Behavior Modification: A Manager's Step-by-Step Procedure

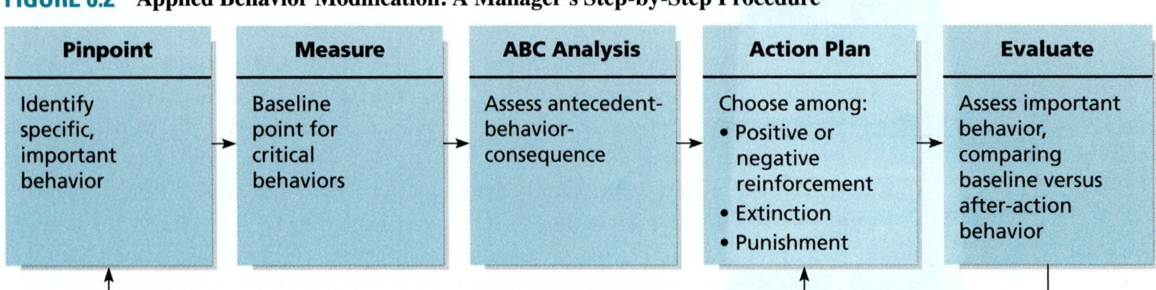

TABLE 6.1
Performance Analysis Questions

Source: Adapted from Thomas K. Connellan, *How to Improve Human Performance: Behaviorism in Business and Industry* (New York: Harper & Row, 1978), p. 51.

Explore Antecedents

Does the employee know what is expected?
Are the standards clear?
Have they been communicated?
Are they realistic?

Identify Behaviors

Can the behavior be performed?
Could the employee do it if his or her life depended on it?
Does something prevent its occurrence?

Assess Consequences

Are the consequences weighted in favor of performance?
Are improvements being reinforced?
Do we note improvement even though the improvement may still leave the employee below the company standards?
Is reinforcement specific?

1. Managers must identify and define the important behavior. A behavior is pinpointed when it can be accurately observed and reliably recorded. To be pinpointed as an important behavior, there must be positive answers to these questions: (*a*) Can it be seen? (*b*) Can it be measured?

2. Managers must measure or count the occurrences of the pinpointed behavior. This count provides managers with a clear perspective on the strength of the behavior under the present, or before-change, situation. The count serves as the means of evaluating any later changes in behavior. Managers can graph these data to determine whether the behavior is increasing, decreasing, or remaining the same.[26]

ABC analysis
Analysis of antecedents, behavior, and consequences when investigating work- or job-related issues.

3. Managers conduct an analysis of the ABCs of the behavior,[27] also called *functionally analyzing the behavior*.[28] In **ABC analysis**, referred to earlier, the **A** designates analyzing the antecedents of **B,** the pinpointed critical behaviors; and the **C** indicates the associated consequence. Specific analyses of the ABCs attempt to determine where the problems lie. Thomas Connellan has developed a set of performance analysis questions to get at the problem source (Table 6.1).[29] The ABC analysis permits managers to consider performance analysis questions important in formulating any specific program. In analyzing absenteeism, for example, managers using a question format and the type of framework displayed in Table 6.2 are systematically viewing the problem of absenteeism in terms of antecedents, behaviors, and consequences.

TABLE 6.2
Using the ABC Analysis on an Absenteeism Problem

Source: Adapted from Fred Luthans and Mark Martinko, "An Orgaizational Behavior Modification Analysis of Absenteeism," *Human Resource Management*, Fall 1976.

A. Antecedent(s)	B. Behavior(s)	C. Consequence(s)
Family problems (spouse; children)	Staying home	Public reprimand
Personal health/illness	Shopping	Private reprimand
Jury duty	Oversleeping	Written record and reprimand
No transportation	Getting up late	Reduction in pay
Company policies	Attending sporting	Suspension
Group norm	Working at home	Firing
Friends visiting	Visiting others	Social isolation from group
Injured on way to work	Serving on jury	
Hangover	In emergency room at hospital	
No child care facilities	At doctor's office	
Lack of proper tools or clothing		

4. The first three steps in an applied behavior modification program set the stage for the actual actions by the manager. The goal of operant conditioning is to strengthen desirable and observable critical performance behaviors and to weaken undesirable behaviors. The fourth step involves the strategies for accomplishing these goals, which are discussed earlier in this section. They are positive reinforcers, negative reinforcers, punishment, and extinction. Managers prefer to use positive reinforcement in most applied behavior modification programs. But identifying positive reinforcers isn't always easy. The most obvious approach for managers to take is to ask subordinates what rewards they prefer. Another identification method is to use attitude surveys asking job reward preferences questions. Note also that punishment and extinction by themselves often do not give guidance to employees as to how they can improve their performance.

5. The fifth step involves evaluation. A major weakness in many applied motivational programs is that formal evaluations aren't conducted. Another weakness is the fact that evaluations tend to place too much focus on the negative aspects of employees' performance.[30] The evaluation of an applied program permits the manager to trace and review changes in behavior before and after the implementation of an action program. Evaluation permits managers to measure performance on an ongoing basis.[31] Furthermore, evaluation can provide feedback to managers on the behaviors exhibited. This feedback enables managers to make necessary and timely corrections in the program.

Employees in the next OB at Work feature emphasize how important it is to receive feedback.

Research on Reinforcement Theory

The sample list of organizational behavior modification users includes Weight Watchers, Michigan Bell Telephone, Ford Motor Co., American Can Company, United States Postal Service, Warner-Lambert Company, Chase Manhattan Bank, Procter & Gamble, and Standard Oil. A survey of empirical research on organizational behavior modification (OBM) examined research involving quantity of performance, quality of performance, absenteeism, employee safety, employee energy conservation and theft, and customer service.[32] The researchers found generally strong evidence that OBM is making and can make a positive contribution to organizational behavior. Absenteeism rates, quality of production, reduction in workplace violence, and employee safety behaviors appear to improve more often than not when organizations use OBM.

Criticisms of Behavior Modification

Critics have attacked behavior modification on a number of grounds. A frequent concern with the use of reinforcers is that there's no "real" change in behavior: the person is just being "bribed" to perform. Bribery refers to the illicit use of rewards to corrupt someone's conduct. In reinforcement, however, outcomes are typically delivered for behaviors designed to benefit the person and the organization. Thus, this criticism, although logical, really doesn't apply to the reinforcers usually used in organizations.

Another perspective is offered by Locke, who believes that to view reinforcements as modifying responses automatically, independent of a person's beliefs, values, or mental processes, is simply a wrong way to view human behavior. He says that this theory is simple and appealing but that the facts don't support it. He claims that people can learn by seeing others get reinforcement and by imitating those who are reinforced (see social learning, discussed earlier). There's also self-reinforcement, which operant conditioning theorists ignore.[33]

Another criticism focuses on the point that individuals can become too dependent on extrinsic reinforcers (e.g., pay). Thus, behavior may become dependent on the reinforcer and may never be performed without the promise of the reinforcer. For example, if a firm's salespeople

OB AT WORK Feedback Is Motivational

Employees are so hungry for guidance in today's pressure-filled workplace that many would prefer ongoing input from the manager to a hike in pay.

Sure, cash bonuses and raises are welcome rewards. But they're rarely enough. Scant feedback can lead to turnover, a concern that has employers increasing both the amount and quality of job critiques.

"I like to know there's something to the workplace that's more than just a paycheck," says Bob, 29, an investment advisor in Wauwatosa, Wisconsin. "I'd rather be someplace I enjoy being, and feedback just goes along with it."

A survey for American Express looked at what workers most want from employers. It found the number one desire, at 46 percent, was personal feedback. That compares with the 32 percent who said they most wanted financial rewards.

Some trends behind the demand:

- **Worker autonomy.** Today's employees have more decision-making authority, but the increased responsibility also means many want to know where they stand.

  "You get uncomfortable day to day not knowing how you're doing," says Randolph, 58, a computer operations manager in Providence, Rhode Island. "The feeling that someone cares far outweighs a money value."
- **Decreasing loyalty.** In an age of job-hopping and mass layoffs, employees are looking for ways to document their worth to future employers. Companies that provide employees with opportunities for promotions and good performance reviews can motivate (and retain) employees more than with just high pay.
- **Fewer guarantees.** Promotions and pay raises no longer are granted to workers solely based on years of service. Performance has become the catalyst for getting ahead.

"As employees see this, they naturally want to know how they're doing," says a management consultant in Princeton, New Jersey.

The feedback can have an effect on productivity and boost morale. A survey by Menlo Park, California–based staffing service OfficeTeam found that 66 percent of respondents believe performance review sessions have a favorable impact on job motivation.

"There is a sense that employees aren't getting enough mentoring as organizations get flatter," says Peter Cappelli, author of *The New Deal at Work,* on managing a mobile workforce. "People are hungry for it."

Aware of the need, employers are turning to frequent job reviews, daily chats, and performance appraisals that include input from co-workers, customers, and subordinates.

Managers may be ranked on nontraditional goals such as fostering work–family balance and encouraging teamwork.

But getting stuck with bad managers can leave some wary of any feedback at all. Others argue that talk is cheap.

"I've been around long enough to know that you must put your money where your mouth is," says Lisa, 40, a factory worker in Island Pond, Vermont. "How many times have people said meaningless things? I want to take what somebody tells me to the bank."

That's not to say guidance doesn't last.

More than 20 years ago, Walter was a young chemical engineer toiling in a laboratory, when his boss walked in. "You're doing a wonderful job," he remembers the supervisor saying, "I'm so glad you're part of the department."

It was just a few words, but the input was such a valuable motivator that Walker, now 61 and retired, still talks of the lesson he learned: It takes more than cash to buy loyalty.

"Many other bosses have just taken my contributions for granted and felt that their response was more money," says Walter. "The real motivator was genuinely realizing my successes and telling me so."

Sources: Karen Auby, "A Boomer's Guide to Communicating With Gen X and Gen Y," *Businessweek,* August 14, 2008, pp. 63–64; Paul Falcone, "Preserving Restless Top Performers," *HRMagazine* 51, no. 3 (March 2006), pp. 117–22; Annette Simmons, "When Performance Reviews Fail," *Training and Development 57,* no. 9 (September 2003): pp. 47–51; Stephanie Armour, "Cash or Critiques: Which Is Best?" *USA Today,* December 16, 1998, p. 6B; and Anne Faircloth, "How to Recover from a Firing," *Fortune,* December 7, 1998, pp. 239–40.

work hard only when commissions are large, what will happen to productivity during slow periods when the company can't afford to pay large commissions? A last criticism, especially in the case of positive reinforcement, is that its utilization may be more perceived than actual.[34]

Surveys on interpersonal relations find that while more than 80 percent of supervisors claim they frequently use forms of positive reinforcement (such as praise, recognition, and rewards), less than 20 percent of employees report that their supervisors express forms of appreciation more than occasionally. This is especially important given that some younger Gen Y employees (born after 1978) seek higher levels of feedback at work than do Gen X (born between 1965 and 1978) and Baby Boomer (born between 1946 and 1964) employees.[35] In light of these concerns, managers should remember three important principles when expressing appreciation and reinforcing good behavior:

1. Describe the desired behavior in specific terms, avoiding sweeping generalizations.
2. Explain why the behavior was helpful to the organization.
3. Regardless of the type of positive reinforcement given, it should always be accompanied by a personal expression of thanks.

When considering these criticisms, we must keep in mind that the relevance and impact of any management approach may be greatly affected by the national culture where that approach is used. An excellent example of this is the study by Welsh, Luthans, and Sommer, in which they had managers in the largest textile plant in Russia use three different motivational styles toward their employees.[36] They found that while extrinsic rewards and behavioral management produced positive results, a strategy involving participation on the part of the workers (an approach endorsed and desired in the United States) not only did not increase performance but may have actually decreased production. Although more work is needed in this area, the significance of cultural and related factors on the appropriateness of managerial activities has to be carefully evaluated.

Behavioral Self-Management

Quitting smoking, dieting, experiencing personal growth and development, and sticking with an exercise regimen each involve the notion of self-control. Regulating one's own motivation has received some attention in the organizational literature.[37] The concepts of self-motivation have evolved primarily from the social learning theory literature and related work in self-control. In the organization literature, this process has been referred to as **behavioral self-management (BSM)**.

behavioral self-management (BSM)
Process whereby a person faces immediate response alternatives involving different consequences; and selects or modifies behavior by managing cognitive processes, causes, or consequences.

Self-management, which is often called self-control, is defined as follows: "A person displays self-control when, in the relative absence of immediate external constraints, he engages in behavior whose previous probability has been less than that of alternatively available behaviors."[38]

In essence, this suggests that there are times when individuals will choose behaviors that they have not chosen consistently in the past, and this selection may be based on the expectation of positive outcomes in the future from this course of action. For example, a college student may decide that it's time to "buckle down" and begin applying himself to his courses with the hope that he can earn higher grades (and increase his GPA). Several features of self-management need to be noted. Self-management is a process whereby a person is faced with immediate response alternatives (e.g., to work moderately hard or to work very hard to complete the job) involving different consequences. Self-management behavior may include personal performance goals, self-instructions on how to achieve goals, self-administered consequences, a plan to behave in a particular manner, or a strategy for personally developing a set of skills.

In BSM, a person is assumed to have some control over her behavior, cognitive processes, and contingent consequences. Indeed, this control is the basis for the notion of empowerment, a broad movement toward providing workers and teams with greater input into their jobs.[39] At the workplace or outside of it, everyone practices BSM to some degree,[40] and it appears to have an important impact on performance within various groups such as managers of joint ventures.[41] Usually we set certain behavior standards and reward or punish ourselves according to personal judgments we make about how our behavior relates to these standards. Similar to the example above, when a student works hard all semester in a challenging course in college and ends up earning an A, he's likely to feel that hard work pays off (i.e., disciplined study behavior leads to a high grade).

FIGURE 6.3
Kanfer's Self-Regulation Methods

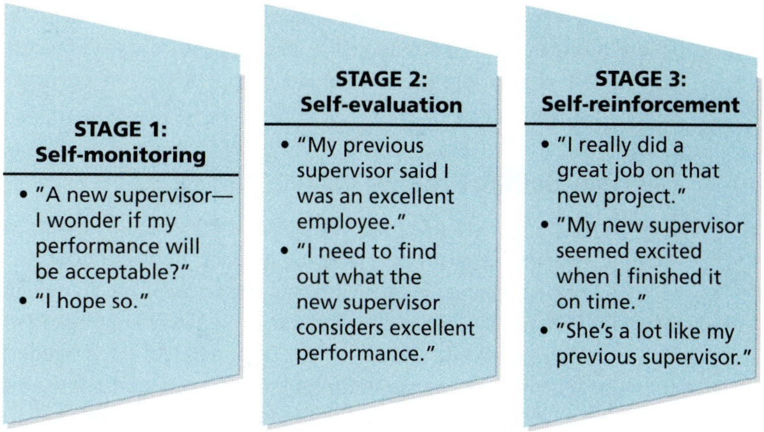

STAGE 1: Self-monitoring	STAGE 2: Self-evaluation	STAGE 3: Self-reinforcement
• "A new supervisor—I wonder if my performance will be acceptable?" • "I hope so."	• "My previous supervisor said I was an excellent employee." • "I need to find out what the new supervisor considers excellent performance."	• "I really did a great job on that new project." • "My new supervisor seemed excited when I finished it on time." • "She's a lot like my previous supervisor."

A Self-Regulation Model

Because effective self-management appears to offer potential benefits to employees and organizations, a general framework could prove useful. Frederick Kanfer has proposed a three-stage model that has managerial application value. Figure 6.3 shows the Kanfer model of self-regulation as applied to a work situation.

According to the model, when a nonroutine event (e.g., new boss, unexpected Web site crash) disrupts the normal work pattern, a person begins to practice self-examination (what Kanfer designates as self-regulation).

Being assigned to a new supervisor doesn't happen every day, so it would be considered a nonroutine occurrence. The event would initiate such thoughts as: What does the new supervisor expect from me? How am I currently performing? How will I need to perform to project a good impression on the new supervisor? This is stage 1, self-monitoring. Self-evaluation (stage 2) would involve comparing the previous supervisor with the new one and deciding whether previous performance will be sufficient to impress the new supervisor. In stage 3, self-reinforcement, the person would exercise his own reinforcement for performing at an acceptable level. Kanfer proposes that self-regulation occurs quickly and without much awareness by a person.[42]

goal setting
The process of establishing goals. In many cases, it involves superior and subordinate working together to set subordinate's goals for specified period.

BSM may appear to be simply another variant of organizational behavior modification. However, there's a distinct difference in terms of the importance of cognitive processes in BSM, as it combines the principles of learning with an emphasis on human interactions in a social setting. In contrast to OBM, which focuses specifically on antecedents, behavior, and consequences, the behavioral self-management approach places more stress on the uniquely human cognitive processes involved in acquiring and maintaining patterns of behavior without the input of other people.

Goal-Setting Theory

conscious goals
Main goals that a person is striving for and is aware of when directing behavior.

Since 1968, when Edwin Locke presented what's now considered his classic paper,[43] there has been considerable and growing interest in applying goal setting to organizational problems and issues. Locke proposed that **goal setting** was a cognitive process of some practical utility. His view was that an individual's **conscious goals** and intentions are the primary determinants of behavior. That is, "one of the commonly observed characteristics of intentional behavior is that it tends to keep going until it reaches completion."[44] Once a person starts something (e.g., a job, a new project), she pushes on until a goal is achieved. Intent plays a prominent role in goal-setting theory.[45] Also, the theory places specific emphasis on the importance of conscious goals in explaining motivated behavior. Locke has used the notion of intentions and conscious goals to propose and provide research support for the thesis that harder conscious goals result in higher levels of performance if these goals are accepted by the individual.

The Goal-Setting Process

goal
Specific target that an individual is trying to achieve; the target (object) of an action.

A **goal** is the object of an action; it's what a person attempts to accomplish. For example, landing five new customers, training twenty new employees, cutting direct costs by $10,000, or decreasing absenteeism in a department by 12 percent is a goal. Many examples could be given of the successful use of goal-setting techniques in achieving important organizational outcomes, such as safety improvement.[46] Frederick W. Taylor has had a direct influence on the current thinking about goals and goal-setting practices.

Locke stated that Taylor used assigned goals as one of his key techniques of scientific management. Each employee was assigned a challenging but attainable goal based on the results of time and motion study. The individual's methods for achieving the assigned goal (e.g., the tools used, the work procedures followed, the pacing needed to do the job) were spelled out in detail.[47]

Thus, Locke pointed out the significant influence of Taylor in his formulation of goal setting. Locke also carefully described the attributes of the mental (cognitive) processes of goal setting. The attributes he highlighted are goal specificity, goal difficulty, and goal intensity.

goal specificity
Degree of quantitative precision of goal.

goal difficulty
Degree of proficiency or level of goal performance being sought.

goal intensity
The process of setting a goal or determining how to reach it.

goal commitment
Amount of effort actually used to achieve goal.

Goal specificity is the degree of quantitative precision (clarity) of the goal. **Goal difficulty** is the degree of proficiency or the level of performance sought. **Goal intensity** pertains to the process of setting the goal or of determining how to reach it.[48] To date, goal intensity hasn't been widely studied, although a related concept, **goal commitment**, has been considered in some studies. Goal commitment is the amount of effort used to achieve a goal.

Figure 6.4 portrays applied goal setting from a managerial perspective, showing the sequence of events for such a goal-setting program. The key steps in goal setting are (1) *diagnosing* whether the people, the organization, and the technology are suited for goal setting; (2) *preparing* employees via increased interpersonal interaction, communication, training, and action plans for goal setting; (3) *emphasizing* the attributes of goals that should be understood by a manager and subordinates; (4) *conducting* intermediate reviews to make necessary adjustments in established goals; and (5) *performing* a final review to check the goals set, modified, and accomplished. Each step needs to be carefully planned and implemented if goal setting is to be an effective motivational technique. In too many applications of goal setting, steps outlined in or issues suggested by Figure 6.4 are ignored.

Goal-Setting Research

Locke's 1968 paper contributed to a considerable increase in laboratory and field research on goal setting. Another force behind the increase in interest and research was the demand of managers for practical and specific techniques that they could apply in their organizations. Goal setting offered such a technique for some managers.[49] The degree of support for goal setting as a viable motivational technique is captured best by the authors of a review of the effects of goal setting on task performance. They stated,

> If there is ever to be a viable candidate from the organizational sciences for elevation to the lofty status of a scientific law of nature, then the relationships between goal difficulty, specificity, commitment, and task performance are most worthy of serious consideration.[50]

Research has shown that specific goals lead to higher output than do vague goals such as "Do your best."[51] Field experiments using clerical workers, maintenance technicians, marketing personnel, truckers, engineers, typists, and manufacturing employees have

FIGURE 6.4 Goal Setting as Applied in Organizations

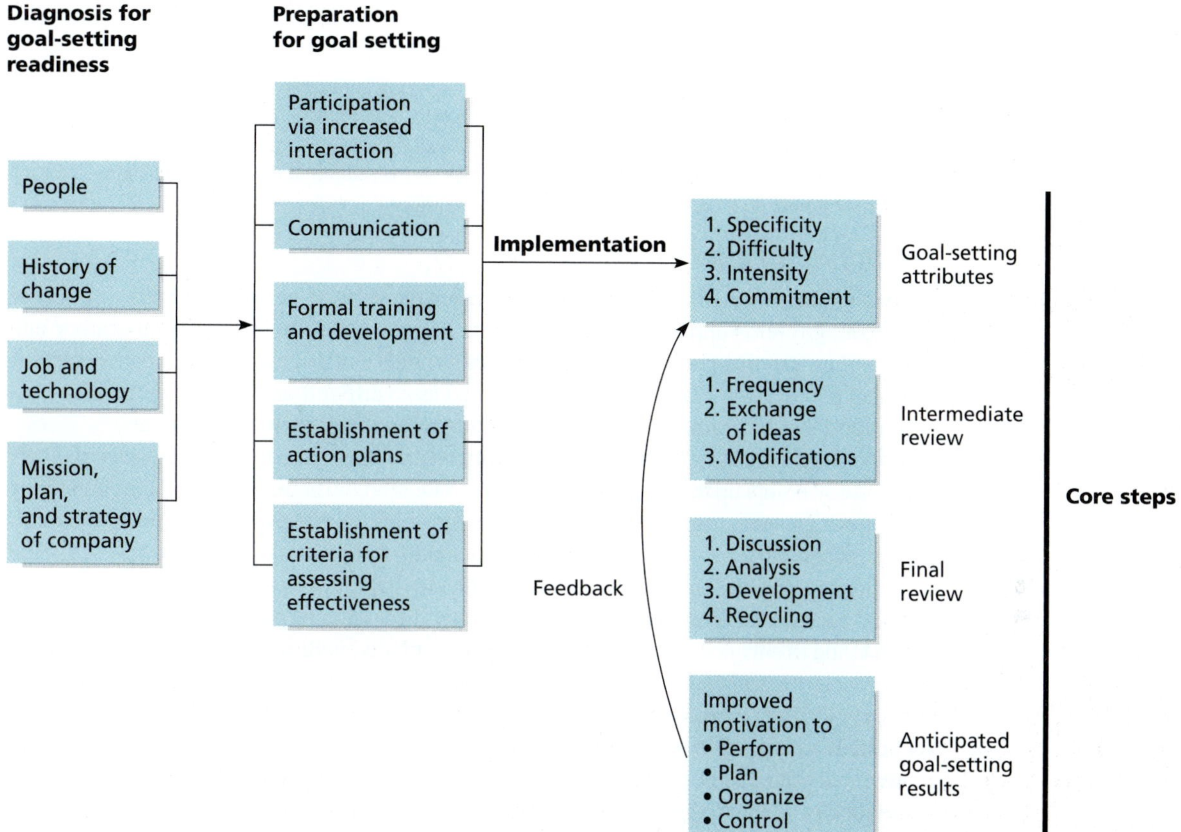

compared specific versus do-your-best goal-setting conditions.[52] The vast majority of these studies support, partly or in total, the hypothesis that specific goals lead to better performance than do vague goals. In fact, in 99 out of 100 studies reviewed by Locke and his associates, specific goals produced better results.[53]

One study in particular highlights the practical significance of setting specific goals.[54] As part of a logging operation, truck drivers had to load logs and drive them to a mill for processing. Analysis of each trucker's performance showed that the truckers often weren't filling their trucks to the maximum allowable weight. For the three months in which underloading was being studied, trucks were seldom loaded in excess of 58 to 63 percent of capacity.

Researchers believed that underloading resulted from management's practice of simply instructing the truckers to do their best in loading the trucks. Researchers concluded that setting a specific goal could be the operational impetus needed to improve the situation. They assigned a specific goal of 94 percent of capacity to the drivers. No driver, however, was disciplined for failing to reach the assigned goal. No monetary rewards or fringe benefits other than praise from the supervisor were given for improvements in performance. No specific training or instruction was given to the managers or drivers.

Within the first month after the goal was assigned, performance increased to 80 percent of the truck's limit. After the second month, however, performance decreased to 70 percent. Interviews with drivers indicated that they were testing management's promise not to take disciplinary action if goals weren't met. After the third month, performance exceeded 90 percent of capacity. This performance was being maintained seven years after the original research.

The results of this field experiment are impressive. They suggest that setting specific goals can be a powerful force. The value of goal setting is reflected in a statement of the researchers:

> The setting of a goal that is both specific and challenging leads to an increase in performance because it makes it clearer to the individual what he is supposed to do. This in turn may provide the worker with a sense of achievement, recognition, and commitment, in that he can compare how well he is doing now versus how well he has done in the past and, in some instances, how well he is doing in comparison to others.[55]

The Difficulty Factor

Generally, the more difficult the goal, the higher the level of performance. But a point of diminishing returns appears to be a real issue in goal difficulty. Although laboratory and field studies find that people with high (difficult) goals consistently perform better, there is a critical point.[56] If and when a goal is perceived as so difficult or threatening that it's virtually impossible to attain, the result is often frustration rather than achievement.

For example, an assessment of the difficulty level of the United Way's fund-raising goals in one study points up the issue of frustration.[57] The more difficult the goal, the more money was raised. This was true, however, only when the goals were seen as attainable by the fund-raisers. When the goals were viewed as unreachable, fund-raisers' morale suffered. On the other hand, goals must be of a realistic difficulty so that they are not set too low.[58]

Goal acceptance is extremely important to any discussion of goal setting's effectiveness. One method to enhance goal acceptance is to permit individuals to participate in goal setting. Researchers suggest that when an individual faces a difficult goal, participative goal setting enhances goal acceptance more than assigned goal setting. In a two-part study, researchers found that participative and representative goal setting (in which group-elected members represented others in negotiating goals) significantly increased individual goal acceptance; consequently, individual goal acceptance significantly contributed to performance.[59]

Locke has contrasted goal setting with the expectancy and need-for-achievement explanations of motivation.[60] Figure 6.5 highlights differences in the explanations of the goal difficulty–performance relationship proposed by these three theories.

Expectancy theory predicts that increased performance will result from easier goals, since the probability of success (and also the probability of being rewarded) increases. The need-for-achievement prediction is that difficult goals improve performance up to a point but that when goals are too difficult, performance suffers.

One explanation of the goal difficulty–performance relationship is presented as graph III in Figure 6.5. Locke predicts that a person's performance (A) will increase as goal difficulty increases (assuming that the person is committed and has the ability to perform), until a ceiling of performance (B) is reached. Individuals who lack commitment to difficult goals have decreasing or poor performance (C).

Adding the Participation Factor

In one of the more interesting studies of goal setting, a jointly designed series of experiments was conducted to study the effect of participation on goal commitment and performance.[61]

Locke served as a third-party mediator of two views held by Latham and Erez. Latham proposed that when goal difficulty is held constant, there are virtually no differences in goal commitment or performance, regardless of whether the goal was assigned or set participatively. Erez believed that participation in goal setting is crucial to goal commitment; that is, if a person doesn't participate, there's little commitment to accomplish the goal.

A series of four experiments by researchers at the University of Maryland and the University of Washington tested the two viewpoints of goal setting. The results indicated that there was no effect of value for participation on goal commitment or performance in

FIGURE 6.5 **The Goal Difficulty–Performance Relationship: Three Motivation Views**

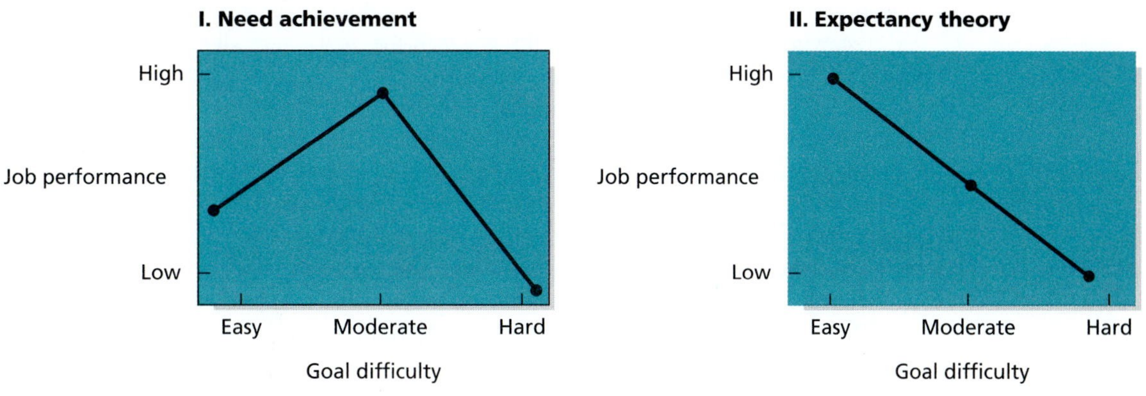

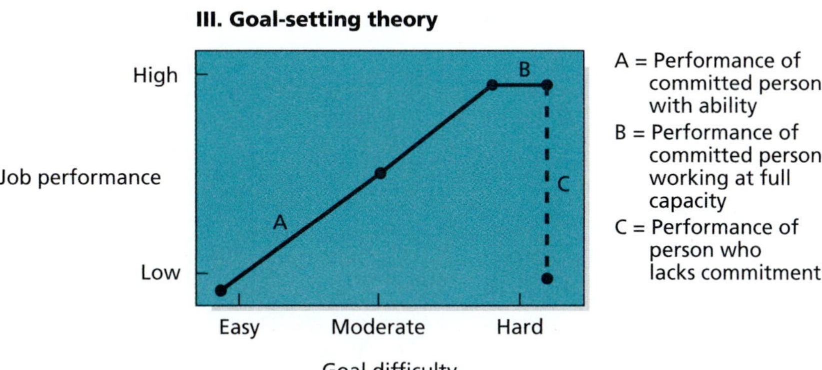

any of the four experiments. The study is commendable for its completeness, the participation of researchers who disagreed with each other's previous findings, and the use of a third-party mediator. Each of these features contributes to improved public confidence in organizational research. But despite Locke's comments that the results of laboratory studies generalize well to the field, the laboratory setting is a weakness of the study.[62] Organizational practitioners would pay more attention to the results of such an innovative study if employees and work settings were used.

Can these results be confirmed in organizations in the United States and around the world? As Eastern European countries attempt to improve the performance of their economies and enterprises, will goal setting be effective? The economies of Hungary, Poland, and Russia may not be prepared for participative goal setting. The past cultures of these and other countries may significantly moderate the effects, if any, of goal-setting programs. After years of having decisions handed down from top-level administrators and bureaucrats, when they were told what to do, many individuals aren't used to participating in goal setting or prepared to do so.

Individual Differences

Scattered throughout the goal-setting literature are studies that examine the effects of individual differences on goal setting. Most of these studies have dealt with the effects of education, race, and job tenure on the goal-setting process. A study involving electronics technicians found that goal difficulty (challenge) was significantly related to performance only for those technicians with 12 or more years of education. For technicians with less education, goal clarity (i.e., having a clear understanding of the goal) and goal feedback (i.e., receiving feedback on how results matched the goal) were significantly related to performance.[63]

In a field experiment, loggers working under assigned, participative, and do-your-best conditions were compared. Researchers found that participative goal setting affected the performance of the less educated loggers but not of the more educated loggers.[64]

One study examined three explanations of why participation in goal setting may increase job performance: the social factor of group discussion, the motivational factor of being involved in the goal-setting process, and the cognitive factor of information sharing.[65] Results of this study of white-collar employees indicated that the social and motivational factors increased performance quantity, learning the task, goal acceptance, group commitment, and satisfaction.

Another recent study examined conflict as a goal-setting variable. Both a laboratory experiment and a field study of college professors suggested that conflicting goals can lead to decreases in performance.[66] These findings were not related to how committed subjects were to the goal, which goals were most important, or the strategies used to approach the task. This research points out the need to pay attention to the total situation experienced by employees who are faced with many (and sometimes contradictory) goals. It also suggests that consideration should be given to the kinds of goals that employees set for themselves.

Criticisms of Goal Setting

It is important to recognize that there are arguments against using goal setting or becoming too enthusiastic about it.[67] For example, researchers have found that when goals are very difficult and compensation or other organizational rewards are tied to goal attainment, then some employees may engage in unethical behaviors to accomplish them.[68] In the early 1990s, Sears Automotive service advisors in California were accused of engaging in unethical practices with customers as a way to meet internal goals and receive incentive compensation.[69] Some managers and researchers have leveled other criticisms against goal setting, including:

Goal setting is rather complex and difficult to sustain.

Goal setting works well for simple jobs (clerks, typists, loggers, and technicians), but not for complex jobs. Goal setting with jobs in which goals aren't easily measured (teaching, nursing, engineering, accounting) has posed some problems.

Goal setting encourages game playing. Setting low goals to look good later is one game played by subordinates who don't want to be caught short. Managers play the game of setting an initial goal that's generally not achievable and then finding out how subordinates react.

Goal setting is used as another check on employees. It's a control device to monitor performance.

Goal accomplishment can become an obsession. In some situations, goal setters have become so obsessed with achieving their goals that they neglect other important areas of their jobs.

Under the right conditions, goal setting can be a powerful technique for motivating employees. When used correctly, carefully monitored, and actively supported by managers, it can improve performance. (Goal difficulty and goal acceptance are two attributes that management must consider.) The clear implication for managers is that getting employees to set and strive to attain specific, relatively hard goals can generate a strong motivational force.

Reviewing Motivation

Chapters 5 and 6 to this point have portrayed a number of popular, empirically tested, and practical theories of motivation. That the theories are typically pitted against one another in the literature is unfortunate, since each theory can help managers better understand workplace motivation. Each theory attempts to organize, in a meaningful manner, major variables associated with explaining motivation in work settings.

The *content* theories concentrate on individuals, placing primary emphasis on people's characteristics. Each of the *process* theories has a specific orientation. Reinforcement theory focuses on the work environment, virtually ignoring the notion of individual needs and attitudes. Expectancy theory emphasizes individual, job, and environmental variables; it recognizes differences in needs, perceptions, and beliefs. Equity theory primarily addresses the relationship between attitudes toward inputs and outcomes and toward reward practices. Goal-setting theory emphasizes the cognitive processes and the role of intentional behavior in motivation.

Each of the theories presented has something to offer managers if used correctly, and various parts of the theories are complementary in many respects. The psychologists and social psychologists who formulated these theories were articulate in explaining needs, motives, and values. They weren't, however, so astute at explaining what managers could do to motivate employees. And despite the abundance of complementary theories and research, many managers still choose to ignore the academically generated theories of motivation.

If anything, the discussion of theories and research indicates that instead of ignoring motivation, managers must take an active role in motivating their employees. Nine specific conclusions have been reached:

1. Managers can influence employees' motivation. If performance needs to be improved, then managers should intervene and help create an atmosphere that encourages, supports, and sustains improvement. Motivation can be managed.

2. Managers must remember that ability, competence, and opportunity all play a role in motivation. A person with little ability or few skills will have a difficult time being productive.

3. Managers need to be sensitive to variations in employees' needs, abilities, and goals. They must also consider differences in preferences (valences) for rewards.

4. Continuous monitoring of employees' needs, abilities, goals, and preferences is each individual manager's responsibility. The only constant is change.

5. Managers must attempt to channel self-motivated behavior into productive results. Some individuals practice a high degree of self-regulation and personal motivation.

6. Managers as role models can be influential in motivating employees. Social learning occurs on a regular basis, and managers must be aware that their style, techniques, and work behavior are being observed and can be easily imitated.

7. Managers need to provide incentives for their employees. When employees note that valued outcomes can be achieved through performance, a major part of the motivation strategy has succeeded.

8. Establishing moderately difficult goals to direct behavior is an important part of any motivational program.

9. Managers should try to provide employees with jobs that offer equity, task challenge, variety, and opportunities for need satisfaction.

If motivation is to be energized, sustained, and directed, managers have to understand needs, intentions, preferences, goals, reinforcement, and comparison. Failure to learn about these concepts results in many missed opportunities to motivate employees in a positive manner.

TABLE 6.3 The Predictive Power of Selected Motivation Theories*

	Theories					
	Need-Based†	Reinforcement	Behavioral Self-Management	Expectancy	Equity‡	Goal Setting
Productivity	6§	6	6	7	7	9
Absenteeism		8	8ƒ	8	8	
Job satisfaction	6				6	6#

*Ratings are based on a scale of 1 to 10 with 10 the highest.
†Includes theories of Maslow, Herzberg, Aldefer, and McClelland.
‡Based primarily on studies of pay issues.
§Primarily found for employees with a high need for achievement.
ƒLimited number of studies.
#Satisfaction levels are higher if goal program is considered fair, meaningful, and more than control mechanism.

Table 6.3 briefly summarizes how well the various themes and approaches predict productivity, absenteeism, and job satisfaction. Ratings are based on available empirical research conducted in organizations primarily in the United States and Canada. Ratings also use the judgments of researchers, anecdotal information, and managerial opinions.[70] While the data presented aren't scientifically validated in every instance, they're based on multiple sources of information. The knowledge and insight provided by summarizing theories, empirical studies, and opinions can provide the basis for developing motivational reward programs.

Organizational Reward Systems

Managers who understand and are comfortable with a number of motivational approaches are better prepared to design effective and motivational reward programs. Theories set the tone and the direction of how to create a motivational atmosphere. Applying the theoretical principles to the work environment is what an organizational reward system attempts to accomplish.

Numerous changes are taking place in how performance is evaluated and rewards are distributed. Requests to eliminate piece rate incentive systems,[71] convert all reward systems to group-based approaches, shift risk from employers to employees by making a greater percentage of compensation variable in nature (e.g., bonuses), and legislate how much executives can earn are being presented as universally perfect ways to address rewards. Although parts of each suggestion have some validity, such radical proposals are unlikely to influence the majority of managers. Instead of radical changes and across-the-board debunking, progressive approaches are likely to draw more attention. Pay systems based on competencies and contributions made, team-based incentives, and rewards focusing on improved results are becoming more widely considered and implemented systems. As organizations become more involved in global transactions, business pay and rewards will be more closely linked to overall unit and total company results.[72]

Instead of eliminating individual reward systems and accepting group-based reward systems, it's better to examine the positive and negative motivational features of various reward systems.

A Model of Individual Rewards

The main objectives of reward programs are (1) to attract qualified people to *join* the organization, (2) to *keep* employees coming to work, and (3) to *motivate* employees to achieve

FIGURE 6.6 **The Reward Process**

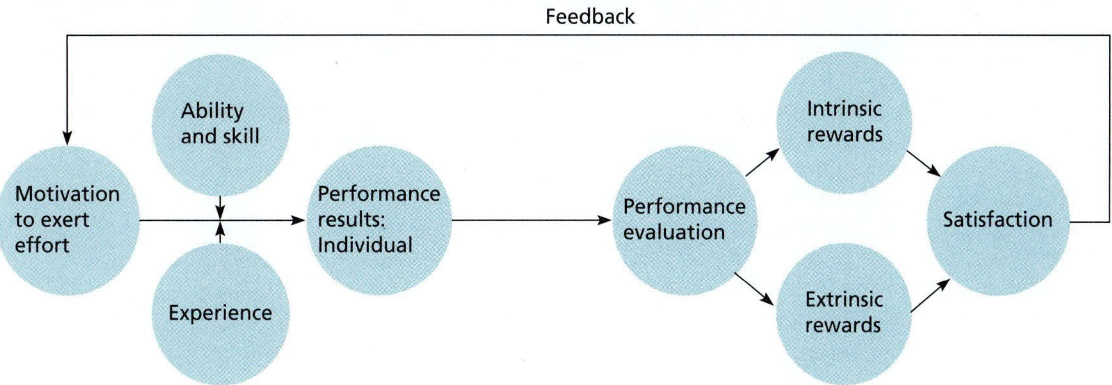

high levels of performance. A model illustrating how rewards fit into an organization's overall policies and programs is useful to managers. Figure 6.6 presents a model that integrates motivation, performance, satisfaction, and rewards. It suggests that the motivation to exert effort isn't enough to cause acceptable performance. Performance results from a combination of the effort of an individual and that person's ability, skill, and experience. Management evaluates each individual's performance either formally or informally. As a result of the evaluation, management distributes extrinsic rewards. The rewards are evaluated by the individual. Individuals also receive or derive intrinsic rewards from the job. To the extent that rewards are adequate and equitable, the individual achieves a level of satisfaction.

A significant amount of research has been done on what determines whether individuals are satisfied with rewards. Edward Lawler has summarized five conclusions based on the behavioral science research literature:[73]

1. *Satisfaction with a reward is a function of both how much is received and how much the individual feels should be received.* This conclusion is based on the comparisons that people make. When individuals receive less than they feel they should, they're dissatisfied.

2. *An individual's feelings of satisfaction are influenced by comparisons with what happens to others.* People tend to compare their efforts, skills, seniority, and job performance with others'. They then attempt to compare rewards; that is, they compare their own inputs with others' inputs relative to the rewards received. Chapter 5 discussed this input–outcome comparison when introducing the equity theory of motivation.

3. *Satisfaction is influenced by how satisfied employees are with both intrinsic and extrinsic rewards.* Intrinsic rewards are valued in and of themselves; they're related to performing the job. Examples would be feelings of accomplishment and achievement. Extrinsic rewards are external to the work itself; they are administered externally. Examples would be salary and wages, fringe benefits, and promotions. There's debate among researchers as to whether intrinsic or extrinsic rewards are more important in determining job satisfaction. Most studies suggest that both rewards are important.[74] One clear message from the research is that extrinsic and intrinsic rewards satisfy different needs.

4. *People differ in the rewards they desire and in the relative importance different rewards have for them.* In fact, preferred rewards vary at different points in a person's career, at different ages, and in various situations.

5. *Some extrinsic rewards are satisfying because they lead to other rewards.* For example, a large office or an office that has carpeting or drapes is often considered a reward because it indicates the individual's status and power. Money is a reward that leads to such things as prestige, autonomy, security, and shelter.

OB AT WORK Rewarding a Diverse Workforce

With an increasingly diverse workforce, managers are finding that they may have to consider employees' cultural heritage when it is time to reward them. In fact, there are those who believe that many of our management and leadership models are culture-bound; that is, they do not consider the possibility that different personalities may flourish in different national cultures. There are also those who believe that national cultural differences are overstated. Having said all of this, let us consider the following:

- Employees from banks in Hong Kong prefer financial rewards such as salary, salary increases, and individual, team and organizational performance incentives; whereas bank employees from Finland prefer more support-oriented rewards like job security, relationships with colleagues and customers, and work/life balance.
- Asians are often taught traditions such as *enryo,* which requires, among other things, modesty in the presence of one's superiors. Deference and reserved behavior are highly valued. As a result, they may feel reluctant to ask for rewards and may also be less likely to complain or ask questions. They may often not respond positively to recognition.
- The manager of a Native American was so impressed with his work that he honored him in a visible ceremony in front of his peers. The employee did not return to work for several days because he was very uncomfortable with public praise, especially in front of his Native American peers.
- Sales executives often accompany their praise of members of the sales force with well-intentioned touching on the arms and pats on the back. Unfortunately, many Asian Americans feel extremely uncomfortable with this behavior.
- A manager asked her primarily Filipino staff to let her know of any problems they were having with some new equipment that had recently been installed in the company's warehouse. The manager assumed that by delegating this responsibility to the group, positive feelings would result. Instead, the employees used every possible means including makeshift remedies to ensure that she never found out any problems existed. To the group, their inability to handle equipment problems meant losing face.
- When doing business in China, American expatriate managers need to be careful regarding how they reward Chinese employees. In the United States, it is not uncommon for an individual to receive a clock after working for the same company for a certain number of years. If American expatriate managers were to transfer this tradition of reward to China, they would be very surprised at the outcome. The Chinese word for "clock" is related to funeral or death. Thus, the message behind such a "reward" may be interpreted as "drop dead."

If managers consciously seek to learn about the cultural differences among groups, it seems that unintentional mistakes such as the above can be avoided. It is clear that managers have made mistakes in the past in their assumptions about males and females, minorities and whites, and old versus young. As our workforce continues to diversify, empathy and sensitivity to differences among people will be a critical managerial skill.

Sources: Flora F. T. Chiang and Thomas A. Birtch, "An Empirical Examination of Reward Preferences within and across National Settings," *Management International Review* 46, no. 5 (2006): 573–596; Irwin Speizer, "Incentives Catch On Overseas, But Value of Awards Can Too Easily Get Lost in Translation," *Workforce Management* 84, no. 13 (November 2005): 46–49; Patricia Digh, "One Style Doesn't Fit All," *HRMagazine* 47, no. 11 (November 2002), pp. 79–82; Marlene Duchatelet, "Cultural Difference and Management/Leadership Models," *American Business Review,* June 1998, pp. 96–99; Livia Markoczy, "Us and Them," *Across the Board,* February 1998, pp. 96–99; Taylor Cos, Jr., *Cultural Diversity in Organizations: Theory, Research, and Practice* (San Francisco: Berrett Koehler, 1993); and Kenneth N. Wexley and Stanley B. Silverman, *Working Scared: Achieving Success in Trying Times* (San Francisco: Jossey-Bass, 1993).

The relationship between rewards and satisfaction isn't perfectly understood, nor is it static. It changes because people and the environment change. But there are important considerations that managers can use to develop and distribute rewards. First, rewards must be sufficient to satisfy basic human needs. Federal legislation, union contracts, and managerial fairness have provided at least minimal rewards in most work settings. Second, individuals tend to compare their rewards with those of others. People make comparisons regardless of the quantity of the rewards they receive. If inequities are perceived, dissatisfaction occurs. Finally, as the OB at Work illustrates, managers distributing rewards must recognize individual differences. Unless individual differences are considered, the reward process invariably is less effective than desired. Any reward package should (1) be sufficient to satisfy basic needs (e.g., food, shelter, clothing), (2) be considered equitable, and (3) be individually oriented.[75]

Extrinsic and Intrinsic Rewards

extrinsic rewards
Rewards external to the job, such as pay, promotion, or fringe benefits.

intrinsic rewards
Rewards that are part of the job itself: the responsibility, challenge, and feedback characteristics of the job.

Figure 6.6 classifies rewards into two broad categories: extrinsic and intrinsic. **Extrinsic rewards** are rewards external to the job, such as pay, promotion, or fringe benefits; **intrinsic rewards** are those that are part of the job itself, such as the responsibility, challenge, and feedback characteristics of the job. In either category, the first consideration is how the rewards are *valued* by employees. Individuals put forth little effort unless the reward has *value.* Both extrinsic and intrinsic rewards can have value.[76]

Extrinsic Rewards

Financial Rewards: Salary and Wages

Money is a major extrinsic reward. It has been said that "although it is generally agreed that money is the major mechanism for rewarding and modifying behavior in industry . . . very little is known about how it works."[77] To really understand how money modifies behavior, the perceptions and preferences of the person being rewarded must be understood, which of course is a challenging task for managers. Success requires careful attention and observation of employees. In addition, managers must be trusted, so that workers freely communicate their feelings about financial rewards.

Unless employees see a connection between performance and merit increases, money isn't a powerful motivator. In some cases, a well-designed appraisal system can make the pay–performance connection clear to employees. This clarity doesn't just happen; managers must work hard at communicating the performance–financial reward connection.[78]

Increasingly, critics charge that the pay–performance relationship should be strengthened for chief executives in large corporations and that *Fortune* 500 chief executive officers (CEOs) are grossly overpaid.

Executive compensation has become a controversial issue. Experts use different statistical techniques to illustrate which executive is the "best bargain" and who's the "worst buy."[79] Front-page stories contrasting million-dollar paychecks for executives and more layoffs for employees are painful and emotion laden.

Critics contend that American executives are paid too much and that their salaries aren't related to their companies' performance.[80] This inequity is considered to be one reason the United States is competitively being challenged. One study of corporate business units determined that a small difference in pay between lower-level employees and upper echelon managers is associated with high product quality.[81] The researchers suggested that the smaller differential may have resulted in higher commitment to organizational goals.

The federal government has on a number of occasions reviewed laws to influence executives' pay. The most controversial suggestions would limit the amount that an executive can be paid by capping it at some absolute level or at some multiple of what the lowest paid worker earns. For example, in 2010, a salary cap of $500,000 was imposed on most of the 45 highest paid employees from several of the companies that received government stimulus funding, including American International Group (AIG), General Motors, Chrysler Group, Chrysler Financial, and General Motors Acceptance Corporation (GMAC).[82] The effect of legislation on executives' motivation to work hard, take risks, and even enter the profession needs to be considered by any politician introducing bills in Congress. Differences across jobs and industries also need to be cautiously considered before executive compensation becomes dictated by law.

Financial Rewards: Fringe Benefits

In the United States, organizations spend 35 to 40 percent of their total compensation amount on employee benefits. A Conference Board–Gallup Poll survey indicated that

74 percent of all workers in America say that employee benefits are crucial to job choice. If limited to only one benefit (beyond money), 64 percent say to provide them with health care.[83] In most cases, fringe benefits are primarily financial. But some (such as software maker SAS's on-site gymnasium) aren't entirely financial. A major financial fringe benefit in many organizations is the pension plan. Fringe benefits such as pension plans, health insurance, and vacations aren't usually contingent on employees' performance. In most cases, they're based on seniority or length of employment.

Interpersonal Rewards

interpersonal rewards
Extrinsic rewards such as receiving recognition or being able to interact socially on the job.

The manager has some power to distribute such **interpersonal rewards** as status and recognition. Managers and co-workers both play roles in granting job status. By assigning individuals to prestigious jobs, the manager can attempt to improve or remove a person's status. But if co-workers don't believe that an employee merits a particular job, status isn't likely to be enhanced. In some situations, by reviewing performance, managers can grant what they consider to be job changes that improve status.

recognition
Management's acknowledgment of work well done.

Much of what was just stated about status also applies to recognition. In a reward context, **recognition** refers to managerial acknowledgment of employee achievement that could result in improved status. Recognition from a manager could include public praise, expressions of a job well done, or special attention.[84] The extent to which recognition is motivating depends, as do most rewards, on its perceived value and on the connection that the individual sees between it and behavior. Examples of how performance is recognized at People's Bank, LifeScan, and Johnson Controls Inc. (Table 6.4) illustrate the vast array of recognition opportunities.

Promotions

For many employees, promotions don't happen often; some never experience even one in their careers. Managers making promotion reward decisions attempt to match the right persons with the jobs. Criteria often used to reach promotion decisions are performance and seniority. Performance, if it can be accurately assessed, is often given significant weight in promotion reward allocations.

Intrinsic Rewards

Completion

The ability to start and finish a project or job is important to some individuals. These people value *task completion.* The effect that completing a task has on them is a form of self-reward. Opportunities that allow such people to complete tasks can have a powerful motivating effect.

Achievement

Achievement is a self-administered reward derived from reaching a challenging goal. David C. McClelland has described individual differences in those striving for achievement.[85] Some seek challenging goals, while others seek moderate or low goals. In goal-setting programs, difficult goals may result in a higher level of individual performance than do moderate goals. Even in such programs, however, individual differences must be considered before reaching conclusions about the importance of achievement rewards.

Autonomy

Some people want jobs providing the right to make decisions; they want to operate without being closely supervised. A feeling of autonomy could result from the freedom to do what the employee considers best in a particular situation. In jobs that are highly

TABLE 6.4
Recognition Approaches

Source: Excerpted and adapted from company brochures and Web sites.

At People's Bank, Connecticut:

All award winners receive the following:

- Recognition gift.
- Newsletter announcement.
- Letter from the president.
- Managers' meeting announcement.
- Letter for their personnel file.

In addition, Excellence and Quality Award winners get their photo and more detailed descriptions of their achievement in the employee newsletter.

At LifeScan, a Johnson & Johnson company:

What do I receive if I earn a Quality Excellence Award?

Achieving a significant improvement in quality is rewarding in itself—it means you've helped our products or services better meet our customers' requirements, and in the process made your job and your co-workers' more hassle-free.

In appreciation for your outstanding quality achievement, you'll receive a very special dinner for two at any of the Bay Area's finest restaurants, plus a sweater embroidered with the LifeScan quality logo. In addition, your photo will appear on *LifeScan's Quality Wall of Fame* along with photos of other award recipients.

Who will present the Quality Excellence Award? Where will it be presented?

Your Quality Excellence Award will be presented by one of LifeScan's officers at a Quarterly Employee Meeting. Your achievement will also be featured in a *LifeScan Monitor* article.

At Johnson Controls Inc.:

Chairman's Award

The Chairman's Award was established in 1985 to recognize employees who continually exceed customers' expectations. "Customer" includes anyone outside of the company who purchases Johnson Controls' goods and services, as well as those individuals within the firm who work with the award-winning employees. The Chairman's Award program is the most prestigious companywide employee recognition program and has the goal of inspiring excellence throughout the firm.

The Award is given on an annual basis to those employees who meet or exceed the goals of increasing sales or reducing costs in the following areas:

- Quality.
- Service.
- Productivity.
- Time compression.

Results are achieved through innovation; cross-functional teamwork and activity; and Six Sigma, *kaizen,* and benchmarking.

structured and controlled by management, it's difficult to create tasks that lead to a feeling of autonomy.

Personal Growth

The personal growth of any individual is unique. Individuals experiencing such growth can sense their development and see how their capabilities are being expanded. By expanding their capabilities, employees can maximize or at least satisfy skill potential. Some become dissatisfied with their jobs and organizations if not allowed or encouraged to develop their skills. The rewards included in this section are distributed or created by managers, work

OB AND YOUR CAREER — Find the Right Job with the Right Rewards

There are several sources of information that individuals can tap to learn whether a given job provides desired extrinsic (e.g., pay and benefits) and intrinsic (e.g., meaningful work) rewards. In terms of learning about extrinsic rewards, job candidates should pour over the organization's website, annual reports, and other publically available information to learn about benefits, and career advancement and promotion opportunities. Although information about pay will usually be provided either during the selection process or once an offer is extended, some candidates are successful in getting pay information from current or previous employees. Also, candidates should also check for relevant pay and benefits information that is posted in similar job openings from the organization on several Web-based job search sites like Monster.com, CareerBuilder.com, CollegeReporter.com, Jobfox.com, Linkup.com, and Indeed.com.

Learning about intrinsic rewards may be more challenging because it takes time after starting a new job to assess realistically how much responsibility, feedback, and challenge is associated with the position. That being said, candidates should ask the following questions of interviewers, and current or past employees to learn more about the extrinsic rewards related to the job in question:

1. Can you please describe what a typical day in this job is like?
2. What are the primary responsibilities associated with this position?
3. What are some of the key challenges that need to be addressed in order to perform well in this job?

Also, job seekers should consult the myriad of resources that help individuals identify and match their personal values and work preferences to those of an organization. The CareerBuilders' Web site has a work values checklist that might provide job seekers with some insight into which intrinsic, extrinsic, and lifestyle values they want in a job. Also, the classic job seekers' guide: *What Color Is Your Parachute? 2010* by Richard N. Bolles has helped countless individuals for nearly 40 years. With over 10,000,000 copies sold, this book helps guide readers to develop a personalized step-by-step plan (called the Flower Exercise) to help them define the parameters of a job that fits them. By understanding such key factors as what a person likes to do on a daily basis, with whom, where, and so on, they are much more likely to find a job that fits well. Without this personal awareness, then it will be much harder for a job seeker to find a job that provides them with meaningful extrinsic rewards.

Sources: See http://career-advice.monster.com/job-search/career-assessment/work-values-check-list/article.aspx (accessed on May 13, 2010); Brian Burnsed, "Is Your Next Job a Click Away: Know Which Sites Will Be most Beneficial," *U.S. News & World Report*, 147(5), 31; Richard N. Bolles, *What Color Is Your Parachute? 2010:* A Practical Manual for Job Hunters and Career Changers (Berkeley, CA: Ten Speed Press, 2009).

groups, or individuals. The OB and Your Career above discusses some tips for finding jobs that provide individuals with desired extrinsic and intrinsic rewards. Table 6.5 summarizes the rewards we've discussed. As the table indicates, managers can play either a direct or an indirect role in developing and administering rewards.

The Interaction of Intrinsic and Extrinsic Rewards

The general assumption has been that intrinsic and extrinsic rewards have an independent and additive influence on motivation. That is, motivation is determined by the sum of the person's intrinsic and extrinsic sources of motivation.[86] This straightforward assumption has been questioned by several researchers.[87] Some have suggested that in situations in which individuals are experiencing a high level of intrinsic rewards, the addition of extrinsic rewards for good performance may cause a decrease in motivation.[88] Basically, the person receiving self-administered feelings of satisfaction is performing because of intrinsic rewards. Once extrinsic rewards are added, feelings of satisfaction change because performance is now thought to be due to the extrinsic rewards. The addition of extrinsic rewards tends to reduce the extent to which the individual experiences self-administered intrinsic rewards.[89]

The argument concerning extrinsic rewards' potential negative effects has stimulated a number of research studies. Unfortunately, these studies report contradictory results. Some researchers report a reduction in intrinsic rewards following the addition of extrinsic

TABLE 6.5
Types and Sources of Selected Extrinsic and Intrinsic Rewards

	Sources		
Type	**Manager**	**Group**	**Individual**
Extrinsic			
Financial			
Salary and wages	D		
Fringe benefits	D		
Interpersonal	D	D	
Promotion	D		
Intrinsic			
Completion	I		D
Achievement	I		D
Autonomy	I		D
Personal growth	I		D

Note: D = Direct source of the reward.
I = Indirect source of the reward.

rewards for an activity;[90] others have failed to observe such an effect.[91] A review of the literature found that 14 of 24 studies supported the theory that extrinsic rewards reduce intrinsic motivation;[92] 10 didn't support it. Of the 24 studies reviewed, only two used actual employees as subjects. All of the other studies used college students or grade school students.

Rewards, Turnover, and Absenteeism

Managers may assume that low turnover is a mark of an effective organization. However, some organizations would benefit if disruptive and low performers quit. Thus, the issue of turnover needs to focus on *who* is leaving as well as on frequency.

Ideally, if managers could develop reward systems that retained the best performers and caused poor performers to leave, the overall effectiveness of an organization would improve. To approach this ideal state, an equitable and favorably compared reward system must exist. The feelings of *equity* and *favorable comparison* have an external orientation. That is, the equity of rewards and favorableness involves comparisons with external parties. This orientation is used because quitting most often means that a person leaves one organization for an alternative elsewhere.

merit rating
A formal rating system applied to employees.

No perfect means exist for retaining high performers. A reward system based on **merit ratings** should encourage most better performers to remain with the organization. Also, the reward system needs some differential that discriminates between high and low performers. High performers must receive significantly more extrinsic and intrinsic rewards than low performers.[93]

presenteeism
Refers to the act of employees who attend work but, due to illness or other medical reasons, tend to underperform their jobs.

Absenteeism, no matter for what reason, is a costly and disruptive problem facing managers.[94] It's costly because it reduces output and disruptive because it requires that schedules and programs be modified. Absenteeism in the United States is estimated to cost over $70 billion per year.[95] On a related note, a concept known as **presenteeism** refers to employees who show up to work but due to illness or other medical reasons, tend to underperform in their jobs.[96] Some estimates place the cost of presenteeism to U.S. companies at more than $150 billion annually.[97]

Employees go to work because they're motivated to do so; the level of motivation remains high if an individual feels that attendance leads to more valued rewards and fewer negative consequences than alternative behaviors.

Managers appear to have some influence over attendance behavior. They have the ability to punish, establish bonus systems, and allow employee participation in developing plans. Whether these or other approaches reduce absenteeism is determined by the value of the rewards perceived by employees, the amount of the rewards, and whether employees perceive a relationship between attendance and rewards. These same characteristics appear every time we analyze the effects of rewards on organizational behavior.

Rewards and Job Performance

Researchers and managers agree that extrinsic and intrinsic rewards can be used to motivate job performance. It's also clear that certain conditions must exist if rewards are to actually motivate: The rewards must be *valued* by the person, and they must be related to a specific level of job performance.

Chapter 5 presented expectancy motivation theory. According to that theory, people associate every behavior with certain outcomes or rewards or punishments. In other words, an assembly-line worker may believe that by behaving in a certain way she'll get certain things. This is a description of the *performance–outcome expectancy.* On one hand, another worker may expect that a steady performance of 10 units a day will eventually result in a transfer to a more challenging job. On the other hand, a worker may expect that a steady performance of 10 units a day will result in his being considered a rate buster by co-workers.

Each outcome has a *valence,* or value, to the person. Because each person has different needs and perceptions, outcomes such as pay, a promotion, a reprimand, or a better job have different values for different people. Thus, in considering which rewards to use, a manager has to be astute in considering individual differences. If valued rewards are used to motivate, they can result in the exertion of effort to achieve high levels of performance.

Rewards and Organizational Commitment

commitment
A sense of identification, loyalty, and involvement expressed by an employee toward the organization or unit of the organization.

There's limited research on the relationship between rewards and organizational commitment.[98] **Commitment** to an organization involves three attitudes: (1) a sense of identification with the organization's goals, (2) a feeling of involvement in organizational duties, and (3) a feeling of loyalty for the organization. Research evidence indicates that the absence of commitment can reduce organizational effectiveness.[99] Committed people are less likely to quit and accept other jobs. Thus, costs of high turnover aren't incurred. In addition, committed and highly skilled employees require less supervision. Close supervision and a rigid monitoring control process are time-consuming and costly. Furthermore, a committed employee perceives the value and importance of integrating individual and organizational goals. The employee thinks of his goals and the organization's goals in personal terms.

Intrinsic rewards are important for developing organizational commitment. Organizations able to meet employees' needs by providing challenging opportunities, giving feedback, encouraging employee participation and by recognizing achievement when it occurs have a significant impact on commitment.[100] Thus, managers need to develop intrinsic reward systems that focus on personal importance or self-esteem to integrate individual and organizational goals and to design challenging jobs.

Reward Systems in High-Performing Organizations

The typical list of rewards that managers can and do distribute in organizations has been discussed. We all know that pay, fringe benefits, and opportunities to achieve challenging goals are considered rewards by most people. It's also generally accepted that rewards are administered by managers through such processes as reinforcement, modeling, and expectancies. Some managers are experimenting with new, innovative, yet largely untested,

TABLE 6.6 Four Reward Approaches: A Summary and Comparison

Reward Approach	Major Strengths	Major Weaknesses	Research Support
Flexible benefits	Because employees have different desires and needs, programs can be tailored to fit individuals.	Administration can become complex and costly. The more employees involved, the more difficult it is to efficiently operate the approach.	Limited, because only a few programs have been scientifically examined.
Banking time off	Can be integrated with performance in that time-off credits can be made contingent on performance achievements.	Organization needs a valid, reliable, and equitable performance appraisal program.	Extremely limited.
Skill-based pay	Employees must clearly demonstrate skill before receiving pay increases.	Training costs to upgrade employee skills are higher than under conventional pay systems. Labor costs increase if employees learn many skills. Employees may "top out."	Very limited, with no direct skill-based versus conventional pay compensation studies available.
Gainsharing	Can enhance teamwork. Employees focus on objectives, learn more about the organization, and may be more productive.	If plans focus only on productivity, employees may ignore other important objectives.	Limited, but a distinct increase in studies is being reported.

reward programs. Four different reward approaches that aren't widely tested are flexible benefits, banking time off, skill-based pay, and gainsharing. Table 6.6 summarizes their strengths and weaknesses.

Flexible Benefits

Sometimes referred to as cafeteria-style plans, flexible benefit plans allow employees to choose benefits from a menu of options that suit them.[101] Having to stay within a given cost limit, employees develop individualized, personally attractive benefit packages that fit their preferences and life stage. Many organizations are shifting from standardized, one-size-fits-all benefit packages to flexible benefit plans as a response to increasing diversity among employees.[102] For example, some younger employees in their 20s may choose more vacation time over higher levels of medical insurance. Older employees with families may opt for greater medical coverage for their dependents and more flextime to attend their children's school events and soccer games. Other employees may take all of the benefits in cash. These programs are growing in popularity as companies attempt to use flexible benefits as a way to attract and retain valued employees.[103] For example, Google states the following with regard to their benefits philosophy:

> "We strive to be innovative and unique in all services we provide both to customers and employees, including our benefits and perks offerings. We realize and celebrate that our employees have diverse needs, and that this diversity requires flexible and individually directed support. Our priority is to offer a customizable program that can be tailored to the specific needs of each individual, whether they enjoy ice climbing in Alaska, want to retire by age 40, or plan to adopt 3 children."[104]

flexible benefit plans Provide individuals with the ability to choose the benefits they prefer rather than a standardized package of benefits that someone else establishes for them.

Using a **flexible benefit plan** offers some distinct advantages. First, it allows employees to play an active rather than a passive role in deciding on the allocation of fringe benefits. Second, employees receive the benefits of greatest personal value to them. This provides many people with a psychologically uplifting feeling. Third, flexible benefit plans make the economic value of fringe benefits obvious to each employee because they force employees to review all of the benefits offerings as they make choices. In many situations, employees grossly underestimate the value of the fringe benefits their employers provide.

Some administrative problems are associated with cafeteria plans.[105] Because of employees' different preferences, records become more complicated. For a large organization with a cafeteria plan, a computer system is almost essential to do the recordkeeping. Another problem involves group insurance premium rates. Most life and medical insurance premiums are based on the number of employees participating. It's difficult to predict the participation level under a flexible benefits plan.

TRW Corporation placed approximately 12,000 employees on a flexible benefits plan. It allows employees to rearrange and redistribute their fringe benefit packages every year. More than 80 percent of the TRW participants have changed their benefit packages since the plan was initiated.[106]

Banking Time Off

banking time off
A reward practice of allowing employees to build up time-off credits for such behaviors as good performance or attendance.

Time off from work is attractive to most people. In essence, most companies have a time-off system built into their vacation programs. Employees receive different amounts of time off, based on the years they've worked for the organization. **Banking time off**, an extension of such a time-off reward, is the practice of granting time off for such behaviors as good performance or attendance. That is, a bank of time-off credits could be built up contingent on performance.

Today, some organizations are selecting their best performers to attend educational and training programs. One company in Houston selects the best performers and provides them with an opportunity to attend a preferred executive educational program. There is excess demand to attend the program and having the time available allows the selected individuals to attend. Being eligible is largely contingent on the individual's performance record. Those ultimately selected are given two Fridays off a month to attend classes.

Skill-Based Pay

skill-based pay
Wages paid at a rate calculated and based on the skills employees possess, display, and develop in performing their jobs.

In traditional compensation systems, characteristics of the job performed (e.g., its difficulty and complexity) and local market rates determine an employee's pay rate and range. But in **skill-based pay** programs, the employee's pay depends not on the job, but on her level and number of job-related skills. The skill-based approach attempts to take into account efficiency, or the value added by the worker's performance.[107]

In skill-based programs, employees work as members of semiautonomous teams. When hired, an employee is paid a starting rate and receives pay increases as she learns new skills required by the team. Once an employee learns all of the team skills, opportunities are provided to learn skills outside the unit and throughout the organization. Pay increases accompany each new set of skills the employee masters. In skill-based programs that don't use teams, an employee moves up one pay grade for each job learned, and jobs can be learned in any sequence. Often, pay raises are the same size regardless of the content of jobs learned.[108]

A five-year study into the effectiveness of skill-based compensation systems found that they encourage employees to acquire and maintain job-related skills.[109] Another study by the American Compensation Association found that 33 percent of respondents have skill-based pay systems. Procter & Gamble has implemented such plans in 30 plants, and Polaroid is attempting to become the first organization to pay virtually all employees through skill-based plans.[110] Also, Tennessee Eastman Division (the largest unit of Eastman Chemical Co.) allows team members to participate in a "pay-for-applied-skills-and-knowledge" plan that has six levels of learning that cover technical, business, and team interaction skills.[111]

Skill-based pay programs afford several benefits. The key advantage is a more highly skilled and flexible workforce. Productivity can increase, and supervisory costs are often reduced. Employees are more motivated to gain and use their skills; they often perceive their pay as being more equitable; and they have a better understanding of how their jobs fit into the organization.[112]

Pay levels and training costs, however, often increase. Employees can be frustrated when no openings are available in job areas for which they're newly trained. And a long-term problem may arise if employees have "topped out"—they've learned all the skills needed by the organization and so have nowhere to go. Dissatisfaction and turnover may result.[113] Overall, a careful cost–benefit analysis should be conducted before implementing a skill-based pay program.

Gainsharing

gainsharing
A formula-based group incentive plan in which employees share in an organization's financial gain from improved performance.

Gainsharing is a formula-based group incentive plan in which employees share in an organization's financial gain from its improved performance.[114] Gainsharing plans generally include the following three characteristics:[115] (1) gainsharing links a percentage of employees' pay to the achievement of performance goals; (2) a portion of the gains or rewards are shared with all members of the gainsharing unit; and (3) a process is in place so that suggestions for improving productivity can be generated, selected, and implemented. Traditional forms of gain-sharing are the Scanlon Plan, Rucker Plan, and Improshare. These plans are differentiated by the measures discussed in Table 6.7.

Gainsharing is the fastest growing incentive program in the United States, partly because of a widespread belief that gainsharing spurs motivation and teamwork. About 26 percent of U.S. companies use the program, with 75 percent of the plans installed since 1980.[116]

TABLE 6.7
Gainsharing Models

Sources: Adapted from Haig Nalbantian, Richard Guzzo, Dave Kieffer, and Jay Doherty, *Play to Your Strengths: Managing Your Internal Labor Markets for Lasting Competitive Advantage* (New York: McGraw-Hill, 2003); and David Beck, "Implementing a Gainsharing Plan: What Companies Need to Know," *Compensation & Benefits Review* (January–February 1992): 22.

Formula	Model
$\frac{\text{(\$)(Labor costs)}}{\text{(\$)(Revenue)}}$	**Scanlon Plan.** Scanlon formulas measure the labor costs required to produce services in a given base period; that is, labor costs are compared with sales volume. Assume, for example, that it requires $500,000 in labor costs to generate $1 million in sales. This 0.50 ratio (500,000/1,000,000) becomes the standard for determining incentive awards. In future periods, if labor costs are less than 50% of sales, savings are allocated among employees and the organization on the basis of a preestablished formula.
$\frac{\text{(\$)(Labor Costs)}}{\text{(\$)(Adj. revenue)}}$	**Rucker Plan®.** Rucker plans also use labor costs as the numerator. The Rucker Plan, however, attempts to adjust for the effects of inflation by subtracting from sales the costs associated with materials and supplies. The assumption is that in this way inflationary effects are roughly accounted for because increased sales value of goods is offset by the increased material and supply costs. As with the Scanlon plan, any improvements in the ratio are subsequently used to calculate the incentive award.
$\frac{\text{(Earned hours)}}{\text{(Available hours)}}$	**Improshare®.** This approach establishes a standard that identifies the expected hours required to produce an acceptable level of output. The standard is derived from a time and motion study and/or from an analysis of the group's historical experience. Any savings resulting from an increase in output in fewer than expected hours are shared between the organization and the employee group on the basis of a preestablished formula.
	Profit sharing. A profit-sharing plan allows employees to participate in the organization's profits. A qualified plan must provide a definite predetermined formula for allocating the contributions made to the plan among the participants and for distributing the funds accumulated under the plan after a fixed number of years, after the attainment of a stated age, or upon the prior occurrence of some event, such as layoff, disability, retirement, or severance of employment.

Researchers conducting a four-year study of a gainsharing program at an auto parts manufacturing plant in the U.S. reported that the implemented employee suggestions contributed to lower production costs.[117]

Carrier (the heating and air-conditioning equipment manufacturer and a subsidiary of United Technologies) provides an example of how gainsharing works. Carrier set as a benchmark the 1.8 hours that production employees take to make a finished product. When employees beat this benchmark with acceptable-quality products, the labor savings are split 50–50 between the subsidiary and every employee in the plant, from machinists to secretaries to managers. To keep employees informed, plant productivity information is posted daily on the plant bulletin boards, and employees are encouraged to provide time-saving ideas.[118]

Although many observers believe that an effective gainsharing program can boost productivity, lower production costs, cut absenteeism and turnover, and improve product quality, some critics assert that these effects aren't long lasting and that research on results is still limited. But most agree that gainsharing is most effective in business units with fewer than 500 employees and when rewards are based on results that employees can directly affect.[119]

The increased interest and attention paid to group incentive plans is likely to continue. Team performance, evaluation, and reward systems will grow in importance as a shifting away from predominately individually based rewards to a mix of individual and group reward systems gains momentum.[120] Since people are being encouraged, directed, and motivated to work more closely together, reward systems must keep pace.[121] The strict individual-based systems don't encourage teamwork.

At Johnsonville Foods in Sheboygan Falls, Wisconsin, the 600-member workforce is divided into 14 cross-functional teams. Employees receive base pay according to the market value of their jobs. When a team member believes she's ready to receive a salary increase, a request to peers is made. Peers decide whether an employee has mastered the skills needed to contribute more. If peers answer yes, a raise is approved. In addition to base pay, employees are eligible for individual and/or team bonuses based on performance. Only if the entire team is profitable and adds value will its members receive a bonus.

At Eaton Corporation, team members study daily sales results. Money saved for Eaton is shared by all team members.[122] Understanding sales, costs, and profitability helps Eaton team members earn more pay. The team bonus approach has caught on as teams look for bottlenecks and ways to become more efficient and attack waste. A sharing of financial data with management helps each Eaton team to study its performance. Individuals can also earn bonuses for perfect attendance and skill improvement.

The link between the performance evaluation system and reward distribution was shown in Figure 6.6. The discussion of this and other linkages in the reward process suggests the complexity of using rewards to motivate better performance. Managers need to use judgment, diagnosis, and the resources available to reward their subordinates individually or as part of a team. Administering rewards is perhaps one of the most challenging and frustrating tasks that managers around the world must perform.

Kohn's Criticism of Performance-Based Rewards

The use of rewards has come to be very natural in work, school, and child rearing at home. Researcher Alfie Kohn (www.alfiekohn.org) offers a compelling set of criticisms of performance-based rewards. He contends that rewards and punishments are just two sides of the same coin—and the coin doesn't buy very much.[123] He suggests that managers must move beyond the use of rewards or punishments. Kohn raises some interesting arguments based on his review and interpretation of the research literature. His arguments are provocative enough that managers should at least be aware of the points he raises.

These are a few of Kohn's criticisms:

- *Rewards injure relationships*. Individual rewards for performance create jealousies, envy, competition, and shame. The person not rewarded feels bad. There are always comparisons of what each person received. The result is less interpersonal goodwill and working together.
- *Rewards are really punishment.* An individual who is extrinsically rewarded is reminded each time he or she receives something that the "boss" is in control. Pleasing the boss, being politically correct, and staying in a subservient role are forms of punishment.
- *Rewards have a Skinner bias*. B. F. Skinner is a behaviorist who conducted most of his experiments on rodents and pigeons and wrote most of his books about people. Easy reinforcement application that works on pigeon- and rodent-dominated research is absurd. Emotions in employees are powerful, yet they are ignored by Skinner.
- *Rewards ignore reason*. What makes incentive pay plans and other forms of extrinsic rewards so appealing is that they are quick fixes. Issuing these kinds of rewards does not require managers to pay any attention to why a particular behavior occurred. Why was John's bonus larger than Mark's bonus? What were the behavioral differences between John and Mark?
- *Rewards discourage risk taking*. When people are driven by rewards, their focus become narrower, their creativity wanes, and they are not inclined to take risks. Taking risks may distract them from receiving a reward. Keeping a narrower, less risky orientation becomes preferred.

Managers should think about the points Kohn raises in his critique. It is unlikely in the foreseeable future to expect performance-based rewards to vanish in work organizations.[124]

One of Kohn's limitations is that he provides no organizational suggestions or prescriptions for replacing rewards. His emphasis on child rearing and raising good children without "goodies" (rewards) is not applicable to work organizations without much more compelling translation work on his part. Kohn's criticisms notwithstanding, it is fair to assume that rewards play an important role in motivating most employees. The most important challenge facing managers is to devise reward schemes that are equitable, reasonable, and meaningful to employees.

Summary of Key Points

- A central part of Bandura's social learning theory is the concept of self-efficacy, that is, the belief that a person knows that he can perform adequately in a particular situation.
- Reinforcement theory relies on applying the principles of operant conditioning to motivate people. A major assumption of operant conditioning is that behavior is influenced by its consequences.
- The nature of reinforcements and punishments and how they're employed influences behavior. Thus, reinforcement scheduling, or the timing of consequences, is an important feature of motivation.
- A concept that has evolved from social learning theory is called self-motivation. The concept of self-control is at the core of what's now called behavioral self-management in the organization literature.
- The expectancy theory of motivation is concerned with the expectations of a person and how they influence behavior. This theory provides managers with a means for pinpointing desirable and undesirable outcomes associated with task performance.
- Equity theory focuses on comparisons, tension, and tension reduction. To date, most research work on equity theory has involved pay. Equity theory is a more straightforward and understandable explanation of employee attitudes about pay than is expectancy

theory. The manager should be aware that people compare their rewards, punishments, tasks, and other job-related dimensions to those of others.

- Goal-setting theory proposes that an individual's goals and intentions are the primary determinants of behavior. Perhaps the most empirically supported approach to motivation, goal setting continues to be refined and studied in laboratory and field settings.
- Despite impressive supportive studies, goal setting has been criticized as working primarily for easy jobs, encouraging game playing, and operating as another control check on employees.
- Reward systems seek to attract people to join the organization, to keep them coming to work, and to motivate them to perform at high levels.
- Organizations typically provide two types of rewards. *Extrinsic* rewards are those external to the job, such as promotions, fringe benefits, and pay. *Intrinsic* rewards are associated with doing the job. They include responsibility, challenge, and meaningful work.
- An individual's satisfaction with a reward is influenced by: how much is received and how much the person feels should be received; comparisons with what happens to others; how satisfied the person is with both intrinsic and extrinsic rewards; the relative importance of different rewards; and whether the reward leads to other rewards.
- If effectively used, rewards can affect such individual behaviors as turnover, absenteeism, performance, and commitment. Research evidence showing how rewards influence these behaviors is becoming increasingly available.
- Nontraditional reward strategies include cafeteria-style fringe benefits, banking time off, skill-based pay, and gainsharing. These nontraditional reward systems each have strengths and weaknesses and are currently being used in many organizations.

Discussion and Review Questions

1. Feedback helps employees form perceptions of their self-efficacy on the job. Based on what you learned in this chapter, why is important that employees develop a sense of self-efficacy? Explain.
2. As a manager, which type of reinforcement would you most likely use with your employees: positive or negative reinforcement? Discuss the pros and cons of each approach.
3. Why is it exceptionally difficult to distribute rewards based on merit?
4. Describe a situation you've previously encountered where reinforcement theory could have been successfully applied. What type of reinforcement schedule would you have used?
5. What ethical considerations should be considered before using a behavior modification program in a work setting?
6. Goal setting is a powerful tool that managers can use to direct employee behavior. However, under what conditions can goal setting lead to undesirable employee outcomes?
7. Are there any intrinsic rewards for students? Discuss any that you believe apply to you.
8. Of the nontraditional reward systems described in the chapter, which system in your opinion would be the most challenging to successfully implement and maintain? Explain.
9. Why is Alfie Kohn's critique incomplete and not likely to result in the elimination of pay-for-performance reward programs?
10. What can a manager do to increase the intrinsic motivational factors associated with a job?

Taking It to the Net

How about Noncash Rewards?

"Show me the money!" A large number of managers assume that money is the primary motivator for most employees. However, research with each new generation shows that while money affects people's decisions to accept or leave a position, it is not always the strongest motivator when a person is on the job.

Noncash rewards are used more and more by organizations. By using the Internet and your searching skills, find 10 creative noncash rewards that firms are using as part of their reward strategy. Next, determine three noncash rewards that are important to you in terms of being motivational. Finally, find companies that use the three noncash rewards that you prefer.

Case for Analysis: *Jack Welch of General Electric: A Neutron Bomb or a Motivator?*

Jack Welch, now the ex-chairman of General Electric (GE), has been referred to as "Neutron Jack"—when he enters a GE facility, the building remains standing, but the workers are wiped out. Welch picked up the nickname by cutting more than 100,000 workers from GE's payroll in his first five years (1981–1986). He eliminated the jobs through layoffs, attrition, and the sale of businesses. When Welch took over at age 45 in 1981, he was GE's youngest chairman. GE was referred to as a "GNP company," one whose growth and prosperity never exceeded that of the overall economy. By the time Welch stepped down in the fall of 2001, he had devastated 289 lackluster businesses such as consumer electronics. He bought companies worth $19 billion and sold companies worth $10 billion.

Welch set out to create a company that could outpace the economy and thrive even in the toughest times. He utterly transformed GE, reshaping the corporate culture to reflect his relentless energy and informal but rigorous style. Welch sorted operations according to a simple criterion: to keep from being sold or shuttered, each had to be No. 1 or No. 2 in its market. He grouped businesses that he said met the test into a number of groups: services, such as GE Credit Corp. and a unit that maintains nuclear power plants; technology products in high-growth markets, such as jet engines and plastics; and what Welch calls the core businesses. These are the classic big players in such mature industries as light bulbs and electric motors. Currently, GE is a global market leader in 12 large-scale businesses.

Welch is a sensitive but no-nonsense man who views the world as competitively tough. He sees global markets coming to be dominated by a few powerful steam-rollers like Philips, Siemens, and Toshiba. To compete, a firm like GE must be bold, free of bureaucratic red tape, and staffed by self-motivated, proud, and quick-moving managers and employees. People who don't personally know Welch may fear his blunt, somewhat abrasive style. But those who spend time around him tend to like his intelligence, humor, and openness.

GE can be enormously exciting for those in the right places or attuned to the Welch mentality. By all accounts, Welch has transformed the company's bureaucratic culture to an astonishing degree. In eliminating managerial layers, Welch moved authority for most decisions down to the operating division level. He promotes a feeling of what he calls ownership, urging managers to act like entrepreneurs instead of hired help. Welch says he also promotes free communication: "We are out to get a feeling and a spirit of total openness. That's alien to a manager of 25 or 30 years who got ahead by knowing a little bit more than the employee who works for him." Welch says he wants to instill in managers "the confidence to lead and the confidence to share."

Welch's emphasis on communication and camaraderie is demonstrated by the long hours put in by GE's corporate officers commenting on drafts of a statement of corporate values that Welch titled, "What We Want to Be." These values—such as breaking down boundaries within the company, sharing good practices, emphasizing ownership—are more than just paperwork, however, as managers at GE are evaluated using the "Welch matrix"—namely, assessing the attainment of bottom-line results and the level of commitment to these company values. Greater weight is given to the values dimension, as these are difficult to teach and will ultimately produce the numbers desired.

Welch is not shy about expressing his opinions on how to manage and motivate people. Here are a few of his thoughts:

On being a tough manager:

> I got a raw deal with all those things about tough-guy Jack—fear, intimidation, guns and sticks and whips and chains. If you're mean, you don't belong at General Electric. Let me tell you why the name Neutron Jack is wrong. Competitiveness means taking action. Nuking somebody means you kill him. We start a renewal process. When people leave our company, we provide a soft landing. People who have been removed for not performing may be angry, but not one will say he wasn't treated with dignity. I don't think anyone would say he was treated unfairly, other than that bad management might have messed up the strategy. We can look ourselves in the mirror every morning and say we did what we could.

On anxiety among employees left at GE:

> If you're a middle manager who's not going anywhere, not trained in tomorrow's technology, it's a tough issue, tough all across America. If you look at what we did as a nation and what companies like GE did over the last 25 years, a lot of people didn't stay current as we went from electromechanical to electronic technology. A lot of methods changed, and a lot of people didn't change with them. If you're a middle manager in General Electric who is pretty well plateaued out, do you like what's happening to you? Probably you're concerned.

On the role of GE's top management:

> [Vice chairman] Larry Bossidy (currently the CEO of GE Credit) knows GE Credit. He built it. I know the plastics business. [Vice chairman] Ed Hood knows jet engines. After that, we start to get into very shallow water. But we know people. We know how to spot good ones more often than we spot bad ones—we don't bat 1,000—and we know how to allocate resources.

On freedom in the American system:

Welch believes that the U.S. system of free enterprise is an advantage that Americans have over the Japanese:

> It allows people like me to become chairman of GE in one generation; it allows the talented young employees in our company to move up fast. . . . The idea of liberation and improvement for our workforce is not enlightenment—it's a competitive necessity.

The need for leaders:

> Call people managers and they are going to start managing things, getting in the way. The job of a leader is to take the available resources—human and financial—and allocate them rigorously. Not to spread them out evenly, like butter on bread. That's what bureaucrats do. . . . You clearly want somebody who can articulate a vision. They have to have enormous energy and the incredible ability to energize others. If you can't energize others, you can't be a leader.

On self-confidence:

> Self-confidence is the fuel of productivity and creativity, decisiveness and speed.

GE has not only has survived under Welch's leadership but is looking youthfully exuberant. During his 20-year reign as CEO, Welch has infused the company with a sense of entrepreneurship, and in doing so has become one of the country's most admired CEOs. The quality Welch seems to value most in people is self-confidence, and he works hard to inspire it in others. He's a believer that people must control their own destinies or others will.

Welch's successor is Jeffrey Immelt, who is working to continue GE's successful performance. Following in Welch's footsteps is a challenging job that Immelt faces each day.

DISCUSSION QUESTIONS

1. Welch practices a hard-nosed management style. How can such a no-nonsense approach create a motivational atmosphere? Does Jack Welch use negative reinforcement, goal setting, or behavioral self-management? Or does he use a combination of techniques?
2. Jack Welch has set goals to be number one in various markets. Assume that it's both a difficult and an assigned goal. What does goal-setting research say about the effect of such goals on performance?
3. Why does Jack Welch value self-confidence so highly? Does his style of management inspire it in others?
4. What actions does Jack Welch take to encourage employee self-management?

Sources: Justin Baer and Francesco Guerrera, "Circuit failure," *Financial Times*, November 2008, p. 7; Diane Brady and Kerry Capell, "GE Breaks the Mold to Spur Innovation," *Businessweek*, April 26, 2004, p. 88; "Life After GE?" *Businessweek*, March 8, 2004, p. 76; Harris Collingwood and Diane L. Coutu, "Jack on Jack," *Harvard Business Review* 80, no. 2 (February 2002): 88; Warren Bennis, "Will the Legacy Live On?" *Harvard Business Review* 80, no. 2 (February 2002): 95; Carol Hymowitz, "Jack Welch Confronts a Difficult Final Act to End a Legendary Career," *The Wall Street Journal*, June 19, 2001, p. B1; John Huey and Geoffrey Colvin, "The Jack and Herb Show," *Fortune*, January 11, 1999, pp. 163–66; John A. Byrne, "Jack," *Businessweek*, June 8, 1998, pp. 91–108; and Thomas O'Boyle, *At Any Cost: Jack Welch, General Electric, and the Pursuit of Profit* (New York: Knopf, 1998).

Experiential Exercise: *Making Choices about Rewards*

OBJECTIVES

1. To illustrate individual differences in reward preferences.
2. To emphasize that both extrinsic and intrinsic rewards are considered important.
3. To enable people to explore the reasons for the reward preferences of others.

RELATED TOPICS

Because rewards are so pervasive in organizational settings, they tend to be linked to merit, seniority, and attendance. In fact, they're so related to organizational behavior that few issues of work life can be discussed without mentioning rewards.

STARTING THE EXERCISE

After reviewing Exhibit 1, individuals should work alone to establish their own lists of reward preferences. The instructor should set up groups of four to six students to examine individual preferences and complete the exercise.

THE FACTS

It's possible to develop an endless list of on-the-job rewards. Exhibit 1 identifies some rewards that could be available to employees.

COMPLETING THE EXERCISE

PHASE I: 25 MINUTES

1. Using Exhibit 1, each individual should make lists of extrinsic and intrinsic rewards.
2. Each person should then rank the items on her list from the most important to least important.
3. From the two lists, rank the eight most important rewards. How many are extrinsic, and how many are intrinsic?

PHASE II: 30 MINUTES

1. The instructor sets up groups of four to six individuals.
2. The individual lists in which the extrinsic and intrinsic categories were developed should be discussed within the groups.
3. The final rank orders of the eight most important rewards decided on within the groups should be placed on a board or chart at the front of the room.
4. Rankings should be discussed within the groups. Which major differences between individual-generated and group-generated lists were found?

EXHIBIT 1
Some Possible Rewards for Employees

Company picnics	Smile from manager	Participation in decisions
Watches	Feedback on performance	Stock options
Trophies	Feedback on career progress	Vacation trips for excellent performance
Piped-in music	Larger office	Manager asking for advice
Job challenge	Most prestigious job	Informal leader asking for advice
Achievement opportunity	More job involvement	Office with a window
Vacation	Use of company recreational facilities	The privilege of completing a job from start to finish
Autonomy	Bonus	Paid sabbatical
Pay increase	Paid health insurance	Financial counseling
Recognition	Health club membership	College tuition grants
Company car	Day care services	
Entertainment expense account		

Experiential Exercise: *Valuing Diversity*

The modern workplace is fast becoming a microcosm of the American population. Minority groups that previously have not had access to management and leadership positions in organizations are now a significant proportion of the overall workforce. Organizations must be able to take advantage of this broader talent pool, ensuring that all people have the opportunity to contribute to the extent of their potential.

Not all organizations have evolved to the point where they are able to see beyond a person's gender or ethnic status and to appreciate people for what they are able to contribute. Eliminating barriers to merit-based advancement is a central part of valuing diversity in the modern workplace.

PURPOSES

To heighten your awareness of the issues that companies are facing as the workplace becomes more diverse and to help you understand the issues faced by individuals who work there.

PROCEDURE

In this exercise, you will identify and interview a corporate diversity officer, and you will identify and interview a person employed in a business or nonprofit organization whose ethnic or gender status differs from your own to learn about the issues he or she faces in the workplace.

1. *Identify and interview a corporate diversity officer:* Many organizations today have designated a staff position to handle diversity issues for the firm. You should identify a person who serves this function in a medium to large organization. Contact this person and arrange a one-hour informational interview. Besides developing your own set of questions for the diversity officer, your interview should cover the following issues:
   - What type of diversity training program does the company have?
   - What are the major diversity issues the company faces?
   - What are the major problems faced by women and minorities in the organization?
   - Does the company recruit in a way that increases its diversity?
   - Does the company have an active affirmative action program?
2. *Identify and interview a person of different gender or ethnicity.* Identify and interview a person of managerial rank or better in a medium to large company who is different in gender or ethnicity from you. This person should *not* be directly involved in the organization's diversity function and preferably should be in a line position. Arrange a one-hour informational interview with this person to learn more about the challenges he or she perceives as directly related to his or her gender or ethnicity. This could be a sensitive issue for some people, so you may have to guarantee anonymity to the person you are interviewing. What you want to learn from this interview is how the individual believes her or his career has been affected because of gender or ethnicity. Several issues to explore include these:
   - Has the person ever been passed up for career advancement based on gender or ethnic status?
   - Has the person ever felt that he or she has been given special consideration based on gender or ethnic status?
   - What kinds of organizational barriers does the person feel as a function of her or his gender or ethnic status?
   - What strategies does the person use to overcome these barriers?
3. *Report your findings to the class:* After conducting your two informal interviews, be prepared to discuss your findings with the class. You should be able to summarize the types of diversity training programs the organization you identified is using and to describe the effect of this training on the organization. You should also be able to summarize your interview with the individual of different gender or ethnic status. What are the key issues as this person sees them? Has this person benefited from or been harmed by corporate diversity programs?

CHAPTER SEVEN

Managing Workplace Stress

Learning Objectives

After completing Chapter 7, you should be able to

Understand
The differences between stressors, stress, and outcomes.

Distinguish
Among four different categories of stressors.

Explain
The effects of stress on health.

Identify
The relationship between stress and social support.

Describe
The objectives of individual and organizational wellness approaches for the reduction and prevention of stress.

The Need for Work/Life Balance

Once, only the salaried elite enjoyed what are now called work/life balance programs. However, demographics indicate that U.S. companies can expect rising demand for flextime and child and elder care programs. By 2020, there will be 27.7 persons aged 65 or older for every 100 working adults, a 28.5 percent increase in just two decades. The more than 75 million Generation Yers (in their 20s to early 30s) representing more than 29 percent of the U.S. population have started their families, and from 2001 to 2011 birth rates could reach 4.3 million annually, equaling the number of births in 1957, the peak year of baby boom births.

The work and personal lives of employees are interconnected. Two explanations have been offered regarding the linkage between work and personal lives. The first, the compensation effect, suggests that job and personal life satisfaction are negatively related. That is, a person is assumed to compensate for low work satisfaction by seeking satisfying activities in the personal domain, and vice versa.

The second explanation, a spillover view of work and personal life, seems to have more research support than the compensation effect. The spillover view suggests that job satisfaction or dissatisfaction spills over into one's personal life and vice versa. For example, if an employee has a satisfying job, then this contentment is theorized to exert a positive influence over home and personal life. Organizations are paying more attention to work and family-friendly programs such as child care perks, time off with pay for elder care, flexible work schedules, flexible benefit plans, telecommuting, workout facilities at work, and even laundry and cleaning services.

Organizations are watching research results emerge on work/family balance programs. To date, the research evidence in general suggests that employee morale, satisfaction, health, and performance are improved among employees who have received work/life program activities such as onsite child care, time off for elder care, or opportunities to work primarily out of their homes (telecommuting). These programs also reduce the level and intensity of stress that employees face.

Sources: K. Gurchiek, "Research Links Workplace Practices, Employee Health," *HRMagazine*, December 2009, p. 15; "The Boomers and Gen-Xers," accessed at www.bhq.com/boomrgenz.htm on April 23, 2007; C. S. Bruck, T. D. Allen, and P. E. Spector, "The Relations between Work-Family Conflict and Job Satisfaction: A Finer-Drained Analysis," *Journal of Vocational Behavior* 60 (2002): 226–53; Fred Harmon, *Business 2010* (Washington, D.C.: Kiplinger Books, 2001); Charlotte Garvey, "Teleworking HR," *HR Magazine,* August 2001, pp. 56–60; and Holly Weeks, "Taking the Stress Out of Stressful Conversations," *Harvard Business Review,* July–August 2001, pp. 112–19.

The experience of work and life stress is certainly not new. Our cave-dwelling ancestors faced stress every time they left their caves and encountered their enemy, the saber-toothed tigers.[1] The tigers of yesteryear are gone, but they have been replaced by other predators—work overload, a nagging boss, computer problems, time deadlines, downsizing, mergers, poorly designed jobs, elder care, marital disharmony, financial crises, terrorism, and accelerating rates of change. These work and nonwork predators interact and create stress for individuals on and off the job.

This chapter focuses on the workplace and the stress created in this setting. Much of the stress experienced by people in our industrialized society originates in organizations; much of the stress that originates elsewhere affects our behavior and performance in these same organizations. Thus, work/life balance issues will be reviewed. Research has clearly shown that workplace stress spills over into one's personal, family, and community life. The opening vignette discussed this work/life balance issue.

This chapter focuses on how to reduce and manage stress more effectively. The elimination of stress in a modern society is impossible and beyond the capability of managers in work settings. Experiencing stress every day is a normal routine. What is not routine is stress that is so intense that it becomes unhealthy, dysfunctional, and dangerous. High levels of stress can decrease the satisfaction and productivity of employees, which ultimately prevents many organizations from reaching and maintaining high levels of effectiveness.

What Is Stress?

Stress means different things to different people. From a layperson's perspective, stress can be described as feeling tense, anxious, or worried. Scientifically, these feelings are all manifestations of the stress experience, a complex programmed response to perceived threat that can have both positive and negative results. The term *stress* itself has been defined in literally hundreds of ways in the literature. Virtually all of the definitions can be placed into one of two categories, however; stress can be defined as either a *stimulus* or a *response.*

A stimulus definition treats stress as some characteristic or event that may result in a disruptive consequence. It is in that respect an engineering definition of stress borrowed from the physical sciences. In physics, stress refers to the external force applied to an object, for example, a bridge girder. The response is strain, which is the impact the force has on the girder.

stressor
A potentially harmful or threatening external event or situation.

stress
An adaptive response, mediated by individual differences, that is a consequence of any action, situation, or event that places special demands on a person.

In a response definition, stress is seen partially as a response to some stimulus called a **stressor**. A stressor is a potentially harmful or threatening external event or situation. Stress is more than simply a response to a stressor, however. In a response definition, stress is the consequence of the interaction between an environmental stimulus (a stressor) and the individual's response. That is, stress is the result of a unique interaction between stimulus conditions in the environment and the individual's predisposition to respond in a particular way. Using a response definition, we will define **stress** as an adaptive response, mediated by individual differences, that is a consequence of any action, situation, or event that places special demands on a person.

We think it is useful to view stress as the response a person makes and to identify stimulus conditions (actions, situations, and events) as stressors. This allows us to focus attention on aspects of the organizational environment that are potential stress producers. Whether stress is actually felt or experienced by a particular individual will depend on that individual's unique characteristics. Furthermore, note that this definition emphasizes that stress is an adaptive response. Because the great majority of stimuli in the work environment do not require adaptation, they are not really potential stress sources.

In the context of the definition of stress, it is important to understand that stress is the result of dealing with something placing special demands on us. *Special* here means unusual, physically or psychologically threatening, or outside our usual set of experiences. Starting a new job assignment in another country, changing bosses, missing a plane, having the computer system fail in the middle of a crucial project, having a performance evaluation meeting with the boss—all of these are actions, situations, or events that may place special demands on you. In that sense, they are *potential* stressors. We say potential because not all stressors will always place the same demands on people. For example, starting a new job assignment in Beijing or Bangalore may be very stressful to one new expatriate manager and not be stressful at all to another expatriate manager.[2]

For an action, situation, or event to result in stress, it must be perceived by the individual to be a source of threat, challenge, or harm. If there are no perceived consequences—good or bad—there is no potential for stress. Three key factors determine whether an experience is likely to result in stress. These factors are importance, uncertainty, and duration. *Importance* relates to how significant the event is to the individual. For example, let us suppose that you are facing a job layoff. The more significant that layoff is to you, the more likely you are to find it stressful. If you expect the layoff to be followed by a period of prolonged unemployment, you will probably view it as a more important event than if immediate reemployment is assured.

Uncertainty refers to a lack of clarity about what will happen. Rumors of an impending layoff may be more stressful to some people than knowing for certain they will be laid off. At least in the latter case, they can make plans for dealing with the situation. Frequently, "not knowing" places more demands on people than does "knowing," even if the known result is perceived as negative.

Finally, *duration* is a significant factor. Generally speaking, the longer special demands are placed on us, the more stressful the situation. Being given a distasteful job assignment that lasts only a day or two may be mildly upsetting, while the same assignment lasting for six months may be excruciating. Most people can endure short periods of strenuous physical activity without tiring; prolong the duration, however, and even the most fit among us will become exhausted. The same holds true for stressors. Stress of short duration is sometimes referred to as acute stress. It may last for a few seconds, a few hours, even a few days. Long-duration stress, on the other hand, is sometimes referred to as chronic stress. Chronic stress may last for months and years. It is the ongoing tension experienced by people of the Middle East and by U.S. soldiers deployed for tours of duty in war-torn Iraq and Afghanistan.[3] It may also be the unrelenting pressure of a job one finds no satisfaction in performing, the constant demands made by an unreasonable boss, or the never-ending struggle to advance in one's chosen career.

Hans Selye pointed out the importance of learning about the concept he designated as *eustress* (i.e., good stress). When stress evokes a positive or uplifting outcome, it is referred to as eustress (from the concept of euphoria). In this chapter, the focus will be on stress that evokes negative outcomes. However, it is reasonable to consider both positive and negative stress when determining how to manage stress effectively in the work setting.

Organizational Stress: A Model

For most employed people, work and work-related activities and preparation time represent much more than a 40-hour-a-week commitment. Work is a major part of our lives, and work and nonwork activities are highly interdependent. The distinction between stress at work and stress at home has always been an artificial one at best. With the explosive increase of dual-career couples and individuals who work from home offices, even this artificial distinction has become blurred. The primary concern here, however, is with direct, work-related stressors. This is due to the emphasis in the book on work-related behavior and performance. Certainly, nonwork stressors are factors in the lives of employees that managers must tune into when and if workers want to discuss them privately.

FIGURE 7.1
A Model of Stressors, Stress, and Outcomes

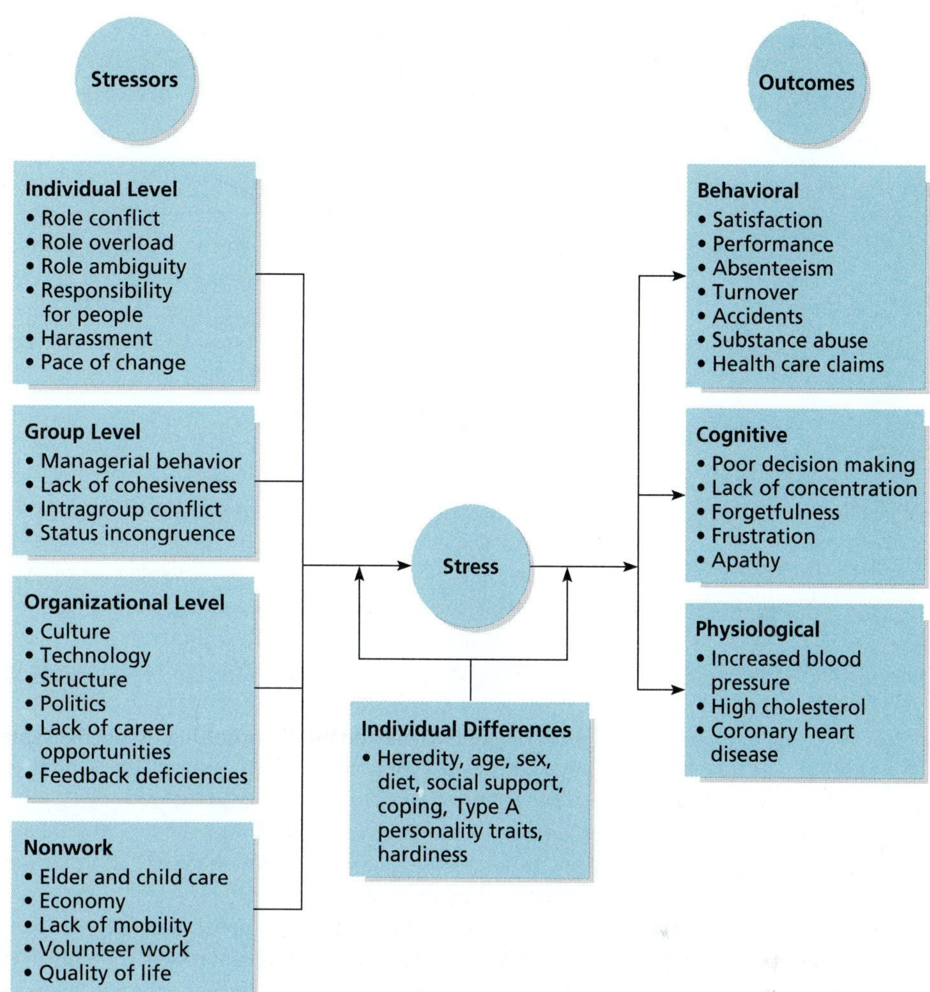

The model in Figure 7.1 is designed to help illustrate the link among organizational stressors, stress, and outcomes. Recall from the definition that stress is a response to an action, situation, or event that places special demands on an individual. These occurrences are represented in Figure 7.1 as *stressors.* We have divided these stressors into four main categories: individual, group, organizational, and extraorganizational. The first three stressor categories are work related.

The experience of work-related and extraorganizational stress produces behavioral, cognitive, and physiological outcomes. The model suggests that the relationship between stress and outcomes (individual and organizational) is not necessarily direct; similarly neither is the relationship between the stressors and stress. These relationships may be influenced by stress moderators. Individual differences such as age, social support, and personality are introduced as potential moderators. A moderator is a valuable attribute that affects the nature of a relationship. While numerous moderators are extremely important, we focus our attention on three representative ones: personality, Type A behavior, and social support.

This framework provides managers with a way of thinking about stress in the workplace. Consequently, it suggests that interventions may be needed and can be effective in improving negative stress consequences. Stress prevention and management can be initiated by individuals or the organization. The intention of most preventive programs is to reduce the occurrence, intensity, and negative effect of stress. The management of stress attempts to eliminate or minimize negative consequences of stress.[4] The prevention of and management of stress are difficult, as will be illustrated later in this chapter.

Work Stressors: Individual, Group, and Organizational

Stressors are those actions, situations, or events that place special demands on a person. In the right circumstances, virtually any occurrence can place special demands on a person; thus, the list of potential stressors is almost infinite. We will examine a sample of the numerous stressors that are relatively common in each of the model's three work-specific categories (e.g., individual, group, organizational).

Individual Stressors

role conflict
Occurs when an individual's compliance with one set of expectations conflicts with compliance with another set of expectations.

Stressors at the individual level have been studied more than any other category presented in Figure 7.1. Role conflict is perhaps the most widely examined individual stressor.[5] **Role conflict** is present whenever compliance by an individual with one set of expectations about the job is in conflict with compliance with another set of expectations. Facets of role conflict include being torn by conflicting demands from a supervisor about the job and being pressured to get along with people with whom you are not compatible. Regardless of whether role conflict results from organizational policies or from other persons, it can be a significant stressor for some individuals. For example, a study at Goddard Space Flight Center (www.nasa.gov/centers/goddard) determined that about 67 percent of employees reported some degree of role conflict. The study further found that Goddard employees who experienced more role conflict also experienced lower job satisfaction and higher job-related tension.[6] It is interesting to note that the researchers also found that the greater the power or authority of the people sending the conflicting messages, the greater was job dissatisfaction produced by role conflict.

An increasingly prevalent type of role conflict occurs when work and nonwork roles interfere with one another. The most common nonwork roles involved in this form of conflict are those of spouse and parent. Balancing the demands of work and family roles is a significant daily task for a growing number of employed adults.[7] Pressure to work late, to take work home, to spend more time traveling, and to frequently relocate in order to advance are a few examples of potential sources of conflict between work and family. When both spouses are employed, added conflict potentially exists when one partner's career progress may be negatively affected by the career progression of the other.

qualitative overload
Occurs when people feel they lack the ability to complete a job or that performance standards are too high.

quantitative overload
Results from having too many things to do or insufficient time to complete a job.

Virtually everyone has experienced work overload at one time or another, and the incident rate is increasing.[8] Overload may be of two types: qualitative and quantitative. **Qualitative overload** occurs when people feel they lack the ability needed to complete their jobs or that performance standards have been set too high. **Quantitative overload**, on the other hand, results from having too many things to do or insufficient time to complete a job. As organizations attempt to increase productivity, while decreasing work-force size, quantitative overload increases (as does stress). New York law firm Cleary, Gottlieb, Steen & Hamilton was sued by the father of an associate at the firm. The associate, unable to cope with the overload, committed suicide by jumping off the roof of the firm's building.[9]

From a health standpoint, numerous studies have established that quantitative overload might cause biochemical changes, specifically elevations in blood cholesterol levels. One study examined the relationship of overload, underload, and stress among 1,540 executives. Those executives in the low and high ends of the stress ranges reported more significant medical problems.[10] The underload–overload continuum is presented in Figure 7.2. The optimal stress level provides the best balance of challenge, responsibility,

FIGURE 7.2
The Underload–Overload Continuum

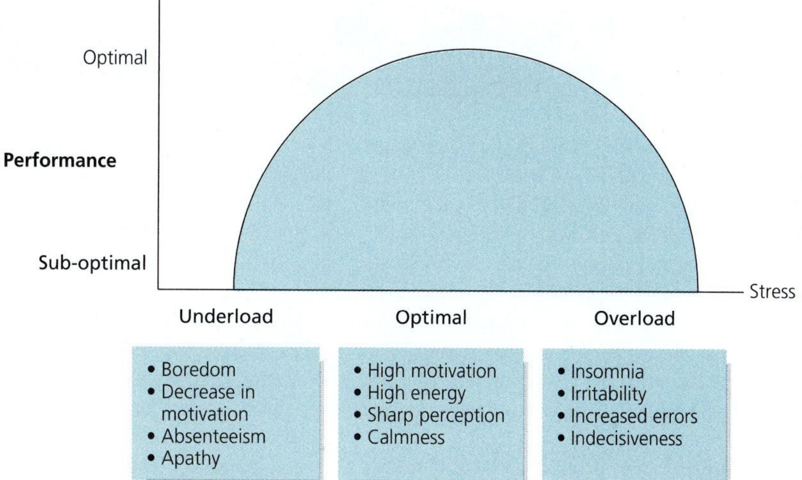

and reward. The potential negative effects of overload can be increased when overload is coupled with low ability to control the work demand.[11] Research suggests that when individuals experience high work demands with little or no control over these demands, the physiological changes that occur persist even after the individual has left work.[12] The next OB at Work feature suggests that general pain may be linked to underload or monotonous work.

Perhaps the most pervasive individual stressor of all is the unrelenting pace of change that is part of life today. At no other point in the history of industrialized society have we experienced such rapid change in the world around us. The past 50 years or so included the advent of such wonders as electronic communications, satellites, moon landings, organ transplants, laser technology, nuclear power plants, pilotless aircraft, supersonic transportation, artificial hearts, and many other space-age developments. The pace of change within organizations has been no less remarkable. Radical restructuring, offshoring, new technologies, the stunning emergence and demise of many dot-com firms, mergers, acquisitions, internationalization, financial scandals, and renewed emphasis on teams support this commonsense conclusion. On the other hand, many people who experience a great deal of change show absolutely no subsequent health problems. For some reason, these people are strong enough to withstand the negative consequences of large doses of change while others are not.

hardiness
Personality trait that enables a person who possesses it to cope with stressors in such a way that they have minimal impact on the person's health.

Why responses to change differ is an intriguing question. One organizational researcher, Suzanne Kobasa, proposes that individuals who experience high rates of change without consequently suffering health problems might differ in terms of personality from those who do. She refers to the personality characteristic as ***hardiness***.[13] People with the hardiness personality trait seem to possess three important characteristics. First, they believe that they can control the events they encounter. Second, they are extremely committed to the activities in their lives. Third, they treat change in their lives as a challenge. In a longitudinal study to test the three-characteristic theory of hardiness, managers were studied over a two-year period. The study found that the more managers possessed hardiness characteristics, the smaller the effect of life changes on their personal health. Hardiness appeared to offset, or buffer, the negative impact of change.

Hardiness is proposed as a factor to reduce stress by changing the way stressors are perceived. The hardy person is able to work through and around stressors, while the less hardy person becomes overwhelmed and unable to cope. The hardy respond by coping, attempting to control, and taking on the stressors as a challenge. This type of response typically results in better behavioral, cognitive, and physiological consequences.[14]

OB AT WORK Monotonous or Underloaded Pain and Stress

What causes pain to the body independent of physical signs of disease? This question has long interested investigators studying conditions with widespread body pain, including fibromyalgia—a syndrome marked by chronic, unexplained, and severe pain, fatigue, and sleep problems. Some experts ascribe these conditions to a psychological predisposition. Other experts trace its roots to physical trauma, such as a traffic accident. But until recently, no one has explored what happens with a combination of ongoing physical strain and psychological distress—particularly when endured in the line of work.

A team of researchers at the University of Manchester in England devoted two years to conducting the first long-term study of widespread pain in relation to taxing labor and lack of job satisfaction. This groundbreaking study focused on the persistent pain experienced by a large, young, healthy cross-section of newly employed individuals.

Representing 12 different work environments, jobs ranged from the physically demanding and routinely dangerous (shipbuilder, firefighter, police officer, army officer, forest ranger, soldier) to the relatively safe, but not without pressure (postal worker, retail worker, nurse, dentist, podiatrist, army clerk). The majority of the 896 subjects were all in their 20s. Roughly one-third were men.

At the start of the study, coinciding with the start of employment (the first full-time job for many), the participants were all pain-free. After one year of work, 15 percent of the participants had developed widespread pain. After two years, an additional 12 percent of the workers developed widespread pain. At the one-year mark, the rate of new widespread pain was significantly higher in women than in men, but this difference did not persist. Strikingly, there was no significant difference in the proportion of subjects reporting widespread pain by the follow-up period for any occupational group.

Through extensive questionnaires, the researchers identified several factors for the onset of widespread pain. The most significant physical risks were pulling heavy weights and prolonged squatting. In addition to these physical culprits, the team found a strong correlation between widespread pain and two psychosocial factors: low social support and monotonous work (e.g., underload).

Lead researcher Elaine F. Harkness, Ph.D., stated: "Monotonous work may lead to increased psychological *job stress*, which might explain the adverse health outcomes, including the onset of musculoskeletal pain."

Harkness and colleagues suggest that reconstituting work may be a tool at our disposal and one that, given the high prevalence of work disability associated with pain syndromes, is worth a try.

Source: Adapted from http://www.fmaware.org (accessed May 12, 2010); "Link between Widespread Pain and Physical Psychological Stress on the Job," *Obesity, Fitness, and Wellness*, May 29, 2004, p. 845.

Individual stressors abound. Not only can they cause stress but also a number of negative consequences as well. As we will see later in the chapter, stress consequences can affect both health and a variety of job performance variables.

Group and Organizational Stressors

The list of potential group and organizational stressors is a long one. Chapter 8 discusses a number of group characteristics. These include group norms, leadership, and the status hierarchy. Each of these can be a stressor for some group members, as can the different types of group conflict discussed in Chapter 9. One problem in discussing group and organizational stressors is identifying which are the most important ones. In the paragraphs that follow, we briefly highlight what we feel are the more significant stressors.

Participation

Participation refers to the extent that a person's knowledge, opinions, and ideas are included in the decision-making process. It is an important part of working in organizations for some people. Groups and organizations that do not encourage or allow participation will be a source of frustration to those who value it. Likewise, others will be frustrated by the delays often associated with participative decision making. Others may view shared decision making as a threat to the traditional right of a manager to have the final say. Participation will act as a stressor for those people.

Intra- and Intergroup Relationships

Poor relationships within and between groups can be a source of stress. For example, several members of the customer service team may not get along, or a firm's salespeople may make commitments that the installation team can't honor, which can lead to friction between these two groups. Poor relationships may include low trust, lack of cohesion, low supportiveness, and lack of interest in listening to and dealing with the problems that confront a group or group member. Problem relationships can lead to communication breakdowns and low job satisfaction, further increasing the likelihood of stress.

Organizational Politics

High levels of political behavior in organizations can be a source of stress for many employees. Office politics are consistently cited as a primary stressor in organizations. Political activity, game playing, and power struggles can create friction, heighten dysfunctional competition between individuals and groups, and increase stress.

Friction, stress, and hard-driving style are exemplified by the action of Al Dunlap, a designated turnaround chief executive officer. Dunlap was given credit for turning around troubled American Can, Crown Zellenbach, and Scott Paper. On the other hand, he was a failure at Sunbeam and was eventually fired.[15] He had a reputation for being political, gruff, and demeaning. One of his first meetings at Sunbeam was described as follows: "It was like a dog barking at you for hours. He just yelled, ranted, and raved. He was condescending, belligerent, and disrespectful."[16] Many managers left Sunbeam because it became a highly politicized and stressful place to work. Al Dunlap was himself a stressor for many of the managers who wouldn't tolerate his behavior and style.

In contrast to Dunlap's and Zellenbach's aggressive styles, Jun Haraguchi, president and CEO of Konica Minolta's Business Solutions U.S.A., follows a "work hard, be nice" philosophy. He practices yoga on a daily basis, plays his guitar with performers at company functions, tells jokes at company meetings, and tries to be approachable to his employees. Haraguchi believes a less stressful environment at the workplace is better for everyone, including himself.

Organizational Culture

Like individuals, organizations have distinct personalities. The personality of an organization is shaped largely by its top executives. A tyrannical and autocratic executive team is able to create a culture that is filled with fear. Ernest Gallo is credited with being the stress producer at Gallo Winery because of the culture he established with his hard-driving style, unrelenting insistence on superior performance, and low tolerance for failure.[17] Charles Wang, co-founder and former CEO of Computer Associates (CA), was accused of instilling a "culture of fear" throughout the company following its creation. Years later, a subsequent CEO, John Swainson, helped to lift the veil of fear by instilling openness, courage to speak honestly, and humor into the CA culture.[18]

Lack of Performance Feedback

Most people want to know how they are doing and how management views their work. All too often, however, meaningful performance evaluation information is lacking, or the information is provided in a highly authoritarian or critical manner. Performance feedback information must be provided, and if it is to be provided in a way that minimizes stress, it must take place in an open two-way communication system.

Inadequate Career Development Opportunities

Career development opportunity stressors are those aspects of the organizational environment that influence a person's perception of the quality of his or her career progress. Career variables may serve as stressors when they become sources of concern, anxiety, or frustration. This can happen if an employee is concerned about real or imagined obsolescence, feels that promotion progress is inadequate, or is generally dissatisfied with the match between career aspirations and the current position.

Downsizing

Downsizing is primarily associated with the reduction of human resources, layoffs, attrition, redeployment, or early retirement.[19] As some organizations strive to become "lean and mean," increasing numbers of employees are either downsized or fear being downsized.[20] In either case, downsizing is a potent stressor. It can have negative effects for both individuals and organizations. Studies have shown, for example, that disability claims can increase as much as 70 percent in companies that have recently downsized.[21] This increase comes both from employees who have been dismissed as well as from those who remained. That is probably why many companies like Novell, Wachovia, and ReliaStar Bankers Security Life Insurance Co. have established programs to help employees cope with the stress of reorganizations and layoffs.[22]

Nonwork Stressors

Nonwork stressors are those caused by factors outside the organization. Although the emphasis in the chapter is on work, nonwork stressors should not be ignored. Raising children, caring for elders, volunteering in the community, taking college courses, and balancing family and work life are stressful situations for numerous people.[23] The stress produced outside work is likely to affect a person's work performance and work behavior in general. The distinction between work and nonwork is blurred, overlaps, and is significant in any discussion or analysis of stress.

As more consideration of nonwork versus work balance continues, it is likely that nonwork/work interaction of stressors research is going to increase. For example, the individual who is attempting to balance her family needs, work requirements, and taking care of an elderly mother is likely to be faced with interactive stressors. That is, it is difficult to separate these three categories of stressors.

Stress Outcomes

The effects of stress are many and varied. Some effects, of course, are positive, such as self-motivation and stimulation to satisfy individual goals and objectives. Nonetheless, some stress consequences are disruptive, counterproductive, and even potentially dangerous. Additionally, as was discussed earlier (see again Figure 7.2), there are consequences associated with *too little* stress as well as too much.

Not all individuals will experience the same outcomes. Research suggests, for example, that one of many factors influencing stress outcomes is type of employment. In one study, conducted at the Institute for Social Research at the University of Michigan, a sample of 2,010 employees was chosen for 23 occupations to examine the relationship between stress and consequences. The occupations were combined into four specific groups: skilled and unskilled blue-collar workers and professional and nonprofessional white-collar workers.

Blue-collar workers reported the highest subjective effects, including job dissatisfaction; white-collar workers, the lowest. The unskilled workers reported the most boredom and apathy with their job conditions. They specifically identified a number of major stressors that created their psychological state: underutilization of skills and abilities, poor fit of the job with respect to desired amounts of responsibility, lack of participation, and ambiguity about the future. Skilled blue-collar workers share some of these stressors and consequences with their unskilled counterparts, but not all; they reported above-average utilization of

OB AT WORK Karoshi: Stress and Death in Japan

Have you ever felt or heard someone else express the feeling, "This job is going to kill me!" Chances are you—or the person you heard—didn't literally believe that. If you were a Japanese worker, however, you might be very serious. Polls indicate that more than 40 percent of Japanese workers aged 30 to 60 believe they will die from the stress of overwork, what the Japanese call *karoshi.* The victims of karoshi are known in their companies as *moretsu shain* (fanatical workers) and *yoi kigyo senshi* (good corporate soldiers). Death by overwork is not as rare as it sounds. In 2002, Kenichi Uchino, a Toyota quality control manager, died at the age 30 of *karoshi.* During each of the six months preceding his death, Kenichi worked more than 80 hours of overtime. Another case was when Ichiro Oshima, an overworked employee of Dentsu, Japan's largest advertising agency, committed suicide. There are many other cases of karoshi, and the incidence is on the rise in many Asian countries like Japan.

In spite of recent revisions to the Japanese labor standard law that reduced the length of the average workweek, Japanese workers spend on average about six weeks (or about 250 hours per year) more on the job than most Americans. A Japanese Health Ministry report identified karoshi as the second-leading cause of death among workers (the first is cancer). Fierce competition among employees, as well as a strong sense of responsibility to their companies, leads many workers to stay at the office well into the night. When they do go home, they are tense and anxious because they feel that they should really be back at work. Some workers deal with the pressure by disappearing. As many as 10,000 men disappear a year, choosing to drop out rather than face the pressure of their jobs.

There are signs, however, that things are changing. The government has funded a multimillion-dollar study of karoshi. Some of Japan's leading firms, such as Sony Corporation, have begun to require employees to take vacations whether they want to or not. Also, more companies are closing on Saturday, part of a national drive toward a five-day workweek. Traditions die hard in Japan, however, and no one believes fear of karoshi will disappear any time soon.

Sources: Adapted from Audrey H.H. Tsui, "Asian Wellness in Decline: A Cost of Rising Prosperity," *International Journal of Workplace Health Management* 1, no. 2 (2008): 123–135; A. Kanai, "Karoshi (Work to Death)" in Japan," *Journal of Business Ethics: Supplement* 84 (2009): 209–216; and "Asia: Jobs for Life; Death by overwork in Japan," *The Economist*, December 2007, p. 98.

their skills and abilities but had less responsibility and more ambiguity. White-collar professionals reported the fewest negative consequences. In all groups, however, there were indications that job performance was affected.[24]

In examining stress outcomes, the distinction in our model between organizational and individual outcomes is somewhat arbitrary. For example, a decline in job performance due to stress is clearly an individual outcome. It is the individual's performance that is being affected. Just as clearly, however, the organization experiences important consequences from employees' stress-related performance decrements.

Individual Outcomes

The emergence or evolution of stress outcomes takes time to identify or pinpoint. Eventually, evidence is available upon which to reach a number of conclusions. For example, a promoted employee develops an uncharacteristic pattern of Friday and Monday absences. A salesperson begins to lose repeat business; departed customers complain that he has become inattentive and curt in his dealings with them. A formerly conscientious nurse forgets to administer medications, with potentially serious consequences for her patients. An assembly worker experiences a significant increase in the percentage of her production rejected by a quality-control unit. A software designer displays sudden, apparently unprovoked outbursts of anger. Each of these individuals is experiencing the effects, or consequences, of excessive stress.

Stress can produce a variety of *psychological consequences,* including anxiety, frustration, apathy, lowered self-esteem, aggression, and depression.[25] With respect to depression, a comprehensive survey of American workers concluded that a third of them experienced job-related depressions. Such consequences are not restricted to American workers, as the accompanying OB at Work feature about Japan demonstrates.[26]

There is a stigma associated with depression.[27] Part of the stigma is that most people lack an understanding of depression and its frequency. Unfortunately, most managers are not aware of these facts:

- According to Mental Health America, the cost of depression is $44 billion a year in medical bills, lost productivity, and absenteeism.[28]
- The World Health Organization estimates that by 2020 depression will be the second-leading cause of premature death and disability worldwide.[29]
- Depression is difficult to detect, especially within the present health care system.[30]

The Diagnostic and Statistical Manual of Mental Disorders (DSM-IV) is the diagnostic tool used to detect depression. The DSM-IV indicates that the diagnosis of depression requires the presence of either a depressed mood or diminished interest in all or most activities, marked psychomotor retardation, significant appetite or weight change, changes in sleep, fatigue or loss of energy, problems thinking or concentrating, feelings of worthlessness, excessive feelings of guilt, or thoughts of suicide or death. These signs must be persistent over the course of two weeks.

Managerial understanding of these symptoms can help organizations, especially when the manager requests an intervention from professional counselors. Managers are not skilled or qualified to intervene themselves, yet mild and moderate cases of depression can be treated over time. Being aware of depression symptoms and situations that precipitate it are the first line of intervention. Unfortunately, the stigma of depression results in a lack of understanding of its pervasiveness, costs, and treatment possibilities.[31]

Some outcomes of stress may be cognitive. Cognitive outcomes include poor concentration, inability to make sound decisions or any decisions at all, mental blocks, and decreased attention spans. Other effects may be behavioral. Such manifestations as being prone to accidents, impulsive behavior, alcohol and drug abuse, and explosive temper are examples. Finally, *physiological outcomes* could include increased heart rate, elevated blood pressure, sweating, hot and cold flashes, increased blood glucose levels, and elevated stomach acid production.

Among the individual outcomes of stress, those classified as physiological are perhaps the most dysfunctional because they can in turn contribute to physical illness. One of the more significant of the physiological consequences and illness relationships is that of coronary heart disease (CHD). Although virtually unknown in the industrialized world a century ago, CHD now accounts for almost two out of every five deaths in the United States. Traditional risk factors such as obesity, smoking, heredity, and high cholesterol can account for approximately 25 percent of the incidence of CHD. There is growing medical opinion that job and life stress may be a major contributor to the remaining 75 percent.[32] Several studies have found, for example, a relationship between changes in blood pressure and job stress.[33]

Some stress outcomes combine effects from several of the categories of consequences described earlier. Consider, for example, the following two scenarios:

> Benjamin works as a teacher in an inner-city high school. He barely remembers the time when he could not wait for the start of each school day; now, he cannot wait until each day ends. As much as he could use the money, he quit teaching optional summer school three summers ago. He needs that break to recharge his batteries, which seem to run down earlier with each passing school year. Many of his students are moody, turned off to society, and abusive to others. Benjamin is beginning to realize that he himself is becoming moody, turned off to society, and abusive to others.
>
> Cecilia works as an air traffic controller in the second-busiest airport in the country. Every day, the lives of literally thousands of people depend on how well she does her job.

Near misses are an everyday occurrence; avoiding disaster requires quick thinking and a cool head. At 31 years of age, Cecilia is the third-oldest controller in the tower. She knows there are few controllers over the age of 45, and she is certain she will never be one. To make matters worse, she is in the final stages of a divorce. Cecilia was told after her most recent physical that she had developed a stomach ulcer. She is thinking of going into the nursery business with her sister. Having responsibility for the well-being of shrubs and trees, rather than people, is very attractive to her.

Burnout
A psychological process resulting from work stress that results in emotional exhaustion, depersonalization, and feelings of decreased accomplishment.

Benjamin and Cecilia are both experiencing job burnout. **Burnout** is a psychological process, brought about by unrelieved work stress, which results in emotional exhaustion, depersonalization, and feelings of decreased accomplishment.[34] Table 7.1 displays some of the indicators of these three burnout outcomes. Burnout tends to be a particular problem among people whose jobs require extensive contact with other people, responsibility for them, or both. Indeed, much of the research that has been conducted on burnout has centered on the so-called helping professions: teachers, nurses, counselors, physicians, social workers, therapists, police, and parole officers.[35] The next OB at Work feature presents some of the myths that surround the burnout concept.

A very important idea implicit in this conceptualization of burnout relates to job involvement. A high degree of involvement in, identification with, or commitment to one's job or profession is a necessary prerequisite for burnout. It is unlikely that one would become exhausted without putting forth a great deal of effort. Thus, the irony of burnout is that those most susceptible are those most committed to their work; all else being equal, lower job commitment equals lower likelihood of burnout. Various individual variables also affect the likelihood of developing burnout. For example, women are more likely to burn out than men, younger employees are more susceptible than older ones (particularly beyond age 50), and unmarried workers are more likely to burn out than married ones.

Organizations contribute to employee job burnout in a variety of ways. Researchers have identified four factors that are particularly important contributors to burnout: high levels of work overload, dead-end jobs, excessive red tape and paperwork, and poor communication and feedback, particularly regarding job performance. In addition, factors that have been identified in at least one research study as contributing to burnout include role conflict and ambiguity, difficult interpersonal relationships, and reward systems that are not contingent upon performance. A recent meta-analysis (a study of several other research studies) found that dimensions of one's personality are correlated with job burnout; and that burnout is linked to higher levels of absenteeism and turnover, as well as reduced job performance.[36]

A consistent theme found in analyzing burnout is the problematic relationship between the person and the work environment. This is typically described in terms of lack of fit. For example, the demands of the job may exceed the capacity of the individual to cope effectively, or the individual's efforts may not be met with equitable rewards. This framework

TABLE 7.1
Indicators of Burnout

Emotional Exhaustion	Depersonalization	Low Personal Accomplishment
Feel drained by work	Become hardened or cynical about job	Can't deal with problems effectively
Feel fatigued in the morning	Treat others like objects	Don't have positive influence on others
Frustrated	Don't care about what happens to others	Can't understand or identify with others' problems
Avoid working with other people	Feel other people blame you	No longer excited by your job

OB AT WORK Preventing Burnout

Burnout among employees should be avoided at all costs. Managers who push employees over the edge into burnout are causing harm to their employees and impeding their ability to do high-quality work. If burned-out employees decide to leave the organization, then managers will need to invest time and financial resources to replace them. Thus, we can conclude that burnout can reduce an organization's effectiveness.

Some organizations have taken steps to prevent employee burnout, including the following examples:

1. Deloitte & Touche has implemented a policy that limits their employees' travel time. It is no longer company policy for employees to spend all five working days of the week at clients' offices. At a maximum, employees are to spend only three nights (four working days) away from home and work the fifth day in their own home offices each week, even when on lengthy assignments.
2. Ernst & Young has a committee that monitors its staff accountants' workloads to head off burnout situations. The company says that its policies are raising retention rates and improving client service. A senior manager at Ernst observed that employees typically won't admit to burning out; thus, having some compassionate, objective overview is useful.
3. Wachovia Bank managers can award their employees with up to three extra paid days off. One manager of the bank's call center operations has awarded 35 percent of his 5,500 call center employees with paid days off the job.
4. Washington-based accounting and consulting firm, Clark Nuber, is helping its tax specialists avoid burnout during busy tax seasons by limiting their schedules to 55 hours per week (which is lower than the industry standard). By working fewer hours, the specialists, the company hopes, will do a better job for clients.

These programs are representative of the steps some organizations are taking to help their employees be more productive. As more managers become aware of the negative effects of burnout, perhaps these programs will become more common across all types of organizations.

Sources: Adapted from Terence F. Shea, "Employees First," *HRMagazine*, July 2008, 36–38; Sue Shellenbarger, "Companies Retool Time-Off Policies to Prevent Burnout, Reward Performance," *Wall Street Journal*, January 5, 2006, p. D.1; and Sue Shellenbarger, "The Myths That Make Managers Push Staff to the Edge of Burnout," *Wall Street Journal*, March 17, 1999, p. B1.

with its focus on explaining behavior in terms of the interaction of the person and environment offers promise in understanding job burnout.[37]

Organizational Consequences

As illustrated in Figure 7.1, a number of the behavioral, cognitive, and physiological outcomes that are linked also have organizational consequences. While the organizational consequences of stress are many and varied, they share one common feature: stress costs organizations money. Although precise figures are lacking, based on a variety of estimates and projections from government, industry, and health groups, we place the costs of stress at approximately $150 billion annually. This estimate, which probably is conservative (some estimates are as high as $300 billion annually),[38] attempts to take into account the dollar effects of reductions in operating effectiveness resulting from stress. The effects include poorer decision making and decreases in creativity. The huge figure also reflects the costs associated with mental and physical health problems arising from stress conditions, including hospital and medical costs, lost work time, turnover, sabotage, and a host of other variables that may contribute to organizational costs. When you consider that employers pay approximately 80 percent of all private health insurance premiums and that workers' compensation laws increasingly include provisions for awarding benefits for injuries stemming from stress in the workplace, it is clear that organizational consequences are significant.

The OB at Work feature on the following page indicates that stress costs American organizations about $7,500 per employee annually.

OB AT WORK The Costs of Job Stress

Scott is founder and president of a rapidly growing downtown custom software development firm. His company, which he estimates has grown by more than 50 percent in the past few years, takes up more time than he likes to admit. "I don't want to think about how many hours I put in a week," he chuckles.

Combine those pressures of building a tech firm in Cleveland with the time commitments of his growing family, and you end up with what most executives continually battle: stress. Stress isn't always a bad thing. Without what doctors call "acute" stress, you wouldn't be able to perform to the level your company expects. A little adrenaline in your blood helps you land that contract or finish that project on deadline. But when the stress is chronic—when you just can't relax—that's when it's a problem. It's an obstacle that will not only affect your business and family relationships, but shorten your life as well.

Stress is linked to the six leading causes of death: heart disease, cancer, lung ailments, accidents, cirrhosis of the liver, and suicide, according to the American Psychological Association (APA). And as many as 90 percent of all physician office visits are for stress-related illnesses and complaints. All this stress isn't good for the business, either. In terms of lost hours due to absenteeism, reduced productivity, and workers' compensation benefits, stress costs American industry more than $7,500 per worker per year, according to the APA. Luckily, there are steps you can take to manage the stress. Exercise, yoga, and deep-breathing exercises are helpful, but what will help the most is simply to get away from work. "There has to be a balance," Scott says. "You always have to have a mix of work, family, and exercise."

Dr. Richard Lang is the executive stress guru of Cleveland. He manages the Executive Health Program at The Cleveland Clinic. The program provides a full-day cornucopia of physical and psychological exams to detect health problems in professionals and executives. Lang says the typical executive he sees is a male around age 50, who is at the senior-management level in his company and the head of a family. Often, the pressures of those responsibilities start to weigh too heavily on the patient. Making the effects of stress worse is how these executives focus on helping others with their problems but lack the necessary support network to help with their own family and business problems.

When work and family pressures build, there are almost always physical symptoms, according to the doctors. The physical signs of chronic stress vary and range in severity. Usually they include symptoms like difficulty focusing or concentrating, disorganization, insomnia and nervousness, and more noticeable physical signs like frequent headaches, chest pain, difficulty breathing, upset stomach, and back pain.

Unfortunately, some executives cope with the stress in dangerous ways like drinking, overeating, and smoking, which create even more of a health problem. There are simple alternatives that will not only lower stress but also improve executives' overall health.

Regardless of what is causing the stress, the doctors explain, almost every stress management program includes some form of regular exercise, whether it is running or lifting weights, or lower-impact activities like deep-breathing exercises, yoga, or progressive muscle relaxation. In addition, many organizations offer employee assistance programs (EAPs) that provide counseling; and wellness and health plans that include information and resources to reduce the effects of stress.

Doctors say many executives who complain they don't have time for exercise are usually surprised that once they get on a regimen they often stick with it due to the stress-reduction effects and other health benefits.

Sources: Adapted from Kristen Gerencher, "MarketWatch: Relax, You Can Beat That Stress," *Wall Street Journal*, January 3, 2010; and Morgan Lewis Jr., "Under Pressure: Stress Defines the Executive's Life But Don't Let It Become a Dangerous Problem," *Inside Business*, April 2004, pp. 72–74.

Excessive stress increases job dissatisfaction. As we saw in Chapter 4, job dissatisfaction can be associated with a number of dysfunctional outcomes, including increased turnover, absenteeism, and reduced job performance. If productivity is reduced just 3 percent, for example, an organization employing 1,000 people would need to hire an additional 30 employees to compensate for that lost productivity. If annual employee costs are $40,000 per employee including wages and benefits, stress is costing the company $1.2 million just to replace lost productivity. This doesn't include costs associated with recruitment and training. Nor does this consider that decreases in *quality* of performance may be more costly for an organization than quantity decreases. Customer dissatisfaction with lower-quality goods or services can have significant effects on an organization's growth.

Stress Moderators

Stressors evoke diverse responses from different people. Some people are better able to cope with a stressor than others. They can adapt their behavior in such a way as to meet the stressor head-on. On the other hand, some people are predisposed to stress; that is, they are not able to adapt to the stressor.

The model presented in Figure 7.1 (on page 197) suggests that various factors can moderate the relationships among stressors, stress, and consequences. A moderator is a condition, behavior, or characteristic that influences the relationship between two variables. The effect may be to intensify or weaken the relationship. The relationship between the number of gallons of gasoline used and the total of miles driven, for example, is moderated by driving speed. At very low or very high speeds, gas mileage declines; at intermediate speeds, mileage increases. Thus, driving speed affects the relationship between gasoline used and miles driven.

Many conditions, behaviors, and characteristics may act as stress moderators, including such variables as age, gender, and the hardiness factor discussed earlier in the chapter. In this section, we will briefly examine three representative types of moderators: (1) personality, (2) Type A behavior, and (3) social support.

Personality

As discussed in Chapter 4, the term *personality* refers to a relatively stable set of characteristics, temperaments, and tendencies that shape the similarities and differences in people's behavior. The number of aspects of personality that could serve as stress moderators is quite large. We will confine our attention to those aspects of personality previously identified in Chapter 4: the Big Five model, locus of control, and self-efficacy.

As you recall from Chapter 4, the Big Five model of personality is made up of five dimensions: extroversion, emotional stability, agreeableness, conscientiousness, and openness to experience. Of these, *emotional stability* is most clearly related to stress. Those high on this dimension are most likely to experience positive moods and feel good about themselves and their jobs. While they certainly experience stress, they are less likely to be overwhelmed by it and are in a better position to recover from it. To a somewhat lesser degree, those high on extroversion are also more predisposed to experience positive emotional states. Because they are sociable and friendly, they are more likely to have a wider network of friends than their introverted counterparts; consequently, they have more resources to draw on in times of distress.

If you are low on agreeableness, you have a tendency to be antagonistic, unsympathetic, or even rude toward others. You are also probably somewhat mistrusting of others. These attributes increase the likelihood that individuals will find other people to be a source of stress, and because others are more likely to find interacting with these individuals stressful as well, an interpersonal relationship environment full of stressful situations is created. *Conscientiousness* is a Big Five dimension most consistently related to job performance and success. To the extent that good performance leads to satisfaction and other rewards, those high on conscientiousness are less likely to experience stress with respect to these aspects of their jobs. Those low on this dimension, however, are more likely to be poorer performers, receive fewer rewards, and generally be less successful in their careers—not a recipe for low stress levels! Finally, those high on *openness to experience* are better prepared to deal with stressors associated with change because they are more likely to view change as a challenge, rather than a threat.

Beliefs people have about where control over their lives resides relates to *locus of control*. As discussed in Chapter 4, "internals" perceive themselves to be in control of the events that shape their lives to a greater extent than "externals," who feel that control is external to them. The traditional assumption is that if people feel they have control in a situation, they will be less likely to assess the situation as threatening or stressful.

While this assumption may be valid in a general sense, the relationship between locus of control and stress is not always that straightforward. A more inclusive depiction suggests that internals are more likely to experience stress when they are unable to exercise the control they believe they should, while externals will be threatened (and, consequently, stressed) in situations where they can exercise some degree of control over what is happening. Viewed from this perspective, the locus of control–stress relationship is a function of personal beliefs and environmental realities. When a person's beliefs about where control resides are congruent with the actual locus of control in a given situation, there is less likelihood stress will result. When beliefs and reality are not the same, the likelihood of experiencing stress increases.

Self-efficacy is another personality attribute that is an important moderator variable. Individuals with high levels of self-efficacy feel confident in their abilities and in their job performance. They are more likely to perceive potential stressors as challenges and opportunities, rather than threats and problems. Those with low levels of self-efficacy, on the other hand, are less confident in their abilities and more likely to assume they will fail. Because they believe they will fail, they will likely exert less effort, thereby ensuring that their assessment of their abilities is correct! Even when a situation is perceived as threatening, those with high self-efficacy are more likely to deal with the threat quickly, effectively, and with fewer negative outcomes.

The relationship between self-efficacy and stress is not confined to one part of the stress process. Self-efficacy may moderate the process from the perception of stressors (e.g., workers with low self-efficacy are more likely to experience work overload) to consequences (e.g., low self-efficacy has been associated with increased incidence of coronary heart disease risk). Thus, as a moderator, self-efficacy plays a pervasive role.

Type A Behavior Pattern

In the 1950s, two medical cardiologists and researchers, Meyer Friedman and Ray Rosenman, discovered what they called the Type A behavior pattern (TABP).[39] They searched the medical literature and found that traditional coronary risk factors such as dietary cholesterol, blood pressure, and heredity could not totally explain or predict coronary heart disease (CHD), the name given to cardiovascular diseases that are characterized by inadequate supply of oxygen to the heart. Other factors seemed to be playing a major role in CHD. Through interviews with and observation of patients, they began to uncover a pattern of behavior or traits. They eventually called this the Type A behavior pattern. The person with TABP demonstrates certain characteristics: he or she

- Chronically struggles to get as many things done as possible in the shortest time.
- Is aggressive, ambitious, competitive, and forceful.
- Speaks explosively and rushes others to finish what they are saying.
- Is impatient, hates to wait, and considers waiting a waste of precious time.
- Is preoccupied with deadlines and is work oriented.
- Is always in a struggle with people, things, and events.

The converse, the Type B individual, mainly is free of the TABP characteristics and generally feels no pressing conflict with either time or persons. The Type B may have considerable drive, want to accomplish things, and work hard, but the Type B has a confident style that allows him or her to work at a steady pace and not to race against the clock. The Type A has been likened to a racehorse; the Type B, to a turtle.

More recent research into TABP suggests that not all aspects of the behavior pattern are equally associated with negative consequences. Specifically, hostility has been identified as being a TABP subcomponent (not identified by Friedman and Rosenman) most predictive of the development of coronary heart disease among Type As.[40] Nor is CHD the only negative outcome: TABP has been associated with a number of health-related consequences including ulcers, insomnia, and depression. As researchers learn more about the individual components that comprise Type A behavior, further refinements in our understanding of this moderator can be expected.

Social Support

social support
The comfort, assistance, or information received through formal or informal contacts with individuals or groups.

Both the quantity and quality of social relationships individuals have with others appear to have a potentially important effect on the amount of stress they experience and on the likelihood that stress will have adverse effects on their mental and physical health. **Social support** can be defined as the comfort, assistance, or information one receives through formal or informal contacts with individuals or groups. A number of studies have linked social support with aspects of health, illness, and stress.[41]

Social support may take the form of *emotional support* (expressing concern, indicating trust, boosting esteem, listening), *appraisal support* (providing feedback and affirmation), or *informational support* (giving advice, making suggestions, providing direction). People who can serve as sources of social support at work include supervisors, co-workers, subordinates, and customers or other non-organizational members with whom an employee might have contact. Nonwork support sources include family members (immediate and extended), friends, neighbors, caregivers (e.g., ministers), health professionals (physicians, psychologists, counselors), and self-help groups (Alcoholics Anonymous, Weight Watchers).

A co-worker listening to a friend who failed to receive a desired promotion, a group of recently laid-off workers helping each other find new employment, or an experienced employee helping a trainee learn a job are all examples of providing support. Social support is effective as a stress moderator because it buffers the negative effect of stressors by providing a degree of predictability, purpose, and hope in upsetting and threatening situations. Almost everyone has experienced feeling "better" (calmer, less anxious, or concerned) after having talked about a problem with a spouse, friend, or co-worker. Similarly, almost everyone has provided support to someone else, and this support has had positive effects for that person. Thus, virtually all of us know from first-hand experience the moderating role social support can play.

A number of studies reinforce what we know to be true for our experiences. Social support has been shown to reduce stress among employed individuals ranging from unskilled workers to highly trained professionals; it is consistently cited as an effective stress coping technique, and it has been associated with fewer health complaints experienced during periods of high stress.[42]

Stress Prevention and Management

An astute manager never ignores a turnover or absenteeism problem, workplace drug abuse, a decline in performance, hostile and belligerent employees, reduced quality of production, or any other sign that the organization's performance goals are not being met. The effective manager, in fact, views these occurrences as symptoms and looks beyond them to identify and correct the underlying causes. Yet most managers likely will search for traditional causes such as poor training, defective equipment, or inadequate instructions regarding what needs to be done. In all likelihood, stress will not be on the list of possible problems. Thus, the very first step in any attempt to deal with stress so that it remains within tolerable limits is recognition that it exists. Once that is accomplished, a variety of approaches and programs for preventing and managing organizational stress are available.

FIGURE 7.3
Organizational Stress Management Program Targets

Source: John M. Ivancevich, Michael T. Matteson, Sara M. Freedman, and James S. Phillips, "Worksite Stress Management Intervention," *American Psychologist,* 1990, p. 253.

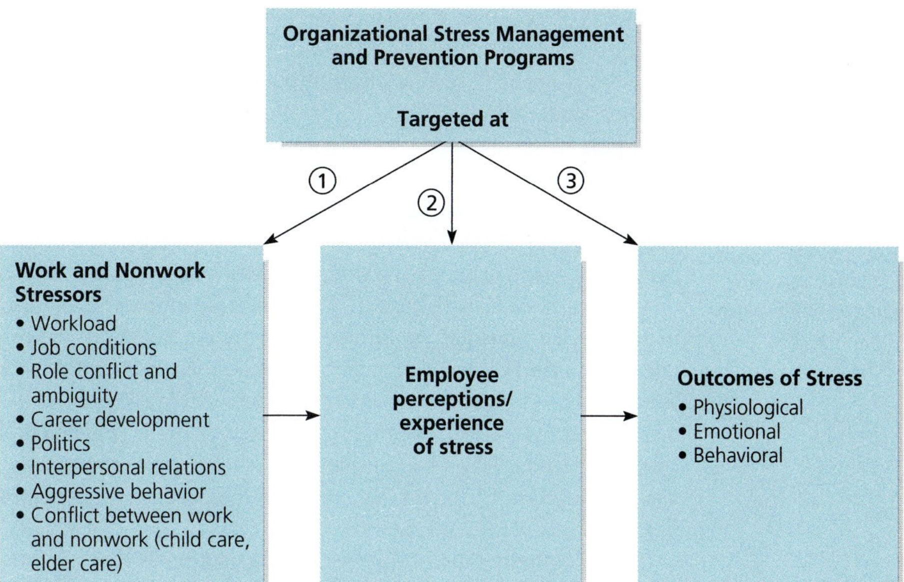

Figure 7.3 presents how organizational stress management programs can be targeted. Programs are targeted to (1) identify and modify work stressors, (2) engage employees in understanding and modifying stress and its effect, and (3) provide employees with support to cope with the negative effect of stress. In a rapidly changing work environment, this type of targeting is difficult to accomplish. However, a trained, educated, and knowledgeable workforce can make modifications with the help of management in how work is performed. Some of the targeted, corrective programs include the following:

- Training programs for managing and coping with stress.
- Redesigning work to minimize stressors.
- Changes in management style to one of more support and coaching to help workers achieve their goals.
- Creating more flexible work hours and paying more attention to work/life balance with regard to child and elder care.
- Better communication and team-building practices.
- Better feedback on worker performance and management expectations.

These and other efforts are targeted to prevent and manage stress. The potential for success of any prevention or management of stress program is good if there is a true commitment to understanding how stressors, stress, and outcomes are interrelated.

The distinction between preventing stress and managing it is very important. Stress prevention focuses on controlling or eliminating stressors that might provoke the stress response. Stress management suggests procedures for helping people cope effectively with or reduce stress that is already being experienced. In this concluding section of the chapter, we examine organizational programs for and individual approaches to stress prevention and management, with the emphasis on *management.* First, however, we will look at a way of thinking about organizational stress prevention.

Maximizing Person–Environment Fit

In defining stress earlier in the chapter, we emphasized that stress is the consequence of the interaction between an environmental stimulus (a stressor) and the individual's response.

From this perspective, stress may be viewed as a consequence of the relationship between the individual and the work environment. While there are many ways of thinking about individual–organizational relationships and stress, the concept of person–environment fit is the most widely used.[43]

person–environment (P–E) fit
The extent to which work provides rewards that meet the person's needs and to which the employee's skills match the requirements of the job.

A **person–environment (P–E) fit** approach generally focuses on two dimensions of fit.[44] One is the extent to which work provides formal and informal rewards to meet or match (fit) the person's needs. Misfit on this dimension results in stress. For example, a job may provide too little job security, insufficient compensation and reward for the effort expended, or inadequate recognition to meet the individual's needs or preferences. The second type of fit deals with the extent to which the employee's skills, abilities, and experience match the demands and requirements of the employer. To the extent that the individual's talents are insufficient for or underutilized by job requirements, stress results. By improving the quality of or maximizing the fit between the employee and the organizational environment, potential stressors are eliminated and stress is prevented. This P–E fit approach is somewhat similar to—and consistent with—the concept of the psychological contract that was developed in Chapter 4. Violations of the psychological contract represent breakdowns in P–E fit.

There are numerous strategies for maximizing P–E fit. Ideally, the process begins before an individual even joins the organization. Employee recruitment programs that provide realistic job previews help potential employees to determine whether the reality of the job matches their needs and expectations. Selection programs that are effective in ensuring that potential employees possess the requisite skills, knowledge, experience, and abilities for the job are key elements in maximizing fit.

Job skills and knowledge are not the only important factors to consider in employee selection, however. Fit can be maximized by closely linking personal predispositions to relevant aspects of the work environment as well. For example, as suggested earlier, individuals with a low tolerance for ambiguity and who find themselves in jobs or organizational environments in which there is little structure will very likely experience stress. There are many other examples: an individual who is by nature authoritarian will experience stress in a participative organization; those wishing autonomy will be distressed by tight controls and managers who micromanage; and individuals with a high need for performance feedback will be stressed by supervisors who never communicate performance information.

socialization
The process by which organizations bring new employees into the culture.

Once in the organization, a critical variable in maximizing fit and preventing stress is effective socialization. **Socialization** is the process by which the individual learns and internalizes the values, expected behaviors, and social knowledge that are important for becoming an effective organizational member. The stages and characteristics of effective socialization were discussed in detail in Chapter 2, and you may wish to refer to that discussion in the present context of maximizing P–E fit.

Organizational Stress Prevention and Management Programs

In addition to the variety of activities that may be undertaken to improve person–environment fit, an increasing number of organizations have developed very specific programs for stress prevention and stress management. Some of these programs focus on a specific issue or problem, such as alcohol or drug abuse, career counseling, job relocation, or burnout. The United States Postal Service, for example, has developed a workplace violence prevention program. Each district has a Threat Assessment Team (TAT) that assesses threatening situations and develops risk reduction plans to minimize the potential risk of future violence at post offices throughout the country. The TATs promote violence awareness and prevention to ensure a safe working environment for all employees and a secure business climate for

Postal Service customers.[45] This program, the most comprehensive one in existence, represents an attempt to reduce the employee-initiated violence that characterized the service in the past.[46]

Still other programs may target a specific group within the organization. An example is pharmaceutical manufacturer GlaxoSmithKline PLC that created a "team resilience program" to help team members discuss and cope with job-related stress like changing deadlines, isolation, and work overload.[47] Approximately 18,000 employees have participated in the program, and the firm reports several positive outcomes from the program between 2003 and 2006: a 60 percent reduction in job-related mental health illness and a 29 percent decrease in mental-health-related absences. The reduction in absences saved the company more than $1.4 million over those four years.[48]

Another example is the Resident Assistance Program in place at Baylor College of Medicine. This program was designed to help medical residents cope successfully with the multitude of stressors they encounter.[49] Some programs may focus on a particular technique, such as developing relaxation skills. Others are more general in nature, using a variety of approaches and geared to a cross-section of employees, such as the Employee Assistance Program at B. F. Goodrich, the Coors Brewing Company Wellness Program, and the Emotional Health Program at Equitable Life. Two specific types of organizational programs have become particularly popular during the past two decades: employee assistance programs and wellness programs.

Employee Assistance Programs (EAPs)

employee assistance programs (EAPs)
Programs designed to assist with a wide range of work- and nonwork-related stress-induced problems.

Originally conceived as alcohol abuse programs, most current **employee assistance programs (EAPs)** are designed to deal with a wide range of stress-related problems, both work and nonwork related, including behavioral and emotional difficulties, substance abuse, excessive debt, family and marital discord, and other personal problems. IBM, Blue Cross and Blue Shield of North Carolina, Alcoa in Evansville, Indiana, and Telemundo Network in Miami, Florida, are examples of companies with such programs.[50] As a result of the recent recession, demand for EAP services has increased. For example, EAP Corporate Counseling Associates of New York City has reported a 21 percent increase in calls to its counselors.[51] EAPs tend to be based on the traditional medical approach to treatment. General program elements include the following:

- *Diagnosis:* An employee with a problem asks for help; EAP staff attempts to diagnose the problem.
- *Treatment:* Counseling or supportive therapy is provided. If in-house EAP staff is unable to help, the employee may be referred to appropriate community-based professionals.
- *Screening:* Periodic examination of employees in highly stressful jobs is provided to detect early indications of problems.
- *Prevention:* Education and persuasion are used to convince employees at high risk that something must be done to assist them in effectively coping with stress.

An increasing number of employers believe that good health among employees is good for the organization. Blue Cross Blue Shield determined that every dollar spent on the psychological care of employees with breast cancer saved $2.50 to $5.10 in overall medical expenses. The public school system of Orange County, Florida, found that the cost of medical claims dropped by 66 percent over five years for employees who used the EAP. At the end of five years, the same employees were taking 36 percent fewer sick leaves. At McDonnell-Douglas (now called Boeing), workers treated for alcohol and drug problems missed 44 percent fewer days of work after the EAP was set up.[52]

EAPs may be internal, company-run programs or external efforts in which the organization contracts with a private firm to provide services to company employees. The previously cited Emotional Health Program at Equitable Life is typical of such programs. It is concerned with prevention, treatment, and referral of employees. Staffed with a clinical psychologist, physician, psychology intern, and counselor, it focuses on individual intervention. Offered are biofeedback, relaxation training, and counseling. When appropriate, referrals are made to external health practitioners and hospitals.

Within the past five years, EAP programs have emerged that help employees understand and manage their personal finances. At IBM, over 60,000 employees have participated in the MoneySmart program that provides individualized planning sessions, seminars, and online tools that educate employees on managing debt and housing expenditures, budgeting for college, and planning for retirement.[53]

Crucial to the success of any EAP is trust. Employees must trust that (1) the program can and will provide real help, (2) confidentiality will be maintained, and (3) use of the program carries no negative implications for job security or future advancement. If employees do not trust the program or company management, they will not participate. EAPs with no customers cannot have a positive effect on stress prevention and management.

Wellness Programs

wellness programs
Activities that focus on an employee's overall physical and mental health.

Wellness programs, sometimes called health promotion programs, focus on the employee's overall physical and mental health. Simply stated, any activity an organization engages in that is designed to identify and assist in preventing or correcting specific health problems, health hazards, or negative health habits can be thought of as wellness related. This includes not only disease identification but lifestyle modification as well. Among the most prevalent examples of such programs are those emphasizing hypertension identification and control, smoking cessation, physical fitness and exercise, nutrition and diet control, and job and personal stress management.

As the following OB at Work feature suggests, many managers believe that organizations have a responsibility to provide wellness programs to their most important asset, employees.

It might appear strange that we would include wellness programs in a discussion of stress management. There are several reasons we do. First, stress prevention and management is a vital part of wellness, and, as we have already noted, it is frequently a component of wellness programs. Second, many of the concerns of wellness programs are at least partially stress related. Stress has been cited as the greatest cause of poor health habits,[54] and poor health habits are what wellness programs attempt to change. Third, a major reason organizations are interested in stress management is that it contributes to healthier, more productive, and more effective organizations. Corporate wellness programs simply extend these payoffs. Fourth, it is impossible to divorce the topic of stress from health. In a sense, wellness programs represent a broad-based, contemporary extension of stress programs; their focus is concern for employee health and quality-of-life issues.

Well Workplace University is a learning center where organizational leaders, health care professionals, and wellness professionals meet to discuss, analyze, and work to build world-class wellness programs. The central benchmarks used to build wellness programs are to (1) build senior-level support, (2) create wellness teams, (3) collect data to drive programs, (4) craft an operating plan, (5) choose best interventions, (6) create supportive culture, and (7) evaluate outcomes. Two recent success stories include Union Pacific Railroad, which achieved a net savings of $1.26 million through a medical self-care program, and Lincoln Plating, a small employer of 210 people that invested $85,000 in a wellness program and reduced annual turnover from 70 to 35 percent in less than two years.[55] Well Workplace University has worked with hundreds of firms, including Mutual of Omaha, Florida Power and Light, and Vistakon (a Johnson & Johnson company).[56]

OB AT WORK The Costs of Job Stress, Part 2

Do organizations have a responsibility to encourage wellness among employees? Seventy-one percent of executives say yes, according to the American Management Association's (AMA) 2003 Survey on Health and Wellness Programs. However, less than half of the companies that responded offer educational programs on self-care topics, including exercise and fitness (47 percent), weight management (34 percent), or nutrition (25 percent).

The AMA surveyed its members and customers at 354 U.S. companies about the wellness programs they offer their employees. According to the findings, 41 percent of the organizations offer programs on smoking cessation, 36 percent offer blood pressure management programs, 33 percent offer stress management programs, and 27 percent offer cholesterol management programs.

Q. In your opinion, . . do corporations have a responsibility to promote wellness among employees?

Yes 71%
No 22
Don't know 7

EDUCATION:

Q. Does your organization sponsor programs on any of the following self-care topics?

Exercise and fitness .... .47%
Smoking cessation .... .41
Blood pressure management .... .36
Weight management.................... .34
Stress management .... .33
Cholesterol management................ .27

Q. In the past year, has the number of company-sponsored health and wellness programs increased, remained the same, or decreased?

Increased 31%
Remained the same 47
Decreased 6
Don't know 16

PARTICIPATION:

More than a third of respondents (36 percent) say they do not attend these programs when the company sponsors them. Only 29 percent of those companies that offer these programs extend some incentive for employees to participate.

Q. If your company offers any of these health and wellness programs, do you attend?

Yes 63%
No................. 36
Don't know 2

Q. If your company sponsors these programs do they offer incentives for employees to attend?

Yes 29%
No................. 71

EXERCISE AND FITNESS:

More than half (52 percent) of the companies surveyed offer discounts or corporate memberships to health clubs for their employees, and 25 percent have exercise facilities available on the company's premises. Another 62 percent of respondents said their organizations participate in community- or corporate-sponsored athletic activities, such as softball leagues, bowling teams, or fund-raiser walks/runs.

Q. Are exercise facilities available to employees on the company's premises?

Yes 25%
No................. 75

Q. Are discounts or corporate memberships to health clubs extended to employees?

Yes 52%
No................. 47
Don't know 1

Q. Does your organization participate in community- or corporate-sponsored athletic activities (e.g., softball leagues, bowling teams, fund-raiser walks or runs)?

Yes 62%
No................. 37
Don't know 1

NUTRITION:

Nearly 30 percent of respondents say their companies have cafeterias that provide or sell meals for employees, and 90 percent say that the selection offered are healthy, including fruits, vegetables, and low-fat entrees. In addition, 92 percent of the companies have vending machines that sell

(*continued*)

fast food and beverages, including candy, snacks, and soft drinks.

Q. Does your organization hire a cafeteria that provides or sells meals for employees?

Yes 29%
No. 71

PREVENTION:

Thirty-eight percent of companies offer corporate-sponsored, comprehensive annual physicals: 22 percent say they are extended to executives only, and 16 percent say they are for all staff members. Seventy-one percent of respondents say their companies provide flu shots.

Q. Does your organization offer corporate-sponsored, annual comprehensive physicals?

Yes, for executives only 22%
Yes, for all staff members. 16
No. 59
Don't know 2

Q. Does the organization provide annual flu shots?

Yes 71%
No. 29

Source: *Annual Survey of the American Management Association* (New York: AMA, 2003).

Another example of success with wellness programs is Hoffman-La Roche Pharmaceuticals of Nutley, New Jersey, which found that it spent only 3 percent of medical benefits dollars on preventive health measures, although 39 percent of the health claims submitted were the result of preventable conditions. Roche management concluded that focusing on prevention would mean healthier, more productive, less stressed, more creative, and less absent employees. Roche named its wellness program "Choosing Health."[57]

Choosing Health starts at the individual level by assessing employee health risks via a 76-item survey. The form takes 15 minutes to complete. A health profile then is sent directly to the employee's home. All employees' responses and profiles are confidential and not released to a third party. The company also provides onsite screening for such ailments as high blood pressure, high cholesterol, and breast and skin cancers. Roche's human resource management (HRM) group receives only aggregated data showing risks with the general population. HRM then patterns preventive health programs after the health risks and education needs of employees as a group. Almost 100 percent of Roche employees participate in Choosing Health.

A part of Choosing Health is an evaluation process to measure the impact of the program. In two years, the average lifestyle score has increased from 63 to 68 (100 is the optimal score). Roche is constantly working to align prevention, intervention, employee health, and productivity.

DuPont Corporation has for several years been dedicated to health promotion.[58] Cost effectiveness studies at DuPont indicate that fitness programs work. DuPont estimates that for every dollar invested in the health promotion program at least two are received in return. One analysis at DuPont indicates the annual costs per person at risk cost a company as follows:

Smokers	$960
Overweight	401
Excess alcohol use	389
High cholesterol	370
High blood pressure	343

DuPont has determined that reducing absenteeism annually by about 6.8 percent would pay for the firm's entire health promotion effort.

Sustaining a Wellness Strategy

Whether you own a company or serve as a manager, it is advisable to work on creating a healthier workplace. Investing in human assets through a concerned effort and strategy is a long-term investment.[59] There is no perfect or "one best" approach to managing stress and burnout. However, there is a general step-by-step approach that appears to be worth consideration.

Briefly, it is recommended that:

1. The health and well-being of employees should be a part of the organization's mission and strategic plans.
2. A written policy statement about health, the promotion of health, and the importance of well-being should be produced.
3. A wellness plan should be developed that has executive commitment, union commitment, and employee commitment. Improving the wellness of employees should be a goal.
4. The "improving wellness" goal should be used as a vehicle for executives, union representatives, and employees to create specific and actionable plans.
5. Organizational resources (e.g., funds, space, time) should be committed to accomplish the wellness plan.
6. A best-practice case file should be created to circulate around the organization. Report successes and celebrate them publicly.
7. Managers should be encouraged and rewarded for their involvement in wellness programs, successes, and working to bring about better work/life balance.[60]

These are general steps that will call attention to and encourage wellness. The effort should start at the managerial level. When managers display through their behaviors a commitment to employee wellness, there is a message being communicated to nonmanagers that the organization cares.

Individual Approaches to Stress Prevention and Management

Organization members do not have to—nor should they—rely on formal organizational programs to assist in stress prevention and management. There are many individual approaches to dealing with stressors and stress.[61] To see this, all you have to do is visit any bookstore onsite or online (e.g., www.amazon.com, www.barnesandnoble.com) and look at the self-improvement section. It will be stocked with numerous how-to books on reducing stress. A popular topic aimed at helping employees reduce stress while increasing their productivity is time management, which is discussed in the next OB and Your Career.

We briefly examine a few more of the popularly cited and frequently used approaches for individual stress prevention and management next. It is not unusual for any of these approaches to be included in the range of options available within an organizational stress management or wellness program. It should also be noted that there is a great deal of variation in the effectiveness of these techniques. What one person finds useful, another may not. There is still a great deal we do not know regarding the effects of individual differences on stress management outcomes.[62]

Cognitive Techniques

The basic rationale for some individual approaches to stress management, known collectively as *cognitive techniques,* is that a person's response to stressors is mediated by cognitive processes or thoughts. The underlying assumption of these techniques is that people's thoughts, in the form of expectations, beliefs, and assumptions, are labels they apply to situations, and these labels elicit emotional responses to the situation. For example, if an individual labels

OB AND YOUR CAREER

Reduce Stress: Be More Efficient with Your Time

Most everyone struggles with the stress associated with staying organized, working smarter and faster, and meeting multiple deadlines. Needless to say, employees who are perceived as organized and efficient will reap more career-related benefits than those who fail to master how to use their time wisely. To help sharpen one's time management skills, experts have offered several suggestions:

1. *Identify what's most important in your work.* Every job has "must dos" and "nice to dos." Sometimes individuals do nonimportant tasks first because they tend to be easier and require less thought. This approach can waste time. Employees need to identify and complete the critical duties (on time) even if it means being late with the noncritical tasks.
2. *Plan your schedule the evening before.* Arriving to the office with a clear idea of what needs to get done can help employees "hit the ground running" each day. This head start helps employees be more organized and less stressed.
3. *Manage the time spent on responding to text messages, e-mails and voice-mails.* Try not to stop working on an important project every time a text, e-mail, or voice-mail is received. These interruptions are disruptive and can break one's train of thought. One expert suggests creating an autoreply message that states that e-mails will be replied to at three times (i.e., 9:00 a.m., 2:00 p.m. and 4:00 p.m.) each day. The same kind of message can be included in a recorded voice-mail message.
4. *Make daily and weekly "to do" lists and update the lists frequently.* One expert recommends starring those activities that must be done this week and then highlighting those from the list that must be done today. As the activities are completed, a line can be drawn through them. This act provides individuals with a sense of accomplishment and progress.
5. *Delegate nonimportant activities.* All noncritical activities should be delegated to others whenever possible.
6. *Set aside an hour or so each day for paperwork and other administrative chores.* By setting aside an hour or so each day for "paperwork," employees will become more efficient or will decide that some of it is less critical and can be delegated.
7. *Know at what times of the day you work most efficiently.* Some individuals do their "heavy mental lifting" in the mornings, whereas others do their best thinking at other times during the day. Try to divide and work on job activities during those parts of the day that fit the task. For example, one of the authors of this book prefers to write in the mornings and evenings, while teaching, making phone calls, grading, and answering e-mail and voice-mails in the afternoons.

Sources: Adapted from John Boe, "Time Is Money," *The American Salesman* 55, no. 1 (January 2010): 7–10; Jena McGregor, "Making Every Hour Count," *Businessweek*, August 25, 2008, p. 67; and "Running a Business: Balancing Work & Life, Five Tips to Boost Productivity," *WSJ.com*, November 29, 2007 (accessed on May 17, 2010).

the loss of a promotion a catastrophe, the stress response is to the label, not to the situation. Cognitive techniques of stress management focus on changing labels or cognitions so that people appraise situations differently. This reappraisal typically centers on removing cognitive distortions such as magnifying (not getting the promotion is the end of the world for me), overgeneralizing (not getting promoted means my career is over; I'll never be promoted in any job, anywhere), and personalization (because I didn't get the promotion, it's clear I'm a terrible person). All cognitive techniques have a similar objective: to help people gain more control over their reactions to stressors by modifying their thought processes.

Evaluative research on cognitive techniques to stress management is not extensive, although the studies reported are generally positive. Representative occupational groups in which research has indicated positive outcomes with the use of cognitive approaches include nurses, teachers, athletes, and air traffic controllers.[63] The positive research results, coupled with the wide range and scope of situations and stressors amenable to such an approach, make cognitive techniques particularly attractive as an individual stress management strategy.

Relaxation Training

The purpose of this approach is to reduce a person's arousal level and bring about a calmer state, both psychologically and physiologically. Psychologically, successful relaxation results in enhanced feelings of well-being, peacefulness and calm, a clear sense of being in control, and a reduction in tension and anxiety. Physiologically, decreases in blood pressure, respiration, and heart rate should take place. Relaxation techniques include breathing exercises; muscle relaxation; autogenic training, which combines elements of muscle relaxation and meditation; and a wide variety of mental relaxation strategies, including imagery and visualization.

Conditions conducive to achieving relaxed states include a quiet environment, a comfortable physical position, and closed eyes. Simply taking a few moments of "mental rest" from job activities can be effective relaxation activity. Short, more frequent breaks of this sort are more relaxing than fewer, longer breaks.[64]

Meditation

Many of the meditative forms that have achieved some degree of popularity in this country are derivatives of Eastern philosophies. Included in this category are Zen meditation and Nam Sumran, or Sikh meditation. Perhaps the most widely practiced in the United States is transcendental meditation, or TM. Its originator, Maharishi Mahesh Yogi, defines TM as turning the attention toward the subtler levels of thought until the mind transcends the experience of the subtlest state of thought and arrives at the source of thought.[65] The basic procedure used in TM is simple, but the effects claimed for it are extensive. One simply sits comfortably with closed eyes and engages in the repetition of a special sound (a mantra) for about 20 minutes twice a day. Studies indicate that TM practices are associated with reduced heart rate, lowered oxygen consumption, and decreased blood pressure.[66]

John Kabat-Zinn, of the Mindfulness-Based Stress Reduction Clinic at the University of Massachusetts Medical School, suggests in a research study that happiness may be a byproduct of meditation. He reported that after eight weeks of training in mindfulness-based stress reduction, individuals activated more of the left side of the brain, which aided them in being easy-going, relaxed, and happy.[67] In other words, meditation increased the left-side activities and reduced the right-side activity.

Biofeedback

Individuals can be taught to control a variety of internal body processes by using a technique called *biofeedback*. In biofeedback, small changes occurring in the body or brain are detected, amplified, and displayed to the person. Sophisticated recording and computer technology make it possible for a person to attend to subtle changes in heart rate, blood pressure, temperature, and brain-wave patterns that normally would be unobservable. Most of these processes are affected by stress.

The potential role of biofeedback as an individual stress management technique can be seen by looking at the bodily functions that can, to some degree, be brought under voluntary control. These include brain waves, heart rate, muscle tension, body temperature, stomach acidity, and blood pressure. Most if not all of these processes are affected by stress. The potential of biofeedback is its ability to help induce a state of relaxation and restore bodily functions to a nonstressed state. One advantage of biofeedback over nonfeedback techniques is that it gives precise data about bodily functions. By interpreting the feedback, individuals know how high their blood pressure is, for example, and discover, through practice, means of lowering it. When they are successful, the feedback provides instantaneous information to that effect.

Biofeedback training has been useful in reducing anxiety, lowering stomach acidity (and thus reducing the likelihood of ulcer formation), controlling tension and migraine headaches, and, in general, reducing negative physiological manifestations of stress. Despite these positive results, people looking to biofeedback for stress control should understand that success requires training and the use of equipment that may be very expensive.

Summary of Key Points

- Stress may be viewed as either a stimulus or a response. We view it as an adaptive response moderated by individual differences, that is, a consequence of any action, situation, or event that places special demands on a person.
- Major variables in the model of organizational stress presented in this chapter are (1) work stressors (individual, group, and organizational), (2) stress itself, (3) stress consequences (organizational and individual), (4) stress moderators (personality, Type A behavior, and social support), and (5) stress prevention and management (maximizing person–environment fit, organizational programs, and individual approaches).
- Stressors are actions, situations, or events that place special demands on a person. Three important categories of stressors are (1) work environment (e.g., noise, temperature), (2) individual stressors (e.g., role conflict, work overload, change), and (3) group and organizational stressors (e.g., politics, culture, interpersonal relationships, downsizing).
- While some consequences of stress are positive, many are dysfunctional. Negative individual consequences include accident proneness, poor concentration, drug and alcohol abuse, and burnout. Organizational consequences may include absenteeism, turnover, increased health and medical costs, and quantitative and qualitative decrements in productivity.
- Some factors affect the nature of the stress response. These are called *stress moderators*. Three important moderators are personality (e.g., locus of control and self-esteem), Type A behavior, and social support.
- Stress prevention and management strategies include (1) maximizing person–environment fit; (2) organizational programs such as employee assistance and wellness; and (3) individual approaches such as cognitive techniques, relaxation training, meditation, and biofeedback.
- Although there is no "one best" strategy for managing stress and preventing burnout, there are specific proactive steps organizations can take. Establishing health and well-being as important strategic goals is the first recommended proactive step.

Discussion and Review Questions

1. Research suggests that stress affects people differently. What are three reasons why this is true?
2. Why should managers not counsel or provide advice to any employee suspected of being depressed?
3. Why have some organizations accepted the responsibility for promoting employee wellness and other firms largely ignored the notion of a job contributing to an individual's stress?
4. What types of jobs or organizations are a better fit for Type A individuals? For Type B individuals? Explain.
5. Why do service or help professions (e.g., social work, addiction counseling) result in high amounts of burnout?
6. What type of social support can a manager initiate in a work setting to help moderate the stress among employees?
7. What kinds of things can a manager do to better maximize employee–environment fit?
8. What is the relationship between stress and personality? What aspects of personality might tend to increase stress? Decrease it?
9. What are some of the costs of unmanaged, chronic stress?
10. Why is benchmarking the wellness programs of other organizations a recommended practice?

Taking It to the Net

The Annual Physical Exam

Pricey annual physicals for employees are available at many clinics. Some organizations are trying to decide whether paying for the physicals is really worth the expense. Using the Internet, investigate the following:

1. The types of physicals that organizations provide.
2. The cost of various physical exam options.
3. A comparison of cost across different clinics or providers.
4. An evaluation of which is the best of four clinics to use for an annual physical.

Visit and learn more about wellness programs:

- Cooper Clinic (Dallas): www.cooperaerobics.com
- Mayo Health Program (Rochester, MN): www.mayo.edu
- Wellness Junction (Allenwood, NJ): www.wellnessjunction.com
- Mission Hospitals (Asheville, NC): www.missionhospitals.org

Case for Analysis: *Stressed Out at Work? Help Is on the Way*

Nowadays, it seems more and more employees are increasingly stressed at work. As discussed earlier in the chapter, high levels of intense stress can have serious consequences for individuals and their organizations. There are many possible explanations for this increase in employee stress, including a stubborn recession, intense global competition, persistently high unemployment and demanding performance work cultures. Compounding the problem is that many employees are struggling with personal and financial issues at home. When a spouse or partner loses a job or is forced to accept fewer hours or less pay by his employer, the reduction in family income is stressful. Many employees still have to pay their mortgages, subsidize living and healthcare expenses for elderly parents, pay for their children's education, have their automobiles repaired, and so forth. Even though these personal issues occur outside of work, they still affect the employee as these stressors can spill over into the employee's work domain.

Another source of stress for employees is related to layoffs. During the most recent recession, several companies and organizations have let go of tens of thousands of employees. Although layoffs are exceptionally hard on the "victims" who are let go, there is also evidence that the "survivors" of layoffs (i.e., those employees who stay with the organization and do not get laid off) experience high levels of stress regarding all of the changes and fear over the future of their own jobs. Some layoff survivors feel guilt over seeing the firing of their co-workers and friends. Also, these surviving employees often have to absorb the work of their co-workers who are no longer with the organization. And, many survivors wonder if (and when) they'll be "next." Research suggests that some of these survivors may ultimately experience lower levels of commitment to and trust in their organizations, a drop in motivation and satisfaction levels, and possibly reduced work performance. Also, some survivors of layoffs may quietly initiate job searches with other organizations. Research suggests that after a layoff occurs, the percent of employees who voluntarily leave the organization can increase by 31 percent. Also, employees who engage in job searches (while in their current jobs) will be more distracted and less focused on their actual jobs. This lack of focus has serious implications for the overall effectiveness of their organizations.

High-performance work cultures can also take a toll on employees' stress levels and mental health. Within a period of about six months, three engineers who worked for the Renault plant outside of Paris, France, committed suicide. It was alleged that prior to their deaths, each of them complained about the "unreasonable workloads, high-pressure management tactics, exhaustion, and humiliating criticism in front of colleagues during performance reviews." Performance reviews have been the source of stress for employees at other companies, as well. General Electric has stopped calling its lower performers "bottom 10s" (as in bottom 10 percent in performance rankings) and instead has begun referring to them as "less effectives." At Goldman Sachs Group, managers were fond of setting unobtainable "stretch goals" in the past. Recently, these managers were counseled to set both achievable and stretch goals with employees. This way, employees can feel a sense of accomplishment while simultaneously being pushed to do more than they thought possible.

What are organizations doing to combat stress among their employees? Many encourage their people to use employee assistance programs (EAPs) or wellness programs. Within the past year or so, there has been an increase in employee requests for financial planning, debt counseling, and legal assistance. Also, many employees are taking advantage of phone and in-person counseling services; a common request is for family and relationship counseling. In addition, experts recommend that organizations modify their cultures so as to decrease the prevalence and harmful effects of stress. For example, managers should encourage employees to share their concerns with teammates or trusted co-workers, ask for help and not keep problems inside, minimize blame when good ideas don't pan out, and create a listening environment where minor issues are identified before they morph into major issues.

To help decrease employees' stress levels, some firms are offering their current employees additional perquisites and benefits as a way to keep them from jumping ship. For example, USAA, the financial services company based in San Antonio, Texas, helps relieve employees' stress by offering concierge service (i.e., someone who runs chores for employees while they're at work). Similarly, General Mills provides its employees with "personalized services" at its headquarters' location to relieve employees of having to do a lot of chores on the weekend. The company hopes that instead, employees will rest and spend time with family. Discovery Communications of Silver Spring, Maryland, recently opened a subsidized childcare center for employees' children. Yum! Brands (which owns KFC and Taco Bell) will follow suit and open a new childcare center at its corporate office in Irvine, California. Intel is offering its employees' children educational scholarships in the amount of $4,000. The company hopes this and other generous benefits will help keep good employees through these stressful times.

Are these prerequisites and extra benefits enough to significantly lower employees' stress levels during these challenging economic times? Probably not, but they might just signal to surviving employees that their organizations care about them; and this in itself is a positive result that may help boost employee retention and morale.

DISCUSSION QUESTIONS

1. What are the primary reasons why many employees are experiencing high levels of stress at work nowadays? Identify and describe these reasons.
2. Why do many of the survivors of layoffs experience stress? Conventional wisdom would suggest that these employees should be happy that they didn't get laid off. Explain your answer.
3. What are companies doing to decrease the stress levels of their employees? To what degree do you think that these steps will help them retain valued employees?

Sources: M.P. McQueen, "Health Costs; Recession's Mental Toll," *Wall Street Journal*, March 7, 2010, p. 2; Kristen Gerencher, "Marketplace: Relax, You Can Beat That Stress," January 3, 2010, *Wall Street Journal*, p. 3; Sue Shellenbarger, "Perking Up: Some Companies Offer Surprising New Benefits," *Wall Street Journal*, March 18, 2009, p. D.1; Elizabeth Bernstein, "When a Co-Worker Is Stressed Out," *Wall Street Journal*, August 26, 2008, p. D.1; Kenneth Levitt, Terry Wilson, and Edna Gilligan, "Corporate Downsizing: An Examination of the Survivors," *Journal of Global Business Issues* 2, no. 2 (Summer 2008): 13–22; and Jenna Gouldreau, Gail Edmondson, and Michelle Conlin, "Dispatches From the War on Stress: Business Begins to Reckon with the Enormous Costs of Workplace Stress," *Businessweek*, August 6, 2007, p. 74.

Experiential Exercise: *Behavior Activity Profile—A Type A Measure*

Each of us displays certain kinds of behaviors, thought patterns, and personal characteristics. For each of the 21 sets of descriptions below, circle the number that you feel best describes your position between each pair. The best answer for each set of descriptions is the response that most nearly describes the way you feel, behave, or think. Answer these in terms of your regular or typical behavior, thoughts, or characteristics.

1. I'm always on time for appointments.	7	6	5	4	3	2	1	I'm never quite on time.
2. When someone is talking to me, chances are I'll anticipate what they are going to say by nodding, interrupting, or finishing sentences for them.	7	6	5	4	3	2	1	I listen quietly without showing any impatience.

3. I frequently try to do several things at once.	7	6	5	4	3	2	1	I tend to take things one a time.
4. When it comes to waiting in line (at banks, theaters, etc.), I really get impatient and frustrated.	7	6	5	4	3	2	1	It simply doesn't bother me.
5. I always feel rushed.	7	6	5	4	3	2	1	I never feel rushed.
6. When it comes to my temper, I find it hard to control at times.	7	6	5	4	3	2	1	I just don't seem to have one.
7. I tend to do most things like eating, walking, and talking rapidly.	7	6	5	4	3	2	1	I do things slowly.

TOTAL SCORE 1–7 __________ = S

8. Quite honestly, the things I enjoy most are job-related activities.	7	6	5	4	3	2	1	I most enjoy leisure-time activities.
9. At the end of a typical workday, I usually feel like I needed to get more done than I did.	7	6	5	4	3	2	1	I accomplished everything I needed to.
10. Someone who knows me very well would say that I would rather work than play.	7	6	5	4	3	2	1	I would rather play than work.
11. When it comes to getting ahead at work, nothing is more important.	7	6	5	4	3	2	1	Many things are more important.
12. My primary source of satisfaction comes from my job.	7	6	5	4	3	2	1	I regularly find satisfaction in non-job pursuits, such as hobbies, friends, and family.
13. Most of my friends and social acquaintances are people I know from work.	7	6	5	4	3	2	1	My friends are not connected with my work.
14. I'd rather stay at work than take a vacation.	7	6	5	4	3	2	1	Nothing at work is important enough to interfere with my vacation.

TOTAL SCORE 8–14__________ = J

15. People who know me well would describe me as hard driving and competitive.	7	6	5	4	3	2	1	People see me as relaxed and easygoing.
16. In general, my behavior is governed by a desire for recognition and achievement.	7	6	5	4	3	2	1	I do what I want to do rather than trying to satisfy others.
17. In trying to complete a project or solve a problem, I tend to wear myself out before I'll give up on it.	7	6	5	4	3	2	1	I tend to take a break or quit if I'm feeling fatigued.
18. When I play a game (tennis, cards, etc.), my enjoyment comes from winning.	7	6	5	4	3	2	1	I like the social interaction.
19. I like to associate with people who are dedicated to getting ahead.	7	6	5	4	3	2	1	I prefer people who are easygoing and take life as it comes.
20. I'm not happy unless I'm always doing something.	7	6	5	4	3	2	1	Frequently, "doing nothing" can be quite enjoyable.
21. What I enjoy most are competitive activities.	7	6	5	4	3	2	1	I prefer noncompetitive pursuits.

TOTAL SCORE 16–21 __________ = H

Impatience (S)	**Job Involvement (J)**	**Hard Driving and Competitive (H)**	**Total Score (A) = S + J + H**

The Behavior Activity Profile attempts to assess the three Type A coronary-prone behavior patterns, as well as provide a total score. The three priority types of Type A coronary-prone behavior patterns follow:

Items	Behavior Pattern	Characteristics
1–7	Impatience (S)	• Is anxious to interrupt • Fails to listen attentively • Gets frustrated by waiting (e.g., in line, for others to complete a job)
8–14	Job Involvement (J)	• Focal point of attention is the job • Lives for the job • Relishes being on the job
15–21	Hard driving/competitive (H)	• Is hardworking, highly competitive • Is competitive in most aspects of life—sports, work, etc. • Races against the clock
1–21	Total score (A)	• Total of S + J + H represents your global Type A behavior

Score ranges for total score are

Score	Behavior Type	Score	Behavior Type
122 and above	Hard-core Type A	70–79	Low Type B
100–121	Moderate Type A	50–69	Moderate Type B
90–99	Low Type A	40 and below	Hard-core Type B
80–89	Type X		

Now you can compare your score to a sample of more than 1,200 respondents.

Percentile Score	Raw Score	
Percent of Individuals Scoring Lower	Males	Females
99%	____140	____132
95	____135	____126
90	____130	____120
85	____124	____112
80	____118	____106
75	____113	____101
70	____108	____95
65	____102	____90
60	____97	____85
55	____92	____80
50	____87	____74
45	____81	____69
40	____75	____63
35	____70	____58
30	____63	____53
25	____58	____48
20	____51	____42
15	____45	____36
10	____38	____31
5	____29	____26
1	____21	____21

Experiential Exercise: *Health Risk Appraisal*

The Health Risk Appraisal form was developed by the Canadian Department of Health and Welfare. The department's initial testing program indicated that approximately one person out of every three who completed the form would modify some unhealthy aspects of lifestyle for at least a while. Figuring the potential payoff was worth it, the government mailed out more than 3 million copies of the questionnaire to Canadians who were receiving social security benefits. A subsequent follow-up indicated that the initial projections of the number of recipients who altered their behavior were correct. Perhaps you will be among the one-third who make lifestyle changes as well.

Choose from the three answers for each question the one answer that most nearly applies to you. The plus and minus signs next to some numbers indicate more than (+) and less than (−). Note that a few items have only two alternatives.

Exercise

_____1. Physical effort most often expended during the workday:
(a) significant; (b) some; (c) none

_____2. Participation in physical activities—skiing, golf, swimming, etc., or lawn mowing, gardening, etc.?
(a) daily; (b) weekly; (c) seldom

_____3. Participation in vigorous exercise program?
(a) three or more days a week; (b) less than one; (c) seldom

_____4. Average miles walked or jogged per day?
(a) one or more; (b) less than one; (c) none

_____5. Flights of stairs climbed per day?
(a) 10; (b) less than 10; (c) none

Nutrition

_____6. Are you overweight?
(a) no; (b) 5 to 19 lbs. (c) 20 lbs. or more

_____7. Do you eat a wide variety of foods, including something from each of the following five food groups: (1) meat, fish, poultry, dried legumes, eggs, or nuts; (2) milk or milk products; (3) bread or cereals; (4) fruits; (5) vegetables?
(a) each day; (b) three times weekly; (c) less than three times weekly

Alcohol

_____8. Average number of bottles (12 oz.) of beer per week?
(a) 0 to 7; (b) 8 to 15; (c) 16

_____9. Average number of hard liquor (1 1/2 oz.) drinks per week?
(a) 0 to 7; (b) 8 to 15; (c) 16

_____10. Average number of glasses (5 oz.) of wine or cider per week?
(a) 0 to 7; (b) 8 to 15; (c) 16

_____11. Total number of drinks per week including beer, liquor, or wine?
(a) 0 to 7; (b) 8 to 15; (c) 16

_____12. Do you take drugs illegally?
(a) no; (b) yes

_____13. Do you consume alcoholic beverages together with certain drugs (tranquilizers, barbiturates, illegal drugs)?
(a) no; (b) yes

_____14. Do you use painkillers improperly or excessively?
(a) no; (b) yes

Tobacco

_____15. Cigarettes smoked per day?
(a) none; (b) 1 or 2; (c) 2

_____16. Cigars smoked per day?
(a) none; (b) 1 or 2; (c) 2

_____17. Pipe tobacco pouches per week?
(a) none; (b) 1 or 2; (c) 2

Personal Health

_____18. Do you experience periods of depression?
(a) seldom; (b) occasionally; (c) frequently

_____19. Does anxiety interfere with your daily activities?
(a) seldom; (b) occasionally; (c) frequently

_____20. Do you get enough satisfying sleep?
(a) yes; (b) no

_____21. Are you aware of the causes and danger of VD?
(a) yes; (b) no

_____22. Breast self-examination? (If not applicable, do not score)
(a) monthly; (b) occasionally; (c) never

Road and Water Safety

_____23. Mileage per year as driver or passenger?
(a) less than 10,000; (b) more than 10,000

_____24. Do you often exceed the speed limit?
(a) no; (b) by 10 mph; (c) by 20 mph

_____25. Do you wear a seatbelt?
(a) always; (b) occasionally; (c) never

_____26. Do you drive a motorcycle, moped, or snowmobile?
(a) yes; (b) no

_____27. If yes to the above, do you always wear a regulation safety helmet?
(a) yes; (b) no

_____28. Do you ever drive under the influence of alcohol?
(a) never; (b) occasionally

_____29. Do you ever drive when your ability may be affected by drugs?
(a) never; (b) occasionally

_____30. Are you aware of water safety?
(a) yes; (b) no

_____31. If you participate in water sports or boating, do you wear a life jacket?
(a) yes; (b) no

General

_____32. Average time watching TV per day (in hours)?
(a) 0 to 1; (b) 1 to 4; (c) 4

_____33. Are you familiar with first-aid procedures?
(a) yes; (b) no

_____34. Do you ever smoke in bed?
(a) no; (b) occasionally; (c) regularly

_____35. Do you always make use of equipment provided for your safety at work?
(a) yes; (b) occasionally; (c) no

Total Score

A *total score* of 35–45 is **excellent.** You have a commendable lifestyle based on sensible habits and a lively awareness of personal health.

A *total score* of 46–55 is **good.** With some minor changes, you can develop an excellent lifestyle.

A *total score* of 56–65 is **risky.** You are taking unnecessary risks with your health. Several of your habits should be changed if potential health problems are to be avoided.

A *total score* of 66 and over is **hazardous.** Either you have little personal awareness of good health habits or you are choosing to ignore them. This is a danger zone.

PART THREE

Behavior within Organizations: Groups and Interpersonal Influence

CHAPTER EIGHT

Group and Team Behavior

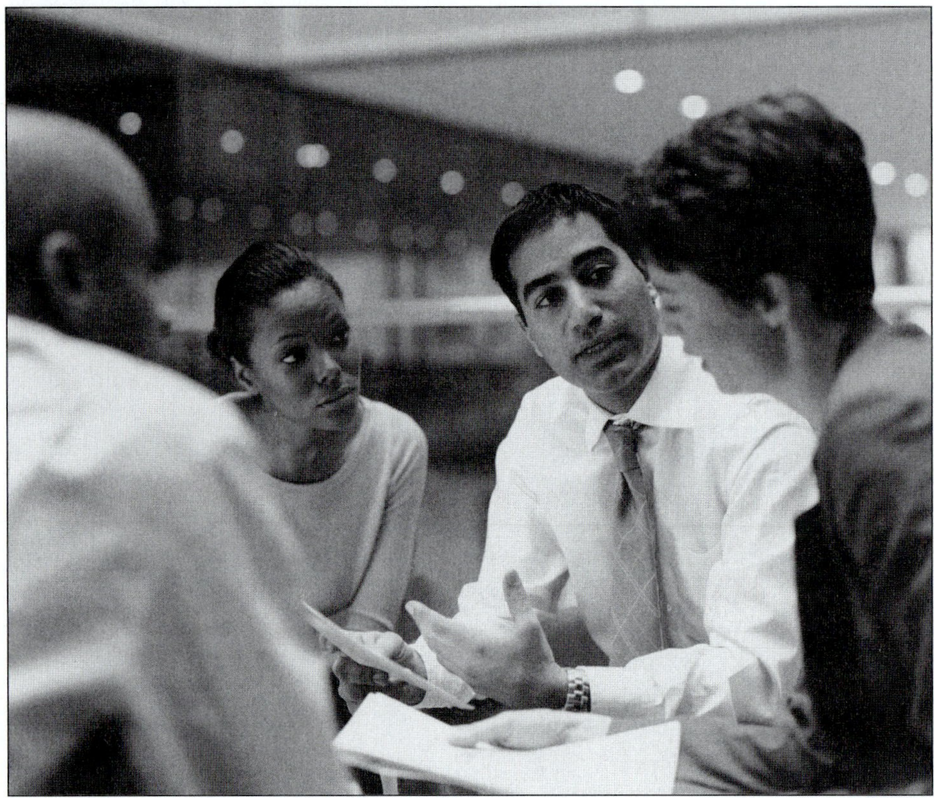

Learning Objectives

After completing Chapter 8, you should be able to

Define
The terms *group* and *team.*

Describe
The difference in groups and teams.

Discuss
Why people form groups and managers form teams.

Compare
The various stages of group development.

Identify
The characteristics associated with virtual teams.

Teams Can Change the World

Effective, hard-working, and cohesive teams can have a long-lasting impact on organizations, society, and the global marketplace. A few examples of the power and impact of teams are in the following newsworthy stories.

The Invention Team

Charles Batcheldor was an English machinist. John Kruesi was a Swiss clockmaker. Ludwig Boehm was a German glassblower. Francis Upton was a Princeton-trained mathematician.

They were drawn to the then-isolated New Jersey hamlet of Menlo Park by the force of Thomas Edison's genius. But it was Edison's unique ability to tap into their skills that turned his half-formed visions into an astonishing stream of workable products. "He was never the lone inventor," says Bill Pretzer, a curator of the Edison collection at the Henry Ford Museum.

"Edison himself moves about, first to one bench, then to another, examining here, instructing there," wrote the *New York Herald.* A sketch handed to Kruesi unexpectedly yielded the phonograph. The work was "strenuous but joyous," one lab hand wrote. The boss (Edison) got as dirty as his workmen. And there was the day when the team rode Edison's miniature locomotive to a nearby fishing hole. "The strangest thing to me is the $12 that I get each Saturday," Upton wrote his father, "for my labor does not seem like work but like study."

It was Upton who bought the instruments that led to a breakthrough insight on electric lighting. It was Batcheldor's nimble hands that threaded a carbon filament into a bulb that Boehm evacuated to a millionth of an atmosphere. And on October 22, 1879, when the bulb finished a 14-hour burn, the darkness filled with the cheers of five men and four nationalities.

The Twitter Team

In 2006, Jack Dorsey, Biz Stone, and Evan Williams were working for a new organization called Odeo, which was a podcasting service. Dorsey and the others thought that a short message service would add a creative spark by letting everyone in the company communicate with each other. So, they built a simple Web application that would allow members of the team to send short 140-character messages to everyone else in the company and vice versa. Thus, Twitter was born. The service grew rapidly in 2009, when it expanded tenfold. Twitter continues to grow. In the first half of 2010, visitors to the U.S. website reached approximately 21 million.

The Apple Team

They were known as dropouts, artists, evangelists, geniuses, iconoclasts, pirates—and friends. Sometimes even best friends. The early team of four, which grew to dozens, wanted to make a personal computer easy enough for anyone to use without fear or loathing and inexpensive enough to be affordable. But the happy few who worked on the Mac also saw in the new world of computing a potentially profound force. Their ultimate goal was to unleash, in themselves and others, limitless individual creativity.

The Mac team, headed by Apple cofounder Steve Jobs, operated like a superstealth startup within the company. Holed up in a two-story building near a gas station dubbed the "Texaco Towers," the team was intensely competitive with other Apple divisions, such as the Lisa computer.

Jobs set challenging goals and deadlines: the caffeine-fueled software team once debugged for 48 hours straight rather than face him without having finished the task. There were epic battles and broken friendships—Jef Raskin, who started the Mac research project in 1979, got frustrated and left Apple in 1982. But Jobs's famous rebel yell—"It's better to be a pirate than join the Navy"—captured the renegade spirit that saw the team through 90-hour work-weeks at stunningly low pay.

In 1983, after three years of labor, the Mac was born. Priced at $2,495, it featured a clean, intuitive graphic user interface that allowed nonprogrammers to use it almost instantly, without geek supervision. When it was turned on, a friendly little icon smiled out at the world. And the world smiled back—the Mac sold faster than any PC that came before.

Although the Mac went on to a difficult adolescence, it was the collective expression of a cohesive, hard-working team who loved it—and marked a turning point in the history of the PC.

The Magic of an Idea Team

For 10 years, MasterCard maxed out five advertising campaigns—and failed to narrow the gap with Visa. So when the company decided to get a new ad agency, it looked like desperation. To McCann Erickson, it looked like opportunity.

McCann assigned a core creative team of three—Joyce King Thomas, Jeroen Bours, and Jonathan Cranin—to prepare a pitch. The trio, who had been working together for two years, conferred with the strategy team and brainstormed intensively for a month. "We were very comfortable working together, so we debated everything freely," says Thomas.

The breakthrough came to Cranin: the tag line "some things money can't buy" to anchor the ad. Back at the office, Thomas caught the spark and began crafting a spot around it. Inspiration struck two weeks later, as Thomas and Bours batted around ideas over coffee and bagels on a Sunday morning. The first ad would be set at a baseball game, feature a list of ordinary transactions, and lead to the setup: "Priceless." Recalls Thomas: "We knew we had it."

MasterCard agreed, even after a different spot tested better in research. "Intuitively, we knew the insights made it more than just another ad," says chief marketing officer Larry Flanagan, then head of U.S. advertising. Gut feeling proved right. Over the past ten years or so, MasterCard has added new U.S. credit cards at a higher rate than Visa.

And the award-winning campaign's versatile format and simple appeal have also made it a global winner: spots have been tweaked for audiences in 105 countries and 48 languages.

Sources: Adapted from Jessica E. Vascellaro and Emily Steel, "Twitter Rolls Out Ads," *Wall StJ*.com, April 14, 2010; J. Mullins and R. Komisar, "A Business Plan? Or a Journey to Plan B?" *MIT Sloan Management Review* 51, no. 3 (2010): 1–5; "Six Teams That Changed the World," CNN Money.com, accessed at http://money.cnn.com/ 2006/05/31/magazines/fortune/sixteams_greatteams_fortune_061206/index.htm (contributions made by Jerry Useem, Ellen McGirt, Eugenia Levenson); and Jeffrey S. Young and William S. Simon, *iCon Steve Jobs: The Greatest Second Act in the History of Business* (New York: Wiley, 2006).

This chapter examines groups and teams in organizations. As the opening vignette illustrates, teams can have a long-lasting impact on organizational effectiveness. Groups and teams in organizations can alter the individual's motivations or attitudes and can influence the behavior of individuals in an organizational setting. Organizational behavior is more than the logical composite of the behavior of individuals; it is also the behavior of groups that interact and the activities within groups. This chapter provides a model for understanding the nature of groups in organizations. The chapter begins by defining the various types of groups, reasons for their formation, and characteristics of groups. Next, a particular type of task group, a team, is defined and reasons managers form teams are given, as are requirements for forming effective teams. Finally, the concepts of roles and role conflict are discussed.

group
Collection of individuals in which behavior and/or performance of one member is influenced by behavior and/or performance of other members.

The Meaning of a Group

In this book, a **group** is defined as

> Two or more employees who interact with each other in such a manner that the behavior and/or performance of a member is influenced by the behavior and/or performance of other members.[1]

Types of Groups

An organization has technical requirements that arise from its stated goals. Accomplishment of these goals requires that certain tasks be performed and that employees be assigned to perform these tasks.[2] As a result, most employees are members of a group based on their positions in the organization; these are **formal groups**. In addition, whenever individuals associate on a fairly continuous basis, groups tend to form whose activities may be different from those required by the organization; these are **informal groups**. Both formal groups and informal groups exhibit common characteristics.

formal groups
Groups created by managerial decision to accomplish stated goals of the organization.

informal groups
Groups that arise from individual efforts and develop around common interests and friendships rather than deliberate design.

Formal Groups

The demands and processes of the organization lead to the formation of two types of formal groups: command and task.

Command Group

The command group, specified by the organization chart, comprises the subordinates who report directly to a given supervisor. The authority relationship between a department manager and the supervisors or between a senior nurse and her subordinates exemplifies a command group.

Task Group

A task group comprises the employees who work together to complete a particular task or project. For example, activities of clerks in an insurance company are required tasks. When an accident claim is filed, several clerks must communicate and coordinate with one another if the claim is to be handled properly. These required tasks and interactions facilitate the formation of a task group.[3] Nurses assigned to duty in the emergency room of a hospital usually constitute a task group because certain activities are required when a patient is treated. A special type of task group is called a *team.* Team performance is affected by all the factors that influence groups, but teams are also affected by additional factors that do not affect the productivity of other sorts of groups. For this reason, the concept of teams will be discussed separately later in the chapter.

Informal Groups

Informal groups are natural groupings of people in the work situation who come together in response to social needs. In other words, informal groups do not arise as a result of deliberate design but rather evolve naturally. Two specific informal groups exist: interest and friendship.

Interest Groups

Individuals who may not be members of the same command or task group may affiliate to achieve some mutual objective. The objectives of such groups are not related to those of the organization but are specific to each group. Employees banding together to present a unified front to management for more benefits and waiters pooling their tips are examples of interest groups.

Friendship Groups

Many groups form because members have something in common, such as age, gender, political beliefs, desire to play the same sport, or ethnic background. These friendship groups often extend their interaction and communication to off-the-job activities.

If employees' affiliation patterns were documented, it would become readily apparent that they belong to numerous and often overlapping groups. A distinction has been made between two broad classifications of groups: formal and informal. The major difference between them is that formal command and task groups are designated by the formal organization as a means to an end. Informal interest and friendship groups are important for their own sake. They satisfy a basic human need for association.[4]

Even though friendship groups are informal, managers should make efforts to become aware of and, if possible, positively influence such groups, directing efforts toward organizational goals.[5] Indeed, in some organizations, the associations that individuals form through friendship groups are more powerful than formal affiliations.[6] Some suggested ways to influence these groups are through building good relations with the informal group's leader, providing group behavior and human relations training for the leader, and supporting members' efforts in sustaining the group relationship.

Why People Form Groups

Formal and informal groups form for various reasons.[7] Some reasons involve needs, proximity, attractions, goals, and economics.

The Satisfaction of Needs

The desire for need satisfaction can be a strong motivating force leading to group formation.[8] Specifically, some employees' security, social, esteem, and self-actualization needs can be satisfied to a degree by their affiliation with groups.

Security

Without the group to lean on when various management demands are made, certain employees may feel they are standing alone, facing management and the entire organizational system. This feeling can be even stronger for new employees. This "aloneness" leads to a degree of insecurity. By being a member of a group, the employee can become involved in group activities and discuss management demands with other employees who hold supportive views. In situations solely affecting the individual employee, the member can still count on the group to support her actions.[9] Interaction and communication among the group's members serve as a buffer to management demands. The need for a buffer may be especially strong in two cases. First, a new employee may depend heavily on the group for aid in correctly performing his job. Second, as a result of many corporate downsizing efforts, individuals depend on group support as a means to adjust to new demands and overcome feelings of insecurity.[10]

Social

The gregariousness of people stimulates their need for affiliation; a desire to be part of a group points out the intensity of social needs. The need to socialize exists not only on the job but away from the workplace, as evidenced by the vast array of social, political, civic, and fraternal organizations people can join.

Esteem

For a variety of reasons, a certain group in a particular work environment may be viewed by employees as having a high level of prestige (technical competence outside activities, etc.). Consequently, membership in this group carries with it a certain status not enjoyed by nonmembers. For employees with high esteem needs, membership in such a group can provide much-needed satisfaction.[11]

Proximity and Attraction

Interpersonal interaction can result in group formation. Two important facets of interpersonal interaction are proximity and attraction. Proximity involves the physical distance between employees performing a job. Attraction designates the degree to which people are drawn to each other because of perceptual, attitudinal, performance, or motivational similarity.[12]

Individuals who work in proximity have numerous opportunities to exchange ideas, thoughts, and attitudes about various on- and off-the-job activities. These exchanges often result in some type of group formation. Proximity also makes it possible for individuals to learn about the characteristics of other people. To sustain the interaction and interest, a group is often formed.

For example, space station crews need to be trained in interpersonal, emotional support, and group interaction skills.[13] Because of proximity and attraction due to the nature of the work task, group formation is inevitable. Whole-crew training is indispensable for crew productivity and well-being. Such training circumvents many problems faced by long-duration space flights, where reliance on ground-based professionals is impractical.

Group Goals

A group's goals, if clearly understood, can be the reasons an individual is attracted to that group. For example, an individual may join a group that meets after work to become familiar with new production methods to be implemented in the organization over the next year. The person who voluntarily joins the after-hours group believes that learning the new system is a necessary and important goal for employees.

Identifying group goals is not always possible. The assumption that formal organizational groups have clear goals must be tempered by the understanding that perception, attitudes, personality, and learning can distort goals.[14] For example, a new employee may never be formally told the goals of the unit that he's joined. By observing the behavior and attitudes of others, individuals may conclude what they believe the goals to be. These perceptions may or may not be accurate.

Economics

In many cases, groups form because individuals believe that they can derive greater economic benefits from their jobs if they organize. Indeed, group pay incentives can be extremely valuable in supporting the way management wants to run the company.[15] For example, individuals working at different points on an assembly line may be paid on a group incentive basis in which the group's production determines each member's wages. By working and cooperating as a group, the individuals may obtain higher economic benefits. Conversely, by paying for individual performance, the structure may get in the way of group productivity by stressing individual, versus group, dependencies.[16] By matching incentive plans with a company's work culture and the type of group being used, the group's processes can be better aligned with those of the organization.[17]

Stages of Development

Groups learn, just as individuals do. Group performance depends both on individual learning and on how well members learn to work with one another.[18] For example, a new-product committee formed to develop a response to a competitor may evolve into an effective team, with the interests of the company being most important; however, it may be ineffective if its members are more concerned about their individual departmental goals than about developing a response to a competitor. This section describes some general stages through which groups evolve and points out the sequential developmental process involved.

Behavioral scientists and managers are interested in how groups develop. A number of models attempt to trace the group development process. Two models stand out in the explanations offered for group development: a five-stage model and the punctuated equilibrium model.

The Five-Stage Model

This model explains the group development process in terms of a maturity cycle.[19] The five stages are referred to as follows:

1. *Forming*. This is the breaking the ice, getting acquainted stage. Group members are trying out behaviors, testing their position, and asking questions of other group members. The group is establishing loose, but specific, ground rules.

2. *Storming*. This stage is characterized by conflict because members are arguing, debating, and experimenting with roles, advice offered by other members, and attempts to move into leadership roles. The group's hierarchy starts to take shape.

3. *Norming*. The group starts to work more effectively together. There is a sense of togetherness or attraction to being a part of a group. This is the beginning of cohesiveness. A set of group-driven expectations is communicated within the group.

4. *Performing*. A group structure, hierarchy, and norms are in place. The group is focused on accomplishing goals and being an efficient unit. This is an important stage in that the group is mature.

5. *Adjourning*. The group prepares to disband. The goals have been accomplished and tasks finished. Some members will be saddened over the loss of member contact and cohesiveness in the future.

There is no set time limit for progressing along the five-stage cycle.[20] In fact, some groups may engage in more than one stage at a time. For example, storming (debating, arguing) may be occurring at the same time the group is performing. The boundaries between the various stages are not clear.[21] The five-stage model should be used as a general framework but not a perfectly accurate snapshot of how groups develop.

The Punctuated Equilibrium Model

Some believe that the five-stage model is too static and unrealistic. The punctuated equilibrium model (PEM) presents group development as a three-phase concept.[22] The first phase occurs when groups define tasks, establish goals, and consider various ways to execute the steps of the plan or project. Somewhere along a time continuum, the group decides to change its perspectives and take action. The group reaches its own point of inertia or equilibrium. The group reaches the point of equilibrium when it realizes that time is running out. After this realization phase, there is then a final phase to accomplish tasks.

Research has found that the movement from phase 1 to phase 2 is about halfway between the first meeting and the final deadline. A sudden sense of urgency seems to take over and motivates members. The pattern of PEM is displayed in Figure 8.1. As illustrated, the first phase takes about half of a group's cycle. Then a burst of energy to make progress on the tasks occurs.[23] Finally, there is a "last ditch" push to complete the project on a positive note. The PEM is more applicable to project teams and temporary groups than is other models. An example of a temporary group would be a student team with a class project due at the end of the semester. A recent study found support for the PEM with college students who after receiving feedback regarding their initial exam grades in a course increased their effort (i.e., increased their attendance and took advantage of extra credit opportunities) to achieve a grade that was more in line with their goals.[24]

FIGURE 8.1
Approximation of the Punctured Equilibrium Model

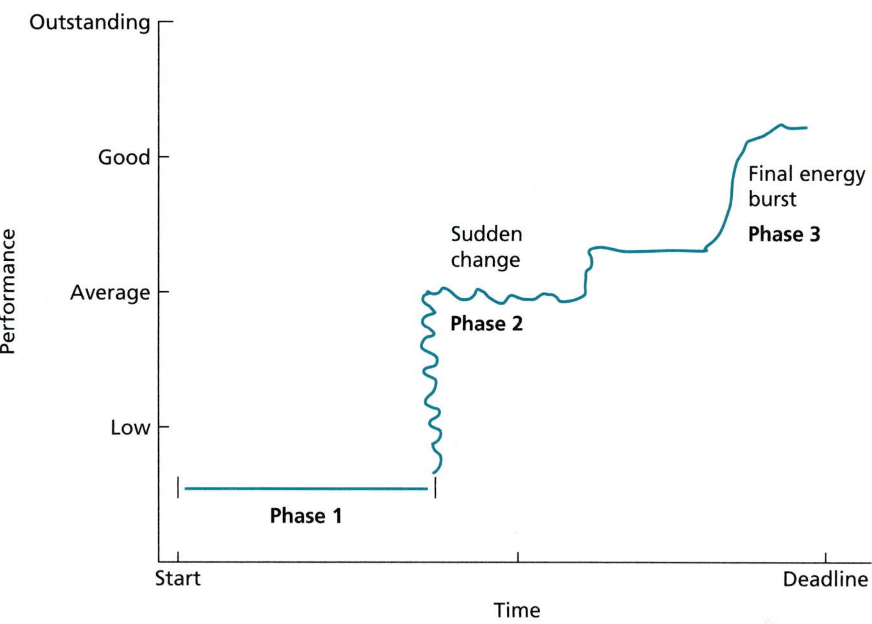

Characteristics of Groups

As groups evolve through their various stages of development, they begin to exhibit certain characteristics: structure, status hierarchy, roles, norms, leadership, cohesiveness, and conflict. Conflict in groups is such an important topic that it will be the subject of the next chapter. This section examines the other characteristics of groups. Understanding group behavior requires an awareness of these general characteristics.[25]

Structure

Within any group, some type of structure evolves over time. Group members are differentiated on the basis of such factors as expertise, aggressiveness, power, leadership skills, and status; each member occupies a position in the group. The pattern of relationships among the positions constitutes a group structure.[26] Members of the group evaluate each position's prestige, status, and importance of the group. In most cases, status differences among positions create a hierarchical group structure.

Status in formal groups is usually based on positioning in the formal organization, while status in informal groups can be based on anything relevant to the group (e.g., golf scores, ability to communicate with management). Other members expect the occupant of each position to enact certain behaviors. The set of expected behaviors associated with a position in the structure constitutes the role of that position's occupant.

Status Hierarchy

Status and position are so similar that the terms are often interchangeable. The status assigned to a particular position is typically a consequence of certain characteristics that differentiate one position from other positions. In some cases, a person is assigned status because of such factors as job seniority, age, or ability. For example, the oldest worker may be perceived as being more technically proficient and is therefore attributed status by a group of technicians. Whenever the other engineers need help with a particularly complicated technical issue, they may consult this "guru" for useful advice. Thus, assigned status may have nothing to do with the formal status hierarchy.

Roles

Each person in the group structure, including its leaders, has an associated role that consists of the expected behaviors of the occupant of that position.[27] The director of nursing services in a hospital is expected to organize and control the department of nursing and to assist in preparing and administering its budget. A nursing supervisor, on the other hand, is expected to supervise the activities of nursing personnel engaged in specific nursing services, such as obstetrics, pediatrics, and surgery. These expected behaviors generally are agreed to not only by the occupants but also by members of the nursing group and other hospital personnel.

In addition to the *expected role,* there is a perceived role and an enacted role. The *perceived role* is the set of behaviors that a person in a position believes he should enact. (In some cases, the perceived role may correspond to the expected role.) The *enacted role,* in contrast, is the behavior that a person actually carries out. Fairly stable or permanent groups typically foster good agreement between expected and perceived roles. But conflict and frustration may result from difference in the three roles. When the enacted role deviates too much from the expected role, the person can either become more like the expected role or leave the group.

An interesting prison experiment that illustrates the powerful nature of expected and enacted roles was conducted by Philip Zimbardo at Stanford University. He and his associates created a prison in the basement of a Stanford University building. Students were hired and paid $15 per day to serve as either a prisoner or a guard.[28] The local police department was brought into the experiment to arrest each prisoner, bring prisoners from their homes or dorm rooms to the prison, and create a record of their arrest. The prisoners then began to serve a two-week sentence. The guards operated the prison as the authority in charge. Physical violence was not permitted. The guards worked eight-hour shifts, but the prisoners remained in jail 24 hours each day. The prisoners and guards took on their roles quickly. The guards became forceful, authoritative, and abusive. The prisoners became passive, obedient, and depressed. The experiment was so realistic and powerful that researchers had to stop the simulation after six days. The roles were accepted and acted out so thoroughly that the stop was ordered to protect everyone involved from further psychological and emotional distress.

Norms

norms
Generally agreed-upon standards of individual and group behavior developed as a result of member interaction over time.

Norms are the standards shared by the members of a group.[29] They have certain characteristics that are important to group members. First, norms are formed only with respect to things that have significance for the group. They may be written, but they're often communicated orally to members. In many cases, they are never formally stated but somehow are known by group members. Second, norms are accepted in various degrees by group members. Some are accepted completely, others only partially. And third, norms may apply to every group member or to only some group members.

Both formal and informal groups may have a variety of norms. For example, most groups have loyalty norms fostering the development of a strong degree of loyalty and commitment from their members. Members are expected to do certain things (e.g., work late, accept transfers, help out other members) to prove they are loyal. Other groups have formal or informal dress norms. Company salesforce members may all dress similarly (e.g., in suits) to present the company's desired image to customers; people working in a customer support call center for online retailers like Overstock.com, eBay, or Amazon.com work away from customers and may come to work in very casual clothing. Finally, groups have resource allocation norms and performance norms. Resource allocation norms of a formal organization relate to how pay, promotions, and status symbols (e.g., office size, reserved parking, assistant) should be allocated. Informal groups may also have allocation

TABLE 8.1
Examples of Positive and Negative Norms

Positive Norms	Negative Norms
1. People defend the company when others criticize it.	1. In our company, they're always trying to take advantage of us.
2. Our people always try to improve, even when things are going well.	2. There's no point in trying to work harder; nobody else does.
3. Around here, people are good listeners and seek out the opinions of others.	3. Around here, it's dog-eat-dog and always watch your back.
4. Our managers and supervisors really care about their employees.	4. In our organization, it's best to hide your problems and avoid your supervisor.

norms regarding such informal rewards as who works with whom or who gets helped and who does the helping. Performance norms relate to evaluating satisfactory performance. In formal groups, this may be made relatively clear by management; but as we shall see, performance norms may not be accepted by the informal group. In fact, informal groups may have performance norms of their own. Table 8.1 contains examples of some positive and negative norms, as expressed in one study.[30] Managers must take into account both formal and informal norms when they try to assemble high-performance groups.[31]

An example of negative group pressure and norms is illustrated in an experiment reported by Asch.[32] He devised a study of groups of eight to ten college students who evaluated pairs of cards such as the example presented in Figure 8.2.

In Asch's experiment, the students in each group were seated around a table. All but one of them were actually the researcher's confidants. The group was shown a series of cards of vertical lines of different lengths (Figure 8.2), and each person was asked to say which of the lines (Card B) was the same length as the line displayed in Card A. One after the other, the members announced their decision. The confidants had been instructed to give an incorrect response. The subject sat in the next to last seat so that all but one had given the incorrect answer before he or she provided his or her response. The average student conformed to every group response on 32 percent of the trials, and 74 percent of the subjects conformed to the incorrect response at least once.

The results of the Asch experiment were astonishing, especially since the correct answer was entirely obvious. Subjects had to override the evidence they observed or provide an answer that conformed to the others.

When interviewed afterward, subjects said that they had been influenced by group pressure, not wanting to appear silly, and the need to avoid criticism from others. Each student perceived the group as a reference group that provided information through their responses on the group norms.

In Asch's later experiments, he introduced others who disagreed with the consensus. This disagreement led to a significant increase in the subject's readiness to disagree with the

FIGURE 8.2
Asch Comparison Cards

dominant view. Because the subject had some social support (e.g., one, two, or three other individuals), he or she was more likely to resist conformity, pressure, and perceived norms.

The Asch experiment has been repeated around the world. In collectivist countries, where the group approach dominates over the individual approach, there were higher levels of conformity.[33] Managers should be aware that blindly accepting group conformity can pose serious problems in attempting to optimize performance in a work setting.

Leadership

The leadership role in groups is a crucial group characteristic because the leader plays an important role in determining group success.[34] The leader of a group exerts some influence over group members. In the formal group, the leader can exercise legitimately sanctioned power. That is, the leader can reward or punish members who don't comply with directives, orders, or rules.

The leadership role is also a significant factor in an informal group. The person who becomes an informal group leader is generally a respected, high-status member who

1. Contributes to the group in accomplishing its goals.
2. Enables members to satisfy needs.
3. Embodies the values of the group. In essence, the leader is a personification of the values, motives, and aspirations of the members.
4. Is the choice of the group members to represent their viewpoint when interacting with other group leaders.
5. Is a facilitator of group conflict, an initiator of group actions, and concerned with maintaining the group as a functioning unit.

Leaders are rare. Often, members of a group look for someone to follow.[35] Becoming an effective group leader doesn't necessarily require charm or a library of theories waiting to be applied. It does, however, require vision, creativity, clear goals, a willingness to work horizontally and vertically, and good communication skills.[36] A good leader focuses on engaging in conversations that create, take care of, and initiate new commitments toward actions leading to common goals—especially on conversations that secure effective cooperative action within an organization.[37] At W.L. Gore & Associates (the maker of GORE-TEX), there are no managers or formal chain of command. In this leadership environment, anyone can be a team leader based on her particular "knowledge, skill, enthusiasm, track record and ability to attract followers."[38]

Whether in charge of a formal or informal group, the leader must be both open (encouraging members to participate) and authoritarian (intervening when necessary to accomplish group goals).[39] Indeed, a good leader must play social, spanning, and organizing roles.[40]

Cohesiveness

cohesiveness
Strength of group members' desires to remain in the group and their commitment to the group.

Formal and informal groups seem to possess a closeness or commonness of attitude, behavior, and performance. This closeness, referred to as **cohesiveness**, is generally regarded as a force acting on the members to remain in a group that is greater than the forces pulling members away from a group. Joining a group allows an individual to have a sense of belonging and feelings of morale.[41] A cohesive group, then, involves individuals who are attracted to one another. A group that is low in cohesiveness doesn't possess interpersonal attractiveness for the members.

There are, of course, numerous sources of attraction to a group. A group may be attractive to an individual because[42]

1. The goals of the group and the members are compatible and clearly specified.
2. The group has a charismatic leader.
3. The reputation of the group indicates that the group successfully accomplishes its tasks.

TABLE 8.2 Relationship between Group Cohesiveness and Agreement with Organizational Goals

		Agreement with Organization Goals	
		Low	**High**
Degree of Group Cohesiveness	**Low**	Performance probably oriented away from organizational goals.	Performance probably oriented toward achivement of organizational goals.
	High	Performance oriented away from organizational goals.	Performance oriented toward achievement of organizational goals.

4. The group is small enough to permit members to have their opinions heard and evaluated by others.
5. The members are attractive in that they support one another and help each other overcome obstacles and barriers to personal growth and development.

Because highly cohesive groups consist of individuals who are motivated to be together, there's a tendency to expect effective group performance. This logic isn't supported conclusively by research evidence. In general, as the cohesiveness of a work group increases, the level of conformity to group norms also increases. But the group norms may be inconsistent with those of the organization.

Cohesiveness and Performance

The concept of cohesiveness is important for understanding groups in organizations. A group's degree of cohesiveness can have positive or negative effects, depending on how well group goals match those of the formal organization. Four distinct relationships are possible, as Table 8.2 shows.

The table indicates that if cohesiveness is high and the group accepts and agrees with formal organizational goals, then group behavior will be positive from the formal organization's standpoint. However, if the group is highly cohesive but its goals aren't congruent with those of the formal organization, then group behavior will be negative from the formal organization's standpoint.

Table 8.2 indicates that if a group is low in cohesiveness and members have goals not in agreement with those of management, then the results probably are negative from the organization's standpoint. Behavior is more on an individual basis than on a group basis because of the low cohesiveness. A group can be low in cohesiveness and yet have members' goals agree with those of the formal organization. Here, the results are probably positive, although again more on an individual basis than on a group basis.

Groupthink

Highly cohesive groups are important forces in organizational behavior. In other words, the organization should place people with many similarities in an isolated setting, give them a common goal, and reward them for performance. On the surface, this may look like a good idea. However, one author has provided a provocative analysis of highly cohesive groups.[43]

Irving Janis studied foreign policy decisions made by several presidential administrations and concluded that these groups were highly cohesive and close-knit. He labeled their decision-making process *groupthink*. Janis defines **groupthink** as the "deterioration of mental efficiency, reality testing, and moral judgment" in the interest of group solidarity. In his book, he described the following characteristics associated with groupthink:

groupthink
A cohesive group's desire for agreement interferes with the group's consideration of alternative solutions.

1. *Illusion of invulnerability.* Members of groups believe that they are invincible.
2. *Tendency to moralize.* Any opposition to group views is characterized by members as weak, evil, or unintelligent.

OB AT WORK Groupthink and War

The theory of groupthink remains influential in analyzing how groups make decisions. Prior to Janis, social psychologists explored the implications of small group settings. Janis's analysis has expanded the groupthink analysis into studies of organizational and foreign affairs decision making.

Applications of groupthink analysis have been applied to presidential decisionmaking. Presidents Kennedy, Nixon, Carter, Reagan, and Bush have provided interesting insight into how different styles fare in group settings. Presidential decision making in the 1990–1991 Persian Gulf crisis after Iraq's August 2, 1990, invasion of Kuwait provides a glimpse of how President George H. W. Bush operated in group settings.

Group cohesiveness was important to President Bush. The camaraderie was exceptional despite a few confrontations between John Sununu and C. Boyden Gray. Brent Scowcroft was the president's long-standing confidant. The president's inner cohesive circle was referred to as the "gang of eight."

While President Bush was cordial and at times encouraged open discussions and debates, he did not place a high priority on each group member airing doubts or raising objections. Nor did he assign anyone the devil's advocate role. The gang of eight didn't follow any particular process for evaluating alternatives. This is in stark contrast to President John F. Kennedy's decision-making group during the Cuban Missile crisis (1962). His group laid out at least 10 alternatives and discussed them methodically. President Bush, supported by Scowcroft, knew what he wanted to do and took the lead in any discussions.

President Bush's team was homogeneous in terms of social and ideological views. Maintaining harmony was made easier because of the similar backgrounds and friendly atmosphere. This resulted in few challenges of the consensus reached about how to deal with Saddam Hussein's invasion of Kuwait.

Although groupthink existed in President Bush's gang-of-eight meetings, the end result was the accomplishment of reversing Iraq's acquisition of Kuwait. The president's leadership and ability overcame the potential groupthink problems. He was able to assemble world leaders and build a U.S.–led coalition that engaged in a ground war that proved easier than even the gang of eight anticipated.

Groupthink existed in President Bush's team, and there was a positive outcome. But it is not always the case. Groupthink can generate negative or positive outcomes, as history has illustrated in organizations and in political situations.

Sources: Marcus Goncalves, *Team Building* (New York: American Society of Mechanical Engineers, 2007); and Steve A. Yetiv, "Groupthink and the Gulf Crisis," *British Journal of Political Science* 33 (2003): 419–442.

3. *Feeling of unanimity.* Each member of the group supports the leader's decisions. Members may have reservations about decisions but do not share their views. Rather than appearing weak, members keep views to themselves. This indicates how pressure toward group solidarity can distort individual members' judgments.

4. *Pressure to conform.* Formal and informal attempts are made to discourage discussion of divergent views. Groups exert great pressure on individual members to conform.

5. *Opposing ideas dismissed.* Any individual or outside group that criticizes or opposes a decision receives little or no attention from the group. Group members tend to show strong favoritism toward their own ideas in the manner by which information is processed and evaluated, thus guaranteeing that their ideas will win out.

Certainly, some level of group cohesiveness is necessary for a group to tackle a problem. If seven individuals from seven different organizational units are assigned a task, the task may never be completed effectively. The point, however, is that when it comes to cohesiveness, more may not necessarily be better. While members of task groups may redefine solving a problem to mean reaching agreement rather than making the best decision, members of cohesive groups may redefine it to mean preserving relations among group members and preserving the image of the group. Groupthink illustrates the impact of group dynamics and cohesiveness of group performance. The accompanying OB at Work feature examines George H. W. Bush's close-knit group meetings involving Iraq's invasion of Kuwait in 1990.

A study examined effects of group loyalty and distortion tendencies in management teams.[44] Results showed that once groups have worked together on a few successful group activities, the resultant group cohesion manifests itself in the form of in-group loyalty, whereby members related their best ideas to a measure of their group's value and status. Loyalty to the group decision overwhelmed logic and denied the existence of value in ideas from other sources.

The groupthink phenomenon has been used to explain such events as the subprime mortgage meltdown that contributed to a U.S. (and worldwide) recession, the Ford Explorer-Bridgestone/Firestone rollover debacle which led to several vehicle operators' deaths and the recall of 6.5 million tires, Merck's delay in recalling their drug Vioxx even after the firm allegedly had evidence that the drug increased some patients' risk of having a heart attack and stroke, and ethically questionable decisions in many other large organizations. Indeed, one researcher reviewing the situation surrounding the decision to launch the space shuttle Challenger blames groupthink for the disaster.[45] Leaders had a preferred solution and engaged in behaviors designed to promote the launch rather than to critically appraise other alternatives. Figure 8.3 presents a groupthink framework that managers could use to evaluate their own situation.

FIGURE 8.3 Janis's Groupthink Framework

Source: Based on Irving Janis and Leon Mann, *Decision Making* (New York: The Free Press, 1977).

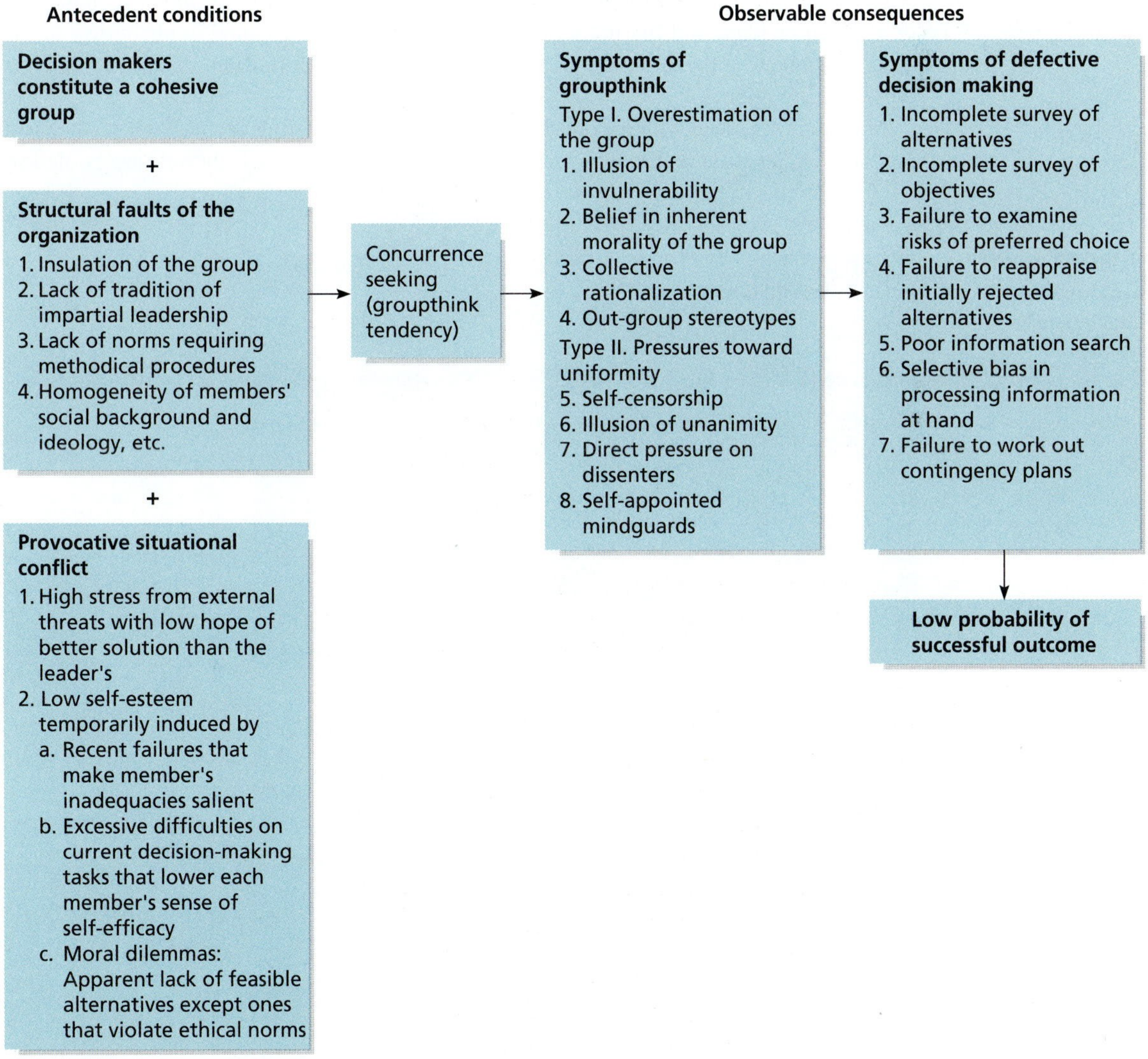

Antecedent conditions

Decision makers constitute a cohesive group

+

Structural faults of the organization
1. Insulation of the group
2. Lack of tradition of impartial leadership
3. Lack of norms requiring methodical procedures
4. Homogeneity of members' social background and ideology, etc.

+

Provocative situational conflict
1. High stress from external threats with low hope of better solution than the leader's
2. Low self-esteem temporarily induced by
   a. Recent failures that make member's inadequacies salient
   b. Excessive difficulties on current decision-making tasks that lower each member's sense of self-efficacy
   c. Moral dilemmas: Apparent lack of feasible alternatives except ones that violate ethical norms

→ Concurrence seeking (groupthink tendency) →

Observable consequences

Symptoms of groupthink
Type I. Overestimation of the group
1. Illusion of invulnerability
2. Belief in inherent morality of the group
3. Collective rationalization
4. Out-group stereotypes

Type II. Pressures toward uniformity
5. Self-censorship
6. Illusion of unanimity
7. Direct pressure on dissenters
8. Self-appointed mindguards

→

Symptoms of defective decision making
1. Incomplete survey of alternatives
2. Incomplete survey of objectives
3. Failure to examine risks of preferred choice
4. Failure to reappraise initially rejected alternatives
5. Poor information search
6. Selective bias in processing information at hand
7. Failure to work out contingency plans

↓

Low probability of successful outcome

When considering how groupthink affects decision making, start with a cohesive group. Structural and situational issues also enter the decision-making arena. As displayed in Figure 8.3, there are several symptoms of groupthink and defective decision making, which contribute to a low probability of a successful outcome. Janis theorized that the symptoms presented in Figure 8.3 require leadership to overcome their effect on reaching optimal decisions.

Social Loafing

social loafing
When individuals within a group hold back what they contribute to the group's effort and performance.

In strong and cohesive social groups and teams, each member's attraction to remain a member is much stronger than the desire to leave. The tendency to shirk responsibilities and not to carry a fair share of the load is not an issue in cohesive teams and groups. When individuals shirk or contribute less than their optimal effort, there exists a **social loafing** effect. This effect has also been referred to as the free rider problem or slacking.

In an experiment, Ringelmann, a French agricultural engineer, noticed that as you added more and more people to a group pulling on a rope, the total force exerted by the group rose, but the average force exerted by each group member declined. The *Ringelmann effect* (e.g., designated as *social loafing*) thus describes the *inverse relationship* between the size of a group or team and the magnitude of the members' individual contribution to the accomplishment of the task.[46] The social loafing effect based on Ringelmann's research is presented in Figure 8.4.

Managers are faced with the question: Why does social loafing occur? Perhaps the most probable explanation is that when members "work together," their outputs are pooled so

FIGURE 8.4
Social Loafing (Ringelmann's Findings)

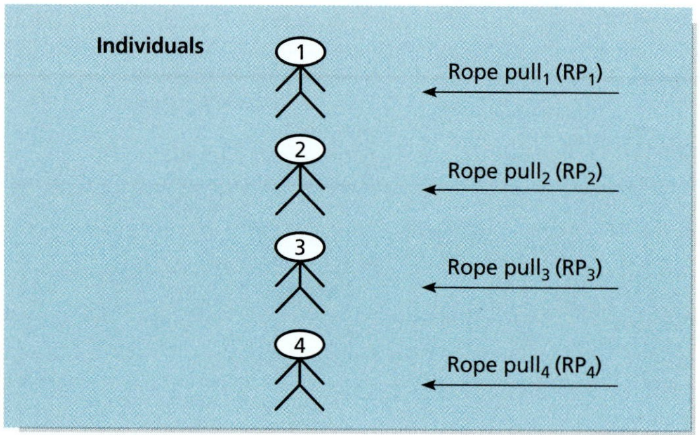

Total rope pull (G) $< RP_1 + RP_2 + RP_3 + RP_4$

that evaluation of individual output is not possible. Thus, they can receive neither credit nor blame for their performances. In essence, they can hide within the group or team.

Recognizing the existence of this phenomenon is useful, but managers need to ask how social loafing can be minimized. If the work being done can actually be reconfigured so that individuals do receive credit or blame for their separate inputs, then social loafing is less likely to occur.

Of course, it is easier to state this than to actually operationalize it—how do we assign credit or blame to the individuals working on a project with a deadline? If and when possible, managers would like to dispense rewards. However, in many situations it is difficult to pinpoint the workers and the loafers.[47]

Unique and challenging tasks have been shown to minimize social loafing. This is consistent with motivational theories pertaining to the nature of work. In general, it has been shown that people are motivated by interesting work (e.g., varied, significant, autonomous, unique). When motivated, individuals are less inclined to engage in social loafing.[48]

The Nature and Types of Teams

Work groups and teams are not the same in terms of development and maturity. Teams are small in size (e.g., 2 to 20 individuals) and have members with complementary skills who have reached what is referred to as the mature or performing stage. The structure, hierarchy, and norms of a team are in place. Many groups never reach this stage of development.[49]

The use of teams has become an increasingly popular work design in all types of organizations, both domestically and globally.[50] As discussed earlier, teams are a special type of task group, consisting of two or more individuals responsible for the achievement of a goal or objective. All teams exist to solve problems. Thus, it is accurate to state that problem solving is an activity that teams practice continuously. Teams can be classified in a number of ways based on their duration and objectives: problem-solving, virtual, cross-functional, skunkworks, and self-directed work teams.

Problem-Solving Teams

Problem-solving teams are formed on a temporary basis to address a specific problem that is confronting the organization. For example, teams of engineers, geologists, and other experts from British Petroleum PLC and the U.S. government worked to contain the massive oil leak about one mile beneath in the Gulf of Mexico caused by the sinking of the Deepwater Horizon drilling rig on April 22, 2010.[51] In less dramatic circumstances, a marketing manager may assemble a team to evaluate the effects a competitor's new advertising campaign may have on company sales. As seen by the examples, the duration of a problem-solving team's existence is usually short in nature. For the most part, problem-solving teams are composed of individuals from the same department or area of an organization who meet together to address and solve a specific problem. Once the problem is solved, the team disbands.

Virtual Teams

As organizations aggressively pursue ways to cut costs, decrease product cycle times, increase customer responsiveness, and integrate more fully with suppliers, many are creating and using *virtual teams* to help achieve these objectives. Other benefits of virtual teams include the ability to offer employees more flexible work arrangements (e.g., telecommuting) that provide 24-hour-a-day, 7-day-a-week customer service for geographically dispersed customers in different time zones and decrease the amount of travel time and expenses that team meetings often require.[52]

Defined as "a team that relies on interactive technology to work together when separated by physical distance,"[53] virtual teams can draw on a variety of interactive technology that includes traditional e-mail, instant messaging, teleconferencing, videoconferencing, Web casts, meeting managers, white boards, and bulletin boards.[54]

A recent study analyzed 80 software development teams (with up to nine members on each team) from 28 laboratories based throughout the world in such countries as Brazil, China, Germany, India, and the United States.[55] The researchers reported the following best practices related to managing dispersed virtual teams:

1. *Focus on social skills.* Virtual team members are usually chosen because of their technical skills and work experience. However, team members also need to possess strong social and teamwork skills to help them collaborate in a virtual environment.
2. *Encourage self-leadership across team.* Geographically distant team members can't walk over to the next office to seek the advice of the team leader whenever a problem or conflict with another team member arises. So, team members need to be self-sufficient and aware of their own strengths and weaknesses.
3. *Arrange face-to-face meetings.* Even though the team is dispersed, members need to come together for face-to-face meetings at key points during a project's life cycle. For example, at least one or two initial face-to-face meetings are needed at the start of the project to identify the scope and nature of the project, and to help team members develop trust with one another.
4. *Foster a global mindset among team members.* Team members need to see themselves as part of a global network and develop a global skill set and perspective that will help them transfer knowledge throughout the global organization. Nestlé, IBM, and SAP use international virtual assignments to help employees develop a global mindset.

General Electric is in the process of rolling out a variety of real-time collaboration tools to its 340,000 employees and to several of its customers and suppliers.[56] Included in the rollout are tools that will allow employees to do the following:

- Use instant messaging and real-time conferencing and application sharing.
- Create shared Web workspaces, even if the user is not technically proficient.
- Break down projects into tasks and track progress.
- Transfer best practices from completed projects to new projects.

In addition, customers and suppliers will have access to real-time data and internal processes within GE's intranet. Officials at GE argue that these features will help revolutionize the company as it continues into the 21st century.[57]

Other organizations are not moving as quickly as GE into the world of virtual teams and collaborative technology. For such work arrangements to be successful, several factors need to be considered. First, the technology should fit the purpose of the collaboration. If all members of a group need to receive the same information quickly, then a bulletin board or group e-mail is appropriate. If training needs to be done, then a Web conference with real-time white board and data sharing may be more suitable. Second, virtual team members must be carefully selected. Choosing members who have the necessary skills, experience, work ethic, and interpersonal skills is critical to effective team functioning. Third, trust between team members should be cultivated early in the process. Face-to-face meetings, team-building training exercises, or both should be used during the initial periods of team formation to facilitate the development of trust. This trust will be critical later in the process when problems, disagreements, and deadlines stress the relationships of members who can't just walk down the hallway to "work things out." Last, teams need to develop a sense of purpose and shared goals. Leaders must be able to set a vision for the team and

OB AND YOUR CAREER

Want Some International Experience? Get Assigned to a Global Virtual Team

Successful organizations like Microsoft rely on virtual teams. Everyone in Microsoft is involved in virtual teams in one way or another, which spans all aspects of day-to-day working—from formal project teams focused on internal and external clients to informal networking with colleagues. At TRW Automotive, a global manufacturer of automotive components based in Michigan, a large number of its 66,000 employees worldwide engage in online virtual meetings and team projects with other employees from different cultures and host country markets.

Joining or getting assigned to a virtual team that has members from different countries and getting assigned to tasks that extend beyond the home country are good ways to begin acquiring international skills and a global perspective. As a member of a global virtual team, you'll be interacting frequently (via face-to-face meetings, Web conferences, phone calls, e-mails, and instant messages) with members from all over the world. Although the experience will not afford members the same level of cross-cultural learning as moving to and working in a host country, work in a global virtual team can expose participants to a wide variety of perspectives, languages, work styles, and creative nontraditional approaches to problem solving. As an added bonus, team members might be able to leverage their experience on the global virtual team to a more in-depth, long-term international assignment that requires relocation to a host country. If the team member's organization is like Nestlé, IBM, and General Electric, all of which value international experience acquisition by their employees, then joining a global virtual team and taking international assignments can enhance one's career prospects within the organization in the long run.

Sources: F. Siebdrat, M. Hoegl, and H. Ernst, "How to Manage Virtual Teams," *MIT Sloan Management Review* 50, no. 4 (2009): 63–68; H. Duckworth, "How TRW Automotive Helps Global Virtual Teams Perform at the Top of Their Game," *Global Business and Organizational Excellence* 28, no. 1 (November 2008): 6; Annie Garfoot, "Virtual Team Case Study: Microsoft," *IT Training*, June 2, 2004, pp. 1–2; and Wally Bock, "Some Rules for Virtual Teams," *The Journal for Quality and Participation* (Fall 2004): 43.

be able to help resolve conflicts between members and assist members in overcoming obstacles.[58]

Microsoft is another company that embraces the virtual team approach. As the accompanying OB and Your Career feature suggests, employees can acquire some international experience by joining a global virtual team.

As companies like Microsoft, GE, Alcoa, AT&T, Pfizer, Ernst & Young, Shell Oil, and Sun Microsystems continue to experiment with and use virtual teams across their global businesses, such practices will become increasingly commonplace in organizations of all types and sizes.[59]

Cross-Functional Teams

Recently, a growing number of organizations have begun using teams that are composed of individuals from different departments or work areas that come together on a task or project basis. These groups, called *cross-functional teams,* monitor, standardize, and improve work processes that cut across different parts of the organization. For example, a computer company may form a cross-functional team made up of members from marketing, sales, research and development, engineering, and human resources to design and develop marketing plans for a new project. In a similar vein, some innovative colleges of business are bringing together professors from various departments such as marketing, finance, management, and operations to plan and teach integrated principles of business courses. Cross-functional teams can have a life span of indeterminate length. A general rule associated with the use of cross-functional teams is that the longer the duration, the more the team members rotate in and out.

An effective cross-functional team can reduce the amount of time a project might otherwise take to complete if it consists of representatives of departments critical to the project's completion. Many cross-functional teams run best without an established boss, as the team itself provides a basis for various individuals to exhibit leadership skills.[60]

OB AT WORK The Earliest Skunkworks

The SR-71 Blackbird is a delta-wing reconnaissance aircraft designed and built by Lockheed for the U.S. Air Force more than 40 years ago. Made almost entirely of titanium, it can fly more than 2,200 mph (Mach 3.2), at altitudes of greater than 85,000 feet.

One of the most impressive characteristics of the history of the SR-71 Blackbird is that a skunkworks team designed it before the introduction of supercomputers. Originally envisioned by Lockheed designer and skunkworks founder Clarence "Kelly" Johnson, the team of engineers—using slide-rules, intelligence, and creativity—built an airplane capable of flying faster and higher than any aircraft before or since.

The skunkworks team faced unique challenges in designing and building the Blackbird. The aircraft's flight profile demanded that structural materials be able to withstand prolonged exposure to high temperatures from excessive heating. The Lockheed engineering team pioneered new inspection, test, quality, control, and manufacturing techniques. The skunkworks culture permitted, encouraged, and rewarded trying out new ideas.

Creative solutions emerged from the team to develop the parts, fuselage, flight control, and fuel systems, and to engineer materials problems and challenges. The ability to experiment, the acceptance of full responsibility, the removal of bureaucratic authority, and the complete autonomy to make decisions were contributing factors to the skunkworks team's success—the creation of the SR-71 Blackbird.

The team was allowed to focus solely on the SR-71; was empowered to do their work as they planned, scheduled, and reviewed; was not hemmed in by standard policies and procedures; and was allowed to analyze customers' needs and requests. The lessons learned suggest that a skunkworks team that is not boxed in by rules and procedures can be very creative and successful. The SR-71 Blackbird is still unsurpassed in its design, speed, and capabilities. It is one of the most spectacular aircraft ever built.

Sources: Adapted from http://www.lockheedmartin.com/aboutus/history/SR71Blackbird.html (accessed May 20, 2010); Peter W. Merlin, "SR-71 Blackbird," *Advanced Materials and Processes*, May 2003, pp. 27–29; and Michael Bommer, Renee De La Porte, and James Higgins, "Skunkworks Approach to Project Management," *Journal of Management in Engineering* (January 2002): 21–28.

When establishing a cross-functional team, management should be concerned with more than just getting representation from all relevant departments. Rather, a focus should be placed on recruiting open-minded individuals who can take the long view of situations and who are not afraid of confrontation and change. It should be realized that cross-functional teams can take a longer time to develop than problem-solving teams because, initially, there may be feelings of mistrust between members from differing departments. In fact, the early stages of most cross-functional team-building efforts emphasize the building of trust and teamwork.

Skunkworks

Originally created at Lockheed as a team-based approach to rapidly develop innovative aeronautical engineering products, *skunkworks* refers to a small team of engineers, technicians, and designers who are placed on a team that has the goal of developing innovative new products. Generally, skunkworks are part of a larger organization that shields the team from barriers or bureaucratic obstacles. Often separated from mainstream employees within the firm, this approach allows for fast communications and rapid turnaround times for experiments, and it fosters a high degree of group identity and loyalty. The first Lockheed skunkworks product is described in the OB at Work feature.

In addition to Lockheed, other companies have made use of the skunkworks concept: IBM's first profitable PC was the product of a skunkworks initiative, and Steve Jobs developed Apple's popular Macintosh computer from a skunkworks operation. More recently, Jaguar has developed the XKR-S; a supercharged high-performance model that was quietly developed by a skunkworks team led by Mike Cross, a dynamics expert, and Russ Varney, chief program engineer.[61] In sum, the skunkworks approach presents companies that embrace it with a rapid entrée into the world of innovation and high-performance teams. Although skunkworks is an interesting concept, a major challenge facing companies is how to diffuse the spirit of innovation throughout the entire organizational culture.[62]

Self-Directed Work Teams

The third type of team, self-directed work teams, usually comprises 10 to 15 individuals who take on the long-term responsibilities of their former supervisors while retaining their prior responsibilities. It's important to note that teams of this type should not be considered unmanaged teams; rather, they should be viewed as differently managed teams—those run by the workers themselves. Typically, the self-directed work team holds control over the determination and assignment of work to be performed, choice of operating procedures, and allocation of resources. Some self-directed teams even select individuals who will serve on the teams and have members evaluate each other's performance in order to assign rewards or pay incentives. Many major companies, including Boeing, Caterpillar, Cummins Engine, Digital Equipment, Ford, General Electric, LTV Steel, and Tektronix, have begun using self-directed work teams. It is estimated that today up to 50 percent of all companies, both large and small, are using some form of self-directed work teams.

It should be noted that self-directed work teams are not appropriate for every organization or culture. Before designing these teams and establishing expectations for them, the organization should conduct an environmental analysis to determine if self-directed work teams are consistent with: (1) the organization's business requirements, values, and goals; (2) the organization's competencies; and (3) the culture in which the organization is operating.[63] Success in implementing and using self-directed work teams is usually contingent on whether the organization is ready for such a team and whether teams are consistent with the cultural practices of the host country.[64]

Why Teams Are Formed

There is no simple explanation for the increased usage of teams in organizations, especially those that are self-directed. There are a number of reasons managers of organizations form teams, including enhanced productivity, flattening of organizations, need for flexibility and quicker decisions, workforce diversity, improved quality, and increased customer satisfaction (see Figure 8.5).

Enhanced Productivity

In a nutshell, the single most important reason teams are formed is to enhance organizational productivity. Organizations throughout the world have realized that team performance

FIGURE 8.5
Reasons Why Teams Are Formed

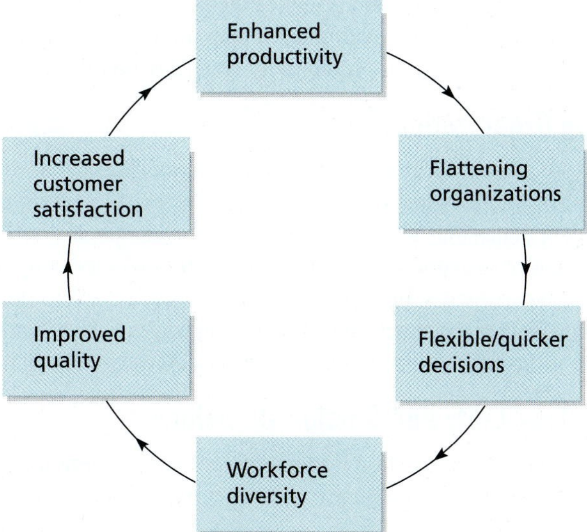

leads to higher productivity levels than what would be achieved by many individuals working individually. This is primarily because teams bring together complementary skills that can fall into one of three categories: technical or functional expertise, problem-solving and decision-making skills, and interpersonal skills.

Technical or Functional Skills

It would make little sense for a marketer to design technical specifications for a new type of smart phone. Likewise, it would make little sense for an engineer to try to guess what features consumers find most important in making decisions as to which type of smart phone to purchase. However, teams of engineers and marketing personnel often work together to identify and design smart phones that are widely accepted by the buying public. In this case, product development groups that consist only of marketers or engineers are less likely to succeed than those with the complementary skills of both.

Problem-Solving and Decision-Making Skills

Teams must possess the ability to identify problems and opportunities their organization faces, to identify feasible decision alternatives and trade-offs, and to make necessary decisions leading to optimum results. Most individuals do not possess the necessary skills needed to perform all these tasks effectively. However, among a well-chosen team, it is likely that taken together, the requisite skills are present and can be used in the organization's best interests.

Interpersonal Skills

Common understanding and knowledge of problems faced and decisions needed cannot arise without effective communication and constructive conflict, which greatly depend on interpersonal skills. These include risk taking, helpful criticism, objectivity, active listening, giving the benefit of the doubt, support, and recognizing the interests and achievement of others. An effective team is made up of members who, in total, possess each of these skills. Individual members, at various times, will be called on to use their unique skills to lead the team forward. Thus, it is critical that team members are chosen based on skills and skill potential, not solely on personality.

The effective use of the complementary skills teams possess can lead to extraordinary results for organizations. For example, Xerox plants using work teams are more than 25 percent more productive than conventionally organized plants. Likewise, General Motors reports more than 20 percent productivity gains in plants that use team-based manufacturing systems. Examples of this type are cropping up in news stories on a weekly basis as an increasing number of organizations realize the power unleashed by teams. Indeed, organizations as diverse as the U.S. government, Federal Express, Home Depot, and Fresh Choice restaurants have all seen their productivity benefit from the use of teams.

Flattening Organizations

Businesses around the world are restructuring, reorganizing, and downsizing their companies to eliminate waste and to better serve their constituencies. As a result, there has been a continual flattening of organizations wherein entire levels of management have been eliminated. In turn, front-line teams of workers are assuming many of the tasks formerly performed by supervisors, midlevel managers, and support staff. Work teams provide the flexibility to trim unneeded forms of redundant bureaucracy. In fact, some companies believe that any function that does not support the efforts of front-line work teams can be considered an option for elimination.

Need for Flexibility and Quicker Decisions

To thrive in today's increasingly competitive markets, organizations must be capable of producing small runs of tailored products on a tight schedule to meet growing demands in emerging markets. This ability calls for innovative technical procedures and bright workers who are flexible and can move from assignment to assignment. Self-directed work teams have the skills, the knowledge, and the motivation to quickly adapt to change. As a result, managers who traditionally spent a large portion of their time supervising workers and fighting mini-crises can be freed up to perform more strategic-type thinking. In total, the use of teams provides the best of both worlds: long-term vision coupled with greater flexibility for quicker short-term decisions.

Workforce Diversity

As the overall workforce becomes more diverse, individuals who possess different backgrounds, perspectives, values, and functional expertise are increasingly staffing work groups. Diversity in team membership is often perceived as a critical antecedent for achieving important outcomes such as enhanced group performance and member morale, satisfaction, intent to remain, and commitment. Contrary to this perception, reviews of the research into diversity management have produced mixed results.[65] While some research studies have reported that heterogeneous groups outperformed less diverse groups, other studies have found the opposite effect.[66] A recent research study attempted to clarify these mixed results by analyzing 108 previous studies that looked at the processes and performance of 10,632 teams.[67] The study's authors concluded that cultural diversity negatively affects team performance in the areas of task conflict and lower levels of social integration among team members. However, team diversity had some positive effects, also. Diversity on teams leads to higher levels of satisfaction and creativity.

One explanation for these mixed results is that diversity in outward appearances such as gender and race does not improve group performance in and of itself, but rather diverse group members contribute unique information and perspectives, which do ultimately enhance group functioning under certain conditions.[68] In addition, these mixed results may be due to the fact that earlier research often treated team diversity as a singular concept when in fact it likely comprises several subcomponents.[69]

In studying 92 work groups in a field research study, Jehn and associates defined the concept of diversity as comprising three types: informational diversity, social category diversity, and value diversity. These different types of diversity displayed unique effects on important work/group outcomes. High levels of *information diversity*—the differences in knowledge bases and perspectives that members bring to a group—have been shown to contribute to overall group effectiveness. High levels of *social category diversity,* the explicit differences among group members in terms of race, gender, and ethnicity, were associated with higher levels of member morale—satisfaction, intent to remain, commitment, and perceived performance. In contrast, groups with high levels of *value diversity*—members' opinions about what the group's real task, goal, or mission should be—may experience major decreases in both group performance and employee morale.[70]

Based on research highlighted here, managers who are contemplating whether or how best to reorganize their human resources into teams or work groups should not just assume that team diversity will automatically lead to higher performance. Instead, careful matching of potential members' informational contributions, social backgrounds, and value preferences should be made so as to help ensure that teams live up to their potential and deliver expected results. In addition, organizations can help prepare employees to deal effectively with group diversity issues. The next OB at Work feature illustrates the role that group diversity can play in the quality of the decisions made by groups.

Improved Quality

Individuals can and will assume responsibility only for the distinct component or part of a project or product they work on. On the other hand, teams assume responsibility for entire projects

OB AT WORK Group Diversity: Some Points to Consider

When it comes to group decision-making processes, diversity generally helps generate better, fairer, and more thorough decisions. Dr. Samuel R. Sommers of Tufts University conducted a study of racial diversity and the performance of decision-making groups. He found that in a mock jury, placing white jurors in diverse groups raised their performance level, encouraging them to cite more facts, make fewer mistakes, deliberate longer, and conduct broader and more accurate discussions—compared with peers in all-white mock juries. Racially mixed juries were much more willing to discuss issues of racism.

Sommers was interviewed about his study and its implications for other groups facing controversial issues.

Interviewer: Your study observed the behavior of mock jurors in an all-white and racially mixed juries as they deliberated a case involving a black defendant. The results were interesting and somewhat unexpected. What did you discover?

Sommers: Traditional assumptions about how diversity influences decision making focus on the idea that having nonwhite individuals in a group will lead to different perspectives being raised in the group. But one of the interesting and somewhat counterintuitive findings that the study produced is that white participants behave very differently when they're in diverse settings versus in all-white settings. [In diverse settings] they raise more facts regarding the trial. They make fewer factual inaccuracies in their statements about the case.

Interviewer: Does group diversity act as a performance enhancer?

Sommers: At the group level, that seems to be a reasonable conclusion. I think people would agree that you want juries to raise a wide range of perspectives and information. You want them to be true to the facts of the case and accurate in their fact-finding. You want them to be open-minded. And on all those counts, diverse groups seem to be doing better than all-white groups.

When society talks about diversity, much of the conversation focuses on ideology and the morality and constitutionality of how to achieve diversity. I think that looking at the observable effects of diversity on a group's performance is a really fruitful way to get a sense of what diversity really means.

Interviewer: Diversity appears to raise the awareness levels and attention to detail of white jurors; does it have a similar effect on black jurors?

Sommers: Would a diverse group perform better than an all-black group? You could probably predict that yes, it would. But we don't know that from this study. We didn't study all-black groups, but it's a very important question. Being in a diverse setting has a motivational influence on the white jurors; it gets them scrutinizing information more carefully knowing that they're going to have to discuss it with a diverse group.

Interviewer: In your study, some of the changes in the behavior of white jurors took place before there was any interaction between the jurors. Was it simply a question of seeing the make-up of the group?

Sommers: Absolutely. Before they even open their mouths or have any form of interaction at all, the racial composition of the group seems to be exerting an influence on the white jurors.

Interviewer: So, do you think that we operate under different default settings depending upon who's in our group?

Sommers: I do think you could make a case, and again we need to do further studies to test this, that in the all-white setting—maybe the default setting for the white participants—they're a little bit more relaxed or content to rely on cognitive shortcuts. They don't engage the information at quite the same level that they feel they need to when they're in a diverse group. So, I think that's a really provocative idea that somehow, at least when discussing a race-related issue, just knowing who you're going to be interacting with can very well lead you to change the information-processing strategy that you use.

Interviewer: How does this research extend beyond jury composition?

Sommers: This should be relevant in any context in which you have groups of people making decisions and have issues of diversity at the forefront of the organization's mind. Whether you're talking about the classroom, the boardroom and the workplace, or decision-making committees in a variety of different fields, there are potential implications. Again, the study was run in a legal setting, but I think the issues that it raises are important for all group types. The fact that whites behave very differently in an all-white versus a diverse setting, and at least in this study, seem to be performing better in the diverse setting, has some profound implications and potential usefulness.

But I don't think there's a simple conclusion here of diversity always leading groups to do better. There's research that suggests that there are potential downsides to diversity, many of them relating to morale and group cohesion. Sometimes those are overcome with time, but sometimes they're hard to overcome. So, it's a much more nuanced issue, but I do think that studying it from a performance perspective is a really useful way to go.

Sources: Adapted from Samuel R. Sommers, "On Racial Diversity and Group Decision Making: Identifying Multiple Effects of Racial Composition on Jury Deliberations," *Journal of Personality and Social Psychology* 90 (2006): 597–617; and Anne Sasso, "Group Diversity: Mock Juries Reveal Surprising Effects of Diversity on Groups," *MiSciNet,* May 5, 2006, accessed at http:sciencecareers.sciencemag.org on May 10, 2006.

or products. When teams assume responsibility, they develop an appreciation of the nuances associated with all aspects of their work. As a result, it becomes a matter of professional pride for team members to search out and act on opportunities for quality improvements. In addition, because team members perform both technical and administrative functions, they gain the commitment, experience, and skills required to improve the interface between the two functions. In contrast, team members who act on their own behalf and fail to work together for the overall "good" of the team can decrease the overall quality of the team effort.[71]

Increased Customer Satisfaction

Customer satisfaction is the key to organizational success for it is the satisfied customer who accounts for the repeat business that organizations need to survive and thrive. The energy, commitment, and flexibility associated with work teams promote customer satisfaction through quick response and improved quality.

Obstacles to Effective Teams

Organizations have increasingly turned to teams to improve the quality and timeliness of decision making, to achieve more cost-effective work processes, and to increase the morale and creativity of employees.[72] Unfortunately, this transition to teams has not been a smooth one for many organizations.[73] One of the major problems is that some companies are "jumping on the bandwagon" and placing people into teams without fully assessing whether a team is needed in the first place.[74] This "teamwork by force" can be counterproductive and result in employee backlash directed toward the increased use of teams in their company.[75] Teams should be used when the following factors are present:

- A complicated problem that requires employees with diverse talents and functional expertise.
- Goals focus on improving an existing product, service, or process.
- A task that lends itself to a division of labor.
- A situation in which making the wrong decision is too costly.[76]

Before placing employees into teams, decision makers at companies should ask themselves the following questions:

- Can the work be performed better by more than one individual?
- Does the work lend itself to a common set of goals for the members in a team?
- Are members of the team interdependent?
- Do members have the appropriate skill mix to excel?[77]

If the answers to these questions are yes, then it would make sense to organize employees into work teams.

Another problem with teams occurs when they are created in a vacuum without the simultaneous addition of any corresponding support systems.[78] For example, if a company wants to achieve greater efficiencies through the use of virtual teams, then it needs to ensure that the proper technology infrastructure (e.g., instant messaging) is in place to support these geographically dispersed teams. In addition, changes in the compensation system are also required. For example, organizations that do not want to make major changes to their compensation system can add a section to individuals' performance appraisals that assesses teamwork skills and attitudes.

The leadership style of team leaders can also be a problem to the effective functioning of teams. For example, team leaders who display too much of an autocratic leadership style may actually undermine team productivity by ignoring or downplaying the contributions and ideas of team members. Also, team leaders who constantly seek compromise may end up encouraging average solutions and outcomes. In contrast, those leaders who encourage integrative or synergistic teamwork solutions in which members' views and contributions are combined in a unique way produce a team solution that is bigger than the sum of members' individual contributions.[79] Also, team leaders who have excellent timing regarding when and how to assist team members are helpful in enhancing their teams' effectiveness.[80]

Although certainly not a cure-all for organizational decision-making and problem-solving dilemmas, when used and managed properly, teams can contribute to increases in productivity, morale, and innovation.[81]

Building Effective Teams

Teams are incapable of performing miracles on their own. Much like individuals, teams need the nurturing and support of management. Toward this end, there are several requirements for building effective teams. These requirements include top-level commitment and provision of clear goals; management–employee trust; willingness to take risks and share information; and time, resources, and a commitment to training. Each of these factors is needed to create effective and focused work teams. Team leaders must play a role in ensuring that these factors are in place and continually updated.

Top-Level Commitment and Provision of Clear Goals

Top-performing organizations have leaders who are deeply committed to the team concept. Through their time, attention, and other behavior, leaders continually express and reinforce the notion that the use of teams is the only means to succeed. Truly committed leaders inspire confidence that team performance is the single best path to economic and personal fulfillment. When teams are motivated to pursue clear and difficult goals, superior performance can be achieved.[82]

Management–Employee Trust

Managers must trust that, given time, workers will actively support the massive changes in responsibility and authority bestowed on them as team members. Conversely, employees need to know and believe that management is serious about wanting people (as team members) to take risks and express their opinions and that the formation of teams is not just a new mechanism to gain additional work from employees.

On a team level, there must exist a high level of trust among members. Members must believe in integrity, character, and abilities. As we are all well aware, trust takes a long time to build and can be jeopardized by a single careless action. The climate of trust within a team seems to be highly dependent on members' perceptions of management's trust of the group as a whole and therefore the level of management trust can serve to enhance or detract from members' trust. Organizations that value employee honesty, openness, and collaborative processes with high employee involvement are more likely to stimulate trusting cultures than those who do not.

Willingness to Take Risks and Share Information

Teams, by acknowledging their existence, must accept the willingness to take risks, while simultaneously being held accountable for their actions. In this respect, the risk of self-direction is personal. Workers and supervisors must be willing to trade their safer, traditional jobs for ones that are less clear-cut and more demanding, time consuming, and challenging. Management must accept the notion that their daily routines and activities will probably be changed forever as teams begin to assume more responsibility for the running of the organization. In other words, change, once started, is difficult to reverse.

OB AT WORK Team-Building Pointers (Learning from Geese)

Fact #1—As each bird flaps its wings, it creates uplift for the bird following. By flying in a "V" formation, the whole flock adds 71 percent greater flying range than if one bird flew alone.

Lesson Learned—People who share a common direction and sense of community can get where they are going quicker and easier because they are traveling on the strength of one another.

Fact #2—Whenever a goose falls out of formation, it suddenly feels the drag and resistance of trying to fly alone and quickly gets back into formation to take advantage of the lifting power of the bird immediately in front.

Lesson Learned—If we have as much sense as geese, we will stay in formation with those who are ahead of where we want to go and be willing to accept their help as well as give ours to others.

Fact #3—When the lead goose gets tired, it rotates back into the formation and another goose flies at the point position.

Lesson Learned—It pays to take turns doing the hard tasks and sharing leadership.

Fact #4—The geese in formation honk from behind to encourage those up front to keep up their speed.

Lesson Learned—We need to make sure our honking from behind is encouraging and not something else.

Fact #5—When a goose gets sick or wounded or shot down, two geese drop out of formation and follow it down to help and protect it. They stay with it until it is able to fly again, or dies. Then they launch out on their own with another formation, or they catch up with their flock.

Lesson Learned—If we have as much sense as geese do, we too will stand by each other in difficult times as well as when we are strong.

Source: Author unknown.

Likewise, if teams are to take responsibility and assume risk in making decisions, they will need detailed information about the organization's overall operations, including financial information concerning individual members and departments. To manage themselves, teams need information that was once the exclusive domain of management. Armed with information, it is inevitable that teams will begin asking questions of management that, in turn, will lead to revealing more sensitive, detailed information. As teams evolve, the point is eventually reached where team knowledge of certain facets of operations is as great or greater than management's. For teams to succeed, management must be willing to accept and actively encourage this knowledge equality.

Time, Resources, and a Commitment to Training

Successful work teams can take months, even years, to mature to a level commensurate with the responsibilities they must take on. Management needs to recognize that the rewards of self-direction and self-management depend on massive planning, intense and prompt access to resources (financial and other), and often the physical redesigning of plants and offices. Internally, the team needs to be provided with a sound and understandable measuring system with which team members can evaluate their performance, an incentive system that rewards team activities, and supportive management that encourages team-building exercises.

In addition, work teams can either succeed or fail based on the amount, intensity, and duration of training they receive. In working as a team, individuals have to put aside personal privileges and contribute to the group well-being. For many individuals this represents a massive change from either just giving or receiving orders. Team members therefore need proper, long-term training in the interpersonal, administrative, and technical skills that may counteract habits, attitudes, and work styles left over from years of employment in a more traditionally run organization.

The OB at Work feature presents five lessons about team building that are simply points to reflect upon when thinking about what it takes to build and nurture an effective team.

Intergroup Behavior and Conflict

Few trends have so affected organizations as that of the movement toward group-based systems. The successful transition from a time where employees worked alone to one where individuals are dependent on others require employees to share information, cooperate with each other, address personal differences, and share a desire to work for the greater good of the entire organization. The emphasis in this chapter has been on this *intragroup* behavior.

An equally important characteristic of groups is that they frequently conflict with other groups in the organization. Groups conflict with others for many reasons, and the resulting outcomes can either be good or negative for the organization. What happens between groups (*intergroup* behavior) is the subject of the next chapter.

The Role Concept

role
An organized set of behaviors expected of an individual in a specific position.

The concept of role was discussed earlier as being vital to understanding group behavior. **Role** refers to the expected behavior patterns attributed to a particular position in an organization. The roles of physician and patient are familiar to everyone. Those roles are culturally defined expectations associated with particular positions.

A role may include attitudes and values as well as specific kinds of behavior. It is what an individual must do to validate her occupancy of a particular position. In other words, what kind of physician or patient an individual is depends a great deal on how he performs the culturally defined role associated with the position. Consider your own perceptions of the roles associated with law enforcement officers, military officers, politicians, college professors, and business executives.

In a formal organization, every position has certain activities that are expected. These activities constitute the role for the position from the standpoint of the organization. The organization develops job descriptions that define the activities of each particular position and how it relates to other positions in the organization. However, for both formal (task and command) and informal (interest and friendship) groups, roles may not be set forth explicitly and yet are clearly understood by group members. For example, members of the marketing department in a bank may know that only the director of marketing represents the bank at national conventions and that they have no chance of attending, even though this has never been explicitly stated. Thus, whether they are formally or informally established, status hierarchies and accompanying roles are integral parts of every organization.

Multiple Roles and Role Sets

multiple roles
Roles performed simultaneously because the individual holds many positions in a variety of organizations and groups.

role set
Others' expectations for behavior of a person in a particular role.

Most of us perform **multiple roles**. We occupy many different positions in a variety of organizations (home, work, church, civic groups, and so forth). Within each of these organizations, we occupy and perform certain roles. We may simultaneously be playing the role of parent, mate, supervisor, and subordinate. Each position involves different role relationships. For example, the position of college professor involves not only the role of teacher in relation to students but also numerous other roles relating the position to administrators, peers, the community, and alumni. Each group may expect different things: students may expect good classroom performance, research, and publication; the college community may expect community service; and alumni may expect help in recruiting students and athletes. This we term **role set**. A role set refers to others' expectations for the behavior of the individual in the particular role. The more expectations, the more complex is the role set.

Multiple roles refer to different roles, while role set refers to the different expectations associated with one role. Therefore, an individual involved in many different roles, each with a complex role set, faces the ultimate in complexity of individual behavior. Multiple roles and role sets are important concepts because of possible complications that make defining specific roles extremely difficult, especially in organizational settings. This can often result in *role conflict* for the individual.

Role Perception

Different individuals have different perceptions of the behavior associated with a given role. In an organizational setting, accuracy in role perception can have a definite impact on performance. This matter is further complicated because, within the organization, there may be different perceptions of the same role: the formal organization's, the group's, and the individual's. For example, a college dean, the students, and the professors themselves have perceptions of the role of professor. But as we saw in the preceding discussion of role sets, students' perceptions of the role of a professor may be very different from college administrators' perceptions. These differences in perception increase even further the possibility of role conflict.

Role Conflict

Because of the multiplicity of roles and role sets, an individual may face a complex situation of simultaneous role requirements where performance of one role precludes the performance of the others. As a group member, the individual faces tremendous pressures to give up his self-identity and accountability in exchange for in-group loyalty.[83] When this occurs, the individual faces a situation known as **role conflict**. Several forms of this conflict can occur in organizations.

role conflict
Occurs when an individual's compliance with one set of expectations conflicts with compliance with another set of expectations.

Person–Role Conflict

Person–role conflict occurs when role requirements violate the basic values, attitudes, and needs of the individual occupying the position. A supervisor who finds it difficult to dismiss a subordinate with a family and an executive who resigns rather than engage in some unethical activity reflect person–role conflict.[84]

Intrarole Conflict

Intrarole conflict occurs when different individuals define a role according to different sets of expectations, making it impossible for the person occupying the role to satisfy all of them. This is more likely to occur when a given role has a complex role set (many different role relationships). The supervisor in an industrial situation has a rather complex role set and thus may face intrarole conflict. On the one hand, top management has a set of expectations that stresses the supervisor's role in the management hierarchy. On the other hand, the supervisor may have close friendship ties with members of the command group who may be former working peers. This is why supervisors are often described as being "stuck in the middle."

Interrole Conflict

Interrole conflict can result from facing multiple roles.[85] It occurs because individuals simultaneously perform many roles, some with conflicting expectations. A scientist in a chemical plant who's also a member of a management group might experience role conflict of this kind. In such a situation, the scientist may be expected to behave in accordance with the expectations of management as well as the expectations of professional chemists.

The next chapter describes how this type of role conflict often causes conflict between groups in many organizations.

Results of Role Conflict

An individual confronted with role conflict experiences psychological stress that may result in emotional problems and indecision.[86] Research has shown that role conflict occurs frequently and with negative effects on performance over a wide spectrum of occupations and contexts.[87]

While managers can do little to avoid certain kinds of role conflict, many kinds can be minimized. For example, some role conflict (especially intrarole conflict) can result from violations of the classical principles of chain of command and unity of command. In other words, when individuals are faced with conflicting expectations or demands from two or more sources, the likely result is a decline in performance.

In addition, interrole conflict can be generated by conflicting expectations of formal or informal groups, with results similar to those of intrarole conflict. Thus, a highly cohesive group whose goals are not consistent with those of the formal organization can cause a great deal of interrole conflict for its members.

Summary of Key Points

- A group consists of employees who interact in such a manner that the behavior or performance of one group member is influenced by the behavior or performance of other group members.
- By being aware of group characteristics and behaviors, managers can be prepared for the potential positive and negative results of group activities. A manager can proactively intervene to modify the perceptions, attitudes, and motivations that influence the results.
- People are attracted to groups because of their potential for satisfying needs, their physical proximity and attraction, and the appeal of group goals and activities. In essence, people are attracted to one another; that is a natural process.
- Groups develop at different rates and with unique patterns that depend on the task, the setting, the members' individual characteristics and behavior patterns, and the manager's style of managing.
- Characteristics of groups include structure, status hierarchy, roles, norms, leadership, cohesiveness, and intergroup conflict. These characteristics pervade all groups. In an informal group, they emerge from within the unit; in a formal group, they are established by the managerial process.
- Group characteristics provide a degree of predictability for the members that is important to the group and to the outside (e.g., management, other groups). An unstable or unpredictable group is a problem for its members and for others who interact with it.
- Each group possesses some degree of cohesiveness. This attractiveness of the group can be a powerful force in influencing individual behavior and performance.
- Research studies indicate that cohesive groups can formulate goals and norms that may not agree with those of management. When a group's goals and norms are incongruent with the organization's, some form of managerial intervention is necessary.
- Groupthink is the desire among cohesive group members to be in agreement, which supersedes considering solutions to problems or situations that are controversial or in which unanimous agreement is not possible.
- Teams are a special type of task group. Three common categories of teams exist in organizations: (1) problem-solving teams, (2) cross-functional teams, and (3) self-directed work teams.

- Managers form teams predominantly to enhance productivity. Teams also form due to flattening organizations, need for flexibility and quick decisions, workforce diversity, improved quality, and increased customer satisfaction.
- The requirements for effective teams include top-level commitment and provision of clear goals; management–employee trust; willingness to take risks and share information; and time, resources, and a commitment to training.
- The concept of role is vital to an understanding of group behavior. A role consists of the expected behavior patterns attributed to a particular position. Most individuals perform multiple roles, each with its own role set (others' expectations for the role). An individual involved in many different roles, each having a complex role set, faces the ultimate in complexity of individual behavior.
- In organizations, there may be as many as three perceptions of the same role: the organization's, the group's, and the individual's. When an individual faces two or more simultaneous role requirements for which the performance of one precludes performance of the other(s), she experiences role conflict.
- Three different types of role conflict—person–role, intrarole, and interrole—can occur in organizational settings. Research has shown that consequences of role conflict to the individual include increased psychological stress and other emotional reactions. Management can minimize certain types of role conflicts and should be continually aware that the consequences of conflict to the organization can include ineffective performance by individuals and groups.

Discussion and Review Questions

1. Imagine you are project manager of a crucial product design team project to develop a schedule whereby each member takes a specific role in finishing the required daily tasks. How would you accomplish the desired work?
2. As a manager of a virtual team, what qualifications and characteristics would you look for in potential team members so that the team's work would be exceptional?
3. Why are some group and team members willing to socially loaf on work assignments?
4. Think of a group project you were involved in for a particular class. Describe how the group evolved or did not evolve.
5. Describe a team of which you are/were a member. What type of team was it, and why was the team formed?
6. Regarding the team you discussed in question 5, were the requirements for effective teams fulfilled? Why or why not?
7. Give an example of when you have experienced person–role conflict, intrarole conflict, and interrole conflict.
8. What is the problem with a high degree of conforming behavior among group members?
9. There are critics of the five-stage group development model. Their main point is that this presentation of a group's development is too static. Do you agree with the criticism? Why or why not?
10. You are a manager, and a member of one of your task groups comes to you and says that his group is engaging in groupthink and he is being pressured to conform to their rules. You can't disclose this information to anyone, yet you want to discourage this group's cohesiveness. What would you do?

Taking It to the Net

Team Building

You have just been appointed to lead a 10-person team within your department. Knowing that several of these team members have not worked well together on previous group assignments, you decide to put everyone through a series of team-building training programs. You believe this will help get the group off to a good start. Use the following Web sites to choose three different training sessions that will help your team members to become more cohesive and function effectively.

1. www.terrapinadventures.com/ (click on "team building")
2. www.buildteamwork.com (click on "training")
3. www.corporategames.com/ (click on "team building adventures and activities")

Case for Analysis: *Leading a Virtual Team*

Ellen Johnson had just completed her first month as manager for a successful company that provides a variety of Web-based services and solutions. Last week, she was informed that she would be the new leader of a team that included 10 individuals. To her surprise, not only were these team members diverse in terms of their functional training and expertise, but they also represented a variety of cultural backgrounds and only three were located in her office building. She quickly learned that 7 of the 10 individuals actually worked from their home countries, which included Japan, China, Mexico, Australia, Germany, Colombia, and Egypt. Up until this point, this "virtual team" collaborated on projects by using a variety of communication tools, including instant e-mail messaging, telephone calls, videoconferencing, document sharing, and occasional meetings at headquarters. After reviewing some of the past meeting notes and communication transcripts among the group members, Johnson realized that many of the team members had very different communication styles and levels of proficiency in English.

The team's new assignment was an important one. The 10 members needed to develop and roll out a new product within the next six weeks. This was in direct response to a new product just launched by a major competitor. To complicate matters, a six-week product development cycle was unheard of; until this point, the company's turnaround time for a new product offering was approximately three months. The company had no choice. If they did not counter the competitive threat immediately, then the company risked losing some key customers and market share.

Johnson researched the past performance of her newly inherited virtual team. Although the overall quality of past decisions was quite high, the team seemed to take several months to make those decisions. This was a potential problem for Johnson. Time was no longer a luxury. She had to figure out a way to encourage the team to move faster without compromising quality. Through a combination of analyzing past team meeting notes and transcripts and speaking one-on-one with team members, she started to accumulate some facts that might be useful in solving the decision-making speed issue.

First, Johnson discovered that the Japanese and Chinese team members did not participate much in the videoconferences or telephone conference calls; rather, they preferred written communication in the form of faxes and e-mail. In contrast, the Australian and Mexican team members seemed to thrive on telephone calls and face-to-face meetings. Second, there appeared to be some infighting among the three members of the group who were domiciled at headquarters. Most of the past arguments seemed to be about the group's mission. Each had a very different idea in mind in terms of what the group needed to accomplish. The comments in written communications didn't get personal, but there were definitely heated debates about what objectives the group should be focusing on. The third potential obstacle to faster decision making had to do with the sporadic use of face-to-face meetings. To her surprise, Johnson discovered that such meetings rarely occurred and that there was no attempt to bring the group together when it was first formed last year. Johnson expected that the team would have met and perhaps engaged in some team-building exercises to build trust and rapport among team members. This was not the case. In addition, the team did not receive any form of decision-making or group conflict resolution training.

Johnson sat back in her office and thought about the problem at hand. She needed her team to develop and launch a new product within six weeks. To produce a high-quality product, each of the 10 virtual team members had to contribute their knowledge and effort in a cooperative and timely manner.

DISCUSSION QUESTIONS

1. What is Johnson's most pressing problem? Why?
2. What can Johnson do to help her team launch the new product within the six-week timeframe? Be specific?
3. Assume Johnson will select a new team to launch another Web-based product after this product is complete. What do you recommend she do differently next time? Explain.

Experiential Exercise: *Participation in and Observation of Group Processes*

OBJECTIVES

1. To provide experience in participating in and observing groups undertaking a specific task.
2. To generate data that can be the focus of class discussion and analysis.

STARTING THE EXERCISE

The situation: You're appointed to a human resource management committee in charge of selecting a manager for the department that provides administrative services to other departments. Before you begin interviewing candidates, you're asked to develop a list of the personal and professional qualifications the manager needs. The list will be used as the selection criteria.

SELECTION CRITERIA

- Strong institutional loyalty.
- Ability to give clear instructions.
- Ability to discipline subordinates.
- Ability to make decisions under pressure.
- Ability to communicate.
- Stable personality.
- High intelligence.
- Ability to grasp the overall picture.
- Ability to get along well with people.
- Familiarity with office procedures.
- Professional achievement.
- Ability to develop subordinates.

COMPLETING THE EXERCISE

1. Select five to seven members to serve on the committee.
2. Ask the committee to rank the items in the above list of selection criteria in their order of importance in selecting the department head.
3. The students not on the committee should observe the group process. Some should observe the whole group; others should observe individual members. The observers can use observation guides A and B.
4. The observers should provide feedback to the participants.
5. The class should discuss how the committee might improve its performance.

A. GROUP PROCESS OBSERVATION GUIDE

Instructions: Observe the group behavior on the following dimensions. Prepare notes for feedback.

Group Behaviors	Description	Impact
Group goal: Are group goals clearly defined?		
Decision procedure: Is the decision procedure clearly defined?		
Communication network: What kind of communication network is used? Is it appropriate?		
Decision making: What kind of decision process is used? Is it appropriate?		
Group norm: Observe the degrees of cohesiveness, compatibility, and conformity.		
Group composition: What kind of group is it?		
Other behavior: Is there any behavior that influences the group process?		

B. INDIVIDUAL ROLE OBSERVATION GUIDE

Initiating ideas: Initiates or clarifies ideas and issues.	**Confusing issues:** Confuses others by bringing up irrelevant issues or by jumping to other issues.
Managing conflicts: Explores, clarifies, and resolves conflicts and differences.	**Mismanaging conflicts:** Avoids or suppresses conflicts, or creates "win or lose" situations.
Influencing others: Appeases, reasons with, or persuades others.	**Forcing others:** Gives orders or forces others to agree.
Supporting others: Reinforces or helps others to express their opinions.	**Rejecting others:** Deflates or antagonizes others.
Listening attentively: Listens and responds to others' ideas and opinions.	**Showing indifference:** Does not listen to or brushes off others.
Showing empathy: Shows the ability to see things from other people's viewpoint.	**Self-serving behavior:** Exhibits self-serving behavior.
Exhibiting positive nonverbal behaviors: Pays attention to others, maintains eye contact, keeps composure, and other signs.	**Exhibiting negative nonverbal behaviors:** Tense facial expression, yawning, little eye contact, and other behaviors.

CHAPTER NINE

Conflict and Negotiation

Learning Objectives

After completing Chapter 9, you should be able to

Define
Functional conflict and *dysfunctional* conflict.

Understand
How to manage conflict though negotiation.

Describe
The effect of intergroup conflict on organizational performance.

Discuss
Why intergroup conflict occurs.

Compare
The consequences of intergroup conflict within groups and between groups.

Identify
How group conflict can be resolved through team-building.

How Intergroup Conflict Can Affect an International Startup Team

Working for a large financial services firm, Rich Johnson is part of a seven-person team responsible for establishing new international ventures (i.e., "startups") in China, Brazil, and India. To successfully launch new subsidiaries overseas, Johnson's team relies on the company's operations management and sales divisions to furnish the new startups with the infrastructure and training necessary to be successful.

Recently, the groups have not been able to work well together; it seems that whenever Johnson's team needs help with onsite problems overseas, no one is available from the operations management or sales divisions to help out. On the rare occasions that they do return e-mails and phone calls, these other group members often give the excuse that they are too short-handed to leave their regular domestic responsibilities. Johnson's group is reacting angrily to the situation. His teammates are beginning to bad-mouth the members of these other groups and try to avoid them in the hallways and the cafeteria, leading to a near total breakdown in communication. Johnson has also noticed that his group has taken the attitude of "we don't need anyone else to get the job done." Unfortunately, he knows differently and has become pessimistic regarding his team's ability to set up successful, functional overseas ventures in a timely manner.

What did Johnson do to break down these barriers between the international startup team and the key people from operations management and sales division back at headquarters? He organized a team-building exercise. He brought all of the employees to a NASCAR race track in North Carolina for a three-day, company-sponsored, team-building exercise. The employees were divided into 10 different pit crews (teams) with seven members in each crew: a person to work the jack, a front and rear tire changer, a person to add the gas, another to catch any gas that spills, and a front and rear tire carrier. Johnson made sure that each team had representatives from operations management, sales, and the international startup team on it. Each seven-person pit crew was assigned to a different race car. The race was organized specifically for this team-building exercise. Whichever pit crew could service their car in the least amount of time during the race would win the competition. The winners would be awarded all-expenses-paid weekend vacations to a Caribbean island. So, the stakes were high, and each crew practiced refueling its race car, jacking up the vehicle, removing tires, putting on new tires, and so forth.

By the end of the race and the three-day team-building activity, the employees were beginning to work really well together and started to get to know each other on a more personal level. They began to see each other as people, as opposed to just "those lazy guys from sales" or "those international prima donnas," and so forth. Johnson hoped that the company's investment in the pit crew competition would pay off in terms of a significant increase in intergroup functioning and performance over the long run.

For any organization to perform effectively, interdependent individuals and groups must establish working relationships across organizational boundaries, between individuals, and among groups. Individuals or groups may depend on one another for information, assistance, and coordinated action. In general, as cooperation increases across different individuals and groups, so does the level of organizational effectiveness. However, this interdependence may foster either cooperation or conflict.

For example, a firm's production and marketing executives may meet to discuss ways to deal with foreign competition. Such a meeting may be reasonably free of conflict. Decisions get made, strategies are developed, and the executives return to work. Thus, there is intergroup cooperation to achieve a goal. However, this may not be the case if sales decline because the firm is not offering enough variety in its product line. The marketing department desires broad product lines to offer more variety to customers, while the production department desires narrow product lines to keep production costs manageable and to increase productivity. Conflict is likely to occur at this point because each function has its own goals, which in this case are in opposition. Thus, groups may cooperate on one point and conflict on another.

Intergroup problems aren't the only conflicts that can exist in organizations[1]; indeed, that interpersonal conflict is a pervasive and fundamental aspect of organizational life has been well documented.[2] Conflict between individuals, however, can usually be more easily resolved through existing mechanisms. For example, troublesome employees can be fired, transferred, or given new work schedules. The next OB at Work feature assesses how you handle interpersonal conflict.

This chapter focuses on conflict between groups in organizations. As Rich Johnson witnessed in the opening vignette, intergroup conflict can have serious implications for an organization. We begin by examining attitudes toward conflict. Reasons for intergroup conflict and its consequences are also presented. Finally, we outline techniques for successfully managing intergroup conflict.

A Realistic View of Intergroup Conflict

Conflict is inevitable in organizations. However, because it can be both a positive and a negative force, management should not strive to eliminate all conflict, only that which has disruptive effects on the organization's efforts to achieve its goals. Some type or degree of conflict may prove beneficial if it is used as an instrument for change or innovation. Thus, the critical issue appears to be not conflict itself but rather how it's managed. Using this approach, we can define conflict in terms of the *effect it has on the organization.* In this respect, we discuss both functional and dysfunctional conflict.[3]

Functional Conflict

functional conflict
From the organization's standpoint, confrontation between groups that results in benefits to the organization.

A **functional conflict** is a confrontation between groups that enhances and benefits the organization's performance. When conflict focuses on tasks, constructive debate can improve decision making and work outcomes.[4] For example, two departments in a hospital may conflict over the most efficient method of delivering health care to low-income rural families. The two departments agree on the goal but not on the means to achieve it. Whatever the outcome, low-income rural families will probably end up with better medical

OB AND YOUR CAREER

How Do You Handle Interpersonal Conflict?

Are you the kind of person who thrives on arguing with other people, regardless of the topic that's being discussed? Or do you tend to shy away from disagreements to maintain harmony? Understanding your preferred conflict management style can help you to be a more effective co-worker and manager. As a student, such knowledge will help you work better with other students on group projects, especially at the end of the semester when multiple deadlines can stress everyone's patience.

Complete the following self-assessment by circling one of the numbers from the following scale to describe your reaction to each of the statements below:

1 = Never 2 = Rarely 3 = Sometimes 4 = Often 5 = Very often

Statement	Circle One				
1. I work to come out victorious, no matter what.	1	2	3	4	5
2. I try to put the needs of others above my own.	1	2	3	4	5
3. I look for mutually satisfactory solution.	1	2	3	4	5
4. I try not to get involved in conflicts.	1	2	3	4	5
5. I strive to investigate issues thoroughly and jointly.	1	2	3	4	5
6. I never back away from a good argument.	1	2	3	4	5
7. I strive to foster harmony.	1	2	3	4	5
8. I negotiate to get a portion of what I propose.	1	2	3	4	5
9. I avoid open discussions of controversial subjects.	1	2	3	4	5
10. I openly share information with others in resolving disagreements.	1	2	3	4	5

Scoring and Interpretation

Competing Q1 _____ + Q6 _____ = Total _____

Collaborating Q5 _____ + Q10 _____ = Total _____

Avoiding Q4 _____ + Q9 _____ = Total _____

Accommodating Q2 _____ + Q7 _____ = Total _____

Compromising Q3 _____ + Q8 _____ = Total _____

Your preferred conflict-handling style is ______(category with highest score).
Your backup conflict-handling style is ______(category with second-highest score).

Competing: High scores on Q1 and Q6 indicate that your preferred style is to focus on winning in a negotiation setting. Conflict is seen as a part of the negotiation process, a means to receive what you desire. You enjoy the negotiation process. Trial attorneys fit this type of conflict management style.

Collaborating: People who have high scores on Q5 and Q10 tend to enjoy the negotiation process because it gives them an opportunity to probe deeply into difficult problems and help produce solutions that are acceptable to multiple parties. Real estate brokers tend to handle conflict in this manner.

Avoiding: Scoring high on Q4 and Q9 indicates that you prefer to avoid conflict and opportunities to negotiate. Although avoidance of conflict can help keep teams functioning when interpersonal difficulties arise, it can also lead to a variety of problems and dysfunctional behavior if issues are left unaddressed and unresolved. Professional politicians tend to be avoiders.

Accommodating: People with high scores on Q2 and Q7 use their relationship-building skills and empathy toward other people's emotions to help solve other people's problems. High accommodators place a good deal of emphasis on the needs of others. These types of negotiators are good in sales-based roles, where relationships are critical. An example of this would be the account manager of a large natural gas company who is assigned to one large account for a three-year period.

Compromising: High scores on Q3 and Q8 indicate that your preferred conflict resolution style is to try to "close the gap" in two parties' desires by using some type of fair criteria that appear reasonable to both sides. Compromisers tend to want to preserve the relationship between parties. An example of a compromiser would be a team leader who is trying to work out a problem between two of her direct reports. She wants to resolve the problem quickly and have both parties feel that the outcome was fair.

Sources: Adapted from G. Richard Shell, "Bargaining Styles and Negotiation: The Thomas-Kilmann Conflict Mode Instrument in Negotiation Training," *Negotiation Journal* 17, no. 2 (April 2001): 155–74, and K. W. Thomas, "Conflict and Conflict Management," in M. Dunnette (ed.), *Handbook of Industrial Psychology and Organizational Psychology*, vol. II (Chicago: Rand McNally, 1976), pp. 889–935.

care once the conflict is settled. Without such conflict in organizations, there would be little commitment to change; most groups would probably become stagnant. Thus, functional conflict can be thought of as a type of creative tension.

Dysfunctional Conflict

dysfunctional conflict
From the organization's standpoint, confrontation between groups that hinders organizational performance.

A **dysfunctional conflict** is any confrontation or interaction between groups that harms the organization or hinders the achievement of organizational goals. Management must seek to eliminate dysfunctional conflicts because such conflict can negatively influence performance by shifting group members' attention away from important tasks.[5]

Beneficial conflicts can often turn into harmful ones. The very same level of stress and conflict that creates a healthy and positive movement toward goals in one group may prove extremely disruptive and dysfunctional in another group (or at a different time for the same group). A group's tolerance for stress and conflict can also depend on the type of organization it serves. Auto manufacturers, professional sports teams, and crisis organizations such as police and fire departments have points at which functional conflict becomes dysfunctional that differ from those of universities, research and development firms, and movie production firms.

After reviewing the research literature on workplace conflict, one author suggests there are three hidden costs associated with dysfunctional workplace conflict[6]:

1. Conflict resolution diverts managers' time away from business opportunities. As managers spend time resolving conflicts among their employees, between departments, and so forth, they are not working on new products, helping customers, or engaging in other important business-related activities.
2. Someone ends up paying for the solution. When two parties negotiate a compromise, some other party may end up paying for it. For example, if a union gains significant concessions from management in terms of pay raises and enhanced benefits coverage for its members, then it's possible that customers could end up paying for part of these concessions in the form of higher prices.
3. Employee health and well-being. Conflict in organizations is stressful and employees are not immune to such reactions. As was discussed in Chapter 7, employee stress can lead to a wide variety of negative behavioral (e.g., absenteeism), cognitive (e.g., frustration), and/or physiological outcomes (e.g., increased blood pressure). It is reasonable to assume that some of the emergency response teams of British Petroleum and the U.S. government experienced high levels of stress related to figuring out how to stop the flow of crude oil from the broken well 5,000 feet below the surface in the Gulf of Mexico.[7]

Conflict and Organizational Performance

Conflict may have either a positive or a negative effect on organizational performance, depending on the nature of the conflict and how it is managed.[8] For every organization, an optimal level of conflict exists that can be considered highly functional; it helps generate positive performance. On one hand, when the conflict level is *too low,* performance can suffer. Innovation and change are difficult, and the organization may have difficulty in adapting to change in its environment. If this low conflict level continues, the organization's very survival can be threatened. On the other hand, if the conflict level becomes *too high,* the resulting chaos can also threaten its survival. An example is dissension among two strong and competing departments in an organization and its effect on performance. Fighting between departmental rivals (e.g., marketing and finance) that becomes too great can render the organization less effective in pursuing its mission of furthering its stakeholders' interests. The proposed relationship between level of intergroup conflict and organizational performance is presented in Figure 9.1 and explained for three hypothetical situations.

FIGURE 9.1 **Proposed Relationship between Intergroup Conflict and Organizational Performance**

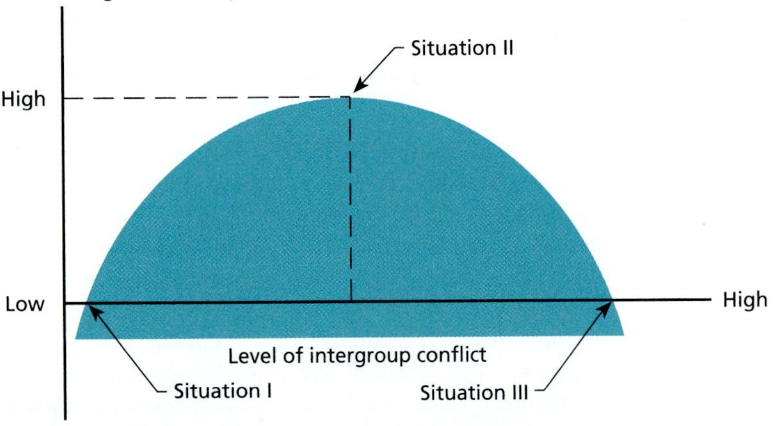

	Level of Intergroup Conflict	Probable Impact on Organization	Organization Characterized By	Level of Organizational Performance
Situation I	Low or none	Dysfunctional	Slow adaptation to environmental changes Few changes Little stimulation of ideas Apathy Stagnation	Low
Situation II	Optimal	Functional	Positive movement toward goals Innovation and change Search for problem solutions Creativity and quick adaptation to environmental changes	High
Situation III	High	Dysfunctional	Disruption Interference with activities Coordination difficult Chaos	Low

Views on Intergroup Conflict in Practice

Some organizational researchers contend that dysfunctional conflict should be eliminated and functional conflict encouraged. But this isn't what actually happens in most organizations. In practice, most managers attempt to eliminate all types of conflict, whether dysfunctional or functional. But why? Some reasons include the following:

1. Anticonflict values have historically been reinforced in the home, school, and place or worship. Traditionally, conflict between children or between children and parents has been discouraged. In school systems, too, conflict was discouraged; teachers had all the answers, and both teachers and children were rewarded for orderly classrooms. Finally, most religious doctrines stress peace, tranquility, and acceptance without questioning.

2. Managers are often evaluated on and rewarded for the lack of conflict in their areas of responsibility. Anticonflict values, in fact, become part of the culture of the organization. Harmony and satisfaction are viewed positively, while conflicts and dissatisfaction are viewed negatively. Under such conditions, managers seek to avoid conflicts—functional or dysfunctional—that could disturb the status quo.

Intragroup Conflict and Group Productivity

As teams become more and more popular in the workplace, the productivity both of the overall group and individual group members is receiving considerable attention from managers and researchers alike.[9] Although not universally accepted, one factor that may influence the overall functioning of teams is conflict between team members. Some have argued that intragroup conflict can lead to improvements in overall group performance, decision quality, strategic planning, financial performance, and organizational growth.[10] In contrast, other researchers have found that certain types of intragroup conflict have an overall negative effect on teams in that it contributes to lower levels of productivity and satisfaction in groups.[11] Taken as a whole, our assumption is that some types of intragroup conflict are beneficial at certain times throughout the life cycle of a group or team.

Researchers have identified three types of conflict that can influence group functioning.[12] The first, *task conflict,* refers to members having differences in viewpoints and opinions pertaining to what the group's task is. For example, two members of a strategic planning task force of a company may have very different opinions regarding what the group needs to accomplish. These differences may originate from a variety of areas including differences in work values, functional area experience, years in the industry, and the like. The second type of intragroup conflict is known as *relationship conflict.* This concept has been defined as being aware of interpersonal incompatibilities between group members that can lead to feelings of dislike, tension, irritation and frustration. The third and more recent type of intragroup conflict to be researched, *process conflict,* is defined as an awareness of controversies regarding how tasks will be accomplished. Process conflict deals with the delegation of tasks and responsibilities to different team members.

Although not conclusive, recent research on the influence of intragroup conflict on individual and group performance has improved the understanding of the topic. Studying the pattern of intragroup conflict over time, researchers have found several differences in how conflict affects high-performing teams compared with low-performing teams.[13] Three-person teams were studied over a three-phase period. High-performing teams, overall, experienced less task, relationship, and process conflict than low-performing teams. The only exception occurred in the middle period during which the high-performing team experienced a higher increase in task conflict. The researchers argued that this conflict serves an important purpose in that it helps a high-performing team determine the specific content of the final product and/or decision.

Previous research has corroborated that a point of reevaluation and transition occurs around the midpoint of a project.[14] It was also reported that process conflict increased steadily across the three periods (though not reaching the levels experienced by the lower-performing team). And, the high-performing team did experience an increase in relationship conflict in the last period before the project was due. The reason for the increased conflict was thought to be the pressure of the due date and the interdependence of the team members. This was in contrast to the low-performing team, which experienced an escalating pattern of relationship conflict throughout all three periods.

Why Intergroup Conflict Occurs

Every group comes into at least partial conflict with every other group with which it interacts. In this section, we examine four factors that contribute to group conflict: work interdependence, differences in goals, differences in perceptions, and the increased demand for specialists.

Work Interdependence

Work interdependence occurs when two or more organizational groups depend on one another to complete their tasks. Conflict potential in such situations is high. Three distinct types of interdependence among groups have been identified.[15]

Pooled Interdependence

pooled interdependence
Interdependence that requires no interaction among groups except through the total organization.

Pooled interdependence requires no interaction among groups because each group, in effect, performs separately. However, the pooled performances of all the groups determine how successful the organization is. For example, the staff of an Apple sales office in one region may have no interaction with their peers in another region; similarly, two Bank of America branches may have little or no interaction. In both cases, however, the groups are interdependent because the performance of each must be adequate if the total organization is to thrive. The conflict potential in pooled interdependence is relatively low, and management can rely on standard rules and procedures developed at the main office for coordination.

Sequential Interdependence

sequential interdependence
Interdependence that requires one group's output to serve as another group's input, thereby providing the basis for great potential conflict.

Sequential interdependence requires one group to complete its task before another group can complete its task. Tasks are performed in a sequential fashion. For example, Chrysler Group LLC is considering a plan to assemble the Fiat 500 subcompact in Mexico.[16] Parts will first be made in the U.S. and other countries and then shipped to Mexico for final assembly.

Under circumstances in which one group's output serves as the input for another, conflict between groups is more likely to occur. Coordinating sequential interdependence involves effective planning by management.[17]

Reciprocal Interdependence

reciprocal interdependence
Interdependence that requires each group's output to serve as input to other groups in the organization.

Reciprocal interdependence requires each group's output to serve as input to other groups in the organization. Consider the relationships among the anesthesiology staff, nursing staff, technicians, and surgeons in a hospital operating room; such relationships create a high degree of reciprocal interdependence. The same interdependence exists among groups involved in space launchings. Another example is the interdependence between airport control towers, flight crews, ground operations, and maintenance crews. Clearly, the potential for conflict is great in any of these situations. Effective coordination involves management's skillful use of the organizational processes of communication and decision making.

All organizations have pooled interdependence among groups. Complex organizations also have sequential interdependence. The most complicated organizations experience pooled, sequential, and reciprocal interdependence among groups. The more complex the organization, the greater is the potential for conflict and the more difficult is the task facing management. The accompanying OB at Work feature illustrates the concept of interdependence in team sports.

Differences in Goals

As the subunits of organization become specialized, they often develop dissimilar goals. A goal of a production unit may include low production costs and few defective products. A goal of the research and development unit may be innovative ideas that can be converted into commercially successful new products. These different goals can lead to different expectations among the members of each unit: Production engineers may expect close supervision, while research scientists may expect a great deal of participation in decision making. Because of the different goals, conflict can result when these two groups interact.

Finally, marketing departments usually have a goal of maximum gross income; in contrast, credit departments seek to minimize credit losses. Depending on which department prevails, different customers might be selected. Here again, conflict can occur because

OB AT WORK Interdependence in Sports

Sports teams are good examples of organizations where members must depend on one another if the entire group is to succeed. Examples of work interdependence in three team sports are shown in the table.

	Baseball Team	Football Team	Basketball Team
1. What is the nature (and degree) of task-based interaction among unit members?	Pooled (low).	Sequential (moderate).	Reciprocal (high).
2. What is the geographical distribution of unit members?	Widely dispersed.	Somewhat clustered.	Highly concentrated.
3. Given team objectives and constraints, where does autonomy reside?	Within each unit member.	Above the unit (that is, within unit management).	Among unit members (that is, within the unit as a whole).
4. How is coordination achieved?	Through unit design in which the sum of individual unit members' objectives approximates unit objectives.	Through complex protocols that clearly and tightly specify the roles and responsibilities of each unit member.	Through continuous self-regulation and responsibility sharing among unit members.
5. What sports expression metaphorically sums up the operating management task?	Fill out (revise) the lineup card.	Prepare (execute) the game plan.	Influence the game's flow.

Sources: Robert W. Keidel, *Seeing Organizational Patterns: A New Theory and Language of Organizational Design* (San Francisco: Berett-Koehler Publishers, 1995). Adapted from Robert W. Keidel, "Baseball, Football and Basketball: Models for Business," *Organizational Dynamics,* (Winter 1984): 12–14.

each department has a different goal. Because of differences in goals, certain conditions (such as resource availability and reward structures) foster intergroup conflict.

Limited Resources

When limited resources must be allocated, mutual dependencies increase, and any differences in group goals become more apparent. If money, space, labor, and materials were unlimited, each group could pursue (at least to a relative degree) its own goals. But resources must be allocated and shared. Groups seek to lower pressure on themselves by gaining control over critical resource supplies, thus reducing the uncertainty of gaining these supplies.[18] For example, when a college is undergoing an overall reduction in its operating budget, the departments of the college will sometimes try to protect their own budget allocations even if this means other departments might experience deeper funding cuts. What often occurs in limited-resource situations is a win–lose competition that can easily result in dysfunctional conflict if groups refuse to collaborate.

Reward Structures

Intergroup conflict is more likely to occur when the reward system is related to individual group performance rather than to overall organizational performance. This potential for conflict escalates even further when one group has primary responsibility for distributing rewards. The group will tend to show strong partiality toward its own members in allocating favorable outcomes and strong partiality toward the out group in distributing negative outcomes.[19]

When rewards are aimed at individual groups, performances are viewed as an independent variable even while the group's performance is in reality very interdependent. For example, in the marketing versus credit situation just described, suppose that the marketing group is rewarded for sales produced and that the credit group is also rewarded for minimizing credit losses. In such a situation, competition is directly reinforced and dysfunctional conflict is inadvertently rewarded.

Intergroup conflict arising from differences in goals may be not only dysfunctional to the organization as a whole, but also dysfunctional to third-party groups—usually the organization's clients. An example is conflict in many teaching hospitals between meeting the goals of quality health care for patients and meeting future physicians' learning needs.

Differences in Perceptions

Differences in goals can be accompanied by differing perceptions of reality; disagreements over what constitutes reality can lead to conflict. For instance, a problem in a hospital may be viewed in one way by the administrative staff and in another way by the medical staff; or alumni and faculty may have different perceptions concerning the importance of a winning football program. Many factors cause groups in organizations to form differing perceptions of reality.[20] Major factors include different goals, different time horizons, status incongruency, and inaccurate perceptions.

Different Goals

Differences in group goals are an obvious contributor to differing perceptions. For instance, if the goal of marketing is to increase market shares and sales throughout the world, that department's personnel would not appreciate a reorganization task force goal to reduce expansion of the company's products to the Pacific Rim. Marketing perceives the Pacific Rim as important, and the task force perceives the Pacific Rim as too far from the home office to control and manage.

Different Time Horizons

Time perspectives influence how a group perceives reality. Deadlines influence the priorities and importance that groups assign to their various activities. Research scientists working for pharmaceutical manufacturers like Bayer or Abbott Laboratories may have a time perspective of several years, while the same firm's manufacturing engineers may work within time frames of less than a year. The CEOs of Google or Facebook might focus on one- and five-year time spans, while middle managers at those organizations might concentrate on much shorter spans. With such differences in time horizons, problems and issues deemed critical by one group may be dismissed as unimportant by another, setting the stage for conflict.

Status Incongruency

Usually, many different status standards, rather than an absolute one, are found in an organization. The result is many status hierarchies. Conflicts concerning the relative status of different groups are common and influence perceptions. For example, status conflicts are often created by work patterns—which group initiates the work and which group responds. A production department may perceive a change as an affront to its status because it must accept a salesperson's initiation of work. This status conflict may be aggravated deliberately by salespeople. Another example involves the academic snobbery that's certainly a fact of

TABLE 9.1
Common Causes of Line–Staff Conflict

Perceived diminution of line authority. Line managers fear that specialists will encroach on their jobs and thereby diminish their authority and power. As a result, specialists often complain that line executives don't make proper use of staff specialists and don't give staff members sufficient authority.
Social and physical differences. Often major differences exist between line managers and staff specialists with respect to age, education, dress, and attitudes. In many cases, specialists are younger than line managers and have higher educational levels of training in a specialized field.
Line dependence on staff knowledge. Since line generalists often don't have the technical knowledge necessary to manage their departments, they are dependent on specialists. The resulting gap between knowledge and authority may be even greater when the staff specialist is lower in the organizational hierarchy than the manager, which is often the case. As a result, staff members often complain that line managers resist new ideas.
Different loyalties. Divided loyalties frequently exist between line managers and staff specialists. The staff specialist may be loyal to a discipline, while the line manager may be loyal to the organization. The member of the product development group may be a chemist first and a member of the organization second. The production manager's first loyalty, however, may be to the organization. When loyalties to a particular function or discipline are greater than loyalties to the overall organization, conflict is likely.

campus life at many colleges: Members of a particular academic discipline perceive themselves, for one reason or another, as having higher status than others.

Inaccurate Perceptions

Inaccurate perceptions often cause one group to develop stereotypes about other groups. While the differences between groups may actually be small, each group tends to exaggerate them. Thus, you hear that "all women executives are aggressive" or "all bank officers behave alike." When differences between the groups are emphasized, stereotypes are reinforced, relations deteriorate, and conflict develops.

Increased Demand for Specialists

Conflicts between staff specialists and line generalists are probably the most common intergroup conflict. Line and staff persons simply view one another and their roles in the organization from different perspectives. For example, a marketing manager (line generalist) may have a different approach to interviewing candidates than an HR manager (staff specialist). The marketing manager may want to ask some interview questions that the HR manager would find unacceptable. The HR manager's job is to ensure the hiring process is done in a professional, fair, and legally defensible manner. These competing goals can sometimes lead to conflict between the two parties. With the growing necessity for technical expertise in all areas of organizations, staff roles might be expected to expand, and line and staff conflicts might be expected to increase. Table 9.1 summarizes some causes of conflict between staff specialists and generalists.[21] The increased sophistication, specialization, and complexity in most organizations make line–staff conflicts a major concern in managing organizational behavior.

Consequences of Dysfunctional Intergroup Conflict

Researchers have spent more than four decades researching and analyzing how dysfunctional intergroup conflict affects those who experience it.[22] They have found that groups placed in a conflict situation tend to react with fairly predictable changes within groups and between groups as a result of dysfunctional intergroup conflict.

Changes within Groups

Many changes are likely to occur within groups involved in intergroup conflict. Unfortunately, these changes generally result in either continuance or escalation of the conflict.

Increased Group Cohesiveness

Competition, conflict, and external threat usually result in group members putting aside individual differences and closing ranks. Members become more loyal to the group, and group membership becomes more attractive.

Rise in Autocratic Leadership

In extreme conflict situations, when threats are perceived, democratic methods of leadership are likely to become less popular; members want strong leadership. Thus, leaders are likely to become more autocratic. In a National Basketball Association strike, the union head has tremendous negotiating authority from the players to do what he believes is best for them.

Focus on Activity

When a group is in conflict, its members usually emphasize doing what the group does and doing it very well. The group becomes more task oriented. Tolerance for members who "goof off " is low, and there's less concern for individual member satisfaction. Emphasis is on accomplishing the group's task and defeating the "enemy" (the other group in conflict).

Emphasis on Loyalty

Conformity to group norms tends to become more important in conflict situations. Group goals take precedence over individual satisfaction, as members are expected to demonstrate their complete loyalty. In major conflict situations, interaction with members of "the other group" may be prohibited.

Changes between Groups

During conflicts, certain changes occur between the groups involved.

Distorted Perceptions

During conflicts, the perceptions of each group's members become distorted. Group members develop stronger opinions of the importance of their units. Each group sees itself as superior in performance to the other and as more important to the survival of the organization than other groups. In a conflict situation, nurses may conclude that they are more important to a patient than physicians, while physicians may consider themselves more important than hospital administrators. The marketing group in a business organization may think, "Without us selling the product, there would be no money to pay anyone else's salary." The production group meanwhile says, "If we don't make the product, there's nothing to sell." Ultimately, none of these groups is more important, but conflict can cause their members to develop gross misperceptions of their self-importance.

Negative Stereotyping

As conflict increases and perceptions become more distorted, all of the negative stereotypes that may have ever existed are reinforced. A management representative may say, "I've always said these union members are just plain greedy. Now they've proved it." The head of a local teacher's union may say, "Now we know that politicians are interested only in getting reelected, not in the quality of education." When negative stereotyping is a factor in a conflict, members of each group see fewer differences within their unit than actually exist and greater differences between the groups than actually exist.

Decreased Communication

Communication between the groups in conflict usually breaks down. This can be extremely dysfunctional, especially where sequential interdependence or reciprocal interdependence relationships exist. The decision-making process can be disrupted, and customers or others the organization serves can be affected. Consider the possible consequences to patients, for instance, if a conflict between hospital technicians and nurses continues until it lowers the quality of health care.

While not the only dysfunctional consequences of intergroup conflict, these are the most common; they're well documented in the research literature.[23] Other consequences, such as violence and aggression, occur less commonly. When intergroup conflicts take place, some form of managerial intervention is usually necessary. The next sections address how managers can deal with these situations.

Managing Intergroup Conflict through Resolution

Managers spend more than 20 percent of their time in conflict management.[24] Because managers must live with intergroup conflict, they need to confront the problem of managing it.[25] Failure to do so can lead to disastrous results. Conflict can rip an organization apart by creating walls between co-workers, leading to poor performance and even resignations.[26]

Managers must realize that because causes of conflict differ, the means of resolving conflict will also differ, depending on circumstances.[27] Choice of an appropriate conflict resolution method depends on many factors, including reasons why the conflict occurred and the specific relationship between the manager and the conflicting groups. This section presents techniques for resolving intergroup conflict that has reached levels dysfunctional to the organization.[28]

Problem Solving

The confrontation method of problem solving seeks to reduce tensions through face-to-face meetings of the conflicting groups. The purpose of the meetings is to identify conflicts and resolve them. The conflicting groups openly debate various issues and bring together all relevant information until a decision is reached. For conflicts resulting from misunderstandings or language barriers, the confrontation method has proved effective. For solving more complex problems (e.g., conflicts where groups have different value systems), the method has been less successful.

Superordinate Goals

superordinate goals
Goals that cannot be achieved without cooperation of conflicting groups.

In the resolution of conflicts between groups, the **superordinate goals** technique involves developing a common set of goals and objectives that can't be attained without the cooperation of the groups involved. In fact, they are unattainable by one group singly and supersede all other goals of any of the individual groups involved in the conflict.[29] For example, in recent years several unions in the auto and airline industries have agreed to forgo pay increases, and in some cases to accept pay reductions, because the survival of their firm or industry was threatened. When the crisis was over, demands for higher wages were again made.

Expansion of Resources

As noted earlier, a major cause of intergroup conflict is limited resources. Whatever one group succeeds in obtaining is gained at the expense of another group. The scarce resource may be a particular position (e.g., presidency of the firm), money, or space. Expansion of resources may be one way of solving such problems. For example, when one major publishing firm decided to expand by establishing a subsidiary firm, most observers believed that the major reason for the expansion was to allow the firm to become involved in other segments of the market. While this was partially correct, a stronger reason was to enable the firm to stem the exit of valued personnel. By establishing the subsidiary, the firm was able to double its executive positions because the subsidiary needed a president, various vice presidents, and other executives. Expanding resources is potentially a successful technique for solving conflicts in many cases, because this technique may enable almost everyone to be satisfied. But in many cases, resources usually aren't expanded.

Avoidance

Frequently, managers can find some way to avoid conflict. While avoidance may not bring any long-term benefit, it can certainly work as a short-run solution. However, avoiding a conflict could be misinterpreted as agreement with group actions or lack of fortitude on the manager's part.[30] Avoiding a conflict neither effectively resolves it nor eliminates it. Eventually, the conflict has to be faced. But in some circumstances, avoidance may be the best temporary alternative. For example, a top-performing employee asks for a large raise at a time when the organization is struggling financially. The manager doesn't agree or disagree with the employee, but rather asks the employee to discuss the raise issue again in about six months. The manager is avoiding an immediate decision (and potential conflict) in order to wait for the firm to have more resources to fund a large raise for the star performer. Of course, the risk of this avoidance behavior is that the employee will look for another job or a transfer to a different department or division that has more resources.

Smoothing

The technique known as *smoothing* emphasizes the common interests of the conflicting groups and deemphasizes their differences. The basic belief behind smoothing is that stressing shared viewpoints on certain issues facilitates movement toward a common goal. The manager must explain to the conflicting groups that the organization's work will be jeopardized if the groups won't cooperate with each other.[31] As long as both groups see that the manager isn't taking sides, they may rise to the occasion and agree, at least, to a limited truce. But if differences between groups are serious, smoothing—like avoidance—is at best a short-run solution.

Compromise

Compromise is a traditional method for resolving intergroup conflicts. With compromise, there's no distinct winner or loser, and the decision reached is probably not ideal for either group. Compromise can be used effectively when the goal sought (e.g., money) can be divided equitably. For example, assume a company can afford to rent only an additional 20 offices to accommodate part of its expanding growth; half of these offices are allocated for use by the sales department and the other half by the customer service group. Both departments need more office space, but the compromise gives both departments an equal number (i.e., 10) of new offices. When such compromise isn't possible, one group must give up something of value as a concession.

Managers who endorse compromise as a conflict resolution tactic send out a message that they're sympathetic to both groups' demands. If used effectively, the manager can simultaneously take an aggressive approach to conflict resolution while exhibiting concern for those involved.[32] Compromise may also involve third-party interventions, as well as total group or representative negotiating and voting.[33] The process of negotiation will be examined in detail later in the chapter.

Authoritative Command

The use of authority may be the oldest, most frequently used method for resolving intergroup conflict. Using this method, management simply resolves the conflict as it sees fit and communicates its desires to the groups involved. Subordinates usually abide by a superior's decision, whether or not they agree with it. Thus, authoritative command usually works in the short run. As with avoidance, smoothing, and compromise, however, it doesn't focus on the cause of the conflict but rather on its results. If the causes remain, conflict will probably recur. Also, if employees feel they were forced to do something with which they disagreed, then it's only a matter of time before this approach backfires and the employees find alternative ways of doing things (or, stop doing the activity altogether), quit, or reduce effort on the job.

Altering the Human Variable

Altering the human variable involves trying to change group members' behavior. This method focuses on the cause or causes of the conflict and on the attitudes of the people involved. While the method is certainly difficult, it does center on the cause of the conflict. Part 6 of this book focuses specifically on changing behavior. In it, we show that, although slower than other methods and often costly, altering the human variable can have significant long-run results.

Altering the Structural Variables

Another way to resolve intergroup disputes is to alter the structural variables. This involves changing the formal structure of the organization. Structure refers to the fixed relationships among the jobs of the organization and includes the design of jobs and departments. Altering the structure of the organization to resolve intergroup conflict involves such things as transferring, exchanging, or rotating members of the groups or having a coordinator, liaison, or go-between who keeps groups communicating with one another.

Identifying a Common Enemy

In some respects, identifying a common enemy is the negative side of superordinate goals. Groups in conflict may temporarily resolve their differences and unite to combat a common enemy. The common enemy may be a competitor that has just introduced a clearly superior product. Conflicting groups in a bank may suddenly work in close harmony when government bank examiners make a visit. The common-enemy phenomenon is very evident in domestic conflicts. Most police officers prefer not to become involved in heated domestic conflicts because, in far too many cases, combatants close ranks and turn on the police officer.

The most commonly used methods for managing intergroup conflict each have strengths and weaknesses and are effective or ineffective in different situations. What this chapter has said thus far about intergroup conflict is summarized in Figure 9.2. The figure illustrates the relationship between causes and types of intergroup conflict, the consequences of intergroup conflict, and techniques for resolution.

Whatever the techniques utilized to deal with intergroup conflict (and there undoubtedly are others not in the figure), managers must learn how to recognize the existence and causes of intergroup conflict. They must also develop skills to effectively deal with it.

FIGURE 9.2 An Overview of Intergroup Conflict

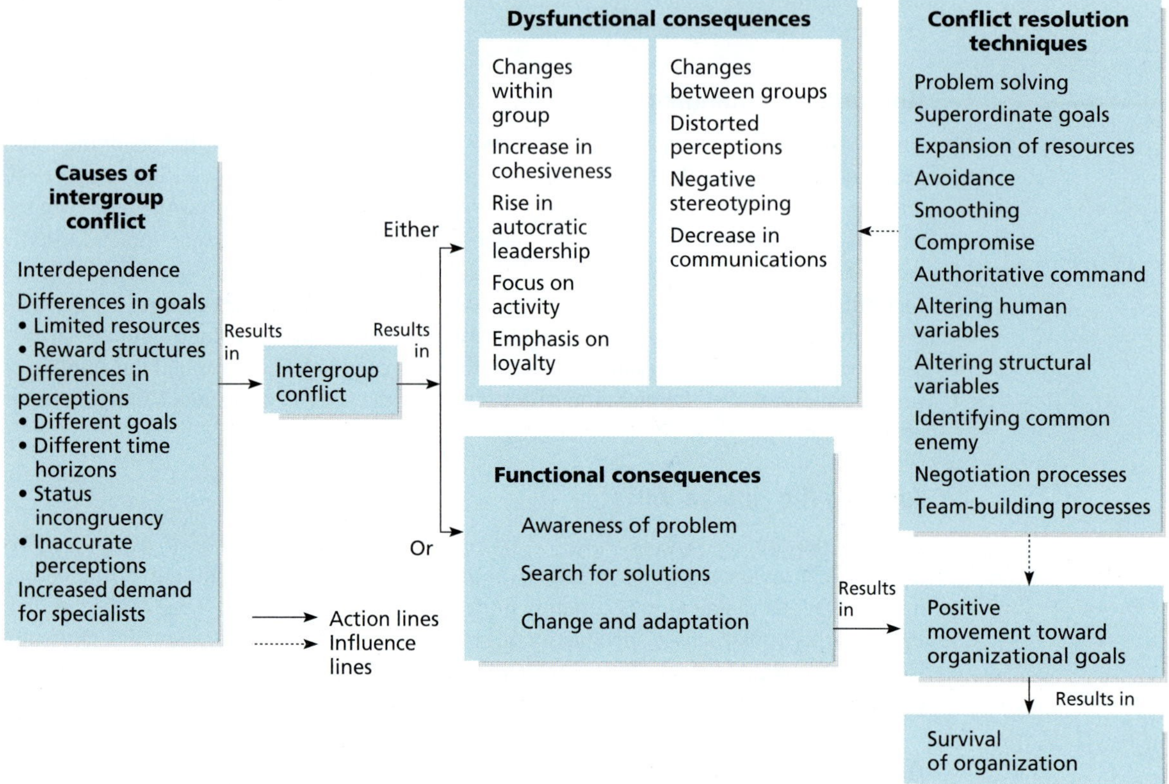

Managing Intergroup Conflict through Negotiation

A widely used yet often less recognized method of managing intergroup conflict is the process of negotiation. Despite its importance, the process is often misunderstood and poorly executed.[34] If done effectively, the negotiation process can be called a collaborative pursuit of joint gains and a collaborative effort to create value where none previously existed.[35] If done poorly, the process can be described as a street fight.

Negotiation entails having two sides with differing or conflicting interests come together to forge an agreement. Usually, each side will bring to the process a series of proposals that then are discussed and acted on. Everyone is familiar with the importance of bargaining to settle union disputes, formulate trade pacts, handle hostage situations, and reach arms agreements. Managers in organizations perform the same function on a continuing basis, negotiating with subordinates, superiors, vendors, and customers daily.

Cross-Cultural Negotiations

Intel Corporation decided to train its employees in interpreting cultural nuances in order to improve their cross-cultural negotiation skills. Helping businesses to avoid committing intercultural errors has become a $100 billion industry in the United States.[36] Research in the area of international negotiations has focused primarily on making cross-cultural comparisons of negotiations in different cultural contexts and on the influence that cultures exert on negotiation practices.[37] One explanation for the linkage between culture and negotiation has to do with the role of cultural values. Defined as desirable goals that serve as guiding principles that are shared by members of a culture, cultural values encourage individuals from a particular culture to employ those negotiation strategies that will achieve results that are compatible with the cultural environment.[38] For example, Chinese negotiators tend to favor negotiation strategies that avoid conflict while preserving trust, social harmony, and face.[39] Thus, global managers need to incorporate these factors when developing an effective Chinese negotiation strategy.

Although the list of factors that differentiate cultures is extremely long, the following are a few of the more critical dimensions that managers can use to assist in the development of a cross-cultural negotiation strategy. First, the cultural framework developed by Hofstede is a good starting point for understanding different cultural perspectives and values (see Chapter 3 for a review). The degree to which one's culture is characterized by individualism, uncertainty avoidance, power distance, and masculinity can help explain the type of negotiation approach and outcomes that will fit within the cultural context.[40] For example, the goals of a negotiator from a highly individualist culture (e.g., the United States) will tend to focus on personal needs and as such will be more likely to use a win–lose or competitive negotiation strategy.[41]

In addition to cultural values, differences in communication style can also influence the outcomes of cross-cultural negotiations.[42] When language barriers exist between two or more participants, comprehension difficulties can impede the progress of the negotiations. Also, nonverbal cues can take on very different meanings for individuals from different cultures. For example, shaking one's head up and down in the United States signifies "yes." In England, the same motion indicates that one is being heard, not that one is necessarily in agreement. To say "no," Americans shake their heads back and forth whereas Middle Easterners jerk their heads back forcefully, and Far Easterners wave a hand in front of their faces.[43]

Group Negotiations

Group negotiations take place whenever one group's work depends on the cooperation and actions of another group over which the first group's manager has no control.[44] Negotiations between marketing and production departments regarding order deliveries, between finance and engineering groups over research and development funding, and between maintenance and manufacturing functions over machine maintenance are all examples of the group process. Another example is related to the distribution of the 2009 movie *Inglourious Basterds*. The Weinstein Company, which produced it, hoped to acquire a larger share of the profits from the hit movie, but had to enter into a deal (and share profits) with a studio partner, Universal Pictures, to release and distribute it.[45]

For most Americans, negotiation differs from compromise in that the only really successful negotiations are those in which all the affected parties walk away feeling like they've won.[46] Several tasks and tactics can be undertaken by managers prior to and during the negotiation process to increase the probability of achieving mutually beneficial results.

Prenegotiation Tasks

Understanding the Other Side

Prior to sitting down and negotiating with managers and/or representatives of other groups, managers must thoroughly understand the other side's needs and positions regarding the issues to be resolved.[47] A product manager who desperately wants a customer order filled by manufacturing within the next two weeks should be aware of other obligations currently being placed on manufacturing. Likewise, a sales group negotiating with a customer over a major purchase should know how the customer uses the product or service, how important it is to the customer's business, what elements of the purchase (e.g., delivery date, training, warranty, price) are critical to the customer, and what alternatives are available to the customer. Regardless of whether the customer is internal (a more frequent occurrence as a result of departmentalization and decentralization efforts undertaken by organizations) or external to the organization, the same procedures apply.

To gain this information, the manager must ask questions. Although positions are usually up-front, underlying interests or problems often aren't.[48] A manager's goal should be to come to the negotiations with a full appreciation of the values, beliefs, and wants that drive the other side's actions. By freely exchanging information with the other group and performing as much outside or third-party research as possible, the manager can come prepared for the process. The element of surprise, which can prove to be of value in many business tactics, only serves to delay and hinder the negotiation process.

Knowing All the Options

Perhaps more important than the accumulation of information is its use in developing, understanding, and evaluating options available to resolve the conflict. Although the same issue may be negotiated over and over again, the outcomes may differ, depending on the parties involved or the timing of the negotiations.[49] One instance of a negotiation between two groups in an organization would be funding a capital investment. For example, discussions between finance and manufacturing may lead to the funds becoming available immediately, contingent on manufacturing's formulation of a detailed spending plan. A second outcome may consist of the funds being allocated over time, with the capital investment project being completed on a piecemeal basis. A third possible outcome would be the allocation of a certain percentage of the funding, with the remainder coming from the sale of the assets being replaced. The important point is that the greater the number of options that can be identified, the greater is the likelihood that both groups can benefit from the negotiation process.

Negotiation Tactics

A countless number of specific negotiation tactics can be employed by managers involved in the process (see Figure 9.3).[50] Several of the most often used ones will be discussed.

1. *Good-guy/bad-guy team.* Anyone who has read a detective story or seen a TV police show is familiar with this tactic. The bad-guy member of the negotiating group advocates positions so much out of line that whatever the good guy says sounds reasonable.

FIGURE 9.3
Negotiation Tactics

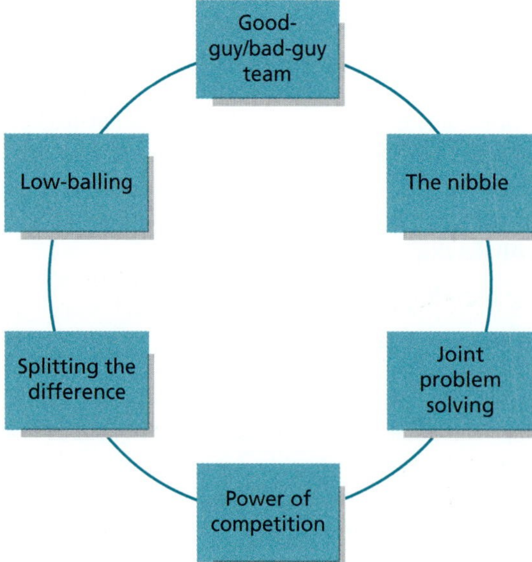

2. *The nibble.* This tactic involves getting an additional concession or perk after an agreement has been reached. An example would be the request for an additional staff position by a marketing manager after an agreement was reached between her group and another marketing group regarding division of market research duties.

3. *Joint problem solving.* A manager should never assume that the more one side wins, the more the other loses. Feasible alternatives not yet considered may exist. For instance, can manufacturing provide earlier completion dates on products if the sales department increases the order size and reduces the order frequency?

4. *Power of competition.* Tough negotiators use competition to make opponents think they don't need them. A line manager may use this tactic by threatening that his group will procure computer services outside the organization if the headquarters computer staff doesn't comply with demands. The most effective defense against this tactic is for a manager to remain objective. Don't commit quickly to unfavorable terms because of the fear of quick action on the other group's part.

5. *Splitting the difference.* This can be a useful technique when two groups come to an impasse. Managers should be careful, however, when the other group offers to split the difference too early. It may mean the other group has already gotten more than it thinks it deserves.

6. *Low-balling.* Ridiculously low offers and/or concessions are often used to lower the other group's expectations. A manager shouldn't let this type of offer lower her expectations or goals, nor should the manager walk out assuming the other group's position is inflexible. The communications process should continue.

Different situations call for different tactics. A manager should be aware of the options available and strive to understand the rationale behind the options.

The Effect of Personalities on the Negotiation Process

The process of negotiating is a very people-oriented experience. In addition to understanding the goals, needs, and wants of the other side, the successful negotiator tries to understand the relevant personality traits of the other individual(s) negotiating.[51] Negotiators come to the bargaining session from varied backgrounds; their experiences, like their perspectives, differ. Their propensities to take risk vary, and their personalities and attitudes are diverse. All this affects behavioral actions.[52] Managers must stop and look beneath the roles the other party to a negotiation is playing and ask what really motivates the individual(s).[53] Knowing these traits allows the manager to "read" and understand the opposing side, a valuable tool in negotiations.

Four of the most common types of personalities a manager will face at the negotiation table are[54]

1. *The power seeker*—task and results oriented, seeking challenges and opportunities, and potentially confrontational. A good decision maker.
2. *The persuader*—outgoing, socially oriented, ambitious, and tough under a cloak of amiability, likability, and affability. A dangerous opponent at the negotiating table.
3. *The reliable performer*—solid, dependable, comfortable in supportive surroundings, and resistant to sudden change. Dependent on past precedents for confidence in decision making.
4. *The limited performer*—lacking in self-confidence, in need of a sheltered environment, nondecisive, and introverted. Likely to crack under pressure.

The degree of a manager's ability to successfully understand and handle people will ultimately determine his or her success at negotiating.

The Role of Trust

This chapter has defined *functional conflict* as a confrontation between groups that enhances and benefits the organization's effectiveness. In the negotiation process, there will be a greater likelihood of a beneficial outcome for the organization if a high degree of trust exists between the conflicting groups.[55] Negotiators tend to regard making statements about their group's needs, wants, and priorities as risky and therefore are only willing to make them if there's mutual trust (i.e., they believe that the other side is also cooperatively motivated).[56] A high level of trust between the two conflicting parties will lead to greater openness and sharing of information.

Managers tend to expect some deception when negotiating.[57] Even relatively cooperative bargainers often inject straw issues or exaggerate minor problems' importance to gain concessions on what really matters.[58] In nearly all bargaining encounters, a negotiator's key skill is the ability to communicate that she is firm on positions when, in fact, the negotiator is flexible—in short, bluffing about one's intentions. But bluffing doesn't constitute lying or fraud—managers should be well aware of the difference. One researcher suggests there are several ways to protect oneself against lies during a negotiation, including[59]:

- Before the negotiation commences:
    - Research and prepare carefully. Search for and review all possible sources of information about the other party and his/her organization. Use Yahoo! or your library's research databases, recent news articles, press releases, Better Business Bureau, etc.
- During the negotiation process:
    - Monitor the other party for deceitful behavior. Ask questions to which one already knows the answers. Also, observe the other party's verbal and nonverbal behaviors for changes (e.g., changes in breathing, decreased eye contact, etc.).
    - Take detailed notes of the negotiation. To make sure each side understands and agrees to what was said, notes should be typed up after each meeting and agreed to as the negotiation progresses.
    - Include a "contingency" provision in the final deal. This basically states that if either party misled the other during the negotiation process, then the deceiving party will be held to agreed-upon consequences (e.g., financial damages) after the agreement is signed.

In addition, a good negotiator will never place the other party in a position from which he can't move without losing face.[60] By offering choices between alternatives (sometimes done by following mild demands with stronger ones), the other side will be more likely to view the process as cooperative and thus be more willing to reach an agreement.

Alternatives to Direct Negotiations

Occasionally, groups are unable to resolve their differences through direct negotiations. Likely candidates are groups that conflict often or are led by managers of equal rank. Groups can reach a point where they feel stuck in disagreement. Rather than letting the conflict evolve into a long, nasty battle, the two sides should seek outside help. A third party, often a CEO or other top executive, can be called in to mediate the dispute.[61] Use of a mediator allows an impartial person to work with the two sides to reach an agreement that benefits both sides and the organization as a whole. Bringing in a mediator early enough in the process allows conflicts to be resolved before group hostilities set in, which could lead to dysfunctional results.

An option to mediation is arbitration, in which groups are bound by the arbitrator's decision. Some companies set up formal committees of high-ranking executives whose sole purpose is to resolve disputes between groups.[62] These committees have the authority to render a clear-cut decision in favor of one group, to provide for a mutually agreeable resolution, or to ask the involved parties to collect more information before a decision is reached. A benefit of this approach is that disagreeing parties don't have to compromise themselves in order to settle an issue. Once a decision is reached, both groups are able to return to a cooperative status.

Resolving Group Conflict through Team Building

In the previous chapter, we focused a great deal of attention on teams as groups. We discussed the rationale for teams and various types of teams such as cross-functional teams and self-managed teams. Obviously one of the rationales for developing teams is to enable the work of the organization to be accomplished more effectively. We saw the many claimed benefits associated with teams such as improved productivity, streamlining, flexibility, quality, increased employee commitment, and improved customer satisfaction. The causes of intergroup conflict discussed in this chapter indicate that the potential for this type of conflict is present in every type of organization. Thus, there is great interest in team building as a means to reduce intergroup conflict. In fact, many people believe that the development of teams is the wave of the future for American and multinational organizations.[63] In fact, its widespread acceptance in the United States is also being accompanied by similar acceptance in Europe.[64]

team building
Encouraging people who work together to meet as a group in order to identify common goals, improve communications, and resolve conflicts.

The purpose of **team building** is to enable work groups to more effectively get their work done or to work through difficult situations; ultimately, improving their performance.[65] It involves people who work together meeting as a group in order to examine such issues as these:

- Is there an understanding of and commitment to common goals?
- Are we using all of the skills and abilities of group members?
- Is there trust and communication among group members?
- Are we continually improving our performance as a group?

The most popular team-building program focuses on helping members of different departments cooperate and work better with each other.[66] Other popular team-building exercises include improving communication skills, developing trust, encouraging feedback, and navigating office politics.[67]

There is a wide variety of team building exercises in which employees can participate, including having a group of employees go white-water rafting, climbing rock walls, and crossing elevated ropes courses.[68] At Wells Fargo, 73 executives (including CFO Howard Atkins) spend time doing team-building exercises such as helping each other cross "two wobbly wooden planks stretched between two boxes."[69]

At Seagate Technology, approximately 200 engineers and other high-performing employees participate in the annual "Eco Seagate" challenge, a $2 million extreme team-building event that includes hiking, kayaking, and adventure racing in the mountains of New Zealand.[70] Some companies send their employees to participate in professional cooking classes or wine-tasting dinners with executive chefs at the Hyatt Lake Las Vegas, the JW Marriott Las Vegas Resort or the Bellagio Resort.[71] A dispersed sales team from a pharmaceutical company was brought together for a team-building session in which they were divided into groups of five and then given a handheld GPS unit and set of clues. The teams competed to see which team could solve a series of puzzles and complete the course in the shortest amount of time.[72]

Groups of employees that participate in such team-building activities may be an existing or relatively new command or task group. Global organizations have found team building

TABLE 9.2
Where Team Building Might Work in Reducing Intergroup Conflict

1. The work is extremely complex. One individual cannot be expected to make every decision.
2. Group members have the knowledge and expertise about how it should be done.
3. Working as individuals or separate groups has not been productive.
4. External demands often require quick response and decisions.
5. Group members want to assume responsibility for the processes/products of their efforts.
6. The work requires different groups to interact frequently. One group often doesn't know what the other's doing.
7. External demands from competition or technology require a flexible and responsive organization.

Source: Adapted from Nancy Hatch Woodward, "Make the Most of Team Building," *HRMagazine,* September 2006, pp. 72–77; M. D. Maginn, *Effective Teamwork* (Burr Ridge, IL: Irwin Professional Publishing, 1994), pp. 5–7; and J. D. Orsburn, L. Moran, E. Musselwhite, J. Zenger, and C. Perrin, *Self-Directed Work Teams* (Burr Ridge IL: Irwin Professional Publishing, 1990), Chapter 2.

particularly useful when management groups consist of individuals from various national and cultural backgrounds.[73] Research has shown that highly diverse transnational teams outperform moderately diverse groups in the long run.[74] Table 9.2 presents some conditions under which team building may be successful.

The specific aims of team building include setting goals and priorities, analyzing how the group does its work, examining the group's norms and processes for communicating and decision making, and assessing the interpersonal relationships within the group. As each of these aims is undertaken, the group is placed in the position of having to recognize explicitly the contributions, positive and negative, of each group member.[75]

Team Building as a Process

Team building is not a short-term strategy to reduce intergroup conflict. It requires a long-term commitment because it is an ongoing process that is really never completed. Ordinarily, the process begins with a series of *diagnostic* meetings. These meetings, which may last an entire day, allow all of the members of the groups to share their perceptions of problems and causes of conflict with all other members. If the groups are large, subgroups can be formed to discuss the issues and report their ideas to the larger group. Clearly, the purpose of these sessions is to obtain the views of all members and to make these views public. Thus, the ultimate purpose of the diagnostic phase is to openly confront issues and problems that previously were talked about in relative secrecy. Organizations such as DuPont have used the diagnostic step in their successful implementation of team building.[76]

Identifying problems and causes of conflict and reaching consensus as to their priority are important initial steps in the process of team building. Then a *plan of action* must be agreed on. The action plan should require each group member or members to undertake a specific action to alleviate one or more of the problems. If, for example, an executive committee agrees that a major cause of conflict is a lack of understanding and commitment to a set of goals, a subgroup can be appointed to recommend goals to the total group at a subsequent meeting. Other group members can work on other problems. For example, if causes of conflict are identified in the relationships among the members, another subgroup can initiate a process for examining the roles of each member. However, team-building activities do not always require a complex process of diagnostic and plan-of-action meetings, as is illustrated in the next OB at Work, which describes a relatively simple and successful application of team building in a small manufacturing firm.

Management's Role in Building Teams

In the previous chapter, we saw the benefits that can result from the successful implementation of teams. It should be clear that major changes are required in most organizations if teams are to succeed. Teams require resources and authority if they are to gain the flexibility and

OB AT WORK

Resolving Conflict through Team Building in a Small Computer Organization

The chief executive officer of a small computer firm recognized that conflict within his executive group was creating tension between the functional departments. He also realized that his practice of dealing on a one-to-one basis with the executive group members (each of whom headed a functional department) contributed to the tension and conflict. Rather than viewing themselves as team members having a stake in the organization, the functional heads viewed each other as competition. The chief executive's practice of dealing with them individually confirmed their beliefs that they managed relatively independent units.

To counteract the situation, the CEO decided to require the top group to meet twice weekly. One meeting focused on operating problems, the other on personal problems. The ground rule for these meetings was that the group must reach consensus on decisions. After one year of such meetings, the CEO group routinely made company-oriented decisions and the spirit of cooperation replaced the climate of interdepartmental conflict.

The CEO believes that the team-building efforts were a success and overcame certain problems, including

1. Confusion as to roles and relationships within the team.
2. Members having a fairly clear understanding of short-term functional goals but vague understanding of long-term organizational goals.
3. Individuals having technical skills, which puts them on the team, but lacking interpersonal skills, which prevents them from contributing to the team.
4. Members often paying more attention to the tasks of the team than to the relationships among the team members.

The CEO believes that had he not initiated team-building meetings, the group would have continued to focus on task problems, while ignoring the relationship issues.

commitment from members. If team building is to succeed, the following elements are critical to its success:[77]

- *Management commitment.* Team building cannot be "this year's thrust." It requires the commitment of management to understand the early-stage problems that often occur in any transition, such as resistance to change, as well as to ensure the availability of the necessary resources. Team building will fail without a committed management group with a long-term focus.
- *Trust.* Mutual trust between management and employees is a prerequisite for success in team building. Managers must trust that, given sufficient time, employees will support the changes necessary to effectively implement team building. Employees must trust that management really wants to know their opinion. Where there is a great deal of mistrust of management, employees may cynically look at the team-building effort as just another management ploy to get more work done with fewer people.
- *Sharing information.* Obviously, if teams are to support the goals of the organization, they will require information about overall results, including financial information. Here again, mutual trust is critical. Secrecy in many organizations has done little to nurture an environment in which information is willingly shared by management with employees and by managers with other managers. A willingness to share information is critical to successful team building.
- *Training.* Most teams cannot manifest on their own. They usually require training because individuals are being asked to put aside personal concerns and contribute to a group effort. Members therefore usually need training in team building, listening, and communication, which will counteract habits and attitudes left over from the previous work environment.
- *Union partnership.* If the organization is unionized, the union must be an active participant and partner in the team-building effort. Here again, trust and the sharing of information will be critical.

Managing Intergroup Conflict through Stimulation

Throughout this chapter, we have stressed that some conflict is beneficial. This point was made again in Figure 9.2, which includes functional consequences of intergroup conflict. The figure indicates that, out of conflict, change can develop from an awareness of problems and from a creative search for alternative solutions. We've already examined a situation where conflict is dysfunctional because it's too high and requires resolution. But it's also possible that intergroup conflict may be too low and require stimulation to generate action.

While lack of conflict may prove beneficial in the short run, it could lead to situations where one group holds tremendous influence over another. For example, observers of the Japanese style of participative management question whether the lack of conflict between managers and employees in Japanese firms is healthy.[78] This section provides techniques that have stimulated conflict to a functional level, where it contributes positively to organizational performance.[79]

Communication

By intelligent use of the organization's communication channels, a manager can stimulate beneficial conflict. Management can carefully place information into formal channels to create ambiguity, reevaluation, or confrontation. Information that's threatening (e.g., a proposed budget cut) can stimulate functional conflict in a department and improve performance. Carefully planted rumors can also serve a useful purpose. For example, a hospital administrator may start a rumor about a proposed reorganization of the hospital. The purpose is twofold: (1) to stimulate new ideas on how to more effectively carry out the mission of the hospital and (2) to reduce apathy among the staff.

Bringing Outside Individuals into the Group

A technique widely used to bring a stagnant organization or subunit of an organization "back to life" is to hire or transfer in individuals whose attitudes, values, and backgrounds differ from those of the group's present members. Many college faculties consciously seek new members with different backgrounds, often discouraging the hiring of graduates of their own programs. This is to ensure a diversity of viewpoints on the faculty. The technique of bringing in outsiders is also widely used in government and business. Recently, a bank president decided not to promote from within for a newly created position of marketing vice president. Instead, he hired a highly successful executive from the very competitive consumer products field. The bank president felt that while the outsider knew little about marketing financial services, her approach to and knowledge of marketing were what the bank needed to become a strong competitor.

Altering the Organization's Structure

Changing the structure of the organization not only helps resolve intergroup conflict; it also *creates* conflict. For example, suppose a school of business has one large department. The Department of Business Administration includes all faculty members who teach courses in management, marketing, finance, production management, and information systems. Accordingly, the department is rather large, with 32 members under one department chairperson, who reports to the dean. A new dean has recently been hired, and he's considering dividing the business administration unit into several separate departments (e.g., marketing, finance, management), each with five or six members and a chairperson. The reasoning is that reorganizing in this manner will create competition among the groups for resources, students, faculty, and so forth, where none existed before because there was only one group. The question is whether this restructuring will improve organizational performance.

Stimulating Competition

Many managers use various techniques to stimulate competition among groups. Incentives, such as awards and bonuses for outstanding performance, often stimulate competition. If properly utilized, such incentives help maintain a healthy atmosphere of competition that may result in a functional level of conflict. Incentives can be given for least defective parts, highest sales, best teacher, or most new customers as well as in any area where increased conflict is likely to lead to more effective performance.

Managing intergroup conflict through stimulation is a difficult challenge for a manager. It can easily backfire and quickly become dysfunctional conflict.

Summary of Key Points

- Conflict between groups is inevitable in organizations. This conflict may be positive or negative, depending on its impact on the organization's goal achievement.
- Functional conflict represents a confrontation between groups that enhances and benefits the organization's performance.
- Dysfunctional conflict results from a confrontation or interaction between groups that hinders the achievement of organizational goals.
- While most managers try to eliminate conflict, evidence indicates that for most organizations an optimal level of conflict can positively influence organizational performance.
- Intergroup conflict results from such factors as work interdependence, differences in goals, differences in perceptions, and the increasing demand for specialists.
- Dysfunctional conflict causes changes to take place within and between the groups involved. Within the group, there may be an increase in group cohesiveness, a rise in autocratic leadership, a focus on the task, and an emphasis on loyalty. Changes occurring between the groups include distorted perceptions, negative stereotyping, and a decrease in communication.
- One difficult task a manager must confront is diagnosing and managing intergroup conflict. Techniques for resolving intergroup conflict include problem solving, superordinate goals, expansion of resources, avoidance, smoothing, compromise, authority, changing either the people or the organization's structure, and identifying a common enemy. The processes of negotiation and team building are also valuable conflict management techniques. Each of these techniques is useful in specific situations and circumstances and both are becoming increasingly popular among managers.
- Conflict management techniques also exist for situations where the manager diagnoses a level of conflict that's dysfunctional because it's too low. Conflict stimulation techniques include using the communication channels, hiring or transferring in differently oriented individuals, changing the organization's structure, and stimulating competition. The important point is that effective conflict management involves both resolution and stimulation.

Discussion and Review Questions

1. Should the process of negotiation such as the one described in this chapter be implemented to resolve student–faculty conflicts? Why?
2. Think about a time when your department at work or one of your groups at school (for a group project) experienced a conflict with another department or group. How did your group respond?
3. Some individuals believe that compromise isn't a good conflict resolution technique because there's no distinct winner and the decision reached is probably not ideal for either group. What are your beliefs about compromise as a conflict resolution technique?

4. Describe how the three types of work interdependence could each lead to conflict between two groups within a specific student organization you're familiar with.
5. How can team building help develop trust between members of different departments or groups at an organization?
6. Is competition for grades among students functional or dysfunctional? Why?
7. Some individuals believe that conflict is necessary for change to take place. Comment.
8. Why do you think many managers avoid confrontations with their employees? Is this a functional and effective way to behave as a manager? Explain.
9. After completing the self-assessment in the OB and Your Career feature at the start of this chapter, were you surprised at the results of your preferred conflict-handling style? Do you agree with the findings? Explain.
10. What is meant when it's said that a manager must be able to diagnose intergroup conflict situations? How can a manager obtain these diagnostic skills?

Taking It to the Net

Negotiating Tips

Due to a sluggish economy and slashed travel budgets, the chemical manufacturing company you work for has experienced a 10 percent decrease in sales over the past six months. As the new vice president of purchasing, you have been asked to negotiate a 10 percent discount from each of the vendors that supply your firm with raw materials. If successful, your company will achieve its year-end profit goals. Knowing how important it is to understand the dynamics of negotiations (e.g., the other side's personality, the different types of negotiation tactics, and so on), you turn to the following Web sites on the Internet to learn more about how to succeed in negotiating a reduction in vendor prices:

1. www.bizhelp24.com/personal/negotiation-skills.html (click on "2", "3" and "4" under Article Index section)
2. www.batna.com (click on "powerful tips")
3. www.brodow.com/Articles/NegotiatingTips.html (see ten tips for negotiating)

Case for Analysis: *A Successful Partnership at Ford-Mazda*

While international joint ventures among auto manufacturers make great sense, often they don't make great profits. For example, for many years, auto giant General Motors bailed out loss-plagued Isuzu, in which at one point it owned a 49 percent stake. The list of cross-cultural disappointments goes on: Chrysler-Mitsubishi, Daimler-Chrysler, and Fiat-Nissan have all produced as much rancor as rewards.

Ford-Mazda is the exception. Their marriage has weathered disagreements over specific projects, trade disputes between Japan and the United States, and even allegations by the Big Three that Mazda and other Japanese rivals were dumping minivans in the United States. The alliance, founded when Ford stepped in to rescue the struggling Japanese carmaker in 1979, has stood firm for over 30 years. With Ford owning 11 percent of Mazda, the two companies have cooperated on several new vehicles and exchanged valuable expertise—Ford in international marketing and finance, Mazda in manufacturing and product development.

Ford and Mazda have worked jointly on several auto models; usually Ford would do most of the styling and Mazda would make key engineering contributions. Jointly worked cars include the Ford Escort and Mercury Tracer models, the subcompact Festiva, the sporty Ford Probe and Mercury Capri, and the Tribute and Explorer SUVs. The Ford-aided Mazdas are the MX-6, 323, Protégé, and Navajo. In all, approximately one of every four Ford cars sold in the United States has benefitted from some degree of Mazda involvement—everything from manufacturing methods to steering designs—whereas two of every five Mazdas has some Ford influence. The Ford-Mazda relationship extends beyond U.S. borders. In 2010, a joint venture between Ford and Mazda in Thailand began producing passenger cars export to several Asian countries.

Ford and Mazda can call on some hard-learned principles for managing a successful strategic alliance, many of which would apply to ties in any industry. The secrets to the Ford-Mazda success are

Keep top management involved. The boss must set a tone for the relationship. Otherwise, middle managers will resist ceding partial control of a project to a partner.

Meet often, and often informally. Meetings should be at all levels and should include time for socializing. Trust can't be built solely around a boardroom table.

Use a matchmaker. A third party can mediate disputes, suggest new ways of approaching the partner, and offer an independent sounding board.

Maintain your independence. Independence helps both parties hone the areas of expertise that made them desirable partners in the first place.

Allow no "sacrifice deals." Every project must be viable for each partner. Senior management must see that an overall balance is maintained.

Appoint a monitor. Someone must take primary responsibility for monitoring all aspects of the alliance.

Anticipate cultural differences. Differences may be corporate or national. Stay flexible and try to place culturally sensitive executives in key posts.

Underlying these principles is the idea that benign neglect is no basis for a partnership. Or, as Ford president Phillip E. Benton Jr. stated, "There's a lot of hard work in making it work."

DISCUSSION QUESTIONS

1. Why might there be high potential for conflict in relationships such as the one enjoyed by Ford-Mazda?
2. What means of managing group conflicts, as discussed in Chapter 9, are used in the Ford-Mazda partnership?
3. Why do you think the Ford-Mazda partnership has been so successful, while many others (including those listed at the beginning of the case) haven't been?

Sources: "Ford to Invest in Thai Car Plant Amid Demand in Asia," *WSJ.com,* June 24, 2010; "Autos: Why Japan's B-Team is Hot," *Businessweek,* December 28, 2009, p. 33; "Mulally Says Ford to Maintain Good Ties with Mazda," *Knight Ridder Tribune Business News,* February 27, 2007, p. 1; Norihiko Shirouzu, "Mazda Motor Looks to Plug Midsize Hole in U.S. Lineup," *Wall Street Journal,* March 4, 2004, p. D.5; Todd Zaun, "Mazda Retools, as Its President Gets More Calls for a Quick Fix," *Wall Street Journal,* November 20, 2000, p. A16; "The Partners," *Businessweek,* February 10, 1992, pp. 102–7; Stratford Shersan, "Are Strategic Alliances Working?" *Fortune,* September 21, 1992, pp. 77–78; and Arvind Parkhe, "Interfirm Diversity, Organizational Learning, and Longevity in Global Strategic Alliances," *Journal of International Business Studies* (Winter 1991): 579–602.

Experiential Exercise: *The Old Stack Problem*

OBJECTIVES

1. To closely examine the dynamics of intergroup competition.
2. To illustrate a group's effectiveness in solving a problem.

STARTING THE EXERCISE

Step 1: Group problem solving (30 minutes). Divide into groups of four to six persons each. Each group member should read "The Problem" (next page). The best procedure is for each person to develop a solution independently and for the group to spend time discussing these solutions without evaluating them. Then solutions should be evaluated and the best solution adopted.

The problem may be assigned in advance of class to give students more time to develop solutions. However, the final discussion and selection process should be done as a group in the classroom.

Step 2: Select judges and spokespeople (5 minutes). Each group should select one member to serve on a panel of judges to select the best solution. A spokesperson must also be selected to present the solution to the panel of judges.

Step 3: Present solutions (15 minutes). Spokespeople for each group will present their group's solution to the judges and the remainder of the class. A chalkboard or flip chart should be used to illustrate the solution along with the spokesperson's explanation. The explanation should be brief and concise, and spokespeople may not criticize other solutions. Spokespeople should provide quality arguments in support of their solutions.

Step 4: Straw vote (5 minutes). After all group solutions have been presented, the judges may think about the solutions for one or two minutes. Then judges will state in turn which solution they prefer. *Judges must make their judgments independently, without discussion among themselves.* Judges are asked simply to state the solution they prefer. They don't explain their reasons for voting. The instructor should record the number of votes given for each solution on the chalkboard or flip chart next to that solution.

Step 5: Modified problem solving (10 minutes). Student groups re-form and discuss their approach. Judges and spokespeople return to their original groups. At this time, the groups may not change the basic strategy of their solution, but they may provide refinements. Groups are encouraged to compare their solution to other solutions at this point and may instruct the spokesperson to present weaknesses in other solutions as well as strengths of their own. The group also has the freedom to nominate a new spokesperson or judge at this time.

Step 6: Restate solutions (10 minutes). The group spokespeople briefly restate the solutions using the earlier illustration. Minor modifications can be made. Spokespeople are encouraged to point out the strengths of their group's solutions and to criticize other solutions. Spokespeople's goal is to persuade the judges that their group's solution is best.

Step 7: Final vote. The judges are given one or two minutes to individually decide which solution to vote for. Judges may not discuss the solutions among themselves, and they must state their vote out loud. The instructor will indicate the number of votes next to each solution's illustration. The solution that receives the most votes is the winner.

EXHIBIT 1

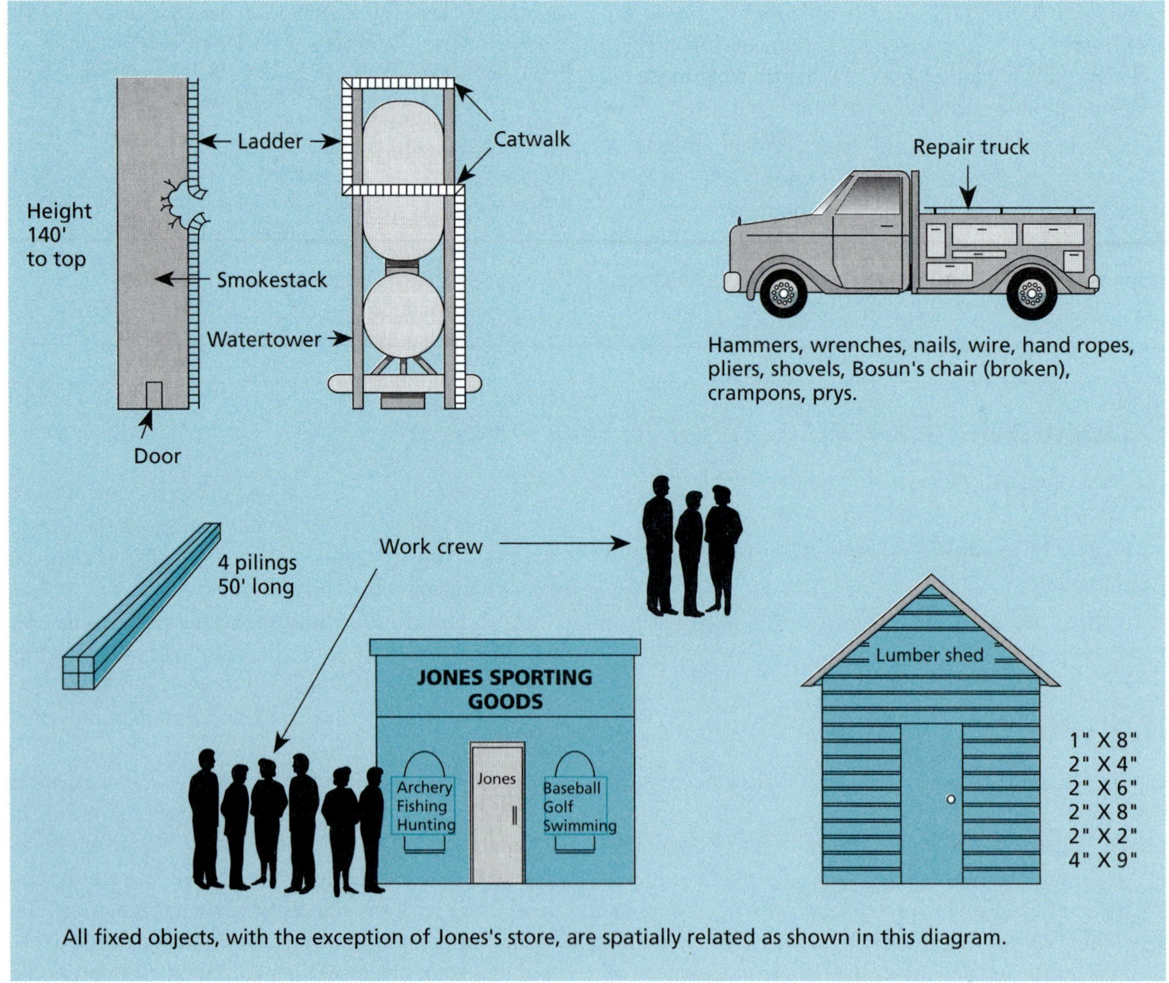

All fixed objects, with the exception of Jones's store, are spatially related as shown in this diagram.

Step 8: Discussion (15 minutes). The class as a whole should reflect on their experience and discuss what happened. Students are encouraged to be self-reflective about their feelings toward their own group's solution, toward the judges, and so on. Judges are encouraged to express their feelings about any pressures they felt from the group to vote in a certain way. The instructor or students may also wish to compare their observations to theories of intergroup behavior as illustrated in lectures or readings. The following questions may help guide that discussion.

1. Did any examples of scapegoating occur? Did losing groups express dissatisfaction or unfairness with the judges or the evaluation process?
2. Did any groups pressure the judges to act as a representative of their group rather than to vote in an unbiased fashion? Did judges feel pressure to represent their group even if pressure was not overtly expressed?
3. Did any groups develop a superiority complex, wherein they truly believed that their own group solution was best although from an objective perspective the solution may not have been best?
4. What were the reactions of the winning group and losing groups? Did winners seem happy and satisfied while losers seemed discontented with one another or with the exercise?
5. During the second round of presentations, were certain solutions singled out for more criticism? Were these solutions the ones that received the most votes in the straw ballot, as if people were trying to tear down the strongest contender?
6. How does this group exercise compare to functioning of groups in the real world?

These groups existed temporarily, while groups in the real world engage in real competitions and have strong and lasting commitments. Would representatives of real-world groups tend to reflect group wishes or to reach unbiased decisions? How might intergroup difficulties be overcome in organizations?

THE PROBLEM

An explosion has ripped a hole in a brick smokestack. The stack appears to be perfectly safe, but a portion of the access ladder has been ripped away and the remainder loosened. Your engineers need to inspect the damage immediately to determine whether the stack may collapse. How do you get one of your engineers up to inspect the hole safely and efficiently?

The smokestack is 140 feet high. The structure next to the smokestack is a water tower. Your solution should use only those materials shown in Exhibit 1, including what you assume to be in the truck and sporting goods store.

CHAPTER TEN

Power and Politics

Learning Objectives

After completing Chapter 10, you should be able to

Understand
The difference between power and authority.

Describe
The five interpersonal power bases.

Discuss
How subunits within an organization acquire and use power.

Identify
When an individual is using impression management tactics.

Comprehend
The reasons perceived authority can influence a person's behavior.

The Personal Power of Great Business Leaders

Great leaders have one thing in common: they realize that having a vision is not enough to achieve the kinds of revolutionary and large-scale ideas they dream of. To make things happen and to influence others, great leaders need to be passionate about their vision and have the *personal power* to enact it. For example, such business leaders as Warren Buffet of Berkshire Hathaway, Michael Dell of Dell Computer, Meg Whitman of eBay, Sir Richard Branson of Virgin Atlantic Airways, Oprah Winfrey of Harpo Productions, Steve Chen and Chad Hurley of YouTube, Jeff Bezos of Amazon.com, Jack Dorsey of Twitter, Henry Ford of Ford Motors, Katharine Graham of The Washington Post, and Sam Walton of Walmart had strong visions of what could be. They were able to make their visions into reality because they had acquired and used the necessary power to do so. Great leaders make things happen by utilizing four different types of personal power. These include the power to

Overcome resistance to change.

Mobilize resources in the required direction.

Manage their own ambitions so they don't lose perspective in the process of leading.

These areas of power can come from a variety of sources, including a leader's personal characteristics (e.g., amount of charisma or emotional intelligence), position within an organizational hierarchy, and/or ability to reward or punish other people's behavior. When used in an appropriate way, personal sources of power can make the difference between seeing a dream come true or forever wondering what could have been if the idea got off the ground.

Sources: Adapted from Chris Nuttall, "How Twitter Inventor's Square Is Taking Shape," *Financial Times*, December 23, 2009, p. 10; Bill Joy, "The Google Guys," *Time*, April 18, 2005, pp. 80–81; Ronald Grover, "Move Over, MySpace," *Businessweek*, December 26, 2005, p. 24; Eric J. Bolland, "Mastering Power," *Executive Excellence* 20, no. 10 (2003): pp. 15–20; and Jeffrey Gandz, "Global Leadership and Personal Power," *Ivey Business Journal* (May/June 2000): 10–12.

Power is a pervasive part of the fabric of organizational life.[1] Getting things done requires power.[2] Every day, managers in public and private organizations acquire and use power to accomplish goals and, in many cases, to strengthen their own position. A person's success or failure at using or reacting to power is largely determined by understanding power, knowing how and when to use it, and being able to anticipate its probable effects.

This chapter explains power and its uses in organizational settings. We also examine the bases of power, the need for power, and the relationship between power and organizational politics. The chapter indicates that power is not a dirty secret but is actually a mechanism used continually to achieve organizational, group, and individual goals.

Power and Authority

power
Ability to get others to do what one wants them to do.

The study of power and its effects is important to understanding how organizations operate. Every interaction and every social relationship in an organization involves an exercise of power.[3] How organizational subunits and individuals are controlled is related to the issue of power. In an organizational setting, **power** is simply the ability to get others to do what one wants them to do.[4] When used for the good of the organization, power can be a positive force for higher levels of organizational effectiveness. However, when power is used in selfish or destructive ways, it can dramatically decrease the morale and productivity of employees in an organization.

Power involves a relationship between two or more people. Robert Dahl, a political scientist, captures this important relational focus when he defines power as "A has power over B to the extent that he can get B to do something B would not otherwise do."[5] A person or group cannot have power in isolation; power has to be exercised or have the potential for being exercised in relation to some other person or group.

Some feel that power is best used in isolation by one person over other people. Conversely, the power-sharing argument asserts that unless some power is shared, productivity, quality, and customer satisfaction will never reach their highest potential levels. However, this raises the problem of determining how to implement power sharing. Power sharing requires time to develop within an organization's culture. It cannot be forced on people, and proper leadership and vision are needed to implement the process.[6] Time is needed to develop (1) better lines of communication, (2) more trust, and (3) openness between the power sharers—managers and subordinates or subunits. Because organizations have for many years relied on authority hierarchies to accomplish goals, it is unreasonable to expect managers simply to begin sharing their power with others without some resistance.

The literature distinguishes between power and authority. Max Weber was the first to call attention to differences between these two concepts.[7] He believed that power involves force and coercion. Authority, however, is a subset of power. Much narrower in scope, authority does not carry the implication of force. Rather, it involves a "suspension of judgment" on the part of its recipients. **Authority** is the formal power that a person has because of the position in the organization. Directives or orders from a manager in an authoritative position are followed because they must be followed. That is, persons in higher positions have legal authority over subordinates in lower positions. In the authority hierarchy, the chief executive officer (CEO) is above the district manager, who is above the salesperson. Authority has the following characteristics:

authority
Formal power a person holds because of his or her position in the organizational hierarchy.

1. It is vested in a person's position. An individual has authority because of the position that he holds, not because of any specific personal characteristics.
2. It is accepted by subordinates. The individual in an official authority position exercises authority and can gain compliance because she has a legitimate right.
3. Authority is used vertically and flows from the top down in the hierarchy of an organization.

Influence is a word we often come across when studying power. We agree with Henry Mintzberg and others that making a distinction between *influence* and *power* adds little to understanding.[8] Therefore, we use the terms influence and power interchangeably throughout this chapter.

Power can be derived from many sources. How it's obtained in an organization depends to a large extent on the type of power being sought. Power can be derived from interpersonal, structural, and situational bases. John French and Bertram Raven suggested five interpersonal bases of power: legitimate, reward, coercive, expert, and referent.[9]

Interpersonal Power

Legitimate Power

legitimate power
A person's ability to influence others by being in a more powerful position.

Legitimate power is a person's ability to influence because of position. For example, a vice president at a company has more power than middle managers, first-line supervisors, and entry-level employees. In theory, organizational equals (e.g., all first-line supervisors) have the same amount of legitimate power. However, each person with legitimate power uses it with a personal flair. Legitimate power is similar to the concept of authority.

Subordinates play a major role in the exercise of legitimate power. If subordinates view the use of power as legitimate, they comply. However, the culture, customs, and value systems of an organization determine the limits of legitimate power.[10] Some boards of directors at publically traded corporations like AIG, Hewlett-Packard, Disney, and Fannie Mae removed CEOs (thus stripping them of their legitimate power) in the past for "not delivering promised shareholder value, committing ethical or accounting lapses, or a combination of both."[11]

Reward Power

reward power
A person's ability to reward the behavior of others.

A person derives power from the ability to reward compliance. **Reward power** is often used to back up the use of legitimate power. If followers value the rewards or potential rewards that the person can provide (recognition, a good job assignment, a pay raise, or a promotion), they are more likely to respond to orders, requests, and directions. For example, a sales manager who can reward salespeople with large cash bonuses, expanded client lists, or additional entertainment funds can exert reward power. Reward power works best when employees understand how they can achieve rewards and are kept abreast of their status toward earning the reward.[12] A type of reward becoming more prevalent is granting ownership through issuing stock shares to employees when they reach certain milestones. In this way, employees are further encouraged to work harder and smarter as the value of their ultimate reward is dependent on organizational results.[13]

Of course, reward power that reinforces the wrong behaviors (e.g., pay-for-performance financial incentives that reward short-term profits instead of prudent long-term decisions) has the potential to motivate employees to take actions that may not be in the best interest of the organization. For example, well-established financial institutions such as Lehman Brothers and Merrill Lynch failed during the recent financial crisis partly due to their executives taking extreme risks to receive large financial incentives for meeting or exceeding performance targets.[14]

Coercive Power

coercive power
Capability to punish noncompliance of followers.

The opposite of reward power is **coercive power**, the power to punish subordinates. Followers may comply because they fear the individual who has power over them. A manager may block a promotion or fire a subordinate for poor performance. These practices, and the fear that they'll be used, constitute coercive power. Although punishment may result in some unexpected side effects, it's a form of coercive power that's still used to bring about compliance or to correct nonproductive behavior in organizations. For example, when he was CEO of General Electric, Jack Welch fired 10 percent of the company's employees each year during his reign due to his discontent with their job performance.[15] For this and similar actions with other organizations, Welch earned the name "Neutron Jack." Managers tend to use coercive power in situations where large numbers of employees are being supervised.[16]

Expert Power

expert power
The power to influence others based on special expertise.

A person with special expertise that's highly valued has **expert power**. Experts have power even when their rank is low. An individual may possess expertise on technical, administrative, or personal matters. The more difficult it is to replace the expert, the greater the expert power she possesses.

Expert power is a personal characteristic, while legitimate, reward, and coercive power are largely prescribed by the organization. An administrative assistant who has a relatively low-level organizational position may have high expert power because she knows the details of operating the business—where everything is or how to handle difficult situations. Another example of someone with expert power would be a co-worker who's exceptionally skilled at making high-impact presentations. Her co-workers might ask her to help whenever they have to make a major presentation for clients.

Referent Power

referent power
Power based on charisma due to personality or style of behavior.

Many individuals identify with and are influenced by a person because of the latter's personality or behavioral style. The charisma of the person is the basis of **referent power**.

A person with charisma is admired because of her personality, vision, and the means she uses to speak from her heart.[17] The strength of a person's charisma is an indication of her referent power. *Charisma* is a term often used to describe the magnetic personalities of some politicians, entertainers, or sports figures. Some managers are also regarded by their subordinates as charismatic. For example, Lee Iacocca, the former CEO of Chrysler, was voted in a survey of 7,000 business executives as one of the most charismatic business leaders over the past 100 years. At a time when the U.S. automobile industry was undergoing dramatic changes, Iacocca responded by introducing radical changes in the way the company did business (e.g., adding union members to the board of directors and launching the minivan) and taking a $1 a year salary until the firm returned to profitability.[18] However, some critics contend that charasmatic individuals do not always make the best leaders.[19]

The five bases of interpersonal power can be divided into two major categories: organizational and personal. Legitimate, reward, and coercive power are primarily prescribed by the organization, the position, formal groups, or specific interaction patterns. A person's legitimate power can be changed by transferring the person, rewriting the job description, or reducing the person's power by restructuring the organization. In contrast, expert and referent power are very personal. A person has expertise, or he develops a set of credentials or the image characteristics of an expert. A person has or does not have charisma. It can't be tampered with, modified, or developed through training programs. It's a personal style that's quite individualized.

The five types of interpersonal power aren't independent. On the contrary, managers can use these power bases effectively in various combinations in differing circumstances. Several studies have examined issues related to contextual uses of power. One study of organizations found that legitimate, expert, and referent power were the three most important reasons employees reported for doing what a peer or boss requested.[20] Two other studies identified a strong correlation between managers' levels and use of expert and referent power and employees' emotional involvement and commitment to their jobs.[21] A related study described how gossip, or informal communication, can either increase or decrease the interpersonal power of an employee.[22]

An interesting study conducted in three organizations investigated whether gender differences existed in subordinates' perceptions of managers' power.[23] Results indicated that male and female managers did not show significant differences in reward, coercive, legitimate, and referent bases of power. However, subordinates rated female managers higher than male managers on expert power. Male managers with female subordinates were rated lower on expert power than other gender combinations. Thus, sex-role stereotypes appear not to bias perceptions of power possession. Rather, it appears that an individual manager's level in the organizational power structure has a greater effect on employee perceptions of power than does the manager's gender.[24]

An interesting aspect about interpersonal power is the fact that it can be cultivated and developed not only by managers, but also by entry-level employees and first-line supervisors. The OB and Your Career feature on the next page examines how this can be accomplished.

Need for Power

Throughout history, human beings have been fascinated by power. In ancient Chinese writings, concern about power is clearly expressed—the taming power of the great, the power of light, the power of the dark. Early religious writings contain numerous references to persons who possess or acquire power. Historical records show differences in the extent to which individuals have pursued, feared, enjoyed, and misused power. Some have been

OB AND YOUR CAREER Build Your Interpersonal Power

Some entry-level employees feel controlled at times by rigid organizational policies, strict senior managers, ambiguous departmental politics, and other factors over which they feel they have no control. In some ways, these relative newcomers may feel powerless to control key aspects of their jobs. In the extreme, this powerlessness was captured by the 1998 comedy *Office Space* by 20th Century Fox. In the movie, Peter Gibbons (played by Ron Livingston) is a software programmer with a dull, thankless job, who is convinced that every day of his life is even worse than the one before it. His supervisor, William "Bill" Lumbergh (played by Gary Cole) tried to keep tight control over his every movement.

Do you have to wait until you're a supervisor or manager before you gain interpersonal power? No, starting right away as an entry-level employee, you can begin building your interpersonal power within an organization. This way, you can avoid becoming like Peter Gibbons in *Office Space*.

You can develop each of the following sources of interpersonal power:

1. **Expert power:** *Become as proficient as possible in key aspects of your job.* Learn everything there is to know about what you're responsible for doing each day. If you're a customer service representative, learn everything you can about your customers' needs, the organization's services and products, and the organization's policies for solving customers' problems. These same principles apply to every job, whether you're an auditor, sales representative, analyst, assistant, or programmer. Learn as much as you can and become the "go-to" person (i.e., co-workers, customers, and supervisors go to you to get answers to their problems).
2. **Reward power:** *Reward people around you in nonfinancial ways.* You can reward co-workers, customers, and others without showering them with money and promotions. If you see a few co-workers who stayed at work all weekend to get an important assignment finished on time, you can point out to their supervisor how hard they worked to get the job done. You are providing an indirect reward for your colleagues. It usually carries more weight when a third party (in this case, you) provides an unsolicited compliment about the hard work of others (your colleagues).
3. **Referent power:** *If you have a way with people, then use it.* If people would describe you as influential or always able to get your way, then you already have referent power. This power can be used to persuade customers to purchase your firm's services or products or to convince your supervisor to increase the budget of your section of the department. If you're in the process of becoming more persuasive, then continue to build this skill. A good way to build your referent power is to watch how someone who already has this type of power uses it to get things done within the organization. This person can serve as a role model and with observation and practice, you can also become more influential with those around you.

known to use power in a destructive manner that harms their organizations.[25] The image of those who seek power is, for the most part, quite negative. For example, power seekers have been portrayed in the following ways:[26]

Neurotics covering up feelings of inferiority, anxiety, or hatred.

Persons substituting power for lack of affection, being alone, or being deprived of friendship.

Those attempting to compensate for some childhood deprivation.

need for power (n Pow)
Desire to influence others.

David McClelland proposes that power can be responsibly sought and used.[27] The **need for power** (or **n Pow** as he refers to it) is defined by McClelland as the desire to have an effect on others. This effect may be shown basically in three ways: (1) by strong action, by giving help or advice, by controlling someone; (2) by action that produces emotion in others; and (3) by a concern for reputation.

Research has attempted to determine how people high in n Pow behave as contrasted with people low in n Pow. In general, individuals high in n Pow are competitive and aggressive, are interested in prestige possessions (e.g., an expensive car), prefer action situations, and join a number of groups. In an organizational setting, results of a recent study somewhat surprisingly found that the degree of a manager's need for power is correlated with success.[28]

The most effective managers disciplined and controlled their desire for power so that it was directed toward the organization as a whole—not toward their own personal aggrandizement. These individuals tended not to display personal insecurity; rather, they possessed great emotional maturity and a democratic, coaching managerial style.[29]

Structural and Situational Power

Power is primarily prescribed by the structure of the organization.[30] The organization's structural arrangements allocate decision-making discretion to various positions. Structure also establishes patterns of communication and the flow of information. Thus, organizational structure creates formal power and authority by specifying certain individuals to perform specific jobs and make certain decisions.

We've already discussed how formal position is associated with power and authority. Certain rights, responsibilities, and privileges accrue from a person's position. Other forms of structural power exist because of resources, decision making, and information.[31]

Resources

Rosabeth Kanter argues convincingly that power stems from access to resources, information, and support and from the ability to get cooperation in doing necessary work.[32] Power occurs when a person has open channels to resources (money, workers, technology, materials, and customers). In organizations, vital resources are allocated downward along the lines of the hierarchy.[33] The top-level manager has more power to allocate resources than do managers further down in the managerial hierarchy. The lower-level manager receives resources granted by top-level managers. To ensure compliance with organizational goals, top-level managers (e.g., presidents, vice presidents, directors) allocate resources on the basis of performance and compliance. Thus, a top-level manager usually has power over a lower-level manager, who must receive resources from above to accomplish goals.

The *dependency* relationship exists because of limited resources and division of labor.[34] The division of labor (e.g., positions in the hierarchy) grants upper management, by position, the privilege of allocating limited resources.[35] Without adequate compliance with top management's goals and requests, a lower-level manager cannot receive the necessary resources to do the job. On the other hand, a wise top management team knows that to improve performance, lower-level managers must be given adequate power and resources to control their destinies.[36]

Decision-Making Power

The degree to which individuals or subunits (e.g., a department or a special project group) can affect decision making determines their level of power. A person or subunit with power can influence how the decision-making process occurs, what alternatives are considered, and when a decision is made. For example, conscientious employees who are closer to the details of a complicated issue (e.g., risk losing a customer over a misunderstanding about pricing terms) can help their bosses avoid making hasty decisions—first by describing the issue in full and then by explaining why the decision needs to be made carefully.[37] Conversely, managers need to provide employees with parameters for making decisions, thereby simultaneously delegating power and guiding the use of it toward organizational objectives.[38]

Information Power

There is an old saying that "information is power." Having access to relevant and important information gives power. Information is the basis for making effective decisions. Thus, those who possess information needed to make optimal decisions have power. The accountant's position in the organization structure may not accurately portray the power she wields. Accountants do not generally have a particularly strong or apparent interpersonal power base in an organization; however, they actually have a significant amount of power because they control important information such as an organization's tax liabilities, profits, losses, expenses and capital expenditures. Likewise, a person's power may be weakened by sharing too much information, for it reduces his relative share of this valuable commodity.[39]

A true picture of a person's power is provided not only by the person's position but also by the person's access to relevant information.

Many organizational situations illustrate how different sources can create powerful and powerless managers. Powerful managers exist because they allocate required resources, make crucial decisions, and have access to important information. Powerful managers also seek out and use information from all their employees.[40] For example, a secretary in charge of registering volunteers in a clinical trial for a new antihistamine drug noticed the volunteers who came in for their routine medical check ups were acting unusually cheerful. She reported this observation to the managers of the trial, who concluded that, although the drug did not work as an antihistamine, it had the potential to be marketed as an antidepressant drug.[41] Although this secretary did not hold a powerful position, she possessed the "right" information that helped inform important managerial decisions at her organization. Powerful managers are adept at using information in a similar manner.

Powerless managers, however, lack the resources, information, and decision-making prerogatives needed to be productive. Here are two examples that demonstrate the powerlessness of managers.[42] Line supervisors may supervise too closely, fail to train subordinates, or jump in and try to do the job themselves. In contrast, staff professionals (e.g., HR specialists) may isolate themselves from the rest of company and resist change, making them conservative risk takers. In both cases, the line supervisors and staff professionals are acting in a manner that decreases their power within the organization.

Upward Flow of Power

Most people think of power as being exerted in a downward direction. It's true that individuals in positions at the lower end of the power hierarchy generally have less power than do individuals in higher-level positions. However, power can also be exercised up the organization.[43] In sociological terms, a person exerting power upward has personal power but no authority.

The discussion of legitimate authority suggests that individuals in higher-level positions (supervisors) can exert only as much power as individuals in lower-level positions (subordinates) accept. The concept of subordinate power can be linked to expertise, location, and information. Significant upward power or influence can sometimes be exerted by a relatively low-ranking administrative assistant, computer programmer, or sales associate who possesses expertise, is in a position to interact with important individuals, or has access to and control of important information.[44] Expertise, location, and information control are important determinants of the power potential of employees at lower levels of the hierarchy.

Two important sources of upward influence have been referred to as manipulative persuasion and manipulation.[45] *Manipulative persuasion* is a person's direct attempt to disguise the true persuasion objective. This is the hidden-agenda ploy. Through persuasive skills, the individual accumulates power to gain an objective. For example, a manager trying to have a poor worker transferred may present only the strengths of the worker to a project manager looking for people for a new assignment. Although the manager's true objective is to unload the worker on someone else, that objective is hidden within the manager's persuasive presentation of the employee's strengths.

Manipulation refers to the form of influence in which both the objective and the attempt are concealed. For example, instead of providing customer complaints to a manager as they're received, the clerk receiving the complaints may arrange them in such a way as to place other employees or a department in a more or less favorable light.[46] If the clerk arranges the incoming complaints so that the manager in charge reprimands a departmental supervisor whom the clerk doesn't like, the clerk's action would be considered manipulation in the upward direction. A recent example of upward influence would be how Bernie Madoff allegedly evaded for years the U. S. Securities and Exchange Commission while he engaged in a $65 billion fraud scheme.[47] He was eventually caught and is currently serving a multi-decade prison term for his manipulative actions.

Organizational level has been found to be inversely related to a manager's propensity to use upward influence appeals.[48] This makes sense as managers at higher levels would likely feel they have enough authority to exercise influence, while managers and other employees lower down in an organizational hierarchy may feel less confident about exercising influence without the backing of higher authority.

Interdepartmental Power

To this point, the primary focus has been on individual power and how it's obtained. However, interdepartmental power is also important. Even though all vice presidents of departments at the same level in the managerial hierarchy are supposed to have the same amount of power, this isn't usually the case. Some vice presidents have more power than others by virtue of being in a particular unit or department.[49] For example, in some companies, marketing may wield the most power. In others, production or engineering might have the upper hand.

strategic contingency
Event or activity of crucial importance to completing a project or accomplishing a goal.

The strategic contingency theory focuses on subunit power. A **strategic contingency** is an event or activity that's extremely important for accomplishing organizational goals.[50] Hinnings and associates studied the strategic contingency explanation of power in 28 subunits of seven manufacturing organizations in Canada and the United States.[51] Engineering, marketing, production, and accounting departments were studied. Each subunit interacted with the three others. The researchers examined various indicators of power, such as substitutability (ability of the subunit to obtain alternative performance for its activities), work flow pervasiveness (the degree to which the work flows of a subunit were linked to the work flows of other subunits), uncertainty (the lack of information about future events), and work flow immediacy (the speed and severity with which the work flow of a subunit affected the final outputs of the organization). Researchers found that only a combination of high values on all the power indicators gave a subunit dominant, first-rank power. Thus, being able to deal with uncertainty alone or possessing substitutability power alone does not provide a subunit with dominant power over other subunits. The model in Figure 10.1 suggests that subunit power, the power differential between subunits, is influenced by (1) the ability to cope with uncertainty, (2) the centrality of the subunit, and (3) the substitutability of the subunit.

Coping with Uncertainty

Unanticipated events can create problems for any organization or subunit. Therefore, the subunits most capable of coping with uncertainty typically acquire power:

> Uncertainty itself does not give power; coping gives power. If organizations allocate to their various subunits task areas that vary in uncertainty, then those subunits that cope most effectively with the most uncertainty should have the most power within the organization.[52]

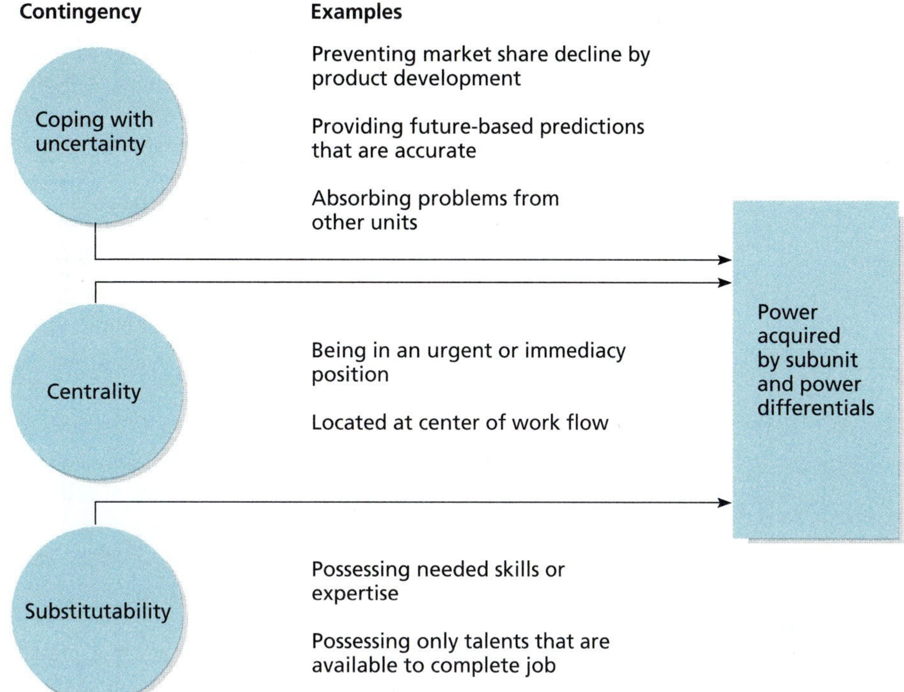

FIGURE 10.1
A Strategic Contingency Model of Subunit Power

Sources: This figure is based on the early research work conducted by D. J. Hickson, C. R. Hinnings, C. A. Lee, R. E. Schneck, and J. M. Pennings. See Hickson et al., "A Strategic Contingency Theory of Intraorganizational Power," *Administrative Science Quarterly* (June 1971): 216–29; and C. R. Hinnings, D. J. Hickson, J. M. Pennings, and R. E. Schneck, "Structural Conditions of Intraorganizational Power," *Administrative Science Quarterly* (March 1974): 22–44.

Coping activities comprise three types. In *coping by prevention,* a subunit works at reducing the probability that some difficulty will arise. For example, designing a new product to prevent lost sales because of new competition in the marketplace is a coping technique. Another example would be to hire two individuals when only one is actually needed, because of expected turnover.

Coping by information is another type. For example, changes to national tax laws would create uncertainty regarding how much more an organization would have to pay in taxes over the next several years. The organization's accounting department could cope with this uncertainty by learning the new laws and estimating the impact of these changes on the organization's tax liabilities.

Coping by absorption, the third type, involves dealing with uncertainty as it impacts the subunit. For example, one subunit might take a problem employee from another subunit and then attempt to retrain and redirect that employee. This is done as a favor, so that the other subunit does not have to go through the pain of terminating or continuing to put up with the employee. The subunit that takes in the problem employee gains the respect of other subunits, which results in an increase in power. Regarding the relation of coping with uncertainty to power, the more a subunit copes with uncertainty, the greater its power within the organization.[53]

Centrality

The subunits most central to the flow of work in an organization typically acquire power. For example, the research and development employees at Apple are powerful because the company thrives on new product releases, with each new product perceived as "better" than the previous one. No subunit has zero centrality since all are somehow interlinked with other subunits. A measure of centrality is the degree to which the work of the subunit contributes to the final output of the organization.[54] A subunit in a position to affect other subunits has some degree of centrality and, therefore, power.

A subunit also possesses power if its activities have a more immediate or urgent impact than that of other subunits. For example, Ben Taub is a major public hospital in Houston. The emergency and trauma treatment subunit is crucial. Because failures in this subunit could result in the death of emergency victims, it possesses significant power within the hospital. The psychiatric subunit does important work that's not as crucial and immediate. Therefore, it has significantly less subunit power than the emergency and trauma treatment subunit. This leads to two main centrality propositions:

1. The higher the pervasiveness of the work flows of a subunit, the greater is its power within the organization,
2. The higher the immediacy of the work flows of a subunit, the greater is its power within the organization.[55]

Substitutability

Substitutability
Extent to which other subunits can perform the job or task of a subunit.

Substitutability refers to other subunits' ability to perform activities of a particular subunit. If an organization has or can obtain alternative sources of skill, information, and resources to perform the job done by a subunit, the subunit's power is diminished. On one hand, training subunits lose power if training work can be done by line managers or outsourced to consultants. On the other hand, a subunit with unique skills and competencies is hard to duplicate or replace; this increases the subunit's power over other subunits.

Changes in the labor market may result in changes in a subunit's power. Today, there's a shortage of robotic technical specialists. Since robotic technicians are difficult to replace, train, and substitute for, the robotic subunit of an organization possesses inordinate power. Of course, other reasons exist for the emergence of powerful robotics subunits, such as their access to technical information, their centrality, and the productivity improvements that they bring about.

Hinnings and associates captured the importance of substitutability power when they proposed that the lower the substitutability of the activities of a subunit, the greater is its power within the organization.[56]

In summary, the first step a subunit may take to increase its power is to assume responsibility for activities critical to the organization.[57] The subunit may then seek to increase its pervasiveness, ability to cope with uncertainty, nonsubstitutability, or all three. Eventually, the subunit will possess enormous levels of power in relation to other subunits in the organization.

Obedience to Authority

Admittedly, some individuals and subunits have vast amounts of influence to get others to do things the way they want them done. However, there is also obedience to perceived authority. Imagine that one afternoon your supervisor says, "You know, we're really losing money using that Beal stamping machine. I'd like you to do a job for the company. I want you to destroy the machine and make it look like an accident." Would you comply with this request? After all, this is your supervisor, and he's in charge of everything: your pay, your promotion opportunities, and your job assignments. You might ask, "Does my supervisor have this much influence over me?"

Where a person's or a subunit's influence starts and stops is difficult to pinpoint. One might assume that the supervisor in the hypothetical example has the specific influence to get someone to do this unethical and illegal "dirty work." However, even individuals who seemingly possess only minor authority can influence others. A series of classic studies by Stanley Milgram focused on the illusion of power.

Milgram conducted highly controversial experiments on "obedience to authority."[58] Subjects in the experiments were adult men from a variety of occupations and social positions in the New Haven, Connecticut, area. Upon arriving at the laboratory, each subject was introduced to his supposed co-subject, a man of about 50 who was actually working with Milgram. The two were asked to draw lots to determine who would be the "teacher" and who the "learner." The drawing was rigged. The real subject always became the teacher.

The experiment was ostensibly designed to find out about the effects of punishment on learning. Whenever the learner made a mistake, he was to be punished with an electric shock. A shock-generating machine was used. It had 30 switches on it, the first delivering 15 volts, the second 30, and so on up to 450 volts, where the switch was labeled, "Danger—Severe Shock—XXX."

The teacher (the real subject) then took his place at the shock-generating machine, where he could not see the learner (Milgram's confederate). The plan was for the learner to make many mistakes in repeating words given to him by the teacher. With each mistake, the teacher was told to increase the shocks. At 75 volts, the teacher could hear grunts coming from the learner, who was actually faking as instructed by Milgram. At 150 volts, the learner shouted, "Let me out," and said his heart couldn't stand the pain. He began to yell. He let out an agonizing scream at 285 volts and refused to go on, but seemingly kept trying and made even more mistakes.

Most teachers became very upset. Some asked the experimenter whether it was proper to continue. No matter what the teacher asked or how he protested, the experimenter said only, "The experiment requires that we go on." The subjects were also told, "You have no other choice; you must go on." Milgram wanted to know how many subjects would defy the orders to go on and how many would continue. Before these experiments were conducted, 40 psychiatrists were asked their opinions about whether the subjects would quit. Only 4 percent of the subjects, the psychiatrists predicted, would continue to shock learners who failed to respond. But look at Figure 10.2 to see what actually happened.

Out of a total of 40 subjects, 26 (65 percent) obeyed the experimenter all the way to the very highest voltage level on the shock generator (XXX). These men weren't abnormal. In fact, most showed extreme signs of emotional strain and psychological conflict during the experiment. They trembled, bit their lips, and dug their fingernails into the palms of their hands. They repeatedly asked for the experimenter's permission to stop. Yet, they continued increasing the voltage. Milgram stated:

> I observed a mature and initially poised businessman enter the laboratory, smiling and confident; within 20 minutes he was reduced to a twitching, stuttering wreck, who was rapidly approaching a point of nervous collapse . . . yet he continued to respond to every word of the experimenter and obeyed to the end.[59]

Why did the subjects obey the experimenter? Although he possessed no specific authority over the subjects, he appeared to be a powerful person. The experimenter created an illusion of power: he dressed in a white lab coat, was addressed by others as "doctor," and was very stern. The subjects perceived him as possessing legitimacy to conduct the study. The experimenter apparently did an excellent job of projecting the illusion of having power.

The Milgram experiments indicate that exercising power in an authoritative way isn't the only way that power can be exerted. Power is often exerted by individuals who have only minimum or no actual power. An individual may be able to significantly influence others simply because she's perceived to have power. The "eye of the beholder" plays an important role in the exercise of power.[60]

FIGURE 10.2
Results of Milgram's Classic Experiment on Obedience

Source: Based on descriptions and data presented by Stanley Milgram.

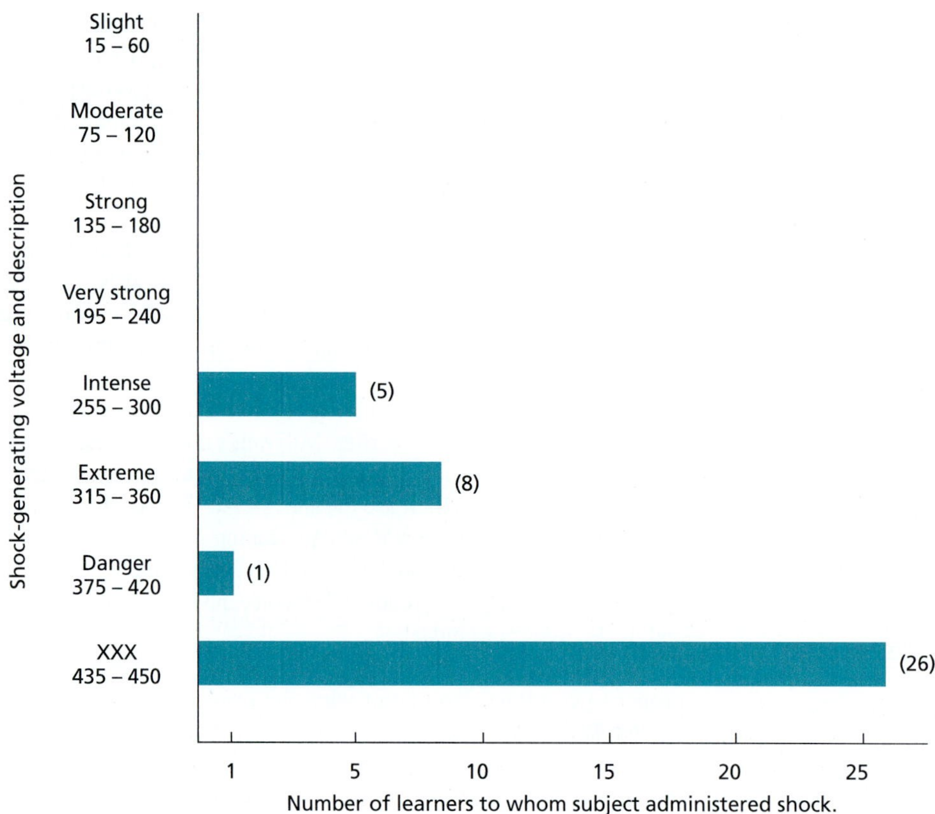

Political Strategies and Tactics

political behavior
Behavior outside the normal power system, designed to benefit an individual or a subunit.

Individuals and subunits continually engage in **political behavior**. By political behavior, we mean

1. Behavior that is usually outside the legitimate, recognized power system.
2. Behavior that is designed to benefit an individual or subunit, often at the expense of the organization in general.
3. Behavior that is intentional and is designed to acquire and maintain power.

As a result of political behavior, the formal power that exists in an organization is often sidetracked or blocked. The accompanying OB at Work feature outlines some of the negative effects of political behavior.

Research on Politics

A number of studies have explored political behavior and perceptions in organizations.[61] An early study of 142 purchasing agents examined their political behavior.[62] Their job objective was to negotiate and fill orders in a timely manner. However, the purchasing agents also viewed their jobs as being a crucial link with the environment—competition, price changes, and market shifts. Thus, they considered themselves information processors. This vital link between each purchasing agent and the external environment placed them in conflict with the engineering department. As a result of the conflict, attempts to influence the engineering subunit were a regular occurrence.

OB AT WORK The Neighborhood Bully Is Back—At Your Workplace

Bullying is a real problem that affects many employees in the workplace. Research on bullying has been conducted in several countries, including the United States, Sweden, Norway, Finland, Ireland, England, Korea, Japan, Germany, Italy, Australia, New Zealand, and Mexico. Why is this issue important for organizations? Employees who experience repetitive bullying are more apt to suffer from physical and psychological problems, the net result of which is a reduction in productivity, increased absenteeism, and turnover. Organizations, to avoid such negative and expensive outcomes, need to understand bullying and be prepared to manage it effectively.

What is bullying at the workplace? It's a pattern of destructive and intentional (or unconscious) behavior that demeans coworkers and subordinates. Bullying can result in the victim feeling humiliated, distressed, and uncomfortable. A considerable amount of bullying is done by individuals who are in positions of higher power than the bullied employee. A typical example would be that of a supervisor at a call center who continuously picks on one of her customer service representatives in front of everyone in the call center. Although this representative does a good job, the supervisor still berates him for not resolving customers' problems quickly enough, for having a squeaky voice on the phone, or for not being as professional as the other representatives on the floor. The representative, after three months of this "unfair" treatment, begins having stomach problems, headaches, and hates coming to work. His productivity begins to drop because the representative has trouble focusing on the work and becomes very nervous whenever the supervisor walks up to his workspace. He ends up quitting and finding a new job.

What are some facts about bullying? Some studies suggest that up to 90 percent of the workforce has experienced bullying at some point during their careers; between 10 and 20 percent experience incidents of bullying each year. Bullies can be either male or female and are bosses 81 percent of the time. Bullies frequently misuse their power, treat employees in an inconsistent manner, put self-interest before the organization, and tend to have emotional outbursts. In terms of the health of the victims, 41 percent are diagnosed with depression, 94 percent suffer severe anxiety, and more than 80 percent of victims report that bullying has made them less productive at work. Victims often report that support is not received from co-workers, superiors, or HR personnel, and less than 10 percent of bullies were disciplined or terminated.

Is there a "typical victim" that bullies target? Although bullies may target a co-worker who is perceived as a threat, many bullies target subordinates who possess less power than they do. Some research has suggested that many victims suffer from low self-esteem, are not assertive, and are not members of the in-group of the department.

Why is bullying becoming more common? Bullies are a fact of life. Most people, when thinking back to their childhood, can remember one or two bullies who instilled discomfort and, possibly, terror in them. Some individuals' personalities make them prone to being bullies at the workplace. Famous examples include Henry Ford, Walt Disney, and Armand Hammer. Also, other factors contributing to the increase in bullying include compressed deadlines, the threat of being laid off or downsized, the ever-changing business landscape due to competition and globalization, and poorly defined codes of conduct and behavioral norms at many organizations.

What should organizations do? The leaders of organizations and departments need to set a good example and not bully subordinates and co-workers. Also, policies and guidelines regarding bullying need to be developed and enforced. Violators must be disciplined. Management training programs should contain a module that defines bullying and clearly states that such behavior will not be condoned. New-employee orientations need to address the issue of bullying, and reporting procedures for violations need to be discussed.

In sum, bullying is a major problem for many employees and their organizations. Employees need to speak up and report such bad behavior to protect their health and long-term standing in the organization. Companies must step up and deal with this harmful behavior to prevent significant productivity loss, absenteeism, and turnover among their employees.

Sources: Adapted from T. Daniel, "Tough Boss or Workplace Bully?" *HRMagazine*, June 2009, pp. 82–86; Michael G. Harvey, Joyce T. Heames, R. Glenn Richey, and Nancy Leonard, "Bullying: From the Playground to the Boardroom," *Journal of Leadership and Organizational Studies* 12, no. 4 (2006): 1–11; Randy Hodson, Vincent J. Roscigno, and Steven H. Lopez, "Chaos and the Abuse of Power," *Work and Occupations* 33, no. 4 (November 2006): 382–416; Nikola Djurkovic, Darcy McCormack, and Gian Casimir, "Neuroticism and the Psychosomatic Model of Workplace Bullying," *Journal of Managerial Psychology* 21, no. 1 (2006): 73–88; Gina Vega and Debra R. Comer, "Sticks and Stones May Break Your Bones, but Words Can Break Your Spirit: Bullying in the Workplace," *Journal of Business Ethics* 58 (2005): 101–9; and C. Raynor, H. Hoel, and C. L. Cooper, *Workplace Bullying: What We Know, Who Is to Blame, and What Can We Do?* (London: Taylor and Francis, 2002).

This study found a variety of political tactics used by purchasing agents:

1. *Rule evasion*—evading the organization's formal purchasing procedures.
2. *Personal-political*—using friendships to facilitate or inhibit the processing of an order.
3. *Educational*—attempting to persuade engineering to think in purchasing terms.
4. *Organizational*—attempting to change the formal or informal interaction patterns between engineering and purchasing.

These four political tactics were outside the legitimate power system, occasionally benefited the purchasing agent at the expense of the rest of the organization, and were intentionally developed so that more power was acquired by the purchasing agent.

Another classic study of political behavior was conducted in the electronics industry in southern California.[63] A total of 87 CEOs, high-level staff managers, and supervisors were interviewed and asked about political behavior. The political behaviors and tactics mentioned most frequently by these individuals included attacking or blaming others, using information, image building/impression management, developing a base of support, and praising others (ingratiating). The same study also identified the personal characteristics of effective politicians: articulate, sensitive, socially adept, competent, and popular.

A related study developed a profile of individuals active in office politics, based on a survey completed by 225 managers.[64] The results indicated that managerial level, job function, and sex were unrelated to managers' levels of political activity. However, certain personality traits corresponded highly with the individual manager's propensity to engage in office politics. The profile that emerged characterized the "political player" as a highly self-monitoring man who viewed the world as difficult and as posing complex (possibly unsolvable) problems, or as a woman with high need for power.

Another study in the 1990s focused on forms of defensive political behaviors exhibited by managers.[65] Defensive behaviors included avoiding action via overconforming, passing the buck, playing dumb, and stalling; avoiding blame via bluffing, justifying, scapegoating, and misrepresenting; and avoiding change via resisting change and protecting one's turf. Personality traits of managers who exhibited defensive behavior included insecurity and anxiety, emotional exhaustion, work alienation, self-monitoring, and low self-efficacy.

Impression Management

Impression management refers to the behaviors individuals use to preserve their self-image and influence the ways in which others perceive them.[66] In other words, individuals who engage in impression management attempt to control information about themselves so as to create a favorable impression with important others in the workplace.[67] Impression management can also be used by organizations that attempt to influence constituents' impressions to gain specific rewards; such rewards can include regaining stakeholder confidence after a controversial event.[68]

Although impression management tactics have been categorized in a number of different ways, we will refer to them as falling into one of two categories: *self-presentation strategies* are employed by an individual in an attempt to make himself more appealing to important others and are accomplished through verbal and nonverbal means (e.g., smiling, eye contact); and *other-enhancement* tactics focus on agreement with important others in order to positively influence them. Typical other-enhancement behaviors include doing favors, flattery, and opinion conformity.[69] Table 10.1 includes a more complete list of impression management tactics.

Much of the research regarding impression management has focused on the types of and motivations behind the use of strategies that employees use to influence others, characteristics of the individuals who employ such tactics, and reactions of the recipients of such impression management tactics.[70]

TABLE 10.1
Impression Management Tactics

Self-Presentation	Other-Enhancement
Smiling	Doing favors for others
Making eye contact	Using flattery
Positive tone of voice	Showing interest in others
Appropriate dress	Being an active listener
High level of energy	Agreeing with others' opinions

By managing the impressions that others will form, an individual can gain an advantage in a variety of different workplace scenarios.[71] For example, one research study concluded that a subordinate's impression management behavior exerted an indirect influence on the supervisor's performance ratings.[72] Several other research studies have corroborated these findings.[73] By controlling information about themselves, subordinates are able to receive higher performance evaluations from supervisors. Impression management tactics can also influence whether a job applicant is successful or not. Research studies have explored the relationship between impression management tactics employed by job applicants during job interviews and the interview outcomes. It was reported that impression management tactics had a positive effect on interviewers' evaluations and whether applicants received invitations for site visits.[74]

Employees and job applicants are two groups of individuals that can benefit from the judicious use of impression management tactics. Of course, one should be cautious so as not to overuse such behaviors as smiling, flattery, and opinion conforming. An individual who overuses these behaviors can be perceived as superficial, overly ingratiating, or not trustworthy.

Playing Politics

If anything, the available research indicates that politics exists in organizations and that some individuals are very adept at political behavior. Mintzberg and others describe these adept politicians as playing games.[75] The games that managers and nonmanagers engage in are intended to resist authority (e.g., the insurgency game); counter the resistance to authority (e.g., the counterinsurgency game); build power bases (e.g., the sponsorship game and coalition-building game); defeat rivals (e.g., the line versus staff game); and affect organizational change (e.g., the whistle-blowing game). In all, Mintzberg describes and discusses 13 political games. Figure 10.3 shows the six that are briefly presented here.

Insurgency Game

This game is played to resist authority. For example, suppose that a plant supervisor is instructed to reprimand a particular worker for violating company policies. The reprimand can be delivered according to the supervisor's feelings and opinions about its worth and legitimacy. A reprimand delivered in a halfhearted manner will probably have no noticeable effect. However, if delivered aggressively, it may be effective. Insurgency in the form of not delivering the reprimand as expected by a higher-level authority would be difficult to detect and correct. Insurgency as a game to resist authority is practiced in organizations at all levels.

Counterinsurgency Game

Often, a person in an authority position fights back when faced with insurgency. The supervisor's superior may have to carefully monitor whether policies concerning the reprimand are being followed. One tactic is to occasionally follow up requests given to subordinates with a detailed checking system. For example, the person with ultimate authority could ask the supervisor on occasion whether the reprimand had been given, when it was given, what the person's reaction was, and how the supervisor would make presentation improvements in the future. The superior could also check with the person reprimanded to determine when and how the reprimand was given. The purpose of periodic monitoring is to encourage the supervisor to deliver the reprimand according to company procedures.

FIGURE 10.3
Sample of Political Games That Managers Play

Sources: Henry Mintzberg, *Power in and around Organizations* (Englewood Cliffs, NJ: Prentice-Hall, 1983), p. 5; and Henry Mintzberg, "Power and Organization Life Cycles," *Academy of Management Review* (April 1984): 207–24.

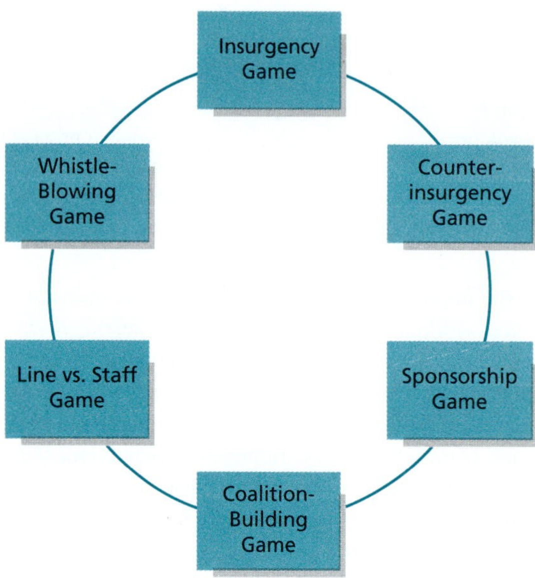

Sponsorship Game

In this rather straightforward game, a person attaches herself to someone with power. The sponsor is typically the person's boss or someone else with higher power and status. Typically, individuals attach themselves to someone who is on the move up in the organization. A few rules are involved in playing this game. First, the person must be able to show commitment and loyalty to the sponsor. Second, the person must follow each sponsor-initiated request or order. Third, the person must stay in the background and give the sponsor credit for everything. Finally, the person must be thankful and display gratitude to the sponsor. The sponsor is not only a teacher and trainer but also a power base. Some of the sponsor's power tends to rub off on the person through association.

Coalition-Building Game

A subunit such as a personnel/human resources department or a research and development department may be able to increase its power by forming an alliance, or coalition, with other subunits. The strength-in-numbers idea is encouraged by coalition building.[76] When such alliances are formed within the organization, common goals and common interests are emphasized. However, forming coalitions with groups outside the organization can also enhance the power of a subunit.

Line versus Staff Game

The line manager versus the staff advisor game has existed for years in organizations. In essence, this game pits line authority to make operating decisions against staff advisors' expertise. There are also value differences and personality clashes. On the one hand, line managers are typically more experienced, more oriented to the bottom line, and more intuitive in reaching decisions. Conversely, staff advisors tend to be younger, better educated, and more analytical decision makers. These differences result in the two groups viewing the organizational world from different perspectives.

Withholding information, having access to powerful authority figures, creating favorable impressions, and identifying with organizational goals are tactics used by line and staff personnel. The line versus staff clash must be controlled in organizations before it reaches the point at which, because of the disruption, organizational goals aren't being achieved.

Whistle-Blowing Game

whistle-blowing
Informing someone about an organizational practice or behavior that violates the law or conflicts with a personal value or belief.

An action is taken to bring about organizational change. It takes place when a person in an organization identifies a behavior that violates his sense of fairness, morals, ethics, or law and then blows the whistle. **Whistle-blowing** means that the person informs someone—a newspaper reporter, a government representative, a competitor—about an assumed injustice, irresponsible action, or violation of the law.

The whistle-blower, who may come from any level in the organization, attempts to correct the behavior or practice by bypassing the authority system within the organization. This is viewed in a negative light by managers with position power. For example, when a pilot complained to management first and then to the public about defects in his plane's automatic pilot mechanisms, his complaints were attacked by management as being groundless. A senior vice president of Lehman Brothers Holdings Inc. voiced his concerns about the firm's "valuations of illiquid investments and the quality of its accounting controls" on May 16, 2008.[77] He was later fired from the firm. An engineer complained about the O-rings of the *Challenger* booster rockets—which later cracked, leading to the death of seven astronauts.[78] The engineer's complaints weren't given a high enough priority to be checked out. In another example, a biologist reported to the Environmental Protection Agency that his consulting firm had submitted false data to the agency on behalf of an electric utility company. As a result, he was fired.

Although federal law protects whistle-blowers' rights and some innovative organizations encourage valid internal whistle-blowing, most organizations continue to retaliate against an informant.[79] In fact, a recent study found that identified whistle-blowers were as likely to experience retaliation after the passage of the federal law protecting them as they were prior to its passage.[80] As a result, whistle-blowing is often done secretly to avoid retribution by the authority system.

Ethics, Power, and Politics

Issues of power and politics often involve ethical issues as well. For example, if power is used within the formal boundaries of a manager's authority and within the framework of organizational policies, job descriptions, procedures, and goals, it's really nonpolitical power and most likely doesn't involve ethical issues. But use of power outside the bounds of formal authority, politics, procedures, job descriptions, and organizational goals is political in nature. When this occurs, ethical issues are likely to be present. Some examples might include bribing government officials, lying to employees and customers, polluting the environment, and a general "ends justify the means" mentality. Can ethics be taught in business schools? The next OB at Work feature discusses this difficult question.

Managers confront ethical dilemmas in their jobs because they frequently use power and politics to accomplish their goals. Each manager, therefore, has an ethical responsibility. Recently researchers have developed a framework that allows a manager to integrate ethics into political behavior. Researchers recommend that a manager's behavior must satisfy certain criteria to be considered ethical:[81]

1. *Utilitarian outcomes.* The manager's behavior results in the optimal satisfaction of people both inside and outside the organization. In other words, it results in the greatest good for the greatest number of people.
2. *Individual rights.* The manager's behavior respects the rights of all affected parties. In other words, it respects basic human rights of free consent, free speech, freedom of conscience, privacy, and due process.
3. *Distributive justice.* The manager's behavior respects the rules of justice. It treats people equitably and fairly, not arbitrarily.

OB AT WORK Can Business Schools Teach Ethics?

In the wake of multiple waves of corporate scandals (e.g., Enron) and fraudulent behaviors (e.g., the Bernie Madoff Ponzi scheme) that were caused either directly or indirectly by unethical leadership, poor decision making, outright greed, or all three, business schools have been put under a microscope. The issue at hand is whether business schools have a responsibility and the ability to teach ethical behavior to business students. This is not a new concept. Harvard Business School offered a business ethics course—"Social Factors in Business Enterprise"—nearly 100 years ago. Keeping pace with this tradition, starting in January 2004, Harvard Business School requires all students to take an ethics course—"Leadership, Governance, and Accountability." Other schools, such as Indiana University's Kelley School of Business, are also taking steps to ensure that students abide by ethical standards. Students of the Kelley Business School must follow a 20-page code of conduct that prohibits cheating, fabrication, and plagiarism, while promoting professional conduct with recruiters.

Experts and professors differ in their opinions about whether ethical behavior can be taught. Some believe that students' values are already formed, and no amount of classroom training will make an individual behave ethically. Others believe that educating students about the severe consequences of unethical business decisions will help deter unethical behavior in the future. For example, at the Tuck School of Business at Dartmouth College, students attend a panel that features an ex-convict involved in a $100 million dollar fraud.

Should business schools require all students to take a specific ethics course? Is it better to add an ethics component to all required courses, like accounting, management, and marketing?

What does a manager do when a potential behavior cannot pass the three criteria? Researchers suggest that it may still be considered ethical in the particular situation if it passes the criterion of *overwhelming factors.* To be justified, the behavior must be based on tremendously overwhelming factors in the nature of the situation, such as conflicts among criteria (e.g., the manager's behavior results in both positive and negative results), conflicts within the criteria (e.g., a manager uses questionable means to achieve a positive result), and/or an incapacity to employ the first three criteria (e.g., the manager acts with incomplete or inaccurate information).

Summary of Key Points

- *Power* is defined as the ability to get things done in the way that one wants them done.
- Authority is a much narrower concept than power. Authority is a form of power that is made legitimate because it is accepted by subordinates or followers.
- There are five interpersonal power bases: legitimate (position-based), reward, coercive (punishment-based), expert, and referent (charismatic).These five bases can be divided into two major categories: organizational and personal. Legitimate, reward, and coercive power bases are primarily prescribed by an organization, while expert and charismatic power bases accrue from personal qualities.
- Structural and situational power bases also exist. An organization's structural arrangement establishes patterns of communication and information flow that play an important role in power formation and use.
- Many managers with a high need for power are effective, use their power to accomplish organizational goals, and are involved heavily in coaching subordinates.
- Power and influence can flow from the bottom to the top in an organization. Lower-level employees can have significant power because of expertise, location, and access and control of information. Some lower-level employees acquire power through persuasion and manipulation skills.
- Subunits within organizations acquire and use power. The strategic contingency approach addresses subunit power. A strategic contingency is an event or activity that is important for accomplishing organizational goals.

- Individuals can sometimes exercise power because people perceive that they have authority.
- Politics is present in all organizations. Politics comprises those activities used to acquire, develop, and use power and other resources to obtain one's preferred outcome when there is uncertainty or disagreement about choices.
- Mintzberg introduced the notion of political game playing. Examples of political games are the insurgency and counterinsurgency games, the sponsorship game, the coalition-building game, the line versus staff game, and the whistle-blowing game.
- Issues of power and politics often involve ethical issues, especially when the use of power is political in nature.

Discussion and Review Questions

1. If you could have only one type of interpersonal power, which would it be and why?
2. Think of a co-worker, fellow student, or friend who seems to have a high need for power. What methods or tactics does this person use to try to influence others? Explain.
3. There's an old saying that "information is power." What strategies should you follow to acquire and use information in a politically powerful manner? Describe.
4. Given the seemingly limitless amount of information on the Internet and the fact that anyone can access it with a few keyword searches in Google, do you believe that "information power" is easier or harder to develop nowadays? Explain your answer.
5. Within the context of a hospital, what makes such subunits as the emergency room and critical care units so powerful? Explain.
6. Subunit power is an important topic for many managers. Assume you are the CEO of Facebook or some other social networking Web site. Which of the following two subunits would likely be more powerful within the company: the subunit responsible for designing the Web site? Or the subunit responsible for packaging and marketing user information to companies for commercial purposes? Choose one subunit and defend your answer.
7. Why is it unrealistic to assume that little or no political game playing exists in an organization such as McDonald's or Google?
8. The sponsorship game has also been referred to, in a more negative tone, as "riding someone's coattails." Why do you think some view this game in a negative way?
9. If someone blows the whistle on his company's actions because the actions endanger lives, do you believe he should be fired? If not, what do you think should happen to this employee?
10. Do you believe there is any type of organization that frequently operates *without* ethical standards to maintain success and profitability? Why or why not?

Taking It to the Net

Office Politics 101

The phrase "office politics" is often associated with nasty, backstabbing activities that can ruin careers, create dictators, and distract employees from doing their jobs. In reality, office politics is not as bad as it's perceived to be, but rather a necessary part of working in an office environment. Go to the Web site listed below and read the articles on rules for office politics, avoiding common pitfalls, and how to deal with your boss. After reading the articles, prepare a brief presentation that summarizes the major points from each of the articles. Which points do you agree with? Which points do you disagree with?

Access the Web site http://labmice.techtarget.com/career/politics.htm. Then,

1. Click on links under "Where to start" tab.
2. Click on links under "Avoiding common pitfalls" tab.
3. Click on links under "Dealing with your boss" tab.

Case for Analysis: *Terry's Dilemma*

Terry has worked for Dutchman Enterprises for seven years. Dutchman is a call center that handles customer service inquiries (e.g., questions about bills) for several major credit card companies. Since staring with the company, Terry has progressed from mailroom worker to customer service representative, and he is now senior customer service specialist in the call center. Terry's technical skills are unmatched, and there is not a customer service problem in the department that he doesn't know how to fix. Terry's supervisor, Frank, is a new college graduate, and while Frank is fine with the department's everyday administration, when something out of the ordinary happens, he has the sense to seek out Terry for advice. Truth be told, not a thing happens in the department without Terry's informal approval.

Terry enjoys the attention and respect he gets as the go-to person in the department. Even though it's technically against the rules, Terry, not Frank, writes the work schedules (Frank admits that Terry knows who does what best). Not surprisingly, Terry has been known to use the schedule to recognize or punish his fellow colleagues in the department.

Terry didn't always have such an enviable position. He failed to graduate from high school and the neighborhood "club" of which he was president was characterized by many, including the police, as a gang. At the urgings of Terry's parents, a close family friend—"Uncle Jake"—took a personal risk and got Terry the job at Dutchman. Jake set up a weekly lunch appointment with Terry to help him set his priorities and focus on his future. Through these mentoring sessions, Jake encouraged Terry to get his GED and then his associate's degree at the local community college. Jake was proud of what Terry had accomplished and the strong bond that they had formed.

Although Jake retired from Dutchman last year, he still keeps in touch with Terry and the various other employees whom he had mentored over the years. To his great pleasure, he receives several calls each month from this group, some just checking in, and others asking for his opinion and advice. Just last week Jake received a call from the HR director. "There's going to be a supervisor opening in the marketing department. Do you know anyone who may be ready for this challenge?" Jake responded that he might and as soon as he hung up the phone, he called Terry to set up a meeting.

Terry always enjoyed these get-togethers with Jake. Although their meetings were now less frequent than when he was a "rebel kid," he still appreciated hearing Jake's insights. On more than one occasion, Terry shared that it was more than likely he'd be dead if it weren't for Jake's intervention. Terry was honored when Jake told him about the new supervisor opportunity and how Jake thought he was the man for the job. Jake's statement, "it will be a hard transition but you can do it and it's time for you to move on," echoed in Terry's mind on his drive home.

Moving to another area like marketing would be difficult. Terry was "the man" in the call center. He had spent years crafting his skills and had the respect of his fellow workers and management alike. If he made the move, he'd be starting fresh. He wondered if his workers would make the same jokes about him that he and his buddies did whenever they got a new supervisor. There was also the salary issue. If he was to take the job as supervisor, he'd no longer get his overtime, and in some weeks his take-home pay could even be less than it is now.

Jake had told Terry to think long term. They were scheduled to meet again tomorrow to talk about the specifics on how to apply for the supervisory position. With Jake's endorsement, Terry was a "shoo-in" to get the job, but he still wasn't sure if he really wanted to take the new supervisor position.

DISCUSSION QUESTIONS

1. Apply French and Raven's bases of power to Jake and Terry. Explain your answer.

2. If Terry takes the job of supervisor, his bases of power may shift. Explain this change.
3. The chapter reintroduces McClelland's need for power. How would you rate Jake's and Terry's "n Pow"? Referring back to the chapter on motivation, how else might you apply McClelland's theory to these two individuals? Explain your answer.
4. What actions would you suggest to Terry for him to be successful in his new position? Be sure to include political tactics in your answer.

Source: Written by Dr. Michael Dutch, Greensboro College, Greensboro, North Carolina (2007).

Experiential Exercise: *Office Diplomacy: The Dos and Don'ts*

OBJECTIVES

1. To examine situations where power and office politics impact social decisions.
2. To illustrate the difficulties of office etiquette.

STARTING THE EXERCISE

Phase I (20 minutes). Here are four tricky situations dealing with office diplomacy that managers commonly encounter. Read through each scenario and the alternative answers. Choose the answer that most closely matches the response you feel a manager should make. Write down why you chose this particular response and not the others, supporting your choice with material contained in this chapter.

Scenario 1. At a meeting with your boss and others, you're asked your opinion concerning a problem. You offer your ideas but see right away that your boss is upset and surprised. After the meeting, you should

1. Tell your boss that you made a mistake, and you'll be sure to discuss your ideas with her before a meeting.
2. Elaborate on your ideas in a report that you personally deliver to the committee.
3. Say nothing. These things happen.

Scenario 2. The newly appointed manager of another department has adopted an aggressive attitude toward you. Your department and the new manager's department work together closely, and you realize that your department's success is in jeopardy unless you can resolve the problem. Each time you try to communicate directly with the other manager, all you get is hostility. You should

1. Confront the manager head-on. Explain that like it or not, you two will be working together.
2. Work around the other manager. Avoid talking to him directly whenever possible.
3. Make your relationship more personal. Invite him to lunch, but avoid trying to talk business.

Scenario 3. Having been hired from the outside, you've just started your new job as manager when one employee in your department comes to you and states that she should have been promoted to your position. You should

1. Help her to transfer to another department where her abilities will be better appreciated.
2. Tell her that, like it or not, you hold the position and she had better get used to it.
3. Give her more responsibility by putting her in charge of a major project.

Scenario 4. An employee asks you, his manager, to lunch to discuss a work-related issue. Which one of you should pick up the tab?

1. The employee should pay since he arranged the lunch.
2. You, as the manager who was invited, should pay.
3. The tab should be split evenly.

Scenario 5. You and one of your employees are in the middle of a meeting in your office when the telephone rings. You don't have an assistant to pick up your calls. You should

1. Ignore the phone. Eventually it will stop ringing.
2. Answer the phone, excuse yourself to your employee, and then give the call your full attention.
3. Answer the call. Say you're in a meeting and can't talk, but will call back as soon as possible.

Phase II (15 minutes). The instructor will form small groups of four, six, or eight students to discuss their choices and the rationale behind their choices.

Phase III (15 minutes). The instructor will wrap the session up and discuss the various alternatives.

Source: Michael C. Thomsett, "How's Your Office Diplomacy?" *Executive Female,* March–April 1992, pp. 68–69.

CHAPTER ELEVEN

Leadership: Fundamentals

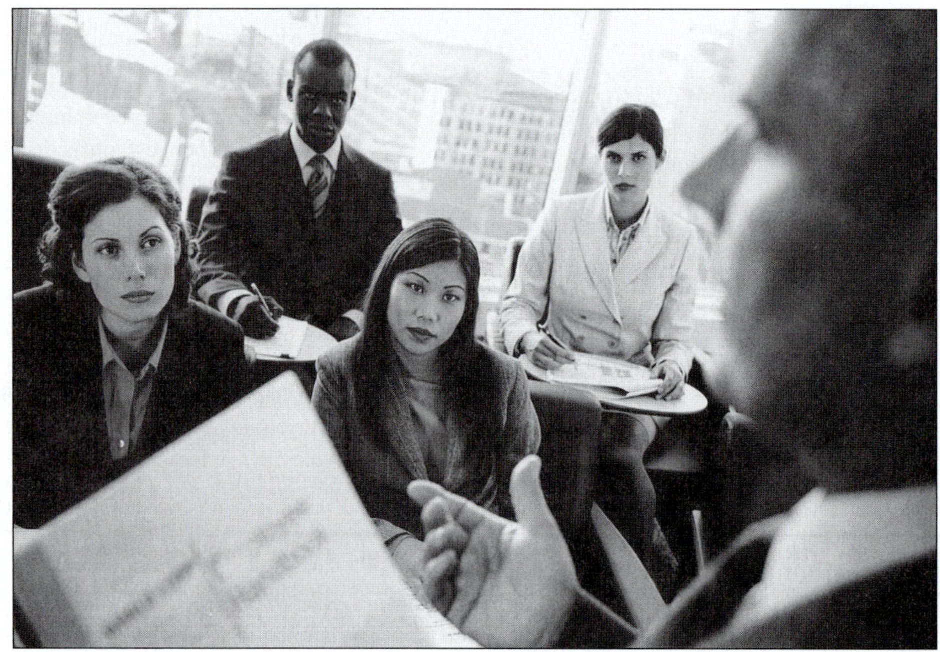

Learning Objectives

After completing Chapter 11, you should be able to

Define
The term *leadership.*

Describe
Why managers appear to prefer the Hersey-Blanchard situational leadership theory.

Discuss
Whether employees can develop into effective leaders.

Compare
The situational factors used in discussions of the contingency and path–goal approaches to leadership.

Identify
The assumptions made about followers of the path–goal and the leader–member exchange theories.

Business Leaders: Born or Made?

As we enter the second decade of the 21st century, there is a perception that corporate America is running out of good leaders. Regardless of whether this claim is true, leadership is becoming increasingly critical in this era of economic recessions, hypercompetition, shortened product life cycles, and globalization. Companies of all sizes are faced with the question of how to ensure that the future supply of leaders has the right skills, abilities, and strategic vision to achieve success. Ignoring the school of thought that some individuals are born to lead, many firms believe that leadership can be developed in a proactive, systematic fashion.

Acting on this belief, organizations like Home Depot, Burger King, General Electric, Wells Fargo, Walgreens, Ford Motor, Johnson & Johnson, and PepsiCo spend considerable time and money to develop leadership skills in many of their most promising employees. Home Depot's Store Leadership Program (SLP) is a demanding 24-month program that combines classroom learning, four different job rotations, and mentoring by company leaders. Home Depot also has a business leadership program, a future leaders program, and a merchandising leadership program.

General Electric addresses corporate learning with their Crotonville Management Development Institute. Designed to expose "students" to real-world problems such as global product and service strategies, strategic alliances, cross-border coordination and integration, and global staffing and development, Crotonville has a $1 billion training and development budget to prepare managers to assume leadership positions. In addition, Burger King offers a "Leaders of Tomorrow" program in which high-potential IT professionals at the company participate in training sessions each month for a year to learn technical and nontechnical skills. Ford Motor uses its Leadership Development Center to engender leadership skills in thousands of managers within the huge automaker. Johnson & Johnson's Executive Quality Leadership Program prepares future leaders by challenging participants to develop leadership skills by finding solutions to real business problems. Senior leaders from the company interact with, mentor, and provide feedback to the leadership trainees. Pepsi takes a slightly different approach to leadership training by encouraging its employees to volunteer after work and on weekends. By taking leadership roles in extracurricular volunteer activities, employees learn new management and leadership skills that ultimately enhance their job performance.

Sources: Adapted from: https://careers.homedepot.com/cg/content.do?p=/leadership (accessed on June 2, 2010); C. Crosby and G. Zlevor, "Developing Leaders," *Leadership Excellence* 27, no. 1 (January 2010): 16–17; Fay Hansen, "Building Better Leaders . . . Faster," *Workforce Management* 87, no. 10 (June 2008): 25–28; Raj Rewal, "Beyond Technology, A Focus on People," *InformationWeek*, April 21, 2008, pp. 55–56; Mica Schneider, "If It Was Good Enough for Jack Welch . . ." *Businessweek*, October 15, 2001, pp. 114–15; Martin Delahoussaye, "Leadership in the 21st Century," *Training*, August 2001, pp. 50–59; Ron Zemke and Susan Zemke, "Where Do Leaders Come from?" *Training*, pp. 44–48; and Stewart Friedman, "Leadership DNA: The Ford Motor Story," *Training & Development*, March 2000, pp. 22–29.

Every group to which you've belonged—family, sports, social, study, work—doubtlessly included one person you considered to be more influential than others. When this person spoke, others listened; when this person suggested or directed action to be taken, others took that action. You thought of and perhaps referred to this person as a leader. Perhaps you yourself have been such a person—a leader. Maybe you enjoyed the experience of being a leader. Maybe you didn't. In any event, you recognize the circumstance. You also recognize the importance of leaders in groups, organizations, institutions, nations, and alliances of nations.

Leaders play important roles and often work behind the scenes to promote the well-being and effectiveness of efforts undertaken by groups and teams of individuals who alone could not accomplish their intended purposes. Good leadership enables organizations to be effective and accomplish their goals. Because of the importance of leaders in society, they have been the subjects of countless studies, novels, stories, and films, all attempting to say something about what leaders do, what leadership is, and even how a leader should treat others. Certainly a text that seeks to prepare students for careers in organizations would have to include considerable attention to leaders and leadership. Are individuals born to be leaders? Can individuals learn how to apply leadership behavior? Or does the question of who will become a leader depend entirely on the situation?

This and the next chapter will present the main contemporary ideas about leadership from the perspective of behavioral science theory and research. We will be keenly interested in arriving at well-founded understandings of leadership not only from the perspective of science but also from the perspective of practice and application. Yet we will have to deal with considerable ambiguity because, even though scientists have studied leadership for decades, it remains something of a mystery. Even after thousands of studies, the experts still lack consensus on exactly what leadership is and how it should be applied.

Generally speaking, however, we can say that leaders are individuals who influence other individuals to do what they might not do in the absence of the leader's influence. We will examine somewhat more complete ideas about leaders in the following pages, but we can certainly appreciate at this point the difficulty of understanding how and why certain individuals become leaders and what they do to exercise their influence. What personal characteristics distinguish leaders from nonleaders? What personal characteristics distinguish effective leaders from ineffective leaders? How do they behave as leaders, and what distinguishes the behavior of effective leaders from ineffective ones? What role do followers play in leadership? Is each leader better suited to influence some types of individuals over others? What can we say about the context, or situation, within which leadership occurs? For that matter, do all situations involving group effort require leadership? These questions present some of the ideas that we will be discussing in the following pages.

The discussion will begin with a definition of leadership as we will use the term. The reader should be alert to the ambiguity of the terms *leader* and *leadership* and recognize that discussions of them often result in confusion because of differing definitions. We will then direct our attention to the studies of leaders and leadership beginning with those studies that attempt to identify the particular *traits* that leaders share that distinguish them from nonleaders. Next, we will discuss the ideas associated with leader *behavior,* specifically the behaviors associated with effective leaders. The discussion concludes with an introduction to the idea that effective leadership depends on the interaction between the leader's traits and behavior and the *situation* in which the leadership occurs.

Leadership Defined

Leadership
An attempt to use influence to motivate individuals to accomplish some goal.

The authoritative source of leadership theory and research, the *Handbook of Leadership,* defines **leadership** as "an interaction between members of a group. Leaders are agents of change; persons whose acts affect other people more than other people's acts affect them. Leadership occurs when one group member modifies the motivation or competencies of others in the group."[1] The leadership definition implies that it involves the use of influence and that all interpersonal relationships can involve leadership. A second element in the definition involves the importance of being a change agent—being able to affect followers' behavior and performance. Finally, the definition focuses on accomplishing goals. The effective leader may have to deal with individual, group, and organizational goals.

Leader effectiveness is typically measured by the accomplishment of one or a combination of these goals. Individuals may view the leader as effective or ineffective according to the satisfactions they derive from the total work experience. In fact, acceptance of a leader's directives or requests rests largely on the followers' expectations that a favorable response can lead to an attractive outcome.

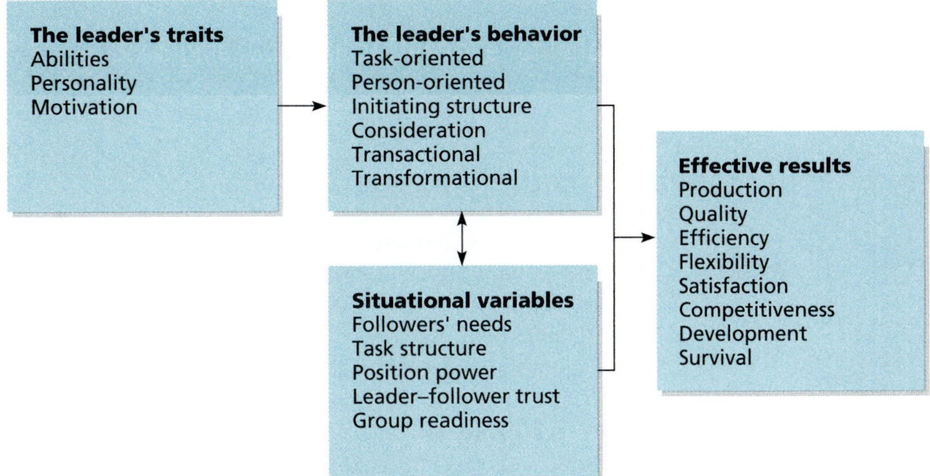

FIGURE 11.1
A Framework for Studying Leadership

The central interest of this textbook is to prepare individuals to manage in organizations. Thus we should here distinguish between managing and leading. Leadership is a narrower concept than management. A manager in a formal organization is responsible for and entrusted with such functions as planning, organizing, and controlling, but not necessarily leading. A manager may or may not engage in leadership. For example, if the manager does not have to interact in any way with other individuals and thus does not have to influence their behavior, that manager would not be a leader in the sense of our definition.

A useful framework for organizing ideas and theories about leadership is presented in Figure 11.1. This figure indicates many of the terms and concepts of leadership ideas and theory. It includes the various traits, behavioral styles, and situational variables found in the leadership literature. This and the following chapter will rely heavily on Figure 11.1 for our discussion.

As Figure 11.1 suggests, a leader can make a difference in measures of organizational effectiveness: production, efficiency, quality, flexibility, satisfaction, competitiveness, and development. However, scholars and practitioners of leadership have a long way to go before they will be able to measure the exact degree of difference that leaders can and do make in any organization. There are several reasons why this is so. First, organizations tend to select their leaders from those with similar backgrounds, experiences, and qualifications. The similarity across selected individuals reduces the range of characteristics exhibited by leaders. The similarity of leaders also can produce a self-selection bias: leaders select individuals similar to themselves. Second, leaders at even the highest levels do not have unilateral control over resources. Major decisions require approval, review, and suggested modification by others. Third, leaders cannot control or modify many important factors in a situation. Labor markets, environmental factors, and policies are often outside a leader's direct control. External factors may be overwhelming and uncontrollable, no matter how astute, insightful, and influential a leader may be in a job situation.[2]

Despite some studies that dispute the claim that leadership makes a difference, there's plenty of evidence that leadership can affect performance.[3] Leaders don't always make a difference, but they can and do in enough cases. Did Ray Kroc make a difference at McDonald's? Did Meg Whitman make an impact on eBay? Did Andy Grove make a difference for Intel? Did Katharine Graham make a difference at The Washington Post? In these and similar cases, there's no clear-cut answer. However, a majority of people would likely conclude that Kroc, Whitman, Grove, and Graham were leaders who made a difference.

Thus, we can safely conclude that leaders and leadership are important and that we should be interested in what sets apart those individuals who become leaders from those who do not. We should be interested in the distinctive traits of leaders.

Traits That Appear to Identify Leaders

As the opening vignette illustrates, organizations are investing in a considerable amount of time and resources to identify and develop future leaders. This investment is motivated partly by previous research on leadership that focused on identifying intellectual, emotional, physical, and other personal traits of effective leaders. This approach assumed that a finite number of individual traits of effective leaders could be found. To a significant extent, the personnel testing component of scientific management supported the **trait theory of leadership**. In addition to being studied by personnel testing, the traits of leaders have been studied by observation of behavior in group situations, by choice of associates (voting), by nomination or rating by observers, and by analysis of biographical data.

trait theory of leadership
Theory that attempts to identify specific characteristics (physical, mental, personality) associated with leadership success. Relies on research that relates various traits to certain success criteria.

Those who study these traits have correlated nearly every measurable characteristic of leaders.[4] We will here review some of the findings associated with the most often studied characteristics.

Abilities

Effective leaders share certain abilities and skills that enable them to do their job, although the exact importance of a particular ability cannot be known with certainty. For example, early studies of the relationship between intelligence (as measured on intelligence tests) and leadership have resulted in some mixed results. One early review of these studies found that leaders were more intelligent than followers.[5] One significant finding was that extreme intelligence differences between leaders and followers might be dysfunctional. For example, a leader with a relatively high IQ attempting to influence a group whose members have average IQs may be unable to understand why the members don't comprehend the problem or the leader's proposed solutions. In addition, such a leader may have difficulty in communicating ideas and policies. *Intelligence,* in the larger sense of the term, involves judgment, knowledge, and fluency of speech.

Some of the more important abilities associated with leadership effectiveness include the ability to get along with people. This interpersonal skill includes persuasiveness, tact, and diplomacy. The effective leader must demonstrate more than passing technical knowledge relevant to the task undertaken by the followers. These abilities no doubt vary in importance from situation to situation, but research confirms their importance in most leader–follower situations.

Because organizations exist to get work done, we should expect that the most effective leaders exhibit the ability to cause their followers to accomplish the desired work. This ability, termed *supervisory ability,* involves setting objectives, planning work, assigning people to do the work, and following up on the results of the work. Citing the research of Edwin Ghiselli, we can state with some assurance that leaders exhibit this ability. Ghiselli also reports that this ability becomes more pronounced as a person moves up the organizational hierarchy, although the nature of the work becomes more abstract and distant from the individual. First-line managers see daily the work their subordinates perform, whereas CEOs rarely see the actual work they initiate.[6]

Personality Traits

Some research results suggest that such personality traits as alertness, energy level, tolerance for stress, emotional maturity, originality, personal integrity, and self-confidence are associated with effective leadership.[7] Ghiselli reported several personality traits associated with leader effectiveness.[8] Ghiselli studied leaders in organizations and was particularly interested in differences among leaders at different levels in organizations. He contrasted supervisors, middle managers, and CEOs and found some differences in certain personality traits. For example, he found that the ability to initiate action decisively was related to the individual's level in the organization. The higher the person went in the organization, the more important this trait became; CEOs were more decisive than middle managers, who were more decisive than supervisors. Ghiselli also found that self-assurance was related to hierarchical position in the organization.

Additional reviews of the trait theory literature conclude that achievement, motivation, ambition, tenacity, initiative, self-confidence, and positive (and negative) personality traits are associated with leadership.[9] Although these traits do not identify actual or potential leaders in every instance, they do appear to have sufficient validity as predictors to warrant continued study. Certainly the testing activities of human resource departments in major organizations continue to use measures of these personality traits to identify employees with leadership potential.

Motivation

Leaders seem to exhibit a relatively high need for power, but they act on that need in socially acceptable ways. Effective leaders work within the system to accomplish socially desirable outcomes. This particular orientation to use power for constructive purposes, termed *socialized power orientation,* has been well established as one of the motivations of leaders. Another motivation that sets leaders apart is a relatively high need for achievement, particularly as reflected in the fields of their interest. Also, effective leaders have a relatively weak need for affiliation, suggesting that they would be more motivated by getting a task completed than by interacting with other people. However, the weak need for affiliation does not preclude the effective leader from using and perfecting interpersonal skills.

Table 11.1 summarizes a number of the most researched traits of leaders (traits found most likely to characterize successful leaders). Some studies have reported that these traits contribute to leadership success. However, leadership success is neither primarily nor completely a function of these or other traits.[10]

Synopsis of Trait Theory

Although some studies conclude that traits such as those in Table 11.1 differentiate effective from ineffective leaders, research findings are still contradictory for a number

TABLE 11.1
Traits Associated with Leadership Effectiveness

Personality	Motivation	Ability
• Energy level	• Socialized power orientation	• Interpersonal skills
• Stress tolerance	• Strong need for achievement	• Cognitive skills
• Self-confidence	• Self-starter	• Technical skills
• Emotional maturity	• Persuasiveness	
• Integrity		

OB AT WORK Wanted: Global Leaders

Globalization requires leaders with a unique skill set. As such, a typical want ad for a global leader would most likely read something like this: "*Wanted: An individual who speaks two or more languages, adapts quickly to different cultures, is curious, is able to apply creative global-centric leadership behaviors, and has a strong sense of adventure and desire to experience new things . . . in short, a cosmopolitan individual with a global mindset.*"

Now more than ever, multinational companies have to fight to survive in the increasingly global marketplace. Despite the rapid increases in competition in home and overseas markets and the ever-increasing complexity of doing business on a global scale, there is a dearth of globally literate leaders who can help multinational companies navigate these dangerous waters to survive and succeed internationally. The results of a survey of *Fortune* 500 firms found that 85 percent of respondents indicate that their firms do not have enough global leaders. The respondents went on to rank the scarcity of competent global leaders as an extremely important issue for the company, followed by such factors as adequate financial resources, improved international communication technology, a higher-quality local workforce, and greater political stability in developing countries. Exacerbating the shortage problem is that many managers and executives have excellent track records in their home countries but lack the appropriate international skills and attitudes to apply their talents in the global marketplace.

What characteristics do global leaders need to possess to be successful? Here is a brief list of some of the more important qualifications:

1. *Inquisitiveness*—Despite the physical demands of travel (jet lag, different languages and cultures, etc.), global leaders are driven by a sense of adventure and a desire to have novel experiences.
2. *Emotional connection*—Global leaders must have a genuine human connection with employees and stakeholders throughout the company's worldwide operations. This includes making an effort to listen to and understand other people and their viewpoints.
3. *Integrity*—International leaders must display ethical behavior and loyalty to the company's agreed-upon values and strategy. Such consistent and integrity-based leadership helps in the development of trust with stakeholders of the organization.
4. *Capacity for managing uncertainty*—Global managers face higher levels of uncertainty than their domestic counterparts, including incomplete market data, foreign currency fluctuations, unpredictable government intervention in trade, and the like. Successful leaders must be aware of such variables and learn to make decisions in the midst of constantly changing environmental conditions.
5. *Business and organizational savvy*—Global leaders must be able to recognize and seize market opportunities, know their firm's strengths and weaknesses, and understand how to navigate their company through the challenges of dealing with different cultures, languages, government regulations, increased geographic distances, unclear lines of authority, and different time zones.
6. *Extroversion*—Global leaders need to be outgoing and sociable as they make contact and develop trust-based relationships with local nationals from different countries. By taking challenging assignments that require high levels of contact with people from different cultures, leaders will develop effective global leadership skills.

Leadership in a domestic environment is difficult enough, but leaders of 21st-century multinational companies must develop the skills and experiences highlighted here to guide their organizations successfully.

Sources: Paula Caligiuri and Ibraiz Tarique, "Predicting Effectiveness in Global Leadership Activities," *Journal of World Business* 44, no. 3 (2009): 336–346; Christina Moro Bueno and Stewart L. Tubbs, "Identifying Global Competencies: An Exploratory Study," *Journal of American Academy of Business* (September 2004): 80–87; Ruth E. Thaler-Carter, "Whither Global Leaders?" *HRMagazine,* May 2000, pp. 82–88; Robert H. Rosen, "What Makes a Globally Literate Leader?" *Chief Executive,* April 2000, pp. 46–48; and Hal B. Gregerson, Allen J. Morrison, and J. Stewart Black, "Developing Leaders for the Global Frontier," *Sloan Management Review* (Fall 1998): 21–32.

of possible reasons. First, the list of potentially important traits is endless. Every year, new traits, such as the sign under which a person is born, handwriting style, and order of birth are added to personality, physical characteristics, and intelligence. This continual "adding on" results in more confusion among those interested in identifying leadership traits. Second, trait test scores aren't consistently predictive of leader effectiveness. Leadership traits alone don't influence followers; rather, they act in combination with contextual and other factors. This interaction influences the leader–follower relationship. Third, patterns of behavior depend largely on the situation: leadership behavior that's effective in a bank may be ineffective in a company that operates a social networking website. Finally, the trait approach fails to provide insight into what the effective leader does on the job. Observations are needed that describe the behavior of effective and ineffective leaders.

Despite its shortcomings, the trait approach is not completely invalid. Kirkpatrick and Locke find evidence that effective leaders are different from other people.[11] Their studies show that leaders don't have to be great intellects to succeed. However, leaders need to have the "right stuff" or traits to have a good chance to be effective. Simply put, leaders are not like all people, but the ways in which they differ are not altogether known or understood. The appeal of the trait theory of leadership has global implications as the OB at Work feature on the previous page suggests.

Stogdill concisely captures the value of the trait approach:

> The view that leadership is entirely situational in origin and that no personal characteristics are predictive of leadership . . . seems to overemphasize the situational and underemphasize the personal nature of leadership.[12]

Thus, our view of leadership must include the ideas that leaders differ from nonleaders and that effective leaders differ from ineffective leaders.

The Behaviors of Effective Leaders

In the late 1940s, researchers began to explore the idea that how a person acts determines that person's leadership effectiveness. Instead of searching for traits, these researchers examined behaviors and their impact on measures of effectiveness such as production and satisfaction of followers. The preponderance of theory and research along these lines has depended on the idea that leaders must cope with two separate but interrelated aspects of their situations: they must accomplish the task, and they must do so through the efforts of those they lead. Thus, even though a variety of different terms have been used to identify these two facts of leadership, all can be understood as relating to tasks and people. Leadership behavior can be studied by analyzing what leaders do in relation to accomplishing the task and to maintaining the effort of people doing the task. As we will see, researchers and theorists (and leaders) use several different terms to refer to these two important foci of leadership behaviors.

Job-Centered and Employee-Centered Leadership

In 1947, Rensis Likert began studying how best to manage the efforts of individuals to achieve desired production and satisfaction objectives.[13] The purpose of most leadership research of the Likert-inspired team at the University of Michigan (UM) was to discover the principles and methods of effective leadership. The effectiveness criteria used in many of the studies included

1. Productivity per work-hour, or other similar measures of the organization's success in achieving its production goals.
2. Job satisfaction of members of the organization.
3. Turnover, absenteeism, and grievance rates.
4. Costs.
5. Scrap loss.
6. Employee and managerial motivation.

OB AND YOUR CAREER Becoming More Employee-Centered

Managers and supervisors can increase employee-centered behaviors in a variety of ways. Some suggestions for doing this include:

1. Try to use rewards (e.g., special assignments, bonuses) rather than punishments for reinforcing and modifying subordinates' behaviors.
2. Be an open and frequent communicator. Share information with subordinates and others to develop and maintain trust.
3. Listen carefully. Employees want to be heard and feel that what they have to say is taken seriously.
4. Mentor employees. Provide them with advice and job opportunities to achieve their career goals.
5. Admit mistakes and correct them with a positive attitude. This behavior will let employees know you're human while contributing to a more supportive and positive work environment.

Source: Adapted from John M. Ivancevich, Robert Konopaske, and Michael T. Matteson, *Organizational Behavior and Management,* 9th ed. (Burr Ridge, IL: McGraw-Hill/Irwin, 2011).

Studies were conducted in a wide variety of organizations: chemical, electronics, food, heavy machinery, insurance, petroleum, pubic utilities, hospitals, banks, and government agencies. Data were obtained from thousands of employees doing different job tasks, ranging from unskilled work to highly skilled research and development work.

job-centered leader
A person who closely supervises and observes the work of others.

Through interviewing leaders and followers, researchers identified two distinct styles of leadership, referred to as *job-centered* and *employee-centered.* The **job-centered leader** focuses on completing the task and uses close supervision so that subordinates perform their tasks using specified procedures. This leader relies on coercion, reward, and legitimate power to influence the behavior and performance of followers. Leaders exhibiting this leadership style seemed to view concern for people as an important luxury that they couldn't always afford.

employee-centered leader
A person who supervises only generally the work of others. He or she attempts to permit others to sense autonomy and support.

The **employee-centered leader** focuses on the people doing the work and believes in delegating decision making and aiding followers in satisfying their needs by creating a supportive work environment. Employee-centered leaders concerned themselves with followers' personal advancement, growth, and achievement. Such leaders emphasized individual and group development with the expectation that effective work performance would naturally follow. The OB and Your Career above provides suggestions as to how managers and supervisors can become more employee-centered.

Although the findings of this extensive research effort are quite complex, we can credit it with making a very strong case for the relative advantage of employee-centered over job-centered leadership. However, the studies suggest that a leader must be either one or the other; an individual cannot be both job- and employee-centered. The seeming inability to be both job-centered and person-centered and be an effective leader stimulated other studies to test that conclusion.

Initiating Structure and Consideration Leadership

initiating structure
Leadership acts that imply the structuring of job tasks and responsibilities for followers.

Among the several large leadership research programs that developed after World War II, one of the most significant was undertaken at Ohio State University (OSU). This program resulted in the development of a two-factor theory of leadership and indicated that leaders could be both job- and employee-centered.[14] A series of studies isolated two leadership behaviors, referred to as *initiating structure* and *consideration.* **Initiating structure** (or job-centered in Likert's terms) involves behavior in which the leader organizes and defines the relationships in the group, tends to establish well-defined patterns and channels of

FIGURE 11.2
Scores of Five Leaders: Initiating Structure and Consideration

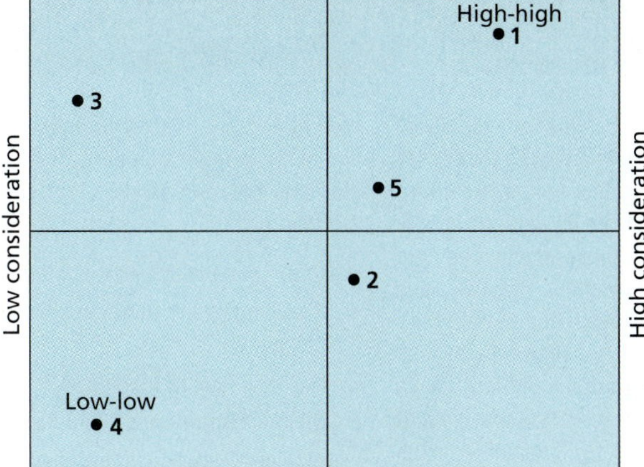

consideration
Acts of the leader that show supportive concern for the followers in a group.

communication, and spells out ways of getting the job done. The leader with a high initiating structure tendency focuses on goals and results. **Consideration** (or employee-centered in Likert's terms) involves behavior indicating friendship, mutual trust, respect, warmth, and rapport between the leader and the followers. The leader with a high consideration tendency supports open communication and participation.

The OSU researchers measured leaders' tendencies to practice these two leadership behaviors and were able to depict them graphically. Figure 11.2 shows behaviors of five different leaders. Individual 1 is high on both initiating structure and consideration; individual 4 is low on both dimensions.

The original premise was that a high degree of consideration and a high degree of initiating structure (high-high) was the most effective of the four possible combinations. Since the original research undertaken to develop the questionnaire, there have been numerous studies of the relationship between these two leadership dimensions and various effectiveness criteria. In a study at International Harvester, researchers began to find some more complicated interactions of the two dimensions. Supervisors who scored high on initiating structure not only had high proficiency ratings from superiors, they also had more employee grievances. A high consideration score was related to lower proficiency ratings and fewer absences.[15]

Other studies have examined how male and female leaders use initiating structure and consideration. A review of the literature reporting the results of such studies found that male and female leaders exhibit equal amounts of initiating structure and consideration and have equally satisfied followers.[16]

The OSU theory has been criticized for simplicity (e.g., only two dimensions of leadership), lack of generalizability, and reliance on questionnaire responses to measure leadership effectiveness. Despite these limitations, the MU and OSU studies made considerable headway in our understanding of effective leadership behavior. In particular, they broke from the traditional thinking that a leader must focus on either tasks or people. The researchers found that leaders could behave in ways that gave equal attention to both factors in any and all leadership situations—the task to be done and the people to do the task.

The search for answers regarding the most effective leadership behavior has known no national boundaries. The next OB at Work feature reports how Indian leaders receive high marks for treating their employees well.

OB AT WORK Indian Business Leaders Focus on Their People

A recent survey by Kenexa Research Institute of over 20,000 employees from several companies found that 69 percent of Indian employees rated their global senior leaders as effective. This stands in stark contrast to the 34 percent of U.S. employees and the 53 percent of Chinese employees who rated their respective senior global leaders as effective. Why are Indian business leaders rated so much higher than their American and Chinese counterparts? A research team from the Harvard Business School (HBS) conducted interviews at 98 large Indian-based firms that provide some insight into this question. After interviewing top executives from such companies as Mahindra & Mahindra, Tata, Aventis Pharma, and Reliance Industries, the HBS researchers reported that Indian leaders put their employees first and emphasize that their people are the main cause of their companies' competitive advantage. The researchers reported other employee-centric practices that Indian leaders follow to be successful, including: pursuing a long-term view of the business, linking the business's success to social missions and priorities, and investing in the development and training of employees.

With median job tenure at just two years and turnover rates among young Indian employees averaging between 15 and 30 percent per year, such people-focused practices as those outlined above are meant to retain valued employees in a tight, competitive labor market. Infosys, a $4.8 billion global leader in outsourcing and consulting services, is not immune to the problems of retaining talented employees. The company's turnover rate is about 15 percent. Although high by U.S. standards, turnover at Infosys is on the lower end of the industry standard. The company takes a variety of steps to make employees feel engaged and committed to the organization:

- Offering above-market salaries, benefits, and perquisites;
- Providing opportunities to advance rapidly within the company;
- Having a female-friendly and diverse work environment;
- Maintaining a strong value-based organization culture;
- Allocating awards for excellence in a variety of functional areas;
- Supporting an employee grievance program; and,
- Inviting five or six young, high-potential employees to join the management council on a rotational basis.

Indian business leaders believe that their competitive advantage lies in their employees. Perhaps business leaders from other countries could improve their organizations' effectiveness by following a similar "people first" approach to leadership.

Sources: Aparna Nancherla, "Trickle-Down Engagement," *T+ D* 64, no. 4 (April 2010): 22–23; Peter Cappelli, Harbir Singh, Jitendra V. Singh, and Michael Useem, "Leadership Lessons from India," *Harvard Business Review* 88, no. 3 (March 2010): 90–97; Elaine Appleton Grant, "How to Retain Talent in India," *MIT Sloan Management Review* 50, no. 1 (Fall 2008): 6–7; and Julian Birkinshaw, "Infosys: Computing the Power of the People," *Business Strategy Review* 19, no. 4 (Winter 2008): 18.

Comparisons of Effective Leadership Behavior Theories

The two theories of leadership behavior are compared and contrasted in Table 11.2. These two theories have provided practitioners with information on what behaviors leaders should possess. This knowledge has resulted in the establishment of training programs for individuals who perform leadership tasks. Each approach is associated with highly respected theorists, researchers, or consultants, and each has been studied in different organizational settings. Yet, the linkage between leadership and such important performance indicators as production, efficiency, and satisfaction hasn't been conclusively resolved by either of the two personal behavioral theories.

The simplicity of the initiating structure and consideration view of leadership is appealing. However, most researchers believe that environmental variables play some role in leadership effectiveness. For example, when successful initiating structure behavior is found, what other variables in the environment are at work? A worker who prefers to have a structured job and needs to have a job is likely to perform effectively under high initiating structure. What situational variables need to be considered? Neither the Ohio State nor the University of Michigan approach points out situational factors.

TABLE 11.2 A Review of Two Theories of Effective Leadership Behavior

Leadership Factors	Prime Initiator(s) of the Theory	Method of Measurement	Subjects	Principal Conclusions
Employee-centered and job-centered	Likert	Interview and questionnaire responses of groups of followers.	Formal leaders and followers in public utilities, banks, hospitals, food, manufacturing, and government agencies.	Employee-centered and job-centered styles result in production improvements. However, soon after, the job-centered approach style creates pressure that is resisted through absenteeism, turnover, grievances, and poor attitudes. The best style is *employee-centered.*
Initiating-structure and consideration	Fleishman, Stogdill, and Shartle	Questionnaire responses of groups of followers, peers, the immediate superior, and the leader.	Formal leaders and followers in military, education, public utilities, manufacturing, and government agencies.	The combination of initiating structure and behavior that achieves individual, group, and organizational effectiveness depends largely on the situation.

The Effects of Situational Differences

situational theories of leadership
An approach to leadership that advocates that leaders understand their own behavior, the behavior of their subordinates, and the situation before utilizing a particular leadership style. This approach requires the leader to have diagnostic skills in human behavior.

The search for the "best" set of traits or behavior has failed to discover an effective leadership mix and style for all situations. Thus, **situational theories of leadership** evolved that suggest leadership effectiveness depends on the fit between personality, task, power, attitudes, and perceptions.[17] A number of situation-oriented leadership approaches have been publicized and researched. Two of the earliest ones are the Fiedler contingency model and the path–goal theory. In this section, we will discuss these two theories as well as two other prominent situational theories: Hersey and Blanchard's situational leadership model (SLM) and leader–member exchange (LMX) theory.

Only after inconclusive and contradictory results evolved from much of the early trait and personal behavior research was the importance of the situation studied more closely by those interested in leadership. Eventually, researchers recognized that the leadership behavior needed to enhance performance depends largely on the situation: what's effective leadership in one situation may be disorganized incompetence in another. The situational theme of leadership, while appealing, is certainly a challenging orientation to implement.[18] Its basic foundation suggests that an effective leader must be flexible enough to adapt to the differences among subordinates and situations.

Deciding how to lead other individuals is difficult and requires an analysis of the leader, the group, and the situation.[19] Managers who are aware of the forces they face are able to modify their styles to cope with changes in the work environment. Three factors of particular importance are (1) forces within the managers, (2) forces in the subordinates, and (3) forces in the situation.[20] Tannenbaum and Schmidt state the situational theme in this way:

> Thus, the successful manager of men can be primarily characterized neither as a strong leader nor as a permissive one. Rather, he is one who maintains a high batting average in accurately assessing the forces that determine what his most appropriate behavior at any given time should be and in actually being able to behave accordingly.[21]

As the importance of situational factors and leader assessment of forces became more recognized, leadership research became more systematic, and contingency models of leadership began to appear in the organizational behavior and management literature. Each model has its advocates and each attempts to identify the leader behaviors most appropriate for a series of leadership situations. Also, each model attempts to identify the leader-situation patterns important for effective leadership.

Contingency Leadership Model

Developed by Fiedler,[22] the contingency model of leadership effectiveness postulates that the performance of groups is dependent on the interaction between leadership style and situational favorableness.

Leader's Style

Fiedler's studies led him to believe that leaders practice one or the other of two styles: *task-oriented leadership* or *relationship-oriented leadership*. He and his colleagues spent many years developing a way to measure an individual's tendency to practice these two styles, eventually settling on a method that relies on psychological reasoning. According to Fiedler, individuals whose personality favors task completion and a sense of accomplishment would more likely practice task-oriented leadership. An individual whose personality values warm, supportive relationships with others would likely practice relationship-oriented leadership.

Moreover, Fiedler's studies convinced him that individuals cannot be both task- and relationship-oriented. Individuals in leadership positions will be more comfortable, sincere, and effective practicing the leadership behavior that supports their own underlying personality. Thus, the most important leadership issue is to match leaders' personalities and styles to the situation in which they will be effective.

Situational Factors

leader–member relations
A factor in the Fiedler contingency model that refers to the degree of confidence, trust, and respect that the leader obtains from the followers.

task structure
Factor in Fiedler contingency model that refers to how structured a job is with regard to requirements, problem-solving alternatives, and feedback on job success.

Fiedler proposes three situational factors that determine whether a task- or relationship-oriented style is more likely to be effective: leader–member relations, task structure, and position power. From theoretical as well as intuitive points of view, interpersonal leader–follower relationships are likely to be the most important variable in a situation.

The **leader–member relations** factor refers to the degree of confidence, trust, and respect that followers have in the leader. This situational variable reflects acceptance of the leader. The leader's influence depends in part on acceptance by followers. If others are willing to follow because of charisma, expertise, or mutual respect, the leader has little need to rely on task-oriented behavior; the followers willingly follow the leader. If, however, the leader isn't trusted and is viewed negatively by followers, the situation would likely, but not necessarily, call for task-oriented behavior.

The second most important situational factor is referred to as **task structure**. This factor refers specifically to the characteristics of the work to be done. Some of the important work characteristics include

1. The degree to which the job's tasks and duties are clearly stated and known to the people performing the job.
2. The degree to which problems encountered in the job can be solved by a variety of procedures. An assembly-line worker solves problems within a systematic framework, while a scientist has many different ways to solve a problem.
3. The degree to which the "correctness" of the solutions or decisions typically encountered in a job can be demonstrated by appeal to authority, by logical procedure, or by feedback. A quality control inspector can show defective parts and clearly indicate why a part is sent back for reworking.
4. The degree to which there's generally more than one correct solution. An accountant preparing a balance sheet has few choices, while a research scientist may have numerous potentially correct alternatives to choose from.

If we think of combining these four characteristics to describe any job, task, or assignment, we can conclude that they do indeed vary from high structure (those clearly known and understood, with relatively few solutions to any encountered problem, whose correctness can be demonstrated) to low task structure (those vaguely known and understood, with many possible solutions to encountered problems, whose correctness cannot be demonstrated). Thus, the second most important situational variable refers to the nature of the task assigned to the leader and the group.

position power
A factor in the Fiedler contingency model that refers to the power inherent in the leadership position.

Position power in the contingency model refers to the power inherent in the leadership position. This situational characteristic takes into account that leadership occurs in a variety of different organizations and groups differentiated according to how much formal authority the leader has to make decisions and to exact obedience from subordinates. To determine leader position power, we ask questions such as[23]

1. Can the supervisor recommend subordinate rewards and punishments to the boss?
2. Can the supervisor punish or reward subordinates on her own?
3. Can the supervisor recommend promotion or demotion of subordinates?

Fiedler contends that such questions provide a profile of strong or weak position power.

Favorableness of the Situation

The three situational factors can now be combined to describe different situations. These situations will differ in the degree to which they are favorable to the leader's influence attempts. Ask yourself this question: would you rather be a leader in a situation where leader-member relations are good, the task is relatively structured, and your position power is relatively strong or in the opposite situation with poor leader–member relations, an unstructured task, and weak position power? Chances are you selected the first situation because it would be more *favorable* to your leadership efforts. Figure 11.3 combines the three situational factors such that we now have eight different situations ranging from situation 1, which is very favorable to the leader, to situation 8, which is very unfavorable to the leader.

Which Leader for Which Situation?

We can use the figure to classify any particular situation if we know about leader–member relations, task structure, and position power. And as we have also seen, leaders have a preference for either task-oriented behavior or relationship-oriented behavior. With this information, research can be undertaken that identifies situations as one of the eight possibilities, and, with sufficient samples of different situations and leaders, we could determine whether a particular style of leadership is more effective leadership.

FIGURE 11.3
Summary of Fiedler's Situational Variables and Their Preferred Leadership Styles

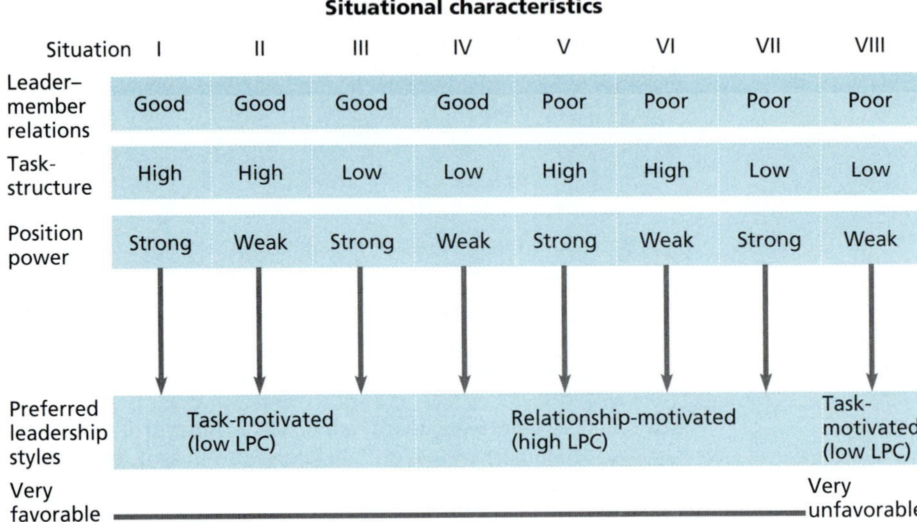

Over the past three decades, Fiedler and advocates of the contingency model have studied military, educational, and industrial leaders. In a summary of 63 studies based on 454 separate groups, Fiedler suggests the kind of leadership that's most appropriate for the situational conditions.[24] Figure 11.3 summarizes these studies. As noted in the figure, task-oriented leaders perform better than relationship-oriented leaders in intermediately favorable situations (4, 5, 6, and 7). These findings support the notion that each type of leader is effective in certain situations.

Consider the following situations:

Office manager. This individual has eight subordinates who like her. She structures the job by making work assignments and by setting goals for required outputs. She is also responsible for reviewing the work of subordinates and is the main spokesperson for and evaluator of the employees at merit review time.

Project engineer. This individual was appointed as the leader of a five-person project study group. None of the assigned members really want to serve in the group; they have other, more pressing jobs. As the appointed leader, the project engineer was actually given no power. His calls for meetings are generally unanswered. And when he gets the assigned members together, they're hostile, negative, and discourteous.

Registered nurse (supervisor). This individual is well liked by her subordinates, but the physicians have almost total control of the work. They won't permit the registered nurse to perform what she feels are nursing activities. This nurse is in a constant battle with the physicians to let her do the job and to stop interfering.

Figure 11.3 classifies these three individuals based on what we know about the situation in which they lead. The officer manager is in situation 1, in which she is liked, has a structured task, and has position power. The project engineer is in situation 8, with poor leader–member relations, low task structure, and weak position power. The registered nurse is in situation 4. She's well liked, but she has no task-structure opportunities and no position power because of the physicians. The situation is more favorable for the situation 1 leader than for the situation 8 leader.

When the situation is highly favorable or highly unfavorable, a task-oriented approach generally produces the desired performance. The well-liked office manager, who has power and has clearly identified the performance goals, is operating in a highly favorable situation.

The project engineer, who faces a group of suspicious and hostile subordinates and has little power and vague task responsibilities, needs to be task-oriented in this highly unfavorable situation.

Changing Situations to Fit the Leader

Fiedler recommends that organizations should concentrate on changing situations to fit their leaders, rather than changing (training) leaders to fit their situations. Thus, individuals who prefer task-oriented behavior will not benefit from training in human relations skills. The reverse also holds; relationship-oriented leaders will not respond to training to make them more task-oriented. He also suggests that leaders can make changes that result in more favorable situations. Table 11.3 presents some of his suggestions for changing particular situational factors.

A practical application of Fiedler's contingency approach is the training program LEADER MATCH.[25] Most training programs try to change the leader's personality to fit the situation, but this programmed learning system trains leaders to modify their leadership situation to fit their personalities. In LEADER MATCH, training participants read a workbook, assess their preferred leadership style, discuss and analyze leadership situations, and evaluate their performance in analyzing the situations.

TABLE 11.3
Leadership Actions to Change Situations

Modifying Leader–Member Relations

1. Spend more—or less—informal time (lunch, leisure activities, etc.) with your subordinates.
2. Request particular people for work in your group.
3. Volunteer to direct difficult or troublesome subordinates.
4. Suggest or affect transfers of particular subordinates into or out of your unit.
5. Raise morale by obtaining positive outcomes (e.g., special bonuses, time off, attractive jobs) for subordinates.

Modifying Task Structure

If you wish to work with less structured tasks:

1. Ask your boss, whenever possible, to give you the new or unusual problems and let you figure out how to get them done.
2. Bring the problems and tasks to your group members and invite them to work with you on the planning and decision-making phases of the tasks.

If you wish to work with more highly structured tasks:

1. Ask your superior to give you, whenever possible, the tasks that are more structured or to give you more detailed instructions.
2. Break the job down into smaller subtasks that can be more highly structured.

Modifying Position Power

To raise your position power:

1. Show your subordinates who's boss by exercising fully the powers that the organization provides.
2. Make sure that information to your group gets channeled through you.

To lower your position power:

1. Call on members of your group to participate in planning and decision-making functions.
2. Let your assistants exercise relatively more power.

Critique of Fiedler's Contingency Model

Fiedler's mode and research have elicited pointed criticisms and concerns. First, Graen and associates present evidence that research support for the model is weak, especially if studies conducted by researchers not associated with Fiedler are examined.[26] The earlier support and enthusiasm for the model came from Fiedler and his students, who conducted numerous studies of leaders. Second, researchers have called attention to the questionable measurement of preferred leadership style; these researchers claim that the reliability and validity of the questionnaire measures are low.[27] Third, the meaning of the variables presented by Fiedler isn't clear. For example, at what point does a *structured* task become an *unstructured* task? Who can define or display this point? Finally, critics claim that Fiedler's theory can accommodate nonsupportive results. This point is specifically made by one critic who states, "Fiedler has revealed his genius twice; first in devising the model, which stands like calculus to arithmetic compared with previous leadership models, and second, in his ability to integrate new findings into his models."[28]

Despite supporters and detractors, Fiedler's contingency model has made significant contributions to the study and application of leadership principles. Fiedler called direct attention to the situational nature of leadership. His view of leadership stimulated numerous research studies and much-needed debate about the dynamics of leader behavior. Certainly, Fiedler has played one of the most prominent roles in encouraging the scientific study of leadership in work settings. He pointed the way and made others uncomfortably aware of the complexities of the leadership process.

Path–Goal Model

path–goal leadership model
Theory that suggests a leader needs to influence followers' perceptions of work goals, self-development goals, and paths to goal attainment.

Like the other situational or contingency leadership approaches, the **path–goal leadership model** attempts to predict leadership effectiveness in different situations. According to this model, developed by Robert J. House, leaders are effective because of their positive effect on followers' motivation, ability to perform, and satisfaction. The theory is designated *path–goal* because it focuses on how the leader influences the followers' perceptions of work goals, self-development goals, and paths to goal attainment.[29]

The foundation of path–goal theory is the expectancy motivation theory discussed in Chapter 5. Some early work on the path–goal theory asserts that leaders become effective by making rewards available to subordinates and by making those rewards contingent on subordinates' accomplishment of specific goals.[30] It is argued that an important part of the leader's job is to clarify for subordinates the behavior most likely to result in goal accomplishment. This activity is referred to as *path clarification.*

Leadership Behavior

The early path–goal work led to the development of a complex theory involving four specific leader behaviors (directive, supportive, participative, and achievement) and three subordinate attitudes (job satisfaction, acceptance of the leader, and expectations about effort-performance-reward relationships).[31] The *directive leader* tends to let subordinates know what's expected of them. The *supportive leader* treats subordinates as equals. The *participative leader* consults with subordinates and considers their suggestions and ideas before reaching a decision. The *achievement-oriented leader* sets challenging goals, expects subordinates to perform at the highest level, and continually seeks improvement in performance. As is evident, these four behaviors are more refined conceptualizations of the two general behaviors we have been discussing throughout the chapter: directive and achievement-oriented behaviors are but two distinct dimensions of task-oriented behavior; supportive and participative behaviors are two distinct dimensions of person-oriented behavior.

A study of professional employees from research and development organizations examined the path–goal model.[32] The results indicated that need for clarity moderated the relationship between a leader's path clarification and employees' satisfaction. The higher the need for clarity among subordinates, the stronger the relationship between the leader's initiating structure and job satisfaction.

Research studies also suggest that these four behaviors can be practiced by the same leader in various situations. These findings are contrary to Fiedler's notion concerning the difficulty of altering style. The path–goal approach suggests more flexibility than the Fiedler contingency model.

The Main Path–Goal Propositions

The path–goal theory has led to the development of two important propositions:[33]

1. Leader behavior is effective to the extent that subordinates perceive such behavior as a source of immediate satisfaction or as instrumental to future satisfaction.
2. Leader behavior is motivational to the extent that it makes satisfaction of subordinates' needs contingent on effective performance and that it complements the environment of subordinates by providing the guidance, clarity of direction, and rewards necessary for effective performance.

According to the path–goal theory, leaders should increase the number of kinds of rewards available to subordinates. In addition, the leaders should provide guidance and counsel to clarify the manner in which these rewards can be obtained. This means that the leader should help subordinates clarify realistic expectancies and reduce the barriers to the accomplishment of valued goals. For example, counseling employees on their chances for promotion and helping them eliminate skill deficiencies so that a promotion becomes a more realistic possibility are appropriate leadership behaviors. The leader works at making the path to goals as clear as possible for subordinates. The style best suited to accomplish this is selected and applied. Thus, the path–goal approach requires flexibility from the leader to use whichever style is appropriate in a particular situation.

Situational Factors

Two situational, or contingency, variables are considered in the path–goal theory: *personal characteristics of subordinates* and *environmental pressures and demands* with which subordinates must cope to accomplish work goals and derive satisfaction.

An important personal characteristic is subordinates' *perceptions of their ability.* The higher the degree of perceived ability relative to task demands, the less likely the subordinate is to accept a directive leader's style. This directive style of leadership would be viewed as unnecessarily close. In addition, a person's *locus of control* also affects responses. Individuals with an internal locus of control (they believe that rewards are contingent upon their efforts) are generally more satisfied with a participative style, while individuals who have an external locus of control (they believe that rewards are beyond their personal control) are generally more satisfied with a directive style.

Environmental variables include factors that aren't within the control of the subordinate but are important to satisfaction or to the ability to perform effectively. These include the tasks, the formal authority system of the organization, and the work group. Any of these environmental factors can motivate or constrain the subordinate. Environmental forces may also serve as rewards for acceptable levels of performance. For example, the subordinate could be motivated by the work group and receive satisfaction from co-workers' acceptance for doing a job according to group norms.

FIGURE 11.4
The Path–Goal Model

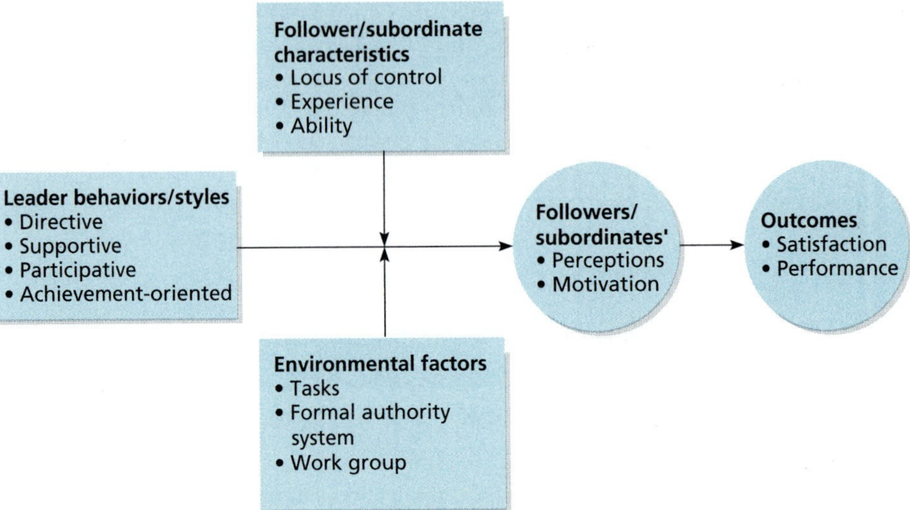

The path–goal theory proposes that leader behavior is motivational to the extent that it helps subordinates cope with environmental uncertainties. A leader who reduces the uncertainties of the job is considered to be a motivator because he increases subordinates' expectations that their efforts lead to desirable rewards.

Figure 11.4 presents the path–goal approach. The total path–goal approach has not been subjected to a complete test. Parts of the model, however, have been examined in field settings. One study found that when task structure (the repetitiveness or routineness of the job) was high, directive leader behavior was negatively related to satisfaction; when task structure was low, directive leader behavior was positively related to satisfaction. Also, when task structure was high, supportive leadership was positively related to satisfaction; under low task structure, there was no relationship between supportive leader behavior and satisfaction.[34]

Critique of the Path–Goal Model

There is some question about the predictive power of the path–goal model. One researcher suggested that subordinate performance might be the cause of changes in leader behavior instead of, as predicted by the model, the other way around.[35] A review of the path–goal approach suggested that the model had resulted in development of only a few hypotheses. These reviewers also point to the record of inconsistent research results associated with the model. They agree that research has consistently shown that the higher the task structure of subordinate jobs, the higher the relationship between supportive leader behavior and subordinate satisfaction. However, they maintain that the second main hypothesis of the path–goal model hasn't received consistent support. This hypothesis—the higher the task structure, the lower the relationship between directive leader behavior and subordinate satisfaction—has received only some support.[36]

On the positive side, one must admit that the path–goal model is an improvement over the trait and personal behavioral theories. It attempts to indicate which factors affect motivation to perform. In addition, the path–goal approach introduces both situational factors and individual differences when examining leader behavior and outcomes such as satisfaction and performance. The approach makes an effort to explain why a particular style of leadership works best in a given situation. As more research accumulates, this type of explanation will have practical utility for those interested in the leadership process in work settings.

Hersey-Blanchard Situational Leadership Model

Managers often complain that esoteric theories don't help them do a better job on the production line, in the office, or in a research and development lab. They request something they can apply and use. Hersey and Blanchard developed a situational leadership model (SLM) that has appealed to many managers.[37] Large firms and small businesses have used the SLM and enthusiastically endorse its value.

SLM's emphasis is on followers and their level of maturity.[38] The leader must properly judge or intuitively know followers' maturity level and then use a leadership style that fits the level. **Readiness** is defined as the ability and willingness of people (followers) to take responsibility for directing their own behavior. It's important to consider two types of readiness: job and psychological. A person high in job readiness has the knowledge and abilities to perform the job without a manager structuring or directing the work. A person high in psychological readiness has the self-motivation and desire to do high-quality work. Again, this person has little need for direct supervision.

readiness
The followers' skills and willingness to do a job.

Leadership Behavior

Hersey and Blanchard used the Ohio State studies to further develop four leadership styles available to managers:

1. *Telling.* The leader defines the roles needed to do the job and tells followers what, where, how, and when to do the tasks.
2. *Selling.* The leader provides followers with structured instructions but is also supportive.
3. *Participating.* The leader and followers share in decisions about how best to complete a high-quality job.
4. *Delegating.* The leader provides little specific, close direction or personal support to followers.

By determining followers' readiness level, a manager can choose from among the four leadership styles. Figure 11.5 depicts the important elements of the SLM.

The next OB at Work feature illustrates how people learning to sail over a period of time could use all four styles of the SLM. Eventually, the sailors use a participating (S3) and a delegating (S4) approach as they conquer the tasks of sailing.

FIGURE 11.5
The Hersey-Blanchard Situational Leadership Model

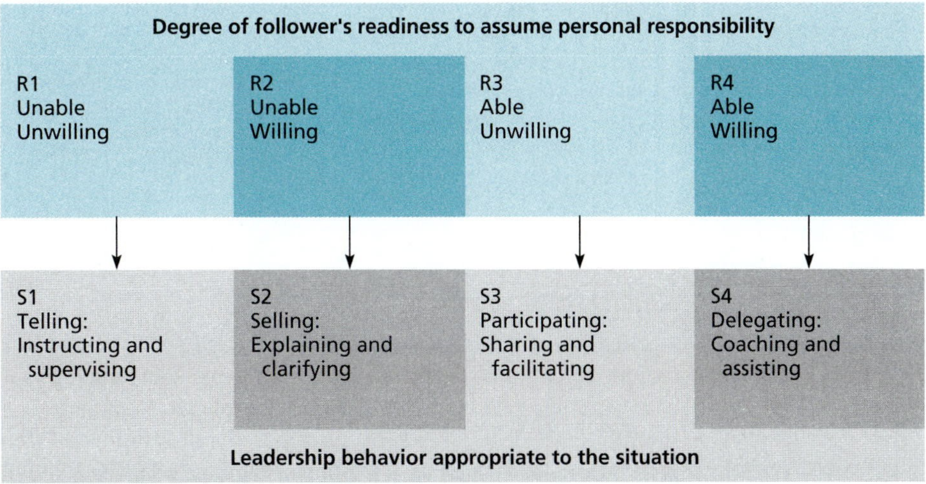

OB AT WORK Helping Women Become Leaders

Katherine Souka is a real estate broker from Brick, New Jersey. Her boyfriend took her out for her first sailing experience. He made the mistake of taking her out sailing in 26-knot winds and racing the boat almost entirely on one side, like a daredevil motorcyclist leaning into a sharp curve. While he was having the time of his life, Souka was terrified of losing hers. To get over her fear and learn how to handle a sailboat herself, she enrolled at Womanship, a sailing school based in Annapolis, Maryland that is "designed by women for women," as founder and president Suzanne Pogell likes to say.

It's mid-May. The afternoon sun darts through ashen clouds, and the wind dapples the Severn River, at the edge of the Chesapeake Bay, with whitecaps. Suddenly, the wind speed doubles to 22 knots, and Syrenka starts to heel, or tilt to one side. Perched at the stern, where she is manning one of the winches used to crank the ropes that control the main sails, Souka looks uneasy.

"I want to show you how not to be afraid," says instructor Kathy McGraw, known as Captain Kathy by her four-woman crew. With some difficulty, the crew members slowly reef, or reduce, the sail. It works. With less sail exposed to the wind, the boat slows down and tilts less. "Isn't that better?" she says.

Souka looks relieved but annoyed. "So you can control the heel in high winds," she says, shaking her head. "He could have made it heel less!"

The following week, having completed the three-day class, Souka exudes the zeal of a convert. She's shopping for her first sailboat and looking to join a local yacht club. "The whole experience helped me gain confidence in myself," she says. "I can do this. Nothing's mysterious about it anymore." As a divorced woman, she found the independence of sailing intoxicating—no relying on a noisy engine, or on men. "It was such a good reminder that you're in control of a lot of your destiny," says Souka, who plans to take a Womanship cruise in the Virgin Islands and to teach her 11-year-old daughter how to sail. "You can set your course, adjust your sails to what comes, and keep moving forward."

At Womanship, teaching sailing is only part of the mission. Handling a boat in high wind, problem solving with other women, overcoming fear—these experiences instill confidence and a sense of accomplishment. Tacking and jibing are means to a greater end. "We're not a typical sailing school," says Pogell. "We're using sailing to empower women, although I usually don't come out and use that word. I want them to discover the empowerment for themselves."

When Pogell launched Womanship in 1984, an all-woman sailing school was unheard of. This was years before the United States fielded the first all-female America's Cup team; before the adventure-vacation industry exploded and made women-only hiking, rafting, and rock-climbing excursions as common as Starbucks; and only four years after the Naval Academy admitted its first female cadet. It's not that women didn't sail. They just didn't have their hands on the wheel much, if ever. "The men were in charge, and the women were along for the ride," says Pogell.

Few women owned boats, and few yacht clubs allowed women to be members, says sailing historian John Rousmaniere. "What Suzanne recognized is that women wanted to learn how to sail," Rousmaniere says, "and the last people who should be teaching them were their husbands."

If anyone was going to rock the boat, it was Pogell, an outspoken former government consultant, public affairs manager, and environmentalist. She characterizes herself as an industry outsider, despite the fact that she has built one of the most successful sailing schools in the country. Womanship offers some 400 courses per year at 16 destinations around the globe, including the British Virgin Islands, the Florida Keys, New England, southern California, Vancouver, Greece, New Zealand, and, of course, Annapolis, which bills itself as the U.S. sailing capital. To date, more than 35,000 students have taken Womanship classes, from two-day daytime courses ($500) to 12-day live-aboard cruises ($3,250 for Greece).

Teaching women how to sail, take responsibility, work as a team, and lead are outcomes that emerge from the sailing school experience. Problem solving and decision making are important in sailing and managing and leading assets in an organization.

Sources: Adapted from "Womanship" at www.womanship.com (accessed on June 2, 2010); Wendi Winters, "The Language of Sailing," accessed at www.whatsupmag.com/apr06/sailing.shtml on April 6, 2007; and Chuck Salter, "Putting Winds in Their Sails," *Fast Company*, August 2003, pp. 92–94.

Situational Factors

Application of the model works as follows. Suppose that a manager determines that his recently hired followers are unable to do the work and unwilling to take the risk associated with learning to do it. The followers are at the (R1) readiness state. By moving vertically from R1 to the leadership behavior appropriate for this state, we see that telling is the appropriate style. That is, an R1 follower requires a leader who is high on task orientation, gives direct instructions, and is low in support behavior. Task behavior is more needed than supportive behavior. In fact, research is available to support the S1 style over any of the others.[39] Some may assume that a participative (S3) style is best. However, asking an insecure follower to participate may result in more insecurity about making a mistake or saying something that's considered dumb.

A follower will be more ready to take on additional responsibility as other leadership styles become more effective. For example, an R&D lab with expert, experienced scientists who are totally able and willing to do the job would flourish under a delegative (S4) style of leadership. Using the readiness indicator with the four-style model helps the manager conceptualize what's best for followers.

Blanchard has responded to some critics of the SLM by revising the original model.[40] He retitled various terms, calling task behavior *directive behavior* and relationship behavior *supportive behavior.* The four leadership styles are now called S1-directing, S2-coaching, S3-supporting, and S4-delegating. Readiness is now called the *development level of followers.* The development level is defined in terms of followers' current competence and commitment to do the job.

In training programs, Hersey and Blanchard use the Leader Behavior Analysis[41] survey scale to assess participants' attitudes about leadership. It consists of 20 questions that have training participants judge what leadership style is best suited. Here's one question:

> Recently, you have begun to have trouble with one of the people you supervise. He has become lackadaisical, and only your constant prodding has brought about task completion. Because of past experience with him, you suspect he may not have all the expertise needed to complete the high-priority task you have given him. You would
>
> a. Continue to direct and follow up on his efforts to complete the task.
> b. Continue to supervise his work and try to draw out his attitudes and feelings concerning the task assignment.
> c. Involve him in problem solving with his task, offer support, and use his ideas in the task completion.
> d. Let him know that this is an important task and ask him to contact you if he has any questions or problems.

The experts state that a selling leadership style is best. This is reflected in the (b) response. The follower has a motivation problem. He also isn't knowledgeable about how best to do the job. The worst style to use would be a delegation approach (d). The person isn't ready to be given responsibility to complete this important task. By analyzing and critiquing trainees' responses to this type of questions, trainers attempt to improve managers' judgments about which leadership style is best.

Although managers are attracted to the SLM, there are some serious unanswered questions. The most important may be, does it really work? Testing of the model, more than 40 years after its inception, is still limited. Even the originators, Hersey and Blanchard, have failed to provide evidence that predictions can be made or of which style is best. Another issue revolves around the notion that a leader can change or adapt his style to fit a follower or group. Are people in leadership positions this adaptable? Again, research is needed to validate the flexibility possibility among leaders.[42]

Despite the words of caution about limited research and flexibility, many managers like the SLM. It's thought to be practical, meaningful, and visible in training settings. As leadership continues to command attention in organizations, the SLM appears to remain a popular way to express what leaders should be doing at work.

Leader–Member Exchange Theory

Personal behavioral explanations of leadership suggest that the leader's behavior is the same across all followers.[43] This thinking is similar to assuming that a parent treats or interacts with each of her children the same. However, Graen has proposed the leader–member exchange (LMX) theory of leadership, which proposes that there's no such thing as consistent leader behavior across subordinates.[44] A leader may be very considerate toward one subordinate and very rigid and structured with another. Each relationship has a uniqueness, and it's the one-on-one relationships that determine subordinates' behaviors.

The LMX approach suggests that leaders classify subordinates into *in-group members* and *out-group members*. In-group members share a common bond and value system, and they interact with the leader. Out-group members have less in common with the leader and don't share much with her. The Leader-Member Exchange Questionnaire partially presented in Table 11.4 measures in-group versus out-group status.[45]

The LMX explanation suggests that in-group members are likely to receive more challenging assignments and more meaningful rewards. Research indicates that in-group members are more positive about the organization culture and higher job performance and satisfaction than employees in the out-group.[46] An out-group member isn't considered to be the type of person the leader prefers to work with, and this attitude is likely to become a self-fulfilled prophecy. Out-group members receive less challenging assignments, receive little positive reinforcement, become bored with the job, and often quit. They experience a lower quality relationship with their leader.[47]

The LMX approach rests on the assumption that the leader's perception of followers influences the leader's behavior, which then influences the follower's behavior. This exchange or mutual influence explanation is also found in the equity theory explanation of motivation.

Comparing the Situational Approaches

The four models for examining situation leadership have some similarities and some differences. They are similar in that they (1) focus on the dynamics of leadership, (2) have stimulated research on leadership, and (3) remain controversial because of measurement problems, limited research testing, or contradictory research results.

The themes of each model are summarized in Table 11.5. Fiedler's model, the most tested, is perhaps the most controversial. His view of leader behavior centers on task- and

TABLE 11.4
Items That Assess Leader–Member Exchange

Source: G. Graen, R. Liden, and W. Hoel (1982), "Role of Leadership in the Employee Withdrawal Process," *Journal of Applied Psychology*, 67, no. 6, p. 869.

1. How flexible do you believe your supervisor is about evolving change in *your* job? 4 = Supervisor is enthused about change; 3 = Supervisor is lukewarm to change; 2 = Supervisor sees little need to change; 1 = Supervisor sees no need for change.
2. Regardless of how much formal organizational authority your supervisor has built into his position, what are the chances that he would be personally inclined to use his power to help you solve problems in your work? 4 = He certainly would; 3 = Probably would; 2 = Might or might not; 1 = None.
3. To what extent can *you* count on your supervisor to "bail you out," at her expense, when *you* really need her? 4 = Certainly would; 3 = Probably; 2 = Might or might not; 1 = None.
4. How often do you take suggestions regarding your work to your supervisor? 4 = Almost always; 3 = Usually; 2 = Seldom; 1 = Never.
5. How would *you* characterize *your* working relationship with your supervisor? 4 = Extremely effective; 3 = Better than average; 2 = About average; 1 = Less than average.

The five items are summed for each participant, resulting in a possible range from 5 to 20.

TABLE 11.5 Summary Comparison of Four Important Situational Models of Leadership

	Fiedler's Contingency Model	House's Path–Goal Model	Hersey-Blanchard Situational Leadership Model	Leader–Member Exchange (LMX) Approach
Leadership qualities	Leaders are task- or relationship-oriented. The job should be engineered to fit the leader's style.	Leaders can increase follower's effectiveness by applying proper motivational techniques.	Leader must adapt style in terms of task and relationship behavior on the basis of followers.	Leader must be adaptive since there is no such thing as consistent leader behavior across subordinates.
Assumptions about followers	Followers prefer different leadership styles, depending on task structure, leader–member relations, and position power.	Followers have different needs that must be fulfilled with the help of a leader.	Followers' maturity (readiness) to take responsibility and ability influence the leadership style that is adopted.	Followers are categorized as in-groups (which share a common bond and value system, and interact with the leader) and out-groups (which have less in common with the leader).
Leader effectiveness	Effectiveness of the leader is determined by the interaction of environment and personality factors.	Effective leaders are those who clarify for followers the paths or behaviors that are best suited.	Effective leaders are able to adapt directing, coaching, supporting, and delegating style to fit the followers' levels of maturity.	The perceptive leader is able to adapt her style to fit followers' needs.
History of research problems	If investigations not affiliated with Fiedler are used, the evidence is contradictory on the accuracy of the model.	Model has generated very little research interest in past two decades.	Not enough research is available to reach a definitive conclusion about the predictive power of the theory.	Approach has generated a limited amount of research to support its assumptions and predictions.

relationship-oriented tendencies and how these interact with task and position power. The path–goal approach emphasizes the instrumental actions of leaders and four styles for conducting these actions (directive, supportive, participative, and achievement-oriented).

The situational variables discussed in each approach differ somewhat. There is also a different view of outcome criteria for assessing how successful the leader behavior has been: Fiedler discussed leader effectiveness, and the path–goal approach focuses on satisfaction and performance.

Summary of Key Points

- As the ability to influence followers, leadership involves the use of power and the acceptance of the leader by the followers. This ability to influence followers is related to the followers' need satisfaction.
- The trait approach has resulted in attempts to predict leadership effectiveness from physical, sociological, and psychological traits. The search for traits has led to studies involving effectiveness and such factors as height, weight, intelligence, and personality.

- There continues to be a great deal of semantic confusion and overlap in the definition of leadership behavior. Such terms as *employee-centered, job-centered, initiating structure,* and *consideration* are classified as descriptions of what the leader does.
- The *situational approach* emphasizes the importance of forces within the leader, the subordinates, and the organization. These forces interact and must be properly diagnosed if effectiveness is to be achieved.
- The *contingency model* proposes that groups' performance is dependent on the interaction of leadership style and situational favorableness. The three crucial situational factors are leader–member relations, task structure, and position power.
- The *path–goal model* deals with specific leader behaviors and how they might affect employee satisfaction.
- The *Hersey-Blanchard situational leadership theory* is popular among managers. It proposes that by determining followers' readiness level, a manager can choose the best leadership style. It assumes that a manager can readily learn to adapt his style to each follower.
- The *leader–member exchange (LMX) theory* approach suggests that each superior–subordinate relationship is unique. The theory assumes that a leader can behave in different ways with different followers.

Discussion and Review Questions

1. Compare the trait, behavioral, and situational approaches to leadership in terms of practical value to organizations seeking to identify and develop present and future leaders.
2. In your experience, can leaders relate to followers both as members of the group and as individuals? What are the implications for leadership theory and practice if you decide that leadership is essentially a one-on-one interaction?
3. Explain the path–goal theory of leadership. Now apply the main ideas of this theory to a different setting, perhaps the case of a parent attempting to help her daughter improve her college study habits and grades.
4. Leader–member exchange theory suggests that subordinates who are part of the leader's in-group will receive better treatment than out-group members. As a member of the out-group, what steps can you take to increase your chances of becoming an in-group member?
5. Is leadership a characteristic a person is born with, or can it be developed through professional experiences, training, and mentoring? Explain.
6. Under what circumstances are authoritative or top-down directives as or more effective than a more participative style of leadership?
7. According to the contingency theory, an alternative to modifying the style of leadership through training is changing the favorableness of the situation. What is meant by changing the favorableness of the situation?
8. Think about a current or previous supervisor's leadership style. Which type of supervisor would you prefer to work for: one who leads by displaying consideration or one who leads by initiating structure? Discuss your preference.
9. In your experience, are leaders flexible enough to adapt leadership styles to the situation or followers? Explain.
10. Would it be difficult for a manager to accurately determine a follower's readiness level? Explain.

Taking It to the Net

Using Facts, Not Gossip

A number of opinions about leaders are popularized in the literature. Use your favorite library portal or public search engine (e.g., www.google.com or www.yahoo.com) to conduct a search for articles of the following:

- Leaders are born, not made.
- Leaders are effective because of what they know.
- Effective leadership is scarce.
- Women are less effective leaders than men.

Are these statements true or false? Is there research evidence to support or refute these statements?

Case for Analysis: *A New Leadership Position*

At Dancey Electronics company in a suburb of Dallas, management forecasts have indicated that the company should enjoy moderate growth during the next 10 years. This growth rate would require the promotion of three employees into newly created general manager positions. These individuals would then be required to spend most of their time working with departmental managers and less time on production, output, and cost issues.

A majority of the candidates for the three new positions have been with the company for at least 15 years. They're all skilled in the production aspects of operations. Company vice president Don Kelly believed, however, that none of the candidates had the training or overall insight into company problems to move smoothly into the general manager positions. Despite these anticipated problems, the board of directors decided that the three new general managers would be recruited from within Dancey.

In attempting to find the best candidates for the new positions, Dancey hired a consulting firm, Management Analysis Corporation (MAC), to perform an internal search for qualified individuals. Through interviews, testing, and a review of company records, the consulting firm generated a list of six candidates.

One candidate was Joe Morris. The analysis used to assess Joe involved the study of environmental variables and his current style of leadership. Exhibit 1 profiles Joe's leadership style and various environmental factors that have some effect on this style.

EXHIBIT 1
Morris Profile of Leadership

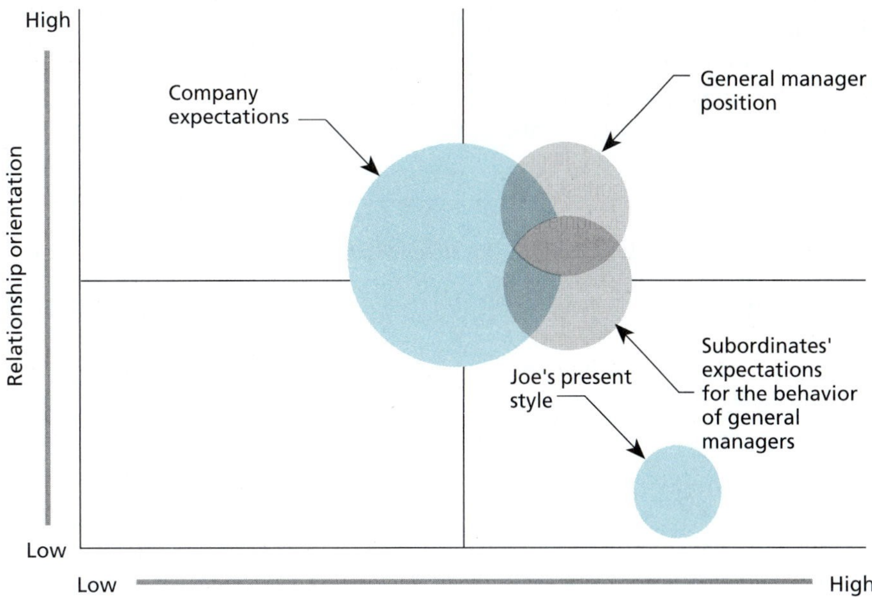

Joe's present leadership style, which is high in task orientation and low in relationship orientation, is similar to the leadership styles of the other five general manager candidates. The expectations of the company, the potential subordinates of the general manager, and the new position of general manager aren't consistent with any of the candidates' present leadership styles. The intersecting area indicates where the expectations of the company, the new position, and the subordinates would be consistent. According to MAC, this is the ideal leadership style for candidates to use as the general manager. If Joe or any other candidate were to accept the general manager job, he would have to significantly increase his relationship orientation. If he didn't, the probability of failure, according to the consulting firm, would be high.

Don Kelly was adamant about not going outside Dancey to find three potentially successful managers. He and the entire board of directors wanted to use a recruitment-from-within policy to secure the three best general managers. It was Don's belief that a leader could modify his style of leadership to meet new situational demands. This belief and the internal recruitment plan led Don to call a meeting to discuss a program to improve the compatibility between the three general managers finally selected (Joe Morris, Randy Santiago, and Ann Shumate) and the environmental factors (the company, the subordinates, and the requirements of the new position).

DISCUSSION QUESTIONS

1. Do you believe that the diagnosis and resulting profile prepared by Management Analysis Corporation were necessary steps in the process of finding a potentially successful group of general managers? Explain.
2. What alternatives are available to modify Joe Morris's potential effectiveness in the new general manager position?
3. Why will it be difficult for Joe Morris to modify his style of leadership?

Experiential Exercise: *Personal and Group Leadership Hall of Fame*

DIRECTIONS

1. Individually establish a list of three living "great leaders" and three dead "great leaders." Each person on the list should be from different fields: business, government, politics, humanitarian work, education, religion, military, sports, and so on.
2. Identify traits, skills, and contributions made by each of the six great leaders.
3. Groups of five or more participants will be formed to discuss the individually prepared lists.
4. From the group discussion, pick the best three living and best three dead great leaders. This list will be the group's final choices.
5. One person from the group should present the group's choices and summarize the reasons why these six great leaders stand out.
6. Are there any similarities across the groups' choices and reasons the leaders were selected?

Experiential Exercise: *Leadership Coach: Are Employees BOBs or WOWs?*

OBJECTIVES

1. To analyze a leadership failure applying relevant leadership theory.
2. To plan and practice a leadership coaching intervention.

RELATED TOPICS

Motivation, performance rewards, diversity, and communication are covered in this exercise.

STARTING THE EXERCISE

Each student in the class is to read the following passage and then answer the questions at the end.

BACKGROUND

You're a management consultant and have just spent the day observing Mike, the president of New Electronics Development Inc. Mike, who has been with the firm for just over a year, called you in to help him figure out why several of his product development employees who are responsible for creating new electronic products are such low performers. Mike is in the process of taking over the day-to-day operations and leadership from the founder and owner, who is looking forward to retirement. The company, while currently healthy, is facing an uncertain future in the rapidly evolving world of electronics. Mike knew the future of the firm, and his personal success, rested on the ability of the firm to develop truly innovative electronics devices. Within the past six months, more than a dozen new products were in the process of being developed and tested. The owner was ecstatic, but Mike, while pleased, thought his product development teams could do even better.

With input from his marketing and finance groups, Mike recently developed a complex metric to look at research group output and productivity. This measure was based on the projects the groups were working on and incorporated time to market, five-year revenue estimates, market share projections, resource requirements to bring the products to market, potential for after-sales service revenue, and a subjective measure of "fit" with Mike's vision of the firm. Mike used this overall output measure in the evaluation of product development team members' output and the allocation of research resources.

While Mike had the time to inform several of his "star" product development teams in advance, the companywide rollout of the measure was made at a staff retreat. Mike posted two lists: the "BOBs" (best of the best) and "WOWs" (worst of the worst). The BOBs were treated to rounds of golf, while the WOWs were instructed to use the time away from the office to improve the creativity of their new product ideas.

Since the retreat, Mike has had weekly "BOB Council" meetings to expedite research allocations and foster further innovative research. Mike explained this process as, "I want to spend my time where it will be the most productive." While there was initially some movement on and off the BOB and WOW listings, the groupings have remained relatively stable over the past three months. Mike's "problem children" are two product development groups that have been on the WOW list since its inception. Mike cannot understand these groups. He told you he would personally rather resign than be perennially on a "loser list."

On the way to your car this afternoon, you were stopped by Leslie, the leader of one of these WOW list groups. Leslie has been the group leader for 10 years, and while she admits her group has had a few "flops," she quickly lists numerous successes that she states are the foundation of the firm's current product group. She firmly and adamantly states that "the revenue from the products developed by my group are paying for that egotist's inflated salary, and he has the gall to make me communicate in memo rather than take my calls. If he had any experience in the industry he would know his BOB measure is bogus."

Leslie goes on to tell you that she never had any problem with the owner and suspects that Mike is trying to push her out because, in his world, women should be at the club playing tennis, not leading product development teams. She states that she and Carlos, the other "permanent" WOW member, are tired of being called "Loser Listers" and are fed up with Mike's abusive treatment.

COMPLETING THE EXERCISE

After you have read the background information, please answer individually the following questions:

1. Based on the material in the Chapters 11 and 12, which leadership model(s) may be used to best describe the situation?
2. What, if anything, can Mike do to improve the performance of New Electronics Development?
3. If you were coaching Mike, what pointers or suggestions would you offer him in terms of improving his leadership approach?

After addressing these questions individually, form small groups to discuss your answers. Take turns playing Mike and the coach, and role-play the five-minute debriefing.

Source: Written by Dr. Michael Dutch, Greensboro College, Greensboro, North Carolina (2007).

CHAPTER TWELVE

Leadership: Emerging Perspectives

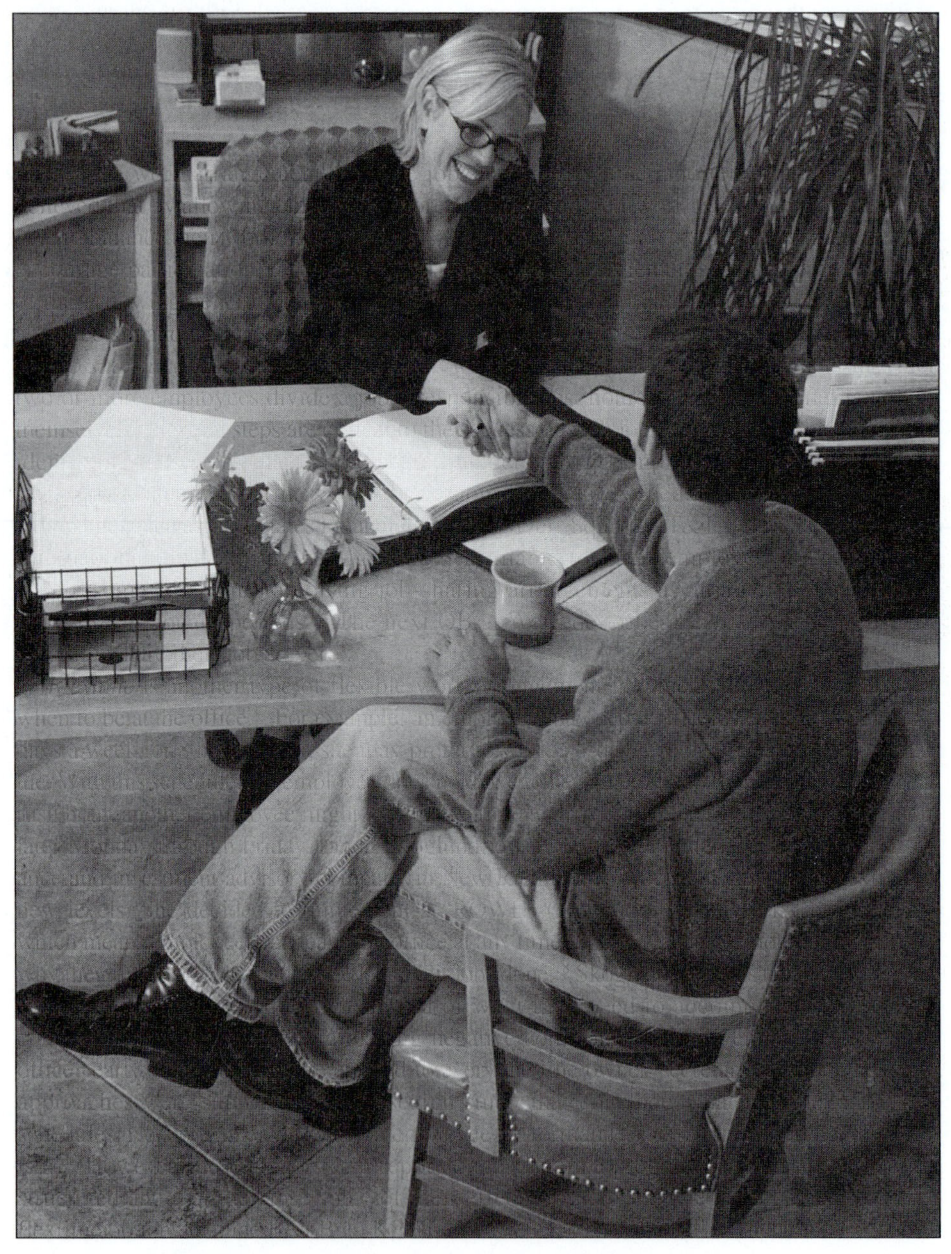

Learning Objectives

After completing Chapter 12, you should be able to

Define
What is meant by a prescriptive model of leadership.

Describe
The type of research needed to further develop a clearer explanation of charismatic leadership.

Discuss
Why leaders make attributions about employee performance problems.

Compare
The differences between transformational and transactional leaders.

Identify
Situations and settings in which self-managed groups and self-leadership would be useful and effective.

Leadership Cultures at Successful Companies

What do Zappos, Proctor & Gamble, and Southwest Airlines all have in common? All of these companies proactively use their organizational cultures to shape and develop future leaders. Tony Hsieh, CEO of Zappos (derived from the Spanish term for shoes, *zapatos*), has created a passionate, cooperative, fun-loving, and team-oriented culture that has helped the online shoe and apparel business grow to over $1 billion in sales in about 10 years. Hsieh encourages associates at the call center to deliver exceptional customer service. Given that there are no time limits placed on how long call center service representatives can talk to customers, one employee spent about two hours on the phone with a customer to ensure that she had an exceptional "wow" experience. By celebrating (and rewarding) such positive interactions with customers, Hsieh wants to instill the firm's core values and positive team spirit into all future leaders who may one day take over his position.

Proctor & Gamble prepares its future leaders by continuously moving them across geographic regions and different countries. Also, rising stars are given the responsibility of managing a small business with considerable growth potential. Proctor & Gamble calls these developmental opportunities "accelerator experiences" because they give future leaders a great deal of experience in a relatively short amount of time.

Southwest Airlines exposes employees at all levels to leadership opportunities. Leaders share their thinking with employees with the hope that informal mentoring and role modeling will inspire those employees to show their leadership potential by going the extra mile for a passenger who needs help or by coming in to help on the weekend during busy times. The organizational culture, which encourages employees to be themselves and work hard, creates fertile ground from which leaders from all levels of the organization can "spread their wings" and develop into tomorrow's leaders.

Sources: Adapted from "Getting a Foothold," *Wall Street Journal*, June 7, 2010, p. A. 17; Patricia O'Connell and John Larrere, "Develop Great Leaders," *Leadership Excellence* 27, no. 4 (April 2010): 12–14; Christopher Palmeri, "Now For Sale, The Zappos Culture," *Businessweek*, January 11, 2010, p. 57.

Examination of the host of theories presented in Chapter 11 discloses concerns about tasks, people, and situations. The terms used are often stated in complex language, but the themes are similar across theories. The issue of flexibility is not accepted by all theories. Can a person really be as flexible as the Hersey-Blanchard theory requires? It seems that some individuals can be flexible, but others are dry, rigid, and inflexible. Determining a leader's flexibility would seem like a worthwhile endeavor for an organization. How can this be done? In work settings, it must be done by observation, discussion, and actual behavior monitoring.

Leadership appears to play an important role in helping individuals and groups attain performance goals and organizations achieve high levels of effectiveness. Some leaders are better at performance enhancement than others. Effective leaders provide a coordination and control function that seems to bring people together, to chart the direction, and to provide verbal encouragement and recognition. Certainly there are many factors outside a leader's control.[1] For example, a department manager must work with the pool of employees available to complete projects. If the pool is self-motivated, achievement-oriented, and positively inclined toward accomplishing organizational goals, the leader's job will be easier than if faced with a lethargic, antagonistic, and negatively oriented group.

Even in situations involving self-managed groups, signs of leadership are present. Self-managed groups have a responsibility to complete an entire task. The members possess the skills to do the whole job and have the power to schedule work, evaluate performance, and sanction nonperformers. Someone in the group may take the lead in reprimanding nonperformers. That person may ask nonperformers to try to do better or may express the group's displeasure with the nonperformance. A little bit of leadership is creeping in, even in the self-managed situation.

The concept of self-leadership involves workers motivating themselves to perform tasks.[2] Is this the wave of the future? In some situations, yes. Some individuals don't like authority and control systems imposed on them. They prefer to manage their own work and build rewards into completing a high-quality job. W. L. Gore & Associates (makers of GORE-TEX and medical products) uses a self-leadership approach. Everyone in the firm has a sponsor responsible for seeing that Gore's four guiding principles are followed: fairness, freedom, commitment, and discretion. The sponsors guide new employees, help them find answers to questions, and show them how goals can be accomplished. The sponsor certainly has characteristics of a leader but is not the traditionally discussed leader. At Gore & Associates, the message is that self-leadership is important, encouraged, and recognized.[3]

Self-managed groups, self-leadership, situational approaches transformational leaders, contingency leadership, and no leadership at all are all possible in a changing world. In our opinion, the least likely occurrence is that no leaders at all will exist in work settings in the 21st century. We believe that leaders will continue to be important, will be constantly trained, and will have to experiment with how to best lead followers. There simply is no one universally accepted model or approach.[4] Although unnecessarily isolating effective leadership traits or behaviors seems impossible, it's likely that sets of characteristics do, in fact, fit with situations and followers. Chapters 11 and 12 encourage identifying and experimenting with the set. As the environment, competition, technology, and demographics of the workforce change, we'll need experimentation. Understanding and applying these two chapters should aid such experimentation.

A frequently heard complaint about the study of leadership is that it's simply a list of traits, behaviors, and situational concepts. This chapter presents theories and research that have stimulated the criticisms. The scarcity of exceptional leaders and ambiguities of leadership have fueled the problem. There is a scarcity when we compare our present-day leaders to world-class figures, executives, and social leaders of yesterday: Abraham Lincoln, Mother Teresa, Winston Churchill, Mahatma Gandhi, Susan B. Anthony, Nelson Mandela, and Alfred Sloan.

To develop more precision about leadership as we know it today, researchers have proposed a number of approaches. They do not answer the past-versus-today leadership comparison.

However, the approaches are informative, meaningful, and realistic in that they often use job-related or task-oriented settings and examples. This chapter examines what we refer to as emerging leadership models, research, and applications. Are these approaches the final answer, the most refined, or the most rigorously studied views of leadership? No. They are, however, interesting, progressive, and integrative explanations of leadership. As the opening vignette illustrates, the United States needs strong leadership from a variety of key individuals and organizations, who will undoubtedly draw on their own unique leadership styles to help guide the country forward during difficult and uncertain times.

As this chapter illustrates, leaders can command respect, transform organizations from lagging to successful units, and find the best combination of persuasion and authority to complete the job. As you review each of the approaches in this chapter, think about the role that diagnosis and listening play. A leader who doesn't encourage communication is at a disadvantage. In using the Vroom-Yetton, attribution, or transformational approach, the effective leader must be skilled in diagnosis and communication. Do you possess these skills?

Vroom–Jago Leadership Model

Vroom and Yetton initially developed a leadership and decision-making model that indicates the situations in which various degrees of participative decision making are appropriate.[5] In contrast to Fred Fiedler, Vroom and Yetton attempted to provide a normative model (prescriptive) that a leader can use in making decisions. Their approach assumes that no one particular leadership style is appropriate for each situation. Unlike Fiedler, they assume that leaders must be flexible enough to change their leadership styles to fit situations. It was Fiedler's contention that the situation must be altered to fit an individual's leadership style.

In developing their model, Vroom and Yetton made these assumptions:

1. The model should be of value to leaders or managers in determining which leadership styles they should use in various situations.
2. No single leadership style is applicable to all situations.
3. The main focus should be the problem to be solved and the situation in which the problem occurs.
4. The leadership style used in one situation should not constrain the styles used in other situations.
5. Several social processes influence the amount of participation by subordinates in problem solving.

Vroom-Yetton model
Leadership model that specifies leadership decision-making procedures most effective in each of several different situations: two autocratic (AI, AII); two consultative (CI, CII); one oriented toward joint decisions of the leaders and group (GII).

Applying these assumptions resulted in the initial model that was concerned with leadership and decision making. The **Vroom-Yetton leadership model** generated interest among researchers, practitioners, and trainers. However, to improve the accuracy and predictability of the initial model, Vroom and Jago have developed a modified model.[6]

Nature of the Vroom-Yetton-Jago Model

The new model shares two key features with its predecessor. First, it employs the same decision processes as those of the original Vroom-Yetton model. The terms for describing decision processes—AI, AII, CI, CII, and GII, with the addition of GI and DI for individual problems—are carried over intact from the previous model. These are presented in Table 12.1.

TABLE 12.1
Decision Styles for Leadership: *Individuals* and *Groups*

Individual Level	Group Level
AI. You solve the problem or make the decision yourself.	**AI.** You solve the problem or make the decision yourself.
AII. You obtain information from a subordinate, then decide on the solution to the problem yourself.	**AII.** You obtain information from subordinates, then decide on the solution to the problem yourself.
CI. You share the problem with a subordinate, getting ideas and suggestions. Then you make the decision.	**CI.** You share the problem with subordinates individually, getting ideas and suggestions. Then you make the decision.
GI. You analyze the problem with a subordinate, and together arrive at a mutually satisfactory solution. Each one's contribution is based on knowledge rather that formal authority.	**CII.** You share the problem with subordinates in a group meeting, and obtain their ideas and suggestions. Then you make a decision, which may or may not reflect the subordinates' input or influence.
DI. You delegate the problem to a subordinate, providing him/her with relevant information that you possess. The subordinate has the responsibility for solving the problem alone. You accept and support the subordinate's solution.	**GII.** You analyze the problem with your subordinates in a group meeting and together, you generate and evaluate alternatives and reach a consensus. Your role is to facilitate the group's discussion and keep the group focused on the problem. You don't force "your solution" but instead accept and implement the solution put forth by the group.

Second, the new model also retains the criteria against which the effects of participation are evaluated. Like the earlier model, the new model concerns evaluating the effects of participation on decision quality, decision acceptance, subordinate development, and time.

Decision Effectiveness

The new model retains the concept of decision effectiveness (D_{Eff}). As shown in the following equation, D_{Eff} is dependent on decision quality (D_{Qual}) and decision commitment (D_{Comm}). **Decision quality** refers to the technical aspects of a decision. A decision is considered to be of high quality to the extent that it's consistent with the organizational goals to be attained and with potentially available information. **Decision commitment** refers to the acceptance of decisions by subordinates. Participation in decisions by subordinates tends to produce feelings of commitment and joint ownership.

decision quality
An important criterion in the Vroom-Yetton model that refers to objective aspects of a decision that influence subordinates' performance, aside from any direct impact on motivation.

decision commitment
The degree to which subordinates accept a particular decision. Participation in decisions often tends to increase the commitment of subordinates.

$$D_{Eff} = D_{Qual} + D_{Comm} - DTP$$

However, there is a third term in the equation, DTP (*decision time penalty*). This term acknowledges that having sound thinking and a committed group to implement the decision is often not all that is needed to produce effective decisions. Decisions must also be made in a timely manner. Many decisions are made under severe time constraints. For example, an air traffic controller has limited time to place airplanes in various zones before increasing the risk of an accident. DTP takes on a value of zero whenever no stringent time constraints limit the process chosen.

Decision effectiveness is the criterion to use if there are no values attached to either time or development or if those values are completely unknown. However, a more comprehensive criterion called *overall effectiveness* (O_{Eff}) is introduced. O_{Eff} is greatly influenced by decision effectiveness, but as shown in the following equation, its values reflect the remaining two criteria affected by degree of participation. Both consequences pertain to effects of the decision process on available "human capital." Independent of the effectiveness of the decisions produced, a decision process can have effects, either positive or negative or both, on the energy and talent available for subsequent work.

$$O_{Eff} = D_{Eff} - \text{Cost} + \text{Development}$$

Negative effects on human capital occur because decision processes use time and energy, even in the absence of a time constraint. An executive group meeting including a senior executive and five subordinates and lasting two hours would consume 12 work-hours. The value of time is certainly not zero, although its precise cost varies with the opportunity costs of the meeting. Which other activities did each manager forsake to participate in that meeting? When critically important activities are not carried out because of time spent in meetings, costs are incurred that must, at the very least, be "traded off " against the benefits of the meeting. In the preceding equation, cost represents the value of time lost through use of a given decision process.

On the other hand, participation can *contribute* to human capital. Participation in decision making can build teamwork, strengthen commitment to organizational goals, and contribute to the development of participants' technical and managerial skills. In the O_{Eff} equation, development is intended to represent organizational benefits that extend beyond the individual decision under consideration. The extent to which these gains from participative leadership can be realized depends on the leader's ability to facilitate teamwork. The next OB at Work feature describes one approach to team leadership.

Situational Variables

One of the biggest differences between the traditional Vroom-Yetton model and the new one lies in the problem attributes. Vroom-Yetton used seven problem attributes; the new model continues the use of these seven and adds five.

The most important additional problem attribute takes into consideration the information and expertise possessed by subordinates. This additional attribute pertaining to information was included because the original Vroom-Yetton model performed somewhat better in accounting for differences in the acceptance of decisions than it did in predicting decision quality. Incorporating information possessed by subordinates and that possessed by the leader is expected to improve predictions about the quality of decisions and to further enhance the validity, or batting average of the model.[7]

A second new problem attribute pertains to the existence of stringent time constraints that could restrict opportunities to involve subordinates. The third involves geographical restrictions on interactions among subordinates. The original Vroom-Yetton model envisioned managers and subordinates located, if not in adjacent offices, at least sufficiently proximate to one another so that interaction could take place relatively easily. Thus, the Vroom-Yetton model prescribed group meetings of managers separated by thousands of miles. Without denigrating the usefulness of such meetings, the benefits that the Vroom-Yetton model predicted from joint decision making may not outweigh the costs of assembling far-flung managers in one central location. The revised model addresses this issue by ascertaining not only the existence of geographical constraints but also whether the expected benefits outweigh the costs.

Finally, the other two new attributes concern the importance of time and development. In the new model, these are not either-or judgments introduced after the fact to guide the choice among equally feasible alternatives. Instead, they are independent judgments obtained simultaneously with judgments of other problem attributes; taken together, they affect the benefits and costs of employing participative methods.

OB AT WORK The Roles of Leaders in Self-Managed Teams

The roles of leaders in self-managed teams have not been well understood either in theory or in practice. A self-managed team is a group of people working together at their decided pace to accomplish specific goals. Those organizations undertaking the change to self-managed teams have found the change somewhat difficult as leaders held to their historical roles. One organization, Metropolitan Life Insurance Company (Met Life), has undertaken the change, and the experience of this organization provides some insights.

Met Life begins by defining a team as a group of people with specific roles and responsibilities organized to work together toward common goals or objectives in which each member depends on others to carry out responsibilities to reach those goals and objectives. Met Life managers say the key word in the definition is *depends.* A team must be able to depend on its members to carry out their tasks, to communicate effectively, to put team needs first, and to help each other. Good teams also depend on good team leadership.

Met Life's managers recommend that team leadership be divided into two roles: client and facilitator. The client is the team leader who asks for help to solve a problem. This person is responsible for what team meetings are supposed to address. The facilitator is responsible for how the meeting goes. Facilitators have four basic responsibilities: helping other team members keep time commitments, keeping group members on track, remaining neutral about the meeting's content, and clarifying group members' ideas and making sure other members' ideas are protected from attack.

These two roles bear a sharp relationship to the behaviors of participative and considerate leaders, as noted in many leadership theories. The problem seems to be not so much with the existence of ideas on how leaders should act generally; rather the problem seems to be how they should act in a particular situation—as self-managed work teams.

Sources: Adapted from Mark M. Chatfield, "Self-Directed and Self-Managed Teams," accessed at http://arism.com/selfteam.htm on April 6, 2007; Richard Cooney, "Empowered Self-Management and the Design of Work Teams," *Personnel Review* (Fall 2004): 677–92; Rudy M. Yandrick, "A Team Effort," *HRMagazine*, June 2001, pp. 136–41; Joe Singer and Steve Duvall, "High-Performance Partnering by Self-Managed Teams in Manufacturing," *Engineering Management Journal* (December 2000): 9–15; Milan Moravec, Jan Johannessen, and Thor A. Hjelmas, "The Well-Managed Self-Managed Team," *Management Review* (June 1998): 56–59; Evan Lembke and Marie G. Wilson, "Putting the 'Team' into Teamwork: Alternative Theoretical Contributions for Contemporary Management Practice," *Human Relations* (July 1998): 927–45; and Yvette DeBow, "Met's IT Set for Continuous Improvement," *Insurance and Technology,* December 1994, p. 48.

Continuous Scales

The original Vroom-Yetton model used dichotomous (yes–no) judgments in generating the prescriptions of the model: do you have enough information to make a high-quality decision? Of the 12 problem attributes in the new model, 10 have been designed to be expressed at five-point scales. The four attributes dealing with importance (quality, commitment, time, and development) are answered on scales ranging from "no importance" to "critical importance." Another six attributes (leader information, problem structure, commitment probability, goal congruence, conflict, and subordinate information) are expressed as probability estimates. For example, the question "Do you have sufficient information to make a high-quality decision?" can now be answered no, probably no, maybe, probably yes, or yes. Table 12.2 shows 1 of the 12 attributes, an example of the questions used to measure them, and the permissible responses for each.

Application of the New Model

Using the manager's analysis of the situation represented by that manager's responses to the diagnostic questions, the formulas predict the most appropriate way of handling the

TABLE 12.2
QR: Quality Requirement

How important is the technical quality of this decision?

(1)	(2)	(3)	(4)	(5)
No import	Low import	Average import	High import	Critical import

situation, the second-best way, and so forth. However, the equations' complexity precludes their pencil-and-paper application.

Vroom and Jago offer two alternatives for the application of their new model to actual managerial problems. The first is a computer program that guides the manager through the analysis of the situation and, with speed and accuracy, solves the relevant equations. The second method, more familiar to users of the original Vroom-Yetton model, employs a decision tree that represents the operation of the complex equations if certain simplifying assumptions are made.[8]

Figure 12.1 shows one of these decision trees. The first simplifying assumption is that each problem attribute can be given a clear yes or no (or high or low) response. This restricts the application of the model to relatively unambiguous situations. The second simplifying assumption is that 4 of the 12 problem attributes are held constant. Severe time constraints and the geographical dispersion of subordinates (relatively infrequent occurrences) are assumed not to exist. Additionally, it's assumed that the manager's motivation to conserve time and to develop subordinates doesn't change. Figure 12.1 depicts what Vroom and Jago label the "time-driven" decision tree. It's designed for the manager who places maximum weight on saving time and minimum weight on developing subordinates.

Validity of the Vroom-Jago Model

As was the case with the original Vroom-Yetton model when it was first introduced, the revised model currently lacks complete empirical evidence establishing its validity. Certainly, the model is thought to be consistent with what we now know about the benefits and cost of participation and represents a direct extension of the original 1973 model. Nonetheless, without extensive evidence that use of the new model can improve decision effectiveness—and, by extension, leadership success—its value as a theoretical contribution and as a practical tool remains open to question.

International Research

A valuable aspect of the Vroom-Yetton and Vroom-Jago approaches to leadership is that research has been conducted both in and outside of the United States. In an increasingly interdependent world, it's increasingly important not to reach conclusions about a theory or an approach based solely on domestic samples of leaders.

One study of Austrian managers uses real decisions made by the participants.[9] Small discussion groups of managers reviewed each situation and provided the decision process used by the manager and an analysis of the problem attributes present in the situation. The study results indicated that small-group judgments were more accurate than a single person's judgments in analyzing written descriptions of the situations.

Another study looked at owner-operated cleaning franchises in the United States and Canada.[10] Leadership behavior of American and Canadian owner-managers was assessed through problem sets. The results indicated that U.S. and Canadian managers who had above-average conformity to what the model prescribes had significantly more profitable businesses and more satisfied employees.

Limitations of the Model

After a thorough review of leadership theories, models, and concepts, one behavioral scientist concluded that the Vroom-Yetton approach is unsurpassed in terms of scientific validity and practical usefulness.[11] Nevertheless, the model has limitations.

The model forces a person to make a definite response. Because it fails to permit a "probably yes" or a "probably no," a yes or no response must be made. Work situations aren't that easy to categorize; in many situations, neither yes nor no is accurate. The model

FIGURE 12.1 **Time-Driven Decision Tree**

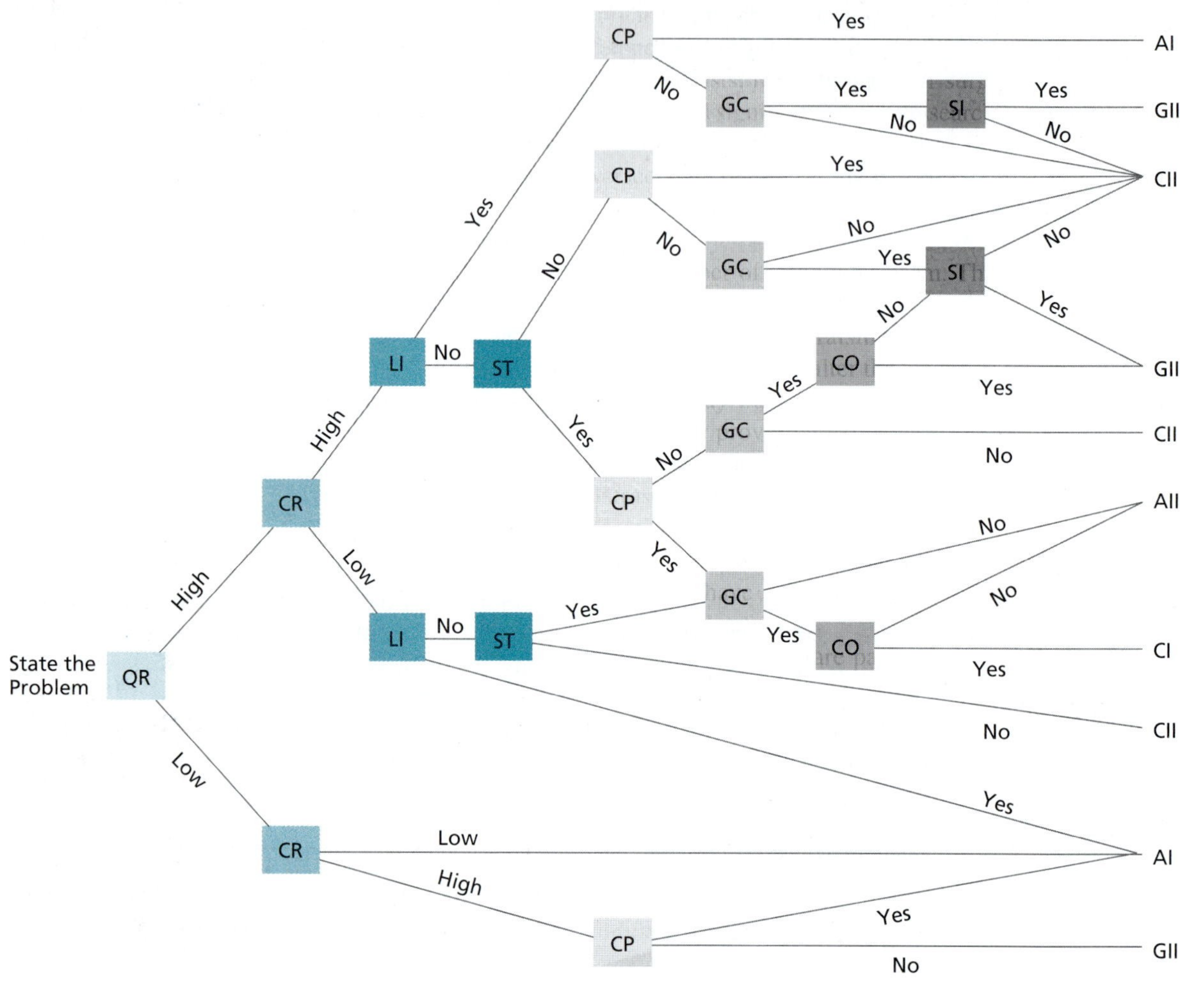

Quality requirement

QR — How important is the technical quality of this decision?

Commitment requirement

CR — How important is subordinate commitment to the decision?

Leader's information

LI — Do you have sufficient information to make a high-quality decision?

Problem structure

ST — Is the problem well structured?

Commitment probability

CP — If you were to make the decision by yourself, is it reasonably certain that your subordinate(s) would be committed to the decision?

Goal congruence

GC — Do subordinates share the organizational goals to be attained in solving this problem?

Subordinate conflict

CO — Is conflict among subordinates over preferred solutions likely?

Subordinate information

SI — Do subordinates have sufficient information to make a high-quality decision?

is also criticized for being too complex. It includes decision trees, ratings, and problem sets. Although the model is complex, we believe this criticism is not warranted. The model is precise and specific, which means that some complexity is likely to be needed. Instead of discussing complexity, we might better state that the model, like most leadership explanations, simplifies how managers think and process stimuli.

Finally, organizational life is complex, and the way individual managers think is complex. The model, according to some critics, fails to deal with the realities of what today's managers face in terms of change, technological advancement, and international competition. Can any model deal with every contingency of leading and remain understandable and useful? Perhaps critics are expecting too much.

Attribution Theory of Leadership

Chapter 4 used attribution theory to explain how managers assign causes or motives to peoples' behavior. Attribution theory also has application value as an explanation and analysis of leadership. Attribution theory mainly concerns the cognitive process by which a person interprets behavior as being caused by (attributed to) certain cues in the relevant environment.[12]

Because most causes of subordinate, or follower, behaviors are not directly observable, determining causes requires reliance on perception. In attribution theory, individuals are assumed to be rational and to be concerned about the causal linkages in their environments.

The attributional approach starts with the position that the leader is essentially an *information processor.*[13] In other words, the leader searches for information cues as to "why" something is happening and then attempts to construct causal explanations that guide her leadership behavior. The process in simple terms appears to be follower behavior → leader attributions → leader behavior.

Leader's Attributions

The leader's primary attributional task is to categorize the cause of follower, or subordinate, behavior into one of three source dimensions: person, entity, or context. That is, for any given behavior, such as poor quality of output, the leader's job is to determine whether the poor quality was caused by the person (e.g., inadequate ability), the task (entity), or some unique set of circumstances surrounding the event (context).

The leader seeks three types of information when forming attributions about a follower's behavior: distinctiveness, consistency, and consensus. For any behavior, the leader first attempts to determine whether the behavior is *distinctive* to the task—that is, whether the behavior occurs on this task but not on other tasks. Next, the leader is concerned about *consistency,* or how frequently the behavior occurs. Finally, the leader estimates *consensus,* the extent to which others behave in the same way. A behavior unique to one follower has low consensus; if it is common to other followers, this reflects high consensus.

Leader's Perception of Responsibility

The judgment of responsibility moderates the leader's response to an attribution. Clearly, the more a behavior is seen as caused by some characteristic of the follower (i.e., an internal cause) and the more the follower is judged to be responsible for the behavior, the more likely the leader is to take some action toward the follower.

attribution leadership theory
Explains how a leader makes references about and responds to a follower's behavior.

Attributional Leadership Model

Attribution theory offers a framework for explaining leader behavior more insightfully than either trait or personal behavioral theories. **Attribution leadership theory** attempts to

FIGURE 12.2
An Attributional Leadership Model

Source: Adapted from Terence R. Mitchell and Robert E. Wood, "An Empirical Test of an Attributional Model of Leader's Responses to Poor Performance," *Academy of Management Proceedings*, ed. Richard C. Huseman, 1979, p. 94.

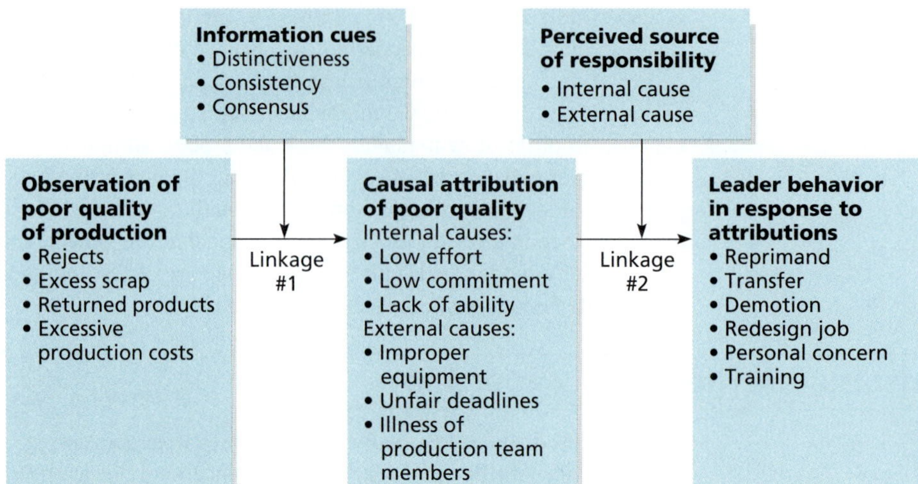

explain why behaviors are happening; trait and personal behavioral theories are more descriptive and don't focus on the why issue.[14] Furthermore, attribution theory can offer some predictions about a leader's response to a follower's behavior. Attributions are more likely to be made when failures or problems occur.[15] However, successful outcomes also can trigger the question, Why did this success occur?

Figure 12.2 presents an attributional leadership model that emphasizes two important linkages. At the first linkage point, the leader attempts to make attributions about poor performance. These attributions are moderated by the three information types: distinctiveness, consistency, and consensus. The second linkage point suggests that the leader's behavior, or response, is determined by the attributions that he makes. This relationship between attribution and leader behavior is moderated by the leader's perception of responsibility. Is the responsibility internal or external?

As discussed previously, distinctiveness, consistency, and consensus influence a leader's attributions. For example, a study of nursing supervisors found that leaders who made attributions of internal causes (e.g., lack of effort) tended to use more punitive behaviors, and leaders tended to make more internal attributions and to respond more harshly when the problems were serious.[16]

An interesting research approach has been to include gender effects in the attributional model of leadership. Research regarding the sex of the leader and the sex of the subordinate has been largely neglected. A study of college students examined whether sex of the leader, sex of the subordinate, and the interaction between these two factors would affect both the attributions made for employees' poor performance and the corrective action taken by leaders.[17] The researchers concluded that the sex composition of the leader–subordinate dyad was a critical and neglected variable in attributional research.

Research support for the attributional theory of leadership is limited. There is a need to test the theory in more organizational settings.[18] Understanding the causes of leader behavior or at least searching for those causes seems more promising for managerial use than does simply adding another trait or descriptive theory to the leadership literature.[19]

Leader Behavior: Cause or Effect?

We have implied that leader behavior has an effect on the follower's performance and job satisfaction. However, a sound basis exists for proposing that follower performance and satisfaction cause the leader to vary his leadership style. It has been argued that people develop positive attitudes toward objects that are instrumental in satisfying their needs. This argument can be extended to leader–follower relationships. For example, organizations reward leaders (managers) based on the performance of followers (subordinates). Leaders might then be expected to develop positive attitudes toward high-performing followers.[20]

Let us say that employee Miguel's outstanding performance enables his boss, Jean, to receive a $1,000 management practice excellence award. The expectation then is that Jean would think highly enough of Miguel and reward him with a better work schedule or job assignment In this case, Miguel's behavior leads to Jean being rewarded, and she in turn rewards Miguel.

In a field study, data were collected from first-line managers and from two of each manager's first-line supervisors. The purpose of this research was to assess the direction of causal influence in relationships between leader and follower variables. The results strongly suggested that leader consideration behavior caused subordinate satisfaction and that follower performance caused changes in the leader's emphasis on both consideration and the structuring of behavior–performance relationships.[21]

reciprocal causation
Argument that follower behavior affects leader behavior and leader behavior influences follower behavior.

Research on the cause-effect issue is still quite limited. To conclude that all leader behavior or even a significant portion of such behavior is a response to follower behavior would be premature. However, an examination of the leader–follower relationship in terms of **reciprocal causation** is needed. In reciprocal causation, leader behavior causes follower behavior, and follower behavior causes leader behavior. Japanese management techniques suggest that the reciprocal causation view has some validity. Leaders and followers are emphasized in the Japanese consensus approach to managing.

Charismatic Leadership

charismatic leadership
The ability to influence followers based on a supernatural gift and attractive powers. Followers enjoy being with the charismatic leader because they feel inspired, correct, and important.

Individuals such as John F. Kennedy, Winston Churchill, Mikhail Gorvachev, and Walt Disney possessed an attractiveness that enabled them to make a difference with citizens, employees, and followers. Their leadership approach is referred to as **charismatic leadership**. Max Weber suggested that some leaders have a gift of exceptional qualities—a charisma—that enables them to motivate followers to achieve outstanding performance.[22] Such a charismatic leader is depicted as being able to play a vital role in creating change.

Sam Walton is considered by many to have possessed charismatic qualities. He worked hard to explain his vision of retailing and serving the customer. He would visit Wal-Mart stores to continually inform his associates (the employees) that customer service is the first, second, and third priority that must be accomplished so that the firm can be recognized as the top retailer. As people responded to his vision and goals, Walton kept up a fast pace to meet other people and express his viewpoint. He paid attention to his employees and his customers—the human assets of business. Walton had a "gift" for making other people feel good about working for him and buying his products and service.

Steven Jobs, cofounder of Apple Computer, provides another example of how charisma inspires others. Jobs's impact, attraction, and inspiration have been described as follows:

> When I walked through the Macintosh building with Steve, it became clear that he wasn't just another general manager bringing a visitor along to meet another group of employees. He and many of Apple's leaders weren't managers at all; they were impresarios. . . . Not unlike the director of an opera company, the impresario must cleverly deal with the creative temperaments of artists. . . . His gift is to merge powerful ideas with the performance of his artists.[23]

FIGURE 12.3
Stages in Charismatic Leadership

Source: Adapted from Jay A. Conger and Rabindra N. Kanungo, "Behavioral Dimensions of Charismatic Leadership," in *Charismatic Leadership*, ed. Jay A. Conger, Rabindra N. Kanungo, and associates (San Francisco: Jossey-Bass, 1988), p. 27.

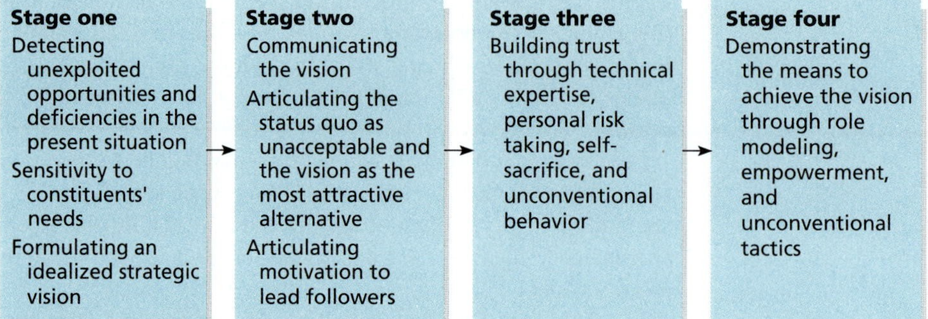

Stage one
Detecting unexploited opportunities and deficiencies in the present situation
Sensitivity to constituents' needs
Formulating an idealized strategic vision
Stage two
Communicating the vision
Articulating the status quo as unacceptable and the vision as the most attractive alternative
Articulating motivation to lead followers
Stage three
Building trust through technical expertise, personal risk taking, self-sacrifice, and unconventional behavior
Stage four
Demonstrating the means to achieve the vision through role modeling, empowerment, and unconventional tactics

Defining Charismatic Leadership

Charisma is a Greek word meaning gift. Powers that couldn't be clearly explained by logical means were called charismatic. Presently, no definitive answer has been given on what constitutes charismatic leadership behavior.[24] House suggests that charismatic leaders are those who have charismatic effects on their followers to an unusually high degree.[25]

Conger's Model

Jay Conger has proposed a model that illustrates how charisma evolves.[26] Figure 12.3 presents his four-stage model of charismatic leadership. In stage one, the leader continuously assesses the environment, adapts, and formulates a vision of what must be done. The leader's goals are established. In stage two, the leader communicates his vision to followers, using whatever means are necessary. Stage three is highlighted by working on trust and commitment. Doing the unexpected, taking risk, and being technically proficient are important to this stage. In stage four, the charismatic leader serves as a role model and motivator. The charismatic leader uses praise and recognition to instill within followers the belief that they can achieve the vision.

What Constitutes Charismatic Leadership Behavior?

What behavioral dimensions distinguish charismatic leaders from noncharismatic leaders? A criticism of the early work on charismatic leadership is that explanations of it lacked specificity. Limited attempts have been made to develop and test specific charismatic qualities such as vision, acts of heroism, and the ability to inspire.[27] However, in most cases, clarifying what specifically constitutes charismatic behavior has been generally ignored.

A number of empirical studies have examined behavior and attributes of charismatic leaders, such as articulation ability, affection from followers, ability to inspire, dominating personality, and need for influence.[28] However, no specific set of behaviors and attributes is universally accepted by theorists, researchers, and practitioners. A descriptive behavioral framework that builds on empirical work has been offered. The framework, presented in Table 12.3, assumes that charisma must be viewed as an attribution made by followers within the work context.

Two Types of Charismatic Leaders

Discussions of charismatic leadership identify two types based on the leader's emphasis on the future: *visionary charismatic leaders* focus on the long term; *crisis-based charismatic leaders* focus on the short term. Through communication ability, the visionary charismatic leader links followers' needs and goals to job or organizational long-term goals and possibilities. Through the exercise of communication skill, the visionary leader links followers'

TABLE 12.3 Behavioral Components of Charismatic and Noncharismatic Leaders

Sources: Adapted from John W. Gettings, David Johnson, Borgna Brunnon, and Chris Frantz, "Wonder Women," accessed at www.infoplease.com/spot/womenceo1.html on May 20, 2007; and Jay A. Conger and Rabindra N. Kanungo, "Toward a Behavioral Theory of Charismatic Leadership in Organizational Settings," *Academy of Management Review* (October 1987): 637–47.

Component	Charismatic Leader	Noncharismatic Leader
Relation to status quo	Essentially opposed to status quo and strives to change it (Steve Jobs at Apple).	Essentially agrees with status quo and strives to maintain it.
Future goal	Idealized vision highly discrepant from status quo (Tom Monaghan with the Domino's Pizza concept).	Goal not too discrepant from status quo.
Likableness	Shared perspective and idealized vision makes leader a likable and honorable hero worthy of identification and imitation (Meg Whitman at eBay).	Shared perspective makes leader likable.
Expertise	Expert in using unconventional means to transcend the existing order (Anne Mulcahy at Xerox).	Expert in using available means to achieve goals within the framework of the existing order.
Environmental sensitivity	High need for environmental sensitivity for changing the status quo (Edgar Woolard at DuPont).	Low need for environmental sensitivity to maintain status quo.
Articulation	Strong articulation of future vision and motivation to lead (Ross Perot at EDS).	Weak articulation of goals and motivation to lead.
Power base	Personal power, based on expertise, respect, and admiration for a unique hero (Jan Carlzon at Scandinavian Airlines System—SAS).	Position power and personal power (based on reward, expertise, and liking for a friend who is a similar other).
Leader–follower relationship	Elitist, entrepreneur, an exemplary (Mary Kay Ash of Mary Kay Cosmetics).	Egalitarian, consensus-seeking, or directive.
	Transforms people to share the radical changes advocated (Edward Land, inventor of Polaroid camera).	Nudges or orders people to share leader's views.

needs and goals with those of the organization. Linking followers' goals with the organization's is easier if the followers are dissatisfied or not challenged by the current situation.

Crisis-based charismatic leaders have an impact when the system must handle a situation for which existing knowledge, resources, and procedures are not adequate.[29] The crisis-produced charismatic leader communicates clearly what actions need to be taken and what their consequences will be.

Crisis management is a growing field of study and inquiry.[30] The crises managers face enable charismatic leadership to emerge. First, under conditions of stress, ambiguity, and chaos, followers give power to individuals who have the potential to correct the crisis situation. The leader is empowered to do what's necessary to correct the situation or solve the problem. In many cases, the leader is unconstrained and is allowed to use whatever she thinks is needed.[31] This relatively high degree of freedom to act without constraints raises important ethical issues related to charismatic leadership as discussed in the next OB at Work feature.

A crisis also permits the leader to promote nontraditional actions by followers. The crisis-based charismatic leader has greater freedom to encourage followers to search for ways to correct the crisis. Some methods, procedures, and tactics adopted by followers may be disorderly, chaotic, and outside the normal boundary of actions. However, the

OB AT WORK Ethical Leadership During a Crisis

When faced with overwhelming and daunting problems, leaders are expected to be at the forefront to inspire their organizations to rise up to meet these challenges. In 1982, Johnson & Johnson, one of the world's largest health care companies, found itself in a very difficult situation. Jim Burke, then CEO of the corporation, was informed that an unknown number of bottles of Extra Strength Tylenol capsules had been laced with cyanide. In the Chicago area, seven people died as a result of taking the altered over-the-counter pain reliever. The result was catastrophic for a company that had always prided itself on product safety.

Investigators ruled out the possibility that cyanide had been introduced into Tylenol capsules during production. Police believed that someone bought or stole the medication from a store, tampered with it, and put it back on the shelves. Unfortunately, the perpetrator was never caught.

Tough decisions had to be made that would have major effects on the long-term stability and survival of the company The Tylenol brand was expected to command nearly $500 million in sales that year, roughly 8 percent of the firm's total revenue. What should Johnson & Johnson do? As the market leader in over-the-counter, nonprescription pain relievers, what steps should the company take to protect its customers while simultaneously protecting its 37 percent market share? Should it even be thinking about financial and competitive issues at a time like this? What about the doctors, nurses, patients, and families who had come to trust and rely on Tylenol for product safety and pain relief? Should Johnson & Johnson consider such a drastic step as recalling millions of bottles of Tylenol so that safer, tamper-resistant versions of the products could be offered instead? This last option could cost the company millions of dollars and untold losses in market share.

What did Jim Burke and his crisis management team decide? Adhering to the principles of the Johnson & Johnson credo, a long-standing corporate ethics statement, the firm ordered a massive nationwide recall of 31 million bottles of Tylenol, costing the company approximately $100 million. In addition, the company quickly disclosed information about the tampering to the media so as to accurately alert the public to the potential risk associated with the product. Also, scientists were sent to the Chicago area to pinpoint the exact locations and/or manufacturing sites in which the tampering took place. The leadership team also took out full-page newspaper ads in 300 markets offering to switch Tylenol capsules for the tablet form of the pain reliever. Also as a result of Burke's leadership, new tamperproof bottles were put on the market.

In the initial days of the crisis, Jim Burke and the other leaders of Johnson & Johnson took immediate and courageous steps to make the right decisions in the midst of a very bad situation. They put their customers' safety ahead of any financial concerns. Many critics thought that they had overreacted, considering that the affected parties were limited to the Chicago area. Others thought that this would mark the end of the Tylenol brand. However, a vast majority of observers believe that Jim Burke's actions not only saved the brand from imminent doom but also captured the respect and goodwill of the many stakeholders that continued to see the Tylenol brand as a safe and effective pain relief medication. This support was made evident when Tylenol's share of the analgesic market recovered to a similar level as before the tragedy.

Sources: Jia Lynn Yang, "Getting a Handle on a Scandal," *Fortune*, May 2007, p. 26; Sean Teacful, yahoo.com, January 23, 2003; William Power, "Tylenol Maker Must Bear Cost of 1982 Recall," *Wall Street Journal*, September 18, 1986, p. 1; Dennis Kneale, "Tylenol Orders Fall 25% but Competitors Lack Enough Products to Fill Market Gap," *Wall Street Journal*, October 13, 1982, p. 56; and Michael Waldholz, "Johnson & Johnson Officials Take Steps to End More Killings Linked to Tylenol," *Wall Street Journal*, October 4, 1982, p. 16.

charismatic leader in a crisis situation encourages, supports, and usually receives action from followers.[32]

Our knowledge about charismatic leadership is still relatively abstract and ambiguous. Despite Weber's concept of charismatic authority, Conger's framework of how charismatic leadership evolves, House's definition and propositions about the characteristics of charismatic leaders, and some limited research results, much more theoretical and research work needs to be done. There is a void in understanding about whether charismatic leaders can be harmful in expressing visions that are unrealistic or inaccurate or in the way they attack a crisis problem. Management scholar and writer Peter Drucker claims, "Charisma becomes the undoing of leaders." How accurate is Drucker? No one knows at this time. However, evidence suggests that charismatic leaders (e.g., Adolf Hitler, Joseph Stalin, Jim Jones) can secure greater commitment to failing, personally demeaning, and tragic goals than can the average leader.[33]

Transactional and Transformational Leadership

Each of the leadership theories discussed emphasizes that leadership is an exchange process. Followers are rewarded by the leader when they accomplish agreed-upon objectives. The leader helps followers accomplish the objectives.

Transactional Leadership

transactional leadership
Leader identifies what followers want or prefer and helps them achieve a level of performance that results in rewards that satisfy them.

The exchange role of the leader has been referred to as *transactional*. Figure 12.4 presents the **transactional leadership** roles. The leader helps the follower identify what must be done to accomplish the desired results: better quality output, more sales or services, and reduced cost of production. In helping the follower identify what must be done, the leader takes into consideration the person's self-concept and esteem needs. The transactional approach uses the path–goal concepts as its framework.

In using the transaction style, the leader relies on contingent reward and on management by exception. Research shows that contingent reinforcement can influence a variety of employee attitudes, perceptions, and behaviors such as job performance; followers believe that accomplishing objectives will result in their receiving desired rewards.[34] Using management by exception, the leader won't be involved unless objectives aren't being accomplished.

Researchers have suggested that there are a number of misconceptions surrounding the use of a transactional leader's use of rewards and punishments to motivate subordinates.[35] A sample of those myths include the following:

> *Myth:* To be effective, leaders need to reward all employees. Rewards should be given to those employees and teams who produce and accomplish organizational goals. By providing rewards to everyone, a sense of entitlement can develop and a mentality that if employees show up to work, they'll be rewarded regardless of their performance.

FIGURE 12.4
Transactional Leadership

Source: Bernard M. Bass, *Leadership and Performance Beyond Expectations* (New York: Free Press, 1985), p. 12.

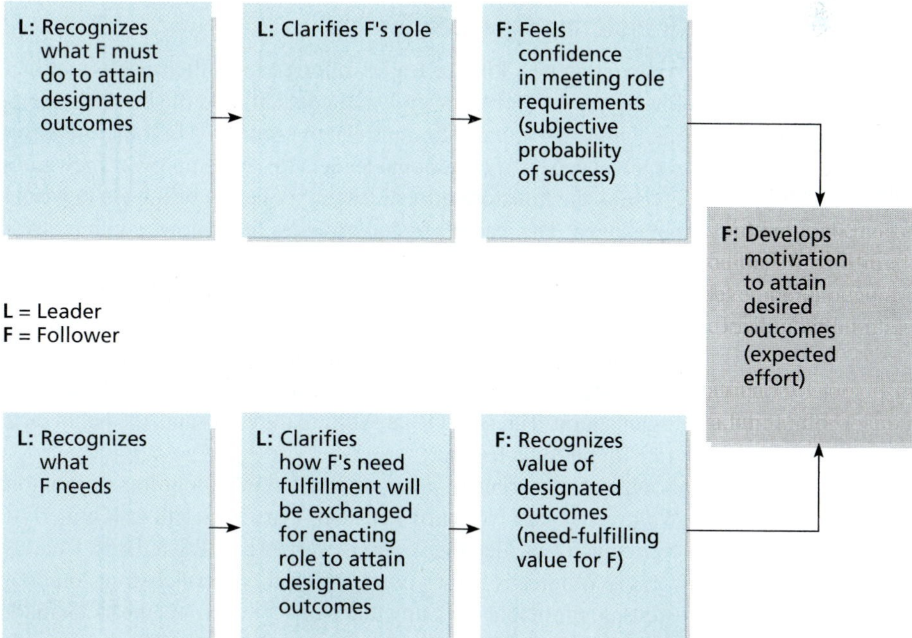

Myth: Leaders need to "reward publically, punish privately." When a leader uses constructive criticism to correct a performance problem of an employee in front of other employees, then that will become a learning moment for everyone within earshot. This can save leaders time and energy from having to repeat themselves.

Myth: In the current economy, organizations lack the resources and budgets to offer meaningful rewards to employees. Even though large bonuses and pay raises are highly motivational for most employees, there are several low- or no-cost rewards that can be used to recognize outstanding employee performance. For example, reward can come in the form of a personalized thank-you note from the president of the company, a day off with pay, a description of the employee's effort in the company newsletter, and so on.

Myth: Annual performance reviews provide sufficient positive and/or negative feedback for employees. Most employees want to know where they stand at various points throughout the year. After completing a challenging and high-profile project, many employees want to be recognized right away. If employees' performance is lacking, then immediate constructive feedback could help them get back on track before it's too late.

Transactional leadership is not often found in organizational settings. One national sample of U.S. workers showed that only 22 percent of the participants perceived a direct relationship between how hard they worked and how much pay they received.[36] That is, the majority of workers believed that good pay was not contingent on good performance. Although workers prefer a closer link between pay and performance, it was not present in their jobs. Why? There are probably a number of reasons, such as unreliable performance appraisal systems, subjectively administered rewards, poor managerial skills in showing employees the pay–performance link, and conditions outside a manager's control. Also, managers often provide rewards that aren't perceived by followers to be meaningful or important.

A small pay increase, a personal letter from the boss, or a job transfer may not be what employees want in the form of a contingent reward. Until managers understand what the employee wants, administer rewards in a timely manner, and emphasize the pay–performance link, there's likely to be confusion, uncertainty, and minimal transactional impact in leader–follower relationships.

Transformational Leadership

An exciting new kind of leader, referred to as the transformational leader,[37] motivates followers to work for transcendental goals instead of short-term self-interest and for achievement and self-actualization instead of security.[38] In **transformational leadership**, viewed as a special case of transactional leadership, the employee's reward is internal. By expressing a vision, the transformational leader persuades followers to work hard to achieve the goals envisioned. The leader's vision provides the follower with motivation for hard work that is self-rewarding (internal).

transformational leadership
Ability to inspire and motivate followers to achieve results greater than originally planned for internal rewards.

Transactional leaders will adjust goals, direction, and mission for practical reasons. Transformational leaders, on the other hand, make major changes in the firm's or unit's mission, way of doing business, and human resource management to achieve their vision. The transformational leader will overhaul the entire philosophy, system, and culture of an organization. The next OB at Work feature presents the behavior and ethical standards of a transformational leader.[39]

Names that come to mind when we think about transformational leaders are Charles R. Walgreen, Indra Nooyi of PepsiCo, Darwin Smith at Kimberly-Clark, Anne Mulcahy of Xerox, and Lou Gerstner when he served as CEO at IBM. Charles "Cork" Walgreen transformed Walgreens from a nondescript, food-service drugstore to a growing, good-to-great, exciting, profitable company that has outperformed the stock market numerous times in the past two decades. Cork had an ability to pick the right people to hire. He also was a leader who practiced team building, cooperation, and shared decision making. His charisma, ability

OB AT WORK A Leader Who Stands Up and Stands Out

Headline after headline informs the public that there is a crisis in leadership in the executive suite. There are, however, some stories that suggest that courageous leaders who do what is ethically right do exist.

The nation's biggest pension fund, California Public Employees' Retirement System, and other investor-activist groups are mounting more campaigns to oust corporate directors they don't think are acting on behalf of shareholders. Important as these efforts are, however, good corporate governance can't easily be voted into practice.

Consider Michael Leven, who is the current president and chief operating officer of Las Vegas Sands Resort. Until 2006, Leven was the chairman and CEO of U.S. Franchise Systems, Atlanta, which owns and operates three hotel brands. When he realized that he wasn't going to meet his company's year-end earnings forecast, he told his top executives that he wanted to publicly announce it. They urged him to check with the company's lawyer, who told him that because the year-end results were four months away, he wasn't obligated to say anything.

"You don't know what's going to happen yet," the lawyer told him.

"But I know I'm not going to be able to meet the forecast," Leven replied, then went ahead with the announcement.

The company's stock dropped on the news, but Leven never second-guessed his decision. "Not to have made the announcement because the law said I didn't have to would have been wrong," he says.

His stance isn't surprising given an earlier decision he made as president of Days Inn of America that nearly derailed his career. The hotel chain was purchased in 1989 by Stanley Tollman and Monty Hundley, who were Days Inn's largest franchisees. Within a few months of the purchase, Leven realized the company's cash balance was shrinking and the accounting standards he had long upheld were being undermined.

He discovered this problem first from suppliers, who called to tell him they weren't getting paid. "AT&T, my biggest supplier, said they were sorry but might have to turn off our phones," says Leven. The company's new owners had installed a new finance executive at Days Inn's headquarters. Leven, with the help of his own veteran finance executive, discovered the new owners weren't paying the franchise fees and mortgage payments they owed.

Alarmed, Leven consulted an attorney, who told him to resign, or at least to confront the new owners. He chose the latter route at first, and the owners agreed to pay back the money they owed. But after a few weeks, the company's cash funds started declining again. This time, Leven quit without any severance.

By then he suspected the owners were also siphoning funds from Days Inn's accounts. He wrote a letter to his bosses outlining his suspicions and quit the same day, but didn't alert the Securities and Exchanges Commission. Days Inn wasn't a public company but it did have some public bonds.

"I had no idea what to do beyond leaving, and I followed my lawyer's advice," he says.

He landed a new job six months later at Holiday Inn. But he had to take a 25 percent pay cut and a lower-level position as president of franchising.

About a year later, Days Inn, depleted of cash, filed for bankruptcy protection. The company was subsequently purchased by Henry Silverman, now chairman and CEO of Cendant. He also hired most of Leven's former staff.

Tollman and Hundley (of Days Inn) were convicted of fraud, conspiracy to commit bank fraud, and lying to banks. The charges stemmed from an elaborate scheme in which lenders were defrauded of more than $100 million, prosecutors said.

Leven says he isn't angry about how things turned out. "I did what I had to do even though it cost me a significant amount of money," he says. But he does feel angry when CEOs accept huge compensation packages at the same time that they ask their employees for pay cuts, and when directors profit from deals they do with companies they are supposed to be overseeing.

Source: Reprinted with permission from Carol Hymowitz, "Good Leadership Requires Executives to Put Themselves Last," *The Wall Street Journal,* April 20, 2004, p. B1.

to help followers see and solve a problem, and attention to detail are characteristics possessed and used by transformational leaders.[40]

The development of transformational leadership factors has evolved from research by Bass.[41] He identified five factors (the first three apply to transformational and the last two apply to transactional leadership) that describe transformational leaders. They are

1. *Charisma.* The leader is able to instill a sense of value, respect, and pride and to articulate a vision.
2. *Individual attention.* The leader pays attention to followers' needs and assigns meaningful projects so the followers grow personally.

OB AND YOUR CAREER Become a Level 5 Leader

Jim Collins, author of *Good to Great*, and his team selected 11 companies (Abbott Labs, Circuit City, Fannie Mae, Gillette, Kimberly-Clark, Kroger, Nucor, Phillip Morris, Pitney Bowes, Walgreens, and Wells Fargo) from more than 1,400 that had been listed in the *Fortune* 500 at some point or other. Each of the selected companies had mediocre results for 15 years and then went through a transition. From that point, they outperformed the market by at least three to one—and sustained that performance for at least 15 years. Each of these was compared with companies in the same industry and about the same size.

Using hundreds of interviews, Collins identified key factors that enable companies to move from mediocre institutions to great institutions. The comparison companies lacked these factors and failed to become great. Perhaps the most important component of the transition from good to great is what Collins designated as *Level 5 Leadership.*

Level 1 is a highly capable individual who "makes productive contributions through talent, knowledge, skills and good work habits."

Level 2 is a contributing team member who "contributes individual capabilities to the achievement of group objectives and works effectively with others in a group setting."

Level 3 is the competent manager who "organizes people and resources toward the effective and efficient pursuit of predetermined objectives."

Level 4 is an effective leader who "catalyzes commitment to and vigorous pursuit of a clear and compelling vision, stimulating higher performance standards."

Level 5 is the executive who "builds enduring greatness through a paradoxical blend of personal humility and professional will."

Every one of the good-to-great companies had Level 5 leaders in the critical transition phase. None of the comparison companies did. These leaders are described as being timid and ferocious, shy and fearless, and modest with a fierce, unwavering commitment to high standards.

Level 5 leaders rely on instilling inspired standards and not inspiring charisma to motivate. They build a culture of discipline. He or she is not a tyrannical disciplinarian, but one who enables freedom and responsibility. Self-disciplined people are hired who are willing to go to lengths to fulfill their responsibilities. They consistently adhere to what Collins calls the Hedgehog Concept, the intersection of three circles:

1. Brutally and realistically determining at what the company can be the best in the world and pursuing it in light of the next two points.
2. Deciding the most effective way of generating sustained cash flow and profitability, then determining the single most important indicator. In the case of Walgreens, it was profit per customer visit and not the traditional profit per store.
3. The good-to-great company and its employees do only the things they are deeply passionate about. This passion is not stimulated or imposed but discovered.

Level 5 leaders channel their ego needs away from themselves and toward building a great company or organization. They often will sacrifice their own gain for the gain of the company. When things do not go well, Level 5 leaders take responsibility for the failures and never blame other people, external factors, or bad luck. Level 5 leaders can help identify and develop other potential leaders throughout the organization.

Good-to-great companies set out on a path to improve long-term results that go unnoticed by the outside for years. They then suddenly appear, well on their way to becoming great.

All of the good-to-great leaders created standards and doggedly kept to those standards for the years of their tenure.

Sources: Adapted from J. Collins, "Celebrity Leadership," *Leadership Excellence* 25, no. 1 (January 2008): 20; Des Dearlove and Stuart Crainer, "Jim Collins and Level 5 Leadership," accessed at www.management-issues.com/2006/5/24/mentors/jim-collins-and-level5-leadership.asp on May 10 and 20, 2007; and Jim Collins, *Good to Great* (New York: Harper Collins, 2001).

3. *Intellectual stimulation.* The leader helps followers rethink rational ways to examine a situation. He encourages followers to be creative.
4. *Contingent reward.* The leader informs followers about what must be done to receive the rewards they prefer.
5. *Management by exception.* The leader permits followers to work on the task and doesn't intervene unless goals aren't being accomplished in a reasonable time and at a reasonable cost.

One of the most important characteristics of the transformational leader is charisma. However, charisma by itself isn't enough for successful transformational leadership, as Bass states:

> Celebrities are held in awe and reverence by the masses who are developed by them. People will be emotionally aroused in the presence of celebrities and identify with them in their fantasy, but the celebrities may not be involved at all in any transformation of their public. On the other hand, with charisma, transformational leaders can play the role of teacher, mentor, coach, reformer, or revolutionary. Charisma is a necessary ingredient of transformational leadership, but by itself it is not sufficient to account for the transformational process.[42]

In addition to charisma, transformational leaders need assessment skills, communication abilities, and sensitivity to others. They must be able to articulate their vision, and they must be sensitive to the skill deficiencies of followers. Some researchers have suggested that women possess higher levels of these transformational skills and abilities, which provide them with a "leadership advantage" over male leaders. A meta-analysis (i.e., a research study that analyzes and summarizes the results of previous research studies) of 45 studies of male and female leadership styles reported that female leaders have a slight advantage over their male counterparts in their ability to be transformational leaders.[43] However, other researchers suggest that this advantage may be "overstated" and "premature" given the complicated nature of this type of gender research.[44] It goes without saying that the "which gender is better at leading" debate will continue. Regardless of whether males or females make better leaders, we can safely conclude one thing; all successful leaders of contemporary organizations need to possess such skills as cooperation, mentoring, teamwork, conflict resolution, empathetic listening, communication, and understanding of employees' work-family issues.

The aim of transformational and transactional leadership skills is identified in what some refer to as levels of leadership. The OB and Your Career feature on the previous page explains Level 5 characteristics, which are based on the empirical work of Collins presented in his book *Good to Great.*[45]

Substitutes for Leadership

The discussions in Chapters 11 and 12 make a very strong case for leadership that encourages followers to take on self-direction. For example, situational leadership theory suggests that the appropriate leadership behavior for followers able and willing to assume responsibility is coaching and assisting them. Thus, when individuals are fully able to direct themselves, they do not need a leader in the usual sense of the term. In addition to characteristics of followers that reduce the need for leadership, other task and organizational characteristics may have a similar effect. In addition, we should think of instances that neutralize the effects of leadership.[46]

Researchers have identified a wide variety of individual, task, environmental, contextual, and organizational characteristics as leadership substitute factors that influence relationships between leader behavior and follower satisfaction and performance. Some of these variables (e.g., follower expectations of leader behavior) appear to influence which leadership style will enable the leader to motivate and direct followers. Others, however, function as substitutes for leadership. Substitute variables tend to negate the leader's ability to either increase or decrease follower satisfaction or performance.[47]

Substitutes for leadership are claimed to be prominent in many organizational settings. However, the dominant leadership approaches fail to include substitutes for leadership in discussing the leader behavior–follower satisfaction and performance relationship.

TABLE 12.4
Substitutes for Leadership

Source: Reprinted from Steven Kerr and John M. Jermier, "Substitutes for Leadership: Their Meaning and Measurement," *Organizational Behavior and Human Performance* (December 1978): 378, with permission from Elsevier.

	Neutralizes	
Characteristic	**Relationship-Oriented Leadership**	**Task-Oriented Leadership**
Of the subordinate:		
1. Ability, training, experience, knowledge		X
2. Need for independence	X	X
3. "Professional" orientation	X	X
4. Indifference toward organizational rewards	X	X
Of the task:		
5. Unambiguous and routine		X
6. Methodologically invariant		X
7. Provides its own feedback concerning accomplishment		X
8. Intrinsically satisfying	X	
Of the organization:		
9. Formalization (explicit plans, goals, and areas of responsibility)		X
10. Inflexibility (rigid, unbending rules and procedures)		X
11. Highly specified and active advisory and staff functions		X
12. Close-knit, cohesive work groups	X	X
13. Organizational rewards not within the leader's control	X	X
14. Spatial distance between superior and subordinates	X	X

Table 12.4, based on previously conducted research, provides substitutes for only two of the more popular leader behavior styles: relationship-oriented and task-oriented. For each of these styles, Kerr and Jermier present substitutes (characteristics of the subordinate, the task, or the organization) that neutralize the style.[48] For example, an experienced, well-trained, knowledgeable employee doesn't need a leader to structure the task (e.g., task-oriented leader). Likewise, a job (task) that provides its own feedback doesn't require a task-oriented leader to inform the employee how he's doing. Also, an employee in a close-knit, cohesive group doesn't need a supportive, relationship-oriented leader. The group substitutes for this leader.[49]

As Chapters 11 and 12 have illustrated, there is no one best explanation or model of leadership. After years of thinking about, observing, and studying leaders in action, the common theme, set of suggestions, or secret formula (there is none) is not available.

Managers and leaders are responsible for protecting, maintaining, and enhancing the assets and integrity of the project, unit, team, or organization. Leaders and managers who can carry out these responsibilities are highly sought by organizations. As the two leadership chapters illustrate, exactly how to carry out these responsibilities is still being studied and debated.

Summary of Key Points

- Vroom and Yetton originally, and Vroom and Jago more recently, have developed a leadership model to select the amount of group decision-making participation needed in a variety of problem situations. The model suggests that the amount of subordinate participation depends on the leader's skill and knowledge, whether a quality decision is needed, the extent to which the problem is structured, and whether acceptance by subordinates is needed to implement the decision.
- The Vroom-Yetton-Jago explanations are criticized for being too complex. Because leadership is a complex process, a more accurate criticism perhaps is that the explanation is too simplistic with regard to managerial cognition about how to lead and the consequences of leadership behaviors.
- The attribution theory of leadership suggests that a leader's ability to predict how followers will react is enhanced by knowing how followers explain their behavior and performance.
- Leaders attribute followers' behaviors to the person, the task, or a unique set of circumstances called the *context*.
- The word *charisma* comes from a Greek work meaning a gift. An ability to influence people that can't be clearly explained by logical means is called charisma.
- Charisma evolves over time. By assessing, adapting, and formulating goals and actions, articulating a vision, and building and reinforcing commitment, the leader builds his charismatic profile.
- Two types of charismatic leaders have been suggested: one who articulates a vision and one who exercises leadership in a crisis situation.
- Transactional leadership involves engaging in an exchange role in which the leader helps followers accomplish meaningful objectives to achieve satisfactory rewards.
- To achieve a vision, the transformational leader makes major changes in mission, the way of doing business, and how human resources are managed.
- The transactional approach is involved in the more expansive transformational leadership framework. Three main characteristics of transformational leadership are charisma, individual attention to followers, and intellectual stimulation of followers.
- Insufficient research evidence exists to promote charismatic, transactional, or transformational practices in organizations. The romantic aspects of being charismatic or transformational haven't been supported with research evidence. Explanations are interesting but not yet sufficiently supported with scientific facts.
- Despite the seeming necessity for leadership as a factor in achieving organizational effectiveness, we can identify circumstances that neutralize the effects of leadership. Follower initiative, structured tasks, and work group cohesiveness can reduce the necessity for leadership.

Discussion and Review Questions

1. Identify any three individuals (past or present) in any field (e.g., business, government, military, religion) who use/used their leadership abilities to build respected, successful organizations. What type of leadership behaviors do/did they use to accomplish this feat?
2. Compare the available research on the Vroom-Yetton-Jago model of leadership with the transactional explanation. What research is needed in both theories of leadership?
3. Under what circumstances would leadership effects be neutralized in an organization?
4. Is it realistic to search for a universal formula or approach to leadership that is effective at most/all types of organizations? Explain.

5. As you learn more about leadership in this course, what steps can you take to gain more experience as a future leader? Identify three specific ways to gain leadership experience at this point in your life.
6. How could a leader use attribution theory to explain the poor performance of an employee team that always seems to miss important project deadlines ?
7. Many people consider Winston Churchill's leadership of Great Britain during World War II to be an excellent example of how to lead successfully during difficult times. What type of leadership did Churchill display?
8. Which of the theories in Chapters 11 and 12 would be most useful in explaining to someone from India what leadership approaches will be needed to make India more competitive in the international marketplace?
9. To what extent do you believe that women have an advantage over men when it comes to managing in contemporary organizations? Explain.
10. Why is communication such an important skill in charismatic, transactional, and transformational explanations of leadership?

Taking It to the Net

Leaders Need Guidance Too!

The OB at Work feature, "Ethical Leadership During a Crisis," described how the leadership team of Johnson & Johnson turned to the firm's credo to help navigate the difficult situation created by the events surrounding one of their leading company products. Johnson & Johnson is not the only company to rely on a set of guiding principles to help shape the decisions made by its leaders. Using your favorite search engine (www.google.com or www.yahoo.com), go to the Internet and locate five other corporate vision statements, guiding principles, or credos that are designed to provide leaders and employees alike with an ethical standard for their behavior. After locating this information, be prepared to answer the following questions.

1. What does the vision statement focus on most? What appears to be the most important priority of that organization—customers, stockholders, profits, employees, or other factors?
2. If a difficult situation were to arise (like the Tylenol case), how would the leaders of the organization use the guiding principles to help shape their decisions? Would this be possible? Or are the statements too vague and ill defined to be of much help?
3. If you were starting your own business, would you develop a credo for yourself and your employees? If so, what types of statements or ideas would it contain?

Case for Analysis: *Intel Prepares Its Top Leaders*

In the spring of 2005, Paul Otellini was scheduled to become the new CEO of the successful chip powerhouse Intel—but first, earning the lofty title meant submitting to a humble exercise: hitting the books. As the first Intel chief executive without a degree in science or engineering, the soft-spoken 53-year-old didn't have the technical expertise that mentors like ex-CEO Craig Barrett and chairman Andy Grove possessed. Which is why Otellini, the company's then president and COO, crammed in more than 50 tutorials, on everything from next-generation wireless networks to microprocessor design, with many more to come.

The training regimen wasn't some chore handed down by the human resource management department.

It was part of a little-known but deliberate philosophy at Intel to grow and groom its own CEOs and leaders.

In an era of corporate headhunters, celebrity CEOs, and management by "creative destruction," succession at Intel, one of America's most profitable manufacturers, is a rare model of discipline. The company plans orderly regime changes years in advance, without enervating gossip, infighting, or drama over the identity of the new boss.

Otellini was scheduled to become the fifth homegrown CEO to run the company since its launch in 1968, which suggests that there's an "Intel inside" aspect to its management formulas as well as its high-performance chips. The first two leaders, Robert Noyce and Gordon Moore, weren't just founders but legends in their industry. The third was Grove—one of Intel's original employees and considered one of the best executives of the 20th century. Former CEO Barrett, a renowned manufacturing guru, taught materials science at Stanford before joining Intel in 1974.

The long lead times are a hallmark of Intel CEO transitions, mainly because the company's board of directors insists on them. "We discuss executive changes 10 years out to identify gaps," says David Yoffie, an Intel director since 1989 and a professor at Harvard Business School since 1981. Every January, he says, the board receives rankings of two dozen or so senior managers. Then it devotes portions of two or three more board meetings to combing through the list. Choosing the CEO, Yoffie says, "is the single most important role of the board."

Intel's board's obsession with the future helps foster another crucial element of the system—a gradual shift in duties from one CEO to the next. Moore set the example in the mid-1980s, when he allowed Andy Grove, then his second in command, to gradually assume CEO chores; likewise, in the mid-1990s, Grove steadily ceded his authority to Barrett. In effect, says Les Vadasz, an original employee and former director who has witnessed every CEO hire, "The successor gets the job before he gets the title."

Training successors in a methodical and orderly manner is all but unheard of in Silicon Valley, where founders can hold on too long and where talk of life without the chief is often heretical. Steve Jobs, Apple's CEO, remains synonymous with the company he founded—and returned to save in 1997. But how many more years will that be possible? Scott McNealy, the outspoken co-founder and ex-CEO of Sun Microsystems, suffered high turnover in his senior ranks in part because he refused to step aside for more than two decades at the top.

At Intel, CEOs and their apprentices swap roles to streamline performance where it's needed. The practice flows out of a wider Intel ideal, known internally as "two in a box." By encouraging overlapping duties and responsibilities, the thinking goes, Intel managers can better support one another in a crisis.

Hence, another aspect of Otellini's grooming: a 30-year Intel veteran who made his reputation running the company's flagship microprocessor line, Otellini increasingly took charge of Intel's worldwide manufacturing operations and its enormous budget for capital projects—including chip factories that typically cost $3 billion apiece.

Like any management credo, of course, Intel's approach has its drawbacks. The most obvious is that it turns current CEOs into lame ducks sooner than at other companies.

Intel struggles with another familiar trade-off of succession. At a company that broadcasts its succession plans years in advance, talented, loyal managers who don't see a path to the top aren't likely to stick around. In May 2004, one of Intel's most valued execs—Mike Fister, head of its server processor division—left Intel to take the top job at Cadence Design Systems, a long-time supplier of chip-design software. Dave House, another highly regarded Intel executive who was considered CEO material, left when he saw himself losing not only to Barrett but also to Otellini, who had the inside track for the next CEO opening.

DISCUSSION QUESTIONS

1. To recruit the CEO from the inside seems to work well for Intel. Do you believe this is a sound policy? Why?
2. How can a nontechnically oriented leader like Paul Otellini succeed as CEO in a technical company such as Intel?
3. Why do some firms fail to plan effectively for executive succession?

Sources: Adapted from http://drfd.hbs.edu/fit/public/facultyInfo.do?facInfo=bio&facEmId=dyoffie (accessed on June 10, 2010); Chris Nuttall, "Intel Earnings Beat Wall St Forecasts," *Financial Times*, October 14, 2009, p. 19; G. Pascal Zachary, "How Intel Grooms Its Leaders," *Business 2.0*, July 2004, pp. 43–45; *Intel Annual Report*, 2003; and Paul S. Otellini, "Intel Executive Bio," *Intel Information*, 2004.

Experiential Exercise: *Vroom-Jago Leadership Style Analysis*

OBJECTIVES

1. To learn how to diagnose different leadership situations.
2. To learn how to apply a systematic procedure for analyzing situations.
3. To improve understanding of how to reach a decision.

RELATED TOPICS

Decision making and problem solving when given facts about a situation.

STARTING THE EXERCISE

Review the decision tree in Figure 12.1 and in Exhibit 1, below. The instructor will then form groups of four to five people to analyze the following cases. Try to reach a group consensus on which decision style is best for the particular case. Select the best style, based on use of the modified model, available decision styles, and decision rules. Each case should take 30 to 45 minutes to analyze.

CASE I: R&D DIRECTOR

You're head of a research and development (R&D) lab in the nuclear reactor division of a large corporation. Often, whether a particular piece of research has potential commercial interest or is merely of academic interest to the researchers isn't clear. In your judgment, one major area of research has advanced well beyond the level at which operating divisions pertinent to the area could possibly assimilate or use the data being generated.

Recently, two new areas with potentially high returns for commercial development have been promised by one of the operating divisions. The team working in the area referred to in the previous paragraph is ideally qualified to research these new areas. Unfortunately, both new areas are relatively devoid of scientific interest, while the project on which the team is currently engaged is of great scientific interest to all members.

At the moment, this team is, or is close to being, your best research team. It's cohesive, has a high level of morale, and has been productive. You're concerned not only that team members wouldn't want to switch their effort to these new areas but also that forcing them to concentrate on these two new projects could adversely affect their morale, their good intragroup working relations, and their future productivity both as individuals and as a team.

You have to respond to the operating division within the next two weeks, indicating which resources, if any, can be devoted to working on these projects. It would be

EXHIBIT 1 Attribute Analysis

Attribute	Analysis	Ratings on Scales
Quality measurement	Critical importance	(QR 5)
Commitment requirement	High importance	(CR 4)
Leaders information	Yes	(LI 4)
Problem structure	Yes	(ST 5)
Commitment probability	Yes	(CP 5)
Goal congruence	Yes	(GC 5)
Subordinate conflict	Yes	(CO 5)
Subordinate information	Maybe	(SI 3)
Time constraints	No	(TC 1)
Geographical dispersion	No	(GD 1)
Motivation—time	High importance	(MT 4)
Motivation—development	No importance	(MD 1)
Highest overall effectiveness (leadership style choice): ________		

possible for the team to work on more than one project, but each project would need the combined skills of all the members of the team, so fragmenting the team isn't technically feasible. This fact, coupled with the fact that the team is cohesive, means that a solution that satisfies any team member would probably go a long way to satisfying everyone on the team.

CASE II: U.S. COAST GUARD CUTTER CAPTAIN

You're captain of a 210-foot, medium-endurance U.S. Coast Guard cutter, with a crew of 9 officers and 65 enlisted personnel. Your mission is general at-sea law enforcement and search and rescue. At 2 a.m. while en route to your home port after a routine two-week patrol, you received word from the New York Resource Coordination Center that a small plane had ditched 70 miles offshore. You obtained all available information concerning the location of the crash, informed your crew of the mission, and set a new course at maximum speed for the scene.

You've now been searching for survivors and wreckage for 20 hours. Your search operation has been increasingly impaired by rough seas, and a severe storm is building to the southwest. Communication with the New York Rescue Center is impossible. A decision must be made shortly about whether to abandon the search and place your vessel on a northeasterly course to ride out the storm (thereby protecting the vessel and your crew but relegating any possible survivors to almost certain death from exposure) or continuing a potentially risky search.

You've contacted the weather bureau for up-to-date information on the severity and duration of the storm. While your crew is extremely conscientious about its responsibility, you believe that the members would be divided on the decision of leaving or staying.

COMPLETING THE EXERCISE

Phase I: 10–15 minutes. Individually read each case and select the proper decision style using the Vroom-Jago model.

Phase II: 30–45 minutes. Join a group appointed by the instructor and reach a group consensus.

PART FOUR

The Structure and Design of Organizations

CHAPTER THIRTEEN

Work Design

Learning Objectives

After completing Chapter 13, you should be able to

Define
Job design.

Discuss
How job design can help improve work/family balance.

Describe
Alternative job design approaches that organizations use to improve job performance.

Discuss
The various factors and relationships that link job design and job performance.

Understand
The differences between job enrichment and job enlargement design strategies.

Identify
Specific individual differences that account for different perceptions of job content.

Designing Jobs to Allow Work/Family Balance

Many companies in the United States are experimenting with work design and benefit offerings that encourage employees to achieve a balance between their work and personal lives. This trend is being driven by two major forces: first, organizations want to attract, motivate, and retain valued employees owing to skill shortages in several key job categories (e.g., information systems, global marketing, etc.); and second, many employees are working longer hours, enduring longer commutes, and traveling more days out of each month and, as a result, may need flexible work arrangements to maintain and preserve their home life. Responding to these forces, more and more organizations are helping their employees achieve a better work/family balance. For example, Deloitte LLP (the U.S.-based member firm of Deloitte, Touche and Tohmatsu), a leading audit, consulting, financial advisory, tax, and risk management firm, provides flexible work arrangements. James E. Copeland Jr., ex-CEO of the firm, summed up the importance of these flexible work design options by saying: "Flexible work arrangements are one more way to keep talented people in the firm. If we manage our flexible work arrangements well, they'll benefit our firm, our clients, and our people."

The Deloitte LLP program consists of the following aspects of flexible work design:

1. *Reduced hours*—Employees can take advantage of part-time and job sharing arrangements. Job sharing occurs when two individuals share the responsibilities of one position.
2. *Reduced workload*—High-performing senior-level individuals work reduced schedules for a defined period to pursue an advanced degree, care for a newborn or a sick parent, and the like.
3. *Flextime*—Full-time professionals are allowed to design their work schedules to fit their particular needs. Typically, this includes variations in starting and ending times or in the number of hours worked per day.
4. *Telecommuting*—Full-time professionals can elect to work from home for part of the week (no more than 50 percent) to accommodate family or personal needs.
5. *Extended leaves of absence*—Employees who want time off for family (e.g., to raise children or to care for an elderly parent) and other personal reasons can apply for a leave up to five years in duration. During this period, they don't receive pay or benefits, but they are able to stay connected through mentoring, short ad hoc projects, and training opportunities.

Building on these successful work practices, Deloitte LLP has recently launched a "Mass Career Customization" (MCC) program that gives employees the opportunity to either increase or decrease their job responsibilities to fit their personal goals regarding work/life balance. More long-term career-oriented than the flexible work schedule options outlined above, the MCC program is being rolled out to the firm's 46,000 employees in the United States. The goal of the new program is to create a more transparent and formalized system that satisfies the changing work/life needs of employees while continuing to service the needs of its clients. The program is showing early signs of success in that a recent survey found that employee satisfaction with "overall career/life fit" has increased by 25 percent. Also, turnover of high-performing employees at Deloitte LLP has reportedly decreased after the MCC program was introduced.

Sources: Adapted from Jessica Toonkel Markuez, "Tailor-Made Careers," *Workforce Management* 89, no. 1 (January 2010): 16–22; Mai Browne, "Flextime to the Nth Degree," *Journal of Accountancy* 200, no. 3 (September 2005): 95–96; Bryan-Low Cassell, "Deloitte Chief Wrestles to Get Consultants Back in Firm," *Wall Street Journal,* August 15, 2003, p. C1; Lotte Bailyn, Paula Rayman, Dale Bengtsen, Françoise Carré, and Mark Tierney, "Fleet Financial and Radcliffe Explore Paths of Work/Life Integration," *Journal of Organizational Excellence* (Summer 2001): 49–64; Michael Prince, "Work/Life Benefits Growing," *Business Insurance,* May 7, 2001; and Deloitte & Touche Mass Career Customization Web site (http://www.deloitte.com/view/en_US/us/Services/additional-services/mass-career-customization/index.htm).

The jobs that people perform in organizations are the building blocks of all organization structures. In fact, organizations exist to enable people to do work in assigned jobs. The phrase *Let's get organized!* usually means that we need to clarify what job each individual should be doing. But we are also interested in performing jobs effectively and we need to understand the causes of effective and ineffective job performance. Ultimately, an organization's effectiveness hinges on the ability of its employees to perform their jobs effectively.

job design
The process by which managers decide individual job tasks and authority.

A major cause of effective job performance is job design—what we get when we clarify what each employee should be doing. In a more technical sense, **job design** refers to the process by which managers decide individual job tasks and authority. Apart from the very practical issues associated with job design (i.e., issues that relate to effectiveness in economic, political, and monetary terms), we can appreciate its importance in social and psychological terms. Jobs can be sources of psychological stress and even mental and physical impairment. On a more positive note, jobs can provide income, meaningful life experiences, self-esteem, regulation of our lives, and respect from and association with others. Thus, the well-being of organizations and people relates to how well management designs jobs.

job redesign
The process by which managers reconsider what employees are expected to do.

This chapter describes some of the many theories and practices that deal with job design and redesign. We must understand the implication of the term **job redesign** in the context of our discussion. It means that management has decided that it's worthwhile to reconsider what employees are expected to do on the job. In some instances, the redesign effort may be nothing more than requiring the individual to use a computer rather than a calculator to do clerical work. In other instances, the redesign effort may require the individual to work with other employees in a team effort rather than to work alone on the task. The contemporary trend in organizations is to redesign jobs that require individuals to work together in groups. Whether Americans can work effectively in groups is the controversial issue.

In contrast to job redesign, job design refers to the first instance in which management creates a job by specifying its duties and responsibilities. But with the passage of time and the development of new tools and processes, management's expectations for that job will change (i.e., it will be redesigned). We should understand job design to be an ongoing, dynamic process. Thus, we will use the term *job design* to refer to any and all managerial efforts to create jobs, whether initially or subsequently.

We begin the discussion of job design by introducing the issue of quality of work life. As is apparent to anyone who has ever worked, what we do on the job plays a major role in our social, health, and psychological statuses as well as in our economic standing. After introducing the relationships between job design and quality of work life, we'll address the more technical aspects of job design.

Designing Jobs to Enhance Quality of Work Life

quality of work life (QWL)
Management philosophy that enhances employee dignity, introduces cultural change, and provides opportunities for growth and development.

As the opening vignette illustrates, the issue of designing jobs has gone beyond the determination of the most efficient way to perform tasks. The concept of **quality of work life (QWL)** is now widely used to refer to "a philosophy of management that enhances the dignity of all workers; introduces changes in an organization's culture; and improves the physical and emotional well-being of employees (e.g., providing opportunities for growth and development)."[1] Indicators of quality of work life include accident rates, sick leave usage, employee turnover, and number of grievances filed.[2] In some organizations, QWL programs are intended to increase employee trust, productivity, involvement, retention, and problem solving so as to increase both worker satisfaction and organizational effectiveness.[3] Thus, the concept and application of QWL are broad and involve more than jobs, but the jobs that people do are important sources of satisfaction. It is not surprising to find that the quality of work life concept embodies theories and ideas of the human relations movement of the 1950s and the job enrichment efforts of the 1960s and 1970s.

The continuing challenge to management is to provide for quality of work life and to improve production, quality, and efficiency through revitalization of business and industry.

At present, the trade-offs between the gains in human terms from improved quality of work life and the gains in economic terms from revitalization aren't fully known. Some believe that we must defer quality of work life efforts so as to make the American economy more productive and efficient.[4] Others observe that the sense of urgency to become more competitive in domestic and overseas trade presents opportunities to combine quality of life and reindustrialization efforts.[5] To those ends, job design can play a vital role. For example, a recent study analyzed the productivity of approximately 25,000 IBM employees in 75 countries. The researchers reported that employees who had jobs that allowed them to telecommute and work from home were able to work 57 hours per week before experiencing conflict between their work and family lives.[6] For those employees who had traditional office jobs, the "breaking point" for work-family stress was at 38 hours per week.[7] These findings suggest that IBM employees who telecommute are working 50 percent more hours than those who drive to the office each day.

Other companies like Deloitte LLP and PricewaterhouseCoopers have also embraced these virtual workplaces. It has been suggested that as the U.S. economy increasingly shifts to virtual work environments (e.g., more employees working from home), the savings will be substantial: 100 hours per person each year will be saved; 50 million less tons of greenhouse emissions; and $200 billion in productivity gains by American companies.[8]

Job design attempts to identify the most important needs of employees and the organization and to remove obstacles in the workplace that frustrate those needs. Managers hope that the results are jobs that fulfill important individual needs and contribute to individual, group, and organizational effectiveness. Managers are, in fact, designing jobs for teams and groups. Some studies have reported that employees who participate in teams get greater satisfaction from their jobs.[9] But other studies report contrary results.[10] So we're left with the uncomfortable but realistic conclusion that quality of work life improvements through job design cannot be assured in specific instances. Obviously, designing jobs is complex. This chapter reviews the important theories, research, and practices of job design. As will be seen, contemporary management has at its disposal a wide range of techniques that facilitate the achievement of personal and organizational performance.

Work/Family Balance and Job Design

As we progress into the 21st century, organizations will continue to direct more attention and resources toward helping employees balance their work and family demands. Driving this work/family tension is a number of variables related to the economy and changing demographics of the workforce. For example, during the most recent recession, many employers turned to flexible work arrangements as a way to avoid or minimize layoffs.[11] Good for maintaining overall productivity and motivation, such arrangements included shortened workweeks, days off without pay, telecommuting, and job sharing (see Figure 13.1). Also, the number of women and single parents entering the workforce is expected to increase. Often viewed as primary caregivers, these individuals will continue to experience stress as they attempt to balance career and family priorities. Another example of demographic changes includes the increase in dual-career couples. In some cases, caregiving responsibilities may be shared, leading both working spouses to require flexible work arrangements to meet family life and career cycle needs. The aging population will be another factor that requires a response from working-age caregivers. As the baby boom generation begins to retire in larger numbers, this issue will grow in importance.

How are organizations responding to these challenges? Although not as dramatic as originally anticipated, a trend is emerging in which some organizations are trying to accommodate diverse employees' needs by offering flexible work arrangements.[12] Examples

FIGURE 13.1
Examples of Flexible Work Arrangements

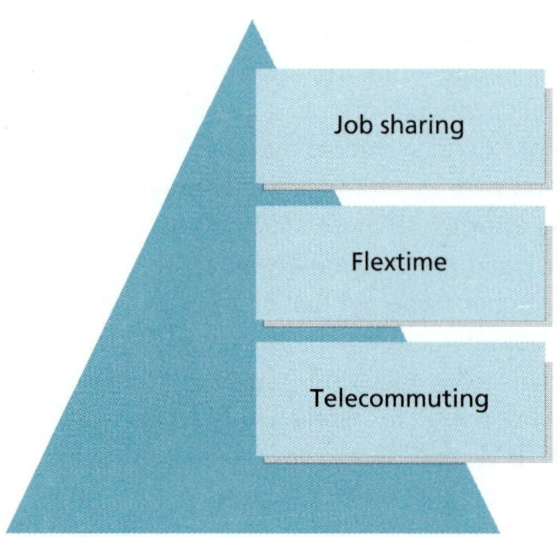

of flexible work arrangements include job sharing, flextime, and telecommuting.[13] It is believed that by allowing employees more control over their work lives, they will be better able to balance their work/home demands. Many have argued that companies that offer and encourage participation in such family-friendly work arrangements will reap one or more of the following benefits: higher recruitment and retention rates, improved morale, lower absenteeism and tardiness, and higher levels of employee productivity.

Job sharing (sometimes referred to as "work sharing") is a work arrangement in which two or more employees divide a job's responsibilities, hours, salary, and benefits among themselves.[14] Several steps are critical to the success of such job-sharing programs, including identifying those jobs that can be shared, understanding employees' individual sharing style, and matching "partners" who have complementary scheduling needs and skills.[15] Companies such as CoreStates Financial, Bristol-Myers Squibb, AT&T, Kraft, and Household International all have job-sharing options available for their employees. As previously stated, some companies are using job-sharing arrangements as an alternative to layoffs during recessionary periods.[16] The next OB at Work describes how two employees successfully share their job at Xerox.

Flextime is another type of flexible work arrangement in which employees can choose when to be at the office.[17] For example, an employee may decide that instead of working five days a week for 8 hours a day, she may prefer to work a 4-day/10-hours-per-day work schedule. With this schedule, the employee does not have to be at the office on Friday. To avoid peak rush hour, another employee might use his flextime to arrive at and leave from work one hour later Monday through Friday. Linda Skoglund, owner of J.A. Counter, a $2.5 million insurance and investment advisory company in New Richmond, Wisconsin, has taken flextime to new levels. She decided to implement a "ROWE" (or Results-Only Work Environment), which means employees can leave the office at any time for any reason (without telling anyone why they're leaving), as long as they get their jobs done.[18] Skoglund suggests that ROWE works as long as employees have a clear idea of what they need to accomplish in their jobs, co-workers are prohibited from making negative comments when an employee leaves the office "early," and the rules are applied to everyone (the owner, secretaries, etc.).[19] Flextime approaches were supported by a research study that concluded that flexible workweek schedules had a positive influence on employee performance, job satisfaction, and absenteeism.[20] However, these authors also reported that flextime programs should not be too unstructured and that they lose some of their effectiveness over time. Companies that offer flextime options include Best Buy, KPMG, Hewlett-Packard, Merrill Lynch, and Cigna.

Telecommuting refers to the work arrangement that allows employees to work in their homes part or full time, maintaining their connection and communication with the office

OB AT WORK — Job Sharing at Xerox: How Two Employees Made It Happen

Barbara Cafero and Robin Como both work for Xerox Corporation. But there's much more that they have in common: Cafero and Como share the same one-hour-long commute to work, both have young children at home, both are in sales, and they share the same job at the company.

Where did the idea for job sharing come from? Cafero and Como had just returned to the company after taking maternity leave and discussed the difficulty of balancing a full-time work schedule with the desire to spend more time with their young children. After considering this challenge, they decided that sharing the same job would be the solution. By following Xerox's quality process training—a process by which employees identify all of the steps necessary to address a problem or concern within the firm—Cafero and Como put together a detailed proposal outlining how the job-sharing idea would work. Included in the proposal were the following: a procedure for how mail would be handled, a recommendation for the number of phone lines that would be required, a list of Xerox employees and managers who would have to be notified, and rough drafts of letters to send to district sales managers to notify them of the job-share arrangement.

How did Cafero and Como's superiors react to the proposal? They supported the proposal and allowed the job-sharing arrangement to be implemented. Since then, Cafero and Como have shared their sales position for more than 10 years. These two employees are satisfied that they were able to strike a balance between their work and home lives, while Xerox is pleased that it was able to retain two productive and experienced employees.

Source: Adapted from Amanda Beeler, "It Takes Two," *Sales and Marketing Management* 155, no. 8 (2003): 3–8.

through a smart phone, laptop, texting, instant messaging, videoconference meeting software, and e-mail.[21] According to a survey by WorldatWork, the number of U.S. employees who worked at home at least one day per month reached 17.2 million in 2008, which represented an increase of 39 percent over 2006.[22] Several companies are expanding their telecommuting programs, including Cisco Systems, Lotus, Northrop & Grumman, and Booz-Allen & Hamilton.[23] For example, Best Buy allows members of its geographically dispersed teams to set their own schedules and meet anywhere they desire; the company also eliminated mandatory meetings and "bases productivity strictly on output rather than hours." Best Buy's telecommuting program seems to be working; voluntary turnover has decreased and employee productivity is up by 35 percent.[24] Although often times resisted by managers who fear loss of control and subordinate accessibility, one company has taken a methodical approach to implementing a telecommuting program. Pfizer Inc., a large health care company, took the following steps to establish their program:

1. Chose a small division to pilot the telecommuting initiative.
2. Limited the number of days to work at home to two per week.
3. Opened the program to all employees of the division.
4. Required interested employees to satisfy a formal proposal and performance standards.
5. Required demonstration that the work could be accomplished offsite and that the employee could sustain and/or enhance performance.

Although organizations like Pfizer and the other family-friendly firms are moving forward to attract, motivate, and retain employees with diverse nonwork needs, organizations need to consider three important issues when developing and implementing such flexible work arrangement options. First, every attempt should be made to open these programs to all employees who could potentially use them. The risk here is that if only certain groups are offered these options, then excluded groups may feel discriminated against. Managers need to be aware that excluded employees can create a backlash against work/family programs.[25] Second, telecommuting does not fit the work style of every employee. Some employees have trouble concentrating at home or feel isolated when they work on their own away from the office.[26] Third, having the CEO of an organization announce these programs is not enough to effect change. Many career-minded employees do not take advantage of job sharing, flextime, or telecommuting for fear of being derailed from their career progression.[27]

Basically, some employees feel too much time working at home reduces the amount of face time they have in front of peers and supervisors. Many employees and career specialists feel that face time is important for career progression because it can signal that they are working hard and are committed to the organization. To make these programs an accepted part of the organization, managers need to be trained and rewarded for encouraging their subordinates to use them without fear of derailing their good standing within the firm. Of course, managers should avoid pressuring employees to use their programs. Some employees prefer to maintain more traditional work arrangements and schedules. Last, organizations need to be mindful of the laws that may affect how these flexible work arrangement policies are developed and managed. Some applicable laws include the Fair Labor Standards Act, workers' compensation, Occupational Safety and Health Act, and others.[28]

The Important Concepts of Job Design

The conceptual model in Figure 13.2 is based on the extensive research literature appearing since the 1970s. The model includes the various terms and concepts appearing in the current literature. When linked together, these concepts describe the important determinants of job performance and organizational effectiveness. The model takes into account a number of sources of complexity. It recognizes that individuals react differently to jobs. While one person may derive positive satisfaction from a job, another may not. It also recognizes the difficult trade-offs between organizational and individual needs. For example, the technology of manufacturing (an environmental difference) may dictate that management adopt assembly-line mass production methods and low-skilled jobs to achieve optimal efficiency. Such jobs, however, may result in great unrest and worker discontent. Perhaps these costs could be avoided by carefully balancing organizational and individual needs.

job performance
The outcomes of jobs that relate to the purposes of the organization such as quality, efficiency, and other criteria of effectiveness.

The ideas reflected in Figure 13.2 are the bases for this chapter. We'll present each important cause or effect of job design, beginning with the end result of job design, **job performance**.

FIGURE 13.2
Conceptual Model of Job Design and Job Performance

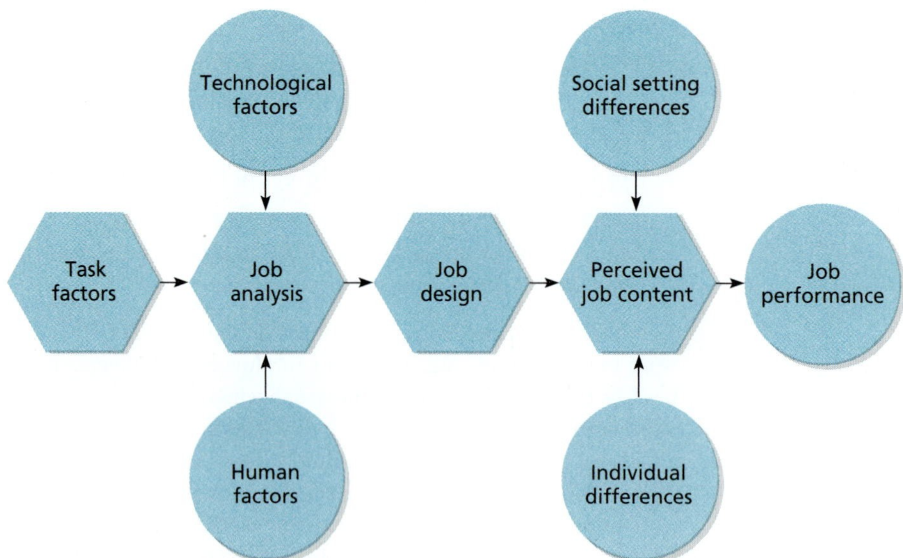

Job Performance Outcomes

Job performance includes a number of outcomes. In this section, we'll discuss performance outcomes that have value to the organization and to the individual.

Objective Outcomes

Quantity and quality of output, absenteeism, tardiness, and turnover are objective outcomes that can be measured in quantitative terms. For each job, implicit or explicit standards exist for each of these objective outcomes. Industrial engineering studies establish standards for daily quantity, and quality control specialists establish tolerance limits for acceptable quality. These aspects of job performance account for characteristics of the product, client, or service for which the jobholder is responsible. But job performance includes other outcomes.

Personal Behavior Outcomes

The jobholder reacts to the work itself. She reacts by either attending regularly or being absent, by staying with the job, or by quitting. Moreover, physiological and health-related problems can ensue as a consequence of job performance. Stress related to job performance can contribute to physical and mental impairment; accidents and occupation-related disease can also result.

Intrinsic and Extrinsic Outcomes

Job outcomes include intrinsic and extrinsic work outcomes. The distinction between intrinsic and extrinsic outcomes is important for understanding people's reactions to their jobs. In a general sense, an intrinsic outcome is an object or event that follows from the worker's own efforts and doesn't require the involvement of any other person. More simply, it's an outcome clearly related to action on the worker's part. Contemporary job design theory defines intrinsic motivation in terms of the employee's "empowerment" to achieve outcomes from the application of individual ability and talent.[29] Such outcomes typically are thought to result solely in the province of professional and technical jobs; yet, all jobs potentially have opportunities for intrinsic outcomes. Such outcomes involve feelings of responsibility, challenge, and recognition; they result from such job characteristics as variety, autonomy, identity, and significance.[30]

Extrinsic outcomes, however, are objects or events that follow from the workers' own efforts in conjunction with other factors or persons not directly involved in the job itself. Pay, working conditions, co-workers, and even supervision are objects in the workplace that are potentially job outcomes but aren't a fundamental part of the work. Dealing with others and friendship interactions are sources of extrinsic outcomes.

Most jobs provide opportunities for both intrinsic and extrinsic outcomes, so we must understand the relationship between the two. It's generally held that extrinsic rewards reinforce intrinsic rewards in a positive direction when the individual can attribute the source of the extrinsic reward to his own efforts. For example, a pay raise (extrinsic reward) increases feeling good about oneself if the cause of the raise is thought to be one's own efforts and competence and not favoritism by the boss. This line of reasoning explains why some individuals get no satisfaction out of sharing in the gains derived from group effort rather than individual effort.

job satisfaction
An individual's expression of personal well-being associated with doing the job assigned.

Job Satisfaction Outcomes

Job satisfaction depends on the levels of intrinsic and extrinsic outcomes and how the jobholder views those outcomes. These outcomes have different values for different people.

For some people, responsible and challenging work may have neutral or even negative value depending on their education and prior experience with work providing intrinsic outcomes.[31] For other people, such work outcomes may have high positive values.[32] People differ in the importance they attach to job outcomes. Those differences alone would account for different levels of job satisfaction for essentially the same job tasks. For example, one company that has initiated management systems intended to provide employees with a great deal of opportunity for exercising judgment and making decisions has found many individuals unable or unwilling to work for it. The company, W. L. Gore & Associates, has been the subject of considerable interest among those who advocate employee empowerment.[33]

Other important individual differences include job involvement and commitment to the organization.[34] People differ in the extent that (1) work is a central life interest, (2) they actively participate in work, (3) they perceive work as central to self-esteem, and (4) they perceive work as consistent with self-concept. Persons who are not involved in their work or the organizations that employ them cannot be expected to realize the same satisfaction as those who are. This variable accounts for the fact that two workers could report different levels of satisfaction for the same performance levels.

A final individual difference is the perceived equity of the outcome in terms of what the jobholder considers a fair reward.[35] If outcomes are perceived to be unfair in relation to those of others in similar jobs requiring similar effort, the jobholder will experience dissatisfaction and seek means to restore the equity, either by seeking greater rewards (primarily extrinsic) or by reducing effort.

Thus, we see that job performance includes many potential outcomes. Some are of primary value to the organization—the objective outcomes, for example. Other outcomes, such as job satisfaction, are of primary importance to the individual. Job performance is without a doubt a complex variable that depends on the interplay of numerous factors. Managers can make some sense of the issue by understanding the motivational implications of jobs through the application of job analysis.[36]

Describing Jobs through Job Analysis

job analysis
Providing a description of how one job differs from another in terms of demands, activities, and skills required.

The purpose of a **job analysis** is to provide an objective description of the job itself[37] and to provide important information for use in a variety of human resource areas in organizations (e.g., job descriptions, selection tests, training programs, and performance appraisals).[38]

Individuals who perform job analysis gather information about three aspects of all jobs: job content, job requirements, and job context. Many different job analysis methods help managers identify content, requirements, and context.

job content
Specific activities required in a job.

O*NET
An online database hosted by the U.S. Department of Labor that provides occupational descriptions and data such as job descriptions, worker knowledge, skills and abilities, and work requirements.

Job Content

Job content refers to the activities required of the job. Depending on the specific job analysis used, this description can be broad or narrow in scope. The description can vary from general statements of job activities down to highly detailed statements of each and every hand and body motion required to do the job. One popular source for content about jobs comes from the U.S. Department of Labor's Occupational Information Network (or O*NET). The **O*NET** (www.onecenter.org) is an online database that "provides occupational descriptions and data for use by job seekers, workforce development offices, human resources professionals, students, researchers and others."[39] A user-friendly and flexible online resource, the O*NET allows individuals to describe work accurately and efficiently. Recently, several "green" or environmentally oriented job descriptions have been added to the massive online database so that job seekers and career counselors can access these increasingly popular occupations.[40]

functional job analysis (FJA)
Method of job analysis that focuses on specific activities, machines, methods, and required output.

Another widely used method, **functional job analysis (FJA)**, describes jobs in terms of

1. What the worker does in relation to data, people, and jobs.
2. What methods and techniques the worker uses.
3. What machines, tools, and equipment the worker uses.
4. What materials, products, subject matter, or services the worker produces.

The first three aspects relate to job activities. The fourth aspect relates to job performance. FJA provides descriptions of jobs that can be the bases for classifying jobs according to any one of the four dimensions. In addition to defining what activities, methods, and machines make up the job, FJA also defines what the individual doing the job should produce. FJA can, therefore, be the basis for defining standards of performance.

Job Requirements

job requirements
The education, experience, licenses, and other personal characteristics an individual needs to perform the job content.

position analysis questionnaire (PAQ)
A method of job analysis that takes into account human characteristics as well as task and technological factors of job and job classes.

Job requirements refer to education, experience, licenses, and other personal characteristics that are expected of an individual if he's to perform the job content. In recent years, the idea has emerged that job requirements should also identify skills, abilities, knowledge, and other personal characteristics required to perform the job content in the particular setting. One widely used method, **position analysis questionnaire (PAQ)**, takes into account these human factors through analysis of the following job aspects:

1. Information sources critical to job performance.
2. Information processing and decision making critical to job performance.
3. Physical activity and dexterity required of the job.
4. Interpersonal relationships required of the job.
5. Reactions of individuals to working conditions.[41]

The position analysis questionnaire can be adapted to jobs of all types, including managerial jobs.

Job Context

job context
Physical environment and other working conditions, along with other factors considered to be extrinsic to a job.

Job context refers to factors such as the physical demands and working conditions of the job, the degree of accountability and responsibility, the extent of supervision required or exercised, and the consequences of error. Job context describes the environment within which the job is to be performed.

Numerous methods exist to perform job analysis. Different methods can give different answers to important questions such as "How much is the job worth?" Thus, selecting the method for performing job analysis isn't trivial—it's one of the most important decisions in job design. Surveys of expert job analysts' opinions bear out the popularity of PAQ and FJA.[42]

Job Analysis in Different Settings

People perform their jobs in a variety of settings—too many to discuss them all. We'll instead discuss two significant job settings: the factory and the office. One has historical significance, the other has future significance.

Jobs in the Factory

Job analysis began in the factory. Industrialization created the setting in which individuals perform many hundreds of specialized jobs. The earliest attempts to do job analysis followed the ideas advanced by the proponents of scientific management. They were industrial engineers who, at the turn of the 20th century, began to devise ways to analyze industrial jobs. The major theme of scientific management is that objective analyses of facts and data collected in the workplace could provide the bases for determining the one best way to design work.[43] F. W. Taylor stated the essence of scientific management as follows:

> *First:* Develop a science for each element of a man's work that replaces the old rule-of-thumb method.
>
> *Second:* Scientifically select and then train, teach, and develop the workman, whereas in the past he chose his own work and trained himself as best he could.
>
> *Third:* Heartily cooperate with the men so as to ensure that all of the work is done in accordance with the principles of the science that has been developed.
>
> *Fourth:* There is almost an equal division of the work and the responsibility between management and workmen. Management takes over all work for which it's better fitted than workmen, while in the past, almost all of the work and the greater part of the responsibility were thrown upon workmen.[44]

These four principles express the theme of scientific management methods. Management should take into account task and technology to determine the best way for each job and then train people to do the job that way.

Scientific management produced many techniques in current use. Motion and time study, work simplification, and standard methods are at the core of job analysis in factory settings. Although the mechanistic approach to job analysis is widespread, many service organizations as well as manufacturers are discovering some of the negative consequences of jobs that are overly routine as the next OB at Work feature suggests.[45]

Consequently, many organizations are turning away from the idea of one person doing one specialized job. As we'll learn later in the chapter, many manufacturing firms are now analyzing jobs to determine the extent to which content and requirements can be increased to tap a larger portion of the individual's talents and abilities.

Jobs in the Office

In the short space of time since the advent of scientific management, the American economy has shifted from factory-oriented to office-oriented work. The fastest growing segment of jobs is secretarial, clerical, and information workers. The growth of these jobs is due to technological breakthroughs in both factory and office settings.

Technological breakthroughs in automation, robotics, and computer-assisted manufacturing have reduced the need for industrial jobs. But that same technology has increased the need for office jobs. Still, the modern office isn't a mere extension of the traditional factory. The modern office reflects the pervasiveness of computer technology. Its most striking feature is the replacement of paper with some electronic medium, usually a personal computer (PC). One individual interacts with the PC to do a variety of tasks that in earlier times would have required many individuals. A significant aspect of job analysis in modern offices is the creation of work modules—interrelated tasks that can be assigned to a single individual.

In recent times, managers and researchers have found that human factors must be given special attention when analyzing jobs in the electronic office. PC users report that they suffer visual and postural problems such as headaches, burning eyes, and shoulder and backaches and repetitive stress injuries such as carpal tunnel syndrome.[46] The sources of these problems seem to be in the design of the workplace, particularly the interaction between the individual and the PC.

Job analysis in the office must pay particular attention to human factors. The tendency is to overemphasize the technological factor—in this case, the computer—and to analyze jobs only as extensions of the technology. As was true of job analysis in factories, it's simply easier to deal with the relatively fixed nature of tasks and technology than to deal with the variable of human nature.[47]

OB AT WORK Six Sigma: Cure-All or Destroyer of Innovation?

Everyone has probably heard of Six Sigma by now. Invented by an engineer at Motorola in 1987, Six Sigma is a quality improvement process that uses data and statistics to improve the efficiency (and cut costs) of business processes. Adapted by approximately 35 percent of companies in the United States (e.g., Sony, Honeywell, Raytheon, Caterpillar, Johnson Controls, Motorola, Bank of America, Sun Microsystems, DuPont, Ford, Dow Chemical, 3M, and Home Depot), the Six Sigma approach has saved firms billions of dollars. For example, Motorola reports that their Six Sigma program has saved the company $16 billion over the past 12 years alone, while Ford credits Six Sigma with savings of more than $1 billion since 2000. Jack Welch, former CEO of GE, stated the following about the Six Sigma results at his firm: "Six Sigma did end up delivering billions of dollars from market share gains and productivity improvements . . ."

How does a Six Sigma program work? The goal is to get most (if not all) of the company's employees and executives trained in the process of quality control. Projects with specific goals and deadlines are identified (e.g., a tire manufacturer wants to make tires with fewer defects so as to decrease the number of recalls and therefore improve customer satisfaction and decrease costs) and then a team is assigned to apply the Six Sigma program of DMAIC (define, measure, analyze, improve, and control).

Who makes up the Six Sigma teams? Starting with the executives, these individuals attend a kickoff event known as an "executive summit." For a couple of days, the executives get a working knowledge of the Six Sigma process and how it will be implemented at the company. Fast-track junior managers who learn the most about the statistical processes are called "blackbelts" who will help lead specific projects. They will receive help from the "greenbelts" who are knowledgeable about Six Sigma but are still learning the nuances of the program.

Is Six Sigma appropriate for every project? Many believe that the Six Sigma quality improvement process is good for organizations that need some "belt tightening" or trimming of waste. However, many experts believe that companies who totally embrace the Six Sigma philosophy cannot simultaneously cultivate innovation, creativity, and risk taking. Six Sigma is about control and minimizing variance. Many believe that innovation is about finding new and unexpected ways to meet customers' needs or to invent a new product that creates a new market (e.g., MySpace Web site and the iPod). For this reason, companies like 3M and Home Depot are rolling back on their total pursuit of Six Sigma. For example, Frank Blake, the CEO of Home Depot, is listening to complaints from store managers that the reporting and measurement demands of their Six Sigma program are draining away time that they could be spending with customers, other managers, and employees in the store.

In sum, Six Sigma has undoubtedly made a major impact on the quality improvement and cost effectiveness of many organizations throughout the United States over the past 20 years. It is also safe to say that many of these and more recent "believers" will continue to use the Six Sigma philosophy well into the 21st century. One major challenge exists, however, and that is how to decide to which parts of the company Six Sigma should be applied and how to do so without undermining the creative and innovative spirit of employees who work there.

Sources: X. Zu and L. Fredendall, "Enhancing Six Sigma Implementation Through Human Resource Management," *The Quality Management Journal* 16, no. 4 (2009): 41–54; Brian Hindo and Brian Grow, "Six Sigma: So Yesterday? In an Innovation Economy, It's No Longer a Cure-All," *Businessweek*, June 11, 2007, p. 11; Jack Welch and Suzy Welch, "The Six Sigma Shotgun: Resistance to Change Requires Blasting Six Sigma into Every Nook and Cranny," *Businessweek*, May 21, 2007, p. 110; Roger O. Crockett and Jena McGregor, "Six Sigma Still Pays Off at Motorola," *Businessweek*, December 4, 2006, p. 50; and Linda Herring, "Six Sigma in Sight," *HRMagazine*, March 2004, pp. 76–81.

Job Designs: The Results of Job Analysis

Job designs are the results of job analysis. They specify three characteristics of jobs: range, depth, and relationships.

job range
Number of tasks a person is expected to perform while doing a job. The more tasks required, the greater the job range.

job depth
Degree of influence or discretion that an individual possesses to choose how a job will be performed.

Range and Depth

Job range refers to the number of tasks a jobholder performs. The individual who performs eight tasks to complete a job has a wider job range than a person performing four tasks. In most instances, the greater the number of tasks performed, the longer it takes to complete the job.

A second characteristic is **job depth**, the amount of discretion an individual has to decide job activities and job outcomes. In many instances, job depth relates to personal influence as well as delegated authority. Thus, an employee with the same job title who's at the same organizational level as another employee may possess more, less, or the same amount of job depth because of the personal influence.

Job range and depth distinguish one job from another not only within the same organization, but also among different organizations. To illustrate how jobs differ in range and depth, Figure 13.3 depicts the differences for selected jobs in firms, hospitals, and universities. For example, business research scientists, hospital chiefs of surgery, and university presidents generally have high job range and significant depth. Research scientists perform a large number of tasks and are usually not closely supervised. Chiefs of surgery have significant job range in that they oversee and counsel on many diverse surgical matters. In addition, they aren't supervised closely and they have the authority to influence hospital surgery policies and procedures.

University presidents have a large number of tasks to perform. They speak to alumni groups, politicians, community representatives, and students. They develop, with the consultation of others, policies on admissions, fund raising, and adult education. They can alter the faculty recruitment philosophy and thus alter the course of the entire institution. For example, a university president may want to build an institution that's noted for high-quality classroom instruction and for providing excellent services to the community. This thrust may lead to recruiting and selecting professors who want to concentrate on these two specific goals. In contrast, another president may want to foster outstanding research and high-quality classroom instruction. Of course, yet another president may attempt to develop an institution that's noted for instruction, research, and service. The critical point is that university presidents have sufficient depth to alter the course of a university's direction.

Examples of jobs with high depth and low range are packaging machine mechanics, anesthesiologists, and faculty members. Mechanics perform the limited tasks that pertain to repairing and maintaining packaging machines, but they can decide how breakdowns on the packaging machine are to be repaired. The discretion means that the mechanics have relatively high job depth.

Anesthesiologists also perform a limited number of tasks. They are concerned with the rather restricted task of administering anesthetics to patients. However, they can decide

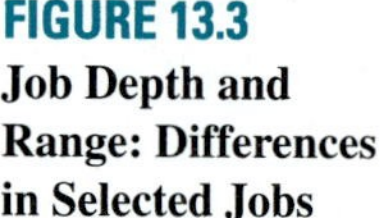

FIGURE 13.3
Job Depth and Range: Differences in Selected Jobs

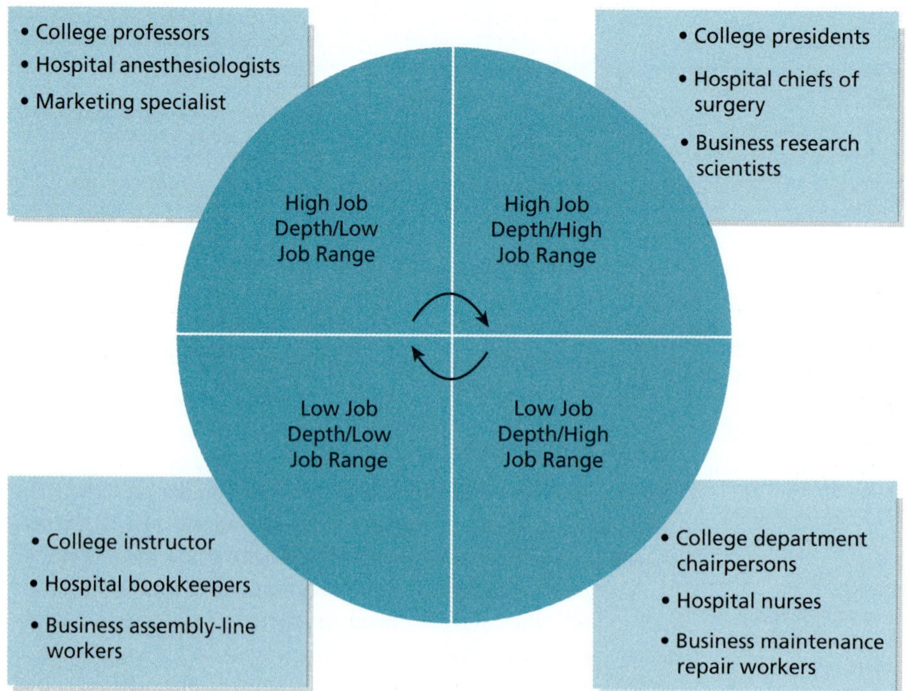

the type of anesthetic to be administered in a particular situation, a decision indicative of high job depth. University professors specifically engaged in classroom instruction have relatively low job range. Teaching involves comparatively more tasks than the work of the anesthesiologist, yet fewer tasks than that of the business research scientist. However, professors' job depth is greater than graduate student instructors' because professors determine how they'll conduct the class, what materials will be presented, and the standards to be used in evaluating students. Graduate students typically don't have complete freedom in the choice of class materials and procedures. Professors decide these matters for them.

Highly specialized jobs are those having few tasks to accomplish by prescribed means. Such jobs are quite routine; they also tend to be controlled by specified rules and procedures (low depth). A highly despecialized job (high range) has many tasks to accomplish within the framework of discretion over means and ends (high depth). Within an organization, there typically are great differences among jobs in both range and depth. Although there are no precise equations that managers can use to decide job range and depth, they can follow this guideline: Given the economic and technical requirements of the organization's mission, goals, and objectives, what is the optimal point along the continuum of range and depth for each job?

Job Relationships

job relationships
Interpersonal relationships required or made possible on the job.

Job relationships are determined by managers' decisions regarding departmentalization bases and spans of control. The resulting groups become the responsibility of a manager to coordinate toward organization purposes. These decisions also determine the nature and extent of jobholders' interpersonal relationships, individually and within groups. As we already have seen in the discussion of groups in organizations, group performance is affected in part by group cohesiveness. The degree of group cohesiveness depends on the quality and kind of interpersonal relationships of jobholders assigned to a task or command group.

The wider the span of control, the larger the group and, consequently, the more difficult the establishment of friendship and interest relationships. Simply, people in larger groups are less likely to communicate and interact sufficiently to form interpersonal ties than people in smaller groups. Without the opportunity to communicate, people will be unable to establish cohesive work groups. Thus, an important source of satisfaction may be lost for individuals who seek to fulfill social and esteem needs through relationships with co-workers.

The basis for departmentalization that management selects also has important implications for job relationships. The functional basis places jobs with similar depth and range in the same groups, while product, territory, and customer bases place jobs with dissimilar depth and range. Thus, in functional departments, people will be doing much the same specialty. Product, territory, and customer departments, however, comprise jobs that are quite different and heterogeneous. Individuals who work in heterogeneous departments experience feelings of dissatisfaction, stress, and involvement more intensely than those in homogeneous, functional departments. People with homogeneous backgrounds, skills, and training have more common interests than those with heterogeneous ones. Thus, it's easier for them to establish satisfying social relationships with less stress, but also with less involvement in the department's activities.

Job designs describe the *objective* characteristics of jobs. That is, through job analysis techniques managers can design jobs in terms of required activities to produce a specified outcome. But yet another factor—perceived job content—must be considered before we can understand the relationship between jobs and performance.

The Way People Perceive Their Jobs

The way people do their jobs depends in part on how they perceive and think of their jobs. Even though Taylor proposed that the way to improve work (i.e., to make it more efficient) is to determine the "best way" to do a task (motion study) and the standard time for completion of the task (time study), the actual performance of jobs goes beyond its technical description.

The belief that job design can be based solely on technical data ignores the very large role played by the individual who performs the job. Individuals differ profoundly, as we noted in the chapter on individual differences. They come to work with different backgrounds, needs, and motivations. Once on the job, they experience the social setting in which the work is performed in unique ways. It's not surprising to find that different individuals perceive jobs differently.

Perceived Job Content

perceived job content
Specific job activities and general job characteristics as perceived by individual performing the job. Two individuals doing the same job may have the same or different perceptions of job content.

Perceived job content refers to characteristics of a job that define its general nature as perceived by the jobholder. We must distinguish between a job's *objective properties* and its *subjective properties* as reflected in the perceptions of people who perform it.[48] Managers can't understand the causes of job performance without considering individual differences such as personality, needs, and span of attention.[49] Nor can managers understand the causes of job performance without considering the social setting in which the job is performed. According to Figure 13.2, perceived job content precedes job performance. Thus, if managers desire to increase job performance by changing perceived job content, they can change job design, individual perceptions, or social settings—the causes of perceived job content.

If management is to understand perceived job content, some method for measuring it must exist. In response to this need, organization behavior researchers have attempted to measure perceived job content in a variety of work settings. The methods that researchers use rely on questionnaires that jobholders complete and that measure their perceptions of certain job characteristics.

Job Characteristics

The pioneering effort to measure perceived job content through employee responses to a questionnaire resulted in the identification of six characteristics: variety, autonomy, required interaction, optional interaction, knowledge and skill required, and responsibility.[50] The index of these six characteristics is termed the Requisite Task Attribute Index (RTAI). The original RTAI has been extensively reviewed and analyzed. One important development was the review by Hackman and Lawler, who revised the index to include the six characteristics shown in Table 13.1.[51]

Variety, task identity, and feedback are perceptions of job range. Autonomy is the perception of job depth; and dealing with others and friendship opportunities reflect perceived job content perceptions of job relationships. Employees sharing similar perceptions, job designs, and social settings should report similar job characteristics. Employees with different perceptions, however, report different job characteristics of the same job. For example, an individual with a high need for social belonging would perceive "friendship opportunities" differently than another individual with a low need for social belonging.[52]

Individual Differences

Individual differences in need strength, particularly the strength of growth needs, have been shown to influence the perception of task variety.[53] Employees with relatively

TABLE 13.1
Six Characteristics of Perceived Job Content

Source: Henry P. Sims, Jr., Andrew D. Szilagyi, and Robert T. Keller, "The Measurement of Job Characteristics," *Academy of Management Journal* (June 1976): 197.

Characteristic	Description
Variety	Degree to which a job requires employees to perform a wide range of operations in their work, and/or degree to which employees must use a variety of equipment and procedures in their work.
Autonomy	Extent to which employees have a major say in scheduling their work, selecting the equipment they use, and deciding on procedures to be followed.
Task identity	Extent to which employees do an entire or whole piece of work and can clearly identify with the results of their efforts.
Feedback	Degree to which employees, as they are working, receive information that reveals how well they are performing on the job.
Dealing with others	Degree to which a job requires employees to deal with other people to complete their work.
Friendship opportunities	Degree to which a job allows employees to talk with one another on the job and to establish informal relationships with other employees at work.

weak higher order needs are less concerned with performing a variety of tasks than are employees with relatively strong growth needs. Thus, managers expecting higher performance to result from increased task variety would be disappointed if the jobholders did not have strong growth needs. Even individuals with strong growth needs cannot respond continuously to the opportunity to perform more and more tasks. At some point, performance turns down as these individuals reach the limits imposed by their abilities and time.

Social Setting Differences

Differences in social settings of work also affect perceptions of job content. Examples of social setting differences include leadership style and what other people say about the job. As more than one research study has pointed out, how one perceives a job is greatly affected by what other people say about it. Thus, if one's friends state their jobs are boring, one is likely to state that his job is also boring. If the individual perceives the job as boring, job performance will no doubt suffer. Job content, then, results from the interaction of many factors in the work situation.

The field of organization behavior has advanced a number of suggestions for improving the motivational properties of jobs. Invariably, the suggestions, termed *job design strategies,* attempt to improve job performance through changes in actual job characteristics. The next section reviews the more significant of these strategies.

Designing Job Range: Job Rotation and Job Enlargement

The earliest attempts to design jobs date to the scientific management era. Efforts at that time emphasized efficiency criteria. With that emphasis, the individual tasks that constitute a job are limited, uniform, and repetitive. This practice leads to narrow job range and, consequently, reported high levels of job discontent, turnover, absenteeism, and dissatisfaction. Accordingly, strategies were devised that resulted in wider job range through increasing the requisite activities of jobs. Two of these approaches are job rotation and job enlargement.

Job Rotation

job rotation
Practice of moving individuals from job to job to reduce potential boredom and increase potential motivation and performance.

Managers of organizations such as Marriott, General Electric, Ford, TRW Systems, and Greyhound Financial Corporation have used different forms of the **job rotation** strategy.[54] This practice involves rotating managers and nonmanagers alike from one job to another. In so doing, the individual is expected to complete more job activities because each job includes different tasks.[55] Job rotation involves increasing the range of jobs and the perception of variety in the job content. Increasing task variety should, according to recent studies, increase employee satisfaction, reduce mental overload, decrease the number of errors due to fatigue, improve production and efficiency,[56] and reduce on-the-job injuries.[57] However, job rotation doesn't change the basic characteristics of the assigned jobs. Some relatively small firms have successfully used job rotation.

One relatively small manufacturing operation, Rohm & Haas Bayport (owned by The Dow Chemical Company), was founded in 1981 to produce specialty chemicals. The plant is located in LaPorte, Texas, and its 67 employees play active roles in management because their jobs are designed with that activity in mind. The company's philosophy is to provide autonomy and responsibility in each individual's job and, consequently, to enable employees to feel a sense of "ownership" of key decisions and actions. Every person in the organization is trained to be and to act like a manager. The 46 process technicians and 15 engineers and chemists report to one of the two manufacturing unit managers who in turn report to the executive team.

The technicians make operating decisions among themselves while working in teams of four to seven people. The company has no shift foremen or line supervisors in the usual sense of these positions. Rather, technicians are expected to be self-managed. Team members rotate jobs with other team members every 4 to 12 weeks to provide task variety and cross-training. They're also trained to do routine maintenance and repairs of their equipment and not to depend on a separate maintenance team for that support. The company's idea is to give individuals near complete control of the conditions that govern work pace and quality. Employees evaluate each other's performance and interview applicants for positions. Job designs at Rohm & Haas Bayport contribute to individual performance, according to company spokespersons.[58]

Critics state that job rotation often involves nothing more than having people perform several boring and monotonous jobs rather than one. An alternative strategy is job enlargement.

Job Enlargement

The pioneering Walker and Guest study[59] was concerned with the social and psychological problems associated with mass production jobs in automobile assembly plants. The study found that many workers were dissatisfied with their highly specialized jobs. In particular, they disliked mechanical pacing, repetitiveness of operations, and a lack of a sense of accomplishment. Walker and Guest also found a positive relationship between job range and job satisfaction. Findings of this research gave early support for motivation theories predicting that increases in job range will increase job satisfaction and other objective job outcomes. **Job enlargement** strategies focus upon the opposite of dividing work—they're a form of despecialization or increasing the number of tasks that an employee performs.[60] For example, a job is designed such that the individual performs six tasks instead of three.

job enlargement
Practice of increasing the number of tasks for which an individual is responsible. Increases job range, but not depth.

Although, in many instances, an enlarged job requires a longer training period, job satisfaction usually increases because boredom is reduced. The implication, of course, is that job enlargement will lead to improvement in other performance outcomes.

The concept and practice of job enlargement have become considerably more sophisticated. In recent years, effective job enlargement involves more than simply increasing task variety. In addition, it's necessary to design certain other aspects of job range, including providing worker-paced (rather than machine- or computer-paced) control. Each of these changes involves balancing the gains and losses of varying degrees of division of labor. Contemporary applications of job enlargement involve training individuals to perform several different jobs, each requiring considerable skill, whether in manufacturing or service organizations.

Some employees can't cope with enlarged jobs because they can't comprehend complexity; moreover, they may not have a sufficiently long attention span to complete an enlarged set of tasks. However, if employees are amenable to job enlargement and have the requisite ability, then job enlargement should increase satisfaction and product quality and decrease absenteeism and turnover. These gains aren't without costs, including the likelihood that employees will demand larger salaries in exchange for performing enlarged jobs. Yet these costs must be borne if management desires to implement the design strategy—job enrichment—that enlarges job depth. Job enlargement is a necessary precondition for job enrichment.

Designing Job Depth: Job Enrichment

job enrichment
Practice of increasing the discretion an individual can use to select activities and outcomes. Increases job depth and accordingly fulfills growth and autonomy needs.

The impetus for designing job depth was provided by Herzberg's two-factor theory of motivation. The basis of his theory is that factors that meet individuals' need for psychological growth (especially responsibility, job challenge, and achievement) must be characteristic of their jobs. The application of his theory is termed **job enrichment**.

The implementation of job enrichment is realized through direct changes in job depth. Managers can provide employees with greater opportunities to exercise discretion by making the following changes:

1. Direct feedback—the evaluation of performance should be timely and direct.
2. New learning—a good job enables people to feel that they are growing. All jobs should provide opportunities to learn.
3. Scheduling—people should be able to schedule some part of their own work.
4. Uniqueness—each job should have some unique qualities or features.
5. Control over resources—individuals should have some control over their job tasks.
6. Personal accountability—people should be provided with an opportunity to be accountable for the job.

The process as implemented at Texas Instruments (TI) is continuous and pervades the entire organization. Every job in TI is subject to analysis to determine if it can be enriched to include managerial activities. Moreover, as the jobs of nonmanagerial personnel are designed to include greater depth, the jobs of managers must emphasize training and counseling of subordinates and de-emphasize control and direction.

As the theory and practice of job enrichment have evolved, managers have become aware that successful applications require numerous changes in how work is done. Important changes include giving workers greater authority to participate in decisions, to set their own goals, and to evaluate their (and their work group's) performance. Job enrichment also involves changing the nature and style of managers' behavior. Managers must be willing and able to delegate authority. Given employees' ability to carry out enriched jobs and managers' willingness to delegate authority, gains in performance can be expected. These positive outcomes are the result of increasing employees' expectations that efforts lead to performance, that performance leads to intrinsic and extrinsic rewards, and that these rewards have power to satisfy needs. These significant changes in managerial jobs, coupled with changes in nonmanagerial jobs, suggest that a supportive work environment is a prerequisite for successful job enrichment efforts.

Job enrichment and job enlargement aren't competing strategies. Job enlargement may be compatible with the needs, values, and abilities of some individuals, while job enrichment may not. Yet job enrichment, when appropriate, necessarily involves job enlargement. A promising new approach to job design that attempts to integrate the two approaches is the job characteristic model. Hackman, Oldham, Janson, and Purdy devised the approach, basing it on the Job Diagnostic Survey.[61]

The model attempts to account for the interrelationships among (1) certain job characteristics; (2) psychological states associated with motivation, satisfaction, and performance; (3) job outcomes; and (4) growth need strength. Figure 13.4 describes the relationships among these variables. Although variety, identity, significance, autonomy, and feedback don't completely describe perceived job content, according to this model they sufficiently describe those aspects that management can manipulate to bring about gains in productivity.

Steps that management can take to increase the core dimensions include

work modules
Whole pieces of work assigned to individuals.

1. Combining task elements.
2. Assigning whole pieces of work (i.e., **work modules**).
3. Allowing discretion in selection of work methods.
4. Permitting self-paced control.
5. Opening feedback channels.

These actions increase task variety, identity, and significance; consequently, the "experienced meaningfulness of work" psychological state is increased. By permitting employee participation and self-evaluation and by creating autonomous work groups, the feedback and autonomy dimensions are increased along with the psychological states "experienced responsibility" and "knowledge of actual results."

Implementing the job characteristics in a particular situation begins with a study of existing job perceptions by means of the Job Description Survey. Hackman and Oldham have reported numerous applications of the model in a variety of organizations.[62] They have also compiled normative data for a variety of job categories so that managers and practitioners can compare the responses of their own employees to those of a larger population.[63]

FIGURE 13.4
The Job Characteristics Model

Source: J. Richard Hackman and Greg R. Oldham, "Development of the Job Diagnostic Survey," *Journal of Applied Psychology* (1975): 159–70.

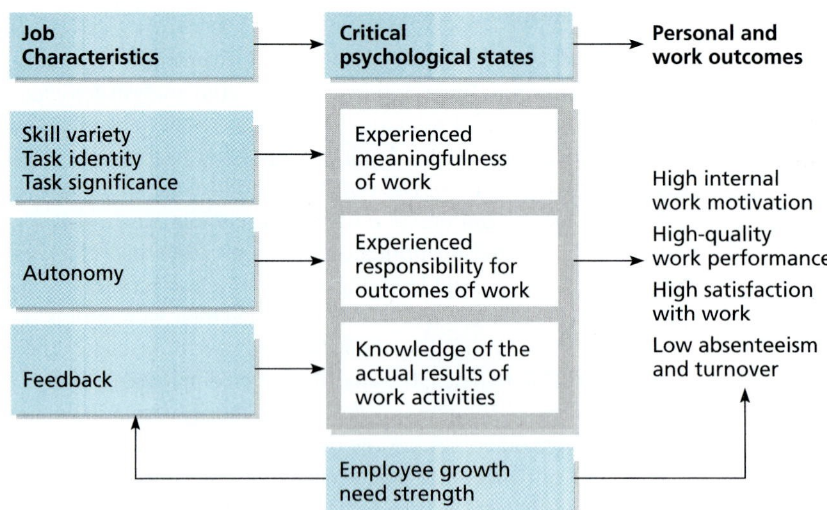

Although the track record of job design efforts is generally positive, some caveats are warranted.

The positive benefits of these efforts are moderated by individual differences in the strength of employees' growth needs. That is, employees with strong need for accomplishment, learning, and challenge will respond more positively than those with relatively weak growth needs. In more familiar terms, employees with high need for self-esteem and self-actualization are the more likely candidates for job design. Employees who are forced to participate in job design programs but who lack either the need strength or the ability to perform designed jobs may experience stress, anxiety, adjustment problems, erratic performance, turnover, and absenteeism. Another potential moderator of successful job design efforts is the changing nature of jobs in the United States (see the OB and Your Career feature on the next page).

The available research on the interrelationships between perceived job content and performance is meager. It's apparent, however, that managers must cope with significant problems in matching employee needs and differences and organizational needs.[64]

Problems associated with job design include the following:

1. The program is time-consuming and costly.
2. Unless lower-level needs are satisfied, people will not respond to opportunities to satisfy upper-level needs. And even though our society has been rather successful in providing food and shelter, these needs regain importance when the economy moves through periods of recession and high inflation.
3. Job design programs are intended to satisfy needs typically not satisfied in the workplace. As workers are told to expect higher-order need satisfaction, they may raise their expectations beyond what's possible. Dissatisfaction with the program's unachievable aim may displace dissatisfaction with the jobs.
4. Job design may be resisted by labor unions who see the effort as an attempt to get more work for the same pay.
5. Job design efforts may not produce tangible performance improvements for some time after the beginning of the effort. One study indicated that significant improvements in effectiveness couldn't be seen until four years after the beginning of the job design program.[65]

Practical efforts to improve productivity and satisfaction through job design have emphasized autonomy and feedback. Relatively less emphasis has been placed on identity, significance, and variety. Apparently, it's easier to provide individuals with greater responsibility for the total task and increased feedback than to change the essential nature of the task itself. To provide identity, significance, and variety often requires enlarging the task to the point of losing the benefits of work simplification and standardization. But within the economic constraints imposed by the logic of specialization, it's possible to design work so as to give individuals complete responsibility for its completion to the end and at the same time to provide supportive managerial monitoring.

In general, one reaches two conclusions when considering the experience of job design approaches. First, they're relatively successful in increasing quality of output. This conclusion pertains, however, only if the reward system already satisfies lower-level needs. If it presently doesn't satisfy lower-level needs, employees can't be expected to experience upper-level need satisfaction (intrinsic rewards) through enriched jobs. In particular, managers can't expect individuals with relatively low growth needs to respond as would those with relatively high growth needs.[66]

Second, successful efforts are the result of the circumstances that initiate the effort and the process undertaken to manage the effort. Organizations under external pressure

OB AND YOUR CAREER The Changing Nature of Jobs in America

Technology, globalization, and a prolonged recession are forces that are changing the nature of jobs and pushing larger amounts of risk onto U.S. workers. About 20–30 years ago, most jobs could have been characterized in the following way: if employees were reliable and did their jobs reasonably well, they would be rewarded with solid base pay and annual pay raises, benefits, and job security. Nowadays, these "permanent jobs" are increasingly being replaced by jobs that are more temporary in nature, characterized by lower base pay, bonuses that have to be renegotiated annually, reduced or no benefits, and little to no job security. Some have labeled this new work design trend temporary or "just-in-time" jobs.

One of the major drivers for this change to treating workers as temporary resources are companies that want to trim labor costs and have the flexibility to adjust their staffing needs (rapidly) to the cyclical ups and downs of their industries. For example, Boeing cut some of its permanent staff in 2009 and replaced them by hiring 1,500 "contract labor" technologists in India. Microsoft has always used temporary staffing firms for well-defined, short-term projects including software development. Once the project is finished, the temporary employees move on to other projects with other companies. Companies like Kelly Services, Robert Half, and Manpower that provide organizations with temporary workers have been growing and have reported large increases in their stock prices in 2009 and 2010.

What's the bottom line? U.S. workers are increasingly taking on more risk in their jobs, compensation, and careers. The following suggestions may help workers increase their job prospects and take advantage of the changes that are occurring regarding the nature of many jobs:

1. Envision yourself as your own brand or company. This mindset will help you take control over your career and point you toward jobs (and projects) that will give you marketable skills and training.
2. Try to work for job-intensive, high-growth industries. Healthcare, financial services, and education are growth industries that offer large numbers of jobs and careers. Do your research to see whether the industries you are interested in are prone to offshoring jobs and using temporary workers.
3. Make education a lifelong process. Research shows that in general, workers with higher levels of education fare better when it comes to job security and earnings. You should strive to continuously update your skill set and education.
4. Be flexible. The mantra for a successful career in the 21st century is to maintain a sense of flexibility. Jobs are continuously changing, and in order to be successful, you need to change with them.
5. Develop and maintain a large network of contacts. From time to time, jobs require collaboration and input from a variety of stakeholders like customers, co-workers, friends and associates in other organizations, and others. So, it's important to maintain an extensive network of people to whom you can turn for advice and recommendations when needed. Also, an extensive network can help you find a new job in case you want to leave your current employer or get laid off.
6. Keep abreast of employment trends. Monitor what your organization and other organizations within the industry are doing with respect to jobs. If your company's competitor announces that it will offshore thousands of jobs over the next 10 years, then it is possible that your organization will follow a similar path. If your job were one that could be offshored, then it would make sense to try to move higher up or move to a different job or division within the organization that has more job security.
7. Develop global skills. The old adage "If you can't beat 'em, join 'em" may make sense as more jobs require global skills and experience. Pursue international job opportunities that will give you relevant cross-cultural, language, and international business skills. For example, a traveling international assignment (where you don't have to relocate overseas) that takes you to China, Brazil, and India four or five times a year could be a great way to try out international assignments. Or, if you're more adventurous, a one- to two-year expatriate assignment to an important new host country market may make sense. The key is to get out in front of the globalization wave before it overtakes your job.

Sources: Adapted from Michelle Conlin, Peter Coy, and Moira Herbst, "The Disposable Worker," *Businessweek*, January 2010, pp. 32–39; Pete Engardio, "Can the Future Be Built in America?" *Businessweek*, September 2009, pp. 46–51; and Michael Mandel, "Which Way to the Future: Globalization and Technology Are Drastically Changing How We Do Our Jobs–And That's Both a Promise and a Problem," *Businessweek*, August, 2007, p. 45.

to change have a better chance of successfully implementing job design than those not under such pressure. Moreover, successful efforts are accompanied by broad-scale participation of managers and employees alike. Since a primary source of organizational effectiveness is job performance, managers should design jobs according to the best available knowledge.[67]

Teams and Job Design

Evolving from the research at the individual level, the concept of job design has also been applied to work groups in organizations. For a variety of reasons, the use of work teams has become common in organizations.[68] Admittedly, work teams do not always achieve high levels of productivity, cooperation, or success. It can be argued that overall team effectiveness can be enhanced through job design methods that increase the motivation of team members. One group of researchers has taken the position that the job characteristics identified and developed by Hackman and colleagues can also be applied to teams.[69] It has been argued that appropriate work team job design can lead to higher levels of team productivity, employee satisfaction, and managers' judgment of effectiveness. Drawing on the Job Characteristics Model presented in Figure 13.4, the following characteristics should be addressed when designing jobs for work teams:

1. *Self-management*—This concept is similar to autonomy at the individual job level and refers to the team's ability to set its own objectives, coordinate its own activities, and resolve its own internal conflicts.
2. *Participation*—This issue refers to the degree to which all members of the team are encouraged and allowed to participate in decisions.
3. *Task variety*—This concept is the extent to which team members are given the opportunity to perform a variety of tasks so as to allow members to use different skills.
4. *Task significance*—This term refers to the degree to which the team's work is valued and has significance for both internal and external stakeholders of the organization.
5. *Task identity*—This concept focuses on the degree to which a team completes a whole and separate piece of work and has control over most of the resources necessary to accomplish its objectives.

Although research investigating these five aspects of team job design is limited, preliminary findings are somewhat promising. After an extensive review of the literature on effective work groups, one set of researchers studied the degree to which work group job design could affect such important effectiveness outcomes as work group productivity, group member satisfaction, and managers' judgments of group effectiveness.[70] They reported that with the exception of task identity, all of the other job design characteristics (self-management, participation, task variety, and task significance) showed positive relationships with one or more of the effectiveness criteria. In a subsequent research study that used a different sample and different measures of effectiveness, similar findings were reported.[71]

In summary, teamwork design appears to be an important issue to the overall functioning and effectiveness of teams. Managers have control over this area and should consider building in several of the job characteristics mentioned above when designing the work that teams will be doing.

Total Quality Management and Job Design

Total quality management (TQM), according to those who espouse and practice it, combines technical knowledge and human knowledge. To deal with the inherent complexity and variability of production and service delivery technology, people must be empowered with authority to make necessary decisions and must be enabled with knowledge to know when to exercise that authority. Aspects of TQM job designs have appeared throughout this discussion. We've discussed job enrichment including provision of autonomy, creation of work modules, and development of trust and collaboration. We've seen these attributes of jobs in the practices of organizations discussed throughout this chapter. But even as we close this chapter, we must raise a fundamental question: Can American workers adjust to the requirements for working together in teams and in collaboration with management? Are the ideas of TQM totally applicable to the American worker? Is TQM the wave of the future? Do American managers have the ability and commitment to implement the necessary changes in jobs required by new technologies and new global realities?[72] Many contemporary observers warn us that the answers to all these questions must be yes because no other choice exists.[73]

Job design strategy focuses on jobs in the context of individuals' needs for economic well-being and personal growth. But let's put the issue in a broader framework and include the issue of the sociotechnical system. Sociotechnical theory focuses on interactions between technical demands of jobs and social demands of people doing the jobs. The theory states that too great an emphasis on the technical system in the manner of scientific management or too great an emphasis on the social system in the manner of human relations will lead to poor job design. Rather, job design should take into account both the technology and the people who use the technology.

Sociotechnical theory and application of job design developed from studies undertaken in English coal mines from 1948 to 1958.[74] The studies became widely publicized for demonstrating the interrelationship between the social system and the technical system of organizations. The interrelationship was revealed when economic circumstances forced management to change how coal was mined (the technical system). Historically, the technical system consisted of small groups of miners (the social system) working together on "short faces" (seams of coal). But technological advancement improved roof control and safety and made longwall mining possible. The new technical system required a change in the social system. The groups would be disbanded in favor of one-person, one-task jobs. Despite the efforts of management and even the union, miners eventually devised a social system that restored many characteristics of the group system. This experience has been completely described in organizational behavior literature and has stimulated a great deal of research and application.

There's no contradiction between sociotechnical theory and total quality management. In fact, the two approaches are quite compatible. The compatibility relates to the demands of modern technology for self-directed and self-motivated job behavior. Such job behavior is made possible in jobs designed to provide autonomy and variety. As worked out in practice, such jobs are parts of self-regulating work teams responsible for completing whole tasks. The work module concept pervades applications of sociotechnical theory.[75]

Numerous applications of sociotechnical design and total quality management are reported in the literature.[76] Some notable American examples include the Sherwin-Williams Paint factory in Richmond, Kentucky, and the Quaker Oats pet food factory in Topeka, Kansas. Both factories were constructed from the ground up to include and allow for specific types of jobs embodying basic elements of autonomy and empowerment. Firms that don't have the luxury of building the plant from scratch must find ways to renovate both their technology and their job designs to utilize the best technology and people. Some of the most influential industrial and service organizations have confronted the necessity to design jobs to take advantage of the rapid pace of technological advance. In the contemporary global environment, sociotechnical system design has been incorporated in the total quality management approach to management.

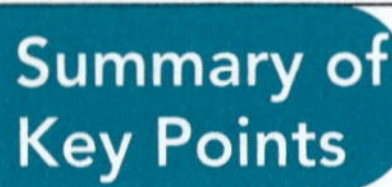

- Job design involves managerial decisions and actions that specify objective job depth, range, and relationships to satisfy organizational requirements as well as the social and personal requirements of jobholders.

- Contemporary managers must consider the issue of quality of work life when designing jobs. This issue reflects society's concern for work experiences that contribute to employees' personal growth and development.
- Strategies for increasing jobs' potential to satisfy the social and personal requirements of jobholders have gone through an evolutionary process. Initial efforts were directed toward job rotation and job enlargement. These strategies produced some gains in job satisfaction but didn't change primary motivators such as responsibility, achievement, and autonomy.
- During the 1960s, job enrichment became a widely recognized strategy for improving quality of work/life factors. This strategy is based on Herzberg's motivation theory and involves increasing jobs' depth through greater delegation of authority to jobholders. Despite some major successes, job enrichment isn't universally applicable because it doesn't consider individual differences.
- Individual differences are now recognized as crucial variables to consider when designing jobs. Experience, cognitive complexity, needs, values, valences, and perceptions of equity are some of the individual differences influencing jobholders' reactions to the scope and relationships of their jobs. When individual differences are combined with environmental, situational, and managerial differences, job design decisions become increasingly complex.
- The most recently developed strategy of job design emphasizes the importance of core job characteristics as perceived by jobholders. Although measurements of individual differences remain a problem, managers should be encouraged to examine ways to increase positive perceptions of variety, identity, significance, autonomy, and feedback. By doing so, the potential for high-quality work performance and high job satisfaction is increased.
- Many organizations, including Citibank, General Motors, and General Foods, have attempted job design with varying degrees of success. The current state of research knowledge is inadequate for making broad generalizations regarding exact causes of success and failure in applications of job design. Managers must diagnose their own situations to determine the applicability of job design in their organizations.
- Sociotechnical theory combines technological and social issues in job design practice. Sociotechnical theory is compatible with job design strategy and in fact emphasizes the practical necessity to design jobs that provide autonomy, feedback, significance, identity, and variety.
- Total quality management (TQM) combines the ideas of job enrichment and sociotechnical theory. Managers who implement TQM design jobs that empower individuals to make important decisions about product/service quality. The empowerment process encourages participative management, team-oriented task modules, and autonomy.

Discussion and Review Questions

1. Many jobs are designed so that employees are rewarded not only for their individual contribution but also for their work in groups and teams. Do you think that rewarding team effort is just as motivational as when an employee is rewarded for his or her own contribution? Explain.
2. Explain the differences between job rotation and job enrichment. Which approach do you feel would be more motivational for the majority of employees?
3. Under what conditions could you see yourself entering into a job-sharing arrangement with a co-worker? Please describe.

4. As a current or future manager, assume that your company could offer only one of the following job design approaches: job sharing, flextime, or telecommuting. Which one would you choose to offer your employees as a way to help them balance their work and personal lives? Justify your choice.
5. What characteristics of jobs can't be enriched? Do you believe that management should ever consider any job to be incapable of enrichment?
6. Explain the relationships between feedback as a job content factor and personal goal setting. Is personal goal setting possible without feedback? Explain.
7. This chapter has described job designs in various service and manufacturing organizations. In which type of organization is job enrichment likely to be more effective as a strategy of increasing motivation and performance? Explain.
8. What do you think of companies such as Motorola and Hewlett-Packard that establish job design policies to help employees balance their work and life commitments? Do you think such policies will help these firms attract and retain more employees? Explain.
9. Think about your current organization or one for which you worked in the past. To what extent would a ROWE (Results-Only Work Environment) fit the organizational culture? Explain.
10. As you understand the idea and practice of total quality management, do you believe that it's the wave of the future in American organizations? Explain.

Taking It to the Net

Searching for a Good Fit? Online Job Descriptions

A common question many job seekers ask themselves is "What kind of a job am I going to get when I graduate/leave my current job?" There are no quick and easy answers to that question since it depends on a variety of factors (experience level, college placement services, health of the economy, and so on). However, a good starting point is to research jobs to see which ones look interesting and could fit with the individual's interests and background. Job descriptions are a quick way to accomplish this task. Job seekers should visit the popular job services Web sites and read over actual job descriptions to get a feel for what organizations are looking for in job applicants. This way, job seekers can discover whether the job is narrowly or broadly defined, what the job content entails, and what the requirements are. This will give job seekers some real-world feedback as to what it takes to get the job of their dreams.

Complete the following steps:

1. Using the Internet, go to www.monster.com.
2. Type in a job title ("sales associate"), skills/keywords ("communication"), or location ("North Carolina").
3. Click on five different job titles that look interesting and answer the following questions about those jobs:
   a. Summarize the content of the job in three or four sentences.
   b. Are most of the job requirements broad or narrow?
   c. If you could modify this job to better suit your personal needs, how would you do it? What type of work design modification would you apply to these jobs (provide three suggestions per job).
4. Repeat the steps above by going to a different job Web site such as www.careerbuilder.com.

Case for Analysis: *Work Redesign in an Insurance Company*

The executive staff of a relatively small life insurance company is considering a proposal to install an electronic data processing system. The proposal is being presented by the assistant to the president, John Skully. He has been studying the feasibility of the equipment after a management consultant recommended a complete overhaul of jobs within the company.

The management consultant had been engaged by the company to diagnose the causes of high turnover and absenteeism. After reviewing the situation and speaking with groups of employees, the consultant recommended that the organization structure be changed from a functional to a client basis. The change in departmental basis would enable management to redesign jobs to reduce the human costs associated with highly specialized tasks.

The current organization includes separate departments to issue policies, collect premiums, change beneficiaries, and process loan applications. Employees in these departments complained that their jobs were boring, insignificant, and monotonous. They had stated that the only reason they stayed with the company was because they liked the small-company atmosphere. They felt that management had a genuine interest in their welfare but that the trivial nature of their jobs contradicted that feeling. As one employee said, "This company is small enough to know almost everybody. But the job I do is so boring that I wonder why they even need me to do it." This and similar comments had led the consultant to believe that the jobs must be altered to provide greater motivation. Recognizing that work redesign opportunities were limited by the organization structure, he recommended that the company change to a client basis. In such a structure, each employee would handle every transaction related to a particular policyholder.

When the consultant presented his views to the members of the executive staff, they were very much interested in his recommendation. In fact, they agreed that his recommendation was well founded. They noted, however, that a small company must pay particular attention to efficiency in handling transactions. The functional basis enabled the organization to achieve the degree of specialization necessary for efficient operations. The manager of internal operations stated, "If we move away from specialization, the rate of efficiency must go down because we'll lose the benefit of specialized effort. The only way we can justify redesigning the jobs as suggested by the consultant is to maintain our efficiency; otherwise, there won't be any jobs to redesign because we'll be out of business."

The internal operations manager explained to the executive staff that despite excessive absenteeism and turnover, he was able to maintain acceptable productivity. The narrow range and depth of the jobs reduced training time to a minimum. It was also possible to hire temporary help to meet peak loads and to fill in for absent employees. "Moreover," he said, "changing the jobs our people do means that we must change the jobs our managers do. They're experts in their own functional areas, but we've never attempted to train them to oversee more than two operations."

A majority of the executive staff believed that the consultant's recommendations should be seriously considered. At that point, the group directed John Skully to evaluate the potential of electronic data processing (EDP) as a means of obtaining efficient operations in combination with the redesigned jobs. He has completed the study and is presenting his report to the executive staff.

"The bottom line," Skully says, "is that EDP will enable us to maintain our present efficiency, but with the redesigned jobs we won't obtain any greater gains. If my analysis is correct, we'll have to absorb the cost of the equipment out of earnings, because there will be no cost savings. So it comes down to what price we're willing and able to pay for improving the satisfaction of our employees."

DISCUSSION QUESTIONS

1. Explain which core characteristics of employees' jobs will be changed if the consultant's recommendations are accepted.
2. Which alternative redesign strategies should be considered? For example, job rotation and job enlargement are possible alternatives. What are the relevant considerations for these and other designs in the context of this company?
3. What would be your decision in this case? What should management be willing to pay for employees' satisfaction? Defend your answer.

Experiential Exercise: *Conducting a Basic Job Analysis*

OBJECTIVES

1. To familiarize students with the initial step of conducting a job analysis.
2. To illustrate the types of information that a job incumbent (person currently in the job) needs to provide a job analyst.
3. To engage students in the actual process of asking another person about the details of his or her job.

RELATED TOPICS

This exercise is related to the topics of job analysis, job content, job requirements, and job context.

JOB ANALYSIS INFORMATION SHEET

Your Job Title ____________________
Class Title ____________________
Your Name ____________________
Supervisor's Title ____________________
Supervisor's Name ____________________

Date ____________________
Department ____________________
Facility ____________________
Prepared by ____________________
Hours Worked ____ a.m./p.m. to ____ a.m./p.m.

1. What is the general purpose of your job?
2. What was your most recent job? If it was in another organization, please name it.
3. To what job would you normally expect to be promoted?
4. If you regularly supervise others, list them by name and job title.
5. If you supervise others, please check those activities that are part of your supervisory duties:

____Hiring
____Orienting
____Training
____Scheduling
____Developing
____Coaching
____Counseling
____Budgeting
____Directing
____Measuring Performance
____Promoting
____Compensating
____Disciplining
____Terminating
____Other ____

6. How would you describe the successful completion and results of your work?
7. *Job Duties.* Please briefly describe what you do and, if possible, how you do it. Indicate those duties you consider to be most important and/or most difficult.
   a. Daily duties ____
   b. Periodic duties (please indicate whether weekly, monthly, quarterly, etc.) ____
   c. Duties performed at irregular intervals ____
   d. How long have you been performing these duties?
   e. Are you performing unnecessary duties? If yes, please describe.
   f. Should you be performing duties not now included in your job? If yes, please describe.
8. *Education.* Please check the blank that indicates the educational requirements for the job, not your *own* educational background.
   a. ____ No formal education required
   b. ____ Less than high school diploma
   c. ____ High school diploma or equivalent
   d. ____ 2-year college degree or equivalent
   e. ____ 4-year college degree
   f. ____ Education beyond undergraduate degree and/or professional license

   Please indicate the education you had when you were placed on this job.
9. *Experience.* Please check the amount needed to perform your job.
   a. ____ None
   b. ____ Less than one month
   c. ____ One month to less than six months
   d. ____ Six months to one year
   e. ____ One to three years
   f. ____ Three to five years
   g. ____ Five to 10 years
   h. ____ Over 10 years

   Please indicate the experience you had when you were placed on this job.

10. *Skills.* Please list any skills required in the performance of your job. (For example, degree of accuracy, alertness, precision in working with described tools, methods, systems, etc.)

    Please list skills you possessed when you were placed on this job.

11. *Equipment.* Does your work require the use of any equipment? Yes ____ No ____ If yes, please list the equipment and check whether you use it rarely, occasionally, or frequently.

Equipment	Rarely	Occasionally	Frequently
a. ______________	________	________	________
b. ______________	________	________	________
c. ______________	________	________	________
d. ______________	________	________	________

COMPLETING THE EXERCISE

Phase I (15–20 minutes). Choose a fellow student with whom to work. Your assignment is to ask this other student the questions (above) and then record his or her answers on the Job Analysis Information Sheet. Your fellow student will play the role of job incumbent (i.e., the person currently in the job). It is acceptable if your partner answers the questions based on a current or previous job that he or she has occupied. If the student who's playing the role of the job incumbent doesn't know the answer to a question, just move on to the next question.

Phase II (10–15 minutes). After the Job Analysis Information Sheet is completed, review the answers with your fellow student and address the following questions:

1. Which of the Job Analysis Information Sheet questions were the most difficult to answer? Why?
2. Which elements or aspects of the job are most important to achieving high performance? Explain.
3. Which elements or aspects of the job are not very important and could possibly be delegated to someone else? Describe.
4. What else does the job incumbent do in the job that isn't captured in the Job Analysis Information Sheet?

Source: Adapted from John M. Ivancevich, *Human Resource Management* (10th ed.), New York: McGraw-Hill/Irwin, 2007, pp. 157–158.

CHAPTER FOURTEEN

Organization Structure

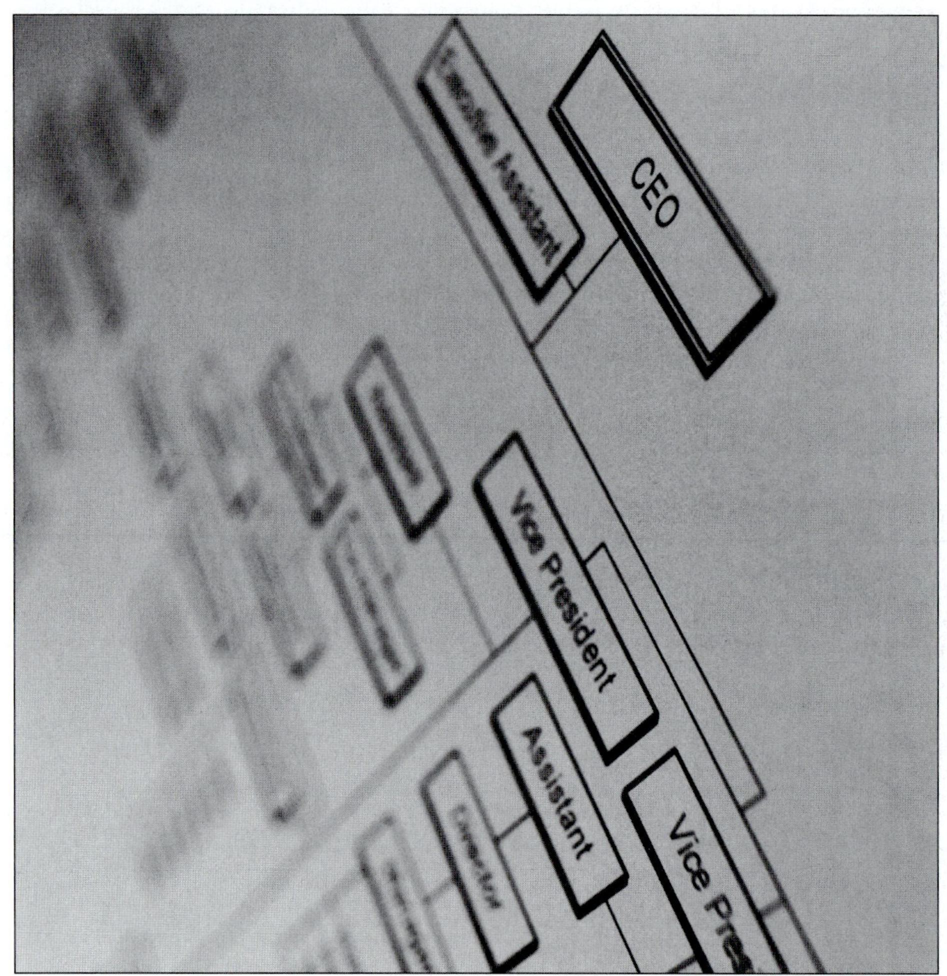

Learning Objectives

After completing Chapter 14, you should be able to

Define
The terms *organization structure* and *organization design.*

Compare
Functional, geographic, product, customer, and matrix departmentalization.

Discuss
The relative advantages and disadvantages of centralization and decentralization of authority.

Identify
The differences between mechanistic and organic designs of organizations.

Understand
Why virtual organizations are becoming more popular.

Organization Structure and Firm Survival

Why do some once-powerful organizations such as Lehman Brothers, Singer, TWA, Pullman, and FAO Schwarz not survive the test of time? Why do other firms such as 3M, Apple, BMW, and GE not only withstand decades of turbulent business conditions, but rather thrive and come to dominate their respective industries? One partial explanation for their success has to do with how well these companies can create, maintain, and modify (when necessary) their organization structure so as to continue to meet the changing demands of their stakeholders and external environments. Some of the more dramatic changes over the past two decades have included increases in hypercompetition due to globalization, rapid advances in technology, and wide-scale deregulation of once-protected industries.

By modifying or reinventing their organization structure, many successful companies have emerged from this topsy-turvy period stronger and more responsive than before. Take, for example, the Sara Lee Corporation. This $12.9 billion consumer products company, known for its brands Hillshire Farm, Ball Park Franks, Jimmy Dean, and Sara Lee, decided to revamp the organization structure of its Food & Beverage sales group so as to encourage a greater focus on its customers. To spearhead this effort, the company created a position called the "chief customer officer" to ensure that Sara Lee Food & Beverage customers would become the primary driving force for the division. What changes took place? Brokers, who previously were the middlepeople between Sara Lee salespeople and retail outlets like Walmart and Safeway, were replaced by Sara Lee's direct salesforce. This allowed greater contact with customers. New salespeople were hired from companies that were very customer-centric. A new organizational structure for the sales division was implemented, and training on the new customer-focused approach was conducted. The results have been positive. Both the volume of sales and profitability have improved since reorganizing the organization structure. Also, companies such as GE, 3M, Ericsson, and Amgen that have made successful adjustments to their organizational structures to meet changing market conditions have realized the following benefits:

1. Leveraged existing and created "new" organizational learning.
2. Became more flexible and responsive to the changing needs and demands of customers, vendors, and other key stakeholder groups.
3. Reduced operating costs while simultaneously boosting productivity.

In sum, companies with the best chance of prospering through the first part of the 21st century will be those that continue to modify their organizational structures on an ongoing basis to navigate the ever-changing shapes of the competitive, technological, and environmental landscapes.

Sources: Julia Chang, "The Sweet Taste of Sales," *Sales and Marketing Management* 159, no. 6 (July/August 2007): 20; Andrew Davies, Tim Brady, and Michael Hobday, "Charting a Path toward Integrated Solutions," *MIT Sloan Management Review* 47, no. 3 (Spring 2006): 39–48; "Toys Were Us: America's Discounters Have Wounded a Category Killer," *Financial Times*, August 16, 2004, p. 16; Paul Hemp, "A Time for Growth: An Interview with Amgen CEO Kevin Sharer," *Harvard Business Review* 82, nos. 7/8 (2004): 66–75; John A. Challenger, "The Transformed Workplace: How Can You Survive," *The Futurist*, November/December 2001, pp. 24–28; Andrew Gold, Arvind Malhotra, and Albert Segars, "Knowledge Management: An Organizational Capabilities Perspective," *Journal of Management Information Systems* 18, no. 1 (Summer 2001): 185–214; Michael Raynor and Joseph Bower, "Lead from the Center: How to Manage Divisions Dynamically," *Harvard Business Review* 79, no. 5 (2001): 92–100; and *Economist*, "Business: A Talent for Longevity," pp. 59–60.

The discussion of organization structure in this section reflects the ideas presented in the opening vignette. Organization structure results from managerial decisions about four important attributes of all organizations: division of labor, bases for departmentalization, size of departments, and delegation of authority. The decisions managers make are influenced by job design factors and organization design factors such as individual differences, task competence, technology, environmental uncertainty, strategy, and certain characteristics of managers themselves. The structure of the organization contributes to organizational effectiveness and that relationship justifies our interest. In this chapter, we focus on the four decisions, discuss mechanistic and organic models of organization design, and evaluate how organization design interacts with technology and the environment.

The Concept of Organization Structure

organization structure
Pattern of jobs and groups of jobs in an organization. An important cause of individual and group behavior.

Organization structure is an abstract concept. No one has ever actually seen one. What we see is the evidence of structure. Then from that evidence we infer the presence of structure. We therefore need to identify what we mean when we discuss structure in this and subsequent chapters.

Structure as an Influence on Behavior

In Chapter 1, we noted the importance of organization structure as an influence on the behavior of individuals and groups who make up the organization. The importance of structure as a source of influence is so widely accepted that some experts define the concept as those features of the organization that serve to control or distinguish its parts. The key word in this definition is *control.* All of us have worked in organizations (we were one of its parts) and we have experienced the way our behavior was controlled. We didn't simply go to work and do what we wanted to do; we did what the organizations wanted and paid us to do. We gave up free choice when we undertook the work necessitated by the jobs we held. Jobs are important features of any organization.

All organizations have a structure of jobs. In fact, the existence of structure distinguishes organizations. While the most visible evidence of structure is the familiar organizational chart, charts are not always necessary to describe the structure. In fact, small organizations can get along very well without them as long as everyone understands what they are to do and who they are to do it with.

But jobs are not the only features of an organization. Again, from experience we know that organizations consist of departments, divisions, units, or any of a number of terms denoting groups of jobs. No doubt, your college is made up of a number of academic departments: management, accounting, and economics if you are in a business school. Each of these departments contains individuals performing different jobs that combine to produce a larger outcome than is possible from the efforts of any single job or department. When you graduate, your education will have been made possible by the combined efforts of individual departments. But the point is not that these departments combine the effects of many different jobs; rather, we're noting here the effect of the departments on the behavior of the individuals in them. As members of departments, individuals necessarily must abide by commonly held agreements, policies, and rules and thereby give up the freedom to act independently.

Structure as Recurring Activities

A second perspective focuses on activities performed as consequences of the structure. According to this perspective, the dominant feature of organization structure is its patterned regularity. This definition emphasizes persistence and regularity of activities. Note that this definition states nothing about the reason for the patterned regularity, only that it exists. This definition points out that within organizations, certain activities can be counted on to occur routinely. For example, people come to work each morning at 8 a.m., clock in, go to their work stations, and begin doing the same work they did the day before. They talk to the same people, they receive information from the same people, they are periodically (but predictably) evaluated for promotion and raises. Without these predictable activities, the work of the organization could not be achieved.

Definitions that focus on regularly occurring organizational activities emphasize the importance of what in this book we term *organizational processes.* The subsequent section of the book discusses the processes of communication, decision making, performance evaluation, career, and socialization. These processes occur with considerable regularity, and it is certainly possible and even useful to analyze the patterns of communication, decision making, and other processes. But it's also useful to distinguish between activity (or processes) and the causes of that activity. Thus, when we discuss structure in the following pages, we refer to a relatively stable framework of jobs and departments that influences the behavior of individuals and groups toward organizational goals.

Designing an Organizational Structure

organizational design
Management decisions and actions that result in a specific organization structure.

Managers who set out to design an organization structure face difficult decisions. They must choose among a myriad of alternative frameworks of jobs and departments. The process by which they make these choices is termed **organizational design**, which means quite simply the decisions and actions that result in an organization structure.[1] This process may be explicit or implicit, it may be "one-shot" or developmental, it may be done by a single manager or by a team of managers.[2] However the actual decisions come about, the content of the decisions is always the same. The first decision focuses on individual jobs, the next two decisions focus on departments or groups of jobs, and the fourth decision considers the issue of delegation of authority throughout the structure.

1. Managers decide how to divide the overall task into smaller jobs of related activities. The effect of this decision is to define jobs in terms of specialized activities and responsibilities. Although jobs have many characteristics, the most important one is their degree of specialization.

2. Managers decide the bases by which to group the individual jobs. This decision is much like any other classification decision and it can result in groups containing jobs that are relatively homogeneous (alike) or heterogeneous (different).

3. Managers decide the appropriate size of the group reporting to each superior. As we have already noted, this decision involves determining whether spans of control are relatively narrow or wide.

FIGURE 14.1
The Four Key Design Decisions

		Continuum	
Division of labor	High	Specialization	Low
Departmentalization	Homogeneous	Basis	Heterogeneous
Span of control	Narrow	Number	Wide
Authority	Centralized	Delegation	Decentralized

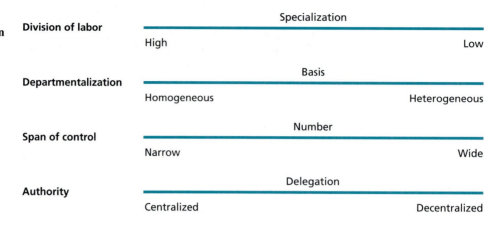

4. Managers distribute authority among the jobs. Authority is the right to make decisions without approval by a higher manager and to exact obedience from designated other people. All jobs contain some degree of the right to make decisions within prescribed limits. But not all jobs contain the right to exact obedience from others. The latter aspect of authority distinguishes managerial jobs from nonmanagerial jobs. Managers can exact obedience; nonmanagers can't.

Thus, organization structures vary depending upon the choices that managers make. If we consider each of the four design decisions to be a continuum of possible choices, the alternative structures can be depicted as in Figure 14.1.

Generally speaking, organization structures tend toward one extreme or the other along each continuum. Structures tending to the left are characterized by a number of terms including *classical, formalistic, structured, bureaucratic, System 1,* and *mechanistic*. Structures tending to the right are termed *neoclassical, informalistic, unstructured, nonbureaucratic, System 4,* and *organic*. Exactly where along the continuum an organization finds itself has implications for its performance as well as for individual and group behavior.[3]

Division of Labor

division of labor
Process of dividing work into relatively specialized jobs to achieve advantages of specialization.

Division of labor concerns the extent to which jobs are specialized. Managers divide the total task of the organization into specific jobs having specified activities. The activities define what the person performing the job is to do. For example, activities of the job of an "assistant store manager" at a retail store at the mall can be defined in terms of the methods and procedures required to recruit, select, train, schedule, compensate, and discipline part and full-time sales associates who work there. Other assistant store managers could use the same methods and procedures to manage their subordinates. Thus, jobs can be specialized both by method and by application of the method.

The economic advantages of dividing work into specialized jobs are the principal historical reasons for the creation of organizations.[4] As societies became increasingly industrialized and urbanized, craft production gave way to mass production. Mass production depends on the ability to obtain the economic benefits of specialized labor, and the most effective means for obtaining specialized labor is through organizations. Although managers are concerned with more than the economic implications of jobs, they seldom lose sight of specialization as the rationale for dividing work among jobs.

Division of labor in organizations can occur in three different ways:[5]

1. Work can be divided into different *personal* specialties. Most people think of specialization in the sense of occupational and professional specialties. Thus, we think of accountants, engineers, scientists, physicians, and the myriad of other specialties that exist in organizations and everyday life.

2. Work can be divided into different activities necessitated by the natural sequence of the work the organization does. For example, manufacturing plants often divide work into fabricating and assembly, and individuals will be assigned to do the work of one of these two activities. This particular manifestation of division of work is termed *horizontal specialization.*

3. Finally, work can be divided along the *vertical plane* of an organization. All organizations have a hierarchy of authority from the lowest-level manager to the highest-level manager. The CEO's work is different from the shift supervisor's.

One dramatic effect of the trend toward downsizing organizations over the past 25 years or so has been to despecialize managerial jobs, particularly middle managers' jobs. For instance, General Electric aggressively pursued a policy of reducing the number of managers in the hierarchy. The result is that managers have more to do and their jobs are less specialized as their spans of control have increased.

The process of defining the activities and authority of jobs is analytical; that is, the total task of the organization is broken down into successively smaller ones. But then management must use some basis to combine the divided tasks into groups or departments containing some specified number of individuals or jobs. We will discuss these two decisions relating to departments in that order.

Departmental Bases

The rationale for grouping jobs rests on the necessity for coordinating them. The specialized jobs are separate, interrelated parts of the total task, whose accomplishment requires the accomplishment of each of the jobs. But the jobs must be performed in the specific manner and sequence intended by management when they were defined. As the number of specialized jobs in an organization increases, there comes a point when they can no longer be effectively coordinated by a single manager. Thus, to create manageable numbers of jobs, they are combined into smaller groups and a new job is defined—manager of the group.

The crucial managerial consideration when creating departments is determining the basis for grouping jobs. Of particular importance is the determination for the bases for departments that report to the top management position. In fact, numerous bases are used throughout the organization, but the basis used at the highest level determines critical dimensions of the organization. Some of the more widely used **departmentalization** bases are described in the following sections.

departmentalization
Process in which an organization is structurally divided by combining jobs in departments according to some shared characteristic or basis.

Functional Departmentalization

Managers can combine jobs according to the functions of the organization. Every organization must undertake certain activities to do its work. These necessary activities are the organization's functions. The necessary functions of a manufacturing firm include production, marketing, finance, information technology, accounting, and human resource management. These activities are necessary to create, produce, and sell a product. Necessary functions of a commercial bank include taking deposits, making loans, and investing the bank's funds. The functions of a hospital include surgery, psychiatry, housekeeping, pharmacy, nursing, and personnel. Each of these functions can be a specific department and jobs can be combined according to them. The functional basis is often found in relatively small organizations

FIGURE 14.2
Functional-Base Organization in Three Settings

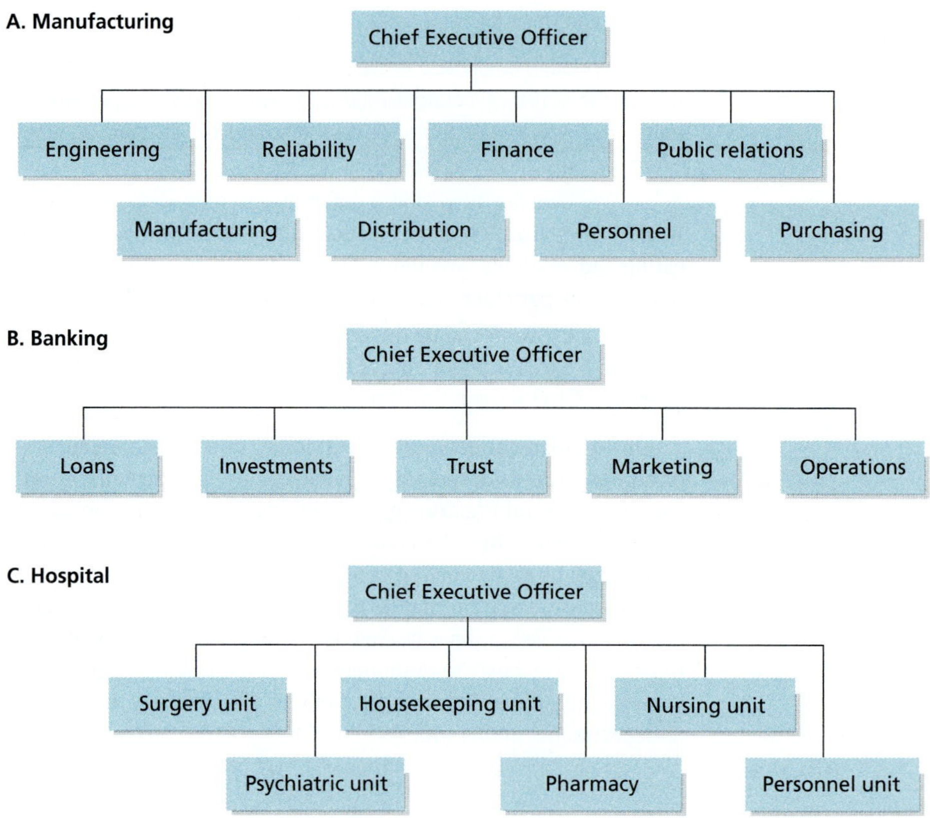

providing a narrow range of products and services. It is also widely used as the basis in divisions of large multiproduct organizations.

Manufacturing organizations are typically structured on a functional basis (Figure 14.2). The functions are engineering, manufacturing, reliability, distribution, finance, personnel, public relations, and purchasing. Organization charts for a commercial bank and a hospital structured along functional lines are also depicted in Figure 14.2. The functional basis has wide application in both service and manufacturing organizations. The specific configuration of functions that appear as separate departments varies from organization to organization.

The principal advantage of the basis is its efficiency. That is, it seems logical to have a department that consists of experts in a particular field such as production or accounting. By having departments of specialists, management creates efficient units. An accountant is generally more efficient when working with other accountants and other individuals who have similar backgrounds and interests. They can share expertise to get the work done. General Motors (GM) attracted considerable attention when it combined traditional product divisions into two functional departments: production and sales. Now under the direction of a new chief operations officer (COO), GM has accelerated consolidation of its auto divisions (including the once-separate Saturn division) into one functionally organized entity.[6] The driving force behind GM's reorganization was a desire to reduce the cost of developing and marketing cars by realizing the efficiencies of function-based organization structure.

A major disadvantage of this departmental basis is that because specialists are working with and encouraging each other in their areas of expertise and interest, organizational goals may be sacrificed in favor of departmental goals. Accountants may see only their problems and not those of production or marketing or the total organization. In other words, the culture of, and identification with, the department are often stronger than identification with the organization and its culture.

Geographic Departmentalization

Another basis for departmentalizing is to establish groups according to geographic area. The logic is that all activities in a given region should be assigned to a manager. This individual would be in charge of all operations in that particular geographic area.

In large organizations, geographic arrangements are advantageous because physical separation of activities makes centralized coordination difficult. For example, it is extremely difficult for someone in New York City to manage salespeople in London. It makes sense to assign the managerial job to someone in the British capital.

Large multiunit retail stores are often organized along territorial lines. Specific retail outlets in a geographic area will constitute units, often termed divisions, which report to a regional manager who in turn may report to a corporate manager. For example, the manager of the Lexington, Kentucky, retail store of a national chain reports to the president, Midwest Division. The Midwest Division reports to the headquarters unit.

Geographic departmentalization provides a training ground for managerial personnel. The company is able to place managers in territories and then assess their progress in that geographic region. The experience that managers acquire in a territory away from headquarters provides valuable insights about how products and/or services are accepted in the field.

Product Departmentalization

Managers of many large diversified companies group jobs on the basis of product. All jobs associated with producing and selling a product or product line will be placed under the direction of one manager. Product becomes the preferred basis as a firm grows by increasing the number of products it markets. As a firm grows, it's difficult to coordinate the various functional departments, and it becomes advantageous to establish product units. This form of organization allows personnel to develop total expertise in researching, manufacturing, and distributing a product line. Concentrating authority, responsibility, and accountability in a specific product department allows top management to coordinate actions.

The organization structure using products as the basis for departments has been a key development in modern capitalism. The term *divisional organization* refers to this form of organization structure. Most of the major and large firms of developed countries use it to some degree. The product-based divisions are often freestanding units that can design, produce, and market their own products, even in competition with other divisions of the same firm.[7] GM pioneered the divisional structure when it evolved into the five separate auto divisions: Chevrolet, Pontiac, Oldsmobile, Buick, and Cadillac. As we noted in our discussion of the functional form, GM has begun a process of moving away from the purely product-based, divisional form.

The Consumer Products Division of Kimberly-Clark reflects product departmentalization. The specific product groups shown in Figure 14.3 include feminine hygiene, household, and commercial products. Within each of these units we find production and marketing personnel. Because managers of product divisions coordinate sales, manufacturing, and distribution of a product, they become the overseers of a profit center. In this manner, profit responsibility is implemented in product-based organizations. Managers are often asked to establish profit goals at the beginning of a time period and then to compare actual profit with planned profit.

Product-based organizations foster initiative and autonomy by providing division managers with the resources necessary to carry out their profit plans. But such organizations face the difficult issue of deciding how much redundancy is necessary. Divisional structures contain some degree of redundancy because each division wants its own research, engineering, marketing, production, and all other functions necessary to do business. Thus, technical and professional personnel are found throughout the organization at the division levels. The cost of this arrangement can be exorbitant.

FIGURE 14.3 Consumer Products Division, Kimberly-Clark Corporation: Organizational Structure

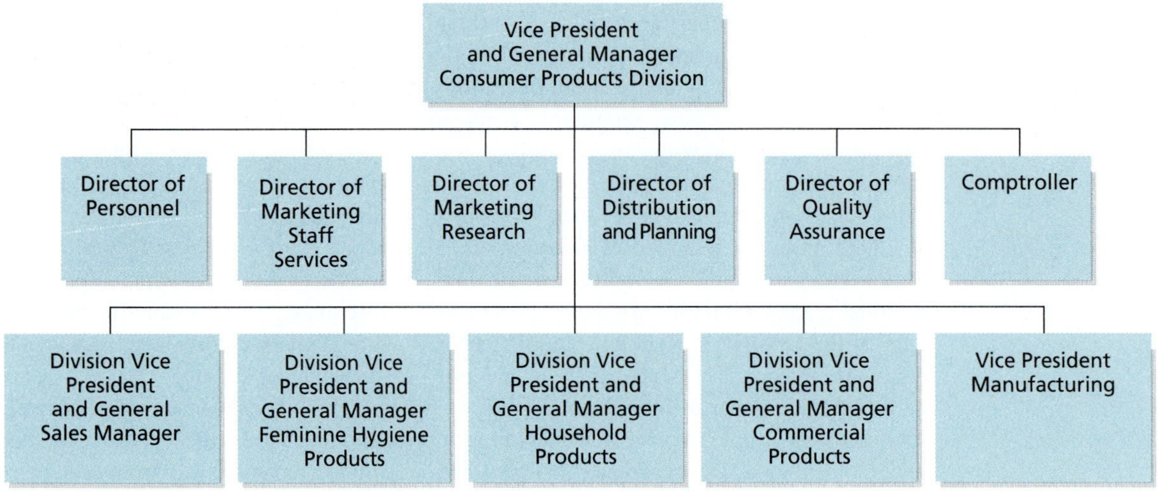

Vice President and General Manager Consumer Products Division

Director of Personnel

Director of Marketing Staff Services

Director of Marketing Research

Director of Distribution and Planning

Director of Quality Assurance

Comptroller

Division Vice President and General Sales Manager

Division Vice President and General Manager Feminine Hygiene Products

Division Vice President and General Manager Household Products

Division Vice President and General Manager Commercial Products

Vice President Manufacturing

Customer Departmentalization

Customers and clients can be a basis for grouping jobs.[8] Examples of customer-oriented departments are the organization structures of some hospitals. Hospitals can be designed with emergency rooms, intensive care units, operating rooms, mental health units, pediatric wings, and baby delivery services. Each unit or department specializes in providing different types of care for patients (i.e., customers) with unique needs.

Another form of customer departmentalization is the loan department in a commercial bank. Loan officers are often associated with industrial, commercial, or agricultural loans. The customer will be served by one of these three loan officers.

The importance of customer satisfaction has stimulated firms to search for creative ways to serve people better. Since the Bell System broke up, competition for customers has forced AT&T to organize into customer-based units that identify with the needs of specific customers. Prior to the breakup, the firm was organized around functions. The move toward customer-based departments at Bell Labs was accompanied by efforts to implement total quality management (TQM), a customer-focused management practice that is reinforced in the customer-based structure.[9] As a result of the current recession, Weyerhaeuser, a $21 billion company, undertook an "extreme makeover" of the way it does business in its wood division.[10] Realizing that their customers, large homebuilders, needed fast deliveries of wood products to help them increase their efficiency and productivity, Weyerhaeuser redesigned the way they managed the wood division to accomplish this feat. This customer focus resulted in higher sales and enabled their customers to cut the time to frame a house from three weeks to five days.[11]

Organizations with customer-based departments are better able to satisfy customer-identified needs than organizations that base departments on noncustomer factors.[12]

Combined Bases for Departmentalization: The Matrix Organization

matrix organization
Organizational design that superimposes product- or project-based design on existing function-based design.

An organization design termed **matrix organization** attempts to maximize the strengths and minimize the weaknesses of both the functional and product bases. In practical terms, the matrix design combines functional and product departmental bases.[13] Companies such as IBM, Proctor & Gamble, BMW, Boeing, American Cyanamid, Caterpillar Tractor, Hughes Aircraft, ITT, Monsanto Chemical, National Cash Register, Prudential Insurance, TWR, and Texas Instruments are only a few of the users of matrix organization.[14] Public sector users include public health and social service agencies. Although the exact meaning of matrix organization varies in practice, it's typically seen as a balanced compromise between functional and product organization, between departmentalization by function and by product.

Matrix organizations achieve the desired balance by superimposing, or overlaying, a horizontal structure of authority, influence, and communication on the vertical structure. For example, manufacturing, marketing, engineering, and finance specialists are assigned to work on one or more projects or products. As a consequence, personnel report to two managers: one in their functional department and one in the project or product unit. The existence of a *dual authority system* is a distinguishing characteristic of matrix organizations. The potential conflict between allegiance to one's functional manager and one's project manager must be recognized and dealt with in matrix organizations.[15]

Matrix structures are found in organizations that (1) require responses to rapid change in two or more environments, such as technology and markets; (2) face uncertainties that generate high information processing requirements; and (3) must deal with financial and human resources constraints. Managers confronting these circumstances are most likely to realize certain advantages with matrix organization.[16]

Matrix organization facilitates the use of highly specialized staff and equipment. Each project or product unit can share the specialized resource with other units, rather than duplicating it to provide independent coverage for each. This is a particular advantage when projects don't require the specialist's full-time efforts. For example, a project may require only half a computer scientist's time. Rather than having several underutilized computer scientists assigned to each project, the organization can keep fewer of them fully utilized by shifting them from project to project.

Such flexibility speeds response to competitive conditions, technological breakthroughs, and other environmental changes. Also, these interactions encourage cross-fertilization of ideas, such as when a computer scientist must discuss the pros and cons of electronic data processing with a financial accounting expert. Each specialist must be able to listen to, understand, and respond to the other's views. At the same time, specialists maintain ongoing contact with members of their own discipline because they are also members of a functional department.

Span of Control

span of control
Number of individuals who report to a specific manager.

The determination of appropriate bases for departmentalization establishes the kinds of jobs that will be grouped together. But that determination doesn't establish the number of jobs to be included in a specific group, the issue of **span of control**. Generally, the issue comes down to the decision of how many people a manager can oversee; that is, will the organization be more effective if the span of control is relatively wide or narrow? During a period of layoffs, however, a manager may have to not only manage a changing number of subordinates who avoid being laid off, but also deal with the employees' survivor guilt or stress. The next OB and Your Career offers some suggestions regarding the management of layoff survivors. The question is basically concerned with determining the volume of interpersonal relationships that the department's manager is able to handle. Moreover, the span of control must be defined to include not only formally assigned subordinates, but also those who have access to the manager. Not only may a manager be placed in a position of being responsible for immediate subordinates, she may also be chairperson of several committees and task groups.[17]

The number of potential interpersonal relationships between a manager and subordinates increases as the number of subordinates increases. This relationship holds because managers

OB AND YOUR CAREER Tips for Managing Survivors of Layoffs

As a result of the recent recession, many U.S. companies have fired large numbers of employees. For example, Ford Motor Company cut 48,000 jobs or about 20 percent of its workforce. Sprint Nextel Corporation cut 40,000 employees or approximately one-third of its workers. Honeywell fired 6,000 or 5 percent of its workforce. Survivors (employees who don't get fired) of such layoffs tend to experience "survivor guilt" in that they can experience a host of negative reactions associated with seeing their colleagues and friends fired and their workloads increased, including decreased trust and loyalty, lowered organizational commitment, and reduced morale, motivation, and performance.

Managers need to address these issues in order to motivate and retain these surviving employees, ultimately trying to make the best out of a difficult situation. Three suggestions include:

1. Communicate often and with transparency. During tough economic times, employees need relevant information delivered on a timely basis. Managers need to explain before, during, and after layoffs why they were necessary, how the layoffs will help ensure the organization's financial health and survival, and what's going to be done differently after the layoffs to help avoid the need for additional layoffs in the future.
2. Set a good example. Try not to show your bitterness and disappointment for having had to lay off several of the employees in your department. This will only perpetuate negative emotions and behaviors in your employees. Apply strong leadership skills to redirect the surviving employees' energies toward future positive behaviors like increasing sales or enhancing customer service.
3. Redeploy and train surviving employees. Given the large number of layoffs, several new positions will need to be filled in order to ensure the proper functioning of the organization. Managers must carefully redeploy surviving employees so that these critical job functions can be filled. Managers must also provide training opportunities to employees to ensure high levels of job performance.

Sources: Scott Thurm, "Recalculating the Cost of Big Layoffs," *Wall Street Journal*, May 5, 2010, p. B1; Carl P. Maertz, Jack W. Wiley, Cynthia LeRouge, and Michael A. Campion, "Downsizing Effects on Survivors: Layoffs, Offshoring, and Outsourcing," *Industrial Relations* 49, no. 2 (April 2010): 275–289; Kristin Burnham, ". . . Manage Survivor Syndrome, Three Management Tips for Helping Employees Cope with Worklife after Layoffs," *CIO*, September 1, 2009, p. 6; "Layoff 'Survivor' Stress: How to Manage the Guilt and the Workload," *HR Focus*, August 2009, pp. 4–7.

potentially contend with three types of interpersonal relationships: direct single, direct group, and cross. Direct single relationships occur between the manager and each subordinate individually (that is, in a one-on-one setting). Direct group relationships occur between the manager and each possible permutation of subordinates. Finally, cross-relationships occur when subordinates interact with one another.

The critical consideration in determining the manager's span of control is not the number of potential relationships. Rather, it's the frequency and intensity of the actual relationships that are important. Not all relationships will occur, and those that do will vary in importance. If we shift our attention from potential to actual relationships as the bases for determining optimum span of control, at least three factors appear to be important: required contact, degree of specialization, and ability to communicate.

Required Contact

In research and development as well as medical and production work, there's a need for frequent contact and a high degree of coordination between a superior and subordinates. Conferences and other forms of consultation often aid in attaining goals within a constrained time period. For example, the research and development team leader may have to consult frequently with team members so that a project is completed within a time period that will allow the organization to place a product on the market. Thus, instead of relying on memos and reports, it is in the best interest of the organization to have as many in-depth contacts with the team as possible. A large span of control would preclude contacting subordinates so frequently, which could impede the project. In general, the greater the inherent ambiguity in an individual's job, the greater the need for supervision to avoid conflict and stress.[18]

OB AT WORK — The Effects of Downsizing on the Spans of Control of Managers

In order to reduce costs and to become more efficient, many firms in the global economy either have downsized or have considered the implications of doing so. Some giants in the basic industries, such as Motorola, Robert Wood Johnson University Hospital, IBM, GM, Ford, Hewlett-Packard, and Chrysler, as well as many of the 21 winners to date of the prestigious Baldrige Award, have already reduced the number of middle managers and increased the spans of control of all managers. This decision is justified by the idea that highly trained individuals throughout the organization, empowered with authority and competence, can manage themselves. The idea isn't new, but its widespread application is. Many firms, large and small, have reported their experiences with wider spans of control—some positive, others negative. Positive experiences stress the renewed commitment of employees who have the benefits of empowerment; negative experiences stress the additional pressures placed on managers to be responsible for the work performance of more employees.

One observer points out that for flattening to reach its full potential, managers and employees must exercise initiative to "add value" to the directives they receive. The idea of adding value implies that individuals take the directive and evaluate its full potential for adding to the organization's well-being and effectiveness. Another observer of flattening in the U.S. banking industry states that whether the practice works depends upon the willingness and ability of employees at the local level to provide quality service and high performance, even peak performance, of their assigned duties. But perhaps the most important factor bearing on the practice's success is the manager's ability to comprehend the new relationship between managers and nonmanagers: No longer can managers set themselves apart from those they manage; they must develop helping and coaching relationships with their subordinates.

Sources: Henry Hornstein, "Downsizing Isn't What It's Cracked Up To Be," *Ivey Business Journal Online*, May/June 2009 (accessed on June 16, 2010); Geoff Colvin, "Undercutting CEO Power," *Fortune*, March 5, 2007, p. 42; http://www.nist.gov/baldrige/ (accessed on July 5, 2007); Janet H. Weakland, "Human Resources Holistic Approach to Healing Downsizing Survivors," *Organization Development Journal* 19, no. 2 (Summer 2001): 59–70; Brian P. Biehoff, Robert H. Moorman, Gerald Blakely, and Jack Fuller, "The Influence of Empowerment and Job Enrichment of Employee Loyalty in a Downsizing Environment," *Group & Organization Management* 11 (March 2001): 93–113; Karen E. Mishra, Gretchen M. Spreitzer, and Aneil K. Mishra, "Preserving Employee Morale during Downsizing," *Sloan Management Review* (Winter 1998): 83–95; Aaron Bernstein, "Oops, That's Too Much Downsizing," *Businessweek*, June 8, 1989, p. 38; and Kim S. Cameron, "Strategies for Successful Downsizing," *Human Resource Management*, Summer 1994, pp. 189–211.

Degree of Specialization

The degree to which employees are specialized is a critical consideration in establishing the span of control at all levels of management. It is generally accepted that a manager at the lower organizational level can oversee more subordinates because work at the lower level is more specialized and less complicated than at higher levels of management. Management can combine highly specialized and similar jobs into relatively large departments because the employees may not need close supervision.

Ability to Communicate

Instructions, guidelines, and policies must be communicated verbally to subordinates in most work situations. The need to discuss job-related factors influences the span of control. The individual who can clearly and concisely communicate with subordinates is able to manage more people than one who can't.

The widespread practice of downsizing and "flattening" organizations of all kinds has direct implications for the span of control decision. As demonstrated recently at Xerox, downsizing reduces the number of all employees, but relatively more managers (usually middle managers) than nonmanagers.[19] This increases the number of nonmanagers per manager; consequently, the average span of control of each manager increases. Whether the factors of required contact, degree of specialization, and ability to communicate have any bearing on the resultant spans of control can be debated. In fact, many middle managers whose spans of control have been widened believe that top management made the decision without regard to these factors. The accompanying OB at Work feature describes experiences with downsizing in American firms.

Even though we can identify some specific factors that relate to optimal spans of control, the search for the full answer continues.[20]

Delegation of Authority

delegation of authority
Process of distributing authority downward in an organization.

Managers decide how much authority should be delegated to each job and each jobholder. As we have noted, authority refers to individuals' right to make decisions without approval by higher management and to exact obedience from others. **Delegation of authority** refers specifically to making decisions, not to doing work. A sales manager can be delegated the right to hire salespeople (a decision) and the right to assign them to specific territories (obedience). Another sales manager may not have the right to hire but may have the right to assign territories. Thus, the degree of delegated authority can be relatively high or relatively low with respect to both aspects of authority. Any particular job involves a range of alternative configurations of authority delegation.[21] Managers must balance the relative gains and losses of alternatives.

Reasons to Decentralize Authority

Relatively high delegation of authority encourages the development of professional managers. Organizations that decentralize (delegate) authority enable managers to make significant decisions, to gain skills, and to advance in the company. By virtue of their right to make decisions on a broad range of issues, managers develop expertise that enables them to cope with problems of higher management. Managers with broad decision-making power often make difficult decisions. Consequently, they are trained for promotion into positions of even greater authority and responsibility.[22] Upper management can readily compare managers on the basis of actual decision-making performance. Advancement of managers on the basis of demonstrated performance can eliminate favoritism and minimize personality in the promotion process.

Second, high delegation of authority can lead to a competitive climate within the organization. Managers are motivated to contribute in this competitive atmosphere because they're compared with their peers on various performance measures. A competitive environment in which managers compete on sales, cost reduction, and employee development targets can be a positive factor in overall organizational performance. Competitive environments can also produce destructive behavior if one manager's success occurs at the expense of another's. But regardless of whether it's positive or destructive, significant competition exists only when individuals have authority to do those things that enable them to win.

Finally, managers who have relatively high authority can exercise more autonomy, and thus satisfy their desires to participate in problem solving. This autonomy can lead to managerial creativity and ingenuity, which contribute to the adaptiveness and development of the organization and managers. As we've seen in earlier chapters, opportunities to participate in setting goals can be positive motivators. But a necessary condition for goal setting is authority to make decisions. Many organizations, large and small, choose to follow the policy of decentralization of authority.

Decisions to decentralize often follow experiences with centralization. For example, over the past 10 years, Best Buy has transformed its business model from a centralized, standardized approach to a customer-focused model that encourages a "unique store approach."[23] Instead of following policies and pricing guidelines developed at the corporate office, store managers and employees of the $10.8 billion consumer-electronics retailer were empowered to learn everything they could about their local customers and then to tailor product offerings, pricing, and other practices to satisfy the unique needs of these customers. More control and autonomy was granted to store managers, and measurement systems and technology were installed that kept track of customer purchasing patterns. Corporate officers gave up some of the control and efficiency that are often associated with centralized decision making so that individual Best Buy store managers and employees could learn how to satisfy and exceed the expectations of their unique customers.[24]

How well is this "customer-centric" business strategy doing for the firm? Although there are many other factors involved, as of March 2010, Best Buy reported a 37 percent increase in quarterly earnings, an increase in market share, and forecasted fiscal year earnings that were higher than Wall Street analysts' predictions.[25] Decentralization at Best Buy appears to be helping its bottom line.

Decentralization of authority has its benefits, but these benefits aren't without costs. Organizations that are unable or unwilling to bear these costs will find reasons to centralize authority.

Reasons to Centralize Authority

Managers must be trained to make the decisions that go with delegated authority. Formal training programs can be quite expensive, which can more than offset the benefits.

Second, many managers are accustomed to making decisions and resist delegating authority to their subordinates. Consequently, they may perform at lower levels of effectiveness because they believe that delegation of authority involves losing control.

Third, administrative costs are incurred because new or altered accounting and performance systems must be developed to provide top management with information about the effects of their subordinates' decisions. When lower levels of management have authority, top management must have some means of reviewing the use of that authority. Consequently, they typically create reporting systems that inform them of the outcomes of decisions made at lower levels in the organization.

The fourth and perhaps most pragmatic reason to centralize is that decentralization means duplication of functions. Each autonomous unit must be truly self-supporting to be independent. But that involves a potentially high cost of duplication. Some organizations find that the cost of decentralization outweighs the benefits.[26]

Decision Guidelines

Like most managerial issues, whether authority should be delegated in high or low degree cannot be resolved simply. Managers faced with the issue should answer the following four questions:

1. How routine and straightforward are the job's or unit's required decisions? The authority for routine decisions can be centralized. For example, fast-food restaurants such as Taco Bell and McDonald's centralize the decision of food preparation so as to ensure consistent quality at all stores. However, the local store manager makes the decisions to hire and dismiss employees. This question points out the importance of the distinction between deciding and doing. The local store prepares the food, but the headquarters staff decides how to prepare it.

2. Are individuals competent to make the decision? Even if the decision is nonroutine (as in the case of hiring employees), if the local manager is not competent to recruit and select employees, then employment decisions must be centralized. This question implies that delegation of authority can differ among individuals depending upon each one's ability to make the decision.

3. Are individuals motivated to make the decision? Capable individuals aren't always motivated individuals. We discussed motivation and individual differences in earlier chapters. Decision making can be difficult and stressful, thus discouraging some individuals from accepting authority. It can also involve a level of commitment to the organization that

an individual isn't willing to make. Motivation must accompany competency to create conducive conditions for decentralization.

4. Finally, to return to the points we made earlier, do the benefits of decentralization outweigh its costs? This question is perhaps the most difficult to answer because many benefits and costs are assessed in subjective terms. Nevertheless, managers should at least attempt to make a benefit–cost analysis.

Like most managerial issues, whether authority should be delegated in high or low degree cannot be resolved simply. As usual, in managerial decision making, whether to centralize or decentralize authority can be guided only by general questions.

Mechanistic and Organic Models of Organization Design

The two models of organizational design described in this section are important ideas in management theory and practice. Because of their importance, they receive considerable theoretical and practical attention. Despite this importance and attention, there's little uniformity in the use of terms that designate the two models. The two terms we use here, *mechanistic* and *organic,* are relatively descriptive of the important features of the models.[27]

The Mechanistic Model

A body of literature that emerged during the early 20th century considered the problem of designing the structure of an organization as but one of a number of managerial tasks, including planning and controlling. These writers' objective was to define *principles* that could guide managers in performing their tasks. An early writer, Henri Fayol, proposed a number of principles that he had found useful in managing a large coal mining company in France.[28] Some of Fayol's principles dealt with the management function of organizing; four of these are relevant for understanding the mechanistic model.

1. *Specialization.* Fayol stated that specialization is the best means for making use of individuals and groups of individuals. At the time of Fayol's writings, the limit of specialization (that is, the optimal point) had not been definitively determined. As the previous chapter showed, scientific management popularized a number of methods for implementing specialization of labor. These methods, such as work standards and motion and time study, emphasized technical (not behavioral) dimensions of work.

2. *Unity of direction.* According to this principle, jobs should be grouped according to specialty. Engineers should be grouped with engineers, salespeople with salespeople, accountants with accountants. The departmentalization basis that most nearly implements this principle is the functional basis.

3. *Authority and responsibility.* Fayol believed that a manager should be delegated sufficient authority to carry out her assigned responsibilities. Because the assigned responsibilities of top managers are considerably more important to the future of the organization than those of lower management, applying the principle inevitably leads to centralized authority. Centralized authority is a logical outcome not only because of top managements' larger responsibilities but also because work at this level is more complex, the number of workers involved is greater, and the relationship between actions and results is remote.

4. *Scalar chain principle.* The natural result of implementing the preceding three principles is a graded chain of managers from the ultimate authority to the lowest ranks. The scalar chain is the route for all vertical communications in an organization. Accordingly, all communications from the lowest level must pass through each superior in the chain of command. Correspondingly, communication from the top must pass through each subordinate until it reaches the appropriate level.

Fayol's writings became part of a literature that, although each contributor made unique contributions, had a common thrust. Writers such as Mooney and Reiley,[29] Follet,[30] and Urwick[31] all shared the common objective of defining the principles that should guide the design and management of organizations. A complete review of their individual contributions won't be attempted here. However, we'll review the ideas of one individual, Max Weber, who made important contributions to the mechanistic model. He described applications of the mechanistic model and coined the term *bureaucracy.*

Bureaucracy

Bureaucracy has various meanings.[32] The traditional usage is the political science concept of government by bureaus but without participation by the governed. In laymen's terms, bureaucracy refers to the negative consequences of large organizations, such as excessive red tape, procedural delays, and general frustration.[33] But in Max Weber's writings, bureaucracy refers to a particular way to organize collective activities.[34] Weber's interest in bureaucracy reflected his concern for the ways society develops hierarchies of control so that one group can, in effect, dominate other groups. Organizational design involves domination in the sense that authority involves the legitimate right to exact obedience from others. His search for the forms of domination that evolve in society led him to the study of bureaucratic structure.

According to Weber, the bureaucratic structure is

> superior to any other form in precision, in stability, in the stringency of its discipline and its reliability. It thus makes possible a high degree of calculability of results for the heads of the organization and for those acting in relation to it.[35]

The bureaucracy compares to other organizations "as does the machine with nonmechanical modes of production."[36] These words capture the essence of the mechanistic model of organizational design.

To achieve the maximum benefits of the bureaucratic design, Weber believed that an organization must have the following characteristics:

1. All tasks will be divided into highly specialized jobs. Through specialization, jobholders become expert in their jobs, and management can hold them responsible for the effective performance of their duties.
2. Each task is performed according to a system of abstract rules to ensure uniformity and coordination of different tasks. The rationale for this practice is that the manager can eliminate uncertainty in task performance due to individual differences.
3. Each member of the organization is accountable for job performance to one, and only one, manager. Managers hold their authority because of their expert knowledge and because it's delegated from the top of the hierarchy. An unbroken chain of command exists.
4. Each employee of the organization relates to other employees and clients in an impersonal, formal manner, maintaining a social distance with subordinates and clients. The purpose of this practice is to assure that personalities and favoritism do not interfere with efficient accomplishment of the organization's objectives.
5. Employment in the bureaucratic organization is based on technical qualifications and is protected against arbitrary dismissal. Similarly, promotions are based on seniority and achievement. Employment in the organization is viewed as a lifelong career, and a high degree of loyalty is engendered.

mechanistic model
Organizational design emphasizing importance of achieving high levels of production and efficiency through extensive use of rules and procedures, centralized authority, and high specialization of labor.

These five characteristics of bureaucracy describe the kind of organizations Fayol believed to be most effective. Both Fayol and Weber described the same type of organization, one that functions in a machinelike manner to accomplish the organization's goals in a highly efficient manner. Thus, the term **mechanistic model** aptly describes such organizations.

The mechanistic model achieves high levels of production and efficiency due to its structural characteristics:

1. It's highly complex because of its emphasis on specialization of labor.
2. It's highly centralized because of its emphasis on authority and accountability.
3. It's highly formalized because of its emphasis on function as the basis for departments.

These organizational characteristics and practices underlie a widely used organizational model. One of the more successful practitioners of the mechanistic model has been United Parcel Service (UPS).[37] This profitable delivery firm competes directly with other delivery firms like FedEx and DHL, as well as the U.S. Post Office, in the delivery of letters and small packages. Even though the Post Office is subsidized and pays no taxes, UPS has been able to compete successfully by stressing efficiency of operations. For example, UPS recently announced that it could save three million gallons of fuel and reduce its carbon emissions by 31,000 metric tons by cutting the number of left turns that the company's drivers take while making deliveries.[38] The company apparently achieves great efficiencies through a combination of automation and organization design. Specialization and formalization are highly visible characteristics of UPS structure. UPS uses clearly defined jobs and an explicit chain of command. The tasks range from truck washers and maintenance personnel to top management and are arranged in a hierarchy of authority consisting of eight managerial levels. The high degree of specialization enables management to use many forms of written reports such as daily worksheets that record each employee's work quotas and performance. Company policies and practices are in written form and routinely consulted in hiring and promotion decisions. Apparently, UPS has found the mechanistic form of organization to be well suited for its purposes.

UPS has more than 1,000 industrial engineers on its payroll. Their job is to design jobs and to set the standards that specify the way UPS employees do their jobs. For example, engineers instruct drivers to walk to the customer's door at the rate of three feet per second and to knock on the door. Company management believes that the standards aren't just a way to obtain efficiency and production but also are a means to provide the employee with important feedback on how he's doing the job. All in all, the company's efficiency bears testimony to its use of mechanistic design principles.

The Organic Model

organic model
Organizational design emphasizing importance of achieving high levels of flexibility and development through limited use of rules and procedures, decentralized authority, and relatively low degrees of specialization.

The **organic model** of organizational design stands in sharp contrast to the mechanistic model due to its different organizational characteristics and practices. The most distinct differences between the two models are a consequence of the different effectiveness criteria each seeks to maximize. While the mechanistic model seeks to maximize efficiency and production, the organic model seeks to maximize satisfaction, flexibility, and development.

The organic organization is flexible to changing environmental demands because its design encourages greater utilization of the human potential. Managers are encouraged to adopt practices that tap the full range of human motivations through job design that stresses personal growth and responsibility. Decision-making, control, and goal-setting processes are decentralized and shared at all levels of the organization. Communications flow throughout the organization, not simply down the chain of command. These practices are intended to implement a basic assumption of the organic model that states that an organization will be effective to the extent that its structure is

> such as to ensure a maximum probability that in all interactions and in all relationships with the organization, each member, in the light of his background, values, desires, and expectations, will view the experience as supportive and one which builds and maintains a sense of personal worth and importance.[39]

An organizational design that provides individuals with this sense of personal worth and motivation and that facilitates satisfaction, flexibility, and development would have the following characteristics:

1. It's relatively simple because of its deemphasis of specialization and its emphasis on increasing job range.
2. It's relatively decentralized because of its emphasis on delegation of authority and increasing job depth.
3. It's relatively informal because of its emphasis on product and customer as bases for departments.

A leading spokesperson and developer of ideas supporting applications of the organic model is Rensis Likert. His studies at the University of Michigan have led him to argue that organic organizations (Likert uses the term *System 4*) differ markedly from mechanistic organizations (Likert uses the term *System 1*) along a number of structural dimensions. The important differences are shown in Table 14.1.

The research literature is filled with reports of efforts to implement and the outcomes of organic designs in actual organizations.[40] Likert himself reports many of these studies. One organization has received considerable attention for its efforts to implement organic principles. Thrivent Financial for Lutherans (TFL) is a large financial services company with 2.6 million members and $67 billion in assets under management.[41] It has transformed its organization from a mechanistic to an organic structure in an effort to take advantage of

TABLE 14.1 Comparison of Mechanistic and Organic Structures

Source: Adapted from Rensis Likert, *The Human Organization* (New York: McGraw-Hill, 1967), pp. 197–211.

Process	Mechanistic Structure	Organic Structure
1. Leadership	Includes no perceived confidence and trust. Subordinates do not feel free to discuss job problems with their superiors, who in turn do not solicit their ideas and opinions.	Includes perceived confidence and trust between superiors and subordinates in all matters. Subordinates feel free to discuss job problems with their superiors, who in turn solicit their ideas and opinions.
2. Motivation	Taps only physical, security, and economic motives, through the use of fear and sanctions. Unfavorable attitudes toward the organization prevail among employees.	Taps a full range of motives through participatory methods. Attitudes are favorable toward the organization and its goals.
3. Communication	Information flows downward and tends to be distorted, inaccurate, and viewed with suspicion by subordinates.	Information flows freely throughout the organization: upward, downward, and laterally. The information is accurate and undistorted.
4. Interaction	Closed and restricted. Subordinates have little effect on departmental goals, methods, and activities.	Open and extensive. Both superiors and subordinates are able to affect departmental goals, methods, and activities.
5. Decision	Relatively centralized. Occurs only at the top of the organization.	Relatively decentralized. Occurs at all levels through group process.
6. Goal setting	Located at the top of the organization, discouraging group participation.	Encourages group participation in setting high, realistic objectives.
7. Control	Centralized. Emphasizes fixing of blame for mistakes.	Dispersed throughout the organization. Emphasizes self-control and problem solving.
8. Performance goals	Low and passively sought by managers, who make no commitment to developing the organization's human resources.	High and actively sought by superiors, who recognize the need for full commitment to developing, through training, the organization's human resources.

the benefits of the *self-directed team* concept. Prior to reorganization, TFL was organized mechanistically according to the traditional functions of the insurance industry, and employees were highly trained to deal with processing, underwriting, valuations, and premium services functions. Specialization resulted in considerable efficiency dealing with customers requiring the attention of one of the functions. But when multiple functions were involved, the organization became bogged down.

TFL's management explored potential benefits of establishing teams of employees that could handle all details of any customer transaction, whether health, life, or casualty insurance. The teams consist of individuals who once were responsible for functions; now they're responsible for customers and take initiatives that once required management prodding. As a result of teams' assumption of responsibility for their own management, three levels of management have been eliminated from the organization. The organization is now simpler and more decentralized than before and, therefore, more organic and less mechanistic.

TFL also implemented a form of employee compensation termed "pay for knowledge" to encourage employees to adopt the new work system. It provides individuals with pay increases for obtaining additional knowledge that enables them to improve their job performance. In the context of TFL's organic organization, employees needed to learn not only new technical knowledge but also new interpersonal knowledge because working with other individuals in teams is critical to the success of the new organizational design.[42]

There is, likewise, no question that proponents of the organic organization believe it is universally applicable; that is, the theory is proposed as the "one best way" to design an organization. In this regard, proponents of both the mechanistic and organic models are equally zealous in their advocacy.

Contingency Design Theories

The demands of a situation are termed *contingencies*. Accordingly, neither the mechanistic nor the organic is necessarily the more effective organization design; either can be better depending on the situation. The contingency point of view provides the opportunity to get away from the dilemma of choosing between mechanistic and organic models. As such, it's an evolution of ideas whose bases are found in the work of earlier writers.

contingency design theory
Organizational design approach that emphasizes the importance of fitting a design to demands of a situation, including technology, environmental uncertainty, and management choice.

The essence of the **contingency design theory** approach is expressed by the question: Under what circumstances and in what situations is either the mechanistic or the organic design relatively more effective? The answer requires the manager to specify the contingencies in a situation that influence a particular design's relative effectiveness. Obviously, the contingency approach is quite complicated because of the necessity to consider so many contingencies, with technology being one of the more important ones.

Technology and Organizational Design

technology
Physical and mental actions by an individual to change the form or content of an object or idea.

The effects of **technology** on organization structure can be readily understood at an abstract level of analysis. Although various definitions of technology exist, it's generally understood as "the *actions* that an individual performs upon an object with or without the aid of tools or mechanical devices, in order to make *some change* in that object."[43] Thus, organization structures reflect technology in the ways that jobs are designed (the division of labor) and grouped (departmentalization).

In recent years, the state of technological knowledge has increased exponentially as computers, the Internet, virtual work, mobile devices, 24/7 connectivity, and robots have entered the workplace. One effect of this new knowledge has been to increase managers' interest in the relationship between organization structure and technology.

The organization theory literature includes a number of studies that examine the relationship between technology and organization structure. We can't possibly survey all these studies here—it would take considerable space and would go beyond the intent of our discussion. Rather, we'll briefly review the classic study that stimulated a number of follow-up studies and has become important in the literature of organizational design.

The Classic Study of Technology and Organizational Design

Joan Woodward gained considerable attention when she released the findings of analyses of 100 manufacturing firms' organization structures in southern England.[44] While she and her colleagues had sought to answer a number of questions regarding contributions of organization structure to organizational effectiveness, it was their conclusions regarding technology and structure that were widely acclaimed.

She and her team of researchers had set out to determine if there were structural differences between the more and less effective firms. They used a number of measures of effectiveness to classify firms into three categories: above average, average, and below average. But when they compared organization structures within each category, no consistent pattern emerged. It was then that the team began analyzing the information relating to technology, "the methods and processes of manufacture."[45] The team measured technology in terms of three related variables:

> (1) stages in the historical development of production processes, (2) the interrelationship between the items of equipment used for these processes, and (3) the extent to which the operations performed in the processes were repetitive or comparable from one production cycle or sequence to the next.[46]

Applying the measure to information about the firm's manufacturing methods resulted in a continuum of technology with job-order manufacturing and process manufacturing methods at the extremes, separated by mass-production manufacturing.

The research team classified firms according to the three categories of technology. It then discovered that the organizational structures of firms within each category were different in comparison to other categories. The important differences were as follows:[47]

1. Organizations at each end of the continuum were more flexible; that is, they resembled the organic model with job duties and responsibilities being less clearly defined. Organizations in the middle of the continuum were more specialized and formalized; that is, they resembled the mechanistic model.

2. Organizations at each end of the continuum made greater use of verbal than written communications; organizations in the middle made greater use of written communications and were more formalized. This pattern is also consistent with distinctions between organic and mechanistic models of design.

3. Managerial positions were more highly specialized in mass production than in either job order or process manufacturing. First-level supervisors engaged primarily in direct supervision, leaving technical decisions to staff personnel. In contrast, managers in job order firms were expected to have greater technical expertise, while managers in process manufacturing were expected to have greater scientific expertise.

4. Consistent with the preceding point, actual control of production in the form of schedule making and routing was separated from supervision of production in mass production firms. The two managerial functions were more highly integrated in the role of the first-level supervisor in organizations at the extremes of the continuum.

Thus, the data indicated sharp organizational differences due to technological differences.

Understanding the Relationship between Technology and Structure

The relationship between technology and organizations can be understood with reference to the natural business functions: product development, production, and marketing. The job order firm produces according to customer specifications; the firm must secure the order, develop the product, and manufacture it. The cycle begins with marketing and ends with production.

This sequence requires the firm to be especially adept at sensing market changes and adjusting to them. But more important, the product development function holds the key to the firm's success. This function must convert customer specifications into products that are acceptable to both the customer and the production personnel. Various approaches exist to facilitate the kinds of interactions and communication patterns required to meet the market and product development problems associated with job order or unit production. The more complicated ones involve interactions better managed in organic-type structures.

At the other extreme of the technological continuum is the process manufacturer. In these firms, the cycle begins with product development. The key to success is the ability to discover a new product through scientific research—a new chemical, gasoline additive, or fabric—that can be produced by already existing facilities or by new facilities once a market is established. The development, marketing, and production functions in process manufacturing all tend to demand scientific personnel and specialized competence at the highest levels in the organization. Because these firms' success depends on adjustment to new scientific knowledge, the organic design is more effective than the mechanistic design.

The mechanistic design is effective for firms that use mass production technology. The market exists for a more or less standardized product—autos, foods, clothing—and the task is to manufacture the product through fairly routine means, efficiently and economically. Workers tend machines designed and paced by engineering standards. Actual control of the work flow is separated from supervision of the workforce. In such organizations, the ideas of scientific management and mechanistic design are applicable.

This explanation of the relationship between technology and structure rests on traditional views of manufacturing technology. Recent advances in computers and robots have initiated new understanding of manufacturing possibilities and organization structures that are compatible with those advances.

Environment and Organizational Design

The relationship between technology and effective organizational design is firmly established. Yet, as we see, interpreting these relationships requires that the organization's environment be taken into account. Thus, the more basic explanation for differences in organization is differences in the environment. This line of reasoning has been pursued by a number of researchers. We'll review one of the classic studies in this section.

The Classic Study of the Relationship between Environment and Organizational Design

Lawrence and Lorsch base their findings on detailed case studies of firms in the plastics, food, and container industries.[48] An initial exploratory study consisted of case studies of six firms operating in the plastics industry. Lawrence and Lorsch analyzed these studies to answer the following questions:[49]

1. How are the environmental demands facing various organizations different and how do environmental demands relate to the design of effective organizations?
2. Is it true that organizations in certain or stable environments make more exclusive use of centralized authority to make key decisions, and, if so, why? Is it because fewer key

decisions are required, or because these decisions can be made more effectively at higher organization levels or by fewer people?

3. Are the same degree of specialization and differences in orientation among individuals and groups found in organizations in different industrial environments?
4. If greater specialization and differences among individuals and groups are found in different industries, do these differences influence problems of coordinating the organization's parts? Do they influence the organization's means of achieving integration?

To answer these four questions, Lawrence and Lorsch studied structure in the three industries. During their investigation, they coined three terms that have become widely used in the theory and practice of organizational design: *differentiation, integration,* and *environment.*

Differentiation

differentiation
Degree of differences among units of an organization due to individual and structural differences.

The "state of segmentation of the organizational system into subsystems, each of which tends to develop particular attributes in relation to the requirements posed by its relevant external environment" is termed **differentiation.**[50] This concept refers in part to the idea of specialization of labor, specifically to the degree of departmentalization. But it's broader and also includes behavioral attributes of employees of these subsystems, or departments. The researchers were interested in three behavioral attributes:

1. They believed that employees of some departments would be more or less task oriented or person oriented than employees in other departments. This belief reflects ideas in Fiedler's situational theory of leadership.
2. They proposed that employees of some departments would have longer or shorter time horizons than members of other departments. They believed these differences could be explained by different environmental attributes, specifically the length of time between action and the feedback of results.
3. They expected to find some employees more concerned with goals of their department than with goals of the total organization.

The organization of each department in the six firms was classified along a continuum from mechanistic to organic. Employees in mechanistically organized departments were expected to be more oriented toward tasks and have shorter time horizons than employees in organic departments.

Integration

integration
Achieving unity of effort among different organizational units and individuals through rules, planning, and leadership.

The "process of achieving unity of effort among the various subsystems in the accomplishment of the organization's task" is labeled **integration**, and it can be achieved in a variety of ways. Proponents of the mechanistic model argued for integration through the creation of rules and procedures to govern subsystem members' behavior. But this method of integration can be effective only in relatively stable and predictable situations.[51] Rules and procedures lose their effectiveness as the environment becomes more unstable; thus, integration by *plans* takes on greater significance. But as we approach the highly unstable environment, integration is achieved by mutual adjustment. Mutual adjustment requires a great deal of communication through open channels throughout the organization, a characteristic of organically designed organizations. In terms of the Lawrence and Lorsch research, the type of integrative devices that managers use should be related to the degree of differentiation. Highly differentiated organizations would tend to use mutual adjustment as a means of achieving integration.

Environment

The independent variable *environment* was conceptualized from the perspective of the organization members as they looked outward. Consequently, the researchers assumed that a

FIGURE 14.4
Conceptualization of the Lawrence and Lorsch Model

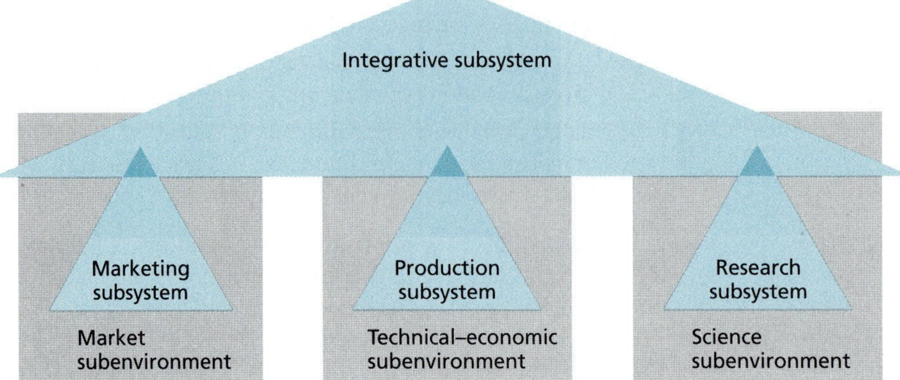

basic reason for differentiating into subsystems is to deal more effectively with subenvironments. Lawrence and Lorsch identified three main subenvironments: the market subenvironment, the technical–economic subenvironment, and the scientific subenvironment. These three subenvironments correspond to the sales, production, and research and development functions within organizations. Most organizations create separate departments for sales, production, and research and development. These departments represent parts of the total organization or, in researchers' terms, subsystems of the total system.

The researchers believed that the degree of differentiation within each subsystem would vary depending on specific attributes of the relevant subenvironment. Specifically, the subenvironment could vary along three dimensions: (1) the rate of change of conditions over time, (2) the certainty of information about conditions at any particular time, and (3) the time span of feedback on the results of employee decisions.[52]

Figure 14.4 depicts the idea that an organization consists of separate parts, usually departments, which must deal with different aspects of the total environment. Lawrence and Lorsch identify the organizational parts, or subsystems, as marketing, production, and research. They identify the environmental parts, or subenvironments, as market, technical–economic, and science. Subsystems must be organized so as to deal effectively with their relevant subenvironments. The greater the differences among the three subenvironments in terms of rate of change, certainty of information, and time span of feedback, the greater will be the differences among the three subsystems in terms of organization structure and behavioral attributes. The greater these differences (i.e., the more differentiated are the three subsystems), the more important is the task of integrating the three subsystems.

Environmental Uncertainty and Organizational Design in the Service Sector

The growing importance of the service sector of the economy has stimulated much interest in understanding how to design service firms for optimal performance.[53] An increasingly promising approach is to use the concept of environmental uncertainty to identify the optimal design. One variation of this approach focuses on the relative uncertainty of two customer attributes: diversity of customer demand for services and variation in customer disposition to participate in the delivery of the service.[54] According to this perspective, a service firm should organize in relatively mechanistic or organic forms depending upon the degree of uncertainty in these two attributes.

Service organizations whose customers demand relatively homogeneous services and have little disposition to participate in the delivery of those services can be managed according to mechanistic principles. Examples of such organizations include retail stores, banks, insurance firms, and airlines. Mechanistic designs provide appropriate mechanisms for integrating activities of relatively undifferentiated functions.

At the far extreme of these types of service firms are those whose customers demand a diverse array of services and are predisposed to participating in the service delivery. Such organizations include medical care, legal advice, and higher education. These organizations are better able to integrate the activities of highly differentiated activities through organic organizations. This is because the organic structure provides the flexibility required to deal with the highly uncertain environment that is characteristic of customers demanding quite different services and desiring to play an active part in their delivery.

In between these two extremes are intermediate levels of uncertainty. The appropriate organizational designs would be less mechanistic and organic than the extremes and would be tailored to deal with different degrees of services demanded and participation expected.

The idea that an organization's structure should enable customers to access its services can be applied at the subunit level as well as at the overall organizational level. For example, we note that banks are examples of organizations whose customers demand relatively homogeneous services and who aren't disposed to participate in delivery of those services. At the overall organizational level of thinking, the typical bank customer may well be so characterized. But within the bank, there may be different units whose customers require more or less diverse services and who desire more or less participation in the delivery of those services. The trust unit of a bank that serves affluent customers with diverse financial and personal needs is quite different from the installment loan unit that serves only short-term credit customers whose sole participation in the delivery of the service is to provide credit-scoring information. The implication for organizational design is that the trust division should reflect relatively more organic characteristics than the installment loan unit.

Understanding the Relationship between Environmental Uncertainty and Structure

The differentiation–integration approach is based on the fundamental viewpoint that organizations must be designed to cope with environmental demands. But this approach goes further to show that different organization designs can and often do exist within a single large organization. A manufacturing firm may find it necessary to design its production department quite differently from its research and development department. In some instances (e.g., in mass production), the production department must be designed according to the mechanistic model, but the research and development department may be designed according to the organic model. Differences in the designs are due to differences in the environmental uncertainty each department confronts. Because the production environment is relatively certain, there's no need to stress adaptability and the department can be designed to achieve high levels of efficiency. But the research and development environment is likely to be highly uncertain with considerable need to cope flexibly with unforeseen changes.

The process of departmentalizing creates the necessity for integrating activities of the departments. Integration of separate, yet interdependent, activities is a familiar problem in managing organizations. Mechanistic design proponents believe that integration can be achieved through the creation of rules, procedures, plans, and a hierarchical chain of command that places managers in the position of integrators. The solutions of organic design proponents, however, differ. They believe that committees, task groups, cross-functional teams, integrators, and group-centered decision making are better approaches. In fact, either approach is appropriate depending upon the situation, according to Lawrence and Lorsch.

Environmental Uncertainty, Information Processing, and Adaptive Design Strategies

The relationships among environment, technology, and organization structure can be synthesized. The key concept is *information* and the key idea is that organizations must effectively receive, process, and act on information to achieve performance.[55] Information flows into the organization from the subenvironments. The information enables the organization to respond to market, technological, and resource changes. The more rapid the changes, the greater the necessity for, and availability of, information.[56]

Organizations in relatively certain and unchanging environments rely on hierarchical control, rules and procedures, and planning to integrate the behavior of subunits. These integrative methods are fundamental features of classical organization designs and are effective as long as the environment remains stable and predictable. Information processing requirements are relatively modest in such environments. For example, firms manufacturing and selling paper containers can plan production schedules with relative assurance that sudden shifts in demand, resource supply, or technology will not disrupt the schedule. Information requirements consist almost solely of projections from historical sales, cost, and engineering data.

Organizations in dynamic and complex environments, however, are unable to rely on traditional information processing and control techniques. Changes in market demand, resource supplies, and technology disrupt plans and require adjustments *during* task performance. On-the-spot adjustments to production schedules and task performance disrupt the organization.

From a managerial perspective, the effect of environmental uncertainty and increased flow of information is to overload the organization with exceptional cases. As a greater number of nonroutine, consequential events occur in the organization's environment, managers are increasingly drawn into day-to-day operating matters. Problems develop as plans become obsolete and as the various functions' coordinating efforts break down.[57]

Some organizations are designed from their inception to deal with information processing demands; most, however, must confront the problem subsequent to their creation. For these organizations that discover that their present design is incapable of dealing with the demands of changing environments, the problem becomes one of selecting an appropriate adaptive strategy. The two general approaches are to (1) reduce the need for information and (2) increase capacity to process information.

Sociotechnical Systems Theory

An influential theory developed in the early 1950s by the researchers of the London-based Tavistock Institute of Human Relations, sociotechnical systems theory suggests that production processes consist of social and technical dimensions.[58] Unique yet interdependent, these two dimensions exert a reciprocal influence on one another. The technical dimension refers to the equipment and methods of production used to create products and services. The social dimension of sociotechnical systems theory consists of the formal and informal work structure that links people to the technology and to each other.[59] Early research showed the benefits of joint-optimization of the technical production system and the social behaviors of workers. These observations encouraged the development of organizational design principles that utilized semiautonomous work groups in the production process.[60]

Considered by some as a precursor to the total quality management (TQM) movement, the Tavistock research on sociotechnical systems theory consistently championed the concepts of teamwork and semiautonomous work groups as critical building blocks of successful production systems. A major tenet of the theory, the "control of variance" concept, suggests that unavoidable variances in the production processes should be controlled as near to the point of the problems as possible.[61] Thus, team involvement in resolving such variances can result in higher levels of productivity, quality, and other key performance criteria.

An example of how technical and social systems interact in a manufacturing environment is the New United Motor Manufacturing Inc. (NUMMI) automotive manufacturing plant in Fremont, California.[62] The NUMMI plant, jointly operated by Toyota and General Motors since 1984, has received numerous accolades in recent years, including the JD Powers Silver Award for being one of the top North American automotive assembly plants and a "recommended buy" endorsement for six consecutive years by *Consumer's Digest*.[63]

Blending state-of-the-art manufacturing processes with comprehensive employee cross-training, simplified job classifications, and increased flexibility of work rules, NUMMI has designed its organization in such a way that it has achieved a fit between its technological and social systems, resulting in higher levels of productivity and quality.[64]

Structuring Virtual Organizations

One of the fastest developing practices in business throughout the world involves firms in cooperative relationships with their suppliers, distributors, and even competitors.[65] These networks of relationships enable organizations to achieve both efficiency and flexibility to exploit advantages of the mechanistic and organic organization designs. Becoming popular in the 1990s, these **virtual organizations** (also called "modular" or "network" organizations) have become so pervasive that some experts refer to them as the models for 21st-century organizations.[66] Early users of this type of virtual organization were Nike and Reebok, which outsourced the manufacturing of their running shoes and sneakers to manufacturers in Southeast Asia about 25 years ago.[67] Flexible organizations outsource noncore processes and the production of component parts and services to take advantage of the latest technologies and to control costs. For example, Porsche uses a virtual approach to produce the Cayenne SUV; the parent company performs the core processes (i.e., engine production, transmission manufacturing, and final assembly) and outsources everything else related to production.[68] Cooperative relationships enable the principal organization to rely upon the smaller, closer-to-the-market partner to sense impending changes in the environment and to respond at the local level, thus relieving the parent organization of that necessity.[69]

virtual organization Achieves efficiency and flexibility by subcontracting some of its operations to members of a network, including suppliers, distributors, customers, strategic alliance partners, and even competitors.

The exact form of the virtual organization varies. Some organizations develop relationships only with key suppliers. For example, Figure 14.5 demonstrates how U.S.-based Bombardier Aerospace produces key components for its business jets in-house in the United States but contracts with companies from around the world to supply the non-core components for the jet aircraft. Other organizations develop relationships with marketers and distributors. In the extreme case, the parent organization functions much like a broker and deals independently with product designers, producers, suppliers, and markets. The critical managerial and organizational decisions involve which of the functions to buy and which to produce and how to manage the relationships with their partners. Managers in these organizations have less environmental uncertainty to deal with because they have, in a sense, subcontracted that responsibility to their counterparts in the network. Such organization structures are, in a sense, boundary-less organizations.[70]

Virtual organizations originated in Japan where firms create alliances with other firms. These alliances take the form of cooperative agreements, consortia, and equity ownerships

FIGURE 14.5
A Virtual Approach to Manufacturing a Bombardier Business Jet

Source: Reprinted from *Organizational Dynamics* 36, no. 4 (December 2006), N. Anand and Richard L. Daft, "What Is the Right Organization Design?" pp. 329–344. Copyright 2011, with permission from Elsevier.

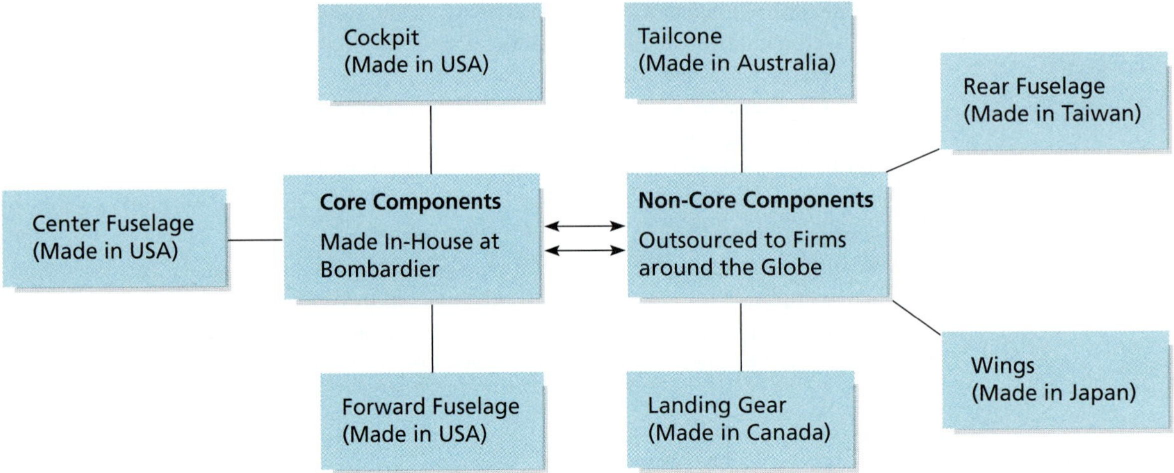

to establish networks of businesses. In Japan, this form of doing business is termed *keiretsu* and involves a very large financial institution, a very large industrial conglomerate, and smaller firms in a network of relationships that enable the large firm to produce the product and the smaller firms to supply components, do research and design, and perhaps distribute and market. The participating bank provides the financial requirements to support the network of cooperative relationships. This form of interorganizational network has enabled Japanese industry to grow without bottlenecks of supply and damaging competition from domestic firms.

How these relationships should be organized and managed is being empirically examined. Although the Japanese experience provides some guidelines, much is left to be learned and put into practice. Studies at the Aston Business School in Great Britain suggest that development of these cooperative relationships represents simply another reaction from organizations that must maintain flexibility to deal with the dynamic changes of the global economy.[71]

Organizational design remains an important issue in the management of organizational behavior and effectiveness. As the 21st century progresses, organizational design is becoming even more important. As is apparent, organizational designs that were successful in the past will prove ineffectual in the face of new international competition, technological change, and the shifting patterns of industrial development.[72] As organizations experiment with new strategies, they will be forced to experiment with new organizational designs. These designs will bear close resemblance to organic designs and virtual organizations.[73]

Summary of Key Points

- The structure of an organization consists of relatively fixed and stable relationships among jobs and groups of jobs. The primary purpose of organization structure is to influence the behavior of individuals and groups to achieve effective performance.
- Four key managerial decisions determine organization structures. These decisions are dividing work, delegating authority, departmentalizing jobs into groups, and determining spans of control.
- Delegating authority enables an individual to make decisions and to exact obedience without approval by higher management. Similar to other organizing issues, delegated

authority is a relative, not absolute, concept. All individuals, whether managers or nonmanagers, in an organization have some authority. The question is whether they have enough to do their jobs.

- Grouping jobs into departments requires the selection of common bases such as function, territory, product, and customer. Each basis has advantages and disadvantages that must be evaluated in terms of overall effectiveness.
- The optimal span of control is no one specific number of subordinates. Although the number of potential relationships increases geometrically as the number of subordinates increases arithmetically, the important considerations are the frequency and intensity of the actual relationships.
- One theory, termed *mechanistic design,* is based on the assumption that the more effective organizational structure is characterized by highly specialized jobs, homogeneous departments, narrow spans of control, and relatively centralized authority. The bases for these assumptions are found in the historical circumstances within which this theory developed. It was a time of fairly rapid industrialization that encouraged public and private organizations to emphasize the production and efficiency criteria of effectiveness. To achieve these ends, classical design theory proposes a single best way to structure an organization.
- Beginning with the human relations era of the 1930s and sustained by behavioral scientists' growing interest in the study of management and organization, an alternative to mechanistic design theory developed. This alternative theory, termed *organic design,* proposes that the more effective organization has relatively despecialized jobs, heterogeneous departments, wide spans of control, and decentralized authority. Such organization structures, it's argued, achieve not only high levels of production and efficiency but also satisfaction, adaptiveness, and development.
- The design of an effective organization structure can't be guided by a "one-best-way" theory. Rather, the manager must adopt the point of view that either the mechanistic or the organic design is more effective for the total organization or for subunits within its organization.
- The manager must evaluate each subenvironment in terms of its rate of change, relative certainty, and time span of feedback. These conditions are the key variables for determining the formal structure of tasks and authority.
- Each subunit structure is designed along the mechanistic–organic continuum in a manner consistent with the state of environmental conditions. Specifically, slower rates of change, greater certainty, and shorter time spans of feedback are compatible with the mechanistic design; the converse is true for the organic design.
- Virtual organizations achieve both efficiency and flexibility by establishing networks of relationships with a variety of groups including suppliers, distributors, customers, strategic alliance partners, and even competitors.

Discussion and Review Questions

1. Assume that you've just started working for a company that does not have an organizational chart that shows reporting relationships. How would you go about determining to whom your boss reports and where your department fits in the overall organization structure?
2. Compare functional and product departmentalization in terms of relative efficiency, production, satisfaction, flexibility, quality, competitiveness, and development. Consider particularly the possibility that one basis may be superior in achieving one aspect of effectiveness, yet inferior in achieving another.

3. Discuss the statement that to manage effectively, a person must have the authority to hire subordinates, assign them to specific jobs, and reward them on the basis of performance. Interview the chairperson of an academic department and determine whether he has this authority.
4. What implications for managerial spans of control can be expected in organizations that downsize? What additional demands will be placed on remaining managers after downsizing?
5. Describe managerial skills and behaviors that would be required to manage effectively in a functional department. Are these skills and behaviors different from those required in a product department? Explain.
6. For what type of organization would you prefer to work? Organic or mechanistic? Explain.
7. What in your experience has been the dominant contingency factor in the design of the organizations in which you have worked? Technology? Environmental uncertainty? Strategy?
8. Use the characteristics of mechanistic and organic organizations to describe two different organizations that you know about. After determining the organizational differences, see if you can relate the differences to technological and environmental differences.
9. Think about the organizational design of your current organization or the school you are attending. Which organizational design discussed in this chapter best describes your current organization or school? Explain the reasons for your choice.
10. Assume that you are starting your own business and want the organizational structure to be a virtual one. What are the advantages and disadvantages of creating such a virtual organization? Explain.

Taking It to the Net

Virtual Organizational Design

Virtual teams are becoming more common as organizations attempt to establish "real-time" relationships with clients, suppliers, and vendors who are based in geographically dispersed locations. Taken to the extreme, sometimes entire organizations operate in a virtual manner (i.e., the organization comprises employees who are based in different geographic locations). Using your favorite search engine, such as www.google.com or www.yahoo.com, search the Internet for at least five organizations that use a virtual organization design. Then, answer the following three questions about the virtual organizations you identified:

1. In your opinion, how can the "leaders" of the organizations exercise control over their geographically dispersed employees?
2. How do you think members of these virtual organizations arrive at decisions?
3. How would you group the members' jobs? By function? By territory? By product? Or by customer?

Case for Analysis: *Defining the Role of a Liaison Officer*

Recently, the governor of a southeastern state created a Department for Human Resources. It combined many formerly distinct state agencies that carried out health and welfare programs. The department's organization chart is shown in Exhibit 1. The functions of each of the bureaus were described in the governor's press release:

> The Bureau for Social Insurance *will operate all income maintenance and all income supplementation programs of the Department for Human Resources.*

EXHIBIT 1
Department for Human Resources: Organization Chart

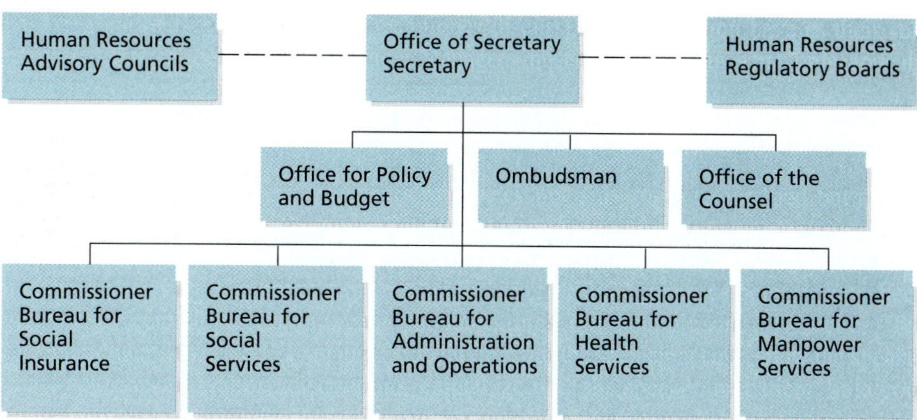

That is, it will issue financial support to the poor, unemployed, and needy, and it will issue food stamps and pay for medical assistance.

The Bureau for Social Services *will provide child welfare services, foster care, adoptions, family services, and all other general counseling in support of families and individuals who require assistance for successful and adequate human development.*

The Bureau for Health Services *will operate all departmental programs that provide health service, including all physical and mental health programs. This bureau will take over the functions of the Department of Health, the Department of Mental Health, and the Commission for Handicapped Children.*

The Bureau for Manpower Services *will operate all labor force development and job placement programs of the department, including all job recruitments and business liaison functions, job training, worker readiness functions, and job counseling and placement.*

The Bureau for Administration and Operations *will consolidate numerous support services, such as preaudits, accounting, data processing, purchasing, and duplicating, now furnished by 19 separate units.*

Soon after the department began to operate in its reorganized form, major problems arose that were traceable to the Bureau for Administration and Operations (BAO). Prior to reorganization, each department had had its own support staff for data processing, accounting, personnel, and budgeting. Those staffs and equipment had all been relocated and brought under the direction of the BAO commissioner. Employees who had once specialized in the work of one area, such as mental health, were now expected to perform work for all the bureaus. In addition, they had to revise forms, procedures, computer programs, accounts, and records to conform to the new department's policies.

Consequently, the department began to experience administrative problems. Payrolls were late and inaccurate; payments to vendors and clients were delayed; and personnel actions got lost in the paperwork. Eventually, the integrity of the department's service programs was in jeopardy.

The executive staff of the department, consisting of the secretary, commissioner, and administrator of the Office for Policy and Budget, soon found itself spending more time dealing with these administrative problems than with policy formulation. Apparently, the department's effectiveness would depend on its ability to integrate the functions of BAO with the needs of the program bureaus. Also, the executive staff was not the appropriate body to deal with these issues. Aside from the inordinate amount of time spent on the administrative problems, a great deal of interpersonal conflict was generated among the commissioners.

The BAO commissioner was instructed by the secretary to give his full-time attention to devising a means for integrating the administrative functions. After consultation with his staff, the idea of an administrative liaison officer was formulated. The BAO commissioner presented the staff paper that described this new job (Exhibit 2) to the executive staff for discussion and adoption. According to the commissioner, there was simply no procedural or planning means for integrating the administrative functions. Rather, it would continue to be a conflict-laden process requiring the undivided attention of an individual assigned to each of the four bureaus.

EXHIBIT 2 **Description of Responsibilities, Administrative Liaison Officer**

Introduction

Executive Order 86-777 abolished the former human resources agencies and merged their functions into a new, single department. A prime element in the organizational concept of the new department is the centralization of administrative and support activities into a Bureau of Administration and Operations, which supports the four program bureaus of the department. While the centralization of these administrative and support activities only included those functions that were located in centralized administrative units in the former human resources agencies, the size of the Department for Human Resources dictates that extra levels of effort be applied to ensure close coordination and cooperation between the four program bureaus and the Bureau for Administration and Operations.

As one element in the comprehensive range of efforts now being applied to ensure a high level of responsiveness and cooperation between the Bureau for Administration and Operations and each program bureau, there will be created within the office of the Commissioner for Administration and Operations four positions for administrative liaison officers, one of which will be assigned responsibility for liaison with each program bureau.

Responsibilities

1. Each administrative liaison officer will provide, to the program bureau commissioner and other officials of the program bureau to which assigned, assistance in the following areas:
   a. Identification and definition of the administrative and operational support needs of that program bureau.
   b. Determination of the relative priorities of those needs for services.
   c. Identification of programmatic and operational requirements of the program bureau that may be assisted by the enforcement of administrative regulations by the Bureau for Administration and Operations.
   d. Identification of resources available within the Bureau for Administration and Operations that may be of value to the program bureau.
   e. Coordination of the delivery of services by the various divisions of the Bureau for Administration and Operations to the program bureau.
   f. Interpretation of data and information provided by the Bureau for Administration and Operations.
   g. Interpretation and distribution of administrative regulations and procedures issued by the Bureau for Administration and Operations with respect to its responsibilities under policies delineated by the secretary and the commissioners of the Department for Human Resources.
2. Each administrative liaison officer will provide assistance to the Commissioner for Administration and Operations and other officials of the Bureau for Administration and Operations in the following areas:
   a. Development of strategies for providing the maximum possible quality and quantity of support services that can be made available to the officer's particular program bureau within budgetary and policy constraints.
   b. Understanding of special needs and problems of respective program bureaus.
   c. Identification of new procedures and systems whereby services rendered to the program bureau can result in improved coordination between all organizational units of the Department for Human Resources.
   d. Identification of inadequacies or gaps in presently available services provided by the Bureau for Administration and Operations.
   e. Direction and/or coordination of task forces and other temporary organizational units created within the Bureau for Administration and Operations assigned to provide resources specific to the program bureau.
   f. Supervision of all personnel of the Bureau for Administration and Operations that may be on a temporary duty assignment to the program bureau to which the officer is assigned.

Operational Arrangement

1. The administrative liaison officer will be appointed to a position within the Office of the Commissioner for Administration and Operations.
2. The assignment of an administrative liaison officer to a program bureau will require the concurrence of the commissioner of that program bureau.
3. The Office of the Administrative Liaison Officer will be physically located within the suite of offices of the program bureau commissioner to whom the officer is assigned.
4. The administrative liaison officer will attend all staff meetings of the commissioner of the program bureau to which assigned and all staff meetings of the Commissioner for Administration and Operations.

DISCUSSION QUESTIONS

1. Evaluate the concept of "administrative liaison officer" as a strategy for achieving integration. Is this an example of the mutual adjustment strategy?
2. How will the officers achieve integration when they will have no authority over either the administrative functions or the programs to be integrated?
3. What would be the most important personal characteristics to look for in an applicant for these positions?

Experiential Exercise: *Identifying and Changing Organization Design*

OBJECTIVES

To increase the reader's understanding of different organization designs.

RELATED TOPICS

Chapters 13, 14, and 15 provide the reader with sufficient information to complete the analysis.

STARTING THE EXERCISE

The instructor will form groups of five to eight individuals toward the end of a class meeting. Each group will meet for 5 to 10 minutes and select a specific organizational unit within your college that will be the focus of the group's analysis. The unit can be an academic department, division, or college or a nonacademic unit such as the athletic department, business affairs office, student housing, or any other formally recognized campus unit.

Before the next class meeting, each group will complete the six steps of the exercise and prepare a report to present to the class.

COMPLETING THE EXERCISE

1. What is the primary purpose of the unit? What functions must be performed to accomplish the mission? What customers does the unit serve with what products or services? What are the primary environments that influence the unit's performance?
2. Describe the unit's primary technology, the relative uncertainty of the primary environments, and the primary information that must be processed.
3. Describe the existing organization structure in terms of the characteristics that distinguish between mechanistic and organic designs.
4. Which organization design more accurately describes the existing organization structure?
5. If the organization structure were changed to be more mechanistic or organic, what would be the effects on jobs, departmental bases, and delegation of authority?
6. Is the existing organization design appropriate for the unit, given its mission, functions, customers, products/services, and environment? Justify your answer.

PART FIVE

The Processes of Organizations

CHAPTER FIFTEEN

Managing Communication

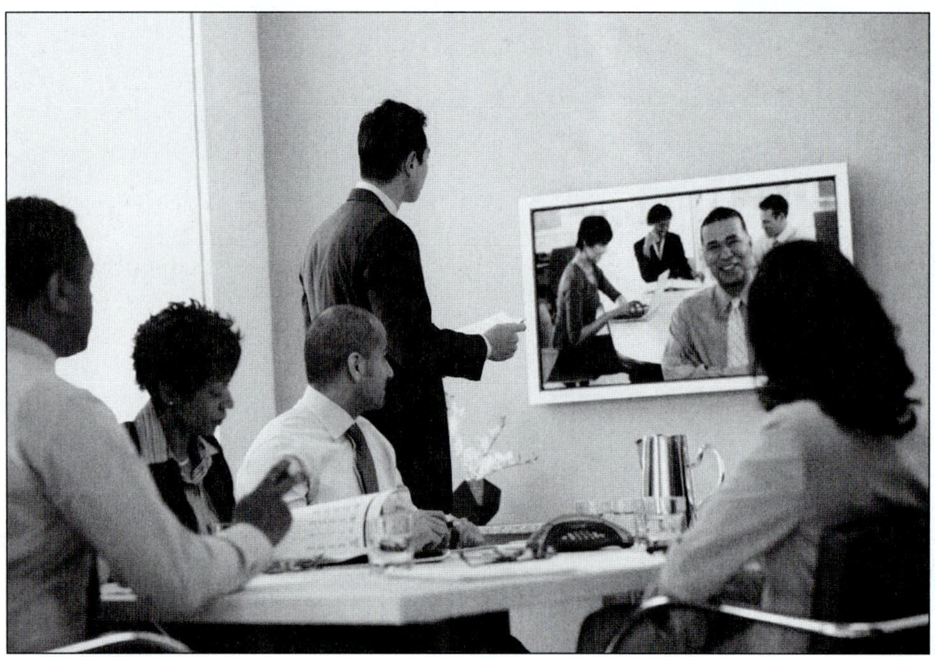

Learning Objectives

After completing Chapter 15, you should be able to

Define
The term *communication.*

Describe
The major elements in the process of communication.

Discuss
How nonverbal cues influence communication effectiveness.

Understand
The intersection between communication and technology.

Identify
The major barriers to effective communication and the means to overcome these barriers.

Communicating in Global Virtual Teams

Global virtual teams are cross-functional teams that operate across time, geographic distance, organizational boundaries, and cultures, whose members communicate mainly through electronic technologies (e.g., smart phone, laptop, texting, e-mail, videoconferencing, etc.). With infrequent face-to-face contact, these teams are faced with the challenge of building and maintaining trust as they work toward accomplishing the team's objectives and goals. In particular, miscommunication between team members from diverse cultures and backgrounds can create a roadblock to the development of trust and, ultimately, effective team functioning. Internationally savvy companies can manage this potential problem by providing each member of its virtual teams with intercultural training that attempts to melt away misperceptions and the "us and them" perceived barriers that are common in the early stages of team formation.

The first part of the intercultural communication training should focus on helping each team member understand her own cultural beliefs, verbal and nonverbal communication styles, and attitudes toward time, space, authority, decision making, work ethic, and the like. The rationale behind this "inward looking" portion of the training is based on the research of Edward T. and Mildred R. Hall, anthropologists and pioneers in the field of culture and communication, who wrote: "Like people all over the world, Americans take their culture for granted. Indeed, it's only in juxtaposition with other cultures that Americans begin to understand the influence of their own culture on their behavior." The second part of the intercultural training for virtual team members focuses on learning how to work effectively with teammates from diverse cultures. Team members will learn how to interpret the verbal and nonverbal communication styles and cultural backgrounds of teammates and how to respond effectively to these unique cues.

For example, assume an American is placed on a global virtual team with individuals from Mexico. First, she would learn about her own cultural biases and communication style. Like many Americans, she prefers the following approaches to business: She likes to tackle projects in monochronic fashion (i.e., one thing at a time); she has a strong work ethic; she favors direct, get-to-the point-communication; and she likes to keep work and home life separate. In contrast, her Mexican counterparts tend to be more polychromatic (i.e., juggle many activities at once), work hard but spend more time with family and friends, prefer a less direct approach to communication (to allow ample time to build trust), and do not refrain from discussing family issues at work.

Without some amount of intercultural communication training, these global virtual team members are going to have a difficult time communicating and building trust. Without such trust, the likelihood of the team's performing at an optimal level will be greatly diminished.

Sources: M. Rabotin, "Reading the World," *T + D* 63, no. 2 (February 2009): 40–43; Arvind Malhotra, Ann Majchrzak, and Benson Rosen, "Leading Virtual Teams," *Academy of Management Perspectives* 21, no. 1 (February 2007): 60–70; Jeanne Brett, Kristin Behfar, and Mary C. Kern, "Managing Multicultural Teams," *Harvard Business Review* 84, no. 11 (November 2006); 84–93; Douglas N. Ross, "Electronic Communications: Do Cultural Dimensions Matter?" *American Business Review,* June 2001, pp. 75–81; Lee Gardenswartz and Anita Rowe, "Cross-Cultural Awareness," *HRMagazine,* March 2001, pp. 139–42; Maurice Cleasby, "Managing Global Contact," *The British Journal of Administrative Management* (March/April 2000): 4–12; Sirkka L. Jarvenpaa and Dorothy E. Leidner, "Communication and Trust in Global Virtual Teams," *Organization Science,* (November/December 1999): 791–815; and Edward T. Hall and Mildred R. Hall, *Understanding Cultural Differences: Germans, French, and Americans* (Intercultural Press: Yarmouth, ME; 1987).

Communication pervades organizational activity; it's the process by which things get done in organizations. Every employee is continually involved in and affected by the communication process. For managers, effectively communicating is a critical skill because the manager's planning, organizing, and controlling functions become operationalized only through communicative activity. Because of its importance to organizational effectiveness, we devote a chapter to providing an understanding of the communication process and to the task of understanding how to become a better communicator.

The Importance of Communication

"You said to get it done as soon as I could. How did I know you meant this minute?" "How did I know she was really serious about quitting and going to work for our competitor?" "Why didn't we listen to the customer when he told us to improve our service? Maybe he'd still be with us today." In these and similar situations, someone usually ends up saying or thinking, "What we have here is a failure to communicate." This statement has meaning for everyone because each of us has faced situations in which the basic problem was communication. Whether on a person-to-person or nation-to-nation basis, in organizations, or in small groups, breakdowns in communication are pervasive.

Finding an aspect of a manager's job that does not involve communication would be extremely difficult. Serious problems arise when directives are misunderstood, when casual joking in a work group leads to anger, or when informal remarks by a top-level manager are exaggerated. Each of these situations results from a breakdown somewhere in the process of communication.

Accordingly, the pertinent question is not whether managers engage in communication because communication is inherent to the functioning of an organization. Rather, the real issue is whether managers communicate well or poorly. In other words, communication itself is unavoidable in an organization's functioning, but *ineffective* communication is avoidable. *Every manager must be a communicator.* In fact, everything a manager does communicates something in some way to somebody or some group. The only question is, "With what effect?" While this may appear an overstatement at this point, it will become apparent as you proceed through the chapter.

Despite the tremendous advances in communication and information technology, communication among people in organizations leaves much to be desired.[1] The opening vignette suggested that despite the existence of information technology, global virtual team members must understand themselves and the other members in order to have effective communication among team members. Communication among people depends not on technology but rather on forces in people and their surroundings. It is a *process* that occurs within people. Recognizing the ever-growing importance of communication, more and more organizations are implementing programs designed to assess managerial communication skills and to provide follow-up training to overcome any deficiencies. Managers who have participated in such programs have been found to possess significantly higher interpersonal skills and problem-solving abilities—leading to higher productivity levels—than those who have not.[2] The next OB at Work feature presents some examples of the benefits of effective communication between management and the rest of the organization.

The Communication Process

The general process of communication contains five elements: the communicator, the message, the medium, the receiver, and feedback (Figure 15.1). It can be simply summarized as: Who says what, in which way, to whom, with what effect?[3] To appreciate each element in the process, we must examine how communication works.

Experts tell us that effective communication is the result of a common understanding between the communicator and the receiver. Communication is successful only if the communicator transmits that understanding to the receiver. In fact, the word **communication** is derived from the Latin *communis,* meaning "common"—the communicator seeks to establish a "commonness" with a receiver. Hence, we can define communication as the transmission of information and understanding through the use of common symbols. The common symbols may be verbal or nonverbal. We'll see later that in the context of an organizational structure, information can flow up and down (vertically), across (horizontally), and down and across (diagonally).

communication
Transmitting information and understanding, using verbal or nonverbal symbols.

OB AT WORK Communication Can Make the Difference

It is not surprising that at management meetings and conferences across the country, a common theme usually emerges: Good communication is the common thread that ties people, plans, strategies, and commitment—in other words, the entire organizational fabric—together. In times of rapid change, organizations need fast adaptation to change. Accomplishing this requires high levels of management and employee trust and cooperation. Effective communication can help to foster trust and cooperation. Let's examine some instances where it appears to be happening.

Capital One is trying hard to improve its employees' ability to control incoming e-mail messages. The problem is that employees average 40 to 50 incoming e-mails each day, often with vague subject lines like "Here's what you asked for." Recipients would spend countless hours each month trying to sort through clogged in-boxes and prioritize the e-mail so as to respond to the most important messages first. So, Capital One has put 3,000 employees through a specially designed training program that helps reduce e-mail overload and strain by teaching senders to write better e-mail messages. Descriptive subject lines are used, along with bullet points and concise messages in the body of the text. Capital One is getting a good return on investment in that the company estimates that this training program is saving the equivalent of 11 workdays per employee per year.

At Martin Marietta Government Electronic Systems, a union facility, a method of communicating change within 48 hours has been instituted. This speeded-up information-sharing process has cut plant grievances from 281 per year to just 12. Management believes this improvement happened because everyone knows what is going on at all times. Thus, there are no surprises.

Organizations like GameStop of Grapevine, Texas, are using communication to help employees become aware and take advantage of their company-provided benefits. Benefits often serve as a good recruiting and retention tool for employees. In the spring of 2009, the company launched a new benefits program for all 12,900 eligible full-time employees. Instead of educating employees on the new benefits with printed brochures and meetings, the company reached all but 20 of its full-time employees by using several communication technologies, including e-mails, automated phone messages, and online videos.

Another organization uses open, direct communication to limit the damage that rumors can do throughout the organization. Shaw Supermarkets, a company with 32,000 employees in the northeastern United States, recently started "The Rumor Buster" newsletter that was published on a weekly basis while the company was experiencing a merger. The newsletter addressed rumors that many employees were worried about (e.g., layoffs) by providing accurate and up-to-date information.

One management consultant, Karen Greenbaum, defines organizational communication as consisting of four activities: leading, informing, listening, and involving. She believes that it is in the last two elements—listening and involving—that most organizational communication efforts fall short. She appears to be correct. Note that in the efforts outlined above, each of the organizations is trying to listen to and involve employees.

Sources: Drew Robb, "Get the Benefits Message Out," *HRMagazine*, October 2009, Vol. 54(10), pp. 69–72; Doug Beizer, "Email is Dead . . . ," *Fast Company*, July/August 2007, pp. 46–47; Lin Grensign-Pophal, "Got the Message," *HRMagazine*, April 2001, pp. 74–79; Mike Miller, "Six Elements of Corporate Creativity," *Credit Union Magazine*, April 2000, pp. 20–22; John Beeson, "Succession Planning," *Across the Board*, February 2000, pp. 38–41; Amanda J. S. Kaufman, "Helping to Build Careers," *Infoworld*, July 13, 1998, pp. 99–100; Peter Lilienthal, "Help Management Really Communicate," *Communication World*, February/March 1995, pp. 19–22; and George Taninecz, "Preaching Winning Practices: America's Best Plants Deliver Secrets of Success," *Industry Week*, June 5, 1995, p. 24.

FIGURE 15.1
The Communication Process

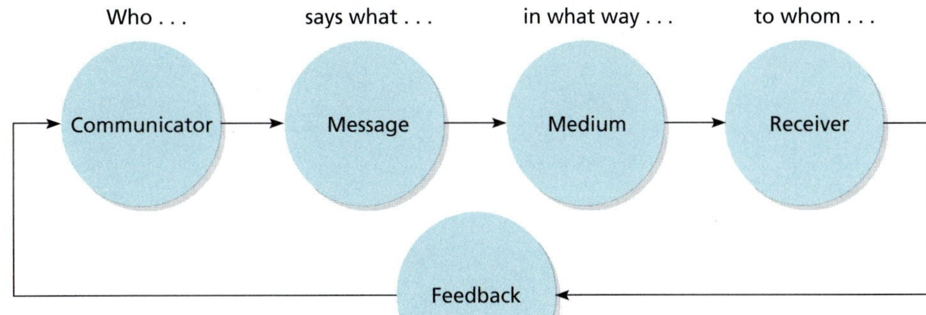

A Classic Model

A widely recognized model of the process of communication has evolved mainly from the early work of Shannon, Weaver, and Schramm.[4] These researchers were concerned with describing the general process of communication in a way that could be useful in all situations. The model that evolved from their work aids our understanding of communication. The basic elements include a communicator, an encoder, a message, a medium, a decoder, a receiver, feedback, and noise (Figure 15.2). Each element in the model can be examined in the context of an organization.

Communicator

In an organizational framework, the communicator is an employee with ideas, intentions, information, and a purpose for communicating. For example, a communicator could be an emergency room nurse who shares an idea with her supervisor on how to decrease the wait time for patients on busy weekend nights. Or, a communicator could be a server at a popular neighborhood restaurant who is planning on asking the supervisor for a pay raise.

Encoding

Given the communicator, an encoding process must take place that translates the communicator's ideas into a systematic set of symbols—into a language expressing the communicator's purpose. The major form of encoding is language. In the restaurant example, the server takes account of his hard work, high customer service scores, number of table turns per hour, and relatively low salary and translates them into one message. The function of encoding, then, is to provide a form in which ideas and purposes can be expressed or packaged as a message.

Message

The result of the encoding process is the message. The purpose of the communicator is expressed in the form of the message—either *verbal* or *nonverbal*. Managers have numerous purposes for communicating, such as to have others understand their ideas, to understand the ideas of others, to gain acceptance of themselves or their ideas, or to produce action.

Not as obvious, however, are *unintended messages* that can be sent by silence or inaction on a particular issue as well as decisions on which goals and objectives not to pursue and which methods not to use. For example, a decision to use one performance evaluation method rather than another may send a message to certain people—an instructor's decision not to give a final exam may send an unintended message to certain students that the course is easy. Or, in the case of the server at the restaurant, the supervisor needs to remain calm and professional after his server asks him for a raise. By acting nervous or agitated, the

FIGURE 15.2 **A Communication Model**

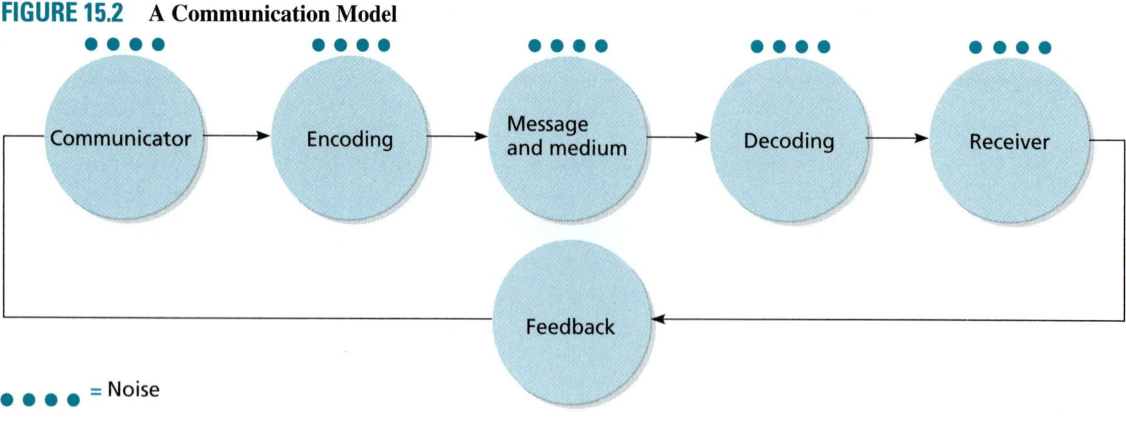

supervisor might send the employee the unintentional message of "I'm busy, don't bother me now," or "You're not worthy of a raise." This is what we meant earlier when we said that everything a manager does communicates.

The message, then, is what the individual hopes to communicate to the intended receiver. The exact form it takes depends to a great extent on the medium used to carry the message. Decisions relating to the two are inseparable.

Medium

The medium is the carrier of the message—the means by which the message is sent. Organizations provide information to members in a variety of ways, including face-to-face communication, telephone conversations, group meetings, texts, e-mails, memos, policy statements, reward systems, production schedules, and video teleconferences. The medium is sometimes a neglected element of the communication process. Often, managers don't adequately consider the impact of the choice of medium on a communication's effectiveness. However, selecting the appropriate medium can have a major impact on communication effectiveness and even managerial performance. In our restaurant example, the server would be wise to deliver his request for a pay raise in a face-to-face meeting. This approach would give the server the ability to react to the supervisor's verbal and nonverbal language, and thus modify the message (i.e., request for a raise) in real time.

Decoding/Receiver

For the process of communication to be completed, the message must be decoded so it's relevant to the receiver. *Decoding,* a technical term for the receiver's thought processes, involves interpretation. Receivers interpret (decode) the message in light of their own previous experiences and frames of reference. Thus, a salesperson will probably decode a memo from the company president differently than a production manager will. A nursing supervisor may decode a memo from the hospital administrator differently than the chief of surgery does. If the restaurant server fits this criterion, then he'll package his message based on his contribution to the success of the restaurant (through excellent customer service or fast table turns) and not argue that he "needs more money" because virtually everyone (including the supervisor) feels they deserve higher compensation for their work. The closer the decoded message comes to the intent desired by the communicator, the more effective is the communication. This underscores the importance of the communicator being "receiver-oriented."

Feedback

One-way communication processes do not allow receiver-to-communicator feedback, increasing the potential for distortion between the intended message and the received message. Provision for feedback in the communication process is desirable.[5] A feedback loop provides a channel for receiver response that enables the communicator to determine whether the message has been received and has produced the intended response. *Two-way* communication processes provide for this important receiver-to-communicator feedback.

For the manager, communication feedback may come in many ways. In face-to-face situations, *direct* feedback through verbal exchanges is possible, as are such subtle means of communication as facial expressions of discontent or misunderstanding. In addition, *indirect* means of feedback (such as declines in productivity, poor production quality, increased absenteeism or turnover, and poor coordination and conflict between units) may indicate communication breakdowns. In the restaurant example, the supervisor may provide the server with direct feedback such as, "Okay, you'll get a five percent raise," or "I can't give you a raise now due to a slump in sales, but I'll reconsider it in six months' time." The supervisor may provide indirect feedback by becoming agitated and upset after the server asks for the pay raise. When this occurs, the server needs to react with his interpersonal skills to try to calm the supervisor and leave on a positive note (e.g., "Let's revisit this when sales are higher in a few months").

Noise

In the framework of human communication, noise can be thought of as all factors that distort the intended message. Noise may occur in each of the elements of communication. For example, a manager under a severe time constraint may be forced to act without communication or may communicate hastily with incomplete information. Or a subordinate may attach a different meaning to a word or phrase than was intended by the manager. In our restaurant example, noise may occur at any point during the exchange. For example, the server may be asking for a pay raise during an especially slow night where sales are down. The supervisor's stress over the low sales numbers that evening may get in the way of his feeling generous and giving a raise to this good employee. Timing is an important part of minimizing noise and being an effective communicator!

The elements discussed in this section are essential for communication to occur. They should not, however, be viewed as separate. They are descriptive of the acts that must be performed for any communication to occur. The communication may be vertical (superior–subordinate, subordinate–superior) or horizontal (peer–peer), or it may involve one individual and a group, but the elements discussed here must be present.

Nonverbal Messages

nonverbal communication
Messages sent with body posture, facial expressions, and hand and eye movements; as important as verbal communication.

The information a communicator sends that is unrelated to the verbal information—that is, nonverbal messages, or **nonverbal communication**—is an area of growing research interest among behavioral scientists.[6] One of the most interesting aspects of nonverbal communication is that it's irrepressibly effective.[7] Try as they might, people cannot refrain from behaving nonverbally. If, for example, a person tries to act as passive as possible, she's likely to be perceived as inexpressive, inhibited, withdrawn, and uptight.

A research study examined the relationship between nonverbal behavior and speaker persuasiveness in a public speaking context.[8] The study suggests that speakers who use practiced and nonspontaneous gestures while delivering a speech will lose the attention of many audience members, ultimately reducing the impact of the speech. Instead, speakers should focus on being open and connecting with the audience, and then observe the audience carefully and use this feedback to modify the speech.[9]

Vocal inflection refers to how a message is transmitted: loudly or softly, quickly or slowly, with controlled or uncontrolled inflection, or with a high or low pitch. The method of transmission adds meaning to the receiver, who assesses these cues. Body expressions are another important source of nonverbal communication. Ekman and Friesen have classified body language into five types of expression: emblems, illustrators, regulators, adaptors, and affect displays.[10]

Emblems are gestures much like sign language (the hitchhiker's thumb, the OK sign with thumb and forefinger, the V sign for victory, and the high-five and closed-fist pump for significant achievement). These movements quickly convey an understood word or phrase. *Illustrators* are gestures that give a picture of what is being said (a raised forefinger to indicate the first point of a sender's position, extended hands to illustrate the size of an object). *Regulators* are movements that regulate a conversation. For example, an upraised palm from the receiver tells a sender to slow down, an arched eyebrow can convey a request for the sender to clarify what has been said, and a nod of the head indicates understanding. Emblems, illustrators, and regulators are consciously used by individuals.

Adaptors and affect displays, on the other hand, are often subconsciously communicated and can reveal much about both the sender's and receiver's feelings and attitudes. *Adaptors* are expressions used to adjust psychologically to the interpersonal climate of a particular situation.[11] Usually learned early in life, adaptors are frequently used to deal with stress in an interpersonal situation. Drumming fingers on a table, tugging a strand of hair, or jiggling a leg or foot are all ways of releasing some degree of stress. *Affect displays,* usually subconscious, directly communicate an individual's emotions. Most affect displays are facial expressions, which are particularly important communicators of a person's feelings. There is a long-held assumption that a person's emotions are mirrored in the face and that these emotions can be "read" with a great deal of accuracy. Affect displays are also expressed in body positions. For example, a "closed posture" (arms folded across the chest, legs crossed) communicates defensiveness and often dislike.

Communicating across Cultures

Culture has been defined as "the collective programming of the mind which distinguishes the members of one human group from another."[12] Stated differently, culture is comprised of the morals, laws, and customs that influence behavior and that is shared by all or almost all members of a social group.[13] When managers from two distant cultures attempt to communicate, misunderstandings can occur (Figure 15.3). For example, when an American says "yeah" to a Japanese person, this message is interpreted as meaning "no" because it sounds like the Japanese word for "no."[14]

Cross-cultural miscommunication can occur for a variety of reasons. Cultural anthropologists Edward T. and Mildred R. Hall theorized that culture is communication and that communication can be divided into several culturally determined parts: words, space, time, and behavior. Within each of these categories, examples of the challenges of communicating across cultures are presented next.[15]

Words

Cultures differ in the amount of contextual information that is necessary when people interact with one another. Individuals from high-context communication cultures do not require a detailed exchange of information, but rather rely on the knowledge they already have about the other individual prior to the interaction. Asian and Latin American cultures tend to fall into this category. In contrast, low-context cultures like in Germany, Australia, and the United States require an explicit, detailed exchange of information when two or more individuals are interacting with one another.[16]

Problems can occur when an individual from a high-context culture must conduct business with a counterpart in a low-context culture. When a Japanese businessman signals to his German counterpart that he is not interested in a particular real estate deal, he will most

FIGURE 15.3
Potential Sources of Cross-cultural Miscommunication

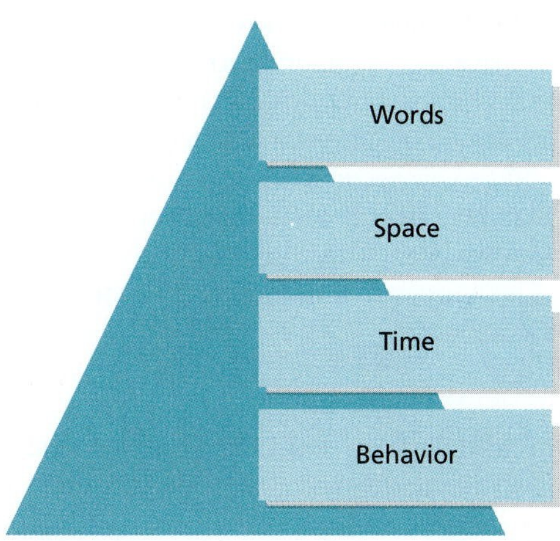

OB AND YOUR CAREER Learning about Different Cultures

Managers can increase their international effectiveness and decrease the risk of cross-cultural misunderstandings by learning as much as possible about the culture and language of the people overseas with which they do business. Below is an initial list of resources to help build cross-cultural knowledge, skills, and networks:

1. *The U.S. Central Intelligence Agency's World Factbook.* This easy-to-use online reference provides information on the history, people, government, economy, geography, communications, transportation, military, and transnational issues for 266 world entities. (See https://www.cia.gov/library/publications/the-world-factbook/.)
2. *Intercultural Press (Nicholas Brealey Publishing Company).* A publisher of books about the principles and practice of cross-cultural communication, Intercultural Press offers resources for living, working, studying, and thriving around the globe. The publisher offers practical and comprehensive guides to international travel and relocation to help individuals develop cultural competency. The company also has a selection of training DVDs, simulations, and activity books that provide resources for trainers and businesspeople and promote cultural awareness and sensitivity. (See http://www.interculturalpress.com/store/pc/home.asp.)
3. *Berlitz.* With over 130 years of experience and 470 offices in 70 countries, Berlitz has an established track record in providing language instruction and cross-cultural training for business and personal enrichment. Private, semiprivate, and group programs are available and total immersion language programs deliver conversational proficiency in as little as two to six weeks' time. (See www.berlitz.com.)
4. *Expatica.com.* A large number of Web sites are available for expatriates and their partners and families. One such resource, Expatica.com, provides local news and information for English-speaking expatriates living in several countries in Europe. Information covers such diverse topics as moving, housing, employment, health and fitness, education, leisure, family and children, and more. (See www.expatica.com.)

likely indicate his disinterest by saying, "This deal will be very difficult" or "I'll have to think about it." The German, interpreting this message as a negotiating tactic to lower the price of the deal, counters with a one-time only offer to lower the asking price by 5 percent. The Japanese, disturbed that his message of "no deal" was not heard, is confused by the behavior of the German.[17] Are employees in multinational organizations also susceptible to cross-cultural misunderstandings? The OB and Your Career above provides a list of suggestions and resources for learning about different cultures. This knowledge will help U.S. managers improve their cross-cultural communication skills and signal to their counterparts in other cultures that they have "done their homework" and learned about their business practices, culture, and language. This in itself can help U.S. managers connect and begin the process of developing trust-based relationships with their international counterparts.

Space

Every person has an invisible boundary of space that surrounds his person. In some cultures (e.g., northern Europe), the boundaries are wide, whereas in other cultures (e.g., Middle Eastern countries), this space can be quite narrow. The amount of personal space maintained by an individual can shift temporarily depending on his physical surroundings (e.g., a crowded elevator) or the degree of intimacy with the person one is interacting with (e.g., spouse). Misunderstandings can occur when a businessman from a culture where men touch and embrace one another as part of normal, everyday life initiates physical contact with his counterpart from a culture where touching between men is rare and only occurs with family members. The latter individual will feel uncomfortable and may misinterpret the intent of the physical contact.[18]

Time

Individuals in Asia, the Middle East, and Latin America tend to view time differently than do most individuals from the United States, Britain, and Germany. Managers from *polychronic* time cultures do many things at once, are subject to interruptions, are committed to human relationships, change plans often, and base promptness on the relationship. However, managers from *monochronic* cultures do one thing at a time, take time commitments seriously, adhere to plans, follow rules of privacy and show respect for private property, and emphasize promptness.[19] The most common example of misunderstandings occurs with regard to appointment times. An American arrives at her Mexican counterpart's office about 10 minutes before their scheduled meeting and discovers that the individual won't be arriving until another hour or so. Infuriated by the lack of respect and casual attitude of the Mexican, she sits and fumes until the meeting takes place. As it turns out, the Mexican businessman bumped into an old friend on the way to the office and could not just rush by him without stopping to say "hello."

Behavior

Reading an individual's body language can be a challenging exercise because it involves subjectively evaluating nonverbal communication. The task becomes more difficult for American employees who work in international environments, where meanings of nonverbal cues often differ strikingly from those back home. Consider, for example, a nod of the head, which means yes in the United States but no in Bulgaria. The OK sign with thumb and forefinger means "money" in France, "worthless" in Japan, and something very obscene in Brazil. Waving, a greeting or farewell in the United States, is a grave insult in Greece and Nigeria.[20]

An interesting study was conducted to determine whether differences existed between how American and Japanese individuals recognized facial expressions.[21] The subjects were 41 American and 44 Japanese college undergraduates. Each group was given 48 posed pictures of six universal emotions (eight each of anger, disgust, fear, happiness, sadness, and surprise) to evaluate. For each emotion, there were two males and two females of both Japanese and American descent pictured.

The study's findings revealed that several differences do indeed exist between the two cultures. First, Americans were more accurate than the Japanese at recognizing four of the six emotions (anger, disgust, fear, and sadness), regardless of the culture or sex of the poser being judged. Second, neither the culture nor sex of the poser affected Americans' judgments of the photos, whereas female emotions were more easily identified than male emotions by the Japanese. Third, both Americans and Japanese agreed that happiness was the easiest emotion to identify and that fear was the hardest.

Communicating within Organizations

Directions of Communication

The design of an organization should provide for communication in four distinct directions: downward, upward, horizontal, and diagonal. These four directions establish the framework within which communication in an organization takes place. Briefly examining each one will enable us to better appreciate the barriers to effective organizational communication and the means to overcome these barriers.

downward communication
Communication that flows from higher to lower levels in an organization; includes management policies, instructions, and official memos.

Downward communication flows from individuals in higher levels of the hierarchy to those in lower levels. The most common forms of downward communication are group or mass distributed e-mails, job instructions, official memos, policy statements, procedures, manuals, and company publications. In many organizations, downward communication often is both inadequate and inaccurate, as reflected in the often-heard statement among organization members that "we have absolutely no idea what's happening." Such complaints indicate inadequate downward communication and individuals' needs for information relevant to their jobs. Absence of job-related information can create unnecessary stress among organization members.[22] A similar situation is faced by a student who hasn't been told an instructor's requirements and expectations.

Many times, the theme of the narrative portion of downward communication is a direct consequence of corporate communication decisions. A study evaluated the message content in the president's letter to stockholders, which is contained in most organizations' annual reports.[23] The purpose of the study was to determine if differences existed between high-performing and low-performing organizations in terms of the themes in presidents' letters. Results of the study indicate that within annual reports, poorly performing firms tend to dwell more on future opportunities than on past financial performance while the opposite is true for the more successful organizations. A recent research study was conducted on the annual report letters written by CEOs of 30 U.S.-based firms and 24 Latin American-based companies listed on the New York Stock Exchange. The researchers found that although there were many similarities between the letters, the Latin American letters were "characterized by a richer mix of topics, a more complex writing style, and evidence of cultural dimensions" that differentiate U.S. and Latin American cultures.[24]

upward communication
Communication flowing from lower to higher levels in an organization; includes suggestion boxes, group meetings, and grievance procedures.

An effective organization needs **upward communication** as much as it needs downward communication. Indeed, research studies have found that, in organizations where upward communication programs were effectively implemented, a majority of managers improved their performance.[25] However, achieving effective upward communication—getting open and honest feedback from employees to management—is an especially difficult task, particularly in larger organizations.[26] Some studies suggest that of the four formal communication channels, upward communication is the most ineffective. Upper-level managers often don't respond to messages sent from lower-level employees, and lower-level employees often are reluctant to communicate upward, especially if the message contains bad news.[27] However, upward communication is often necessary for sound decision making.

Some of the most common upward communication devices are suggestion boxes, group meetings, and appeal or grievance procedures. In their absence, people somehow find ways to adapt to nonexistent or inadequate upward communication channels. One such strategy is the emergence of "underground" employee publications in many large organizations.[28] Other strategies include sending anonymous e-mails, creating unauthorized Web sites, and airing grievances in chatrooms and bulletin boards.

Varying forms of upward communication play a key role in the successful operation of many Japanese businesses.[29] The Japanese place a strong emphasis on face-to-face communication between top-level managers and rank-and-file employees. For example, in companies such as Sony and Toyota, it is common practice for nonmanagerial levels to talk directly to top-level executives on work-related matters. Often, top-level managers participate in orientation and training programs to enable employees to access them. In addition, there are frequently both formal and informal mechanisms to actively solicit suggestions from employees, with rewards given for implemented ideas.

horizontal communication
Communication that flows across functions in an organization; necessary for coordinating and integrating diverse organizational functions.

Often overlooked in the design of organizations is the provision for **horizontal communication**. In a college of business administration, when the chairperson of the accounting department communicates with the chairperson of the marketing department concerning the course offerings, the flow of communication is horizontal. Although vertical (upward and downward) communication flows are the primary considerations in organizational design, effective organizations also need horizontal communication. Horizontal communication—for example, communication between production and sales in a business organization and among the different departments or colleges within a university—is necessary for the coordination and integration of diverse organizational functions. A recent research study found that hospital employees who engage in horizontal communication are likely to identify strongly with their profession, while those employees who communicate vertically are more likely to identify with the organization.[30]

Because mechanisms for ensuring horizontal communication ordinarily do not exist in an organization's design, its facilitation is left to individual managers. Peer-to-peer communication is often necessary for coordination and can also provide social need satisfaction. **Diagonal communication**, while probably the least used channel of communication in organizations, is important in situations where members cannot communicate effectively through other channels. For example, the comptroller of a large organization may wish to conduct a distribution cost analysis. One part of that task may involve having the sales force send a special report directly to the comptroller rather than going through traditional channels in the marketing department. Thus, the flow of communication would be diagonal as opposed to vertical (upward) and horizontal. In this case, a diagonal channel is most efficient in terms of time and effort for the organization.

diagonal communication
Communication that cuts across functions and levels in an organization; important when members cannot communicate through upward, downward, or horizontal channels.

Communication and Technology

Within recent years, several high-tech innovations have contributed to an explosion of communication tools, which has led to a "24/7" mentality among businesspeople today. In general, such innovations as smart phones have made communication faster, easier, and in some cases less expensive. Now an employee can download a video of a company commercial, get directions to a client's office, look at a spreadsheet of travel expenses, take a photo and e-mail an interesting promotional poster, or download a PDF file while waiting for a coffee at a Starbucks via a wireless Internet connection. A review of some of these major innovations in communication technology is presented next.

Internet/Intranet/Extranet

The Internet has become an important part of daily life for millions of people throughout many parts of the world. The Internet is an organization of computer networks connecting everything from large supercomputers at government agencies to mainframes and servers at businesses to PCs at individuals' homes.[31] The Internet allows users to shop on Amazon, find local service providers on Craigslist, download music from iTunes, update personal status on social networking Web sites like Facebook and MySpace, send "tweets" on Twitter, or conduct research for a paper via a library portal. As of December 2009, Internet users in the United States have been estimated at over 234 million (or 76.3 percent) of the population.[32] Some estimates suggest that worldwide Internet usage has grown from 361 million in 2000 to approximately 1.8 billion (or 26.6 percent) of the world population as of December 2009.[33]

The term "Internet" is used to cover many services and information technologies. The World Wide Web is the service that currently has the most applicable communication protocols and technology for business on the Internet. Internet services include electronic mail (e-mail), instant message, intranets, extranets, newsgroups, and chat rooms. The Web brings graphics, interaction, and hyperlinking capabilities to the Internet and allows for multimedia content such as voice and video.

An **intranet** is a private, protected electronic communication system within an organization. If it is connected to the Internet, it has its privacy protected by what are called firewalls. A firewall is a network mode set up internally to prevent external traffic from crossing into the private domain. Intranets are used to communicate such things as proprietary organizational information, company plans, confidential medical records, training programs, compensation data, and company records.

intranet
A private Internet-based network developed and maintained by a particular organization; intranets allow certain stakeholders to gain access to internal organizational information.

An example on an intranet is how American Airlines uses the employee portal "Jetnet" to automate employee travel reservations (employees travel for free) and enrollment in benefits. The use of this intranet has saved the company approximately $3 million per year.[34]

extranet
A private protected electronic communication system that is designed to connect employees with individuals external to the organization such as vendors, customers, or other strategic partners.

An **extranet** is designed to connect employees with individuals external to the organization, such as vendors, customers, and other strategic partners. At Campbell Soup Company, extranet portals are being developed to get retailers and consumers more involved in new product development.[35] At chocolate manufacturer Hershey, IT employees recently built an extranet that will allow customers and retailers to check the status of their orders online.[36]

Electronic Mail, Messaging, Social Networking, and Blogs

The use of e-mail will continue to expand rapidly in the coming years. For example, some estimates indicate the number of e-mail users globally will increase from 1.2 billion in 2007 to 1.6 billion in 2011.[37] In the past, some e-mail users sent out unedited, poorly written messages on the fly. This type of sloppiness has been criticized and is discouraged in organizations. The privacy of e-mail is another serious issue. Supervisors, colleagues, and others can access e-mail messages. Consequently, care must be exercised in properly using e-mails as a communication approach.

The permanency of e-mail messages is another issue that astute users of e-mail communications have learned to consider. Erased messages can remain on disk drives, servers, and social networking sites indefinitely. In the wake of the Enron case, e-mail storage and recordkeeping have become important issues for many companies. For example, federal regulators fined five Wall Street firms a total of $8.25 million for failing to adequately maintain copies of e-mail files that adhere to recordkeeping standards.[38]

A recent survey was conducted by the American Management Association to determine the extent to which companies monitor employees' e-mail, Internet, and phone usage.[39] Results from the survey suggest that nearly one-third of those companies polled had fired workers for improper use of the Internet and one-quarter of responding firms fired employees for misusing e-mail.[40] These are important findings when considering that nearly three-quarters of major U.S. companies are now recording and reviewing employees' communications, including e-mail, telephone calls, and Internet connections. For example, Chevron and Microsoft both settled sexual harassment lawsuits for $2.2 million apiece as a result of internally circulated e-mails that could have created hostile work environments.[41]

E-mail is an effective way of communicating simple messages. Complex data and information should probably be sent in hard copy documents. Think simple. Secure your e-mails. Always use correct and professional language in preparing and sending e-mails.

In addition to e-mail, the growth of instant messaging (IM) has also been explosive within recent years. This has been fueled by free consumer services such as AOL Instant Messenger, Microsoft's MSN Messenger, Google's Talk, Yahoo! Messenger, and Skype. Now, an increasing number of organizations are installing internal IM systems such as IBM's Lotus SameTime software.[42] Corporate use of IM is expected to grow rapidly because IM offers real-time communication among geographically dispersed employees; it is an inexpensive alternative to multiple telephone calls and travel; it creates a document trail for future reference; it offers integration with voice and video; and it demands the immediate attention of its users.[43]

Driven by the increased need to conduct business from anywhere at any time, text messaging from cell phones is also gaining in popularity.[44] Given that most employees, customers, and vendors have cell phones in the United States, many companies are exploring ways to use text messaging to connect with potential customers, increase sales, and enhance customer satisfaction.[45] For example, *American Idol,* ESPN, and Disney encourage viewers to get involved with their televised programs by texting votes and messages to the show. CNN asks viewers to text in questions and opinions about current events.

Texting to reach customers has many advantages compared with the more traditional methods such as TV, radio, newspapers, magazines, or direct mail, including:[46]

- Texting is less expensive than many other forms of advertising and marketing.
- There's less spam because cell phone companies block most of it.
- Texting is the favorite form of communication among young consumers, making them an attractive target market.
- People read 95 percent of text messages because they are generally from known sources and friends.

Another way in which technology is transforming communication is with the explosion in popularity of social networking sites such as Facebook, MySpace, and LinkedIn. Serving a variety of human and business needs, social networking sites are rapidly becoming part of the communication fabric of organizations. Although conventional wisdom suggests these sites are the exclusive domain of teenagers and 20-somethings, this new era of social networking is reaching far and wide. The social networking and microblogging Web site Twitter has been creating a buzz in many circles. For example, the U.S. Department of State, realizing that people were using Twitter to broadcast images of the protests against Iran's election results in 2009, asked the company to delay maintenance to keep the tweets flowing.[47] This was significant given the Iranian government's attempt to censor more traditional news outlets and reporters. An article in *Businessweek* featured the former CEO of General Electric, Jack Welch, and his spouse discussing how the pair "tweets" on a daily basis and sees Twitter as "a high-value way for companies to help brand themselves and microtarget consumer groups, as well as another tool for managers to interact with their people, and vice versa."[48]

Individuals, groups, and organizations use social networking sites and blogs for a variety of purposes. Current or former employees use these Web sites to discuss a company's policy or vent about an unpopular supervisor. A group of customers excited about a new product (e.g., the release of Apple's iPad) could create such a buzz around the launch of that product that its sales get a boost. Accenture has developed its own social networking program called "Performance Multiplier" to enable employees to post updates, photos, and weekly goals related to their performance. The program aims for employees to receive and use informal feedback from managers and employees so that they can improve their performance.[49]

Risks are associated with the oft informal and boundaryless world of social networking sites. For example, Virgin Atlantic fired a cabin crew for complaining on the Internet (while they were off duty) about passengers and making jokes about faulty jet engines.[50] Employers are establishing guidelines to prevent public disclosures that could hurt an organization's reputation or create a social networking scandal.[51] General Electric has set up an internal "Tweet Squad" consisting of young hipster employees who help older employees and managers refine their social networking skills. Also, IBM has established the following guidelines to help its employees understand what they can and cannot say on blogs and social networking sites:[52]

- Employees are personally responsible for all content that is published online.
- What is published might become public for a long time. Keep this in mind.
- Employees should be transparent about their role at IBM in all posts.
- Employees should get permission before reporting on internal or private conversations.
- When necessary, employees should promptly correct mistakes and edit previous posts.

Social networking sites have given individuals a powerful communication tool; once information is posted, it can be accessed within seconds from any Web-enabled smart phone or PC around the globe. E-mail and instant/text messaging are also powerful Internet-based communication tools. Some observers are concerned that employees are becoming overly distracted by frequently stopping their work to check their voice-mail; respond to e-mail, text messages, and tweets; check out the latest videos on YouTube; and update their Facebook or MySpace page. Basex, a New York City-based business research company, estimated, "These distractions consume as much as 28 percent of the average U.S. worker's day . . . and sap productivity to the tune of $650 billion a year."[53] Given the high stakes associated with these technology-based forms of communication, managers and employees will continue to explore and exploit them for the foreseeable future.

Smart Phones

Smart phones will continue to gain in popularity as businesspeople attempt to stay connected at virtually all times. According to market reports, approximately 91 percent or 285 million Americans had cell phone subscriptions in 2009.[54] The success of the mobile phone is being challenged by the "smart phone," such as Motorola's Android, Apple's iPhone, and Research in Motion's BlackBerry, which enables businesspeople to access e-mail, text messages, and videos; download software applications ("apps"); and browse the Internet while they go from city to city. Smart phones allow them to store addresses, phone numbers, customer prices, and other data critical to day-to-day functioning.[55] Such growth reflects the need for managers to stay organized and connected with colleagues, customers, and other important stakeholders from virtually anywhere anytime. Research from Gartner suggests that 139 million people used smart phones worldwide in 2008, and this number increased to 295 million in 2010.[56] Given such a growing market, companies such as Apple, Google, Motorola, Samsung, Nokia, Verizon, Palm, and Microsoft are all competing to take as much market share as possible.

Voice-Mail

Voice-mail, or leaving a recorded message, is the primary method by which employees communicate internally. It accounts for approximately 90 percent of telephone communication within organizations today. Voice-mail, more popular than e-mail, serves many functions, but one of the most important is message storage. Incoming messages are delivered without interrupting receivers and allow communicators to focus on the reason for their call. Voice-mail minimizes inaccurate message taking and differences in time zones. Employees today are encouraged to develop the ability to leave concise, professional, and courteous voice-mail messages. Best practices include the following:[57]

- Organize your thoughts before picking up the telephone.
- Identify a specific, brief request that can be delivered via voice-mail.
- State your name, the time and date, your company name, and purpose of your call.
- Be precise and keep the message simple.
- Say what you would like the receiver to do.
- Give a reason for the request.
- Say "thank you."
- Finish with, "Feel free to call me at the following number. . . ."

Videoconferencing, Teleconferencing, and e-Meetings/Collaboration

Videoconferencing refers to technologies associated with viewing, and teleconferencing refers to technologies primarily associated with speaking. Often the terms are used interchangeably. Both technologies enable individuals to conduct meetings without getting together face-to-face.

These technologies enable participants to interact at the same time even when they are dispersed around the globe. Videoconferencing, in particular, is being used by an increasing number of companies as they attempt to increase productivity and lower travel costs.

For example, W. R. Grace & Company, a $2 billion specialty chemical manufacturer, holds between 40 and 60 videoconferences per month. The firm's $200,000 investment in videoconferencing equipment paid for itself within two months in travel savings.[58]

Another form of conferencing is Webconferencing (or "webinars") in which the Internet is used to conduct real-time e-meetings or presentations of geographically dispersed participants. Participants connect to the Webconference via a personal computer or other Internet-enabled device. In addition to presentations, Webconferencing and online collaboration software allow voice, video, instant messaging, document sharing, and presentations among participants.[59] These capabilities help facilitate on-line collaboration on projects and other work assignments. Several companies including Citrix Systems' "GoToMeeting" and Microsoft's "Office Live Meeting Service" offer online collaboration services.[60]

Electronic meeting software (EMS), or meetingware, uses networked computers to automate meetings. A large screen at the front of the room is the focal point. The screen serves as an electronic flip chart displaying comments, ideas, and responses of participants. Meetingware allows facilitators to poll meeting participants, analyze voting results, and create detailed reports.

Meetingware is helpful when large groups must reach decisions quickly. Instead of one by one, meeting participants can simultaneously provide a vote, an opinion, or an idea. At Hewlett-Packard, meetingware has accelerated new product development by 30 percent.[61] Structured electronic meetings are 20 to 30 percent shorter than face-to-face meetings.

Advancements in information technologies are continuing and are providing organizational members with additional ways to communicate. Technology, however, will not solve all communication problems. Overloading employees with new "toys," additional information, and technologies to learn can result in more distraction and less efficiency. Also, a certain amount of social interaction and personal touch can be lost by relying solely on electronic technologies for communication. Electronic communication omits many verbal and most nonverbal cues that people use to acquire feedback. Guarding against anonymity and depersonalization are concerns when using many of the information technologies such as e-mail, videoconferencing, and electronic meetings.

information richness
Refers to the amount of information that can be transmitted in an effective manner.

There are many different ways to communicate within an organization, to supervisors and co-workers, and externally, to customers and vendors. Communication media differ in their **information richness**. The richness of communication refers to the amount of information that can be transmitted in an effective manner.[62] A medium that enables high richness, such as a face-to-face interaction, is more likely to result in common understanding between individuals or a group when compared with a low-in-richness medium, such as a generalized e-mail to all employees.

The Grapevine: An Informal Communication Channel

The grapevine is a powerful means of communication that cuts across formal channels of communication. Despite the efforts of many companies to limit or disapprove of the grapevine's use, it is still extremely prevalent.[63] Although the nature of its effect on organizational effectiveness is debatable, there's no denying that its effect is real. Many if not most of an organization's employees listen to the assortment of facts, opinions, suspicions, and rumors the grapevine provides. This is information that normally does not travel through the organization's formal channels. According to research, an organization has several grapevine systems, information traveling in a grapevine does not follow an orderly path, and the grapevine is at least 75 percent accurate.[64]

Managers must recognize that a grapevine that serves as a constant source of rumors can be troublesome. Rumors are an everyday part of business and management. In fact, an estimated 33 million-plus rumors are generated in U.S. businesses every day.[65] The best that managers can hope for is that they can manage rumors—keeping them from disrupting organizational activities—rather than eliminate them.[66] A rumor is an unverified belief that is in general circulation inside the organization (an internal rumor) or in the organization's external environment (an external rumor).[67] A rumor has three components: the *target* is the object of the rumor; the *allegation* is the rumor's point about the target; and the *source* is the original communicator of the rumor. Often, individuals will attribute a rumor to a prestigious or authoritative source to give the rumor more credibility.[68]

Some grapevine rumors are true; some are not. Rumors can be divided into four categories.[69]

1. *Pipe dreams or wish fulfillment.* These express the wishes and hopes of those who circulate rumors. These are the most positive rumors, helping to stimulate the creativity of others. Often solutions to work problems are a result of employees verbally expressing desire for change. These improvements sometimes increase efficiency for certain departments within the organization. Even though the tone is positive, they still represent employee concerns.

2. *The Bogie rumor.* This type of rumor comes from employees' fears and anxieties, causing general uneasiness among employees, such as during budget crunches. In this case, employees verbally express their fears to others. These rumors are sometimes damaging (such as a rumor about possible layoffs) and need a formal rebuttal from management.

3. *Wedge drivers.* This is the most aggressive and damaging type of rumor. It divides groups and destroys loyalties. These rumors are motivated by aggression or even hatred. They are divisive and negative rumors. They tend to be demeaning to a company or individual and can cause damage to the reputation of others. A wedge driver rumor may be a tale such as "Louise, the office manager, was seen the other day alone with that new accountant. They were in a car together leaving Motel Six." Or someone may spread the word that "Mary got the promotion because she's sleeping with the boss." Women are more likely to be attacked with the sexual type of rumor.

4. *Home-stretchers.* These are anticipatory rumors. They occur after employees have been waiting a long time for an announcement. There may be just one final thing necessary to complete the puzzle and this, in effect, enhances the ambiguity of the situation.

Grapevines, rumors, and gossip are deeply ingrained in organizational life, so managers must be tuned in to what's being said. Managers must also seek to keep employees informed about what's going on.[70] A formal company newsletter can help. Falsified facts traveling through the rumor mill can be corrected by managers acting promptly, feeding accurate information to primary communicators or liaison individuals. Rumors are more difficult to correct over time because they "harden"—the details become consistent and the information becomes publicly accepted. Informal communications systems, such as the grapevine itself, can provide yet another, albeit weak, communication vehicle to keep the workforce informed about job-related matters. Finally, the organization can conduct training programs for employees on the disruptive nature of damaging rumors.

Interpersonal Communication

interpersonal communication Communications that flow between individuals in face-to-face and group situations.

Within an organization, communication flows from individual to individual in face-to-face and group settings. Such flows, termed **interpersonal communication**, can vary from direct orders to casual expressions. Interpersonal communication is the primary means of managerial communication; on a typical day, over three-fourths of a manager's communications occur in face-to-face interactions.[71] In recent years, managerial supervision has become more challenging given that organizations have become flatter and as a result, managers have more subordinates to oversee.[72]

The problems that arise when managers attempt to communicate with other people can be traced to *perceptual differences* and *interpersonal style differences*. We know that each manager perceives the world according to his background, experiences, personality, frame of reference, and attitude. Managers relate to and learn from the environment (including the people in that environment) primarily through information received and transmitted. And how managers receive and transmit information depends in part on how they relate to two very important *senders* of information: *themselves* and *others*.

Interpersonal Styles

interpersonal style Manner in which we relate to other persons.

Interpersonal style refers to *how an individual prefers to relate to others*. The fact that much of any interpersonal relationship involves communication indicates the importance of interpersonal style.

Let's begin by recognizing that information is held by ourselves and by others but that no one of us fully has or knows that information. The different combinations of knowing and not knowing relevant information are shown in Figure 15.4. The figure, popularly known as the Johari Window, identifies four combinations, or regions, of information known and unknown by the self and others.[73]

1. *The arena*. The region most conducive to effective interpersonal relationships and communication is termed the *arena*. In this setting, both the communicator (self) and the receivers (others) know all of the information necessary to carry on effective communication. For a communication attempt to be in the arena region, the parties involved must share identical feelings, data, assumptions, and skills. Because the arena is the area of common understanding, the larger it becomes, the more effective communication is.

2. *The blind spot*. When relevant information is known to others but not to the self, a *blind spot* results. This constitutes a handicap for the self, since one can hardly understand the behaviors, decisions, and potentials of others without having the information on which these are based. Others have the advantage of knowing their own reactions, feelings, perceptions, and so forth, while the self is unaware of these. Consequently, interpersonal relationships and communications suffer.

3. *The facade*. When information is known to the self but unknown to others, a person (self) may resort to superficial communications—that is, present a "false front," or facade. Information that we perceive as potentially prejudicial to a relationship or that we keep to ourselves out of fear, desire for power, or whatever, makes up the *facade*. This protective front, in turn, serves a defensive function for the self. Such a situation is particularly

FIGURE 15.4
The Johari Window: Interpersonal Styles and Communication

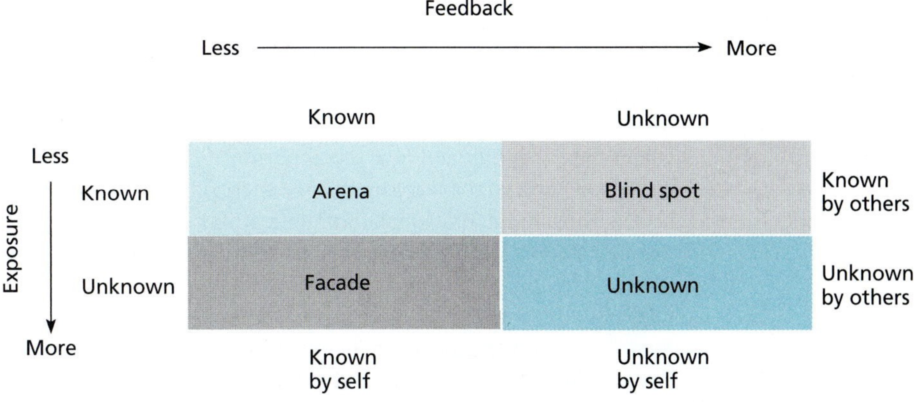

damaging when a subordinate "knows" and an immediate supervisor "does not know." The facade, like the blind spot, diminishes the arena and reduces the possibility of effective communication.

4. *The unknown*. This region constitutes that portion of the relationship where relevant information is known by neither the self nor other parties. As is often stated, "I don't understand them, and they don't understand me." It is easy to see that interpersonal communication is poor under such circumstances. Circumstances of this kind often occur in organizations when individuals in different specialties must communicate to coordinate what they do.

Interpersonal Strategies

An individual can improve interpersonal communication by using two strategies: exposure and feedback.

1. *Exposure*. Increasing the arena area by reducing the facade area requires that the individual be open and honest in sharing information with others. The process that the self uses to increase the information known to others is termed *exposure* because it sometimes leaves the self in a vulnerable position. Exposing one's true feelings by "telling it like it is" often involves risk.

2. *Feedback*. When the self doesn't know or understand, more effective communication can be developed through feedback from those who do know. Thus, the blind spot can be reduced with a corresponding increase in the arena. Of course, whether feedback can be used depends on the individual's willingness to hear it and on the willingness of others to give it. Thus, the individual has less control over the provision of feedback than over the provision of exposure. Obtaining feedback is dependent on the active cooperation of others, while exposure requires the active behavior of the communicator and the passive listening of others.

Managerial Styles

The day-to-day activities of managers are closely tied to effective interpersonal communications. Managers provide *information* (which must be *understood*), they give *commands* and *instructions* (which must be *obeyed* and *learned*), and they make *efforts to influence* and *persuade* (which must be *accepted* and *acted on*). Thus, how managers communicate, both as senders and receivers, is crucial to effective performance.

Theoretically, managers who desire to communicate effectively can use both exposure and feedback to enlarge the area of common understanding, the arena. As a practical matter, such is not the case. Managers differ in their ability and willingness to use exposure and feedback. At least four different managerial styles can be identified.

Type A

Type A
Managers who are autocratic leaders, typically aloof and cold; often poor interpersonal communicators.

Managers who use neither exposure nor feedback are said to have a **Type A** style. The unknown region predominates in this style because such managers are unwilling to enlarge the area of their own knowledge or the knowledge of others. Type A managers exhibit anxiety and hostility and give the appearance of aloofness and coldness toward others. In an organization with a large number of such managers in key positions, expect to find poor and ineffective interpersonal communications and a loss of individual creativity. Type A managers often display characteristics of autocratic leaders.

Type B

Some managers desire some degree of satisfying relationships with their subordinates. Because of their personalities and attitudes, however, these managers are unable to open up and express their feelings and sentiments. Because they cannot use exposure, they must rely on feedback. The facade is the predominant feature of interpersonal relationships when managers overuse feedback to the exclusion of exposure. Subordinates probably distrust such managers, realizing these managers are holding back their own ideas and opinions. **Type B** behavior is often displayed by managers who desire to practice some form of permissive leadership.

Type B
Managers who seek good relationships with subordinates but are unable to openly express feelings; often ineffective interpersonal communicators.

Type C

Managers who value their own ideas and opinions but not the ideas and opinions of others use exposure at the expense of feedback. The consequence of this style is the perpetuation and enlargement of the blind spot. Subordinates soon realize that such managers are not particularly interested in communicating, only in telling, and are mainly interested in maintaining their own sense of importance and prestige. Consequently, **Type C** managers usually have subordinates who are hostile, insecure, and resentful.

Type C
Managers interested only in their own ideas, not ideas and opinions of others; usually not effective communicators.

Type D

The most effective interpersonal communication style balances exposure and feedback. Managers who are secure in their positions feel free to expose their own feelings and to obtain feedback from others. To the extent that a manager practices **Type D** behavior successfully, the arena region becomes larger, and communication becomes more effective.

Type D
Managers who feel free to express feelings to others and to have others express feelings; most effective interpersonal communicators.

To summarize, the importance of interpersonal styles in determining the effectiveness of interpersonal communication cannot be overemphasized. The primary determinant of effectiveness of interpersonal communication is the manager's attitude toward exposure and feedback. The most effective approach is that of the Type D manager. Type A, B, and C managers resort to behaviors that are detrimental to the effectiveness of communication and to organizational performance.

Barriers to Effective Communication

A manager has no greater responsibility than to develop effective communication.[74] Why then does communication break down? On the surface, the answer is relatively easy. We have identified the elements of communication as the communicator, the encoding, the message, the medium, the decoding, the receiver, and the feedback. If noise exists in these elements *in any way,* complete clarity of meaning and understanding does not occur. In this section, we discuss the following barriers to effective communications and how these barriers vary by sender and receiver: frame of reference, selective listening, value judgments, source credibility, semantic problems, filtering, in-group language, status differences, proxemic behavior, time pressures, and communication overload (see Figure 15.5). These sources of noise can exist in both organizational and interpersonal communications.

Barriers Created by the Sender

There are five specific barriers created by senders of communication.

Semantic Problems

Communication has been defined as the transmission of *information* and *understanding* through the use of *common symbols*. Actually, we cannot transmit understanding. We can merely transmit information in the form of words, which are the common symbols. Unfortunately, the same words may mean entirely different things to different people. The understanding is in the receiver, not in the words.

FIGURE 15.5
Barriers to Effective Communication by Sender and Receiver

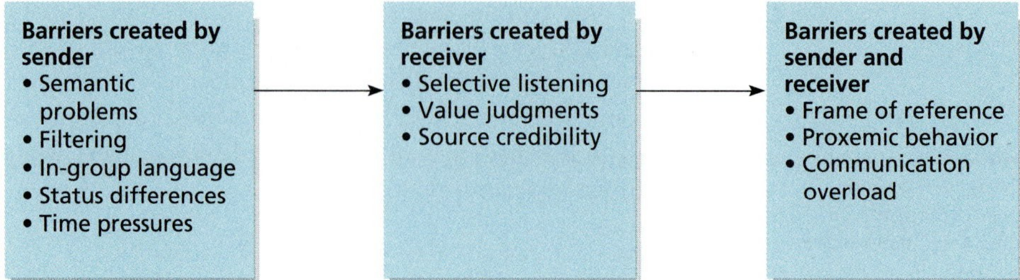

Because different groups use words differently, communication can often be impeded. This is especially true with abstract or technical terms or phrases. "Cost–benefit study" would have meaning to those involved in the administration of the hospital but might mean very little to some staff physicians. In fact, it might even carry a negative meaning. Such concepts as *trusts, profits,* and *Treasury bills* may have concrete meaning to bank executives but little or no meaning to bank tellers. Thus, because words mean different things to different people, a communicator may speak the same language as a receiver but still not achieve the intended goal of the communication.

Filtering

Filtering, a common occurrence in upward communication in organizations, refers to the manipulation of information so that the receiver perceives it as positive. For example, subordinates "cover up" unfavorable information in messages to their superiors. The reason for such filtering should be clear; this is the direction (upward) that carries control information to management. Management makes merit evaluations, grants salary increases, and promotes individuals based on what it receives by way of the upward channel. The temptation to filter is likely to be strong at every level in the organization.

In-Group Language

Each of us at some time has undoubtedly been subjected to highly technical jargon, only to learn that the unfamiliar words or phrases described simple procedures or familiar objects. For example, students may be asked by researchers to "complete an instrument as part of an experimental treatment." The student soon learns that this involves nothing more than filling out a paper-and-pencil questionnaire.

Occupational, professional, and social groups often develop words or phrases that have meaning only to members. Such special language can serve many useful purposes. It can provide members with feelings of belonging, cohesiveness, and (in many cases) self-esteem; it can also facilitate effective communication *within* the group. The use of in-group language can, however, result in severe communication breakdowns when outsiders or other groups are involved. Management, in this case, should provide communication skills training to affected individuals to facilitate effective communication between involved parties.[75]

Status Differences

Organizations often express hierarchical rank through a variety of symbols (titles, offices, carpets, etc.). Such status differences can be perceived as threats by persons lower in the hierarchy, and this can prevent or distort communication. For example, not wanting to look incompetent, a nurse may remain quiet instead of expressing an opinion or asking a question of the nursing supervisor.

In an effort to use their time efficiently, managers often make status barriers more difficult to surmount. The government administrator or bank vice president may be accessible only by appointment or by passing the careful quizzing of a secretary. This widens the communication gap between superiors and subordinates.

Isolation from accurate feedback is particularly pervasive at top levels of an organization. An executive of a company of 20,000 employees may have direct relationships with only 10 or 15 individuals. The personality of the highly successful executive may discourage honest feedback: An executive demeanor of total confidence and command doesn't easily invite criticism from subordinates; a low level of resiliency or "thin skin" when it comes to negative feedback and an abrasive style with subordinates have the same effect.[76]

Upper-level executives also often take on an exaggerated importance. For example, one executive once casually wondered aloud how a proposed law would affect the company, knowing that the bill stood little chance of being passed. Later, he discovered that his subordinates had responded to the casual remark with a thorough, costly—and ultimately useless—analysis of the bill's effect. From then on, the executive was cautious with his comments.[77]

Some organizations are deemphasizing status and power differences to encourage more open supervisor–subordinate communication. Others are actively encouraging employees to ask questions not only about objective facts but also about the reasons and motives behind those facts.[78] At Honda Motors in Marysville, Ohio, for example, visible differences in status and power have been intentionally avoided. The plant has no executive cafeteria or washroom and no special parking spaces, and executives work in open offices with no frills. Management believes that these actions reduce communication barriers between managers of all levels and their subordinates. The Honda Philosophy expresses this concept: "In order for the associates' best work to come forward, they must feel valued and comfortable speaking up and interacting with their work groups. That's where respect comes in. Only in an atmosphere of maximized respect and inclusion can a workforce reach its highest levels of achievement."[79]

Time Pressures

The pressure of time presents an important barrier to communication. Managers don't have time to communicate frequently with every subordinate. However, time pressures can often lead to far more serious problems than this. *Short-circuiting* is a failure of the formally prescribed communication system that often results from time pressures. What it means is simply that someone has been left out of the formal channel of communication who would normally be included. For example, suppose a salesperson needs a rush order for an important customer and goes directly to the production manager with the request, since the production manager owes the salesperson a favor. Other members of the sales force who get word of this become upset over this preferential treatment and report it to the sales manager. Obviously, the sales manager would know nothing of the "deal" having been short-circuited.

In some cases, going through formal channels is extremely costly or even impossible from a practical standpoint. Consider the impact on a hospital patient if a nurse had to report a critical malfunction in life support equipment to the nursing team leader, who in turn had to report it to the hospital engineer, who would instruct a staff engineer to make the repair.

Barriers Created by the Receiver

In some situations barriers are created by receivers.

Selective Listening

In this form of selective perception, the individual tends to block out new information, especially if it conflicts with existing beliefs. Thus, in a directive from management, the receiver notices only things that reaffirm his beliefs. Things that conflict with preconceived notions are either ignored or distorted to confirm those preconceptions.

For example, a notice may be sent to all operating departments that costs must be reduced if the organization is to earn a profit. The communication may not achieve its desired effect because it conflicts with the perceived "reality" of the receivers. Thus, operating employees may ignore or be amused by such information in light of the large salaries, travel allowances, and expense accounts of some executives. Whether such preconceptions are justified is irrelevant; what's important is that they result in breakdowns in communication. In other words, if we only hear what we want to hear, our "reality" can't be disturbed.

Value Judgments

In every communication situation, the receiver makes value judgments. This basically involves assigning an overall worth to a message prior to receiving the entire communication. Value judgments may be based on the receiver's evaluation of the communicator, previous experiences with the communicator, or on the message's anticipated meaning. For example, a college professor, perceiving the department chairperson as not being concerned enough about teaching quality, may consider a merit evaluation meeting with the chairperson as "going through the motions." A cohesive work group may form negative value judgments concerning all actions by management.

Source Credibility

Source credibility is the trust, confidence, and faith that the receiver has in the words and actions of the communicator. The level of credibility that the receiver assigns to the communicator in turn directly affects how the receiver views and reacts to the communicator's words, ideas, and actions. Thus, subordinates' evaluation of their manager affects how they view a communication from her. This, of course, is heavily influenced by previous experiences with the manager. Again, we see that everything done by a manager communicates. Union leaders who view management as exploiters and managers who view union leaders as political animals are likely to engage in little honest communication.

Barriers Created by the Sender, the Receiver, or Both

Senders or receivers also create barriers in organizational communication. For example, there are three specific types of barriers.

Frame of Reference

Different individuals can interpret the same communication differently, depending on previous experiences that result in variations in the encoding and decoding processes. Communication specialists agree that this is the most important factor that breaks down the "commonness" in communications. When the encoding and decoding processes aren't alike, communication tends to break down. Thus, while the communicator actually speaks the "same language" as the receiver, the message conflicts with how the receiver "catalogs" the world. This problem is depicted in Figure 15.6. The interior areas in this diagram represent the accumulated experiences of the participants in the communication process. If they share a large area, effective communication is facilitated. If a large area is not shared—if there has been no common experience—then communication becomes impossible or, at best, highly distorted. Communicators can encode and receivers can decode only in terms of their experiences.

FIGURE 15.6 Overlapping Fields of Experience

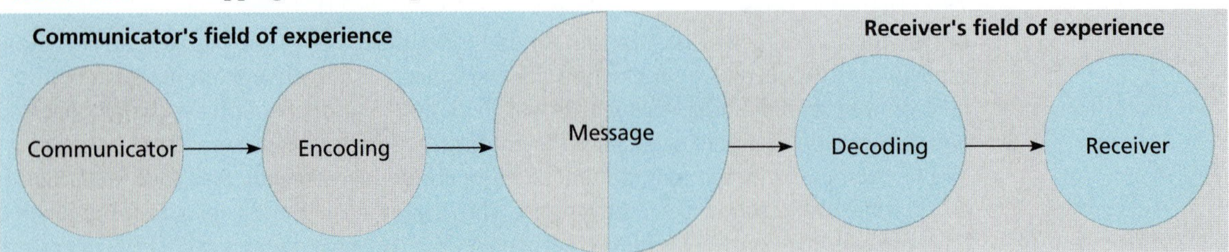

Distortion often occurs because of participants' differing frames of reference. Teenagers perceive things differently than do their parents; college deans perceive problems differently than do faculty members. People in various organizational *functions* can also interpret the same situation differently. A business problem may be viewed differently by the marketing manager than by the production manager. Different *levels* in the organization also have different frames of reference. First-line supervisors' frames of reference differ in many respects from those of vice presidents. Their different positions in the organization structure influence their frames of reference.[80] As a result, their needs, values, attitudes, and expectations differ, often resulting in unintentional distortion of communication.

Effective managerial problem solving depends on the manager adopting the appropriate frame of reference to guide the search for solutions. If the problem is mislabeled or the wrong frame of reference is used, chances for success are lowered.[81] Many other barriers examined in this section also result from variations in encoding and decoding.

Proxemic Behavior

An important but often overlooked element of nonverbal communication is *proxemics,* defined as an individual's use of space when interpersonally communicating with others. According to Edward Hall, a prominent researcher of proxemics, people have four zones of informal space—spatial distances they maintain when interacting with others: the intimate zone (from physical contact to 18 inches), the personal zone (from 18 inches to 4 feet), the social zone (from over 4 to 12 feet), and the public zone (more than 12 feet).[82] For Americans, manager–subordinate relationships begin in the social zone and progress to the personal zone after mutual trust has developed.[83] An individual's personal and intimate zones make up a "private bubble" of space that is considered private territory, not to be entered by others unless invited.

Proxemics creates a significant communication barrier when the proxemic behaviors of the sender and receiver differ. For example, assume that, like most Americans, you stand in the social zone while interacting at a social gathering such as a cocktail party. However, in the South American culture, a personal-zone distance is considered more natural in such situations. When a South American businessperson you're talking with at a cocktail party assumes a personal-zone distance, how do you feel? Typically in such a situation, an individual feels so uncomfortable with the person standing "too close" that any verbal communication isn't heard. Conflicting proxemic behavior can also affect each individual's perceptions of the other—you may view the South American as pushy and aggressive; she may see you as cold and impolite.

Communication Overload

One vital task performed by a manager is decision making. One of the necessary factors in effective decisions is *information.* The past 15 years or so have often been described as the time when information technology radically changed the corporate landscape.[84] Indeed, as seen in the next OB at Work feature, on the development and use of intranets, technology has great potential to improve both the efficiency and effectiveness of organizational communication. Because of the advances, the difficulty does not lie in generating information. Rather, managers often feel buried by a deluge of information and data. As a result, people can't absorb or adequately respond to all of the messages directed to them. They screen out the majority of messages, which in effect means that these messages are never decoded. Thus, in the area of organizational communication, "more" isn't always "better."

The barriers to communication discussed here, while common, are by no means the only ones. Figure 15.7 illustrates these barriers' impact on the process of communication. Examining the barriers indicates that they are either *within individuals* (e.g., frame of reference, value judgments) or *within organizations* (e.g., in-group language, filtering). This point is important because attempts to improve communication must of necessity focus on changing people and/or changing the organizational structure.

OB AT WORK Intranets Improve Internal Communication

Intranets are improving both the efficiency and effectiveness of internal organizational communication. An intranet brings the visually appealing and interactive technology of the World Wide Web inside the organization to network employees in unlimited ways. The potential of personalized Web pages to improve the effectiveness of management–employee communication also appears to be unlimited. Let's examine some innovative uses of this new technology.

One obvious advantage is the savings that result in printing and physically delivering employee communications. The pharmaceutical firm Eli Lilly saved $400,000 by distributing product information online to its offices around the world instead of using mail, fax, and the phone. Motorola Inc., moving its health care provider directory to 700,000 U.S.-based employees online, saved 8 million pieces of paper and $750,000.

More important, the intranet is also improving communication effectiveness. IBM has created an internal version of Facebook or MySpace to connect its 365,000 employees, more than 40 percent of whom work regularly from off-site customer locations or home. Known as "BluePages," the social networking online directory allows employees to connect with fellow IBM employees by pulling up their job title, phone number, location and e-mail, a photo, what teams they're working on, and the names of their co-workers and direct supervisor. These internal technologies are designed to enhance the connectivity of IBM employees worldwide.

In addition to improving communication effectiveness for consulting firms, intranets can assist major airline companies to improve their effectiveness. Continental Airlines has relied on its intranet to communicate flight statuses and airport regulations, as well as to dispel false information that circulates among employees. Also, British Airways, in response to an industry slowdown, redesigned their intranet to make HR transactions simpler and more consistent across all business lines. The effect of these changes was to reduce costs and enhance the user-friendliness of the HR portal.

Companies as diverse as Hallmark, Siemens, and Starbucks are deploying intranets for uses from financial management to more efficient manufacturing operations. National City Bank, with employees in five Midwestern states, developed Gateway, an intranet to foster a sense of community among employees as well as to assist when new banks are purchased in the integration of cultures, product lines, and systems.

These and other organizations are finding that an intranet has tremendous potential as an inexpensive and effective way to communicate within an organization. And not surprisingly, those who have tried it say that the biggest benefits are improved employee communication and increased collaboration between different departments and functions such as marketing, engineering, and research.

Sources: "How Social Networking Increases Collaboration at IBM," *Strategic Communication Management* 14, no. 1 (January 2010): 32–36; J. Arnold, "Improving Intranet Usefulness," *HRMagazine*, April 2008, pp. 103–106; D. Keith Denton, "Using Intranets to Make Virtual Teams Effective," *Team Performance Management* 12, nos. 7/8 (2006): 253–57; Bo Bernhard Nielsen and Francesco Ciabuschi, "Siemens ShareNet: Knowledge Management in Practice," *Business Strategy Review* 14, no. 2 (2003): 33–39; Robin Gareiss, "Continental Uses IT to Chart a New Course," *Information Week,* September 24, 2001, pp. 52–54; Antone Gonsalves, "Employees Share Pearls of Wisdom," *Information Week,* September 10, 2001, pp. 48–50; Larry Greenemeier, "Starbucks Sweetens IT Support for Booming Cafes," *Information Week,* August 20, 2001, pp. 22–23; and Emelie Rutherford, "Is This Any Way to Build an Intranet?" *CIO,* April 1, 2000, pp. 124–36.

FIGURE 15.7 Barriers to Effective Communication

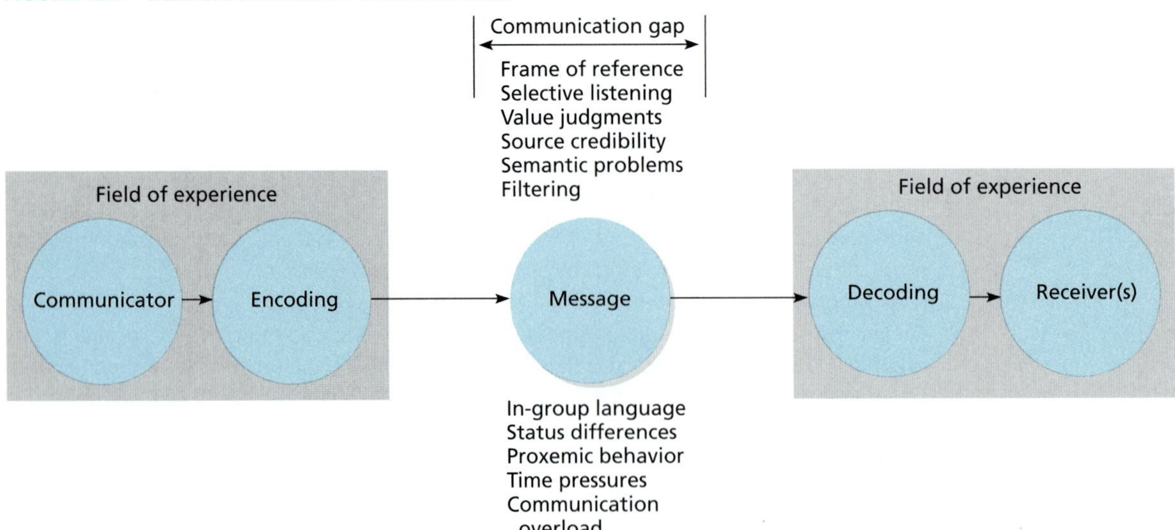

Improving Communication in an Organization

Managers striving to become better communicators must accomplish two separate tasks. First, they must improve their *messages*—the information they wish to transmit. Second, they must seek to improve their own *understanding* of what other people try to communicate to them. In other words, they must become better encoders and decoders. They must strive not only to be understood but also to understand.[85] The following techniques can help accomplish these two important tasks.

Following Up

This technique is used when you assume that you're misunderstood and, whenever possible, attempt to determine whether your intended meaning was actually received. As we've seen, meaning is often in the mind of the receiver. For example, an accounting unit leader in a government office passes on to accounting staff members notices of openings in other agencies. While long-time employees may understand this as a friendly gesture, a new employee might interpret it as an evaluation of poor performance and a suggestion to leave.

Regulating Information Flow

Regulating communication can ensure an optimum flow of information to managers, thereby eliminating the barrier of communication overload. Communication can be regulated in both quality and quantity. The idea is based on the *exception principle* of management, which states that only significant deviations from policies and procedures should be brought to the attention of superiors. In formal communication then, superiors should be communicated with only on matters of importance and not for the sake of communication. In other words, executives should be supplied with diagnostic rather than superfluous information.[86]

Using Feedback

Earlier, the chapter identified feedback as an important element in effective two-way communication. It provides a channel for receiver response that enables the communicator to determine whether the message has been received and has produced the intended response.[87] In face-to-face communication, direct feedback is possible. In downward communication, however, inaccuracies often occur because of insufficient opportunity for feedback from receivers. Distributing a memorandum about an important policy to all employees doesn't guarantee that communication has occurred.

We might expect that feedback in the form of upward communication would be encouraged more in organic organizations, but mechanisms that encourage upward communication are found in many different organizational designs. A healthy organization needs effective upward communication if its downward communication is to have any chance of being effective. The point is that developing and supporting mechanisms for feedback involve far more than following up on communications. Rather, to be effective, feedback needs to be engaging, responsive, and directed toward a desired outcome.[88]

Empathy

Empathy is the ability to put oneself in the other person's role and to assume that individual's viewpoints and emotions. This involves being receiver-oriented rather than communicator-oriented. The form of the communication should depend on what is known about the receiver. Empathy requires communicators to place themselves in the shoes of the receiver to anticipate how the message is likely to be decoded.

Too often, managers perceive themselves to be much better communicators than their subordinates perceive them.[89] Managers must spend more effort understanding and appreciating the process of decoding. In decoding, the message is filtered through the receiver's perceptions. For vice presidents to communicate effectively with supervisors, for faculty to communicate effectively with students, and for government administrators to communicate effectively with minority groups, empathy is often an important ingredient. Empathy can reduce many barriers to effective communication. Remember that the greater the gap between the experiences and background of the communicator and the receiver, the greater the effort needed to find a common ground of understanding where fields of experience overlap.

Repetition

Repetition is an accepted principle of learning. Introducing repetition or redundancy into communication (especially that of a technical nature) ensures that if one part of the message is not understood, other parts carry the same message. New employees are often provided with the same basic information in several different forms. Likewise, students receive much redundant information when first entering a university. This ensures that registration procedures, course requirements, and new terms such as *matriculation* and *quality points* are communicated.

Encouraging Mutual Trust

Time pressures often mean that managers cannot follow up communication and encourage feedback or upward communication every time they communicate. Under such circumstances, an atmosphere of mutual confidence and trust between managers and their subordinates can facilitate communication. Subordinates judge for themselves the quality of their perceived relationship with their superiors. A study of American and Canadian office workers found that only 38 percent of the workers surveyed felt that management was honest with them. Even fewer—27 percent—believed that management cared about them as individuals.[90] Managers who can develop a climate of trust find that following up on each communication is less critical. Because they've fostered high source credibility among subordinates, no loss in understanding results from a failure to follow up on each communication. Some organizations initiate formal programs designed to encourage mutual trust.

Effective Timing

Individuals are exposed to thousands of messages daily. Because of the impossibility of taking in all the messages, many are never decoded and received. Managers must realize that while they are attempting to communicate with a receiver, other messages are being received simultaneously. Thus, the message that the manager sends may not be heard. Messages that do not compete with other messages are more likely to be understood.

Because of this problem, many organizations use "retreats" when important policies or changes are being made. A group of executives may be sent to a resort to resolve an important corporate policy issue, or a college department's faculty may retreat to an off-campus site to design a new curriculum.

On an everyday basis, effective communication can be facilitated by properly timing major announcements. The barriers discussed earlier often arise from poor timing that results in distortions and value judgments.

Simplifying Language

Complex language has been identified as a major barrier to effective communication. University students often suffer when their teachers use technical jargon that transforms simple concepts into complex puzzles. Government agencies are also known for their often incomprehensible communications. And we have already noted instances where professional people use in-group language in attempting to communicate with individuals outside their group. Managers must remember that effective communication involves transmitting *understanding* as well as information. If the receiver does not understand, then the communication has been ineffective. In fact, many techniques discussed in this section have as their sole purpose the promotion of understanding. Managers must encode messages in words, appeals, and symbols that are meaningful to the receiver.

Effective Listening

To improve communication, managers must seek not only to be understood but also to *understand*. This involves listening. One method of encouraging someone to express true feelings, desires, and emotions is to listen. Just listening is not enough; one must listen with understanding. Can managers develop listening skills? Numerous pointers have been given for effective listening in organizational settings. For example, one writer cites "Ten Commandments for Good Listening": stop talking, put the speaker at ease, show the speaker you want to listen, remove distractions, empathize with the speaker, be patient, hold your temper, go easy on argument and criticism, ask questions, and stop talking.[91] Note that "stop talking" is both the first and the last commandment.

Such guidelines can be useful to managers. More important, however, is the *decision to listen*. Guidelines are useless unless the manager makes the conscious decision to listen. Only after the realization that effective communication involves understanding as well as being understood can guidelines for effective listening become useful.

In conclusion, to find any aspect of a manager's job that does not involve communication would be hard. If everyone in the organization had common points of view, communicating would be easy. Unfortunately, such is not the case—each member comes to the organization with a distinct personality, background, experience, and frame of reference. The structure of the organization itself influences status relationships and the distance (levels) between individuals, which in turn influence the ability of individuals to communicate.

This chapter has described basic elements in the process of communication and what it takes to communicate effectively. These elements are necessary whether the communication is face-to-face or written and communicated vertically, horizontally, or diagonally within an organizational structure. We discussed several common communication barriers and several means to improve communication. Figure 15.8 shows techniques that facilitate more effective communication. Often, time does not permit managers to use many of the techniques for improving communication, and skills such as empathy and effective listening are not easy to develop. The figure does, however, illustrate the challenge of communicating effectively and suggests what is required. It shows that communicating involves both transmitting and receiving. Managers must be effective at both; they must understand as well as be understood.

FIGURE 15.8 **Improving Communication in Organization (Narrowing the Communication Gap)**

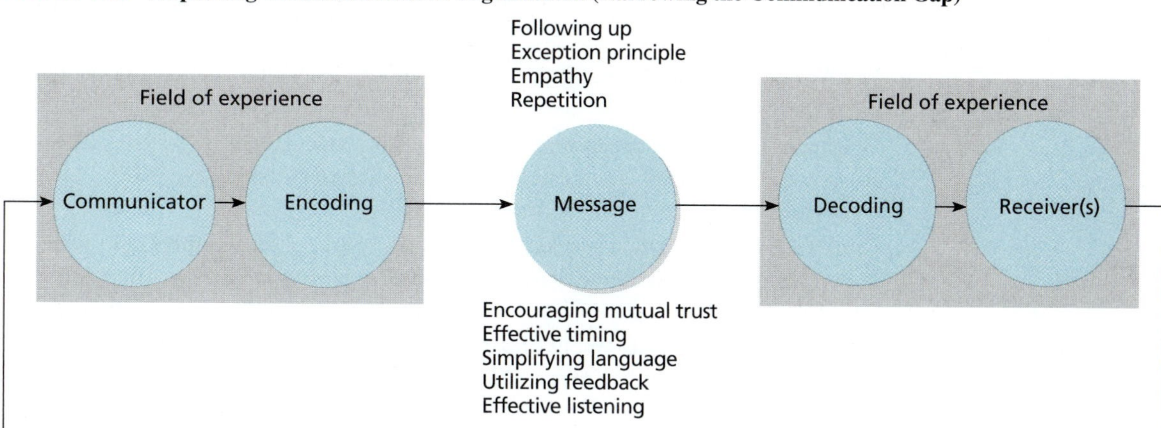

Summary of Key Points

- Communication is the transmission of information and understanding through the use of common symbols.
- The communication process consists of certain basic elements that must always be present if effective communication is to result. These elements are the communicator, the message, the medium, the receiver, and feedback.
- Nonverbal communication is an important source of information about a sender's or receiver's thoughts and feelings. The voice, body expressions, and proxemics are all important mechanisms of nonverbal communication.
- Organizational design and the communication process are inseparable. The design of an organization must provide for communication in three distinct directions: vertical (downward and upward), horizontal, and diagonal.
- The grapevine is an informal communication channel that pervades organizations. In a typical organization, information that's rarely communicated through formal channels is instead passed along through a grapevine.
- Rumors, carried through the grapevine, are an everyday part of organizational life. Regardless of validity, they tend to flourish when they are viewed by the receiver as important, entertaining, ambiguous, or all three.
- Communication effectiveness is enhanced when both the sender and receiver utilize feedback and exposure. Balanced use of both is the most effective approach.
- To alleviate the numerous barriers to communication in organizations, managers should follow up on their messages, regulate information flow, use feedback, develop empathy, use message repetition, encourage mutual trust, simplify their language, effectively time the delivery of their messages, and become effective listeners.

Discussion and Review Questions

1. Assume that you are about to ask your supervisor for a raise. Which communication medium or channel would you use? What steps would you take to decrease the amount of noise that can decrease the effectiveness of your message?
2. With the increase of diversity in the workplace, discuss the additional issues needing to be addressed that may be present in today's organizations in relation to (*a*) the communication process and (*b*) the sending and receiving of nonverbal messages.
3. Assume you are about to meet and negotiate with an individual from a low-context culture. Do you think the person will know a great deal about you before you meet with him or her? Explain.
4. Think back to the last time that you heard a rumor about someone at work or school. What was the content of the rumor? Did it turn out to be accurate? Explain.
5. To what degree do you use upward communication effectively with your supervisor or professors at school? Give a specific example of when you used this type of communication and describe the outcome of the interaction.
6. Think back to a time when you knew a manager, coach, or teacher/professor who was an exceptionally good communicator. Why was this person so effective at communication? Describe.
7. Many individuals carry a variety of personal communication devices with them wherever they go (e.g., a smart phone). Assuming these individuals leave their devices turned on 24/7, do you see any disadvantages associated with this continuous accessibility? Any advantages? Describe.

8. Describe a situation in which you've been the receiver in a one-way communication process. Give some reasons certain individuals might not like it. Why might some people prefer it?
9. In your opinion, which barrier to communication is the most frustrating? What can you do to deal with it in an effective manner?
10. Discuss why organizational design and communication flow are so closely related.

Taking It to the Net

Netiquette: Effectively Communicating with E-Mail

How many times have you wished, right after pressing the "send" button of your e-mail program, that you could take back and soften the message you just launched into cyberspace? What kind of emotion was behind your e-mail? Maybe none, but will the recipient perceive it that way? Maybe, or maybe not. Or, did you ever stop to think that the person you're sending a message to probably receives up to 100 or so e-mails on a daily basis? How much attention will your e-mail receive?

Suffice it to say that most of us could use some polishing when it comes to our use of e-mail communication. Several articles and Web sites can be found on the Internet to help us improve our effectiveness with this ubiquitous communication medium.

Using your favorite search engine (e.g., www.yahoo.com or www.google.com), search for and identify 10 sources that provide tips and advice on how to use e-mail effectively. Summarize the best practices and be prepared to present/write a brief overview. Be sure to include which tips are particularly important to help you improve your own e-mail use.

Case for Analysis: *Leigh Randell*

Leigh Randell is supervisor of in-flight services at the Atlanta base of Omega Airlines, a successful regional air carrier with routes throughout the South and Southwest. In addition to Atlanta, it has bases in six major cities.

Randell's job involves supervision of all in-flight services and personnel at the Atlanta base. She has been with the airline for seven years and in her present job for two years. Although preferring flying to a permanent ground position, she decided to try the management position. In her job, she reports directly to Kent Davis, vice president of in-flight services.

During the past year, Randell has observed what she believes is a great deal of duplication of effort between flight attendants and passenger service personnel in the terminal with respect to paperwork procedures for boarding passengers. This, she believes, has resulted in unnecessary delays in departures of many flights—especially through flights (those that don't originate or terminate in Atlanta). Because most Omega through flights stop in Atlanta, Randell believes that such delayed departures are probably not a major problem at Omega's other bases or at smaller airports. Thus, she has decided to try to coordinate the efforts of flight attendants and passenger service personnel with a simpler, more efficient boarding procedure, thereby reducing ground time and increasing passenger satisfaction through closer adherence to departure times.

In this respect, she has, on three occasions during the past two months, written memos to Tom Ballard, Omega's passenger services representative at the Atlanta base. Each time, Randell has requested information regarding specific procedures, time, and costs for boarding passengers on through flights. She has received no reply from Tom Ballard. His job involves supervision of all passenger service personnel. He has been with Omega for five years, having joined its management training program immediately after graduating from college. He reports directly to Alan Brock, vice president of passenger services at the Atlanta base. Exhibit 1 presents the organization structure for the Atlanta base.

EXHIBIT 1
Omega, Atlanta: Organization Chart

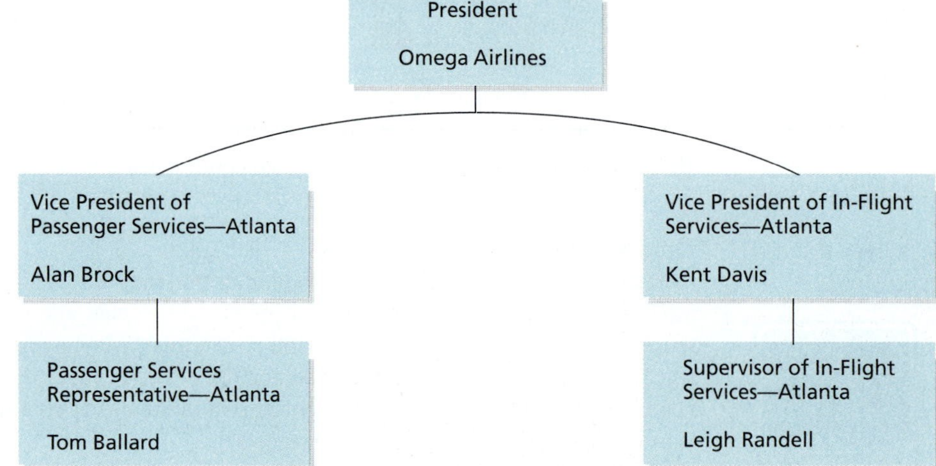

Last week, Leigh wrote a memo to Kent Davis:

> For several months, I have been trying to develop a new method for facilitating the boarding of passengers on through flights by more closely coordinating efforts of In-Flight Services and Passenger Services. The results would be a reduction in clerical work, costs, and ground time and closer adherence to departure times for through flights. Unfortunately, I have received no cooperation at all in my efforts from the passenger services representative. I have made three written requests for information, each of which has been ignored. Needless to say, this has been frustrating to me. While I realize that my beliefs may not always be correct, in this instance I am only trying to initiate something that will be beneficial to everyone involved: Passenger Services, In-Flight Services, and, most important, Omega Airlines. I would like to meet with you to discuss this matter and the possibility of my transferring back to flight duty.

Kent Davis summoned Alan Brock and Tom Ballard to a hastily called conference. Tom Ballard was mildly asked why he had not furnished the information that Randell had requested.

"Too busy," he said. "Her questions were out of sight. There was no time for me to answer this sort of request. I've got a job to do. Besides, I don't report to her."

"But Tom, you don't understand," Kent Davis said. "All Leigh Randell is trying to do is improve the present system of boarding passengers on through flights. She has taken the initiative to work on something that might benefit everyone."

Tom Ballard thought for a moment. "No," he replied, "It didn't look like that to me. You know I've also had ideas on how to improve the system for quite some time. Anyway, she's going about it all wrong."

DISCUSSION QUESTIONS

1. What barriers to effective communication do you detect in this case?
2. Is anyone "wrong" in this situation? By what other means could Randell have requested the information from Tom Ballard? What do you think of Tom Ballard's reaction? Why?
3. While communicating information vertically up or down the organization does not present a major problem, why is horizontal and diagonal communication more difficult to attain? What would you recommend that the management of Omega Airlines do to remedy this situation? How would your recommendations improve communication in the organization?

Experiential Exercise: *Perceptual Differences*

OBJECTIVE

To illustrate how people perceive the same situation differently through the process of selective perception.

RELATED TOPICS

This exercise aptly demonstrates the wide variety of perceptual differences among people when considering a situation where little factual information is provided. The exercise should also indicate that most people selectively perceive the information they're comfortable with in analyzing a situation. Many will also subconsciously fill in gaps of information with assumptions they suppose are facts.

Quiz: The Robbery

The lights in a store had just been turned off by a businessman when a man appeared and demanded money. The owner opened a cash register. The contents of the cash register were scooped up, and the man sped away. A member of the police force was notified promptly.

Answer the following questions about the story by circling T *for true,* F *for false, or* ? *for unknown.*

1.	A man appeared after the owner turned off his store lights.	T	F	?
2.	The robber was a man.	T	F	?
3.	The man who appeared did not demand money.	T	F	?
4.	The man who opened the cash register was the owner.	T	F	?
5.	The store owner scooped up the contents of the cash register and ran away.	T	F	?
6.	Someone opened a cash register.	T	F	?
7.	After the man who demanded money scooped up the contents of the cash register, he ran away.	T	F	?
8.	While the cash register contained money, the story does not state how much.	T	F	?
9.	The robber demanded money of the owner.	T	F	?
10.	A businessman had just turned off the lights when a man appeared in the store.	T	F	?
11.	It was broad daylight when the man appeared.	T	F	?
12.	The man who appeared opened the cash register.	T	F	?
13.	No one demanded money.	T	F	?
14.	The story concerns a series of events in which only three persons are referred to: the owner of the store, a man who demanded money, and a member of the police force.	T	F	?
15.	The following events occurred: someone demanded money, a cash register was opened, its contents were scooped up, and a man dashed out of the store.	T	F	?

Source: William V. Haney, *Communication and Interpersonal Relations: Text and Cases* (Homewood, IL: Richard D. Irwin, 1979), pp. 250–51.

STARTING THE EXERCISE

The instructor will divide the class into groups of four students each. Students will then, as individuals, complete the quiz on the preceding page. Group members shouldn't converse until everyone has finished.

COMPLETING THE EXERCISE

1. Your instructor will provide the answers to the 15 questions. Score your responses.
2. As a group, discuss your members' responses. Focus your discussion on the following questions:
   a. Why did perceptions differ across members? What factors could account for these differences?
   b. Many people don't perform very well with this quiz. Why? What other factors beyond selective perception can adversely affect performance?

CHAPTER SIXTEEN

Decision Making

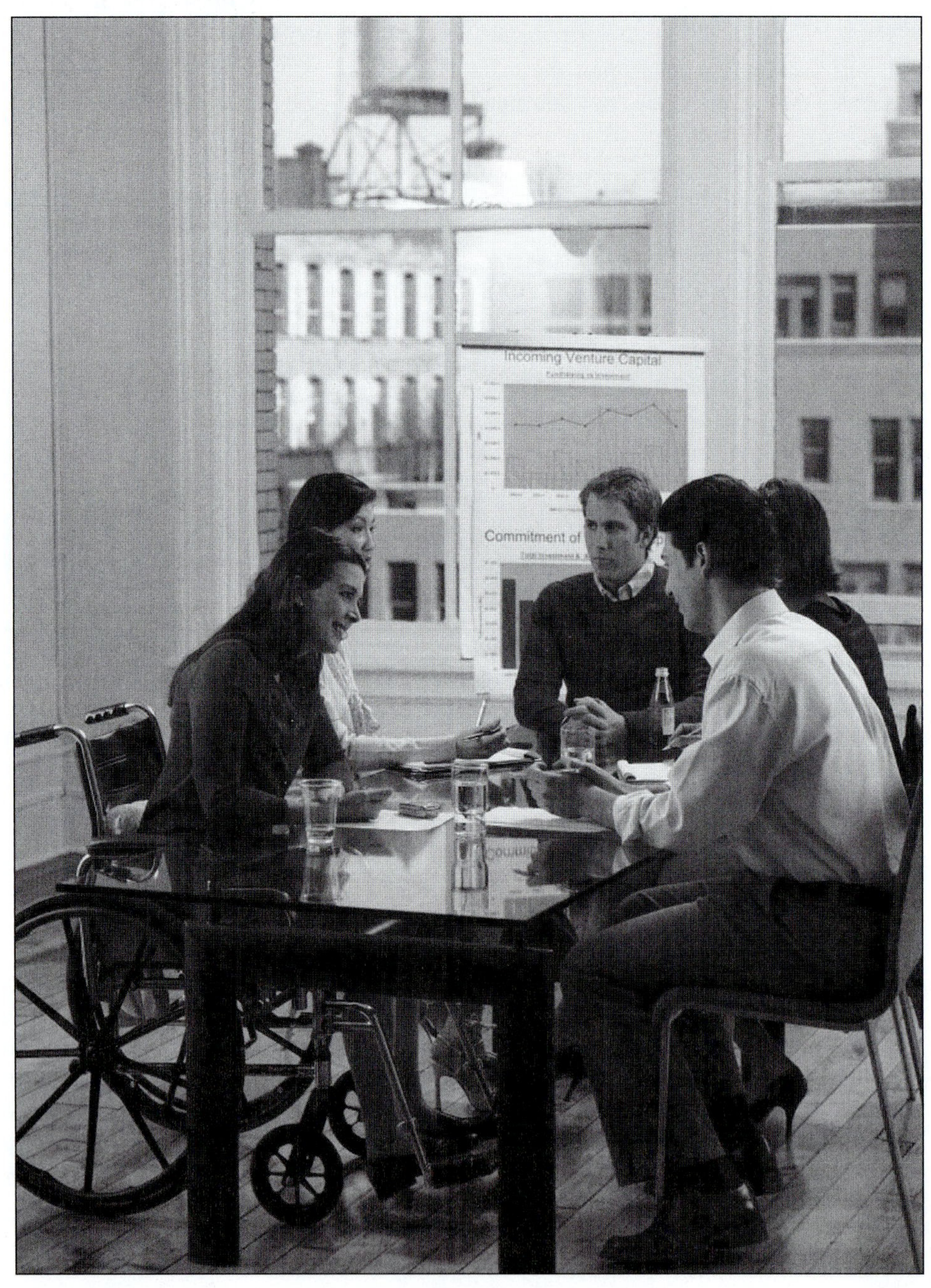

Learning Objectives

After completing Chapter 16, you should be able to

Define
The terms *programmed decision* and *nonprogrammed decision.*

Describe
The various steps in the process of decision making.

Discuss
The major behavioral influences on the process of decision making.

Compare
Group decision making and individual decision making.

Identify
The various methods that managers can use to stimulate creativity in group decision making.

Decision Making: Are You as Good as You Think You Are?

Until today, Pat Jones had always thought of herself as a competent and effective decision maker. As the vice president of human resources for a medium-sized manufacturing firm, she has developed and applied her own personal approach to problem solving. Several times per week, Jones has to "put out a fire" by speaking to the employees who brought up the problem, analyzing it with available data that were at her fingertips on her PC, and then solving the problem quickly; then it's off to the next "fire." For the most part, she believed that her decisions were sound and have worked reasonably well. At least, that's what Jones told herself over the years. Recently, Jones has been seriously reconsidering just how good a decision maker she has been. Her supervisor has just asked her to be the lead trainer in a day-long training program designed to help employees and managers in her 200-person company to improve their decision-making skills. In preparation for the program, Jones reviewed several books, online sources, and training exercises that are designed to improve managerial decision making and problem solving. To her surprise, she discovered that she makes most of her decisions quickly and "on the fly" without thoroughly analyzing the problem or alternatives. Wanting to get a handle on this issue, she found that there are several best practices to follow when making decisions, including

1. Establish specific goals and objectives for the organization and measure results.
2. Identify problems that impede the realization of these goals and objectives.
3. Develop multiple alternatives to solve these problems.
4. Evaluate the alternatives and choose the one that comes closest to optimizing the objectives.
5. Implement the decision by using effective communication.
6. Measure and evaluate the decision on a periodic basis.

After preparing the training seminar, Jones made a commitment to herself that she would try to "practice what she preaches" by being more methodical and thorough when it comes to tackling difficult problems and decisions in the future.

Sources: Sydney Finkelstein, Jo Whitehead, and Andrew Campbell, "The Illusion of Smart Decision Making: The Past Is Not Prologue," *The Journal of Business Strategy*, 30, no. 6 (2009): 36–43. "Do You Manage by the Numbers? Be Careful if You Do: Your Data May Be Playing Tricks on You," *Inc.*, November 2006, pp. 59–60; Ben R. Newell, Tim Rakow, Nicola J. Weston, and David R. Shanks, "Search Strategies in Decision Making: The Success of 'Success,'" *Journal of Behavioral Decision Making* 17, no. 2 (2004): 117–38; Paul C. Nutt, "Context, Tactics, and the Examination of Alternatives during Strategic Decision Making," *European Journal of Operation Research* (July 2000): 159–86; and Paul C. Nutt, "Decision-Making Success in Public, Private, and Third Sector Organizations: Finding Sector Dependent Best Practices," *The Journal of Management Studies* (January 2000): 77–91.

This chapter focuses on decision making. The quality of managerial decisions is a critical determinant of the manager's effectiveness.[1] In order for an organization to function effectively, its managers need to make wise and informed decisions. Thus, the flow of the preceding chapters leads logically to a discussion of decision making—that is, people behave as *individuals* and as members of *groups,* within an *organizational structure,* and they *communicate* for many reasons. One of the most important reasons is to make decisions. As Pat Jones of the opening vignette now realizes, making effective decisions can be a complex process, relying on all the skills and training a manager possesses. This chapter, therefore, analyzes decision making in terms of how people decide as a consequence of the information they receive both through the organizational structure and through the behavior of important persons and groups.

Types of Decisions

While managers in various organizations may be separated by education, position, experience level, age, and lifestyle, sooner or later they must all make decisions.[2] As discussed throughout this book, debate continues on whether managers should encourage subordinates to participate in decision making.[3] Likewise, depending on the organization's size and overall technical complexity, opportunities to involve subordinates in the decision process may vary.[4] However, regardless of organizational variations and the degree of employee participation, managers are ultimately responsible for decision outcomes.[5] That is, they face a situation involving several alternatives, and their decision involves a comparison of alternatives and an evaluation of the outcome. In this section, we move beyond a general definition of a decision and present a system for classifying various decisions.

Specialists in decision making have developed several ways of classifying decisions. Similar for the most part, these systems differ mainly in terminology. We shall use the widely adopted system suggested by Herbert Simon.[6] It distinguishes between two types of decisions: programmed and nonprogrammed.

programmed decisions
Specific procedures developed for repetitive and routine problems.

nonprogrammed decisions
Decisions required by unique and complex management problems.

1. **Programmed decisions**. If a particular situation occurs often, a routine procedure usually can be worked out for solving it. Thus, decisions are *programmed* to the extent that problems are repetitive and routine and a definite procedure has been developed for handling them.

2. **Nonprogrammed decisions**. Decisions are *nonprogrammed* when they are novel and unstructured. No established procedure exists for handling the problem, either because it has not arisen in exactly the same manner before or because it is complex or extremely important. Such problems deserve special treatment.

These two classifications, while broad, make important distinctions. On the one hand, organizational managers face great numbers of programmed decisions in their daily operations. Such decisions should be treated without expending unnecessary organizational resources on them. On the other hand, nonprogrammed decisions must be properly identified as such because they form the basis for allocating billions of dollars of resources in our economy every year. Table 16.1 breaks down the different types of decisions, with examples of each type in different organizations. It indicates that programmed and nonprogrammed decisions apply to distinctly different problems and require different procedures.

TABLE 16.1
Comparison of Types of Decisions

	Programmed Decisions	Nonprogrammed Decisions
Problem	Frequent, repetitive, routine. Certainty regarding cause-and-effect relationships.	Novel, unstructured. Uncertainty regarding cause-and-effect relationships.
Procedure	Dependence on policies, rules, and definite procedures.	Need for creativity, intuition, tolerance for ambiguity, and creative problem solving.
Examples:		
Business firm	Hiring process.	New product launch.
University	Admission policies.	Construction of new business school.
Health care	Procedures to discharge patients.	Unexpected funding reduction.

Unfortunately, we know very little about the human process involved in nonprogrammed decisions.[7] Traditionally, to make programmed decisions, managers use rules, standard operating procedures, and the structure of the organization that develops specific procedures for handling problems. More recently, operations researchers have facilitated such decisions through the development of mathematical models. In contrast, managers make nonprogrammed decisions by general problem-solving processes, judgment, intuition, and creativity.[8] Informal relationships between managers, as well as formal ones, may be used to handle such ambiguous problems.[9] For example, a number of studies have suggested that Japanese organizations can be highly effective at processing information and taking action by relying on unplanned interaction around problems rather than on formal procedures and problem solving. To date, the advances in modern technology haven't improved nonprogrammed decision making nearly as much as they've improved programmed decision making.[10] The next OB at Work feature tells us that while some advances have been made, especially with respect to programmed decisions, we must be careful to evaluate the contributions of technology to decision making.

Ideally, top management's main concern should be nonprogrammed decisions, while first-level managers should be concerned with programmed decisions. Middle managers in most organizations concentrate mostly on programmed decisions, although in some cases they participate in nonprogrammed decisions. In other words, the nature, frequency, and degree of certainty surrounding a problem should dictate at what level of management the decision should be made.

Obviously, problems arise in organizations where top management expends much time and effort on programmed decisions. One unfortunate result is a neglect of long-range planning. It's subordinated to other activities whether the organization is successful or is having problems. Success justifies continuing the policies and practices that achieved it; if the organization experiences difficulty, its current problems have first priority and occupy the time of top management. In either case, long-range planning ends up being neglected. Neglect of long-range planning usually results in an overemphasis on short-run control and, therefore, less delegation of authority to lower levels of management. This often has adverse effects on employee motivation and satisfaction.

OB AT WORK Falling in Love with Technology

It is easy for managers to become enamored with technology. It is easy to admire it for its own sake as well as for the unquestionable productivity gains that it makes possible. But it is also important—in fact, more important—to look further for an evaluation of the real value it delivers. The real potential value of technology will not be realized unless it enables managers to improve the quality of their decisions. It must assist managers in bringing their own expertise to bear on important decisions in their areas and allow them to make better decisions. The challenge to improve the quality of decisions is a difficult one for corporate information systems. The first challenge is to determine what information is relevant. Once determined, the relevant information needs to be routed to those managers who require it. Finally, all of these activities have to be accomplished as quickly and cost efficiently as possible. What follows are some examples of decision-support systems that are improving the quality of decisions and using technology to its full potential.

Sabre Airlines Solutions (part of Sabre Holdings), a $2.6 billion firm that provides technology solutions for the travel industry, developed the "Aircrews" software program for American Airlines. The software helped the airline make crew assignments for its 4,000 daily flights from a pool of 30,000 crew members. The system assigned crews by weighing variables such as crew location, flying time, weather, union rules, and federal regulations. All in all, there are 20 to 30 million variables for deciding a crew flight assignment, which results in billions of combinations. Clearly, it cannot be done manually. In fact, 20 million pairings need to be generated to reach an optimal decision.

In addition to making daily and weekly flight assignments, the system also helped determine the long-term staffing needs of American Airlines over a five-year period. It worked so well that the system was purchased by other organizations such as Federal Express, US Airways, British Airways, and Delta Airlines. It has saved American Airlines more than $20 million and is expected to save the other airlines even more. In 2010, the Sabre system processes more than 19,000 transactions per second or 2 billion per day. It is no wonder that approximately 300 airlines and 100 airports use Sabre's services.

AES, a $14 billion energy company in Arlington, Virginia, has created a unique approach to sharing information within the company. The 27,000 global employees are encouraged to use communication technology (e-mail, voice-mail, etc.) to contact anyone in the company at any time. Because the company lacks a communication hierarchy, formal restrictions regarding who to speak to for certain types of information do not apply. The overriding goal is to gather information rapidly so that just-in-time decisions can be made.

Other companies have taken similar steps to leverage technology in order to improve decision-making speed and quality. To better serve its customers worldwide, Oracle created an enormous data warehouse of solutions of past customer-service problems. To reduce its number of defects in manufacturing, Honeywell established a companywide database to store all of its production statistics. Within Corning's Optical Fiber Group, a competitive analysis team constantly mines Internet data to inform the group's future strategic direction.

The brief examples provided direct our attention to the tremendous potential value of technology for improving both the efficiency and effectiveness of managerial decisions. And it is on these criteria that the value of technology in decision making must ultimately be evaluated, not the glitz of the technology itself.

Sources: http://www.sabreairlinesolutions.com/home/ (accessed July 18, 2010); http://www.aes.com/aes/index?page=about_us (accessed July 18, 2010); James Surwiecki, "Mass Intelligence," *Forbes*, May 24, 2004, p. 48; David Sandahl and Christine Hewes, "Decision Making at Digital Speed," *Pharmaceutical Executive*, August 2001, pp. 62–68; Clinton Wilder, "Sabre to Open Internet Marketplace for Travel Providers," *Information Week*, March 6, 2000, p. 29; and "NCR Launches DSS for ISP Care," *America's Network*, April 15, 1998, p. 45.

The Decision-Making Process

decision
Means to achieve some result or to solve some problem; outcome of a process influenced by many forces.

Decisions should be thought of as means rather than ends. They are the *organizational mechanisms* by which an attempt is made to achieve a desired state. They are, in effect, an *organizational response* to a problem. Every decision is the outcome of a dynamic process that is influenced by a multitude of forces. Although this process is diagrammed in Figure 16.1, it is not a fixed procedure. It is a sequential process rather than a series of steps.[11] This enables us to examine each element in the normal progression that leads to a decision.

Figure 16.1 applies more to nonprogrammed decisions than to programmed decisions. Problems that occur infrequently, with a great deal of uncertainty and risk surrounding the outcome, require that the manager use the entire process. For problems that occur

FIGURE 16.1
The Decision-Making Process

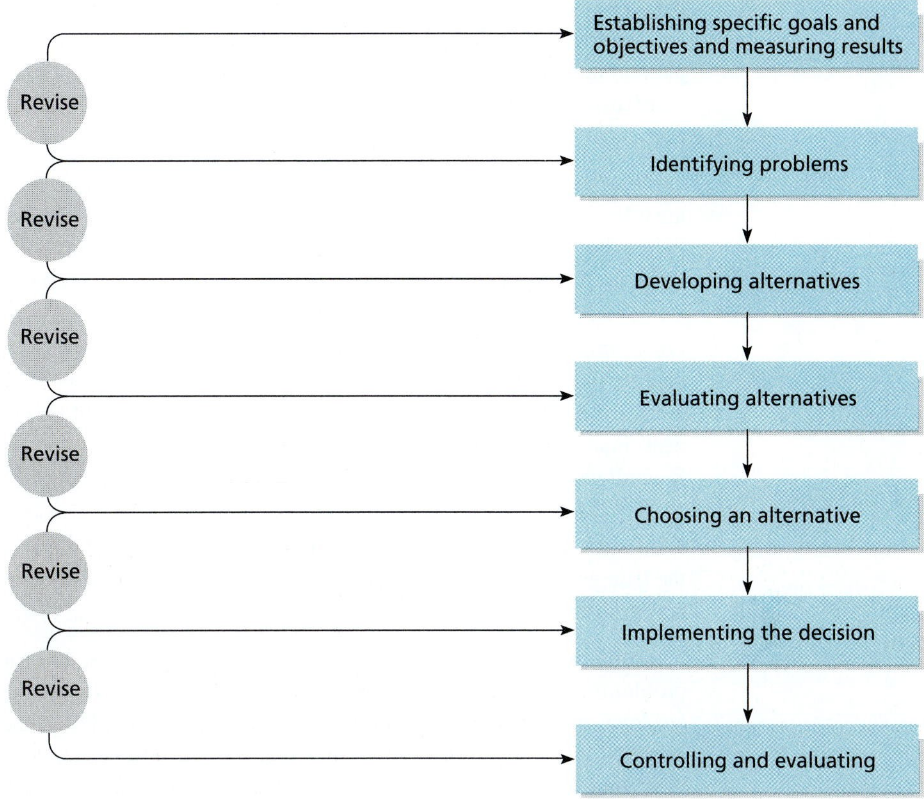

frequently, the entire process is not necessary. If a policy is established to handle such problems, managers don't need to develop and evaluate alternatives each time a problem of this kind arises.

Establishing Specific Goals and Objectives and Measuring Results

Organizations need goals and objectives in each area where performance influences effectiveness. Companies like Marriott and IKEA routinely set goals for their divisions and business units. Adequately established goals and objectives will dictate which results must be achieved and which measures indicate whether those results have been achieved. As part of the goal- and objective-setting process, top management must communicate their tolerance for experimentation and failure on the part of subordinates.[12] In the absence of such communication, middle and lower-level managers will attempt to zero-out risk, a situation that involves avoiding any potential failures (and corresponding successes), thus ensuring the organization of mediocre results.

Identifying Problems

A necessary condition for a decision is a problem.[13] That is, if problems did not exist, there would be no need for decisions. The decision maker is a problem solver, charged with either selecting from available alternatives or inventing an alternative different in meaningful ways from previously existing alternatives.[14] The existence of a problem is indicated by a gap between the organization's goals and objectives and the levels of actual performance. For example, the release of Apple's iPhone 4 on June 24, 2010, was met with customer complaints about reception problems. Although initial demand for the smart phone was strong with a reported 1.7 million phones sold during the first three days of its release, the negative press associated with the phone's reception (and the company's initial response to the complaints) may have dampened sales by creating a public relations problem for Apple.[15]

Identifying the exact problem can be hindered by certain factors:

1. *Perceptual problems.* Our individual perceptions may protect or defend us from unpleasant facts. Negative information may be selectively perceived to distort its true meaning; it may also be totally ignored. For example, a college dean may fail to identify increasing class sizes as a problem while at the same time being sensitive to problems faced by the president of the university in raising funds for the school.

2. *Defining problems in terms of solutions.* This is really a form of jumping to conclusions. For example, a sales manager may say, "The decrease in profits is due to our poor product quality," which suggests a particular solution: the improvement of product quality in the production department. Certainly, other solutions may be possible. Perhaps the sales force has been inadequately selected or trained. Perhaps competitors have a less expensive product. Regardless, one must seek to identify the real cause of problems through careful analysis.

3. *Identifying symptoms as problems.* "Our problem is a 32-percent decline in orders." While it is certainly true that orders have declined, the decline is really only a symptom of the true problem. The manager must identify the *cause* of the decline in order to find the real problem.

Problems are usually of three types: opportunity, crisis, and routine. Crisis and routine problems present themselves and must be attended to by the managers.[16] Opportunities, in contrast, must usually be found; they await discovery.[17] Often they go unnoticed and are eventually lost by an inattentive manager. Because most crises and routine problems, by their very nature, demand immediate attention, a manager may spend a great deal of time handling them and not have time to pursue important new opportunities. Many well-managed organizations try to draw attention away from crises and routine problems and toward longer-range issues through planning activities and goal-setting programs. For example, Educational Testing Service, which administers and scores 50 million tests each year to individuals in 180 million countries, periodically assembles a group of decision makers from within the firm to "make evidence-based decisions about new product offerings."[18]

An alternative view related to identifying problems within organizations can be seen through the lens of *sense making*. Karl Weick, a noted organizational psychologist, coined this expression when he suggested that managers must constantly try to understand the contexts in which they are operating.[19] For example, a CEO of a medium-sized computer programming company might ask herself: "How will outsourcing to India affect my business?" Weick suggests that these types of questions occur when managers' existing expectations of how the world should operate are interrupted by new and ambiguous information (e.g., a trend in outsourcing programmer work to India) and they feel the need to make sense of this new information (e.g., will this trend in outsourcing help or hurt my business?).[20] How do managers make sense out of this new information? They should seek out data from multiple sources (e.g., customers, vendors, employees, investors, consultants) and involve other individuals in the sense-making process. Also, managers should not try to automatically apply their existing problem-solving approaches to the new information; rather, they should be open to trying new approaches to problem solving.[21]

Developing Alternatives

Before a decision is made, feasible alternatives (potential solutions to the problem) should be developed, and the possible consequences of each alternative should be considered. For example, a sales manager may identify an inadequately trained sales force as the cause of declining sales. The sales manager would then identify possible alternatives for solving the problem, such as (1) a sales training program conducted at the home office by management, (2) shifting more of salespeople's compensation from base pay to commission, and (3) more intense on-the-job training.

Developing alternatives is really a search process in which the relevant internal and external environments of the organization are investigated to provide information that can be developed into possible alternatives. Obviously, this search is conducted within certain time and cost constraints; only so much effort can be devoted to developing alternatives.[22]

However, sufficient effort should be made to develop a wide range of alternatives. There's a positive link between the number of alternatives considered and the speed with which decisions can be reached.[23] Not generating enough detailed and varied alternatives can actually wind up costing both time and resources, the very commodities organizations seek to conserve. For example, assume an extremely busy restaurant manager needs to hire a cook. To save time, she hires the first job candidate who she interviews (because he seems "good enough"), instead of taking the time to interview three or four additional applicants. The manager missed the opportunity to consider "alternatives" to the first candidate, which may end up costing her time and money later if the hired individual doesn't work out and a new cook has to be hired and trained.

One means to broaden the development of alternatives is through the use of scenario analysis.[24] Scenarios compel managers to consider what could be, not what has been. Managers explore different future business patterns, not extrapolations of historical behavior. Scenario analysis allows managers to compensate for tunnel vision—the inability to think in abstract patterns.[25] The major advantage of scenario-based development of alternatives is that it allows decision makers to uncover new alternatives that would have been overlooked under traditional alternative generation practices.

Evaluating Alternatives

Once alternatives have been developed, they must be evaluated and compared. In every decision situation, the objective in making a decision is to select the alternative that will produce the most favorable outcomes and the least unfavorable outcomes. This again points to the need for objectives and goals. When selecting among alternatives, the decision maker should be guided by previously established goals and objectives. The alternative–outcome relationship is based on three possible conditions:

1. *Certainty.* The decision maker has complete knowledge of the probability of the outcome of each alternative.
2. *Uncertainty.* The decision maker has absolutely no knowledge of the probability of the outcome of each alternative.
3. *Risk.* The decision maker has some probabilistic estimate of the outcomes of each alternative.

Decision making under conditions of risk is probably the most common situation.[26] It is in evaluating alternatives under these conditions that statisticians and operations researchers have made important contributions to decision making. Their methods have proved especially useful in the analysis and ranking of alternatives, especially in the area of game theory where decision makers put themselves in the shoes of others, trying out all the potential reactions to their actions prior to the decision being made.[27]

Choosing an Alternative

The purpose in selecting an alternative is to solve a problem to achieve a predetermined objective. This point is an important one. It means that a decision is not an end in itself but only a means to an end. While the decision maker chooses the alternative that is expected to result in achieving the objective, the selection of that alternative should not be seen as an isolated act. If it is, the factors that led to and lead from the decision are likely to be excluded. Specifically, the steps following the decision should include implementation, control, and evaluation. For example, once a new car design is chosen, auto manufacturers like Ford, Toyota, and Renault spend a considerable amount of time and money implementing the new design into the manufacturing process. The critical point is that decision making is more than an act of choosing; it is a dynamic process.

Unfortunately for most managers, an alternative rarely achieves the desired objective without having some positive or negative impact on another objective. Situations often exist where two objectives cannot be fully achieved simultaneously. If one objective is *optimized,* the other is *suboptimized.* For example, a university may optimize a short-run objective such as reducing costs (e.g., eliminate several sections of a required introductory management course) at the expense of a long-run objective (e.g., graduating students in a timely manner). Thus, the multiplicity of organizational objectives complicates the real world of the decision makers forcing them, in effect, to continually be wondering "what-if."[28]

In certain situations, an organizational objective may also be at the expense of a societal objective. This is clear in the rise of ecology groups, environmentalists, and the consumer movement. Apparently, these groups question the priorities (organizational against societal) of certain organizational decision makers. After the Deepwater Horizon oil rig exploded on April 20, 2010, and large amounts of oil began flowing into the Gulf of Mexico, critics questioned whether British Petroleum's decision to drill an oil well one mile below the surface of the gulf was a reasonable one from an environmental and ecological perspective.[29] Many observers were surprised that British Petroleum did not appear to have an effective emergency plan in place immediately after the explosion to stop the oil leak. In any case, whether an organizational objective conflicts with another organizational objective or with a societal objective, the values of the decision maker strongly influence the alternative chosen. Individual values were discussed earlier, and their influence on the decision-making process should be clear.

In managerial decision making, optimal solutions are often impossible. The decision maker cannot possibly know all of the available alternatives, the consequences of each alternative, and the probability of these consequences occurring.[30] Thus, rather than being an optimizer, the decision maker is a *satisficer,* selecting the alternative that meets an acceptable (satisfactory) standard.

Implementing the Decision

Any decision that is not implemented is little more than an abstraction. In other words, a decision must be effectively implemented to achieve the objective for which it was made. It is entirely possible for a "good" decision to be hurt by poor implementation. In this sense, implementation may be more important than the actual choice of the alternative.

In most situations, implementing decisions involves people, so the test of a decision's soundness is the behavior of the people affected by the decision. Subordinates can't be manipulated in the same manner as other resources. A technically sound decision can easily be undermined by dissatisfied subordinates. Thus, a manager's job is not only to choose good solutions but also to transform such solutions into behavior in the organization. This is done by effectively communicating with the appropriate individuals and groups.[31]

Control and Evaluation

Effective management involves periodic measurement of results. Actual results are compared with planned results (the objective), and changes must be made if deviations exist.

OB AT WORK Do Good Companies Make Poor Decisions?

When Euro Disney opened Disneyland Paris in the spring of 1992, there was much fanfare that the multimillion-dollar theme park would bring a slice of Americana to the European continent. Unfortunately, several decisions were made that contributed to yearly operating losses at the theme park for the first few years. These decisions included charging expensive admission prices, prohibiting the sale of wine and beer with meals, serving only French sausage (while not offering the neighboring Italian and German varieties), creating pan-European marketing campaigns that were too general to effectively attract tourists from different European nations, and failing to include European travel agents in early marketing programs (many Europeans make their vacation travel plans through agents and tour operators). Although Euro Disney over the years has invested heavily in the park to make it a successful European tourist destination, the park on more than one occasion has failed to meet its performance and profitability goals. In 2009, Euro Disney reported a $93 million net loss despite a record 15.4 million visits.

One of the most successful companies in the United States (and the world) has also had its share of problems due to poor decisions. In 2003, a raid on 60 Walmart stores in 21 states throughout the United States by federal immigration officials led to the discovery of several illegal workers who were cleaning the stores. Many of the illegal immigrants were being housed in crowded conditions and sometimes slept in the back of the Walmart stores. In March 2003, the retailer agreed to pay $11 million to settle the case.

Cisco Systems, a $19 billion company that provides networking and communications products and services for the Internet, announced that it had to write off $2.2 billion for components it ordered but could not use. Decisions were made in the design of the inventory tracking and forecast planning systems that led to this costly mistake. A new multimillion-dollar fix-it project, called *eHub,* is being designed to prevent future problems like this from happening again.

Decision makers at Euro Disney, Walmart, and Cisco Systems have had to endure the effects of less than optimal decision making. These decision makers are not alone. One researcher, Paul C. Nutt, studied hundreds of actual managerial decisions and found that approximately 50 percent of these decisions failed. He analyzed such decisions as the Firestone tire recall, the building of the Denver International Airport, and Quaker's acquisition of Snapple. He concluded that managers who fall victim to any of the following decision-making traps are more likely to make poor or failed decisions:

1. Failing to understand people's concerns and competing claims.
2. Overlooking people's interests and commitments.
3. Defining expectations in an unclear manner.
4. Limiting the search for alternatives and remedies.
5. Misusing evaluations of possible alternatives.
6. Ignoring or downplaying ethical questions.
7. Neglecting to analyze the results of the decision to understand what worked and didn't work.

In conclusion, although decisions are usually made without the benefit of perfect information and unlimited time to search for and evaluate alternative solutions, managers should try to avoid the common decision-making traps that can lead to expensive and time-consuming failed decisions.

Sources: Scheherazade Daneshkhu, "Magic Fades as Paris Theme Park Sinks into Loss," *Financial Times,* November 13, 2009, p. 27; "Affidavit Says Wal-Mart Knew of Illegal Workers," *Washington Post,* November 8, 2005, p. D2; "Wal-Mart Execs Knew of Illegal Workers," *Los Angeles Times,* November 8, 2005, p. C3; Ira Sager and Carol Matlack, "Euro Disney: Looking Euro Dismal," *Businessweek,* December 8, 2003, p. 14; Carol Matlock and David Fairlamb, "Euro Disney: No Joyeux Noël Here," *Businessweek,* December 1, 2003, p. 31; Paul C. Nutt, *Why Decisions Fail: Avoiding the Blunders and Traps That Lead to Debacles* (San Francisco: Berrett-Koehler, 2002); Paulo Prada and Bruce Orwell, "A Certain 'Je Ne Sais Quoi' at Disney's New Park," *Wall Street Journal,* March 12, 2002, p. B1; Paula Kaihla, "Inside Cisco's $2 Billion Blunder," *Business 2.0,* March 2002, pp. 88–90; and "A Faint Squeak from Euro-Mickey," *Economist,* July 29, 1995, p. 44.

Here again, we see the importance of measurable objectives. Without them, there is no way to judge performance. Changes, if necessary, must be made in the solution chosen, in its implementation, or in the original objective if it is deemed unattainable. If the original objective must be revised, then the entire decision-making process is reactivated. The important point is that once a decision is implemented, a manager cannot assume that the outcome will meet the original objective. Some system of control and evaluation is needed to make sure the actual results are consistent with the results planned when the decision was made.

If decision makers in a company follow the preceding steps, does that guarantee they'll make excellent decisions? Not necessarily. The accompanying OB in the Real World feature examines this issue.

Behavioral Influences on Individual Decision Making

Several behavioral factors influence the decision-making process. Some affect only certain aspects of the process, while others influence the entire process. However, each may have an impact and therefore must be understood to fully appreciate the decision-making process in organizations. Six individual behavioral factors—ethics, values, personality, propensity for risk, potential for dissonance, and escalation of commitment—are discussed in this section. Each has a significant effect on the decision-making process.

Ethical Decision Making

Ethics is a system or code that guides individuals' conduct. In terms of decision making, it helps individuals evaluate different alternatives to a problem in terms of right or wrong. Employees and managers often face decisions that have ethical implications. In extreme situations, managerial decisions can have implications of life or death for fellow employees, customers, or citizens. On a day-to-day basis, unethical decisions and behavior from employees, co-workers, and supervisors can lead to distrust, conflict, and a less productive work environment.

Stories and accounts of both types of decisions can be found in the news on any given day. For example, since its initial recall of 6.5 million tires in August 2001, Firestone Tire Company had come under pressure from the U.S. National Highway Traffic Safety Administration to recall additional tires from the U.S. market. In July 2001, the company resisted and turned down the request for the additional recall. This decision to wait had serious implications when considering that several deaths were allegedly linked to the tread separation failures in these tires. Firestone eventually changed its decision and agreed to recall an additional 3.5 million tires in October 2001.[32]

Another example of how ethical decisions can have life or death consequences involves Manville Corporation's manufacture of products with toxic asbestos. Asbestos is a mineral that was once widely used in automotive brakes, piping, and insulation products.[33] Thousands of people claimed to have contracted respiratory diseases as a result of contact with the substance; for many, the diseases did not manifest symptoms until many years after exposure.[34] Complicating this case was that early reports indicated that asbestos dust was harmful to humans; yet, Manville continued to manufacture and sell the products.[35]

Manville's decision to do so not only affected thousands of individuals (i.e., those who became ill and family members of affected parties), but also led to severe product liability judgments against the manufacturer. Manville was ordered to reorganize under Chapter 11 of the Federal Bankruptcy Code in August 1982 and to turn over approximately 80 percent of common stock, $1.6 billion in accounts receivable, and approximately $1 billion in cash.[36] Unfortunately, the asbestos problem is still not resolved. On October 8, 2010, the U.S. Court of Appeals ruled that in some cases, employers are only liable if the employee shows evidence of an asbestos-related illness and are not liable for exposing an employee to asbestos. Given that some asbestos-related illnesses take years to manifest, some victims' groups are upset by the ruling.[37]

In addition to major life-changing decisions such as those made by individuals at Firestone and Manville, decisions are made every day by employees, co-workers, and supervisors that impact organizational effectiveness. A survey by the Society of Human Resource Management and the Ethics Resource Center asked 750 human resource professionals whether they had observed workplace conduct that was in violation of the law or the organization's standards of ethical business conduct. The most common types of workplace misconduct cited by human resource professionals included the following:

- Lying to supervisors (cited by 45 percent of respondents).
- Abuse of drugs and/or alcohol (cited by 36 percent of respondents).

- Lying or falsifying records (cited by 36 percent of respondents).
- Conflicts of interest (cited by 34 percent of respondents).
- Stealing or theft (cited by 27 percent of respondents).

In addition, 89 percent of respondents indicated that the average employee misrepresents information in communication with supervisors.[38]

Based on the findings of this survey and the number of stories found in the pages of newspapers and the business press, it appears that unethical decision making is a pervasive phenomenon that requires more attention from leaders and managers alike. To that end, it is important to review what is known about the factors that influence an individual's tendency to be ethical (or unethical) when making decisions that affect others.

Factors Influencing Ethical Decision Making

Based on a comprehensive review of the empirical research done on ethical decision making in business, several tentative conclusions have been made regarding which factors appear to exert influence over ethical decisions.[39] Some factors that have been studied at the individual level include gender, moral philosophy, values, education, work experience, age, and awareness. Group and organizational factors dealt with influence of significant others (at the workplace), organizational culture and climate, codes of ethics, and rewards and sanctions.

Of the individual factors, gender, education, work experience, and level of awareness have not consistently related to ethical decision making. However, individuals who possess certain moral philosophies and who are older tend to take ethical considerations into account when making decisions. On the group level, significant others within the organization exert a strong influence over peers and co-workers. As for the organizational level, the culture and climate exert a direct influence over how individuals make ethical decisions. Also, companies that publicize codes of ethics succeed in raising employees' awareness regarding appropriate ethical behavior.[40] Employee violations of such codes can result in severe consequences, as in the case of two Fidelity International fund managers who were fired for putting their own interests in front of those of the company.[41]

Instilling Ethical Values

Some individuals believe ethics cannot be taught. Making ethical decisions is a product of one's morals, upbringing, and similar factors. Yet, given the apparent increase in less-than-ethical behavior as illustrated in the previous section, many leaders, managers, and human resource professionals feel the need to do something. For example, Texas Instruments (TI) attacks this problem proactively by doing the following: offering an in-house training program entitled "Decision Making in the New TI" that stresses the importance of corporate ethics and values; issuing a 14-page booklet on values and ethics to every employee; and providing every employee with a tear-out card that encourages managers to think through a series of issues before deciding whether a course of action is ethical. The card includes the following points:

1. Is the action legal?
2. Does it comply with our values?
3. If you do it, will you feel bad?
4. How will it look in the newspaper?
5. If you know it's wrong, don't do it!
6. If you're not sure, ask.
7. Keep asking until you get an answer.

Other examples of companies taking action to improve the overall ethical decision making of their employees include Caterpillar, Bayer, and Johnson & Johnson. Caterpillar puts its 95,000 employees through annual ethics training. Employees are presented with written scenarios and asked to choose the best (and most ethical) way to deal with the situations presented in the scenarios.[42] The 16,600 employees of Bayer's North American operations can contact the company's ombudsman to report (confidentially) unethical behavior such as discrimination, biased performance reviews, and unfair pay decisions.[43] Each year, members of the board of directors and executive officers at Johnson & Johnson are asked to certify that they have complied with the company's Code of Business Conduct & Ethics.[44]

Values

values
Basic guidelines and beliefs that a decision maker uses when confronted with a situation requiring choice.

In the context of decision making, **values** are the guidelines a person uses when confronted with a situation in which a choice must be made. Values are acquired early in life and are a basic (often taken for granted) part of an individual's thoughts. Values' influence on the decision-making process is profound:

In *establishing objectives,* value judgments must be made regarding the selection of opportunities and the assignment of priorities.

In *developing alternatives,* value judgments about the various possibilities are necessary. In *choosing an alternative,* the values of the decision maker influence which alternative is chosen.

In *implementing a decision,* value judgments are necessary in choosing the means for implementation.

In the *control* and *evaluation* phase, value judgments cannot be avoided when corrective action is decided on and taken.

Clearly, values pervade the decision-making process, encompassing not only people's economic and legal responsibilities, but their ethical responsibilities as well.[45] They're reflected in the decision maker's behavior before making the decision, in making the decision, and in putting the decision into effect.[46] Indeed, some researchers state that alternatives are relevant only as a means of achieving managerial values.[47]

Personality

Decision makers are influenced by many psychological forces, both conscious and subconscious. One of the most important of these forces is personality. Decision makers' personalities are strongly reflected in their choices. Studies that have examined the effect of personality on the process of decision making have generally focused on three types of variables:[48]

1. *Personality variables*—the attitudes, beliefs, and needs of the individual.
2. *Situational variables*—external, observable situations in which individuals find themselves.
3. *Interactional variables*—the individual's momentary state that results from the interaction of a specific situation with characteristics of the individual's personality.

The most important conclusions concerning the influence of personality on the decision-making process are as follows:

1. One person is not likely to be equally proficient in all aspects of the decision-making process. Some people do better in one part of the process, while others do better in another part.

2. Certain characteristics, such as intelligence, are associated with different phases of the decision-making process.
3. The relationship of personality to the decision-making process may vary for different groups on the basis of such factors as sex, social status, and cultural background.
4. Individuals facing important and ambiguous decisions may be influenced heavily by peers' opinions.

An interesting study examined the importance of cultural influences on decision-making style differences between Japanese and Australian college students.[49] In Japan, a group orientation exists, while in Australia, the common cultural pattern emphasizes an individual orientation. The results confirmed the importance of the cultural influence. Japanese students reported greater use of decision processes or behaviors associated with the involvement and influence of others, while Australian students reported greater use of decision processes associated with self-reliance and personal ability. In general, the personality traits of the decision maker combine with certain situational and interactional variables to influence the decision-making process.

Propensity for Risk

From personal experience, we're all undoubtedly aware that decision makers vary greatly in their propensity for taking risks. This one specific aspect of personality strongly influences the decision-making process. A decision maker with a low aversion to risk establishes different objectives, evaluates alternatives differently, and selects different alternatives than a decision maker in the same situation who has a high aversion to risk. The latter attempts to make choices where the risk or uncertainty is low or where the certainty of the outcome is high. The best managers need to tread a fine line between making ill-conceived, arbitrary decisions based purely on instinct (low aversion to risk) and becoming too obsessed with a reliance on numbers, analyses, and reports (high aversion to risk).[50]

According to one management researcher, the amount of risk in any given decision depends on three questions: (1) Have clear goals been established? (2) Is information about possible alternatives known? (3) Have future outcomes associated with the possible alternatives been indentified?[51] Depending on the answers to each of these questions, a framework can be used to classify whether decisions are being made under conditions of certainty, risk, or uncertainty. The framework is illustrated in Figure 16.2 and is based on the following definitions: *certainty* is having all the information the decision maker needs to make a decision; *risk* occurs when information about alternatives is available, but little is known about the outcomes associated with these alternatives; and *uncertainty* refers to the situation when managers have little to no information about possible alternatives or their associated outcomes. In general, decisions that are made under conditions

FIGURE 16.2
A Framework for Classifying Decisions

	Probability of Failure: Low ⟵		⟶ High
Characteristics of Decision	**Certainty**	**Risk**	**Uncertainty**
Goals are clearly established	Yes	Yes	Yes
Information about possible alternatives is available	Yes	Yes	No
Future outcomes associated with alternatives are understood	Yes	No	No

of uncertainty are more likely to fail as compared with those made under risk and certainty conditions.

When making decisions, managers who can identify goals in a clear manner and gather relevant information about possible alternative solutions and outcomes related to those alternatives are more likely to make successful decisions. Unfortunately, managers do not always have the time, patience, or resources to gather extensive amounts of information about problems. In addition, decision makers may frame problems in a way such that viable solutions can be discovered. Day-to-day time pressures and deadlines brought about by demanding clients, changing market conditions, and interacting with co-workers and supervisors can encourage managers to make nonoptimal decisions.[52]

To better understand how individuals make decisions under conditions of uncertainty, two researchers developed a theory that includes the role of emotion in the decision-making process.[53] In contrast to the rational model of decision making, prospect theory posits that the ways in which individuals frame problems influence their decisions. When a problem is framed in a positive manner, it was reported that subjects tended to avoid risky choices. The reasoning was that individuals become risk-averse under these conditions because they do not like the idea of losing something of value. In contrast, when individuals framed problems in a negative light, they tended to be more risk oriented in their decisions. The idea here is that they have nothing to lose, so they are more inclined to take risks.[54] For example, a manager of a larger car rental agency may acknowledge that the agency occasionally runs out of cars (leaving its customers without any transportation), but he is quick to say that it only happens once in a while and it is not a large problem (i.e., he frames the problem in a positive manner). Thus, he is not likely to make any decisions to improve the inventory situation.

On the other hand, if the manager framed the problem as being one that could eventually hurt his business (by losing return business, goodwill, etc.), then he would be much more likely to make a decision to improve his inventory management system. Although the research support for this theory has been mixed, prospect theory represents a thought-provoking addition to the understanding of how managers make decisions in everyday life.[55] Suffice it to say that managers should be cognizant of their tendencies to frame problems in either a positive or negative light. By being unduly positive about a given issue, managers may hesitate or avoid a proactive decision. In contrast, those managers who tend to see every problem as a "do or die" scenario will tend to take large risks even when the potential return at times is quite negligible. Framing problems in a balanced, objective manner will help managers improve their overall problem-solving skills.

Potential for Dissonance

Much attention has focused on the forces that influence the decision maker before a decision is made and that impact the decision itself. Only recently has attention been given to what happens after a decision has been made. Specifically, behavioral scientists have focused attention on *postdecision anxiety.*

cognitive dissonance
Anxiety that occurs when there is conflict between an individual's beliefs and reality. Most individuals are motivated to reduce dissonance and achieve consonance.

Such anxiety is related to what Leon Festinger called **cognitive dissonance** more than 35 years ago and what researchers today term *regret theory.*[56] This theory states that there is often a lack of consistency, or harmony, among an individual's various cognitions (attitudes, beliefs, etc.) after a decision has been made. As a result, the decision maker has doubts and second thoughts about the choice. For example, a manager may decide to fire an employee but then (two weeks later) when he realizes how much the ex-employee actually did for the organization, the manager may experience dissonance and regret his decision. In addition, the intensity of the anxiety is likely to be greater in the presence of any of the following conditions:

1. The decision is psychologically and/or financially important.
2. There are a number of forgone alternatives.
3. The forgone alternatives have many favorable features.

Dissonance can, of course, be reduced by admitting that a mistake has been made. Unfortunately, many individuals are reluctant to admit that they've made a wrong decision. These individuals are more likely to reduce their dissonance by using one or more of the following methods:

1. Seek information that supports the wisdom of their decisions.
2. Selectively perceive (distort) information in a way that supports their decisions.
3. Adopt a less favorable view of the forgone alternatives.
4. Minimize the importance of the negative aspects of the decisions and exaggerate the importance of the positive aspects.

Although each of us may resort to some of this behavior in our personal decision making, a great deal of such behavior could easily harm organizational effectiveness.

Personality, specifically the level of self-confidence and persuasibility, heavily influences potential for dissonance. In fact, all of the behavioral influences are closely interrelated and are only isolated here for purposes of discussion.[57]

Escalation of Commitment

Another variation on the rational model of decision making occurs when a decision maker adheres to a course of action even when confronted with negative information concerning the viability of that course of action.[58] It has been observed that after a setback of some sort, decision makers escalate their commitment of resources (e.g., time, money) to the same course of action to recoup the losses.[59] Such a tendency to escalate commitment in light of additional negative consequences can influence a variety of organizational decisions: mergers and acquisitions, hiring and promotion decisions, and investment choices. A classic example of an investment decision that was made and held to despite strong opposition by local residents was the Shoreham Nuclear Power Plant project in Long Island, New York. When the project was announced in 1966, the estimated cost was approximately $75 million with the goal of having the plant on line by 1973.[60] Owing primarily to intense opposition from local groups in Suffolk County, the massive project ended up taking 23 years and over $5 billion to complete.[61] Despite the escalation of commitment involved in this case, the plant was never opened and was eventually dismantled. The entire cost of the project was passed on to consumers of electricity in the region.[62] Another example can be seen in the next OB at Work feature, in which Henry Ford, despite millions of dollars and many years of investment, was unable to produce sufficient quantities of rubber for tire production in the Amazon.

Although numerous theories have been offered to explain this phenomenon, self-justification theory has received a considerable amount of attention.[63] Self-justification theory states that decision makers will escalate their commitment to a course of action because they do not want to admit—to themselves, others, or both—that prior resources were not allocated properly. In other words, individuals stay the course because they do not want to admit that they were incorrect; instead they convince themselves of the correctness of the earlier decisions by continuing to pursue them.[64]

Managers need to be aware of this tendency to justify their past actions by continuing on an ill-fated course of action. It is recommended that managers take a step back periodically

OB AT WORK Henry Ford Established Fordlândia ("Ford Land") in the Amazon!

In the late 1920s, automotive manufacturing legend Henry Ford committed to the idea that he must control the sourcing of the raw material for the millions of tires his cars required, namely *rubber*. Until then, Ford had no choice but to purchase rubber at unacceptably high prices from European companies that harvested rubber from rubber trees on plantations in Southeast Asia. So, Ford reasoned that it would make more sense to source rubber from the Americas, where the material could be shipped to his automotive plants in the United States. With this goal in mind, he bought approximately 2.5 million acres deep in the heart of the Amazon in Brazil. Accessible only by boat, the area was named "Fordlândia" (or "Ford Land" in English), and its primary mission was to produce enough rubber to satisfy the car company's rubber needs. That seemed like an obtainable goal, considering that Brazilian Amazon was home to many native rubber trees.

Henry Ford committed to much more than just rubber production. He transferred an entire slice of "Americana" to the heart of the Amazon. He sent top American engineers and their families to live in Fordlândia. These individuals supervised the building of an American-like town, complete with a state-of-art hospital, generators for electricity, paved streets, spacious homes, wells that pumped fresh water, well-built buildings to house the rubber manufacturing equipment, and even U.S.-style mailboxes to line the streets of this new town.

Unfortunately, this total commitment by Henry Ford to producing rubber in the Amazon led to several crises and the ultimate demise of the $20 million venture. Determined to use U.S. engineers from the Ford Company to make Fordlândia a success, Henry Ford underestimated the specialized knowledge that was necessary to grow rubber trees. The rubber trees did not grow or produce rubber. The land that he purchased turned out to be too moist and hilly for the trees. Also, the U.S. engineers directed the Brazilian workers to plant 1.4 million trees, too many for the acreage. Expert botanists suggested that the reason the trees weren't growing was due to a leaf disease and insects that thrived when the rubber trees' leaves were too close to one another. Contributing to the failure of the enterprise was the Brazilian workers' resistance to Henry Ford's insistence on doing things the "American way." Workers were asked to work a normal day shift (6 a.m. to 3 p.m.) in the fields. Also, the cafeteria served American-style cuisine that was dubbed "healthy" by Henry Ford. The workers preferred to work several hours before sunrise and after sunset due to the scorching sun of the tropics. Also, they preferred their own foods and were annoyed by the American foods that were forced on them.

What did Henry Ford do after three years of trying to grow rubber trees at Fordlândia? Despite the losses and frustrations associated with Fordlândia, he bought a new tract of land in the Amazon which was named "Belterra." The land was flatter and less damp, making it much more suitable to growing rubber trees. He imported seedlings from Southeast Asia that were more resistant to the leaf diseases and had his workers toil for the next 10 years. Although more productive than Fordlândia, the Belterra plantation yielded a peak output of 750 tons of latex in 1942, which was far below that year's goal of 38,000 tons.

Henry Ford's commitment to harvesting rubber at Belterra in the Amazon could have succeeded over time, but the increased popularity of synthetic rubber led to the eventual demise of Ford's vision of bringing American know-how and culture to the Amazon; eventually, the Ford Motor Company sold the land back to the Brazilian government for a nominal amount. With the advantage of 20/20 hindsight, many observers consider this escalation of commitment an unfortunate waste of resources and time.

Sources: Adapted from Greg Grandin, *Fordlandia: The Rise and Fall of Henry Ford's Forgotten Jungle City* (New York: Metropolitan Books, 2009); Mary A. Dempsey, "Fordlandia," *Michigan History*, July/August 1994, pp. 24–33; http://www.michiganhistorymagazine.com/extra/fordlandia/fordlandia.html; Joseph A. Russell, "Fordlandia and Belterra, Rubber Plantations on the Tapajos River Brazil," *Economic Geography* 18, no. 2 (April 1942): 125–45; and http://fordlandia.com/.

and evaluate, as objectively as possible, whether a project or initiative is meeting expectations in terms of satisfactory financial return, expanded markets, and the like. A high level of self-monitoring and seeking feedback will tend to reduce this potential cognitive distortion in decision making.

Group Decision Making

Until now, this chapter has focused on individuals making decisions. In most organizations, however, a great deal of decision making is achieved through committees, teams, task forces, and other groups. Managers frequently face situations in which they must seek and combine judgments in group meetings. This is especially true for nonprogrammed problems, which are novel and involve much uncertainty regarding the outcome. In most organizations, decisions on such problems are rarely made by one individual on a regular basis. The increased complexity of many of these problems requires specialized knowledge in numerous fields—knowledge usually not possessed by one person. This requirement, coupled with the reality that the decisions made must eventually be accepted and implemented by many units throughout the organization, has increased the use of the collective approach to the decision-making process. As a result, many managers spend as much as 80 percent of their working time in committee meetings.

In addition to interorganizational meetings, managers are increasingly being called upon to participate in collaborative efforts between organizations.[65] Collaboration involves "a process of joint decision making among key stakeholders of a problem domain about the future of that domain."[66] Managers participate in many forms of collaborative decision-making efforts, including those that involve dealings with other for-profit organizations and those that consist of partnering with nonprofit or government organizations. Some collaborations concentrate on advancing a shared decision among stakeholders, some focus on solving specific problems, and others are directed toward resolving conflicts among stakeholders.

Individual versus Group Decision Making

Considerable debate has taken place over the relative effectiveness of individual versus group decision making. Groups usually take more time to reach a decision than individuals do, but bringing specialists and experts together has benefits. The mutually reinforcing effect of their interaction results in better decisions, especially when a high degree of diversity among backgrounds exists and the group periodically adjusts its goals and objectives.[67] In fact, a great deal of research has shown that consensus decisions with five or more participants are superior to individual, majority vote, and leader decisions.[68]

Unfortunately, open discussion can be negatively influenced by behavioral factors, such as the pressure to conform. Such pressure may be the influence of a dominant personality in the group—"status incongruity" may cause lower-status participants to be inhibited by higher-status participants and to "go along" even though they believe that their own ideas are superior, or certain participants may attempt to exert influence based on the perception that they are experts in the problem area.[69]

This perception of expertise also inhibits group consideration of outside assistance. Group members may show a negative bias toward advice and guidance given by nongroup members, regardless of value, preferring instead to consider only internally generated solutions to problems.[70]

Certain decisions appear to be better made by groups, while others appear better suited to individual decision making. Nonprogrammed decisions appear to be better suited to group decision making. Such decisions usually call for pooled talent in arriving at a solution; also, the decisions are so important that they are usually made by top managers and to a somewhat lesser extent by middle managers.

In terms of the decision-making process itself, the following points concerning group processes for nonprogrammed decisions can be made:

1. In *establishing objectives,* groups are probably superior to individuals because of the greater amount of knowledge available to groups.
2. In *identifying alternatives,* the individual efforts of group members encourage a broad search in various functional areas of the organization.
3. In *evaluating alternatives,* the collective judgment of the group, with its wider range of viewpoints, seems superior to that of the individual decision maker.

FIGURE 16.3
Probable Relationship between Quality of Group Decision and Method Utilized

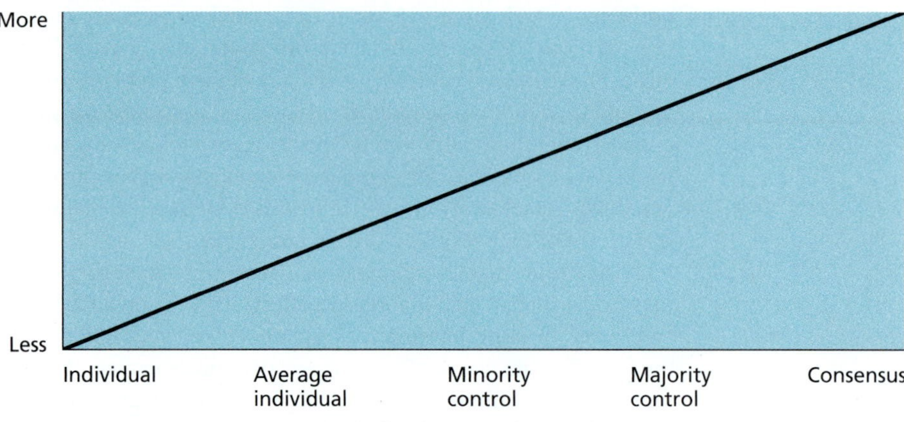

4. In *choosing an alternative*, group interaction and the achievement of consensus usually result in the acceptance of more risk than would be accepted by an individual decision maker. Also, the group decision is more likely to be accepted as a result of the participation of those affected by its consequences.
5. *Implementing a decision*, whether or not it was made by a group, is usually accomplished by individual managers. Thus, individuals bear responsibility for implementing the group's decision.

Figure 16.3 summarizes the research findings on group decision making. It shows the probable relationship between the quality of a decision and the method used to reach the decision. It indicates that as we move from individual to consensus decision making, the quality of the decision improves. Also, each successive method involves a higher level of mutual influence by group members. Thus, for a complex problem requiring pooled knowledge, the quality of the decision is likely to be higher as the group moves toward consensus.

Techniques for Stimulating Creativity in Group Decision Making

Because groups are better suited than individuals to making nonprogrammed decisions, an atmosphere fostering group creativity should be developed. In this respect, group decision making may be similar to brainstorming. Discussion must be free-flowing and spontaneous, all group members must participate, and the evaluation of individual ideas must be suspended in the beginning to encourage participation. However, a decision must be reached, and this is where group decision making differs from brainstorming. The next OB and Your Career provides some tips on how to increase your creativity within a team or group framework.

Group decision making probably is preferable to individual decision making in many instances. However, you may have heard the statement "A camel is a racehorse designed by a committee." While the necessity and benefits of group decision making are recognized, it also can present numerous problems, some of which have already been noted. For example, a recent meta-analysis (a study that analyzes the results of several other research studies) of 108 research studies with 10,632 teams reported that diverse teams have higher levels of creativity and satisfaction, but also experience more task conflict and social integration issues.[71] Practicing managers need specific techniques that enable them to increase the benefits from group decision making while reducing the problems associated with it.

Increasing the creative capability of a group is especially necessary when individuals from diverse sectors of the organization must pool their judgments to create a satisfactory course of action for the organization. When subordinates and peers believe that the manager

OB AND YOUR CAREER Sparking Your Creativity

Most knowledge-based organizations need employees who can be creative problem-solvers both individually and with their fellow team members. The real value and potential competitive advantage of such firms lies not in their physical or financial assets but rather in their intellectual assets—the ideas and insights in the minds of their employees. Such organizations cannot survive without creativity and are discovering that it is a skill that can be developed. Here are some tips for becoming more creative:

1. Get out of the office. Take a walk at a park or mall during lunch. Give your mind a chance to percolate on the problem or issue. Try to minimize phone calls, text messages, and other distracting activities during this quiet thinking time.
2. Be childlike. Try to look at the problem like a child would. Some believe this fresh approach is the most important gateway to thinking outside the box because it frees the mind of conventional "grown up" thinking.
3. Be a maverick. The best ideas and decisions often come from those who don't care about what others are thinking of them.
4. Break your routine. Park on a different side of the building. Talk with people you don't know well. Read a magazine or blog that wouldn't normally interest you. Ideas can come from many different sources.
5. Ask "What if . . . ?" This question can stimulate your thoughts and plenty of discussion in a group.
6. Listen. No one has a monopoly on good ideas. Ask questions, and then listen.

Source: Adapted from John M. Ivancevich, Robert Konopaske, and Michael T. Matteson, *Organizational Behavior and Management*, 9th ed. (Burr Ridge, IL: McGraw-Hill, 2011), p. 426.

in charge of the group is essentially nonbiased or "on their side," group members may express their viewpoints more freely and feel less compelled to protect themselves from potentially nonsupportive or retaliatory responses.[72] When properly utilized, three techniques—brainstorming, the Delphi process, and the nominal group technique—have been extremely useful in increasing the group's creative capability in generating ideas, understanding problems, and reaching better decisions.

Brainstorming

brainstorming
A technique that promotes creativity by encouraging idea generation through noncritical discussion.

In many situations, groups are expected to produce creative or imaginative solutions to organizational problems. In such instances, **brainstorming** often enhances the creative output of the group. Brainstorming includes a strict series of rules to promote the generation of ideas while at the same time removing members' inhibitions that usually stymie face-to-face groups. The basic rules are these:

1. No idea is too ridiculous. Group members are encouraged to state any extreme or outlandish idea.
2. Each idea presented belongs to the group, not to the person stating it. In this way, group members use and build on the ideas of others.
3. No idea can be criticized. The purpose of the session is to generate, not evaluate, ideas.

Brainstorming is widely used in advertising, where it's apparently effective. In some other fields, it has been less successful. Brainstorming groups normally produce fewer ideas than do the equivalent number of individuals working by themselves, and there's no evaluation or ranking of the ideas generated.[73] Thus, the group never really concludes the problem-solving process.

Delphi Process

This technique involves soliciting and comparing anonymous judgments on the topic of interest through a set of sequential questionnaires interspersed with summarized information and feedback of opinions from earlier responses.[74]

Delphi process
A technique that promotes creativity by using anonymous judgment of ideas to reach a consensus decision.

The **Delphi process** retains the advantage of having several judges while removing the biasing effects that might occur during face-to-face interaction. The basic approach has been to collect anonymous judgments by mail questionnaire. For example, the members independently generate their ideas to answer the first questionnaire and return it. The staff members summarize the responses as the group consensus and feed this summary back, along with a second questionnaire for reassessment. Based on this feedback, respondents independently evaluate their earlier responses. The underlying belief is that the consensus estimate results in a better decision after several rounds of anonymous group judgment. However, while continuing the procedure for several rounds is possible, studies have shown essentially no significant change after the second round of estimation.

An interesting application of the Delphi process was undertaken by the American Marketing Association to determine the international issues most likely to have significant impact on the marketing efforts of the organization.[75] Twenty-nine experts on international marketing participated in the study. Major issues the experts identified included the environment, globalization, regional trading blocks, internationalization of service industries, and rising foreign direct investment.

Nominal Group Technique

nominal group technique (NGT)
A technique that promotes creativity by bringing people together in a very structured meeting that allows little verbal communication. Group decision is the mathematically pooled outcome of individual votes.

Nominal group technique has gained increasing recognition in health, social service, education, industry, and government organizations.[76] The term **nominal group technique (NGT)** was adopted by earlier researchers to refer to processes that bring people together but don't allow them to communicate verbally. Thus, the collection of people is a group "nominally" (in name only).

Basically, NGT is a structured group meeting in which 7 to 10 individuals sit around a table but don't speak to one another. Each person writes ideas on a pad of paper. After five minutes, a structured sharing of ideas takes place. Each person presents one idea. A person designated as recorder writes the ideas on a flip chart in full view of the entire group. This continues until all participants indicate that they have no further ideas to share. There is still no discussion.

The output of the first phase is a list of ideas (usually between 18 and 25). The next phase involves structured discussion in which each idea receives attention before a vote is taken. This is achieved by asking for clarification or stating the degree of support for each idea listed on the flip chart. The last stage involves independent voting in which each participant, in private, selects priorities by ranking or voting. The group decision is the mathematically pooled outcome of the individual votes.

Both the Delphi process and NGT have proved to be more productive than brainstorming.[77] Each has had an excellent success record. Basic differences between the Delphi process and NGT are

1. Delphi participants are typically anonymous to one another, whereas NGT participants become acquainted.
2. NGT participants meet face-to-face around a table, while Delphi participants are physically distant and never meet.
3. In the Delphi process, all communication between participants is by way of written questionnaires and feedback from the monitoring staff. In NGT, participants communicate directly.[78]

Practical considerations, of course, often influence which technique is used. For example, such factors as the number of available working hours, costs, and the physical proximity of participants influence selection of a technique.

Rather than making readers experts in the Delphi process or NGT, this section has aimed to indicate the frequency and importance of group decision making in every organization.

The three techniques discussed are practical devices for improving the effectiveness of group decisions.

Decision making is a responsibility shared by all managers, regardless of functional area or management level. Every day, they are required to make decisions that shape the future of their organizations as well as their own futures. Some of these decisions may have a strong impact on the organization's success, while others are less crucial. However, all decisions have some effect (positive or negative, large or small) on the organization. The quality of these decisions is the yardstick of managerial effectiveness. In summary, we remind the reader that decision making is a skill that is gained through experience of trial and error.[79]

In other words, one must make some wrong decisions to learn how to make right ones.

Summary of Key Points

- Decision making is a fundamental process in organizations. Managers make decisions on the basis of the information (communication) they receive through the organization structure and the behavior of individuals and groups within it.
- Decision making distinguishes managers from nonmanagers. The quality of managers' decisions determines their effectiveness as managers.
- Decisions may be classified as programmed or nonprogrammed, depending on the problem. Most programmed decisions should be made at the first level in the organization, while nonprogrammed decisions should be made mostly by top management.
- Decision making should not be thought of as an end but as a means to achieve organizational goals and objectives. Decisions are organizational responses to problems.
- Decision making should be viewed as a multiphased process in which the actual choice is only one phase. The preceding phases are establishing goals, identifying problems, developing alternatives, and evaluating alternatives.
- The decision-making process is influenced by numerous environmental and behavioral factors. Because of different values, perceptions, and personalities, different decision makers may not select identical alternatives in the same situation.
- A great deal of nonprogrammed decision making is carried on in group situations. Much evidence supports the claim that in most instances, group decisions are superior to individual decisions. Three techniques (brainstorming, the Delphi process, and the nominal group technique) improve the effectiveness of group decisions. The management of collective decision making must be a vital concern for future managers.

Discussion and Review Questions

1. Think about a current (or past) supervisor that you have (or had) at a job. What types of programmed decisions did he make? What types of nonprogrammed decisions needed to be addressed? Explain.
2. When looking at the decision-making process (Figure 16.1), do you feel any one step is more important than the others? If so, why?
3. Describe a situation you've encountered where a decision made by an individual would have been better made by a group. Why do you feel this way?
4. Think back to the most recent big decision you had to make about work (e.g., asking for a pay raise), a major financial decision (e.g., buying a car), or a school-related issue (e.g., whether to take a certain course with a certain professor). How many different alternatives did you consider? Did you rush your decision? Explain.
5. Think of a time when you held fast to a decision even after learning that it was probably a wrong or faulty decision. How long did you persist with your original (faulty)

decision? Looking back now, when should you have modified your decision? What could have convinced you to do so? Describe.

6. Some people equate values and ethics. If you were a member of a group and you felt the group was making an unethical decision or one that conflicted with your values, what would you do? How far would you go to stop the unethical action?
7. Describe a situation in which you were forced to make a decision where your values helped make the final choice.
8. Brainstorming can be a very effective method for stimulating creativity for group decision making. Describe a situation where you either used or could have used brainstorming to come up with a creative idea. How did the brainstorming begin or how would you have begun the process?
9. Assume you are about to purchase a used car (i.e., a decision without "perfect" information). How would go about reducing the uncertainty associated with this decision? What specific steps could you take to make sure you are getting a good car for a fair price? Explain.
10. Think of a corporate executive who, you believe, is a good decision maker. What traits make this executive effective?

Taking It to the Net

Can Better Decision Making Be Taught?

Kepner-Tregoe, a management consulting and training firm, thinks so. Specializing in strategic and operational decision making for over 50 years, the firm has instructed thousands of executives and managers in how to make better decisions. Kepner-Tregoe offers seminars to businesses that focus on a step-by-step approach to help people organize information, use experience, and improve judgment to solve complex problems and make informed decisions. The company believes that better decision making helps its clients to reduce costs, increase productivity, and make gains in bottom-line results. For more information, visit their Web site at http://www.kepner-tregoe.com.

Using any search engine (e.g., www.google.com or www.yahoo.com), go online and identify five other consulting companies that offer training seminars that help employees and managers enhance their decision-making skills. After identifying the five Web sites, write and present a brief summary about the types of training programs being offered and the types of clients they are targeting. Do you think you would benefit from these types of training programs? How about your organization? Why or why not?

Case for Analysis: *Breaking the Rules*

Nancy Taggart worked in the customer service department at the Xemas Company. The Xemas Company manufactured industrial air conditioning systems and replacement parts for these systems. Xemas sold its products to large regional distributors, which, in turn, supplied and supported independent dealers throughout the United States and Canada.

One night, Nancy received a call from one of Xemas's dealers who seemed unduly agitated. The dealer said he had a customer who needed a part for his air conditioning system right away and the dealer didn't have the part in stock. He claimed he had tried to reach his distributor for the past two hours, but he was unable to get through on the phone. He asked if Nancy could send the part overnight and then bill the distributor. The charge would then be included on the invoice the distributor sent the dealer at the end of the month.

Because it was past the distributor's normal operating hours, Nancy knew she couldn't reach anyone there. Furthermore, Nancy knew something was amiss, as

Xemas had discontinued this type of shipping and billing practice because distributors had complained. They wanted to control all shipments to reduce the chance of selling to a bad credit risk.

But even though Nancy knew the rules, she decided to break them, based on the seemingly urgent nature of the situation. The dealer said the customer needed the part immediately. Nancy decided customer service was the most important issue involved in the situation, so she sent the part out promptly.

The next day, the local distributor was called. It turned out the dealer wasn't a regular customer of the distributor. Because of this situation, the distributor refused to pay for the part. While Xemas would try to get the dealer to pay directly to them, for the time being the company was out $150, the cost of the part. To make sure the books balanced, Nancy wrote out a personal check for $150 to cover the cost of the part and sent it to billing.

Within days, Nancy received a phone call from one of the firm's executive vice presidents, Ramon Hernandez. Ramon told Nancy that he had received a call from a supervisor in the billing department. The person he spoke to was irate and insisted that something he done about this employee, Nancy Taggart, who had broken company rules. Ramon then asked Nancy for an explanation for her actions. After hearing Nancy's story, Ramon stated that he agreed with the billing supervisor concerning the seriousness of the situation, and that actions did indeed need to be taken. He informed Nancy that she would hear from him the next day regarding those actions.

The next evening, when Nancy arrived at work, a letter awaited her from Ramon. With a feeling of dread, Nancy opened the letter. Inside was a check for $150. Attached to the check was a note from Ramon. The note stated that Nancy was going to be given both a raise and a preferred parking spot.

DISCUSSION QUESTIONS

1. Why was Nancy rewarded for breaking the rules?
2. Describe what type of decision Nancy had to make. What decision alternatives were available to her besides the one she chose?
3. What types of behavioral factors might have influenced Nancy's decision?

Sources: Adapted from David Armstrong, "Management by Storytelling," *Executive Female*, May–June 1992, p. 77; David E. Bowen and Edward E. Lawler III, "The Empowerment of Service Workers," *Sloan Management Review* (Spring 1992): 31–39; and Leonard L. Berry and A. Parasuraman, "Services Marketing Starts from Within," *Marketing Management* (Winter 1992): 25–34.

Experiential Exercise: *Lost on the Moon: A Group Decision Exercise*

OBJECTIVE

To come as close as possible to the "best solution" as determined by experts of the National Aeronautics and Space Administration (NASA).

RELATED TOPICS

Motivation, individual differences, and group development are important topics related to this exercise.

STARTING THE EXERCISE

After reading the following scenario, you will, first individually and then as a member of a team, rank the importance of items available for carrying out your mission.

THE SCENARIO

Your spaceship has just crash-landed on the moon. You were scheduled to rendezvous with a mother ship 200 miles away on the lighted surface of the moon, but the rough landing has ruined your ship and all of the equipment aboard, except for the 15 items listed on the worksheet on the next page. Your crew's survival depends on reaching the mother ship, so you must choose the most critical items available for the 200-mile trip. Your task is to rank the 15 items in the worksheet on page 486 in terms of their importance for survival. Place number 1 by the most important item, number 2 by the second most important, and so on through number 15, the least important.

COMPLETING THE EXERCISE

Phase I: 15 minutes. Read the scenario. Then, in column 2 (Your Ranks) of the worksheet, assign priorities to the 15 items listed. Use a pencil since you may wish to change your rankings. Somewhere on the sheet, you may wish to note your logic for each ranking.

Worksheet Items	1 NASA'S Ranks	2 Your Ranks	3 Error Points	4 Group Ranks	5 Error Points
Box of matches	____	____	____	____	____
Food concentrate	____	____	____	____	____
Fifty feet of nylon rope	____	____	____	____	____
Parachute silk	____	____	____	____	____
Solar-powered portable heating unit	____	____	____	____	____
Two .45-caliber pistols	____	____	____	____	____
One case of dehydrated milk	____	____	____	____	____
Two 100-pound tanks of oxygen	____	____	____	____	____
Stellar map (of the moon's constellation)	____	____	____	____	____
Self-inflating life raft	____	____	____	____	____
Magnetic compass	____	____	____	____	____
Five gallons of water	____	____	____	____	____
Signal flares	____	____	____	____	____
First-aid kit containing injection needles	____	____	____	____	____
Solar-powered FM receiver-transmitter	____	____	____	____	____
Total error points			Individual ____		Group ____

Phase II: 25 minutes. Your instructor will assign you to a team. The task of each team is to arrive at a consensus on the rankings. Share your individual solutions and reach a consensus—the ranking for each of the 15 items that best satisfies all team members. Thus, by the end of phase II, all members of the team should have the same set of rankings in column 4 (Group Ranks). Do not change your individual rankings in column 2.

Phase III: 10 minutes. Your instructor will provide you with the "best solution" to the problem—that is, the set of rankings determined by the NASA experts, along with their reasoning. Each person should note this set of rankings in column 1 (NASA's Ranks). (Note: While it is fun to debate the experts' rankings and their reasoning, remember that the objective of the game is to learn more about decision making, not how to survive on the moon!)

Phase IV (evaluation): 15 minutes. Now, see how well you did individually and as a team. First, find your individual score by taking, for each item, the absolute difference between your ranks (column 2) and NASA's ranks (column 1) and writing it in the first error points column (column 3). Thus, if you ranked "Box of matches" 3 and NASA ranked it 8, you would put a 5 in column 3, across from "Box of matches." Then, add the error points in column 3 and write the total at the bottom in the space for individual total error points.

Next, score your group performance in the same way, this time taking the absolute differences between group ranks (column 4) and NASA's ranks (column 1) and writing them in the second error points column (column 5). Add the group error points and write the total in the space provided. (Note that all members of the team have the same group error points.)

Finally, prepare three pieces of information to be submitted when your instructor calls on your team:

1. Average individual total error points (the average of all group members' individual totals). One team member should add these figures and divide by the number of team members to get the average.
2. Group total error points, as shown on each group member's work sheet.
3. Number of team members who had fewer individual total error points than the group total error points.

Using this information, your instructor will evaluate the results of the exercise and discuss group versus individual performance. Together, you will then explore the implications of this exercise for the group decision-making process.

CHAPTER SEVENTEEN

Managing Organizational Change and Learning

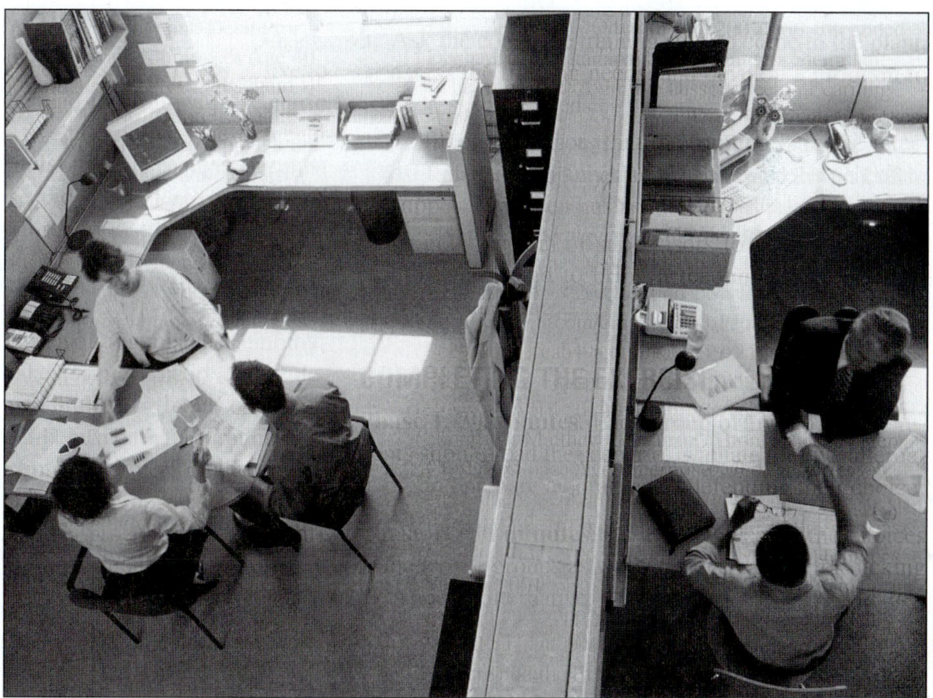

Learning Objectives

After completing Chapter 17, you should be able to

Describe
The seven-step model of organizational change.

Describe
Sources of change and alternative change management.

Discuss
The ethical issues that arise in organizational development practices.

Compare
Alternative interventions that management can implement to improve performance.

Identify
How appreciative inquiry can be used to overcome resistance to change.

Managing Change Is a Proactive Behavior

Lemon feta cheese, fresh basil, artichoke hearts, pepperoni, organic tomato sauce—all are ingredients of a major change on the menu at Round Table Pizza, a franchise restaurant chain headquartered in Concord, California. Because it's thinner and requires some altered cooking methods, the Pepperoni Artisan pizza is a departure from other pizzas Round Table makes.

New menu items, however, account for only some of the changes that Round Table Pizza has been making for business reasons—it is managing with a strong focus on employees. The company's initiatives include implementing a new performance management system and integrating employees in transition from franchised to company-owned stores.

"Thirty years ago, a *Fortune* 100 probably had one or two enterprisewide change initiatives going on; today that number is probably between 20 and 25," says Jeffrey M. Hiatt, CEO of Prosci Inc., a business process reengineering company in Loveland, Colorado, and author of books on change management. Not only have change interventions been on the rise, but the importance of managing individuals through change has been gaining credence as well. Corporate leaders are concluding that it can be costly to fail to manage employees through the process.

An employer who is serious about change management has to use a proactive approach that includes communication, a road map for the sponsors of change, training programs that go along with the overall project, a plan for dealing with resistance, and patience and long-term commitment.

Mutual of Omaha, which until recently offered a class for all employees on how to navigate change, decided it needed a new approach for dealing with change management—in part because of new projects in technology areas. The company is working with Prosci Inc. to help managers and employees understand and navigate the change process in real time. They are using worksheets for the ADKAR change management model, which Prosci publishes. ADKAR stands for awareness, desire, knowledge, ability, and reinforcement—the five stages of personal change management.

The worksheets provide managers first, and then employees, a chance to analyze their feelings about changes taking place in their personal and professional lives. Once they identify areas of resistance, the model helps them find ways to overcome those barriers.

Using this approach with managers first helps them gain an understanding of what their employees may be feeling. Having managers use it with their employees helps those employees make adjustments to their own attitude and provides managers with useful feedback about areas they need to address with their staffs.

Tools such as ADKAR can be useful, but unless managers have developed some of the softer skill sets, they may not be successful in helping their employees through the change process. Unless you build competencies with managers, the conversations they have with their employees will be about managing resistance, not managing change. Inexperienced managers may resort to threats.

Managers at Round Table Pizza are trained in helping employees understand their role in an "ownership" environment and see that what they do is essential to the success of the company and, ultimately, to their own success.

Before a new product or project is rolled at Round Table Pizza, employees meet with their managers and bring any issues they may have to the table. Their concerns could range from an element of a new corporate procedure to the taste of a new pizza flavor, and the company listens.

Feedback can produce a variety of results—from employees' comments on product changes as at Round Table Pizza, to identification of significant problems in adjusting to the change. In some instances, managers may lack the skills necessary for leading their workers into the change. Or they may not have bought into the change—and have let employees know it.

Sources: Adapted from http://www.change-management.com/ (accessed July 10, 2010); Nancy Hatch Woodward, "To Make Changes, Manage Them," *HR Magazine*, May 2007, pp. 63–67; Round Table Pizza, accessed at www.roundtablepizza.com on May 1, 2007; and "Using ADKAR to Manage Change," accessed at www.change-management.com/tutorial-adkar-series-1.htm on April 10, 2007.

As managers contemplate the futures of their organizations in the midst of a prolonged recession and rapidly changing global business environment, they can't escape the inevitability of change. *Change* is certainly among the most frequently used words on the business pages of every newspaper in the world. Not only have entire countries and empires gone through dramatic and wrenching changes, but so have great companies such as IBM, General Motors, and Ford. Some organizations have not survived: Montgomery Ward, Pan-American Airlines, and Circuit City no longer exist. So it makes a great deal of sense for managers to address the issues associated with managing change; the overall effectiveness and survival of their organizations depend on it.

Well-known business writers state that contemporary business organizations confront changing circumstance that put bygone eras of change to shame by comparison. The combination of global competition, computer-assisted manufacturing methods, the Internet, and instant communications has implications more far-reaching than anything since the beginning of the Industrial Revolution.[1] Popular literature, including best sellers, warns managers that their organizations' futures depend on their ability to master change.[2] Other authors state that change is a pervasive, persistent, and permanent condition for all organizations.[3]

Effective managers must view managing change as an integral responsibility, rather than as a peripheral one.[4] But we must accept the reality that not all organizations will successfully make the appropriate changes. Those with the best chance for success are relatively small and compete in industries in which research and development expenditures have traditionally been relatively high and barriers to entry are relatively low. Such firms in these industries have changed to survive and they are likely to be the survivors in the 21st century.[5]

This chapter explores issues associated with managing change through the application of structural, behavioral, and technological change programs and interventions. Our point of view is that the important management responsibility of managing change can best be undertaken and accomplished by applying specific processes and interventions.

Learning Principles and Change

To better understand how changes are brought about in individuals, we must comprehend the various principles of learning discussed in Chapter 6. Managers can design a theoretically sound organizational change program, yet not achieve any of the anticipated results because they overlooked the importance of providing motivation, reinforcement, and feedback to employees.[6] These principles of learning serve to unfreeze old learning, instill new learning, and refreeze that new learning.

Unfreezing old learning requires people who want to learn new ways to think and act. Unfreezing deals directly with resistance to change.[7] Individuals may not accept that they need more skill in a particular job or more understanding of the problems of other units of the firm. Some people recognize this need and are receptive to experiences that will aid them in developing new skills or new empathies. Others reject the need or play it down because learning is to them an admission that they aren't completely competent in their jobs. These kinds of people face the prospect of change with different expectations and motivations. Determining the expectations and motivations of people isn't easy. It is, however, a task that managers must undertake to manage change; it's management's responsibility to show employees why they should want to change.

Movement to new learning requires training, demonstration, and empowerment. Training nonmanagerial employees hasn't been a high priority among many American corporations, but recent losses of market shares to foreign competitors that invest greater resources in training have encouraged American firms to make training a regular part of their employees' assignments. Through training and demonstration of the appropriateness of that training, employees can be empowered to take on behaviors they previously had not imagined possible. New behaviors must be taught in a careful and sensitive manner.

Refreezing the learned behavior occurs through the application of reinforcement and feedback. When people receive encouragement, rewards, supportive information, or acclaim for doing something, they're more likely to do the same thing in a similar situation. The other side of the coin might suggest punishment for not responding to training and new ideas. Punishment will decrease the probability of repeating old behavior but cannot encourage acquiring new methods and views. It is easier to achieve successful change through the use of positive rewards. If the colleagues and superiors of newly trained people recognize and reinforce new ideas or new skills, the people will be encouraged to continue to behave in the new way. Reinforcement can also occur when the knowledge or skill acquired in a training program is imparted a second time through a refresher course.

Management must guard against the possibility that what a person has learned at a training site is lost when that person is transferred to the actual work site. If the training has gone well, only a minimum amount will be lost in this necessary transfer. A possible strategy for keeping the loss to a minimum is to make the training situation similar to the actual workplace environment.

If colleagues and superiors are not supportive, the newly trained people will be discouraged from persisting with attempts to use what they've learned. This is one reason why it has been suggested that superiors be trained before subordinates. The superior, if trained and motivated, can serve as a reinforcer and feedback source for the subordinate who has left the training confines and is now back on the job.

Change Agents

change agent
An intervener who brings a different perspective to a situation and challenges the status quo.

Because managers tend to seek answers in traditional solutions, the intervention of an outsider is often necessary. The intervener, or **change agent**, brings a different perspective to the situation and challenges the status quo. The success of any change program rests heavily on the quality and workability of the relationship between the change agent and the key decision makers within the organization. Thus, the form of intervention is a crucial consideration.[8]

To intervene is to enter into an organization or ongoing relationship among persons or departments, for the purpose of helping them improve their effectiveness. A number of forms of intervention are used in organizations.

External Change Agents

External change agents are temporary employees of the organization because they're engaged only for the duration of the change process. They originate in a variety of organizational types including universities, consulting firms, and training agencies. Many large organizations have individuals located at central offices who take temporary assignments with line units that are contemplating organizational development. At the conclusion of the change program, the change agent returns to headquarters.

The usual external change agent is a private consultant who has training and experience in the behavioral sciences. Such an individual will be contacted by the organization and then engaged after agreement is reached on the conditions of the relationship. Ordinarily, the change agent will have previous intervention experience and graduate degrees in specialties that focus on individual and group behavior in organizational settings. Many change agents are adept at "tuning in" and identifying key issues that need to be addressed with the organizational development intervention.[9] With this kind of experience and training, the external change agent has the perspective to facilitate the change process.

Internal Change Agents

The internal change agent is an individual working for the organization who knows something about its problems.[10] The usual internal change agent is a recently appointed manager or executive of the organization; often, the individual takes the job with the expectation that a major change is necessary. Sometimes, an internal team or entire department might be tasked with creating change throughout the organization. For example, Deustche Bank AG assigned its human resources department to spearhead a companywide change in the way the bank manages its people and processes.[11] How successful internal change agents undertake their roles has been extensively studied.

External–Internal Change Agents

Some organizations use a combination external–internal change team to intervene and develop programs. This approach attempts to use the resources and knowledge base of both external and internal change agents. It involves designating an individual or small group within the organization to serve with the external change agent as spearheads of the change effort. The internal group can come from any level or function in the organization. As a general rule, an external change agent will actively nurture the visible support of top management as a way to emphasize the importance of the change effort.[12]

Each of the three approaches to intervention has advantages and disadvantages. The external change agent is often viewed as an outsider. When this belief is held by employees inside the company, there's a need to establish rapport between the change agent and the decision makers. The change agent's views on the problems faced by the organization are often different from the decision makers' views, which leads to problems in establishing rapport. Differences in viewpoints often result in mistrust of the external change agent by the policy makers or a segment of the policy makers. Offsetting these disadvantages is the external change agent's ability to refocus the organization's relationship to changing environmental demands. In many cases, the external change agent offers a fresh perspective and is less encumbered by organizational baggage or biases. The external change agent has a comparative advantage over the internal change agent when significant strategic changes must be evaluated.[13]

The internal change agent is often viewed as being more closely associated with one unit or group of individuals in the organization. This perceived favoritism leads to resistance to change by those who aren't included in the internal change agent's circle of close friends or associates, but this knowledge can be valuable in overcoming the resistance and preparing for and implementing change. The internal change agent can serve as the champion for change because of enlightened understanding of the organization's capability.[14]

The third type of intervention, the combination external–internal team, is the most rare, but it seems to have an excellent chance for success. In this type of intervention, the outsider's objectivity and professional knowledge are blended with the insider's knowledge of the organization and its human resources. This blending of knowledge often results in increased trust and confidence among the parties involved. The combination external–internal team's ability to communicate and develop a more positive rapport can reduce resistance to any forthcoming change.

Resistance to Change

Most organizational change efforts eventually run into some form of employee resistance.[15] Employee resistance to change is a behavioral and/or emotional response to actual, perceived, or imagined threats brought about by work change. Change triggers rational and irrational emotional reactions because of the uncertainty involved. Instead of assuming that employees will resist change or react in a particular manner, it is better to consider the general reasons why people resist change.

Why People Resist Change

The issue of people resisting change in organizations is inevitable. It is a well-known phenomenon to any manager who has tried to bring about organizational change. A corollary to the view that people resist change is that the greater the magnitude of the change, the greater will be the resistance. The resistance to change can range from passive resignation to deliberate sabotage. Managers need to learn the various manifestations of how people resist change. Research has found there are four primary reasons people resist change (see Figure 17.1).[16]

Parochial Self-Interest

Some people resist organizational change out of fear of losing something they value. Individuals fear the loss of power, resources, freedom to make decisions, friendships, and prestige. In cases of fearing loss, individuals think of themselves and what they may have to give up. The fearful individual has only parochial self-interest in mind when resisting change. The organization and the interests of co-workers are not given much priority.

Misunderstanding and Lack of Trust

When individuals do not fully understand why the change is occurring and what its implications are, they will resist it. Misunderstanding the intent and consequences of organizational change is more likely to occur when trust is lacking between the person initiating the change and the affected individual. In organizations characterized by high

FIGURE 17.1
Reasons Why People Resist Change

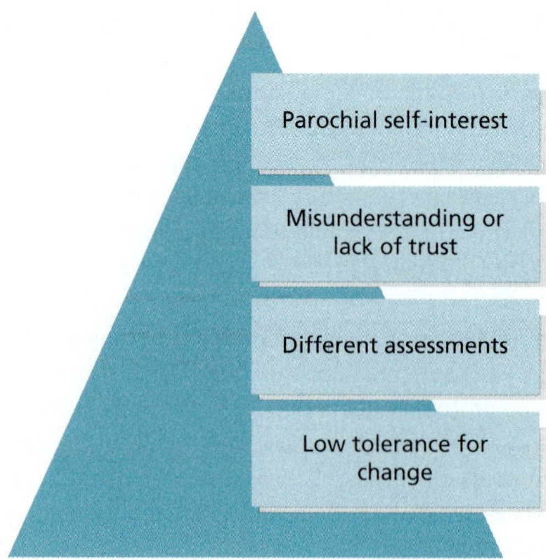

levels of mistrust, misunderstandings likely will be associated with any organizational change.

Different Assessments

Because individuals view change differently—its intent, potential consequences, and personal impact—there are often different assessments of the situation. Those initiating changes see more positive results because of the change, while those being affected and not initiating the changes see more costs involved with the change. Management might consider the change to wireless computing a benefit, but others might consider the introduction of wireless computing to be a signal of wanting employees to be connected to the firm 24/7.

Initiators of change often make two overly broad assumptions: (1) they have all the relevant data and information available to diagnose the situation, and (2) those to be affected by the change also have the same facts. Whatever the circumstances, the initiators and the affected employees often have different data and information. This leads to resistance to change. However, in some cases, the resistance is healthy for the firm, especially in the situation where the affected employees possess more valid data and information than the initiators of change.

Low Tolerance for Change

People resist change because they fear they will not be able to develop the new skills necessary to perform well. Individuals may understand clearly that change is necessary, but they may be emotionally unable to make the transition. For example, this type of resistance is found in offices that introduce cubicles as the workstation, instead of private office spaces. Some individuals, and even their bosses, resist changes that can be interpreted as decreasing individual privacy.

A low tolerance for change also is found in individuals who resist change to save face. Making the necessary adjustments and changes would be, they assume, an open admission that some of their previous behavior, decisions, and attitudes were wrong. For example, a salesperson may react to a reallocation of her largest customers as a result of poor previous performance when in fact the reallocation of customers was a consequence of a strategic decision from corporate headquarters and had nothing to do with her previous performance.

Reducing Resistance to Change

Resisting change is a human response, and management must take steps to minimize it. Reducing resistance can cut down on the time needed for a change to be accepted or tolerated. Also, the performance of employees can rebound more quickly if resistance is minimized.

A number of methods have been useful in decreasing employee resistance to change. Several important methods are listed here:

- Education and communication (explaining and informing).
- Participation and involvement (involving employees in the process).
- Facilitation and support (retraining and providing a range of support).
- Negotiation and agreement (discussions with resisters and negotiation).
- Manipulation and cooptation (bringing in supporters to guide others).
- Explicit and implicit coercion (threats, taking away rewards, job loss).

The next OB at Work feature illustrates a few easy-to-implement pointers for managers to use in reducing resistance to change.

OB AT WORK Overcoming Resistance to Change by Inclusion

People resist anything they don't understand or don't like; this is a normal reaction. In organizations where life is a constant push–pull of new ideas facing off against engrained ways of doing things, the ability to overcome resistance is a critical career skill. S. K. Gupta has learned that lesson the hard way. "I used to be Mr. Know-it-all," he says. "I was way ahead of everybody else." Because of this, says the vice president of operations for Lockheed Martin's space systems company in Denver, he struggled for years against a glass ceiling of his own construction.

But he finally realized that it's "unnatural for people to want change." He started studying why people resisted the ideas he thought were no-brainers and how he could overcome that resistance. Gupta realized that he needed to start including people in the change effort. Now, he has a new philosophy. "Problem solving is good, but helping others solve problems is better," he says. That, he notes, has enabled him to build trust and alliances that have lessened resistance to his ideas. Instead of expecting people to instantly understand and adopt his ideas, he says, he now sees it as his job to "convince, cajole, and coax."

That recognition led to a career turnaround and numerous promotions. He recognized the power of this attitude shift a few years ago when one of his bosses gave him a special assignment that required the ability to effect change. Gupta wondered why he received this assignment, so he asked the boss why he was selected. "He said it was because he saw me change the system from within rather than from the outside," he says.

"I would propose what I thought were brilliant ideas, and I couldn't get people interested," he says. "Yet, other people would go in and say, 'I have an idea' and people would jump at it."

What Gupta learned, through reading and working with a consultant, is that people have three levels of resistance: "I don't get it, I don't like it, or I don't like you." The first level, he says, is the easiest to overcome, because it's based on a shortage of information. The third level—I don't like you—is the toughest, because relationships with co-workers require trust and that can be challenging to maintain.

Here are a few pointers Gupta believes can help reduce resistance:

- *Stop pitching and listen.*

The natural tendency of hotshots with a brilliant idea is to sell it incessantly. But it's just as important to stop and listen to people's reactions to your brilliant idea. "People tend to become totally focused on the idea and presenting it, and they become walking infomercials."

- *Investigate all resistance.*

When you encounter resistance, find out why it's there. Maybe managers are concerned about the business cycle. It isn't likely, for example, that management is going to embark on an expensive new leadership-development program in this kind of economy.

If the resistance is based on personal issues, solutions take more time, because you have to build more trust and credibility.

- *Understand the resister.*

Nine months ago, Gupta arranged for a 30-minute meeting with one of his superiors to discuss his next assignment. But before the meeting, he sat down to assess this executive vice president. "He's a driver," he says. "What he wants to make his decision are options and possibilities. If I went to him with testimonials or guarantees, I would never succeed."

Also, he recognized that the best thing he could do for this results-driven executive was to save him time. So he wrapped up his presentation in 12 minutes. "It was the best 12 minutes I've ever had," he says, noting that the assignment he eventually received included a promotion.

To be a successful change agent like Gupta, you have to slow down and educate people, giving them information that will allow them to recognize the problem you've identified. And sometimes, you just have to give the organization time to accept the concept of change.

Source: Hal Lancaster, "How to Overcome Resistance to Change," *Wall Street Journal*, Career Journal at www.careerjournal.com, July 1, 2004.

A Model for Managing Organizational Change

The process of managing change can be approached systematically. The steps can be portrayed in a logical way as suggested in Figure 17.2. The model consists of specific steps generally acknowledged to be essential to successful change management.[17] A manager considers each of them, either explicitly or implicitly, to undertake a change program. Prospects of initiating successful change can be enhanced when managers actively support the effort and demonstrate that support by implementing systematic procedures that give substance to the process.[18]

FIGURE 17.2 A Seven-Step Model for the Management of Organizational Change

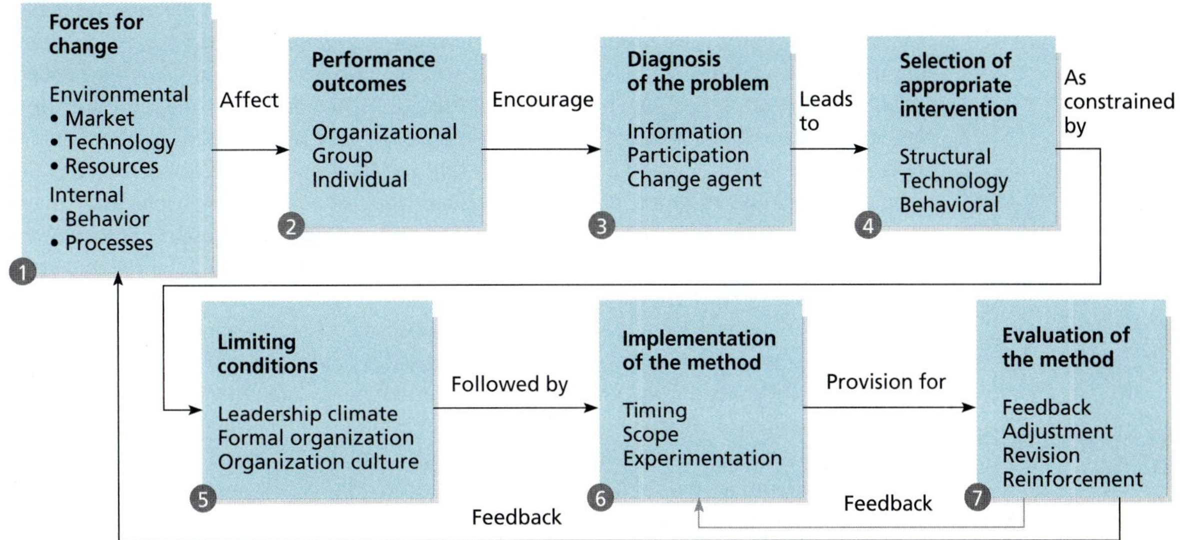

The model indicates that forces for change continually act on the organization; this assumption reflects the dynamic character of the modern world. At the same time, it's the manager's responsibility to sort out the information that reflects the magnitude of change forces.[19] The information is the basis for recognizing when change is needed; it's equally desirable to recognize when change isn't needed. But once managers recognize that something is malfunctioning, they must diagnose the problem and identify relevant alternative techniques.

Finally, the manager must implement the change and monitor the change process and change results. The model includes feedback to the implementation step and to the forces-for-change step. These feedback loops suggest that the change process itself must be monitored and evaluated. The mode of implementation may be faulty and may lead to poor results, but responsive action could correct the situation. Moreover, the feedback loop to the initial step recognizes that no change is final. A new situation is created within which problems and issues will emerge; a new setting is created that will itself become subject to change. The model suggests no final solution; rather, it emphasizes that the modern manager operates in a dynamic setting wherein the only certainty is change itself.

The forces for change can be classified into two groups, environmental forces and internal forces. Environmental forces are beyond management's control. Internal forces operate inside the firm and are generally within the control of management.

Environmental Forces

Organizations seldom undertake significant change without a strong shock from their environment.[20] The external environment includes many economic, technological, and social/political forces that can trigger the change process. Those who study and practice organizational change agree that these environmental triggers are necessary but not sufficient to initiate change. Change also involves managers who are aware of the change and who take action.

The manager of a business has historically been concerned with reacting to *economic forces*. Competitors introduce new products, increase their advertising, reduce their prices, or increase their customer service. In each case, a response is required unless the manager is content to permit the erosion of profit and market share. At the same time, changes occur in customer tastes and incomes. The firm's products may no longer have customer appeal; customers may be able to purchase less expensive higher-quality forms of the same products.

The second source of environmental change forces is *technology*. The knowledge explosion has introduced new technology for nearly every business function. Computers have made possible high-speed data processing and solutions to complex production problems. New machines and new processes have revolutionized how many products are manufactured and distributed. Computer technology and automation have affected not only the technical conditions of work, but the social conditions as well.[21] New occupations have been created, and others have been eliminated. The Internet has revolutionized the ways in which information is gathered and disseminated. It has enabled the creation of e-commerce, virtual working, virtual teams, and the ability to make faster, more informed decisions. Slowness to adopt new technology that reduces cost and improves quality will appear in the financial statements sooner or later.[22] Technological advance is a permanent fixture in the business world. As a force for change, it will continue to demand attention.

The third source of environmental change forces is *social and political* change. Business managers must be tuned in to the great movements over which they have no control but which, in time, influence their firm's fate. Sophisticated mass communications and global markets create great potential for business, but they're also great threats to managers who can't understand these important factors.[23] For example, disgruntled or disappointed customers can vent their frustrations on social networking sites like Twitter and Facebook or post complaint videos on Web sites like YouTube. When such a video goes viral (known as "viral revenge"), it has the potential to create negative public relations for organizations. In 2009, Dave Carroll and his band Sons of Maxwell posted the song "United Breaks Guitars" on YouTube to air his complaint that United Airlines (after the baggage handlers allegedly damaged his guitar) refused for over a year to compensate the singer.[24] Within three days of posting the video, 1.5 million people viewed it and some 10,000 people posted comments, mostly in support of the band.[25] Finally, the links between government and business become more interrelated as regulations are imposed and relaxed.

Comprehending implications of external forces requires *organizational learning* processes.[26] These processes, now being studied in many organizations, involve the capacity to absorb new information, process that information in the light of previous experience, and act on the information in new and potentially risky ways. But only through such learning experiences will organizations succeed in the 21st century.

Internal Forces

Internal forces for change, which occur within the organization, can usually be traced to process and behavioral problems. The process problems include breakdowns in decision making and communications. Decisions aren't being made, are made too late, or are of poor quality. Communications are short-circuited, redundant, or simply inadequate. Because of inadequate or nonexistent communications, a customer order isn't filled, a grievance isn't processed, or an invoice isn't filed and the supplier isn't paid. Interpersonal and interdepartmental conflicts reflect breakdowns in organizational processes.

Low levels of morale and high levels of absenteeism and turnover are symptoms of behavioral problems that must be diagnosed and addressed. A certain level of employee discontent exists in most organizations—it's dangerous to ignore employee complaints and suggestions. But the process of change includes the *recognition* phase—the point where management must decide to act.

In many organizations, the need for change goes unrecognized until some major catastrophe occurs. For example, three major clients within a month announce that they're dropping their business with the firm due to unresolved quality problems. Or, the employees strike or seek the recognition of a union before the management finally recognizes the need for higher wages, better benefits, and improved working conditions. Whether it takes a whisper or a shout, the need for change must be recognized by some means; and once that need has been recognized, the exact nature of the problem must be diagnosed. If the problem isn't properly understood, the impact of misguided change on people can be extremely negative.

Diagnosis of a Problem

Change agents facilitate the diagnostic phase by gathering, interpreting, and presenting data.[27] Although the accuracy of data is extremely important, how the data are interpreted and presented is equally important. First, the data are discussed with a group of top managers, who are asked to make their own diagnosis of the information; or, second, change agents may present their own diagnoses without making explicit their frameworks for analyzing the data. A difficulty with the first approach is that top management tends to see each problem separately. Each manager views his problem as being the most important and fails to recognize other problem areas. The second approach has inherent problems of communication. External change agents often have difficulty with the second approach because they become immersed in theory and various conceptual frameworks that are less realistic than the managers would like.[28]

Appropriate action is necessarily preceded by diagnosis of the problem's symptoms. Experience and judgment are critical to this phase unless the problem is readily apparent to all observers.[29] Ordinarily, however, managers can disagree on the nature of the problem. There's no formula for accurate diagnosis, but the following questions point the manager or change agent in the right direction:

1. What is the problem as distinct from the symptoms of the problem?
2. What must be changed to resolve the problem?
3. What outcomes (objectives) are expected from the change, and how will those outcomes be measured?

Alternative Interventions

The answers to these questions can come from information ordinarily found in the organization's information system. Alternatively, it may be necessary to generate ad hoc information through the creation of committees or task forces.[30] Meetings between managers and employees provide a variety of viewpoints that can be sifted through by a smaller group. Interviewing key personnel is an important problem-finding method. Another diagnostic approach that obtains broader-based information is the attitude survey.

attitude survey
A way to collect data or information about a person's opinion or reaction to an event, person, item, situation, or organization program.

The **attitude survey** is a useful diagnostic approach if the potential focus of change is the total organization. For example, the Fallon Clinic of Worcester, Massachusetts, has its learning and organizational development department conduct a companywide survey each year to assess the training needs of its 1,700 current and new employee and staff members.[31] If smaller units or entities are the focus of change, the survey technique may not be a reliable source of information. For example, if the focus of change is a relatively small work group, diagnosis of the problem is better accomplished through individual interviews followed by group discussion of the interview data. Consequently, the group becomes actively involved in sharing and interpreting perception of problems. However, the attitude survey can pose difficulties for organizations with relatively low levels of trust in management's sincerity to use the information in constructive ways.

In addition to the diagnosis of organizational problems, individual employee issues can be assessed. Identification of individual employees' problems comes about through interviews and human resource management department information. Consistently low performance evaluations indicate such problems, and it's often necessary to go into greater detail. Identifying individuals' problems is far more difficult than identifying organizational problems. Thus, the diagnostic process must stress the use of precise and reliable information.

To summarize, the data collection process can tap information in several ways. A number of widely used approaches are useful for assorted purposes:[32]

1. Questionnaire data can be collected from large numbers of people.
2. Direct observations can be taken of actual workplace behavior.
3. Selected individuals in key positions can be interviewed.
4. Workshops can be arranged with groups to explore different perceptions of problems.
5. Documents and records of the organization can be examined for archival and current information.

intervention
A specific action or program undertaken to focus the change process on particular targets.

An **intervention** is a specific action that a change agent takes to focus the change process. Although the term has a generally used meaning, it has a specific meaning in the context of organizational development where it refers to a formal activity. The choice of a particular intervention depends on the nature of the problem that management has diagnosed. Management must determine which alternative is most likely to produce the desired outcome, whether it be improvement in skills, attitudes, behavior, or structure. As we've noted, diagnosis of the problem includes specifying the outcome(s) that management desires from the change.

The literature of organization development recognizes that different interventions have different effects on organizations, groups, and individuals. The term *depth of intended change* refers to the magnitude of the problem to be addressed and the significance of the change required to address the problem.

Depth and Approach of Intended Change

Depth of intended change refers to the scope and intensity of the organizational change efforts.[33] The idea is depicted in Figure 17.3, which likens the organization to an iceberg. This analogy draws attention to two important components: the *formal* and *informal* aspects of organizations. The formal components of an organization are like that part of an iceberg that's above water; the informal components are observable, rational, and oriented to structural factors. On the other hand, the informal components are not observable to all people, are affective, and are oriented to process and behavioral factors.

Both the formal and informal aspects of organizations can be changed in a methodical, deliberate way. Planned and managed change describes the systematic process of introducing new structures, behaviors, and technologies for accomplishing goals. Organizations can take any of these three approaches.

Structural. The approach focuses on changing or redesigning jobs, workflow, or organizational structure. Organizations can become more organic, virtual, flat, or modular. Jobs and work can be enriched, combined, expanded, or converted to a virtual arrangement.

Behavioral. Some refer to this as organizational development (OD). Team building, diversity training, enhancing/developing leadership skills and attitudes, and modifying employees' knowledge and learning can be included under a behavioral change approach.

Technological. This change could involve computers, intranets, the information technology (IT) infrastructure, materials, techniques, or automation of work processes.

FIGURE 17.3
The Organizational Iceberg

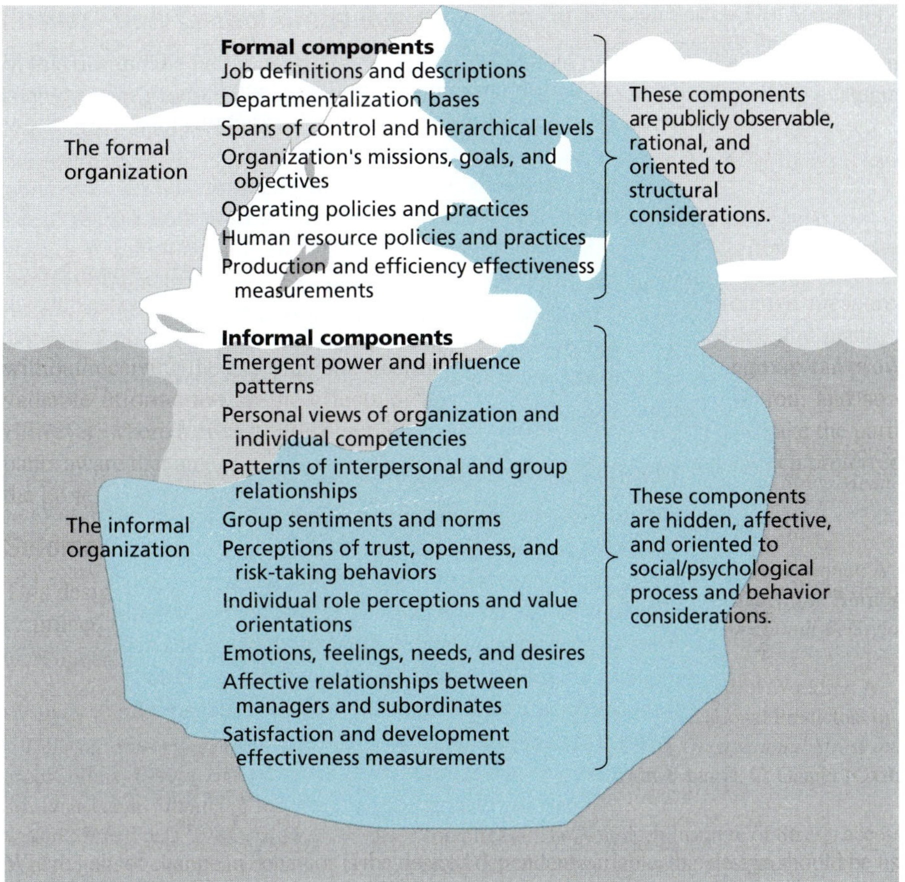

Identifying Alternative Change Techniques

The particular change technique chosen in step 4 in the framework presented in Figure 17.2 depends on the nature of the problem. Management must determine which alternative is most likely to produce the desired outcomes.[34] The three change approaches differ in their focus; namely, to change structure, behavior, or technology.

Structural Change

Logically, organizing follows planning, as the structure is a means for achieving the objective established through planning. *Structural change,* in the context of organizational change, refers to managerial attempts to improve performance by altering the formal structure of task and authority relationships.[35] But because structure creates human and social relationships that members of the organization may value highly, efforts to disrupt these relationships may be resisted.[36]

Structural changes alter some aspects of the formal task and authority system. The design of an organization involves the specification of jobs, the grouping of jobs into departments, the creation of virtual teams and identification of work to be done at remote sites (e.g., the employee's home), the determination of the size of groups reporting to a single manager, and the distribution of authority, including the provision of staff assistance. Changes in the nature of jobs, bases for departmentalization, locations where work tasks are completed, and line–staff relationships are, therefore, structural changes.

Changes in the Nature of Jobs

Changes in the nature of jobs originate with new methods and new machines. Work simplification and job enrichment are two examples of methods changes. Work simplification increases specializations, whereas job enrichment decreases it.

A job can be changed by altering (1) the job description, (2) the role expectations of a position, (3) the relationships among positions, and (4) work flow patterns. For example, a change in a job description means that the duties to be performed and the manager's expectations about the duties are changed.[37] A purchasing agent had his job description changed in an area involving his latitude for making purchasing decisions. After the change, he was able to make any purchasing decision without checking immediately with his manager. This change was structural. His increased authority also meant that he would have to work on Saturday evenings. This was a role expectation for purchasing agents who had full purchasing decision authority.

Changes in the Bases for Departmentalization

Opinion is growing among managers and researchers that grouping jobs on the basis of function, territory, product, or customer does not occur in an orderly fashion.

Departmentalization in some firms is based largely on a contingency perspective. The situation, people, resources, and external organizational forces appear to dictate largely what basis of departmentalization will be used. The multiproducts and multi-industry organization requires a significant amount of managerial coordination. Thus, experiments with different forms of departmentalization and various managerial hierarchies are being conducted.[38]

An increasing number of firms are using teleworkers or individuals performing unit, department, or project jobs away from an office, factory floor, or cubicle. These workers may be a part of a formal department, unit, team, or project, but they receive, complete, and send work via fax, e-mail, video conferencing, or all three. In 2008, there were approximately 17.2 million telecommuters in the United States who spent at least one day per month working from home, and it is likely that there will be a continuing increase in the number of employees working remotely.[39] Effectively coordinating, evaluating, and leading telecommuters is a task that a growing number of managers will have to learn.[40]

Change in Line–Staff Relationships

A common approach to change is to create staff assistance as a temporary or permanent solution. One response of manufacturing firms to the problem of market expansion is to create separate staff and service units. These units provide the technical expertise to deal with the production, financial, and marketing problems posed by expansion.

An illustrative case is a company that had grown quite rapidly after its entry into the fast-food industry. Its basic sources of control were area directors who supervised the operations of the sales outlets of a particular region. During the growth period, the area directors had considerable autonomy in making the advertising decisions for their regions. Within general guidelines, they could select their own advertising media and formats and set their own advertising budgets. But as competitors appeared and markets became saturated, corporate officials decided to centralize the advertising function in a staff unit located at corporate headquarters. Consequently, the area directors' authority was limited, and a significant portion of their jobs was eliminated.

Elements of structural change often include plans, procedures, span of control, and levels of organization. The point that should be taken, however, is not that any list of structural change approaches is incomplete, but that all structural parts are interrelated. Job changes do not take place in a vacuum; on the contrary, the change affects all surrounding jobs. The management of structural change must be guided by the point of view that all things are connected.

Behavioral Change

Behavioral change techniques are efforts to redirect and increase employee motivation, skills, and knowledge bases. The major objective of such techniques is to coordinate performance of assigned tasks. The early efforts to change employee behavior date back to scientific management work-improvement and employee-training methods. These attempts primarily were directed at improving the skills and knowledge bases of employees. The employee counseling programs that grew out of the early studies (the Hawthorne studies) were (and remain) primarily directed at increasing employee motivation.

Training and development programs for managers typically have emphasized interpersonal relationships and technical skills. Because managers are concerned primarily with overseeing the work of others, these traditional programs emphasize techniques for dealing with people problems: how to handle the malcontent, the slacker, the troublemaker, and the complainer. The programs also include conceptual material dealing with communications, leadership styles, conflict resolution, and organizational relationships. The training methods often involve role-playing, discussion groups, lectures, simulations, and organized courses offered by the firm's training department or universities, consultants, and training corporations.

Training continues to be an important technique for introducing behavioral changes.[41] In some applications, training has taken on a form quite different from that which developed under classical management theory. The vast majority of organizational development change techniques have been directed at changing the behavior of individuals and groups through problem solving, decision making, and communication. Team building, sensitivity training, and transactional analysis—the most commonly used change approaches—will be discussed in more detail.

Team Building

The purpose of team building is to enable work groups to do their work more effectively—to improve their performance.[42] The work groups may be established or relatively new command and task groups. The members of the work groups can be both internal and external to the organization.[43] The specific aims of the team-building intervention include setting goals and priorities, analyzing the group's work methods, examining the group's communication and decision-making processes, and assessing the interpersonal relationships within the group.[44] As each of these aims is undertaken, the group is placed in the position of having to recognize explicitly the contributions, positive and negative, of each group member.[45]

The process by which these aims are achieved begins with *diagnostic* meetings. Often lasting an entire day, the meetings enable each group member to share with other members her perceptions of problems. If the group is large enough, subgroups engage in discussion and report their ideas to the total group. These sessions are designed for expression of the view of all members and to make these views public. That is, diagnosis, in this context, emphasizes the value of "open communication" of issues and problems that were previously discussed in secrecy or not discussed at all.

Identifying problems and concurring on their priority are two important initial steps. However, a *plan of action* must be agreed upon. The plan should call on each group member, individually or as part of a subgroup, to act specifically to alleviate one or more of the problems. If, for example, an executive committee agrees that one of the problems is lack of understanding of and commitment to a set of goals, a subgroup can be appointed to recommend goals to the total group at a subsequent meeting. Other group members can work on different problems. For example, if problems are found in the relationships among the members, a subgroup can initiate a process for examining the roles of each member.

Team-building interventions do not always require a complex process of diagnostic and action meetings. For example, the CEO of a large manufacturing firm recognized that conflict within the executive group was breeding defensiveness among the functional departments. She also recognized that her practice of dealing on a one-on-one basis with executive group members, each of whom headed a functional department, contributed to the defensiveness and conflict. Rather than viewing themselves as team members with a stake in the organization, the department heads viewed one another as competitors. The CEO's practice confirmed their belief that they managed relatively independent units.

To counteract the situation, the CEO adopted the simple expedient of requiring the group to meet twice weekly. One meeting focused on operating problems, the other on personnel problems. The ground rule of these meetings was that the group must reach a consensus on each decision. After one year of such meetings, company-oriented decisions were being made, and the climate of interunit competition had been replaced by one of cooperation.

Team building also is effective when new groups are being formed. There are often problems when new organizational units, project teams, or task forces are created. Typically, such groups have certain characteristics that must be altered if the groups are to perform effectively. For example, the following combination of characteristics will lead to real problems:

1. Confusion exists as to roles and relationships.
2. Members have a fairly clear understanding of short-term goals.
3. Group members have technical competence that puts them on the team.
4. Members often pay more attention to the tasks of the team than to the relationships among the team members.

The result is that the new group will focus initially on task problems but ignore the relationship issues. By the time the relationship problems begin to surface, the group is unable to deal with them, and performance begins to deteriorate.

To combat these tendencies, a new group should schedule team-building meetings during the first week of its life. The meetings should take place away from the work site; one- or two-day sessions often are sufficient. The format of such meetings varies, but essentially their purpose is to provide time for the group to work over a reasonable time frame and to clarify the roles of members in reaching the group's objectives. An important outcome of such meetings is to establish an understanding of each member's contribution to the team and of the reward for that contribution. Although the reports of team building indicate mixed results, the evidence suggests that group processes improve through team-building efforts.[46]

This record of success accounts for the increasing use of team building as an organizational development method.[47]

Diversity Training

This form of training attempts to make the participants more aware of themselves and of their effect on diverse others.[48] *Sensitivity* in this context means sensitivity to self and to relationships with others. *Diversity* refers to the growing number of minority groups in the workplace. Diversity training stresses the *process* rather than the *content* of training and *emotional* rather than *conceptual* training. It is clear that this form of training is different from the traditional forms, which stress the acquisition of a predetermined body of concepts with immediate application to the workplace.

The process of diversity training includes a group of managers who, in most cases, meet away from their place of work. Under the direction of a trainer or facilitator, the group usually engages in dialogue, which focuses on why some organizational acts and actions are seen as offensive while others are not.[49] The objective is to provide an environment that produces its own learning experiences. The unstructured dialogue encourages one to learn about the self in dealing with others. One's motives and feelings are revealed through behavior toward others in the group and through the behavior of others.

Managers should examine this technique critically to determine what kinds of behavioral changes are desirable and what kinds are possible. Certain conditions could limit the range of possible changes. In this light, managers must determine whether the changes induced by the training are instrumental for organizational purposes and whether the prospective participant gains a better insight into diversity issues, concerns, and goals.

Technological Change

technological change Any application of new ways of transforming resources into products or services.

Technological change includes any application of new ways of transforming resources into products or services. In the traditional sense of the word, technology means new machines—lathes, presses, computers, and the like. But the concept can be expanded to include all new techniques, whether or not they include new machines. From this perspective, the work improvement methods of scientific management can be considered technological breakthroughs. However, in this section, only those changes that can be linked to the introduction of a machine or worker–machine process are discussed.

The majority of manufacturing and service organizations are implementing technological change in the form of computers and automation.[50] In service firms, computers now either perform or assist employees in performing a wide variety of tasks such as processing customer banking transactions, purchasing airline tickets, purchasing life insurance policies, and filling orders for customers. Manufacturing processes continue to find new and effective ways to apply computer technology. In many plants, computers now control large parts of the manufacturing process such as material handling, quality testing, and assembly. Some companies have created *flexible manufacturing systems*. These systems produce a part or product entirely by automation. From initial design to delivery, the unit is untouched by human hands.[51]

These technological changes have occurred largely because of the potential of high technology to lower production costs, boost productivity, and improve quality. However, although computer and robotics technologies have affected more than half of America's jobs, the rate of high-tech implementation in U.S. organizations has fallen far short of projections. The reason: many high-tech changes haven't delivered expected results.

Many observers believe that the disappointing performance of such technological change is due to management's neglect of the structural and behavioral changes that must accompany technological change. Specifically, employees' jobs have not been redesigned in a way that both makes the best of new technology and addresses the employees' social and psychological needs. A mismatch exists between technology, how workers perform their jobs, and how managers supervise the workers. Consequently, technology's potential isn't realized.[52]

This neglect is costly because computerizing the workplace requires major structural and behavioral changes for success.[53] Changes are necessary in a number of areas, including the following:

Employee training. Workers must be highly skilled to handle the substantial team responsibility for a major part of the manufacturing process. Team members must understand the technology to oversee machine functions and be skilled in diagnostic problem solving and communicating to quickly correct the glitches that sometimes occur. Thus, technological change essentially alters the amount and type of training.

Compensation. Many companies with highly automated manufacturing process and employee teams have implemented a pay-for-knowledge compensation system.

Individualized pay approaches, such as a piece-rate system, don't work because the contributions of individual employees are difficult to measure. The pay-for-knowledge approach boosts team flexibility.

Management style. Because of the nature of their responsibilities, teams working with highly automated processes often have much more authority in performing their tasks than do individuals in more traditional assembly line jobs. This increase in employee autonomy changes the nature of the manager's job. The emphasis shifts from supervision and control to coaching and consultation.[54] Technological change also requires that managers broaden their knowledge to include a thorough understanding of the new technology.

Technological innovations can change other aspects of the workplace. The changes can alter working conditions, the social relations among workers, career patterns, and promotion procedures, to name a few. The degree and extent of any changes in behavior and structure depend on the magnitude of the technological change. Essentially, the decision to adopt a technological change must involve consideration of the numerous behavioral and structural impacts that often occur. These impacts must, in turn, be reconciled with the conditions that limit the scope and magnitude of the proposed change.

As the next OB at Work feature discusses, technological changes in the workplace can often also lead to challenging ethical issues for managers. The three major alternative approaches to change—structural, behavioral, and technological—attempt to improve performance by improving communication, decision making, attitudes, and skills. These approaches are based on the assumption that changes in structure, behavior, and technology can result in improvements for the organization, individuals, and groups. Often changes in one area such as structure are related to changes in the other two areas. The anticipated outcomes of this system of interrelated changes include the factors shown in Figure 17.4. Accomplishing all of the anticipated outcomes would be worthwhile for any manager. However, any successes may be limited because of implementation problems, resistance to change, and various other conditions.

FIGURE 17.4 **Three Change Approaches**

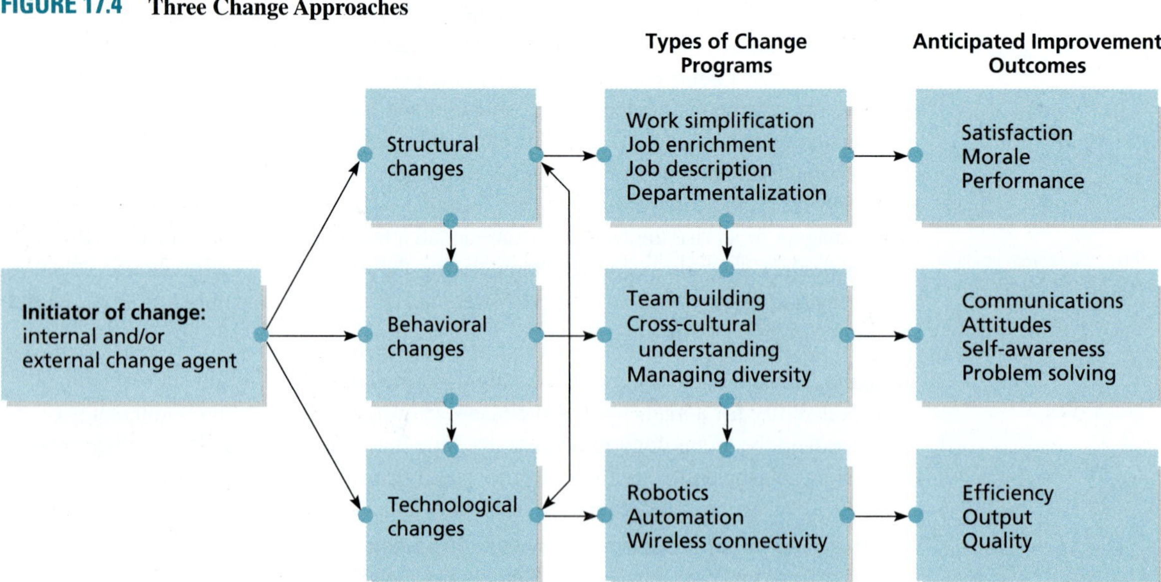

OB AT WORK Technology Change Creates Ethical Issues for Managers

Managers of public and private organizations have several responsibilities related to technology. They must develop and incorporate technological change into their organizations' daily operations. Managers must also make decisions concerning the potential effects of technological change on their workers, their customers, and society. The pace of technological change creates unique and ever-increasing burdens on managers' decision making. Consequently, managers may need help handling ethical issues raised by technology change.

One such issue deals with individual concerns regarding privacy of information. For example, organizations collect a considerable amount of information about applicants (many of whom later become employees), including background checks, work history, credit history, personality, and medical history. Once hired, many employees provide additional personal information to the HR department in the form of Social Security numbers, addresses, bank account numbers for direct deposit, the number, names, and ages of their children, and so on. It is not surprising that one study found that an overwhelming number of individuals reported uneasy feelings and concerns about technology-related problems. The survey found that 89 percent of the respondents felt that computers made it easier for someone to improperly obtain personal and confidential information about them; 76 percent suggested that because of computers, people have lost all control over how personal information is circulated; 69 percent noted that computers represent a threat to their personal privacy; and 66 percent indicated that there are no adequate safeguards to protect the privacy of personal information stored in computers.

Even these brief descriptions of technology-based ethical issues indicate that today's managers face a highly complex ethical arena. To effectively manage their organizations while coping with these ethical issues, managers should employ the following steps:

- Be aware of the issues.
- Develop an ethical framework.
- Be consistent.
- Communicate clearly.
- Stay alert.

Each of the five steps is very important. Yet, the issue of staying alert stands out above all others. The changing nature of technology and technology-based ethical issues requires managers to stay alert for emerging issues from current technologies and for emerging issues from new technologies. Effective management requires the ability to perceive and appreciate the implications of new circumstances and environments. Managers must successfully adapt to change. Ethical decision making is similar to many other management responsibilities: it requires that managers remain flexible and adaptable.

Sources: Adapted from G. Stoney Alder, Marshall Schminke and Terry W. Noel, "The Impact of Individual Ethics on Reactions to Potentially Invasive HR Practices," *Journal of Business Ethics* 75, no. 2 (2007): 201–214; Laura P. Hartman, *Perspectives in Business Ethics* (Burr Ridge, IL: McGraw-Hill, 2002); William P. Cordeiro, "Suggested Management Responses to Ethical Issues Raised by Technological Change," *Journal of Business Ethics,* September 1997, pp. 1393–400; and Richard T. Herschel and Patricia Hayes Andrews, "Ethical Implications of Technological Advances on Business Communication," *Journal of Business Communication* (April 1997): 160–70.

Appreciative Inquiry

appreciative inquiry (AI)
An organizational change process that focuses on diagnosis and presentation of positive characteristics of change, the process, and outcomes.

The bulk of organizational change and development programs start any diagnosis with an emphasis on identifying problems, shortfalls, or deficiencies such as sexual harassment problems, excessive costs or resource limits, and not meeting a previously established performance goal. **Appreciative inquiry (AI)** is a method of focusing on positive or potential opportunities.[55]

Appreciation means to value, see the best in others, and recognize positive potential. The concept of *inquiry* refers to the systematic analysis and the openness to discovery. Used by such diverse organizations as Save the Children, McDonald's, and the U.S. Navy, appreciative inquiry (AI) involves a method for bringing about positive change.[56] AI proposes that organizations and individuals are creative enough to develop programs, relationships, and behaviors that address success, personal growth, and fulfillment. It searches for an attempt to bring out the best in people, the organization, and the external environment. AI uses the art and practice of asking probing questions that can strengthen an individual

FIGURE 17.5
4-D Framework for Appreciative Inquiry

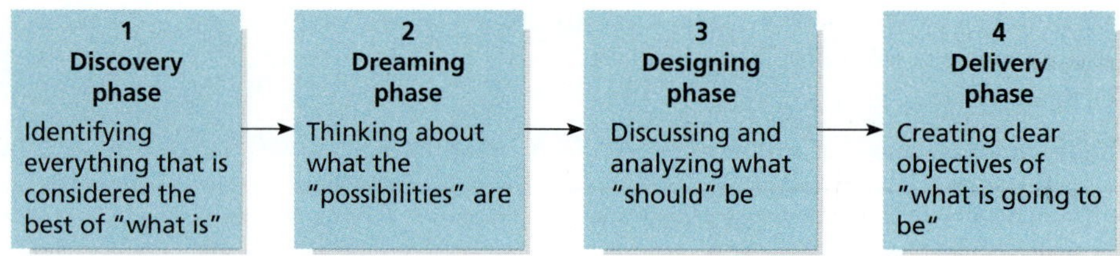

or an organization's ability to anticipate, seize, and initiate positive potential.[57] In a concise form, AI is

- A methodology that takes the idea of social construction of reality by utilizing metaphors and narratives.
- A *positive* approach to change that completely lets go of problems-based management.
- An emphasis on *individual engagement* to bring about creative solutions.

Figure 17.5 outlines what is referred to as the 4-D framework of appreciative inquiry. Pioneering work on refining this framework was conducted by the consulting firm of Marge Schiller and Associates at AVON Mexico.[58]

The 4-D process begins with discovering or appreciating what is the "best" in the current situation being examined. This could involve determining what employees like about their work, unit, or colleagues. As this discussion evolves, the next "D" phase emerges, dreaming. What would make the work, unit, or colleagues ideal? Talking about ideals and the value of being in an ideal situation shifts the process to the third "D" phase: designing or exchanging thoughts and eventually formulating and constructing with others a collective model of what an ideal group, team, or work setting would be in terms of schedules, expectations, roles, responsibilities, rewards, and goals. Once the ideal model is conceptualized, discussed, modified, and produced, the focus shifts to the fourth "D" phase, delivering. Now is the time to establish a plan, an execution strategy, and a set of goals to change the situation being examined. Instead of the "ideal," the theme is now actually altering the real situation or setting.[59]

A key issue regarding AI and change is this: if one wants to inspire, mobilize, and sustain motivation, what is the best way—by focusing on problems, shortfalls, or deficits or by addressing opportunities to build on strengths? AI is positioned to probe and ask about peak, positive events, experiences, and models.

AVON Mexico used AI to develop opportunities for increasing the number of women in top management positions. A team of employees and consultants collected stories that described, analyzed, and portrayed gender equality and fairness at AVON Mexico.[60] These stories were used as the basis of two-day training programs for AVON Mexico employees to devise additional programs and approaches for accomplishing gender equality. The AI process of discovering, dreaming, designing, and delivering served as the change approach used at AVON Mexico. Following its use of the AI training approach, the company won the Catalyst Award for gender equality, and more women are now in senior positions at AVON Mexico.[61] Other examples of how AI is used in organizations are presented in the next OB at Work feature.

Trends in Organizational Change

Forces primarily in the external environment have encouraged various types of change in U.S. organizations: downsizing, empowerment, virtual jobs, and flextime. Each type of change usually brings about changes in the structural, behavioral, and technological aspects of the organization.

OB AT WORK Snapshots of AI Use and Claims

The following are a few examples of how appreciative inquiry (AI) is being used to execute change, identify best practices, and share experiences. The claims are listed, but the type of research conducted, by whom, and in what kind of context is not presented. Thus, it is premature to conclude that AI has been empirically validated in all of these settings.

- *United States Navy*—AI summit including the Chief of Naval Operations, admirals, and all ranks down to seamen; resulted in more than 30 pilot projects for leadership development and operational changes in the Navy. The Center for Positive Change has been established at the Naval Postgraduate School, where naval officers are trained in appreciative inquiry as a component of leadership.
- *Roadway Express*—An AI pilot project focused on building employee involvement, reducing waste, and increasing speed and efficiency of workflow; resulted in creation of eight self-organized "project teams." One team generated savings of $10,000 per month by reducing driver delay and more than $7,000 per year in other cost reductions.
- *Verizon*—Large-scale AI change focusing on customer service, teamwork, and communication; created union–management partnership.
- *McDonald's*—An AI intervention was initiated at the human resources group of the McDonald's Midwest division aimed at cultural change and improved strategic alignment for human resources. Bringing all the important stakeholders into the process created unprecedented opportunities for learning and sharing. Specific initiatives included launching a global AI approach to facilitate the exchange of best practices.
- *Nutrimental (Brazil)*—Large-scale AI summit with more than 700 attendees focused on increased competitiveness in the marketplace by identifying best practices and strengths; average return per worker increased 22 percent and a 27 percent increase in sales volume.
- *Hunter Douglas Windows Fashion Division*—AI initiatives included the workforce, suppliers, customers, and community members; resulted in improvements in strategic planning, business processes, and customer service; resulted in significant increases in productivity and employee retention; eliminated mandatory employee overtime. There was an estimated $3.5 million in savings the first year.
- *Lafarge North America*—After restructuring operations, the largest supplier of construction materials in the United States and Canada used AI to help create a high-performing leadership team; evaluations showed the participants' understanding of the leadership team's purpose increased by 56 percent, trust between team members rose by 47 percent, and members' commitment to how the team would work together to lead the new division increased by 29 percent.
- *Lovelace Hospital*—Short staffing, poor teamwork, and skyrocketing recruiting costs plagued this hospital; an AI approach examined why nurses enjoyed working there; resulted in a 13 percent reduction in turnover the first year, a 30 percent reduction in the nurse vacancy rate, improved morale among nurses, and increased patient satisfaction ratings.

In spite of the lack of easily assessable data, the value of AI could be promising. Its emphasis on positive outcomes, strengths, and success offers a positive perspective on implementing and managing change.

Sources: David L. Cooperrider, Diana Whitney, and Jacqueline M. Stavros, *Appreciative Inquiry Handbook: For Leaders of Change* 2nd ed. (San Francisco: Barrett-Koehler, 2008); D. Cooperrider and M. Avital, eds., *Advances in Appreciative Inquiry: Constructive Discourse and Human Organization* (Mahwah, NJ: Elsevier, 2004); "Yellow Roadway Plans to Add Shipping Terminals," *Kansas City Business Journal*, January 5, 2004, pp. 8–9; and D. Whitney and A. Trosten-Bloom, *The Power of Appreciative Inquiry* (San Francisco: Barrett-Koehler, 2003).

Downsizing

Declining revenues and increasing costs, mergers, and international competition have intensified the need for organizations to reduce costs while being more efficient and productive. Many companies like Yahoo!, American Express, Motorola, General Motors, Merck, and Google have responded to this need by *downsizing*.[62] This major action involves reducing the size of the workforce, and often closing some operations and consolidating others.[63]

The core task of the downsizing effort is determining what operations should be closed and which positions should be eliminated in the organization. Many companies identify units to be closed through an analysis of each unit's financial performance and the company's projected future demand of its services. Market analysis of a product or service's future demand is conduced when a unit's operations are tied to marketed output. Concerning position, the content of jobs is analyzed to identify those that can be eliminated or consolidated with other positions.[64]

Once the downsizing decision has been made, the most traumatic aspect of downsizing occurs—the actual shutdown of operations and employee layoffs. Some companies have attempted to help affected employees through this transition by providing advance notice, severance pay, extended health care benefits, and outplacement services.

However, despite organizational efforts, the period is exceptionally traumatic, both for employees who leave and for those who remain. Many management experts believe that downsizing is the primary contributor to a decline in employee loyalty in organizations.[65] Moreover, research suggests that the downsizing agent, or person who is primarily responsible for reducing the number of employees, might suffer several negative effects, including experiencing stress, feeling stigmatized, fearing for personal safety, and losing personal ties by having to lay off friends.[66]

Thus, once the actual downsizing decisions have been made, the organization is faced with rebuilding the company. Structural changes in job content, workflow, and organizational design must be implemented. Management must also focus on rebuilding commitment among the surviving employees, many of whom question the company's commitment to them. This task can be particularly challenging. Companies have responded in a number of ways.

In sum, downsizing is often an essential organizational change for companies striving to remain competitive in demanding external environments. However, the change is necessarily a painful one in many respects. Effective downsizing requires careful analysis of the companies' operations and a well-planned implementation that minimizes unnecessary human costs.

Empowerment

empowerment
Giving employees permission to make decisions to complete workloads on time.

An increasingly competitive external environment demands that organizations produce better products and services and be more efficient in doing so. To meet this requirement, a rising number of companies are turning to employees, seeking their ideas and inputs, and giving workers more autonomy in doing their jobs. **Empowering** individuals means granting them permission to use their talents, skills, resources, and experience to make decisions about customer relationship management, investments, hiring people, just-in-time inventory management, total quality control, computer purchases, and forming alliances.

Empowerment has occurred by redesigning jobs from an individual to team-based orientation. This structural change gives the responsibility for a major segment of work to a team of employees who often have the authority to schedule their own work, establish and monitor team performance measures, select and train their members, and solve production problems.

Empowerment has been credited with improving production and service quality and efficiency in a number of companies. However, this type of change often encounters several obstacles. A frequent problem is opposition to the change from managers who fear a loss of authority and power.[67] Accustomed to a more authoritative style of management, some supervisors have difficulty in empowering subordinates and adopting a coaching management style to replace a style that emphasizes telling employees what to do. Some employees also have difficulty in assuming the greater responsibility that empowerment requires.

However, when these and other challenges are overcome, empowerment has produced some impressive results.[68]

telecommuting
Performing all or some portion of a job at sites away from the central work site.

Telecommuting

A major structural, behavioral, and technological systems change is **telecommuting**, that is, performing all or some portion of the job at sites (e.g., home) away from the central work site. Virtual employees are connected to their supervisor or office through computer networks. As stated earlier, approximately 17.2 million U.S. employees are considered telecommuters.[69] Sales personnel, consultants, purchasing agents, software programmers, and many other occupational groups use telecommuting.

Organizations are attracted to telecommuting by the reduced overhead costs of providing and maintaining office space and amenities. At AT&T, a sales manager in Virginia manages eight commission-pay sales personnel from her home three days each week.[70] The computer connectivity that permits the sales manager to oversee, review, and change the work of each salesperson saves office space and commuting time.

Telecommuting can help workers deal with work/personal life issues and cope with commuting stress and interruptions in a traditional office by providing more flexibility.[71]

On the other hand, some telecommuters report feeling isolated and out of the loop. Telecommuting can be useful in circumstances where employees prefer not to travel to and from work and want to spend more time with their families.

Telecommuting poses some major challenges for managers in terms of reviewing performance and building cohesive teams and teamwork. There also may be some tension between telecommuters and traditional onsite employees.[72]

Flextime

A work schedule or structure that provides flexible work hours theoretically provides more autonomy and discretion to employees. The most common flextime schedule gives employees a choice of starting and ending times as long as they work a core period. For example, a company might require all employees to be present in the office from 10:00 a.m. to 4 p.m. daily, while allowing these employees to work the remaining 10 hours each week from an offsite location like a home office.

Another form of a flexible schedule is the compressed workweek. This allows employees to work their 35 to 40 hours in a three- or four-day schedule (e.g., four days of 10 hours per day). AVT Document Exchange Software Group, which sells e-document software, allows its general staff to work four 10-hour days and take off three days a week.[73]

Research has found that having flextime schedules positively affects absenteeism and productivity. This work arrangement change from the traditional five-day workweek arrangement is used to recruit and retain employees at Marcel Dekker Inc., a publishing firm.[74]

Recognizing Limiting Conditions

The selection of a change technique is based on diagnosis of the problem, but it is also tempered by the conditions at the time an intervention is to occur. Three such limiting conditions are the *leadership climate*, the *formal organization*, and the *organizational culture*.

Leadership climate refers to the nature of the work environment that results from the leadership style and the administrative practices of managers. Any change program not supported by management has only a minimal chance of success.[75] Management must be at least slightly positive toward the change. By not supporting the change, or by being unenthusiastic about it, a manager can undermine the efforts to change because he or she is in an authority position and, as such, can influence others. The style of leadership itself may be the subject of change: for example, sensitivity training is a direct attempt to move managers toward a certain style—open, supportive, and group centered. But the participants in sensitivity training may be unable to adopt such styles if these are incompatible with the style of their own superiors.

The *formal organization* must be compatible with the proposed change(s). This includes the effects on the organizational environment resulting from philosophy and policies of top management, as well as legal precedent, organizational design, and the system of control. Of course, each of these sources of impact may be the focus of the change effort. For example, a change to technology that eliminates jobs contradicts a policy of guaranteed employment.

The effect of group norms, values, and informal activities on the *organization's culture* can influence the effect of a change program. The effect of traditional behavior, sanctioned by a group but not formally acknowledged, was first documented in the Hawthorne studies. A proposed change in work methods or the installation of an automated device can run counter to the expectations and attitudes of work groups. If such is the case, the manager implementing the change must anticipate resistance and be prepared to overcome it.

When managers evaluate the strength of limiting conditions, they are simultaneously considering the problem of objective setting. Many managers have been disappointed by change efforts that fell short of their expectations.[76] Particularly frustrated are those managers who cannot understand why the simple issue of a directive does not produce the intended response. Thoughtful managers will recognize that even as they attempt to make changes, other conditions reinforce the status quo. The realities of limiting conditions are such that managers often must be content with incremental change or even no change at all.

If a manager implements change without considering the constraints imposed by prevailing conditions within the present organization, the original problem may only get worse. Such change may actually result in further problems. Taken together, these constraints constitute the climate for change—positive or negative.

Overcoming Limiting Conditions

The selection of any developmental intervention should be based on diagnosis of the problem, but as we just said the choice is tempered by certain conditions that exist at the time. Scholars identify three sources of influence on the outcome of management development programs that can be generalized to cover the entire range of organizational development interventions: leadership climate, formal organization, and organizational culture.

Leadership Climate

leadership climate
The nature of work environment in an organization that results from the leadership style and administrative practices.

The nature of the work environment that results from the leadership style and administrative practices of managers is termed the **leadership climate**. It can greatly affect a change program. Any change program that lacks management's support and commitment has only a slim chance of success.[77] We can also understand that the style of leadership may itself be the subject of change. For example, total quality management (TQM) attempts to move managers toward a certain style: open, supportive, and group centered. But we must recognize that participants may be unable to adopt such styles if the styles aren't compatible with their own management style.[78]

Another important factor related to leadership climate that can help facilitate the change process is shared leadership. Shared leadership is when companies like Hewlett-Packard and IBM can call on several leaders at different levels and in different divisions who can help implement change initiatives simultaneously across the organization.[79] Instead of having one change agent who is a "super hero," organizations like IBM spread leadership responsibilities among the employees who are "all connected by a shared sense of identity and purpose." This approach to change management assumes that change is "business as usual" and must be a part of the normal operating strategy of any effective organization.

formal organization
The philosophy, policies, structure, and systems of control of an organization.

Formal Organization

The **formal organization** includes the philosophy and policies of top management, as well as legal precedent, organizational structure, and the systems of control. Of course, each of

OB AND YOUR CAREER Managing Change, Step-by-Step

One day, you may be asked to help make major changes at your organization. Although no absolute guarantees can ensure success in every instance, the accumulated experience of people involved with organizational development offers some guidelines. We share the views of one such individual, William G. Dyer, who has spent 30 years assisting organizations to reach their potential effectiveness. He states that the following conditions must be present if the intervention is to have a chance of bringing about the desired change:

1. Secure commitment from the top. The leadership and top management of the organization must provide strong and visible support for the changes.
2. Inform the change agents. People responsible for changing the organization need to be given information in advance explaining what they need to do and why.
3. Connect the changes to the whole organization. The effort and the modified evaluation and reward systems must be connected to the rest of the organization.
4. Line managers have to implement the effort. Line managers need to lead the implementation of the change effort, with the support of the change agent.
5. Get an accurate diagnosis. The change effort needs to be based on a valid and thorough diagnosis of the organization.
6. Top management needs to remain committed. The leaders of the organization need to remain committed from diagnosis through implementation and evaluation.
7. Evaluate thoroughly. The intervention must be evaluated carefully and needs to be more than just asking employees how they felt about the effort.
8. Align the effort. Employees must see clearly the relationship between the change effort and the organization's mission and goals.
9. Competent change agent. Use a change agent who is experienced and has a strong track record with similar organizational interventions.

These nine conditions combine many of the important points made in this chapter. Organizational development is a major undertaking that managers should pursue in a systematic way. Change is an important part of organizational life. By understanding how to manage change, you can help your organization remain effective and competitive.

Sources: Adapted from William G. Dyer, "Team Building: A History of the Past, Present, and Future OD," *Academy of OD Newsletter*, Winter 1989, pp. 7–8; and John M. Ivancevich, Robert Konopaske and Michael T. Matteson, *Organizational Behavior and Management* 9th ed. (New York: McGraw-Hill/Irwin, 2011), p. 541.

these sources of impact may itself be the focus of the change effort. The important point is that a change in one must be compatible with all of the others.[80] It may be possible to design organizations that not only facilitate change, but also actually welcome it.[81]

Organizational Culture

organizational culture What the employees perceive and how this perception creates a shared sense and pattern of beliefs, values, and expectations.

As we've learned, **organizational culture** refers to the pattern of beliefs resulting from group norms, values, and informal activities.[82] As we said above, the impact of traditional behavior that's sanctioned by group norms but not formally acknowledged was first documented in the Hawthorne studies. A change in work methods or the installation of an automated device can run counter to the attitudes of the work group, and if such is the case, the change strategy must anticipate the resulting resistance.[83]

Resistance to Change

Apparently no matter how smooth or efficient a proposed change may be, there will be some form of resistance. The resistance is a limiting factor because of some real or imagined threat to what is familiar. Concepts of broken promises in the past, fear of change, peer pressure, disruption of regular patterns, and other behavioral and emotional responses can disrupt what looks good on paper or sounds good in planning meetings. Some of the reasons for resistance are individual, while others are part of the work setting or the culture. Managers involved in change programs need to consider and evaluate the individual and context reasons behind any resistance to change.

As the OB and Your Career above suggests, implementing change that doesn't consider the constraints imposed by prevailing conditions within the present organization may, of course, amplify the problem that triggered the developmental process in the first place. If structural, behavioral, or technological change is implemented in this way, the potential for subsequent problems is greater than would ordinarily be expected. Taken together, the prevailing conditions constitute the climate for change, and they can be positive or negative.

Implementing and Evaluating the Change

The implementation of proposed change has two dimensions: *timing* and *scope. Timing* is knowing when to make the change. Introducing a new electronic cash register system in a retail store would not be a good idea during the Thanksgiving season; however, it could be implemented in an off-peak month like February. The matter of timing is strategic; it depends on a number of factors, particularly the organization's operating cycle and the groundwork that has preceded the change. *Scope* is knowing how much of a change to make. A change of considerable magnitude should not compete with ordinary operations. It might be easier to implement during a slack period. On the other hand, if the change is critical to the survival of the organization, then immediate implementation is in order.

The scope of the change depends on the change strategy. The change may be implemented throughout the organization and become established quickly. Or it may be phased into the organization level-by-level, department-by-department. The strategy of successful change uses a phased approach that limits the scope but provides feedback for each subsequent implementation.

The provision of feedback information is termed the *monitoring* phase. Figure 17.2 shows that information is fed back into the forces-of-change phase because the change itself establishes a new situation that might create problems.

The stimulus for change is a deterioration of performance objectives and standards that can be traced to structural, behavioral, or technological causes. The standards may be any number of indicators, including profit, sales volume, productivity, absenteeism, turnover, scrappage, and costs. The major source of feedback on those variables is the firm's management information system. But if the change includes the objective of improving employee attitudes and morale, the usual sources of information are limited, if not invalid.

The Ethical Issues of Organizational Change

Organizational change involves applying powerful behavioral science knowledge by a change agent to bring about performance improvements. The ethical issues turn on the power relationships of the various participants in the change effort.[84] At the most fundamental level, critics note that change is based largely on the existing power relationships in the organization because the effort is initiated by managers. As a managerial technique, change necessarily implements managerial values regardless of the values of the change agent. The change can be inherently unethical because it restricts the range of values that can legitimately be considered in bringing about the change. Even though a change may bring about performance improvements in the organization, the basic power relationships remain unchanged.

Opportunities for unethical behavior can be seen in change-related activities. For example, the purposes of a particular intervention can be misrepresented to the participants to win their participation. Managers may say that they want to implement management by objectives (MBO) to provide greater employee participation when, in fact, they're attracted to MBO as a means of performance evaluation that holds individuals responsible for results rather than activities. A second change activity involves data analysis. Change agents collect and analyze data to diagnose the nature of the problem and to evaluate the solution. The change agents' allegiance to the people who hire them (the organization managers) will inevitably lead to misuse when the data conflict with managers' preferences. Data indicative of management incompetence can be misused so as to indicate employee incompetence. Finally, change may involve manipulation of individuals without informed consent. Employees who are subjects of change interventions aren't given the choice to participate, particularly when the focus of the change is group and organizational performance. Manipulation can, in fact, turn into coercion when the individual must choose between participating in the process or being fired.

Thus, the argument for the unethical nature of change proceeds from the recognition that it inherently reflects but one possible set of values, managerial values. As a consequence, organizational change activities that involve ethical choices will always be guided by the underlying values of management, even when those choices involve misrepresentation, misuse, and manipulation.

The best protection against misrepresentation, misuse, and manipulation is managers who create and foster an organizational culture that encourages ethical behavior. Such a culture would begin with top management's formal declaration that ethical behavior is the norm and that in all actions, individuals—including change agents—are to conduct themselves in an ethical manner, even when such conduct may be costly to the organization in economic and technical terms. Through the actions of top management, ethical behavior can become part of the everyday activities and decisions of everyone in the organization.

Codes of ethics are suggested means for institutionalizing ethical behavior. Top management demonstrates its commitment to the code through its daily behavior. In addition, the organization reinforces ethical behavior through punishment and rewards. Deviants are dealt with swiftly, and adherents are rewarded consistently. The performance evaluation system can be a very important mechanism for demonstrating management's commitment to ethical behavior.

Thus, change itself is not unethical. But individuals can be unethical if rewarded for unethical behavior. Consequently, management must create an environment that fosters ethical conduct. In such an environment, change interventions can proceed in an ethical manner.

The Learning Organization

Because organizations are continuously changing they must learn from the past, competitors, and experts to remain competitive. Learning is a key ingredient in growing, becoming more effective and socially responsible, and sustaining the business's value proposition. Peter Senge, in his best-selling book *The Fifth Discipline,* described a learning organization as proactively creating, using, and transferring knowledge to change its behavior.[85] Sharing knowledge, experience, and ideas becomes a habit in a learning organization.

Buckman Laboratories of Memphis, Tennessee, is held up as an example of a progressive learning organization.[86] The firm uses forums, training, electronic bulletin boards, virtual conference rooms, and presentations to share information and experiences (www.knowledge-nurture.com). By working together and sharing, the entire 1,200-person workforce is able to perform feats that previously were impossible. For example, a Buckman sales representative was attempting to close a deal in Indonesia. The plant's decision-making team wanted a proposal within two weeks—an impossible task. The sales rep went to this online forum, explained his predicament, and within 48 hours had volumes of data, information, and facts to prepare the sales proposal. He made the two-week deadline with time to spare and closed the deal.

Learning Capabilities and Leadership

A number of factors that facilitate organizational learning have been identified. Table 17.1 presents nine different factors and briefly explains each of them. For example, it lists a climate of openness, which involves an openness to information, the encouragement of

TABLE 17.1 A Learning Perspective

Sources: Adapted from Taina Savolainen and Arto Haikonen, "Dynamics of Organizational Learning and Continuous Improvement in Six Sigma Implementation," *TQM Magazine* 19, no. 1, (2007), pp. 6–17; Ivan Marques, "Change: A Concept of Organizational Learning and Change," *Development and Learning Organizations* 21, no. 3, (2007), pp. 6–19; and B. Moingeon and A. Edmondson, *Organizational Learning and Competitive Advantage* (Thousand Oaks, CA: Sage, 1996), p. 43.

1.	Scanning the environment	Interest in external happenings and in the nature of one's environment. Valuing the processes of awareness and data generation. Curious about what is "out there" as opposed to "in here."
2.	Performance issues	Share perception of a gap between actual and desired state of performance. Disconfirming feedback interrupts a string of successes. Performance shortfalls are seen as opportunities for learning.
3.	Metrics	Spend effort to define and measure key factors; strive for specific, quantifiable measures; discourse over metrics is seen as a learning activity.
4.	Experimental philosophy	Support for trying new things; curiosity about how things work; ability to "play" with things. Small failures are encouraged, not punished. See changes in work processes, policies, and structures as a continuous series of graded tryouts.
5.	Transparency	Accessibility of information, relatively open boundaries. Opportunities to observe others; problems/errors are shared, not hidden; debate and conflict are acceptable.
6.	Education	Ongoing commitment to education at all levels; support for growth and development of members.
7.	Operational variety	Variety exists in response modes, procedures, systems; significant diversity in personnel. Pluralistic rather than monolithic definition of valued internal capabilities.
8.	Multiple advocates	Top-down and bottom-up initiatives are possible; multiple advocates and gatekeepers exist.
9.	Engaged leaders and role models	Leadership at significant levels articulates vision and is very actively engaged in its actualization; takes ongoing steps to implement visions; "hands-on" involvement in educational and other implementation steps.

sharing, and debate.[87] This factor is one of the trademarks of Buckman Laboratories, which was just discussed.

Managers who also lead can create or contribute to the learning environment. The building and sustaining of a learning organization requires a commitment to learning, the generation of creative ideas that are implemented, and the desire to build cohesive teamwork, collaboration, and support. Table 17.2 presents a list of activities that can be performed to build learning within an organization.

A major result of an effective learning organization is that knowledge is managed more effectively.[88] Knowledge management is the sharing of information to achieve innovation, competitive advantage, and productive accomplishments. Although a learning organization leads to knowledge management, it is also true that by managing knowledge, organizations will learn.

Learning and managing knowledge are not enough in a constantly changing work environment. Pfeffer and Sutton correctly suggest that many firms have fallen into a knowing–doing gap. What is learned and knowledge gained about change, strategies, and resistance must be converted into action and evaluation. It is easier and more comfortable to talk intellectually about empowerment, converting to more telecommuting, or eliminating layers of management than to actually execute a change.[89] The challenge facing managers who understand change, learning organizations, and knowledge management is to become action oriented and decisive.

TABLE 17.2 Leadership Roles and Activities for Building a Learning Organization

Source: Based in part on D. Ulrich, T. Jick, and M. von Gilnow, "High-Impact Learning: Building and Diffusing Learning Capability," *Organizational Dynamics,* Autumn 1993, pp. 52–66.

Leadership Activities	Role 1: Build a Commitment to Learning	Role 2: Work to Generate Ideas with Impact	Role 3: Work to Generalize Ideas with Impact
Make learning a component of the vision and strategic objectives	X		
Invest in learning	X		
Publicly promote the value of learning	X		
Measure, benchmark, and track learning	X		
Create rewards for and symbols of learning	X		
Implement continuous improvement programs		X	
Increase employee competence through training, or buy talent from outside the organization		X	
Experiment with new ideas, processes, and structural arrangements		X	
Identify mental models of organizational processes		X	
Instill systems thinking throughout the organization		X	
Create an infrastructure that moves ideas across organizational boundaries			X
Rotate employees across functional and divisional boundaries			X

Learning

Senge proposes that the manager's role in the learning organization is that of a designer, teacher, and facilitator who can build shared vision and challenge the traditional model of managing. Managers who view the organization as a system of interrelated parts and communicate a vision of the future can lead others to learn from mistakes and break away from using old patterns of problem solving and decision making.

Converting a traditional organization to a more learning-oriented institution requires changing the way information and experiences are used. Managers must change the way information is sought, used, stored, and reviewed. Information must be shared, available, and transparent. These requirements are resisted because they are not usually the way information is viewed. Managers who believe in the learning organization concept actively work to make information, new ideas, and creativity a part of the culture of their unit, project, or department.

Summary of Key Points

- The need to consider organizational development arises from changes in the inter- and extraorganizational environment. Changes in the input, output, technological, and scientific subenvironments may indicate the need to consider the feasibility of a long-term, systematically managed program for changing the structure, process, and behavior of the organization. Even in the absence of environmental changes, organizational processes and behavior may become dysfunctional for achieving organizational effectiveness.
- The diagnosis of present and potential problems involves the collection of information that reflects the level of organizational effectiveness. Data that measure the current state of production, efficiency, satisfaction, adaptiveness, and development must be gathered and analyzed. The purpose of diagnosis is to trace the cause of the problem. In addition to serving as the basis for problem identification, the diagnostic data also establish the basis for subsequent evaluation of the organizational development effort.
- To diagnose the problem, managers can consider these analytical questions:
  1. What is the problem, and what distinguishes it from the symptoms?
  2. What must be changed to resolve the problem?
  3. What outcomes are expected, and how will these outcomes be measured?
- The managerial response to these questions should be stated in terms of criteria that reflect organizational effectiveness. Measurable outcomes such as production, efficiency, satisfaction, adaptiveness, and development must be linked to skill, attitudinal, behavioral, and structural changes necessitated by problem identification.
- Through diagnosis, management associates the problem with skill, attitudinal, behavioral, and structural causes and selects the appropriate intervention. If employee participation is inappropriate because the necessary preconditions don't exist, management must unilaterally define the problem and select the appropriate method. Whether the problem is related to skill or attitudinal, behavioral, or structural causes, the strategy must include provision of learning principles.
- The last step of the change process is the evaluation procedure. The ideal situation would be to structure the procedure in the manner of an experimental design. That is, the end results should be operationally defined, and measurements should be taken, before and after, both in the organization undergoing development and in a second organization (the control group). If the scope of the program is limited to a subunit, a second subunit could serve as a control group. An evaluation not only enables management to account for its use of resources but also provides feedback. Based on this feedback, corrections can be taken in the implementation phase.

Discussion and Review Questions

1. Why is diagnosis so vital in organizational change programs?
2. Explain the concept of *organization intervention* and why any particular management or organization change can be considered an intervention.
3. Might some managers attempt to implement a particular intervention, such as TQM, without first diagnosing whether the intervention would be appropriate for their organization's problems?
4. Why is it important for managers to reduce the resistance to change openly displayed or covertly practiced by employees?
5. Evaluate the ethical issues associated with downsizing an organization by reducing its labor force to increase the organization's long-run chance of survival. What other ethical issues can you identify in the practice of organizational development as you understand it thus far?
6. Describe the relationships among the steps of the change model depicted in this chapter and the process of unfreezing–new learning–refreezing. Which steps of the model are related to which elements of the relearning process?
7. How is the appreciative inquiry approach to organizational change different from a problem-solving approach?
8. Why is top management support so important for the success of an organizational development and change initiative?
9. Explain the difficulties that you would encounter in attempting to obtain diagnostic information from members of two groups that believe they're competing for scarce resources.
10. Explain why a change program should be evaluated and why such an evaluation is so difficult to conduct.

Taking It to the Net

Monitoring Dramatic Changes

A statement that organizations are undergoing constant change is hardly insightful. It is simply a fact of the life of organizations that changes in behavior, structure, work design, and processes are occurring in rapid-fire order and disorder. Examine the news releases and history on the Internet of any five *Fortune* 500 or *Forbes* 400 companies. Prepare a short report of major changes that can be traced in the five firms you selected.

1. Highlight the most dramatic behavior (people), structure, work design, and process changes reflected for the five companies.
2. In retracing the history of your selected firms, are there more dramatic changes reflected in the most recent five-year period or in earlier periods?
3. Do any of your selected firms have or report on an organizational change task force?

Case for Analysis: *Bayer's Major Changes in One Plant*

Within a period of only seven months prior to Bayer's acquisition of a production facility in Myerstown, Pennsylvania, the plant had changed ownership three times and the workforce seemed to have dissolved as fast as the analgesic tablets rolling off production lines—down from 800 to 360 workers in less than a year. That was a lot of change to absorb in a facility that had been steadily producing over-the-counter and prescription pharmaceuticals for more than half a century.

But there was more: employees were uncertain about what it would be like to work for Bayer, a German-owned company, and the plant manager post had been vacant for a while. Morale among workers plummeted, and job security became a running joke.

Line managers had worries of their own, not the least of which was ramping up to Bayer's expectation for a 24-hour-per-day, seven-day-per-week production schedule with an acquisition-weary workforce. Even more troubling was the fact that the plant was operating in the red and had been a drain on the bottom line for some time.

Bayer management realized that given competitive forces and the rate of change in their industry, they needed to streamline operations to have a more secure future in Bayer Corp.'s newly formed consumer care division. But there was no plant manager at Myerstown from January 1995 until August 1996, so the functional department managers—including the HR manager—worked as a team to manage the plant through that trying time. They soon realized that employees needed to be involved at the heart of any turnaround.

"That's where HR came in and really spearheaded the effort," says Jon Danchisko, manager of human resources and organization development. With the help of Sibson & Co., a global management consulting firm, Danchisko's six-person HR team embarked on a present-state analysis, selecting 93 employees at random to participate in seven focus group meetings to get a clear indication of what was going on at the plant. Employees answered a number of open-ended questions, including "Why do people work here?" and "Why do people leave here?"

Next, HR compiled this information and invited employees who hadn't participated in the first focus groups to comment on the findings. Finally, HR analyzed workers' input. Workers noted several positive workplace attributes, such as pay and benefits, in their feedback. However, they also brought up 30 issues that required attention—too many to respond to without more interpretation and analysis. This kind of involvement was new to employees. Before Bayer's acquisition, the management style at the facility was top-down rather than collaborative and reactive instead of proactive.

Knowing that Myerstown employees were skeptical of new management programs because of past failures, plant manager John O'Neil and the HR team addressed workers at an all-employee meeting about the first initiative—developing a site strategy and goals. In a subsequent meeting, he introduced all five initiatives and the following site strategy: "to be clearly recognized as Bayer Consumer Care's most effective site in the Northern American's region in terms of safety, customer service, value-added manufacturing/packaging, and cost effectiveness."

Myerstown employees felt that communication was so important in getting and receiving information about on-site performance, department projects, and rumors that they initiated the "Myerstown Information Exchange." This electronic newsletter is sent monthly to members of the site management team, who in turn discuss the information with those who report to them.

Not everyone was enthusiastic about the change process. One of the key points uncovered in the initial focus groups and subsequent team meetings was pessimism about starting a new "program." As one employee put it, "It would be nice if [managers] were really sincere in this, but we've all been through this before. I think this is going to be another flavor of the month."

Several employees enumerated the buzzwords and acronyms of programs that previous managers had tried long ago and that invariably fell by the wayside: WQC (work quality circles), JIT (just-in-time manufacturing), SPC (statistical process control), and team-based manufacturing. Indeed, employees had been barraged in the past with T-shirts and coffee mugs for other management programs.

Managers found it refreshing that employees would be so candid about these issues and figured that engaging them in a dialogue about past failures and what needed to be done in the future would help everyone work together to make it happen because they'd all be on common ground.

"As an employee, I felt like the entire process was handled extremely well," says Rick Higley, a pharmaceutical operator who served on the Roadmap for Change Team. "The thing I really appreciated about the process was that the managers listened to what everyone had to say, treated us as equals, and really valued our opinions."

Resistance to change can be overcome by acknowledging not only the business rationale for change but also the hopes, fears, and dreams of those affected, noted the change management experts at Sibson & Co. In the race to make change happen, organizational leaders often fail to tell the straight story to people who then write their best scripts. Progressive companies go to great lengths to involve people in a transformation that affects them, which sends critical messages about validation and involvement.

DISCUSSION QUESTIONS

1. What type of change(s) occurred at Bayer?
2. What type of employee resistance to change did Bayer have to address?
3. What are the positive and negative lessons learned from how change was handled at Bayer?

Sources: Robert J. Sutton, "The Weird Rules of Creativity," *Harvard Business Review,* September 2001, pp. 94–107; and Jennifer Laabs, "Paving the Way to Profitability, *Workforce,* March 2000, pp. 66–70.

Experiential Exercise: *Alternative Ways to Initiate Change*

OBJECTIVE

To evaluate alternative ways to initiate training in the face of possible resistance from both the employees and their supervisors.

RELATED TOPICS

Individual, group, and leadership theories are relevant, along with ideas and concepts from organizational change and development.

STARTING THE EXERCISE

The instructor will divide the class into groups of five to seven. The groups should read the following scenario and decide which of the five alternatives the manager should implement. Although other alternatives are possible, evaluate only those indicated. Each group will prepare and present an oral report justifying its choice.

SCENARIO

A manager faces a problem involving mistakes employees are making. The mistakes occur in nearly every department of the plant in which this particular operation is performed. The manager believes that a training program is necessary to help employees perform better and reduce the errors. He believes that supervisors who report to him will defend existing procedures because the introduction of a training program could imply criticism of the way they've been operating. The manager also thinks that the supervisors fear resistance by employees afraid of not doing well in the training program. Given these facts and considerations, the manager believes that he has five alternative ways to initiate the needed change:

1. Add a recommendation that training be undertaken to the agenda of the weekly meeting with the supervisors.
2. Talk to the supervisors individually and get their ideas about what to do before bringing up the issue in the weekly meeting.
3. Ask the corporate training staff to come to the plant, assess the training needs, and develop a program to address those needs.
4. Tell the supervisors that the training is in the interests of the company and that they are expected to support it with enthusiasm.
5. Appoint a team of supervisors to study the matter thoroughly and to bring a recommendation to the weekly meeting.

COMPLETING THE EXERCISE

Phase I: 30 minutes. Each group of five to seven students should read the scenario, evaluate the five alternatives, and prepare an oral report defending their choice.

Phase II: 30 minutes. As a class, discuss the choices made by the groups as well as their reasons for picking a particular alternative.

APPENDIX

Procedures and Techniques for Studying Organizations: Behavior, Structure, Processes

Sources of Knowledge about Organizations

The vast majority of the research reports and writing on organizations is contained in technical publications known as academic journals. Some of these journals, such as the *Academy of Management Review,* are devoted entirely to topics of management and organization, whereas such journals as *Organizational Behavior and Human Decision Processes* are devoted largely to results of laboratory studies. Such journals as *Harvard Business Review* and *Business Horizons* are general business journals, whereas *American Sociological Review* and *Journal of Applied Psychology* are general behavioral science journals. These general business and behavioral science journals often contain articles of interest to management students.

Table A.1 presents a selective list of journals providing information, data, and discussion about what is occurring within and among organizations. This knowledge base provides managers with available research information that could prove useful in their own organizations or situations.[1]

History

The oldest approach to the study of organization is through the history of organizations, societies, and institutions. Organizations are as old as human history. Throughout time, people have joined with others to accomplish their goals, first in families and later in tribes and other more sophisticated political units. Ancient peoples constructed pyramids, temples, and ships; they created systems of government, farming, commerce, and warfare. For example, Greek historians tell us that it took 100,000 men to build the great pyramid of

TABLE A.1
Selected Sources of Writing and Research about Organizations

1. *Academy of Management Perspectives*
2. *Academy of Management Journal*
3. *Academy of Management Learning and Education*
4. *Academy of Management Review*
5. *Administrative Science Quarterly*
6. *Advanced Management Journal*
7. *Business Horizons*
8. *California Management Review*
9. *Fast Company*
10. *Fortune*
11. *Harvard Business Review*
12. *Health Psychology*
13. *HR Magazine*
14. *Human Relations*
15. *Human Resource Planning*
16. *Industrial Relations*
17. *International Journal of Human Resource Management*
18. *Journal of Applied Behavioral Science*
19. *Journal of Applied Psychology*
20. *Journal of Business Ethics*
21. *Journal of Business Strategy*
22. *Journal of Conflict Resolution*
23. *Journal of International Business Studies*
24. *Journal of Management*
25. *Journal of Management Inquiry*
26. *Journal of Management Studies*
27. *Journal of Occupational Behavior*
28. *Journal of World Business*
29. *Labor Law Journal*
30. *Management Review*
31. *Management Science*
32. *Monthly Labor Review*
33. *Organizational Behavior and Human Decision Processes*
34. *Organizational Dynamics*
35. *Organizational Research Methods*
36. *Organization Science*
37. *Personnel Psychology*
38. *Psychological Bulletin*
39. *Public Administration Review*
40. *Public Personnel Management*
41. *Sloan Management Review*
42. *Strategic Management Journal*
43. *Training*
44. *Training & Development Journal*

Khufu in Egypt. The project took more than 20 years to complete. It was almost as high as the Washington Monument and had a base that would cover eight football fields. Remember that these people had no construction equipment or computers. One thing they did have, though, was *organization.* Although these "joint efforts" did not have formal names such as XYZ Corporation, the idea of "getting organized" was quite widespread throughout early civilizations. The literature of the times refers to such managerial concepts as planning, staff assistance, division of labor, control, and leadership.[2]

The administration of the vast Roman Empire required the application of organization and management concepts. In fact, it has been said, "the real secret of the greatness of the Romans was their genius for organization."[3] This is because the Romans used certain principles of organization to coordinate the diverse activities of the empire.

If judged by longevity, the Roman Catholic Church would have to be considered to be an effective organization. Although its success is the result of many factors, one of these factors is certainly the effectiveness of its organization and management. For example, a hierarchy of authority, a territorial organization, specialization of activities by function, and use of the staff principle were integral parts of early church organization.

Finally, and not surprisingly, some important concepts and practices in modern organizations can be traced to military organizations. Like the church, military organizations were faced with problems of managing large, geographically dispersed groups and adopted the concept of staff as an advisory function for line personnel early on.

Knowledge of the history of organizations in earlier societies can be useful for the future manager. In fact, many of the early concepts and practices are being used successfully today. But we may ask whether heavy reliance on the past is a good guide to the present and future.[4] We shall see that time and organizational setting have much to do with what works in management.

Experience

Some of the earliest books on management and organizations were written by successful practitioners. Most of these individuals were business executives, and their writings focused on how it was for them during their time with one or more companies. They usually put forward certain general principles or practices that had worked well for them. Although using the writings and experiences of practitioners sounds "practical," it has drawbacks. Successful managers are susceptible to the same perceptual phenomena as the rest of us. Their accounts are therefore based on their own preconceptions and biases. No matter how objective the approach, experiential accounts may not be entirely complete or accurate. They may also be superficial, because they are often after-the-fact reflections of situations in which, when the events were occurring, the managers had little time to think about how or why an action was taken. As a result, suggestions in such accounts are often oversimplified. Finally, as with history, what worked yesterday may not work today or tomorrow.[5]

Science

A major focus in this book is the behavioral sciences, which have produced theory, research, and generalizations concerning the behavior, structure, and processes of organizations. Behavioral scientists' interest in the problems of organizations is relatively new, becoming popular in the early 1950s. At that time, an organization known as the Foundation for Research on Human Behavior was established to promote and support behavioral science research in business, government, and other organizations.

Many advocates of the scientific approach believe that practicing managers have, in too many cases, accepted prevalent practices and principles without the benefit of scientific validation. They believe that scientific procedures should be used to validate practice whenever possible. Because of their work, many of the earlier practices and principles have been discounted or modified, and others have been validated.

Behavioral Sciences Research and Methods

Research

Current research in the behavioral sciences varies greatly with respect to the scope and methods used. One common thread among the various disciplines is the study of human behavior through the use of scientific procedures. Thus, it is necessary to examine the nature of science as it's applied to human behavior.

Some critics believe that a science of human behavior is unattainable and that the scientific procedures used to gain knowledge in the physical sciences cannot be adapted to the study of humans, especially humans in organizations. While this is not the appropriate place to become involved in these arguments, we believe that the scientific approach can be applied to management and organizational studies.[6] Furthermore, as we have already pointed out, means other than scientific procedures have provided important knowledge concerning people in organizations.

When asked about nonscientific ideas, physical scientists generally reply, "There is no evidence for anything like that." They point out, for example, that it is difficult to believe in the existence of UFOs when no artifact of extraterrestrial origin has been found. This argument is not very convincing. After all, physical scientists also speculate about ideas that are, as yet, unconfirmed by empirical evidence. If they didn't, progress would slow down or simply stop.[7]

FIGURE A.1
Model for Organizational Research

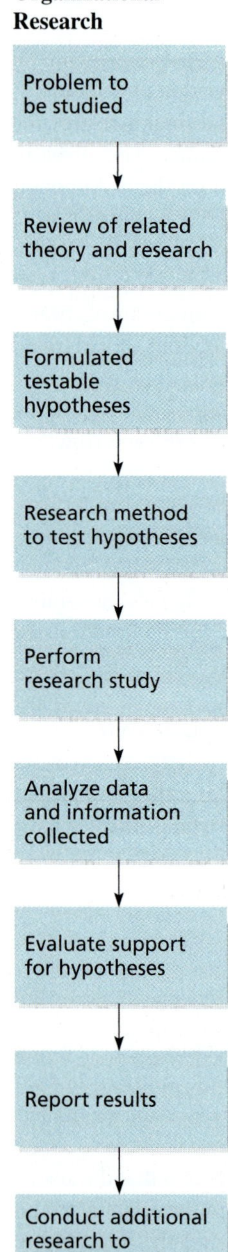

The manager draws from the behavioral sciences just as the physician draws from the biological sciences. The manager must know what to expect from the behavioral sciences, their strengths and weaknesses, just as the physician must know what to expect from bacteriology and how it can serve as a diagnostic tool. However, the manager, like the physician, is a practitioner who must make decisions in the present, whether or not science has all the answers. Neither can wait until he finds them before acting.[8] Neither the physician nor the behavioral scientist has all the answers.

The Scientific Approach

The scientific approach is a process of gathering data to test hypotheses or to explain phenomena. A step-by-step process that is popular among researchers is presented in Figure A.1. Most current philosophers of science define science by what they consider to be its one universal and unique feature: *method.* The greatest advantage of the scientific approach is its characteristics of *self-correction,* which no other method of attaining knowledge has.[9] The approach is an objective, systematic, and controlled process with built-in checks all along the way to knowledge. These checks control and verify the scientist's activities and conclusions to enable the attainment of knowledge independent of the scientist's own biases and preconceptions.

Most scientists agree that rather than use a single scientific method, scientists can and do use several methods. Thus, it probably makes sense to say that there is a scientific *approach.* Table A.2 summarizes the major characteristics of this approach and Figure A.1 graphically presents one approach. While only an "ideal" science would exhibit all of the characteristics in Table A.2, the characteristics are nevertheless the hallmarks of the scientific approach. They exhibit the basic nature—objective, systematic, controlled—of this scientific approach, which enables others to have confidence in research results. What is important is the overall fundamental idea that the scientific approach is a controlled rational process.

Figure A.1 is a series of steps used to build a case to support or reject hypotheses. Each researcher uses his or her own series of steps, but a systematic approach is recommended.

Throughout the book organizational behavior terms, issues, and analyses were used in clarifying how people behave in organizations. A scientific language or vocabulary was used to better understand human resources Assumptions, propositions, and hypotheses about behavior were interjected and formed the basis of debates, controversy, and understanding about OB. For example, the Hawthorne researchers originally hypothesized that "if workers received appropriate rest breaks, then productivity would increase." The hypothesis is a predictive statement presented in an "if–then" context: if (rest break)–then (productivity increase). This hypothesis was not supported in the Hawthorne studies.

The hypothesis in OB research typically illustrates a linkage between what is referred to as an independent variable (presumed to affect a dependent variable) and a dependent variable. The dependent variable is what the researcher is attempting to understand or explain. Rest pauses were independent variables that supposedly affected productivity, the dependent variable.

Methods of Inquiry

How do behavioral scientists gain knowledge about the functioning of organizations? Just as physical scientists have certain tools and methods for obtaining information, so too do behavioral scientists. These are usually referred to as *research designs.* In broad terms, three basic designs are used by behavioral scientists: the case study, the field study, and the experiment.

Case Study

A case study attempts to examine numerous characteristics of one or more people, usually over an extended period. For years, anthropologists have studied the customs and behaviors

TABLE A.2
Characteristics of the Scientific Approach

1. Procedures are public. A scientific report contains a complete description of what was done to enable other researchers in the field to follow each step of the investigation as if they were actually present.
2. Definitions are precise. The procedure used, the variables measured, and how they were measured must be clearly stated. For example, if examining motivation among employees in a given plant, researchers must define what is meant by motivation and how it was measured (e.g., number of units produced, number of absences).
3. Data collection is objective. Objectivity is a key feature of the scientific approach. Bias in collecting and interpreting data has no place in science.
4. Findings must be replicable. This enables another interested researcher to test the results of a study by attempting to reproduce them.
5. The approach is systematic and cumulative. This relates to one of the underlying purposes of science to develop a unified body of knowledge.
6. The purposes are explanation, understanding, and prediction. All scientists want to know "why" and "how." If they determine "why" and "how" and are able to provide proof, they can then predict the particular conditions under which specific events (human behavior in the case of behavioral sciences) will occur. Prediction is the ultimate objective of behavioral science, as it is of all science.

of various groups by actually living among them. Some organizational researchers have done the same thing. They have actually worked and socialized with the groups of employees they were studying.[10]

The reports on such investigations are usually in the form of a case study. A well-known example is when organizational researcher Henry Mintzberg spent time with the senior managers of several organizations to learn about what roles these managers assume on a daily basis.[11]

The chief limitations of the case study approach for gaining knowledge about the functioning of organizations are as follows:

1. Rarely can two cases be meaningfully compared in essential characteristics. In other words, in another firm of another size, the same factors might not have resulted in a strike.
2. Rarely can case studies be repeated or their findings verified.
3. The significance of the findings is left to the subjective interpretation of the researcher. Like the practitioner, the researcher attempts to describe reality, but it is reality as perceived by one person (or a very small group). The researcher's training, biases, and preconceptions can inadvertently distort the report. A psychologist may give an entirely different view of a group of blue-collar workers than would be given by a sociologist.
4. The results of a case study are based on a sample of one. Consequently, the ability to generalize from them may be limited.[12]

Despite these limitations, the case study is widely used as a method of studying organizations.[13] Researchers have suggested a number of best practices that can reduce the impact of these limitations, including use of precise language and a carefully crafted research design; theoretical sampling of cases, interviews that limit informant bias, rich presentation of evidence in tables and appendixes, and clear statement of theoretical arguments.[14]

In sum, case studies are extremely valuable in answering exploratory questions and providing rich information about important topics of study.

Field Study

Attempting to add more reality and rigor to the study of organizations, behavioral scientists have developed several systematic field research techniques, such as personal interviews, observation, archival data, and questionnaire surveys. They use these methods, individually or in combination, to investigate current practices or events. With these methods, unlike some other methods, the researcher does not rely entirely on what the subjects say. She may personally interview other people in the organization—fellow workers, subordinates, and superiors—to gain a more balanced view before drawing conclusions.[15] In addition, archival data, records, charts, and statistics on file may be used to analyze a problem or hypothesis.

A popular field study technique involves the use of expertly prepared questionnaires. Not only are such questionnaires less subject to unintentional distortion than personal interviews, but they also enable the researcher to greatly increase the number of individuals participating. Figure A.2 presents part of a questionnaire used in organizations to evaluate ratee perceptions of a performance appraisal interview program. The questionnaire enables the collection of data on particular characteristics that are of interest (e.g., equity, accuracy, and clarity). The seven-point scales measure ratee perceptions of the degree to which the performance appraisal interviews possess a given characteristic.

FIGURE A.2 Scale for Assessing GANAT Appraisal Interviews

Source: This interview appraisal form was developed by John M. Ivancevich.

Part A: Appraisal Interview

The following items deal with the formal appraisal interview used in conjunction with the GANAT project program. Please circle the number that best describes your opinion of the most recent interview session.

	Very False						Very True
1. The appraisal interview covered my entire job.	1	2	3	4	5	6	7
2. The discussion of my performance during the appraisal interview was covered equitably.	1	2	3	4	5	6	7
3. The appraisal interview was accurately conducted.	1	2	3	4	5	6	7
4. I didn't have to ask for any clarification.	1	2	3	4	5	6	7
5. The interview was fair in every respect.	1	2	3	4	5	6	7
6. The interview really raised my anxiety level.	1	2	3	4	5	6	7
7. The interview's purpose was simply not clear to me.	1	2	3	4	5	6	7
8. The appraisal interview really made me think about working smarter on the job.	1	2	3	4	5	6	7
9. The appraisal interview was encouraging to me personally.	1	2	3	4	5	6	7
10. I dreaded the actual interview itself.	1	2	3	4	5	6	7
11. The boss was totally above board in all phases of the interview.	1	2	3	4	5	6	7
12. The interview gave me some direction and purpose.	1	2	3	4	5	6	7
13. The interview really pinpointed areas for improvement.	1	2	3	4	5	6	7
14. The interview was disorganized and frustrating.	1	2	3	4	5	6	7
15. I disliked the interview because the intent was not clear.	1	2	3	4	5	6	7
16. The appraisal interviewer (boss) was not well trained.	1	2	3	4	5	6	7
17. The interview has been my guide for correcting weaknesses.	1	2	3	4	5	6	7
18. I understood the meaning of each performance area better after the interview.	1	2	3	4	5	6	7
19. The interview time was too rushed.	1	2	3	4	5	6	7
20. I received no advance notice about the interview.	1	2	3	4	5	6	7
21. During the interview, my performance was fairly analyzed.	1	2	3	4	5	6	7
22. I was often upset because the interview data were not accurate.	1	2	3	4	5	6	7
23. My record, as it was introduced in the interview, contained no errors.	1	2	3	4	5	6	7

In most cases, surveys are limited to a description of the current state of the situation. However, if researchers are aware of factors that may account for survey findings, they can make conjectural statements (known as *hypotheses*) about the relationship between two or more factors and relate the survey data to those factors. Thus, instead of just describing ratee perceptions of performance evaluation, the researchers could make finer distinctions (e.g., distinctions regarding job tenure, salary level, or education) among groups of ratees. Comparisons and statistical tests could then be applied to determine differences, similarities, or relationships. Finally, *longitudinal* studies involving observations made over time are used to describe changes that have taken place. Thus, in the situation described here, we can become aware of changes in overall ratee perceptions of appraisal interviews over time as well as those relating to individual managers.[16]

Despite advantages over many of the other methods of gaining knowledge about organizations, field studies are not without problems. Here again, researchers have training, interests, and expectations that they bring with them.[17] Thus, a researcher may inadvertently ignore a vital technological factor while concentrating on only behavioral factors in a study of employee morale. Also, the fact that a researcher is present may influence how the individual responds. This weakness of field studies has long been recognized and is noted in some of the earliest field research in organizations.

Experiment

The experiment is potentially the most rigorous of scientific techniques. For an investigation to be considered an experiment, it must contain two elements: manipulation of some variable (independent variable) and observation or measurement of the results (dependent variable) while maintaining all other factors unchanged. Thus, in an organization, a behavioral scientist could change an organizational factor and observe the results while attempting to keep everything else unchanged in one or two general types of experiments.[18]

In a *laboratory experiment,* the researcher creates the environment. For example, a management researcher may work with a small voluntary group in a classroom. The group may be students or managers. If a student sample is used, it is important to determine (1) if the population of interest is similar to the student sample and (2) if research results can be generalized from a student sample to organizational employees.[19] Samples in a laboratory experiment may be asked to communicate, perform tasks, or make decisions under different sets of conditions designated by the researcher. The laboratory setting permits the researcher to closely control the conditions under which observations are made. The intention is to isolate the relevant variables and to measure the response of dependent variables when the independent variable is manipulated. Laboratory experiments are useful when the conditions required to test a hypothesis are not practically or readily obtainable in natural situations and when the situation to be studied can be replicated under laboratory conditions. For such situations, many schools of business have behavioral science laboratories where such experimentation is done.

In a *field experiment,* the investigator attempts to manipulate and control variables in the natural setting rather than in a laboratory. Early experiments in organizations include manipulating physical working conditions such as rest periods, refreshments, and lighting. Today, behavioral scientists attempt to manipulate a host of additional factors.[20] For example, a training program might be introduced for one group of managers but not for another. Comparisons of performance, attitudes, and so on could be obtained later, either at one point or at several different points (a longitudinal study), to determine what effect (if any) the training program had on the managers' performances and attitudes.

The experimental design is especially appealing to many researchers because it is the prototype of the scientific approach. It is the ideal toward which every science strives. However, while its potential is still great, it has not yet produced a great breadth of knowledge about the functioning of organizations. Laboratory experiments suffer the risk of artificiality: the results of such experiments often do not extend to real organizations. Teams of business administration or psychology students working on decision problems may provide a great deal of information for researchers. Unfortunately, extreme caution must be used in determining whether this knowledge can be extended to a group of managers or nonmanagers making decisions under severe time constraints.[21]

Field experiments also have drawbacks. First, researchers cannot control every possible influencing factor (even if they knew them all), as they can in a laboratory. Also, here again, the presence of a researcher may make people behave differently, especially if they are aware that they are participating in an experiment. Experimentation in the behavioral sciences and, more specifically, in organizations is a complex matter.[22]

In a *true experiment,* the researcher has complete control over the experiment: the who, what, when, where, and how. A *quasi-experiment,* however, is one in which the researcher lacks the degree of control over conditions that is possible in a true experiment. In a vast majority of organizational studies, complete control is impossible. Thus, quasi-experiments are typically the rule when organizational behavior is studied via an experiment.

Finally, with each method of inquiry used by behavioral scientists, some *measurement* is usually necessary. Knowledge, to be meaningful, must often be compared with or related to something else. As a result, research questions (hypotheses) are usually stated to show how differences in the magnitude of some variable are related to differences in the magnitude of some other variable.

The variables studied are measured by research instruments. Those instruments may be psychological tests, such as personality or intelligence tests; questionnaires designed to obtain attitudes or other information, such as the questionnaire shown in Figure A.2; or, in some cases, electronic devices to measure eye movement or blood pressure.

That a research instrument be both *reliable* and *valid* is very important. Reliability is the consistency of the measure. In other words, repeated measures with the same instrument should produce the same results or scores. Validity is concerned with whether the research instrument actually measures what it is supposed to be measuring.[23] A research instrument may be reliable but not valid. For example, a test designed to measure intelligence could yield consistent scores over a large number of people but not be measuring intelligence.

Experiments to study organizational behavior use a number of designs. To illustrate some of the available designs, we use the example of a training program being offered to a group of managers. Suppose that the task of the researcher is to design an experiment that permits the assessment of the degree to which the program influenced the performance of the managers. We use the following symbols in our discussion:[24]

S = The subjects (e.g., the managers or workers participating in the experiment).
O = The observation and measurement devices used by the researcher (e.g., ratings of managers' performance by superiors).
X = The experimental treatment, the manipulated variable (e.g., the training program).
R = The randomization process.

Research Designs

One-Shot Design

If we assume that all managers go through the training program, the researchers will have difficulty evaluating it. This is because the researchers cannot compare the group with another group that did not undergo the training program. This design, called a *one-shot design,* is diagrammed as

X O

The letter X stands for the experimental treatment (e.g., the training program); the letter O stands for the observation of performance on the job. The measure could be in the form of an average score based on ratings of superiors. However, the researchers can in no way determine whether performance was influenced at all by the training program. This experimental design is rarely used because of its weaknesses.

One-Group Pretest–Posttest Design

The previous design can be improved upon by first gathering performance data on the managers, instituting the training program, and then remeasuring their performance. This is diagrammed as

$$O_1\ X\ O_2$$

Thus, a pretest is given in time period 1, the program is administered, and a posttest is administered in time period 2. If $O_2 > O_1$, the differences can be attributed to the training program. Numerous factors can confound the results obtained with this design. For example, if new equipment has been installed between O_2 and O_1, this could explain the differences in the performance scores. Thus, a *history* factor may have influenced the results. The most recurrent factors that could also influence results are listed along with their definitions in Table A.3.[25] Examination of the table indicates that results achieved in this design may be confounded by *maturation* (the supervisors may learn to do a better job between O_2 and O_1, which would increase their performance regardless of training), *testing* (the measure of performance in O_1 may make the supervisors aware that they are being evaluated, which may make them work harder and increase their performance), and *instrumentation* (if the performance observations are made at different

TABLE A.3
Recurring Sources of Error in Experimental Studies

Factor	Definition
1. History	Events other than the experimental treatment (X) that occurred between pretest and posttest.
2. Maturation	Changes in the subject group with the passage of time that are not associated with the experimental treatment (X).
3. Testing	Changes in the performance of the subjects because measurement of their performance makes them aware that they are part of an experiment (i.e., measures often alter what is being measured).
4. Instrumentation	Changes in the measures of participants' performance that are the result of changes in the measurement instruments or the conditions under which the measuring is done (e.g., wear on machinery, boredom, fatigue on the part of the observer).
5. Selection	When participants are assigned to experimental and control groups on any basis other than random assignment, any selection method other than random assignment will result in systematic biases that will result in differences between groups that are unrelated to the effects of the experimental treatment (X).
6. Mortality	If some participants drop out of the experiment before it is completed, the experimental and control groups may not be comparable.
7. Interaction effects	Any of these factors may interact with the experimental treatment, resulting in confounding effects on the results. For example, the types of individuals withdrawing from a study (mortality) may differ for the experimental group and the control group.

times of the day, the results could be influenced by fatigue). Each of these factors offers explanations for changes in performance other than the training program. Obviously, this design can be improved.

Static-Group Comparison Design

In this design, half of the managers would be allowed to enroll for the training. Once the enrollment reached 50 percent of the managers, the training program would begin. After some period of time, the group of managers who enrolled in the program would be compared with those who did not enroll. This design is diagrammed as

$$\begin{array}{c} X\ O \\ O \end{array}$$

The addition of a *control* group (comparison group) has eliminated many of the error factors associated with the first two designs. However, because the managers were not randomly assigned to each group, the managers who enrolled may very possibly be the more highly motivated or intelligent managers. Thus, *selection* is a major problem with this design. Because the subjects were not randomly assigned to the experimental group (undergoing training) and the control group (no training), differences may exist between the two groups that are not related to the training.

The three designs discussed thus far (one-shot, one-group pretest–posttest, static-group comparisons) have been described as "pseudo-experimental" or "quasi-experimental" designs. When true experimentation cannot be achieved, these designs (especially the last two) are preferred over no research at all or over relying on personal opinion. The next three designs can be considered true experimental designs because the researcher has complete control over the situation, determining precisely who will participate in the experiment and which subjects will or will not receive the experimental treatment.

Pretest–Posttest Control Group Design

This design, one of the simplest forms of true experimentation used in the study of human behavior, is diagrammed as

$$\begin{array}{c} R\ O_1\ X\ O_2 \\ R\ O_1 O_2 \end{array}$$

It is similar to the one-group pretest–posttest design except that a control group has been added and the participants have been randomly assigned to both groups, as indicated by R. Which group is to receive the training (experimental group) and which will not (control group) is also randomly determined. The two groups may be said to be equivalent at the time of the initial observations and at the time the final observations are made; they are different only in that one group has received training while the other has not. In other words, if the change from O_1 to O_2 is greater in the experimental group than in the control group, we can attribute the difference to the training program rather than selection, testing, maturation, and so forth.

The major weakness of the pretest–posttest control group design is one of *interaction* (selection and treatment), where individuals are aware that they are participating in an experiment. In other words, being observed the first time makes all of the participants work more diligently, both those who are in the training group and those who are in the control group. Hence, the participants in the training program are more receptive to training because of the pretest. This problem of interaction can be overcome by using a posttest-only control group design.

Posttest-Only Control Group Design

In this design, the participants are randomly assigned to two groups, the training is administered to one group, and the scores on the posttests are compared (performance evaluated). It is diagrammed as

R X O

R O

This eliminates the problem of the previous design by not administering a pretest. However, the dependent variable (performance) is an ultimate rather than a relative measure of achievement. Also, the research does not have a group that was pretested and posttested without receiving the experimental treatment (training program). Such a group can provide valuable information on the effects of history, maturation, instrumentation, and so on. However, where a pretest is difficult to obtain or where its use is likely to make the participants aware that an experiment is being carried on, this approach may be much preferred to the pretest–posttest control group design.

Solomon Four-Group Design

This design, which combines the previous designs, is the most desirable of all the designs examined here. It is diagrammed as

Group 1	R	O_1	X	O_2
Group 2	R	O_1		O_2
Group 3	R		X	O_2
Group 4	R			O_2

Where gain or change in behavior is the desired dependent variable, this design should be used. While it does not control any more sources of invalid results, it permits the estimation of the extent of the effects of some sources of error. In our example, supervisors are randomly assigned to four groups, two of which will receive the training, one with a pretest and one without. Therefore, the researcher can examine, among other things, the effects of history (group 1 to group 2), testing (group 2 to group 4), and testing–treatment interaction (group 2 to group 3). Clearly, this design is the most complex, because it uses more participants, and it is more costly. The added value of the extra information will have to be compared with the additional costs.[26]

Observation and Measurement

In the research design, "O" was used to designate the observation and measurement used. Behavioral science researchers attempt to measure variables so that hypotheses can be tested. Four methods are used to measure variables included in a research study: (1) observation, (2) interviews, (3) surveys, and (4) nonreactive measures.[27]

Observation

Managers are constantly observing the behavior of employees. Through observation, managers can count, infer, and study specific behaviors. One problem of making observations is that inferences must be made. Inferences can be incorrect because the human element is involved. Perceptual inaccuracies, bias, and inexperience can each cause inaccuracies in inferences. Being cautious is advised with any type of measurement and is required when managerial observations are used.

Interviews

This measurement involves face-to-face, telephone, or video-conferencing interactions that ask specific questions. Interviews permit a series of questions and the flexibility to record exact responses. Trained interviewers can use structured or the same questions of every person or an unstructured series of various questions.

Some respondents are uncomfortable with interviews because they are face-to-face. Anonymity is not entirely possible with interviews. Another limitation with interviews is that they are labor intensive. Interviews take away from work.

Questionnaires

These are sets of written or electronically (e-survey) prepared questions asking about attitudes, opinions, demographic characteristics, preferences, and other information. The majority of organizational behavior and management field surveys and experiments use questionnaires.

The use of questionnaires is popular because they are easy to administer, can be completed anonymously, and are relatively inexpensive. On the other hand, questionnaires present a number of problems: low response rates, missing data, and restricted responses. Moreover, they require good reading skills.

Nonreactive Measures

These are measures that yield information without a person's knowledge. Historical records, wear and tear on property (e.g., carpets, wooden floors, door handles, chairs) for measuring use rates, and absenteeism and turnover data are examples. Data on preferences are kept by companies such as Amazon.com. A customer's preferences for a genre of books, music, or other goods purchased are kept up to date.

Instead of using experimental designs and concentrating on measurement issues some researchers also use qualitative research procedures. The notion of applying qualitative research methods to studying behavior within organizations has been addressed in leading research outlets.[28] The term *qualitative methods* describes any array of interpretative techniques that attempt to describe and clarify the meaning of naturally occurring phenomena. It is, by design, rather open-ended and interpretative. The researcher's interpretation and description are the significant data collection actions in a qualitative study. In essence, qualitative data are defined as those (1) whose meanings are subjective, (2) that are rarely quantifiable, and (3) that are difficult to use in making quantitative comparisons.

The quantitative approach to organizational behavior research is exemplified by precise definitions, control groups, objective data collection, use of the scientific method, and replicable findings. These characteristics, presented in Table A.2, stress the importance of reliability, validity, and accurate measurement. On the other hand, qualitative research is more concerned with the meaning of what is observed. Because organizations are so complex, a range of quantitative and qualitative techniques can be used side-by-side to learn about individual, group, and organizational behavior.[29]

Qualitative Research

Qualitative methodology uses the experience and intuition of the researchers to describe the organizational processes and structure being studied. The data collected by a qualitative researcher require her to become very close to the situation or problem being studied. For example, a qualitative method used by anthropologists is the *ethnographic method*.[30] The researcher typically studies a phenomenon for long periods as a *participant–observer*—becoming part of the situation in order to feel what it is like for the people in that situation. The researcher becomes totally immersed in other people's realities.[31]

Participant observation is usually supplemented by various quantitative data collection tools such as structured interviews and self-report questionnaires. A variety of techniques are used so that the researcher can cross-check the results obtained from observation and recorded in field notes.

In training researchers in the ethnographic method, a common practice is to place them in unfamiliar settings. A researcher may sit with and listen to workers on a production line, ride around in a police car to observe police officers, or do cleanup work in a surgical operating room. The training is designed to improve the researcher's ability to record, categorize, and code what is being observed.

An example of qualitative research involvement is presented in John Van Maanen's participant–observer study of a big-city police department. He went through police academy training and then accompanied police officers on their daily rounds; he functioned with police officers in daily encounters. Thus, he was able to provide vivid descriptions of police work.[32]

Other qualitative techniques include content analysis (e.g., the researcher's interpretation of field notes), informal interviewing, archival data surveys and historical analysis, and the use of unobtrusive measures (e.g., data whose collection is not influenced by a researcher's presence). An example of the last would be the wear and tear on a couch in a cardiologist's office. The original measure of the Type A behavior pattern in Chapter 7 was the wear and tear on the edges of the couch where patients sat while waiting for an appointment with the physician. Wear and tear was assumed to suggest anxiety and hyperactive behavior. Qualitative research appears to rely more on multiple sources of data than on any one source. The current research literature suggests the following characteristics are associated with qualitative research:[33]

1. *Analytical induction.* Qualitative research begins with the close-up, firsthand inspection of organizational life.
2. *Proximity.* Researchers desire to witness firsthand what is being studied. If the application of rewards is being studied, the researcher would want to observe episodes of reward distribution.
3. *Ordinary behavior.* The topics of research interest should be ordinary, normal, routine behaviors.
4. *Descriptive emphasis.* Qualitative research seeks descriptions for what is occurring in any given place and time. The aim is to disclose and reveal, not merely to order data and predict.
5. *Shrinking variance.* Qualitative research is geared toward the explanation of similarity and coherence. There is a greater emphasis on commonality and on things shared in organizational settings than on things not shared.
6. *Consumer enlightenment.* The consumer of qualitative research could be a manager. A major objective is to enlighten without causing confusion. Providing coherent and logically persuasive commentary accomplishes this.

Researchers and managers do not have to choose either quantitative or qualitative research data and interpretation. Convincing and relevant agreements exist for using more than one method of research when studying organizational behavior. Quantitative and qualitative research methods and procedures have much to offer practicing managers. Blending and integrating quantitative and qualitative research are what researchers and managers must do in the years ahead to better understand, cope with, and modify organizational behavior.

GLOSSARY

A

ABC analysis The analysis of antecedents, behavior, and consequences when investigating work or job-related issues.

ability A biological or learned trait that permits a person to do something mental or physical.

affect The emotional segment of an attitude.

appreciative inquiry (AI) An organizational change process that focuses on diagnosis and presentation of positive characteristics of change, the process, and outcomes.

Asch's line experiment Showed how group pressure can influence individual decision making and preferences.

attitude Mental state of readiness for need arousal.

attitude survey A way to collect data or information about a person's opinion or reaction to an event, person, item, situation, or organization program.

attribution The process of perceiving the causes of behavior and outcomes.

attribution leadership theory The attributions people make about other individuals.

authority Formal power a person holds because of his or her position in the organization hierarchy. The recognition of authority is necessary for organizational effectiveness and is a cost of organizational membership.

B

banking time off A reward practice of allowing employees to build up time-off credits for such things as good performance or attendance. Employees then receive the time off in addition to regular vacation time granted by the organization.

behavior The behavior segment of an attitude.

behavior modification An approach to motivation that uses the principles of operant conditioning, achieving individual learning by reinforcement. This term can be used interchangeably with the term *organizational behavior modification.*

behavioral self-management (BSM) A process whereby a person is faced with immediate response alternatives involving different consequences. The person selects or modifies his behavior by managing cognitive processes, causes, or consequences.

benchmarking A standard of excellence or achievement against which a firm's products or practices are measured or judged.

Big Five personality factors An individual's traits of agreeableness, conscientiousness, emotional stability, extroversion, and openness to experiences.

boundary-spanning role The role of an individual who must relate to two different systems, usually an organization and some part of its environment.

brainstorming A technique that provides creativity by encouraging idea generation in a group through noncritical discussion.

burnout A psychological process resulting from work stress that results in emotional exhaustion, depersonalization, and feelings of decreased accomplishment.

C

centralization A dimension of organizational structure that refers to the extent to which top management retains authority to make decisions.

change agent An intervener who brings a different perspective to a situation and challenges the status quo.

charismatic leadership The ability to influence followers based on a supernatural gift and attractive powers. Followers enjoy being with the charismatic leader because they feel inspired, correct, and important.

code of ethics An organization's formal document statement of its ethical values and expectations regarding employees' ethical behavior.

coercive power Perceived capability to punish noncompliance of followers.

cognition The perception, opinion, or belief segment of an attitude.

cognitive dissonance A mental state of anxiety that occurs when there's a conflict among an individual's various cognitions (e.g., attitudes and beliefs) after a decision has been made. Most individuals are motivated to reduce dissonance and achieve consonance.

cohesiveness Strength of group members' desires to remain in the group and their commitment to the group.

command group The group of subordinates who report to one particular manager. The command group is specified by the formal organization chart.

commitment A sense of identification, involvement, and loyalty expressed by an employee toward the company.

communication The transmission of information and understanding through the use of common symbols, both verbal and nonverbal.

complexity A dimension of organizational structure that refers to the number of different jobs, units, and authority levels within an organization.

conflict The perceived incompatibility between two or more values, goals, or needs.

Confucian dynamism The extent to which people believe in the importance of the values of persistence, status, thrift, and feeling shame and the unimportance of the values of personal stability, face saving, respect for tradition, and reciprocation of favors and gifts.

conscious goals The main goals that a person is striving for and is aware of when directing behavior.

consideration Acts of the leader that show supportive concern for the followers in a group.

content motivation theories Theories that focus on the factors within a person that energize, direct, sustain, and stop behavior.

contingency approach to management Approach to management that believes there's no one best way to manage in every situation and managers must find different ways that fit different situations.

contingency design theory An approach to organization design that states that the effective structure depends on factors in the situation, including technology, environmental uncertainty, and management choice.

cross-cultural management The study of the behavior of individuals in organizations around the world.

culture shock cycle A three-phase cycle (fascination and interest, frustration and confusion, and adaptation) that most individuals experience when sent to another culture.

D

decision A means to achieve some result or to solve some problem. The outcome of a process that is influenced by many forces.

decision commitment The degree to which subordinates accept a particular decision. Participation in decisions often tends to increase the commitment of subordinates.

decision quality An important criterion in the Vroom-Yetton model that refers to objective aspects of a decision that influence subordinates' performance, aside from any direct impact on motivation.

delegation of authority The process by which authority is distributed downward in an organization.

Delphi process A technique used to improve group decision making that involves the solicitation and comparison of anonymous judgments on the topic of interest through a set of sequential questionnaires interspersed with summarized information and feedback of opinions from earlier responses.

departmentalization The process by which an organization is structurally divided. Some of the more publicized divisions are by function, territory, product, customer, and project.

devil's advocate A person who challenges others in terms of their logic, decisions, and analysis of a situation or problem.

diagonal communication Communication that cuts across functions and levels in an organization; important when members cannot communicate through other channels.

differentiation An important concept in the Lawrence and Lorsch research that refers to the process by which subunits in an organization develop particular attributes in response to the requirements imposed by their particular subenvironments. The greater the differences among the subunits' attributes, the greater the differentiation.

dispositional attributions Emphasize some aspect of the individual, such as ability or skill, to explain behavior.

distributive justice The perception of fairness of the resources and rewards in an organization.

diversity The vast array of physical and cultural differences such as race, gender, ethnicity, age, and other factors that constitute the spectrum of human attributes.

division of labor The process of dividing work into relatively specialized jobs to achieve advantages of specialization.

downward communication Communication that flows from individuals in higher levels of the organization's hierarchy to those in lower levels. It includes management policies, instructions, and official news.

dysfunctional conflict Any confrontation or interaction between groups that hinders the achievement of organizational goals.

E

emotional intelligence (EQ) The ability to accurately perceive, evaluate, express, and regulate emotions and feelings.

emotional labor The effort, energy, and planning that must be used to accomplish desired emotions (e.g., handling customer complaints).

employee assistance programs (EAPs) Programs designed to assist with a wide range of work- and nonwork-related stress-induced problems.

employee-centered leader A person who only generally supervises the work of others. He or she attempts to permit others to sense autonomy and support.

empowerment Giving employees permission to make decisions to complete workloads on time.

equity theory of motivation A theory that examines discrepancies within a person after the person has compared his or her input/output ratio to that of a reference person.

ERG theory of motivation A theory developed and tested by Alderfer that categorizes needs as existence, relatedness, and growth.

escalation of commitment Behavior of decision makers to adhere to a certain course of action in light of negative information about the viability of that course of action.

ethics The study and consideration of moral values and behaviors that distinguish right from wrong activities.

expatriate manager A manager from the firm's home nation who's on a foreign assignment.

expectancy The perceived likelihood that a particular act will be followed by a particular outcome.

expectancy theory of motivation A theory in which the employee is faced with a set of first-level outcomes and selects an outcome based on how this choice is related to second-level outcomes. The preferences of the individual are based on the strength (valence) of desire to achieve a second-level state and the perception of the relationship between first- and second-level outcomes.

expert power The power to influence others based on special expertise.

extinction In a learning situation, the decline in the response rate because of nonreinforcement.

extranet A private protected electronic communication system that is designed to connect employees with individuals external to the organization such as vendors, customers, or other strategic partners.

extrinsic rewards Rewards external to the job, such as pay, promotion, or fringe benefits.

F

flexible benefit plans A compensation approach that allows employees to choose the benefits they prefer rather than receive a standardized package of benefits that is established for them.

flexible manufacturing technology (FMT) Modern manufacturing methods that combine computer and robot to achieve high levels of production as well as high levels of flexibility.

formal groups Groups created by managerial decision to accomplish stated goals of the organization.

formal organization The philosophy, policies, structure, and systems of control of an organization.

formalization A dimension of organization structure that refers to the extent to which rules, procedures, and other guides to action are written and enforced.

functional conflict A confrontation between groups that enhances and benefits the organization's performance.

functional job analysis (FJA) A method of job analysis that focuses on the worker's specific job activities, methods, machines, and output. Widely used to analyze and classify jobs.

G

gainsharing An innovative reward strategy wherein employees share in the financial rewards of achieving set objectives.

global corporation An enterprise structured so that national boundaries become blurred.

globalization The interdependency of transportation, distribution, communication, and economic networks across international boundaries.

GLOBE (Global Leadership and Organizational Behavior Effectiveness) A multiphase and multimethod program of international research that collects and analyzes data from 17,000 managers from 62 countries to understand how cultural variables influence leaders and their organizational cultures.

goal A specific target that an individual is trying to achieve; a goal is the target (object) of an action.

goal approach to effectiveness Perspective on effectiveness that emphasizes the central role of goal achievement as a criterion for assessing effectiveness.

goal commitment The amount of effort that is actually used to achieve a goal.

goal difficulty The degree of proficiency or the level of goal performance that is sought.

goal intensity The process of setting a goal or determining how to reach it.

goal setting The process of establishing goals. In many cases, goal setting involves a superior and subordinate working together to set the subordinate's goals for a specified period.

goal specificity The degree of quantitative precision (clarity) of the goal.

grapevine The informal communication network that transmits gossip, rumor, facts, and different types of information.

group Collection of individuals in which behavior and/or performance of one member is influenced by behavior and/or performance of other members.

groupthink A cohesive group's desire for agreement interferes with the group's consideration of alternative solutions.

H

hardiness Personality trait that enables a person who possesses it to cope with stressors in such a way that they have minimal impact on the person's health.

Herzberg's two-factor theory of motivation The view that job satisfaction results from the presence of intrinsic motivators and that job dissatisfaction stems from not having extrinsic factors.

horizontal communication Communication that flows across functions in an organization; necessary for coordinating and integrating diverse organizational functions.

host-country nationals Workers from the local population.

humanistic personality theories Place emphasis on growth and self-actualization of people.

I

impression management tactics The behaviors individuals use to preserve their self-image and/or influence the ways in which others perceive them.

individual differences Individuals are similar, but they are also unique. The study of individual differences such as attitudes, perceptions, and abilities helps a manager explain differences in performance levels.

individualism–collectivism Individualism emphasizes pursuit of individual goals, needs, and success. Collectivism emphasizes group need, satisfaction, and performance.

informal groups Groups that arise from individual efforts and develop around common interests and friendships rather than deliberate design.

information richness Refers to the amount of information that can be transmitted in an effective manner.

informational diversity The differences in individuals' knowledge base and perspectives that influence group problem solving and overall group effectiveness.

informational justice The perception of fairness of the communication provided to employees from authorities.

initiating structure Leadership acts that imply the structuring of job tasks and responsibilities for followers.

instrumentality In the expectancy theory of motivation, the relationship between first- and second-level outcomes.

integration A concept in the Lawrence and Lorsch research that refers to the process of achieving unity of effort among the organization's various subsystems. The techniques for achieving integration range from rules and procedures, to plans, to mutual adjustment.

intellectual capital The knowledge that resides in an organization.

interpersonal communication Communication that flows from individual to individual in face-to-face and group settings.

interpersonal justice The perception of fairness of the treatment received by employees from authorities.

interpersonal rewards Extrinsic rewards such as receiving recognition or being able to interact socially on the job.

interpersonal style The way in which an individual prefers to relate to others.

intervention A specific action or program undertaken to focus the change process on particular targets.

intranet A private Internet-based network developed and maintained by a particular organization; intranets allow certain stakeholders to gain access to internal organizational information.

intrinsic rewards Rewards that are part of the job itself. The responsibility, challenge, and feedback characteristics of the job are intrinsic rewards.

J

job analysis Process of defining and studying a job in terms of behavior and specifying education and training needed to perform the job.

job-centered leader A person who closely supervises and observes the work of others.

job content The specific activities required in a job.

job context The physical environment and other working conditions, along with other factors considered to be extrinsic to a job.

job depth The amount of control that an individual has to alter or influence the job and the surrounding environment.

job description A summary statement of what an employee actually does on the job.

job descriptive index A popular and widely used 72-item scale that measures five job satisfaction dimensions.

job design The process by which managers decide individual job tasks and authority.

job enlargement An administrative action that involves increasing the range of a job by increasing the number of tasks. Supposedly, this action results in better performance and a more satisfied workforce.

job enrichment An approach, developed by Herzberg, that involves increasing the individual's discretion to select activities and outcomes. It seeks to improve task efficiency and human satisfaction by means of building into people's jobs greater scope for personal achievement and recognition, more challenging and responsible work, and more opportunity for individual advancement and growth.

job performance The outcome of jobs that relates to the purposes of the organization such as quality, efficiency, and other criteria of effectiveness.

job range The number of operations that a job occupant performs to complete a task.

job redesign Redesigning the jobs of individuals, usually along the lines suggested by the job characteristics model of job design, in order to improve performance. May be used as an intervention in organizational development.

job relationships The interpersonal relationships required or made possible on a job.

job requirements Factors such as education, experience, degrees, licenses, and other personal characteristics required to perform a job.

job rotation A form of training that involves moving an employee from one workstation to another. In addition to achieving the training objectives, this procedure is also designed to reduce boredom.

job satisfaction The attitude that workers have about their jobs. It results from their perception of the job.

job sharing A type of flexible work arrangement in which two or more employees divide a job's responsibilities, hours, pay, and benefits among themselves.

K

knowledge management The acquisition, storing, and application of knowledge that can improve the short- and long-term effectiveness of organizations.

L

leader–member relations A factor in the Fiedler contingency model that refers to the degree of confidence, trust, and respect that the leader obtains from the followers.

leadership An attempt to use influence to motivate individuals to accomplish some goal.

leadership climate The nature of work environment in an organization that results from the leadership style and administrative practices.

learned needs theory A theory that proposes that a person with a strong need will be motivated to use appropriate behaviors to satisfy the need. A person's needs are learned from the culture of a society.

learning The process by which a relatively enduring change in behavior occurs as a result of practice.

legitimate power A person's ability to influence others by being in a more powerful position.

level 5 leadership A type of leadership in which the leader displays humility, self-motivation, and a strong professional will to advance the goals of the organization.

locus of control A personality characteristic that describes people who see the control of their lives as coming from inside themselves as *internalizers*. People who believe that their lives are controlled by external factors are *externalizers*.

long-term orientation A cultural dimension that refers to the degree to which a given culture values persistence, thrift (savings), having a sense of shame, and ordering relationships by status.

M

Machiavellianism A term used to describe political maneuvers in an organization. Used to designate a person as a manipulator and power abuser.

masculinity–femininity High masculinity in a culture designates assertiveness, dominance, and independence. High femininity in a culture designates interdependence, compassion, and emotional opinions.

matrix organization An organizational design that superimposes a product- or project-based design on an existing function-based design.

mechanistic model The type of organizational design that emphasizes the importance of production and efficiency. It is highly formalized, centralized, and complex.

media richness The data-carrying capacity of a particular communication medium.

mentor A friend, coach, adviser, or sponsor who supports, encourages, and helps a less experienced protégé.

merit rating A formal rating system that is applied to hourly paid employees.

Minnesota Multiphasic Personality Inventory (MMPI) A widely used survey for assessing personality.

mood contagion Feelings and emotions spread from one person to another person.

motivation A concept that describes the forces acting on or within an employee that initiate and direct behavior.

multinational corporations (MNCs) Firms that do business in more than one country.

multiple roles Roles performed simultaneously because the individual holds many positions in a variety of organizations and groups.

Myers-Briggs Indicator (MBTI) A scale that assesses personality or cognitive style. Respondents' answers are scored and interpreted to classify them as extroverted or introverted, sensory or intuitive, thinking or feeling, and perceiving or judging. Sixteen different personality types are possible.

N

national culture A set of values, attitudes, beliefs, and norms shared by a majority of the inhabitants of a country.

need for power (n Pow) A person's desire to have an impact on others. The impact can occur from such behaviors as strong action, producing emotion, or concern for reputation.

need hierarchy model Maslow assumed that the needs ofa person depend on what he already has. This in a sense means that a satisfied need is not a motivator. Human needs organized in a hierarchy of importance are classified as physiological, safety, belongingness, esteem, and self-actualization.

needs Deficiencies that an individual experiences at a particular point in time.

negative reinforcement Reinforcement that strengthens a response because the response removes some painful or unpleasant stimulus or enables the organism to avoid it.

nominal group technique (NGT) A technique to improve group decision making that brings people together in a very structured meeting that does not allow for much verbal communication. The group decision is the mathematically pooled outcome of individual votes.

nonprogrammed decisions Decisions required for unique and complex management problems.

nonverbal communication Messages sent with body posture, facial expressions, and head and eye movements.

norms Generally agreed-upon standards of individual and group behavior developed as a result of member interaction over time.

O

O*NET An online database hosted by the U.S. Department of Labor that provides occupational descriptions and data such as job descriptions, worker knowledge, skills and abilities, and work requirements.

operant conditioning Learning that occurs as a consequence of behavior.

operants Behaviors amenable to control by altering the consequences (rewards and punishments) that follow them.

organic model The organizational design that emphasizes the importance of adaptability and development. It is relatively informal, centralized, and simple.

organization Entity that enables society to pursue accomplishments that can't be achieved by individuals acting alone.

organization structure The formal patterns of how people and jobs are grouped in an organization. The organization structure is often illustrated by an organization chart.

organizational behavior (OB) The field of study that draws on theory, methods, and principles from various disciplines to learn about *individuals'* perceptions, values, learning capacities, and actions while working in *groups* and within the *organization* and to analyze the external environment's effect on the organization and its human resources, missions, objectives, and strategies.

organizational behavior modification (OB Mod or OBM) An operant approach to organization behavior. This term is use interchangeably with the term *behavior modification.*

organizational citizen behaviors (OCBs) Behaviors that go above and beyond expected behaviors, such as stepping in for a colleague who had an emergency or helping a person in another unit learn how a procedure works in the company.

organizational culture What the employees perceive and how this perception creates a shared sense and pattern of beliefs, values, and expectations.

organizational design A specific organizational structure that results from managers' decisions and actions. Also, the process by which managers choose among alternative frameworks of jobs and departments.

organizational development (OD) The process of preparing for and managing change in organizational settings.

organizational justice The degree to which individuals feel fairly treated within the organizations for which they work.

P

parent-country nationals Individuals sent from the country in which the firm is headquartered. Often called *expatriates.*

path–goal leadership model Theory that suggests a leader needs to influence followers' perceptions of work goals, self-development goals, and paths to goal attainment.

perceived job content The characteristics of a job that define its general nature as perceived by the person who does the job.

perception The process by which an individual gives meaning to the environment. It involves organizing and interpreting various stimuli into a psychological experience.

personality A stable set of characteristics and tendencies that determine commonalities and differences in people's behavior.

personality test Test used to measure emotional, motivational, interpersonal, and attitude characteristics that make up a person's personality.

person–environment (P–E) fit The extent to which work provides rewards that meet the person's needs and to which the employee's skills match the requirements of the job.

person–role conflict A type of conflict that occurs when the requirements of a position violate the basic values, attitudes, and needs of the individual occupying the position.

political behavior Behavior outside the normal power system designed to benefit an individual or a subunit.

pooled interdependence Interdependence that requires no interaction between groups because each group, in effect, performs separately.

position analysis questionnaire (PAQ) A method of job analysis that takes into account human characteristics as well as task and technological factors of jobs and job classes.

position power A factor in the Fiedler contingency model that refers to the power inherent in the leadership position.

positive reinforcement Action that increases the likelihood of a particular behavior.

power Ability to get others to do what one want them to do.

power distance The degree to which members of a society accept differences in power and status among themselves.

presenteeism Refers to the act of employees attending work but due to illness or other medical reasons, tend to underperform their jobs.

procedural justice The perceived equity or fairness of the processes and procedures used to make resource and reward allocation decisions.

process conflict Type of intragroup conflict in which group members disagree as to the best method to accomplish a particular task.

process motivation theories Theories that describe and analyze how behavior is energized, directed, sustained, and stopped.

processes Activities that breathe life into organization structure. Common processes are communication, decision making, socialization, and career development.

programmed decisions Situations in which specific procedures have been developed for repetitive and routine problems.

psychodynamic personality theories Freudian approach that discusses the id, superego, and ego. Special emphasis is placed on unconscious determinants of behavior.

psychological contract An implied understanding of mutual contributions between a person and his or her organization.

psychological contract violation The perception of the person that his or her firm has failed to fulfill or has reneged on one or more obligations.

punishment An uncomfortable consequence for a particular behavior response or the removal of a desirable reinforcer because of a particular behavior response. Managers can punish by application or removal.

Pygmalion effect The enhanced learning or performance that results from others' having positive expectations of us.

Q

qualitative overload Occurs when people feel they lack the ability to complete a job or that performance standards are too high.

quality of work life (QWL) Management philosophy that enhances employee dignity, introduces cultural change, and provides opportunities for growth and development.

quantitative overload Results from having too many things to do or insufficient time to complete a job.

R

readiness The followers' skills and willingness to do a job.

reciprocal causation Argument that follower behavior affects leader behavior and leader behavior influences follower behavior.

reciprocal interdependence Interdependence that requires the output of each group in an organization to serve as input to other groups in the organization.

recognition Management acknowledgement of work well done.

reengineering The redesign of business processes to achieve significant improvement in cost, service, quality, and speed.

referent power Power based on charisma due to personality or style of behavior.

relationship conflict Type of intragroup conflict in which group members are aware of interpersonal incompatibilities among themselves that can lead to feelings of dislike.

reverse mentoring A process by which junior-level employees support, encourage, and help senior-level managers. A common focus of reverse mentoring is technology, an area with which junior-level employees often have more experience and knowledge.

reward power A person's ability to reward the behavior of others.

role An organized set of behaviors expected of an individual in a specific position.

role conflict Occurs when an individual's compliance with one set of expectations conflicts with compliance with another set of expectations.

role set Others' expectations for behavior of a person in a particular role.

S

self-efficacy The belief that one can perform adequately in a situation. Self-efficacy has three dimensions: magnitude, strength, and generality.

sequential interdependence Interdependence that requires one group to complete its task before another group can complete its task.

short-term orientation A cultural dimension that refers to the degree to which a culture values respect for tradition, the exchange of favors and gifts, protecting "face" (i.e., avoiding shame), and personal steadiness and stability.

situational attributions Attributions that emphasize the environment's effect on behavior.

situational theories of leadership An approach to leadership that advocates that leaders understand their own behavior, the behavior of their subordinates, and the situation before using a particular leadership style. This approach requires the leader to have diagnostic skills in human behavior.

skill-based pay Wages paid at a rate calculated and based on the skills employees possess and display in performing their jobs.

skills Task-related competencies.

skunkworks A small group of engineers, technicians, designers, or all three who are placed on a specialized team and isolated from the rest of the organization; the team's goal is to rapidly develop innovative ideas, products, or services.

social category diversity Explicit differences between members of a group based on race, gender ethnicity, age, or all three.

social learning The extension of Skinner's work initiated by noted psychologist Albert Bandura. Bandura views behavior as a function of a continuous interaction between cognitive (person), behavioral, and environmental determinants. Contrary to Skinner, Bandura believes that cognitive functioning must not be ignored in explaining and modifying behavior.

social loafing When individuals within a group hold back what they contribute to the group's effort and performance.

social support The comfort, assistance, or information received through formal or informal contacts with individuals or groups.

socialization The process by which organizations bring new employees into the culture.

span of control The number of subordinates reporting to a specific superior. The span is a factor that affects the shape and height of an organizational structure.

spirituality A state or experience that can provide individuals with direction or meaning, or provide feelings of understanding, support, inner wholeness, or connectedness.

stakeholder approach to effectiveness Perspective that emphasizes the relative importance of different groups' and individuals' interests in an organization.

stereotype An overgeneralized, oversimplified, and self-perpetuating belief about people's personal characteristics.

strategic contingency Event or activity of crucial importance to completing a project or accomplishing a goal.

stress An adaptive response, mediated by individual differences, that is a consequence of any action, situation, or event that places special demands on a person.

stressor A potentially harmful or threatening external event or situation that contributes to perceived stress.

structure Blueprint that indicates how people and jobs are grouped together in an organization. Structure is illustrated by an organization chart.

substitutability Extent to which other subunits can perform the job or task of a subunit.

superordinate goals Goals that cannot be achieved without the cooperation of the conflicting groups.

system A grouping of elements that individually establish relationships with each other and that interact with their environment both as individuals and as a collective.

T

task conflict Type of intragroup conflict in which group members have differences in viewpoints and opinions regarding what the group's task is.

task structure Factor in Fiedler contingency model that refers to how structured a job is with regard to requirements, problem-solving alternatives, and feedback on job success.

team building Encouraging people who work together to meet as a group to identify common goals, improve communications, and resolve conflicts. A traditional intervention focusing on work groups, it has been given renewed interest as organizations rediscover the power of team effort.

technological change Any application of new ways of transforming resources into products or services.

technology Physical and mental actions by an individual to change the form or content of an object or idea.

telecommuting Performing all or some portion of a job at sites away from the central work site.

Thematic Apperception Test (TAT) A projective test that uses a person's analysis of pictures to evaluate such individual differences as need for achievement, need for power, and need for affiliation.

third-country nationals Employees from a country other than where the parent company is headquartered.

360-degree feedback Comparison of feedback evaluations of a person's boss, subordinates, and peers.

trait personality theories Theories based on the premise that predispositions direct the behavior of an individual in a consistent pattern.

trait theory of leadership Theory that attempts to identify specific characteristics (physical, mental, personality) associated with leadership success. Relies on research that relates various traits to certain success criteria.

transactional leadership Leader identifies what followers want or prefer and helps them achieve level of performance that results in rewards that satisfy them.

transformational leadership Ability to inspire and motivate followers to achieve results greater than originally planned for internal rewards.

Type A (managers) Managers who are aloof and cold toward others and are often autocratic leaders. Consequently, they are ineffective interpersonal communicators.

Type B (managers) Managers who seek good relationships with subordinates but are unable to express their feelings. Consequently, they are usually ineffective interpersonal communicators.

Type C (managers) Managers more interested in their own opinions than in those of others. Consequently, they are usually ineffective interpersonal communicators.

Type D (managers) Managers who feel free to express their feelings to others and to have others express their feelings; the most effective interpersonal communicators.

U

uncertainty avoidance The degree to which people are comfortable with ambiguous situations and with the inability to predict future events with accuracy.

upward communication Upward communication flows from individuals at lower levels of the organization structure to those at higher levels. Among the most common upward communication flows are suggestion boxes, group meetings, and appeal or grievance procedures.

V

valence The strength of a person's preference for a particular outcome.

value diversity Differences in group members' opinions regarding what the group's tasks, goals, or mission should be.

values The conscious, affective desires or wants of people that guide their behavior. Basic guidelines and beliefs that a decision maker uses when confronted with a situation requiring choice.

virtual organization Achieves efficiency and flexibility by subcontracting some of its operations to members of a network, including suppliers, distributors, customers, strategic alliance partners, and even competitors.

virtual team A team that uses information technology and telecommunications so that members in remote locations can work together on projects.

Vroom-Yetton model Leadership model that specifies leadership decision-making procedures most effective in each of several different situations: two autocratic (AI, AII); two consultative (CI, CII); and one oriented toward joint decisions of the leaders and group (GII).

W

wellness programs Activities and organizational programs that focus on an employee's overall physical and mental health.

whistle-blowing The process in which an employee, because of personal opinions, values, or ethical standards, concludes that an organization needs to change its behavior or practices and informs an outsider, bypassing the organization's authority system.

work module An important characteristic of job redesign strategies that involves creating whole tasks so that the individual experiences a beginning, middle, and end of the process.

World Wide Web A subset of the Internet, the Web is a retrieval system for a vast amount of information and documents found on individual Web sites or home pages.

ENDNOTES

Chapter 1

1. John Varney, "Leadership as Meaning-making," *Human Resource Management International Digest* 17, no. 5 (2009): 3–5; and Manfred F. R. Kets de Vries, "Decoding the Team Conundrum," *Organizational Dynamics* 36 (2007): 28–44.
2. Robert Konopaske and John M. Ivancevich, *Global Management and Organizational Behavior* (New York: McGraw-Hill/Irwin, 2004).
3. Sherry E. Sullivan and Lisa A. Mainiero, "Kaleidoscope Career: Benchmarking Ideas for Fostering Family-Friendly Workplaces," *Organizational Dynamics* 36 (2007): 45–62.
4. Teresa Brannick, "In Defense of Being 'Native': The Case for Insider Academic Research," *Organization Research Methods* 10 (2007): 59–74.
5. A. Baldonado and J. Spangenburg, "Leadership and the Future: Gen Y Workers and Two-Factor Theory," *Journal of American Academy of Business* 15, no. 1 (2009): 99–103; and Jack Scarborough, *The Origins of Cultural Differences and Their Impact on Management* (Westport, CT: Quorum, 2001).
6. The authors have adapted and utilized this model for classroom and training use in domestic and international settings.
7. Charles C. Lewis, *Synoptic Excellence: Managing Organizational Culture* (New York: Trafford Publishing, 2006).
8. Edgar H. Schein, *The Corporate Culture Survival Guide* (San Francisco: Jossey-Bass, 2009).
9. John M. Ivancevich and William Lidwell, eds., *Guidelines for Excellence in Management* (Cincinnati, OH: South-Western, 2004).
10. Ibid.
11. Linda K. Trevino and Katherine A. Nelson, *Managing Business Ethics* (New York: John Wiley, 2007).
12. R. Audi, "Objectivity Without Egoism: Toward Balance in Business Ethics," *Academy of Management Learning & Education* 8, no. 2 (2009): 263–264; and Ethics Resource Center, *National Business Ethics Survey* (Washington, DC: Ethics Resource Center, 2006).
13. M. Gunther, "Cops of the Global Village," *Fortune,* June 27, 2005, pp. 158–66.
14. Laura P. Hartman, *Perspectives in Business Ethics* (Burr Ridge, IL: McGraw-Hill/Irwin, 2002).
15. Sergio G. Lazzarini, "The Impact of Membership in Competing Alliance Constellations: Evidence on the Operational Performance of Global Airlines," *Strategic Management Journal* 28 (2007): 345–67.
16. Arie Y. Lewin and John W. Minton, "Determining Organizational Effectiveness: Another Look and an Agenda for Research," *Management Science* 32 (1986): 514–538.
17. John R. Kimberly and David B. Rottman, "Environment, Organization, and Effectiveness: A Biographical Approach," *Journal of Management Studies* 24 (1987): 595–622.
18. James Waldroop and Timothy Butler, "Managing Away Bad Habits," *Harvard Business Review,* September–October 2000, pp. 89–101.
19. Discussions of the history of management thought can be found in Daniel A. Wren, *The Evolution of Management Thought* (New York: Ronald Press, 1972); Claude S. George Jr., *The History of Management Thought* (Englewood Cliffs, NJ: Prentice-Hall, 1968); and W. Jack Duncan, *Great Ideas in Management: Lessons from the Founders and Foundation of Management Practice* (San Francisco: Jossey-Bass, 1988).
20. The term *Classical School of Management* refers to the ideas developed by a group of practitioners who wrote of their experiences in management. Notable contributors to these ideas include Frederick W. Taylor, *Principles of Management* (New York: Harper & Row, 1911); Henri Fayol, *General and Industrial Management,* trans. J. A. Conbrough (Geneva: International Management Institute, 1929); James D. Mooney, *The Principles of Organization* (New York: Harper & Row, 1947); and James D. Mooney, *The Elements of Administration* (New York: Harper & Row, 1944).
21. Henry Mintzberg, *The Nature of Managerial Work* (Englewood Cliffs, NJ: Prentice-Hall, 1980).
22. Peter F. Drucker, "Management's New Paradigms," *Forbes,* October 5, 1998, pp. 152–77.
23. Alan M. Rugman and Joseph R. D'Cruz, *Multinationals as Flagship Firms* (Oxford: Oxford University Press, 2000).
24. Michael Watkins, *The First 90 Days: Critical Success Strategies for New Leaders at All Levels* (Boston: Harvard Business School Press, 2003).
25. Katherine J. Klein and Steve W. J. Kozlowski, *Multilevel Theory, Research, and Methods in Organizations: Foundations, Extensions, and New Directions* (San Francisco: Jossey-Bass, 2000).
26. Henry Mintzberg, "Organization Design: Fashion or Fit?" *Harvard Business Review,* January–February 1981, pp. 103–16.

27. Richard B. Chase and Sriram Daser, "Want to Perfect Your Company's Service? Use Behavioral Science," *Harvard Business Review,* June 2001, pp. 78–85.
28. William Q. Judge and Joel A. Ryman, "The Shared Leadership Challenge in Strategic Alliance Lessons from the U.S. Health Care Industry," *Academy of Management Executive* 15 (2001): 71–79.
29. Suzanne C. de Janasz, Karen O. Dowd, and Beth Z. Schneider, *Interpersonal Skills in Organizations* (Burr Ridge, IL: McGraw-Hill/Irwin, 2002).
30. Stephen Stasser, J. D. Eveland, Gaylord Cummins, O. Lynn Denison, and John H. Romani, "Conceptualizing the Goal and System Models of Organizational Effectiveness," *Journal of Management Studies* 18 (1981): 321; Kim Cameron, "Critical Questions in Assessing Organizational Effectiveness," *Organizational Dynamics* 9 (1980): 66–80, identifies two other approaches: the internal process approach and the strategic constituencies approach. The former can be subsumed under the systems theory approach, and the latter is a special case of the multiple-goal approach.
31. Michael C. Jackson, *Systems Approach to Management* (New York: Kluwer, 2000).
32. Chester I. Barnard, *The Functions of the Executive* (Cambridge, MA: Harvard University Press, 1938), p. 55.
33. Edwin A. Locke and Gary P. Latham, *A Theory of Goal-Setting and Task Performance* (Upper Saddle River, NJ: Prentice-Hall, 1990).
34. Gary Ryan Blair, *Goal Setting for Results* (New York: Walk the Talk, 2003).
35. James L. Price and Charles W. Mueller, *Handbook of Organizational Measurement* (Marshfield, MA: Pitman, 1986), pp. 128–30.
36. Ibid.
37. Jackson, *Systems Approach to Management.*
38. Lawrence Mishel, Jared Bernstein, and John Schmitt, *The State of Working America* (Ithaca, NY: Cornell University Press, 2001).
39. William Gareth, "Managing Successful Universities," *Higher Education Quarterly* (April 2007): 223.
40. Amitai Etzioni, "Two Approaches to Organizational Analysis: A Critique and a Suggestion," in *Assessment of Organizational Effectiveness,* ed. Jaisingh Ghorpade (Santa Monica, CA: Goodyear, 1971), p. 36.
41. J. Harrison, D. Bosse, and R. Phillips, "Managing for Stakeholders, Stakeholder Utility Functions, and Competitive Advantage," *Strategic Management Journal* 31, no. 1 (2010): 58–74; and James H. Davis, F. David Schoorman, and Lex Donaldson, "Toward a Stewardship Theory of Management," *Academy of Management Review* 22 (1997): 20–47.
42. Alfie Morgan, *Strategic Leadership: Managing the Firm in a Turbulent World* (Dubuque, IA: Kendall/Hunt, 2001).
43. S. G. Lazzarini, "The Impact of Membership in Computing Alliance Constellations," *Strategic Management Journal* 28, no. 4 (2007): 345–67.
44. Anne S. Tsui, "An Empirical Examination of the Multiple-Constituency Model of Organizational Effectiveness," *Proceedings of the Academy of Management,* 1989, pp. 188–92.
45. Garth Saloner, Andrea Shepard, and Joel Podolny, *Strategic Management* (New York: John Wiley, 2001).
46. Ibid.

Chapter 2

1. J. J. Johnson, "Differences in Supervisor and Non-supervisor Perceptions of Quality Culture and Organizational Climate," *Public Personnel Management* (February 2004): 119–29.
2. B. Gregory, S. Harris, A. Armenakis, and C. Shook, "Organizational Culture and Effectiveness: A Study of Values, Attitudes, and Organizational Outcomes," *Journal of Business Research* 62, no. 7 (2009): 673–679; and C. Yilmaz and E. Ergun, "Organizational Culture and Firm Effectiveness: An Examination of Relative Effects of Culture Traits and the Balanced Culture Hypothesis in an Emerging Economy," *Journal of World Business* 43, no. 3 (2008): 290–306.
3. Nelson Lichtenstein, *The Retail Revolution: How Walmart Created a Brave New World of Business* (New York: Metropolitan Books, 2009).
4. *Wal-Mart 2009 Annual Report*, Walmart, accessed April 9, 2010, http://walmartstores.com/sites/AnnualReport/2009/letter.html.
5. Iivari Juhani and Magda Huisman, "The Relationship between Organizational Culture and the Deployment of Systems Development Methodologies," *MIS Quarterly* 31 (2007): 33–58.
6. Ibid.
7. Edgar H. Schein, *Organizational Culture and Leadership* (San Francisco: Jossey-Bass, 1985), p. 9.
8. "Careers," Pfizer, accessed April 9, 2010, http://www.pfizer.com/careers/working_for_pfizer/mission_values.jsp.
9. "What Makes a Company Great?" *Fortune,* October 26, 1998, p. 218.
10. J. A. Chatman and S. E. Cha, *Leading by Leveraging Culture* (London: Financial Tunes-Prentice-Hall, 2003).
11. Gian Caprara and Patrizia Steca, "Prosocial Agency: The Contribution of Values and Self-Efficacy Beliefs to Prosocial Behavior Across Ages," *Journal of Social & Clinical Psychology* 26 (2007): 218–39.
12. S. Sidle, "Building a Committed Global Workforce: Does What Employees Want Depend on Culture?" *Academy of Management Perspectives* 23, no. 1 (2009): 79–80; and R. House, M. Javidan, P. Hanges, and P. Dorfman, "Understanding Cultures and Implicit Leadership Theories across the Globe: An Introduction to Project Globe," *Journal of World Business* 37 (2002): 3–10.
13. I. Levin and J. Gottlieb, "Realigning Organization Culture for Optimal Performance: Six Principles &

Eight Practices," *Organization Development Journal* 27, no. 4 (2009): 31–46; and L. M. Lesmen, M. A. Shaffer, and E. Snape, "In Search of Sustained Competitive Advantage: The Impact of Organizational Culture, Competitive Strategy, and Human Resource Management Practices on Firm Performance," *International Journal of Human Resource Management* 15 (2004): 17–35.

14. P. Braddy, A. Meade, J. Michael, and J. Fleenor, "Internet Recruiting: Effects of Website Content Features on Viewers' Perceptions of Organizational Culture," *International Journal of Selection and Assessment* 17, no. 1 (2009): 19–34; and Anne B. Fisher, "Where Companies Rank in Their Industries," *Fortune,* March 4, 1996, p. F-2.
15. Michael Zwell, *Creating a Culture of Competence* (New York: John Wiley, 2000).
16. Keom L. Freiberg, "The Heart and Spirit of Transformation Leadership: A Qualitative Case Study of Herb Kelleher's Passion for Southwest Airlines" (PhD diss., University of San Diego, 1987), p. 234.
17. Peg C. Neuhauser, *Corporate Legends and Lore* (New York: McGraw-Hill, 1993).
18. John D. Clemens and Melora Wolff, *Movies to Manage By: Lessons in Leadership from Great Films* (New York: McGraw-Hill, 2000).
19. Ibid.
20. Markus Hauser, "Organizational Culture and Innovativeness of Firms: An Integrative View," *International Journal of Technology Management* 16 (1998): 239–55.
21. Don Hellriegel and John W. Slocum Jr., *Organizational Behavior* (Cincinnati, OH: Thomson, 2007).
22. Ibid.
23. Ibid.
24. Iivari and Huisman, "The Relationship between Organizational Culture and the Deployment of Systems Development of Technologies."
25. Ibid.
26. Edgar H. Schein, *Organizational Culture and Leadership* (San Francisco: Jossey-Bass, 1997).
27. Philip I. Morgan and Emmanuel Ogbonna, "Subcultural Dynamics in Transformation: A Multi-perspective Study of Healthcare Professionals," *Human Relations* 61, no. 1 (2006): 39–65.
28. Schein (1997), *op cit.*
29. Allan A. Kennedy and Terrence E. Deal, *The New Corporate Cultures* (New York: Dimension, 2000).
30. Debra E. Myerson, *Tempered Radicals: How People Use Difference to Inspire Change at Work* (Cambridge, MA: Harvard Business School Press, 2001).
31. Kennedy and Deal, *The New Corporate Cultures.*
32. Ibid.
33. *Harvard Business Review on Mergers and Acquisitions* (Cambridge, MA: Harvard Business School Press, 2001).
34. D. Gebler, "The Ten Merger Commandments," *Risk Management* 56, no. 5 (2009): 10; and Donald De Pamphillis, *Mergers, Acquisitions, and Other Restructuring Activities: An Integrated Approach to Process, Tools, Cases, and Solutions* (New York: Academic Press, 2001).
35. Ken Ramano, "Organizational Culture—Your Company's Personality," *Inside Tucson Business,* April 19, 2004, p. 5.
36. Y. Chuang, R. Church, and J. Zikic, "Organizational Culture, Group Diversity, and Intra-group Conflict," *Team Performance Management* 10 (2004): 26–34.
37. Jeanie Daniel Duck, *The Change Monster: The Human Forces That Fuel or Foil Corporate Transformation and Change* (New York: Crown, 2001).
38. "The History of Research and Innovation at the Center for Creative Leadership," Center for Creative Leadership, accessed April 11, 2010, http://www.ccl.org/leadership/research/history/creation.aspx?pageId=1682.
39. Mary E. Guffey, *Essentials of Business Communication* (Cincinnati, OH: South-Western, 2007).
40. Rob Moll, "Outer Office, Inner Life," *Wall Street Journal*, January 10, 2010, p. A.15; Lake Lambert III, *Spirituality Inc.: Religion in the American Workplace* (New York: NYU Press, 2009).
41. Jonathan A. Smith and John J. Rayment, "The Global SMP Fitness Framework," *Management Decision* 45 (2007): 220.
42. Badrinarayan S. Pawar, "Workplace Spirituality Facilitation: A Comprehensive Model," *Journal of Business Ethics* 90, no. 3 (2009): 375–386; and Badrinarayan S. Pawar, "Two Approaches to Workplace Spirituality Facilitation: A Comparison and Implications," *Leadership & Organization Development Journal* 29, no. 6 (2008): 544–567.
43. L. Fry and J. Slocum, "Maximizing the Triple Bottom Line through Spiritual Leadership," *Organizational Dynamics* 37, no. 1 (2008): 86–96.
44. B. Pawar, "Some of the Recent Organizational Behavior Concepts as Precursors to Workplace Spirituality," *Journal of Business Ethics* 88, no. 2 (2009): 245–261.
45. L. W. Fry, "Towards a Theory of Spiritual Leadership," *The Leadership Quarterly* 14 (2003): 693–727.
46. "Good Business: Heritage," Tom's of Maine, accessed April 15, 2010, http://www.tomsofmaine.com/business-practices/heritage/early-history; and L. E. Reave, "Spiritual Values and Practices Related to Leadership Effectiveness," *The Leadership Quarterly* 16 (2005): 655–87.
47. Tom Chappell, *The Soul of a Business: Managing for Profit and the Consumer Good* (New York: Bantam-Doubleday, 1994).
48. Ibid.
49. R. B. Brown, "Organizational Spirituality: The Sceptic's Version," *Organization* 10 (2003): 393–400.
50. A. Giacolone and C. Jurkiewicz, eds., *The Handbook of Workplace Spirituality and Organizational Performance* (Armonk, NJ: M. E. Sharpe, 2003).

51. M. George, "Clash of Values: Why Spirituality into Business Won't Go!" paper presented at the International Conference on Organizational Spirituality, Surrey University, 2002.
52. R. J. Taormina, "Convergent Validation of Two Measures of Organizational Socialization," *International Journal of Human Resource Management* 15 (2004): 76–94.
53. These stages are identified by Daniel C. Feldman, "A Contingency Theory of Socialization," *Administrative Science Quarterly* 21 (1967): 434–35. The following discussion is based heavily on this work as well as on Daniel C. Feldman, "A Practical Program for Employee Socialization," *Organizational Dynamics* 5 (1976): 64–80; and Daniel C. Feldman, "The Multiple Socialization of Organization Members," *Academy of Management Review* 6 (1981): 309–18.
54. Emmanuel Ogbonna and Lloyd C. Harris, "Organizational Culture: It's Not What You Think," *Journal of General Management* 23 (1998): 35–48.
55. R. Gershon, P. W. Stone, S. Bakken, and E. Larson, "Measurement of Organizational Culture and Climate in Healthcare," *Journal of Nursing Administration* 34 (2004): 34–40.
56. "Calvert Investments," Calvert Group, accessed April 15, 2010, http://www.calvertgroup.com/; and James C. Collins and Jerry I. Porras, *Built to Last* (New York: HarperCollins, 1995).
57. Gareth R. Jones, "Psychological Orientation and the Process of Organizational Socialization: An Interactionist Perspective," *Academy of Management Review* 8 (1983): 464–74.
58. J. Van Maanen, "People Processing: Strategies for Organizational Socialization," *Organizational Dynamics* 7 (1978): 8–36.
59. Ibid.
60. Robert Boice, *Advice for New Faculty Members* (Boston: Allyn & Bacon, 2000).
61. A. De Vos, K. De Stobbeleir, and A. Meganck, "The Relationship Between Career-Related Antecedents and Graduates' Anticipatory Psychological Contracts," *Journal of Business and Psychology* 24, no. 3 (2009): 289–298; and R. Recardo and J. Jolly, "Organizational Culture and Teams," *SAM Advanced Management Journal* 62 (1997): 4–7.
62. H. D. C. Thomas and N. Anderson, "Newcomer Adjustment: The Relationship Between Organizational Socialization Tactics, Information Acquisition and Attitudes," *Journal of Occupational and Organizational Psychology* 75 (2002): 423–37.
63. Marjorie Derven, "Management Onboarding," *T + D* 62, no. 4 (2008): 49–54.
64. J. Johnson-Bailey and R. Cervero, "Mentoring in Black and White: The Intricacies of Cross-Cultural Mentoring," *Mentoring and Tutoring,* April 2004, pp. 7–21.
65. Susan J. Wells and Aleita Johnson, "Tending Talent," *HR Magazine*, May 2009, pp. 53–58.
66. Johnson-Bailey and Cervero, *op cit*.
67. Sarah Boehle, "Millennial Mentors," *Training* 46, no. 6 (2009): 34–36.
68. Bruce Peitier, *The Psychology of Executive Coaching: Theory and Application* (New York: Brumer/Mazel, 2001).
69. S. Mueller, "Electronic Mentoring as an Example of the Use of Information and Communications Technology in Engineering Education," *European Journal of Information and Communications Technology in Engineering Education* 29 (2004): 53–63.
70. Taylor Cox Jr. and Ruby L. Beale, *Developing Competency to Manage Diversity* (San Francisco: Berrett-Koehler, 1997).
71. Bureau of Labor Statistics, U.S. Department of Labor, accessed April 15, 2010, http://www.bls.gov.
72. Ibid.
73. C. F. Fey and D. R. Denison, "Organizational Culture and Effectiveness: Can American Theory Be Applied In Russia?" *Organization Science* 14 (2003): 686–706.
74. Mark A. Williams, Mark W. Williams, and Donald O. Clifton, *The 10 Lenses: Your Guide to Living and Working in a Multicultural World* (New York: Capital Books, 2001).
75. David Jamieson and Julie O'Mara, *Managing Workforce 2000* (San Francisco: Jossey-Bass, 1991), pp. 84–89.
76. A. H. Eagly, M. C. Johannsen-Schmidt, and M. L. van Enger, "Transformational, Transactional, and Laissez-Faire Leadership Styles: A Meta-Analysis Comparing Women and Men," *Psychological Bulletin* 129 (2003): 569–91.
77. Pushkala Prasad, Albert J. Mills, Michael Elmes, and Anshuman Prasad, eds., *Managing The Organizational Melting Pot: Dilemmas of Workforce Diversity* (Thousand Oaks, CA: Sage, 1997).
78. "Commitment to Diversity," Seattle Times Company, accessed April 15, 2010, http://www.seattletimescompany.com/working/diversity.htm.
79. Santosh C. Saha, *The Politics of Ethnicity and National Identity* (New York: Peter Lang Publishing, 2007).

Chapter 3

1. S. Segal-Horn and A. Dean, "Delivering 'Effortless Experience' across Borders: Managing Internal Consistency in Professional Service Firms," *Journal of World Business* 44, no. 1 (2009): 41–50.
2. Harry G. Barkema and Freek Vermeulen, "International Expansion through Start-up or Acquisition: A Learning Perspective," *Academy of Management Journal* 41 (1998): 7–26; and Charles W. L. Hill, *International Business,* 8th ed. (New York: McGraw-Hill/Irwin, 2010).
3. C. Worley and E. Lawler, "Building a Change Capability at Capital One Financial," *Organizational Dynamics* 38, no. 4 (2009): 245–251.

4. J. Clover, "Helping Managers Go Global," *Personnel Today*, January 2008, pp. 24–25.
5. Gabriel J. Byrne and Frank Bradley, "Culture's Influence on Leadership Efficiency: How Personal and National Cultures Affect Leadership Style," *Journal of Business Research* 60, no. 2 (2007): 168–75; Tony Morden, "International Culture and Management," *Management Decision* 33 (1995): 16–21; and P. Christopher Earley and Randall S. Peterson, "The Elusive Cultural Chameleon: Cultural Intelligence as a New Approach to Intercultural Training for the Global Manager," *Academy of Management Learning & Education* 3, no. 1 (2004): 100–15.
6. Robert B. Reich, *The Work of Nations: Preparing Ourselves for 21st-Century Capitalism* (New York, Knopf, 1991), p. 7.
7. Richard Tomkins, "Happy Birthday, Globalisation: 20 Years Ago Theodore Levitt Prophesied the Age of the Global Corporation," *Financial Times,* May 6, 2003, p. 14, and Theodore Levitt, "The Globalization of Markets," *Harvard Business Review,* May–June 1983, p. 94.
8. K. Mäkelä and V. Suutari, "Global Careers: A Social Capital Paradox," *The International Journal of Human Resource Management* 20, no. 5 (2009): 992–1008; Ruth Aguilera and George Yip, "Global Strategy Faces Local Constraints," *Financial Times,* May 27, 2005. p. 2; and Mary Lou Egan and Marc Bendick, Jr., "Workforce Diversity Initiatives of U.S. Multinational Corporations in Europe," *Thunderbird International Business Review* 45, no. 6 (2003): 701–27.
9. Julian Birkenshaw and Neil Hood, "Multinational Subsidiary Evolution: Capability and Charter Change in Foreign-Owned Subsidiary Companies," *Academy of Management Review* 23 (1998): 773–95; and H. V. Perlmutter, "The Tortuous Evolution of the Multinational Corporation," *Columbia Journal of World Business* 4 (1969): 9–18.
10. L. Claus and D. Briscoe, "Employee Performance Management across Borders: A Review of Relevant Academic Literature," *International Journal of Management Reviews* 11, no. 2 (2009): 175–196; Frank Shipper, Richard C. Hoffman, and Denise M. Rotondo, "Does the 360 Feedback Process Create Actionable Knowledge Equally across Cultures?" *Academy of Management Learning & Education* 6, no. 1 (2007): 33–50; and John F. Milliman, Stephen Nason, Kevin Lowe, Nam-Hyeon Kim, and Paul Huo, "An Empirical Study of Performance Appraisal Practices in Japan, Korea, Taiwan and the U.S.," *Academy of Management Journal* (1995): 182–86.
11. David A. Robinson and Michael Harvey, "Global Leadership in a Culturally Diverse World," *Management Decision* 46, no. 3 (2008): 466–480.
12. "About Ford," Ford Motor Company, accessed April 15, 2010, http://corporate.ford.com/about-ford/heritage.
13. John Reed and Daniel Schafer, "Alliance Forged in Green New World," *Financial Times*, April 10, 2010, p. 10.
14. Adler, *International Dimensions,* p. 11.
15. T. Cappellen and M. Janssens, "Characteristics of International Work: Narratives of the Global Manager," *Thunderbird International Business Review* 52, no. 4 (2010): 337–348; Richard S. DeFrank, Robert Konopaske, and John M. Ivancevich, "Executive Travel Stress: Perils of the Road Warrior," *The Academy of Management Executive* 14, no. 2 (2000): 58–71.
16. C. K. Prahalad and Kenneth Lieberthal, "The End of Corporate Imperialism," *Harvard Business Review*, July–August 1998, pp. 69–79.
17. J. Olsen and L. Martins, "The Effects of Expatriate Demographic Characteristics on Adjustment: A Social Identity Approach," *Human Resource Management* 48, no. 2 (2009): 311–328; Soo Min Toh and Angelo S. DeNisi, "Host Country Nationals as Socializing Agents: A Social Identity Approach," *Journal of Organizational Behavior* 28, no. 3 (2007): 281–301; and R. M. Kanter, *World Class: Thriving Locally in the Global Economy* (New York: Simon and Schuster, 1995).
18. Prahalad and Lieberthal, p. 74.
19. Robert B. Giloth, ed., *Jobs and Economic Development: Strategies and Practice* (Thousand Oaks, CA: Sage, 1998); and Christopher A. Bartlett and Sumatra Ghoshal, "What Is a Global Manager?" *Harvard Business Review*, August 2003, pp. 101–10.
20. Pankaj Ghemawat, "Managing Differences," *Harvard Business Review*, March 2007, pp. 58–68; and Teresa J. Domzal and Lynette S. Unger, "Emerging Positioning Strategies in Global Marketing," *Journal of Consumer Marketing* 4 (1987): 23–40.
21. S. Boehle, "Global Sales Training's Balancing Act," *Training*, January 2010, pp. 29–31.
22. Rick Yan, "Short-Term Results: The Litmus Test for Success in China," *Harvard Business Review,* September–October 1998, pp. 61–75.
23. M. Rabotin, "Reading the World," *T + D* 63, no. 2 (2009): 6; Jeanne Brett, Kristin Behfar, and Mary C. Kern, "Managing Multicultural Teams," *Harvard Business Review*, November 2006, pp. 84–91; and Mary Ann Von Glinow, Debra L. Shapiro, and Jeanne M. Brett, "Can We Talk, and Should We? Managing Emotional Conflict in Multicultural Teams," *Academy of Management Review* 29, no. 4 (2004): 578–92; Aparna Joshi, Giuseppe Labianca, and Paula Caligiuri, "Getting Along Long Distance: Understanding Conflict in a Multinational Team through Network Analysis," *Journal of World Business* 37, no. 4 (2002): 277–84; and Jane E. Salk and Mary Yoko Brannen, "National Culture, Networks, and Individual Influence in a Multinational Management Team," *Academy of Management Journal* 43, no. 2 (2000): 191–202.
24. Martha Frase, "Show All Employees A Wider World," *HR Magazine*, June 2007, pp. 98–102; Robert Konopaske

and John M. Ivancevich, *Global Management and Organizational Behavior* (New York: McGraw-Hill/Irwin, 2004), pp. 151–52.

25. Laura Miller, "Two Aspects of Japanese and American Co-Worker Interaction: Giving Instructions and Creating Rapport," *Journal of Applied Behavior Science* 31 (1995): 141–61.
26. M. Teasdale, "Producing a Perfect Blend," *Personnel Today,* January 2009, pp. 24–25.
27. C. Worley and E. Lawler, "Building a Change Capability at Capital One Financial," *Organizational Dynamics* 38, no. 4 (2009): 245–51.
28. J. Shapiro, "Benchmarking The Benchmarks," *HR Magazine,* April 2010, pp. 43–46; and Johnson Edosomwam, "The Baldrige Award: Focus on Total Customer Satisfaction," *Industrial Engineering* (July 1991): 20–24.
29. F. M. Scherer, *International High-Technology Competition* (Cambridge, MA: Harvard University Press, 1992), p. 55.
30. Tomasz Lenartowicz and Kendall Roth, "Does Subculture within a Country Matter? A Cross-Cultural Study of Motivational Domains and Business Performance is Brazil," *Journal of International Business Studies* 2 (2001): 305–25.
31. Adler, *International Dimensions,* p. 27.
32. P. Christopher Earley, "East Meets West Meets Mideast: Further Explorations of Collectivistic and Individualistic Work Groups," *Academy of Management Journal* 36 (1993): 319–48.
33. T. May, "Do Org Charts Still Matter?" *Computerworld*, November 2009, p. 38; Neil Weinberg, "A Fable of Two Companies," *Forbes,* November 30, 1998, pp. 122–27; and John M. Ivancevich, *Human Resource Management,* 9th ed. (New York: McGraw-Hill/Irwin, 2003), p. 157.
34. John Blenkinsopp and Maryam Shademan Pajouh, "Lost in Translation? Culture, Language and the Role of the Translator in International Business," *Critical Perspectives on International Business* 6, no. 1 (2010): 38–52.
35. David A. Ricks, *Blunders in International Business*, 4th ed., (Hoboken, NJ: Wiley-Blackwell, 2006).
36. Craig S. Smith, "Chinese Speak the International Language of Shopping," *New York Times,* November 7, 2006, p. A4.
37. Ashley Dunn, "Cross-Cultural Misunderstanding," *Los Angeles Times,* May 28, 1989, pp. 12, 19.
38. Robin Wigglesworth, "Real Estate Exposure May Be Largest Threat," *Financial Times*, May 6, 2009, p. 2.
39. The description of these four dimensions is based on Geert Hofstede, *Culture's Consequences: International Differences in Work-Related Values* (Beverly Hills, CA: Sage, 1980); Geert Hofstede, "The Cultural Relativity of Organizational Practices and Theories," *Journal of International Business Studies* 14, no. 2 (Fall 1983): 75–89; and Geert Hofstede, "Motivation, Leadership, and Organization: Do American Theories Apply Abroad?" *Organizational Dynamics* 9, no. 1 (1980): 42–63.
40. Simeha Ronen, *Comparative and Multinational Management* (New York: Wiley, 1986), pp. 266–67.
41. Geert Hofstede and Michael Harris Bond, "The Confucius Connection: From Cultural Roots to Economic Growth," *Organizational Dynamics* 16, no. 4 (1988): 4–21.
42. Ibid.
43. Ibid.
44. Geert Hofstede, *Culture's Consequences: Comparing Values, Behaviors, Institutions and Organizations across Nations*, 2nd ed. (Thousand Oaks, CA: Sage Publications, 2003); Geert Hofstede, "Cultural Constraints in Management Theories," paper presented at the annual meeting of the National Academy of Management, Las Vegas, August 11, 1992, pp. 1–21; Norman B. Bryan, Ephraim R. McClean, Stanley J. Smits, and Janice M. Burn, "Work Perceptions among Hong Kong and United States I/S Workers: A Cross-Cultural Comparison," *Journal of End User Computing* 7 (1995): 22–29; and Andrew D. Brown and Michael Humphreys, "International Cultural Differences in Public Sector Management," *International Journal of Public Sector Management* 8 (1995): 5–23.
45. Susumu Ueno and Uma Sekaran, "The Influence of Culture on Budget Control Practices in the U.S.A. and Japan: An Empirical Study," *Journal of International Business* (Winter 1992): 659–74.
46. Ibid.
47. Irene K. H. Chew and Joseph Putti, "Relationship on Work-Related Values of Singaporean and Japanese Managers in Singapore," *Human Relations* 48, no. 10 (1995): 1149–70; for a critique of Hofstede's research, see Brendan McSweeney, "Hofstede's Model of National Cultural Differences and Their Consequences: A Triumph of Faith—A Failure of Analysis," *Human Relations* 55, no. 1 (2002): 89–118; and Geert Hofstede, "Dimensions Do Not Exist: A Reply to Brendan McSweeney," *Human Relations* 55, no. 11 (2002): 1355–61.
48. Harrison M. Trice and Janice M. Beyer, *Cultures of Work Organizations* (Englewood Cliffs, NJ: Prentice-Hall, 1993), p. 338.
49. Ana Maria Soares, Minoo Farhangmehr, and Aviv Shoham, "Hofstede's Dimensions of Culture in International Marketing Studies," *Journal of Business Research* 60, no. 3 (2007): 277–84.
50. Robert House, Mansour Javidan, Paul Hanges, and Peter Dorfman, "Understanding Cultures and Implicit Leadership Theories across the Globe: An Introduction to Project GLOBE," *Journal of World Business* 37 (2002): 3–10.

51. Mansour Javidan, Gunter K. Stahl, Felix Brodbeck, and Celeste P. M. Wilderom, "Cross-border Transfer of Knowledge: Cultural Lessons from Project GLOBE," *Academy of Management Executive* 19, no. 2 (2005): 59–76.
52. House et al., "Understanding Cultures and Implicit Leadership Theories."
53. James H. Donnelly, Jr., James L. Gibson, and John M. Ivancevich, *Fundamentals of Management,* 10th ed. (Burr Ridge: Irwin–McGraw Hill, 1998), pp. 70–71.
54. Robert B. Reich, "Plenty of Knowledge Work to Go Around," *Harvard Business Review* 83, no. 4 (2005): 17; and James Champy, "Deeper Accountability," *Forbes,* November 30, 1998, p. 108.
55. Dora C. Lau and J. Keith Murnighan, "Demographic Diversity and Faultlines: The Compositional Dynamics of Organizational Groups," *Academy of Management Review* 23 (1998): 325–40.
56. Susan Moffat, "Should You Work for the Japanese?" *Fortune,* December 3, 1990, p. 107.
57. Shung J. Shin, Frederick P. Morgeson, and Michael A. Campion, "What You Do Depends on Where You Are: Understanding How Domestic and Expatriate Work Requirements Depend upon the Cultural Context, *Journal of International Business Studies* 38, no. 1 (2007): 64–84; and J. Stewart Black and Lyman W. Porter, "Managerial Behaviors and Job Performance: A Successful Manager in Los Angeles May Not Succeed in Hong Kong," *Journal of International Business Studies* 22 (1991): 99–113.
58. Sheng Wang, Tony W. Tong, Guoli Chen, and Hyondong Kim, "Expatriate Utilization and Foreign Direct Investment Performance: The Mediating Role of Knowledge Transfer," *Journal of Management* 35, no. 5 (2009): 1181–1206; J. Stewart Black, Mark Mendenhall, and Gray Obbou, "Toward a Comprehensive Model of International Adjustment: An Integration of Multiple Theoretical Perspectives," *Academy of Management Review* 16 (1991): 291–317; Roger Darby, "Developing the Euro-Manager Managing in a Multicultural Environment," *European Business Review* 95 (1995): 13–15; and Mike Edkins, "Making the Move from West to East," *Personnel Management,* June 29, 1995, pp. 34–37.
59. Chao C. Chen, Xiao-Ping Chen, and James R. Meindl, "How Can Cooperation Be Fostered? The Cultural Effects of Individualism-Collectivism," *Academy of Management Review* 23 (1998): 285–304.
60. Sarah Dobson, "Overseas Relocations Well Worth the Trip," *Canadian HR Reporter,* September 22, 2008, pp. 13–15.
61. Jane Simms, "Handle with Care," *Human Resources* (2006): 72–75; and PricewaterhouseCoopers, *International Assignments: European Policy and Practices* (A. McErlain, 1999).
62. Mark C. Bolino, "Expatriate Assignments and Intra-organizational Career Success: Implications for Individuals and Organizations," *Journal of International Business Studies* 38, no. 5 (2007): 819–35.
63. Robert Konopaske, Chet Robie, and John M. Ivancevich, "Managerial Willingness to Assume Traveling Short-term and Long-term Global Assignments," *Management International Review* 49, no. 3 (2009): 359–87; and Robert Konopaske, Chet Robie, and John M. Ivancevich, "A Preliminary Model of Spouse Influence on Managerial Global Assignment Willingness," *The International Journal of Human Resource Management* 16, no. 3 (2005): 405–26.
64. J. Stewart Black and Gregory K. Stephen, "The Influence of the Spouse on American Expatriate Adjustment and Intent to Stay in Pacific Rim Overseas Assignments," *Journal of Management,* December 1989, p. 228; and Rosalie Tung, "Selection and Training of Personnel for Overseas Assignments," *Columbia Journal of World Business* 16 (1981): 68–78.
65. Kalervo Oberg, "Cultural Shock: Adjustment to New Cultural Environments," *Practice Anthropology* 7 (1960): 177–82.
66. Robert H. Sims and Mike Schraeder, "An Examination of Salient Factors Affecting Expatriate Culture Shock, *Journal of Business and Management* 10, no. 1 (2004): 73–88; Oberg, "Culture Shock"; Richard G. Linowes, "The Japanese Manager's Traumatic Entry into the United States: Understanding the American Japanese Cultural Divide," *Academy of Management Executive* (November 1993): 21–38; and Joyce Osland, "Working Abroad: A Hero's Adventure," *T + D,* November 1995, pp. 47–51.
67. P. Friedman, L. Dyke, and S. Murphy, "Expatriate Adjustment From the Inside Out: An Autoethnographic Account," *The International Journal of Human Resource Management* 20, no. 2 (2009): 252–68.
68. Cassandra Hayes, "Can a New Frontier Boost Your Career?" *Black Enterprise,* May 1995, pp. 71–74.
69. J. Brandl and A. Neyer, "Applying Cognitive Adjustment Theory to Cross-cultural Training for Global Virtual Teams," *Human Resource Management* 48, no. 3 (2009): 341–53.
70. Stewart J. Black and Mark Mendenhall, "Cross-Cultural Training Effectiveness: A Review and a Theoretical Framework for Future Research," *Academy of Management Review* 15, no. 1 (1990): 113–36.
71. P. Christopher Earley, "Intercultural Training for Managers: A Comparison of Documentary and Interpersonal Methods," *Academy of Management Journal* 30 (1987): 685–98.
72. Rosalie Tung, "Selecting and Training Procedures of U.S., European, and Japanese Multinationals," *California Management Review* 25 (1982): 51–71; and R. L. Desatnick and M. L. Bennett, *Human Resource Management in the Multinational Company* (New York: Nichols, 1978).

73. Jan Selmer, "The Preference for Predeparture or Postarrival Cross-cultural Training: An Exploratory Approach," *Journal of Managerial Psychology* 16, no. 1 (2001): 50–58.
74. Ibid.
75. G. Stahl, C. Chua, P. Caligiuri, J. Cerdin, and M. Taniguchi, "Predictors of Turnover Intentions in Learning-driven and Demand-driven International Assignments: The Role of Repatriation Concerns, Satisfaction with Company Support, and Perceived Career Advancement Opportunities," *Human Resource Management* 48, no. 1 (2009): 89–109; Charlene Solomon, "Repatriation: Up, Down or Out?" *Personnel Journal* 74 (1995): 28–30; and Aimin Yan, Guorong Zhu, and Douglas T. Hall, "International Assignments for Career Building: A Model of Agency Relationships and Psychological Contracts," *Academy of Management Review* 27, no. 3 (2007): 373–91.
76. Steven L. Wartick and Donna J. Wood *International Business and Society* (Malden, MA: Blackwell, 1998).

Chapter 4

1. Melba J. Vasquez and James M. Jones, "Diversity Is a Compelling Interest and Affirmative Action Is an Important Strategy for Achieving It," *American Psychologist* 62 (2007): 146–47.
2. P. Schnorbach, "Gen Y for Hire," *Material Handling Management* 64, no. 3 (2009): 34; and Bill George, *Authentic Leadership: Rediscovering the Secrets for Creating Lasting Value* (New York: John Wiley & Sons, 2004).
3. Mitchell G. Ash, "Cultural Contexts and Scientific Changes in Psychology," *American Psychologist,* February 1992, pp. 198–207; and Kurt Levin, "Environmental Forecast in Child Behavior and Development," in *Handbook of Child Psychology,* ed. (Worcester, MA: Clark University Press, 1931), pp. 94–127.
4. J. R. B. Halbesleben and W. M. Bowler, "Emotional Exhaustion and Job Performance: The Mediating Role of Motivation," *Journal of Applied Psychology* 92, no. 1 (2007): 146–47.
5. Gerald W. Faust, Richard I. Lyles, and Will Phillips, *Responsible Managers Get Results: How the Best Find Solutions—Not Excuses* (New York: Amacom, 1998).
6. Clinton O. Longenecker and Laurence S. Fink, "Key Criteria in Twenty-first Century Management Promotional Decisions," *Career Development International* 13, no. 3 (2008): 241–51; and T. A. Judge, C. L. Jackson, J. C. Shaw, B. A. Scott, and B. L. Rich, "Self-Efficacy and Work-Related Performance: The Integral Role of Individual Differences," *Journal of Applied Psychology* 92, no. 1 (2007): 107–27.
7. Marvin D. Dunnette, "Aptitudes, Abilities, and Skills," in *Handbook of Industrial and Organizational Psychology,* ed. Marvin D. Dunnette (Skokie, IL: Rand McNally, 1976), pp. 481–82.
8. G. F. Gebauer and N. J. Macintosh, "Psychometric Intelligence Dissociates Implicit and Explicit Learning," *Journal of Experimental Psychology: Learning Memory, and Cognition* 33 (January 2007): 34–54.
9. T. Judge, C. Hurst, and L. Simon, "Does It Pay to be Smart, Attractive, or Confident (or All Three)? Relationships Among General Mental Ability, Physical Attractiveness, Core Self-evaluations, and Income," *Journal of Applied Psychology* 94, no. 3 (2009): 742–55.
10. For a complete discussion of job analysis, see John M. Ivancevich, *Human Resource Management: Foundations of Personnel,* 11th ed. (Burr Ridge, IL: McGraw Irwin, 2010), pp. 146–81.
11. Ibid.
12. D. V. Becker, D. T. Kenrick, S. L. Neuberg, K. C. Blackwell, and D. M. Smith, "The Confounded Nature of Angry Men and Happy Women," *Journal of Personality and Social Psychology* (February 2007): 179–90.
13. E. Patton and G. Johns, "Women's Absenteeism in the Popular Press: Evidence for a Gender-specific Absence Culture," *Human Relations* 60, no. 11 (2007): 1579–1612; D. Farrell and C. L. Stamm, "Meta-Analysis of the Correlates of Employee Absence," *Human Relations* 41 (1983): 211–27.
14. L. Paris, J. Howell, P. Dorfman, and P. Hanges, "Preferred Leadership Prototypes of Male and Female Leaders in 27 Countries," *Journal of International Business Studies* 40, no. 8 (2009): 1396–1405.
15. Martin M. Elvira and Lisa E. Cohen, "Location Matters: A Cross-Level Analysis of the Effects of Organizational Sex Composition on Turnover," *Academy of Management Journal* 44 (2001): 591–605.
16. Lawrence Mishel, Jared Bernstein, and John Schmitt, *The State of Working America* (Ithaca, NY: Cornell University Press, 2001).
17. David A. Thomas, "The Truth about Mentoring Minorities," *Harvard Business Review,* April 2001, pp. 98–111.
18. "Employment Projections: 2008–2018," U.S. Bureau of Labor Statistics, accessed April 26, 2010, http://www.bls.gov/news.release/ecopro.nr0.htm.
19. G. M. Walton and G. L. Cohen, "A Question of Belonging: Race, Social Fit, and Achievement," *Journal of Social Psychology* 92 (2007): 82–96.
20. S. Shrivastava and J. Gregory, "Exploring the Antecedents of Perceived Diversity," *Journal of Management and Organization* 15, no. 4 (2009): 526–542; and Nigel Nicholson, "How Hardwired Is Human Behavior?" *Harvard Business Review,* July–August 1998, pp. 134–47.

21. David Krech, Richard S. Crutchfield, and E. L. Ballachey, *Individual and Society* (New York: McGraw-Hill, 1962), p. 20.
22. L. Grimm, A. Markman, W. Maddox and G. Baldwin, "Stereotype Threat Reinterpreted as a Regulatory Mismatch," *Journal of Personality and Social Psychology* 96, no. 2 (2009): 288–304; M. E. Heilman and T. G. Okimoto, "Why Are Women Penalized for Success at Male Tasks?: The Implied Communality Deficit," *Journal of Applied Psychology* 92, no. 1 (2007): 81–92.
23. Scott B. Button, "Organizational Efforts to Affirm Sexual Diversity: A Cross-Level Examination," *Journal of Applied Psychology* 86, no. 1 (2001): 17–28.
24. Todd J. Maurer, Frank G. Barbeite, Elizabeth M. Weiss, and Michael Lippstreu, "New Measures of Stereotypical Beliefs About Older Workers' Ability and Desire for Development: Exploration Among Employees Age 40 and Over," *Journal of Managerial Psychology* 23, no. 4 (2008): 395–418; and Lisa Decarlo, "More Lawsuits Loom for Lucent," *Forbes,* August 16, 2001, pp. 24–25.
25. E. G. Olson, "The Workplace Is High on the Court's Docket," *Businessweek,* October 10, 1988, pp. 88–89.
26. D. M. Amodio and P. G. Devine, "Stereotyping and Evaluation in Implied Race Bias: Evidence for Independent Constructs and Unique Effects on Behavior," *Journal of Personality and Social Psychology* 91, no. 4 (2006): 652–61.
27. Peter F. Drucker, "Managing Oneself," *Harvard Business Review,* March/April 1999, pp. 665–74.
28. Kathryn M. Bartol, Cathy C. Durham, and June M. L. Poon, "Influence of Performance Evaluation Rating Segmentation Motivation and Fairness Perceptions," *Journal of Applied Psychology* 86, no. 6 (2001): 1106–19.
29. K. T. Omivake, "The Relation between Acceptance of Self and Acceptance of Others Shown by Three Personality Inventories," *Journal of Consulting Psychology* 18 (1954): 443–46.
30. J. Anthony Deutsch, W. G. Young, and T. J. Kalogeris, "The Stomach Signals Satiety," *Science,* April 1978, pp. 23–33.
31. H. H. Kelley, *Attribution in Social Interaction* (New York: General Learning Press, 1971).
32. J. Sabini, M. Siepmann, and J. Stein, "The Really Fundamental Attribution Error In Social Psychological Research," *Psychological Inquiry* 12 (2001): 1–14.
33. R. H. Smith and S. H. Kim, "Comprehending Envy," *Psychological Bulletin* 133, no. 1 (2007): 46–64.
34. S. Sidle, "Explaining Performance in Annual Reports: Are American or Japanese Executives More Self-Serving?" *The Academy of Management Perspectives* 23, no. 1 (2009): 81–82.
35. Martin Fishbein and Isek Ajzen, *Belief, Attitude, Intention, and Behavior: An Introduction to Theory and Research* (Reading, MA: Addison-Wesley, 1975).
36. J. J. Rosenberg, "A Structural Theory of Attitudes," *Public Opinion Quarterly* 24 (1960): 319–40.
37. S. G. Barsade and D. E. Gibson, "Why Does Affect Matter in Organizations?" *Academy of Management Perspectives* 21 (2007): 36–59.
38. Leon Festinger, *A Theory of Cognitive Dissonance* (Evanston, IL: Row, Peterson, 1957).
39. Andrew J. Elliot and Patricia G. Devine, "On the Motivational Nature of Cognitive Dissonance: Dissonance as Psychological Discomfort," *Journal of Personality and Social Psychology* 67, no. 3 (1994): 382–94.
40. C. Maertz, A. Hassan, and P. Magnusson, "When Learning Is Not Enough: A Process Model of Expatriate Adjustment as Cultural Cognitive Dissonance Reduction," *Organizational Behavior and Human Decision Processes* 108, no. 1 (2009): 66–78; and Decha Dechawatanapaisal and Sununta Siengthai, "The Impact of Cognitive Dissonance on Learning Work Behavior," *Journal of Workplace Learning* 18, nos. 1/2 (2006): 42–54.
41. Roy Lewicki, Daniel J. McAllister, and Robert J. Bies, "Trust and Distrust: New Relationships and Realities," *Academy of Management Review* 23 (1998): 438–58.
42. Ibid.
43. Emma Jacobs, "20 Questions: Sir Richard Branson," http://www.ft.com/cms/s/0/3cfb1268-fbbc-11de-9c29-00144feab49a.html#axzz19zTEN9yW, January 7, 2010, accessed April 26, 2010; "About Us," Virgin, accessed April 26, 2010, http://www.virgin.com/about-us/; Matthew Garrahan, "Branson Takes Step Closer to Space Age Enterprise," *Financial Times,* December 9, 2009, p. 5.
44. Holly Weeks, "Taking the Stress Out of Stressful Conversations," *Harvard Business Review,* July–August 2001, pp. 112–20.
45. Ibid.
46. H. S. Kim and D. K. Sherman, "Express Yourself: Culture and the Effect of Self-Expression on Choice," *Journal of Personality and Social Psychology* 92 (2007): 1–11.
47. Ibid.
48. Fred E. Fiedler, *A Theory of Leadership Effectiveness* (New York: McGraw-Hill, 1967).
49. J. Senger, "Managers' Perceptions of Subordinates' Competence as a Function of Personal Value Orientations," *Academy of Management Journal,* December 1971, pp. 415–24.
50. J. P. Womack and D. T. Jones, *Lean Thinking: Banish Waste and Create Value in Your Organization* (New York: Simon & Shuster, 2003).
51. D. P. Lipsky, R. L. Seiber, and Richard D. Fincher, Emerging Systems for Managing Workplace Conflict: Lessons from American Corporations for Managers and Dispute Resolution Professionals (San Francisco: Jossey-Bass, 2003).

52. D. J. Schleicher, J. D. Watt, and G. J. Greguras, "Reexamining the Job Satisfaction-Performance Relationship: The Complexity of Attitudes," *Journal of Applied Psychology* 89 (2004): 165–77.
53. M. L. Williams, M. A. McDaniel, and N. T. Nguyen, "A Meta-Analysis of the Antecedents and Consequences of Pay Level Satisfaction," *Journal of Applied Psychology* 91 (2006): 392–413.
54. L. Levy-Garboria and C. Montmarquette, "Reported Job Satisfaction: What Does It Mean?" *Journal of Social Economics* 33 (2004): 135–51.
55. T. A. Judge, C. J. Thoresen, J. E. Bono, and G. K. Patton, "The Job Satisfaction–Job Performance Relationship: A Qualitative and Quantitative Review," *Psychological Bulletin* 127 (2001): 376–402.
56. Ibid.
57. Ibid.
58. Dennis W. Organ, "A Reappraisal and Reinterpretation of the Satisfaction-Causes-Performance Hypothesis," *Academy of Management Review* 2 (1977): 46–53.
59. Dennis W. Organ and Mary Konovsky, "Cognitive versus Affective Determinants of Organizational Citizenship Behavior," *Journal of Applied Psychology* 74 (1989): 157–64.
60. Chi-Sum Wong, Chun Hui, and Kenneth S. Law, "Casual Relationship between Attitudinal Antecedents to Turnover," *Academy of Management Journal* (Best Papers Proceedings), 1995, pp. 342–46.
61. James P. Guthrie, "High-Involvement Work Practices, Turnover, and Productivity: Evidence from New Zealand," *Academy Management Journal* 44 (2001): 180–92.
62. David J. Prottas and Cynthia A. Thompson, "Stress, Satisfaction, and the Work Family Interface: A Comparison of Self-Employed Business Owners, Independent and Organizational Employees," *Journal of Occupational Health Psychology* 11 (2006): 366–79.
63. Jena McGregor, "The 2008 Winners: Overall, Customer Service Has Dipped," *Businessweek*, March 2008, p. 47.
64. A. C. Yeung, T. C. Cheng, and C. Ling-Yau, "From Customer Orientation to Customer Satisfaction: The Gap between Theory and Practice," *IEEE Transactions on Engineering Management* 51 (2004): 85–97.
65. J. Griffith, "Do Satisfied Employees Satisfy Customers? Support-Services Staff Morale and Satisfaction Among Public School Administrators, Students, and Parents," *Journal of Applied Social Psychology* 31 (2001): 1627–58.
66. J. H. Gittell, *The Southwest Airlines Way: Using the Power of Relationships to Achieve High Performance* (New York: McGraw-Hill, 2003).
67. Raymond B. Cattell, *Personality and Mood by Questionnaire* (San Francisco: Jossey-Bass, 1973); and Raymond B. Cattell, *The Scientific Analysis of Personality* (Chicago: Aldine, 1966).
68. Ibid.
69. Ibid.
70. Sigmund Freud, "Psychopathology of Everyday Life," in *The Complete Psychological Works of Sigmund Freud* (Standard Edition), ed. J. Strachey (London: Hogarth Press, 1960), originally published in S. Freud, *The Psychopathology of Everyday Life* (New York: Macmillan, 1904).
71. Phillip G. Zambardo, *Psychology and Life* (Glenview, IL: Scott, Foresman, 1985), p. 382.
72. Carl Rogers, *On Personal Power: Inner Strength and Its Revolutionary Impact* (New York: Delacorte, 1977).
73. Anne Anastasi, *Psychological Testing* (New York: Macmillan, 1976), chaps. 17–19.
74. J. Allick, "Personality Dimensions Across Cultures," *Journal of Personality Disorders* 19 (2005): 212–32.
75. R. R. McCrae and P. T. Costa, "The Structure of Interpersonal Traits: Wiggins' Circumplex and the Five-Factor Model," *Journal of Personality and Social Psychology* 8 (1989): 251–72; and R. R. McCrae and P. T. Costa, "Validation of the Five-Factor Model of Personality Across Instruments and Observers," *Journal of Personality and Social Psychology* 52 (1987): 81–90.
76. Murray R. Barrick and Michael K. Mount, "The Big Five Personality Dimensions and Job Performance: A Meta-Analysis," *Personnel Psychology* 44, no. 1 (1991): 1–26.
77. Timothy A. Judge, Daniel Heller, and Michael K. Mount, "Five-factor Model of Personality and Job Satisfaction: A Meta-analysis," *Journal of Applied Psychology* 87, no. 3 (2002): 530–41.
78. Dishan Kamdar and Linn Van Dyne, "The Joint Effects of Personality and Workplace Social Exchange Relationships in Predicting Task Performance and Citizenship Performance," *Journal of Applied Psychology* 92, no. 5 (2007): 1286–98.
79. Murray R. Barrick and Ryan D. Zimmerman, "Hiring for Retention and Performance," *Human Resource Management* 48, no. 2 (2009): 183–206; and T. Judge and A. A. Erez, "Interaction and Intersection: The Constellation of Emotional Stability and Extraversion in Predicting Performance," *Personnel Psychology* 60, no. 3 (2007): 573–96.
80. H. Zhao, S. Seibert, and G. Lumpkin, "The Relationship of Personality to Entrepreneurial Intentions and Performance: A Meta-Analytic Review," *Journal of Management* 36, no. 2 (2010): 381–404; and N. Bozionelos, "The Big Five of Personality and Work Involvement," *Journal of Managerial Psychology* 19 (2004), pp. 69–81.
81. Julian B. Rotter, "Generalized Expectancies for Internal versus External Control of Reinforcement," *Psychological Monographs* 1, no. 609 (1966): 80.
82. T. R. Mitchell, C. M. Smyser, and S. E. Weed, "Locus of Control: Supervision and Work Satisfaction," *Academy of Management Journal* 18 (1975): 23–31.

83. Carl R. Anderson, "Locus of Control, Coping Behaviors, and Performance in a Stress Setting: A Longitudinal Study," *Journal of Applied Psychology* 62 (1977): 446–51.
84. Debra L. Nelson and Ronald J. Burke, "Women Executives: Health, Stress, and Success," *Academy of Management Executive* 14 (2000): 107–21.
85. B. Strickland, "Internal-External Control Expectancies: From Contingency to Creativity," *American Psychologist* 44 (1989): 1–12.
86. Jui-Chen Chen and Colin Silverthorne, "The Impact of Locus of Control on Job Stress, Job Performance and Job Satisfaction in Taiwan," *Leadership & Organization Development Journal* 29, no. 7 (2008): 572–82; and Michael Frese, Wolfgang Kring, Andrea Soose, and Jeannette Zempel, "Personal Initiative at Work: Differences between East and West Germany," *Academy of Management Journal* 39 (1996): 37–63.
87. Stephen R. Hawk, "Locus of Control and Computer Attitude: The Effect of User Involvement," *Computers in Human Behavior* 5 (1988): 199–206.
88. Kevin Daniels and Andrew Guppy, "Occupational Stress, Social Support, Job Control, and Psychological Well-Being," *Human Relations* 47 (1994): 1523–44; and Adrian Furnham and Barrie Gunter, "Biographical and Personality Predictors of Organizational Climate," *Psychologia* 37 (1994): 199–210.
89. Jacqueline M. Hooper and Louis Veneziano, "Distinguishing Starters from Nonstarters in an Employee Physical Activity Incentive Program," *Health Education Quarterly* 22 (1995): 49–60; and K. A. Wallston and B. S. Wallston, "Health Locus of Control Scales," in *Research with the Locus of Control Construct: Assessment Methods,* ed. H. M. Lefcourt (New York: Academic Press, 1981), pp. 189–43.
90. A. Bandura, *Social Learning Theory* (Englewood Cliffs, NJ: Prentice-Hall, 1977); and A. Bandura, "Self-Efficacy," *Psychological Review* 84 (1977): 191–215.
91. A. Bandura, "Self-Efficacy Mechanism in Human Behavior," *American Psychologist* 37 (1982): 122–47.
92. Michael Bergdahl, *The 10 Rules of Sam Walton: Success Secrets for Remarkable Results* (New York: John Wiley & Son, 2007); and Sam Walton, *Made in America* (New York: Doubleday Inc., 1992).
93. Alan M. Saks, "Longitudinal Field Investigation of the Moderating and Mediating Effects of Self-Efficacy on the Relationship between Training and Newcomer Adjustment," *Journal of Applied Psychology* 80 (1995): 211–25.
94. William S. Silver, Terence R. Mitchell, and Marilyn E. Gist, "Responses to Successful and Unsuccessful Performance: The Moderating Effect of Self-Efficacy on the Relationship between Performance and Attributions," *Organizational Behavior & Human Decision Processes* 62 (1995): 286–99.
95. P. Christopher Earley, "Self or Group? Cultural Effects of Training on Self-Efficacy and Performance," *Administrative Science Quarterly* 39 (1994): 89–117.
96. Richard Christie and Florence L. Geis, eds., *Studies in Machiavellianism* (New York: Academic Press, 1970).
97. Myron Gable and Frank Dangello, "Locus of Control, Machiavellianism, and Managerial Job Performance," *Journal of Psychology* 128 (1994): 599–608; and John R. Sparks, "Machiavellianism and Personal Success in Marketing: The Moderating Role of Latitude for Improvisation," *Journal of the Academy of Marketing Science* 22 (1994): 390–400.
98. J. B. Vancouver, "The Depth of History and Explanation as Benefit and Bane for Psychological Control," *Journal of Applied Psychology* 90 (2005): 38–52.
99. Charles C. Manz and Henry P. Sims, *The New Superleadership: Leading Others to Lead Themselves* (San Francisco: Barrett-Loehler, 2001).
100. Teresa M. Amabile and Mukti Khaire, "Creativity and the Role of the Leader," *Harvard Business Review*, October 2008, pp. 100–9.
101. J. H. Aitken, "Measured Intelligence, Achievement, Openness to Experience, and Creativity," *Personality & Individual Differences* 36 (2004): 913–29.
102. S. B. Kaufman, "Review of Explaining Creativity: The Science of Human Innovation," *Psychology of Aesthetics, Creativity, and The Arts,* February 2007, pp. 47–48.
103. C. Olofson, "So Many Decisions, So Little Time," *Fast Company,* October 1999, pp. 62–63.
104. D. A. Leonard and W. C. Snap, *When Sparks Fly: Igniting Creativity in Groups* (Boston: Harvard University Press, 1999).
105. T. Proctor, *Creative Problem Solving for Managers* (London: Routledge, 1999).
106. Gryskiewicz, "Restructuring," p. 3; and Leonard M. S. Yong, "Managing Creative People," *Journal of Creative Behavior* 28 (1994): 16–20.
107. P. Tierney, S. M. Farmer, and G. M. Graen, "An Examination of Leadership and Employee Creativity: The Relevance of Traits and Relationships," *Personnel Psychology* 52 (1999): 591–626.
108. R. Fuden and E. Lembessis, "The Mozart Effect: Questions about the Seminal Findings of Rauscher, Shaw, and Colleagues," *Perceptual & Motor Skills* 98 (2004): 389–405.
109. Daniel Goleman, "What Makes a Leader?" *Harvard Business Review,* November–December 1998, pp. 93–102.
110. Jeffrey M. Conte, "A Review and Critique of Emotional Intelligence Measures," *Journal of Organizational Behavior* 26, no. 4 (2005): 433–40.
111. H. M. Weiss and R. Cropanzano, "Affective Events Theory," in *Research in Organizational Behavior,* ed. M. Staw and L. L. Cummings (Greenwich, CT: JAI Press, 1996), pp. 17–19.

112. Y. Jung-Soo and S. Park, "Cross-Cultural Differences in Decision Making Style: A Study of College Students in Five Countries," *Social Behavior & Personality: An International Journal* 31 (2003): 35–47.
113. Kevin R. Murphy, *A Critique of Emotional Intelligence: What Are the Problems and How Can They Be Fixed?* (Mahwah, NJ: Lawrence Erlbaum Associates, 2006).
114. Jennifer Laabs, "Emotional Intelligence at Work," *Workforce,* July 1999, pp. 68–72.
115. Some of the most contemporary work on psychological contracts is provided by Denise M. Rousseau, *Psychological Contracts in Organizations* (Thousand Oaks, CA: Sage, 1995) and Denise M. Rousseau, "Psychological and Implied Contracts," *Employee Responsibility and Rights Journal,* Spring 1989, pp. 121–39.
116. T. Ho, "Social Influences on Evaluations of Psychological Contract Fulfillment," *Academy of Management Review* 30 (2005): 113–28.
117. Elizabeth W. Morrison and Sandra L. Robinson, "When Employees Feel Betrayed: A Model of How Psychological Contract Violation Develops," *Academy of Management Review* 22 (1997): 226–56.
118. Ho, "Social Influences."
119. Sandra L. Robinson, M. S. Kratz, and Denise M. Rousseau, "Changing Obligations and The Psychological Contract: A Longitudinal Perspective," *Academy of Management Journal* 37 (1994): 137–52; and Sandra L. Robinson and Denise M. Rousseau, "Violating the Psychological Contract: Not the Exception But the Norm," *Journal of Organizational Behavior* 16 (1994): 245–59.
120. Ellen M. Whitener, Susan E. Brodt, M. Audrey Koreguard, and Jon M. Weiner, "Managers as Initiators of Trust: An Exchange Relationship Framework for Understanding Managerial Trustworthy Behavior," *Academy of Management Review* 23 (1998): 513–39.

Chapter 5

1. C. Zatzick, M. Marks, and R. Iverson, "Which Way Should You Downsize in a Crisis?" *MIT Sloan Management Review* 51, no. 1 (2009): 79–86; and Jason A. Colquitt and Marcia J. Simmering, "Conscientiousness, Goal Orientation, and Motivation to Learn during the Learning Process: A Longitudinal Study," *Journal of Applied Psychology* 83 (1998): 654–65.
2. John P. Campbell, Marvin D. Dunnette, Edward E. Lawler III, and Karl E. Weick, *Managerial Behavior, Performance and Effectiveness* (New York: McGraw-Hill, 1970), p. 340.
3. M. A. Tietjen and R. M. Myers, "Motivation and Job Satisfaction," *Management Decision,* June 1998, pp. 226–32.
4. Dalbir Bindra, *Motivation: A Systematic Reinterpretation* (New York: Ronald Press, 1959).
5. Marchall R. Jones, ed., *Nebraska Symposium on Motivation* (Lincoln: University of Nebraska Press, 1955), p. 14.
6. "NCR History," NCR, accessed June 28, 2010, http://www.ncr.com/about_ncr/company_overview/history.jsp?lang=EN.
7. Mark Bernstein, "John Patterson Rang Up Success with the Incorruptible Cashier," *Smithsonian,* June 1989, pp. 150–66.
8. "Great Moments in Workstyle," *Inc.,* January 1986, pp. 52–53.
9. "George Pullman," *Pullman-Car.com,* accessed June 28, 2010, http://www.pullman-car.com/history/george_pullman.html.
10. Richard S. Allen, "Cross-Cultural Equity Sensitivity: A Test of Differences between the United States and Japan," *Journal of Managerial Psychology* 20, no. 8 (2005): 641–63; Shaker A. Zahra and Hugh M. O'Neill, "Charting the Landscape of Global Competition: Reflections on Emerging Organizational Challenges and Their Implications for Senior Executives," *Academy of Management Executive* (November 1998): 12–21; and Justine Di Cesare and Golnaz Sadri, "Do All Carrots Look the Same? Examining the Impact of Culture on Employee Motivation," *Management Research News* 26, no. 1 (2003), pp. 29–40.
11. Ralph E. Winter, "Lincoln Electric Positioned to Profit," *Wall Street Journal*, May 5, 2010, Eastern edition; and "About Us," Lincoln Electric, accessed May 5, 2010, http://www.lincolnelectric.com/corporate/about/about.asp.
12. George T. Milkovich and Jerry M. Newman, *Compensation,* 9th ed. (Burr Ridge, IL: McGraw-Hill/Irwin, 2008).
13. Richard M. Hodgetts, "A Conversation with Donald F. Hastings of the Lincoln Electric Company," *Organizational Dynamics* (Winter 1997): 68–74.
14. A. H. Maslow and A. R. Kaplan, *Maslow on Management* (New York: John Wiley, 1998).
15. Eilene Zimmerman, "How to Work More Hours and Still Go Home Early," *New York Times,* February 18, 2007, p. 3; and J. Usunier, *International and Cross-Cultural Management Research* (Thousand Oaks, CA: Sage, 1999).
16. Lyman W. Porter, "A Study of Perceived Need Satisfaction in Bottom and Middle Management Jobs," *Journal of Applied Psychology* 45 (1961): 1–10.
17. Lyman W. Porter, *Organizational Patterns of Managerial Job Attitudes* (New York: American Foundation for Management Research, 1964).
18. Lyman W. Porter, "Job Attitudes in Management: Perceived Deficiencies in Need Fulfillment as a Function of Size of the Company," *Journal of Applied Psychology* (December 1963): 386–97.

19. John M. Ivancevich, "Perceived Need Satisfactions of Domestic versus Overseas Managers," *Journal of Applied Psychology,* August 1969, pp. 274–78.
20. Edward E. Lawler III and J. L. Suttle, "A Causal Correlation Test of the Need Hierarchy Concept," *Organizational Behavior and Human Performance,* April 1972, pp. 265–87; Douglas T. Hall and K. E. Nougaim, "An Examination of Maslow's Need Hierarchy in an Organizational Setting," *Organizational Behavior and Human Performance* 3 (1968): 12–35; and Andrew Neher, "Maslow's Theory of Motivation: A Critique," *Journal of Humanistic Psychology* 31 (1991): 89–112.
21. Abraham H. Maslow, "Critique of Self-Actualization Theory," *Journal of Humanistic Education and Development* 29 (1991): 103–8.
22. Clayton P. Alderfer, *Existence, Relatedness, and Growth: Human Needs in Organizational Settings* (New York: Free Press, 1972).
23. Ann Tsui, Jane L. Pearce, Lyman W. Porter, and Angela M. Tripoli, "Alternative Approaches to the Employee–Organization Relationship: Does Investment In Employees Pay Off?" *Academy of Management Journal* 40 (1997): 1089–121.
24. Mark A. Griffin, Malcolm G. Patterson, and Michael A. West, "Job Satisfaction and Teamwork: The Role of Supervisor Support," *Journal of Organizational Behavior* 22 (2001): 537–50.
25. Clayton P. Alderfer, "A Critique of Salancik and Pfeffer's Examination of Need–Satisfaction Theories," *Administrative Science Quarterly* 22 (1977): 658–69.
26. Clayton P. Alderfer and Richard A. Guzzo, "Life Expectancies and Adults' Enduring Strength of Desires in Organizations," *Administrative Science Quarterly* 24 (1979): 347–61.
27. J. P. Wanous and A. Zwany, "A Cross-Sectional Test of Need Hierarchy Theory," *Organizational Behavior and Human Performance* 18 (1977): 78–97.
28. Jeremy B. Fox, K. Dow Scott, and Joan M. Donohue, "An Investigation into Pay Valence and Performance in a Pay-for-Performance Field Setting," *Journal of Organizational Behavior* 14 (1993): 687–93.
29. Frederick Herzberg, B. Mausner, and B. Synderman, *The Motivation to Work* (NewYork: John Wiley & Sons, 1959).
30. R. J. House and L. Wigdor, "Herzberg's Dual-Factor Theory of Job Satisfaction and Motivation: A Review of the Empirical Evidence and a Criticism," *Personnel Psychology* 20 (1967): 369–80; and J. Schneider and Edwin Locke, "A Critique of Herzberg's Classification System and a Suggested Revision," *Organizational Behavior and Human Performance* 6 (1971): 441–58.
31. Abraham K. Korman, *Industrial and Organizational Psychology* (Englewood Cliffs, NJ: Prentice-Hall, 1971), pp. 148–50.
32. Edward E. Lawler III, *Motivation in Work Organizations* (Monterey, CA: Brooks/Cole, 1973), p. 72.
33. Frank Giancola, "Herzberg's Theory Revisited," *Workspan* 48, no. 12 (2005): 68–69; Miriam Lacey, "Rewards Can Cost Nothing? Yes They Can . . . Really!" *Journal for Quality and Participation,* June 1994, pp. 6–8; and Don Merit, "What Really Motivates You?" *American Printer,* January 1995, p. 74.
34. In discussing motivation applications with numerous managers in Europe, the Pacific Rim, and Latin America, the Herzberg explanation is referred to more often than any other theory. Herzberg's writings and explanations have found their way into many countries.
35. Isaac O. Adigun and Geoffrey M. Stephenson, "Sources of Job Motivation and Satisfaction among British and Nigerian Employees," *Journal of Social Psychology* 132 (1992): 369–76.
36. David C. McClelland, "Business Drive and National Achievement," *Harvard Business Review,* July–August 1962, pp. 99–112.
37. R. Murray, *Thematic Apperception Test Pictures and Manual* (Cambridge, MA: Harvard University Press, 1943).
38. David C. McClelland, *Motivational Trends in Society* (Morristown, NJ: General Learning Press, 1971).
39. McClelland, "Business Drive." McClelland proposes that a society's economic growth is based on the level of need achievement inherent in its population.
40. David C. McClelland, "Toward a Theory of Motive Acquisition," *American Psychologist* 20 (1965): 321–33.
41. David C. McClelland and D. Burnham, "Power Is the Great Motivator," *Harvard Business Review,* March–April 1976, pp. 100–11.
42. W. V. Meyer, "Achievement Motive Research," in *Nebraska Symposium on Motivation,* ed. William J. Arnold (Lincoln: University of Nebraska Press, 1968).
43. Barbara Parker and Leonard H. Chusmir, "Development and Validation of a Life-Success Measures Scale," *Psychological Reports* 70 (1992): 627–37.
44. David C. McClelland, "Managing Motivation to Expand Human Freedom," *American Psychologist* 33 (1978): 201–10.
45. David C. McClelland, "Retrospective Commentary," *Harvard Business Review,* January–February 1995, pp. 138–39.
46. Bruce D. Kirkcaldy, Adrian Furnham, and Richard Lynn, "Individual Differences in Work Attitudes," *Personality and Individual Differences* 13, no. 1 (1992): 49–55.
47. U. J. Weirsma, "Gender Differences in Attribute Preferences: Work–Home Role Conflict and Job Level as Mediating Variables," *Journal of Occupational Psychology* 73 (1990): 231–43; and James E. Long, "The Effects of Tastes and Motivation on Individual Income," *Industrial and Labor Relations Review* 48 (1995): 338–51.

48. Ruth L. Jacobs and David C. McClelland, "Moving Up the Corporate Ladder: A Longitudinal Study of the Leadership Motive Pattern and Managerial Success in Women and Men," Special issue, "Issues in the Assessment of Managerial and Executive Leadership," *Consulting Psychology Journal Practice and Research* 46 (1994): 32–41.
49. William D. Spangler, "Validity of Questionnaire and TAT Measures of Need for Achievement: Two Meta-Analyses," *Psychological Bulletin* 112 (1992): 140–54.
50. P. D. Machungiva and N. Schmitt, "Work Motivation in a Developing Country," *Journal of Applied Psychology* 68 (1983): 31–42.
51. McClelland, "Business Drive."
52. See PepsiCo, accessed May 5, 2010, www.pepsico.com; Patricia Sellers, "It's Good to Be the Boss," *Fortune,* October 16, 2006, p. 134; and Dawn Anfuso, "PepsiCo Shares Power and Wealth with Workers," *Personnel Journal,* June 1995, pp. 42–49.
53. Ken C. Snead and Adrian M. Harrell, "An Application of Expectancy Theory to Explain a Manager's Intention to Use a Decision Support System," *Decision Sciences* 25 (1994): 499–513; Cynthia Lee and P. Christopher Earley, "Comparative Peer Evaluations of Organizational Behavior Theories," *Organization Development Journal* 10 (1992): 37–42; David A. Nadler and Edward E. Lawler III, "Motivation: A Diagnostic Approach," in *Perspectives on Behavior in Organizations,* ed. J. Richard Hackman, Edward E. Lawler III, and Lyman W. Porter (New York: McGraw-Hill, 1977), pp. 26–38; Edwin A. Locke, "Personnel Attitudes and Motivation," *Annual Review of Psychology* 26 (1973): 457–80; and Victor H. Vroom, *Work and Motivation* (New York: John Wiley & Sons, 1964).
54. Jeremy B. Fox, K. Dow Scott, and Joan M. Donohue, "An Investigation into Pay Valence and Performance in a Pay-for-Performance Field Setting," *Journal of Organizational Behavior* 14 (1993): 687–93.
55. Dennis W. Organ and Thomas S. Bateman, *Organizational Behavior: An Applied Psychological Approach* (Plano, TX: Business Publications, 1986).
56. Robert D. Pritchard and P. J. DeLeo, "Experimental Test of the Valence–Instrumentality Relationships in Job Performance," *Journal of Applied Psychology* 57, no. 3 (1973): 264–79.
57. H. Garland, "Relation of Effort–Performance Expectancy to Performance in Goal Setting Experiences," *Journal of Applied Psychology* 68 (1984): 79–84.
58. John P. Campbell and Robert D. Pritchard, "Motivation Theory in Industrial and Organizational Psychology," in *Handbook of Industrial and Organizational Psychology,* ed. Marvin D. Dunnette (Skokie, IL: Rand McNally, 1976), pp. 84–95.
59. Carol J. Loomis, "Mr. Lipp Has a Little List," *Fortune,* January 11, 1999, pp. 86–88; and Robert Isaac, Wilfred J. Zerbe, and Douglas C. Pitt, "Leadership and Motivation: The Effective Application of Expectancy Theory," *Journal of Managerial Issues* 13, no. 2 (2001): 212–26.
60. James A. Shepperd, "Productivity Loss in Performance Groups: A Motivation Analysis," *Psychological Bulletin* 113 (1993): 67–81.
61. Mary Jo Ducharme, Parbudyal Singh, and Mark Podolsky, "Exploring the Links between Performance Appraisals and Pay Satisfaction," *Compensation and Benefits Review* 37, no. 5 (2005): 46–53; and Marco Lauriola and Irwin P. Levin, "Relating Individual Differences in Attitude toward Ambiguity to Risky Choices," *Behavioral Decision Making* 14 (2001): 107–22.
62. Piers Steel and Cornelius J. Konig, "Integrating Theories of Motivation," *Academy of Management Review* 31, no. 4 (2006): 889–913; and Nora Wood, "What Motivates Best?" *Sales & Marketing Management,* September 1998, pp. 70–78.
63. Catherine H. Tinsley and Jeannie M. Brett, "Managing Workplace Conflict in The United States and Hong Kong," *Organizational Behavior and Human Decision Processes* 85 (2001): 360–81.
64. Jeffrey Pfeffer, "Producing Sustainable Competitive Advantage through the Effective Management of People," *Academy of Management Executive* 9 (1995): 55–69.
65. J. Stacey Adams, "Toward an Understanding of Equity," *Journal of Abnormal and Social Psychology* (November 1963): 422–36.
66. Richard C. Husemann, John D. Hatfield, and Edward W. Miles, "A New Perspective on Equity Theory: The Equity Sensitivity Construct," *Academy of Management Review,* 12 (1987): 222–34; and Chao C. Chen, Jaepil Choi, and Shu-Cheng Chi, "Making Justice Sense of Local-Expatriate Compensation Disparity: Mitigation by Local Referents, Ideological Explanations, and Interpersonal Sensitivity in China-Foreign Joint Ventures," *Academy of Management Journal* 45, no. 4 (2002): 807–17.
67. Jerald Greenberg, "Setting the Justice Agenda: Seven Unanswered Questions about What, Why, and How," *Journal of Vocational Behavior* 58 (2001): 210–19.
68. Jason A. Colquitt, "On the Dimensionality of Organizational Justice: A Construct Validation of a Measure," *Journal of Applied Psychology* 86, no. 3 (2001): 386–400.
69. J. Harris, "What's Wrong with Executive Compensation?" *Journal of Business Ethics: Supplement* 85 (2009): 147–56.
70. M. Lecker, "The Smoking Penalty: Distributive Justice or Smokism?" *Journal of Business Ethics Supplement* 84 (2009): 47–64; H. Moon, D. Kamdar, D. Mayer, and R. Takeuchi, "Me or We? The Role of Personality and Justice As Other-centered Antecedents to Innovative

Citizenship Behaviors Within Organizations," *Journal of Applied Psychology* 93, no. 1 (2008): 84–94; Maureen L. Ambrose and Russell Cropanzano, "A Longitudinal Analysis of Organizational Fairness: An Examination of Reactions to Tenure and Promotion Decisions," *Journal of Applied Psychology* 88, no. 2 (2003): 266–75; Margaret L. Williams, Stanley B. Malos, and David K. Palmer, "Benefit System and Benefit Level Satisfaction: An Expanded Model of Antecedents and Consequences," *Journal of Management* 28, no. 2 (2002): 195–215; Orlando C. Richard, Edward C. Taylor, Tim Barnett, and Mary Frances Nesbit, "Procedural Voice and Distributive Justice: Their Influence on Mentoring Career Help and Other Outcomes," *Journal of Business Research* 55, no. 9 (2002): 725–39; and Martha C. Andrews and K. Michele Kacmar, "Discrimination among Organizational Politics, Justice, and Support," *Journal of Organizational Behavior* 22, no. 4 (2001): 347–59.

71. Ambrose and Cropanzano, "A Longitudinal Analysis of Organizational Fairness."
72. C. Zapata-Phelan, J. Colquitt, B. Scott, and B. Livingston, "Procedural Justice, Interactional Justice, and Task Performance: The Mediating Role of Intrinsic Motivation," *Organizational Behavior and Human Decision Processes* 108, no. 1 (2009): 93–105; Joerg Dietz, Sandra L. Robinson, Robert Folger, Robert A. Baron, and Martin Schultz, "The Impact of Community Violence and an Organization's Procedural Justice Climate on Workplace Aggression," *Academy of Management Journal* 46, no. (2003): 317–26; Maureen L. Ambrose and Marshall Schminke, "Organization Structure as a Moderator of the Relationship Between Procedural Justice, Interactional Justice, Perceived Organizational Support, and Supervisory Trust," *Journal of Applied Psychology* 88, no. 2 (2003): 295–305; and Daniel P. Skarlicki, and Robert Folger, "Retaliation in the Workplace: Roles of Distributive, Procedural, and Interactional Justice," *Journal of Applied Psychology* 82, no. 3 (1997): 434–443.
73. John M. Ivancevich, Robert Konopaske, and Michael T. Matteson, *Organizational Behavior and Management*, 9th ed. (New York: McGraw-Hill, 2011).
74. Stafanie E. Naumann and Nathan Bennett, "A Case for Procedural Justice Climate: Development and Test of a Multilevel Model," *Academy of Management Journal* 43, no. 5 (2000): 881–889.
75. R. J. Bies and J. F. Moag, "Interactional Justice: Communication Criteria of Fairness," in *Research on Negotiations in Organizations*, ed. R. J. Lewicki, B. H. Sheppard, and M. H. Bazerman (Greenwich, CT: JAI Press, 1986); and J. Greenberg, "The Social Side of Fairness: Interpersonal and Informational Classes of Organizational Justice," in *Justice in the Workplace: Approaching Fairness in Human Resource Management*, ed. R. Cropanzano (Hillsdale, NJ: Erlbaum, 1993).
76. R. J. Bies, "Interactional (In)justice: The Sacred and the Profane," in *Advances in Organizational Justice,* ed. J. Greenberg and R. Cropanzano (Stanford, CA: Stanford University Press, 2001).
77. Bill Leonard, "Study: Bully Bosses Prevalent in U.S.," *HR Magazine,* May 2007, pp. 22–24.
78. Rita Zeidner, "Bullying Worse Than Sexual Harassment?" *HR Magazine,* May 2008, pp. 28–29.
79. Bennett J. Tepper, "Consequences of Abusive Supervision," *Academy of Management Journal* 43, no. 2 (2000): 178–190.
80. Bies and Moag, "Interactional Justice"; and Greenberg, "The Social Side of Fairness."
81. P. S. Goodman and A. Friedman, "An Examination of Adam's Theory of Inequity," *Administrative Science Quarterly* 16 (1971): 271–88; and Linda S. Perry, "Effects of Inequity on Job Satisfaction and Self-Evaluation in a National Sample of African-American Workers," *Journal of Social Psychology,* August 1993, pp. 565–73.
82. Jerald Greenberg, "Equity and Workplace Status: A Field Experiment," *Journal of Applied Psychology* 73 (1988): 606–13.
83. Chera L. Haworth and Paul E. Levy, "The Importance of Instrumentality Beliefs in the Prediction of Organizational Citizenship Behaviors," *Journal of Vocational Behavior* 59 (2001): 64–75.
84. Christina L. Stamper and Linn Van Dyne, "Work Status and Organizational Citizenship Behavior: A Field Study of Restaurant Behavior," *Journal of Organizational Behavior* 22 (2001): 517–36.
85. Edwin A. Locke, "The Nature and Causes of Job Satisfaction," in *Handbook of Industrial and Organizational Psychology,* ed. Marvin D. Dunnette, (Skokie, IL: Rand McNally, 1976), pp. 1297–349.
86. Robert Vecchio, "Predicting Worker Performance in Inequitable Settings," *Academy of Management Review* 7 (1982): 103–10.
87. Richard A. Cosier and Daniel R. Dalton, "Equity Theory and Time: A Reformulation," *Academy of Management Review* 8 (1983): 311–19.
88. Robert Folger, "Reformulating the Preconditions of Resentment: A Referent Cognitions Model," in *Social Comparison, Justice, and Relative Deprivation: Theoretical, Empirical, and Policy Perspectives,* ed. John C. Masters and William P. Smith (Hillsdale, NJ: Erlbaum & Associates, 1987), pp. 153–215.
89. Russell Cropanzano and Robert Folger, "Referent Cognitions and Task Division Autonomy: Beyond Equity Theory," *Journal of Applied Psychology* 74 (1989): 293–99.
90. L. A. Witt, K. Michele Kacmar, and Martha C. Andrews, "The Interactive Effects of Procedural Justice and Exchange Ideology on Supervisor-Rated Commitment," *Journal of Organizational Behavior* 22 (2001): 505–15.

91. For a complete analysis, see E. A. Locke and G. P. Latham, *A Theory of Goal Setting and Task Performance* (Englewood Cliff, NJ: Prentice-Hall, 1990).

Chapter 6

1. Eric de Nijs, "GRACE at Work," *T + D,* March 2006, pp. 47–51; Charlotte Garvey, "The Whirlwind of a New Job," *HR Magazine,* June 2001, pp. 110–18; and Edward E. Lawler III, "What It Means to Treat People Right," *Ivey Business Journal* 68, no. 2 (2003): 1–7.
2. Albert Bandura, *Social Learning Theory* (Englewood Cliffs, NJ: Prentice-Hall, 1977), p. vii.
3. Robert Wood and Albert Bandura, "Social Cognitive Theory of Organizational Management," *Academy of Management Review* 14 (1989): 361–84.
4. For an excellent and concise discussion of social learning theory as applied to organizations, see Robert Kreitner and Fred Luthans, "A Social Learning Approach to Behavioral Management: Radical Behaviorists 'Mellowing Out,'" *Organizational Dynamics* 13 (1984): 47–65.
5. Albert Bandura, "Self-Efficacy: Toward a Unifying Theory of Behavioral Change," *Psychological Review* 83 (1977): 191–215.
6. Narda R. Quigley, Paul E. Tesluk, Edwin A. Locke, and Kathryn M. Bartol, "A Multilevel Investigation of the Motivational Mechanisms Underlying Knowledge Sharing and Performance," *Organization Science* 18, no. 1 (2007): 71–92; Nancy G. Boyd and George S. Vozikis, "The Influence of Self-Efficacy on the Development of Entrepreneurial Intentions and Actions," *Entrepreneurship: Theory and Practice* 18 (1994): 63–77; Tracy McDonald and Marc Siegall, "The Effects of Technological Self-Efficacy and Job Focus on Job Performance, Attitudes, and Withdrawal Behaviors," *Journal of Psychology* 126 (1992): 465–75; and Golnaz Sadri and Ivan T.Robertson, "Self-Efficacy and Work-Related Behaviour: A Review and Meta-Analysis," *Applied Psychology: An International Review* 42 (1993): 139–52.
7. Edwin A. Locke, E. Frederick, Cynthia Lee, and Philip Bobko, "The Effect of Self-Efficacy, Goals, and Task Strategies on Task Performance," *Journal of Applied Psychology* 69 (1984): 241–51.
8. Jia Lin Xie, Jean-Paul Roy, and Ziguang Chen, "Cultural and Individual Differences in Self-rating Behavior: An Extension and Refinement of the Cultural Relativity Hypothesis," *Journal of Organizational Behavior* 27, no. 3 (2006): 341–64; P. Christopher Earley, "Self or Group? Cultural Effects of Training on Self-Efficacy and Performance," *Administrative Science Quarterly* 39 (1994): 89–117; and Simon S. K. Lam, Xiao-Ping Chen, and John Schaubroeck, "Participative Decision Making and Employee Performance in Different Cultures: The Moderating Effects of Allocentrism/Idiocetrism and Efficacy," *Academy of Management Journal* 45, no. 5 (2002): 905–15.
9. Dov Eden, "Leadership and Expectations: Pygmalion Effects and Other Self-Fulfilling Prophecies in Organizations," *Leadership Quarterly* 3 (1992): 271–305; Marilyn E. Gist, "Self-Efficacy: Implications in Organizational Behavior and Human Resource Management," *Academy of Management Review* 12 (1987): 472–85; Paul Loftus, "Expect Yourself," *Canadian Banker,* January–February 1995, pp. 31–33; and Matt Oechsli, "Pygmalion Revisited," *Managers Magazine,* March 1994, pp. 16–21.
10. Xander M. Bezuijen, Peter T. van den Berg, Karen van Dam, and Henk Thierry, "Pygmalion and Employee Learning: The Role of Leader Behaviors," *Journal of Management* 35, no. 5 (2009): 1248–67.
11. Taly Dvir, Dov Eden, and Michal L. Banjo, "Self-Fulfilling Prophecy and Gender: Can Women Be Pygmalion and Galatea?" *Journal of Applied Psychology* 80 (1995): 253–70.
12. Alexander D. Stajkovic and Fred Luthans, "Differential Effects of Incentive Motivators on Work Performance," *Academy of Management Journal* 44 (2001): 580–90.
13. B. F. Skinner, "Whatever Happened to Psychology and the Science of Behavior," *American Psychologist* 42 (1987): 780–86.
14. Fred Luthans, *Organizational Behavior* (Burr Ridge, IL: McGraw-Hill, 2006), pp. 145–49.
15. Ibid.
16. Fred Luthans and Alexander Stajkovic, "Provide Recognition for Performance Improvement," in *Principles of Organizational Behavior,* ed. E. A. Locke (Oxford: Blackwell, 2000), pp. 166–80.
17. Todd Henneman, "What's the Payoff?" *Workforce Management* 84, no. 10 (2005): 41–47; Sara L. Rynes and B. Gerhart, *Compensation in Organizations: Progress and Prospect* (San Francisco: New Lexington Press, 1999); and Jeanie Casison, "The Future Looks Bright," *Incentive* 177, no. 2 (2003): 36–38.
18. Scott A Jeffrey and Victoria Shaffer, "The Motivational Properties of Tangible Incentives," *Compensation and Benefits Review* 39, no. 3 (2007): 44–50.
19. "Our Credo Values," Johnson & Johnson, accessed May 12, 2010, http://www.jnj.com/connect/about-jnj/jnj-credo/?flash=true.
20. P. Whitaker, "What Non-financial Rewards Are Successful Motivators?" *Strategic HR Review* 9, no. 1 (2010): 43–50; Malia Boyd, "Motivating on a Dime," *Performance,* March 1995, pp. 62–65; David Packard, *The HP Way: How Bill Hewlett and I Built Our Company* (New York: HarperBusiness, 1995), and Katherine Sherbrooke, "The Gift of Time," *Executive Excellence* 19, no. 3 (2002): 12–13.
21. Lanse Minkler, "Shirking and Motivations in Firms: Survey Evidence on Worker Attitudes," *International*

Journal of Industrial Organization 22, no. 6 (2004): 863–92; and Shelly Branch, "You Hired 'Em, But Can You Keep 'Em?" *Fortune,* November 9, 1998, pp. 247–50.

22. Barrie E. Litzky, Kimberly A. Eddleston, and Deborah L. Kidder, "The Good, the Bad, and the Misguided: How Managers Inadvertently Encourage Deviant Behaviors," *Academy of Management Perspectives* 20, no. 1 (2006): 91–103; and Linda Klebe Trevino, "The Social Effects of Punishment in Organizations: A Justice Perspective," *Academy of Management Review* 17 (1992): 647–76.
23. Edward L. Thorndike, *Animal Intelligence* (New York: Macmillan, 1911), p. 244.
24. Alexander D. Stajkovic and Fred Luthans, "A Meta-Analysis of the Effects of Organizational Behavior Modification on Task Performance, 1975–1995," *Academy of Management Journal* 40 (1997): 1122–49.
25. Luthans, *Organizational Behavior.*
26. Alexander D. Stajkovic and S. Sommer, "Self-Efficacy and Causal Attributions," *Journal of Applied Social Psychology* 30 (2000): 707–37.
27. Thomas K. Connellan, *How to Improve Human Performance: Behaviorism in Business and Industry* (New York: Harper & Row, 1978), pp. 48–75.
28. Luthans, *Organizational Behavior.*
29. Connellan, *How to Improve Human Performance,* p. 51.
30. K. Cravens, E. Oliver, and J. Stewart, "Can a Positive Approach to Performance Evaluation Help Accomplish Your Goals?" *Business Horizons* 53, no. 3 (2010): 269–279.
31. P. Nick Blanchard and James W. Thacker, *Effective Training* (Englewood Cliffs, NJ: Prentice Hall, 1999), pp. 253–54; and Robert D. Behn, "Why Measure Performance? Different Purposes Require Different Measures," *Public Administration Review* 63, no. 5 (2003): 586–606.
32. Luthans and Stajkovic, "Provide Recognition for Performance Improvement."
33. Edwin A. Locke, "The Motivation to Work: What We Know," in *Advances in Motivation and Achievement,* ed. M. M. Maehr and P. R. Pintrich (Greenwich, CT: JAI Press, 2002), pp. 375–412.
34. David J. Cherrington, "Follow Through on Award Programs," *HR Magazine,* April 1992, pp. 52–55.
35. Erin White, "Age Is as Age Does: Making the Generation Gap Work for You," *Wall Street Journal,* June 30, 2008 , p. B6, Eastern edition.
36. Dianne H. B. Welsh, Fred Luthans, and Steven M. Sommer, "Managing Russian Factory Workers: The Impact of U.S.-Based Behavioral and Participative Techniques," *Academy of Management Journal* 36 (1993): 58–79.
37. T. Sitzmann and K. Ely, "Sometimes You Need a Reminder: The Effects of Prompting Self-regulation on Regulatory Processes, Learning, and Attrition," *Journal of Applied Psychology* 95, no. 1 (2010): 132–144; Babette Raabe, Michael Frese, and Terry A. Beehr, "Action Regulation Theory and Career Self-Management," *Journal of Vocational Behavior* 70, no. 2 (2007): 297–311; Stajkovic and Sommer, "Self-Efficacy"; and Harry Levinson, "Management by Whose Objectives?" *Harvard Business Review,* January 2003, pp. 107–22.
38. C. E. Thoreson and Michael J. Mahoney, *Behavioral Self-Control* (New York: Holt, Rinehart & Winston, 1974), p. 12.
39. X. Zhang and K. Bartol, "Linking Empowering Leadership and Employee Creativity: The Influence of Psychological Empowerment, Intrinsic Motivation, and Creative Process Engagement," *Academy of Management Journal* 53, no. 1 (2010): 107–28; Abhishek Srivastava, Kathryn M. Bartol, and Edwin A. Locke, "Empowering Leadership in Management Teams: Effects on Knowledge Sharing, Efficacy, and Performance," *Academy of Management Journal* 49, no. 6 (2006): 1239–51; and Robert C. Ford and Myron D. Fottler, "Empowerment: A Matter of Degree," *Academy of Management Executive* 9, no. 3 (1995): 21–29.
40. Charles C. Manz, "Self-Leadership: Toward an Expanded Theory of Self-Influence Processes in Organizations," *Academy of Management Review* 11 (1986): 585–600.
41. Colette A. Frayne and J. Michael Geringer, "A Social Cognitive Approach to Examining Joint Venture General Manager Performance," *Group and Organization Management* 6 (1994): 240–62.
42. Frederick H. Kanfer, "Self-Management Methods," in *Helping People Change: A Textbook of Methods,* ed. Frederick H. Kanfer and Arnold P. Goldstein (New York: Pergamon, 1980), p. 339.
43. Edwin A. Locke, "Toward a Theory of Task Motivation and Incentives," *Organizational Behavior and Human Performance,* May 1968, pp. 157–89.
44. Thomas A. Ryan, *Intentional Behavior* (New York: Ronald Press, 1970), p. 95.
45. Mark E. Tubbs and Steven E. Ekeberg, "The Role of Intentions in Work Motivation: Implications for Goal-Setting Theory and Research," *Academy of Management Review* 16 (1991): 180–99.
46. Debra Steele Johnson, Russell S. Beauregard, Paul B. Hoover, and Aaron M. Schmidt, "Goal Orientation and Task Demand Effects on Motivation, Affect, and Performance," *Journal of Applied Psychology* 85 (2000): 724–38.
47. Frederick W. Taylor, *The Principles of Scientific Management* (New York: W. W. Norton, 1947).
48. Edwin A. Locke, K. N. Shaw, L. M. Saari, and Gary P. Latham, "Goal Setting and Task Performance: 1969–1980," *Psychological Bulletin* 90 (1981): 129.

49. Edwin A. Locke, "The Ubiquity of the Technique of Goal Setting in Theories of and Approaches to Employee Motivation," *Academy of Management Review* 3 (1978): 600.
50. Anthony J. Mento, Robert P. Steel, and Ronald J. Karren, "A Meta-Analytic Study of the Effects of Goal Setting on Task Performance: 1966–1984," *Organizational Behavior and Human Decision Processes* 39 (1987): 53.
51. Locke, "Task Motivation and Incentives."
52. For a complete analysis, see Locke et al., "Goal Setting."
53. Ibid.
54. Gary P. Latham and J. J. Baldes, "The Practical Significance of Locke's Theory of Goal Setting," *Journal of Applied Psychology* 60 (1975): 122–24.
55. Ibid, p. 124.
56. S. L. Fisher and J. K. Ford, "Differential Effects of Learner Effort and Goal Orientation on Two Learning Outcomes," *Personnel Psychology* 51 (1998): 397–420; and Anat Drach-Zahavy and Miriam Erez, "Challenge versus Threat Effects on the Goal-Performance Relationship," *Organizational Behavior and Human Decision Processes* 88, no. 2 (2002): 667–82.
57. A. Zander and T. T. Newcomb, "Goal Levels of Aspirations in United Fund Campaigns," *Journal of Personality and Social Psychology* 6 (1967): 157–62.
58. Ibid.
59. Miriam Erez, P. Christopher Earley, and Charles L. Hulin, "The Impact of Participation on Goal Acceptance and Performance: A Two-Step Model," *Academy of Management Journal* 28 (1985): 50–66. See also Miriam Erez and Frederick H. Kanfer, "The Role of Goal Acceptance in Goal Setting and Task Performance," *Academy of Management Review* 8 (1983): 454–63.
60. Edwin A. Locke and Gary P. Latham, *Goal Setting: A Motivational Technique That Works* (Englewood Cliffs, NJ: Prentice-Hall, 1984), p. 22.
61. Gary P. Latham, Miriam Erez, and Edwin A. Locke, "Resolving Scientific Disputes by the Joint Design of Crucial Experiments by the Antagonists: Application to the Erez–Latham Dispute regarding Participation in Goal Setting," *Journal of Applied Psychology* 73 (1988): 753–72.
62. Edwin A. Locke, ed., *Generalizing from Laboratory to Field Settings* (Lexington, MA: Lexington Books, 1986).
63. John M. Ivancevich and J. Timothy McMahon, "Education as a Moderator of Goal-Setting Effectiveness," *Journal of Vocational Behavior* 11 (1977): 83–94.
64. Gary P. Latham and Gary A. Yukl, "Assigned versus Participative Goal Setting with Educated and Uneducated Wood Workers," *Journal of Applied Psychology* 60 (1975): 299–302.
65. Miriam Erez and R. Arad, "Participative Goal Setting: Social, Motivational, and Cognitive Factors," *Journal of Applied Psychology* 71 (1986): 591–97.
66. Edwin A. Locke, Ken G. Smith, Miriam Erez, Dong-Ok Chah, and Adam Schaffer, "The Effects of Intra-Individual Goal Conflict on Performance," *Journal of Management,* 20 (1994): 67–91.
67. L. Ordóñez, M. Schweitzer, A. Galinsky, and M. Bazerman, "Goals Gone Wild: The Systematic Side Effects of Overprescribing Goal Setting," *Academy of Management Perspectives* 23, no. 1 (2009): 6.
68. A. Barsky, "Understanding the Ethical Cost of Organizational Goal-Setting: A Review and Theory Development," *Journal of Business Ethics* 81, no. 1 (2008): 63–81.
69. Ibid.
70. Frank J. Landy and W. S. Becker, "Motivation Theory Reconsidered," in *Research in Organizational Behavior,* ed. Larry L. Cummings and B. M. Stewart (Greenwich, CT: JAI Press, 1987), p. 33.
71. George T. Milkovich and Jerry M. Newman, *Compensation,* 9th ed. (Burr Ridge, IL: McGraw-Hill, 2007).
72. Ibid.
73. Edward E. Lawler III, "Reward Systems," in *Improving Life at Work,* ed. J. Richard Hackman and J. L. Suttle (Santa Monica, CA: Goodyear, 1977), pp. 163–226.
74. Christine Avery and Diane Zabel, *The Flexible Workplace: A Sourcebook of Information and Research* (Westport, CT: Quorum, 2001).
75. Richard B. McKenzie and Dwight R. Lee, *Managing through Incentives* (New York: Oxford University Press, 1998).
76. Scott A. Jeffrey and Victoria Shaffer, "The Motivational Properties of Tangible Incentives," *Compensation and Benefits Review* 39, no. 3 (2007): 44–51; and Kenneth W. Thomas, "Intrinsic Motivation and How It Works," *Training,* October 2000, pp. 130–35.
77. R. L. Opsahl and Marvin D. Dunnette, "The Role of Financial Compensation in Industrial Motivation," *Psychological Bulletin* 66 (1966): 114.
78. J. Shields, D. Scott, R. Sperling, and T. Higgins, "Rewards Communication in Australia and the United States: A Survey of Policies and Programs," *Compensation and Benefits Review* 41, no. 6 (2009): 14–26; Duncan Brown and John Purcell, "Reward Management: On the Line," *Compensation and Benefits Review* 39, no. 3 (2007): 28–35; and Geoffrey Colvin, "The Great CEO Pay Heist," *Fortune,* June 25, 2001, pp. 64–70.
79. Carol J. Loomis, "This Stuff Is Wrong," *Fortune,* June 25, 2001, pp. 73–84.
80. For a discussion, see: S. Kaplan, "Are U.S. CEOs Overpaid?" *Academy of Management Perspectives* 22, no. 2 (2008): 5–20; and J. Walsh, "Are U.S. CEOs

Overpaid? A Partial Response to Kaplan," *Academy of Management Perspectives* 23, no. 1 (2009): 73–75.

81. Douglas M. Cowherd and David I. Levine, "Product Quality and Pay Equity between Lower-Level Employees and Top Management: An Investigation of Distributive Justice," *Administrative Science Quarterly* 37 (1992): 302–20.
82. Darrell A. Hughes, Aparajita Saha-Bubna, and Michael R. Crittenden, " Feinberg Caps Pay at AIG, Others," *WSJ.com,* March 24, 2010, retrieved July 3, 2010 from ABI/INFORM Global.
83. Edward E. Lawler, *Rewarding Excellence* (San Francisco: Jossey-Bass, 2000).
84. Steven Berglas, "How to Keep A Players Productive," *Harvard Business Review,* September 2006, pp. 104–14; and Barbara Mackoff and Gary Wenetz, *The Inner Work of Leaders: Leadership as a Habit of Mind* (New York: Amacom, 2001).
85. David C. McClelland, *The Achieving Society* (New York: Van Nostrand Reinhold, 1961).
86. K. Thomas, "The Four Intrinsic Rewards that Drive Employee Engagement," *Ivey Business Journal Online* 2009, http://wpstage.iveybusinessjournal.com/author/kthomas, retrieved May 13, 2010 from ABI/INFORM Global; and Charles C. Manz and Henry P. Sims, *The New Superleadership: Leading Others to Lead Themselves* (San Francisco: Beirett-Koehler, 2001).
87. Sanford E. DeVoe and Sheena S. Iyengar, "Managers' Theories of Subordinates: A Cross-Cultural Examination of Manager Perceptions of Motivation and Appraisal of Performance," *Organizational Behavior and Human Decision Processes* 93, no. 1 (2004): 47–61; and Xu Huang and Evert Van De Vliert, "Where Intrinsic Job Satisfaction Fails to Work: National Moderators of Intrinsic Motivation," *Journal of Organizational Behavior* 24, no. 2 (2003): 159–79.
88. Edward L. Deci, "The Effects of Externally Mediated Rewards on Intrinsic Motivation," *Journal of Personality and Social Psychology* 31 (1971): 105–15. See also Edward L. Deci, *Intrinsic Motivation* (New York: Plenum, 1975); and Gardiner Morse, "Why We Misread Motives," *Harvard Business Review,* January 2003, p. 18.
89. Barry M. Staw, *Intrinsic and Extrinsic Motivation* (Morristown, NJ: General Learning Press, 1975).
90. Barry M. Staw, "The Attitudinal and Behavioral Consequences of Changing a Major Organizational Reward," *Journal of Personality and Social Psychology* 6 (1974): 742–51; and Edward L. Deci, Richard Koestner, and Richard M. Ryan. "A Meta-Analytic Review of Experiments Examining the Effects of Extrinsic Rewards on Intrinsic Motivation," *Psychological Bulletin* 125, no. 6 (1999): 627–68.
91. Cynthia D. Fisher, "The Effects of Personal Control, Competence, and Extrinsic Reward Systems on Intrinsic Motivation," *Organizational Behavior and Human Performance* 21 (1978): 273–87. See also James S. Phillips and Robert G. Lord, "Determinants of Intrinsic Motivation: Locus of Control and Competence Information as Components of Deci's Cognitive Evaluation Theory," *Journal of Applied Psychology* 65 (1980): 211–18.
92. K. B. Boone and Larry L. Cummings, "Cognitive Evaluation Theory: An Experimental Test of Processes and Outcomes," *Organizational Behavior and Human Performance* 28 (1981): 289–310.
93. Michael Zwell, *Creating a Culture of Competence* (New York: John Wiley, 2000).
94. J. Segal, "Encouraging Absenteeism," *HR Magazine,* October 2008, pp. 103–4: Fred F. Easton and John C. Goodale, "Schedule Recovery: Unplanned Absences in Service Operations," *Decision Sciences* 36, no. 3 (2005): 459–88; and Vivian C. S. Lau, Wing Tung Au, and Jane M. C. Ho, "A Qualitative and Quantitative Review of Antecedents of Counterproductive Behavior in Organizations," *Journal of Business and Psychology* 18, no. 1 (2003): 73–99.
95. Sean Nicholson, Mark V. Pauly, Daniel Polsky, Catherine M. Baase, Gary M. Billotti, Ronald J. Ozminkowski, Marc L. Berger, and Clair E. Sharda, "How to Present the Business Case for Healthcare Quality to Employers," *Applied Health Economics and Health Policy* 4, no. 4 (2005): 209–18.
96. G. Johns, "Presenteeism in the Workplace: A Review and Research Agenda," *Journal of Organizational Behavior* 31, no. 4 (2010): 519–42; D. Baker-McClearn, K. Greasley, J. Dale, and F. Griffith, "Absence Management and Presenteeism: The Pressures on Employees to Attend Work and the Impact of Attendance on Performance," *Human Resource Management Journal* 20, no. 3 (2010): 311–32; Paul Hemp, "Presenteeism: At Work—But Out of It," *Harvard Business* Review, October 2004, pp. 49–58.
97. Ibid.
98. Kibeon Lee, Julie J. Carswell, and Natalie J. Allen, "A Meta-Analytic Review of Occupational Commitment: Relations with Person and Work-Related Variables, *Journal of Applied Psychology* 85 (October 2000): 799–811.
99. Ibid.
100. N. Malhotra, P. Budhwar, and P. Prowse, "Linking Rewards to Commitment: An Empirical Investigation of Four UK Call Centres," *The International Journal of Human Resource Management* 18, no. 12 (2007): 2095–127; J. P. Meyer, N. J. Allen, and L. Topolnytsky, "Commitment in a Changing World of Work," *Canadian Psychology,* February 1998, pp. 83–93.
101. Jenny Keefe, "Flexible Benefits: Beat Challenges of Implementation," *Employee Benefits,* October 2008, p. S5.

102. Tom Washington, "Flexible Benefits: Compelling Evidence," *Employee Benefits,* September 2009, p. S10.
103. Paul Stephens, "Flex Plans Gain in Popularity," *CA Magazine,* January/February 2010, p. 10.
104. "Benefits," Google, accessed May 13, 2010, http://www.google.com/intl/en/jobs/lifeatgoogle/benefits/.
105. Victoria E. Knight, "There's Still Time to Spend '08 Flex-Account Money," *Wall Street Journal,* January 21, 2009, p. B8; and Sarah Rubenstein, "Buying Health Insurance, Cafeteria Style; Some Employers Offer a Menu of Deductibles, Co-Payments, Networks and Prescription Plans," *Wall Street Journal,* October 19, 2004, p. D4.
106. Lawler, "Reward Systems," p. 182.
107. Richard Long, "Paying for Knowledge: Does It Pay?" *Canadian HR Reporter* 18, no. 6 (2005): 12–14; and David B. Balkin, Gideon D. Markman, and Luis R. Gomez-Mejia, "Is CEO Pay in High-Technology Firms Related to Innovation?" *Academy of Management Journal* 43 (2000): 1118–29.
108. H. L. Tosi, S. Werner, J. Katz, and L. R. Gomez-Mejia, "How Much Does Performance Matter: A Meta-Analysis of CEO Compensation Studies," *Journal of Management* 26 (2000): 301–39.
109. Erich C. Dierdoff and Eric A. Surface, "If You Pay for Skills, Will They Learn? Skill Change and Maintenance Under a Skill-Based Pay System," *Journal of Management* 34, no. 4 (2008): 721–43.
110. Mark R. Forehand, "Extending Overjustification: The Effect of Perceived Reward-Giver Intention," *Journal of Applied Psychology* 85 (2000): 919–31.
111. C. James Novak, "Proceed with Caution When Paying Teams," *HR Magazine,* April 1997, pp. 73–77.
112. Glenn Parker, Jerry McAdams, and David Zielinski, *Reward Teams: Lessons from the Trenches* (San Francisco: Jossey-Bass, 2000).
113. Ibid.
114. Jeffrey B. Arthur and Christopher L. Huntley, "Ramping Up the Organizational Learning Curve: Assessing the Impact of Deliberate Learning on Organizational Performance under Gainsharing," *Academy of Management Journal* 48, no. 6 (2005): 1159–70; David Beck, "Implementing a Gainsharing Plan: What Companies Need to Know," *Compensation and Benefits Review* 24 (1992): 21–33; and Jeffrey B. Arthur and Lynda Airman-Smith, "Gainsharing and Organizational Learning: An Analysis of Employee Suggestions Over Time," *Academy of Management Journal* 44, no. 4 (2001): 737–55.
115. Luis R. Gomez-Mejia, Theresa M. Welbourne, and Robert M. Wiseman, "The Role of Risk Sharing and Risk Taking under Gainsharing," *Academy of Management Review* 25, no. 3 (2000): 492–508.
116. J. Fox and B. Lawson, "Gainsharing Program Lifts Baltimore Employees' Morale," *American City and Country,* September 1997, pp. 93–94.
117. Jeffrey B. Arthur and Christopher L. Huntley, "Ramping Up the Organizational Learning Curve: Assessing the Impact of Deliberate Learning on Organizational Performance Under Gainsharing," *Academy of Management Journal* 48, no. 6 (2005): 1159–70.
118. Nancy J. Perry, "Here Come Richer, Riskier Pay Plans," *Fortune,* December 19, 1988, pp. 52–54.
119. "Newsletters," IOMA, www.ioma.com/newsletters/pfp/index.shtml.
120. Milkovich and Newman, *Compensation,* pp. 311–20.
121. Ibid.
122. Thomas F. O'Boyle, "Working Together," *Wall Street Journal,* June 5, 1992, pp. A1, A5.
123. Alfie Kohn, *Punished by Rewards* (Boston: Houghton Mifflin, 1999).
124. T. Kanni, "Why We Work," *Training,* August 1998, pp. 34–39.

Chapter 7

1. Paul M. Lehrer, Robert L. Woolfolk, and Wesley E. Sims, eds., *Principles and Practice of Stress Management* (New York: The Guilford Press, 2007).
2. Michelle Conlin and Dexter Roberts, "Go-Go-Go-Going to Pieces in China: Frazzled Managers Are Displaying all the Classic Signs of Western-Style Stress," *Businessweek,* April 23, 2007, p. 88; Richard S. DeFrank and John M. Ivancevich, "Stress on the Job: An Executive Update," *Academy of Management Executive* 12 (1998): 55–56; and Michael T. Matteson and John M. Ivancevich, *Controlling Work Stress* (San Francisco: Jossey-Bass, 1987).
3. M. Atkinson, A. Guetz, and L. Wein, "A Dynamic Model for Posttraumatic Stress Disorder Among U.S. Troops in Operation Iraqi Freedom," *Management Science* 55, no. 9 (2009): 1454–68.
4. Bruce Cryer, Rollin McCraty, and Doc Childre, "Pull the Plug on Stress," *Harvard Business Review,* July 2003, pp. 102–7.
5. Cary Cooper, "Future Research in Occupational Stress," *Stress Medicine* 11 (2000): 63–65.
6. R. L. Kahan, D. M. Wolfe, R. P. Quinn, J. D. Snoek, and R. A. Rosenthal, *Organizational Stress: Studies in Role Conflict and Ambiguity* (New York: John Wiley & Sons, 1964), p. 94.
7. L. Brummelhuis and T. van der Lippe, "Effective Work-life Balance Support for Various Household Structures," *Human Resource Management* 49, no. 2 (2010): 173–93; and Stewart D. Friedman and Jeffrey H. Greenhaus, *Work and Family—Allies or Enemies?* (London: Oxford University Press, 2000).
8. Lehrer et al., *Principles and Practice.*
9. A. Stevens, "Suit over Suicide Raises Issue: Do Associates Work Too Hard?" *Wall Street Journal,* April 15, 1994, pp. B1, B7.

10. R. L. Payne, *Emotions at Work: Theory, Research, and Applications for Management* (New York: John Wiley, 2007).
11. James C. Quick, Debra L. Nelson, Jonathon D. Quick, and Dusty K. Orman, "An Isomorphic Theory of Stress: The Dynamics of Person-Environment Fit," *Stress and Health* 17 (2000): 147–57.
12. Einar M. DeCroon, Allard J. Van Der Beek, Roland W. B. Blonk, and Monique H. W. Frings-Dresen, "Job Stress and Psychosomatic Health Complaints among Dutch Truck Drivers: A Re-Evaluation of Karasik's Interactive Job Demand-Control Model," *Stress Medicine* (March 2000): 101–7.
13. S. R. Maddi and S. C. Kobasa, *The Hardy Executive: Heath Under Stress* (Homewood, IL: Dow Jones-Irwin, 1984).
14. R. Frank, "Coping: The Psychology of What Works," in *Coping: The Psychology of What Works*, ed. C. R. Synder (New York: Oxford University Press), pp. vii–ix.
15. John Kay, "Corporate 'Saviours' Who Kill Off Their Companies," *Financial Times,* May 24, 2005, p. 19; and Pamela L. Perrewe, Gerald R. Ferris, Dwight D. Frink, and William P. Anthony, "Political Skill: An Antidote for Workplace Stressors," *Academy of Management Executive* 14 (2000): 115–23.
16. J. A. Byrne, *Chainsaw: The Notorious Career of Al Dunlap* (New York: HarperCollins, 1999).
17. M. T. Matteson and J. M. Ivancevich, *Managing Job Stress and Health* (New York: Free Press, 1982), p. 48.
18. Don Tennant, "Banishing Ghosts," *Computerworld,* December 1, 2008, pp. 4–5.
19. Debra Nelson and Cary L. Cooper, *Positive Organizational Behavior* (Thousand Oaks, CA: Sage, 2007).
20. "Layoff 'Survivor' Stress: How to Manage the Guilt and the Workload," *HR Focus,* August 2009, pp. 4–6.
21. Edward E. Lawler and James O'Toole, *America at Work: Choices and Challenges* (New York: Palgrave Macmillan, 2006).
22. Donna M. Owens, "Personalized Transition," *HR Magazine,* March 2008, pp. 45–48.
23. K. Bourne, F. Wilson, S. Lester, and J. Kickul, "Embracing the Whole Individual: Advantages of a Dual-centric Perspective of Work and Life," *Business Horizons* 52, no. 4 (2008): 387–98.
24. Ibid.
25. K. Reivich and A. Shatte, *The Resilience Factor* (New York: Broadway Books, 2002).
26. For a recent discussion about karoshi, see A. Kanai, "Karoshi" (Work to Death) in Japan," *Journal of Business Ethics* 84 (2009): 209–16.
27. "Job Stress," The American Institute of Stress, accessed April 10–24, 2007, www.welcoa.org/consulttrain/wellworkplace.php.
28. Mental Health America, accessed April 23, 2007, www.mentalhealthamerica.net.
29. Ibid.
30. Y. Raj, "How Primary Care Doctors Can Screen for Depression," *Medical Economics* 85, no. 14 (2008): 28–33; K. B. Wells, R. Sturm, C. D. Sherbourne, and L. S. Meredith, *Caring for Depression: A Rand Study* (Cambridge, MA: Harvard University Press, 1996).
31. R. M. Sapolsky, *Why Zebras Don't Get Ulcers* (New York: Henry Holt, 2004).
32. D. C. Schwebel and J. Seels, "Cardiovascular Reactivity and Neuroticism: Results from a Laboratory and Controlled Ambulatory Stress Protocol," *Journal of Personality* 67 (1999): 67–92.
33. D. Paton, C. C. Thomas, J. M. Violante, C. Dunning, and L. M. Smith, *Managing Traumatic Stress Risk: A Proactive Approach* (New York: Charles C. Thomas, 2004).
34. R. J. Burke, "Workaholism in Organizations: Psychological and Physical Well-Being Consequences," *Stress Medicine* 16 (2000): 11–16.
35. Paton et al., *Managing Traumatic Stress Risk.*
36. B. Swider and R. Zimmerman, "Born to Burnout: A Meta-analytic Path Model of Personality, Job Burnout, and Work Outcomes," *Journal of Vocational Behavior* 76, no. 3 (2010): 487.
37. M. P. Leiter and C. Maslaih, "Areas of Worklife: A Structured Approach to Organizational Predictors of Job Burnout," in *Research in Occupational Stress and Well-being*, ed. P. L. Perrewe and D. C. Ganter (Oxford: Elsevier, 2004).
38. "Job Stress," The American Institute of Stress, accessed April 23, 2007, www.stress.org/job.htm.
39. Meyer Friedman and Diane Ulmer, *Treating Type A Behavior and Your Heart* (New York: Alfred A. Knopf, 1984).
40. K. Orth-Gomer and N. Schneiderman, eds., *Behavioral Medicine Approaches to Cardiovascular Disease Prevention* (Mahwah, NJ: Erlbaum, 1996).
41. See, for example, L. Brummelhuis and T. van der Lippe, "Effective Work-life Balance Support for Various Household Structures," *Human Resource Management* 49, no. 2 (2010): 173–93; Fran H. Norris and Krzysztof Kaniasty, "Received and Perceived Social Support in Times of Stress: A Test of the Social Support Deterioration Deterrence Model," *Journal of Personality & Social Psychology* 71 (1996): 498–511.
42. G. Luria and A. Torjman, "Resources and Coping with Stressful Events," *Journal of Organizational Behavior* 30, no. 6 (2009): 685–707; C. R. Synder, "Coping: Where Are You Going?" in *Coping: The Psychology of What Works,* ed. C. R. Synder (New York: Oxford University Press, 1999), pp. 324–33.
43. See, for example, L. Yang, H. Che, and P. Spector, "Job Stress and Well-being: An Examination from the View of Person-Environment Fit," *Journal of Occupational and Organizational Psychology* 81, no. 3 (2008): 567–87; and Jeffrey R. Edwards, "An Examination of Competing Versions of the Person–Environment Fit

Approach to Stress," *Academy of Management Journal* 39 (1996): 292–339.

44. Edwards, "An Examination of Competing Versions," *Academy of Management Journal*, 1996, *op cit*.
45. "Statement of Guy Cottrell," United States Postal Service, accessed May 17, 2010, http://www.usps.com/communications/newsroom/testimony/2010/pr10_cottrell0316.htm.
46. Mark Ames, "Going Postal: Rage, Murder and Rebellion," accessed April 23, 2007, www.stress.org/job.htm.
47. Carola Mamberto, "Companies Aim to Combat Job-related Stress: At Glaxo, Program Uses Teams as Part of Effort to Improve Workplace," *Wall Street Journal,* August 13, 2007, p. B6.
48. Ibid.
49. Ames, "Going Postal," *op cit*.
50. Pamela Babcock, "Workplace Stress? Deal With It!" *HR Magazine,* May 2009, pp. 67–71.
51. Ibid.
52. Vijai P. Shaimi, "Take Advantage of Employee Assistance Programs," *Mindpub,* October 2000, p. 225.
53. P. Weaver and G. Rollins, "Easing the Burden of Employees' Debt," *HR Magazine,* July 2008, pp. 61–64.
54. "Well Workplace University," Workplace Councils of America (Welcoa), accessed April 10–24, 2007, www.welcoa.org/consulttrain/wellworkplace.php.
55. "Well Workplace University," Welcoa, accessed May 17, 2010, http://www.welcoa.org/consulttrain/wellworkplace.php.
56. Ibid.
57. Kelly Dunn, "Roche Chooses Health By Promoting Prevention," *Workforce,* April 2000, pp. 82–84.
58. "DuPont Issues H.E.A.L.T.H. Awards to recognizing workplaces with commendable workplace health promotion programs that encourage employee health," accessed at www2.dupont.com/Media_Center/en_US/daily_news/november/article20061130a.html; and discussion with DuPont Health and Wellness Services manager on October 16, 18, and 20, 2000.
59. Jack Kimball, "Developing a Healthy Workplace Strategy," *San Fernando Valley Business Journal,* January 19, 2004, pp. 13–14.
60. Stephanie Armour, "More Men Seek Better Work-Life Balance," *USA Today,* October 8, 2003, p. D1.
61. Bruce Cryer, Rollin McCraty, and Doc Childre, "Pull the Plug on Stress," *Harvard Business Review,* July 2003, pp. 102–7.
62. David Bunce, "What Factors Are Associated with the Outcome of Individual-Focused Worksite Stress Management Interventions?" *Journal of Occupational and Organizational Psychology* 70 (1997): 1–17.
63. J. R. Abascal, D. Brucato, and L. Brucato, *Stress Mastery: The Art of Coping Gracefully* (Upper Saddle River, NJ: 2001).
64. Ibid.
65. E. E. Solberg, R. Halrorsen, and H. H. Holen, "Effect of Meditation on Immune Cells," *Stress Medicine* 16 (2000): 185–200.
66. Ibid.
67. Jon Kabat-Zinn, *Coming to Our Senses* (New York: Hyperion, 2006).

Chapter 8

1. Marvin E. Shaw, *Group Dynamics* (New York: McGraw-Hill, 1981).
2. R. W. Toseland and Robert F. Rivas, *Introduction to Group Work Practice* (Upper Saddle River, NJ: Allyn & Bacon, 2004).
3. L. L. Ukens, *The New Encyclopedia of Group Activities* (San Francisco: Jossey-Bass, 2004).
4. S. H. Godar and S. P. Ferris, *Virtual and Collaborative Teams* (New York: Idea Group, 2004).
5. M. E. Turner (ed.), *Groups at Work: Theory and Research* (Mahwah, NJ: Lawrence Erlbaum, 2003).
6. E. E. Lawler, *Organizing for High Performance* (San Francisco: Jossey-Bass, 2001).
7. Manual London and Marilyn London, *First-Time Leaders of Small Groups: How to Create High Performing Committees, Tasks Forces, Clubs and Boards* (San Francisco, Jossey-Bass, 2007).
8. Carol Scearce, *122 Ways to Build Teams* (Thousand Oaks, CA: Sage, 2007).
9. London and London, *First-Time Leaders of Small Groups.*
10. Elizabeth Mannix, Margaret A. Neale, and Sally Blount-Lyon, eds., *Time in Groups* (St. Louis, MO: Elsevier, 2004).
11. Ibid.
12. William G. Dyer, W. Gibb Dyer Jr., and Jeffrey H. Dyer, *Team Building: Proven Strategies for Improving Team Performance* (San Francisco: Jossey-Bass, 2007).
13. J. R. Kelly and S. G. Bursade, "Mood and Emotions in Small Groups and Work Teams," *Organizational Behavior and Human Decision Process* 86 (2001): 99–130.
14. K. M. Sheldon and B. A. Bettencourt, "Psychological Need-Satisfaction and Subjective Well-Being Within Social Groups," *British Journal of Social Psychology* 41 (2002): 161–86.
15. London and London, *First-Time Leaders of Small Groups.*
16. Andrew Hede, "The Shadow Group: Towards an Explanation of Interpersonal Conflict in Work Groups," *Journal of Managerial Psychology* 22, no. 1 (2007): 25–39.
17. Ibid.
18. Marshall S. Poole and Andrea B. Hollingshead, *Theories of Small Groups* (Thousand Oaks, CA: Sage, 2004).

19. One early analysis of group development identified four stages similar to the ones discussed here. The author appropriately labeled the four stages as *forming, storming, norming,* and *performing.* Each stage is characterized by features and activities similar to our approach.
20. Mannix, Neal, and Blount-Lyon, *Time in Groups.*
21. E. Romanelli and M. L. Tushman, "Organizational Transformation as Punctuated Equilibrium: An Empirical Test," *Academy of Management Journal* 37 (1994): 1141–66.
22. C. J. G. Gersick, "Time and Transition in Work Teams: Toward a New Model of Group Development," *Academy of Management Journal* 31 (1988): 9–41.
23. M. J. Waller, J. M. Conte, C. B. Gibson, and M. A. Carpenter, "The Effect of Individual Perceptions of Deadlines on Team Performance," *Academy of Management Review* 26 (2001): 586–600.
24. E. Love, D. Love, and G. Northcraft, "Is the End in Sight? Student Regulation of In-Class and Extra-Credit Effort in Response to Performance Feedback," *Academy of Management Learning & Education* 9, no. 1 (2010): 81–97.
25. S. A. Wheelan and T. Williams, "Mapping Dynamic Interaction Patterns in Work Groups," *Small Group Research* 34 (2003): 443–67.
26. P. A. Chansler, P. M. Swanidass, and C. Cammann, "Self-Managing Teams: An Empirical Study of Group Cohesiveness in Natural Work Groups at a Harley-Davidson Motor Company Plant," *Small Group Research* 34 (2003): 101–21.
27. O. Ayoko and V. Callan, "Teams' Reactions to Conflict and Teams' Task and Social Outcomes: The Moderating Role of Transformational and Emotional Leadership," *European Management Journal* 28, no. 3 (2009): 220–35; M. J. Homsey, L. Majkut, D. J. Terry, and B. M. McKimmie, "On Being Loud and Proud: Non-Conformity to Group Norms," *British Journal of Social Psychology* 42 (2003): 319–35.
28. Philip B. Zimbardo, C. Haney, W. C. Banks, and D. Jaffe, "The Mind Is a Formidable Jailer: A Pirandellian Prison," *New York Times,* April 8, 1973, pp. 38–60.
29. Ulrike Cress and Joachim Kimmerle, "Guidelines and Feedback in Information Exchange: The Impact of Behavioral Anchors and Descriptive Norms in a Social Dilemma," *Group Dynamics: Theory, Research, and Practice* 11 (2007): 42–53.
30. Lawler, *Organizing for High Performance.*
31. Florence Stone, "How to Be Part of a High-Performing Team," *Supervisory Management,* November 1994, pp. 12–13.
32. "Solomon Asch Experiment: A Study of Conformity," accessed at www.age-of-the-sage.org/psychology/social/asch_conformity.html; and Solomon G. Asch, *Social Psychology* (Englewood Cliffs, NJ: Prentice Hall, 1952), ch. 16.
33. H. L. Liao, A. Joshi, and A. Chuang, "Sticking Out Like a Sore Thumb: Employee Dissimilarity and Deviance at Work," *Personnel Psychology* 57 (2004): 969–1000.
34. G. J. Gilanes, "In Their Own Words: An Exploratory Study of Bona Fide Group Leaders," *Small Group Research* 34 (2003): 741–70.
35. G. Fisher, T. A. Hunter, and W. D. K. Macrosson, "Belfin's Team Role Theory: For Non-Managers Also?" *Journal of Managerial Psychology* 17 (2002): 14–20.
36. Gilanes, "In Their Own Words."
37. Ibid.
38. C. Manz, F. Shipper, and G. Stewart, "Everyone a Team Leader: Shared Influence at W. L. Gore & Associates," *Organizational Dynamics* 38, no. 3 (2009): 239–44.
39. R. Zimmerman, M. Mount, M. Goff III, "Multisource Feedback and Leaders' Goal Performance: Moderating Effects of Rating Purpose, Rater Perspective, and Performance Dimension," *International Journal of Selection and Assessment* 16, no. 2 (2008): 121–33; and D. A. Wyrick, "Understanding Learning Styles to Be a More Effective Team Leader and Engineering Manager," *Engineering Management Journal* 15 (2003): 27–33.
40. Ibid.
41. B. Brockman, M. Rawlston, M. Jones, and D. Halstead, "An Exploratory Model of Interpersonal Cohesiveness in New Product Development Teams," *The Journal of Product Innovation Management* 27, no. 2 (2010): 201–32; and K. L. Harris, "The Effects of Culture and Cohesiveness on Intragroup Conflict and Effectiveness," *Journal of Social Psychology* 143 (2003): 613–31.
42. C. Cartwright and A. Zander, *Group Dynamics: Research and Theory* (New York: Harper & Row, 1968).
43. Irving Janis, *Victims of Groupthink: A Psychological Study of Foreign Policy Decisions and Fiascos* (Boston: Houghton Mifflin, 1973).
44. G. E. Burton, "The Measurement of Distortion Tendencies Induced by the Win-Lose Nature of In-Group Loyalty," *Small Group Research* 21 (1990): 128–41.
45. Chun Wei Choo, "Information Failures and Organizational Disasters," *MIT Sloan Management Review* 46, no. 3 (2005): 8–10; and G. Moorhead, R. Ference, and C. P. Neck, "Group Decision Fiascos Continue: Space Shuttle Challenger and a Revised Groupthink Framework," *Human Relations* 44 (199): 539–50.
46. D. A. Kravitz and B. Martin, "Ringelmann Rediscovered: The Original Article," *Journal of Personality and Social Psychology* 37 (1986): 936–41.
47. Wilf H. Ratzburg, "Social Loafing," accessed May 2, 2007, www.geocities.com/athensforum/1650/htmlgroups16.html.
48. R. C. Liden S. J. Wayne, R. A. Jaworski, and N. Bennett, "Social Loafing: A Field Investigation," *Journal of Management* 2 (2004): 285–304.

49. J. R. Katzenbach and D. K. Smith, *The Wisdom of Teams: Creating the High-Performance Organization* (New York: HarperBusiness, 1999), p. 45.
50. J. R. Hackman, *Leading Teams: Setting the Stage for Great Performances* (Boston: Harvard Business School Press, 2002).
51. Corey Dade and Brian Baskin, "Slick Hits U.S. Shores as BP Works to Catch Oil; Obama Administration Puts Plans for New Offshore Drilling Permits on Hold," http://online.wsj.com/article/SB10001424052748704370704575227812615975390.html, May 7, 2010,
52. Charlene M. Solomon, "Managing Virtual Teams," *Workforce,* June 2001, pp. 60–65.
53. F. Siebdrat, M. Hoegl, and H. Ernst, "How to Manage Virtual Teams," *MIT Sloan Management Review* 50, no. 4 (2009): 63–68; and Luis R. Gomez-Mejia, David B. Balkin, and Robert L. Cardy, *Managing Human Resources,* 3rd ed. (Upper Saddle River, NJ: Prentice Hall, 2000).
54. Solomon, "Managing Virtual Teams."
55. Siebdrat, Hoegl, and Ernst, "How to Manage Virtual Teams," *op cit.*
56. David Drucker, "Virtual Teams Light Up GE—Customers, Suppliers Linked in Real Time with Collaboration Apps," *InternetWeek,* April 2000, pp. 16–20.
57. Ibid.
58. Solomon, "Managing Virtual Teams."
59. Billie Williamson, "Managing at a Distance," *Businessweek,* July 2009, p. 64; J. Cordery, C. Soo, B. Kirkman, B. Rosen, and J. Mathieu, "Leading Parallel Global Virtual Teams: Lessons from Alcoa," *Organizational Dynamics* 38, no. 3 (2009): 204–6; and Julekha Dash, "Think of People When Planning Virtual Teams," *Computerworld,* February 2001, pp. 34–36.
60. J. O'Brian, "Cross-Functional Teams Build a Big Picture Attitude," *Supervisory Management* 39, no. 10 (1994): 1–2.
61. John Griffiths, "A Big Cat, Purring: The Jaguar XKR- S," *Financial Times,* September 27, 2008, p. 42.
62. This section is based on Michael Schrage, "What's That Bad Odor at Innovation Skunkworks?" *Fortune,* December 20, 1999, pp. 340–46; and James B. Quinn, "Team Innovation," *Executive Excellence,* July 1996, pp. 13–17.
63. Bradley L. Kirkman and Debra L. Shapiro, "The Impact of Cultural Values on Job Satisfaction and Organizational Commitment in Self-Managing Work Teams: The Mediating Role of Employee Resistance," *Academy of Management Journal* 44, no. 3 (2001): 557–69.
64. John R. Hollenbeck, Christopher J. Meyer and Daniel R. Ilgen, "Trait Configurations In Self-Managed Teams: A Conceptual Examination of the Use of Seeding for Maximizing and Minimizing Trait Variance in Teams," *Journal of Applied Psychology* 92 (2007): 883–92.
65. Karen A. Jehn, Gregory B. Northcraft, and Margaret A. Neale, "Why Differences Make a Difference: A Field Study of Diversity, Conflict, and Performance in Workgroups," *Administrative Science Quarterly* 44 (1999): 741–63; Katherine Williams and Charles O'Reilly, "Demography and Diversity in Organizations," in *Research in Organizational Behavior,* ed. Barry M. Staw and Robert M. Sutton (Stamford, CT: JAI Press 1998), pp. 77–140; and Frances Milliken and Luis Martins, "Searching for Common Threads: Understanding the Multiple Effects of Diversity in Organizational Groups," *Academy of Management Review* 21 (1996): 402–33.
66. Susan Jackson, "Team Composition in Organizations," in *Group Process and Productivity,* ed. S. Worchel, W. Wood, and J. Simpson (London: Sage, 1992), pp. 1–12.
67. G. Stahl, M. Maznevski, A. Voigt, and K. Jonsen, "Unraveling the Effects of Cultural Diversity in Teams: A Meta-analysis of Research on Multicultural Work Groups," *Journal of International Business Studies* 41, no. 4 (2010): 690–709.
68. G. Healy and K. Oikelone, "Equality and Diversity Actors: A Challenge to Traditional Industrial Relations," *Equal Opportunities International* 26, no. 1 (2007): 44–65.
69. Tony Simons, Lisa H. Pelled, and Ken A. Smith, "Making Use of Difference: Diversity, Debate, and Decision Comprehensiveness in Top Management Teams," *Academy of Management Journal* 42 (1999): 662–73.
70. John et al., "Why Differences Make a Difference."
71. Jeanne M. Brett, Ray Friedman, and Kristin Behfar, "How To Manage Your Negotiating Team," *Harvard Business Review,* September 2009, pp. 105–9.
72. Laurel Coppersmith and Arlene Grubbs, "Team-Building: The Whole May Be Less Than the Sum of Its Parts," *The Human Resource Professional,* May/June 1998, pp. 10–14.
73. Rob Cross, "Looking Before You Leap: Assessing the Jump to Teams in Knowledge-Based Work," *Business Horizons* 43, no. 5 (2000): 29–36.
74. Allan B. Drexler and Russ Forrester, "Teamwork—Not Necessarily the Answer," *HR Magazine,* January 1998, pp. 55–58.
75. K. Sassenberg, K. J. Jones, and J. Y. Shah, "Why Some Groups Just Feel Better: The Regulatory Fit of Group Power," *Journal of Personality and Social Psychology* 92 (2007): 249–67.
76. Ibid.
77. Suzanne T. Bell, "Deep-Level Composition Variables as Predictors of Team Performance: A Meta-Analysis," *Journal of Applied Psychology* 92 (2007): 595–615.
78. Brian Dumaine, "The Trouble with Teams," *Fortune,* September 1994, pp. 86–90.
79. Raimo Nurmi, "Teamwork and Team Leadership," *Team Performance Management* 2 (1996): 9–13.

80. R. Wageman, C. Fisher, and J. Hackman, "Leading Teams When the Time is Right: Finding the Best Moments to Act," *Organizational Dynamics* 38, no. 3 (2009): 192–203.
81. Bell, "Deep-Level Composition Variables."
82. Cross, "Looking Before You Leap."
83. M. van Viegt and C. M. Hart, "Social Identity as Social Glue: The Origins of Group Loyalty," *Journal of Personality and Social Psychology* 86 (2004): 585–98.
84. C. Senecal, E. Julien, and F. Guay, "Role Conflict and Academic Procrastination: A Self-Determination Perspective," *European Journal of Social Psychology* 33 (2003): 135–95.
85. L. A. Duckurich, K. L. Hamilton, and C. Haas, "Effects of Conflict Management Strategies on Perceptions of Intragroup Conflict," *Group Dynamics: Theory, Research, and Practice* 11 (2007): 66–78.
86. Ibid.
87. S. Gilboa, A. Shirom, Y. Fried, and C. Cooper, "A Meta-Analysis of Work Demand Stressors and Job Performance: Examining Main and Moderating Effects," *Personnel Psychology* 61, no. 2 (2008): 227–71; and S. Alton, G. Burnett, and G. B. Burnett, *Peace in Everyday Relationships: Resolving Conflict in Your Personal and Work Life* (New York: Hunter House, 2003).

Chapter 9

1. Mary Ann Von Glinow, Debra L. Shapiro, and Jeanne M. Brett, "Can We Talk, and Should We? Managing Emotional Conflict in Multicultural Teams," *Academy of Management Review* 29, no. 4 (2004): 578–92; Clayton Alderfer and Ken J. Smith, "Studying Intergroup Relations Embedded in Organizations," *Administrative Science Quarterly* 27 (1982): 35–64; and P. K. Edwards, *Conflict at Work* (New York: Basil Blackwell, 1987).
2. Henri Barki and Jon Hartwick, "Conceptualizing the Construct of Interpersonal Conflict," *International Journal of Conflict Management* 15, no. 3 (2004): 216–44; John G. Oetzel and Stella Ting-Toomey, "Face Concerns in Interpersonal Conflict: A Cross-Cultural Empirical Test of the Face Negotiation Theory," *Communication Research* 30, no. 6 (2003): 599–625; and Philip J. Moberg, "Linking Conflict Strategy to the Five-Factor Model: Theoretical and Empirical Foundations," *International Journal of Conflict Management* 12, no. 1 (2001): 47–56.
3. Stephen P. Robbins, *Managing Organizational Conflict* (Englewood Cliffs, NJ: Prentice-Hall, 1974); and Robert E. Quinn, *Beyond Rational Management: Mastering the Paradoxes and Competing Demands of High Performance* (San Francisco: Jossey-Bass, 1988).
4. Bradley J. Olson, Satyanarayana Parayitam, and Yongjian Bao, "Strategic Decision Making: The Effects of Cognitive Diversity, Conflict, and Trust on Decision Outcomes," *Journal of Management* 33, no. 2 (2007): 196–222; and Karen A. Jehn and Jennifer A. Chatman, "The Influence of Proportional and Perceptual Conflict Composition on Team Performance," *International Journal of Conflict Management* 11, no. 1 (2000): 56–73.
5. E. Liberman, Y. Levy, and P. Segal, "Designing an Internal Organizational System for Conflict Management: Based on a Needs Assessment," *Dispute Resolution Journal* 64, no. 2 (2009): 62–74; Michelle K. Duffy, Jason D. Shaw, and Eric M. Stark, "Performance and Satisfaction in Conflicted Interdependent Groups: When and How Does Self-Esteem Make a Difference?" *Academy of Management Journal* 43, no. 4 (2000): 772–82.
6. C. Dreu, "The Virtue and Vice of Workplace Conflict: Food for (Pessimistic) Thought," *Journal of Organizational Behavior* 29, no. 1 (2008): 5–18.
7. Jeffrey Ball, Isabel Ordonez, and Siobhan Hughes, "U.S. News: BP Criticized for Inability to Assess Oil Flow—EPA Orders Use of Milder Dispersant; Scientists Fear Extensive Damage," *Wall Street Journal*, May 21, 2010, p. A6, Eastern edition.
8. Deanna Geddes and Ronda Roberts Callister, "Crossing the Line(s): A Dual Threshold Model of Anger in Organizations," *Academy of Management Review* 32, no. 3 (2007): 721–46; Karen A. Jehn and Elizabeth A. Mannix, "The Dynamic Nature of Conflict: A Longitudinal Study of Intragroup Conflict and Group Performance," *Academy of Management Journal* 44, no. 2 (2001): 238–51; and Randall S. Peterson and Kristin Jackson Behfar, "The Dynamic Relationship between Performance Feedback, Trust, and Conflict in Groups: A Longitudinal Study," *Organizational Behavior and Human Decision Processes* 92, nos. 1–2 (2002): 102–12.
9. M. Korsgaard, S. Jeong, D. Mahony, and A. Pitariu, "A Multilevel View of Intragroup Conflict," *Journal of Management* 34, no. 6 (2008): 1222–52.
10. Karen Jehn, "A Multimethod Examination of the Benefits and Detriments of Intragroup Conflict," *Administrative Science Quarterly* 42, 1995, pp. 256–82; Kathleen Eisenhardt and Chris Schoovohen, "Organizational Growth: Linking Founding Team, Strategy, Environment, and Growth among U.S. Semiconductor Ventures," *Administrative Science Quarterly* 35 (1990), pp. 504–29; Dave Schweiger, William Sandberg, and Paul Rechner, "Experiential Effects of Dialectical Inquiry, Devil's Advocacy, and Consensus Approaches to Strategic Decision Making," *Academy of Management Journal* 32 (1989): 745–72; and L. J. Bourgeois, "Strategic Goals, Environmental Uncertainty, and Economic Performance in Volatile Environments," *Academy of Management Journal* 28 (1985): 548–73.
11. E. Martínez-Moreno, P. González-Navarro, A. Zornoza, and P. Ripoll, "Relationship, Task and Process Conflicts and Team Performance: The Moderating Role of

Communication Media," *International Journal of Conflict Management,* 20, no. 3 (2009): 251–68; Jehn and Mannix, "The Dynamic Nature of Conflict"; and V. Wall and L. Nolan, "Perceptions of Inequality, Satisfaction, and Conflict in Task Oriented Groups," *Human Relations* 39 (1986): 1033–52.

12. Jehn and Mannix, "The Dynamic Nature of Conflict."
13. Roxanne Wilkens and Manuel London, "Relationships between Climate, Process, and Performance in Continuous Quality Improvement Groups," *Journal of Vocational Behavior* 69, no. 3 (2006): 510–23.
14. Connie Gersick, "Time and Transition in Work Teams: Toward a New Model of Group Development," *Academy of Management Journal* 31 (1988): 9–41; and Gerardo A. Okhuysen and Mary J. Waller, "Focusing on Midpoint Transitions: An Analysis of Boundary Conditions," *Academy of Management Journal* 45, no. 5 (2002): 1056–65.
15. J. Thompson, *Organizations in Action* (New York: McGraw-Hill, 1967).
16. Business and Finance, *Wall Street Journal,* August 17, 2009, p. A1, Eastern edition.
17. For example, see C. B. Chapman, D. F. Cooper, and M. J. Page, *Management for Engineers* (New York: John Wiley & Sons, 1987).
18. See D. J. Wood and B. Gray, "Toward a Comprehensive Theory of Collaboration," *Journal of Applied Behavioral Science* 27 (1991): 139–62, for a comprehensive review of situations where groups and organizations can choose to engage in either conflict or collaboration.
19. A. Mummendey, B. Simon, C. Dietzke, M. Grunert, G. Haeger, S. Kessler, S. Lettgen, and S. Schaferhoff, "Categorization Is Not Enough: Intergroup Discrimination in Negative Outcome Allocation," *Journal of Experimental Social Psychology* 28 (1992): 125–44.
20. Avan R. Jassawalla and Hemant C. Sashittal, "Building Collaborative Cross-Functional New Product Teams," *Academy of Management Executive* 13, no. 3 (1999): 50–63; Karen A. Brown and Terence R. Mitchell, "Influence of Task Interdependence and Number of Poor Performers on Diagnosis of Causes of Poor Performance," *Academy of Management Journal* 29 (1986): 412–23; Reed E. Nelson, "The Strength of Strong Ties: Social Networks and Intergroup Conflict in Organizations," *Academy of Management Journal* 32 (1989): 377–401; and Denis Cormier, Irene M. Gordon, and Michel Magnan, "Corporate Environmental Disclosure: Contrasting Management's Perceptions with Reality," *Journal of Business Ethics* 49, no. 2 (2004): 143–59.
21. Line–staff conflict has been the subject of a great deal of research for over four decades. For representative examples, see J. A. Balasco and J. A. Alutto, "Line and Staff Conflicts: Some Empirical Insights," *Academy of Management Journal* 12 (1969): 469–77; and J. E. Sorenson and T. L. Sorenson, "The Conflict of Professionals in Bureaucratic Organizations," *Administrative Science Quarterly* 19 (1974): 98–106.
22. The classic work is Muzafer Sherif and Carolyn Sherif, *Groups in Harmony and Tension* (New York: Harper & Row, 1953). In a study conducted among groups in a boys' camp, they stimulated conflict between the groups and observed the changes in group behavior.
23. C. Marlene Fiol, Michael G. Pratt, and Edward J. O'Connor, "Managing Intractable Identity Conflicts," *Academy of Management Review* 34, no. 1 (2009): 32–55; Edgar Schein, "Intergroup Problems in Organizations," in *Organization Development: Theory, Practice, Research,* 2nd ed., ed. Wendell French, Cecil Bell, and Robert Zawacki (Plano, TX: Business Publications, 1983), pp. 106–10.
24. M. A. Rahim, J. E. Garrett, and G. F. Buntzman, "Ethics of Managing Interpersonal Conflict in Organizations," *Journal of Business Ethics* 11 (1992): 423–32.
25. Kathleen M. Eisenhardt, "Speed and Strategic Choice: How Managers Accelerate Decision Making," *California Management Review* 50, no. 2 (2008): 102–16; Jeff Weiss and Jonathan Hughes, "Want Collaboration? Accept—and Actively Manage—Conflict," *Harvard Business Review,* March 2005, pp. 92–101; and Oluremi B. Ayoko, Charmine E. J. Hartel, and Victor J. Callan, "Resolving the Puzzle of Productive and Destructive Conflict in Culturally Heterogeneous Workgroups: A Communication Accommodation Theory Approach," *International Journal of Conflict Management* 13, no. 2 (2002): 165–96.
26. J. Firth, "A Proactive Approach to Conflict Resolution," *Supervisory Management,* November 1991, p. 3; and Holmes Miller and Kurt J. Engemann, "A Simulation Model of Intergroup Conflict," *Journal of Business Ethics* 50, no. 4 (2004): 355–70.
27. Geddes and Callister, "Crossing the Line(s)"; M. O. Stephenson, Jr., and G. M. Pops, "Conflict Resolution Methods and the Policy Process," *Public Administration Review* 49 (1989): 463–73; and Wallace Warfield, "Some Minor Reflections on Conflict Resolution: The State of the Field as a Moving Target," *Negotiation Journal* 18, no. 4 (2002): 381–84.
28. Also see Robbins, *Managing Organizational Conflict,* pp. 67–77; and M. Afzalur Rahim, ed., *Managing Conflict: An Interdisciplinary Approach* (New York: Praeger, 1989).
29. Muzafer Sherif and Carolyn Sherif, *Social Psychology* (New York: Harper & Row, 1969), pp. 228–62. Sherif and Sherif conducted sociopsychological experiments to determine effective ways of resolving conflict. Based on this research, they developed the concept of superordinate goals.
30. D. H. Weiss, "Barriers Created by Team Leaders," *Supervisory Management* 37 (1992): 6–8; and Elizabeth

H. Creyer and John C. Kozup, "An Examination of the Relationship between Coping Styles, Task-Related Affect, and the Desire fro Decision Assistance," *Organizational Behavior and Human Decision Processes* 90, no. 1 (2003): 37–52.

31. G. Milite, "When the Team Becomes Too Human," *Supervisory Management* 37 (1992): 9.
32. For a discussion of the link between conflict management strategies and concern for the needs of others, see G. S. Hammock and D. R. Richardson, "Aggression as One Response to Conflict," *Journal of Applied Social Psychology* 22, no. 4 (1992): 298–311.
33. M. A. Neale and Max H. Bazerman, "The Effects of Framing and Negotiator Overconfidence on Bargaining Behavior and Outcomes," *Academy of Management Journal* 28 (1985): 34–49.
34. M. Giacomantonio, C. De Dreu, and L. Mannetti, "Now You See It, Now You Don't: Interests, Issues, and Psychological Distance in Integrative Negotiation," *Journal of Personality and Social Psychology* 98, no. 5 (2010): 761–74; Jeswald W. Salacuse, *The Global Negotiator: Making, Managing and Mending Deals Around the World in the Twenty-First Century* (Hampshire, UK: Palgrave Macmillan, 2003); and D. A. Lax and J. K. Sebenius, *The Manager as Negotiator* (New York: Free Press, 1986), chap. 1.
35. Roy Lewicki, Bruce Barry, and David Saunders, *Essentials of Negotiation* (Burr Ridge, IL: McGraw-Hill Irwin, 2010); T. Anderson, "Step into My Parlor: A Survey of Strategies and Techniques for Effective Negotiation," *Business Horizons* 35, no. 3 (1992): 71–76; and Steven Cohen, *Negotiating Skills for Managers* (New York: McGraw-Hill/Irwin, 2002).
36. Lalita Khosla, "You Say Tomato," *Forbes,* May 2001, pp. 36–37.
37. Yasmin S. Purohit and Claire A. Simmers, "Power Distance and Uncertainty Avoidance: A Cross-national Examination of Their Impact on Conflict Management Modes," *Journal of International Business Research* 5, no. 1 (2006): 1–19; Ana Valenzuela, Joydeep Srivastava, and Seonsu Lee, "The Role of Cultural Orientation in Bargaining under Incomplete Information: Differences in Causal Attributions," *Organizational Behavior and Human Decision Processes* 96, no. 1 (2005): 72–88; and Roger J. Volkema and Maria Tereza Leme Fleury, "Alternative Negotiating Conditions and the Choice of Negotiation Tactics: A Cross-Cultural Comparison," *Journal of Business Ethics* 36, no. 4 (2002): 381–99.
38. Tinsley and Pillutla, "Negotiating in the United States and Hong Kong"; Nancy J. Adler, *International Dimensions of Organizational Behavior* (Boston: PWS-Kent, 1991); and F. R. Kluckhohn and F. L. Stodtbeck, *Variations in Value Orientations* (New York: Row, Peterson, 1961).
39. C. Warden and J. Chen, "Chinese Negotiators' Subjective Variations in Intercultural Negotiations," *Journal of Business Ethics* 88, no. 3 (2009): 529–37; Kam-hon Lee, Guang Yang, and John L. Graham, "Tension and Trust in International Business Negotiations: American Executives Negotiating with Chinese Executives," *Journal of International Business Studies* 37, no. 5 (2006): 623–41; and Xinping, Shi, "Antecedent Factors on International Business Negotiations in the China Context," *Management International Review* 41 (2001): 163–79.
40. Geert Hofstede, *Cultures and Organizations: Software of the Mind,* 2nd ed. (New York: McGraw-Hill, 2004); and Geert Hofstede, *Culture's Consequences: International Differences in Work-Related Values* (Beverly Hills, CA: Sage, 1980).
41. Brett and Okumura, "Inter- and Intracultural Negotiation"; and John G. Oetzel and Stella Ting-Toomey, "Face Concerns in Interpersonal Conflict," *Communication Research* 30, no. 6 (2003): 599–624.
42. Jill E. Rudd and Diana R. Lawson, *Communicating in Global BusinessNegotiations: A Geocentric Approach* (Thousand Oaks, CA: Sage, 2007).
43. David Ricks and Giuseppe Bertola, *Blunders in International Business,* 4th ed. (Malden, MA: Blackwell Publishing, 2006).
44. Lax and Sebenius, *The Manager as Negotiator.*
45. Lauren A. E. Schuker and Ethan Smith, "Rewinding to the Old Miramax," *Wall StreetJournal,* April 19, 2010, p. B5.
46. M. Zetlin, "The Art of Negotiating," *Success!,* June 1986, pp. 34–39; Deborah M. Kolb and Judith Williams, "Breakthrough Bargaining," *Harvard Business Review,* February 2001, pp. 89–99; and Michele J. Gelfand, Lisa H. Nishii, Ken-Ichi Ohbuchi, and Mitsuteru Fukuno, "Cultural Influences on Cognitive Representations of Conflict: Interpretations of Conflict Episodes in the United States and Japan," *Journal of Applied Psychology* 86, no. 6 (2001): 1059–74.
47. Steven Cohen, *Negotiating Skills for Managers* (New York: McGraw-Hill, 2002).
48. J. Grenig, "Better Communication Spells Success in Negotiations," *Impact,* December 2, 1985, pp. 6–7.
49. Zetlin, "The Art of Negotiating."
50. Ibid.
51. M. LaBrosse, "Unleash Your Inner Negotiator," *Employment Relations Today* 35 (2008): 105–9; and C. W. Barlow and G. P. Eisen, *Purchasing Negotiations* (Boston: CBI Publishing, 1983), chap. 5.
52. J. A. Wall, Jr., and M. W. Blum, "Negotiations," *Journal of Management* 17 (1991): 273–303.
53. G. Dangot-Simpkin, "Eight Attitudes to Develop to Hone Your Negotiating Skills," *Supervisory Management,* February 1992, p. 10; and James K. Sebenius, "Six Habits of Merely Effective Negotiations," *Harvard Business Review,* April 2001, pp. 87–99.
54. Barlow and Eisen, *Purchasing Negotiations.*
55. James R. Silkenat, *The ABA Guide to International Business Negotiations: A Comparison of Cross-cultural*

Issues and Successful Approaches, 3rd ed. (Chicago: American Bar Association, 2009).

56. Maurice E. Schweitzer, John C. Hershey, and Eric T. Bradlow, "Promises and Lies: Restoring Violated Trust," *Organizational Behavior and Human Decision Processes* 101, no. 1 (2006): 1–19; and D. G. Pruitt, J. M. Magenau, E. Konar-Goldband, and P. J. Carnevale, "Effects of Trust, Aspiration, and Gender on Negotiation Tactics," *Journal of Personality and Social Psychology* 38, no. 1 (1980): 9–22.
57. Mara Olekalns and Philip L. Smith, "Mutually Dependent: Power, Trust, Affect and the Use of Deception in Negotiation," *Journal of Business Ethics* 85 (2009): 347–65; and J. D. O'Brian, "Negotiating with Peers: Consensus, Not Power," *Supervisory Management,* January 1992, p. 4.
58. G. R. Shell, "When Is It Legal to Lie in Negotiations?" *MIT Sloan Management Review* 32, no. 3 (1991): 93–101.
59. Robert S. Adler, "Negotiating With Liars," *MIT Sloan Management Review,* 48, no. 4 (2007): 69–74.
60. Grenig, "Better Communication."
61. L. G. Greenhaigh, "Secrets of Managing People Much, Much More Effectively," *Boardroom Reports,* November 1, 1989, pp. 13–14; and Corinne Bendersky, "Organizational Dispute Resolution Systems: A Complementarities Model," *Academy of Management Review* 28, no. 4 (2003): 643–56.
62. B. Rodgers, *The IBM Way: Insights into the World's Most Successful Organization* (New York: Harper & Row, 1986).
63. Frederick P. Morgeson, Matthew H. Reider, and Michael A. Campion, "Selecting Individuals in Team Settings: The Importance of Social Skills, Personality Characteristics, and Teamwork Knowledge," *Personnel Psychology* 58, no. 3 (2005): 583–611; and "The Payoff from Teamwork," *Businessweek,* July 10, 1989, pp. 56–60; and David M. Schweiger, Tugral Atamer, and Roland Calori, "Transnational Project Teams and Networks: Making the Multinational Organization More Effective," *Journal of World Business* 38, no. 2 (2003): 127–40.
64. A. Desreumaux, "OD Practices in France: Part I," *Leadership and Organization Development Journal* 6, no. 4 (1985): 29; A. Desremaux, "OD Practices in France: Part II," *Leadership and Organization Development Journal* 7, no. 1 (1986): 10–14; and Joanne C. Preston and Terry R. Armstrong, "Team Building in South Africa: Cross Cultural Synergy in Action," *Public Administration Quarterly* 15 (1991): 65–82.
65. Nancy Hatch Woodward, "Make the Most of Team Building," *HR Magazine,* September 2006, pp. 72–76; Hayley Pinkerfield, "Team Time," *Human Resources,* November 2006, pp. 98–100; Richard W. Woodman and John J. Sherwood, "Effects of Team Development Intervention: A Field Experiment," *Journal of Applied Behavioral Science* 16 (1980): 211–17; and Jean Gordon, "A Perspective on Team Building," *Journal of American Academy of Business* 2, no. 1 (2002): 185–89.
66. Woodward, "Make the Most of Team Building."
67. Ibid.
68. Douglas P. Shuit, "Sound the Retreat," *Workforce Management* 82, no. 9 (2003): 38–45.
69. Ibid.
70. Jeffrey M. O'Brien, "Team Building in Paradise," *Fortune*, May 26, 2008, p. 112.
71. Marc Boisclair, "Stepping Up to the Plate," *Incentive,* April 2005, pp. 26–30.
72. Merrick Rosenberg, "Beyond the Basics," *T + D,* December 2007, pp. 26–29.
73. Mika Gabrielsson, Hannu Seristö and John Darling, "Developing the Global Management Team: A New Paradigm of Key Leadership Perspectives," *Team Performance Management* 15, nos. 7/8 (2009): 308–25; D. Sandy Staples and Lina Zhao, "The Effects of Cultural Diversity in Virtual Teams versus Face-to-Face Teams," *Group Decision and Negotiation* 15, no. 4 (2006): 389–406; and Denice E. Welch, "Globalization of Staff Movements: Beyond Cultural Adjustment," *Management International Review* 43, no. 2 (2003): 149–62.
74. P. Christopher Earley and Elaine Mosakowski, "Creating Hybrid Team Cultures: An Empirical Test of Transnational Team Functioning," *Academy of Management Journal* 43, no. 1 (2000): 26–49.
75. Richard L. Hughes, William E. Rosenbach, and William H. Clover, "Team Development in Intact, Ongoing Work Group," *Group and Organizational Studies* 8 (1983): 161–81.
76. Bernard A. Rausch, "Dupont Transforms a Division's Culture," *Management Review* 78 (1989): 37–42.
77. Adapted from Jack D. Orsburn, Linda Moran, Ed Musselwhite, John H. Zenger, and Craig Perrin, *Self-Directed Work Teams* (Burr Ridge, IL: Irwin Professional Publishing, 1990), p. 23; and Darcy E. Hitchcock and Marsha L. Willard, *Why Teams Can Fail* (Burr Ridge, IL: Irwin Professional Publishing, 1995), chaps. 2–3.
78. R. M. Marsh, "The Difference between Participation and Power in Japanese Factories," *Industrial and Labor Relations Review* 45 (1992): 250–57.
79. Robbins, *Managing Organizational Conflict,* chap. 9.

Chapter 10

1. See Stewart Clegg, David Courpasson, and Nelson Phillips, *Power and Organizations* (London: Sage, 2006); and Iain Mangham, *Power and Performance in Organizations* (New York: Basil Blackwell, 1988), for a discussion of power in organizations. See also David C. McClelland and David H. Burnham, "Power Is the Great Motivator," *Harvard Business Review,* January 2003, pp. 117–29.

2. J. Pfeffer, "Understanding Power in Organizations," *California Management Review* (Winter 1992): 29–50.
3. Anthony T. Cobb, "Political Diagnosis: Applications in Organizational Development," *Academy of Management Review* 11 (1986): 482–96.
4. C. Marlene Fiol, Edward J. O'Connor, and Herman Aguinis, "All for One and One for All? The Development and Transfer of Power across Organizational Levels," *Academy of Management Review* 26 (2001): 224–42; J. Pfeffer, *Managing with Power: Politics and Influence in Organizations* (Boston: Harvard Business School Press, 1996); and John R. P. French and Bertram Raven, "The Bases of Social Power," in *Studies of Social Power,* ed. D. Cartwright (Ann Arbor, MI: Institute for Social Research, University of Michigan, 1959), pp. 150–67.
5. Robert Dahl, "The Concept of Power," *Behavioral Science* 2 (1957): 202–3.
6. Abhishek Srivastava, Kathryn M. Bartol, and Edwin A. Locke, "Empowering Leadership in Management Teams: Effects of Knowledge Sharing, Efficacy, and Performance," *Academy of Management Journal* 49, no. 6 (2006): 1239–51; "The Perils of Inadequate Leadership," *Harvard Business Review,* September/October 1994, p. 137; and Victor H. Vroom, "Educating Managers for Decision Making and Leadership," *Management Decision* 41, no. 10 (2003): 968–81.
7. Max Weber, *Theory of Social and Economic Organization* (New York: Free Press, 1947), pp. 324–28.
8. Henry Mintzberg, *Power in and around Organizations* (Englewood Cliffs, NJ: Prentice-Hall, 1983), p. 5; and Henry Mintzberg, "Power and Organization Life Cycles," *Academy of Management Review* 9 (1984): 207–24.
9. French and Raven, "The Basis of Social Power."
10. Chester I. Barnard, *The Functions of the Executive* (Cambridge, MA: Harvard University Press, 1938).
11. Arthur Levitt, Jr., "The Imperial CEO Is No More," *Wall Street Journal,* March 17, 2005, p. A16.
12. Leslie A. Weatherly, "Performance Management: Getting It Right From the Start," *HR Magazine,* March 2004, pp. 1–11; and A. Halcrow, "Rules of the Game," *Personnel Journal* 74 (1995): 4; and Leslie A. Weatherly, "Performance Management: Getting It Right from the Start," *HR Magazine,* March 2004, pp. 1–12.
13. Edward E. Lawler III and Christopher G. Worley, "Winning Support for Organizational Change: Designing Employee Reward Systems That Keep on Working," *Ivey Business Journal,* March/April 2006, 1–5; J. Blasi, J. Gasawat, and D. Kruse, "Employees and Managers as Shareholders," *Human Resource Planning* 17, no. 4 (1994): 57–67.
14. Wayne Cascio and Peter Cappelli, "Lessons from the Financial Services Crisis," *HR Magazine,* January 2009, pp. 47–50.
15. Justin Baer and Francesco Guerrera, "Circuit Failure," *Financial Times,* November 20, 2008, p. 7.
16. A. J. Stahelski, D. E. Frost, and M. E. Patch, "Uses of Socially Dependent Bases of Power: French and Raven's Theory Applied to Workgroup Leadership," *Journal of Applied Social Psychology* 19 (1989): 283–97.
17. C. Levay, "Charismatic Leadership in Resistance to Change," *Leadership Quarterly* 21, no. 1 (2010): 127–43; Nurcan Ensari and Susan Elaine Murphy, "Cross-Cultural Variations in Leadership Perceptions and Attribution of Charisma to the Leader," *Organizational Behavior and Human Decision Processes* 92, no. 1/2 (2003): 52–66; and J. Warham, "Eight Steps to Charisma," *Across the Board,* April 1994, pp. 49–50.
18. Bill Breen, The 3 Ways of Great Leaders," *Fast Company,* September 2005; Anthony J. Mayo and Nitin Nohria, *In Their Time: The Greatest Business Leaders of the 20th Century* (Cambridge, MA: Harvard Business Press, 2005).
19. Sandra E. Cha and Amy C. Edmondson, "When Values Backfire: Leadership, Attribution, and Disenchantment in a Values-Driven Organization," *Leadership Quarterly* 17, no. 1 (2006): 57–78; Joseph A. Raelin, "The Myth of Charismatic Leaders," *T + D,* March 2003, pp. 46–51; and Rakesh Khurana, "The Curse of the Superstar CEO," *Harvard Business Review,* September 2002, pp. 60–66.
20. G. Yukl and C. M. Falbe, "Importance of Different Power Sources in Downward and Lateral Relations," *Journal of Applied Psychology* 76 (1991): 416–23.
21. J. A. Halpert, "The Dimensionality of Charisma," *Journal of Business and Psychology* 4 (1990): 399–410; and A. M. Rahim, "Relationships of Leader Power to Compliance and Satisfaction with Supervision: Evidence from a National Sample of Managers," *Journal of Management* 15 (1989): 545–56.
22. Nancy B. Kurland and Lisa Hope Pelled, "Passing the Word: Toward a Model of Gossip and Power in the Workplace," *Academy of Management Review* 25 (2000): 428–38.
23. B. R. Ragins and E. Sundstrom, "Gender and Perceived Power in Manager–Subordinate Relations," *Journal of Occupational Psychology* 63 (1990): 273–87.
24. E. A. Fagenson, "Perceived Masculine and Feminine Attributes Examined as a Function of Individuals' Sex and Level in the Organizational Power Hierarchy: A Test of Four Theoretical Perspectives," *Journal of Applied Psychology* 75 (1990): 204–11.
25. Kerry J. Sulkowicz, "Worse than Enemies: The CEO's Destructive Confidant," *Harvard Business Review,* February 2004, pp. 64–71; and Roy Lubit, "The Long-term Organizational Impact of Destructively Narcissistic Managers," *Academy of Management Executive* 16, no. 1 (2002): 127–39.
26. David Kipnis, *The Powerholders* (Chicago: University of Chicago Press, 1976), pp. 149–56. Kipnis doesn't present these characteristics as fitting all power seekers but only as a summarization of the negative face of power seekers.

27. David C. McClelland, *Power: The Inner Experience* (New York: Irvington, 1975), p. 7.
28. D. McClelland and D. Burnham, "Power Is the Great Motivator," *Harvard Business Review,* January/February 1995, pp. 126–39.
29. J. T. Knippen and T. B. Green, "Dealing with an Insecure Boss," *Supervisory Management,* March 1995, p. 14.
30. Jeffrey Pfeffer, *Power in Organizations* (Marshfield, MA: Pitman, 1981), p. 117; and Dean Tjosvold, "Power and Social Context in Superior–Subordinate Interaction," *Organizational Behavior and Human Decision Processes* 35 (1985): 281–93.
31. Pfeffer, *Power,* pp. 104–22; Rosabeth M. Kanter, "Power Failures in Management Circuits," *Harvard Business Review,* July/August 1979, pp. 65–75; and Hugh R. Taylor, "Power at Work," *Personnel Journal* 65 (1986): 42–49.
32. Kanter, "Power Failures in Management Circuits."
33. David Ulrich and Jay B. Barney, "Perspectives in Organizations: Resource Dependence, Efficiency, and Population," *Academy of Management Review* 9 (1984): 471–81.
34. For a study of dependency between organizations, see Steven S. Skinner, James H. Donnelly, Jr., and John M. Ivancevich, "Effects of Transactional Form on Environmental Linkages and Power–Dependence Relations," *Academy of Management Journal* 30 (1987): 577–88.
35. For a discussion of the resource issue in a nonbusiness setting, see William McKinley, Joseph L. C. Cheng, and Allen G. Schnick, "Perception of Resource Criticality in Times of Resource Scarcity: The Case of University Departments," *Academy of Management Journal* 29 (1986): 621–31.
36. Dean Tjosvold and Haifa Sun, "Effects of Power Concepts and Employee Performance on Managers' Empowering," *Leadership & Organization Development Journal* 27, no. 2 (2006): 217–34; R. N. Ashkenas, "Beyond Fads: How Leaders Drive Change with Results," *Human Resource Planning* 17, no. 2 (1994): 25–44; and Heather K. S. Laschinger, Joan E. Finegan, Judith Shamian, and Piotr Wilk, "A Longitudinal Analysis of the Impact of Workplace Empowerment on Work Satisfaction," *Journal of Organizational Behavior* 25, no. 4 (2004): 527–45.
37. J. T. Knippen and T. B. Green, "What to Do about a Boss Who Makes Decisions Too Fast," *Supervisory Management,* April 1994, p. 6.
38. Phred Dvorak, "Theory & Practice: How Understanding the 'Why' of Decisions Matters; Employees More Likely to Embrace Changes when Fully Informed," *Wall Street Journal,* March 19, 2007, p. B3; L. Landes, "The Myth and Misdirection of Employee Empowerment," *Training,* March 1994, p. 116; Scott Beagrie, "How to Delegate," *Personnel Today,* November 25, 2003, p. 25; and Carol Walker, "Saving Your Rookie Managers from Themselves," *Harvard Business Review,* April 2002, pp. 97–106.
39. J. Dobos, M. H. Bahniul, and S. E. Kogler Hill, "Power-Gaining Communication Strategies and Career Success," *Southern Communication Journal* 57 (1991): 35–48.
40. R. Tagiuri, "Ten Essential Behaviors," *Harvard Business Review,* January/February 1995, pp. 10–11; and "The Danger of Becoming Overdependent on a Staff Member," *Supervisory Management,* July 1995, p. 4.
41. G. Day and P. Schoemaker, "Are You a 'Vigilant Leader'?" *MIT Sloan Management Review* 49, no. 3 (2008): 43–51.
42. Kanter, "Power Failures in Management Circuits."
43. Pol Herrmann and James Werbel, "Promotability of Host-Country Nationals: A Cross-Cultural Study," *British Journal of Management* 18, no. 3 (2007): 281–293; Debbie Thorne McAlister and John R. Darling, "Upward Influence in Academic Organizations: A Behavioral Style Perspective," *Leadership & Organization Development Journal* 26, no. 7/8 (2005): 558–73; Gary Yukl and Tom Taber, "The Effective Use of Managerial Power," *Personnel,* March–April 1983, pp. 37–44; and Henry Mintzberg, "The Organization as Political Arena," *Journal of Management Studies* 22 (1985): 135–54.
44. Lyman W. Porter, Robert W. Allen, and H. L. Angee, "The Politics of Upward Influence in Organizations," in *Research in Organizational Behavior,* ed. Larry L. Cummings and Barry M. Staw (Greenwich, CT: JAI Press, 1981), pp. 181–216.
45. For excellent discussions of upward influence, see L. Atwater, P. Roush, and A. Fischtal, "The Influence of Upward Feedback on Self- and Follower Ratings of Leadership," *Personnel Psychology* 48 (1995): pp. 35–59.
46. For an interesting discussion of this and related topics, see Robert C. Liden and Terence R. Mitchell, "Ingratiating Behaviors in Organizational Settings," *Academy of Management Review* 13 (1988): 572–87.
47. Martin Z. Braun, "Can the SEC Get Its Street Cred Back?" *Businessweek,* April 12, 2010, p. 28; Jesse Westbrook, "Why The SEC Keeps Backpedaling," *Businessweek,* January 6, 2010, pp. 28–29; and Greg Farrell and Brooke Masters, "How Madoff Concealed the $65bn Fraud," *Financial Times,* August 12, 2009, p. 14.
48. R. P. Vecchio and M. Sussman, "Choice of Influence Tactics: Individual and Organizational Determinants," *Journal of Organizational Behavior* 12 (1991): 73–80.
49. Fiol et al., "All for One."
50. Michel Crozier, *The Bureaucratic Phenomenon* (Chicago: University of Chicago Press, 1964).
51. C. R. Hinnings, D. J. Hickson, J. M. Pennings, and R. E. Schneck, "Structural Conditions of

Intraorganizational Power," *Administrative Science Quarterly* 19 (1974): 22–44.

52. D. J. Hickson, C. R. Hinnings, C. A. Lee, R. E. Schneck, and J. M. Pennings, "A Strategic Contingency Theory of Intraorganizational Power," *Administrative Science Quarterly* 16 (1971): 216–29.
53. Hinnings et al., "Structural Conditions," p. 39.
54. Richard L. Daft, *Organization Theory and Design* (St. Paul, MN: West, 1983), pp. 392–98. This source contains an excellent discussion of the strategic contingency perspective in terms of managerial and organizational theory. Daft concisely presents the original Hickson et al. theory and research.
55. Hinnings et al., "Structural Conditions," p. 41.
56. Ibid., p. 40.
57. C. S. Saunders, "The Strategic Contingencies Theory of Power: Multiple Perspectives," *Journal of Management Studies* 27 (1990): 1–18.
58. Stanley Milgram, "Behavioral Study of Obedience," *Journal of Abnormal and Social Psychology* 67 (1963): 371–78; and Stanley Milgram, *Obedience to Authority* (New York: Harper & Row, 1974). For another discussion of the concept of obedience, see N. Woolsey, B. Gary, and G. Hamilton, "The Power of Obedience," *Administrative Science Quarterly* 29 (1984): 540–49.
59. Milgram, "Behavioral Study," p. 377.
60. K. Macher, "The Politics of People," *Personnel Journal,* January 1986, pp. 50–53.
61. Kenneth J. Harris, Matrecia James, and Ranida Boonthanom, "Perceptions of Organizational Politics and Cooperation as Moderators of the Relationship between Job Strains and Intent to Turnover," *Journal of Managerial Issues* 17, no. 1 (2005): 26–42; Dan L. Madison, Robert W. Allen, Lyman W. Porter, Patricia A. Renwick, and Bronston T. Mayes, "Organizational Politics: An Exploration of Managers' Perceptions," *Human Relations* 33 (1980): 79–100; Jeffrey Gantz and Victor V. Murray, "The Experience of Workplace Politics," *Academy of Management Journal,* June 1980, pp. 237–51; and Robert W. Allen, Dan L. Madison, Lyman W. Porter, Patricia A. Renwick, and Bronston T. Mayes, "Organizational Politics: Tactics and Characteristics of Its Actors," *California Management Review* (1979): 77–83.
62. George Strauss, "Tactics of the Lateral Relationship: The Purchasing Agent," *Administrative Science Quarterly* 7 (1962): 161–86.
63. Allen et al., "Organizational Politics."
64. For a complete description of the profile of a political manager, see C. Kirchmeyer, "A Profile of Managers Active in Office Politics," *Basic and Applied Social Psychology* 11 (1990): 339–56.
65. B. E. Ashforth and R. T. Lee, "Defensive Behavior in Organizations: A Preliminary Model," *Human Relations* 43 (1990): 621–48.
66. Laura Morgan Roberts, "Changing Faces: Professional Image Construction in Diverse Organizational Settings," *Academy of Management Review* 30, no. 4 (2005): 686–711; Sandy Wayne and Robert Liden, "Effects of Impression Management of Performance Ratings," *Academy of Management Journal* 38 (1995): 232–52; and Barry R. Schlenker, *Impression Management: The Self-Concept, Social Identity and Interpersonal Relations* (Monterey, CA: Brooks/Cole, 1980).
67. Kenneth J. Harris, K. Michele Kacmar, Suzanne Zivnuska, and Jason D. Shaw, "The Impact of Political Skill on Impression Management Effectiveness," *Journal of Applied Psychology* 92, no. 1 (2007): 278–85; Margarette Arndt and Barbara Bigelow, "Presenting Structural Innovation in an Institutional Environment: Hospitals' Use of Impression Management," *Administrative Science Quarterly* 45 (2000): 494–522; Dennis Bozeman and Michele Kacmar, "A Cybernetic Model of Impression Management Processes in Organizations," *Organizational Behavior and Human Decision Processes* 69 (1997): 9–30; and Barry Schlenker and M. Weigold, "Interpersonal Processes Involving Impression Regulation and Management," in *Annual Review of Psychology,* ed. M. R. Rosenzweig and L. W. Porter (Palo Alto, CA: Annual Reviews, 1992), pp. 133–68.
68. Arndt and Bigelow, "Structural Innovation."
69. Wayne and Liden, "Impression Management."
70. Val Singh and Susan Vinnicombe, "Impression Management, Commitment and Gender: Managing Others' Good Opinions," *European Management Journal* 19 (2001): 183–94; William Turnley and Mark Bolino, "Achieving Desired Images while Avoiding Undesired Images: Exploring the Role of Self-Monitoring in Impression Management," *Journal of Applied Psychology* 86 (2001): 351–60; Paul Rosenfeld, "Impression Management, Fairness and the Employment Interview," *Journal of Business Ethics* 16, no. 8 (1997): 801–8; Sandy Wayne and Gerald Ferris, "Influence Tactics, Affect, and Exchange Quality in Supervisor–Subordinate Interactions: A Laboratory Experiment and Field Study," *Journal of Applied Psychology* 75 (1990): 487–500; and James Tedeschi and Valerie Melburg, "Impression Management and Influence in the Organization," in *Research in Sociology of Organizations,* vol. 3, ed. S. B. Bacharach and E. J. Lawler (Greenwich, CT: JAI Press, 1984), pp. 31–58.
71. M. Bolino, M. Kacmar, W. Turnley, and J. Glistrap, "A Multi-Level Review of Impression Management Motives and Behaviors," *Journal of Management* 34, no. 6 (2008): 1080–109; Mark C. Bolino, Jose A. Varela, Belen Bande, and William H. Turnley, "The Impact of Impression-Management Tactics on Supervisor Ratings of Organizational Citizenship Behavior," *Journal of Organizational Behavior* 27, no. 3 (2006): 281–97.
72. Wayne and Liden, "Impression Management."
73. Sandy Wayne and Michele Kacmar, "The Effects of Impression Management on the Performance Appraisal

Process," *Organizational Behavior and Human Decision Processes* 48 (1991): 70–88; Wayne and Ferris, "Influence Tactics"; and David Kipnis, Stuart Schmidt, and Ian Wilkenson, "Intraorganizational Influence Tactics: Exploration of Getting One's Way," *Journal of Applied Psychology* 65 (1980): 440–52; and Chad A. Higgins, Timothy A. Judge, and Gerald R. Ferris, "Influence Tactics and Work Outcomes: A Meta-Analysis," *Journal of Organizational Behavior* 24 (2003): 89–106; and Lyle Sussman, Arthur J. Adams, Frank E. Kuzmits, and Louis E. Raho, "Organizational Politics: Tactics, Channels, and Hierarchical Roles," *Journal of Business Ethics* 40, no. 4 (2002): 313–30.

74. M. Barrick, J. Shaffer, and S. DeGrassi, "What You See May Not Be What You Get: Relationships Among Self-presentation Tactics and Ratings of Interview and Job Performance," *Journal of Applied Psychology* 94, no. 6 (2009): 1394–411; Wei-Chi Tsai, Chien-Cheng Chen, and Su-Fen Chiu, "Exploring Boundaries of the Effects of Applicant Impression Management Tactics in Job Interviews," *Journal of Management* 31, no. 1 (2004): 108–25; and Cynthia Stevens and Amy Kristof, "Making the Right Impression: A Field Study of Applicant Impression Management during Job Interviews," *Journal of Applied Psychology* 80 (1995): 587–606.
75. For a complete and interesting discussion of political games, refer to Mintzberg, *Power in and around Organizations,* chapter 13.
76. William B. Stevenson, Jane L. Pearce, and Lyman W. Porter, "The Concept of Coalition in Organization Theory and Research," *Academy of Management Review* 10 (1985): 256–68.
77. Michael Corkery, "Lehman Whistle-Blower's Fate: Fired—Mr. Lee Raised Red Flags About 'Repo 105' Accounting Device; Let Go for Downsizing, Said Firm," *Wall Street Journal,* March 16, 2010, p. C1.
78. Julianne G. Mahler and Maureen H. Casamayou, *Organizational Learning at NASA: The Columbia and Challenger Accidents* (Washington, D.C.: Georgetown University Press, 2009).
79. Jessica R. Mesmer-Magnus and Chockalingam Viswesvaran, "Whistleblowing in Organizations: An Examination of Correlates of Whistleblowing Intentions, Actions, and Retaliation," *Journal of Business Ethics* 62, no. 3 (2005): 277–97; and M. P. Miceli, J. P. Near, "Whistleblowing: Reaping the Benefits," *Academy of Management Executive* 8 (1994): 65–72.
80. Marcia P. Miceli and Janet P. Near, "The Incidence of Wrongdoing, Whistle-Blowing, and Retaliation: Results of a Naturally Occurring Field Experiment," *Employee Responsibilities and Rights Journal* 2 (1989): 91–108.
81. Gerald F. Cavanagh, Denis J. Moberg, and Manuel Velasquez, "The Ethics of Organizational Politics," *Academy of Management Review* 6 (1981): 363–74; and Manuel Velasquez, Denis J. Moberg, and Gerald F. Cavanagh, "Organizational Statesmanship and Dirty Politics." Also see "Collegians Speak Out on Ethical Issues," *Collegiate Edition Marketing News,* January 1988, pp. 1, 4.

Chapter 11

1. Bernard M. Bass, *Stogdill's Handbook of Leadership* (New York: Free Press, 1990), p. 21.
2. L. Melita Prati, Ceasar Douglas, Gerald R. Ferris, Anthony P. Ammeter, and M. Ronald Buckley, "Emotional Intelligence, Leadership Effectiveness, and Team Outcomes," *The International Journal of Organizational Analysis* 11 (2004): 21–40.
3. J. Hogan and R. Hogan, "Leadership and Sociopolitical Intelligence," in *Multiple Intelligences and Leadership,* ed. R. E. Riggio, S. E. Murphy, and F. J. Pirozzola (Mahwah, NJ: Lawrence Erlbaum, 2002), pp. 75–88.
4. K. Ng, S. Ang, and K. Chan, "Personality and Leader Effectiveness: A Moderated Mediation Model of Leadership Self-efficacy, Job Demands, and Job Autonomy," *Journal of Applied Psychology* 93 (2008): 733–43; Michael Feiner, *Feiner Points of Leadership* (New York: Warner, 2004).
5. Ralph M. Stogdill, *Handbook of Leadership* (New York: Free Press, 1974), pp. 43–44.
6. Edwin E. Ghiselli, *Explorations in Managerial Talent* (Santa Monica, CA: Goodyear, 1971). See also Rob R. Meijer, "Consistency of Test Behavior and Individual Differences in Precision Prediction," *Journal of Occupational and Organizational Psychology* 71 (1998): 147–60, for a report of recent method validation studies.
7. Constance L. Milton, "The Ethics of Personal Integrity in Leadership and Mentorship: A Nursing Theoretical Perspective," *Nursing Science Quarterly* 17 (2004): 116–20.
8. Edwin E. Ghiselli, "The Validity of Management Traits in Relation to Occupational Level," *Personnel Psychology* 16 (1963): 109–13.
9. For recent reviews, see T. Judge, R. Piccolo, and T. Kosalka, "The Bright and Dark Sides of Leader Traits: A Review and Theoretical Extension of the Leader Trait Paradigm," *Leadership Quarterly* 20 (2009): 855–75; Steven J. Zaccaro, "Trait-Based Perspectives of Leadership," *American Psychologist* 62 (2007): 6–16.
10. Craig L. Pearce, Jay A. Conger, and Edwin A. Locke, "Shared Leadership Theory," *Leadership Quarterly* 18 (2007): 281–89.
11. Shelley A. Kirkpatrick and Edwin A. Locke, "Leadership: Do Traits Matter?" *The Executive,* May 1991, pp. 48–60; and Andrew Kinder and Ivan T. Robertson, "Do You Have the Personality to Be a Leader?" *Leadership and Organizational Development* 15, no. 1 (1994): 3–12.
12. Ralph M. Stogdill, "Personal Factors Associated with Leadership," *Journal of Applied Psychology* 25 (1948): 72.

13. Rensis Likert, *New Patterns of Management* (New York: McGraw-Hill, 1961).
14. For a review of the studies, see Stogdill, *Handbook of Leadership,* chap. 11. Also see E. A. Fleishman, "The Measurement of Leadership Attitudes in Industry," *Journal of Applied Psychology* 37 (1953): 153–58; C. L. Shartle, *Executive Performance and Leadership* (Englewood Cliffs, NJ: Prentice-Hall, 1956); and E. A. Fleishman, E. F. Harris, and H. E. Burtt, *Leadership and Supervision in Industry* (Columbus, OH: Bureau of Educational Research, Ohio State University, 1955).
15. Fleishman et al., *Leadership and Supervision.*
16. G. H. Dobbins and S. J. Platz, "Sex Differences in Leadership: How Real Are They?" *Academy of Management Review* 11 (1986): 118–27.
17. Seokhwa Yum, Jonathan Cox, and Henry P. Sims, Jr., "The Forgotten Follower: A Contingency Model of Leadership and Follower Self-Leadership," *Journal of Managerial Psychology* 21, no. 3 (2007): 374–88.
18. Ibid.
19. Gary Yukl and Richard Lepsinger, *Flexible Leadership: Creating Value by Adding Balancing Multiple Challenges* (New York: Pfeiffer, 2004).
20. The discussion that follows is based on R. Tannenbaum and W. H. Schmidt, "How to Choose a Leadership Pattern," *Harvard Business Review,* May/June 1973, pp. 162–80.
21. Ibid., p. 180.
22. Fred E. Fiedler, *A Theory of Leadership Effectiveness* (New York: McGraw-Hill, 1967).
23. Fred E. Fiedler and M. M. Chemers, *Leadership and Effective Management* (Glenview, IL: Scott, Foresman, 1974).
24. Richard L. Miller, Jeanne Butler, and Charles J. Cosentino, "Followership Effectiveness: An Extension of Fiedler's Contingency Model," *Leadership and Organization Development Journal* 25 (2004): 362–68.
25. Fred E. Fiedler, "How Do You Make Leaders More Effective: New Answers to an Old Puzzle," *Organizational Dynamics* 1 (1972): 3–8; and Fred E. Fiedler and M. M. Chemers, *Improving Leadership Effectiveness: The LEADER MATCH Concept* (New York: John Wiley & Sons, 1984).
26. G. Graen, J. B. Orris, and K. M. Alvares, "Contingency Model of Leadership Effectiveness: Some Experimental Results," *Journal of Applied Psychology* 55 (1971): 196–201.
27. Chester A. Schriesheim, Bennett J. Tepper, and Linda A. Tetrault, "Least-Preferred Co-Worker Scale, Situational Control, and Leadership Effectiveness: A Meta-Analysis of Contingency Model Performance Predictions," *Journal of Applied Psychology* 79 (1994): 561–73.
28. Miller, Butler, Consentino, "Followership Effectiveness."
29. Robert J. House, "A Path–Goal Theory of Leadership Effectiveness," *Administrative Science Quarterly* 16 (1971): 321–39; Robert J. House and Terence R. Mitchell, "Path–Goal Theory of Leadership," *Journal of Contemporary Business* 3 (1974): 81–98; Robert J. House, "Path-goal Theory of Leadership: Lessons, Legacy, and a Reformulated Theory," *Leadership Quarterly* 7 (1996): 323–52.
30. M. G. Evans, "The Effects of Supervisory Behavior on the Path–Goal Relationship," *Organizational Behavior and Human Performance* 5 (1970): 277–98.
31. Robert J. House and G. Dessler, "The Path–Goal Theory of Leadership: Some Post Hoc and A Priori Test," in *Contingency Approaches to Leadership,* ed. J. G. Hunt (Carbondale, IL: Southern Illinois University Press, 1974).
32. Robert T. Keller, "A Test of the Path–Goal Theory of Leadership with Need for Clarity as a Moderator in Research and Development Organizations," *Journal of Applied Psychology* 74 (1989): 208–12.
33. House and Mitchell, "The Path–Goal Theory," p. 84.
34. House and Dessler, "The Path–Goal Theory."
35. C. Greene, "Questions of Causation in the Path–Goal Theory of Leadership," *Academy of Management Journal* 22 (1979): 22–41.
36. C. A. Schriesheim and A. DeNisi, "Task Dimensions as Moderators of the Effects of Instrumental Leadership: A Two-Sample Replicated Test of Path–Goal Leadership Theory," *Journal of Applied Psychology* 66 (1981): 589–97.
37. Originally published in Paul Hersey and Kenneth H. Blanchard, *Management of Organizational Behavior: Utilizing Human Resources* (Englewood Cliffs, NJ: Prentice-Hall, 1969). Now in the sixth edition, which discusses readiness.
38. Kenneth H. Blanchard, "Situational Leadership," *Leadership Excellence* 25, no. 5 (2008): 19.
39. Kevin B. Lowe, "Shared Leadership: Reframing the Hows and Whys of Leadership," *Leadership Quarterly* (February 2006): 105–8.
40. John F. Monoky, "What's Your Management Style?" *Industrial Distribution* 3 (1998): 142; and Kenneth H. Blanchard and Bob Nelson, "Recognition and Reward," *Executive Excellence,* April 1997, p. 15.
41. The Leader Behavior Analysis scales and instructions are available from Blanchard Training and Development Inc., 125 State Place, Escondido, CA 92025. See John K. Butler, "Assessing the Situations of the LEAD," *Organization Development Journal* 11 (1993): 33–42.
42. William R. Norris and Robert Vecchio, "Situational Leadership: A Replication," *Group and Organization Management* 17 (1992): 331–42; and Warren Blank, John R. Weitzel, and Stephen G. Green, "A Test of the Situational Theory," *Personnel Psychology* 43 (1990): 579–97.
43. Kathleen Boies and Jane M. Howell, "Leader-Member Exchange in Teams: An Examination of the Interaction Between Relationship Differentiation and Mean LMX in Explaining Team-Level Outcomes," *Leadership Quarterly* 17 (2006): 246–57.

44. G. B. Graen and M. Uhl-Bien, "The Relationship-based Approach to Leadership: Development of LMX Theory of Leadership Over 25 Years: Applying a Multi-level, Multi-domain Perspective," *Leadership Quarterly* 6 (1995): 219–47.
45. George Graen, R. Liden and W. Hoel, "Role of Leadership in the Employee Withdrawal Process," *Journal of Applied Psychology* 70 (1982): 868–72.
46. Steve W. J. Kozlowski and Mary L. Doherty, "Integration of Climate and Leadership Examination of a Neglected Issue," *Journal of Applied Psychology* 74 (1989): 546–53.
47. Antoinette S. Phillips and Arthur G. Bedeian, "Leader–Follower Exchange Quality: The Role of Personal and Interpersonal Attributes," *Academy of Management Journal* 37 (1994): 990–1001.

Chapter 12

1. Giles Hust, Leon Mann, Paul Bain, Andrew Pirola-Merlo, and Andreas Nichver, "Learning to Lead: The Development and Testing of a Model of Leadership Learning," *Leadership Quarterly* 15 (2004): 311–27.
2. Alan D. Boss and Henry P. Sims Jr., "Everyone Fails: Using Emotion Regulation and Self-leadership for Recovery," *Journal of Managerial Psychology* 23, no. 2 (2008): 135–50; C. P. Ncek, H. Nouri, and J. L. Godwin, "How Self-Leadership Affects the Goal-Setting Process," *Human Resource Management Review* 13 (2003): 691–707.
3. Tom Peters, *Thriving on Chaos* (New York: Knopf, 1987), p. 264.
4. Leonard O. Pellicer, *Caring Enough to Lead: How Reflective Practice Leads to Moral Leadership* (New York: Corwin Press, 2007).
5. Victor Vroom and Philip Yetton, *Leadership and Decision Making* (Pittsburgh: University of Pittsburgh Press, 1973).
6. Victor H. Vroom and Arthur G. Jago, *The New Leadership: Managing Participation in Organizations* (Englewood Cliffs, NJ: Prentice-Hall, 1988).
7. Victor H. Vroom and Arthur G. Jago, "On the Validity of the Vroom-Yetton Model," *Journal of Applied Psychology* 63 (1978): 151–62; R. H. G. Field, "A Test of the Vroom-Yetton Normative Model of Leadership," *Journal of Applied Psychology* 67 (1982): 523–32; Arthur G. Jago and Victor H. Vroom, "Predicting Leader Behavior from a Measure of Behavior Intent," *Academy of Management Journal* 21 (1978): 715–21; and William R. Pasewark and Jerry R. Strawser, "Subordinate Participation in Audit Budgeting Decisions," *Decision Sciences* 25 (1994): 281–99.
8. Vroom and Jago, *The New Leadership*. Authors retain all rights for decision trees, cases, and computer software.
9. W. Bohnisch, Arthur G. Jago, and G. Reber, "Zur interkulturellen Validitat des Vroom/Yetton Models," *Bebriebsivirtschaft* (1987): 85–93.
10. C. Margerison and R. Gluf, "Leadership Decision-Making: An Empirical Test of the Vroom and Yetton Model," *Journal of Management Studies* 16 (1979): 45–55.
11. John B. Kelley, "The Validity and Usefulness of Theories in an Emerging Science," *Academy of Management Review* 9 (1984): 296–306. See also F. William Brown and Kenn Finstuen, "The Use of Participation in Decision Making: A Consideration of the Vroom-Yetton and Vroom-Jago Normative Models," *Journal of Behavioral Decision Making* 6 (1993): 207–19.
12. Roger C. Mayer and Edward C. Tomlinson, The Role of Causal Attribution Dimensions in Trust Repair," *Academy of Management Review* 34, no. 1 (2009): 85–104; Glenn D. Reeder, Roos Vonk, Maria J. Ronk, Jaap Ham, and Melissa Lawrence, "Dispositional Attribution: Multiple Inferences about Motive-Related Traits," *Journal of Personality and Social Psychology* 86 (2004): 530–44.
13. Gary Yukl, *Leadership in Organizations* (Upper Saddle River, NJ: Prentice-Hall, 2005).
14. Terence R. Mitchell, S. C. Green, and Robert E. Wood, "An Attributional Model of Leadership and the Poor Performing Subordinate: Development and Validation," in *Research in Organizational Behavior,* ed. Barry M. Staw and Larry L. Cummings (Greenwich, CT: JAI Press, 1981).
15. Henry P. Sims Jr. and Peter Lorenzi, *The New Leadership Paradigm* (Newbury Park, CA: Sage, 1992), p. 221; and James C. McElroy, "Attribution Theory Applied to Leadership," *Journal of Managerial Issues* 3 (1991): 90–106.
16. Terence P. Mitchell and Robert E. Wood, "An Empirical Test of an Attributional Model of Leader's Responses to Poor Performance," in *Academy of Management Proceedings,* ed. Richard C. Huseman, 1979, pp. 94–98.
17. G. H. Dobbins, E. C. Pence, J. A. Organ, and J. A. Sgro, "The Effects of Sex of the Leader and Sex of the Subordinate on the Use of Organizational Control Policy," *Organizational Behavior and Human Performance* 32 (1983): 325–43.
18. Mark J. Martinko, ed., *Attribution Theory: An Organizational Perspective* (Boca Raton, FL: Saint Lucie Press, 1995).
19. Robert E. Ployhart and Ann Marie Ryan, "Toward an Explanation of Applicant Reactions: An Examination of Organizational Justice and Attribution Frameworks," *Organizational Behavior and Human Decision Processes* 72 (1997): 308–35.
20. Peter Earley, "Leaders or Followers?" *Education Management and Administration* (2003): 353–67.
21. C. N. Greene, "The Reciprocal Nature of Influence between Leader and Subordinate," *Journal of Applied Psychology* 60 (1975): 187–93.

22. Henry L. Tosi, Vilnios F. Misangyi, Angelo Faneeli, David A. Waldman, and Frances J. Yammarino, "CEO Charisma, Compensation, and Firm Performance," *Leadership Quarterly* 15 (2004): 405–20.
23. John Sculley, "Sculley's Lessons from Inside Apple," *Fortune,* September 14, 1987, pp. 108–11. Also see James C. Collins and Jerry I. Porras, "Building a Visionary Company," *California Management Review* (Winter 1995): 80–100.
24. Takala Tuomo, "How to Be an Effective Charismatic Leader: Lessons for Leadership Development," *Development and Learning Organizations* 20, no. 4 (2006): 19–21.
25. Min-Ping Huang, Bor-Shiuan and Li-Fong Chou, "Fitting in Organizational Values: The Mediating Role of Person-Organization Fit between CEO Charismatic Leadership and Employee Outcomes," *International Journal of Manpower* 26, no. 1 (2005): 35–49.
26. His views of charismatic leadership are clearly presented in Jay A. Conger, *The Charismatic Leader* (San Francisco: Jossey-Bass, 1989); and Jay A. Conger and Rabindra N. Kanunga, "Charismatic Leadership in Organizations: Perceived Behavioral Attributes and Their Measurement," *Journal of Organizational Behavior* 15 (1994): 439–52.
27. William L. Gardner and Bruce J. Avolio, "The Charismatic Relationship: A Dramaturgical Perspective," *Academy of Management Review* 23 (1998): 12–58.
28. Jaepil Choi, "A Motivational Theory of Charismatic Leadership: Envisioning, Empathy, and Empowerment," *Journal of Leadership & Organizational Studies* 13, no. 1 (2008): 24–43; C. Levay, "Charismatic Leadership in Resistance to Change," *Leadership Quarterly* 21 (2010): 127–43; Jay A. Conger, "The Necessary Art of Persuasion," *Harvard Business Review,* May/June 1998, pp. 84–95; Bernard M. Bass, *Leadership Performance beyond Expectations* (New York: Academic Press, 1985); and Warren G. Bennis and Burt Nanus, *Leaders* (New York: Harper & Row, 1985).
29. R. Khurana, *Searching for a Corporate Savior: The Irrational Quest for Charismatic CEOs* (Princeton, NJ: Princeton University Press, 2002).
30. Sheldene Simola, "Concepts of Care in Organizational Crisis Prevention," *Journal of Business Ethics* 62, no. 4 (2005): 341–53; C. Lalonde, "In Search of Archetypes in Crisis Management," *Journal of Contingencies and Crisis Management* 12 (2004): 76–88.
31. Badrinnaryan Shankar Pawar and Kenneth K. Eastman, "The Nature and Implications of Contextual Influences on Transformational Leadership: A Conceptual Examination," *Academy of Management Review* 22 (1997): 80–109.
32. B. Hedberg, "How Organizations Learn and Unlearn," in *Handbook of Organizational Design,* ed. P. C. Nystrom and W. H. Starbuck (London: Oxford University Press, 1980), pp. 3–37.
33. Daniel Sankowsky, "The Charismatic Leader as Narcissist: Understanding the Abuse of Power," *Organizational Dynamics* 23 (1995): 57–71; and Jane M. Howell and Bruce J. Avolio, "The Ethics of Charismatic Leadership: Submission or Liberation?" *The Executive,* May 1992, pp. 43–54.
34. N. Podsakoff, P. Podsakoff, and V. Kuskova, "Dispelling Misconceptions and Providing Guidelines for Leader Reward and Punishment Behavior," *Business Horizons* 53, no. 3 (2010): 291–303; Allan H. Church and Janine Waclawski, "The Relationship Between Individual Personality Orientation and Executive Leadership Behavior," *Journal of Occupational and Organizational Psychology* 71 (1998): 99–125.
35. N. Podsakoff et al, "Dispelling Misconceptions."
36. D. Yankelovich and J. Immerivoki, *Putting the Work Ethic to Work* (New York: Public Agenda Foundation, 1983).
37. J. C. Wofford, Vicki Goodwin, and J. Lee Whittington, "A Field Study of a Cognitive Approach to Understanding Transformational and Transactional Leadership," *Leadership Quarterly* 9 (1998): 55–84.
38. A. H. Eagly, M. C. Johannesen-Schmidt, and M. L. Van Engen, "Transformational, Transactional, and Laissez-Faire Leadership Styles: A Meta-Analysis Comparing Women and Men," *Psychological Bulletin* 129 (2003): 569–91.
39. Jim Collins, *Good to Great* (New York: HarperCollins, 2001), pp. 32–33.
40. Ibid., pp. 46–47.
41. Bass, *Leadership Performance beyond Expectations.* Deanne N. Den Hartog, Muijap Van, J. Jaap, and Paul L. Koopman, "Transactional versus Transformational Leadership: An Analysis of the MLQ," *Journal of Occupational and Organizational Psychology* 70 (1997): 19–34 tests and extends the underlying methodology to identify these two leadership patterns.
42. Hartog et al., p. 31.
43. Eagly et al., "Transformational, Transactional, and Laissez-Faire Leadership Styles: A Meta-Analysis Comparing Women and Men."
44. Robert P. Vecchio, "In Search of Gender Advantage," *Leadership Quarterly* 14 (2003): 835–50; Robert P. Vecchio, "Leadership and Gender Advantage," *Leadership Quarterly* 13 (2003): 643–71.
45. Collins, *Good to Great.*
46. M. Cole, H. Bruch, and B. Shamir, "Social Distance as a Moderator of the Effects of Transformational Leadership: Both Neutralizer and Enhancer," *Human Relations* 62, no. 11 (2009): 1697–733; D. R. May, A. Y. L. Chan, T. D. Hodges, and B. J. Avolio, "The Moral Component of Authentic Leadership," *Organizational Dynamics* 32 (2003): 247–60.
47. Steven Kerr and John M. Jermier, "Substitutes for Leadership: Their Meaning and Measurement," *Organizational Behavior and Human Performance* 22 (1978): 376–403; and Scott Williams, "Personality

and Self-Leadership," *Human Resource Management Review,* Summer 1997, pp. 139–55.

48. Ibid.
49. Richard S. Lapidus, James A. Chonko, and Lawrence R. Chonko, "Stressors, Leadership Substitutes, and Relations and Supervision," *Industrial Marketing Management,* May 1997, pp. 255–69.

Chapter 13

1. Richard E. Kopelman, "Job Redesign and Productivity: A Review of the Evidence," *National Productivity Review* 4 (1985): 239.
2. Randy Hodson, "Group Relations at Work: Solidarity, Conflict, and Relations with Management," *Work and Occupations* 25 (1997): 426–52; and Simone Grebner, Achim Elfering, Norbert K. Semmer, Claudia Kaiser-Probst, and Marie-Louise Schlapbach, "Stressful Situations at Work and in Private Life among Young Workers: An Event Sampling Approach," *Social Indicators Research* 64, no. 1 (2004): 11–49.
3. Paul Osterman, "How Common Is Workplace Transformation and Who Adopts It?" *Industrial and Labor Relations Review* 47 (1994): 173–88.
4. Marvin R. Weisbord, *Productive Workplaces: Organizing and Managing for Dignity, Meaning and Community* (San Francisco: Jossey-Bass, 1987).
5. Denise M. Rousseau and Rosemary Batt, "Global Competition's Perfect Storm: Why Business and Labor Cannot Solve Their Problems Alone," *Academy of Management Perspectives* 21, no. 2 (2007): 16–23; and Susan G. Cohen, Lei Chang, and Gerald E. Ledford, Jr., "A Hierarchical Construct of Self-Management Leadership and Its Relationship to Quality of Work Life and Perceived Work Group Effectiveness," *Personnel Psychology* 50 (1997): 275–308.
6. Rita Zeidner, "Home Is Where the Productivity Is," *HR Magazine,* July 2010, pp. 20–21.
7. Ibid.
8. M. Chafkin and L. Buchanan, "The Office Is Dead, Long Live the Office," *Inc.*, April 2010, pp. 62–73.
9. Barry M. Staw, Robert I. Sutton, and Lisa H. Pelled, "Employee Positive Emotion and Favorable Outcomes at the Workplace," *Organization Science* 4 (1994): 51–71; and Rosemary Batt, "Who Benefits from Teams? Comparing Workers, Supervisors, and Managers," *Industrial Relations* 43, no. 1 (2004): 103–13.
10. Jean Ann Seago, "Five Pitfalls of Work Redesign in Acute Care," *Nursing Management* 28, no. 10 (1997): 49–50.
11. J. Schramm, "Work Turns Flexible," *HR Magazine,* March 2009, p. 88.
12. Anonymous, "Flexible Hours in the Ranks," *HR Magazine,* January 2010, pp. 16–17.
13. E. Stavrou and C. Kilaniotis, "Flexible Work and Turnover: An Empirical Investigation Across Cultures," *British Journal of Management* 21, no. 2 (2010): 541–54.
14. Luis R. Gomez-Mejia, David B. Balkin, and Robert L. Cardy, *Managing Human Resources,* 6th ed. (Upper Saddle River, NJ: Prentice Hall, 2009).
15. "Have You Considered Job Sharing as a Retention Tool?" *HR Focus* 83, no. 9 (2006): 10–12; Charlene Solomon, "Job Sharing: One Job, Double Headache?" *Personnel Journal,* September 1994, pp. 88–93; and Amanda Beeler, "It Takes Two," *Sales and Marketing Management* 155, no. 8 (2003): 38.
16. D. Cadrain, "Sharing Work—and Unemployment Benefits," *HR Magazine,* July 2009, pp. 40–43.
17. K. Shockley and T. Allen, "Investigating the Missing Link in Flexible Work Arrangement Utilization: An Individual Difference Perspective," *Journal of Vocational Behavior* 76, no. 1 (2010): 131–142; Sue Shellenbarger, "Time on Your Side: Rating Your Boss's Flexible Scheduling," *Wall Street Journal,* January 25, 2007, p. D1; and Gomez-Mejia et al., *Managing Human Resources.*
18. Scott Westcott, "Beyond Flextime Trashing the Workweek," *Inc.*, August 2008, pp. 30–31.
19. Ibid.
20. Boris B. Baltes, Thomas E. Briggs, Joseph W. Huff, Julie A. Wright, and George A. Neuman, "Flexible and Compressed Workweek Schedules: A Meta-Analysis of Their Effects on Work-Related Criteria," *Journal of Applied Psychology* 84 (1999): 496–513.
21. Grant H. Fenner and Robert W. Renn, "Technology-assisted Supplemental Work: Construct Definition and a Research Framework," *Human Resource Management* 43, nos. 2–3 (2004): 179–90.
22. Diana Ransom, "SmartMoney: Six Ways to Manage a Virtual Work Force," http://online.wsj.com/article/SB10001424052748704133804575197901538081896.html *Wall Street Journal* (Online), April 21, 2010 (accessed on June 12, 2010).
23. John A. Pearce II, "Successful Corporate Telecommuting with Technology Considerations for Late Adopters," *Organizational Dynamics* 38, no. 1 (2009): 16–25.
24. Ibid.
25. Sharon Leonard, "The Baby Gap," *HR Magazine,* July 2000, pp. 368–70; and Janet Wiscombe, "Tearing Down the 'Maternal Wall,'" *Workforce* 81, October 2002, p. 15.
26. Michelle Conlin, "The Ideal Virtual Worker?" *Businessweek,* July 24, 2009, p. 65.
27. Keith Hammonds, Roy Furchgott, Steve Hamm, and Paul Judge, "Work and Family," *Businessweek,* September 5, 1997, pp. 96–101.
28. Gillian Flynn and Sarah F. Gale, "The Legalities of Flextime," *Workforce,* October 2001, pp. 62–66.
29. Nigel Bassett-Jones and Geoffrey C. Lloyd, "Does Herzberg's Motivation Theory Have Staying Power?" *The Journal of Management Development* 24, no. 10 (2005): 929–43; and Kenneth W. Thomas and Betty A.

Velthouse, "Cognitive Elements of Empowerment: An 'Interpretive' Model of Intrinsic Task Motivation," *Academy of Management Review* 15, no. 4 (1990): 666–81.

30. Joan R. Rentach and Robert P. Steel, "Testing the Durability of Job Characteristics as Predictors of Absenteeism over a Six-Year Period," *Personnel Psychology* 51 (1998): 163–90.
31. Menachem Rosner and Louis Putterman, "Factors behind the Supply and Demand for Less Alienating Work, and Some International Illustrations," *Journal of Economic Studies* 18, no. 1 (1991): 18–41.
32. Holdsworth and Susan Cartwright, "Empowerment, Stress and Satisfaction: An Exploratory Study of a Call Centre," *Leadership & Organization Development Journal* 24, no. 3 (2003): 131–41; and Jill Kickul, Scott W. Lester, and Jonathon Finkl, "Promise Breaking during Radical Organizational Change: Do Justice Interventions Make a Difference?" *Journal of Organizational Behavior* 23, no. 4 (2002): 469–88.
33. "The Shape of Workplaces to Come: Managing the Future," *Financial Times,* February 6, 2010, p. 3; Frank Shipper and Charles C. Manz, "Employee Self-Management without Formally Designated Teams: An Alternative Road to Empowerment," *Organizational Dynamics* 20, no. 3 (1992): 48–61; and Michael Weinreb, "Power to the People," *Sales and Marketing Management* 155, no. 4 (2003): 30–36.
34. Robert J. Vandenberg and Charles E. Lance, "Examining the Causal Order of Job Satisfaction and Organizational Commitment," *Journal of Management* 18 (1992): 153–67.
35. Sridhar N. Ramaswami and Jagdip Singh, "Antecedents and Consequences of Merit Pay Fairness for Industrial Salespeople," Journal of Marketing 67, no. 4 (2003): 46–66; Glenn Bassett, "The Case against Job Satisfaction," *Business Horizons* 37, no. 3 (1994): 61–68; and Jill Kanin-Lovers and Gordon Spunich, "Compensation and the Job Satisfaction Equation," *Journal of Compensation and Benefits* 7 (1992): 54–57.
36. Robert P. Tett and Dawn D. Burnett, "A Personality Trait-Based Interactionist Model of Job Performance," *Journal of Applied Psychology* 88, no. 3 (2003): 500–17; and Robert Dowless, "Motivating Salespeople: One Order of Empowerment: Hold the Carrots," *Training,* February 1992, pp. 16, 73–74.
37. Frederick P. Morgeson and Michael A. Campion, "Social and Cognitive Sources of Potential Inaccuracy in Job Analysis," *Journal of Applied Psychology* 82 (1997): 627–55, and James P. Clifford, "Job Analysis: Why Do It, and How Should It Be Done?" *Public Personnel Management* 23, no. 2 (1994): 321–40.
38. Michael T. Brannick, Edward L. Levine, and Frederick P. Morgeson, *Job and Work Analysis: Methods, Research, and Applications for Human Resource Management,* 2nd ed. (Thousand Oaks, CA: Sage, 2007).
39. "About O*NET," O*NET Resource Center accessed June 14, 2010, http://www.onetcenter.org/aboutOnet.html.
40. "O*NET Goes 'Green,' *Occupational Outlook Quarterly* 54, no. 1 (2010): 56.
41. Edward L. Levine, Doris M. Maye, Ronald A. Ulm, and Thomas R. Gordon, "A Methodology for Developing and Validating Minimum Qualifications," *Personnel Psychology* 50 (1997): 1009–23.
42. Jai V. Ghorpade, *Job Analysis: A Handbook for the Human Resource Director* (Englewood Cliffs, NJ: Prentice-Hall, 1988).
43. The literature of scientific management is voluminous. The original works and the subsequent criticisms and interpretations would make a large volume. Of special significance are the works of the principal authors, including Frederick W. Taylor, *Principles of Scientific Management* (New York: Harper & Row, 1911); Harrington Emerson, *The Twelve Principles of Efficiency* (New York: Engineering Magazine, 1913); Henry L. Gantt, *Industrial Leadership* (New Haven, CT: Yale University Press, 1916); Frank B. Gilbreth, *Motion Study* (New York: D. Van Nostrand, 1911); and Lillian M. Gilbreth, *The Psychology of Management* (New York: Sturgis & Walton, 1914).
44. Taylor, *Principles,* pp. 36–37.
45. Greg L. Stewart and Kenneth P. Carson, "Moving beyond the Mechanistic Model: An Alternative Approach to Staffing for Contemporary Organizations," *Human Resource Management Review* 7 (1997): 157–84.
46. Patrick Giblin, "RSI @ Home: Long Computer Sessions Can Lead to Big Problems," *Knight Ridder Tribune Business News,* May 18, 2006, p. 1; Douglas R. May and Catherine E. Schwoerer, "Employee Health by Design: Using Employee Involvement Teams in Ergonomic Job Redesign," *Personnel Psychology* 47 (1994): 861–76; Larry Reynolds, "Ergonomic Concerns Stiffen Rules Regarding VDT Use," *Personnel,* April 1991, pp. 1–2; and Connie Vaughn-Miller, "Haven't Got Time for the Pain," *Occupational Health & Safety* 72, no. 6 (2003): 112–16.
47. Theodore W. Braun, "Ergonomics: The Safety Science of the 1990's," *Risk Management,* October 1994, pp. 54–60.
48. Chi-Sum Wong, Chun Hui, and Kenneth S. Law, "A Longitudinal Study of the Job Perception–Job Satisfaction Relationship: A Test of the Three Alternative Specifications," *Journal of Occupational and Organizational Psychology* 71 (1998): 127–46.
49. Timothy A. Judge, Christine L. Jackson, John C. Shaw, Brent A. Scott, and Bruce L. Rich, "Self-Efficacy and Work-Related Performance: The Integral Role of Individual Differences," *Journal of Applied Psychology* 92, no. 1 (2007): 107–27; and Patrick H. Raymark, Mark J. Schmit, and Robert M. Guion, "Identifying Potentially Useful Personality Constructs for

Employee Selection," *Personnel Psychology* 50 (1997): 723–36.
50. Juan I. Sanchez, Alina Samora, and Chockalingam Viswesvaran, "Moderators of Agreement between Incumbent and Non-Incumbent Ratings of Job Characteristics," *Journal of Occupational and Organizational Psychology* 70 (1997): 209–18.
51. J. Richard Hackman and Edward W. Lawler III, "Employee Reactions to Job Characteristics," *Journal of Applied Psychology* 55, no. 3 (1971): 259–86; and J. Richard Hackman and Greg R. Oldham, "Development of the Job Diagnostic Survey," *Journal of Applied Psychology* 60, no. 2 (1975): 159–70.
52. For a recent review on work design, see: Stephen E. Humphrey, Jennifer D. Nahrgang, and Frederick P. Morgeson, "Integrating Motivational, Social, and Contextual Work Design Features: A Meta-analytic Summary and Theoretical Extension of the Work Design Literature," *Journal of Applied Psychology* 92, no. 5 (2007): 1332–56.
53. Robert P. Steel and Joan R. Rentach, "The Dispositional Model of Job Attitudes Revisited: Findings of a 10-Year Study," *Journal of Applied Psychology* 82, no. 6 (1997): 873–79.
54. Amy Kates, "(Re)Designing the HR Organization," *Human Resource Planning* 29, no. 2 (2006): 22–31; and Gregory B. Northcraft, Terri L. Griffith, and Christina E. Shalley, "Building Top Management Muscle in a Slow Growth Environment," *Academy of Management Executive* 6 (1992): 32–41.
55. M. Fiester, A. Collis, and N. Cossack, "Job Rotation, Total Rewards, Measuring Value," *HR Magazine,* August 2008, pp. 33–34; and Michael A. Campion, Lisa Cheraskin, and Michael J. Stevens, "Career-Related Antecedents and Outcomes of Job Rotation," *Academy of Management Journal* 37 (1994): 1518–42.
56. Michael A. Campion and Carol L. McClelland, "Follow-Up and Extension of the Interdisciplinary Costs and Benefits of Enlarged Jobs," *Journal of Applied Psychology* 78, no. 3 (1993): 339–51; and Michael A. Campion and Carol L. McClelland, "Interdisciplinary Examination of the Costs and Benefits of Enlarged Jobs: A Job Design Quasi-Experiment," *Journal of Applied Psychology* 76, no. 2 (1991): 186–98.
57. B. Mirza, "Reporting Rule Change Could Signal a New Ergonomics Standard," *HR Magazine,* April 2010, p. 12; and Lance Hazzard, Joe Mautz, and Denver Wrightman, "Job Rotation Cuts Cumulative Trauma Cases," *Personnel Journal* 71 (1992): 29–32.
58. Don Nichols, "Taking Participative Management to the Limit," *Management Review* 76 (1987): 28–32; and Bob Deierlein, "Team Cuts Costs," *Fleet Equipment,* April 1990, pp. 28–30.
59. Charles R. Walker and Robert H. Guest, *The Man on the Assembly Line* (Cambridge, MA: Harvard University Press, 1952).
60. Michael A. Campion, Troy V. Mumford, Frederick P. Morgeson, and Jennifer D. Nahrgang, "Work Redesign: Eight Obstacles and Opportunities," *Human Resource Management* 44, no. 4 (2005): 367–90.
61. J. Richard Hackman, Greg Oldham, Robert Janson, and Kenneth Purdy, "New Strategy for Job Enrichment," *California Management Review* (Summer 1975): 57–71; and J. Richard Hackman and Greg Oldham, "Development of the Job Diagnostic Survey," *Journal of Applied Psychology* 60, no. 2 (1975): 159–70.
62. J. Richard Hackman and Greg Oldham, *Work Redesign* (Reading, MA: Addison-Wesley, 1980).
63. Tom D. Taber and Elisabeth Taylor, "A Review and Evaluation of the Psychometric Properties of the Job Diagnostic Survey," *Personnel Psychology* 43 (1990): 467–500.
64. Michael J. Handel, "Skills Mismatch in the Labor Market," *Annual Review of Sociology* 29 (2003): 135–66; and Gary Johns, Jia L. Xie, and Yongqing Fang, "Mediating and Moderating Effects in Job Design," *Journal of Management* 18 (1992): 657–76.
65. Ricky W. Griffin, "Effects of Work Redesign on Employee Perceptions, Attitudes, and Behaviors: A Long-Term Investigation," *Academy of Management Journal* 34 (1991): 425–35.
66. Larry A. Pace and Eileen P. Kelly, "TQM at Xerox," *International Journal of Technology Management* 16, nos. 4–6 (1998): 326–35; and Joseph Fiorelli and Richard Feller, "Re-Engineering TQM and Work Redesign: An Integrative Approach to Continuous Organizational Excellence," *Public Administration Quarterly* 18 (1994): 54–63; and Anthony L. Patti, Sandra J. Hartmann, Lilliam Fok, and Wing M. Fok, "Jobs and People in a Total Quality Management Environment: A Survey of Academicians and Practitioners," *International Journal of Management* 18, no. 3 (2001): 359–74.
67. Kimberly D. Elsbach and Andrew B. Hargadon, "Enhancing Creativity through 'Mindless' Work: A Framework of Workday Design," *Organization Science* 17, no. 4 (2006): 470–83; Lloyd Dobyns and Clare Crawford-Mason, *Quality or Else: The Revolution in World Business* (Boston: Houghton Mifflin, 1991); and E. Craig McGee, "The Convergence of Total Quality and Work Design," *Journal of Quality & Participation* 16 (1993): 90–96.
68. A. Mannes, "Are We Wise About the Wisdom of Crowds? The Use of Group Judgments in Belief Revision," *Management Science* 55, no. 8 (2009): 1267–79; John Hollenbeck, Daniel Ilgen, Jeffrey LePine, Jason Colquitt, and Daniel Hedlund, "Extending the Multilevel Theory of Team Decision Making: Effects of Feedback and Experience in Hierarchical Teams," *Academy of Management Journal* 41 (1998): 269–82; and Bradley Kirkman and Debra Shapiro, "The Impact of Cultural Values on Employee Resistance to

Teams: Toward a Model of Globalized Self-Managing Work Team Effectiveness," *Academy of Management Review* 22 (1997): 730–57.

69. Michael Campion, Ellen Papper, and Gina Medsker, "Relations between Work Team Characteristics and Effectiveness: A Replication and Extension," *Personnel Psychology* 49 (1996): 429–52; Michael Campion, Gina Medsker, and C. Higgs, "Relations between Work Group Characteristics and Effectiveness: Implications for Designing Effective Work Groups," *Personnel Psychology* 46 (1993): 823–50; Hackman and Oldham, "Development of the Job Diagnostic Survey"; and Hackman and Lawler, "Employee Reactions to Job Characteristics."
70. Campion, Medsker, and Higgs, "Work Group Characteristics and Effectiveness."
71. Campion, Papper, and Medsker, "Replication and Extension."
72. Willem Niepce and Eric Molleman, "Work Design Issues in Lean Production from a Sociotechnical Systems Perspective: Neo-Taylorism or the Next Step in Sociotechnical Design?" *Human Relations* 51 (1998): 259–87; and Satisha Mehra and Surendra P. Agrawal, "Total Quality as a New Global Competitive Strategy," *International Journal of Quality & Reliability Management* 20, nos. 8/9 (2003): 1009–25.
73. George S. Easton and Sherry L. Jarrell, "The Effects of Total Quality Management on Corporate Performance: An Empirical Investigation," *Journal of Business* 71 (1998): 253–307; and Tom Christensen, "A High-Involvement Redesign," *Quality Progress* 26 (1993): 105–8.
74. Eric Trist, "The Evolution of Sociotechnical Systems," Occasional Paper (Ontario Quality of Working Life Centre, June 1981); and William M. Fox, "Sociotechnical System Principles and Guidelines," *Journal of Applied Behavioral Science* 31 (1995): 91–105.
75. Gensheng Liu, Rachna Shah, and Roger G. Schroeder, "Linking Work Design to Mass Customization: A Sociotechnical Systems Perspective," *Decision Sciences* 37, no. 4 (2006): 519–45; and Fred Emery, "Participative Design: Effective, Flexible and Successful," *Journal of Quality and Participation* 18 (1995): 6–9.
76. T. Kull and R. Narasimhan, "Quality Management and Cooperative Values: Investigation of Multilevel Influences on Workgroup Performance," *Decision Sciences* 41, no. 1 (2010): 81–113; A. B. Shani and James A. Sena, "Information Technology and the Integration of Change: Sociotechnical System Approach," *Journal of Applied Behavioral Science* 30 (1994): 247–70.

Chapter 14

1. Margaret R. Davis and David A. Weckler, *A Practical Guide to Organization Design* (Menlo Park, CA: Crisp Publications, 1997).
2. Ronald A. Heiner, "Imperfect Decisions in Organizations: Toward a Theory on Internal Structures," *Journal of Economic Behavior and Organization* 9 (1988): 25–44; and Michael T. Hannan, Lazlo Polos, and Glenn R. Carroll, "The Fog of Change: Opacity and Asperity in Organizations," *Administrative Science Quarterly* 48, no. 3 (2003): 399–432.
3. P. Rowland and K. Parry, "Consensual Commitment: A Grounded Theory of the Meso-level Influence of Organizational Design on Leadership and Decision-making," *Leadership Quarterly* 20, no. 4 (2009): 535–53; and Greg R. Oldham and J. Richard Hackman, "Relationship between Organizational Structure and Employee Reactions: Comparing Alternative Frameworks," *Administrative Science Quarterly* 26 (1981): 66–83.
4. James C. Dumville and Francisco A. Torano, "Division of Labor, Efficient? Empirical Evidence to Support the Argument," *SAM Advanced Management Journal* (Spring 1997): 16–20.
5. Donald J. Campbell, "Task Complexity: A Review and Analysis," *Academy of Management Review* 13 (1988): 40–52.
6. Alex Taylor III, "GM's Saturn Problem," *Fortune,* December 13, 2004, pp. 119–24; and James R. Treece and John Templeman, "Jack Smith Is Already on a Tear at GM," *Businessweek,* May 11, 1992, p. 37.
7. Joseph T. Mahoney, "The Adoption of the Multidivisional Form of Organization: A Contingency Approach," *Journal of Management Studies* 29 (1992): 49–72.
8. Frank Cornish, "Building a Customer-Oriented Organization," *Long-Range Planning* 21 (1988): 105–7; and Lynette Ryals and Simon Knox, "Cross-Functional Issues in the Implementation of Relationship Marketing through Customer Relationship Management," *European Management Journal* 19, no. 5 (2001): 534–42.
9. Michael Maccoby, "Transforming R&D Services at Bell Labs," *Research-Technology Management* 35 (1992): 46–49.
10. Allan Bradshaw, "How HR Helped Weyerhaeuser's Extreme Makeover," *Human Resource Planning* 30, no. 4 (2007): 46–50.
11. Ibid.
12. Jay R. Galbraith and Robert K. Kazanjian, "Organizing to Implement Strategies of Diversity and Globalization: The Role of Matrix Organizations," *Human Resource Management* 25 (1986): 37–54.
13. Robert S. Kaplan and David P. Norton, "How to Implement a New Strategy without Disrupting Your Organization," *Harvard Business Review,* March 2006, pp. 100–9; Mohammed K. El-Najdawi and Matthew J. Liberatore, "Matrix Management Effectiveness: An Update for Research and Engineering Organizations," *Project Management Journal* 28 (1997): 25–31; and Milton Harris and Artur Raviv, "Organizational Design," *Management Science* 48, no. 7 (2002): 852–66.

14. Jay R. Galbraith, *Designing Matrix Organizations That Actually Work: How IBM,Procter & Gamble, and Others Design for Success* (San Francisco: Jossey-Bass, 2009).
15. Paul B. de Laat, "Matrix Management of Projects and Power Struggles: A Case Study of an R&D Laboratory," *Human Relations* 47 (1994): 1089–119.
16. Christopher A. Barlett and Sumantra Ghosal, "Organizing for Worldwide Effectiveness: The Transactional Solution," *California Management Review* (Fall 1988): 54–74; and James K. McCollum and J. Daniel Sherman, "The Effects of Matrix Organization Size and Number of Project Assignments on Performance," *IEEE Transactions on Engineering Management* 38 (1991): 75–78.
17. Manfred Kling and Charles Davies, "Organization Redesign of DND's Material Group: Operation Excellence," *Optimum* 27, no. 4 (1997): 25–33.
18. Carol Hymowitz, "Today's Bosses Find Mentoring Isn't Worth the Time and Risks," *Wall Street Journal,* March 13, 2006, p. B.1; Ann Altaffer, "First-Line Managers: Measuring Their Span of Control," *Nursing Management* 29 (1998): 36–40; and William A. Kahn, "Managing the Paradox of Self-Reliance," *Organizational Dynamics* 30, no. 3 (2002): 239–56.
19. Pamela L. Moore, "She's Here to Fix the Xerox," *Businessweek,* August 6, 2001, pp. 47–48; and Karen E. Mishra, Gretchen M. Spreitzer, and Aneil K. Mishra, "Preserving Employee Morale during Downsizing," *MIT Sloan Management Review* 39, no. 1 (1998): 83–95.
20. David H. Freedman, "Corps Values," *Inc.,* April 1998, pp. 54–66; and Kenneth M. Meier and John Bohte, "Span of Control and Public Organizations: Implementing Luther Gulick's Research Design," *Public Administration Review* 63, no. 1 (2003): 61–71.
21. Jeffrey A. Alexander, "Adaptive Change in Corporate Control Practices," *Academy of Management Journal* 34 (1991): 162–93.
22. Carolyn G. Friese, Paula J. Fleurant, Sandra S. Hillman, and Kathryn T. Ulmen, "Nursing Council: Coordination within Decentralization," *Nursing Management* 29 (1998): 40–41.
23. Bill Stopper, "Best Buy: Customer-Centric Innovation," *Human Resource Planning* 29, no. 3 (2006): 34–36.
24. Ibid.
25. Donna Kardos Yesalavich, "Best Buy Gains 3.6%; Exxon, Peabody Drop," http://online.wsj.com/article/SB10001424052748703409804575144183166697648.html, *Wall Street Journal* (Online), March 26, 2010, accessed June 16, 2010.
26. Michel Poitevin, "Can the Theory of Incentives Explain Decentralization?" *Canadian Journal of Economics* 33 (2000): 878–906; and Abraham Seidmann and Arun Sundararajan, "Competing in Information-Intensive Services: Analyzing the Impact of Task Consolidation and Employee Empowerment," *Journal of Management Information Systems* 14 (1997): 33–56.
27. Tom Burns and G. M. Stalker, *The Management of Innovation* (London: Tavistock, 1961), are largely responsible for the terms *mechanistic* and *organic.*
28. Henri Fayol, *General and Industrial Management,* trans. J. A. Conbrough (Geneva: International Management Institute, 1929). The more widely circulated translation is that of Constance Storrs (London: Pitman, 1949).
29. James D. Mooney and Allan C. Reiley, *Onward Industry* (New York: Harper & Row, 1939); revised in James D. Mooney, *The Principles of Organization* (New York: Harper & Row, 1947).
30. Henry C. Metcalf and Lyndall Urwick, eds., *Dynamic Administration: The Collected Papers of Mary Parker Follett* (New York: Harper & Row, 1940).
31. Lyndall Urwick, *The Elements of Administration* (New York: Harper & Row, 1944).
32. For a review, see: Eric J. Walton, "The Persistence of Bureaucracy: A Meta-analysis of Weber's Model of Bureaucratic Control," *Organization Studies* 26, no. 4 (2005): 569–600.
33. Michael Crozier, *The Bureaucratic Phenomenon* (Chicago: University of Chicago Press, 1964), p. 3.
34. Max Weber, *The Theory of Social and Economic Organization,* trans. A. M. Henderson and Talcott Parsons (New York: Oxford University Press, 1947).
35. Ibid., p. 334.
36. *From Max Weber: Essays in Sociology,* trans. H. H. Gerth and C. W. Mills (New York: Oxford University Press, 1946), p. 214.
37. Rob Preston, "High Five," *InformationWeek,* May 7, 2007, p. 15; Julia Kirby, "Reinvention with Respect: An Interview with Jim Kelly of UPS," *Harvard Business Review,* November 2001, pp. 116–18; Kent C. Nelson, "Efficiency Wasn't Enough, So We Learned How to Dance," *Computerworld,* March 23, 1992, p. 33; Richard B. Chase and Nicholas J. Aquilano, *Operations Management* (Homewood, IL: Richard D. Irwin, 1992), p. 533; and Paul Lukas and Maggie Overfelt, "United Parcel Service," *Fortune Small Business* 13, no. 3 (2003): 24.
38. Robin Godlwyn Blumenthal, "A Turn for the Better," *Barron's*, February 18, 2008, p. 12.
39. Rensis Likert, *New Patterns of Management* (New York: McGraw-Hill, 1961); and Rensis Likert, *The Human Organization* (New York: McGraw-Hill, 1967).
40. K. Gregory Jin, Ron Drozdenko, and Rick Bassett, "Information Technology Professionals' Perceived Organizational Values and Managerial Ethics: An Empirical Study," *Journal of Business Ethics* 71, no. 2 (2007): 149–59; Amos Drory and Nurit Zaidman, "Impression Management Behavior: Effects of the Organizational System," *Journal of Managerial Psychology* 22, no. 3 (2007): 290–308; Marshall Schminke, "Considering the Business of Business

Ethics: An Exploratory Study of the Influence of Organizational Size and Structure on Individual Ethical Predispositions," *Journal of Business Ethics* 30, no. 4 (2001): 375–90; and Greg L. Stewart and Kenneth P. Carson, "Moving Beyond the Mechanistic Model," *Human Resource Management Review* 7 (1997): 157–84.

41. "About Us," Thrivent Financial for Lutherans, accessed June 16, 2010, https://www.thrivent.com/aboutus/.
42. Donald J. McNerney, "Compensation Case Study: Rewarding Team Performance and Individual Skillbuilding," *HR Focus,* January 1995, pp. 1, 4; Dennis H. Pillsbury, "Team Concept Makes Vorpagel #1 for AAL," *Life & Health Insurance Sales,* October 1993, pp. 10–11; and Fred Luthans, "A Conversation with Charles Dull," *Organizational Dynamics* 21 (1993): 57–70.
43. Charles Perrow, "A Framework for the Comparative Analysis of Organizations," *American Sociological Review* 32 (1967): 195. See Michael Withey, Richard L. Daft, and William H. Cooper, "Measures of Perrow's Work-Unit Technology: An Empirical Assessment and a New Scale," *Academy of Management Journal* 26 (1983): 45–63.
44. Joan Woodward, *Industrial Organization: Theory and Practice* (London: Oxford University Press, 1965).
45. Ibid., p. 35.
46. J. J. Rackham, "Automation and Technical Change—The Implications for the Management Process," *Organizational Structure and Design,* ed. Gene W. Dalton, Paul R. Lawrence, and Jay W. Lorsch (Homewood, IL: Richard D. Irwin, and Dorsey Press, 1970), p. 299.
47. Joan Woodward, *Management and Technology: Problems of Progress in Industry,* no. 3 (London: Her Majesty's Stationery Office, 1958), pp. 4–30; and Gary A. Yukl and Kenneth N. Wexley, eds., *Readings in Organizational and Industrial Psychology* (New York: Oxford University Press, 1971), p. 19.
48. Paul R. Lawrence and Jay W. Lorsch, "Differentiation and Integration in Complex Organizations," *Administrative Science Quarterly* 12 (1967): 1–47; Jay W. Lorsch, *Product Innovation and Organization* (New York: Macmillan, 1965); Paul R. Lawrence and Jay W. Lorsch, *Organization and Environment* (Homewood, IL: Richard D. Irwin, 1969); and Paul R. Lawrence, "The Harvard Organization and Environment Research Program," in *Perspectives on Organization Design and Behavior,* ed. Andrew H. Van de Ven and William Joyce (New York: Wiley Interscience, 1981), pp. 311–37.
49. Lawrence and Lorsch, *Organization and Environment,* p. 16.
50. Lawrence and Lorsch, "Differentiation and Integration in Complex Organizations," pp. 3–4.
51. James D. Thompson, *Organizations in Action* (New York: McGraw-Hill, 1967), p. 56.
52. Lawrence and Lorsch, "Differentiation and Integration in Complex Organizations," pp. 7–8.
53. Sanjib Chowdhury and Grant Miles, "Customer-Induced Uncertainty in Predicting Organizational Design: Empirical Evidence Challenging the Service versus Manufacturing Dichotomy," *Journal of Business Research* 59, no. 1 (2006): 121–29; Ruth N. Bolton, P. K. Kannan, and Mathew D. Bramlett, "Implications of Loyalty Program Membership and Service Experiences for Customer Retention and Value," *Academy of Marketing Science* 28 (2000): 95–108; James L. Heskett, *Managing in the Service Economy* (Boston: Harvard Business School Press, 1986); and Susan A. Mohrman, David Finegold, and Janice A. Klein, "Designing the Knowledge Enterprise: Beyond Programs and Tools," *Organizational Dynamics* 31, no. 2 (2002): 134–50.
54. Martin P. Charns, "Organization Design of Integrated Delivery Systems," *Hospital and Health Services Administration* 42 (1997): 411–32.
55. The development of theory relating information process and organization structure has been discussed in various sources. The most publicized sources are Jay Galbraith, *Designing Complex Organizations* (Reading, MA: Addison-Wesley, 1973); and Jay Galbraith, *Organization Design* (Reading, MA: Addison-Wesley, 1977).
56. M. Barton and K. Sutcliffe, "Learning When to Stop Momentum," *MIT Sloan Management Review* 51, no. 3 (2010): 69–76; Joseph P. Forgas, "Affective Influences on Judgments and Behavior in Organizations: An Information Processing Perspective," *Organizational Behavior and Human Decision Processes* 86 (2001): 3–24; and Shouhong Wang, "Impact of Information Processing on Organizations," *Human Resources Management,* 16, no. 2 (1997): 83–90; and G. Tomas M. Hult, David J. Ketchen, Jr., and Stanley F. Slater, "Information Processing, Knowledge Development, and Strategic Supply Chain Performance," *Academy of Management Journal* 47, no. 2 (2004): 241–53.
57. Miles H. Overholt, "Flexible Organizations: Using Organization Design as a Competitive Advantage," *Human Resource Planning* 20, no. 1 (1997): 22–32; and Yasin Sankar, "Designing the Learning Organizations as an Information-Processing System," *International Journal of Organization Theory and Behavior* 6, no. 4 (2003): 501–22.
58. Eric L. Trist, "The Sociotechnical Perspective: The Evolution of Sociotechnical Systems as a Conceptual Framework and as Action Research Program," in *Perspectives on Organization Design and Behavior,* ed A. Van de Ven and W. F. Joyce (New York: John Wiley, 1981); and Eric L. Trist and Ken W. Bamforth, "Some Social and Psychological Consequences of the Longwall Method of Coal-Getting," *Human Relations* 4 (1951): 6–24.
59. Gensheng Liu, Rachna Shah, and Roger G. Schroeder, "Linking Work Design to Mass Customization: A Sociotechnical Systems Perspective," *Decision Sciences*

37, no. 4 (2006): 519–45; Markham T. Frohlich and J. Robb Dixon, "Information Systems Adaptation and the Successful Implementation of Advanced Manufacturing Technologies," *Decision Sciences* 30, no. 4 (1999): 921–57; and Thomas G. Cummings, "Self-Regulating Work Groups: A Sociotechnical Synthesis," *Academy of Management Review* 11 (1978): 625–35.

60. Harry Hummels and Jan de Leede, "Teamwork and Morality: Comparing Lean Production and Sociotechnology," *Journal of Business Ethics* 26, no. 1 (2000): 75–88.
61. H. Scarbrough, "The Social Engagement of Social Science: A Tavistock Anthology," *Human Relations* 28 (1995): 23–31.
62. J. Shook, "How to Change a Culture: Lessons From NUMMI," *MIT Sloan Management Review* 51, no. 2 (2010): 63–68.
63. Matt Nauman, "GM-Toyota Auto Plant in Fremont, Calif., Ranks Near Top in Efficiency," *Knight Ridder Tribune Business,* June 10, 2004, p. 1; and General Motors, "General Motors and Toyota Announce All-New Vehicle," General Motors, http://www.gm.com/cgi-bin/pr_display.pl?1938.
64. Hummels and de Leede, "Teamwork and Morality."
65. Sandhya Shekhar, "Understanding the Virtuality of Virtual Organizations," *Leadership & Organization Development Journal* 27, no. 5 (2006): 465–483.
66. For a review, see N. Anand and Richard L. Daft, "What is the Right Organization Design?" *Organizational Dynamics* 36, no. 4 (2007): 329–344.
67. Ibid.
68. Ibid.
69. J. Crispim and J. de Sousa, "Partner Selection in Virtual Enterprises," *International Journal of Production Research* 48, no. 3 (2010): 683.
70. Robert L. Cross, Amin Yan, and Meryl R. Louis, "Boundary Activities in 'Boundaryless' Organizations: A Case Study of a Transformation to a Team-Based Structure," *Human Relations* 53, no. 6 (2000): 841–68; Raymond E. Miles, Charles C. Snow, John A. Malthus, Grant Miles, and Henry J. Coleman Jr., "Organizing in the Knowledge Era: Anticipating the Cellular Form," *Academy of Management Executive,* 11 (1997): 7–20; and Ronald N. Ashkenas, Dave Ulrich, C. K. Prahalad, and Todd Jick, *The Boundaryless Organization: Breaking the Chains of Organizational Structure* (San Francisco: Jossey-Bass, 2002).
71. Abbe Mowshowitz, "Virtual Organization: A Vision of Management in the Information Age," *Information Society* 10, no. 4 (1994): 267–88; Heather Ogilvie, "At the Core, It's the Virtual Organization," *Journal of Business Strategy* 15 (1994): 29; and "Learning from Japan," *Businessweek,* January 27, 1992, pp. 52–55, 58–59.
72. Anthony M. Townsend, Samuel DeMarie, and Anthony R. Hendrickson, "Virtual Teams: Technology and the Workplace of the Future," *Academy of Management Executive* 12 (1998): 17–29.
73. William F. Joyce, Victor E. McGee, and John W. Slocum, Jr., "Designing Lateral Organizations: An Analysis of the Benefits, Costs, and Enablers of Nonhierarchical Organizational Forms," *Decision Sciences* 28 (1997): 1–25; and Paul R. Sparrow, "New Employee Behaviours, Work Designs and Forms of Work Organization: What Is in Store for the Future of Work?" *Journal of Managerial Psychology* 15, no. 3 (2000): 202–18.

Chapter 15

1. Adi Katz and Dov Te'eni, "The Contingent Impact of Contextualization on Computer-Mediated Collaboration," *Organization Science* 18, no. 2 (2007): 261–79; Klaus Krippendorf, "An Epistemological Foundation for Communication," *Journal of Communication* 34 (1984): 21–36; and Beth A. Bechky, "Sharing Meaning across Occupational Communities: The Transformation of Understanding on a Production Floor," *Organization Science* 14, no. 3 (2003): 312–30.
2. M. J. Papa and E. E. Graham, "The Impact of Diagnosing Skill Deficiencies and Assessment-Based Communication Training on Managerial Performance," *Communication Education* 40 (1991): 368–84.
3. These five questions were first suggested in H. D. Lasswell, *Power and Personality* (New York: W. W. Norton, 1948), pp. 37–51.
4. Claude Shannon and Warren Weaver, The Mathematical Theory of Communication (Urbana, IL: University of Illinois Press, 1948); and Wilbur Schramm, "How Communication Works," in *The Process and Effects of Mass Communication,* ed. Wilbur Schramm (Urbana, IL: University of Illinois Press, 1953), pp. 3–26. These works are considered classics in the field of communication.
5. Wing Lam, Xu Huang, and Ed Snape, "Feedback-Seeking Behavior and Leader-Member Exchange: Do Supervisor-Attributed Motives Matter? *Academy of Management Journal* 50, no. 2 (2007): 348–63; Susan Ashford, "Feedback-Seeking in Individual Adaptation: A Resource Perspective," *Academy of Management Journal* 29, no. 3 (1986): 465–87; and Sherry E. Moss and Juan I. Sanchez, "Are Your Employees Avoiding You? Managerial Strategies for Closing the Feedback Gap," *Academy of Management Executive* 18, no. 1 (2004): 32–45.
6. "Science and Technology: Gestures of Intent," *Economist,* May 5, 2007, p. 89; Dale A. Level, Jr., and William P. Galle, Jr., *Managerial Communications* (Plano, TX: Business Publications, 1988); and Erik P. Bucy, "Emotional and Evaluative Consequences of Inappropriate Leader Displays," *Communication Research* 27, no. 2 (2000): 194–226.
7. For a detailed review of research associated with non-verbal communication, see B. M. DePaulo, "Nonverbal

Behavior and Self-Presentation," *Psychological Bulletin* 11, no. 2 (1992): 203–43.

8. Nick Morgan, "How to Become an Authentic Speaker," *Harvard Business Review,* November 2008, pp. 115–119.
9. Ibid.
10. Paul Ekman and W. V. Friesen, *Unmasking the Face* (Englewood Cliffs, NJ: Prentice-Hall, 1975).
11. Level and Galle, *Managerial Communications,* p. 66.
12. Geert Hofstede, *Cultures and Organizations: Software of the Mind* (London: McGraw-Hill, 1991).
13. Nancy Adler, *International Dimensions of Organizational Behavior,* 4th ed. (Cincinnati, OH: South-Western Publishing, 2002); and Robert Konopaske and John M. Ivancevich, *Global Management and Organizational Behavior* (New York: McGraw-Hill/ Irwin, 2004).
14. David Ricks, *Blunders in International Business,* 3rd ed. (Oxford: Blackwell Publishers, 1999).
15. Edward T. Hall and Mildred R. Hall, *Understanding Cultural Differences: Germans, French, and Americans* (Yarmouth, ME: Intercultural Press, 1989).
16. Ibid.
17. Adler, *International Dimensions of Organizational Behavior.*
18. Hall and Hall, *Understanding Cultural Differences.*
19. Ibid.
20. C. Barnum and N. Wolniansky, "Taking Cues from Body Language (International Business Transactions)," *Management Review* (June 1989): 59–60.
21. D. Matsumoto, "American–Japanese Cultural Differences in the Recognition of Universal Facial Expressions," *Journal of Cross-Cultural Psychology* 23 (1992): 72–84.
22. Jonny Gifford, "Information on a Plate," *Personnel Today,* January 24, 2006, pp. 28–29; and Nicholas Smeed, "A Boon to Employee Communications: Letters of Understanding," *Personnel* 62 (1985): 50–53.
23. G. F. Kohut and A. H. Segars, "The President's Letter to Stockholders: An Examination of Corporate Communication Strategy," *Journal of Business Communication* 29, no. 1 (1992): 7–21.
24. R. Conaway and W. Wardrope, "Do Their Words Really Matter? Thematic Analysis of U.S. and Latin American CEO Letters," *Journal of Business Communication* 47, no. 2 (2010): 141–68.
25. M. Kroumova, M. Lazarova, "Broad-based Incentive Plans, HR Practices and Company Performance," *Human Resource Management Journal* 19, no. 4 (2009): 355–374; W. Smither, M. London, R. R. Reilly, and R. E. Millsap, "An Examination of an Upward Feedback Program over Time," *Personnel Psychology* 48 (1995): 1–34.
26. Charles E. Beck and Elizabeth A. Beck, "The Manager's Open Door and the Communication Climate," *Business Horizons* 29, no. 1 (1986): 15–19.
27. Dennis Tourish and Paul Robeson, *Journal of Management Studies* 43, no. 4 (2006): 711–30; and Allan D. Frank, "Trends in Communication: Who Talks to Whom?" *Personnel* 62 (1985): 41–47.
28. For two excellent example of company efforts to enhance communication (and the pitfalls of such attempts), see Ruth G. Newman, "Polaroid Develops a Communications System—But Not Instantly," *Management Review* 79 (1990): 34–39; and M. M. Petty, James F. Cashman, Anson Seers, Robert L. Stevenson, Charles W. Barker, Grady Cook, "Better Communication at General Motors," *Personnel Journal* (September 1989): 40–53.
29. M. Erez, "Interpersonal Communication Systems in Organizations, and Their Relationships to Cultural Values, Productivity, and Innovation: The Case of Japanese Corporations," *Applied Psychology: An International Review* 41, no. 1 (1992): 43–64.
30. Jos Bartels, Oscar Peters, Menno de Jong, Ad Pruyn, and Marjolijn van der Molen, "Horizontal and Vertical Communication as Determinants of Professional and Organisational Identification," *Personnel Review* 39, no. 2 (2010): 210–26.
31. Preston Gralla, *How the Internet Works,* 6th ed. (Indianapolis, IN: Que—A Division of Macmillan Computer Publishing, 2001).
32. "Internet Usage and Popluation in North America," Internet World Stats, accessed June 22, 2010, http://www.internetworldstats.com/stats14.htm.
33. Ibid.
34. Bill Roberts, "Portal Takes Off," *HR Magazine,* February 2003, pp. 95–99.
35. Mary Hayes, "Hungry for Bottom-Line Results," *InformationWeek,* September 22, 2003, pp. 107–8.
36. "Gambits & Gadgets in the World of Technology," *Wall Street Journal,* June 5, 2003, p. B4.
37. "Number of E-Mail Users Worldwide to Reach 1.6 Billion in 2011," *The Radicati Group Report*, http://software.tekrati.com/research/9512/ (accessed June 28, 2009).
38. Tim Paradis, "Message to Wall Street: Save E-Mail," *Wall Street Journal,* December 4, 2002, p. C5.
39. Aparna Nancherla, "Surveillance Increases in Workplace," *T + D,* May 2008, p. 12.
40. Ibid.
41. Michelle Conlin, "Workers, Surf at Your Own Risk," *Businessweek,* June 12, 2000, pp. 105–6.
42. Roger Cheng, "Corporate News: Yahoo-Google Messaging May Drive Growth," *Wall Street Journal,* June 17, 2008, p. B4; D. Greenfield, "Permission to Speak Freely," *InformationWeek,* March 2008, pp. 56–60; and William M. Bulkeley, "Instant Message Goes Corporate; 'You Can't Hide'," *Wall Street Journal,* September 4, 2002, p. B1.
43. David Strom, "Managing Your Instant Messaging Frontier," *Business Communications Review* 36, no. 4 (2006): 62–65; and Michael D. Osterman, "Instant Messaging in he Enterprise," *Business Communications Review* 33, no. 1 (2003): 59–63.

44. Mary Hayes Weier, "Business Gone Mobile," *InformationWeek,* March 30, 2009, pp. 23–27.
45. Bart Perkins, "Texting Rules!" *Computerworld,* May 11, 2009, p. 26.
46. Ibid.
47. Daniel Dombey and Chris Nattall, "Twitter Delays Service Breaks after State Department Talks," *Financial Times,* June 17, 2009, p. 2.
48. Jack and Suzy Welch, "Why We Tweet," *Businessweek,* June 15, 2009, p. 76.
49. Jena McGregor, "Job Review in 140 Keystrokes," *Businessweek,* March 23, 2009, p. 58.
50. Michelle Conlin and Douglas MacMillan, "Managing the Tweets," *Businessweek,* June 1, 2009, p. 20.
51. Bill Roberts, "Stay Ahead of the Technology Use Curve," *HR Magazine,* October 2008, pp. 57–61.
52. Conlin and MacMillan, "Managing the Tweets."
53. Maggie Jackson, "May We Have Your Attention, Please? With the Workplace Ever More Full of Distractions, Researchers Are Developing Tools to Keep Us on Task," *Businessweek,* June 12, 2008, http://www.businessweek.com/magazine/content/08_25/b4089055162244.htm, accessed May 15, 2010.
54. "USA Mobile Penetration: 91%," wireless.org, accessed June 23, 2010, http://www.dailywireless.org/2010/03/29/usa-mobile-penetration-91/.
55. Stephen Manes, "The Sound of One Hand E-Mailing," *Forbes,* October 27, 2003, p. 216; and "Business: PDA, RIP, Handheld Computers," *Economist,* October 18, 2003, p. 87.
56. Reena Jana and Peter Burrows, "An All-Out Online Assault on the iPhone," *Businessweek,* April 6, 2009, p. 74.
57. Adapted from Elizabeth Guilday, "Voicemail Like a Pro," *T + D,* October 2000, pp. 68–69.
58. Tony Kontzer, "Victory for Videoconferencing," *InformationWeek,* December 15, 2003, p. 58.
59. Paul Taylor, "Seats at the Virtual Table: Personal Technology," *Financial Times,* April 24, 2009, p. 16.
60. Ibid.
61. See www.hp.com and Hewlett-Packard, *Annual Report 2002.*
62. B. Donabedian, S. M. McKinnon, and W. J. Bruns, "Task Characteristics, Managerial Socializations, and Media Selection," *Management Communication Quarterly* 11, no. 3 (1998): 372–400.
63. John Tierney, "As the Grapevine Withers, Spam Filters Take Root," *New York Times,* May 22, 2007, p. Fl; and David Cathmoir Nicloo, "Acknowledge and Use Your Grapevine," *Management Decision* 32, no. 6 (1994): 25–30.
64. K. M. Watson, "An Analysis of Communication Patterns: A Method for Discriminating Leader and Subordinate Roles," *Academy of Management Journal* 25 (1982): 107–22.
65. Robert Levy, "Tilting at the Rumor Mill," *Dun's Review,* December 1981, pp. 52–54.
66. Lisa A. Burke and Jessica Morris Wise, "The Effective Care, Handling, and Pruning of the Office Grapevine," *Business Horizons* 46, no. 3 (2003): 71–76; and Akande Abebowale and Funmilayo Odewale, "One More Time: How to Stop Company Rumors," *Leadership and Organizational Journal* 15, no. 4 (1994): 27–30.
67. R. L. Rosnow, "Psychology in Rumor Reconsidered," *Psychological Bulletin* 89 (1980): 578–91.
68. Frederick Koenig, *Rumor in the Marketplace* (Dover, MA: Auburn House, 1985).
69. J. Mishra, "Managing the Grapevine," *Public Personnel Management* 19 (1990): 213–28.
70. Phillip G. Clampitt and M. Lee Williams, "Decision Downloading," *MIT Sloan Management Review* 48, no. 2 (2007): 77–82.
71. Fred Luthans and Janet K. Larsen, "How Managers Really Communicate," *Human Relations* 39, no. 2 (1986): 161–78. See also Larry E. Penley and Brian Hawkins, "Studying Interpersonal Communication in Organizations: A Leadership Application," *Academy of Management Journal* 28 (1985): 309–26.
72. Hymowitz, "Today's Bosses Find Mentoring Isn't Worth the Time and Risks."
73. Joseph Luft, "The Johari Window," *Human Relations and Training News,* January 1961, pp. 6–7. The discussion here is based on a later adaptation. See James Hall, "Communication Revisited," *California Management Review* (Fall 1973): 56–67.
74. Walter D. St. John, "You Are What You Communicate," *Personnel Journal* 64 (1985): 40–43; and David A. Griffith, "The Role of Communication Competencies in International Business Relationship Development," *Journal of World Business* 37, no. 4 (2002): 256–65.
75. Owen Hargie and Dennis Tourish, "Communication Skills Training: Management Manipulation or Personal Development?" *Human Relations* 47 (1994): 1377–89.
76. Bob Wall, "Being Smart Only Takes You So Far," *T + D,* January 2007, pp. 64–68; Michael Laff, "Middle Managers Have Thickest Skin," *T + D,* October 2006, pp. 18–19; and Robert E. Kaplan, Wilfred H. Drath, and Joan R. Kofodimos, "Why Some Managers Don't Get the Message," *Across the Board,* September 1985, pp. 63–69.
77. William Hennefrund, "Fear of Feedback," *Association Management,* March 1986, pp. 80–83.
78. Chris Argyris, "Good Communication That Blocks Learning," *Harvard Business Review,* July/August 1994, pp. 77–85.
79. "Honda Philosophy," Honda of America, accessed June 23, 2010, http://ohio.honda.com/CompanyInfo/philosophy.cfm.
80. Watson, "An Analysis of Communication Patterns," p. 111; and John M. Hunthausen, Donald M. Truxillo, Tayla N. Bauer, and Leslie B. Hammer, "A Field Study of Frame-of-Reference Effects on Personality Test Validity," *Journal of Applied Psychology* 88, no. 3 (2003): 545–51.

81. F. W. Nickols, "How to Figure Out What to Do," *Training,* August 1991, pp. 31–34, 39.
82. Edward Hall, *The Hidden Dimension* (Garden City, NY: Doubleday, 1966).
83. Phillip L. Hunsaker, "Communicating Better: There's No Proxy for Proxemics," *Business,* March–April 1980, pp. 41–48.
84. Andrew McAfee, "Mastering the Three Worlds of Information Technology," *Harvard Business Review,* November 2006, pp. 141–49; Liz Thach and Richard W. Woodman, "Organizational Change and Information Technology: Managing on the Edge of Cyberspace," *Organizational Dynamics* 23, no. 2 (1994): 30–46; and Samuel M. DeMarie and Michael A. Hitt, "Strategic Implications of the Information Age," *Journal of Labor Research* 21, no. 3 (2000): 419–30.
85. Ernest G. Bormann, "Symbolic Convergence Theory: A Communication Formulation," *Journal of Communication* 35 (1985): 128–38.
86. Peter F. Drucker, "The Information Executives Truly Need," *Harvard Business Review,* January/February 1995, pp. 54–62.
87. Robert C. Liden and Terence R. Mitchell, "Reactions to Feedback: The Role of Attributions," *Academy of Management Journal* 28 (1985): 291–308.
88. K. Cravens, E. Oliver, and J. Stewart, "Can a Positive Approach to Performance Evaluation Help Accomplish Your Goals?" *Business Horizons* 53, no. 3 (2010) 269–79; and Harriet V. Lawrence and Albert K. Wiswell, "Feedback Is a Two-Way Street," *T + D,* July 1995, pp. 49–52.
89. M. E. Schnake, Michael P. Dumler, Dan Cochran, and Timothy Barnett, "Effects of Differences in Superior and Subordinate Perceptions of Superiors' Communication Practices," *Journal of Business Communication* 27 (1990): 37–50; and Merna Skinner, "Training Managers to be Better Communicators," *Employment Relations Today* 27, no. 1 (2000): 73–81.
90. G. W. Kemper, "Managing Corporate Communication in Turbulent Times," *IABC Communication World,* May–June 1992.
91. Keith Davis, *Human Behavior at Work* (New York: McGraw-Hill, 1980), p. 394.

Chapter 16

1. Max H. Bazerman, *Judgment in Managerial Decision Making,* 6th ed. (Hoboken, NJ: Wiley, 2005); and Bernard M. Bass, *Organizational Decision Making* (Homewood, IL: Richard D. Irwin, 1983).
2. Danny Samson, *Managerial Decision Making* (Homewood, IL: Richard D. Irwin, 1988); and Paul C. Nutt, *Why Decisions Fail* (San Francisco: Berrett-Koehler Publishers, 2002).
3. Richard L. Daft, "Theory Z: Opening the Corporate Door for Participative Management," *Academy of Management Executive* 18, no. 4 (2004): 117–21; and John L. Cotton, David A. Vollrath, and Kirk L. Froggatt, "Employee Participation: Diverse Forms and Different Outcomes," *Academy of Management Review* 13 (1988): 8–22.
4. Patrick E. Connor, "Decision-Making Participation Patterns: The Role of Organizational Context," *Academy of Management Journal* 35 (1992): 218–31.
5. Roger L. Martin, "The Execution Trap," *Harvard Business Review,* July 2010, pp. 66–71.
6. Herbert A. Simon, *The New Science of Management Decision* (New York: Harper & Row, 1960), pp. 5–6.
7. Neil M. Agnew and John L. Brown, "Executive Judgment: The Intuition/Rational Ratio," *Personnel,* December 1985, pp. 48–54.
8. Stephen D. Brookfield, *Developing Critical Thinkers: Challenging Adults to Explore Alternative Ways of Thinking* (San Francisco: Jossey-Bass, 1987).
9. William B. Stevenson and Mary C. Gilly, "Information Processing and Problem Solving: The Migration of Problems through Formal Positions and Networks of Ties," *Academy of Management Journal* 34 (1991): 918–28.
10. Weston Agor, "The Logic of Intuition: How Top Executives Make Important Decisions," *Organizational Dynamics* 14 (1986): 5–18.
11. Paul C. Nutt, "Types of Organizational Decision Processes," *Administrative Science Quarterly* 29 (1984): 414–50; and S. Pokras, *Strategic Problem Solving and Decision Making* (Los Altos, CA: Crisp, 1989).
12. Richard Farson and Ralph Keyes, "The Failure-Tolerant Leader," *Harvard Business Review,* August 2002, pp. 64–69; Norman Augustine, "Is Any Risk Acceptable Today?" *Across the Board,* May 1994, pp. 14–15; and Tunia Cherian George, "How FedEx Gets Staff to Deliver," *Businessline,* September 2, 2003, p. 1.
13. Russell L. Ackoff, *The Art of Problem Solving* (New York: John Wiley & Sons, 1987).
14. Allen R. Solem, "Some Applications of Problem-Solving versus Decision-Making to Management," *Journal of Business and Psychology* 6 (1992): 401–11.
15. Yukari Iwatani Kane and Niraj Sheth, "Apple Knew of iPhone Issue—Engineers Aware of Antenna Risks Before Release, but CEO Jobs Liked Design," *Wall Street Journal,* July 16, 2010, p. B1, Eastern edition.
16. Markus C. Becker and Thorbjorn Knudsen, "The Role of Routines in Reducing Pervasive Uncertainty," *Journal of Business Research* 58, no. 6 (2005): 746–57; and DeanTjosvold, "Effects of Crisis Orientation on Managers' Approach to Controversy in Decision Making," *Academy of Management Journal* 27 (1984): 130–38.
17. Donald Sull, "Are You Ready to Rebound?" *Harvard Business Review,* March 2010, pp. 70–74.
18. "About ETS," ETS, accessed July 26, 2010, http://www.ets.org/about; and Thomas H. Davenport, "Make Better

Decisions," *Harvard Business Review,* November 2009, pp. 117–23.

19. Karl E. Weick, *Sensemaking in Organizations* (London: Sage, 1995).
20. Jane Seiling and Gina Hinrichs, "Mindfulness and Constructive Accountability as Critical Elements of Effective Sensemaking: A New Imperative for Leaders as Sensemanagers," *Organization Development Journal* 23, no. 3 (2005): 82–88.
21. Deborah Ancona, Thomas W. Malone, Wanda J. Orlikowski, and Peter M. Senge, "In Praise of the Incomplete Leader," *Harvard Business Review,* February 2007: 92–100.
22. Paul Shrivastava, "Knowledge Systems for Strategic Decision Making," *Journal of Applied Behavioral Science* 21 (1985): 95–108; and Tilmann Betsch, Susanne Haberstroh, Beate Molter, and Andreas Glockner, "Oops, I Did It Again—Relapse Errors in Routinized Decision Making," *Organizational Behavior and Human Decision Processes* 93, no. 1 (2004): 62–74.
23. William Q. Judge and Alex Miller, "Antecedents and Outcomes of Decision Speed in Different Environmental Contexts," *Academy of Management Journal* 34 (1991): 449–63.
24. F. Buytendijk, T. Hatch, and P. Micheli, "Scenario-based Strategy Maps," *Business Horizons* 53, no. 4 (2010): 335–347; David H. Mason, "Scenario-Based Planning: Decision Model for the Learning Organization," *Planning Review* 22 (1994): 6–11.
25. Paul J. Shoemaker, "Scenario Planning: A Tool for Strategic Thinking," *MIT Sloan Management Review* 36, no. 2 (1995): 25–40.
26. Pino G. Audia and Henrich R. Greve, "Less Likely to Fail: Low Performance, Firm Size, and Factory Expansion in the Shipbuilding Industry," *Management Science* 52, no. 1 (2006): 83–94; Kenneth R. MacCrimmon and Donald A. Wehrung, *The Management of Uncertainty: Taking Risks* (New York: Free Press, 1986); and Christian Gollier and Nicolas Treich, "Decision-Making under Scientific Uncertainty: The Economics of the Precautionary Principle," *Journal of Risk and Uncertainty* 27, no. 1 (2003): 77–103.
27. For a detailed explanation of game theory, see Adam Brandenburger and Barry Nalebuff, "The Right Game: Use Game Theory to Shape Strategy," *Harvard Business Review,* July/August 1995, pp. 57–71.
28. Jeffrey E. Kottemann, Fred D. Davis, and William E. Remus, "Computer-Assisted Decision Making: Performance, Beliefs, and the Illusion of Control," *Organizational Behavior and Human Decision Processes* 57 (1994): 26–37.
29. "Black Storm Rising; The Gulf of Mexico Oil Spill," *Economist,* May 6, 2010, pp. 69–71.
30. Paul Shrivastava and I. I. Mitroff, "Enhancing Organizational Research Utilization: The Role of Decision Makers' Assumptions," *Academy of Management Review* 9 (1984): 18–26.
31. Charles R. Schwenk, *The Essence of Strategic Decision Making* (Lexington, MA: Lexington Books, 1988); and Sue Myburgh, "Strategic Information Management: Understanding a New Reality," *Informational Management Journal* 36, no. 1 (2002): 36–41.
32. Cindy Skrzycki, "The Secret Auto-Safety Files," *Washington Post,* November 21, 2006, p. D1; and Kenneth N. Gilpin, "Firestone Will Recall an Additional 3.5 Million Tires," *New York Times,* October 2001, p. C3.
33. Maura Reynolds, "Senate Deal for Asbestos Victims Trust Fund Announced," *Los Angeles Times,* April 20, 2005, p. A31; Cynthia F. Mitchell, "Trustees Named for Manville's Asbestos Fund—Action Puts Concern Closer to Leaving Chapter 11," *Wall Street Journal,* June 12, 1986, p. 1; and Andrew Schneider, "Asbestos Remains Major Problem Despite White House Efforts to Bar Litigation," *Knight Ridder/Tribune Business News,* February 1, 2004, p. 1.
34. Mitchell, "Trustees Named for Manville's Asbestos Fund."
35. W. Thomas Stephens, "Manville-Asbestos Ethical Issues Shaping Business Practice," *Financier,* January 1988, pp. 33–37.
36. George C. Dillon, "Does It Pay to Do the Right Thing?" *Across the Board,* July/August 1991, pp. 15–19.
37. "Asbestos Victims Left in Limbo after Ruling," *The Safety & Health Practitioner* 28, no. 11, November 2010, pp. 8–9.
38. "Lack of Formal Ethics Programs Connected to Workplace Problems," survey from Society for Human Resource Management (SHRM) and Ethics Resources Center (ERC), www.shrm.org; and Susan J. Wells, "Turn Employees into Saints?" *HR Magazine,* December 1999, pp. 48–58.
39. David Fritzsche and E. Oz, "Personal Values' Influence on the Ethical Dimension of Decision Making," *Journal of Business Ethics* 75, no. 4 (2007): 335–43; Shannon Bowen, "Organizational Factors Encouraging Ethical Decision Making: An Exploration into the Case of an Exemplar," *Journal of Business Ethics* 52, no. 4 (2004): 311–24; and Terry W. Low, Linda Ferrell, and Phylis Mansfield, "A Review of Empirical Studies Assessing Ethical Decision Making in Business," *Journal of Business Ethics* 25, no. 3 (2000): 185–204.
40. Kathie L. Pelletier and Michelle C. Bligh, "Rebounding from Corruption: Perceptions of Ethics Program Effectiveness in a Public Sector Organization," *Journal of Business Ethics* 67, no. 4 (2006): 359–74; Low et al., "A Review of Empirical Studies"; and Bruce R. Gaumnitz and John C. Lere, "A Classification Scheme for Codes of Business Ethics," *Journal of Business Ethics* 49, no. 4 (2004): 329–35.

41. Ellen Sheng, "Fidelity Fires Two Fund Managers," *Wall Street Journal Online,* http://online.wsj.com/article/SB10001424052748704240004575086390253589472.html, accessed July 18, 2010.
42. Jean Thilmany, "Supporting Ethical Employees," *HR Magazine,* September 2007, pp. 105–12.
43. E. Frauenheim, "Blowing the Whistle at Bayer," *Workforce Management* 88, no. 1 (2009): 8.
44. "Code of Business Conduct and Ethics for Members of the Board of Directions and Executive Officers," Johnson & Johnson, accessed July 18, 2010, http://www.investor.jnj.com/governance/boardconduct.cfm.
45. Kelly C. Strong and G. Dale Meyer, "An Integrative Descriptive Model of Ethical Decision Making," *Journal of Business Ethics* 11, no. 2 (1992): 89–94; and Christine A. Hemingway and Patrick W. Maclagan, "Managers' Personal Values as Drivers of Corporate Responsibility," *Journal of Business Ethics* 50, no. 1 (2004): 33–44.
46. Linda Klebe Trevino, "Ethical Decision Making in Organizations: A Person–Situation Interactional Model," *Academy of Management Review* 11 (1986): 601–17.
47. Ralph L. Keeney, "Creativity in Decision Making with Value-Focused Thinking," *MIT Sloan Management Review* 35, no. 4 (1994): 33–41.
48. D. Ghosh, "Corporate Values, Workplace Decisions and Ethical Standards of Employees," *Journal of Managerial Issues* 20, no. 1 (2008): 68–87; P. A. Renwick and H. Tosi, "The Effects of Sex, Marital Status, and Educational Background on Selected Decisions," *Academy of Management Journal* 21 (1978): 93–103; and A. A. Abdel-Halim, "Effects of Task and Personality Characteristics on Subordinate Responses to Participative Decision Making," *Academy of Management Journal* 26 (1983): 477–84. For an interesting cross-cultural study, see Frank Heller, Peter Drenth, Paul Koopman, and Veljko Rus, *Decisions in Organizations: A Three-Country Comparative Study* (Newbury Park, CA: Sage, 1988).
49. Mark H. Radford, Leon Mann, Yasuyuki Ohta, and Yoshibumi Nakane, "Differences between Australian and Japanese Students in Reported Use of Decision Process," *International Journal of Psychology* 26, no. 1 (1991): 35–52.
50. Stephen Overell, "Learning to Trust that Gut Feeling: Management Intuition," *Financial Times,* August 18, 2000, p. 12; and Ann Langley, "Between Paralysis by Analysis and Extinction by Instinct," *MIT Sloan Management Review* 36, no. 3 (1995): 63–76.
51. Adapted from Richard L. Daft, *Management,* 5th ed. (Ft. Worth, TX: Dryden Press, 2000).
52. Ibid.
53. Amos Tversky and Daniel Kahneman, "The Framing of Decisions and the Psychology of Choice," *Science,* January 30, 1981, pp. 453–58.
54. Peter L. Bernstein, "How We Take Risks," *Across the Board,* February 1997, pp. 23–26; N. S. Fagley and Paul M. Miller, "The Effects of Decision Framing on Choice of Risky vs. Certain Options," *Organizational Behavior and Human Decision Processes* 39 (1987): 264–80; and Daniel Kahneman and Amos Tversky, "Prospect Theory: An Analysis of Decision under Risk," *Econometrica* 47 (1979): 263–91.
55. A. Glöckner and T. Betsch, "Do People Make Decisions Under Risk Based on Ignorance? An Empirical Test of the Priority Heuristic Against Cumulative Prospect Theory," *Organizational Behavior and Human Decision Processes* 107, no. 1 (2008): 75–95; Kin Fai Ellick Wong and Jessica Y. Y. Kwong, "Between-Individual Comparisons in Performance Evaluation: A Perspective from Prospect Theory," *Journal of Applied Psychology* 90, no. 2 (2005): 284–94; Glen Whyte, "Escalating Commitment in Individual and Group Decision Making: A Prospect Theory Approach," *Organizational Behavior and Human Decision Processes* 54 (1993): 430–56; Tatsuya Kameda and James H. Davis, "The Function of the Reference Point in Individual and Group Risk Decision Making," *Organizational Behavior and Human Decision Processes* 46 (1990): 55–77; Fagley and Miller, "The Effects of Decision Framing"; and Tversky and Kahneman, "The Framing of Decisions."
56. Leon Festinger, *A Theory of Cognitive Dissonance* (New York: Harper & Row, 1957), chap. 1; and Richard P. Larrick and Terry L. Boles, "Avoiding Regret in Decisions with Feedback: A Negotiation Example," *Organizational Behavior & Decision Process* 63 (1995): 87–97.
57. J. Richard Harrison and James C. March, "Decision Making and Postdecision Surprises," *Administrative Science Quarterly* 29 (1984): 26–42. Also see James C. March, *Decisions and Organizations* (New York: Basil Blackwell, 1988).
58. M. Keil, G. Depledge, and A. Rai, "Escalation: The Role of Problem Recognition and Cognitive Bias," *Decision Sciences* 38, no. 3 (2007): 391–421; Xin He and Vikas Mittal, "The Effect of Decision Risk and Project Stage on Escalation of Commitment," *Organizational Behavior and Human Decision Processes* 103, no. 2 (2007): 225–37; and Mark Keil, "Escalation of Commitment in Information Systems Development: A Comparison of Three Theories," *Academy of Management Journal* (1995): 348–55.
59. Kin Fai Ellick Wong and Jessica Y. Y. Kwong, "The Role of Anticipated Regret in Escalation of Commitment," *Journal of Applied Psychology* 92, no. 2 (2007): 545–53; Barry M. Staw, "Knee-Deep in the Big Muddy—A Study of Escalating Commitment to a Chosen Course of Action," *Organizational Behavior and Human Performance* 16 (1976): 27–44; and Henry Moon, "Looking Forward and Looking

Back: Integrating Completion and Sunk-Cost Effects within an Escalation of Commitment Progress Decision," *Journal of Applied Psychology* 86, no. 1 (2001): 104–13.

60. Dan Fagin, "Lights Out at Shorham," *Long Island History Online,* November 2001, pp. 1–5, www.lihistory.com/9/hs9shore.htm.
61. Jerry Ross and Barry M. Staw, "Organizational Escalation and Exit: Lessons from the Shoreham Nuclear Power Plant," *Academy of Management Journal* 36 (1993): 701–32.
62. Fagin, "Lights Out at Shorham."
63. Joel Brockner, "The Escalation of Commitment to a Failing Course of Action: Toward Theoretical Progress," *Academy of Management Review* 17 (1992): 39–61.
64. Ibid.
65. Bill McEvily and Alfred Marcus, "Embedded Ties and the Acquisition of Competitive Capabilities," *Strategic Management Journal* 26, no. 11 (2005): 1033–55.
66. For examples, see B. Gray, *Collaborating: Finding Common Ground for Multi-Party Problems* (San Francisco: Jossey-Bass, 1989).
67. Martha L. Maznevski, "Understanding Our Differences: Performance in Decision-Making Groups with Diverse Members," *Human Relations* 47 (1994): 531–32; and Gerardo Andres Okhuysen, "Structuring Change: Familiarity and Formal Interventions in Problem-Solving Groups," *Academy of Management Journal* 44 (2001): 794–808.
68. For examples, see Barry M. Staw, "The Escalation of Commitment to a Course of Action," *Academy of Management Review* 6 (1981): 577–88; Max H. Bazerman and Alan Appelman, "Escalation of Commitment in Individual and Group Decision Making," *Organizational Behavior and Human Performance* 33 (1984): 141–52; Barbara Bird, "Implementing Entrepreneurial Ideas: The Case for Intention," *Academy of Management Review* 13 (1988): 442–53; and Warren E. Watson, Larry K. Michaelsen, and Walt Sharp, "Member Competence, Group Interaction, and Group Decision-Making: A Longitudinal Study," *Journal of Applied Psychology* 76 (1991): 803–9.
69. Richard A. Guzzo and James A. Waters, "The Expression of Affect and the Performance of Decision-making Groups," *Journal of Applied Psychology* 67 (1982): 67–74; Dean Tjosvold and R. H. G. Field, "Effects of Social Context on Consensus and Majority Vote Decision Making," *Academy of Management Journal* 26 (1983): 500–6; and Fredrick C. Miner, Jr., "Group versus Individual Decision Making: An Investigation of Performance Measures, Decision Strategies, and Process Losses/Gains," *Organizational Behavior and Human Performnce* 33 (1984): 112–24.
70. Diane M. Mackie, M. Cecilia Gastardo-Conaco, and John J. Skelly, "Knowledge of the Advocated Position and the Processing of In-Group and Out-Group Persuasive Messages," *Personality and Social Psychology Bulletin* 18 (1992): 145–51.
71. G. Stahl, M. Maznevski, A. Voigt, and K. Jonsen, "Unraveling the Effects of Cultural Diversity in Teams: A Meta-analysis of Research on Multicultural Work Groups," *Journal of International Business Studies* 41, no. 4 (2010): 690–709.
72. Kathleen J. Krone, "A Comparison of Organizational, Structural, and Relationship Effects on Subordinates' Upward Influence Choices," *Communication Quarterly* 40 (1992): 1–15.
73. Richard P. McGlynn, Dennis McGurk, Vicki Sprague Effland, Nancy L. Johll, and Deborah J. Harding, "Brainstorming and Task Performance in Groups Constrained by Evidence," *Organizational Behavior and Human Decision Processes* 93, no. 1 (2004): 75–87; and R. Brent Gallupe, Lana M. Bastianutti, and William H. Cooper, "Unblocking Brainstorms," *Journal of Applied Psychology,* February 1991, pp. 137–42.
74. Norman Dalkey, *The Delphi Method: An Experimental Study of Group Opinion* (Santa Monica, CA: Rand Corporation, 1969). This is the classic groundbreaking work on the Delphi method.
75. "Study Spots Global Marketing Trends (Global Marketing 2000: Future Trends and Their Implications, A Delphi Study)," *Marketing News,* October 14, 1991, p. 9.
76. See Andre L. Delbecq, Andrew H. Van de Ven, and David H. Gustafson, *Group Techniques for Program Planning* (Glenview, IL: Scott, Foresman, 1975), for a work devoted entirely to techniques for group decision making. See also Evan W. Duggan and Cherian S. Thachenkary, "Integrating Nominal Group Technique and Joint Application Development for Improved Systems Requirements Determination," *Information & Management* 41, no. 4 (2004): 399–411.
77. Leigh Thompson, "Improving the Creativity of Organizational Work Groups," *Academy of Management Executive* 17, no. 1 (2003): 96–111; and Brian Mullen, Craig Johnson, and Eduardo Salas, "Productivity Loss in Brainstorming Groups: A Meta-Analytic Integration," *Basic and Applied Social Psychology* 12 (1991): 3–23.
78. Delbecq, Van de Ven, and Gustafson, *Group Techniques for Program Planning,* p. 18.
79. "Making Good Decisions," *Supervisory Management,* January 1995, pp. 10–11.

Chapter 17

1. Michael A. Beitler, *Strategic Organizational Change* (New York: PPI, 2006).
2. Alexander Grashow, *The Practice of Adaptive Leadership: Tools and Tactics for Changing Your Organization and the World* (Boston: Harvard Business School Publishing, 2009). D. Abrashoff, *It's Your Ship:*

Management Techniques from the Best Damn Ship in the Navy (New York: Warner, 2005).

3. Thomas G. Cummings and Christopher G. Worley, *Organizational Development and Change*, 9th ed. (Boston: South-Western College Publishing, 2008).
4. Janice A. Klein, *True Change: How Outsiders on the Inside Get Things Done in Organizations* (San Francisco: Jossey-Bass, 2004).
5. Davis Dyer and Daniel Gross, *Generations of Corning: The Life and Times of a Global Corporation* (New York: Oxford University Press, 2001).
6. Robert E. Quinn, *Building the Bridge as You Walk on It: A Guide for Leading Change* (San Francisco: Jossey-Bass, 2004).
7. Mark Jenkins, Nick Henry, and Steven Pinch, "Knowledge, Clusters, and Competitive Advantage," *Academy of Management Review* 29 (2004): 258–71.
8. Jordi Trullen and Jean M Bartunek, "What a Design Approach Offers to Organization Development," *The Journal of Applied Behavioral Science* 43, no. 1 (2007): 23–40; and Kurt Lewin, "Group Decisions and Social Change," in *Readings in Social Psychology,* ed. Eleanor E. Maccobby, Theodore M. Newcomb, and Eugene L. Hartley (New York: Holt, Rinehart & Winston, 1985).
9. Michael Jarrett, "Tuning Into the Emotional Drama of Change: Extending the Consultant's Bandwidth," *Journal of Change Management* 4, no. 3 (2004): 247–58.
10. Klein, *True Change.*
11. Michael Svoboda and Silke Schroder, "Transforming Human Resources in the New Economy: Developing the Next Generation of Global HR Managers at Deutsche Bank AG," *Human Resource Management* 40, no. 3 (2001): 261–73.
12. Timothy A. Pine, *Enabling Excellence: The Seven Elements Essential to Achieving Competitive Advantage* (Milwaukee, WI: ASQ Quality Press, 2007).
13. Jagdish N. Sheth, *The Self-Destructive Habits of Good Companies . . . And How to Break Them* (Philadelphia, PA: Wharton School Publishing, 2007).
14. Michael Beer and Anna Elise Walton, "Organization Change and Development," in *Organization Development: Theory Practice, and Research,* ed. Wendell L. French, Cecil H. Bell Jr., and Robert A. Zawacki (Homewood, IL: Richard D. Irwin, 1989), p. 73.
15. Dennis G. Erwin and Andrew N. Garman, "Resistance to Organizational Change: Linking Research and Practice," *Leadership & Organization Development Journal* 31, no. 1 (2010): 39–56.
16. Ari Ginsberg and Eric Abrahamson, "Champions of Change and Strategic Shifts: The Role of Internal and External Change Advocates," *Journal of Management Studies* 28 (1991): 173–90.
17. Jeanie Daniel Duck, *The Change Monster: The Human Forces That Foil Corporate Transformation and Change* (New York: Crown Business, 2001).
18. Ibid.
19. Ralph H. Kilmann, "Toward a Complete Program for Corporate Transformation," in *Corporate Transformation,* eds. Ralph H. Kilmann, Teresa Joyce Covin, and Associates (San Francisco: Jossey-Bass, 1998), pp. 302–29.
20. Ron Zemke, "How Change Really Happens," *Training,* October 2000, pp. 122–26.
21. Morten Levin, "Technology Transfer in Organizational Development," *International Journal of Technology Management* 14, nos. 2, 3, 4 (1997).
22. A. Arora, A. Foster, and A. Gambardella, *Markets for Technology* (Boston: MIT Press, 2004).
23. H. G. Berkema, J. A. C. Baum, and E. A. Mannix, "Management Challenges in a New Time," *Academy of Management Journal* 45 (2002): 916–30.
24. Bart Perkins, "The Power of Viral Revenge," *Computerworld,* July 27, 2009, pp. 40–41.
25. Ibid.
26. David A. Garvin, *Learning in Action* (Boston: Harvard Business School Press, 2000).
27. Rich Teerlink and Lee Ozley, *More Than a Motorcycle: The Leadership Journey at Harley-Davidson* (Boston: Harvard Business School Press, 2001).
28. Ibid.
29. Peter Burrows, "The Radical: Carly Fiorina's Bold Management Experiment at HP," *Businessweek,* February 19, 2001, pp. 70–80.
30. Gordon L. Lippitt, Peter Longseth, and Jack Mossop, *Implementing Organizational Change* (San Francisco: Jossey-Bass, 1985), pp. 53–74.
31. J. Salopek, P. Harris, P. Ketter, M. Laff, J. Llorens, A. Nancherla, and A. Pace , "Linking Training to Care," *T + D,* October 2009, pp. 64–66.
32. S. Kudyba, ed., *Managing Data Mines* (Hershey, PA: Idea Group, 2004).
33. The relationship between depth of organization and intended change is popularly termed *depth of intervention.* We have chosen to term it *degree of intended change* to highlight the issues associated with change rather than those related to intervention. See Roger Harrison, "Choosing the Depth of Organizational Intervention," *Journal of Applied Behavioral Science* 6 (1970): 181–202, for the original discussion of the concept; and also Wendell L. French and Cecil H. Bell Jr., *Organizational Development: Behavioral Science Interventions for Organizational Improvement* (Englewood Cliffs, NJ: Prentice-Hall, 1984).
34. John Arnes, Trevor Slack, and C. R. Henings, "The Pace, Sequence, and Linearity of Radical Change," *Academy of Management Journal* 47 (2004): 15–39.
35. Mark Hoogendoom, Catholijn Jonker, Martijn Schut, and Jan Treur, "Modeling Centralized Organization of Organizational Change," *Computational & Mathematical Organization Theory* 13, no. 2 (2007): 147–84.

36. Richard L. Daft, *Organizational Theory and Design* (Cincinnati, OH: South-Western, 2000).
37. Denise M. Rousseau and S. A. Tijoriwala, "What's a Good Reason to Change? Motivated Reasoning and Social Accounts in Promoting Organizational Change," *Journal of Applied Psychology* 84 (1999): 514–28.
38. Oreg Shaul, "Personality, Context and Resistance to Organizational Change," *European Journal of Work and Organizational Psychology* 15, no. 1 (2006): 73–101.
39. Ryan M. Johnson, CCP, "Telework Trendlines 2009," A Survey Brief by WorldatWork Data collected by The Dieringer Research Group Inc., February 2009 (see www.worldatwork.org/waw/adimLink?id=31115; accessed on July 10, 2010).
40. Alain Verbeke, *Moving Toward the Virtual Workplace* (Cheltenham, UK: Edward Elgar, 2004).
41. N. Franz, "Catalyzing Employee Change With Transformative Learning," *Human Resource Development Quarterly* 21, no. 1 (2010): 113–18.
42. Carole A. Beatty and Brenda Barker, *Building High Performance Teams* (Thousand Oaks, CA: Sage, 2004).
43. Peter Senge, *The Dance of Change: The Challenges to Sustaining Momentum in Learning Organizations* (New York: Doubleday, 1999).
44. Nancy Hatch Woodward, "Make the Most of Team Building," *HR Magazine,* September 2006, pp. 72–76; Donald L. Kirkpatrick, *How to Manage Change Effectively* (San Francisco: Jossey-Bass, 1985), pp. 101–6.
45. John P. Kotter, "Leading Change: The Eight Steps to Transformation," in *The Leader's Change Handbook,* ed. J. A. Conger, G. M. Spreitzer, and E. E. Lawler III (San Francisco: Jossey-Bass, 1999), pp. 87–99.
46. Beatty and Barker, *Building High Performance Teams.*
47. David A. Whetten and Kim S. Cameron, *Developing Management Skills* (Upper Saddle River, NJ: Prentice-Hall, 2004).
48. R. Anand and M. Winters, "A Retrospective View of Corporate Diversity Training From 1964 to the Present," *Academy of Management Learning & Education* 7, no. 3 (2008): 356–72; W. B. Swann Jr., J. T. Polzer, D. C. Seyle, and S. J. Ko, "Finding Value in Diversity: Verification of Personal and Social Self-Views in Diverse Groups," *Academy of Management Review* 29 (2004): 9–27.
49. Carol Saunders, Craig Van Slyke, and Douglas R. Vogel, "My Time or Yours? Managing Time Visions in Global Virtual Teams," *Academy of Management Executive* 18 (2004): 19–31.
50. M. Walzer, "Making the Leap from R&D to Manufacturing," *Chemical Engineering* 116, no. 12 (2009): 44–46; and T. B. Anderson, *Technological Change and the Evolution of Corporate Innovation* (Cheltenham, UK: Edward Elgar, 2001).
51. P. Waurzyniak, "Automating Automotive," *Manufacturing Engineering* 141, no. 3 (2008): 75–86; and M. A. Schilling and H. K. Steensma, "The Use of Modular Forms: An Industry-Level Analysis," *Academy of Management Journal* 44 (2001): 1149–68.
52. Theresa Morris, "Internal and External Sources of Organizational Change: Corporate Form and Banking Industry," *Sociological Quarterly* 48, no. 1 (2007): 119–40.
53. F. Levy and R. J. Murnane, *The New Division of Labor: How Computers Are Creating the Next Job Market* (Princeton, NJ: Princeton University Press, 2004).
54. Jan P. Muczyk and Bernard Reimann, "MBO as a Complement to Effective Leadership," *Academy of Management Executive* 3 (1989): 131–38.
55. J. M. Watkins and B. J. Mohr, *Appreciative Inquiry: Change at the Speed of Imagination* (New York: John Wiley, 2001).
56. David L. Cooperrider, Diana Whitney, and Jacqueline M. Stavros, *Appreciative Inquiry Handbook: For Leaders of Change,* 2nd ed. (San Francisco: Barrett-Koehler, 2008).
57. J. D. Ludema, D. Whitney, T. J. Griffin, and B. J. Mohr, *The Appreciative Inquiry Summit: A Practitioner's Guide for Leading Large-Scale Change* (San Francisco: Barrett-Koehler, 2003).
58. Watkins and Mohr, *Appreciative Inquiry.*
59. M. O. Carlson, K. S. Reinhardt, and G. E. Humphrey, *Weaving Science Inquiry and Continuous Improvement* (Thousand Oaks, CA: Sage, 2003).
60. Joanne C. Preston and Kenneth L. Murell, "The Efficacy of Appreciative Inquiry Is Building Relational Capital in a Transnational Strategic Alliance," *Academy of Management Proceedings,* pp. E1–E5.
61. M. Hammer and J. Champy, *Reengineering the Corporation* (New York: HarperCollins, 1993).
62. C. Zatzick, M. Marks, and R. Iverson, "Which Way Should You Downsize in a Crisis?" *MIT Sloan Management Review* 51, no. 1 (2009): 79–86; and Judith A. Clair, Nicole Jackson, Ronald Dufresne, and Jamie Ladge, "Being the Bearer of Bad News: Downsizing Agents in Organizations," *Organizational Dynamics,* 35, no. 2 (2006): 131–44.
63. J. Stringham and D. R. Workman, *The Unemployment Survival Guide* (New York: Gibbs Smith, 2004.
64. A. Ross, *No Caller: The Human Workplace and Its Hidden Costs* (Philadelphia: Temple University, 2004).
65. D. Roth, "10 Companies That Get It: Southwest Airlines," *Fortune,* November 8, 1999, p. 115.
66. Clair et. al., "Being the Bearer of Bad News: Challenges Facing Downsizing Agents in Organizations."
67. Peter K. Mills and Gerardo R. Ungson, "Reassessing the Limits of Structural Empowerment: Organizational Constitution and Trust as Controls," *Academy of Management Review* 28, no. 1 (2003): 143–53.
68. Matthew Mariani, "Telecommuters," *Occupational Outlook Quarterly* 44 (2000): 10–17.
69. N. B. Kurland and D. E. Bailey, "Telework: The Advantages and Challenge of Working Here, There,

Anywhere, and Anytime," *Organizational Dynamics* 28, no. 2 (1999): 53–68.
70. J. Robinson, *Work to Live: The Guide to Getting a Life* (New York: Trade Perigee).
71. "Flexible Hours in the Ranks," *HR Magazine: SHRM's 2010 HR Trend Book,* January 2010, pp. 16–17; and N. H. Woodward, "TGI Thursday," *HR Magazine,* July 2003, pp. 72–76.
72. Woodward, "TGI Thursday."
73. Sarah Fister Gale, "Formalized Flextime: The Perk That Brings Productivity," *Workforce,* February 2001, pp. 39–42.
74. Arnis et al., "The Pace, Sequence, and Linearity of Radical Change."
75. Peter Senge, *The Fifth Discipline* (New York: Doubleday, 1990).
76. G. L. Stewart, Charles C. Manz, and H. P. Sims, Jr., *Team Work and Group Dynamics* (New York: Wiley, 1999).
77. Harold J. Leavitt, *Top Down: Why Hierarchies Are Here to Stay and How to Manage Them More Effectively* (Boston: Harvard Business School Press, 2004).
78. J. Lipman-Blumen and Harold J. Leavitt, "Hot Groups 'With Attitude': A New Organizational State of Mind," *Organizational Dynamics* 27, no. 4 (1999): 63–73.
79. Christopher G. Worley and Edward E. Lawler III, "Designing Organizations That Are Built to Change," *MIT Sloan Management Review* 48, no. 1 (2006): 19–23.
80. N. M. M. Lorenze and R. T. Riley, *Managing Technological Change* (New York: Springer-Verlag, 2004).
81. Joanne Martin, *Organizational Culture: Mapping the Terrain* (Thousand Oaks, CA: Sage, 2002).
82. E. H. Schein, *Organizational Culture and Leadership* (San Francisco: Jossey-Bass, 2004).
83. Ibid.
84. Stewart et al., *Team Work and Group Dynamics.*
85. Schein, *Organizational Culture and Leadership.*
86. Senge, *The Fifth Discipline.*
87. "Knowledge Nurture," Buckman Laboratories, accessed July 11, 2010, www.knowledge-nurture.com/.
88. Darlene Russ-Eft and Hallie Preskell, *Evaluation in Organizations: A Systematic Approach to Enhancing Learning, Performance, and Change* (New York: Perseus Books, 2001).
89. Senge, *The Fifth Discipline.*
90. Jeffrey Pfeffer and Robert I. Sutton, *The Knowing-Doing Gap: How Smart Companies Turn Knowledge into Action* (Cambridge, MA: Harvard Business School Press, 2000).

Appendix

1. F. Lee, A. C. Edmondson, S. Thomke, and M. Worline, "The Mixed Effects of Inconsistency on Experimentation in Organizations," *Organizational Science* 15 (2004): 310–26.
2. C. S. George, Jr., *The History of Management Thought* (Englewood Cliffs, NJ: Prentice-Hall, 1968).
3. J. D. Mooney, *The Principles of Management* (New York: Harper & Row, 1939).
4. Teresa Brannick and David Coghlan, "In Defense of Being Native: The Case for Insider Research," *Organizational Research Methods* 10 (2007): 59–74.
5. M. L. Mitchell and J. M. Jolley, *Research Design Explained* (Pacific Grove, CA: Wadsworth, 2001).
6. Donald P. Schwab, *Research Methods for Organizational Studies* (Mahwah, NJ: Erlbaum, 1999).
7. John Brockman, *Doing Science* (Englewood Cliffs, NJ: Prentice-Hall, 1991), p. 155.
8. Edward E. Lawler III, A. M. Mohrman, S. A. Mohrman, G. E. Ledford Jr., and T. G. Cummings, *Doing Research That Is Useful for Theory and Practice* (San Francisco: Jossey-Bass, 1985).
9. G. P. Hodgkinson, A. J. Maule, and N. J. Brown, "Causal Cognitive Mapping in the Organizational Strategy Field: A Comparison of Alternative Elicitation Procedures," *Organizational Research Methods* 7 (2004): 3–26.
10. D. Remenyi, B. Williams, A. Money, and E. Swartz, *Doing Research in Business and Management* (Thousand Oaks, CA: Sage, 1998).
11. Henry Mintzberg, *The Nature of Managerial Work* (New York: Harper & Row, 1973).
12. Kathleen M. Eisenhardt, "Building Theories from Case Study Research," *Academy of Management Review* 14 (1989): 532–50.
13. Nicolaj Siggelkow, "Persuasion with Case Studies," *Academy of Management Journal* 50, no. 1 (2007): 20–24.
14. Kathleen M Eisenhardt and Melissa E Graebner, "Theory Building from Cases: Opportunities and Challenges," *Academy of Management Journal* 50, no. 1 (2007): 25–32.
15. J. Carpenter, G. W. Harrison, and J. A List, *Field Experiments in Economics* (New York: JAI Press, 2005).
16. A. H. Church and J. Waclawski, *Designing and Using Organizational Survey* (Hampshire, UK: Gower 1998).
17. David Klahr and Herbert Simon, "Studies of Scientific Discovery: Complementary Approaches and Convergent Findings," *Psychological Bulletin* 125 (1999): 524–43.
18. Kimberly Kempf-Leonard, *Encyclopedia of Social Measurement* (San Francisco: Elsevier, 2004).
19. Ibid.
20. See an account of the classic Hawthorne studies in F. J. Roethlisberger and W. J. Dickson, *Management and the Worker* (Boston: Harvard Business School, 1939). The original purpose of the studies, which were conducted at the Chicago Hawthorne Plant of Western Electric, was to investigate the relationship between productivity and physical working conditions.

21. Karl E. Weick, "Laboratory Experimentation with Organizations: A Reappraisal," *Academy of Management Review* 2 (1977): 123–27.
22. J. P. Campbell, "Labs, Fields, and Straw Issues," in *Generalizing from Laboratory to Field Settings,* ed. Edwin A. Locke (Lexington, MA: Lexington Books, 1986), pp. 269–74.
23. James L. Price and Charles W. Mueller, *Handbook of Organizational Measurement* (Marshfield, MA: Pitman, 1986).
24. R. H. Helmstader, *Research Concepts in Human Behavior* (New York: Appleton-Century-Crofts, 1970); and D. W. Emery, *Business Research Methods* (Homewood, IL: Richard D. Irwin, 1980).
25. Larry V. Hedges and Therese D. Pagott, "The Power of Statistical Tests in Meta-Analysis," *Psychological Methods* 6 (2001): 203–17.
26. Katherine J. Klein, Amy Buhl Conn, and Joann Speer Sorra, "Implementing Computerized Technology: An Organizational Analysis," *Journal of Applied Psychology* 86, no. 5 (2001): 811–24.
27. Leland Wilkinson, "Statistical Methods in Psychology Journals: Guidelines and Explanations," *American Psychologist* 54, no. 8 (1999): 594–604.
28. R. Adcock and D. Collier, "Measurement Validity: A Shared Standard for Qualitative and Quantitative Research," *American Political Science Review* 95 (2001): 529–46.
29. N. K. Denzin and Y. S. Lincoln, eds., *The Handbook of Qualitative Research* (Thousand Oaks, CA: Sage, 2005).
30. P. Chamberlayne, J. Bornat, and T. Wengraf, eds., *The Turn to Biographical Methods in the Social Sciences* (London: Routledge, 2000).
31. Ibid.
32. John Van Maanen, J. M. Dobbs Jr., and R. R. Faulkner, *Varieties of Qualitative Research* (Beverly Hills, CA: Sage, 1982).
33. Barbara Czarniawska, *Narratives in Social Science Research* (London: Sage, 2004).

NAME/COMPANY INDEX

SUBJECT INDEX